International Encyclopedia of the SOCIAL SCIENCES

International Encyclopedia of the SOCIAL SCIENCES

DAVID L. SILLS EDITOR

VOLUME 3

The Macmillan Company & The Free Press

International Encyclopedia of the SOCIAL SCIENCES

C

[CONTINUED]

COLONIALISM

I. POLITICAL ASPECTS   *Rupert Emerson*
II. ECONOMIC ASPECTS   *D. K. Fieldhouse*

I
POLITICAL ASPECTS

Colonialism is the establishment and maintenance, for an extended time, of rule over an alien people that is separate from and subordinate to the ruling power. It is no longer closely associated with the term "colonization," which involves the settlement abroad of people from a mother country, as in the case of the ancient Greek colonies or the Americas. Colonialism has now come to be identified with rule over peoples of different race inhabiting lands separated by salt water from the imperial center; more particularly, it signifies direct political control by European states or states settled by Europeans, as the United States or Australia, over peoples of other races, notably over Asians and Africans. To this category should be added Japan's rule over her dependent territories, lost after World War II.

Some further features of the "colonial situation" are: domination of an alien minority, asserting racial and cultural superiority, over a materially inferior native majority; contact between a machine-oriented civilization with Christian origins, a powerful economy, and a rapid rhythm of life and a non-Christian civilization that lacks machines and is marked by a backward economy and a slow rhythm of life; and the imposition of the first civilization upon the second (Balandier 1951, p. 75).

The Belgians attempted in the earlier years of the United Nations to broaden the concept of colonialism to include all ethnically distinct minorities discriminated against in their home countries. Contending that such minorities were often in greater need of UN attention than the people in overseas dependencies, the Belgian thesis proposed their acceptance as nonself-governing peoples under Chapter XI of the Charter. This interpretation was generally rejected in the UN and by the colonial and former colonial peoples themselves. The most serious shortcomings of the narrower interpretation are that it excludes the Asian and other non-Russian peoples in the Soviet Union, alleged to be dominated by the Great Russians, and the Africans and Asians of South Africa, barred from the main stream of the country's life by the apartheid doctrine. South Africa lacks the geographic separation of colonies from the imperial center but can be at least partially brought within the colonial rubric because the dominant group is white European whereas the ruled are of different race and color. The Asian peoples of the Soviet Union are usually placed outside the traditional colonial category even though Western observers often accuse the U.S.S.R. of being *the* colonial power par excellence.

Definitions of colonialism couched in terms of value and emotion take quite a different form. This is most true of those left-wing analysts who can find nothing but evil in colonialism. Thus the "Great Soviet Encyclopaedia" of 1953 speaks of colonization as the military or economic enslavement of any dependent country and sees it as accompanied by bestial exploitation and extermination of the indigenous population. The more leftward-inclined Asian and African leaders frequently denounce colonialism in similar terms.

1

Historical evolution of modern colonialism

Modern colonialism started with the fifteenth-century voyages of the Portuguese along the west coast of Africa, which in 1498 brought Vasco da Gama to India. The Portuguese and Spaniards were the first to establish their dominions overseas and clung to them long after their imperialist drive had lost its forward thrust. The Americas were wholly taken over as European domains, the Dutch and British began to stake out their claims in India and the Indies, and France had won and lost more than one empire by 1815. The first blows for anti-colonialism were struck by the American Revolution and the subsequent liberation of most of Latin America.

Although Europe's imperial expansion and growth in power continued during the first three-quarters of the nineteenth century, the circumstances of the times tended to discourage the extension of colonial holdings. Britain's command of the seas and its industrial head start gave it a virtual monopoly of access to the world overseas, making unnecessary the kind of exclusive control that colonialism offered. The abandonment of mercantilism and the swing to laissez-faire and free trade made colonies less attractive than they had been before. Bentham had pleaded that Britain and France should rid themselves of their dependencies; Turgot saw colonies falling from the tree like ripe fruit; and Disraeli, assuming the colonies would soon be independent, regarded them in 1852 as "millstones around our neck."

China was opened to the penetration of the West but was not subjected to colonial rule. Only in India did the British more or less consistently expand their colonial sway, and France took over Algeria and made its first encroachments in Indochina. In Britain it was even seriously proposed, not long before the start of the scramble for Africa, that there should be a withdrawal from African holdings.

A very different climate of opinion and range of action prevailed in the last quarter of the century. The restraints on colonialism were swept away in the new imperialist flood that speedily completed the partition of the world between the imperial powers. Africa was almost totally divided into European dependencies. In other areas as well, new colonies were carved out or old ones consolidated and extended, as in southeast Asia, where the Dutch, French, and British greatly expanded the scope and intensity of their rule in the Indies, Indochina, Malaya, and Burma. Changing power relationships brought a redivision of territories in the Spanish–American War, in the Boer War, and after World War I with the transfer of German and Turkish holdings.

To assess the causes of the change in the last decades of the nineteenth century would involve the whole range of theories of imperialism, but certain elements particularly related to colonialism may be singled out. Such men as Jules Ferry, Joseph Chamberlain, and Cecil Rhodes justified the revival of colonialism in terms of the needs of the new industrial system and by the demands of a Darwinian struggle between nations and races. The entry of France, Germany, and Italy, followed by Japan and the United States, into the imperial rivalry, not to mention Russia's expansive mood, seemed to substantiate Lenin's dictum that only colonial possession gave a complete guarantee against the risks of competitive struggle. The new wave of protectionism and governmental intervention at home restored validity to the assertion of direct political control overseas. Such control seemed particularly justified in tropical Africa, where it was arguable that only the assumption of full responsibility by a Western government could establish the conditions under which modern enterprise could function. This position found powerful support in the prevalent theories holding that certain races, notably the Teutonic or Anglo–Saxon, had a peculiar genius for government.

The transition away from colonialism. Western imperialism reached its highest point before World War I, although several decades went by before World War II brought a full rejection of colonialism. The Spanish–American War marked the beginning and the end of any large-scale American involvement with colonialism, and the Boer War crystallized the hostility of many, in Britain and elsewhere, to imperialism. The years preceding World War I were the last in which a complacent colonialism could flourish as a part of what seemed the natural order of things. Liberal and socialist attacks on colonialism were growing, although the belief in white supremacy lingered on. The adoption of the mandates system in the Versailles peace settlement was one significant expression of the doubts that were beginning to undermine colonialism. The only significant additions to the colonial domains between the two world wars were short-lived: Mussolini's anachronistic seizure of Ethiopia and Japan's drive on China and, later, southeast Asia.

All the forces opposed to colonialism and sapping its vitality grew in strength in the interwar years. The success of the Russian Revolution brought into being a world-wide network of agitation against imperialism, and nationalist activities and organizations were multiplying in the dependent territories themselves. In the imperial centers the will to maintain empire steadily declined with the spread of ideas hostile to racialism and colonial domination. World War II greatly hastened the process through the Japanese displacement of the colonial powers in southeast Asia, the further weakening of those powers at home, the intensification of anti-imperialist opinion throughout the world, and the atmosphere of change that permeated many of the colonies.

After 1945 the flood tide of anticolonialism swept away the colonial system with a speed and thoroughness that matched colonialism's advance at the close of the nineteenth century. The possession of colonies, so long a matter of pride and prestige, now became a sin to be expiated only, if at all, by the granting of immediate independence. The League of Nations' indifference to the problem was replaced by the profound involvement of the United Nations in the process of decolonization.

Attitudes toward colonialism

Attitudes toward colonialism have varied greatly from time to time and from place to place. Most frequently, colonialism has been accepted as merely one manifestation of the ever-present truth that the strong dominate the weak. Although the missionary element has rarely been wholly absent, the usual presumption has been that every colony does or ought to exist for the benefit of the mother country.

The justifications of colonial rule cover a wide range, often resting upon the right of the conqueror, perhaps bolstered by a claim of racial superiority. Where the interests of the dependent peoples are taken into account, it is held that an extended period of guardianship is necessary to enable them to "stand by themselves under the strenuous conditions of the modern world." Here the *mission civilisatrice* and the "white man's burden" come into play. Some French spokesmen for colonialism acclaim it as the universal instrument for the spread of civilization, pointing to themselves and many of their neighbors as products of Roman colonization.

The defense of colonialism is likely to adopt some variant of the criterion laid down by John Stuart Mill, who, in the case of peoples not yet ready for representative government, defended alien rule on the ground that the colonial mode of government was as legitimate as any other if it was the one which in the existing state of civili-

zation of the subject people most facilitated their transition to a higher stage of improvement. Lord Lugard (1922) introduced another element in proposing that the colonial powers were under a dual mandate obligating them to secure the advancement of their dependent territories and to develop them in the interest of the world at large.

The assumptions on which such defenses of colonialism rest have been increasingly subject to challenge in recent decades. The more moderate present-day approach tentatively accepts colonial rule if the authorities devote themselves to preparing their wards for independence, but growing skepticism as to the trustworthiness of the colonial powers has led to the insistence that they accept international supervision in so doing. The UN Charter looked to independence or self-government for all dependent peoples, tightened control over the trust territories surviving from the mandates system, and brought all nonself-governing territories into the international public domain.

The more radical approach denounces the imposition of alien rule as always evil under all circumstances. This starting point eliminates all controversy as to whether one colonial system or policy is better than another by blanket condemnation of all, leaving immediate independence as the only way out. Building on the anticolonial resolution of the 1955 Bandung Conference, the UN General Assembly in its 1960 Declaration on the Granting of Independence gave this position international recognition. This declaration denounced the alien subjugation of peoples as a denial of human rights and an impediment to peace, proclaimed the right of all peoples to self-determination without conditions or reservations, and repudiated the doctrine of tutelage by asserting that inadequacy of political, economic, social, or educational preparedness shall never serve as a pretext for delaying independence. Asian and African opinion has constantly been moving toward this radical position, pillorying colonialism as the source of most of the world's troubles and proclaiming that the higher law of anticolonialism renders all remnants of the era of European colonialism illegitimate and open to attack.

The anticolonialists project such doctrines into the future through the use of the concept of neocolonialism, which accuses the imperialists, among whom the Americans figure prominently, of regarding the independence that the colonial peoples have wrung from them as only the occasion to adopt more subtle tactics of domination and exploitation. Overt colonial rule is thus replaced by economic and other forms of control, including the provision of aid, and the nominally free countries are Balkanized and manipulated in the imperial interest.

The colonial and former colonial powers see what has been happening in recent decades in a very different light. They reject the charge of being oppressors and exploiters and point to their accomplishments in advancing their dependent peoples in every sphere, including the granting of independence to hundreds of millions since 1945. However, they differ greatly in the way in which they have envisaged their colonial mission. The position of four of them—Britain, France, Belgium, and Portugal—may be briefly sketched to indicate the wide range of variation.

Varying colonial policies

Great Britain. With the exception of the United States, whose colonial holdings were far smaller, Great Britain could adapt itself more easily to the new dispensation than any of the other colonial powers. The entire British policy of regarding colonies not as integral parts of the mother country but as countries with their own distinctive ways of life facilitated autonomous development. The colonial peoples were given an increasing share in the governing councils, public service, and judiciary and thus were started on what came to be a standard cycle culminating in self-government and then independence. This was a cycle through which the older dominions had passed and which was tested again in India, Ceylon, and elsewhere in the interwar decades. World War II brought both a heightening of the belief that colonial rule imposed responsibility for the well-being of dependent peoples and an acceptance of the need to move speedily to end colonialism. India's independence, in 1947, started a process of decolonization that dismantled the British empire in Asia and most of Africa and the West Indies; and although difficulties have cropped up where there is a substantial amount of white settlement or race mixture, as in the Rhodesias, Kenya, and British Guiana, the British have been able to transform most colonies into independent states within the framework of long-established policies that were already in operation.

France. France, on the other hand, was forced to undertake a basic reversal in direction. In contrast to the British, the French inclined always to a policy of cultural, economic, and political assimilation. It was characteristic of French policy that the 1944 Brazzaville conference of leading colonial officials decreed that France's work of civilization in her colonies excluded any idea of autonomy or of evolution outside the French empire, "even in the distant future." French aid for the colonies was greatly increased after World War II, and many reforms were introduced, but the bonds linking the colonies to France were not relaxed until the eve of independence. The Indochinese and Algerian wars demonstrated French reluctance to accept colonialism's end. Even in 1958, when Guinea opted for independence by voting "no" in the referendum on de Gaulle's constitution, Guinea was treated as an outlaw. Yet in the succeeding months de Gaulle reconciled himself and the French people to African independence on terms of intimate collaboration between France and the newly freed countries—terms often so intimate as to lead to charges that a French neocolonialism had been instituted, rendering independence nominal.

Belgium. Belgian rule over the Congo, which came to an abrupt end on July 1, 1960, was an unusual combination of elements. The Belgians concentrated power in Brussels, as did the French in Paris, but they did not follow France in associating Africans with them in the imperial center nor Britain in drawing the Congolese into the local administration and governing councils. The great triumvirate—the Belgian government, the giant corporations, and the church—made tremendous strides in economic development, and to a lesser extent in welfare and education, laying the foundation for what would have been a solid structure if uninterrupted decades of colonial rule had stretched ahead. The Belgian philosophy of colonialism explicitly excluded the creation of an elite on the French or British model until mass education would have spread widely and a middle class come into being. The haste with which Belgium moved to sever its formal ties with the Congo following the riots in Leopoldville in January 1959 gave no opportunity to bridge the immense gap between its patronizing paternalism and the responsibilities suddenly assumed by the Congolese, who were left with a government lacking trained African leaders and officials and an army lacking African officers.

Portugal. The Portuguese offer a fourth variant of colonialism, ruling over an empire shorn of Goa but still reaching from Macao to Mozambique and Angola. Oldest of the Western colonial powers, Portugal continues to protest vigorously that she has no nonself-governing peoples but only equal provinces of a single indivisible realm. The Portuguese boast that they are free of racial prejudice, but their African colonies are marked by the cleavage between the few thousands of "civilized" or "assimilated" Africans and the millions of "uncivilized." The 1961 rising in Angola led the Portuguese government to announce a number of reforms, including the abolition of the *regime do indigenato* and the establishment of a single status for all within the Portuguese domain, but the overwhelming majority of the Africans remain illiterate and touched by little more of modernity than pressure to work as laborers for the Europeans. Furthermore, embittered competition has inevitably broken out between the advancing African elements and the thousands of Portuguese peasants and workers officially encouraged to emigrate to Portuguese Africa with the double purpose of relieving home poverty and establishing the Portuguese presence so firmly as to make it unchallengeable. The heart of the problem is that Portugal is itself only a partially developed country, having lived for many years under a dictatorship and being unable to overcome its own poverty and mass illiteracy. Its ability to secure the advancement of millions of people overseas is obviously questionable.

The literature of colonialism

The literature dealing with colonialism is wide-ranging and diverse and reflects the changing nature of the colonial problem. For the most part it consists of studies of particular dependencies or groups of dependencies, but a substantial body of literature dealing with general aspects of colonialism has also been built up. Several studies have undertaken to compare the colonial policies of the powers in terms of the goals that have been set, the success with which these goals have been reached, and the administrative and other machineries that have been employed. At both ends of the spectrum the motives lying behind the acquisition of dependencies and the evaluation of the forces leading to the present surge of decolonization open challenging vistas to inquiry. Among the themes that have recurred regularly in the examination of colonialism are the relative values of direct and indirect rule, centralization and decentralization, varying types of economic policy, the acceptability and effects of white settlement, pressures of different kinds to aid in recruiting a labor force, and the scope and nature of the educational system.

In the interwar decades there appeared in the literature of colonialism the relatively new theme of international control over the colonial powers, but since 1945 this has been superseded by the processes and problems of decolonization and the means of securing economic and political development. The transition through the last stages of colonial rule to independence has been studied in a number of instances but still offers an unusually rich field of inquiry. Africa, achieving independence almost overnight, has come in for unprecedented attention. Now that colonialism is virtually at an end, it becomes possible to explore in depth and in detail what type of colonial system has produced the best results, but before this question can be meaningfully explored it is necessary to determine the scale of values by which colonialism in its various guises is to be measured.

The era of colonialism is far too close to us for any definitive and objective assessment of it to be possible. A few salient points may, however, be tentatively put forward.

(1) Colonialism imposed alien and authoritarian regimes on subordinate societies. These regimes tended to train a few of their subjects in bureaucratic management and required passive acquiescence from the remainder.

(2) Although for long periods passive acquiescence was indeed largely attained, as colonialism advanced it also stimulated nationalist agitation and organization and came to be more and more passionately detested, particularly by those among the colonial people who came into closest contact with the European superiors.

(3) The anticolonial forces have derived their inspiration and ideas primarily from the teachings of the colonial powers themselves, have for the most part adopted Western forms of organization and action, and have been led by men intimately acquainted with the West.

(4) For good or ill, colonialism has been the primary channel through which the ideas and techniques, the spiritual and material forces of the West, have impinged upon the rest of mankind.

RUPERT EMERSON

[See also IMPERIALISM; MODERNIZATION; NATION; NATIONALISM.]

BIBLIOGRAPHY

BALANDIER, GEORGES 1951 La situation coloniale: Approche théorique. *Cahiers internationaux de sociologie* 11, no. 51:44–79.

BURNS, ALAN 1957 *In Defence of Colonies: British Colonial Territories in International Affairs.* London: Allen & Unwin; New York: Macmillan.

EASTON, STEWART C. 1964 *The Rise and Fall of Western Colonialism: A Historical Survey From the Early Nineteenth Century to the Present.* New York and London: Praeger.

FURNIVALL, JOHN S. 1948 *Colonial Policy and Practice: A Comparative Study of Burma and Netherlands India.* Issued in cooperation with the International Secretariat, Institute of Pacific Relations. New York: Macmillan; Cambridge Univ. Press.

GIRAULT, ARTHUR (1895) 1938 *Principes de colonisation et de législation coloniale.* 7th ed. Revised by Louis Milliot. Paris: Sirey.

HAILEY, MALCOLM (1938) 1957 *An African Survey: A Study of Problems Arising in Africa South of the Sahara.* Issued under the auspices of the Royal Institute of International Affairs. Rev. ed. New York and London: Oxford Univ. Press.

KAT ANGELINO, A. D. DE (1929–1930) 1931 *Colonial Policy.* 2 vols. The Hague: Nijhoff; Univ. of Chicago Press. → Abbreviated translation from the Dutch. Volume 1: *General Principles.* Volume 2: *The Dutch East Indies.* First published as *Staatkundig beleid en bestuurszorg in Nederlandsch-Indië.*

LUGARD, FREDERICK J. D. (1922) 1929 *The Dual Mandate in British Tropical Africa.* 4th ed. Edinburgh and London: Blackwood.

MANNONI, DOMINIQUE O. (1950) 1956 *Prospero and Caliban: The Psychology of Colonization.* New York: Praeger; London: Methuen. → First published in French as *Psychologie de la colonisation.*

MAUNIER, RENÉ (1932–1946) 1949 *The Sociology of Colonies.* 2 vols. Edited and translated by E. O. Lorimer. London: Routledge. → Volume 1: *An Introduction to the Study of Race Contact: Psychology of Expansion.* Volume 2: *The Progress of Law.* First published in French in three volumes.

NKRUMAH, KWAME 1965 *Neo-colonialism: The Last Stage of Imperialism.* London: Nelson.

PANIKKAR, KAVALAM MADHAVA (1953) 1959 *Asia and Western Dominance: A Survey of the Vasco da Gama Epoch of Asian History, 1498–1945.* New ed. London: Allen & Unwin.

PERHAM, MARGERY F. 1962 *The Colonial Reckoning: The End of Imperial Rule in Africa in the Light of British Experience.* New York: Knopf.

PLAMENATZ, JOHN P. 1960 *On Alien Rule and Self-government.* London: Longmans.

ROYAL INSTITUTE OF INTERNATIONAL AFFAIRS 1937 *The Colonial Problem.* Oxford Univ. Press.

II
ECONOMIC ASPECTS

This article will deal with the economic theories propounded and the practices adopted at different times during the four and a half centuries of European colonization and with the effects these had on the colonies. It will examine what difference the end of formal empires in the mid-twentieth century made to the economic relations between metropolitan powers and former colonies.

The primary fact about colonialism as a historical phenomenon is that precast theories seldom dictated or even strongly influenced practice. At every stage the economic relationships between colonies and metropolis were determined pragmatically, according to current European practices and needs and conditions in the colonies. Theories were secondary, designed to justify or attack existing practice. Even in the case of Adam Smith's *Wealth of Nations* (1776), when a new approach seems to have had demonstrable effects, it is clear that changed colonial policies resulted more from altered circumstances than from an intellectual acceptance of his arguments.

Economic theories of colonialism. Theories of colonialism may be placed into four periods of time: prior to 1660; from 1660 to 1776; from 1776 to 1870; and from 1870 onward. Such divisions are arbitrary, but they provide a primitive framework for analysis.

Before 1660. During the two centuries before 1660 colonial economic theories were of minimal importance. The expansion of colonial territories proceeded experimentally, reflecting a wide diversity of aims: crusading zeal against Islam, the missionary impulse, geographical curiosity, the desire for bullion and for luxury trades in the East, and land hunger. None of these objectives required theoretical justification—though men like Bartolomé de Las Casas might denounce particular aspects of Spanish native policy in America—and the economic systems imposed on American settlements and Eastern trading bases were derived from the simple premise that each colonizing country was entitled to any advantages its new possessions offered. The northern European countries that came to colonization later—England, France, and Holland—had more time to theorize before acting; but no one produced a general theory of colonialism, and contemporary attitudes must be deduced from passing references. Most French and English commentators, such as Bodin, Antoine de Montchrétien, Marc Lescarbot, Bacon, and Richard Hakluyt, mixed economic with other rewards of colonization indiscriminately: the need for a route to the East via a northwest passage, the utility of American bases in the war with Spain, the interests of transatlantic fishermen, the possibility of finding gold and silver, the support a maritime empire would give the navy, the value of outlets for unemployed people, the possibility of new markets and sources of raw materials, and the Christian mission to convert the heathen. Most of these were commonplaces of Iberian writers: there was no attempt to select or to provide a rationale of colonialism.

The mercantilist era. During the period after about 1660, however, colonial theories became more sophisticated. This was the classical age of mercantilist thought, though it must be remembered that the multiplicity of arguments and practices it embraced were first dubbed a "system" by Adam Smith in 1776 [*see* ECONOMIC THOUGHT]. The essence of mercantilism was that it projected current metropolitan preoccupations into the colonies and assumed that dependencies existed solely to serve these particular interests. There was still some diffusion of aims, but the primary considerations were now economic advantage and the value of colonial trade for supporting an artificially large merchant marine. The economic possibilities of colonies were categorized. As producers of raw materials they served their owners by freeing them from dependence on European supplies, which might be cut off during war and for which monopoly prices were often charged. Colonial products could, moreover, be paid for in exported manufactures, saving foreign exchange, and could be re-exported to Europe to help the balance of trade. Conversely, colonies provided uniquely favorable markets for European exports, since they were monopolies, and thus helped to maintain employment in metropolitan industries. Since they were subordinate, they could be prevented from building competing industries, and their economies could be made entirely complementary. These arguments, based on observation of established practices, were the staple of pamphleteers and statesmen from the second quarter of the seventeenth into the early nineteenth century: of Richelieu, Colbert, and Vauban in France; of Child, Petty, Davenant, Defoe, Arthur Young, and many others in Britain. Though never brought together into a coherent academic "system," they formed a well understood and only occasionally criticized corpus of concepts, conveniently summarized as the *pacte colonial*.

Adam Smith: free trade.   Attacks on these principles became significant only in the mid-eighteenth century, led by the French physiocrats and Encyclopedists; the first because they disapproved of overemphasis on industrial production for the colonies, the second because they disliked all monopoly [see ECONOMIC THOUGHT]. But it was Adam Smith (1776), normally taken to be the first academic economist, who first attacked mercantilism root and branch and provided an alternative theory of colonial economics. He did this by applying his theory of the division of labor to colonial production and trade. The value to Europe of colonies in America (he largely ignored possessions elsewhere) was merely that they provided new articles for international trade and extended the market for European manufactures. Such advantages were independent of any colonial system and were diminished to the extent that any state tried to monopolize its colonial trade. Monopoly raised the cost to consumers both in America and Europe; discouraged foreign capital from colonial investment; raised the profits of metropolitan capital and so reduced each country's competitiveness; and made the metropolis dangerously dependent on colonies of uncertain loyalty. In addition, the higher profits allegedly made by European merchants on the monopoly trade of the colonies had to be set against the costs of imperial government and defense, which were paid by the general taxpayer. Hence a better colonial system would be one in which there was no monopoly and in which common costs were shared between colonies and metropolis. Better still, all colonies should be liberated, for once their trade was open to the world, the principle of the division of labor could be fully applied, and Europe would no longer bear the unrewarding cost of imperial organization.

Smith was rightly pessimistic about Europe's willingness to admit the truth of these facts. For half a century his arguments convinced only the minority, and no colony was liberated voluntarily, for there were always enough traditionalists to argue that the benefits of colonialism were real and to run against colonial monopoly and therefore purely economic rewards. But the trend of economic theory, as expounded in England by men like David Ricardo and the Benthamites, continued to run against colonial monopoly and therefore against colonies, for the two were still assumed to be inseparable. In any case the question had become almost academic by the 1830s, for once the United States, Spanish America, and Brazil were independent the British alone retained a substantial empire, compensating by gains in India for what they had lost in America. But in the 1820s, the British, as they moved toward international free trade, were also losing interest in their colonies, which were increasingly criticized as fields of government expenditure unrequited by economic advantages. India and trading bases in the East were generally accepted, because they were economically self-supporting and were an increasingly valuable market for British manufactures; but settlement colonies were falling into disrepute.

Modern period: capital outlet.   In the century after 1830 two distinct theories were developed to justify or rationalize colonies as economic phenomena under the new conditions. The first theory applied only to colonies of white settlement in North America, South Africa, and Australasia and concerned only the British. Against those who denounced such possessions, E. G. Wakefield, in a series of publications starting with his *Letter From Sydney* in 1829 and culminating in his *Art of Colonization* in 1849 argued that suitable colonies were valuable to the parent state, even under free trade conditions, provided they were correctly organized. Denying the precepts of Ricardo, he argued that an industrialized state could generate surplus capital which it was unprofitable to invest at home either in agriculture (because of the declining profitability of marginal lands) or in industry (because foreign markets did not expand fast enough to absorb its products). Adopting Smith's theory of "new equivalents," he held that this capital would be more profitably employed if it were exported to places where fertile land was in good supply. Provided ample labor was made available by emigration, capital would be more productive in these new lands and at the same time would expand the market for British manufactures and increase the supply of cheap foodstuffs and industrial raw materials. Colonies would provide these advantages better than independent states because colonies could be forced to be free-trading, and the new settlements would remain primary producers for the indefinite future.

Wakefield's theory and the detailed prescriptions he laid down for new settlements were never fully tested; but his basic argument carried conviction and constituted the main justification for settlement colonies under free trade conditions. But since only Great Britain possessed important settlement colonies in the nineteenth century, Wakefield's theory had limited applicability. The vast majority of new European colonies in the period after 1830 were tropical territories in Africa, Asia, and the Pacific that did not fit his formula. By the last quarter of the century new theories were necessary to justify these acquisitions to the mass electorates of Europe.

Modern period: market outlet.   Thus the second main theory of colonialism in the modern period was specially adapted to the facts of tropical dependencies. Significantly, no leading economist dared challenge Adam Smith by formulating a comprehensive doctrine; the new "neomercantilist" theories were evolved by politicians and businessmen rather than academic economists. Theory followed the fact of new colonies and had to justify them. As propounded and widely disseminated by such statesmen as Jules Ferry of France and Joseph Chamberlain of Britain, the new argument was that tropical colonies were essential as markets (*débouchés*) for the surplus products of European industry as it expanded under the influence of renewed domestic protectionism—necessary safety valves for industrial capitalism—without which Europe faced social chaos and perhaps revolution. As a secondary point it was held that industrial states needed guaranteed sources of cheap industrial raw materials and food and that colonies ensured that any one country could not be made to pay monopoly prices for them. In addition, some argued that Europe had surplus capital that was best invested in tropical plantations, mines, and communications. Thus, in general, such colonies

provided the solution to most of the economic and social problems of industrial Europe under conditions of protectionism.

Twentieth-century criticism.   By the early twentieth century these arguments were widely accepted, even to the extent that many believed tropical colonies actually did provide these projected advantages and that they had been deliberately acquired for these functions. Seldom were any of these assumptions true: the irony was that critics of the new colonization accepted them and founded their new anticolonialist arguments on these alleged facts. Critics had been vocal throughout the later nineteenth century, mostly on financial or humanitarian grounds. After about 1900 they divided into two groups: those who believed the profits of tropical empire to be real but deplored them; and those who believed the rewards to be illusory. The first school was led by European Marxists who regarded the export of capital to the tropics as evidence that Europe was entering a new phase of "monopoly capitalism" when it was no longer profitable to invest in protected domestic markets because they were dominated by a few great trusts. Europe had to export surplus capital or allow capitalism itself to stagnate. Ultimately the nations would compete for the limited supply of colonies, and the resulting wars for imperial redivision would inaugurate the socialist revolution and the end of capitalism. This was the basic argument propounded by V. I. Lenin in his influential pamphlet *Imperialism, the Highest Stage of Capitalism* (1916). Others, like Rosa Luxemburg, produced variants on the same theme.

The rival school of critics was led by J. A. Hobson, whose *Imperialism: A Study* (1902) stated the case against the profitability of tropical colonization. Hobson accepted the propagandists' argument that colonies were the product of surplus capital seeking fields for investment but held that this surplus existed only because the social and economic systems of Europe denied the masses sufficient consumer capacity to justify increased investment in home industry. Hobson was wrong in thinking that the bulk of the exported capital had gone to the new dependencies: in fact most was going to the old settlement colonies, India and the independent American countries. But he rightly pointed out that most of the new colonies were too poor to provide valuable markets for manufactured exports and held that the cost of defense and administration, coupled with the moral degradation resulting from most of Europe's activities in Africa and Asia, outweighed any advantages such colonies might provide. His conclusion was that Europe's best interest was to invest at home; to stick to free trade; and to place undeveloped tropical territories, whose raw materials were needed by the West, under international supervision. He thus brought the debate over colonization back to the position taken by Adam Smith. During the remaining half century of European colonialism no one satisfactorily demonstrated that tropical empire was either necessary or profitable to the Western powers.

The "practice" of colonialism. The practice of colonialism (taking this to mean the devices actually employed to provide economic advantages to the owners of colonial dependencies) can be described as having evolved through three stages of unequal length: from the foundation of the first colonies to the 1830s; from that time to near the end of the century; and from about 1890 to the period of decolonization after 1945. In each period imperial arrangements closely followed contemporary practices in the parent states and owed very little to theory.

Before 1830: the mercantilist period. During the first period—the era of mercantilism—the pattern was set by Spain and Portugal as the pioneers of overseas colonization. They in turn instinctively applied the protectionist and monopolistic practices current in sixteenth-century Europe to their new possessions. Later-starting imperial states adopted most, though not all, of these techniques, so that by the later seventeenth century there was a "system" largely common to all empires, varying mainly according to whether colonies were in America or the East. There were practices common to all: foreign ships were entirely excluded from colonial ports; virtually all colonial exports and imports were routed through the ports of the metropolis; and specified manufactures or processing of raw materials were banned in the dependencies. Spain and Portugal went further than others by insisting, until late in the eighteenth century, that American trade should be carried only in annual convoys and be restricted to a single metropolitan port. Spain also banned most intercolonial trade in America and restricted the Pacific trade from Mexico to the Philippines. By these means it was hoped that each metropolis would have a monopoly of colonial bullion and raw materials and a guaranteed colonial market for manufactures; that metropolitan merchants would be ensured a middleman profit on trade passing through the parent state; and that the colonies would be preserved as primary producers, ideal markets for industrial Europe. In addition, production of the most wanted colonial products was encouraged by complex systems of bounties and preferential tariffs in the home markets. Trade with Africa and the East was dealt with rather differently. Until after 1640 Portugal excluded even her own nationals from dealing in the more valuable Eastern commodities, leaving a monopoly to the crown. England, France, and Holland also imposed monopolies on their Eastern trade but granted them to privileged chartered companies with full administrative powers.

The main imperial "profit" from these mercantilist practices arose from commercial monopoly. This is practically impossible to estimate quantitatively but almost certainly existed, at least to the extent that colonists had to pay a higher price for their imports and received lower returns for their exports than under a free trading system. This metropolitan profit varied inversely with the economic capacity of the parent state, favoring economically uncompetitive countries like Spain, who would otherwise have had little share in the trade of their own colonies, more than a country like Britain, which, by the eighteenth century, possessed the greater economic potential. For Britain it has been estimated that in 1773 the gross "profit" of mercantile controls in North America lay between $2.5 and $7 million, ignoring the ancillary costs involved in empire. But in addition to such commercial profits, Spain and Portugal made substantial fiscal profits from their American colonies by transferring surplus revenue to the metropolitan exchequer. Portugal was receiving thereby some £900,000 annually in the mid-eighteenth century. No other colonial power used this device. The French subsidized their colonies. The British conceded the principle of fiscal autonomy until after 1763 and then attempted to impose taxes on the colonies, not to make a profit but to offset the cost of colonial defense and administration. This attempt failed, although it had considerable importance in the course of events leading to American independence.

Nineteenth-century trend to free trade. The first and longest era of colonialism ended effectively during the first half of the nineteenth century—more because the colonies that had made it meaningful were now independent than because colonial theory had changed. The British, who possessed the only large empire, gradually adopted free-trade practices at home and extended them to the colonies. British colonies were virtually open to the world by 1830 and by 1860 the last vestiges of shipping controls and preferences on colonial products had gone. Other colonial powers slowly followed suit. The Dutch threw open their colonial trade after 1815 but created a special monopoly of the carriage and sale of certain commodities that the Batavian government collected as part of the "culture system" from 1830 to the 1870s. France preserved the colonial shipping monopoly together with preferences and certain exclusive regulations until the 1860s but had abolished them by 1870. Spain and Portugal never completely removed mercantile controls but largely liberalized them for their few dependencies. By 1870 the era of mercantilism seemed over, in that no imperial power then obtained economic advantages from its dependencies that were not available to the world.

Resurgence of limited protectionism. The period of colonial free trade was very short-lived. The revival of protectionism in most parts of Europe in the last quarter of the century led naturally to its extension to the new tropical empires. France adopted a strongly protectionist domestic tariff in 1892 and extended it to all her colonies except West Africa, the Congo, and the Pacific, which had to have separate tariff systems because of international treaties or local economic conditions. Even so all colonies gave and received preferences. The Russians enclosed their new possessions in central Asia and the Far East within their metropolitan tariffs and gave bounties and preferences on selected colonial products. The United States incorporated most new dependencies in the Caribbean and Pacific within the metropolitan tariff, leaving only the Panama canal zone and Samoa open to international trade on the open-door principle. Portugal, Spain, and Italy either assimilated their colonies to the metropolis or imposed preferences. But not all states reverted to mercantile concepts. The Dutch abolished their semimonopoly of Indonesia in the 1870s and maintained an open door, although using quotas on imports in the 1930s. Germany before 1914 and Belgium also preserved the open door with moderate tariffs in their colonies. Britain resisted demands from pressure groups at home and from some settlement colonies and did not drop free trade until 1932, though the self-governing colonies indulged in protection and, after 1899, gave Britain limited preferences. Some preferences were given to colonial products in the British market during and after World War I. Britain reverted to protection in 1932, and the Ottawa agreements of that year led to a preferential system throughout the empire, coupled with quotas on some products and financial control by means of the sterling area.

During the last phase of European colonialism, therefore, most colonial powers adopted some form of preferential system: hence the term "neomercantilist" to describe the new pattern. Yet it never approximated in its severity the mercantilism of the first period. No power excluded foreign ships or goods from its colonies, forced colonial trade to pass through metropolitan ports, forbade colonial manufactures that might compete with its own or, with the sole exception of Holland between 1830 and 1877, transferred colonial revenues to the metropolitan treasury.

Significance of colonial trade. Moreover, few colonial powers obtained anything approaching a monopoly of the overseas trade of their dependencies or found their chief market or source of imports in their empires. Russia and the United States took most of the exports and supplied most of the imports of their possessions; but for both colonial trade was of marginal importance. Britain's share in her empire's overseas trade declined steadily from about 49 per cent in the decade after 1854 to 35 per cent in 1929–1933, rising only slightly thereafter as a result of imperial preferences. But the colonies' share in British total overseas trade rose from about 28 per cent in the 1850s to 51 per cent between 1950 and 1954. France continued to furnish a high proportion of her colonies' imports—always more than half (except during the world wars)—but the proportion of colonial exports to France declined fairly steadily. On the other hand the colonies' share of France's total overseas trade was always relatively small: about 10 per cent until 1914, then rising to 28 per cent in 1934. Belgian territories in central Africa took 51 per cent of their imports from Belgium in 1928 and 46 per cent in 1938. They sent 70.6 per cent of their exports in 1928 and 80.7 per cent in 1938 to Belgium. But the Congo played a very small part in Belgian overseas trade, supplying 2.4 per cent and 6.6 per cent of Belgian imports in 1928 and 1938 respectively and taking less than 2 per cent of Belgian exports in each year. The trade of the Netherlands Indies was not monopolized by Holland and played a minor part in Dutch overseas trade. In 1928 only 5.3 per cent of Dutch imports came from Indonesia, 7.2 per cent in 1938. In the former year 8.9 per cent of Dutch exports went to Indonesia and 9.5 per cent in 1938. Indonesian exports to Holland declined from 78.3 per cent in 1850 (during the period of the "culture system") to 15.3 per cent in 1930; and Indonesian imports from Holland fell from 41.9 per cent to 16.8 per cent in the same period.

Although not comprehensive, these figures point to a firm conclusion about modern colonialism on its commercial side. Most colonial powers took a large proportion of the overseas trade of their colonies; but with the sole exception of Britain, whose empire was far larger and provided uniquely favorable markets and varied sources of raw materials, the colonies were of small importance to the world trade of their owners. Artificial factors, such as tariffs, preferences, and currency systems, probably affected the pattern of colonial trade to some extent, but never as much as mercantile controls had done before 1830. Since, moreover, there was never a total ban on foreign trade or shipping, and therefore no monopoly, it cannot be said that "neomercantilism" exploited dependencies; in fact, bounties, preferences, and quotas on colonial products probably favored the colonial producer more than colonial tariffs helped the metropolitan producer. The old *pacte colonial* was indeed revived, but it was no longer exclusive and was reasonably two-sided in its benefits.

Advantage of colonial investments.   There remains the question of metropolitan advantage from capital investment in the colonies. Did political controls, especially of non-European labor, create especially favorable conditions for European capital in the dependencies, providing a "super-profit" for European "finance-capitalists"? The question is too complex to unravel briefly; but two points are reasonably certain. First, the great bulk of European investment in colonies was in government bonds or in fixed interest debentures in public utility companies. On both, the interest paid was only very slightly higher than that from comparable stocks in Europe or America, so that colonies were not forced to provide artificially high returns to metropolitan investors. Second, the return on some risk stocks—equities—was often high, and probably higher than could be obtained at most times on industrial equities in Europe or the United States. But this was due less to the fact of colonial subordination than to the intense world demand for certain products possessed by some tropical colonies, for example, metals and rubber; and the return on capital invested in such ventures was not evidently different from that invested in independent countries of similar economic type that lacked the capacity to develop their own natural endowments, notably those in the Middle East and Latin America. In short, the special profitability of capital investment attracted to the tropical colonies reflected the inherent advantages of the strong world demand at particular times for their particular types of product, the scarcity of capital there, and the strong bargaining position of Western countries when dealing with politically or economically weak societies. Colonial investments did not depend on formal imperial control to provide excess profits.

This fact is the key to understanding the economic relations between the industrialized Western powers and the new ex-colonial countries in the period after decolonization in the 1960s. The phenomenon denounced by Marxists and by nationalists in the new states as "neocolonialism" was the continued economic dependence of the ex-colonies on their previous masters or on other Western powers. This could take the form of special commercial relations, such as exist between France and several ex-dependencies in west Africa and elsewhere; between Britain and many members of the sterling area; and between the United States and the Philippines or Puerto Rico. Alternatively, "neocolonialism" might consist in the "exploitation" of these "developing" societies through their reliance on foreign capital, which tends to place segments of their economies under the control of foreign companies or governments. In either case "neocolonialism" implies that the advanced countries are continuing to interfere in the economic life of onetime colonies as if they had not been liberated.

It remains debatable how much truth there is in these allegations; but in fact "neocolonialism" is as imprecise a concept as colonialism. Facts are in any case more important than accusations. Most developing countries, like most earlier colonies, are primary economies, and depend heavily on more advanced states for markets, imported manufactures, capital, technical skills, and opportunities to train their own nationals. If they prefer to avoid contacts of these kinds in order to retain their entire freedom of action, the choice is now open to them, strengthened by the possibility of obtaining the same amenities from Russia or China as "non-imperialist" states. In practice, however, the balance of advantage almost certainly lies with the receiving countries. In the 1960s they have been given much capital in the form of "aid"—i.e., grants or capital on noncommercial terms—and many have benefited substantially from preferential markets for their products in France, the Common Market, Britain, or the United States. [*See* FOREIGN AID, *article on* ECONOMIC ASPECTS; INTERNATIONAL INTEGRATION, *article on* ECONOMIC UNIONS; INTERNATIONAL TRADE CONTROLS, *article on* TARIFFS AND PROTECTIONISM.] If "neocolonialism" exists, it is the inevitable product of an inherent imbalance between the advanced and the developing economies, irrespective of the political factors involved. This one-sided relationship will disappear only when the new states reach the position already achieved by Japan and become as powerful economically as the ex-colonial powers on whom they continue to depend. Evidence provided by eastern

Europe after 1945 does not suggest that the economic status of nominally independent countries associated with socialist Russia differs substantially from that alleged to exist between the ex-colonial territories of Africa and the East with their one-time masters.

D. K. FIELDHOUSE

BIBLIOGRAPHY

BODELSEN, CARL A. G. (1924) 1960 *Studies in Mid-Victorian Imperialism.* 2d ed. London: Heinemann.

BROWN, MICHAEL B. 1963 *After Imperialism.* London: Heinemann.

CAIRNCROSS, ALEXANDER K. 1953 *Home and Foreign Investment, 1870–1913: Studies in Capital Accumulation.* Cambridge Univ. Press.

The Cambridge History of the British Empire. Edited by J. Holland Rose. 8 vols. (1929–1959) 1963 Cambridge Univ. Press.

CLARK, GROVER 1936 *The Balance Sheets of Imperialism: Facts and Figures on Colonies.* New York: Columbia Univ. Press.

COLE, CHARLES W. (1939) 1964 *Colbert and a Century of French Mercantilism.* Hamden, Conn.: Shoe String Press.

DESCHAMPS, LÉON 1891 *Histoire de la question coloniale en France.* Paris: Plon.

EMERSON, RUPERT 1960 *From Empire to Nation: The Rise to Self-assertion of Asian and African Peoples.* Cambridge, Mass.: Harvard Univ. Press. → A paperback edition was published in 1962 by Beacon.

FURNIVALL, JOHN S. (1939) 1944 *Netherlands India: A Study of Plural Economy.* Cambridge Univ. Press.

HANCOCK, WILLIAM K. 1950 *Wealth of Colonies.* Cambridge Univ. Press.

HECKSCHER, ELI F. (1931) 1955 *Mercantilism.* 2 vols. Rev. ed. London: Allen & Unwin; New York: Macmillan. → First published in Swedish.

HOBSON, JOHN A. (1902) 1948 *Imperialism: A Study.* 3d ed. London: Allen & Unwin.

KNORR, KLAUS E. (1944) 1963 *British Colonial Theories: 1570–1850.* Toronto Univ. Press.

KOEBNER, RICHARD; and SCHMIDT, HELMUT D. 1964 *Imperialism: The Story and Significance of a Political World, 1840–1960.* Cambridge Univ. Press.

KOLARZ, WALTER (1952) 1955 *Russia and Her Colonies.* New York: Praeger.

LANNOY, CHARLES DE; and LINDEN, HERMAN V. 1907–1921 *Histoire de l'expansion coloniale des peuples européens.* 3 vols. Brussels: Lamertin. → Volume 1: *Portugal et Espagne.* Volume 2: *Néerlande et Danemark.* Volume 3: *Suède.*

LENIN, VLADIMIR I. (1916) 1964 *Imperialism, the Highest Stage of Capitalism: A Popular Outline.* Volume 22, pages 185–304 in Vladimir I. Lenin, *Collected Works.* 4th ed. Moscow: Progress.

MYINT, HLA 1964 *The Economies of the Developing Countries.* London: Hutchinson.

PARRY, JOHN H. 1940 *The Spanish Theory of Empire in the Sixteenth Century.* Cambridge Univ. Press.

PARRY, JOHN H. 1963 *The Age of Reconnaissance.* Cleveland: World.

ROBERTS, STEPHEN H. (1929) 1963 *History of French Colonial Policy: 1870–1925.* Hamden, Conn.: Shoe String Press.

SCHUYLER, ROBERT L. 1945 *The Fall of the Old Colonial System: A Study in British Free Trade, 1770–1870.* New York: Oxford Univ. Press.

SEMMEL, BERNARD 1960 *Imperialism and Social Reform: English Social–Imperial Thought, 1895–1914.* Cambridge, Mass.: Harvard Univ. Press.

SMITH, ADAM (1776) 1952 *An Inquiry Into the Nature and Causes of the Wealth of Nations.* Chicago: Encyclopaedia Britannica. → A two-volume paperback edition was published in 1963 by Irwin.

SOUTHWORTH, CONSTANT 1931 *The French Colonial Venture.* London: King.

THORNTON, ARCHIBALD P. 1959 *The Imperial Idea and Its Enemies: A Study in British Power.* New York: St. Martins.

TOWNSEND, MARY E. 1930 *The Rise and Fall of Germany's Colonial Empire: 1884–1918.* New York: Macmillan.

VIEKKE, BERNARDUS H. M. (1943) 1960 *Nusantara: A History of Indonesia.* Rev. ed. Chicago: Quadrangle Books.

WINCH, DONALD N. 1965 *Classical Political Economy and Colonies.* London: Bell; Cambridge, Mass.: Harvard Univ. Press.

COLOR VISION
See under VISION.

COMBINATIONS AND PERMUTATIONS
See PROBABILITY, *article on* FORMAL PROBABILITY.

COMMISSIONS, GOVERNMENT

The term "commission" covers several usages: (1) the document, signed and sealed, that evidences an official appointment, such as a captain's commission; (2) the term of office of an appointee, as in the phrase appended to a notary's acknowledgment, "My commission expires on . . . (date)"; (3) the title of the heads of various departments or divisions of national, state, or municipal governments, for example, commissioner of patents or county commissioner; (4) the name of an official agency or institution headed by a collegial body of commissioners. This article is confined to the last of these usages, excluding unofficial bodies (often self-constituted) that call themselves commissions and that may indeed perform some more or less analogous functions in the larger political system of society. Even so understood, the terminology is arbitrary: an agency called a commission may be otherwise indistinguishable from something elsewhere called a board, a council, a committee, a tribunal, or a court. Nuances of emphasis that in certain cases would support distinctions between these terms—resting on the source of the powers (president's commission), the larger or higher body from which the membership is drawn (judicial committee of the privy council), or the nature of the mandate given (board of examiners)—break down in the indiscriminate usage the words have received. The distinction attempted in the *Encyclopaedia of the Social Sciences* (1930–1935), between commissions as regulatory bodies (Dickinson 1931) and boards as administrative (Fairlie 1930) or advisory (Macmahon 1930), has not caught on. The one common feature of all such bodies that is pertinent here is the plural headship of the institution, in contrast with agencies having a single chief. This feature is usually, if not inevitably, accompanied by a certain degree of autonomy within the surrounding governmental structure.

Government commissions, formally constituted, appear to be rare among the institutions of relatively primitive societies. But they occur frequently in the governments of advanced countries, whether the regimes are federal or unitary, presidential or parliamentary, one-, two-, or multiparty, or democratic in the Eastern or the Western sense. In Britain, official bodies formally commissioned to carry out various governmental tasks, and empowered in so doing to adjudge rights and impose penalties, date back at least to the time of Henry VIII. During the sixteenth and seventeenth centuries, some of these (for example, the Court of High Commission) were seen as encroachments on the common law courts and gave "government by commission" a bad name as a threat to liberties —a reputation that lingered there in conservative legal quarters as late as Lord Hewart's attack on administrative justice in *The New Despotism* (1929) and in the United States in the American Bar Association's anti-New Deal campaign that culminated in the Administrative Procedure Act of 1946. Meanwhile, during the nineteenth century in Britain, royal commissions of inquiry became favored instruments leading to major advances in social legislation, such as the Factory Acts. In the United States, administrative and regulatory commissions were created sporadically in state and local governments as early as the 1830s as a means of giving added competence, vigor, or impartiality to various governmental functions. They multiplied in number during the post-Civil War decades and gained in prestige when Congress copied the model in establishing the Interstate Commerce Commission in 1887. After Galveston, Texas, experimented with it in 1901, the "commission plan" enjoyed wide popularity as a model form of municipal government. Reliance on commissions became an article of the Progressive faith.

On the Continent, commissions were formed around the monarchical establishments of the leading European powers in the sixteenth and seventeenth centuries. Peter the Great introduced them into Russia, and the Soviet Union employs them in its budgeting and planning processes.

Types and functions of commissions

Two preliminary distinctions, if not too sharply drawn, are useful in sorting out types of commissions and the various functions they may perform. One is temporal, between bodies convened *ad hoc* to deal with a specific situation and those permanently established to handle a class of business arising regularly or intermittently. Thus, a boundary commission expires when its determination has been made; a truce commission is finished when a treaty of peace has been concluded; a claims commission is temporary if the claims it is set up to hear relate to a single episode, like the Philippines War Damage Commission, and permanent if the claims are of a class that will recur indefinitely. Very different considerations may enter into the appointments made to temporary commissions from those applicable to replacements in an ongoing body. For the same reason, structure, powers, and procedure may also vary considerably.

The second kind of distinction turns on the overt purposes commissions may be established to serve: (1) an arbitral commission to reach a decision binding on the parties to a dispute, such as the Electoral Commission that settled the outcome of the Hayes–Tilden election in 1876; (2) a commission of inquiry to investigate, report findings, and perhaps pass judgment on the responsibility of individuals for an event—often a disaster or a scandal—that has transpired, such as the Warren Commission following the assassination of President Kennedy in 1963; (3) a ceremonial commission to mark an occasion of moment, such as the George Washington Bicentennial Commission, in 1932; (4) a study commission to make plans or recommendations for future public policy, such as the two Hoover Commissions on Organization of the Executive Branch of the Government, in 1949 and 1955; (5) an operating commission to conduct a branch of public enterprise, such as the Atomic Energy Commission, or to administer a subsidy system, such as the Federal Maritime Commission; (6) an advisory commission to maintain liaison between a governmental agency and some of its clientele publics, such as the Advisory Commission on Intergovernmental Relations; (7) a regulatory commission to supervise some field of public or private activity, such as the Civil Service Commission or the Federal Communications Commission. These categories are suggestive rather than exhaustive. Clearly, most of the tasks they comprise could be—and in apparently similar circumstances often are—performed by single-headed agencies or by a single official with a suitable staff. A single judge can arbitrate a dispute or conduct an inquiry, as Justice Spence of the Supreme Court of Canada did in 1966 into the sex-and-security scandal charges brought by the Liberal government against members of the previous Diefenbaker government. A cabinet minister can organize a study, recommend policies, oversee a departmental operation, and regulate an industry: the secretary of the treasury, for example, does all these things every year.

To understand the prevalence of commissions, therefore, it is helpful to employ a third sort of classification that looks at their latent functions and, hence, the ulterior purposes they may serve. For example, a collegial body may lend added dignity, authority, or apparent impartiality to official action and thus tend to legitimize both the action itself and the regime that established the commission. A hard decision from such a source may be easier for its subject to accept, and in that case the beneficial effects accrue to all concerned. Similarly, the award of a tribunal or a rule adopted by a commission—the product of deliberation—may be more acceptable than the decree of a single official that smacks of whim or patronage. The effect of a united front may indeed be deemed so important as to warrant a caucus procedure, binding all the members of a commission to give an outward expression of unanimity to the decision of a majority. Alternatively, a commission that announces divided decisions, and publishes majority and dissenting opinions, may nevertheless legitimize its work by its evident reliance on rationality to justify its actions.

Again, when an unpleasant duty is to be done, for which no one involved wants personal responsibility, the task may be given to a commission. To take an extreme example: when a man is sentenced to be shot, the means usually used is a firing squad and not a single executioner so that no one may know whose bullet did the deed. More generally, a collegial body, meeting *in camera* and acting collectively and impersonally, shields the responsibility of the members in anonymity. Here the benefits accrue to the members rather than to the regime.

A commission is indispensable if its chief function is representational, to assure a voice in deliberations to each of several parties with diverse interests. International bodies, domestic intergov-

ernmental agencies (established, for example, under an interstate compact), and tripartite tribunals to handle labor–management disputes fall into this category. Ex officio memberships, as on an interagency commission, are a mark of the representational function.

Commissions have other latent functions, notably, bargaining, public education, delay, patronage, appeasement, frustration, and rubber-stamping. A commission composed of representatives of contending economic, sectional, or ethnic interests, with or without additional members as "impartial" mediators or referees, may provide the means of working out internally the compromises essential in reaching a decision acceptable to all the interests. An interdepartmental or intergovernmental commission, or a mixed commission of officials and private parties, may function similarly as a forum for bargaining. In all these situations, successful bargaining contains conflicts that otherwise would result in stalemate or would spill over into a wider political arena. Where acquiescence in a decision rests basically on agreement between recognized representatives, for instance, in settling strikes, fixing prices, or allocating markets, the bargaining function reinforces the legitimacy of the commission as an institution.

A further constructive function is educational. Commission studies, reports, and recommendations, clarifying issues and marshalling evidence, are important elements in the political process of building public support for many policy changes. In Britain this historic role of royal commissions and of parliamentary select committees has lately been more often performed by departmentally appointed committees. In the United States it is a role of temporary commissions, regulatory commissions, and congressional committees.

The delaying function scarcely needs elaboration. Unsuccessful bargaining leads to a deadlock that it may be inconvenient to acknowledge. Indecision in the face of uncertainties over the costs and benefits of alternative policies may be equally awkward to confess. Controversies that cut across party lines endanger the stability of coalitions and jeopardize other objectives. So when an intractable problem evidently admits of no agreed or clear solution at present, tacit or explicit agreement may nevertheless (or therefore) be reached that the issue need not be settled now. Creating a study commission to report later may be a face-saving form of inaction that postpones the timetable for decision. The Wickersham Commission on Law Enforcement, established during the Hoover administration to temporize with the prohibition issue, was a classic instance. The tactics of delay may boomerang, of course, as they did in that case.

The patronage function is equally plain. Multimember commissions afford a multiplicity of appointments. Some of these, because of their prominence or the policy stakes that hang on them, will be filled according to tests of merit and fitness. But the more numerous (and hence obscure) the places or the more honorific the assigned duties, the more likely it is that they will be used to satisfy patronage claims. It would be a mistake to suppose that all the patronage accrues necessarily to the formal appointing authority. Commission appointments may reflect demands, or serve to co-opt support, from quarters within the political system that are apparently unrelated to a commission's overt scope of activities. In the United States, for instance, ex-congressmen frequently find shelter in federal commissions.

Finally, a commission may serve to pacify some clamorous group for whom nothing more will actually be done: a study project will keep the members occupied and symbolize their concerns. This, as it turned out, proved to be the main function of the Kestnbaum Commission on Intergovernmental Relations in 1954–1955, some of whose sponsors and members appeared to desire a return to the Articles of Confederation. A policy proposal may also be given to a study commission hostile to its main thrust as a means of killing it or to a tame group for a foreordained approval.

The study of commissions

The universe of commissions, doing business under that name or another, is too heterogeneous for systematic study as a single category, apart from the initial difficulties of definition and collection in compiling an inventory. Research in the field, accordingly, has generally taken one or another of at least three broad paths, not altogether mutually exclusive: historical, topical, and comparative, all dealing with selected fragments.

Case studies have dealt with commissions individually, or in groups, or with significant episodes in the life of single agencies. Their emphasis may be on the agency as an institution or, more broadly, on policy development in its field. Such studies range in bulk from Sharfman's bland four-volume account, *The Interstate Commerce Commission* (1931–1937)—which, though the work of an economist, is devoid of economic analysis—to articles and pamphlets, for example, the Inter-university Case Program's publication, *The Public Advisory*

Board and the Tariff Study (1956). Well-done case studies have the merits of realism and depth and the disadvantages of using history as a basis for theoretical generalizations. Henderson's (1924) still-classic examination of the disillusioning first decade of the Federal Trade Commission's experience illustrates the value of this type of work.

Topical studies in Britain and the United States during the 1920s and 1930s were dominated by the concerns of public law—the scope of delegated powers of commissions in dealing with individuals and business firms and the extent of judicial review of administrative decisions. These concerns entailed a concentration on regulatory authorities and made more or less irrelevant the question of single-headed or multimember agencies. In Britain the *Report of the Committee on Ministers' Powers* of 1932 defended existing trends toward delegation of power against Lord Hewart's attack. In the United States the controversy lasted longer and produced a voluminous legal literature on evolving judicial doctrines of due process and on the combinations of powers that make a regulatory agency at once prosecutor-and-judge and legislator-and-judge.

The U.S. Attorney General's Committee on Administrative Procedure, headed by Dean Acheson and supported by staff work under the direction of Walter Gellhorn, issued a report (1941) that was a landmark: it covered all federal agencies having regulatory powers and examined in detail the procedures each employed in exercising them —thereby getting into matters of internal organization and permitting systematic comparisons. World War II postponed action on the report, while it multiplied the number of regulatory agencies and the activities to be regulated. The Administrative Procedure Act of 1946 effected a compromise of the contending political forces. Treating rule-making and adjudicatory powers separately, it prescribed procedural safeguards for each but in language sufficiently general and with saving clauses sufficiently broad as not to prevent any substantive action previously authorized. Perhaps its most notable feature was the requirement, in formal adjudication, of the use of independent hearing examiners. Its symbolic success is attested by the fact that the whole topic has ever since remained largely in the province of specialists in administrative law, while the practice of regulation employs more lawyers and more red tape.

The related topic of investigatory powers, involving the compulsory appearance of witnesses and the production of records and reports, is in Britain mainly an aspect of administrative or ministerial action, since royal commissions ordinarily are limited to voluntary testimony and the courts are bound by statutory delegations. In the United States this topic, important as it is in the work of regulatory and enforcement agencies, including commissions, has aroused widespread political and scholarly interest chiefly in connection with congressional investigating committees, which are beyond the scope of this article. [*See* LEGISLATION, *article on* LEGISLATURES.]

The report of the U.S. President's Committee on Administrative Management (1937), although its attack on the "headless fourth branch" proved abortive, ushered in a fresh range of more rewarding issues for study: the internal structure and workings of commissions; and the relations of commissions, and in particular the ten principal regulatory commissions, to the president, to the Congress and its committees, to cognate executive departments, and to organized clientele groups. The U.S. Supreme Court's decision in *Humphrey's Executor* v. *United States*, 295 U.S. 602 (1935), sustaining a statutory limit on the president's power to remove a member of the Federal Trade Commission, had already raised the issue of commission independence, but the focus of research thereafter shifted to, and has remained on, commission behavior rather than judicial doctrine about the separation of powers. Once the rule-making, adjudicatory, and enforcement powers of the commissions were held constitutionally valid, it was futile to argue whether these agencies were *in* the executive branch or somewhere else.

Independence has several facets. Presidents rarely attempt to influence the outcome of particular commission decisions; this would seem improper when private rights are being adjudicated. But presidents freely use their appointing power to bring about changes in prevailing commission viewpoints. The scope for such changes depends on the frequency of vacancies, which varies considerably even though the terms of office are staggered and outrun the president's own. The practice of reappointing incumbents is equally uncertain; President Eisenhower in his first term reappointed none. The Board of Governors of the Federal Reserve System had only 3 chairmen in the 30 years following its reorganization in 1935; and Chairman William M. Martin, a Truman appointee, survived into the Johnson administration. The Federal Trade Commission, by contrast, had 41 different chairmen in the first 50 years of its existence; only 4 lasted as long as 2 years.

The other side of the coin of independence is political isolation. Without administration support it is seldom possible for a commission to get needed changes in its organic statute or larger appropriations. It is difficult also to arrange top-level interagency coordinating mechanisms for policy purposes across a broad economic front, such as transportation, water resources, or finance, when an independent commission is one of the agencies with jurisdiction in the premises. This was less of a problem in the pre-World War II days, when the segments of the economy subject to commission regulation seemed relatively self-contained.

One ameliorating step followed a recommendation of the first Hoover Commission and was justified at the time chiefly on grounds of administrative efficiency. A series of reorganization plans in the 1940s and 1950s, affecting all the commissions except the ICC and the Federal Reserve System (where practice already conformed), concentrated in the chairman's office authority over all administrative affairs of a commission and authorized the president to designate the chairman. This is a milder form of a remedy previously urged and partially applied in the fields of shipping and civil aeronautics: segregating, as far as practicable, the adjudicatory aspects of a commission's job from its other functions, namely, promotion, subsidy, and operations, and assigning a regular executive department to handle the operations.

A special case is the Civil Service Commission, which combines an immense administrative and record-keeping task with a reviewing function in connection with personnel grievances. Its clientele consists of federal civilian employees and their unions. Since the Hoover Commission's reports it has moved from a tradition of regulation to a position as champion of employee interests, while its chairman, wearing a second hat, has been drawn into the the White House staff as the president's adviser on personnel matters. Here the trend toward increasing judicialization, so characteristic of many regulatory commissions, has been reversed.

Commission relations with clientele interests raise the issue of independence in another aspect, relevant to both regulatory and advisory bodies. A degree of intimacy breeds expertise and ease of communication on the part of the commission and confidence and voluntary compliance on the part of the clientele. Carried too far, it jeopardizes a commission's reputation for impartiality and invites conflicts of interest, if not outright corruption. Short of that, it fosters a parochial view that excludes interests which are affected but not represented in the immediate arena, as when banks and bank supervisors stand together against, say, savings and loan associations. How much intimacy is enough? In the Progressive era, when the commission movement arose, the expressed ideal was an impartiality that forbade all but formal and public contacts. A later and more realistic judgment would usually tolerate or welcome considerably closer relationships. Where the line is to be drawn depends importantly upon the degree to which a commission is engaged in adjudication or must rely on persuasion to accomplish its tasks. But the disillusioned note the tendency of intimacy to grow as time passes. This is the basis for Bernstein's probably oversimplified concept (1955) of a "life-cycle of regulatory commissions," according to which the missionary zeal that attends the birth of a commission is dissipated as the clientele interests infiltrate their supposed governor and ultimately make it their captive. [*See* LOBBYING.]

One other theoretical formulation may prove fruitful in further research on the politics of economic policy, including the policies entrusted to commissions. This is Lowi's three-way categorization (1964) of domestic economic policies as either "distributive" (for example, the disposal of the public domain), or "regulatory," or "redistributive" (for example, a graduated income tax), and his association of each of these categories with its characteristic type of politics—the politics of patronage, the politics of interest-group conflict, and the politics of class conflict. It may be that the categories are not so distinct as he supposes, but they are suggestive of ways of ordering more precise insights into the workings of commissions as well as of other governmental agencies.

Finally, a word is in order about the comparative approach to the study of commissions. It is one thing —and a thing often done—to collect and describe seriatim a number of instances more or less similar. It is something else again to devise analytical categories that will yield illuminating comparisons across a broad array of cases. Wheare's revealing study (1955) of committees in British government is a systematic and methodologically sophisticated effort of this sort. It identifies seven "characters" —chairman, secretary, official, expert, layman, party member, and interested party—and examines each in the context of six types of committees— committees to advise, to inquire, to negotiate, to legislate, to administer, and to scrutinize and control. Some of his committees are commissions, and his categories are applicable generally.

HARVEY C. MANSFIELD

[*See also* ADMINISTRATION; ADMINISTRATIVE LAW; PRESIDENTIAL GOVERNMENT.]

BIBLIOGRAPHY

BERNSTEIN, MARVER H. 1955 *Regulating Business by Independent Commission.* Princeton Univ. Press.

CLOKIE, HUGH McD.; and ROBINSON, J. WILLIAM 1937 *Royal Commissions of Inquiry: The Significance of Investigations in British Politics.* Stanford Univ. Press.

CUSHMAN, ROBERT E. 1941 *The Independent Regulatory Commissions.* New York: Oxford Univ. Press.

DICKINSON, JOHN 1931 Commissions. Volume 4, pages 36–40 in *Encyclopaedia of the Social Sciences.* New York: Macmillan.

FAIRLIE, JOHN A. 1930 Boards, Administrative. Volume 2, pages 607–609 in *Encyclopaedia of the Social Sciences.* New York: Macmillan.

FESLER, JAMES W. 1942 *The Independence of State Regulatory Agencies.* Chicago: Public Administration Service.

FRANKFURTER, FELIX (1930) 1964 *The Public and Its Government.* Boston: Beacon.

GREAT BRITAIN, COMMITTEE ON MINISTERS' POWERS 1932 *Report.* Papers by Command, Cmd. 4060. London: H.M. Stationery Office.

HANSER, CHARLES J. 1965 *Guide to Decision: The Royal Commission.* Totowa, N.J.: Bedminster Press.

HENDERSON, GERARD C. (1924) 1925 *The Federal Trade Commission: A Study in Administrative Law and Procedure.* New Haven: Yale Univ. Press.

HERRING, E. PENDLETON 1936a *Federal Commissioners: A Study of Their Careers and Qualifications.* Cambridge, Mass.: Harvard Univ. Press.

HERRING, E. PENDLETON 1936b *Public Administration and the Public Interest.* New York: McGraw-Hill.

HEWART, GORDON 1929 *The New Despotism.* New York: Cosmopolitan.

HYNEMAN, CHARLES S. 1950 *Bureaucracy in a Democracy.* New York: Harper. → See especially Chapters 21–24.

INTER-UNIVERSITY CASE PROGRAM 1956 *The Public Advisory Board and the Tariff Study,* by David S. Brown. ICP Case Series, No. 30. University: Univ. of Alabama Press.

LANDIS, JAMES M. 1938 *The Administrative Process.* New Haven: Yale Univ. Press.

LIEBER, FRANCIS (1853) 1874 *On Civil Liberty and Self-government.* 3d ed., rev. Philadelphia: Lippincott.

LOWI, THEODORE J. 1964 American Business, Public Policy, Case-studies, and Political Theory. *World Politics* 16:677–715.

MACMAHON, ARTHUR W. 1930 Boards, Advisory. Volume 2, pages 609–611 in *Encyclopaedia of the Social Sciences.* New York: Macmillan.

REDFORD, EMMETTE S. 1965 The President and the Regulatory Commissions. *Texas Law Review* 44:288–321.

SHARFMAN, ISAIAH L. 1931–1937 *The Interstate Commerce Commission: A Study in Administrative Law and Procedure.* 4 vols. New York: Commonwealth Fund.

SMITH, J. TOULMIN 1849 *Government by Commissions Illegal and Pernicious.* London: Sweet.

U.S. ATTORNEY GENERAL'S COMMITTEE ON ADMINISTRATIVE PROCEDURE 1941 *Administrative Procedure in Government Agencies.* 77th Congress, 1st Session. Senate Document No. 8. Washington: Government Printing Office.

U.S. COMMISSION ON ORGANIZATION OF THE EXECUTIVE BRANCH OF THE GOVERNMENT 1949 *Report to the*

Congress. Appendix N: Committee on Independent Regulatory Commissions. Washington: Government Printing Office.

U.S. President's Committee on Administrative Management 1937 *Report . . .: With Studies of Administrative Management in the Federal Government.* Washington: Government Printing Office.

Wheare, Kenneth C. 1955 *Government by Committee: An Essay on the British Constitution.* Oxford: Clarendon.

COMMODITY AGREEMENTS, INTERNATIONAL

International commodity agreements (ICA's) are essentially multilateral instrumentalities of governmental control that support the international price of individual primary commodities, especially through such arrangements as export quotas or assured access to markets. Accordingly international commodity agreements are to be distinguished from commodity study groups, which are entirely lacking in operational responsibility; from international cartels of a nongovernmental character; and from the Combined Food Board (1942–1945) or the International Materials Conference (1951–1953), which involved international allocative machinery for a considerable number of primary commodities during periods of war-induced shortage. The proposed definition also excludes the following "near" forms of international undertakings: (1) bilateral bulk-purchase agreements; (2) multilateral control arrangements governing the market outlets for manufactured products, such as the International Cotton Textile Agreement negotiated in 1961; (3) arrangements for sectoral integration, in the pattern of the European Coal and Steel Community or the Common Agricultural Policy of the European Economic Community; (4) plans for a commodity-reserve currency; (5) proposals for international food reserves; and (6) measures for the reduction of tariffs or nontariff restrictions against the international movement of goods or services. International commodity agreements, in their modern form, may be dated from the Brussels Sugar Convention (1902), under whose terms the major contemporary exporters of beet sugar undertook to support the international market by abandoning national systems of export subsidies. The most important agreement of the 1920s was the Stevenson Rubber Scheme, implemented by the British and Dutch governments on behalf of their respective colonial territories in Malaya and the Netherlands East Indies. This scheme, which resulted in a sharp but short-lived price increase (Whittlesey 1931), was frankly restrictionist in character, and experience under it was the major reason for certain safeguards incorporated in chapter 5 of the Havana Charter for an international trade organization (United Nations 1947).

Since the end of World War II, agreements have been successfully negotiated for wheat, sugar, tin, coffee, and olive oil. The International Wheat Agreements (IWA) of 1949 and 1953, and the postwar International Sugar Agreements (ISA) are prototypes, respectively, of two forms of commodity agreements—the multilateral contract and the variable export quota. Floor and ceiling prices were established for sugar and enforced essentially by regulating the permissible exports of member countries; the sugar agreement provided, further, that stocks in exporter hands neither exceed nor fall short of stated percentages of export quotas. An entirely different instrumentality was used for wheat. Importers agreed to accept specified quantities if the price fell to the minimum level stated in the agreement, and exporters agreed to provide specified quantities to member countries whenever the price was at the contract ceiling. At prices between the floor and the ceiling, the wheat agreement was to be essentially inoperative. In the tin agreement (ITA), successively higher price thresholds were specified, at which a buffer-stock agency (*a*) had to purchase, (*b*) might purchase, (*c*) could not purchase or sell without specific authorization, (*d*) might sell, and (*e*) was required to sell. The agreement also provided for imposition of export controls after buffer accumulations exceeded specified amounts. The major sanction involved in the agreement for coffee, negotiated at a prolonged conference in 1962, was the certificate of origin, to be required of importing countries as a means of limiting their takings from any exporters electing to "go it alone."

Historically, U. S. policy with respect to international commodity agreements has been characterized by a certain degree of ambivalence. Avoiding agreements on industrial raw materials subject to wide fluctuations in demand, it has, until very recently, participated only in agreements in which the United States has predominantly a producer interest, notably the International Wheat Agreement. Even in the case of sugar (of which the United States remains a net importer), it has acted more in a producer than in a consumer capacity; too large a differential between domestic prices and those prevailing abroad would embarrass the continuation of the domestic sugar-control system. From time to time the United States has toyed with the idea of an agreement for lead and zinc, as a means of terminating an existing system of unilaterally imposed import quotas, which was the source of considerable irritation in trade relations with Mexico, Peru, Australia, and Canada.

Prerequisites for negotiation. Empirically, if not in theory, the following would seem to be among the primary conditions to be met if an international commodity conference is to materialize into an agreement:

(1) *Inelastic demand.* Clearly, if close substitutes are available, supporting the market price of any individual commodity is certain to have immediately and sharply adverse effects. The existence of synthetic rubber explains the complete lack of any postwar agreement for the natural product; restrictive agreements for individual oilseeds are ruled out by the existence of a considerable list of alternative seeds, as well as by competition from butter; but sugar has lent itself to a continuous succession of agreements since 1937.

(2) *Reasonably stable market shares.* Since export quotas generally divide up markets proportionately to the national shares prevailing in some base period, difficulties arise whenever there are either abrupt or longer-term shifts in the proportions contributed by various producing countries. The progressive displacement of exports of raw cotton from the United States by those originating elsewhere, compounded by the development of synthetic fibers, precluded the successful negotiation of an international cotton agreement in the postwar period, and the rising volume of exports from African countries seriously complicated the negotiation of the International Coffee Agreement of 1962.

(3) *Distress price levels.* As is best illustrated by the breakdown in negotiations for a revised sugar agreement in 1951 and for a cocoa agreement in 1963, exporting countries are not prepared to accept the necessary compromises unless prevailing prices are extremely low.

(4) *Mixed producer–consumer interest.* The longest-lived agreements currently in effect involve commodities concerning which the major industrial countries have rather mixed motives. Thus the United Kingdom is interested, as an importing country, in relatively low prices for sugar; but as champion of the Commonwealth countries in the West Indies as well as Oceania, the United Kingdom does not wish world sugar prices to fall to disastrous levels. In pre-Castro days, the United States sought a higher price for Cuba's sugar shipments to non-U.S. destinations than did even the Cubans, who were rather more impressed with the desirability of maintaining export volume. Even the new

agreement for coffee reflects some mutuality of producer and consumer interest within the major importing countries: no domestic sources of supply exist, but the temperate zone industrial nations are broadly concerned for the well-being of less developed countries in tropical regions of Latin America and Africa, which supply most of the world's coffee exports.

Obsolete principles versus realities. Prominent in the chapter of the Havana Charter dealing with intergovernmental commodity-control agreements were provisions purporting to benefit the consumer, especially via (a) equal representation for importing and exporting countries; (b) participation by all countries "substantially interested" in the particular commodity; (c) the checkreins of publicity in the form of an annual report; and (d) the assurance of increasing market outlets for supplies originating in the regions of most efficient production.

A wide gulf separates the principles underlying these provisions from the hard realities of the agreements actually negotiated in the postwar period. The U.S.S.R. continues to vote in the International Sugar Agreement and the International Wheat Agreement as an exporting country, although the dynamics of international trade are such that it has recently become a heavy net importer of both. Under present circumstances, the United States, while not itself a member of the ITA, in effect imposes a ceiling on international tin prices by regulating the rate at which tin disposals are made out of that nation's strategic stockpiles. Similarly in the case of wheat, the international market has been governed less by the IWA than by oligopolistic pricing practices on the part of the Canadian Wheat Board and the U.S. Commodity Credit Corporation. Membership of a host of nations in present-day international commodity agreements may merely complicate the processes of administration and decision making, while in at least one instance—the decision of the United Kingdom *not* to affiliate with the IWA of 1953—the absence of a major wheat-importing country may have had a salutary effect in moderating the exercise of oligopolistic power.

The Organization of Petroleum Exporting Countries (OPEC), established in 1960, is a special case. It violates, thus far without challenge, the Havana Charter provisions requiring consumer representation. It utilizes a process of collective bargaining—not with importing *countries*, but with producing and marketing *companies* largely controlled by citizens of the advanced industrial countries, notably the United States, the United Kingdom, the

Netherlands, and France. Perhaps the time is becoming ripe for a truly international undertaking concerning petroleum. An internal system of prorationing in the United States, on behalf of domestic producing groups, has already, and inevitably, given rise to a system of import controls, and a strong case can be made for having import quotas enforced by a multilateral, rather than a unilateral, instrumentality. Germany, Italy, and Japan, for example, have very little direct control over petroleum supplies but are major consumers and importers. The further fact that the petroleum-exporting countries include relatively wealthy members of the less developed world, while poorer members are heavily dependent on petroleum imports, also argues for a degree of restraint in the exercise of bargaining power by the OPEC.

Economic effects.   The international commodity agreements suffer from the various limitations that characterize all efforts to support artificially the market position of individual commodities. In particular, price targets tend to be set too high, long-run elasticities in demand as well as in supply tend to be underestimated, and cost structures tend to be built up so that any favorable effects on producer income are at best transitory. Longevity in the agreements, accordingly, is not necessarily a virtue and in the case of sugar has been achieved only by making inoperative the key provisions governing export quotas during periods (especially of high prices) when agreement on market shares has proved impossible.

It has been argued that stabilization of the price paid for only a portion of world export sales tends, broadly, to destabilize the price of the remainder (Johnson 1950). The general case for this theoretical position has not, however, been definitively proved. An important consideration is the inelasticity of demand in the stabilized portion of the market relative to that in the unstabilized sector. Thus, the assurance of adequate supplies of sugar to the United States and of wheat to the United Kingdom, under successive international agreements or national control programs, has tended, on balance, to be stabilizing.

Moreover, while it is generally true that prices in national markets tend to fluctuate less widely than those of commodities sold without protection in residual "free" markets, it by no means follows that free market prices as a group are necessarily less stable than prices of primary commodities subject to world market conditions (i.e., primary commodities for which prices throughout the noncommunist world tend to differ chiefly by transporta-

tion costs together with nominal tariffs). Chiefly for reasons of supply inelasticity, compounded in the case of cocoa by demand inelasticity and in the case of natural rubber and wool by rather wide cyclical fluctuations in demand, cocoa, natural rubber, and wool have historically tended to be among those commodities experiencing the widest fluctuations in market price. While sterling-area producers are dominant exporters of all three, and the foreign-exchange reserves of the sterling area accordingly tend to fluctuate in keeping with their current market strength or weakness, none has been governed by an agreement in the postwar period. Moreover, the fact that the price swings experienced by these commodities have by and large been reversible has led the major exporting countries to introduce various devices—from national marketing boards, through variable export taxes to prepayment of producers' income taxes—that do have the effect of "stabilizing" producer income from year to year (although not the nation's total foreign-exchange earnings). This approach represents an adjustment toward living with instability (Nurkse 1958).

Controls over the market price of individual commodities have undesirable side effects, politically as well as economically. The severity of export quotas imposed under the tin agreement from December 1957 through September 1960 appears to have had a long-term effect on productive capacity; when export restrictions on tin were relaxed, output failed to revive in step with a strong recovery in consumption, and, accordingly, this commodity provides a classic example of the irreversible supply curve. One possible lesson to be learned from the Cuban experience under Fidel Castro is that there is a relationship, subtle and indirect rather than overt, between economic forms of market control and a degree of political tyranny. Such a philosophy was shared by the supporters of the Anti-Corn-Law League in nineteenth-century England, who built their case on a presumed linkage between freer trade and world peace.

Current pressures favoring agreements.   Serious disadvantages notwithstanding, the number of international commodity agreements has been tending to proliferate, and there are good reasons for expecting that trend to continue. For one thing, the United States has moved, by a succession of moderate steps, from a position of doctrinaire opposition to these agreements to one where official policy has become that of willingness, in the words of President Kennedy, "to cooperate in serious, case-by-case examinations of commodity market problems." Such agreements tend to be strongly favored by the less developed countries as a means of "stabilizing" (i.e., raising) the foreign exchange earned by their major exports. In Europe, international market-sharing arrangements have enjoyed the active support of French authorities for more than a decade. The German Federal Republic, as the major importer of agricultural commodities within the European Economic Community, favors agreements as instrumentalities for maintaining a place for overseas suppliers within the Common Market. On similar grounds, an agreement for grains has also received some scholarly support (Coppock 1963). Moreover, the United Kingdom, which has until recently relied on a policy of cheap food imports together with a program of direct payments to its domestic agricultural producers, has begun to develop a series of agreements with major overseas suppliers of grain and meat, in order to reduce the budgetary burden resulting from a combination of direct payments, unrestricted domestic production, and unlimited imports. International commodity agreements have considerable appeal to all external suppliers favorably impressed with the short-term advantages, and prepared to overlook the longer-run disadvantages, of having market outlets assured on a quota basis.

Alternatives. Various efforts have been made to invent mechanisms other than international commodity agreements for transferring purchasing power to less developed countries whose earnings have been either cyclically or chronically depressed. Certain of these alternatives, such as proposals for a commodity-reserve currency (United Nations 1964a), would serve the ends of foreign aid and international monetary "reform" at the expense of undermining the role of the price system as the major instrument of economic management in (relatively) free-enterprise societies. Others, operating through overt financial transfers (United Nations 1964b; Swerling 1964), have the major advantage of leaving the price system largely unaffected as the allocator of economic resources. Finally, the International Monetary Fund—although with considerable reluctance and after some delay (Fleming & Lovasy 1960)—has acted to make one extra tranche (i.e., one-fourth of the nation's IMF quota) available for compensating shortfalls in export proceeds of less developed countries, when those shortfalls arise for reasons not within the control of the country experiencing the balance-of-payments difficulties (International Monetary Fund 1963). Such an approach has the important virtue of taking into account fluctuations

in export volume rather than responding exclusively to variations in commodity prices.

BORIS C. SWERLING

[*See also* CARTELS AND TRADE ASSOCIATIONS; INTERNATIONAL TRADE; INTERNATIONAL TRADE CONTROLS.]

BIBLIOGRAPHY

BAUER, P. T.; and YAMEY, B. S. 1964 Organized Commodity Stabilization With Voluntary Participation. *Oxford Economic Papers* 16:105–113.

BLAU, GERDA 1963 International Commodity Arrangements and Policies. Part I. *Monthly Bulletin of Agricultural Economics and Statistics* 12, Sept.: 1–9.

CAINE, SYDNEY 1963 *Prices for Primary Producers.* London: Institute of Economic Affairs.

COPPOCK, JOHN O. 1963 *North Atlantic Policy: The Agricultural Gap.* New York: Twentieth Century Fund.

DAVIS, JOSEPH S. 1947 *International Commodity Agreements: Hope, Illusion, or Menace?* New York: Carnegie Endowment for International Peace.

FLEMING, J. MARCUS; and LOVASY, GERTRUD 1960 Fund Policies and Procedures in Relation to the Compensatory Financing of Commodity Fluctuations. *International Monetary Fund Staff Papers* 8:1–76.

HAVILAND, WILLIAM E. 1963 *International Commodity Agreements.* Montreal: Private Planning Association of Canada, Canadian Trade Committee. → Contains a useful bibliography.

INTERNATIONAL MATERIALS CONFERENCE 1953 *Final Report on Operations.* Washington: The Conference.

INTERNATIONAL MONETARY FUND 1963 *Compensatory Financing of Export Fluctuations: A Report on Compensatory Financing of the Fluctuations in Exports of Primary Exporting Countries.* Washington: The Fund.

JOHNSON, HARRY G. 1950 The De-stabilising Effect of International Commodity Agreements on the Prices of Primary Products. *Economic Journal* 60:626–629.

NURKSE, RAGNAR et al. 1958 The Quest for a Stabilization Policy in Primary Producing Countries: A Symposium. *Kyklos* 11:139–265.

POLITICAL AND ECONOMIC PLANNING 1964 Commodity Agreements and EEC Farm Policy. *Planning* 30:149–209.

ROBERTSON, W. 1960 The Tin Experiment in Commodity Market Stabilization. *Oxford Economic Papers* 12:310–335.

Rubber Statistical Bulletin. → Issued since 1946.

STERN, ROBERT M. 1964 *Policies for Trade and Development.* New York: Carnegie Endowment for International Peace.

SWERLING, BORIS C. 1964 Financial Alternatives to International Commodity Stabilization. *Canadian Journal of Economics and Political Science* 30:526–537.

UNITED NATIONS, INTERIM COORDINATING COMMITTEE FOR INTERNATIONAL COMMODITY ARRANGEMENTS 1947 *Review of International Commodity Arrangements.* New York: United Nations.

UNITED NATIONS CONFERENCE ON TRADE AND DEVELOPMENT 1964a *The Case for an International Commodity Reserve Currency.* Contributed Paper No. 7, prepared by Albert G. Hart, Nicholas Kaldor, and Jan Tinbergen. Geneva: United Nations.

UNITED NATIONS CONFERENCE ON TRADE AND DEVELOP-

MENT 1964b *International Commodity Problems*. Contributed Paper No. 1, prepared by James E. Meade. Geneva: United Nations.

UNITED NATIONS CONFERENCE ON TRADE AND DEVELOPMENT, GENEVA, 1964 1964c *Towards a New Trade Policy for Development*. New York: United Nations.

WALLICH, HENRY C. 1961 Stabilization of Proceeds From Raw Material Exports. Pages 342–365 in Howard S. Ellis (editor), *Economic Development for Latin America*. New York: St. Martins.

WHITTLESEY, CHARLES R. 1931 *Government Control of Crude Rubber: The Stevenson Plan*. Princeton Univ. Press.

COMMODITY EXCHANGES

See SPECULATION, HEDGING, AND ARBITRAGE.

COMMON LAW

See under LEGAL SYSTEMS.

COMMONS, JOHN R.

As an adventurous economic historian and theorist, John Rogers Commons (1862–1945) was a leader in the development of a number of vital areas of investigation, especially industrial relations and monetary economics. His academic talents, along with a sanguine temperament and a gift for economic statesmanship, made him a major architect of economic reform in the period of American history that covers Theodore Roosevelt's Square Deal, Woodrow Wilson's New Freedom, and Franklin D. Roosevelt's New Deal.

Commons was born in Hollandsburg, Ohio, in 1862; his parents were active abolitionists. His religious Calvinist mother, hoping that he would become a minister, sent him, in 1882, to her alma mater, Oberlin College. He paid part of his expenses by working as a printer, at which time he became interested in trade-unionism and Henry George's single-tax movement.

After receiving a B.A. in 1888, he attended The Johns Hopkins University for two years of graduate study. There he was attracted to the two leading movements for the reform of the dominant classical economics. His teacher, Richard T. Ely, was a prominent figure in one, namely, the infusion into classical economics of the viewpoint of the German historical school, which emphasized the use of history, statistics, comparative economic development, jurisprudence, and ethics. The objective was to develop a sound economics for social guidance. The other movement was the marginalist, or utility, approach, in which some of Commons' friends among the graduate students took a prominent part. This school he viewed as providing a more logically unified theory of price determination than did classical economics. Thus armed with the latest tools of inquiry and an overwhelming interest in practically all the controversial social and economic issues of the day, in 1890 he began his academic career. Before the decade was over he had taught at four schools—Wesleyan, Oberlin, Indiana, and Syracuse. The abolition of his chair of sociology at Syracuse in 1899 temporarily ended his academic career. In 1904, Ely, who had moved to the University of Wisconsin, brought his protégé there. The period at Wisconsin proved to be Commons' most creative one.

Commons soon made a reputation as the leading student of American labor problems. With the collaboration of disciples, he published the pioneering *A Documentary History of American Industrial Society* (1910–1911) and *History of Labour in the United States* (1918–1935). His theory of the origin and development of the American trade-union movement as a response to the scope of product markets, which he presented most clearly in "American Shoemakers, 1648–1895: A Sketch of Industrial Evolution" (1909), is still the most widely accepted one. The trade-union movement, he held, arose out of the efforts of individual workmen to protect their job rights against cheaper labor. The effectiveness of unions in improving wages and other major terms of employment depends upon their ability to control and standardize conditions within the product market areas in the industry in which they operate. The market area for some goods and most services is local; for others the region is important; for most goods the market area has become the entire nation, and in such cases success of the union depends on its ability to organize the whole industry.

Commons had extraordinary success as a policy maker. He helped prepare most of the legislation that made Wisconsin the laboratory in social and economic reform for other states and the federal government. This included, notably, legislation for civil service, public utility and railroad regulation, workmen's accident compensation, and unemployment insurance. He not only helped to draft the bill creating the Wisconsin Industrial Commission to supervise the state's labor laws but also was a member of the first commission, from 1911 to 1913. He did similar work for the federal government in 1901 as a member of the Industrial Commission, which made the first comprehensive inquiry into the American economy, and in 1914–1915 as a member of President Woodrow Wilson's Industrial Relations Commission. The major designers of the epoch-making Social Security Act of

1935 were his students. He also played a leading role in the development of the notion of having the federal authority manage the monetary system, to maintain, as he put it in the famous Strong Bill of 1928, "the stability of commerce, industry, agriculture, and employment, . . . and a more stable purchasing power of the dollar . . ." (H.R. 11806).

Commons wrote three major treatises in economic theory. The first, *The Distribution of Wealth* (1893), was an ingenious attempt to combine marginalist economics with the emphasis of the German historical school on the fundamental importance of jurisprudence for achieving sound economic growth and equitable distribution of income. In the other two, *Legal Foundations of Capitalism* (1924) and *Institutional Economics* (1934a), which should be read with his early essay "A Sociological View of Sovereignty" (1899–1900), he sought to demonstrate the importance for economic theory of collective action in all its varieties. These included not only the state but also a host of voluntary associations, such as the corporation and the trade union; in fact, collective action conceptually embraced all institutions, since Commons defined an institution as "collective action in control of individual action."

From the standpoint of the theory of collective action, he developed, as the basic economic unit of investigation, "the transaction," which included both social and individual action. He borrowed from Thorstein Veblen the concept of transactions performed by going concerns, but he broadened it so that it applied to any form of desirable organized economic activity, containing conflicting but reciprocal interests. The principles of the going concern are the network of "working rules," or customs. To Commons, these controls are "laws" broadly conceived; they are the outgrowth of experience and make possible the orderly growth of individual action. Some type of judge ultimately determines the appropriateness of the working rule. Thus, he viewed the Supreme Court of the United States as "the supreme faculty of political economy" for the nation.

A major pivot in Commons' analysis was the role of the administrative process. The germ of this idea dates back to his *Proportional Representation* (1896). He believed that the sound enactment of new working rules takes place through "collective bargaining" between the representatives of the affected organized group interests. His model was the Wisconsin Industrial Commission with its advisory committees. Such quasi-judicial commissions, he maintained, were a fourth branch of government and had as their ideal "reasonable regulation through constructive investigation." With the world-wide growth of collective action and the consequent problems of adjusting conflicts between organized groups, or "blocs," Commons' institutional theory has been found increasingly relevant, and his economic statesmanship continues to be admired.

JOSEPH DORFMAN

[*For the historical context of Commons' work, see* ECONOMIC THOUGHT, *article on* THE INSTITUTIONAL SCHOOL. *See also* ELY; SELIGMAN, C. G.]

WORKS BY COMMONS

1893   *The Distribution of Wealth.* New York and London: Macmillan; New York: Kelley Reprints.
(1896) 1907   *Proportional Representation.* 2d ed. New York: Macmillan.
1899–1900   A Sociological View of Sovereignty. *American Journal of Sociology* 5:1–15, 155–171, 347–366, 544–552, 683–695, 814–825; 6:67–89.
(1899–1913) 1913   *Labor and Administration.* New York: Macmillan. → Contains essays and speeches previously published in various publications.
1909   American Shoemakers, 1648–1895: A Sketch of Industrial Evolution. *Quarterly Journal of Economics* 24:39–84.
(1910–1911) 1958   COMMONS, JOHN ROGERS et al. (editors) *A Documentary History of American Industrial Society.* 10 vols. New York: Russell.
1918–1935   *History of Labour in the United States.* 4 vols. New York: Macmillan.
(1924) 1959   *Legal Foundations of Capitalism.* Madison: Univ. of Wisconsin Press.
1929   Jurisdictional Disputes. Pages 93–123 in *Wertheim Lectures on Industrial Relations.* Cambridge, Mass.: Harvard Univ. Press.
(1934a) 1959   *Institutional Economics: Its Place in Political Economy.* 2 vols. in 1. Madison: Univ. of Wisconsin Press.
(1934b) 1963   *Myself.* Madison: Univ. of Wisconsin Press.
1936   Institutional Economics. *American Economic Review* 26:237–249.
(1950) 1956   *The Economics of Collective Action.* Edited by K. H. Parsons. New York: Macmillan. → Contains a bibliography of Commons' writings.

WORKS ABOUT COMMONS

CHAMBERLAIN, NEIL W. 1963   The Institutional Economics of John R. Commons. Pages 63–94 in Joseph Dorfman et al., *Institutional Economics: Veblen, Commons, and Mitchell Reconsidered.* Berkeley: Univ. of California Press.
DORFMAN, JOSEPH 1949   The Saga of John Rogers Commons. Volume 3, pages 276–294 in Joseph Dorfman, *The Economic Mind in American Civilization.* New York: Viking.
DORFMAN, JOSEPH 1959a   John R. Commons and the Economics of Collective Action. Volume 4, pages 377–395 in Joseph Dorfman, *The Economic Mind in American Civilization.* New York: Viking.
DORFMAN, JOSEPH 1959b   Response of the Elders. Volume 5, pages 664–673 in Joseph Dorfman, *The Economic Mind in American Civilization.* New York: Viking.

HARTER, LAFAYETTE G. JR. 1962 *John R. Commons: His Assault on Laissez-faire.* Corvallis: Oregon State Univ. Press.

PERLMAN, MARK 1958 John Commons: Theorist as Policy Maker. Pages 173–190 in Mark Perlman, *Labor Union Theories in America.* Evanston, Ill.: Row, Peterson.

COMMUNICATION

This article is a generalized description of the communication process as a multichannel system. For articles on specific systems of communication, see the articles listed under ART *as well as* COMMUNICATION, ANIMAL; LANGUAGE; KINESICS; PARAPSYCHOLOGY; *and* PERCEPTION, *article on* SPEECH PERCEPTION. *Approaches to the study of communication are discussed in* ATTITUDES, *article on* ATTITUDE CHANGE; COGNITIVE THEORY; COMMUNICATION, MASS; COMMUNICATION, POLITICAL; LINGUISTICS; *and* PROPAGANDA.

The communicative process involves areas of human behavior that have long been of interest to the publicist, the humanist, and the politician. Social scientists have generally accepted the communicative process as a given and have concerned themselves primarily with its success or failure, its effects, or its improvement. More recently, struck by the barriers to the flow of information between societies, between teachers and students, between the politician and the electorate, between parents and children, between husbands and wives, and between the professional and his clientele, a number of disciplines have focused both thought and research effort upon the mechanisms of information transmission. By and large, increased interest has not been accompanied by a departure from earlier preoccupation with normative evaluation of the process or by a shift from earlier preconceptions about its central dynamic.

Two relatively unquestioned fallacies have served as deterrents to the development of theories about communication and to the organization of research to test such theories. The first of these has been the dominating dyadic frame into which communication research has been forced. Communication has been studied as a process identified by the passage of information through the transmission of more or less meaningful symbols from one individual to another, from one group or representative of a group to another group or representative. Thus, the ideal model for the communicative process is based on the dyad: a knowledgeable monadic father or teacher who emits knowledge-carrying symbols that enter into the head of a less knowledgeable or nonknowledgeable monadic child. Such a conception is deceptively familiar, and it has the absolute support of common sense. This model has strong underpinnings provided by our attitude toward teaching and learning, superordination and subordination, wisdom and ignorance. It is reified by the writing and reading process and by the derivations of literacy represented by books, newspapers, motion pictures, and radio and television. The dyadic model is part of cultural tradition. As such it has impeded the systematic investigation of the larger system of which the dyadic situation is little more than incidental. The dyadic view forces research into Ptolemaic structure. Communication behavior is masked by definitions of communication as "that process whereby encapsulated particles of meaning are transmitted between individual organisms by means of specialized sending and receiving devices."

Literate man's anthropocentric and ethnocentric predilection to locate the avenue of transmission in the aural–audio channel or in derivative channels concerned with the transportation of the written word or with the vocalized written word has been equally misleading. Enamored of the almost limitless capacity of language to store cues to accumulated experience, some scholars have confused language, culture, and social interaction. In societies that stress vocal performance and have confidence in the reliability of lexicalized information, a storehouse of social experience is available, in verbal form, to the investigator. It is, however, methodologically dangerous to extrapolate from this special situation to statements about mankind as essentially a vocally communicating species. Review of carefully drawn ethnographic reports reveals that societies vary widely in their rules of evidence, in the extent to which, for example, tangibility takes preference over visibility or audibility or some combination of these. It is both naive and ethnocentric to define communication in terms based upon the self-view of talk-oriented societies.

Human society, wherever examined and of whatever order of development, has language and is dependent upon it. We have been unable to detect any comparable development among other animals. Yet, at the moment we can only theorize about the importance of this distinction between nonhuman and human interactional behavior. We have no data whatsoever that can give us security about when it is that the men in any society talk or listen and when they do not. More significantly, we have only the most poetic conception of what portion of experience is shared when man in any society vocalizes or listens. And, until we do know more about the distinctive, the exclusive, functions of speech, comparisons of the relative efficiency of human and animal communication must remain broadly theoretical and, usually, invidious. However, even at this early stage of descriptive investigation of either animal or human communication, one thing stands out clearly: Man's possession of language and the absence (if true) of such a system among his prehominid forebears need not be predicated upon or used as proof of the fact that man has abandoned, lost, or suppressed the multisensory reinforcement mechanisms that enable him to be as continuously social as the nonhominids. The too narrow view of communication behavior and the word-centered conception of communication has been based upon, and feeds into, an unnecessarily restricted view of the relationship between biological and social processes.

Preconditions for communication. Man is an occupant of multiple niches, physiographic and social. He lives in, has reconstructed, and adapts to the most diverse range of environments of any of the animals. This environmental diversity combines with man's long gestation period, extended infancy, lengthy maturation, and low birth rate to make him specifically dependent upon sustaining relationships with his fellows. Having evolved over millions of years from socially dependent forebears, man has demonstrated a special capacity for intricate subdivisions of task and role assignment and regulation. As in lower animals, his relationship to his group mates is more than sequences of trial and error, action and reaction. His interactive behavior is not mechanical but interdependently systemic. Because of a complex division of labor, man's performances are seldom isolated actions in themselves. The social performance of a given member of society is by definition incomplete; task accomplishment is dependent upon continuative, coordinate, parallel, or complementary individual or subgroup behaviors. These are rarely ritualized, mechanical, conjoint performances. Flexibility and adaptability demand continuous and reliable feedback, contribution, and correction between the performing membership; and this is never apart from the capacities and behavior of the performers.

To support social organization, a society, human or animal, must, in the sense of G. H. Mead, be composed of "significant symbolizers" (1934). Society depends upon predictability and regularity. Every human society finds it necessary to kill, specially define, regulate, rehabilitate, or isolate unreliable or unpredictable symbolizers. Sanity or reliable symbolization (as measured by a particular society within its own special thresholds of significant symbolization) must be maintained if that society is not to be destroyed by accumulating discrepancy and misinformation.

It seems logical, but hardly obvious, that a single channel, the auditory–aural or any other, has too narrow and too specialized a range and is too easily adulterated to be entrusted with social regulation, a task so critical to survival. Man must, except in the nonexample of "wolf-men," maintain contact with other men throughout life. He must engage in communicative activity in the light and in the dark, upwind and downwind, in situations of dyadic intimacy and at audibility-absorbing distance, in situations that require absolute quiet, and in situations where competitive wave lengths drown out or distort his own oral contributions or reception. He must deal with others who are only confused by his oral productions: to the speaker they are sensible utterances; to the listener they are but nonsense in his ears. He must be predictable after long separations. And, above all, he must not destroy the conditions whereby the young can incorporate a language that he, as an adult, neither understands nor is able to teach. With all of these preconditions it should not be surprising that man (like his animal forebears) is a regulated multisensory station in a transmission system, a multichannel interactor.

Intercorporeal influence.   The theoretical structure presented here is appropriate to the extra-individual province shared by biology, sociology, and anthropology. One theoretical point regarding sense perceptions, however, is cogent. We will assume that animals do not "see," "hear," "feel," and so on, as separate operations, even though neural terminals may seem to be specifically stimulated by light, sound, heat, cold, pressure, and chemical activity. This is in agreement with Cherry: "It is even questionable whether the various 'senses' are to be regarded as separate, independent detectors. The human organism is one integrated whole, stimulated into response by physical signals; it is not to be thought of as a box, carrying various independent pairs of terminals labeled 'ears,' 'eyes,' 'nose,' *et cetera*" (Cherry 1957, pp. 127–128).

At first sight this may seem nihilistic. However, such a position concerning physiological or psychological processes in no way denies the fact that the structural properties of vocalic language and of nonlexical body motion language may be abstracted from their behavioral matrices. Structural properties must be isolated for description and analysis prior to the investigation of the relationships of these to each other and to other communicative modalities in the communicational system.

By means of kinesic analysis we have been relatively successful in recent years in isolating structured and patterned communicative elements in visible aspects of human body motion. These have been tested and found necessary to the social activity of a variety of human situations (Birdwhistell 1961; 1962; Scheflen 1965). This encourages us to postulate that other, and perhaps all, directly or indirectly influenceable somatic systems within the living body provide potentials for human interconnectedness. Interconnectedness is used in the sense of the structural aspects of interaction. The capacity for interconnectedness is a consequence of, and the necessary condition for, the flow of viable influence within the membership of a social group. The capacity for interconnectedness provides the social group with the potential for adaptability and continuity. It is the regulated flow of this influence that has given society a history at least as long as bisexuality and viviparous birth.

Influence is a term used to cover all intercorporeal processes of patterned somatic sensitization and response. It is postulated that the relative stability of adaptations leads to a patterned intercorporeal influence structure. This constitutes a vital reservoir of regular and variable behavior, from which the society "selects" for iconic representation and coding at the social level. It is not easy to think about matters such as these and remain disciplined about levels of organization. Customarily, "the ladder of organization levels" is stated in terms that characterize cells that are within a corporeal field as interacting with cells within that given field to form organs; these organs interact within that corporeal field to form a physiological system that is somehow integrated to engage, but only at the next higher level, with other physiological systems. I would not argue for a moment with this model as a source of canons to prevent reductionistic "explanation." However, to take too simplistic a view of the organizational ladder may blind us to relationships, to interdependencies, that exist at lower levels of organization. And this can easily occur if we somehow impose on our material an implicit framework that defines physiological processes as a level above biological processes and, logically enough, psychological processes as a level above physiological process—and then, finally, sociological processes as an abstraction of combinations of these psychological processes.

The speciational grouping, the multicorporeal environment, is the natural and necessary field of all complex organisms. And this environment is not merely, if ever, an organization of organic wholes. The division of labor, of whatever complexity, necessary to maintain a multicorporeal environment cannot be explained exhaustively by the description of action–reaction sequences between total organisms. I am positing that there exists a pattern of somatic influence composed of ordered partials within the somatic structure of the component organisms. These partials emergently combine to form interdependent patterns that are distributed regularly in the multicorporeal field. Thus, the viability of the particular organism is dependent upon appropriate somatic activity of other organisms within the multicorporeal field. In the viable social grouping there exists a series of biological acts that are necessarily intercorporeal if the given organism and, in consequence, the multicorporeal field are to survive. Thus, the individual incorporates part of a pattern that requires the activity of several organisms to gain completion. I am not restricting these generalizations to such deceptively apparent intercorporeal operations as are involved in the successful or unsuccessful delivery of fertile sperm to fertilizable ovum, of mother's milk to neonate, or of body warmth to the chilled other. These are but climactic incidents in a far more complex and far-reaching structuralization of intracorporeal partials which in context become intercorporeal transactions, extraindividual and essentially biological acts.

Timing and structure. The achievement of readiness for, and the accomplishment, completion, and abandonment of interdependent action is dependent upon intricate and reliable timing operations of readiness within both the operative individual and the multicorporeal systems. These timing operations are integral, if not central, to all communicative activities. Timing operations are present in all observed interactive systems. They are not necessarily of greater or lesser priority in a theoretical hierarchy of importance in communication. In one sense, timing is an integral function of, and evidence for, the existence of communicative structure.

In certain species, seasonal timing and coordination of readiness seem to be maintained by external contexts of influence. For example, a wide range of organisms are coordinated by a complex dependence upon light or heat variations as occasioned by regular earth–solar relationships. Specialized diets that are weather dependent provide further controls for coordination. Other more omnivorous organisms may be further regulated from within at one level by nutritional requirements and at another level by the oestrous cycle.

As ethology continues its productive investigation of animal interactive behavior, we should get increased perspective upon the range of regulatory systems.

There is no need to postulate that man is more, or less, subject to such timing systems than are other animals. Nor do we need to assume that in man such operations have been assigned to, or surrendered to, culture. There is no need to be caught with false paradoxes of nature and nurture. At the moment, all of our evidence here is suggestive and circumstantial, and any generalization must be tentative. It is literally true that we still do not know how the membership of any animal grouping monitors its interactional patterning, how the component relationships remain sufficiently stable to permit continuity (membership replacement), or how the membership organizes and accumulates reaction to change permitting adaptation in a changing milieu. However, it is clear even from our limited data that intercorporeal timing is, for mammals at least, more than a mechanical response of a genetically precalibrated system in a physiographically regular environment. There is every evidence that complex organisms remain influenceable, that they incorporate dependent partials throughout life. This is the biological context in which human communication becomes comprehensible. And it is not a context abandoned in the evolutionary leap from prehominid to man. It remains active beyond the lives of individual men.

It has been pointed out that (a) complex organisms are organically dependent upon other organisms; (b) each organism has patterned partials whose activation or suppression is necessary to its survival and to its emergent contribution to biological continuity; and (c) these partials gain completion by regularity calibration at a series of levels. Only extended research can isolate and describe the mechanisms by means of which these partials are incited, triggered, released, suppressed, and modified by information flowing in the intercorporeal interstices.

Up to this point we have been discussing the relationship between incorporated partials of influence and intercorporeal interconnectedness. There is a temptation to relegate all activities of this nature to a special area of investigation, perhaps to be described as "biological or intercorporeal communication." Such a move inevitably would serve to reinstate earlier preconceptions, which see such events of interconnectedness as distinct from and both phylogenetically and ontogenetically prior to social communication. The latter, by such definition, would be assigned concern with the stimulation and regulation of interpersonal activity in the form of social partials. It would seem inadvisable to give up the methodological advantage gained by the recognition of structured partials by arbitrarily dividing behavior into that to be termed biological as contrasted with a remainder assigned to society. It would seem more economical to search the interactional situation for communicative activity through all apparent avenues and channels of influence and to recognize that, at least in this framework of behavior, biological and social events coexist. At the least, if we are concerned with problems of the regulation of change and dynamic continuity, they are practically inseparable. There is no need to distinguish between biological and social communication. Communication can serve to cover all such events.

Multichannel communication. It is not profitable to use the term "precommunication" for intercorporeal connectedness and influence partials or to describe them as the "raw materials of communication." Such phrasing is more appropriately applied to organic, physiological, and psychological processes. Communication is the dynamic aspect of interconnection and is only indirectly related to these individuative processes. As soon as the membership of a grouping is subject to and dependent upon intermembral influence and mechanisms are operative to reduce the likelihood of the individual organism being comparably influenced by members of alien groups and species, it can be said that we have a society and that communication is taking place. A decipherable social code exists whenever a pattern of behavior presented in regularly structured contexts of behavior will serve regularly to trigger, regulate, or modify the behavior of an influenced membership. The minimal meaningful variation of behavior (of whatever size and carried along whatever channel) within the pattern may be termed a cue. The cue is always both an event in itself and an aspect of structure; that is, it always both carries identity and instructs the participant in locating the relevant contexts of its occurrence. Parenthetically, a cue need not be a direct derivation from the behavioral complex of the incorporated partial. Indeed, we know that in language the discriminating cues are arbitrary and bear no discoverable generic relationship to the activity that they signal. Kinesic cues also have this same quality of being arbitrary. In body motion as in spoken language, the cue is iconic for the partial. We may make the working assumption that the other channels operate in the same manner. However, only reliable data about the other modalities will permit us to conclude safely that this arbitrary cue-and-experience association is characteristic of all communicative activity.

As soon as a group develops even the most rudimentary system of triggering cues, communication becomes continuous. These cues, of whatever shape or degree of conspicuousness, constitute a finite segment or structure of segments. Communication is a continuous process made up of these discontinuous and related elements. The cue signals some kind of change in the environment. However, the absence of a specific and discernible cue does not create a situation of nonsociety, of noncommunication. In the absence of a cue a "steady" state can be said to be signaled; the ordered activity within the state is in itself cueful.

The concept of the steady state in its contrast with activating cues can be fatally obscurantist as an idea if it prevents recognition of the fact that it is only a heuristic simplification of, or an observational slice from, the very complex ordering of interpersonal and group relationships present in all societies. For example, the membership of a viviparous and bisexual grouping is not, by definition, homogeneous. Every observation of group behavior, either animal or human, leads us to the conclusion that intermembral cues cannot appear in isolation, are never things-in-themselves. They are always cross-referenced. Cues of whatever shape or duration are always modified by the signature of the sender and, usually, by the identification of the addressees. Thus, even the most context-specific or event-specific cue is bound to complex modification cues, which serve to signal the reliability of the cue by transmitting information about the context, the sender, and the intended receiver of the signal. "To whom it may concern" messages undoubtedly occur within a social grouping, but they are probably sufficiently rare as to constitute special cases. At the same time, while certain situations of urban life may permit a period of relative anonymity in the message sender, these are certainly of short duration and are usually, as in the case of mob action, socially defined as a serious threat to the society.

By the mid 1950s it had become obvious from observation of even the most ritualistic interactional sequences, that is, within the most explicit of contexts, that signature and address was a complex communicational procedure. Preliminary inspection and analysis showed that much of the material loosely assembled under the rubrics of "social identity" and "social status and role" was of communicative consequence. These systematic observations, when coupled with some of the insights supplied by Goffman (1956) and given depth of biological perspective by ethological data, dissipated any confidence that sign–symbol dichotomies were useful in communication theory. There do not seem to be instances of phenomena so restricted or so isolated as to be designated as signs. Elaborate, signaled contextual redundancy is required for sign reliability. This insight serves several purposes. First, it relieves communication theory of the problem of dealing with isolated units of meaning, which are unrelated to the communicative stream; that is, the cue, when seen as effective in a variety of contexts, always signals the presence of a code to which the cue belongs. Second, it clarifies the necessarily continuous nature of the communicative process. And, finally, supported by an increasing body of evidence indicating the ultimate inseparability of linguistics and kinesics in communicative systems, it makes manifest the inadequacy of any theory of communication based on monochannel message transmission.

Inspection of any extensive body of interactional data offers proof that humans vocalize but a very small percentage of their interactional time. Furthermore, such vocalizations do not characteristically take place in a situation devoid of tactile contact, shielded against olfactory and gustatory sensation, shaded to obscure visual experience or in a situation of such anesthetic force as to prevent proprioceptive and automatic feedback. It is not necessary to depreciate the role of language or even of words and sentences in the communicative process. However, from the point of view of the behavioral scientist concerned with communication, language is an infracommunicational system. I am convinced that neither language nor communication can be either studied or understood so long as we assume that either subsumes the other. A monochannel analysis of communication must ignore or deny too much evidence to gain support unless the definition of communication is limited to the wholly aware, completely purposive transmission of commonly held, explicit, and denotative verbal information between interactants.

RAY L. BIRDWHISTELL

[*Directly related are the entries* COMMUNICATION, ANIMAL; KINESICS; LANGUAGE, *article on* LANGUAGE AND CULTURE; SEMANTICS AND SEMIOTICS. *Other relevant material may be found in the biographies of* SAPIR; WHORF.]

BIBLIOGRAPHY

BIRDWHISTELL, RAY L. 1961 Paralanguage: 25 Years After Sapir. Pages 43–63 in Conference on Experimental Psychiatry, Western Psychiatric Institute and Clinic, 1959, *Lectures on Experimental Psychiatry.* Univ. of Pittsburgh Press.

BIRDWHISTELL, RAY L. 1962 Critical Moments in the Psychiatric Interview. Pages 179–188 in Tenth Anniversary Symposium on Biological, Psychological and Sociological Approaches to Current Psychiatric Problems, State Research Hospital, Galesburg, Ill., 1960, *Research Approaches to Psychiatric Problems: A Symposium.* New York: Grune.

CHERRY, COLIN (1957) 1961 *On Human Communication: A Review, a Survey, and a Criticism.* New York: Wiley. → A paperback edition was published in 1963.

GOFFMAN, ERVING 1956 *The Presentation of Self in Everyday Life.* Social Science Research Centre, Monograph No. 2. Univ. of Edinburgh, Social Science Research Centre. → A paperback edition was published by Doubleday in 1959.

MEAD, GEORGE H. 1934 *Mind, Self and Society From the Standpoint of a Social Behaviorist.* Edited by Charles W. Morris. Univ. of Chicago Press.

MEAD, MARGARET 1964 *Continuities in Cultural Evolution.* New Haven: Yale Univ. Press.

SCHEFLEN, ALBERT E. 1965 *Stream and Structure of Communicational Behavior: Context Analysis of a Psychotherapy Session.* Behavioral Studies Monograph No. 1. Philadelphia: Eastern Pennsylvania Psychiatric Institute.

COMMUNICATION, ANIMAL

I. SOCIAL AND PSYCHOLOGICAL
   ANALYSIS   *Jarvis Bastian*
II. COMMUNICATION MODELS AND
    SIGNALING BEHAVIOR   *Thomas A. Sebeok*

I

SOCIAL AND PSYCHOLOGICAL ANALYSIS

It is not easy to mark the boundaries of the subject of animal communication. Some quite good reasons might be offered for viewing the subject as encompassing all phenomena of life, for the very notion of biological adaptation can be said to involve an animal population's or, more to the point, a gene pool's communication with its environment. Even when biological adaptation is considered only at the behavioral level, this broad view may seem increasingly appropriate as we come to appreciate heretofore unsuspected ways by which animals communicate with their environments—such as the echo-ranging systems of the dolphins. But however impressive the echo-ranging systems of dolphins, bats, eared seals, and so on, are, they are no more (nor less) marvelous than, say, the olfactory systems of carnivores or the visual system of higher primates. An active wresting of adaptively pertinent information, rather than a mere reacting to environmental changes, is a characteristic feature of all higher modes of adaptation.

Thus, there is usually little advantage to be gained from viewing animal communication as extending across all of an animal population's interactions with every aspect of its environment, and it is common to restrict most discussions of the subject to what may be called social communication. This is a valuable restriction, for with the exploitation of social modes of adaptation, an additional range of environmental information becomes significant, namely, that arising from the social environment. The problems associated with these adaptations are quite special because the reciprocity of influence and concomitant fluidity in social interactions is usually much greater than in the interactions between animals and their nonsocial environments. This is not to say that the processes and mechanisms of social interaction are necessarily different in kind from those involved in interaction with nonsocial environments but only to point out that pressures related to social factors have been involved in their evolution (Wynne-Edwards 1963). It is because of this that it is especially reasonable to distinguish social communication as a special part of the more general problem of the communication of animals with their environments.

However, in making this distinction we must be careful not to make social communication conceptually more special than it really is. Most often social communication is considered a subordinate part of social behavior. This is clearly wrong, for, basically, social communication and social behavior are identical. At bottom, can anything more be said of social behavior than that it is the partial, and mostly reciprocal, determination of one or more animals' actions by other animals? And, reversing the coin, can the occurrence and reception of communicative signals be something more than just this social behavior? There are probably many reasons why social communication has been mistakenly thought to be a subject set apart from the rest of social behavior. No doubt some are related to the apparent ease with which we seem to distinguish man's linguistic actions from the rest of his social interactions. But man's linguistic activities constitute an exceedingly specialized form of animal communication, and it is well to bear constantly in mind that it is extremely risky to apply generalizations and ideas having their basis in what we feel to be the properties of linguistic communication to nonlinguistic communication. (Caution in proceeding in the reverse direction is at least equally warranted.) Actually, nonlinguistic modes of communication are exploited as much by humans as by any other social fauna, and if we were to attend only to these, the inclination to separate communication from social interaction would surely diminish.

The distinction between social communication and social behavior is also promoted by the feeling, again prompted by a presumed analogy to human linguistic actions, that successful communication involves the transmission of information or some other commodity. That is, it is thought that in communication something is literally made common to both signaler and recipients that would otherwise remain the private possession of the signaler. This notion is also linked with the idea that communication occurs only when one animal, the signaler, performs some sort of action and by this action generates the signal whose reception by others constitutes the information transmission. One of the difficulties with this formulation of animal communication is that there are many situations in which an animal may affect the conduct of others in its group, not through any actions of its skeletal musculature, but simply by sensory attributes of its body over which it in no sense can be said to have control, such as the coloring of its feathers or of its beak. Even when the communicative events derive from particular behavioral acts, the applicability of the notion of information transmission is open to question, although to whatever extent it is applicable it is just as much so to all of social behavior. In animal communication the information that might be said to be transmitted is precisely the social significance of any attribute, behavioral or otherwise, of the participants in any social interaction.

Signaling systems

Nonetheless, specializations in social modes of adaptation do occur very widely, even in species not routinely living in groups, in which specific actions by one participant appear to function primarily to produce patterns of stimulation that characteristically evoke regular changes in the behavior of others. Such conventionalization of the means of integrating animal social behavior can well be regarded as signaling systems, always appreciating that we are only referring to especially systematic, regularized episodes of social interaction. Social specializations of this sort, as with any biological specialization, are the more pronounced the more directly they contribute to the integrity of a species, and thus, animal signaling systems appear most often in the government of social episodes relating to biologically critical areas, such as reproduction and infant care, species and group integration, spacing and population control, predator defense, cooperative foraging, etc.

There are many questions about any animal signaling system that require answers if we are to develop an understanding of these parts of biology. To date none have been more than partially answered for any single species, and as the answers can certainly be expected to be interrelated not only with each other but also with the immense numbers of other questions remaining to be answered about any species' mode of adaptation, we can view our current state of knowledge only with despair. But however woefully lacking in answers, we will discuss these questions in three very much overlapping groups, relating in turn to the structures, functions, and mechanisms of animal signaling systems.

Structural aspects. The most basic structural question concerns the physical nature of the signals. For any species this depends on the nature of the afferent and efferent adaptations and on the demands of the habitat. In principle every available avenue of exteroception is potentially exploitable for mediating social intercourse, and in fact, all are exploited by one animal form or another. There are, of course, restrictions imposed by sensitivities of the receptor systems and by glandular and motor capabilities for generating signals commensurate with these sensitivities. For instance, exposure of colored surfaces could have no value for intraspecific signaling in color-blind species. But many other factors (carefully reviewed by Marler 1961*a*) may participate in the selection of signaling modes that are perhaps less apparent—as for instance, the time and distance over which social interactions occur, the sources of signal distortion in the signaling medium, and the exposure to predation associated with signaling actions. Because signaling systems are intrinsically social phenomena, their adaptive exploitation requires the characteristics of signal emission, transmission, and reception to be well matched, to insure the effective mediation of social episodes.

This brings us to questions concerned with the nature of the particular signals, where similar degrees of complexity must be faced. Only detailed, systematic investigation can reveal which features of a given signal possess social significance, i.e., are critical in determining the results of signal reception. Fortunately there have been some very notable successes in developing appropriate methods for identifying the critical stimulus features governing social interactions, such as are described by Tinbergen (1951; 1953*a*). Ideally, the most effective procedure exposes animals to models incorporating stimulus variations of the features of the naturally occurring signals and measures the effects of such variations on the conduct of recipients. This has been practicable in a number of instances where the natural signal involves only a single sensory mode and remains relatively stable for long durations, such as the chemical signals that have been isolated as parts of the social adaptations of various insects (Wilson 1963). Even with auditory signals, which are usually much briefer and less steady, advances in recording and reproducing techniques have made it possible to employ a close approximation to the model-manipulation approach by selective filtering of recordings of the original signals in order to determine the behavioral effects (Busnel 1963; Falls 1963); and it can be expected that before long the very close parallels to the model-manipulation procedures that have been so productively used in the analysis and synthesis of human speech sounds (e.g., Liberman 1957) will begin to be used with equal effect by animal behaviorists concerned with acoustical signaling.

Unfortunately, the full power of the model-manipulation method can perhaps never be fully brought to bear on the problem of identifying the significant features of many kinds of animal signals. This is because, especially in social episodes involving close proximity of the participants, the signals may involve several sensory modalities simultaneously. The difficulties are further intensified when the features of the signals are produced by many different concurrent motor adjustments, as in the signals of some carnivores and terrestrial primates (Hinde & Rowell 1962; DeVore 1965).

When the signals are shifting patterns of multimodal stimulus combinations, the determination of the contribution made by each aspect to the significance of the total complex may never be complete. Nevertheless, the ingenuity of investigators and the prospects for exploitable technological developments in manipulating complex stimulus events in the field or laboratory, if not limitless, are at least sufficiently unpredictable to permit the hope that much progress can be made in analyzing the constituents of even the most complex and fluid signals, for we know that signal complexity cannot exceed the socially effective resolution capacities of its recipients. We appear to be further aided in meeting this problem of signal complexity by the seeming absence of gestalt properties in their reception (Hess 1962). That is, the social effects of parts of a signal complex may interact in simply an additive fashion, so that the effects of subsets of the total complex may be studied separately. This possibility is well illustrated in studies by Miller and his associates (1959) in which they compared the stimulus values of (1) fearful monkeys, (2) life-size still photographs of fearful monkeys, and (3) life-size still photographs of just the facial regions of fearful monkeys in evoking conditioned avoidance responses in other monkeys. They found that all three different stimulus complexes were effective, which suggests that such conditioning procedures, together with advanced techniques of stimulus manipulation, might very well be valuable in analyzing critical features of even the most complex social signals.

Perhaps an even more imposing barrier to the exploitation of the model-manipulation method is raised by the evidently very important role played by context effects in determining the behavioral consequences of the signals, especially the more elaborate modes of social adaptation. Thus, apparently, the same signal emitted in different social contexts (Schaller 1963) or following different prior signaling actions (Altmann 1962) does not evoke the same behavioral effects. As a result of such difficulties, this extremely valuable technique of analyzing the stimuli that control general animal behavior may be of limited use in studying many kinds of signals operating in social interactions.

But there is no reason for pessimism. Careful field observation by competent (ecologically oriented) workers aided by good cinematic and audio field recording can be expected not only to yield precise identifications of the signals occurring in conventional behavioral interactions but also to disclose what are their more or less invariant features —though perhaps not the particular contribution made by each, nor their interactions, in determining the behavioral effects of signal reception. These prospects are heightened by the relative stability of animal signals. In profound contrast to human linguistic signals, which change incessantly and with great rapidity, nonlinguistic signals of man and other animals tend to be steady and to remain so for long periods of time. And since even the fluctuating auditory displays of songbirds (Thorpe 1961a) and dolphins (Dreher & Evans 1964) tend to occur as repetitive trains, we can hope to attain rather close specifications of these signals.

Not only must extended observation of free-ranging animals be relied on to furnish much of the information needed for determining the particular physical characteristics; it is also required to provide additional structural data essential to understanding the functioning of any signaling system. We need to know the features of as many of the signals as possible, how variable each is, and to what degree the different classes of signals intergrade. We also need to know their distributions of occurrence in an animal population, in terms of their grading by age, sex, and social status and in terms of the presence and ranges of "dialectical" differences.

Another very important question is whether signals or their constituent features occur in different simultaneous or sequential combinations. That is, do these systems possess syntactical properties? So far only very few combinatorial phenomena have been found that are loosely analogous to the syntactic operations of intensification in human languages. However, the foremost advantage of syntactic systems is the large number of different events provided by a few combinatorial elements, and as far as is known, nonlinguistic signaling systems involve impressively small numbers of different signals.

Functional aspects. Once some degree of resolution can be provided for questions concerning the structural properties of animal signaling systems, combined observation and experimentation in the field and laboratory is also indispensable for answering the next broad set of questions—those addressed to the functioning of the systems. These questions occur on at least two levels. The first is concerned with the functional determinants of the glandular–muscular actions of the participants in a particular social episode; the other is concerned with the functioning of such episodes on an ecological level, that is, in the contribution that these conventionalized behaviors make to the species' over-all mode of adaptation. Questions on both levels must be posed in terms relevant to the social and ecological settings into which the evolution of these signaling processes has fitted them. Although it is completely clear that deep understanding of functional problems cannot be achieved without recourse to experimental methods, the scientific value of the uses of such methods is directly proportional to their degree of congruence with information concerning the nature of the ecological adaptations of animal populations.

Before pursuing these functional considerations of animal signaling systems any further, we should pause briefly to immunize what is to follow against some of the conceptual poisons that so easily infect discussions of this kind. Fortunately, most of the deleterious aspects of the biologist's notion of function have been removed by the recognition of the worthlessness of teleological explanations for the teleological mechanisms that so pervade the phenomena of life. But they continue to pose a threat when the functioning of communicative acts is considered, because of the seductive qualities of thinking about signaling actions in terms of the purposes or intentions of the signaler. It is quite easy to avoid such thinking by thoroughly appreciating that animal signaling actions, such as the "waggle" dance performed by workers of some species of bees, are purposive in exactly the same way as a shark's kidneys or a sparrow's hemoglobin. Some day, perhaps, a behavioral theory will be developed in which the notion of purposive actions appears in a way that goes beyond the general idea of biological adaptation and that sharply distinguishes, say, only some kinds of human actions as purposive in this special sense. Until then the term "purposive" will be a predicate more of features of biological populations than of specific actions, and we might do better just to use the term "adaptive" and get on with the task of discovering the specific features of particular signaling, neuromuscular, renal, and biochemical systems and how they function to confer selective advantage on their possessors.

On the behavioral level two principal questions about the functioning of signaling systems confront us. The first is concerned with the circumstances of an animal's environment (external and internal) that determine its signaling actions and can be taken as concerning the *reference* of the signals generated by such actions. The second question concerns the behavior changes contingent upon signal reception, or what may be called the *significance* of the signal. Because the reference of a signal may be only indirectly connected to its significance, describing the functions of signaling systems in terms of transferring information or conveying meaning may often be quite strained. Even when the reference and significance of a signaling action can be specified, nothing is added on the behavioral level of analysis by assertions about the information transmitted or the message conveyed, although these may be warranted, and indeed important, considerations on an ecological level of analysis.

The emotional components. In examining the events of signal emission from a viewpoint somewhere between the glandular–muscular and ecological levels of analysis, one gets, along with Darwin and many others, a strong impression of their fundamentally emotional character. That is, signal emission is associated with shifts in the levels of arousal of emotional or drive states in the animal, induced by the environmental changes to which the signal refers. This characterization is, of course, flagrantly anthropomorphic and becomes increasingly objectionable as the signaling systems of animal forms below the birds and mammals are considered. At present there is not much meaning to discussions of the emotional qualities of a spider's courtship behaviors. Nevertheless, to the degree that the term "emotional" can be provided any technical meaning with respect to human behavior, this anthropomorphistic usage does have some measure of justification, because of the emotional character of much of man's nonlinguistic signals, particularly those emitted by human infants, and their apparent homology with the signals of other animal forms (Andrew 1963; Schaller 1963). Actually, a more forceful objection to the emphasis on the emotional qualities involved in the processes of animal signal emission might be that they are quite unexceptional in this regard. If the bulk of all animal behavior, man's included, were organized and activated by emotional processes, then accounting for the apparent exceptions would present the most challenging problems. Perhaps the most notable of such exceptions would be those forms of human interaction, mediated by linguistic signaling systems, that appear to be specifically protected, though often only flimsily, against emotional influences by traditional conventions (Hebb & Thompson 1954). But even when linguistic signals do not refer to emotional processes (though they very often do), much of the variation in their linguistically nonsignificant features is subject to emotional determination.

Not only do animal signaling actions appear to be associated with emotional processes in the emitter; their significance, that is, their effect on their receivers, is largely emotional as well. Characteristically, the consequences of signal reception involve changes in the emotional status of the receiver, frequently leading to its emission of signaling actions in turn, which evoke further emotional changes in the initial signaler, and so on, until sometimes quite elaborate interaction episodes, such as the courtship patterns of many birds, are sequentially unfolded in this way. Obviously, there is more that transpires in such episodes than just exchanges of signals, but the important point is that the actions of the participants are steered by the emotional changes arising from signal reception.

Mechanisms. The strength of these restrictions is unknown, but it has an important bearing on the kinds of answers that might be proposed to questions about the mechanisms governing signal emission, the behavior consequences of signal reception, and the development of these mechanisms in species and their members. The specific features of these mechanisms have not been established for any species, but gratifying progress has been made in determining the general nature of neurochemical components of the mechanisms and their dynamics, particularly for some avian species (as, for instance, in the work of Lehrman 1962; Schein & Hale 1959; Holst & Saint Paul 1962).

This work suggests that whatever the various mechanisms may be, we should be prepared to expect them to be no different from the mechanisms governing other, nonsocial behavior. Similarly, we can expect the development of their components to involve interactions of various sorts between genetic and experiential factors (Marler 1963). And we should not be surprised to find, especially for the more advanced forms, that different developmental histories underlie the mechanisms governing the emission of different signals or the responses to them in a given species. For instance, it could very well be that for a particular signal hereditary factors are more penetrant in the development of the mechanisms governing its emission than the behavioral results of its reception, or vice versa. Because of this we may find that certain signaling mechanisms in some animals are highly plastic, not only in terms of their references, but also in the physical form of the signals they produce. This is already well established for phonatory signaling of certain species of "talking" birds (Ginsburg 1960; Grosslight et al. 1962), but more surprisingly, the techniques of operant conditioning have also been used to manipulate vocalization of some nonhuman mammals, such as the domestic dog (Salzinger & Waller 1962), the house cat (Molliver 1963), the bottlenose dolphin (Turner 1964), and the chimpanzee (Hayes & Hayes 1950).

However, it is far from clear that any of the above cases represents a departure from the emotional character of these signaling actions. The degree to which the activation of these signaling mechanisms may be divorced from emotional processes is a particularly exciting question, for the answers may yield a better understanding of the basis of this independence in human speech (Geschwind 1964).

JARVIS BASTIAN

[Other relevant material may be found in EMOTION; ETHOLOGY; IMPRINTING; INSTINCT; KINESICS.]

BIBLIOGRAPHY

The bibliography for this article is combined with the bibliography of the article that follows.

II

COMMUNICATION MODELS AND SIGNALING BEHAVIOR

To understand the ways whereby animals communicate with each other requires the cooperative attack of a wide variety of disciplines, ranging from bioacoustics and biochemistry through anatomy to sensory physiology and neurophysiology, and from comparative psychology and zoology to anthropology and linguistics. The diverse lines of research that have converged on the study of animal communication—which, in turn, seems so far to have constituted the principal axis of synthesis in the entire field of animal behavior—may together be subsumed under the label *zoosemiotics*. This word was coined (Sebeok 1963*a*, p. 465) to emphasize the necessary dependency of this emerging field on a science that involves, broadly, the coding of information in cybernetic control processes and the consequences that are imposed by this categorization where living animals function as input–output linking devices in a biological version of the traditional information-theory circuit, with a transcoder added. Thus, the science of zoosemiotics lies at the intersection of general semiotics, the doctrine of signs, and ethology, the biological study of behavior [*see* ETHOLOGY; SEMANTICS AND SEMIOTICS].

Zoosemiotics

The essential unity of a zoosemiotic event may be decomposed, for a field observer's or laboratory experimenter's convenience, into six aspects, and the sphere of animal communication studies has in practice tended to divide roughly in accordance with these dimensions. The hexagonal model which is suggested here (Broadhurst 1963, chapters 2, 3) entails a communication unit in which a relatively small amount of energy or matter in one animal, the *source*, brings about a relatively large redistribution of energy or matter in another animal, the *destination*, and postulates a *channel* through which the participants are capable of establishing and sustaining contact. Every source requires a transmitter, which serves, by a process called encoding, to reorganize the messages it produces into a form that the channel can accommodate; and a receiver is required to reconvert, by a process called decoding, the incoming messages into a form that can be understood by the destination. The source and the destination are therefore said to share, at least partially, a *code*, which may be defined as that set of transformation rules whereby messages can be converted from one representation to another. An ordered selection from a conventional set of signs is a *message*. The physical embodiment of a message is a signal, which is usually mixed with noise. (The term "noise" here refers to variability at the destination not predictable from variability introduced at the source.) Finally, to be operative, the message presupposes a *context* referred to and apprehensible by the destination.

The origin, propagation, and effect of signs can be studied by an examination of the manner in which an animal encodes a message, how this is transmitted in a channel, and how the user decodes it. Since any form of physical energy can be exploited for purposes of communication, a primary task is to specify the sensor or constellation of sensors employed among the members of a given species or among members of different species. Organisms may have sensors for chemicals in solution or dispersed in air (taste and smell), sensors for light (vision), sensors for pressure changes (tactile perception or hearing), or still other sensors involving, for example, parts of the electromagnetic spectrum besides the visual portion. Many animals employ multiple sense organs: thus, communication among bees involves olfactory, optical, acoustic, and other mechanical signals; a herd of mule deer achieves social integration by hearing, vision, smell, and touch.

Chemical systems provide the dominant means of communication in most animal species (Wynne-Edwards 1962, chapter 6; Wilson & Bossert 1963; Bossert & Wilson 1963) and perhaps even in birds. Information is transferred by substances referred to as pheromones (Wilson 1963). Chemical signals may be emitted by an animal's entire body cover, the skin, by special scent glands (e.g., as in ruminants), and by still other parts of the body. They may be received throughout the body (e.g., as in some aquatic invertebrates) or by specialized structures called chemoreceptors, that is, by the distal organs of smell and the proximal organs of taste. It is as yet unknown whether any animal can modulate the intensity or pulse frequency of pheromone emission to formulate new messages. Pheromones tend to function as yes–no signals: a particular scent either is produced or it is not; once emitted, however, the odor is very likely to persist and, thus, convey a message after the departure of its source from the site. The one great advantage, therefore, of chemical signals is their capacity— exploited for social integration by terrestrial mammals especially—to serve as vehicles of communication into the future. This function whereby an individual can leave messages for another to find in his absence or, by a delayed feedback loop, even leave messages for himself, is analogous to the human use of script (Haldane 1955). Its overwhelming evolutionary value is confirmed by the fact, for example, that herbivores usually leave telltale trails, at the risk of revealing their whereabouts to carnivores, while some of the latter broadcast a strong smell advertising their presence, at the sacrifice of part of the surprise element in hunting.

Optical systems (Marler 1961*b*; Wynne-Edwards 1962, chapter 2; Tinbergen 1964) presuppose reflected daylight in the case of diurnal species and bioluminescence (McElroy & Seliger 1962) in those species that dwell in dark but transparent media. Patterns of visual activity are highly variable as to shape and color, duration, and range of intensity; they can also be actively displayed by movements and postures, as in three-spined sticklebacks (Tinbergen 1953*a*); by facial expressions, as in the primates (Andrew 1964); or by intermittent flashing, as in fireflies. Thus, visual signs are both flexible and transient: they can be rapidly switched on or off. These capacities allow for precise coding of information and may even be exploited to misdirect, as in protective displays involving "eyespots" in moths (Blest 1957). Ethologists, concerned with the origin and evolution of visual and other forms of signaling behavior, have described and provisionally classified them into three principal categories: movements signifying intention, that is, those which seem to be preparatory or incomplete versions of functional acts (such as choking in kittiwakes); autonomic effects (such as piloerection in dogs); and so-called displacement movements, that is, those which appear to be irrelevant in the context in which they are delivered (such as preening in pigeons during courtship). Ethologists think that there has been an evolutionary process of increased adaptation to visual signaling behavior; they call this modification ritualization.

Tactile systems include rather disparate phenomena, from all sectors of the animal world. They all have in common the requirement that the individuals communicating by such means must be in physical contact: suckling, copulating, fighting, social grooming or mutual preening. Although communication in this channel is thereby limited to relatively short distances, its effective range can be increased somewhat by the use of elongated feelers, such as antennae, tentacles, barbels, fin rays, or the like, and considerably further by, for example, lines of silk, as in many spiders (Wynne-Edwards 1962, chapter 7). Since tactile signals are subject to wide variations in duration and intensity, they are particularly useful for the transmission of quantitative information, such as distances. The nature of topographic discriminations achieved through an animal's body surface or through more or less sensitive contact receptors is not well understood; the possibilities of cutaneous message processing are, however, being explored (Geldard 1960).

Partly because it has an immediate appeal to the imagination of men and partly because it was stimulated by technological refinements that be-

came available in the decades after World War II, the study of the mechanical vibrations by which some animals communicate constitutes one of the most advanced branches of zoosemiotics (Symposium on Animal Sounds and Communication 1960; Busnel 1963). Bioacoustical systems may operate in the air, as with insects and with birds, which as a class are the most vocal of animals. The mammals that communicate this way are the bats (Griffin 1958), shrews, rodents, deer, seals (Bartholomew & Collias 1962), the carnivores, especially Felidae (Moelk 1944) and Canidae (Hafez 1962, pp. 442–443), and the monkeys and anthropoid apes (Yerkes & Learned 1925; Altmann 1966). Bioacoustical systems for social communication and display may also operate underwater (Wynne-Edwards 1962, chapter 4; Symposium on Marine Bio-acoustics 1964) and have been variously recognized among Crustacea, aquatic insects, fishes, and Cetacea; in recent years whale communication has been receiving increased attention (Sebeok 1963*a*). Finally, rhythmic changes of density in a solid may also form an acoustical system, e.g., the quacks of queen honeybees are transmitted directly through the hive material (Wenner 1962). Although both visual and auditory perception occur in space and time, vision is pre-eminently the spatial sense, just as audition is the temporal. In acoustic communication, reaction times are typically fast (the speed of response in the avian ear is estimated to be about ten times that in the human: Thorpe 1963*a*) and sound signals can be received at as great distances as chemical ones. The emission of sounds involves a minute output of energy, and their transient character makes accurate timing possible. If perceived by the proper receiving organs, sounds—especially those in the higher frequencies—can be directional, when it is advantageous that information about the sender's location be broadcast; on the other hand, with the use of lower frequencies the sender's whereabouts may be kept concealed. Sound fills the entire space around the source and therefore does not require a straight line of connection with the receiver: a signal can travel around corners and is not usually interrupted by obstacles. This flexibility in frequencies, intensities, and patterns is important in that it allows for considerable specific differentiations, as well as, within a species, for individual variation with many shadings and emphases.

Echolocation—where the encoder and decoder of an acoustic (or, sometimes, electrically coded) message is the same living animal in a situation of rapid feedback—may be regarded as a special case of communication. This phenomenon was first discovered in bats (Griffin 1958) but has since been found in all sorts of other animals, including gyrinid beetles, the South American oilbird, the southeast Asian swiftlet, and some seals and porpoises (Kellogg 1961). It has also been shown that moths of the family Arctiidae emit noisy ultrasonic pulses when they detect insectivorous bats pursuing them and that these bursts may function to mislead their predators (Dunning & Roeder 1965).

It is well known that certain fishes generate electric fields. It seems probable that some of the feebler impulses are employed for signaling, at least in those species (such as a number of mormyrids and gymnotids) where the frequencies and patterns of discharge are distinct (Wynne-Edwards 1962, chapter 5). Such electric rhythms have even been compared to the song displays of birds and ascribed an analogous territorial function. While it is suspected that thermal sensation, also, is employed as a communication channel among certain animals, there is as yet insufficient evidence to substantiate this.

Matter, as well as energy, may serve as a message conductor, as in honeybees, ants, and termites, where processes that bring food and water also transport information vital to the survival of the colony. This form of semiotic biosocial facilitation of interindividual stimulative relationships is known as trophallaxis (Wheeler 1926; Lindauer 1962).

Context and significance of signals

Although it is both necessary and proper to distinguish the several channels of animal communication and to study each in isolation, the redundancy that prevails among the multiplicity of bands in natural systems—an effect sometimes referred to as the law of heterogeneous summation—must soon become an object of both theoretical and practical concern. The over-all code that regulates an animal communication network often seems to consist of a set of subcodes grouped in a hierarchy. Fluctuations that occur in these subcodes are determined by such factors as the kind of information to be transmitted, the availability of alternative channels, and the distance between source and receiver. Thus, in the mountain gorilla, vocalizations employed when the individual is hidden from view by dense vegetation serve to draw attention to the animal emitting them; these sounds notify other gorillas of the specific emotional state of the performer and alert them to watch for gestures, which then communicate further information. Postures and gestures, especially facial expressions, coordinate behavior within the group when the distance between the members decreases; the vis-

ual subcode is in turn replaced by the tactile subcode when distance is still further diminished, as between a female and her small infant (Schaller 1963).

In each species the source of a message must share a code with its destination. This is the critical element of communicative commerce; it constitutes a particularized version of the universal "need to know." Every emitting organism's selection of a message out of its species-consistent code, as well as the receiving organism's apprehension of it, proceeds either in accordance with a "closed" genetic program, automatically and predictably shaping a wholly prefabricated set of responses, or with reference to the animal's unique memory store, which then directs the way in which the genetically precoded portion of the total behavior program is acted out. Even in "open" behavior programs certain releaser mechanisms can begin to function only at predetermined stages of maturation. The relationship of learning to instinct in animals in general has been reviewed by Thorpe (1963b), and the relative influence of inheritance and learning in the development of vocalizations by Marler (1963), while the question of learning from alien species, especially the capacity of certain birds and mammals to imitate human speech—the phenomenon of mimicry—has been examined by Andrew (1962). As one would expect, the higher vertebrates tend to be increasingly malleable through learning experience—certain domesticated species can even be motivated by verbal instruction (elephants, for example, can be trained to distinguish between up to 24 different commands by purely auditory perception).

The basic assumption of zoosemantics is that in the last analysis all animals are social beings, each species with a characteristic set of communication problems to solve. All organic alliances presuppose a measure of communication: protozoa interchange signals; an aggregate of cells becomes an organism by virtue of the fact that the component cells can influence one another. Creatures of the same species must locate and identify each other; moreover, they must convey information as to what niche they occupy, in territory as well as status, in the social hierarchy and also as to their momentary mood. Intraspecific and interspecific messages furthering ends such as these can be coarsely categorized in terms of their ecological or functional contexts, and different scholars have devised roughly comparable, but all more or less subjective, schemes to classify the supposed signification of the signals they have observed. Thus, it is possible to note intraspecific expressions of threat, warning, fear, pain, hunger, and—at least in the highest of animals—such feelings as defiance, well-being, superiority, elation, excitement, friendliness, submission, dejection, and solicitude and interspecific warning signals, intimidating signals, decoying signals, and positive or negative masking signals (Wynne-Edwards 1962, pp. 24–25). Frings and Frings (1964) have noted species identification in aggregational systems (cellular, sessile, mobile, social, and interspecific) and dispersal systems (ritualized fighting, aggressive displays, and territorial behavior); social cooperation, involving such items of information as alarm signals (subclassified as indicators of departure, distress, warning, and the like) and food signals; sexual attraction and recognition; courtship and mating; and communication in the parent–young relationship. Collias (1960, p. 387) relates all acoustic messages to five contexts: food gathering, predatism, sexual and allied fighting behavior, parent–young interrelations, and aggregations and group movements. Armstrong, with due cautioning about difficulties and uncertainties, lists the categories required to cover the range of context in the auditory communication of birds (see Table 1).

Table 1

Identity	Motivation	Environment
Species	Sexual need	Location
Sex	Need (other than sexual)	(a) individuals
Individuality	Escape or alarm	(b) objects
Status		Territory
		Predators

Source: Adapted from Armstrong 1963, p. 6.

The associative ties between signals and their meanings are often arbitrary (as opposed to iconic): thus, tail movements in a dog denote friendship; in a cat, hostility; and in a horse, the presence of flies. Some signals are "shifters" (Sebeok 1965a), whose meaning differs according to the situation: thus, the honeybee's tail-wagging dance has more than one denotatum, for it designates either a food source or a nesting site; the gesture pattern is identical, its pragmatic import depending, not upon variation in the form of the expression, but solely upon the attendant physical context. The herring gull's head tossing has more than one function: it occurs as a precoital display, but this is indistinguishable from the head tossing exhibited by a female begging for food (Tinbergen [1953b] 1961, p. 112).

The importance of compiling a complete inventory of the behavior of every species studied has been stressed by, among others, Tinbergen (1951),

who called collections of raw materials of this sort "ethograms." An ethogram should, of course, incorporate a description of the zoosyntactic properties of the codes peculiar to each species. In this respect an ethographer plays the role of a cryptanalyst, receiving messages not destined for him and ignorant of the pertinent transformation rules. Although there are perhaps 700,000 animal species extant, virtually none of the codes in use is fully understood, not even the one regulating the remarkable communication system honeybees have developed. While the fact that these bees perform intricate movements—the famous "dances"—in directing their hivemates to a source of food supply or to new quarters has been widely reported and is now a familiar story, it is not so well known that these insects transmit information through acoustic means as well. It has been amply demonstrated that the length of the train of sound emitted during the straight run of the dance tells the distance of the find (Wenner 1964), but this discovery is bound to be only a first step in the comprehensive unfolding of the auditory subcode of the bees; researchers in several laboratories are now investigating this hardly anticipated facet of the apiarian ethogram.

Following certain distinctions noted by Morris (1946, pp. 219–220), it seems useful to mark three possible approaches to zoosemiotics: pure, descriptive, and applied.

Pure zoosemiotics is concerned with the elaboration of theoretical models or, in the broadest sense, with the development of a language designed to deal scientifically with animal signaling behavior.

Descriptive zoosemiotics comprehends the study of animal communication as a natural and as a behavioral science, in its pragmatic, semantic, and syntactic aspects, as briefly outlined in this article.

Finally, *applied zoosemiotics* aims to deal with the exploitation of animal communication systems for the benefit of man. Utilitarian applications—tasks, in the main, for the future—may be confidently envisaged in wildlife management (e.g., control of the coyote by input of its own or its prey's distress calls); agriculture (e.g., pollination of orchard trees by electronically programmed bees); and pest control (e.g., the prevention of woodpecker damage to wooden utility poles by use of repellent chemical and auditory signals). Our knowledge of basic zoosemiotic processes may also be put to practical uses to supplement existing human information-handling devices (in aiding the deaf and the blind, in assisting communication with man in outer space), and to advance bionics, the science of converting living systems into mechanical and electrical analogues. Linguists and psycholinguists who are concerned with animal communication are interested chiefly in disclosing the biological and anthropological origins of human communication. They seek answers to particular questions such as these: what are the anatomical and physiological correlates of verbal behavior and what sensory and cognitive specializations are required for language perception? what motivates the onset and accomplishment of language learning in the development of human infants? why do subhuman forms lack the capacity to acquire even the beginnings of language? how can present evolutionary theory account for the unique form and behavior of language in man? what is the genetic basis for language propensity, man's species-specific biological endowment? Zoosemiotics, although still in its infancy, provides the scientist with a simpler setting in which to search for solutions than does the far more complex sociobiological environment that constitutes the framework of man's communicative behavior.

THOMAS A. SEBEOK

[See also ETHOLOGY; SEMANTICS AND SEMIOTICS; SOCIAL BEHAVIOR, ANIMAL.]

BIBLIOGRAPHY

ALTMANN, STUART A. 1962 Social Behavior of Anthropoid Primates: Analysis of Recent Concepts. Pages 277–285 in Eugene L. Bliss (editor), *Roots of Behavior: Genetics, Instinct, and Socialization in Animal Behavior.* New York: Harper.

ALTMANN, STUART A. (editor) 1966 Social Communication Among Primates. Unpublished manuscript.

ANDREW, R. J. 1962 Evolution of Intelligence and Vocal Mimicking. *Science* New Series 137:585–589.

ANDREW, R. J. 1963 Evolution of Facial Expression. *Science* New Series 142:1034–1041.

ANDREW, R. J. 1964 The Displays of the Primates. Volume 2, pages 227–309 in John Buettner-Janusch (editor), *Evolutionary and Genetic Biology of Primates.* New York: Academic Press.

ARMSTRONG, EDWARD A. 1963 *A Study of Bird Song.* Oxford Univ. Press.

BARTHOLOMEW, GEORGE A.; and COLLIAS, NICHOLAS E. 1962 The Role of Vocalisation in the Social Behaviour of the Northern Elephant Seal. *Animal Behaviour* 10:7–14.

BLEST, A. D. 1957 The Evolution of Protective Displays in the Saturnioidea and Sphingidae (Lepidoptera). *Behaviour* 11:257–309.

BLEST, A. D. 1961 The Concept of "Ritualisation." Pages 102–124 in W. H. Thorpe and O. L. Zangwill (editors), *Current Problems in Animal Behaviour.* Cambridge Univ. Press. → Discusses the process whereby "derived" movements have arisen.

BORST, ARNO 1963 *Der Turmbau von Babel: Geschichte der Meinungen über Ursprung und Vielfalt der Sprachen und Völker,* Vol. 4. Stuttgart (Germany): Hiersemann.

BOSSERT, WILLIAM H.; and WILSON, EDWARD O. 1963 The Analysis of Olfactory Communication Among Animals. *Journal of Theoretical Biology* 5:443–469.

BROADHURST, PETER L. 1963 *The Science of Animal Behaviour.* Baltimore: Penguin.

BUSNEL, RENE G. (editor) 1963 *Acoustic Behaviour of Animals.* New York: American Elsevier.

COLLIAS, N. E. 1960 An Ecological and Functional Classification of Animal Sounds. Pages 368–391 in Symposium on Animal Sounds and Communication, Indiana University, 1958, *Animal Sounds and Communication.* Edited by Wesley E. Lanyon and W. N. Tavolga. Washington: American Institute of Biological Sciences.

DARWIN, CHARLES (1872) 1965 *The Expression of the Emotions in Man and Animals.* Edited by Francis Darwin. Univ. of Chicago Press. → Modern developments stem largely, if indirectly, from this classic work.

DEVORE, IRVEN (editor) 1965 *Primate Behavior: Field Studies of Monkeys and Apes.* New York: Holt.

DREHER, J. J.; and EVANS, W. E. 1964 Cetacean Communication. Pages 373–393 in Symposium on Marine Bio-acoustics, Lerner Marine Laboratory, 1963, *Marine Bio-acoustics.* Edited by William N. Tavolga. New York: Pergamon.

DUNNING, DOROTHY C.; and ROEDER, KENNETH D. 1965 Moth Sounds and the Insect-catching Behavior of Bats. *Science* New Series 147:173–174.

ETKIN, WILLIAM 1963 Communication Among Animals. Pages 149–165 in Jon Eisenson et al., *The Psychology of Communication.* New York: Appleton. → A survey article which concludes that the essential difference between human and animal communication lies in the capacities of the mind.

ETKIN, WILLIAM 1964 Theories of Socialization and Communication. Pages 167–205 in William Etkin (editor), *Social Behavior and Organization Among Vertebrates.* Univ. of Chicago Press.

FALLS, J. B. 1963 Properties of Bird Song Eliciting Responses From Territorial Males. Pages 259–271 in International Ornithological Congress, Thirteenth, *Proceedings.*

FRINGS, HUBERT; and FRINGS, MABLE 1964 *Animal Communication.* New York: Blaisdell: → Intended primarily for nonspecialists; reviewed in Sebeok 1965b.

FRINGS, MABLE; and FRINGS, HUBERT 1960 *Sound Production and Sound Reception by Insects: A Bibliography.* University Park: Pennsylvania State Univ. Press.

FRISCH, KARL VON 1950 *Bees: Their Vision, Chemical Senses, and Language.* Ithaca, N.Y.: Cornell Univ. Press.

GELDARD, FRANK A. 1960 Some Neglected Possibilities of Communication. *Science* New Series 131:1583–1588. → Deals with messages transmitted over the cutaneous channel.

GESCHWIND, NORMAN 1964 The Development of the Brain and the Evolution of Language. Georgetown University, Washington, D.C., Institute of Languages and Linguistics, *Monograph Series on Languages and Linguistics* 17:155–169.

GINSBURG, NORMAN 1960 Conditioned Vocalization in the Budgerigar. *Journal of Comparative and Physiological Psychology* 53:183–186.

GRIFFIN, DONALD R. 1958 *Listening in the Dark.* New Haven: Yale Univ. Press. → On the acoustic orientation of bats and men.

GROSSLIGHT, JOSEPH H.; HARRISON, P.; and WEISER, C. 1962 Reinforcement Control of Vocal Response in the Mynah Bird (Gracula Religiosa). *Psychological Record* 12:193–201.

HAFEZ, E. S. E. (editor) 1962 *The Behaviour of Domestic Animals*. Baltimore: Williams & Wilkins.

HALDANE, J. B. S. 1955 Animal Communication and the Origin of Human Language. *Scientific Progress* 43:385–401.

HASKELL, PETER T. 1961 *Insect Sounds*. Chicago: Quadrangle.

HASKELL, PETER T.; and FRASER, F. C. (editors) 1962 *Biological Acoustics*. Symposia of the Zoological Society of London, No. 7. London: The Society.

HAYES, KEITH J.; and HAYES, CATHERINE 1950 Vocalization and Speech in Chimpanzees [motion picture]. University Park: Pennsylvania State Univ., Psychological Cinema Register.

HEBB, D. O.; and THOMPSON, W. R. 1954 The Social Significance of Animal Studies. Volume 1, pages 532–561 in Gardner Lindzey (editor), *Handbook of Social Psychology*. Cambridge, Mass.: Addison-Wesley.

HESS, ECKHARD H. 1962 Ethology: An Approach Toward the Complete Analysis of Behavior. Pages 157–266 in *New Directions in Psychology*, by Roger Brown et al. New York: Holt.

HINDE, R. A. 1964 Intraspecific Communication in Animals. Pages 62–84 in David McK. Rioch and Edwin A. Weinstein (editors), *Disorders of Communication*. Baltimore: Williams & Wilkins.

HINDE, R. A.; and ROWELL, T. E. 1962 Communication by Postures and Facial Expression in the Rhesus Monkey (Macaca Mulatta). Zoological Society of London, *Proceedings* 138:1–21.

HOCKETT, CHARLES F. (1958) 1963 *A Course in Modern Linguistics*. New York: Macmillan. → See especially section 64.

HOCKETT, CHARLES F. 1959 Animal "Language" and Human Language. Pages 32–39 in Symposium on the Evolution of Man's Capacity for Culture, Chicago, 1957, *The Evolution of Man's Capacity for Culture: Six Essays*. Edited by James N. Spuhler. Detroit, Mich.: Wayne State Univ. Press. → Discusses seven crucial design features of human language.

HOCKETT, CHARLES F. 1960a The Origin of Speech. *Scientific American* 203, no. 3:88–96. → Discusses 13 design features shared by all the languages of the world.

HOCKETT, CHARLES F. 1960b Logical Considerations in the Study of Animal Communication. Pages 392–430 in Symposium on Animal Sounds and Communication, Indiana University, 1958, *Animal Sounds and Communication*. Edited by Wesley E. Lanyon and W. N. Tavolga. Washington: American Institute of Biological Sciences. → A more extensive and more technical presentation than Hockett 1960a.

HOCKETT, CHARLES F. 1963 The Problem of Universals in Language. Pages 1–22 in Conference on Language Universals, Dobbs Ferry, N.Y., 1961, *Universals of Language*. Edited by Joseph H. Greenberg. Cambridge, Mass.: M.I.T. Press.

HOCKETT, CHARLES F.; and ASCHER, ROBERT 1964 The Human Revolution. *Current Anthropology* 5:135–168.

HOLST, ERICH VON; and SAINT PAUL, URSULA VON 1962 Electrically Controlled Behavior. *Scientific American* 206, no. 3:50–59.

HUXLEY, JULIAN; and KOCH, LUDWIG 1964 *Animal Language*. New York: Grosset & Dunlap.

INDIANA UNIVERSITY, CONFERENCE ON PARALINGUISTICS AND KINESICS, BLOOMINGTON, 1962 1964 *Approaches to Semiotics: Cultural Anthropology, Education, Linguistics, Psychiatry, Psychology*. Edited by Thomas A. Sebeok et al. Janua linguarum, Series Maior, No. 15. The Hague: Mouton.

KAINZ, FRIEDRICH 1961 *Die "Sprache" der Tiere: Tatsachen, Problemschau, Theorie*. Stuttgart (Germany): Enke. → Reviewed in Sebeok 1964.

KELLOGG, WINTHROP N. 1961 *Porpoises and Sonar*. Univ. of Chicago Press. → Reviewed in Sebeok 1963a.

LEHRMAN, DANIEL S. 1962 Interaction of Hormonal and Experiential Influences on Development of Behavior. Pages 142–156 in E. L. Bliss (editor), *Roots of Behavior: Genetics, Instinct, and Socialization in Animal Behavior*. New York: Harper.

LENNEBERG, ERIC H. 1964 A Biological Perspective of Language. Pages 65–88 in Eric H. Lenneberg (editor), *New Directions in the Study of Language*. Cambridge, Mass.: M.I.T. Press.

LIBERMAN, ALVIN M. (1957) 1961 Some Results of Research on Speech Perception. Pages 142–153 in Sol Saporta (editor), *Psycholinguistics: A Book of Readings*. New York: Holt. → First published in Volume 29 of the *Journal of the Acoustical Society of America*.

LINDAUER, MARTIN 1961 *Communication Among Social Bees*. Cambridge, Mass.: Harvard Univ. Press. → Reviewed in Sebeok 1963a.

LINDAUER, MARTIN 1962 Ethology. *Annual Review of Psychology* 13:35–70.

LINSDALE, JEAN M.; and TOMICH, P. QUENTIN 1953 *A Herd of Mule Deer: A Record of Observations Made on the Hastings Natural History Reservation*. Berkeley: Univ. of California Press.

McELROY, WILLIAM D.; and SELIGER, HOWARD H. 1962 Biological Luminescence. *Scientific American* 207, no. 6:76–89.

MARLER, PETER 1959 Developments in the Study of Animal Communication. Pages 150–206 in Peter R. Bell (editor), *Darwin's Biological Work: Some Aspects Reconsidered*. Cambridge Univ. Press.

MARLER, PETER 1961a The Logical Analysis of Animal Communication. *Journal of Theoretical Biology* 1:295–317.

MARLER, PETER 1961b The Evolution of Visual Communication. Pages 96–121 in Conference on Vertebrate Speciation, University of Texas, 1958, *Vertebrate Speciation: A University of Texas Symposium*. Edited by W. Frank Blair. Austin: Univ. of Texas Press.

MARLER, PETER 1963 Inheritance and Learning in the Development of Animal Vocalization. Pages 228–243 in Rene G. Busnel (editor), *Acoustic Behaviour of Animals*. New York: American Elsevier. → See also pages 794–797.

MASON, WILLIAM A.; and RIOPELLE, A. J. 1964 Comparative Psychology. *Annual Review of Psychology* 15:143–180. → Reviews the literature concerning primate behavioral research.

MATTHEWS, L. HARRISON; and KNIGHT, MAXWELL 1963 *The Senses of Animals*. London: Museum Press.

MILLER, ROBERT E. et al. 1959 Non-verbal Communication of Affect. *Journal of Clinical Psychology* 15:155–158.

MILNE, LORUS J.; and MILNE, MARGERY J. 1962 *The Senses of Animals and Men*. New York: Atheneum.

MOELK, MILDRED 1944 Vocalizing in the House-cat: A Phonetic and Functional Study. *American Journal of Psychology* 57:184–205.

MOLLIVER, MARK E. 1963 Operant Control of Vocal Behavior in the Cat. *Journal of the Experimental Analysis of Behavior* 6:197–202.

MORRIS, CHARLES W. 1946 *Signs, Language and Behavior.* Englewood Cliffs, N.J.: Prentice-Hall. → Attempts to develop a language with which to talk about the signs of both animals and men.

RENSCH, B.; and ALTEVOGT, R. 1954 Zähmung und Dressurleistungen indischer Arbeitselefanten. *Zeitschrift für Tierpsychologie* 11:497–510. → On the taming and training of Indian elephants.

SALZINGER, KURT; and WALLER, MARCUS B. 1962 The Operant Control of Vocalization in the Dog. *Journal of the Experimental Analysis of Behavior* 5:383–389.

SCHALLER, GEORGE B. 1963 *The Mountain Gorilla: Ecology and Behavior.* Univ. of Chicago Press.

SCHEIN, M. W.; and HALE, E. B. 1959 The Effect of Early Social Experience on Male Sexual Behavior of Androgen Injected Turkeys. *Animal Behaviour* 7:189–200.

SEBEOK, THOMAS A. 1962 Coding in the Evolution of Signalling Behavior. *Behavioral Science* 7:430–442. → Examines two differences between speech and communication in subhuman species: the different types of information that each species can communicate and the different methods by which they code information.

SEBEOK, THOMAS A. 1963a [Reviews]. *Language* 39:448–466. → Discusses Kellogg 1961 and Lindauer 1961 among others.

SEBEOK, THOMAS A. 1963b The Informational Model of Language: Analog and Digital Coding in Animal and Human Communication. Pages 47–64 in Paul L. Garvin (editor), *Natural Language and the Computer.* New York: McGraw-Hill. → A revised version of Sebeok 1962.

SEBEOK, THOMAS A. 1964 [Review of] *Die "Sprache" der Tiere: Tatsachen, Problemschau, Theorie* (1961), by Friedrich Kainz. *American Anthropologist* New Series 66:954–956.

SEBEOK, THOMAS A. 1965a Animal Communication. *Science* 7:1006–1014.

SEBEOK, THOMAS A. 1965b [Review of] *Animal Communication* (1964), by Hubert Frings and Mable Frings, *Science* New Series 147:492–493.

SYMPOSIUM ON ANIMAL SOUNDS AND COMMUNICATION, INDIANA UNIVERSITY, *1958* 1960 *Animal Sounds and Communication.* Edited by Wesley E. Lanyon and W. N. Tavolga. Washington: American Institute of Biological Sciences. → Includes chapters on sound communication in Orthoptera and Cicadidae; sound production and underwater communication in fishes; the influence of sound on the behavior of amphibians and reptiles; the ontogeny of vocalizations in birds; bird songs and mate selection; an ecological and functional classification of animal sounds; and Hockett 1960b.

SYMPOSIUM ON MARINE BIO-ACOUSTICS, LERNER MARINE LABORATORY, *1963* 1964 *Marine Bio-acoustics.* Edited by William N. Tavolga. New York: Pergamon.

TEMBROCK, GÜNTER 1959 *Tierstimmen: Eine Einführung in die Bioakustik.* Wittenberg (Germany): Ziemsen.

THORPE, WILLIAM H. 1961a *Bird-song: The Biology of Vocal Communication and Expression in Birds.* Cambridge Monographs in Experimental Biology, No. 12. Cambridge Univ. Press.

THORPE, WILLIAM H. 1961b Comparative Psychology. *Annual Review of Psychology* 12:27–50.

THORPE, WILLIAM H. 1963a Antiphonal Singing in Birds as Evidence for Avian Auditory Reaction Time. *Nature* 197:774–776.

THORPE, WILLIAM H. 1963b *Learning and Instinct in Animals.* 2d ed., rev. & enl. Cambridge, Mass.: Harvard Univ. Press. → The first edition was published in 1956.

TINBERGEN, NIKOLAAS 1951 *The Study of Instinct.* Oxford: Clarendon. → Experimental ethological methods.

TINBERGEN, NIKOLAAS 1953a *Social Behaviour in Animals, With Special Reference to Vertebrates.* London: Methuen.

TINBERGEN, NIKOLAAS (1953b) 1961 *The Herring Gull's World: A Study of the Social Behavior of Birds.* Rev. ed. New York: Basic Books.

TINBERGEN, NIKOLAAS 1963 On Aims and Methods of Ethology. *Zeitschrift für Tierpsychologie* 20:410–433.

TINBERGEN, NIKOLAAS 1964 The Evolution of Signaling Devices. Pages 206–230 in William Etkin (editor), *Social Behavior and Organization Among Vertebrates.* Univ. of Chicago Press.

TURNER, R. N. 1964 Methodological Problems in the Study of Cetacean Behavior. Pages 341–350 in Symposium on Marine Bio-acoustics, Lerner Marine Laboratory, 1963, *Marine Bio-acoustics.* Edited by William N. Tavolga. New York: Pergamon.

WENNER, ADRIAN M. 1962 Communication With Queen Honey Bees by Substrate Sound. *Science* 138:446–447.

WENNER, ADRIAN M. 1964 Sound Communication in Honeybees. *Scientific American* 210, no. 4:116–124.

WHEELER, WILLIAM M. (1926) 1928 *The Social Insects: Their Origin and Evolution.* New York: Harcourt. → First published in French.

WILSON, EDWARD O. 1963 Pheromones. *Scientific American* 208, no. 5:100–114. → Discusses chemical substances secreted by animals that influence the behavior of other animals of the same species.

WILSON, EDWARD O.; and BOSSERT, WILLIAM H. 1963 Chemical Communication Among Animals. Volume 19, pages 673–716 in Laurentian Conference, *Recent Progress in Hormone Research: Proceedings.* Edited by G. Pincus. New York: Academic Press.

WOOD-GUSH, D. G. M. 1963 Comparative Psychology and Ethology. *Annual Review of Psychology* 14:175–200.

WYNNE-EDWARDS, V. C. 1962 *Animal Dispersion in Relation to Social Behaviour.* Edinburgh and London: Oliver & Boyd; New York: Hafner.

WYNNE-EDWARDS, V. C. 1963 Intergroup Selection in the Evolution of Social Systems. *Nature* 200:623–626.

YERKES, ROBERT M.; and LEARNED, BLANCHE W. 1925 *Chimpanzee Intelligence and Its Vocal Expressions.* Baltimore: Williams & Wilkins.

COMMUNICATION, INTERPERSONAL

See COMMUNICATION; DIFFUSION, *article on* INTERPERSONAL INFLUENCE; INTERACTION; KINESICS; PERCEPTION, *article on* PERSON PERCEPTION.

COMMUNICATION, MASS

I. THE STUDY OF MASS COMMUNICATION	*Morris Janowitz*
II. CONTROL AND PUBLIC POLICY	*Wilbur Schramm*
III. TELEVISION AND ITS PLACE IN MASS CULTURE	*Richard Hoggart*
IV. AUDIENCES	*Leo Bogart*
V. EFFECTS	*Joseph T. Klapper*

I
THE STUDY OF MASS COMMUNICATION

Urbanization, industrialization, and modernization have created the societal conditions for the development of mass communications. In turn, these processes of social change produce societies that are highly dependent on mass communications. Mass communications comprise the institutions and techniques by which specialized social groups employ technological devices (press, radio, films, etc.) to disseminate symbolic content to large heterogeneous and widely dispersed audiences. In other words, mass communications perform essential functions for a society that uses complex technology to control the environment. These functions of mass communications include the transmission of a society's heritage from one generation to another, the collection of information for the surveillance of the environment, and the correlation of the various parts of the society in response to changes in the environment. Social science research on mass communications seeks an objective understanding of the institutions that fashion mass communications and the consequences of communication and mass persuasion for human society.

The social scientific perspective. In surveying the extensive research on mass communications, one finds that there are great gaps between the orientations of social scientists and those of mass media personnel and their critics. First, there is a great difference in estimates of the effectiveness and potency of the mass media based on the findings of social scientists as compared with the viewpoints of those directly involved in operating the channels of mass communications. Mass media personnel, as well as their critics, tend to contend that the mass media are all-pervasive influences and powerful agents of social change. Thus they point to the individual and dramatic impact of specific programs and campaigns, such as the publication in Germany of President Woodrow Wilson's Fourteen Points early in 1918, or Orson Welles's dramatization of H. G. Wells's *War of the Worlds* over the CBS radio network in 1938 (for which see Cantril 1940). They point to the long-term consequences of the mass media in fashioning tastes and moral standards and in creating images of political leaders. While social scientists continue to differ in their particular inferences and conclusions, in general they tend to view the impact of the mass media as circumscribed. They see the mass media as limited agents of social change and as only one element among others, such as technological progress, organizational controls, cultural and ideological forms, and the processes of socialization and personality development.

In part, this gap is due to the different questions being asked by mass media personnel and by social scientists. Professional practitioners in the mass media are seeking specific and pragmatic answers to practical communications problems, while research workers are more concerned with general principles and hypotheses. In part, this gap is due to the weaknesses and limitations of social science research on mass communications, which, because of its highly fragmented character, is often not cumulative and therefore unable to supply valid answers to basic issues.

Second, the mass media have been subjected to uninhibited social criticism by some intellectuals and practitioners who see them as contributing to the demise of civilization. These critics hold the view that the growth of the mass media, in and of itself, deteriorates moral and intellectual standards. This point of view stands in contrast to the aspiration of intellectuals at the turn of the century, who hoped that with the proliferation of the mass media, modern society, however large and complicated, could yet fulfill the requirements of the democratic process. It was in the mass media that hopeful thinkers saw a new opportunity for mass education and the elevation of men's minds. Modern political history has undermined such intellectual hopes, and in the contemporary world the mass media are seen by critics as speeding up the development of a mass society and the destruction of individuality. But the social scientific point of view must reject the notion that the growth of the mass media necessarily produces an undifferentiated society with a general lack of articulation and an inability to make collective decisions. Researchers must see the mass media as instruments of social control and social change that may have either positive or negative consequences, depending upon their organization and content.

Popular images of the pervasive effects of the mass media were generated by the use of propaganda during World War I, by the growth of mass advertising in the United States during the 1920s, and by the use of mass techniques of agitation in the rise of European totalitarian movements. Thus, it is understandable that the first results of empirical research were to challenge such perspectives and to debunk popular notions. For example, although the pioneering studies on the impact of the movies carried out under the auspices of the Payne Foundation (Charters 1933) showed definite and discernible consequences of moviegoing for youth behavior—often socially undesirable consequences

—the over-all conclusions hardly attributed a pervasive influence to the film in shaping youth culture. Specific studies on totalitarian states conducted during World War II and thereafter also revealed that after the seizure of power by dictators mass persuasion became less important as a basis of control in these political systems. The image of limited communication effect was, in particular, reinforced by research on the basis of civilian and military morale in Germany and Japan (see, for instance, Shils & Janowitz 1948), which showed that ideology was of limited significance and that hostile propaganda could operate only within specific confines. In addition, laboratory studies on the impact of the mass media, as well as studies using the sample survey technique, also tended to produce findings that highlighted the limitations of mass effects, especially since these research procedures were used mainly to study specific messages and short-term effects.

Nevertheless, students of mass communications recognize that available research describes only part of a complex process and that the findings of specific empirical studies need to be evaluated and integrated by means of a more systematic frame of reference that takes into consideration the fundamental nature of personality and the broader process of social change. This frame of reference includes, first, the assumption that the mass media both reflect the social structure and social values of a society and operate as agents of social change. Because of the diffuse nature of communications processes, the mass media are both causes and effects; or, in the language of social research, they are both independent and dependent variables. Therefore, the full range of effects can only be understood by making inferences about causal processes. Second, the analysis of mass communications involves not only a study of the continuous process of transmitting symbols and their effect on audiences but also the equally complex and subtle process by which the audience communicates with and influences the communicator. In fact, this assumption implies that the analysis of mass communications is incomplete unless this two-way process is included. Third, mass communication systems invariably involve an interplay with interpersonal communications. Again, a comprehensive analysis requires the study of how interpersonal communications condition the communicator as he produces messages and content and, in turn, how interpersonal communications negate or increase the impact of mass communications on audiences.

As a result of the complexity of the mass communication process, most research has been oriented toward probing one or another phase of the total process. Harold Lasswell's phrase, "Who says what to whom with what effect?" has been the general format in which specific research proceeds: The "who" question includes the study of the organization and personnel of the mass media; "what" refers to the content of the mass media; "to whom" points to the structure of the audience and various audience characteristics; and the "with what effect" aspect has received attention in the studies of mass media impact and audience response. Although this format was coined over thirty years ago (Lasswell 1932), it still presents a highly useful approach for integrating the large number of diverse approaches to the study of the mass media of communications and their effects. But the study of each element must be thought of as a step in understanding the total process and especially in estimating the long-run consequences of mass media.

Personnel and organizational structure

The "who" question has been investigated through two different but highly interrelated approaches. First, who are the people—the managers, directors, writers, performers—who produce and transmit mass communications? This is the sociology of an occupational and professional group. What are the social origins, educational backgrounds, career lines, and professional organizations of mass media personnel? What type of personalities are attracted to work in the mass media, and what are their self-images and social perspectives?

Second, since mass communications must inevitably be produced by large organized collectivities rather than by individual persons or small groups, what are the decision-making processes in mass media enterprises? How are these enterprises structured in terms of status, power, and other elements of social control? What consequences do the technological characteristics of the various media have on their internal organization? How does the control of the mass media relate to the economic and political organization of the society?

Personnel and professionalization have been the least explored aspects of the mass media. However, two comprehensive studies by Leo Rosten—one on the Washington corps of correspondents (1937) and the other on the Hollywood movie colony (1941)—reveal several central issues. The Washington correspondents represent a case of the highly developed but informal type of professionalization, where rules and regulations concerning standards of performance have evolved and are enforced by colleague pressures so as to raise the level of performance. On the other hand, Hollywood, as a movie colony and subsequently as a television center, represents an extreme case of the type of media establishment that has a high level of social and interpersonal tensions; in such communications enterprises the demand for spontaneity and creativity necessarily outruns human energies. The popular stereotype of Hollywood as a frenzied, schizoid community staffed by persons with constant fears of failure and frequent feelings of self-hatred is a caricature that is apparently not without support in fact.

The limited number of studies of the sociology of the creative arts in the mass media, together with astute observations of participants who have written on the subject, such as James T. Farrell (1946), suggest that one major source of discontent and "alienation" among mass media personnel derives from the organizational need to bureaucratize creative effort. The result is a divorce of creative workers from control over and identification with the end products of their work. The term "bureaucratization" must be used with reservation, for a considerable number of productive activities in the mass media have not become rationalized. Therefore, sociological observations about alienation among the producers of mass aesthetics are difficult to translate into precise conclusions. These notions apply to the very small numbers of truly creative personalities and not to the vast bulk of symbol handlers and technicians. Moreover, it would appear to be an error to assume that inevitably the essence of creativeness is lost in organized group effort. We need merely to recall the corps of assistants who worked with Michelangelo and Rubens or the monuments to collective artistic creativity such as the Sainte-Chapelle and the cathedrals of Chartres and Milan.

The significant point is not that artistic and creative work has been collectivized in the mass media for the first time in human experience, but that it has been extensively collectivized on a scale never before possible. The technological requirements of the mass media and the exaggerated pressure to create rapidly under deadlines force a high degree of specialization and a detailed review of each person's efforts. In the setting of a massive and complex organization, as is to be found in many of the mass media, it is not difficult for the individual worker, whether artist or not, to lose or otherwise abnegate his sense of personal responsibility for the quality of the work eventually produced. Nevertheless, against this response must be weighed the pressures of creativity or of profes-

sional responsibility to maintain areas of individuality even in these large-scale organizations. One of the reasons that such pressures continue to exist is that the pervasive demand for new ideas and new content insures a constant and ever increasing search for talent.

It is also important to distinguish between genuine creativity and professional responsibility among mass media personnel. Social research has little to say about the conditions under which genuine creativity appears, but it is clear that the organization of the mass media has tended to inhibit or at least dampen the development of professional responsibility. It is very difficult to apply the concept of professionalism to the mass media personnel in a one-party state, while in nations with multiple-party systems and relatively autonomous communications institutions, the status of mass media personnel is more that of employees of a large-scale organization than that of practicing professionals. Even in Great Britain, where the organization of journalists is highly developed, the professional associations are more concerned with conditions of work than with professional standards. In democratic societies there are no bodies for enforcing professional standards among journalists or even quasi-public bodies for reviewing and evaluating their performance. Professionalization therefore takes the more limited form of an emphasis on more adequate educational preparation (a topic about which there is little agreement), a concern with informal relations among specialists, and the development of devices such as the increased reliance on the "by-line" in order to identify mass media products with individual producers and writers [see JOURNALISM].

The absence of higher levels of professionalization in the mass media is a result of the structure and process of decision making within the mass media. Because of the presumed importance of the mass media as instruments of social and political control, these institutions become fused with the basic control structure of any society. In a totalitarian state, this control is comprehensive but not without inherent limitations. If the media of such political systems are to serve more than merely to reaffirm basic societal loyalties, and if they are to disseminate information and contribute to collective problem solving, then some limited degree of independence is required. Alex Inkeles, in his *Public Opinion in Soviet Russia* (1950), a research study that describes the organization of the Soviet mass media, points to such devices as letters to the editors and reports of self-criticism as efforts to increase the validity and acceptance of mass media content. In some one-party socialist societies there have been modifications of central party controls, including the development of limited areas of professional responsibility for mass media personnel. Often the modification takes the form of creating specialized periodicals with limited circulation to reach specialized groups without disturbing the larger process of mass media control via precensorship.

In multiparty states with mixed forms of media ownership and control, the historical development of the mass media shows a trend toward greater freedom from government control. In such states there is typically an emphasis on the necessity of an independent and competitive mass media system. However, political theorists have come more and more to recognize that the removal of governmental interference does not necessarily, or in fact, produce mass media systems that meet all the requirements of a free society. There have been a small number of penetrating studies of the control structure of the mass media in the United States and Great Britain. Most of these studies were undertaken by foundations, universities, and, in a few notable cases, governmental agencies. They all concluded that certain technological, economic, and organizational factors may prevent competition from supplying an effective basis for high levels of mass media performance. One of the most important of these studies was conducted in the United States under the aegis of a quasi-public sponsor, the Commission on the Freedom of the Press. It is noteworthy that the principal financial supporter of this commission was Henry Luce, head of the Time–Life publishing corporation.

The work of the commission included historical surveys of the radio, motion picture, and book industries, as well as a comprehensive review of the role of the government in the mass media process. The policy recommendations of the commission (Commission on Freedom of the Press 1947) were afterward closely paralleled by the findings of the British Royal Commission on the Press (Great Britain . . . 1947–1948). In short, while government interference was rejected by both reports, the view they set forth was that traditional conceptions of competition would not guarantee adequate media performance. Instead, it was recommended that the mass media accept public responsibility for presenting a comprehensive and meaningful interpretation of contemporary events and that the government would have to take a positive role in this process.

Underlying these recommendations was a series of empirical observations that were documented in the 1940s and have been repeatedly confirmed by subsequent research. For the United States, these studies point to a drift of the major media toward increasing centralization in their decision-making processes, but none has even suggested that complete monopolistic control is or will be the outcome in any of the mass media industries. The evolving pattern is rather that which appears to obtain in many other areas of mass production, namely, that a limited number of very large units dominate a wide sector of a particular medium or even a combination of media. That a degree of competition has characterized the relations among these organizational giants cannot be denied. This competition is to a considerable extent enhanced by the fact that the audience can choose between various media.

Moreover, technological changes do not inherently move in the direction of supporting more and more concentration. For example, frequency modulation (FM) radio has introduced a new network of decentralized units; and even in the newspaper field in the United States, the trend toward consolidation has leveled off as new reproduction techniques have been introduced. Equally apparent, however, is the fact that the large producers of mass communications have often cooperated with each other in generally successful efforts to fend off attempts by other, supposedly countervailing, power groups (such as the government, the churches, and other public or private interest organizations) to influence decisions regarding the structure and content of the mass media.

In assessing the consequences of this drift toward power concentration, simple stereotyped conclusions are not warranted. For the United States, there is considerable evidence that the larger and more all-embracing these industries become, the more they come to resemble public institutions and the more sensitive they grow to the shifting imperatives of public opinion, public relations, and public responsibility. Of course, the mass media have developed codes of performance to protect themselves from the extreme excesses of public pressure. These codes have tended to be negative in outlook and to neglect the needs of specialized audiences. It has been suggested that in some circumstances the fewer the units of mass communications the less they are susceptible to the dictates of particular outside vested interest groups. Thus it is argued, for example, that publishers in a community with only one newspaper are relatively immune to the pressures of advertisers, inasmuch as the latter have no recourse to the threat of taking their business elsewhere.

To make these observations is not to suggest, however, that where mass media are operated as business enterprises a community of interests with other business enterprises fails to operate. Nor is it to argue that the mass communicators' growing consciousness of the attitudes of the public means that the control of the mass media is inevitably becoming more responsible. The meaning of public opinion and public responsibility may be read and interpreted in different ways. Recourse to the dictates of public taste and opinion may quite conceivably mean little more than the misuse of survey data to justify existing tastes, rather than stimulate new and more enlightened interests. Furthermore, an easy acquiescence to the amorphous and often ambiguous desires of the audience may simply reinforce those pressures and opportunities for the abdication of leadership responsibility for change.

If in the democratic societies the issues of media control focus on professional and organizational responsibility, throughout wide sectors of the world the basic issue is still the establishment of greater autonomy of the press. Raymond Nixon's investigation of the freedom of the press throughout the world indicates that there is a gradual trend toward broader freedom. He linked this development to higher levels of education and economic development (Nixon & Ward 1961). However, there is no reason to believe in the inevitability of such a trend or to assume that specific variables are at work. This issue involves the most fundamental and complex processes of political development.

Content of mass communications

The symbols and messages of the mass media are available for widespread consumption. The sheer availability of mass communications content has stimulated a considerable body of research into the "what" aspect of Harold Lasswell's four-faceted question. Research into mass media content, or content analysis, as it has come to be called, has been particularly influenced by the recognition that such content is amenable to quantitative treatment (see especially Lasswell & Leites 1949; Berelson 1952). As a result, content analysis procedures, both quantitative and qualitative, have been applied to all types of media content, most frequently for descriptive purposes and to a lesser extent as an analytical tool for analyzing the communications process and its impact. First, content analysis has been an effective instrument for describing both short-term and long-term trends in media content. The range of topics covered by descriptive trend studies is indeed broad: for example, such studies have traced the decline in prophetic religious themes in popular sermons (Hamilton 1942), the growth of scientific authority as a basis of child-rearing advice in women's magazines (Mead &

Wolfenstein 1955), and the trend in propaganda, from World War I to World War II, toward a less emotional, less moralistic, and more truthful orientation (Kris & Leites 1947). Second, content analysis supplies an approach for comparing the same material as presented in different media within a nation or the contents of the same media as between different nations. For example, Asheim (1949) found that in converting dramatic fiction into movies the result was not to produce "happy" ends but rather indeterminate endings. For cross-national purposes, school textbooks have supplied a convenient device for revealing societal differences (Walworth 1938).

Third, the procedures of content analysis are also particularly appropriate for comparing media content with some explicit set of standards or abstract categories. For example, studies have been done to determine whether newspapers conform in their content to particular standards. In this vein, content analysis is also used as a form of propaganda detection or propaganda analysis. The objective may be to identify the use of particular propaganda devices, such as simplification, glittering generalities, testimonials, and the like. Alternatively, the objective may be to uncover propaganda strategies by the use of such analytical categories as distortion, parallel presentations, or patterns of imbalance. Propaganda analysis can be based on comparing a suspect source with a set of categories derived from a source identified as representing a biased or propaganda outlet. This particular technique was applied during World War II by the Organizations and Propaganda Analysis Section of the U.S. Department of Justice to compare native fascist publications in the United States with Axis media content. Findings based on these procedures were admitted in court trials of Nazi agents and native fascists and had the consequence of absolving many suspect newspapers and radio stations from charges that were based on only a few examples of bias in their presentation of news or in their editorial comments.

Fourth, content analysis offers a relatively precise technique for describing the diffusion of scientific and scholarly knowledge and for observing the process of popularization of scientific materials. A leading example of this aspect of content analysis is the readability test (Flesch 1951); such tests have been developed to help editors and publishers judge the difficulty of a particular communication and to estimate the type and size of audiences that can readily understand the message.

On the basis of the existing body of quantitative and qualitative research, several broad generalizations may be made about the contents of mass communications. First, what is communicated by the mass media is a highly selected, nonrepresentative sample of all that is available for communication. Likewise, the content that is received and consumed by the potential audience is a highly selected sample of all that is communicated. Second, considerably more communications content is entertaining than informative; there is more of the sort that distracts and diverts attention and less of the quality that stimulates consideration of the central social, economic, and political problems of living. However, notwithstanding the demonstrable difference between the contents of mass communications and the contents of human existence, there remains in the mass media a quantity of the sober and serious, the educational and informational, so considerable that it has served, in the view of some experts (see, for instance, Schramm 1954), to confound and confuse rather than to educate and inform segments of the mass audience. Third, because mass communications are commonly aimed at the largest possible audience, most of them are simple in form and uncomplicated in content. In their desire to be understood by the overwhelming majority of their audiences, mass communicators have tended to de-emphasize intricate presentations, the meanings of which may be unclear and may be misinterpreted. However, with the growth of mass literacy and with ever larger segments of the population receiving college-level education, counter trends have developed. As a society enters the phase of advanced industrialization, there is a trend within the general mass media toward devoting a portion of their content to high-level material, just as there is a trend toward higher quality in those media, such as FM radio and certain publishing houses, that cater to more specialized audiences.

If content analysis procedures are to produce more than descriptive findings, it is necessary to address the simple but basic question, "What does the content of mass communications mainly reflect —the characteristics of the mass audience or the characteristics and intentions of the communicator?" Undoubtedly, the contents of most mass communications reflect both of these elements. In any particular study it is difficult to separate out the relevant importance of each element, and therefore the significance and validity of content analysis remains decidedly problematic. But it is precisely by making assumptions about the conditions under which the contents of the mass media serve either as indicators of the intentions of the communicators or as reflections of the interests and values of the audiences that content analysis

is transformed from a descriptive tool to a device for analyzing the process of mass communications.

The use of content analysis in order to infer the intentions of the communicator is best applied to highly purposive communications such as political content. Nathan Leites (1951) speaks of the "operational code," that is, the basic assumptions and directives underlying the communications of political elites. The more knowledge an analyst has about the organizational setting of political communication the more feasible is such content analysis. Thus, Gabriel Almond, in his study *The Appeals of Communism* (1954), is concerned with the contrast between the pattern of internal communications among Communist party leaders and their core members, on the one hand, and the content of their communications to larger external audiences, on the other. Leo Lowenthal and Norbert Guterman, in *Prophets of Deceit* (1949), analyze the content of fascist output in order to probe its underlying intentions and to assess the limited extent to which these agitators propose an explicit program. This approach also makes the assumption that agitational propagandists have the ability to reflect the repressed aspirations of their particular publics. While their format and appeals may be extreme and their audiences small, their content reflects a measure of potential political desires of the larger society and therefore warrants the closest scrutiny.

By contrast, if content analysis is to be used as a measure of the underlying values and sentiments of the audience, it is appropriate to use mass media content with wide appeals and to trace changes through time or to make comparisons between different countries. We are dealing here with the notion of the "focus of attention." One of the earliest efforts in this regard was that of Hornell Hart (1933), who studied changes in social attitudes and interests through analyses of selected popular magazines published from 1900 to 1930; he found a general decline for this period in the status of religion and religious sanctions, which he took as a measure reflecting changing attitudes toward religion. Leo Lowenthal (1961) has reported on the change in the heroes of popular magazine fiction from idols of production to idols of consumption. Martha Wolfenstein and Nathan Leites (1950) have used the movies as an indicator for the comparative analysis of sexual attitudes in Great Britain, France, and the United States, while McGranahan and Wayne (1948) studied dramatic plays to compare the *Zeitgeist* of the United States with that of Germany. Content analysis of the mass media has become an element in the cultural analysis of traditional societies that are in the process of modernization. Because of the problems involved in making inferences about causality in content analysis, the burden of the task of analyzing the impact of mass media has shifted to the direct study of audience structure and audience response. [See CONTENT ANALYSIS.]

Audience research

One aspect of the direct investigation of the impact of the mass media is the description of the size and structure of the audience for each particular medium of communication. There is a large amount of material, especially from the industrialized nations of Europe and North America, but also increasingly from all the nations of the world, that describes the "to whom" of mass communications in terms of gross characteristics and media preferences. The Department of Mass Communications of UNESCO has an active program for collecting basic statistical data on the development of the mass media and the size of audiences throughout the world. These world-wide reports rely mainly on statistical data about the number and circulation of newspapers, radio receiving sets, movie theaters, published books, and other measures of audiences that derive from production figures. Important aspects of audience size can also be measured from such "built-in" or automatic measures of consumption as ticket sales, newsstand circulation, or subscription sales. However, a basic impetus to audience research has come from those media, such as radio and television, which lack such simple measures; the managers of these media frequently want to know more about the social characteristics of their audiences and to find out what particular segments of their output receive the greatest attention.

Interest in audience research is particularly strong in the United States, where the mass media are heavily supported by commercial advertising revenues. Paul F. Lazarsfeld has been one of the leading experts in the development of such research. Although various mechanical and electronic devices as well as self-reporting questionnaires and diaries have been used, the standard approach is to make use of sample surveys to measure audience size and composition. Frequently these surveys are conducted by telephone and involve elaborate and rapid field work in order to measure the relative position of leading mass media performers. For the United States, Handel (1950) has summarized movie audience research, and Bogart (1956) has done the same for television.

In countries where radio and television are operated by the government, audience research is carried out for the purpose of understanding audience reactions and as an aid to program planning. Thus, for example, the British Broadcasting Corporation and the various West German regional networks have extensive audience research programs. Even in such one-party socialist states as Poland, radio audience research is undertaken both for scientific purposes and in order to take into account consumer preferences and tastes.

A summary of the more quantitative findings of audience surveys will show some of the changes that have taken place as the content and roles of the media have changed. Although American audiences are by no means typical, they do reflect the pattern existing in those countries where there is an increasingly high level of mass media penetration together with some choice between alternative offerings. In the United States television has emerged as the dominant medium, and national surveys in the mid-1960s reveal that the typical American family watches as much as four hours of television daily. Despite this extensive exposure to television, 85 per cent of the families read one or more newspapers regularly, and 60 per cent read one or more magazines regularly. As newspapers have transformed themselves from essentially political journals to purveyors of news, human interest features, and amusement materials, their readership ranks have been broadened to become more representative of the whole population. Television has captured large segments of the former radio audience; however, radio broadcasting of music and news has re-emerged in response to more specialized demands. The movies have suffered the most from the impact of television; but film attendance is still extensive among young people, and "super-features" attract mass adult audiences. The number of comic books sold each month exceeds the number of children in the country. Clearly, the term "mass audience" is no misnomer.

Researchers have also devoted energy to the question of whether mass media exposure is competitive or cumulative (Columbia University . . . 1946). Is exposure to one medium associated with exposure to others, or does one medium crowd out the next? No clear-cut answers are available, for at least two patterns can be discerned. In one sense, exposure is cumulative: with an increase in level of education, persons who are exposed to one medium (including television) are likely to expose themselves to newspapers, magazines, and books. In other words, as a person's field of interest is broadened by more education, his interests in the mass media also grow. However, there is a point at which competition sets in, for even with the growth of leisure there are limits to available time. Especially among better educated persons, extensive involvement with television reduces the time spent on and interest in other mass media. For these groups, there appears to be some competition between the printed media (newspapers, magazines, and books) and the electronic media (television and radio).

By contrast, the development of the mass media and audience exposure in the so-called new nations reflects limited levels of literacy and scarcity of technological facilities. However, most of these nations make large investments to increase literacy and to expand the mass media as part of the processes of economic development and the formation of central political control. In many of them literacy has risen at a faster rate than was the case for Europe during the nineteenth century. While these new mass media systems are not developed in depth, after a country achieves independence there is characteristically a striking increase in the capacity of these media to disseminate messages from the central political authority. In these nations the media and audience structures that develop are different from those of Western industrialized nations. Newspapers and magazines supply crucial but limited channels of communication between elite groups, especially in the urban centers, while radio emerges as the national mass medium because of its low cost and because it does not depend on the prior development of literacy.

Audience research has developed in the direction of seeking to describe more precisely the social and psychological characteristics and the specific content preferences of the persons who make up the audiences of particular media. Routine surveys of audience structure, especially those sponsored by commercial groups, proceed in terms of basic categories such as age, sex, education, occupation, and income. But these categories are not refined enough to capture the complexities of contemporary social structure. Nor do the categories focus sharply enough on the web of group and associational life through which a person is integrated into the larger society. As a result, the explanatory power of conventional research into audience structure is not very great.

Emerging lines of research are reflected in the work of university-based scholars, such as Harold Wilensky (1964), who have sought to classify audience membership in terms of more refined categories, such as career patterns and work settings. This approach focuses on the content as well as on the amount of education. Emphasis is placed on the bureaucratic setting in which the person follows his profession or occupation and on the role of voluntary associations in conditioning media exposure.

Audience research has also come progressively to concentrate on social-psychological and personality characteristics. Both from a theoretical point of view and in the practical application of research findings, it is not enough to know the gross characteristics of those persons who are exposed to a particular channel of communication. It is equally important to isolate those social-psychological predispositions that can be appealed to in order to mobilize new audiences or to change the exposure patterns of existing ones.

Walter Lippmann's classic book, *Public Opinion* (1922), in which he developed the term "stereotype," still remains a basic point of departure for the analysis of audiences. Human personality has a powerful capacity to simplify social reality and to select congenial elements from the media content. The oversimplification of social reality, especially when it is rigidly rooted in personal and social needs, is the essence of the process of stereotyping. Following up on these basic insights and broadening the perspective to include the observations of psychoanalysis resulted in a series of brilliant studies by Herzog (1943), Warner and Lunt (1941), and Henry (1947).

In recent years, advertisers have shown considerable interest in the study of the motive structures underlying exposure to various types of sale messages. The term "motivation research" has been loosely used to refer to studies that seek to understand the social psychology of audience exposure to advertisements. Popular accounts of these developments (see, for instance, Packard 1957) have attracted widespread public attention, but they have not answered the question of the extent to which such audience research has increased the power of advertising beyond that produced by forceful and imaginative practitioners operating without benefit of systematic research.

At some point research on audience characteristics blends with the direct study of audience reactions and media impact. Audience research includes studies of media preferences, interest in particular types of content and messages and in the mass imagery of the media, and the level of confidence and trust that the audience places in different media sources. These dimensions are not only audience characteristics but also indicators of the ongoing impact of the mass media. Thus in the United States, for example, surveys indicate that popular trust in television as a news source has gradually risen to a level comparable to that for newspapers. The increased confidence in television as a news source is concentrated among young people who have grown up in a television culture and thus accept this channel with fewer reservations than their parents.

In the United States audience research sponsored by commercial television companies also documents extensive audience criticism of television content, including complaints about the great amount of violence and the heavy emphasis on advertising. While such criticism reflects a popular culture that encourages critical remarks about television, and while this criticism does not lead to marked resistance to television exposure or articulated demands for changes in programming, these attitudes are noteworthy. These findings underline the conclusion of careful observers that television no longer has a single mass audience but, like the film audience, is becoming more specialized. According to Steiner (1963) there are at least two major segments in the television audience. On the one hand, there is the mass audience that is satisfied with a common fare and that exercises little or no selectivity in its viewing habits. On the other hand, there is another segment that consumes massive dosages of television but that actively searches for a more subtle media fare. (The distinction is between the viewers of the nondescript westerns and those who require westerns that have historical, revealing, or thoughtful contents, such as "High Noon" or "Gunsmoke"; another example is the distinction between the viewers of an anthology of light drama and those who watched the "Play of the Week.") Nevertheless, these same findings on audience structure indicate that as the national levels of education rise, there are marked changes in the mass media, but that because of the economic and organizational reasons described above in the section on media control, a lag persists in the capacity of the mass media to supply the demands of more discerning audience tastes and standards.

Communications effects

The findings of studies of communications effects are strongly influenced by the research methods that are employed. The three basic approaches are experimental studies, both laboratory and quasi-laboratory experiments; surveys based on interviews or questionnaires; and intensive case studies employing participant observation, informal and group interviews, personal documents, and other sources of documentation. While the technical aspects of effect studies have been greatly refined and improved, these methodologies were already employed in the Payne Foundation studies of films which were completed during the early 1930s.

The first two methods are the most extensively utilized because of their presumed quantitative precision. In the experimental technique, persons are given controlled exposure to a communication, and the effects are evaluated on the basis of the measurement of attitudes before and after such exposure. This method also requires comparison with a control group that is not exposed to the message. In the sample survey method, data are collected by means of questionnaires or interviews dealing with media exposure and attitudes, opinions, and behavior. The goal is to derive conclusions from correlations obtained between the degree or conditions of exposure to various communications and the measured attitudes and behavior. A sample survey can be a type of field experiment if the interviews are repeated during the period in which the population studied is exposed to the mass media. The third approach, that of the case study in depth, has emerged less as a specific method of research than as a strategy of evaluation and synthesis of material from a variety of sources.

From the thousands of laboratory experiments, it has been demonstrated that under contrived conditions even brief messages can produce measurable changes in attitudes among selected groups. Because experiments deal with persons removed temporarily from their social group attachments, it is understandable that experimental findings are formulated as psychological and social-psychological propositions without regard to the cultural and social setting. Under the stimulation of Carl Hovland and his associates (e.g., Hovland et al. 1953), this form of experimentation has become highly sophisticated, and the theoretical assumptions have been made explicit. This approach has generated some illustrative findings with regard to the conditions under which communications tend to be effective, for example: communications are more effective when they seek to alter peripheral rather than central attitude patterns, when they are cumulative, and when they seek to reinforce rather than to convert existing attitudes. However, it is recognized that there are limiting conditions that are not included in the experimental design.

Experiments have demonstrated a "sleeper" effect, namely, that the consequences of exposure to even a brief message can be delayed and become manifest some time after the exposure. Considerable research has been done on such topics as the credibility and prestige of the source, the order of presentation of items, and the manner of presentation of controversial issues. For example, experiments have shown that among better educated persons the presentation of both sides of an issue produces more attitude change than the presentation of only one side, while less educated persons are more influenced by communications that employ one-sided arguments (Hovland et al. 1949).

Investigation of the question of whether attitudes are changed more by arguments that diverge a little or by ones that diverge a great deal from a person's opinion has led to contradictory findings. The importance of the issue or its salience to the person may be an intervening variable; that is, for important issues arguments that diverge slightly may produce more change in attitudes than do marked differences (Hovland et al. 1957). Psychologists have been particularly concerned with the role of anxiety in producing or inhibiting the receipt of information and modifying attitudes, since a great deal of mass communication makes use of "scare" techniques. Laboratory research indicates that there is a point at which the anxiety produced by such appeals becomes so great that it actually inhibits attitude change (Janis & Feshbach 1953).

The findings from experiments seem to show evidence of attitude changes that are greater than those reported by survey research studies. This discrepancy is due to the differences in the research technology and the research objectives, for neither approach supplies definitive and comprehensive answers. Experiments deal with specific delimited messages, while surveys must of necessity focus on broader flows of communications. The experimental situation is seen as contrived, and therefore the results have been labeled by some specialists as unreal. In particular, because the experimental situation deals with specific messages, it rules out those contradictory messages that a person encounters in the real world of communications. In other words, because the subjects are "forced" to be exposed to a message, the process of self-selection of content is weakened. It is precisely this mechanism of self-selection of material congruent with one's existing opinion that reduces the impact of mass communication. Sample survey findings are better able to cope with this process of self-selection. Moreover, experiments generally tend to deal with immediate reactions to mass communications, while surveys cover a longer period of time and therefore include the extinction effect.

Experimental studies tend to deal with relatively unimportant issues as compared with surveys.

Again, this would lead to uncovering greater impact in the case of experiments, but there have been efforts to introduce important substantive issues into experimental work. Perhaps the most important difference between the two methods is that in experimental work the salience of social group affiliation is eliminated and the audience is reduced to a collection of individuals, a form of mass so to speak, and therefore becomes more liable to persuasion. Some experiments have built-in group process variables and have found that communication effects are therefore reduced. An alternative formulation of the issue is the contention that most experiments deal with university undergraduates in an educational setting, that is, a population and a setting predisposed to change, and that this is not an adequate representation of social reality.

Nevertheless, the experimental approach has important advantages because of its precision and ability to focus on specific variables. In contrast, because the survey approach cannot focus on specific messages, it may overlook particular forms of mass media impact. For example, survey work on the impact of television has followed the same pattern as the earlier work on the impact of movies. In Great Britain, Hilda Himmelweit and her associates (Himmelweit et al. 1958) found that television did not have a profound effect on children's behavior and academic achievement; its effect was more discernible on a small minority of overexposed children for whom there was reason to believe that television served as a form of defense, as a result of social and personal difficulties. However, experimental studies of exposure to television programs containing aggressive materials give a clearer indication that exposure to such content produces disruptive and socially undesirable effects. It is as if the experimental approach operates as a magnifying glass in revealing subtle reactions that become obscured by more diffuse research tools.

If the experimental method is subject to criticism because of its contrived and oversimplified character, the survey approach has the pervasive difficulty of adequately analyzing the host of intervening variables between the communications "input" and the resulting attitudes and social behavior. However, the strength of the survey method rests in its concern with group process, that is, both with primary group structures and the role of the opinion leader. Mass communication research has been influenced by observational and case studies, particularly in industrial sociology, which have underlined the crucial importance of primary groups (face-to-face intimate associations) in fashioning attitudes and morale. The impact of research findings on military morale during World War II served to refine and extend this type of sociological analysis. In particular, Edward Shils and Morris Janowitz (1948) observed that the German *Wehrmacht* was relatively immune to Allied propaganda appeals because of the effectiveness of primary group cohesion, which protected the rank and file from the appeals of outside sources. The hard-core noncommissioned officers constituted a cadre of "opinion leaders" who supported the control structure; direct attachment to and trust in Hitler served as the basis of secondary attachments. Only when the primary group structure was disrupted were German military personnel accessible to the symbols of Allied propaganda.

There has been a variety of survey researches that have elaborated the importance of primary groups and of rank-and-file opinion leaders in conditioning the impact of the mass media. Preoccupation with these concepts has led to an interpersonal or "two-step" theory of mass communications. As set forth by Elihu Katz and Paul F. Lazarsfeld (1955), this theory asserts that the mass media have influence through informal leaders who have high exposure to the mass media and who in turn make their interpersonal influence felt on their close associates. In this view, the innovation of new practices takes place because the mass media supply ideas to these opinion leaders, who then rely on face-to-face contact as the mechanism of diffusion [see DIFFUSION, *article on* INTERPERSONAL INFLUENCE].

Undoubtedly this is one process of audience response, but there are other processes through which the mass media have an impact. First, there is considerable research evidence that some persons are directly accessible to the mass media because they have weak rather than strong group attachments (see Daugherty & Janowitz 1958). These are persons characterized by a high degree of "anomie" and a limited degree of social integration. Often these individuals verbalize their distrust of societal institutions and the mass media; nevertheless, they come to depend heavily on selected channels for their opinions and social support. Second, on certain issues, certain persons will find themselves under conflicting primary group pressures, especially during political campaigns (Janowitz & Marvick 1956). These persons are likewise more accessible to the mass media than those persons who live in a politically homogeneous culture. Third, there are both temporary and more chronic social and psychological conditions, especially during periods of stress and crisis, that weaken the effectiveness of informal face-to-face pressures and controls; under such circumstances the mass media

can more directly impinge on the individual's attitudes, values, and behavior [see BRAINWASHING; PERSUASION].

The two-step theory of communication is neither precise enough in its conceptualization of opinion leaders nor detailed enough in the accumulation of empirical materials. The term "opinion leader" might best be reserved for the limited number of top-level figures in journalism, politics, economic, and professional life who are strategic in the introduction of new ideas. For the United States, the number would be in the hundreds at most, and such persons are not to be located by sample surveys. In addition, one can speak of mid-level and local community level opinion leaders of increasing numbers but of decreasing influence. Even local community level opinion leaders are limited in number and not identifiable by conventional sample surveys. Forms of sociometric and reputational designation have been used to describe these leaders, especially in studies of community power structures. These researches indicate that, while there are general opinion leaders, leadership can vary on the basis of the specific issues involved. Moreover, formal office and official position also have elements of opinion leadership, since power to influence opinion is not confined to informal and interpersonal networks [see COMMUNITY, *article on* THE STUDY OF COMMUNITY POWER].

The persons identified in sample surveys as opinion leaders might best be described as local "activists." They do have higher levels of exposure to the mass media and greater involvement in local community affairs than other people. These activists also tend to be better educated and of higher socioeconomic status than the population in general. Therefore, one important research task is to understand the dynamics of opinion formation in low income groups and in marginal groups, where the penetration of local activists is incomplete and fragmentary. There is reason to believe that for these groups such functionaries as trade union officials, teachers, and political party officials are more crucial than informal "opinion leaders." Moreover, because lower income people characteristically have weak networks of social contact outside their familial settings, their incomplete views of the larger social order tend to be fashioned by the mass media.

Mass media and social control

The emphasis on discovering specific reactions and changes generated by media content tends to produce a basic distortion or limitation in their findings. The bulk of the content of the mass media is not designed to challenge or modify the social and political structure of a nation, either in a one-party state or in a democratic society. This is not to underemphasize the ability of minority groups to have their points of view presented in the mass media; rather, this is to emphasize that a fundamental impact of the mass media is to contribute to the patterns of social control. Therefore, the impact of the mass media must be judged not only in terms of the changes in attitudes and behavior produced but also in terms of the *reinforcing* effect on social norms and social behavior.

To study mass media as a system of social control, it is essential to encompass all of the elements of Lasswell's formula. This requires the use of the case study, despite all of its scientific limitations. W. I. Thomas' and Znaniecki's classic study, *The Polish Peasant in Europe and America,* includes one of the first major theoretical and empirical analyses of the functional significance of the press as an instrument of social control (1920). Thomas demonstrated that for the submerged Polish community under alien rule in Europe or in minority status in Chicago the native language press supplied an important element of group integration and a linkage to the wider community. Robert E. Park continued this sociological perspective in his study *The Immigrant Press and Its Control* (1922). Lasswell and Kaplan (1950), in their analysis of political power, also assigned to mass communications a crucial role in maintaining and fashioning the symbols of legitimate government.

Theorists with such widely diverse formulations of contemporary social structure as Louis Wirth and Talcott Parsons have emphasized the importance of mass communications systems as instruments of social control (see Wirth 1948; Parsons 1942). Within this general frame of reference, research studies of the structure of industrial societies have taken various forms. For example, Riley and Riley (1959) have sought to probe peer group structure and the consumption of the mass media as elements of normative structure among youngsters. In his study *The Community Press in an Urban Setting,* Morris Janowitz (1952) sought to fuse within a single work analyses of several aspects of the press: its historical development, ownership and control, the social role of the publisher, the image of the community as reflected by the contents of the press, and the functions of the local press for its readers. This research viewed the community press as one of the social mechanisms through which the individual is integrated into the urban social structure. Harold Wilensky (1964) has traced out the role of the mass media in leisure in order to distinguish those occupational

groups for whom the mass media operate to strengthen their associational integration and those for whom the mass media serve as a substitute for group membership. This perspective has also penetrated studies of political communication. The emphasis of such research is less on the study of audience reactions to specific messages and the specific political decisions that are presumed to be generated than it is on the role of the mass media in defining the political issues of the day and in fashioning the relevance of politics for the individual (see, for instance, Lang & Lang 1959).

The social control perspective also supplies a basis for the development of the comparative analysis of mass media systems, a research theme that is likely to grow in importance in the years ahead. The first of such analyses were case studies of the Nazi social system by Harold Lasswell, Ernst Kris and Nathan Leites, and others, who analyzed the declining role of mass communications as the Nazis shifted to a heavier reliance on organizational pressure and terror. Alexander Inkeles and Barrington Moore have studied the Soviet Union during different periods of political control and have emphasized the manner in which the elites have utilized the apparatus of mass agitation, not only as propaganda devices but also as imperfect and fragile channels for informing themselves about popular attitudes and loyalties [*see* PROPAGANDA].

In the comparative analysis of mass communications, the use of mass communications in the rise to power and the consolidation of power by the Chinese Communist party present fundamental issues for communications research. Historians will debate the question whether the Chinese communists' seizure of power and their consolidation of power took place with less terror than in the case of the Russian Revolution. If there was less resistance to their consolidation of power, and consequently less need for terror, this may have been the result of the greater decay of the traditional Chinese social structure. But in the process of political revolution, mass agitation and effective propaganda of the deed appear to be important techniques. While the rise of "thought reform" (brainwashing in popular jargon) is not confined to China, it has been practiced in China on such an immense scale that it has contributed to common understandings and therefore has effectively articulated with organizational controls. As a result, during the first fifteen years after their seizure of power, the Chinese communists were able to rule without the mass purges that characterized the Russian Communist party.

Social scientists have made efforts to integrate the study of the mass media as instruments of control with the study of political and economic developments in the so-called new nations of Africa and Asia. For example, Daniel Lerner (1958) has emphasized the general pattern of increase in standard of living, urbanization, literacy, and exposure to the mass media during the process of transition from traditional to modern society. Social research must guard against the danger of imposing categories grounded in Western experience on these mass communication processes. While there is a heavy emphasis on the expanding of the mass media in developing societies, the penetration of the central authority into the daily consciousness of the mass of the population has to overcome profound resistances. In this process of modernization, the resulting forms are not inevitably Western or European but are likely to include important neo-traditional elements, especially in the area of mass media and mass culture.

The responsibility of social scientists

Finally, research into mass communications has led to extensive debate about the moral implications of social research and the professional responsibility of social scientists. A minority of social scientists, as well as outside observers, have expressed concern that the findings might create the basis for extensive mass manipulation that would weaken and destroy democratic freedoms and values. By contrast, the typical opinion among social scientists working in this field is that knowledge accumulates slowly and that this fear is greatly exaggerated. They rest their position on the historical observation that even without the benefit of scientific research political agitators intuitively have succeeded in the worst imaginable forms of mass manipulation.

A more careful and reasoned defense is to be found among those social scientists who are concerned with a "sociology of knowledge" position. These persons hold that the pursuit of scientific knowledge is a valid and legitimate human goal, provided the research procedures are carried out with due regard for human dignity. They accept the notion that agitators have succeeded without scientific knowledge, but they do not claim that this observation relieves the social scientist from both personal and professional responsibility about the use of his findings. Obviously, in a free society there is a limit to his control over the use of his findings, but he must take reasonable steps to protect both himself and society. These steps involve seeking to insure that his findings are accurately reported in both the professional and popular media and that his research is not made the permanent private property of a particular group or sponsor. He must also seek through professional associations to establish and enforce adequate standards of performance.

The "sociology of knowledge" position rests not merely on personal and professional responsibility but also on a theory of knowledge as well. In this view, the accumulation of knowledge is designed to assist understanding of the power, and therefore of the limits, of mass communications. It assumes that a deeper understanding of social and political processes can serve to reinforce a pluralistic society. In fact, research into mass communication has served to reduce the image of the omnipotence of communications. Mass communications operate within definable parameters, and when mass manipulation becomes excessive, although the results can be disruptive and disastrous, there are other social processes at work as well. In short, research into mass communications has served to emphasize the underlying issue that "institutional building" is required for effective social change. There is no logical or demonstrated reason that it must of necessity create a basis for mass manipulation.

MORRIS JANOWITZ

[See also COMMUNICATION, POLITICAL; FILM; LITERATURE; PROPAGANDA.]

BIBLIOGRAPHY

The amount of monographic research literature on mass communication is vast and will doubtless continue to increase. A number of comprehensive bibliographic volumes have been prepared on the available scientific and semi-scientific literature: for instance Smith, Lasswell & Casey 1946; *and* Bureau of Social Science Research 1956. *As convenient guides to the analysis of mass communications, a series of research and source books has been published for use by students and practitioners. Among them are* Berelson & Janowitz 1950; Schramm 1954; *and* Society for the Psychological Study of Social Issues 1954. *Joseph T. Klapper's* The Effects of Mass Communication 1960, *and Wilbur L. Schramm's* The Science of Human Communication 1963, *supply convenient bibliographic essays.*

ALMOND, GABRIEL A. 1954 *The Appeals of Communism.* Princeton Univ. Press.
ASHEIM, LESTER 1949 From Book to Film: A Comparative Analysis of the Content of Novels and the Motion Pictures Based Upon Them. Ph.D. dissertation, Univ. of Chicago. → Partially reprinted in Berelson & Janowitz (1950) 1966.
BARGHOORN, FREDERICK C. 1964 *Soviet Foreign Propaganda.* Princeton Univ. Press.
BERELSON, BERNARD 1952 *Content Analysis in Communication Research.* Glencoe, Ill.: Free Press.
BERELSON, BERNARD; and JANOWITZ, MORRIS (editors) (1950) 1966 *Reader in Public Opinion and Communication.* 2d ed., rev. & enl. New York: Free Press.

BERKOWITZ, LEONARD; CORWIN, R.; and HEIRONIMUS, M. 1963   Film Violence and Subsequent Aggressive Tendencies. *Public Opinion Quarterly* 27:217–229.

BOGART, LEO (1956) 1958   *The Age of Television: A Study of Viewing Habits and the Impact of Television on American Life.* 2d ed. New York: Ungar.

BUREAU OF SOCIAL SCIENCE RESEARCH, WASHINGTON, D.C. 1956   *International Communication and Political Opinion: A Guide to the Literature,* by Bruce L. Smith and Chitra M. Smith. Princeton Univ. Press.

CANTRIL, HADLEY 1940   *Invasion From Mars: A Study in the Psychology of Panic.* Princeton Univ. Press.

CHAFEE, ZECHARIAH 1947   *Government and Mass Communications.* Univ. of Chicago Press.

CHARTERS, W. W. 1933   *Motion Pictures and Youth: A Summary.* New York: Macmillan.

COLUMBIA UNIVERSITY, BUREAU OF APPLIED SOCIAL RESEARCH 1946   *The People Look at Radio: Report on a Survey Conducted by the National Opinion Research Center.* Chapel Hill: Univ. of North Carolina Press.

COMMISSION ON FREEDOM OF THE PRESS (1947) 1958   *A Free and Responsible Press: A General Report on Mass Communication . . .* Univ. of Chicago Press.

CONFERENCE ON COMMUNICATION AND POLITICAL DEVELOPMENT, DOBBS FERRY, N.Y., *1961* 1963   *Communications and Political Development.* Edited by Lucian W. Pye. Princeton Univ. Press.

DAUGHERTY, WILLIAM E.; and JANOWITZ, MORRIS (compilers) 1958   *A Psychological Warfare Casebook.* Baltimore: Johns Hopkins Press.

DEUTSCH, KARL W. 1953   *Nationalism and Social Communication: An Inquiry Into the Foundations of Nationality.* Cambridge, Mass.: M.I.T. Press; New York: Wiley.

DOOB, LEONARD W. 1961   *Communication in Africa: A Search for Boundaries.* New Haven: Yale Univ. Press.

FARRELL, JAMES T. 1946   *The Fate of Writing in America.* New York: New Directions.

FLESCH, RUDOLF F. 1951   *How to Test Readability.* New York: Harper.

GREAT BRITAIN, ROYAL COMMISSION ON THE PRESS 1947–1948   *Minutes of Evidence.* 1–38. London: H.M. Stationery Office.

HAMILTON, THOMAS 1942   Social Optimism and Pessimism in American Protestantism. *Public Opinion Quarterly* 6:280–283.

HANDEL, LEO A. 1950   *Hollywood Looks at Its Audience.* Urbana: Univ. of Illinois Press.

HART, HORNELL (1933) 1934   Changing Social Attitudes and Interests. Pages 382–443 in President's Research Committee, *Recent Social Trends in the U.S.: Report.* New York: McGraw-Hill.

HENRY, WILLIAM E. 1947   Art and Culture Symbolism: A Psychological Study of Greeting Cards. *Journal of Aesthetics and Art Criticism* 6:36–44.

HERZOG, HERTA (1943) 1950   What Do We Really Know About Day-time Serial Listeners? Pages 352–365 in Bernard Berelson and Morris Janowitz (editors), *Reader in Public Opinion and Communication.* Enl. ed. Glencoe, Ill.: Free Press.

HIMMELWEIT, HILDE; OPPENHEIM, A. N.; and VINCE, PAMELA 1958   *Television and the Child: An Empirical Study of the Effect of Television on the Young.* Oxford Univ. Press.

HOGGART, RICHARD 1957   *The Uses of Literacy: Changing Patterns in English Mass Culture.* Fair Lawn, N.J.: Essential.

HOVLAND, CARL I.; HARVEY, O. J.; and SHERIF, MUZAFER 1957   Assimilation and Contrast Effects in Reactions to Communication and Attitude Change. *Journal of Abnormal and Social Psychology* 55:244–252.

HOVLAND, CARL I.; JANIS, IRVING L.; and KELLEY, HAROLD H. 1953   *Communication and Persuasion: Psychological Studies of Opinion Change.* New Haven: Yale Univ. Press.

HOVLAND, CARL I.; LUMSDAINE, ARTHUR A.; and SHEFFIELD, FREDERICK D. 1949   *Experiments on Mass Communication.* Studies in Social Psychology in World War II, Vol. 3. Princeton Univ. Press.

INKELES, ALEX (1950) 1958   *Public Opinion in Soviet Russia: A Study in Mass Persuasion.* 3d printing, enl. Russian Research Center Studies, No. 1. Cambridge, Mass.: Harvard Univ. Press.

JANIS, IRVING L.; and FESHBACH, SEYMOUR 1953   Effects of Fear-arousing Communications. *Journal of Abnormal and Social Psychology* 48:78–92.

JANIS, IRVING L.; and HOVLAND, CARL I. (editors) 1959   *Personality and Persuasibility.* New Haven: Yale Univ. Press.

JANOWITZ, MORRIS 1952   *The Community Press in an Urban Setting.* Glencoe, Ill.: Free Press.

JANOWITZ, MORRIS; and MARVICK, DWAINE (1956) 1964   *Competitive Pressure and Democratic Consent: An Interpretation of the 1952 Presidential Election.* 2d ed., Michigan, University of, Governmental Studies, No. 32. Chicago: Quadrangle Books.

KATZ, ELIHU; and LAZARSFELD, PAUL F. 1955   *Personal Influence: The Part Played by People in the Flow of Mass Communications.* Glencoe, Ill.: Free Press. → A paperback edition was published in 1964.

KLAPPER, JOSEPH T. 1960   *The Effects of Mass Communication.* Glencoe, Ill.: Free Press.

KRIS, ERNST; and LEITES, NATHAN C. (1947) 1953   Trends in Twentieth Century Propaganda. Pages 278–288 in Bernard Berelson and Morris Janowitz (editors), *Reader in Public Opinion and Communication.* Enl. ed. Glencoe, Ill.: Free Press.

LANG, KURT; and LANG, GLADYS E. (1959) 1966   The Mass Media and Voting. Pages 455–472 in Bernard Berelson and Morris Janowitz (editors), *Reader in Public Opinion and Communication.* 2d ed. New York: Free Press. → This article was first published in 1959 in *American Voting Behavior.*

LASSWELL, HAROLD D. 1932   The Triple-appeal Principle: A Contribution of Psychoanalysis to Political and Social Science. *American Journal of Sociology* 37:523–538.

LASSWELL, HAROLD D.; and KAPLAN, ABRAHAM 1950   *Power and Society: A Framework for Political Inquiry.* Yale Law School Studies, Vol. 2. New Haven: Yale Univ. Press. → A paperback edition was published in 1963.

LASSWELL, HAROLD D.; and LEITES, NATHAN 1949   *Language of Politics: Studies in Quantitative Semantics.* New York: Stewart.

LEITES, NATHAN C. 1951   *The Operational Code of the Politburo.* New York: McGraw-Hill.

LERNER, DANIEL 1958   *The Passing of Traditional Society: Modernizing the Middle East.* Glencoe, Ill.: Free Press. → A paperback edition was published in 1964.

LIPPMANN, WALTER (1922) 1944   *Public Opinion.* New York: Macmillan. → A paperback edition was published in 1965 by Free Press.

LOWENTHAL, LEO 1961   *Literature, Popular Culture and Society.* Englewood Cliffs, N.J.: Prentice-Hall.

LOWENTHAL, LEO; and GUTERMAN, NORBERT 1949

Prophets of Deceit: A Study of the Techniques of the American Agitator. New York: Harper.

McGRANAHAN, D. V.; and WAYNE, I. 1948 German and American Traits Reflected in Popular Drama. *Human Relations* 1:429–455.

MEAD, MARGARET; and WOLFENSTEIN, MARTHA (editors) 1955 *Childhood in Contemporary Cultures.* Univ. of Chicago Press.

NIXON, RAYMOND B.; and WARD, JEAN 1961 Trends in Newspaper Ownership and Inter-media Competition. *Journalism Quarterly* 38:3–12.

PACKARD, VANCE O. 1957 *The Hidden Persuaders.* New York: McKay. → A paperback edition was published in 1958 by Pocket Books.

PARK, ROBERT E. 1922 *The Immigrant Press and Its Control.* New York: Harper.

PARSONS, TALCOTT 1942 Propaganda and Social Control. *Psychiatry* 5:551–572.

Personality and Persuasibility, by Irving L. Janis et al. Yale Studies in Attitude and Communication, Vol. 2. 1959 New Haven: Yale Univ. Press.

RILEY, JOHN W. JR.; and RILEY, MATILDA W. (1959) 1962 Mass Communication and the Social System. Pages 537–578 in American Sociological Society, *Sociology Today: Problems and Prospects.* Edited by Robert K. Merton et al. New York: Basic Books.

ROSTEN, LEO C. 1937 *The Washington Correspondents.* New York: Harcourt.

ROSTEN, LEO C. 1941 *Hollywood: The Movie Colony, the Movie Makers.* New York: Harcourt. → See especially Part 2.

SCHRAMM, WILBUR L. (editor) 1954 *The Process and Effects of Mass Communication.* Urbana: Univ. of Illinois Press.

SCHRAMM, WILBUR L. (editor) 1963 *The Science of Human Communication: New Directions and New Findings in Communication Research.* New York: Basic Books.

SHILS, EDWARD A.; and JANOWITZ, MORRIS (1948) 1966 Cohesion and Disintegration in the Wehrmacht in World War II. Pages 402–417 in Bernard Berelson and Morris Janowitz (editors), *Reader in Public Opinion and Communication.* 2d ed. New York: Free Press. → First published in Volume 12 of the *Public Opinion Quarterly.*

SMITH, BRUCE L.; LASSWELL, HAROLD D.; and CASEY, RALPH D. 1946 *Propaganda, Communication and Public Opinion: A Comprehensive Reference Guide.* Princeton Univ. Press.

SOCIETY FOR THE PSYCHOLOGICAL STUDY OF SOCIAL ISSUES (1954) 1962 *Public Opinion and Propaganda: A Book of Readings.* Edited by Daniel Katz et al. New York: Holt.

STEINER, GARY A. 1963 *The People Look at Television: A Study of Audience Attitudes.* New York: Knopf.

THOMAS, WILLIAM I.; and ZNANIECKI, FLORIAN (1920) 1958 The Wider Community and the Role of the Press. Volume 2, pages 1367–1396 in William I. Thomas and Florian Znaniecki, *The Polish Peasant in Europe and America.* New York: Dover.

UNITED NATIONS EDUCATIONAL, SCIENTIFIC AND CULTURAL ORGANIZATION, DIVISION OF FREE FLOW OF INFORMATION 1959— *Professional Association in the Mass Media: Handbook of Press, Film, Radio, Television Organizations.* Paris: UNESCO.

WALWORTH, ARTHUR C. JR. 1938 *School Histories at War: A Study of the Treatment of Our Wars in the Secondary School History Books of the United States and in Those of Its Former Enemies.* Cambridge, Mass.: Harvard Univ. Press; Oxford Univ. Press.

WARNER, W. LLOYD; and LUNT, PAUL S. (1941) 1950 *The Social Life of a Modern Community.* New Haven: Yale Univ. Press.

WILENSKY, HAROLD L. 1964 Mass Society and Mass Culture: Interdependence or Independence? *American Sociological Review* 29:173–197.

WIRTH, LOUIS 1948 Consensus and Mass Communication. *American Sociological Review* 13:1–15.

WOLFENSTEIN, MARTHA; and LEITES, NATHAN 1950 *Movies: A Psychological Study.* Glencoe, Ill.: Free Press.

II
CONTROL AND PUBLIC POLICY

Every society controls its mass media in accordance with its policies and needs. The controls may be legal and political (that is, laws and censorship), economic (ownership and support), or social (criticism and the giving or withholding of patronage). They may be positive, designed to obtain a desired kind of performance from the media, or negative, intended to prohibit a given kind of performance that might endanger the state, the rights of individuals, or the norms of society. The patterns and degree of control depend upon the political and economic orientation of the society.

Government and the mass media

All constitutional systems affirm the principle of freedom of expression. Thus, for example, the United States bases its policy in regard to the mass media on the first amendment to the constitution, "Congress shall make no law . . . abridging the freedom of speech, or of the press," and the fourteenth amendment, "No state shall make or enforce any law which shall abridge the privileges or immunities of citizens of the United States." Article 12 of the Spanish charter of July 13, 1945, proclaims that "all Spaniards may freely express their ideas as long as they do not advocate the overthrow of the fundamental principles of government." Article 125 of the constitution of the Soviet Union states that "the citizens of the U.S.S.R. are guaranteed by law (a) freedom of speech; (b) freedom of the press." According to article 19 of the Universal Declaration of Human Rights, adopted by the UN General Assembly in 1948: "Everyone has the right to freedom of opinion and expression; this right includes freedom to hold opinions without interference and to seek, receive and impart information through any media and regardless of frontiers." Obviously such unanimity of principle would not give rise to such differences in practice unless freedom of expression was differently defined and understood in the several cultures.

The historical background. The first mass media came into being in western Europe under authoritarian governments that were already concerned over the emergence of an ambitious middle class and justifiably worried over what printed matter might do to rouse the people against the power centers. Therefore, steps were soon taken to control the new media. Patents, or licenses to publish, were given only to persons regarded as politically "safe," and these people were permitted to exercise the privilege of publishing only as long as they refrained from rocking the ship of state. In the seventeenth century many books and periodicals in the areas of politics and religion were censored before publication. When licensing and censorship became cumbersome, in the late seventeenth century, the governments found it more convenient to rely on the threat of punishment *after* publication —for example, prosecutions for treason or seditious libel, the former charge, as Siebert says, being "reserved for activities which shook the foundations of the state; sedition . . . for the irritating flea-bites of the dissident and the nonconformist" (Siebert et al. [1956] 1963, p. 23).

These controls, of course, were aimed at preserving the government in power. But in a deeper sense they grew out of a long tradition of authoritarian philosophy, from Plato, who thought the state was safe only in the hands of wise men (*Republic*, especially books 6 and 8; *Apology*; *Crito*), to Hobbes, who argued that the power to maintain order is sovereign and not subject to individual objection (*Leviathan*, 1651), to Hegel, for whom "this substantial unity is an absolute unmoved end in itself, in which freedom comes into its supreme right. On the other hand this final end has supreme right against the individual, whose supreme duty is to be a member of the State" (*Philosophy of Right*, 1821).

Freedom of expression—the classic doctrine. As the rulers of Europe had feared would happen, printed materials were in the forefront of a series of democratic revolutions in the seventeenth and eighteenth centuries. These revolutions brought in governments that based their information policies on the philosophy of the European Enlightenment, the concept of natural rights of man, and the confidence that rational man, given a fair chance, can distinguish truth from error. Thus France wrote into article 11 of its Declaration of the Rights of Man, in 1789 (and confirmed it in the preamble to the constitution of October 27, 1946), that "the unrestrained communication of opinion being one of the most precious rights of man, every citizen may speak, write, and publish freely." John Milton (*Areopagitica*, 1644) spoke confidently of a self-righting process if free expression were permitted: "Let her [Truth] and Falsehood grapple; who ever knew Truth put to the worse, in a free and open encounter?" John Stuart Mill (*On Liberty*, 1859) said: "If all mankind minus one were of one opinion (and only one person were of the contrary opinion), mankind would be no more justified in silencing that one person, than he, if he had the power, would be justified in silencing mankind."

Out of such doctrine, in the eighteenth and nineteenth centuries, grew a private-enterprise press, accustomed to publishing and criticizing freely, and with it the concept of a "free market place of ideas" from which the public could freely select what it felt to be right and true. The relation of mass media to government was almost precisely reversed. Instead of existing by sufferance as long as they supported and advanced the policies of government, the media now came to be considered representatives of the public in keeping watch on government, and therefore to be kept as free as possible from control by government.

Freedom of expression—modern variations. In the late nineteenth and the twentieth centuries extreme libertarianism has been modified in practice, for a number of reasons. For one thing, modern psychology identified many areas of irrationality in "rational man" and cast considerable doubt on his ability to distinguish truth from skillful propaganda. Furthermore, the growing concentration of ownership of the media made it more doubtful that all viewpoints would be adequately expressed in a free-enterprise market place. The emergence of films and the broadcast media presented new control problems, because of their supposed influence on morals and beliefs and because the allocation of broadcast channels could not be left to uninhibited competition—someone had to referee. Therefore, even in countries where libertarianism had been strongest, owners and operators of the media were asked to assume greater responsibility for their actions, and more controls were placed on the newer media—film, radio, and television—than on the press.

However, nations in the modern world have so combined libertarian and authoritarian doctrine and practice that among the noncommunist states it is possible to discern almost a complete spectrum of systems, from the most libertarian to the most authoritarian—let us say, from England, where the doctrines of Milton and Mill still keep the government's hands as much as possible off the media, to Spain, where the law of April 22, 1938, is still in force, saying that because of the essential functions of the press it "could not be suffered to continue to exist in independence of the State . . . it is for the State to organize, supervise, and control that national institution, the periodical press."

Totalitarian control of mass media.   Since 1917 another type of mass-media system has developed, beginning in the Soviet Union and based on the thinking of Hegel (*Philosophy of Right*, 1821), Marx (*Capital*, 1867–1894), and Lenin (1901). Lenin argued that private ownership is incompatible with freedom of the press. "Freedom is a sham," he said, "as long as the best printing plants and the huge stocks of paper are in the possession of the capitalists" ([1919] 1935–1938, vol. 7, pp. 226–227). Therefore, said the Soviet delegate to the fifth session of the United Nations Economic and Social Council, "in order to enjoy effective freedom of the press, the highly complex technical means of modern information must be controlled. . . . Only when the resources necessary for the control of the press are public property do the people enjoy effective freedom of the press." What is the press to be free to do? Its purpose, said a Soviet theorist, "is not to trade in news but to educate the great mass of the workers and to organize them, under the sole guidance of the Party, to achieve clearly defined aims." "We must and shall transform the press," said Lenin in 1918, "into an instrument for the economic re-education of the masses" (last three quotations are from Terrou & Solal 1951, p. 51).

In the Soviet Union and other communizing countries, the press is thus intended to serve an instrumental purpose under the close control of the Communist party, which thinks of itself as a kind of general staff for the proletariat. None of the media are privately owned; they are either parts of the government or operated by an official organization. The result is a planned and systematic press, in contrast to the somewhat less systematic ones of countries where private competition alone has determined where a newspaper should survive. Needless to say, the entire media structure is very closely supervised and integrated, and controversial events are reported and discussed for the Soviet citizen with a unanimity of interpretation to which a Western reader is unaccustomed.

Methods of political and legal control

The Commission on Freedom of the Press (1947*d*, vol. 1, pp. 62–68) has listed most political and legal controls that have commonly been applied to the media. They include licensing in advance; censorship of offending material before publication; seizure of offending material; injunctions against publication of a newspaper or book or of specified content; requirement of surety bonds against libel or other offense; compulsory disclosure of ownership and authority; postpublication criminal penalties for objectionable matter; postpublication collection of damages in a civil action; postpublication correction of libels and other misstatements; discrimination in granting access to news sources and facilities; discrimination and denial in the use of communications facilities for distribution; taxes; discriminatory subsidies; and interference with buying, reading, and listening.

Almost any mass-media system will, of course, be subject to certain basic statutory controls, among them a law designed to protect individuals or groups against defamation, a copyright law to protect authors and publishers, a basic statute designed to preserve the common standard of decency and morality against infraction by the mass media, and another basic statute to protect the state against treasonable and seditious utterances. Where the systems chiefly diverge is in the extent to which they are subordinate to political authorities and the extent to which in their controls they go beyond the statutory restrictions just listed.

Subordination to political authorities.   There are different degrees of subordination, of course. But clearly subordinate to political authorities are communizing media systems like those of the U.S.S.R., classical authoritarian systems like those of Spain and Portugal, and new-nation systems like that of Ghana. Clearly not subordinate are systems like those of the United States, Great Britain, France, Australia, and other countries of Europe and the Americas where libertarian philosophy has been strong and of new states like India where an effort has been made to maintain libertarian ideas despite the stresses and strains with which all new governments have to contend. Between the two extremes are a very large number of countries in which the media are partly subordinate, partly not.

Mass media subordinate to the political authorities are ordinarily subject to the classical authoritarian controls: licensing, censorship, and punishment for issuing material offensive to the government or the prevailing norms. Most systems have an official organization of some sort to supervise the media and enforce the controls.

In the Soviet Union, for example, there is Glavlit, a directorate established by an order of June 9, 1931, "to exercise every form of politico-ideological, military and economic supervision of printed works, manuscripts, photographs, pictures, etc., intended for publication and distribution, and also to supervise broadcasts, lectures, and exhibitions." There are local branches of Glavlit, and their representatives are placed in press and printing establishments (Terrou & Solal 1951, p. 119). Glavlit has the right to authorize a new periodical and to close it. A book or pamphlet must bear the imprimatur of Glavlit, and every page of proof must be approved and signed by a representative of Glavlit before it may be printed. Furthermore, mass media in the communizing states are generally official enterprises, the editors of many papers are appointed by the Central Committee of the Communist party at the appropriate level, and party propagandists and theoreticians are placed with influential publications. Thus, the mass media in such a system are integrated into the official structure in a way that builds control into their every operation.

In noncommunist authoritarian systems, ownership of the press may or may not be public, but as Terrou and Solal (1951, pp. 127–128) say of Spain, it makes no difference because "the management of the enterprise is subject to a 'power of oversight' and publishing is hemmed in by a network of obligations and restrictions which make it quite unnecessary to lay down special provisions for the formation or operation of the enterprise. . . . The supervision to which it is subjected places it, in relation to the authorities, in a state of absolute hierarchical subordination." The mechanism for this subordination, in the case of Spain, includes a state organization for management and supervision, empowered to fix the size of circulation, intervene in appointment of members of the managerial staff, oversee the work of the staff, censor where necessary, and issue rules for the journalistic profession.

Thus, at the authoritarian end of the political control spectrum it is perhaps less appropriate to speak of state intervention than of state integration, inasmuch as the media are so completely interwoven with public policy and the administrative machinery of the state.

Control in nonsubordinate countries. At the other end of the spectrum, however, in the countries where the media are not subordinate to political authorities, there is a conscious attempt to keep state intervention at a minimum. This is reflected in a high proportion of private ownership in the media, a minimum of prior authorization, a maximum of freedom to criticize and to argue opposing viewpoints, and an attempt to keep official controls, if at all possible, in the courts.

In the United States, for example, the newspaper, magazine, and book press, radio and television, and films are mostly privately owned; a variety of enterprises and a high degree of competition are encouraged. In most of the other countries where the media are not subordinate to political authorities, the press and films (at least the entertainment film industry) are likely to be privately owned and operated.

Radio and television broadcasting. Broadcasting is organized in a great variety of patterns. In many of the Latin American countries, as in the United States, it is private enterprise. In such countries as Great Britain, Japan, Canada, and Australia private and public broadcasting enterprises operate side by side. In these countries special efforts are made to keep the public broadcasting system free of governmental political influence. The British Broadcasting Corporation (BBC), for example, is a public corporation—neither a private nor a state enterprise—responsible to a board of distinguished citizens (Briggs 1961). In a majority of countries, however, broadcasting is a state monopoly. In Belgium it is a public foundation; in France, a public service with its own budget; in Germany, a public establishment operating typically under a large broadcasting council, representing many cultural, religious, and professional organizations, that appoints the board of governors; in Italy, a company operating under concession from the state; in India and numerous other countries, an administrative service.

Broadcasting, however, by its very nature is hard to keep completely free of government. Even in the United States, where every effort is made to keep the government's hands off radio and television content, it is still necessary for the government, through the Federal Communications Commission (FCC), to choose among applicants for channels—which it does chiefly on the basis of their experience and financial soundness and the programs they promise. Many other countries, because broadcasting is so important for reaching all the people, have felt it necessary to keep it a national service, under government management.

Motion pictures and the press. Motion pictures are censored on moral grounds even in countries where the media are not subordinate to political authorities. In the United States this censorship has usually occurred at the state or municipal level; in some other countries, at the national level (Commission 1947c; Lyon-Caen & Lavigne 1957). The continuing economic crisis of the film industry in some countries has made it the beneficiary of government loans and subsidies to an extent unmatched by any other privately owned mass medium, but the prime motive of this government intervention (whatever its eventual results) is to make the industry profitable, as well as a source of national prestige (Political and Economic Planning 1952).

The press, in nonsubordinate countries, is generally quite free from official control beyond the statutory ones mentioned earlier. It is not usually required to obtain a license to publish, beyond, perhaps, registering the names of the journal and the responsible persons. In peacetime, at least, it is ordinarily free of government censorship (for discussion of these issues, see especially Johnson 1958; Williams 1957).

Freedom of political comment. The media of the nonsubordinate countries are typically quite free to criticize or oppose government policies. In time of war or national crisis, of course, any government is edgy about criticism or uninhibited circulation of news. In World War II, for example, U.S. news media accepted a voluntary censorship of news, presided over by a well-known newsman, Byron Price, but overseas the military services censored news originating in areas under their control. A sense of national crisis leads many young and developing countries to restrict criticism from the media even in peacetime. However, in the case of older and more solid states in peacetime, a truly extraordinary amount of criticism is permitted— even encouraged. France provides an excellent example of a press full of vigorous and conflicting viewpoints (although under President de Gaulle there has been a large number of prosecutions for printing comments offensive to the chief of state), and during at least twenty of the last thirty years two-thirds or more of the daily newspapers in the United States have been editorially opposed to the president in office. In the United States Justice Holmes' doctrine that "clear and present danger" to the country must be proved (*Schenck* v. *United States*, 1919) stands between most critics of the government and punishment for harsh words.

Even in countries where criticism is encouraged, however, governments are frequently accused of controlling the release of and access to official news in the government's best interest (Rourke 1961). This is generally called "managing the news."

Economic controls

When a Western newspaperman says that the Soviet press is not free, he is likely to mean that it is not *politically* free. When a Soviet newspaperman says that the U.S. and western European press is not free, he is likely to mean that it is not *economically* free. Thus, Vyshinskii ([1938] 1948, pp.

612–613) charged that the London *Times* "is the organ of banks, connected through its directors with Lloyd's Bank, with the largest railroad companies, with insurance companies." Hearst, he said, was "a big American capitalist." The Western press, he charged, was free for capitalists only; true freedom "consists essentially in the possibility of freely publishing the genuine, not the falsified, opinions of the toiling masses, rather than in the absence of preliminary censorship."

Patterns of ownership. In a private-enterprise system, of course, control does go with ownership, and Breed (1952) and Rosten (1937) have shown how the wishes of the owner and top management, even when not directly expressed as orders, are still reflected in the performance of the enterprise. For this reason, and because of the importance, in libertarian theory, of representing a wide range of viewpoints in a "free market place of ideas," some observers have been concerned over trends toward bigness and fewness in the United States media and also in the media of some other countries. Whereas newspaper competition was the rule fifty years ago, now less than 5 per cent of U.S. cities and towns with daily newspapers have competitive ownership (for a description of this trend, see Nixon 1949). Starting a city daily in the United States is now so costly that it is seldom attempted. The result is that ownership has been increasingly restricted and has come to represent the wealthier and usually more conservative strata of society. For example, although a majority of United States voters are registered in the Democratic party, over two-thirds of the newspapers that endorse presidential candidates usually endorse the Republican candidate.

There has been no decrease in the number of broadcasting stations, as there has been in newspapers, but much of their programming is provided by three television and four radio networks (Bricker 1956). To prevent further concentration, the government permits each network to own no more than five stations. Until recent years there was a concentration of film making in a few gigantic enterprises, which owned both studios and theaters. Government antitrust action requiring the separation of studio and theater enterprises and the growth of new companies to make films for television have reversed the trend toward concentration in the movie industry (Bernstein 1960). The wire news services to newspapers and broadcasting stations are provided mostly by two large news agencies, the Associated Press, a cooperative, and United Press International, a privately owned company. In a famous case in 1945 the Associated

Press was required, under antitrust legislation, to accept clients for its services even though the new clients might be in competition with older ones; it thus became, in effect, a common carrier for news (*Associated Press* v. *United States*, 1945).

Influence of advertisers. Directly or indirectly, advertisers have the power to affect private mass-media enterprises. Efforts to influence newspaper policy by withholding advertising have more often failed than succeeded in the United States (Schramm 1957, pp. 132–133), but the economic decisions of advertisers and agencies, quite apart from any political intent, have sometimes held the power of life and death over very large enterprises. For example, the decisions of many large firms to advertise elsewhere, especially on television rather than in print, together with rising costs, have caused the closing of some of the largest magazines in the United States and of the New York *Mirror* in 1963, when it had the second largest circulation among newspapers in the United States.

In the case of commercial broadcasting, advertisers can exercise a certain amount of influence on content by deciding whether or not to sponsor a particular program. Some countries (Great Britain, for example) do not permit the sponsorship of a program and sell only the time *between* programs (see Wilson 1961 for the background to this compromise). A certain amount of indirect economic influence on the content of broadcasting arises out of the importance of audience ratings (U.S. Congress, House Committee on Interstate and Foreign Commerce 1961). It is important to provide many advertisers with the largest possible markets, and this so-called tyranny of ratings tends to result in more attention to large-audience programs than to the needs of smaller audience groups and in a flood of imitations of successful programs.

Other economic restrictions. Import restrictions, basically economic but sometimes used also as political controls, decrease the flow of information and informational materials across many national borders.

In countries where the mass media are not financially sound, economic control is sometimes exerted by allocation of newsprint or other scarce resources to favored enterprises. In some countries bribes to reporters and editors are reported to be common. And one of the most common economic controls where the press is new or weak is subsidization by a political group or individual.

Social controls

Public opinion, especially when reflected in subscriptions, audience ratings, or film attendance, is a powerful control on private-enterprise media and to some extent a control on publicly owned media. Thus, for example, the BBC, although a public corporation, has continually modified its television programming as a direct result of comparisons between its audience ratings and those of commercial stations.

Because feedback to the mass media is usually slight, these enterprises are often influenced by letters or telephone calls from the public. A few hundred letters and calls about an offensive statement have been known to result in putting a U.S. network program off the air (Schramm 1957, p. 152). Some critics are influential. The criticism of books is more highly developed than that of films or broadcasts, and there is almost no regular criticism of newspapers. The scarcity of such criticism led the Commission on Freedom of the Press, in the United States, to recommend "the establishment of a new and independent agency to appraise and report annually upon the performance of the press" (Commission [1947b] 1958, p. 100).

Opinion has proved especially effective when it represents large organized groups. The Catholic Legion of Decency, for example, has influenced the movie industry with its recommendations of acceptable and unacceptable films and the implied threat of boycott by a large group of consumers (Facey 1945). Members of opinion groups have sometimes been effective in influencing the selection and display of books in libraries (Fiske 1959). Trade associations and other affiliated groups have been alert to what they consider unfair treatment of their members, especially in films. Indeed, it has been remarked that if the film industry fully heeded the protests of special groups, it might very well not be able to make movies with people in them. More recently, however, the American film industry, doubtless as part of its attempt to recapture the audiences lost to television, but also encouraged by the commercial success of some imported "art" movies, has taken a more aggressive attitude toward the censors. How far this trend will continue and whether it is supported by a genuine change in public taste remain matters for speculation.

Some public policy problems

A high proportion of the mass media's public policy problems grow out of either an attempt to balance freedom and responsibility in media performance or a conflict of rights. Countries where libertarian roots are deep and where most media are not subordinate to political authorities are likely to be preoccupied with keeping their media *free*; whereas authoritarian countries (although many of them would deny that their media are not free) are more likely to be concerned with keeping the media *responsible.*

In the United States this relationship between freedom and responsibility raises continuing policy problems. There is no great desire to return to the unbridled and irresponsible political writing of the early nineteenth century, which Mott called "The Dark Ages of Partisan Journalism" ([1941] 1962, pp. 167–180). Libertarianism of that kind is obsolete. But many observers and critics feel that the media should not only be free *from* something; they should also be free *for* something. What the mass media should be free for, the kind of responsible performance to be expected of them, has been studied during the last twenty years by a number of expert commissions, notably the Commission on Freedom of the Press, in the United States, and a series of royal commissions in the United Kingdom, Canada, Australia, and Sweden, among others. Many of the problems before these commissions have dealt also with conflicting rights: the public's "right to know" versus individual rights, such as privacy and fair trial; the public's right to protect moral standards versus the artist's right to be heard or seen and the adult public's right to receive adult media; the media owners' right to free expression versus the public's right to a variety and balance of viewpoints and interpretations; and so forth. It is generally agreed that the best hope of resolving such conflicts in the public interest (in a country like the United States) is for the owners and operators of the media to assume the responsibility for providing a free market place of ideas and a vigorous service sensitive to individual rights and minority as well as majority needs.

Freedom and responsibility. If the media are not responsible, said the Commission on Freedom of the Press (1947*b*), someone will have to enjoin responsibility upon them. The implication is that the government would have to do this. And yet there has been the greatest reluctance on the part of critics, media, and government alike to permit the federal government to move into control of media content. For example, the so-called Blue Book of the FCC (see Siepmann [1950] 1956, pp. 37–40) became a *cause célèbre* in 1946 chiefly because it implied that the FCC, having granted a license partly on the basis of an applicant's promise to deliver a certain kind of programming, should check up on whether he keeps his promise. The United States federal courts have more often proved themselves a resource for overturning local and state censorship than for confirming any government controls on content. Indeed, perhaps the most

successful control a government agency has been able to place on content has been through the Federal Trade Commission, which monitors television and radio advertisements for false claims.

Self-regulation—some dilemmas. The emergence of professional organizations and of professional codes of good practice has sometimes been hailed as a recognition of responsibility by the media. The newspaper code ("Canons of Journalism," adopted by the American Society of Newspaper Editors) is a highly generalized statement, requiring no specific adherence. The Production Code of the Motion Picture Association of America, on the other hand, contains a detailed list of specifications for avoiding offense to moral sensibilities and pressure groups. It is administered by an office supported by film makers, which is empowered to require changes in films, if deemed necessary, before awarding a Seal of Good Practice. The radio and television codes are less specific. They are administered by an agency of the National Association of Broadcasters, which, so far as is known, has never dropped a member for nonadherence to the code. In both the film and the broadcasting industries some enterprises do and some do not subject themselves to the code. A number of schools of journalism have, in a sense, established self-regulation by joining in a program to evaluate their curricula by professional standards.

Whereas self-regulation is an evidence of responsibility, still the working of the codes and regulating programs illustrates one of the problems of nations and media that operate in the libertarian tradition: it is relatively easier to apply negative than to apply positive controls. It is easier for a society to ensure that what it dislikes is *not* done by the media or to the media than to ensure that what it feels it needs from the media it gets.

WILBUR SCHRAMM

[*See also* CENSORSHIP; COMMUNICATION, MASS, *article on* TELEVISION AND ITS PLACE IN MASS CULTURE; CONSTITUTIONAL LAW.]

BIBLIOGRAPHY

BERNSTEIN, IRVING 1960 *Economics of Television Film Production and Distribution.* A report to the Screen Actors Guild. Sherman Oaks, Calif.: The Guild.

BLANSHARD, PAUL 1955 *The Right to Read: The Battle Against Censorship.* Boston: Beacon.

BOURQUIN, JACQUES 1950 *La liberté de la presse.* Paris: Presses Universitaires de France.

BREED, WARREN 1952 The Newspaperman, News and Society. Ph.D. dissertation, Columbia Univ., New York.

BRICKER, JOHN W. 1956 *The Network Monopoly.* Report prepared for use of the Committee on Interstate and Foreign Commerce. Washington: Government Printing Office.

BRIGGS, ASA 1961 *The History of Broadcasting in the United Kingdom*. Vol. 1. Oxford Univ. Press. → Volume 1: *The Birth of Broadcasting*. This volume is intended to be the first of a three-volume history of broadcasting in the United Kingdom.

BRITISH BROADCASTING CORPORATION 1946 *Broadcasting Policy: 1945–1946*. Papers by Command, Cmd. 6852. London: H.M. Stationery Office.

CHAFEE, ZECHARIAH JR. 1941 *Free Speech in the United States*. Cambridge, Mass.: Harvard Univ. Press. → Supersedes Chafee's *Freedom of Speech*, 1920.

CHENERY, WILLIAM L. 1955 *Freedom of the Press*. New York: Harcourt.

CLAUSSE, ROGER 1951 *L'information à la recherche d'un statut*. Université Libre de Bruxelles, Cahiers de l'Institut de Sociologie Solvay, No. 5. Brussels: Librairie Encyclopédique.

COMMISSION ON FREEDOM OF THE PRESS 1946 *Peoples Speaking to Peoples: A Report on International Communication*. Univ. of Chicago Press.

COMMISSION ON FREEDOM OF THE PRESS 1947a *The American Radio: A Report on the Broadcasting Industry in the United States*. Univ. of Chicago Press.

COMMISSION ON FREEDOM OF THE PRESS (1947b) 1958 *A Free and Responsible Press: A General Report on Mass Communication*. Univ. of Chicago Press.

COMMISSION ON FREEDOM OF THE PRESS 1947c *Freedom of the Movies: A Report on Self-regulation*. Univ. of Chicago Press.

COMMISSION ON FREEDOM OF THE PRESS 1947d *Government and Mass Communication*, by Zechariah Chafee, Jr. 2 vols. Univ. of Chicago Press.

COOPER, KENT 1956 *The Right to Know: An Exposition of the Evils of News Suppression and Propaganda*. New York: Farrar, Straus.

CRAIG, ALEC (1962) 1963 *Suppressed Books: A History of the Conception of Literary Obscenity*. New York: World. → First published as *The Banned Books of England and Other Countries: A Study of the Conception of Literary Obscenity*.

CROSS, HAROLD L. 1953 *The People's Right to Know: Legal Access to Public Records and Proceedings*. A report . . . to the American Society of Newspaper Editors. New York: Columbia Univ. Press. → A *Second Supplement*, which supersedes *Cumulative Supplement 1*, was published in 1959.

DAWSON, THOMAS (1927) 1947 *The Law of the Press*. 2d ed. London: Staples.

EEK, HILDING 1953 *Freedom of Information as a Project of International Legislation: A Study of International Law in Making*. Uppsala Universitets Arsskrift, No. 6. Uppsala (Sweden): Lundequistska Bokhandeln.

ERNST, MORRIS L. 1946 *The First Freedom*. New York: Macmillan.

FACEY, PAUL W. 1945 The Legion of Decency: A Sociological Analysis of the Emergencies and Development of a Social Pressure Group. Ph.D. dissertation, Fordham Univ., New York.

FISKE, MARJORIE 1959 *Book Selection and Censorship: A Study of School and Public Libraries in California*. Berkeley: Univ. of California Press.

FLIESS, PETER J. 1955 *Freedom of the Press in the German Republic, 1918–1933*. Louisiana State University Studies, Social Science Series, No. 4. Baton Rouge: Louisiana State Univ. Press.

GENERAL COUNCIL OF THE PRESS 1954 *The Press and the People*. London: The Council. → See also the Council's later annual reports.

GERALD, J. EDWARD 1948 *The Press and the Constitution, 1931–1947*. Minneapolis: Univ. of Minnesota Press.

GERALD, J. EDWARD 1963 *The Social Responsibility of the Press*. Minneapolis: Univ. of Minnesota Press.

GREAT BRITAIN, BROADCASTING COMMITTEE 1950–1951 *Report*. Papers by Command, Cmd. 8116. London: H.M. Stationery Office.

GREAT BRITAIN, ROYAL COMMISSION ON THE PRESS 1947–1948 *Minutes of Evidence*. 1–38. London: H.M. Stationery Office.

HAGEMANN, WALTER 1948 *Publizistik im dritten Reich: Ein Beitrag zur Methodik der Massenführung*. Hamburg (Germany): Hansischer Gildenverlag.

HOCKING, WILLIAM E. 1947 *Freedom of the Press: A Framework of Principle*. A report from the Commission on Freedom of the Press. Univ. of Chicago Press.

HUETTIG, MAE D. 1944 *Economic Control of the Motion Picture Industry: A Study in Industrial Organization*. Philadelphia: Univ. of Pennsylvania Press; London: Oxford Univ. Press.

ICKES, HAROLD L. 1939 *America's House of Lords: An Inquiry Into the Freedom of the Press*. New York: Harcourt.

INDIA (REPUBLIC) PRESS COMMISSION 1954–1955 *Report*. 2 vols. New Delhi: Government of India Press.

INKELES, ALEX (1950) 1958 *Public Opinion in Soviet Russia: A Study in Mass Persuasion*. 3d printing, enl. Russian Research Center Studies, No. 1. Cambridge, Mass.: Harvard Univ. Press.

INNIS, HAROLD A. 1949 *The Press; A Neglected Factor in the Economic History of the Twentieth Century*. Oxford Univ. Press.

JOHNSON, GERALD W. 1958 *Peril and Promise: An Inquiry Into Freedom of the Press*. New York: Harper.

KAWABE, KISABURŌ 1921 *The Press and Politics in Japan: A Study of the Relation Between the Newspaper and the Political Development of Modern Japan*. Univ. of Chicago Press.

KAYSER, JACQUES 1952 Les procédés actuels de l'information compromettent-ils la paix? *Politique étrangere* 17:499–508.

KECSKEMETI, PAUL 1950 Totalitarian Communications as a Means of Control: A Note on the Sociology of Propaganda. *Public Opinion Quarterly* 14:224–234.

KINGSBURY, SUSAN M. et al. 1937 *Newspapers and the News: An Objective Measurement of Ethical and Unethical Behavior by Representative Newspapers*. Bryn Mawr College Series in Social Economy, No. 1. New York: Putnam.

KONVITZ, MILTON R. 1963 *First Amendment Freedoms: Selected Cases on Freedom of Religion, Speech, Press, Assembly*. Cornell Studies in Civil Liberty. Ithaca, N.Y.: Cornell Univ. Press. → Based in part on the author's *Bill of Rights Reader: Leading Constitutional Cases*.

LENIN, VLADIMIR I. (1901) 1929 Where to Begin. Volume 4, book 1, page 114 in Vladimir I. Lenin, *Collected Works*. New York: International Publishers.

LENIN, VLADIMIR I. (1919) 1935–1938 Theses and Report on Bourgeois Democracy and the Dictatorship of the Proletariat. Volume 7, pages 223–240 in Vladimir I. Lenin, *Selected Works*. New York: International Publishers.

LIPPMANN, WALTER 1955 *Essays in the Public Philosophy.* Boston: Little.

LYON-CAEN, GÉRARD; and LAVIGNE, P. 1957 *Traité théorique et pratique de droit du cinéma français et comparé.* 2 vols. Paris: Librairie Générale de Droit et de Jurisprudence.

MALHAN, P. N. 1953 Liberty of the Press in India. *Indian Journal of Political Science* 14:39–49.

MARTIN, KINGSLEY 1947 *The Press the Public Wants.* London: Hogarth.

MOCK, JAMES R. 1941 *Censorship 1917.* Princeton (N.J.) Univ. Press.

MOTT, FRANK L. (1941) 1962 The Dark Ages of Partisan Journalism. Pages 167–180 in Frank L. Mott, *American Journalism: A History, 1690–1960.* 3d ed. New York: Macmillan.

MOTTIN, JEAN 1949 *Histoire politique de la presse, 1944–1949.* Paris: Bilans Hebdomadaires.

NIXON, RAYMOND B. (1949) 1960 The Problem of Newspaper Monopoly. Pages 241–250 in Wilbur Schramm (editor), *Mass Communications: A Book of Readings.* 2d ed. Urbana: Univ. of Illinois Press.

PAULU, BURTON 1956 *British Broadcasting: Radio and Television in the United Kingdom.* Minneapolis: Univ. of Minnesota Press.

POIRIER, PIERRE 1945 *Code de la presse et de l'imprimerie: Droit national et international des journalistes.* Brussels: Larcier.

POLITICAL AND ECONOMIC PLANNING 1952 *The British Film Industry: A Report on Its History and Present Organisation, With Special Reference to the Economic Problems of British Feature Film Production.* London: Political and Economic Planning.

LA PRENSA, BUENOS AIRES 1952 *Defense of Freedom.* New York: Day.

RAZI, G. M. 1952 *Le droit sur les nouvelles: Agences d'informations, enterprises de presse.* Institut de Droit Comparé de l'Université de Paris, Nouvelle série de monographies de droit public et de droit pénal. Paris: Sirey.

RIVERS, WILLIAM L. 1965 *The Opinionmakers.* Boston: Beacon. → This is in part a replication of Leo C. Rosten's study of Washington correspondents.

ROSTEN, LEO C. 1937 *The Washington Correspondents.* New York: Harcourt.

ROTHENBERG, IGNAZ 1946 *The Newspaper: A Study in the Workings of the Daily Press and Its Laws.* New York and London: Staples.

ROURKE, FRANCIS E. 1961 *Secrecy and Publicity: Dilemmas of Democracy.* Baltimore: Johns Hopkins Press.

SCHRAMM, WILBUR 1957 *Responsibility in Mass Communication.* New York: Harper.

SIEBERT, FREDERICK S. 1952 *Freedom of the Press in England, 1476–1776: The Rise and Decline of Government Controls.* Urbana: Univ. of Illinois Press.

SIEBERT, FREDERICK S.; PETERSON, THEODORE; and SCHRAMM, WILBUR (1956) 1963 *Four Theories of the Press: The Authoritarian, Libertarian, Social Responsibility, and Soviet Communist Concepts of What the Press Should Be and Do.* Urbana: Univ. of Illinois Press.

SIEPMANN, CHARLES (1950) 1956 *Radio, Television and Society.* New York: Oxford Univ. Press.

SMEAD, ELMER E. 1959 *Freedom of Speech by Radio and Television.* Washington: Public Affairs Press.

SOLAL, LUCIEN 1959 *Dictionnaire du droit de la presse.* Paris: Syndicat National de la Presse Quotidienne Régionale.

STRASCHNOV, GEORGES 1948 *Le droit d'auteur et les droits connexes en radiodiffusion.* Brussels: Bruylant.

SUMMER INSTITUTE ON INTERNATIONAL AND COMPARATIVE LAW, UNIVERSITY OF MICHIGAN 1955 *Lectures on Communication Media: Legal and Policy Problems.* Ann Arbor: Univ. of Michigan Law School.

TERROU, FERNAND 1951 La liberté de l'information sur le plan international. *Études de presse* New Series 3, no. 1:11–22.

TERROU, FERNAND 1953 Aspects législatifs et règlementaires de l'intervention de l'état dans le domaine de l'information. *Revue administrative* 6:259–264; 371–378.

TERROU, FERNAND; and SOLAL, LUCIEN 1951 *Legislation for Press, Film, and Radio.* UNESCO Publication No. 607. Paris: UNESCO.

U.S.S.R. LAWS, STATUTES, ETC. (1927) 1937 *Osnovnye direktivy i zakonodatel'stvo o pechati: Sistematicheskii zbornik.* (Basic Regulations and Legislation Concerning the Press: Systematic Collection). Compiled by L. G. Fogelevich. 6th ed. Moscow: OGIZ.

U.S. CONGRESS, HOUSE COMMITTEE ON INTERSTATE AND FOREIGN COMMERCE 1961 *Evaluation of Statistical Methods Used in Obtaining Broadcast Ratings.* 87th Congress, 1st Session, House Report No. 193. Washington: Government Printing Office.

U.S. CONGRESS, SENATE, COMMITTEE ON COMMERCE 1961–1962 *Freedom of Communications: Final Report.* 6 parts, 87th Congress, 1st Session, Senate Report No. 994. Washington: Government Printing Office.

VILLARD, OSWALD G. 1944 *The Disappearing Daily: Chapters in American Newspaper Evolution.* New York: Knopf.

VYSHINSKII, ANDREI IA. (editor) (1938) 1948 *The Law of the Soviet State.* New York: Macmillan. → First published in Russian.

WILLIAMS, FRANCIS 1946 *Press, Parliament and People.* London: Heinemann.

WILLIAMS, FRANCIS (1957) 1958 *Dangerous Estate: The Anatomy of Newspapers.* London: Readers Union; New York: Macmillan.

WILSON, H. HUBERT 1961 *Pressure Group: The Campaign for Commercial Television in England.* New Brunswick, N.J.: Rutgers Univ. Press.

YOUNG, EUGENE J. 1938 *Looking Behind the Censorships.* New York: Lippincott.

III

TELEVISION AND ITS PLACE IN MASS CULTURE

It is notoriously difficult to define mass communications precisely, but television, among all the media, is likely to have the highest proportion of those characteristics which feature in any reasonable definition. It has by far the largest audiences of all forms of communication; indeed, it sometimes reaches virtually the entire population of a nation—as, for example, in the United Kingdom during telecasts of great national interest, such as a royal message, a state funeral, or a football final. Radio, too, can have most of a nation for its audience, but it cannot cross language barriers. Television, being visual, does just that. Through the use of satellites it is now multiplying its audiences several times over. The same program that can be seen in the United States can also reach huge audiences across the countries of Europe up to the iron curtain or sometimes even beyond it. Furthermore, it reaches these audiences at the same time or, give or take a few seconds, at virtually the same time; these enormous audiences are not made up of successive audiences, as are those of the cinema.

Television's audiences are more amorphous and less self-selected than those of the other media of communication. Most of its audiences are made up of general consumers of television, that is, people who sit down ready to be entertained for the greater part of an evening, without necessarily having chosen a specific program at a particular time out of a feeling that it has a special appeal to them as differentiated individuals. They do not divide themselves, nor are they often divided by the providers of television, according to age, sex, class, or region. By comparison, the readership of the national press in Great Britain, for example, is still roughly assignable to social class, though this characteristic is weakening under the impact of the newer "classless" media.

Television reaches right into the living rooms of its amorphous audience. It seeks to hold them and to retain that hold, rather than being content to be reached for as the mood arises. This becomes less true if there is more than one channel and if the programs on those channels are arranged so as to contrast with each other and encourage selective viewing. However, where the funds for television come from advertising, the point holds even where there are several channels: they all narrow their programming toward those items which seem likely to keep the average consumer–viewer from switching off or over.

Television is an archetypal form of mass communication also because it is an industry—an industry whose products are recreation, ideas, and education. Further, the men who produce the programs—authors, scriptwriters, visual artists, directors, producers, actors, program controllers—are physically and to some extent culturally separated from their audiences, and that separation is progressively increasing. Mass-communication industries, comprising large bodies of highly endowed and intensely professional people with more than average articulateness, inevitably become narcissistic toward their own trade; they progressively worship the machine that draws on their talents

and increasingly prefer not to ask searching questions about their more complex interrelations with their society and the individuals who compose it. Their link with the audiences is indirect; they put their programs into the camera, and the engineers beam them into millions of separate homes; there is no one-to-one relationship. The programs themselves become consumer products for which the producers have a sort of pure professional or aesthetic love; around them accrue much of the folklore and legend common to all such highly sophisticated mysteries.

Like all major mass communications, television has a continuous production belt. It is a recreational, cultural, educational, and informational "sausage machine," which must be fed day after day so as to produce at roughly the same times roughly the same amounts and proportions of material. Inevitably and progressively (unless the process is deliberately resisted) it turns out the same *kind* of material, which is all of the same density and texture although it appears with different packaging—material that is predigested, homogenized, sterilized, artificially colored and seasoned each and every day. The pressures toward this kind of uniformity arise from the persistent need to deliver interesting goods day after day, to meet the schedules, and to keep up the ratings. The servants of the machine may and do change, as the shifts rotate daily and weekly, and as personnel come and go over the years in the great factory. But the consumer product has built into it a range of established and recurrent characteristics, partly because of the necessary organizational structure of the factory, partly because of the inherent qualities of the medium itself, and partly because of pressure from the audience to provide them with what they have come to expect. There is, of course, more variation than has been suggested; however, there is much less than one might have expected.

Questions about television's possibilities for growth as well as its dangers are, then, questions about all mass communications. Moreover, these are not only questions about the medium in itself. No medium of mass communication can be adequately discussed solely in terms of itself; such a discussion inevitably leads to a discussion of the society which television reflects and affects and which uses it in this way rather than that. However, this important outer area can be touched on only peripherally within the limits of this article.

Television's relation to its audiences

Although television is important and pervasive in its effects on attitudes and behavior, it is probably not as important as it is commonly thought to be. There are not a great many reliable psychological studies on the effects of television, though the number is fast increasing, nor are their results in all respects definitive. All that we can say at present is that television probably cannot change taste radically or upset deep-seated assumptions, but that where it follows the grain of personal or social predispositions, it can reinforce them. Recurrent violence on television seems likely to encourage acts of violence only in the psychotic or mentally disturbed, and television programs which go along with the tastes and interests of a particular social group are most easily assimilated and tend to strengthen those tastes. These effects are increased when a given theme recurs often, is dramatically presented, and provides the viewer with the opportunity to identify himself with a character on the screen (see Klapper 1960; Halloran 1964).

Even these limited findings have important indications for program planning. To what extent can one risk further unbalancing the unbalanced? Should a program planner settle for meeting the existing expectations of the largest majority? However, these are small questions in comparison with those about which we are still almost wholly in the dark. For example, it may have been proved that television is likely to cause the *acting out* of violence only in those who are already disturbed: but is it also true that exposure to repeated violence—as a thing simply to be enjoyed—has *no* effect, at the deepest levels of the psyche, on the millions of "normal" viewers?

Patterns of programming. What should television offer its audiences? There can be no simple answer. In practice, answers differ from country to country according to prevailing ideologies; these ideologies determine the administrative and financial structure of the various television systems and so determine their patterns of programming.

In Britain, both the British Broadcasting Corporation and the commercially financed but publicly controlled channels (ITV) are required by law to "inform, educate, and entertain." In practice, both systems entertain first, inform next, and educate least of all (in terms of time given to specific formal education). In the United States the place of entertainment is manifestly more prominent; in totalitarian countries information and education have a more important place than in Britain or the United States and tend, insofar as both are colored by ideological purpose, to be run into one another.

But what functions in relation to their audiences might be said to be more or less fundamental to any television system in a democracy? First, it should provide a good deal of reasonably straightforward services for the known needs of the majority of the population. The broadcasters have to amuse most of us in the periods when we most seek amusement, and they have to keep us (though it can only be sketchily) abreast of what has been happening in the world. Thus they have to provide entertainment ranging from the equivalent of a variety show to that of a concert hall, as well as a range of informational sources varying from the equivalent of a morning newspaper to that of a weekly journal of opinion. Moreover, all this must be done in the light of the fact that television is very expensive and that therefore the number of channels available (so far as we can see at present) is not likely to be sufficient to allow very fine breakdowns by audience taste. For much of its time, television will have to think, if not of absolute majorities, at least of sizable minorities.

But even this approach is a different concept of programming from the one dominant in those countries in which the audience sought most of the time was the largest possible majority of the total population. It is not sensible to oppose this view with the notion of television as the servant of small minorities; but even with only one channel, a television system can serve a range of overlapping sizable minorities much of the time. This is the promise of educational television in the United States (Schramm et al. 1963). The word "overlapping" is important. Large minorities are not discrete sections of the total population. The same people can belong to different large minorities at different times, depending on how they are feeling. Of course, programming can be so arranged as to hit the dead center of average taste most of the time and so discourage any form of selectivity in viewing. If the broadcasters are successful in obtaining this kind of consistent attention, then they are tempted to decide that their audiences are as uniform in tastes as their own programs. The history of some unexpectedly successful programs (for instance, in Great Britain), which were not designed for the "mass audience" but which nevertheless got a surprisingly hefty minority audience, challenges that thinking.

One can extend this idea that the taste of today's audiences is actually more varied than program planners are led to think or lead themselves to think. The existing tastes of most of us are not simply a product of irremovable hereditary factors; they are to a large extent a product of our opportunities, education, social class, available money, and where we happen to be born. It seems reasonable to ask whether broadcasters should simply *reflect* the average range of interests which a great number of other environmental forces have together produced at any particular time. If they decide to do this, they should realize that their role only appears to be a passive one. They will, in fact, be harnessed to the service of, and made to pull in the same direction as, many other powerful forces whose aim—in commercial democracies—is to exploit the existing range of tastes and interests. In that apparently passive role, television will therefore not be passive at all; as seen above, it will by its nature reinforce the existing narrowness in range of taste and the existing assumed limits. Should the broadcasters not be free, within sensible limits, to cater also to the potential as well as to the actual tastes of their audiences? Thus they might decide to offer programs which some people, though not as yet a large majority or even a sizable minority, find imaginatively and intellectually exciting, in the hope that others, who might otherwise never have had a chance to know of such possible interests, may become interested too.

This part of the argument is much confused by the clash of slogans. Shall broadcasters "give the people what the people want," or shall they "give the people what they ought to have"? This fruitless contrast was usefully dismantled by the British Committee on Broadcasting (the Pilkington Committee) in its report published in 1962.

The choice is not between *either* giving the public what it wants, *or* giving the public "what someone thinks is good for it," and nothing else. There is an area of possibility between the two; and it is within this area that the choice lies. The broadcasting authorities have certainly a duty to keep sensitively aware of the public's tastes and attitudes as they now are and in all their variety; and to care about them. But if they do more than that, this is not to give the public "what someone thinks is good for it." It is to respect the public's right to choose from the widest possible range of subject matter and so to enlarge worth while experience. Because, in principle, the possible range of subject matter is inexhaustible, all of it can never be presented, nor can the public know what the range is. So, the broadcaster must explore it, and choose from it first. This might be called "giving a lead": but it is not the lead of the autocratic or arrogant. It is the proper exercise of responsibility by public authorities duly constituted as trustees for the public interest. (Great Britain 1962, p. 18)

Any decision to put on programs other than those apparently justified by simple "feedback" from the market or by plain consonance with existing taste can be called paternal, patronizing, or propagandist. Indeed, such a decision is danger-

ous. Program planners are also mortal men with circumscribed views and assumptions that are not always examined. Their interpretation of the need to offer their audiences the chance to widen taste may, for example, amount to no more than the desire to make as many people as possible into "middlebrows"; they may have very simple views of the relations between social class and cultivation.

Criteria of value in programming. It is extremely difficult to define a "good" program. "Good in relation to what?" is a useful question, but it is only the first question; relied on for long, it becomes the motto for an evasive relativism. "Counting heads" is not a sufficient test of a program's success, but it is not irrelevant. When a program attracts an unexpectedly small audience, this may indicate that, though the producer did all he could to make it interesting without compromising the integrity of his subject, only a tiny minority of people are at present willing to be interested; on the other hand, it may indicate that not enough thought—at least, not enough of the right kind of thought—went into the effort to communicate widely. Again, technical competence is important and technical brilliance admirable. But, in the face of the difficulty of defining "good television" without seeming either patronizing or a victim of the market, many television producers hold on to technical virtuosity or "professionalism" as an end in itself. There are certain programs where the possibilities of the medium are being extended through a fascinating exploration of its inherent characteristics. However, in general, technical skill is and must be the servant of the particular subject or theme which is being presented.

In presenting that material, the broadcasters must aim at "objectivity" and "balance." This is often said, and although it sounds easy, it is in fact difficult. The two words are not synonymous. "Objectivity" means the decision not to push a particular editorial line, but rather to present the rough and qualified contours of truth as accurately as possible. "Balance" means ensuring that all sides have a fair and a reasonable chance to be heard. Both "objectivity" and "balance" have to be *positively* and flexibly interpreted, or they will become polite synonyms for sitting on the fence and for balancing one side against the other so nervously that all sides lose their force. The problem—which can be solved—is to avoid propaganda or partiality, to suggest the complextity of truth, and to allow the sense of the importance of making choices to be felt.

"Objectivity" and "balance" are not sufficient criteria of value in programs. Furthermore, though remembering that tastes do differ provides a useful check to narrow-mindedness, it still leaves virtually all the difficult questions about standards unanswered. We have seen that thinking in terms of fixed sociocultural hierarchies does not help much either. There is no room here to do more than has been done: to point to the complexity of the problems, indicate some of their elements, and reiterate their importance. As a coda, another quotation from the Pilkington Report may be useful:

Triviality is not necessarily related to the subject matter of a programme; it can appear in drama, current affairs programmes, religious programmes or sports programmes just as easily as in light comedy or variety shows. One programme may be gay and frivolous and yet not be trivial. Another programme may seek prestige because it deals with intellectual or artistic affairs —and yet be trivial in its grasp or treatment; it may, for example, rely for its appeal on technical tricks or the status of its compere, rather than on the worth of the subject matter, and the depth of its treatment. Triviality resides in the way the subject matter is approached and the manner in which it is presented. (Great Britain 1962, paragraph 98)

On the more practical aspects of the relations between television and its audiences, the question is, What links should exist between the two? This question is best discussed in the final section of this article, which deals with structures. The point of mentioning it here is that it underlines once again television's inherent trend toward centralization and thus its separation from its audiences. We have already noted that separation increases as television's practitioners become more internally engrossed in their work, because by definition the practitioners are self-consciously professional and most members of their audiences are not. Television is not a home industry or a folk industry. Even its conventional art has to be carefully planned; it doesn't just happen because someone just happens to feel that way. Television is a many-layered industry with stage after stage interposed between an original idea and what eventually appears on the screen. Inevitably, it produces an ethos—a mystique—of its own.

The qualities of the medium itself

Television production is a several-stage process, and thus it is an even more complicated process than that of producing a finished performance of a dramatist's final script in the live theater. Moreover, this medium often uses several writers at the same time on the same script or teams of writers working concurrently on a number of scripts or a series; in other instances a story line

and thematic pattern are established and different men take over the script writing at different times, or the relationship between a writer and his producer is a continuous dialectic. All these differences between television and live theater need not mean loss to a dramatist used to the ways of the theater; he may gain from them so long as he recognizes their possibilities as well as their limits.

The medium has qualities which restrict those who use it or at least closely define their areas of movement, but so do all art forms and channels for the expression of art. As in other fields of art, the tension between the given limitations of the medium and its new and peculiar possibilities challenges the imagination of a writer and suggests different ways of exploring experience. The restrictions of budget for any particular program, as well as problems of available space and personnel, are similar in kind to those technical and commercial pressures which were felt, say, in the development of the novel during the nineteenth century. The relevant considerations here can range from the simple and obvious to the most psychologically obscure: from merely circumventing a shortage of cameras to discovering new possibilities within the medium by means of a creative response to the challenge of that shortage. The parallels with, for example, the writing of sonnets are obvious.

About the qualities of the medium itself not a great deal that is authoritative has been written, but there are some useful hints and guesses. Television has a peculiar "immediacy" and "fluidity": it strongly suggests a sense that "it's all happening"—a sense of "thereness," "thisness," and "nowness"—and it tends to break down pre-existing categories. It resists stage acting and even cinema acting, breaks through the picture frame or mental proscenium arch, and merges the spectator with the picture, on its sidelines if not at the center. On television everything tends to become a form of documentary. Television tends to seek "personalities" of its own. Of course, television personalities help to build up "channel loyalty" and link disparate items, and so program planners like them. But the power of personalities is more than that: they are part of the self-validating and self-sufficient immediacy of television in its own right.

Television has an exceptional sense of immediate history. When a great public occasion—for example, a state funeral such as Sir Winston Churchill's—is seen on television, the sense of immediate historical presence is overwhelming. Furthermore, television can make a funeral in a back garden seem heavy with the meaning of life. It heightens even the most "ordinary" ordinariness of life and seems to give it dramatic significance. Because of its sense of actuality, of its Brechtian breaking of distance, we are all sidewalk spectators of the drama of life when we watch television. Sometimes one really believes in the reality of an event only because it has been validated through being seen on television.

We know little about what all this really means yet; it is too early to determine how far television may be encouraging a more plastic and fluid psychic responsiveness, or how far it may be the agent of a disconnected, discontinuous flow of value-free sensations (see McLuhan 1964). When it is not simply providing routine servicing, television is constantly seeking its own forms—its own kinds of drama, comedy, current affairs, and educational programs. Much has been done, but television programming is still at no more than the end of the beginning. This exploration, plus the assumption, already discussed, that an audience's potential range is greater than its actual range, requires the emphasis to be put on openness and experimentation in program planning. About both the medium itself and its deepest relationships with its audiences we still know too little to be dogmatic.

The formal structures of television

There are three main kinds of formal structure for television, as for all broadcasting: the state-controlled, the commercially impelled, and the in-between, or—as I would prefer to call it—the potentially democratic.

In the first, the communications system is an arm of government and so at bottom propagandist, no matter what its apparent face. It can be found in one form or another in communist countries, fascist countries, and in other types of authoritarian countries, especially those in which the Roman Catholic church is strong. It stresses the party line and the national philosophy, and keeps a tight hold on the channels for debate. Under this system the greatest sufferers are information and education, since both are consistently distorted. Television is regarded chiefly as a channel through which things are done *to* people rather than as a medium with its own possibilities and characteristics. Therefore state-controlled television tends not to be experimental either about what the medium can best do or about what audiences might enjoy if they had the chance.

In the second system—the commercially impelled—television is tied to commerce, usually because it makes its money by selling advertising time. Such systems can vary from those in which advertising is regarded (or said to be regarded) chiefly as a convenient means for financing the programs to systems in which (public professions notwithstanding) the main feature is advertising. In the former type of system, the programs are still the most important thing, whereas in the latter type they are regarded as carriers or bait for the commercials; however, in the end, the pressures on all such systems are very much the same. This emphasis on commercial values can happen under any system which allows advertisements but obviously is likely to be more extreme under direct sponsorship.

The drive is to maximize profit by increasing the number of impacts delivered or persons reached; the audience is seen as a vast number of possible consumers whom it would be advantageous to hold as one large mass. The basic urge of this kind of television is, therefore, to keep the largest possible number of people content for the largest possible amount of time. Its natural drive is the reverse of that of state-controlled systems; it stresses entertainment rather than information and education. It tends to narrow the range of programs offered, so as to concentrate on types of programs considered likely to attract a mass audience. Thus it tends to ignore minorities, because minorities are subdivisions of the potential single mass audience. A good example of this self-defeating concentration on a narrow range of programs known to be popular can be seen in the programming of New York City's numerous television channels during prime time. The commercially impelled system also reduces the urge to experiment, whether in regard to the potential tastes of the audiences or to the more freely imaginative possibilities of the medium itself; it inherently seeks to exploit existing tastes.

The "potentially democratic" system. I called the third system the "potentially democratic" because I doubt that a full-fledged democratic broadcasting system exists anywhere in the world. At its best, the British Broadcasting Corporation sometimes gets near to it. In such a system the state does not have day-to-day supervision or any executive control (though in the public interest there must be some overriding guardianship); nor is the advertiser able to distort the uses of the medium, since there is no advertising.

The two chief difficulties in such a system are paying for it and providing the necessary minimum of supervision without inhibiting the broadcasters. Advertising—with the advertisement revenue-receiving body formally and genuinely separated from the program-providing body—might just be possible at one end of the financial spectrum; the danger here is the steady spread of the pressures of advertising into the planning of programs. Mass-media advertising is like a seamless garment, and to think you can seal off a part of it is to be like the young lady of Riga who thought she could ride a tiger with impunity. At the other end of the financial spectrum is a system of direct payment from public funds to the broadcasting authority, who would be entrusted to use it for broadcasting in the public interest, with "public interest" not too restrictively defined. This has various possible forms, too, and some are less tricky than others. But obviously the danger here is that the state will exercise increasing, creeping pressure, as the direct provider of funds.

In between these two ends of the financial spectrum there are, again, several different ways of paying for broadcasting. On the whole, the most successful is the license fee, because it gives most scope for the broadcasters to serve the public interest in the wide and flexible sense described earlier. Although there are arguments against this approach —for example, that it is a form of "poll tax," or that it is too expensive because the money has to be collected in millions of small packets—the arguments in its favor seem overwhelming. The license fee falls on all, and almost all use broadcasting; furthermore, it multiplies and subdivides the sources of money so that no one large agency is tempted, because it is footing the bill, to try to exercise consistent strong pressure or feels cheated if things do not go in just the way it wants. However, once practically every family has a television set, the ceiling on new licenses has been reached, and from that time on, the amount of the license, if it is to serve its purpose, must be tied to increases in wages and incomes.

The supervision of a "democratic" (nonstate and noncommercial) broadcasting system is even trickier than the problem of paying for it. There must be a buffer between the broadcasting professionals and whatever party happens to be in power at any one time—a buffer which allows the broadcasters to stand on their own professional feet and exercise proper editorial independence but which also stops them from too narrowly, too remotely, or less than responsibly defining the public interest. Countries trying to operate this system vary in the buffer they use, but the British Broadcasting Corporation's board of governors, for both its strengths and its weaknesses, is an interesting particular instance (for the problems of educational television in the United States, see National Educational Television 1960).

Below the government level, it is important that broadcasters be kept responsive to public need. But "public need" is not easy to define, and some large-scale bodies which claim to speak for "ordinary opinion" are no more than philistine and restrictive. There seems to be a need for a range of responsive and well-informed bodies forming links between the producers and their audiences: not pressure groups in a political or economic sense but interest groups, specialist groups, and professional groups —all helping to form a texture of relevant critical understanding and of challenge and response between the two sides of the operation.

In all this, the overriding need is to find a structure that will let professionalism in broadcasting (in the sense defined above) grow and become, as far as possible, responsible for itself. The fully democratic broadcasting system which might emerge if the twin pressures of the state and the advertisers were thus avoided is difficult to define precisely (and even more difficult to put into practice), but a rough workable definition is certainly possible. Such a system would not assume an automatic and close correlation between "cultivation" and social class; it would not think of itself as offering some fixed sociocultural status symbols *downward* to the masses. Nor would it reject the standards of civilization in the pursuit of popular support. Nor would it peddle "culture" as a form of marginal differentiation in the "affluent society." It would be a very varied and pluralist organization with a strong but dispersed life. Furthermore, it would be highly professional in that it would be not only technically efficient but also would devote a great deal of thought to the possibilities of the medium and to its own varied and changing relationships with its audiences; and it would regard its audiences, too, as varied and changing. It would be editorially objective but not inhibitedly given to fence sitting. Finally, it would combine a very high degree of freedom with a relevant sense of responsibility.

RICHARD HOGGART

[*See also* FILM; MASS SOCIETY.]

BIBLIOGRAPHY

Research on television by social scientists has so far concentrated on audiences. Leading studies include Lang & Lang 1953; Belson 1959; Steiner 1963; Glick & Levy 1962. Bogart 1956; Klapper 1960; *and Halloran 1964 summarize much other research in this field. For the structure of the television industry in the United States it is still necessary to consult journalistic accounts such as* Opotowsky 1961 *and* Paul 1962, *as well as trade sources such as* Variety. *The structure and social responsibilities of television have been examined in* Great Britain, Broadcasting Committee 1962; Canada, Committee on Broadcasting 1965. *In the United States, some of the same issues were raised in a more acute form by the hearings in* U.S. Congress 1960. *Schools of journalism and public communica-*

tion, especially in the United States, have shown an increasing interest in mass-media research; the best-known outlet for articles from this source is the Journal of Broadcasting. McLuhan 1964 *is a brilliant and idiosyncratic philosophical treatise on the mass media. Developments in educational television in the United States are dealt with in* National Educational Television and Radio Center 1960 *and* Schramm et al. 1963.

BELSON, WILLIAM A.   1958   Measuring the Effects of Television: A Description of Method. *Public Opinion Quarterly* 22:11–18.

BELSON, WILLIAM A.   1959   Effects of Television on the Interests and Initiative of Adult Viewers in Greater London. *British Journal of Psychology* 50:145–158.

BOGART, LEO   (1956) 1958   *The Age of Television: A Study of Viewing Habits and the Impact of Television on American Life.* 2d ed., rev. & enl. New York: Ungar.

CANADA, COMMITTEE ON BROADCASTING   1965   *Report.* Ottawa: Queen's Printer.

GLASER, WILLIAM A.   1965   Television and Voter Turnout. *Public Opinion Quarterly* 29:71–86.

GLICK, IRA O.; and LEVY, SIDNEY J.   1962   *Living With Television.* Chicago: Aldine.

GREAT BRITAIN, BROADCASTING COMMITTEE   1962   *Report.* London: H.M. Stationery Office.

HALLORAN, J. D. L.   1964   *The Effects of Mass Communication.* Television Research Committee, Working Paper No. 1. Leicester Univ. Press.

Journal of Broadcasting. → Published since 1956/1957 by the Association for Professional Broadcasting Education.

KLAPPER, JOSEPH T.   1960   *The Effects of Mass Communication.* Glencoe, Ill.: Free Press.

LANG, KURT; and LANG, GLADYS E.   1953   The Unique Perspective of Television and Its Effect: A Pilot Study. *American Sociological Review* 18:3–12.

LOVE, RUTH L.   1965   The Business of Television and the Black Weekend. Pages 73–86 in Bradley S. Greenberg and Edwin B. Parker (editors), *The Kennedy Assassination and the American Public: Social Communication in Crisis.* Stanford Univ. Press.

McLUHAN, MARSHALL   1964   *Understanding Media: The Extensions of Man.* New York: McGraw-Hill. → A paperback edition was published in 1965.

MILLER, MERLE; and RHODES, EVAN   1964   *Only You, Dick Daring! Or, How to Write One Television Script and Make $50,000,000: A True-life Adventure.* New York: Sloane. → A factual account of what it is like to be a writer for a major U.S. television network.

NATIONAL EDUCATIONAL TELEVISION AND RADIO CENTER   1960   *The Impact of Educational Television.* Edited by Wilbur L. Schramm. Urbana: Univ. of Illinois Press.

OPOTOWSKY, STAN   1961   *TV, the Big Picture.* New York: Dutton.

PAUL, EUGENE   1962   *The Hungry Eye.* New York: Ballantine.

SCHRAMM, WILBUR L. et al.   1963   *The People Look at Educational Television: A Report of 9 Representative ETV Stations.* Stanford Univ. Press.

STEINER, GARY A.   1963   *The People Look at Television: A Study of Audience Attitudes.* New York: Knopf.

U.S. CONGRESS, HOUSE COMMITTEE ON INTERSTATE AND FOREIGN COMMERCE, SPECIAL SUBCOMMITTEE ON LEGISLATIVE OVERSIGHT   1960   *Investigation of Television Quiz Shows: Hearings.* Washington: Government Printing Office.

Variety. → The leading weekly journal of show business, published in New York since 1905; its TV section is a mine of basic information.

WEINBERG, MEYER   1962   *TV in America: The Morality of Hard Cash.* New York: Ballantine. → A well-documented account of the TV quiz show scandal in 1959 and the subsequent congressional hearings.

IV

AUDIENCES

The rise of the mass media has been inseparably linked to the growth of national cultures with a linguistic unity, to the increase of literacy, and to key events in the technological revolution—from movable type to the transistor. In these relationships, cause and effect intermingle. The rise of literacy in the Western world was accompanied by the birth of the first inexpensive newspapers, but mass literacy was required before any of the print media could win a wide public. Mass literacy in turn depends on an organized system of mass education, inconceivable in a purely feudal or tribal society.

"Mass," in this context, suggests an absence of social structure, although not necessarily of group identity. A principal characteristic of the mass audience is that it is dispersed. An audience for an FM radio broadcast may be far smaller than one for an open-air concert, but the former constitutes a mass audience in the sense that its members perceive themselves (and are perceived by the radio station's manager) as *potentially* consisting of all persons within range of the station's transmitter. The audience at a "live" concert quite evidently does not see itself in this way. The reason is that the messages of mass communication are open to all. The oldest form of such open communication is the public proclamation—a form that includes the public poster and the wall news bulletin. Yet, public announcements of this kind, with their implicit reliance on secondary transmission of the news by word of mouth, are not ordinarily thought of within the framework of the great mass media of today.

Traditionally, the mass media have been regarded as "merely means of transmission" (Hall & Whannel 1964). But as McLuhan (1964) points out, "the medium is the message," in the sense that its own peculiar attributes help to determine the very meaning of the communication. In short, the essence of any medium is that it mediates. It is not so much a neutral channel through which a message flows as it is a distinctive material in which the message is recast. Such mediation is already performed by the written word as it appears in any society that has evolved beyond the level of folk culture; indeed, the transmission of culture depends first and foremost upon the written word. In this sense, the scribes of antiquity were the precursors of Caxton and Gutenberg. The printing press was essentially a mechanical means for achieving on a larger scale what the medieval manuscript copyists (whose work, organized in the monasteries on a group basis, had some of the features of mass production) had already assured in principle.

The invention of movable type did not in itself make the book into a mass medium, since two necessary conditions were absent: mass literacy and the means for widespread dissemination of identical communications content. The latter condition did not really come into existence until the arrival of mass-produced and inexpensive newspapers in the mid-nineteenth century. These were made possible by the high-speed rotary press and cheap wood-pulp paper and were later made still cheaper by the introduction of automatic typecasting machines. The dramatic effect of these innovations can be inferred from the fact that from 1846 to 1850 daily newspaper circulation nearly doubled.

The first newspapers, in the seventeenth century, had been feeble affairs by modern standards, in terms of both content and number of readers. Yet, only an arbitrary cutoff point can be used to state when their circulations reached proportions that would justify calling them mass media. According to one authority, in 1704 the average daily sale of all London newspapers combined was 7,300, or about 2.7 million a year (Altick 1957, pp. 47–48). Whether this circulation is considered large or small for a country where the population hardly exceeded 6 million depends on the historical perspective from which it is viewed. At any rate, it is certain that the number of newspapers sold in England almost doubled between 1753 and 1780. Individual newspapers, however, had not reached appreciably larger circulations by the end of the century; over-all sales were greater simply because there were more newspapers (ibid., p. 48). Moreover, the stamp duty on English newspapers made them too expensive for the average member of the public, although copies were available free to habitués of the clubs and coffeehouses that flourished in the larger cities. It was not until the nineteenth century that newspapers became as cheap and as widely circulated as they are today. In the period 1860–1870, for instance, most daily newspapers in New York sold for four cents or less, and by 1872 at least three of them were credited with daily circulations in the range of 90,000 to 100,000;

comparable circulations were achieved by London and Paris newspapers during the same period (Mott [1941] 1962, pp. 403–404).

Radio, in the days before tape recording, extended the concept of what makes a mass medium beyond the criterion of mere reproducibility of communications content. Unlike the telephone (a medium of private communication made possible by mass facilities), radio has the same ability as print or cinema to put the same message before many people at the same time. It is precisely the direct extension of the communicator's message beyond the scope of interpersonal contact that transforms private communication into a mass medium. Thus, the enormous distribution of phonograph records, for instance, makes them a mass medium, particularly in the area of popular music, where fashions in style and in the fortunes of individual performers show sharp fluctuations and strong susceptibility to organized promotion.

The great twentieth-century inventions—film, radio, phonograph records, and television—have made literacy unnecessary for understanding mass communication, but the spread of the mass media presupposes a society that has attained a degree of affluence, in which mass literacy is taken for granted. The mass media are in evidence throughout the mid-twentieth-century world, but the size of media audiences varies enormously from place to place.

Current media statistics, such as those in UNESCO's World Communications, are rapidly outdated, particularly in the case of the newer media. In 1955 there were about 6 million television sets in use in western Europe. By 1960 the number had quadrupled, and by 1965 it had grown eightfold. By contrast, in the relatively stagnant economies of Latin America and Africa the number of television sets showed only a very slow rate of growth (for these and related figures see U.S. Information Agency 1966, p. 4, table 1).

It is highly tempting, but also misleading, to classify countries according to the incidence of radio or television sets, cinemas, or newspaper or magazine circulation per capita. The penetration of a medium may be diffused or concentrated in terms of either geography or social class.

In certain countries of Africa, Asia, and South America the mass media are in full use only among upper-class and upper-middle-class urban elements, who represent a small part of the total population. However, if the absolute size of this minority is substantial (as in India), the media may still represent a considerable cultural and political force. For instance, the news of President Kennedy's assassination was soon known by a very large proportion of the Indian people, even those in villages far from a radio set. As is documented by Lerner (1958), even in a folk society of illiterate peasants close to the ancestral soil and without access to radio, television, movies, or the printed word, there are usually found geographically dispersed members of the extended mass society. Deep in the jungle or on the plains, surrounded by villagers or tribesmen, there is always a trader, a government administrator, a teacher, a medical technician, an agricultural specialist, or an itinerant peddler. Anyone who has ties to the outer world sustained by reading, by radio, or by occasional excursions to the urban centers can act as a relay point through which new information and ideas reach those who live by the traditional order.

But the newer media, which do not depend on the printed word, have direct effects quite independent of such secondary diffusion. In remote hamlets throughout the world the agents of governmental and international welfare organizations erect their movie screens each night to show training films on health, agriculture, sanitation, or politics. In ten thousand tropical open-air cafes the radio blares from dawn to late at night, within hearing range of all who pass by. In the big cities of even the most backward lands crowds of slum dwellers gather each night in taverns and clubs and before the windows of radio stores to watch the television shows. They constitute a regular television audience even though the price of a set is well beyond their means.

The very universality of the mass media appears to serve contradictory functions. The diffusion of the same information to different groups enforces social cohesion by creating common heroes and symbolic reference points. At the same time, this very diffusion may be a socially divisive force insofar as it emphasizes particular subcultural interests in a complex and heterogeneous society. Mass media may help a group to define its own distinctive character, as may be seen in the cases of the French-speaking audience of the Canadian Broadcasting Corporation, the native readers of *Drum* in the Republic of South Africa, or audiences of Negro weekly newspapers and radio stations in the United States.

The institutions of modern political democracy are inconceivable without mass media, through which political information and opinion can be disseminated and discussed. Yet, paradoxically, the totalitarian governments of the twentieth century could not have established or maintained themselves in power without making use of press,

film, and radio. Autocracy, whether in eighteenth-century France or nineteenth-century Russia, has long used censorship of the media as a device for stifling dissident voices. But only recently have state-controlled media been used, as in the Germany of Goebbels or the Ghana of Nkrumah, to create mass support for the ideology of the regime in power.

In countries with representative governments radio and television have added significant new dimensions to the operations of the political process by introducing new criteria for evaluating candidates—their ability to project their personalities with charm and vigor, in a context dominated by professional entertainers. Broadcasting has also brought a vicarious sense of direct participation in the political process to a broadly scattered electorate that relied in the past on the more impersonal contacts of print. The intrusion of cameras and microphones into political meetings, demonstrations, and conventions has brought a new self-consciousness to the behavior of the participants and altered the very character of such events.

Comparative mass media systems

If nations are to be classified according to the prevalence of mass media, we must first set aside countries such as Yemen or Mali, which lack indigenous media and therefore depend on radio signals or occasional publications that cross their national boundaries. Other countries can be ranked according to the level of their print culture, as measured by the rate of literacy and the figures for circulation and readership of newspapers and magazines.

The highest per capita readership of newspapers is found in the United Kingdom, where a newspaper is sold for every two people every day (United Nations . . . 1964, p. 331). Short distances enable the morning national newspapers of that country to attain overnight distribution throughout the nation. Thus, the distinctions between the newspapers tend to be based on politics and social class differences rather than on local interests, although some national dailies publish regional editions. In contrast, the United States has no national newspapers and the major part of even the big-city dailies is made up of local news and advertising.

In general, areas with a strongly developed print culture, as in Europe, North America, and Japan, are also those with the most advanced broadcasting culture. But this is not always the case. Some Asiatic and South American countries emerged into the age of radio and television, while bypassing the spread of universal literacy. In many Latin American slums television antennas are marks of social status, which sprout from the roofs of dismal shanties whose illiterate inhabitants lack running water and other basic necessities. In some countries (e.g., Israel and the Republic of South Africa) reasons of politics or economic need have kept out television as a matter of official policy, in spite of public demand.

The relative importance of the various mass media in any country cannot be judged by the extent to which people have access to them. Countries with comparable populations (including comparable literacy rates) vary substantially in the number of newspapers or magazines actually read by the average reader. Broadcast listening and viewing hours vary with national cultural values, tastes, and behavior styles even when the proportions of set ownership are comparable. Listening patterns also reflect government action and the state of the economy, which together determine the hours of the broadcast day, the number of stations on the air, the quality of programming output, and the intensity of competition. It should also be remembered that the penetration of a mass medium extends beyond its physical presence, through messages relayed by word of mouth—the "two-step flow," described by Katz and Lazarsfeld (1955). The number of copies printed may give no clue to the real influence of a publication. Addison and Steele's *Spectator* may have had a far greater number of readers per copy than any newspaper or magazine in England today. In many areas of the world publications are still passed from hand to hand or, as in the Soviet Union and China, placed on billboards for all to see.

The extent of media penetration in a country cannot be predicted solely from knowledge of its educational or economic level. For instance, in the Congo, where a third of the population could read in 1950, two newspapers were circulated for every 1,000 people, and there were six radios for the same number (United Nations . . . 1964, p. 80). But in Nigeria, with a lower level of literacy (about 11 per cent), the penetration of the press was four times as great and of radio twice as great (p. 102). Other contrasts may be found in Latin America. Argentina, with 86 per cent literacy, had 155 copies of the press for every 1,000 people (p. 177). Uruguay, with the same proportion of literates, had 260 copies per 1,000 (p. 194). While Argentina had 167 radios for every 1,000 people, Uruguay had 354, but Argentina, which introduced television earlier, had 42 sets per 1,000 people (p. 177) and Uruguay only 24 (p. 195). Venezuela, with half its population illiterate, had only 96

newspapers circulating per 1,000 population but had 194 radios and 60 television sets, more than Argentina (p. 196). Another interesting contrast in rival economic systems was afforded by East Germany and West Germany, both with virtually universal literacy. The number of newspapers per 1,000 people was much higher in East Germany (456) than in West Germany (307). The proportion of radios was about the same (about 3 for every 10 people), but West Germany led in television sets—139 per 1,000, compared with 90 per 1,000 in East Germany (pp. 286, 290).

The concept of audience

Comparative studies of mass media are somewhat obscured by ambiguous terminology, which reflects changing uses of the word "audience" itself. The term audience (Latin *audientia*) connotes a situation in which a powerful, but passive, auditor (such as a king or magistrate) listens to an advocate or suppliant actively presenting his case. Hence comes its later application to the theater. In the classic tradition drama exists only in relation to the audience. That heightening and purging of the emotions of which Aristotle wrote in his *Poetics* is inconceivable except in the mutual empathic relation of actors and onlookers bound together in an interplay of feeling, even though the words and gestures are all on one side of the stage. Since the audience is an integral part of the dramatic spectacle, it must also be regarded as a body that is collective in nature and that has social characteristics of its own apart from the characteristics of its individual members. Aristotle was no doubt describing an "ideal type" rather than rendering a literal description of the Athenian theatergoers of his day. By definition, an audience, in the Aristotelian sense, must be conscious of its presence and purpose in being where it is and of its own reactions. There is a social cohesion among the members of the audience, but this rises out of the spectacle, which is their common experience. Their unity is forged by the spectacle and exists only as long as the spectacle continues. Drama arouses the feelings of awe and pity only to the degree that it can play on those universals in human experience and aspiration which are intensified in a collective setting.

From its early associations with the sense of hearing, the word "audience" in the nineteenth century began occasionally to be applied to the reading public as well. To Charles Dickens on the lecture platform there may hardly have seemed to be a major distinction between the people who read his books in serial form and those who gathered to hear his readings. But it was only with the motion picture that the term "audience" became applicable to a mass medium in the classical (i.e., theatrical) meaning. The movie theater is, after all, superficially identical with the legitimate theater in its seating arrangements, its fixed spatial relationship between spectacle and public, and its rule that the audience must sit in darkness and for the most part in silence.

There are two new elements in the motion picture experience. In the first place, the movies can do without the conventions that ordinarily distinguish the world of the drama from the world of reality. Events on the theatrical stage are always directly perceived as re-enactment, as fiction. The very presence of flesh-and-blood actors makes it impossible for the audience to confuse the depicted action with the truth. But movie photography, with its ability to collapse time and to broaden scenic perspectives to take in all the complex settings, landscapes, backgrounds, and moving multitudes of the real world, *can* create the illusion that what is being shown is somehow a direct representation of something that actually did happen. The second critical difference between the cinema and the theater (and the one that most concerns us in this context) lies in the absence of feedback. The communication is disembodied, it flows in one direction. Except for the long-range influence of box-office receipts, fan mail, and the articles of critics, there is no way for actors, directors, or producers to know at first hand whether they have succeeded or failed, because there is no regular way for the audience to express itself either during or immediately after the performance.

Radio and television, like the movies, are derivations of the theater inasmuch as they are spectacles arranged for the benefit of a specific group. Also like the movies, they communicate content in an order and at a rate over which the audience has no control (often with a time lag between the original performance and the exposure) and reach people who cannot transmit their reactions directly to the performers. The listeners to a particular broadcast (and to some extent the regular listeners to a series of broadcasts) share a common experience and a certain consciousness of each other's presence. Quite early in the evolution of radio programming the studio audience was introduced as a device to promote empathy on the part of the scattered listeners. It also served to provide the live entertainers with the feedback reactions considered necessary to evoke their best efforts. As technology became more sophisticated, the latter aspect was given less importance. But it was still found necessary to produce the illusion of a studio audience, in order to stimulate the response of the unseen listeners or viewers. This was made possible by the use of recorded applause and laughter that could be adjusted to specified degrees of loudness and enthusiasm.

There is a fundamental difference between the feedback from audience to producers of films or broadcasts and that from audience to writers or editors of print media. Newspapers have a long-standing tradition of publishing a selection of letters from readers; eight per cent of the people in the United States report they have written at least one letter to a newspaper (Audits and Surveys Company, Inc. 1961). The reader who writes in does so, not so much to enlighten the editor or to convince him to change his mind, as to see his own opinions in print and presumably to influence other readers. In this sense, he is aiming at a mass audience for his opinions.

In the case of mail from listeners, viewers, or movie-goers, the writer wants to communicate directly with the star or producer to whom his letter is addressed. Not always is he merely approving, complaining, or suggesting changes, as a fan or critic. Often the fan letter is a device for achieving human contact with the admirable or powerful figures he imagines stars to be. He may ask for help with his personal problems; he maintains the illusion that the star feels as close to him as he does to the star, whose private life may be a matter of public record and interest (Bogart 1949).

The letters column on the editorial page provides the newspaper editor with a mechanism by which to evade concern with the letters' content. Since broadcasters do not have a comparable mechanism, they are bound to take letters more seriously, particularly critical letters, to which they often assign a weight beyond true proportion. This tendency is supported by the apparatus of commercial broadcasting, in which the sponsor of a program—and the whole business establishment of the broadcasting industry—normally finds it both unnecessary and commercially distasteful for even a single viewer to be antagonized. The media producer's perceptions and preoccupations with the public's reaction to his efforts have been better described in thinly disguised "fictional" narratives, such as Foreman's (1958), than by professional sociologists.

Broadcast-audience measurement

The measurement of audiences for television and radio programs is a major industry in the United States and is carried out on a highly systematic and continuing basis in western Europe, Japan, and several countries of Latin America. Identical techniques are generally applicable to television and radio, although the advent of the easily portable transistor radio has created a highly mobile audience, which is difficult to measure.

Audience as a measurement concept for radio evolved some years after the term "radio audience" had become a conventional part of the broadcaster's vocabulary. Initially, the yardstick of radio penetration was the count of receiving sets. This paralleled the use of a tangible unit of measurement for newspaper and magazine circulation: printed sold copies. Later, various formulas were used to estimate the number of listeners in ratio to the number of letters, and surveys were made to measure just what stations people could receive on their sets.

The measurement of program audiences by the survey method was a by-product of commercial broadcasting in the United States, as described by Head (1956) and documented in the Harris Committee hearings (U.S. Congress . . . 1963). Stations and networks sold air time to advertisers in units which appeared to be fixed, but which actually varied greatly in the size and character of the listener groups they yielded. The sponsor was not really buying an hour of time on a station or a half-hour on a network, but rather the opportunity to present a sales message to a certain number of listeners. That number would vary according to the signal strength and popularity of the station and the timing and appeal of the sponsor's program.

As advertisers made larger and larger investments in radio, they became increasingly concerned with the need for accurate measurement. Thus, radio research in the United States evolved from one-shot, unsystematically done surveys to continuing studies, first directly sponsored by the broadcasting industry and then produced as syndicated services by individual research firms, which in some cases developed into institutions of considerable wealth and power. Curiously enough, the evolution of audience research by the noncommercial British Broadcasting Corporation underwent a parallel evolution, from special to continuing studies (Paulu 1956).

What was encompassed in the term "audience" could only be defined pragmatically, in terms of the statistics yielded by particular research methods. "Audience" could be the number of people who said they "ever" listened to a particular show, or it could be the number who said they had listened to that show last week. It could be the number who reported they were listening to the show at the very time they were interviewed in person or on the telephone. It could be the number who selected the show from a roster of programs that had been on the air the previous night or who listed the show in a radio-listening diary. "Audience" could encompass not only the respondents, who were the source of information, but the other family members on whose listening the respondents also reported. "Audience" could be the people who listened to *any* part of the program, those who listened for at least five minutes, or only the average number listening per minute of program.

An enormous range of statistics was produced by such a variety of definitions and research methods. Each measurement assigned a single quantitative value to the term "audience," yet what was being measured represented more than a single kind of listening experience. The members of the audience are continually drifting in and drifting out; some of them are more attentive than others. A rather considerable variety of media-exposure patterns were thus lumped together only for the sake of convenience. Measurement now consisted of estimating the intangible "listening experience" rather than the tangible quantities of radio sets or of letters to the station.

In most countries where broadcast-audience measurement exists it is provided either for an entire nation or for one or a few principal cities where receivers are concentrated. In the United States the highly competitive system of commercial broadcasting has created a number of services which measure audiences nationally and locally in hundreds of cities. Measurements are made of total set usage at various times of the day, the size of the total audience for a program, and the number of people listening or watching at a particular minute. Still further measurements are made to ascertain the composition or characteristics of the viewers and the audience stability (that is, the degree to which the audience shifts over time from show to show).

Distinctions may also be made between different levels of viewing interest. These correspond to the difference between the primary audience (the actual subscribers or purchasers) of print media and the secondary, or "pass-along," audience. As more television families have come to own more than one television set—21 per cent in the United States as of August 1965 (Advertising Research Foundation 1965, p. 10)—viewing has tended to get more and more remote from its original character as a group experience. This is comparable to the evolution of radio from its central position in the family living room to a personal, highly portable instrument. The degree to which people like individual programs does not show a consistent relationship to audience size, as measured by ratings.

Print-audience measurement

The evolution of broadcast-audience research had a profound effect upon the study of print media, in which the established criteria of measurement involved that most tangible of yardsticks, paid circulation.

The drive for measurement of audiences for print media was, as in broadcasting, a by-product of the sale of advertising. The editorial vitality or political influence of a publication, like that of a broadcast program, has generally reflected, not its size, but rather the fire, talent, and ingenuity that go into it. Advertising, however, has tended to be most responsive to sheer numbers, although environment is of course not neglected. But circulation alone is no longer generally considered an adequate yardstick of a publication's appeal. In the United States a large part of the circulation of print media is today delivered to the people who buy their subscriptions on a long-term basis, often at vastly reduced rates. This stems from the continuous drive to gain greater and greater numbers of "guaranteed" readers to sell to the advertisers.

Years after the newspapers and magazines of the United States had found advertisers satisfied with audited paid circulation as the basis for comparing one publication with another, they suddenly found that the audience figures for radio programs were of a magnitude that few publications could match. The term "audience" was applied to print media in an effort to match these large figures by demonstrating that a newspaper or magazine normally had several readers for every copy printed and placed in circulation. The rise of mass-circulation magazines, particularly the picture magazines with large "pass-along" or casual readership, made it possible to use the general opinion survey as a way to locate readers and to compare their total numbers from one publication to the next. It was through these competitive demands of American advertising media that audience became a commonplace concept in the field of communications research. The overwhelming preponderance of effort and expenditure in the study of mass media in Europe and the United States has been devoted to the measurement of the size and characteristics of media audiences. In the United States a number of "syndicated services" report on a variety of different media through periodic surveys. Personal interviews and self-administered questionnaires have been used to measure the extent to which different magazines are read by the same people or to which individual programs are watched by readers of certain periodicals.

In an economy where the mass communications media are operated privately for profit, measurements of audience size are inevitably the basis of decisions that affect media content. Other things being equal, most mass media operators seek to broaden rather than restrict their coverage. They would prefer that their influence be greater rather than less.

Differentiation of audiences

"Audience" has been commonly used as a term that aggregates units of equivalent value, so that a major research interest has been to count these units rather than to differentiate them. Audience figures for print and broadcast media are dealt with comparatively, as though communication in space and time could somehow be reduced to a common basis, and audience figures for each medium have been lumped together without regard to the setting in which different people experience each one or the different qualities of communication each may represent to different groups.

In the United States one of the problems in evaluating audience data on the mass media is that surveys are not usually designed to permit subgroups to be distinguished except in a very coarse way. Survey samples are usually not large enough to isolate the small segments of the population that represent the true market for elite culture. The conventional way of dividing an audience into income or education groups may isolate the upper fourth or the upper fifth under each heading, while the key target of elite culture may be no more than the top 1 or 2 per cent. When these people are averaged in with the others the results may appear to suggest that income and education have less effect on audience taste or choice than they in fact do. For example, a study made by W. R. Simmons for Harper–Atlantic Sales, Inc., in 1965 found that readers of *Harper's* magazine differ markedly in travel and consumption styles from other persons of "identical" income, education, etc. (Blair 1965).

Media audiences may be differentiated at three levels: exposure to the medium, to the vehicle, and to its content. At the first level an analyst must deal largely in terms of broad-scale demographic generalizations. Certain kinds of people may be said to be strong newspaper readers or television watchers or the first to acquire a television set when the medium is new. Within this framework it becomes necessary to further differentiate the audiences for individual publications or programs, whose exposure patterns may be quite different from those of the average user of the medium. Further, different kinds of people vary in their selective attention to the features or articles of a periodical or to the segments of a broadcast; a publication will not be read with the same degree of thoroughness by every reader and not every item in it will be read by the same kinds of people.

Media audiences or publics are often thought of as mutually exclusive (as in the case of programs which come on the air at the same time on different stations or of rival periodicals with radically opposite political viewpoints). But far more commonly, mass media audiences really consist of different aggregations or combinations, into which the same people may be shuffled, regrouped, or subdivided. Such subdivisions may occur for many different reasons. For instance, they may reflect stages in the life cycle. In an advanced media culture young children are exposed to broadcast media before print media and begin to select their own radio and television programs before their parents begin to read newspaper items or cartoon captions aloud to them. In the United States 44 per cent are reading newspapers themselves by the age of seven (Schramm et al. 1960).

Studies done by the Japanese Ministry of Education have shown that 11 per cent of the children in Tokyo were watching television by the age of two, 40 per cent were watching by the age of three, and among five-year-old children the percentage rose to 96 (Furu 1965, p. 61). As children mature, both their media habits and their preferences for different types of media content undergo substantial change. This is illustrated in a classic study of small children's shift from animal to human fantasy in comic book preferences (Wolf & Fiske 1949), as well as in numerous studies of shifting preferences for various types of television program content (summarized in Bogart 1956).

Adults also differ in their characteristic media patterns. For example, a study of workers in Leningrad, reported by Durham (1965), found weekly television viewing among young adults to be under five hours a week, while older persons watched nearly two hours more per week. A study by the English Institute of Practitioners in Advertising found that 44 per cent of the 16–24 age group saw a film at least once a week, as compared with only 5 per cent among those over 65 (Hall & Whannel [1964] 1965, p. 346). The Newsprint Information Committee's study of newspaper reading in the United States found that the percentage reading a paper on the average weekday increased from 72 per cent among teen-agers to 83 per cent in the 40–54 age group and then declined to 78 per cent

among those 55 and older (Audits and Surveys Company, Inc. 1961). A high proportion of popular recordings are bought by adolescents, particularly in the affluent postwar society of the United States or western Europe. The volatile musical tastes of the adolescent subculture have thus come to dominate popular music in general.

Audience differences may also reflect the mere distribution of access to a medium and the economic forces that affect it. Thus, in a country where television sets are expensive and radios are relatively cheap, the typical audiences for television and radio will have different incomes. The audiences for different media may also be sharply differentiated by social class; indeed, social class may be one determinant of the degree of reliance on different media. For example, Steiner (1963, p. 75) reports average daily television viewing in the United States ranges from under 3 hours among the college educated to nearly 4½ hours among those with less than four years of high school. There may also be ethnic or religious differences in the audiences of different media vehicles. According to an unpublished survey made by Data Inc. in 1964, each of the three afternoon papers then published in New York drew its readers preponderantly from the members of a different religious group.

Moreover, people who are identical in income and education may choose different media for psychological reasons. For example, it has been found that blue-collar workers who watch educational television are more apt than their neighbors to identify themselves as members of the middle class, as "opinion leaders," and as individuals with cultural and civic interests (Schramm et al. 1963).

Broadly speaking, the great mass media in most countries strive for popular appeal to all sectors of society. But in practice their appeal is differentiated both with respect to specific media vehicles (individual programs, films, publications) and to the different types of content (sports, finance, food, fashion) presented by each medium. Curiously, since television is a pastime activity, the number of hours spent viewing appears to be independent of the number of different programs available at the same time (Bogart [1956] 1958, chapter 4). The differentiation of media audiences cannot, therefore, be explained wholly in terms of economic opportunity and direct consumption cost; the role of different tastes and interests is equally important.

There are also variations in physical opportunity for exposure to media—variations that correspond to different specialized sex, age, or interest roles. A magazine sold only at the check-out counter of supermarkets is bought primarily by the shopping housewife; a television program that comes on in the late afternoon, when the mother is preparing dinner and the father has not yet returned from work, attracts a great many young children regardless of its content. In Muslim countries religious tradition keeps most women, apart from the urban elite, out of the motion picture theater.

Content and physical opportunity are likely to complement each other. Broadcast programs aimed at uplifting the morale of the housewife are placed on the air in the morning precisely because the housewives will make up the bulk of the listeners or viewers.

But content also determines audience appeal, inasmuch as there may be a symbolic identification between the roles or interests of the audience and those of the protagonists and characters, fictional or real. Clearly, the level of taste or intellectual complexity of media content will also influence audience composition. Everyone is more or less conscious of his own interests and exposes himself to the mass media accordingly. In effect, people read the publications and watch or listen to the programs that are most in conformity with their tastes, predilections, and opinions (Berelson et al. 1954, chapter 11). But the audience is also selective at a level below the threshold of consciousness, inasmuch as it selectively perceives and retains in its memory the most relevant, congruent, or comfortable part of the media content to which it is exposed [see COMMUNICATION, MASS, *article on* EFFECTS; *see also* Bogart & Tolley 1964].

Audiences may also be differentiated in terms of political orientation. This has been a traditional function of the press in most democratic countries, where a variety of viewpoints are available. In much of the Western world, choice of a newspaper is an act of political self-expression. At the same time, it may indeed relate to social status just as political party alignments do. The reader of *The Times* of London, of *Le Monde* of Paris, of Rio de Janeiro's *Correio da Manhã* is apt to be conservative not merely because of what is on the editorial pages of those papers but because their total substance and tone appeals to the conservative business communities of those cities. In the United States the reduction of competition in all but the very largest cities has altered the traditional role of newspapers as organs of conflicting opinion. But many newspapers that enjoy a monopoly position offer a diversity of viewpoints through the syndicated columnists on their editorial or magazine pages.

All the mass media have in common an ability to provide information, to stimulate or to relax, to pass time or to kill it, to persuade, to act as rallying points for diverse bodies of taste and opinion. There are, however, profound differences between print and the audio–visual media, with regard to their communicatory capacities.

In the time-bound media (broadcasting and film) the audience has no control over the rate of input as it does with print. Thus, the selective separation of irrelevant "noise" from meaningful information takes place at a slower pace and with more focused attention. The reader must "work harder" than the listener or viewer, but he remains in control and sets his own pace. This helps explain why print-oriented people tend to be better educated than those who are broadcast-oriented, both in the heyday of radio and in the age of television. It may also explain why empathy, identification, and catharsis appear to be the peculiar properties of the time-bound media, while reflection, internal rehearsal, and fantasy are the attributes of the print media (Wright 1960).

Mass culture and mass media

By common definition, mass media are those that attract people over a broad range of intellectual or cultural levels. Yet media-audience differentiation often carries an implicit classification of media content as "mass" or "elite" in terms of classical aesthetic canons. In this area, it is impossible to make sharp conceptual distinctions.

One broad distinction that is often made is between generalized and specialized organs of mass communication. Under the latter heading might be included trade publications, local periodicals, and broadcast programs or publications in such relatively specialized areas as fashion, sports, or education; many such publications or programs may reach vast audiences, yet their appeal is consciously directed or restricted. A good example of the former would be the kind of lavishly produced film epic, pioneered by Cecil B. De Mille, that aims to include something to suit every taste, while offending none. But even this distinction is hard to apply consistently. If an opera singer cuts a recording of an operatic aria in an edition of twenty thousand pressings, this would generally be conceded to fall into the realm of elite culture. But if she appears on a television variety program and sings the same aria before millions of viewing families, this might be said to bring the same content into the domain of mass culture. Similarly, a scholarly publication with five thousand readers might not ordinarily be considered a mass medium, but a community weekly newspaper with the same circulation would fall under that heading.

It therefore seems more appropriate to characterize as mass media *all* media that use techniques making for a loss of direct personal communication between the communicator and his public. This would include all printed publications, including some with highly restricted publics: hard-cover books, "little" magazines, the specialized organs of voluntary associations, corporations, trade unions, and other groups. Under the same heading, "art" films, educational television, phonograph recordings, FM radio, and other audio–visual media with limited appeal would have to be considered mass media, in contrast to the plastic and live performing arts, even though all of these are a part of elite culture.

The popular culture manifested in the mass media is quite distinct from folk culture; for instance, the existence of a folk culture implies direct personal participation in art forms such as music or the dance. The "high culture" elite that preserves the traditional spirit of the arts is to be distinguished from the power elite that controls the content and distribution of the mass media. Of course, it is possible to be a member of both these elites at once; the well-educated television producer who refuses to have a television set in his house is not a wholly mythical figure.

The relation of the mass media to contemporary popular culture is commonly conceived in terms of dissemination from the elite (masters of the media) to the mass (consumers). There are periods when this process is reversed, when popular culture in its most vulgar aspects enters into the culture of the elite as a display of disenchantment with prevailing social forms or symbols. During the eighteenth century it was the utmost chic for the aristocrats of the French court to assume the guise of shepherds and peasants in their festive outings, as immortalized in the paintings of Boucher and Fragonard. Somewhat reminiscent of this studied reversal of social-class roles, fashions in the 1960s have included the celebration of the horrendous, the commercialized cliché, or the recently outmoded under the rubric "camp." The high prices commanded by pop art or the craze in fashionable society for the *discothèque* symbolize the transformation of popular culture into an elite genre; they offer a counterpoise to the spectacle of hillbilly pop tunes composed in Times Square office buildings by white-collar suburbanites.

Elite culture varies in physical accessibility, according to the medium through which it is diffused. Good bookstores, art cinemas, and other specialized channels of dissemination tend to be restricted geographically to major cities and intellectual centers, while periodicals and broadcasts are more widespread. In most countries, whether or not the broadcasting system is state-run, elite culture on television is confined to the very early or very late parts of the broadcast day or to those parts of the weekend during which most people do not watch television at all, because of its limited audience appeal.

In any given week a substantial number of program hours may be devoted to elite-culture material, but as Minow points out (1964), this is usually isolated in time, so that the interested viewer must search for it. He must expend energy to find interesting programs just as he would to find the particular books he wants to read, the motion pictures he wants to see, or the art exhibits, plays, or concerts he wants to attend. Most members of the elite-culture audience presumably do not want to expend this kind of energy, because they view television as a pastime, much like anyone else. At any rate, it is known that high-brows on the whole do not watch mainly high-brow shows. This has been documented in several studies of the educational television audience (see, for instance, Schramm et al. 1963). Similarly, more upper-income New Yorkers read the *Daily News* than the *New York Times* (Simmons . . . [1955] 1964, p. 38), and among upper-income Londoners, 36 per cent read the *Daily Express* and only 10 per cent *The Times* (Hall & Whannel [1964] 1965, p. 234).

The relation between critical success and popular success is difficult to trace in any mass medium, but in television it does not seem to exist at all. The reason is that the functions of the critic have been transferred to the audience, whose choice of program is recorded and analyzed by commercial rating organizations such as the A. C. Nielsen Company. The influence of these ratings on program content can be inferred from the fact that about two-thirds of United States network television shows are replaced each season on the basis of ratings rather than of press notices.

In a highly developed mass-media culture like that of the United States the audiences for all the major media reflect the general distribution of population, even though individual vehicles are directed at one sex or age group. Mass-media content tends to be pegged at a level that appeals to the largest number of people and is correspondingly inoffensive or uncritical of the established order. Its hallmarks are the familiar, the hackneyed, and the stereotyped.

In most countries with a commercial system of broadcasting, audience measurements indicate that public choice in programming comes very close to the entertainment formula established years ago by American radio and motion pictures. Countries with a state-operated system of broadcasting face the continuing problem of balancing programs aimed at social uplift with others that will assure the presence, night in and night out, of a large body of attentive viewers. This is complicated when commercial and state-operated or educational channels exist side by side. A kind of Gresham's law of popular preference operates to make no more than a minority available for an elite-interest or educational program when it competes with less demanding amusements. The BBC's famous "Third Programme" draws 1 per cent of the audience (Paulu 1961).

At the same time, the minority audience for elite culture purveyed by the mass media may encompass far more people than would be reached by the same content through traditional means or forms. Berelson (1964) estimates that the average United States college graduate spends nearly twelve hours per month "in the presence of culture," while the person who has not completed high school spends two or less. He estimates that commercial television accounts for 22 per cent of the total amount of time spent in this way by all segments of the population.

Educational television in the United States has not been able to attain massive audiences in competition with commercial television. Only 10 per cent of the people in areas covered by ETV watch it at all in the course of a week (National Educational Television and Radio Center 1966, p. 7). Yet, in many countries ETV has demonstrated its value both as an adjunct to regular classroom instruction in schools and universities and as a means of independent adult education. In eastern Europe substantial audiences are assured for educational telecasts at times when they are the only programs available to the viewer.

In commercial broadcasting, advertising may become an important influence over programming decisions, since it is in the interest of broadcasters and advertisers alike to attract large audiences to the advertising messages and so obtain the largest possible yield for the advertiser's investment. Advertising also occupies a substantial amount of broadcast time and thereby becomes an important element in the actual symbolic content of the medium. The information advertising conveys and the fantasies and desires it generates are also significant factors in the substance of print publications throughout the noncommunist world. As McLuhan (1964) suggests, advertisements are often prepared with more thought than the material that surrounds them.

The mass media have brought the members of diverse societies into a common universe of discourse and have been an increasingly powerful force for the international unification of ideas and values. Certain symbols (Mickey Mouse, the Shell sign, the cowboy) have been diffused and universalized to the point where they lack any specific cultural reference. Schramm (1959), analyzing fourteen prestige newspapers around the world, found the proportion of news originating outside the country or area ranged between 14 per cent and 50 per cent, with a median of 32 per cent. Even though news media in nearly all countries are highly parochial and nationalistic in perspective, major news events are perceived as having broad general significance, regardless of their immediate relevance to the particular country.

But if the mass media tend to break down barriers to international understanding, they also tend to create new ones. The media have made possible the emergence of specialized bodies of lore and information which are by-products of an increasingly complex technology and a more intensive division of labor.

The growth of the mass media in Europe and the United States makes increasing demands on leisure time, which is itself increasing. This tends to deepen the chasm between the commonplace and the exceptional, between the popular culture of comic strips, pop records, and soap opera, and the elite culture of fine opera, drama, poetry, and the visual arts. At the same time, the broad-scale dissemination of the elite culture through the mass media makes its character at least superficially familiar to vast populations to whom it would otherwise be utterly unknown.

LEO BOGART

[See also FILM; JOURNALISM; MASS SOCIETY.]

BIBLIOGRAPHY

ADVERTISING RESEARCH FOUNDATION 1965 National Survey of Television Sets in U.S. Households . . . August 1965. New York: The Foundation.

ALTICK, RICHARD D. 1957 The English Common Reader: A Social History of the Mass Reading Public, 1800–1900. Univ. of Chicago Press.

AUDITS AND SURVEYS COMPANY, INC. 1961 A National Study of Newspaper Reading. New York: Newsprint Information Committee. → This study was supervised by the Bureau of Advertising of the American Newspaper Publishers Association, for the Newsprint Information Committee; the Audits and Surveys Company (New York) carried out the survey on which the study is based.

BERELSON, BERNARD 1949 What "Missing the Newspaper" Means. Pages 111–129 in Paul F. Lazarsfeld and Frank N. Stanton (editors), Communications Research: 1948–1949. New York: Harper.

BERELSON, BERNARD 1964 In the Presence of Culture. Public Opinion Quarterly 28:1–12.

BERELSON, BERNARD; LAZARSFELD, PAUL F.; and McPHEE,

WILLIAM N. 1954 *Voting: A Study of Opinion Formation in a Presidential Campaign.* Univ. of Chicago Press. → A paperback edition was published in 1966.

BLAIR, WILLIAM S. 1965 Does Profile Matching Work? *Mediascope* 9, no. 9:82–86.

BOGART, LEO 1949 Fan Mail for the Philharmonic. *Public Opinion Quarterly* 13:423–434.

BOGART, LEO (1956) 1958 *The Age of Television: A Study of Viewing Habits and the Impact of Television on American Life.* 2d ed., rev. & enl. New York: Ungar.

BOGART, LEO; and TOLLEY, B. STUART 1964 The Impact of Blank Space: An Experiment in Advertising Readership. *Journal of Advertising Research* 4:21–27.

COLUMBIA UNIVERSITY, BUREAU OF APPLIED SOCIAL RESEARCH 1946 *The People Look at Radio: Report on a Survey Conducted by the National Opinion Research Center,* by Harry Field and Paul F. Lazarsfeld. Chapel Hill: Univ. of North Carolina Press.

COLUMBIA UNIVERSITY, BUREAU OF APPLIED SOCIAL RESEARCH 1948 *Radio Listening in America; The People Look at Radio—Again: Report on a Survey Conducted by the National Opinion Research Center,* by Paul F. Lazarsfeld and Patricia Kendall. Englewood Cliffs, N.J.: Prentice-Hall.

DURHAM, F. GAYLE 1965 Radio and Television in the Soviet Union. Unpublished research report, Massachusetts Institute of Technology, Center for International Studies.

FOREMAN, ROBERT 1958 *The Hot Half-hour.* New York: Criterion.

FURU, TAKEO 1965 Research on "Television and the Child" in Japan. Pages 51–81 in Nippon Hoso Kyokai, *Studies in Broadcasting.* No. 3. Tokyo: Nippon Hoso Kyokai.

GLICK, IRA O.; and LEVY, SIDNEY J. 1962 *Living With Television.* Chicago: Aldine.

HALL, STUART; and WHANNEL, PADDY (1964) 1965 *The Popular Arts.* New York: Pantheon.

HANDEL, LEO A. 1950 *Hollywood Looks at Its Audience.* Urbana: Univ. of Illinois Press.

HEAD, SYDNEY W. 1956 *Broadcasting in America: A Survey of Television and Radio.* Boston: Houghton Mifflin.

KATZ, ELIHU; and LAZARSFELD, PAUL F. 1955 *Personal Influence: The Part Played by People in the Flow of Mass Communications.* Glencoe, Ill.: Free Press. → A paperback edition was published in 1964.

LERNER, DANIEL 1958 *The Passing of Traditional Society: Modernizing the Middle East.* New York: Free Press. → A paperback edition was published in 1964.

MacLEAN, MALCOLM S. JR. 1952 Mass Media Audiences: City, Small City, Village and Farm. *Journalism Quarterly* 29:271–282.

McLUHAN, MARSHALL 1964 *Understanding Media: The Extensions of Man.* New York: McGraw-Hill. → A paperback edition was published in 1965.

MINOW, NEWTON W. 1964 *Equal Time: The Private Broadcaster and the Public Interest.* Edited by Lawrence Laurent. New York: Atheneum.

MOTT, FRANK L. (1941) 1962 *American Journalism: A History, 1690–1960.* 3d ed. New York: Macmillan.

NATIONAL EDUCATIONAL TELEVISION AND RADIO CENTER 1966 *A Fact Book.* New York: The Center.

PAULU, BURTON (1956) 1957 *British Broadcasting: Radio and Television in the United Kingdom.* Oxford Univ. Press.

PAULU, BURTON 1961 *British Broadcasting in Transition.* Minneapolis: Univ. of Minnesota Press.

SCHRAMM, WILBUR L. (editor) (1949) 1960 *Mass Communications: A Book of Readings.* Urbana: Univ. of Illinois Press.

SCHRAMM, WILBUR L. 1959 *One Day in the World's Press: Fourteen Great Newspapers on a Day of Crisis, November 2, 1956.* Stanford Univ. Press.

SCHRAMM, WILBUR L. 1964 *Mass Media and National Development: The Role of Information in the Developing Countries.* Stanford Univ. Press.

SCHRAMM, WILBUR L.; LYLE, JACK; and PARKER, EDWIN B. 1960 Patterns in Children's Reading of Newspapers. *Journalism Quarterly* 37:35–40.

SCHRAMM, WILBUR L.; LYLE, JACK; and POOL, ITHIEL DE SOLA 1963 *The People Look at Educational Television: A Report of Nine Representative ETV Stations.* Stanford Univ. Press.

SIEPMANN, CHARLES (1950) 1956 *Radio, Television and Society.* New York: Oxford Univ. Press.

SIMMONS (W. R.) AND ASSOCIATES RESEARCH, INC. (1955) 1964 *Profile of the Millions: A Study of the New York Market and Adult Readers of Six Daily and Five Sunday Newspapers and Adult Viewers of Evening Television.* 4th ed. New York: Simmons and Associates.

SMITH, ROGER H. (editor) (1963) 1964 *The American Reading Public: What It Reads, Why It Reads; From Inside Education and Publishing. . . .* New York: Bowker.

STEINER, GARY A. 1963 *The People Look at Television: A Study of Audience Attitudes.* New York: Knopf.

UNITED NATIONS EDUCATIONAL, SCIENTIFIC, AND CULTURAL ORGANIZATION, DEPARTMENT OF MASS COMMUNICATIONS 1964 *World Communications: Press, Radio, Television, Films.* 4th ed., rev. New York: UNESCO.

U.S. CONGRESS, HOUSE, COMMITTEE ON INTERSTATE AND FOREIGN COMMERCE 1963 *Broadcast Ratings: Hearings.* 88th Congress, 1st Session on The Methodology, Accuracy, and Use of Ratings in Broadcasting. Washington: Government Printing Office.

U.S. INFORMATION AGENCY, RESEARCH AND REFERENCE SERVICE 1966 *Overseas Television Growth in 1965.* Washington: Government Printing Office.

WOLF, KATHERINE M.; and FISKE, MARJORIE 1949 The Children Talk About Comics. Pages 3–50 in *Communications Research: 1948–1949.* Edited by Paul F. Lazarsfeld and Frank N. Stanton. New York: Harper.

WRIGHT, CHARLES R. (1960) 1964 Functional Analysis and Mass Communication. Pages 91–109 in Lewis A. Dexter and David M. White (editors), *People, Society, and Mass Communications.* New York: Free Press.

V

EFFECTS

The effects, alleged effects, and possible effects of mass communication are numerous and varied, direct and indirect. The development and extent of modern radio and television networks and the growth of the media industries have obviously affected the technological and economic nature of modern society and have nurtured revolutions in the use of leisure time and in processes ranging from pedagogy to marketing. The mere classification of the effects of mass communication presents a formidable methodological problem, which has as yet defied attempts to construct exhaustive schemata.

No such range of effects can be discussed within the scope of this article. The effects that are here considered are those with which the behavioral sciences are perhaps most concerned, namely, the effects of modern mass communication upon the attitudes and behavior of its audiences.

Even within this area, certain exclusions have been necessitated by limitations of space and by the specialized treatment which such discussions would require. Thus, the article does not deal with the use of mass media in formal pedagogy, whether presented in classrooms or on closed or open broadcast systems. Relatively little mention is made of either the effects of mass communication in international psychological warfare or the effects of domestic mass communication in countries other than the United States; the various and dissimilar ways in which foreign communications systems are organized and controlled, and the different cultural milieus in which their audiences exist, preclude casual generalization of the processes here described to foreign arenas.

Finally, no attempt is here made to deal with the effects of mass media as instruments of consumer advertising. The goals of such advertising and the psychological significance to the audience member of the decisions involved are often so unlike the goals and decisions of the kind of persuasive communications here discussed that generalizations from the one topical area to the other are hardly permissible.

The article will first consider the effects of mass communication as an agent of persuasion. The principles established by findings in this area will be found to be reflected in the topical areas here discussed, namely, the effects of mass media upon audience views of public issues, the effects of mass media upon public taste, and the effects of depictions of crime and violence. Some of the vast areas of ignorance about the effects of mass communication are noted, along with some suggestions as to how some of them might be explored.

The research literature here cited includes both surveys and laboratory studies that bear upon the press, motion pictures, radio, television, and, in some cases, laboratory approximations of such media. No attempt is made to indicate precisely what medium is under discussion in reference to every cited finding. Many of the studies bear on mass communication as a whole rather than on any one medium, and in any case the findings here cited are believed by the author to be applicable,

except when otherwise noted, to any or all of the media.

Persuasive mass communication

It has been repeatedly demonstrated that by far the most common effect of mass communication is to reinforce its audience's pre-existing interests, attitudes, and behavior and that the least common effect is to convert audience attitudes and behavior. In addition, pertinent attitudes of a considerable proportion of the audience are modified in intensity or salience but not in direction, that is, not to the point of conversion.

The relative frequency of these types of attitude change was first documented in a now classic study (Lazarsfeld et al. 1944) of the origin and fate of vote intentions during the 1940 U.S. presidential campaign. Employing panel techniques, these researchers interviewed several hundred residents of Erie County, Ohio, prior to the nominating conventions and at approximately monthly intervals thereafter, right up to election day. The study found that after exposure to months of mass media campaigning and partisan propaganda, 53 per cent of the respondents voted exactly as they said they would in May, before the candidates were even nominated. To whatever degree mass communication affected these voters, it did so in the service of reinforcement. By contrast, less than 10 per cent had been converted to the opposition candidate. Practically all the other respondents had undergone minor attitude changes short of conversion.

Later research has gone beyond the identification of effects and is able to describe much of the dynamics of their occurrence. Central to the study of these processes is the fact that mass communications rarely work directly upon their audiences but function within a nexus of other factors that mediate the potential effects. These mediating factors tend, for the most part, to make mass communication an agent, but not the sole cause, of reinforcement.

It is not possible within the scope of this article to cite and discuss all such factors. Nor, indeed, are all of them yet known. Among the most basic and most important, however, are audience predispositions and certain selective processes they engender; the influence of group norms; the operation of a process variously called the two-step flow, personal influence, and opinion leadership; and the position of mass media in a free enterprise society.

Predispositions and selective processes. The term "predisposition" requires little if any explanation. As used here, it carries its common denotation as a "tendency toward." More precisely, "predisposition" can be viewed as an attitude "set" that is pertinent to the issue at hand and that exists prior to the audience member's exposure to whatever mass communication is under surveillance. Thus, a person may be predisposed to vote Republican, to enjoy classical music, or to commit acts of violence. It is the substance of such predispositions which mass communication tends to reinforce, not in and of itself alone but rather as a contributory agent, working through the selective processes noted below.

Selective exposure. Research has repeatedly shown that people tend to expose themselves to mass communication material that is in accord with their existing attitudes or interests and to avoid communications that express contrary attitudes or are outside their fields of interest. Persons who do not like classical music, for example, are most unlikely to expose themselves to broadcasts of classical music and will tend to avoid them in favor of others more in accord with their existing tastes (see, e.g., Suchman 1941). By the same token, persons with Republican predispositions are more likely to expose themselves to Republican campaign propaganda than to Democratic campaign propaganda, and the same is true of Democrats (see, e.g., Lazarsfeld et al. 1944 and, in reference to television, Schramm & Carter 1959). In brief, the audience member uses the medium much as he would a large supermarket: he selects from its many offerings the fare he knows he likes, and he does not as a rule purchase products which he dislikes or with which he is unfamiliar. The process of selective exposure is thus a process of feeding existing appetites and thus reinforcing dietary preferences. Applied to mass communication, selective exposure minimizes the likelihood of the predisposed audience member's being exposed to the other side of the issue and maximizes his continued exposure to sympathetic communications. It is therefore a cause of behavior that tends to make mass communication a reinforcing rather than a converting influence.

Selective retention. The tendency of audience members who have been exposed to unsympathetic material to recall it less well than they recall sympathetic material, and to forget it more rapidly, is known as selective retention. The phenomenon was well documented as early as 1943, when Levine and Murphy observed such effects following the exposure of students to political tracts variously supporting and attacking the students' own points of view. The occurrence of selective retention in

at least some degree has been widely regarded as obvious and has aroused little research curiosity in recent years. Its occurrence continues to be documented, however, among the findings of studies devoted to other objectives (e.g., Zimmerman & Bauer 1956, later replicated by Schramm without published report).

This kind of subconscious erasure obviously tends, like selective exposure, to reinforce the audience member's existing views and to minimize the likelihood of his being converted.

Selective perception. The audience member's court of last resort is selective perception, or the tendency to perceive material as sympathetic to his predispositions, even when the material presented is not, in fact, sympathetic. Since it occurs both concurrently with and after exposure to unsympathetic communication, it is hard to disentangle chronologically from selective retention. Having been exposed to unsympathetic communications that they recall reasonably well, audiences tend so to distort the content as to render it, in their own minds, supportive (and thus reinforcive), even though it is in fact a statement of opposition. Thus, communications designed to advance racial tolerance have been perceived by prejudiced persons as affirmations of ethnic inequality (Columbia University . . . 1946; Cooper & Jahoda 1947). In the course of informal inquiry, the present author personally observed that a poster proclaiming "It takes all races to make our city run" was perceived by prejudiced persons as a confirmation of their views that minority group members were needed to perform the menial chores necessary for the majority groups to live in comfort. More recently, persons who witnessed the Kennedy–Nixon debates were found able to recall statements or views with which they disagreed but to assign such statements to the candidate they shunned, regardless of which candidate actually made the statement (Katz & Feldman 1962). Thus, selective perception, like selective exposure and selective retention, is another phenomenon that mediates the effects of mass communication and does so in the direction of reinforcement.

Group norms. Social psychologists have repeatedly demonstrated the profound influence that group norms assert upon the attitudes and opinions of individuals who are or wish to be members of the group in question (an excellent review of the basic pertinent literature will be found in Katz & Lazarsfeld 1955).

Briefly, membership in groups has been found to serve as an anchoring point of many attitudes and, for the most part, to act in a variety of ways as a deterrent to opinion change. Both formal and informal groups tend to possess or develop considerable homogeneity of values, attitudes, and opinions in reference to specific issues. Persuasive mass communications that take positions alien to those of the group are therefore likely to be resisted by the individual member, not only because they are in conflict with his own predispositions but also because conversion would endanger such psychological and social benefits as he derives from good standing in the group. Discussion of issues with other group members has been found likely to reinforce both the individual's original attitudes and his resistance to the unsympathetic communication. Such discussion has also been shown to exercise a "refresher" function: by making the norms more conspicuous, the discussion serves to draw unconscious drifters back to orthodoxy (McKeachie 1954).

By way of example, predispositions on the part of respondents toward opinions characteristic of their family groups, and even a readiness to adhere to a given point of view for no other reason than that it is family-anchored, have been noted in various studies, including the previously mentioned investigation of the 1940 U.S. election campaign by Lazarsfeld and others (1944). So strong was the tendency toward family homogeneity found in this study that "only 4% of the 413 panel members who voted claimed that someone in their families had voted differently" (Lazarsfeld et al. [1944] 1960, p. 141). Similar if less marked homogeneity was found among co-workers and among comembers of formal organizations.

It would seem logical that the strength of these tendencies would be correlated both with the salience of the question to the group and with the degree to which the audience member values his membership. Pertinent research, however, has indicated that this is not always the case. Experiments are reported, for example, in which the correlation appears in reference to one issue and one group but fails to appear in reference to another issue of presumably equal salience or among members of a presumably similar group (Kelley 1955; Kelley & Volkart 1952). To the best knowledge of the author, this anomaly has not yet been clarified or resolved.

The two-step flow of communication. A phenomenon often integral to the influence of mass communication has been called *personal influence, interpersonal influence, the two-step flow of communication,* and *opinion leadership.* The process

and its history are described in detail by Katz (1957) and will here be treated only as necessary to establish its influence as a mediator of mass communication effects.

The important aspect of the phenomenon, from this point of view, is that in reference to decisions in various areas of attitude and behavior, people have been found to be influenced by specific other individuals as strongly or more strongly than they have been influenced by mass communication. These "others" have variously been termed *opinion leaders, gatekeepers, influentials, initiators, innovators,* and *taste makers.* They do not usually occupy formal positions of leadership, being characteristically neither political officeholders, teachers, preachers, nor any other type of elite. Their chief demographic characteristic is that they have no distinctive demographic characteristics. They are simply people who, consciously or unconsciously, critically influence the attitudes and opinions of a handful of people demographically like themselves. Their following is characteristically small, involving only a handful of persons; their influence is typically exerted in informal face-to-face discourse and may or may not be purposive; and their leadership is characteristically exercised within a limited topical sphere. The opinion leader in reference to public issues, for example, is not likely to be an opinion leader in reference to aesthetic issues or in reference to fashion.

Where opinion leadership exists, it has been found typically much involved with mass communications. Thus, the opinion leader is usually more exposed to topically appropriate mass communications than are his followers, to whom he may or may not pass on the information he has gleaned. (This capability is reflected in the term "gatekeeper" and in the concept of the two-step flow of communication.) The opinion leader may direct followers to mass communication to document or promote his opinions or, vice versa, he may interpret to his followers what mass communication on a given topic really means. The essential point is that where personal influence exists, it often mediates the effects of mass communication.

The direction of this mediation was long obscured by the fact that the phenomenon first came under research scrutiny in reference to change: changes in vote intention, changes in fashion, the adoption of new agricultural techniques, and the like. Studies of the role of the opinion leader in such circumstances led to his being widely if implicitly conceived as primarily an agent of change. It has recently become apparent, however, that personal influence probably functions more often as an agent of stasis than as an agent of change. Thus, the opinion leader has been found to be an embodiment of group norms, whose leadership is effective precisely because it provides satisfaction in terms of the shared values of the informal groups to which both leader and follower belong. Even the nature of personal influence in certain processes of change appears to be more a matter of counteracting departures from the norm than of initiating such departures: for example, personal influence in changing vote intentions appears to be primarily exerted on persons who had previously changed away from group norms, and the effective exercise of opinion leadership apparently serves in the main to bring such persons back into homogeneity with the group. In sum, recent re-evaluation of earlier research suggests that opinion leadership, or interpersonal influence, probably works in the direction of stability and reinforcement more often than it does in the interests of change. Insofar as this is true, and insofar as it touches on mass communication, personal influence (or opinion leadership, or the two-step flow) appears to be another of the factors that mediate the effects of mass communication in such a way as to render the media primarily agents of reinforcement. [See DIFFUSION, article on INTERPERSONAL INFLUENCE.]

Mass media in a free enterprise society. Mass media that function as profit-making enterprises in a free, competitive economy must strive to please enormous and highly variegated audiences and to avoid offending any significant proportion of the population. Although a sizable portion of media offerings—particularly news, commentaries, documentaries, and other informational programs—deal with highly controversial subjects, the major portion of mass media offerings are designed to serve an entertainment function. These entertainment products generally tend to avoid controversial issues and, implicitly or explicitly, to reflect beliefs and values already sanctified by the mass audience. To whatever degree this occurs, the media themselves serve to reinforce such beliefs and values. This course is the more likely to be followed by those media, such as television networks, whose investment and production costs are high. Small-budget media, such as specialized magazines or individual radio stations, can afford to address themselves exclusively to selected, small audiences, but national television networks cannot do so and remain economically viable. Put another way, mass communication that is profit-oriented must be directed primarily to mass tastes and must reflect mass values. When a mass medium ceases to do this, it ceases to be a mass medium.

The creation of opinion on new issues. Reinforcement and conversion can, of course, occur only where there is an opinion to reinforce or oppose. It cannot occur in the absence of opinion. Although there has been relatively little research on the subject, the media appear to be extremely effective in creating opinions. By way of a common-sense example, a few months before Fidel Castro came to power, probably less than 2 per cent of the American people so much as knew his name, let alone his political leanings. A year thereafter, however, the American public knew a great deal about him and his political behavior and were rather homogeneous in their opinions about him. The source of their knowledge and the bases of their opinions were obviously restricted, for all practical purposes, to the mass media.

It is not difficult to see why the mass media are extremely effective in creating opinions on new issues. In such a situation the audiences have no existing opinions to be guarded by the conscious or subconscious play of selective exposure, selective retention, or selective perception. Their reference groups are likewise without opinion, and opinion leaders are not yet ready to lead. In short, the factors that ordinarily render mass communication an agent of reinforcement are inoperative, and the media are thus able to work directly upon their audiences. The attitudes that the audiences derive from the media thereafter enjoy the reinforcive effects described above.

Areas of public concern

Persuasion on public issues. Data revealing the vast predominance of reinforcement over conversion in the area of political persuasion have been noted above (see Lazarsfeld et al. 1944). Similar findings have emerged from research on the influence of mass communication in many political campaigns (see especially Berelson et al. 1954). A modest study pursued by Schramm and Carter (1959) revealed that the audience for a Republican-sponsored election eve telecast contained twice as many Republicans as Democrats and succeeded in changing the vote intention of only one person among the hundred or so respondents. Star and Hughes (1950) found that a multimedia campaign designed to increase knowledge and approval of the United Nations attracted an audience consisting for the most part of persons who knew a good deal about the United Nations and were already favorably disposed toward it. Wiebe (1958) found that the broadcasts of the Army–McCarthy hearings were selectively perceived by most of the audience, whose existing opinions about the senator and the issues were accordingly reinforced. Other similar findings are numerous.

It must not be assumed, however, that reinforcement, which involves no change in opinion, is synonymous with lack of effect. Reinforcement *is* an effect, and an extremely important one. It strengthens the resolve in question, produces a type of immunity to counterpropaganda, and nurses straying sheep back into the fold (see, for instance, Lazarsfeld et al. 1944; Berelson et al. 1954; Katz & Feldman 1962).

Furthermore, none of the foregoing is to gainsay the fact that conversions *do* occur. It is, rather, to suggest that conversion occurs infrequently and usually under very special conditions, and it is often a kind of indirect reinforcement. In brief, convertees are often found to have been, as it were, predisposed to conversion. An excellent example occurs in research literature bearing upon the effects of Voice of America broadcasts to European satellite countries (International Public Opinion Research, Inc. 1953). Defectors from these countries to the "free world" were found, in many instances, to have lived for years in relative contentment under Stalinistic communism and either not to have listened to the Voice of America enough to make a difference or in any case to have been unaffected by the broadcasts. At first blush, it appeared that exposure to the Voice of America had suddenly become effective among persons for whom it had been previously ineffective and had rapidly made them not only intense anticommunists but warm and knowledgeable exponents of Western views as well. Deeper research revealed that many of them had become disaffected for wholly nonpolitical reasons. Some, for example, were young men facing the draft. Some were factory managers who had been demoted for not achieving their production quotas. The future of life at home had suddenly become unattractive. Seeking a better future, they began searching about. At this point the Voice of America became a convenient and effective *agent* of conversion. Put in other words, these people had become predisposed to change, and the Voice of America was available to help them implement the change. Somewhat similar findings have been reported in reference to the effect of Allied propaganda appeals to Nazi soldiers (Shils & Janowitz 1948) and in reference to the effect of UN information campaigns upon communist troops participating in the Korean conflict (Schramm & Riley 1951).

Public taste. Concern over the effects of mass communication on the level of public taste has been expressed in reference to virtually all American mass media. Social critics have variously feared that mass communication would hinder the development of good taste among children and debase the existing tastes of adults. The mass media have also been called upon to assume the primary responsibility for developing the aesthetic tastes of their audiences.

Research indicates that mass communication, in and of itself, neither raises nor lowers the tastes of any significant portion of the audience (see, for example, Lazarsfeld 1940; Suchman 1941; Wolf & Fiske 1949; Klapper 1949; Himmelweit et al. 1958). Here again, as in reference to persuasion, mass communication serves primarily as an agent that reinforces whatever levels of aesthetic taste its audience members bring to it. Persons who do not like classical music, or do not like programs on relatively high cultural levels, simply do not expose themselves to such programs and are in fact often unaware of their existence. Increasing the incidence of such programs is thus unlikely to change the tastes of any significant portion of the audience.

Research reveals, however, that given a predisposition to develop cultural and aesthetic tastes, people can and have done so by watching or listening to appropriate media offerings. A now classic study (Suchman 1941) revealed, for example, that persons who were not particularly interested in classical music were sometimes impelled to listen to it on the air because they felt that their ignorance was inappropriate to some status they had recently attained. Their motivation to begin listening to the classical music was totally extraneous to the aesthetic quality of the music itself. By and by, however, they came to like the music for its own sake.

The interesting question also arises as to whether group norms serve to debase aesthetic tastes. It is conceivable, for example, that some persons who like media material on a high aesthetic level may find such tastes a subject of ridicule and thus a social handicap in groups that are otherwise congenial. The norms of such groups may demand familiarity with material of a lower quality. The individuals concerned may therefore undertake to view such aesthetically inferior material at the cost of the higher-quality material they prefer, and in the course of time they may come to like such material for its own sake. It seems unlikely that such a process would actually kill anyone's taste for aesthetic material, but it might decrease his exposure to it. The phenomenon, if it occurs at all, does not seem so likely to involve an actual negation of existing tastes as, rather, to produce a broadening of tastes in a downward direction. Several authors have suggested, in speculative essays, that some such process occurs (e.g., Friedan 1963; Tamiment Institute 1961). Others (in particular Steiner 1963; Berelson 1964; Wilensky 1964) have documented the universal participation, by intellectuals as well as nonintellectuals, in mass culture and mass media products. But no research known to the author really faces the question of whether any change in the communication consumption habits of cultural elites has occurred since the development of the media of mass entertainment.

In any case, however, it is clear that mass communication serves for the most part to reinforce existing tastes. While it is not usually the prime mover, it can play a major role in taste development by providing a means of implementing such predisposition to change as may derive from extramedia sources. Accordingly, research into the operation of these extramedia sources would appear to be a prerequisite, or at least a necessary and integral part, of any campaign aimed at the development of audience taste.

Crime and violence. The American public, and indeed other publics as well, has always feared that media depictions of crime and violence would lead children to commit violence or at least to regard its commission with equanimity. The concern has been expressed not only in reference to television but, before that, in reference to comic books, movies, radio, and even newspapers.

The effect of depictions of violence on attitudes and behavior (as opposed to immediate emotional effects) has been the topic of inquiry of several studies, and additional studies are now being pursued. Prior to about 1960, this research typically consisted of surveys in which children who were heavy media users or heavy consumers of media depictions of crime and violence were compared with children who did not rate heavily on either count. These surveys typically resulted in one of two sets of findings. Either the two groups of children were found not to differ in reference to such criteria as were employed in the study, or the heavy users were found to differ in regard to characteristics that for the most part antedated or were irrelevant to their exposure to the media material. Thus, an elaborate study of the effects of television on British children (Himmelweit et al. 1958, p. 215) "found no more aggressive, maladjusted, or delinquent behavior among viewers than among [nonviewing] controls." These findings are in accord with earlier studies, for example, that of Lewin (1953), who found no differences among heavy and light violence consumers in tendencies toward delinquency, school attitude or achievement, or conduct.

As noted above, other studies did find differences between heavy and light consumers of violence. Ricciuti (1951), for example, found that children who particularly liked programs containing crime and violence scored somewhat lower than their colleagues on IQ and school achievement and were slightly below average in general happiness and interpersonal adjustments. At the same time, Ricciuti found no differences between the groups in nervous habits, fears, daydreams, and frustration reactions. A complex study by Bailyn (1959) revealed that certain types of depicted violence were particularly liked by boys (not girls) who were both highly exposed to such depictions *and* who exhibited certain psychological characteristics, including numerous problems relative to themselves, their family, and their peers, as well as a tendency to blame difficulties on others rather than themselves. Bailyn considers that these factors antedate the children's partiality for the aggressive material and thus "would not logically be thought of as effects of exposure" (*ibid.*, p. 3). She notes that these psychological characteristics are very similar to traits that were previously found by Sheldon Glueck and Eleanor Glueck to play a role in the "causal complex of delinquency" (*ibid.*, p. 37). She points out, however, that these characteristics do not in themselves differentiate between high and low exposure and that it is only those boys who are *both* highly exposed *and* possess these characteristics who are especially partial to the media material involved. High exposure, she found, was primarily associated with lack of parental restrictions on media usage and with low IQ.

Various other studies suggest that preference for crime and violence material is not a cause but a correlate of maladjustment. Eleanor Maccoby, for example, found that children who were mildly frustrated immediately before viewing films remembered more of the aggressive content than did the nonfrustrated children (unpublished study, described in Bogart 1956, p. 154).

The most extensive study of television in the lives of American children supports the findings of the earlier studies cited above and concludes "that the kind of child we send to television, rather than television itself, is the chief element in delinquency . . . . [The] most that television can do is to feed the malignant impulses that already exist" (Schramm et al. 1961, pp. 165–166).

Within the last few years, the survey literature has been supplemented by a host of laboratory experiments whose findings are regarded by some people as indicating that media depictions of violence or aggression elicit aggressive behavior on the part of children or young adults. The typical procedure involves the exposure of subjects, usually for not over ten minutes, to a film clip depicting "aggression" and thereafter seeking the effect of the exposure as manifested by predetermined criterional behavior (see, for instance, Bandura et al. 1961; Lövaas 1961; Mussen & Rutherford 1961).

In almost all the experiments involving child subjects, both the stimulus material and the criterional behavior involve laboratory simulations of "aggression" which are so distant from aggression in the consensual sense of that term that generalization to the topics of social concern seems quite unjustified. Thus, stimulus materials have included films of adults attacking a plastic doll, cartoons in which animals wrestle, and the like. Criterional behavior has also typically involved the rough handling of toys or even, in one instance, a statement that it would be fun to see a balloon popped. The occurrence of effects is sought immediately after exposure, and the persistence of any observed effects is very rarely an object of inquiry.

In one of the experiments which involved children and in which some approach to interpersonal aggression was undertaken (Bandura 1963), the child subjects were exposed to a stimulus film in which one adult, dressed like a child, seized the toys of another adult, who was also dressed like a child, precipitating a mild fight. A significant degree of spontaneous imitative aggression occurred among children who saw a version of the film in which the aggressor won, but not among those who saw a version in which the victim was triumphant. These data are regarded by Bandura and others as an indication that children will imitate depicted violence if it is shown to be fruitful. However, the only study in which children were enabled during criterional behavior to "attack" each other with rubber daggers or similar play weapons revealed no significant increase in violent or aggressive behavior, as these terms are commonly understood (Siegel 1956).

Several experimenters have pursued parallel laboratory studies with adult subjects (e.g., Berkowitz 1962; Berkowitz et al. 1963; Walters et al. 1962; Walters et al. 1963; Walters & Thomas 1963). In many of these, the stimulus films portrayed real interpersonal violence. However, the criterional behavior involved, in its most "violent" form, very small increments in the duration and intensity of electric shocks, which the subjects had been told to administer in the first place. [*See* AGGRESSION, *article on* PSYCHOLOGICAL ASPECTS.]

The vast difference between the types of "violence" or "aggression" in these studies and the commission of real physical violence has led many researchers, including the authors of one of the studies (Mussen & Rutherford 1961), to deny the validity of generalizing the experimental results to the likelihood of committing real violence in a naturalistic situation. The present author agrees with this (see also Hartley 1964 for a review and critique of experiments in this tradition).

Other areas of effect. The scope of this article does not permit discussion of all the attitudinal and behavioral effects that have been subjects of social comment, concern, or, in some cases, hope. Prominent among the questions we are thus unable to discuss is whether television viewing promotes passivity or, conversely, whether it stimulates new interests and activities; another common concern is that it reduces time spent on reading. In general, the pattern of effect that has been described throughout this article appears applicable to these other areas. Thus, research indicates that television neither changes active children into passive children nor changes passive children into active ones (Himmelweit et al. 1958). Rather, it provides an easy way for passive children to be passive, and it is a source of new interests and activities for children who are naturally curious and active (Himmelweit et al. 1958; Schramm et al. 1961). Although the data are not completely clear, the effects of television on reading appear to follow a similar pattern (see, for example, Himmelweit et al. 1958; Witty 1966). In those areas, as in others, reinforcement appears to be the dominant effect.

Research needs

Despite all that has been said above, our knowledge of the effects of mass communication is still limited, and there is need for additional research. Perhaps the most crucial need is for a series of inquiries on what children of various ages actually perceive when they look at the cinema or television screen or when they view or read other mass communications. It is only in the last three or four years that communication researchers have begun rigorously to question the frequent if implicit view that children perceive either what adults perceive or what adults think children perceive. These assumptions, once made explicit, appear to be obviously naive and probably invalid.

A second topic demanding research might be called the fate of minor attitude change. It has been noted above that such changes, falling far short of conversion, are quite common. But, for all we now know, these minor changes may be steppingstones on the path to major changes that have been neither sought nor documented. The concept of "sleeper effects," that is, the possibility that major effects will become visible only weeks or months after exposure to the communications, was first formulated by Hovland, Lumsdaine, and Sheffield (1949), but the conditions promoting or inhibiting such effects and the patterns of their development have not as yet been adequately described. The recently developing interest in "learning without involvement," perhaps best set forth by Krugman (1965), seems likely to be found pertinent to this general area, as does also the recent work pursued by Festinger and Maccoby on "resistance to persuasive communications" (1964).

A third area of ignorance is closely connected to the second. Much research has been devoted to determining the effects of a specific mass communication program, or of a series of such programs, on audience attitudes and behavior. But in actual life the audiences of mass media are exposed to hundreds or thousands of communications, many of them similar in content or point of view to the few specific programs whose effects are assayed. Our knowledge of the over-all effects of mass communication will remain limited unless and until research can be directed upon the effects of cumulative exposure to mass communications. This is tantamount to saying that there is urgent and critical need for "longitudinal studies" that keep audience members under scrutiny for years or decades. The methodological problems involved in the pursuit of such a study are formidable and have not yet been reduced to malleable proportions.

There is need also for inquiry into the variety of functions that the same communication may serve for different members of its audience. By the same token, there is equal need for inquiry into the apparent ability of diverse and dissimilar types of communications to serve the same functions for specific audience members. The old methods of classifying programs as "informative" or "entertaining," or in such gross categories as "light drama" and "serious drama," are beginning to appear somewhat naive. The classification of audiences primarily or exclusively in terms of such time-honored demographic categories as sex, age, educational achievement, and the like is probably equally naive. The development of our knowledge as to how mass communication affects its mass audiences will probably be handicapped until functional patterns of communication can be identified and defined and until audience subgroups can be defined in terms of the functions that various types

of mass communication serve for them. The potential fruitfulness of such a research approach has been discussed by Wright (1960), Klapper (1960), and Katz and Foulkes (1962).

JOSEPH T. KLAPPER

[*See also* ADVERTISING; ATTITUDES, *article on* ATTITUDE CHANGE; COMMUNICATION, POLITICAL; MARKET RESEARCH, *article on* CONSUMER RESEARCH; PERSUASION; PROPAGANDA.]

BIBLIOGRAPHY

BAILYN, LOTTE 1959 Mass Media and Children: A Study of Exposure Habits and Cognitive Effects. *Psychological Monographs* 73, no. 1:1–48.

BANDURA, ALBERT 1963 What T.V. Violence Can Do to Your Child. *Look* 27, no. 21:46–48, 52.

BANDURA, ALBERT; ROSS, DOROTHEA; and ROSS, SHEILA A. 1961 Transmission of Aggression Through Imitation of Aggressive Models. *Journal of Abnormal and Social Psychology* 63:575–582.

BERELSON, BERNARD 1964 In the Presence of Culture . . . . *Public Opinion Quarterly* 28:1–12.

BERELSON, BERNARD; LAZARSFELD, PAUL F.; and MCPHEE, WILLIAM N. 1954 *Voting: A Study of Opinion Formation in a Presidential Campaign.* Univ. of Chicago Press.

BERKOWITZ, LEONARD 1962 *Aggression: A Social Psychological Analysis.* New York: McGraw-Hill.

BERKOWITZ, LEONARD; CORWIN, R.; and HEIRONIMUS, M. 1963 Film Violence and Subsequent Aggressive Tendencies. *Public Opinion Quarterly* 27:217–229.

BOGART, LEO (1956) 1958 *The Age of Television: A Study of Viewing Habits and the Impact of Television on American Life.* 2d ed., rev. & enl. New York: Ungar.

COLUMBIA UNIVERSITY, BUREAU OF APPLIED SOCIAL RESEARCH 1946 *The Personification of Prejudice as a Device in Educational Propaganda: An Experiment in Product Improvement,* by Patricia L. Kendall and Katherine M. Wolf. New York: The Bureau.

COOPER, EUNICE; and JAHODA, MARIE 1947 The Evasion of Propaganda: How Prejudiced People Respond to Anti-prejudice Propaganda. *Journal of Psychology* 23: 15–25.

FESTINGER, LEON; and MACCOBY, NATHAN 1964 On Resistance to Persuasive Communications. *Journal of Abnormal and Social Psychology* 68:359–366.

FRIEDAN, BETTY 1963 *The Feminine Mystique.* New York: Norton.

HARTLEY, RUTH E. 1964 *The Impact of Viewing "Aggression": Studies and Problems of Extrapolation.* New York: Columbia Broadcasting System, Office of Social Research.

HIMMELWEIT, HILDE; OPPENHEIM, A. N.; and VINCE, PAMELA 1958 *Television and the Child: An Empirical Study of the Effect of Television on the Young.* Oxford Univ. Press.

HOVLAND, CARL I.; LUMSDAINE, ARTHUR A.; and SHEFFIELD, FREDERICK D. 1949 *Experiments on Mass Communication.* Studies in Social Psychology in World War II, Vol. 3. Princeton Univ. Press.

INTERNATIONAL PUBLIC OPINION RESEARCH, INC. 1953 *Media of Communication and the Free World as Seen by Czechoslovak, Hungarian and Polish Refugees.* New York: International Public Opinion Research, Inc. → The organization that compiled this report is now known as International Research Associates, Inc.

KATZ, ELIHU 1957 The Two-step Flow of Communication: An Up-to-date Report on an Hypothesis. *Public Opinion Quarterly* 21:61–78.

KATZ, ELIHU; and FELDMAN, JACOB J. 1962 The Debates in the Light of Research: A Survey of Surveys. Pages 173–223 in Sidney Kraus (editor), *The Great Debates: Background, Perspective, Effects.* Bloomington: Indiana Univ. Press.

KATZ, ELIHU; and FOULKES, DAVID 1962 On the Use of the Mass Media as "Escape": Clarification of a Concept. *Public Opinion Quarterly* 26:377–388.

KATZ, ELIHU; and LAZARSFELD, PAUL F. 1955 *Personal Influence: The Part Played by People in the Flow of Mass Communications.* Glencoe, Ill.: Free Press. → A paperback edition was published in 1964.

KELLEY, HAROLD H. 1955 Salience of Membership and Resistance to Change of Group-anchored Attitudes. *Human Relations* 8:275–283.

KELLEY, HAROLD H.; and VOLKART, EDMUND H. 1952 The Resistance to Change of Group-anchored Attitudes. *American Sociological Review* 17:453–465.

KLAPPER, JOSEPH T. 1949 *The Effects of Mass Media.* New York: Columbia Univ., Bureau of Applied Social Research.

KLAPPER, JOSEPH T. 1960 *The Effects of Mass Communication.* Glencoe, Ill.: Free Press.

KRUGMAN, HERBERT E. 1965 The Impact of Television Advertising: Learning Without Involvement. *Public Opinion Quarterly* 29:349–356.

LAZARSFELD, PAUL F. 1940 *Radio and the Printed Page: An Introduction to the Study of Radio and Its Role in the Communication of Ideas.* New York: Duell.

LAZARSFELD, PAUL F.; BERELSON, BERNARD; and GAUDET, HAZEL (1944) 1960 *The People's Choice: How the Voter Makes Up His Mind in a Presidential Campaign.* 2d ed. New York: Columbia Univ. Press.

LEVINE, JEROME M.; and MURPHY, GARDNER 1943 The Learning and Forgetting of Controversial Material. *Journal of Abnormal and Social Psychology* 38:507–517.

LEWIN, HERBERT S. 1953 Facts and Fears About the Comics. *Nation's Schools* 52:46–48.

LÖVAAS, O. IVAR 1961 Effect of Exposure to Symbolic Aggression on Aggressive Behavior. *Child Development* 32:37–44.

McKEACHIE, WILBERT J. 1954 Individual Conformity to Attitudes of Classroom Groups. *Journal of Abnormal and Social Psychology* 49:282–289.

MUSSEN, PAUL H.; and RUTHERFORD, ELDRED 1961 Effects of Aggressive Cartoons on Children's Aggressive Play. *Journal of Abnormal and Social Psychology* 62:461–464.

RICCIUTI, EDWARD A. 1951 Children and Radio: A Study of Listeners and Non-listeners to Various Types of Radio Programs in Terms of Selected Ability, Attitude, and Behavior Measures. *Genetic Psychology Monographs* 44:69–143.

SCHRAMM, WILBUR; and CARTER, RICHARD F. 1959 Effectiveness of a Political Telethon. *Public Opinion Quarterly* 23:121–127.

SCHRAMM, WILBUR; LYLE, JACK; and PARKER, EDWIN B. 1961 *Television in the Lives of Our Children.* Stanford Univ. Press.

SCHRAMM, WILBUR; and RILEY, JOHN W. JR. 1951 Communication in the Sovietized State, as Demonstrated in Korea. *American Sociological Review* 16:757–766.

SHILS, EDWARD; and JANOWITZ, MORRIS 1948 Cohesion and Disintegration in the Wehrmacht in World War II. *Public Opinion Quarterly* 12:280–315.

SIEGEL, ALBERTA E. 1956 Film-mediated Fantasy Aggression and Strength of Aggressive Drive. *Child Development* 27:365–378.

STAR, SHIRLEY A.; and HUGHES, HELEN MACGILL 1950 Report on an Educational Campaign: The Cincinnati Plan for the United Nations. *American Journal of Sociology* 55:389–400.

STEINER, GARY A. 1963 *The People Look at Television: A Study of Audience Attitudes.* New York: Knopf.

SUCHMAN, EDWARD A. 1941 Invitation to Music: A Study of the Creation of New Music Listeners by the Radio. Pages 140–188 in Paul F. Lazarsfeld and Frank N. Stanton (editors), *Radio Research: 1941.* New York: Duell.

TAMIMENT INSTITUTE 1961 *Culture for the Millions? Mass Media in Modern Society.* Edited by Norman Jacobs. Princeton, N.J.: Van Nostrand.

WALTERS, RICHARD H.; LEAT, MARION; and MEZEI, LOUIS 1963 Inhibition and Disinhibition of Responses Through Empathetic Learning. *Canadian Journal of Psychology* 17:235–243.

WALTERS, RICHARD H.; and THOMAS, EDWARD L. 1963 Enhancement of Punitiveness by Visual and Audiovisual Displays. *Canadian Journal of Psychology.* 17:244–255.

WALTERS, RICHARD H.; THOMAS, EDWARD L.; and ACKER, C. WILLIAM 1962 Enhancement of Punitive Behavior by Audio–Visual Displays. *Science* 136:872–873.

WIEBE, GERHART D. 1958 The Army–McCarthy Hearings and the Public Conscience. *Public Opinion Quarterly* 22:490–502.

WILENSKY, HAROLD L. 1964 Mass Society and Mass Culture: Interdependence or Independence? *American Sociological Review* 29:173–197.

WITTY, PAUL 1966 Studies of Mass Media. *Science Education* 50:119–126.

WOLF, KATHERINE M.; and FISKE, MARJORIE 1949 The Children Talk About Comics. Pages 3–50 in Paul F. Lazarsfeld and Frank N. Stanton (editors), *Communications Research: 1948–1949.* New York: Harper.

WRIGHT, CHARLES R. 1960 Functional Analysis and Mass Communication. *Public Opinion Quarterly* 24:605–620.

ZIMMERMAN, CLAIRE; and BAUER, RAYMOND A. 1956 The Effect of an Audience Upon What Is Remembered. *Public Opinion Quarterly* 20:238–248.

COMMUNICATION, NONLEXICAL
See KINESICS.

COMMUNICATION, POLITICAL

I. INTRODUCTION — *Ithiel de Sola Pool*

II. INTERNATIONAL ASPECTS — *Charles A. McClelland*

I
INTRODUCTION

Definition. Both the word "communication" and the word "political" may be defined in various ways. A broad definition of "communication" is any transmission of signs, signals, or symbols between persons. A broad definition of "political" is of or pertaining to a process whereby intentional changes are effected in the rules governing the relations between individuals. By such broad definitions "political communication" is a category that includes a large proportion of all deliberative and hortatory activities that take place outside of the household. An international ultimatum or the speeches of a candidate are, of course, political communications; but so, by this definition, are an employee's request that his superior address him as "Mr." rather than by his first name, or a letter from a club to its members telling them that the dues are to be raised.

By a narrower definition, however, "political communication" refers only to the activity of certain specialized institutions that have been set up to disseminate information, ideas, and attitudes about governmental affairs. This narrow definition is often implicit in institutional studies of political communication. For example, studies of psychological warfare may focus on across-the-lines broadcasts and leaflet distribution (Lasswell 1927; Lerner 1949; Daugherty & Janowitz 1958). Studies of election campaigns may focus on the use of television, posters, and speeches (Herring 1940; Ostrogorskii 1902; Childs 1965). Studies of legislative communication may focus on letters to the Congress, committee documents, and floor speeches (Schattschneider 1935). Studies of administrative management may focus on office memoranda and letters (Simon [1947] 1961, chapter 8).

Implicit in such studies is the notion that certain institutions have as their primary function the facilitation of the exchange and dissemination of messages, and that the characteristics of such institutions constitute the special province of the student of communications. But it is equally clear that although the rate of flow of political messages may be distinctly lower in other environments than these institutions it is not nil. Some students of political communications expand their scope to consider under that rubric much more than just the characteristics of specialized communications institutions (Berelson et al. 1954; Hovland et al. 1953; A Plan of Research . . . 1954; Schramm 1964).

To report the infinity of facts that make up even the smallest social event is impossible. Every phenomenological statement about society is, as historiographers are fond of pointing out, really a report of certain selected indices that are believed to reflect what is happening in the whole. The particular indices that a scholar selects to report is a matter of his style and his discipline. Yet some indices are more widely useful than others. In its broad definition "communication" belongs among that limited set of concepts which provides convenient handles for describing social life in its entirety.

Just as the economist focuses his antenna on exchange relations (either in the particular institution, the market, where such relations are most active or, alternatively, as a way of conceptualizing any or all of social life), and just as the political scientist focuses his antenna on power relations (either solely in the state or as a way of conceptualizing any or all of social life), so too the student of communication may use the exchange of messages either as an index by which to describe institutions (such as the press) that are specifically set up for the purpose of message dissemination or may use the universal social act of communicating as a powerful index for describing any and all aspects of social life. The domain of the study of communication can thus legitimately be the entire domain of the social sciences.

If one takes the communications approach to the study of society as a whole, then the study of political communication becomes just one particular approach to the study of all of politics.

Some classical contributions. One can document the breadth of the topics that may be analyzed as political communication by reviewing some of the classical contributions to the field. Among works prior to 1914 that a student of communication would have to consider as major contributions to his field would be Plato's *Gorgias*, which considers morality in propaganda; Aristotle's *Rhetoric* and Mill's *System of Logic*, which analyze the structure of persuasive argumentation; Machiavelli's *The Prince* and Lenin's *What Is to Be Done?* which are handbooks of political communication for the securing of power; Milton's *Areopagitica* and Mill's *On Liberty*, which consider the systemic effects of permitting individual variation in the flow of political messages; Dicey's *The Development of Law & Opinion in England in the 19th Century*, which considers the effect of the ideological context on public actions; and Marx's *German Ideology*, Sorel's *Reflections on Violence*, and Pareto's *The Mind and Society*, which distinguish the social function from the true value of beliefs.

Propaganda and persuasion

The study of political comunication underwent a major efflorescence after World War I. A number of factors stimulated that growth. The Allies, particularly after Wilson's Fourteen Points, had undertaken a substantial psychological warfare effort against Germany (Lasswell 1927). The German ultra-right, unwilling to admit the facts of defeat, perpetrated the myth that the German soldier had been undefeated on the field of battle but had had victory snatched away by an Allied propaganda "Schwindel" that fooled Germany into giving up. This myth was expressed in a large body of German literature that overestimated the power of propaganda (Thimme 1932).

Such illusions about the vast powers of the "hidden persuaders" (Packard 1957) were in the same period reinforced in the United States by the growth of advertising and public relations. The men in these new businesses, eager to win clients, overstated their own powers over the public mind. They acted as propagandists for propaganda.

While the illusion that clever propagandists with the aid of the mass media could achieve great manipulation of the public became widespread, both research and experience were showing how painfully hard it was to educate the public to preferred civic attitudes. Notable was the National Opinion Research Center's study (1948) of a large-scale United Nations week in Cincinnati, which despite Herculean efforts affected an almost unnoticeable segment of the population. Such observations of the ineffectuality of propaganda led students of political communication to seek by field and experimental studies to understand the conditions under which persuasion does change attitudes and the conditions under which it does not.

Among the field studies perhaps the most notable were the studies by Lazarsfeld, Berelson, and others, of the impact of election campaigns. They demonstrated that relatively few minds are truly changed by a campaign but that a campaign serves other important functions; it may define the issues and mobilize interest and partisanship.

Communication has many effects besides that of persuading people of the thing said. It also affects attention, information, interest, and action. It often does so without causing a person to decide that what he previously thought to be false is true, or vice versa (Lerner 1951; Pool et al. 1956). Nonetheless, a large part of the sociological and psychological literature on political communication has dealt with the conditions of persuasion.

Laboratory studies, most notably those of Carl Hovland and his associates at Yale, have shed substantial light on the conditions under which messages persuade. Certain individuals show a general tendency to be more easily persuaded than others. Informed and intelligent persons are more apt to be persuaded permanently by a presentation that refutes the arguments on the other side as well as presenting its own arguments, while uninformed and unintelligent persons are moved more by a one-sided presentation. Threatening communica-

tions, where circumstances permit, are apt to be disregarded and forgotten more than communications that present encouraging information. Arguments on matters of attitude (not fact) when presented to persons already predisposed to accept the arguments are apt to have more effect on the hearer's attitude after a passage of time than they did immediately after the presentation. Factual information and also attitudinal material that goes against the hearer's predisposition lose part of their impact with time (Hovland 1959).

Psychological experiments have also shown that when a person's opinion structure is dissonant or unbalanced, his opinions are apt to change. If a person simultaneously believes two things that are hard to reconcile, and if circumstances force attention to this imbalance, then a person is apt to change an attitude or redefine the situation to avoid such imbalance (Abelson & Rosenberg 1958; Brown 1962; Festinger 1964; Attitude Change 1960). The classic political case is cross-pressure in an election campaign, when a voter favors a candidate in one respect and dislikes him in another (Berelson et al. 1954). Balance may be restored by deciding that only one of those aspects is important, or by forgetting one of them, or by reversing one of the perceptions of the candidate, or by changing one's own evaluation on one of the points.

However, the results of laboratory studies of attitude change, as Hovland pointed out (1959), diverge from the results of field surveys in one important respect. In the laboratory the messages communicated usually have an effect on the subject; in the field the usual finding is that propaganda makes little discernible difference in any democratic, that is, competitive communication situation. That is because the paid or otherwise controlled subject in the laboratory is in a forced communication situation. In real life, on the other hand, exposing oneself to communication is generally a voluntary act. Persons listen and read selectively, and they do not readily expose themselves to communications that will change their minds. In politics voters attend primarily to their own candidate. They seldom listen to the opposition and even when they do so may selectively misperceive or forget things that are said that they disagree with. So, in real-life situations the directly persuasive effects of political communication are much less cogent than they are in the laboratory. A book that summarizes comprehensively and well what social scientists know about the impact of communications on their receivers is Joseph Klapper's *The Effects of Mass Communication* (1960).

Contents of communications

Political scientists have long been interested in effects of communications other than their immediate persuasive power over their receivers. They have often been interested in describing, for example, the contents of the information flow permeating a society. Dicey's study of the spread of collectivist ideas in England is a classic example. Perhaps the foremost contemporary exponent of such studies is Harold Lasswell, who has either made or instigated the most systematic attempts to provide surveys of the social distribution of attention. In the 1930s he initiated the use of content analysis to compare the political propaganda output at different times and places (Lasswell & Blumenstock 1939), an effort expanded at the Library of Congress during World War II. The studies at the Hoover Institute, originated by him, produced comparisons of the political symbols used in editorials in major papers in five countries over a sixty-year period (Lasswell et al. 1952; Pool et al. 1952).

A study of the contents of political communications in a country may be motivated by purely descriptive purposes. It is interesting to note, for example, the growth of attention to world affairs in the United States or the decline of attention to economics in political campaigns as the great depression has receded into the past. But study of the distribution of attention in society can have more than just descriptive interest. Content analysis of political media can be useful both for intelligence purposes and for social scientific purposes.

During World War II content analysis of enemy broadcasts was effectively used by both British and American agencies to decipher Nazi military plans (George 1959). Kremlinology is a present version of the same technique (Griffith 1963; Rush 1958). The order in which leaders are named, the disappearance of one formula and the appearance of another, or the allusion to some past analogical event may provide clues to major political developments. Needless to say, this kind of analysis is superfluous when a political movement is willing to engage in free discussion of its problems and precluded when it can afford total silence.

The deciphering of Aesopian meanings becomes important when a political group feels simultaneously obliged to communicate and constrained not to communicate frankly. That happens under a variety of circumstances. It happens when dissidents attempt to express their views in ways that will avoid repression by the powers that be. It happens when elites wish to communicate to fellow cognoscenti without revealing their hand to naive hearers. It happens when a politician wishes to convey a message without unduly disturbing established conventions.

Historical examples of such Aesopian political communication have been analyzed most extensively by Leo Strauss (1948). The logic of such analysis has been most fully dissected by Alexander George (1959). Actual analyses of Soviet covert debates are many, but little careful attention has been given to just why it is that the Soviets choose to engage in a mode of political communication that is probably no longer well adapted to their needs. It reveals much that they would like to keep secret, while making the conduct of their policy discussions inefficient. Various relevant factors may be adduced to account for their discussion of policy questions in covert but revealing ways in their major public organs. Among these are the heritage of an illegal revolutionary past, but also a past full of ideological debate; the heritage of the authoritarian tsarist past; and an irrational reaction-formative preoccupation with secrecy in the Russian culture. There is also the need to give directives to thousands of middle-echelon persons on how to behave, for a complex society, even a centralized planned one, must find a way to have millions of independent decisions made in a socially functional way. Finally, informal communications are so severely hampered by Soviet fear of uncontrolled social action that discussion in major media often becomes just as easy as more private kinds of informal discussion. For example, only one central mimeograph facility is allowed in each major department, all stencils are numbered, and a card on the use of each kept by the police authorities.

Effects of political communication

The ways in which Aesopian political material can provide insights into a political system may also demonstrate how the distribution of communication content can be a matter of interest to social scientists concerned with the effects of communication. Clearly, there are both systemic and individual consequences to the distribution of attention, quite different from the persuasive consequences of individual messages.

One example is the emergence of political alienation when the contents of communications in the official and the mass media do not correspond to the perceptions and the interest of their audiences (Kris & Leites 1947; Levin 1962). Modern totalitarian societies, unlike historical authoritarian ones, are very public-opinion conscious and put out vast amounts of political communication to the public. The publics, however, may learn to consider such communications unreliable, often trusting more to rumor (Bauer et al. 1956); they then become less involved in political matters and devote minimum attention to the mass of material thrown at them. But the depolitization is, of course, never complete, and people who are given highly censored versions of the news acquire great skill at reading between the lines and become quite energetic at seeking information by such means as listening to foreign broadcasts. The non-Asian communist countries are now virtually covered by short-wave radios (about twenty million in the Soviet Union); and listening to foreign broadcasts is fairly universal. A very different situation exists, of course, in some underdeveloped countries, where large parts of the public do not know about major outside world events and trends. Nowadays, since every major nation broadcasts internationally the latest trends in culture, art, and popular music, political matters too become universally known, among interested persons, without much delay. The political consequences of such a change in the attention situation have already been profound and may be accentuated as communication satellites make international communication even easier.

Practicing propagandists are generally aware that it is much easier to change people's distribution of attention than to change their values and attitudes. Virtually all propaganda efforts serve only to focus people's attention on certain issues rather than to reverse their previous views on those issues. Advertisers seldom seek to change the desires of the public; they try to convince the public that their product meets those desires. Successful psychological warriors do not try to convert the enemy nationals into rejecting their own fatherland and joining in the cause of the propagandists. They succeed only when their target forces are falling apart anyway and they can simply focus the attention of the enemy troops on that fact and inform them how to save themselves (Lerner 1949; Shils & Janowitz 1948). In general, it may be said that persuasion as such is only a small part of political communication. Most of it consists of modifying the information on which people will act, given their own values and preferences.

The mass media.   The growth of the mass media has had a major impact on the conduct of political activity. In the United States, for example, radio and, even more, television have significantly reduced the power of the local political machine and drastically reduced the use of rallies and mass meetings. Since Franklin Roosevelt's fireside chats on radio in the 1930s it has been possible for the president or the presidential candidate to establish a direct campaign relationship with every individual voter. In a presidential campaign this relationship is far more significant than the remarks of a local politician. Television, of course, adds an extra element of visibility and probably some extra impact. There is some evidence that different political personalities are more effective on radio than on television, but this has not been much investigated (Pool 1959). Both media certainly give an opportunity for the exercise of political charisma.

Furthermore, the cost-effectiveness of the mass media is likely to be greater than that of more individualized campaign methods, at least in terms of spreading information. Expensive as television time may be, it is apt to be cheap per person reached. This is true even if one disregards the mammoth audiences reached on such special occasions as the Kennedy–Nixon debates in the 1960 presidential campaign.

However, it would be a mistake to make any simple comparative statement about the relative political effectiveness of the mass media versus face-to-face organization. They serve different functions and for maximum effectiveness they must be linked together. That is a principle that skillful political organizers have generally understood. In *What Is to Be Done?* Lenin developed the notion of a disciplined party of professional revolutionists, but in the same pamphlet he also strongly advocated the establishment of an all-Russian newspaper to serve as a "collective organizer." Even today in the Soviet Union, the several million oral agitators are serviced by a special magazine, *Bloknot agitatora* ("The Agitator's Notebook").

Indeed, the growth of political parties and the growth of the press went hand in hand in most countries of the world until recent decades. One of the difficulties of establishing effective party systems in some of the newly emerging nations is that the newer mass media, particularly radio, cannot meet the needs of the small partisan group as well as the revolutionary newspaper put out in a small print shop.

A number of major social science studies have dealt with the relationship of word-of-mouth communication to the mass media. It has been fairly well established in a variety of cultures that whereas the mass media serve effectively to diffuse information, people seldom act on that information without confirming their impulse by checking with an opinion leader with whom they are in face-to-face contact (Katz & Lazarsfeld 1955; Rogers 1962; Pool 1963). In India, for example, villages in which people listened to agricultural broadcasts in groups and then discussed them were compared with similar villages that received the same broadcasts but had no organized listening groups. In both sets of villages learning of the information was comparable, but only where there were organized listening groups with face-to-face discussion was there any significant amount of adoption of the new practices that were learned (Mathur & Neurath 1959). The implications for the complementarity of the mass media and political organization are clear.

ITHIEL DE SOLA POOL

[*Directly related are the entries* PROPAGANDA; PSYCHO-LOGICAL WARFARE. *Other relevant material may be found in* ATTITUDES; COMMUNICATION, MASS; PERSUASION; PUBLIC OPINION; PUBLIC RELATIONS.]

BIBLIOGRAPHY

ABELSON, R. P.; and ROSENBERG, M. J. 1958 Symbolic Psycho-logic: A Model of Attitudinal Cognition. *Behavioral Science* 3:1–13.

Attitude Change. 1960 *Public Opinion Quarterly* 24: 163–365.

BAUER, RAYMOND; INKELES, ALEX; and KLUCKHOHN, CLYDE 1956 *How the Soviet System Works.* Cambridge, Mass.: Harvard Univ. Press.

BERELSON, BERNARD; LAZARSFELD, PAUL F.; and McPHEE, WILLIAM N. 1954 *Voting: A Study of Opinion Formation in a Presidential Campaign.* Univ. of Chicago Press.

BROWN, ROGER 1962 Models of Attitude Change. Pages 1–85 in Roger Brown et al., *New Directions in Psychology.* New York: Holt.

CHILDS, HORWOOD L. 1965 *Public Opinion.* Princeton, N.J.: Van Nostrand.

DAUGHERTY, WILLIAM E.; and JANOWITZ, MORRIS (compilers) 1958 *A Psychological Warfare Casebook.* Baltimore: Johns Hopkins Press.

FESTINGER, LEON 1964 *Conflict, Decision, and Dissonance.* Stanford Studies in Psychology, No. 3. Stanford (Calif.) Univ. Press.

GEORGE, ALEXANDER L. 1959 *Propaganda Analysis: A Study of Inferences Made From Nazi Propaganda in World War II.* Evanston, Ill.: Row, Peterson.

GRIFFITH, WILLIAM E. 1963 *Albania and the Sino–Soviet Rift.* Cambridge, Mass.: M.I.T. Press.

HEIDER, FRITZ 1958 *The Psychology of Interpersonal Relations.* New York: Wiley.

HERRING, EDWARD P. 1940 *The Politics of Democracy.* New York: Norton.

HOVLAND, CARL I. 1959 Reconciling Conflicting Results Derived From Experimental and Survey Studies of Attitude. *American Psychologist* 14, no. 1:8–17.

HOVLAND, CARL I.; JANIS, IRVING L.; and KELLEY, HAROLD H. 1953 *Communication and Persuasion: Psychological Studies of Opinion Change.* New Haven: Yale Univ. Press.

KATZ, ELIHU; and LAZARSFELD, PAUL F. 1955 *Personal Influence: The Part Played by People in the Flow of Mass Communications.* Glencoe, Ill.: Free Press. → A paperback edition was published in 1964.

KLAPPER, JOSEPH T. 1960 *The Effects of Mass Communication.* Glencoe, Ill.: Free Press.

KRIS, ERNST; and LEITES, NATHAN C. (1947) 1953 Trends in Twentieth Century Propaganda. Pages 278–288 in Bernard Berelson and Morris Janowitz (editors), *Reader in Public Opinion and Communication.* Enl. ed. Glencoe, Ill.: Free Press.

LASSWELL, HAROLD D. (1927) 1938 *Propaganda Technique in the World War.* New York: Smith.

LASSWELL, HAROLD D.; and BLUMENSTOCK, DOROTHY 1939 *World Revolutionary Propaganda: A Chicago Study.* New York: Knopf.

LASSWELL, HAROLD D.; LERNER, DANIEL; and POOL, ITHIEL DE SOLA 1952 *The Comparative Study of Symbols.* Stanford (Calif.) Univ. Press.

LAZARSFELD, PAUL F.; BERELSON, BERNARD; and GAUDET, HAZEL (1944) 1960 *The People's Choice: How the Voter Makes Up His Mind in a Presidential Campaign.* 2d ed. New York: Columbia Univ. Press.

LERNER, DANIEL 1949 *Sykewar: Psychological Warfare Against Germany, D-Day to VE-Day.* New York: Stewart.

LERNER, DANIEL (editor) 1951 *Propaganda in War and Crisis: Materials for American Policy.* New York: Stewart.

LEVIN, MURRAY B. 1962 *The Compleat Politician: Political Strategy in Massachusetts.* Indianapolis: Bobbs-Merrill.

MATHUR, JAGDISH CHANDRA; and NEURATH, PAUL M. 1959 *An Indian Experiment in Farm Radio Forums.* Paris: UNESCO.

NATIONAL OPINION RESEARCH CENTER 1948 Cincinnati Looks Again, Report 37A. Unpublished manuscript.

OSTROGORSKII, MOISEI IA. 1902 *Democracy and the Organization of Political Parties.* 2 vols. London and New York: Macmillan. → An abridged edition was published in 1964 by Quadrangle Books.

PACKARD, VANCE O. 1957 *The Hidden Persuaders.* New York: McKay. → A paperback edition was published in 1958 by Pocket Books.

A Plan of Research in International Communication: A Report. 1954 *World Politics* 6:358–377.

POOL, ITHIEL DE SOLA 1959 TV: A New Dimension in Politics. Pages 236–261 in Eugene Burdick, Arthur J. Brodbeck (editors), *American Voting Behavior.* Glencoe, Ill.: Free Press.

POOL, ITHIEL DE SOLA 1963 The Mass Media and Politics in the Modernization Process. Pages 234–253 in Conference on Communication and Political Development, Dobbs Ferry, New York, 1961, *Communications and Political Development.* Princeton Univ. Press.

POOL, ITHIEL DE SOLA et al. 1952 *The "Prestige Papers": A Survey of Their Editorials.* Stanford (Calif.) Univ. Press.

POOL, ITHIEL DE SOLA; KELLER, SUZANNE; and BAUER, RAYMOND A. 1956 The Influence of Foreign Travel on Political Attitudes of American Businessmen. *Public Opinion Quarterly* 20, no. 1:161–175.

ROGERS, EVERETT M. 1962 *Diffusion of Innovations.* New York: Free Press.

RUSH, MYRON 1958 *The Rise of Khrushchev.* Washington: Public Affairs Press.

SCHATTSCHNEIDER, ELMER E. 1935 *Politics, Pressures, and the Tariff: A Study of Free Private Enterprise in*

Pressure Politics; as Shown in the 1929–1930 Revision of the Tariff. New York: Prentice-Hall.

SCHRAMM, WILBUR L. 1964 *Mass Media and National Development: The Role of Information in the Developing Countries.* Stanford (Calif.) Univ. Press.

SHILS, E.; and JANOWITZ, M. 1948 Cohesion and Disintegration in the Wehrmacht in World War II. *Public Opinion Quarterly* 12, no. 3:280–315.

SIMON, HERBERT A. (1947) 1961 *Administrative Behavior: A Study of Decision-making Processes in Administrative Organization.* 2d ed. New York: Macmillan. → A paperback edition was published in 1965 by the Free Press.

STRAUSS, LEO (1948) 1963 *On Tyranny: An Interpretation of Xenophon's "Hiero."* New York: Free Press.

THIMME, HANS 1932 *Weltkrieg ohne Waffen: Die Propaganda der Westmächte gegen Deutschland.* Stuttgart (Germany): Cotta.

II
INTERNATIONAL ASPECTS

The international system can be conceived in the terms of reference of a very large and complicated communication network. The prime argument for viewing international relations in this way is that the communication approach reveals aspects of the subject that hitherto have been neglected; and, therefore, it promises to advance knowledge of international behavior.

A simple communication system consists merely of a message, a sender of the message, a channel through which the message can travel, and a receiver of the message. There are, however, some further requirements if this simple structure is to be made to work. The system must be in contact with an environment changeful enough to give the sender the occasion for transmitting a message; the sender must have the ability to scan and select from the variety of things produced by a changeful environment; and both sender and receiver need to have somewhat comparable capabilities to engage in encoding and decoding the messages that are sent and received. From the standpoint of the interested social scientist, a means for observing is an essential part of the system (Cherry 1957, p. 89).

Beyond these requirements, a communication system can be elaborated almost endlessly by the incorporation of additional components. For example, the system may be equipped in some way to discover if the messages sent were received as intended. Filtering and condensing parts can be added to diffuse the transmissions to many receivers and to gather the messages from many senders to a single receiver. Provision may be made for storing the records of past communications and for retrieving them when they are again needed. Multiple channels may be used or a single channel can be arranged to carry several different streams of messages. In brief, the opportunities to enlarge and elaborate a simple communication structure usually appear to be limitless.

Scope

It may be thought that to characterize a part or the whole of social phenomena such as the relations among nations is merely to carry over an analogy to social science from the realms of mechanics and electronics. This is not the case, however; because relations among nations are carried along on a flood of words, both written and spoken. Further, many international events that are more physical than the acts of speaking and writing are symbolic in their purposes and effects and fall, therefore, into the category of communication. The communication aspects of international relations may be appreciated more fully by the consideration of a comprehensive definition of international communication and of the topics that fit within that definition.

Let us define international communication as including both the structure and the content of the stream of social messages transmitted over time and across national boundaries. Diplomatic exchanges and negotiations between national governments come easily within the definition. No conflict between states could be carried on without a flow of information bearing ideas, feelings, and intentions between the antagonists. To make a proposal, to issue a warning, or to deliver a protest in international politics is to commit a communicative act. The essential purpose of moving a fleet to a troubled area or of sending the head of state abroad on a good-will tour is generally to relay some specific information to other peoples and countries. The traditional functions of diplomacy are to gather and evaluate information from abroad and to carry on conversations and negotiations with foreign governments. Unquestionably, international communication is pervasive in the practices of international politics. It extends well beyond official relations of governments, however. Smith has illustrated eloquently what else is encompassed in international communication. He includes the following:

. . . the relatively disinterested activities of international newsgathering agencies; the creation of impressions abroad by tourists and other migrants; the probably massive but generally unplanned impact of books, art works, and movies distributed in foreign countries; the international contacts of students, educators, scientists and technical assistance experts; the negotiations and correspondence of international business interests; the activities of international missionaries and religious movements; the work of international pressure groups, such as trade unions, chambers of commerce, and political parties; international philanthropic activities, like the Ford Foundation's "private Point Four" program in India; the "propaganda of the deed" implicit even in the *un*publicized activities of leaders and collectivities, as perceived by various audiences; and a great many other processes by which information and persuasion are consciously or unconsciously disseminated across national and cultural boundaries. (Smith 1956, pp. 183–184)

Recent research

The foregoing illustrates the types of subjects that come within the scope of international communication or that can be considered in a communication context. Next we shall consider the question of what has been added in recent years to the store of knowledge of international affairs through research on communication. It is difficult, for several reasons, to offer a compact survey of the research accomplishment. No effective theory of communication in international relations has emerged to organize and simplify the facts and to locate the various constituting segments of the subject. Researchers from several disciplines, including political science, psychology, sociology, education, anthropology, and journalism, have engaged in relevant work; but the different interests and perspectives of these fields complicate the task of summarization. Nor are the theoretical foundations of international relations sufficiently stable to offer a satisfactory organizing framework. What seems most reasonable under the circumstances is to discuss, from more than a single vantage point, some of the scholarly literature on international communication. It is best to view the subject according to several sets of organizing categories. The situation is somewhat puzzling because large expanses of the subject have been investigated very little but, at the same time, the volume of the literature has become very large. In a survey covering the period 1943–1955, Smith and Smith (Bureau . . . 1956) identified over 2,500 articles, books, and reports of substantial character on international communication.

Senders, channels, and receivers. The simple communication system structure that was described at the beginning of this article has been used frequently to guide reporting on the areas of communication research. Thus, one may think in terms of studies of senders, messages, channels, and receivers. The senders, or communicators, of international messages have been studied less frequently than the receivers, i.e., the audiences or "targets," of communication. Cohen's (1957) analysis of

John Foster Dulles' activities in the negotiating of the Japanese peace treaty is an outstanding example of the study of international communicators. The conceptual scheme of Snyder et al. (1962) for foreign-policy decision-making analysis stresses the importance of the communication elements that influence decision-making groups in the formulation of policy. The Snyder and Paige (1958) study of the 1950 U.S. decision on Korea provides numerous data for understanding the actions of international communicators. Nevertheless, only a sketchy knowledge exists of how communicators scan, select, and encode information from the international environment for the transmission of messages to others. About the same situation exists in the area of channel studies.

The channels of international communication are complex systems in their own right and are highly specialized for the particular functions they serve. Most of the research that has been done has centered on two topics: (a) the flow of world news through the mass media and (b) the growth of national communications in transitional and modernizing societies. UNESCO has sponsored studies of how different parts of the world are served by the news agencies, the press, and other mass circulation media. Schramm (1959) and Kayser (1953) have provided some materials for studying the content of the news in the press of different countries, and Pool et al. (1952) have shown the role played in international relations by certain "prestige" newspapers. Analyses have been made to determine how much international and foreign news appears in newspapers, and a beginning has been made in studying the relay stages and selection processes in the transmission of world news from the point of occurrence of a significant international event to the newspaper on the breakfast table. It is clear that the public channels of international communication are highly selective so that some message flows are let through the system while others are turned back through choices made by "gatekeepers" located at various points in the transmission chain (Carter 1958).

Some of the most important work of recent years has centered on studies of the growth patterns of communication networks in countries changing from traditional social forms to modern national organization. The spread of the mass media and the changes in the habits of social communication have been considered an indicator of national development and also a vital ingredient that must combine with other social, economic, and psychological elements if national development is to continue (Lerner 1958; Conference on Communication . . . 1963). The pioneering work that brought attention to the forms and the structures of social communication and their importance in the building of political communities was that of Karl Deutsch (1953).

As one might anticipate, the effects of communication on audiences have interested researchers perhaps more than any subject in the field. The result is that a great mass of information is available about public opinion on many international issues, about popular views on war and peace, and about attitudes and images concerning foreign peoples and foreign governments. The specific results of educational efforts in world affairs, of propaganda campaigns, and of different kinds of people-to-people communications have been reported in large numbers. Several volumes of the series of studies "Citizen Participation in International Relations" (Hero 1959a; 1959b; 1960a; 1960b) assemble much of the data about American audiences and foreign affairs.

The expansion to world-wide dimensions of survey research on public opinion has made increasingly apparent the possibilities of carrying on periodic cross-national samplings of opinion on international matters and of charting long-term trends of opinion change. Indeed, valuable cross-national comparative studies have already been reported, for example, those of Buchanan and Cantril (1953), Gillespie and Allport (1955), Almond (1954), and Free (1959). As yet no approach has been sufficiently developed to bring together the data of thousands of surveys of opinion on foreign affairs that have been collected over the years in dozens of countries. Pool (1961) has urged that these idle resources be put to use and has suggested some methods for establishing systematic and quantitative criteria for assembling this knowledge.

Some general conclusions concerning audiences and international relations can be set forth on the basis of the research that has been done on public and international affairs. There is overwhelming testimony to the low state of factual knowledge about foreign affairs in mass publics in all countries and to the lack of understanding in national populations of the meanings of even very important international events. The early insight (Lasswell 1935; Lasswell et al. 1952) that in all nations foreign affairs enlist the attention, knowledge, skills, and participation of small elites has, in general, been supported by the results of audience research. A modification of elite theory has been made, however, in recognition of the fact that national populations are organized in large numbers of special publics and special interest groupings.

Thus, the concept of a single small elite group largely in charge of foreign relations has been widened somewhat to encompass numbers of special publics and their "opinion influentials."

In recent years, the outstanding hypothesis advanced to explain both the apparent insensitivity of mass publics and the role of leaders and influentials in the communication process is the concept of the "two-step flow" (Katz & Lazarsfeld 1955; Katz 1957). This hypothesis states that the effects of communication from the mass media take place among relatively few people but that among those affected are persons who convey opinions and ideas to others by direct and personal conversation. The first step of the communication flow is via the mass media, and the second step operates through face-to-face communicating and personal influence. The failures of many vigorous world affairs programs to educate the general public (for an example, see the study of Star & Hughes 1950) may be related to the slighting of the second step of communication.

Communication and foreign policy. In locating additional research on international communication, it is advantageous to make reference to the categories now commonly employed in describing the general field of international relations. When the study of international relations is divided into two parts, one concerned with the making of foreign policy and the other with the interactions and organization of the international political system, it will be found that some communication studies occupy both sectors. The framework of Snyder et al. (1962), which was mentioned previously, is a major guide to the study of the making of foreign policy, and it calls for careful attention to the processes of communication within national societies. Rosenau (1961) has made a significant contribution in his conceptualization of the foreign-policy process as a system of mutual influence involving the government, the influentials, and the attentive publics, carried forward by means of a circular flow of communication. Data supporting this conceptual scheme have been published by Rosenau (1963). The place of the press in the making of foreign policy has been discussed frequently but studied rarely. An analysis of the press and foreign policy by Cohen (1963) has partially corrected the situation. Almond's study (1950) still stands as the best general treatment of public opinion and its relationship to U.S. foreign policy.

A novel approach to the communication aspects of the exchanges and interactions between nations in the international system has been developed by North and his associates (1963). By devising a program of content analysis for a large computer, the North group has been producing measures of the kinds of perceptions and the amount of emotion being carried, during crises, in the statements and messages of national decision makers. The practices of diplomacy, otherwise, have received little attention from the communication research standpoint. Proceedings of international conferences offer rich materials for content analysis, but little work has been done in this direction. Spanier and Nogee (1962) have interpreted recent disarmament negotiations from the propaganda angle, however.

Governments are interested in persuasive communication as one of the instruments of foreign policy. Many studies have been done under government auspices to evaluate information programs and propaganda campaigns conducted abroad. Wartime needs to counter enemy propaganda and to explore all avenues of propaganda and psychological warfare were instrumental in stimulating propaganda analysis. Surveys of these wartime accomplishments and of the progress of the art and science of propaganda are readily available (Lerner 1951; George 1959; Holt & van de Velde 1960; Daugherty & Janowitz 1958).

Psychological factors. Two clusters of theory and research that are contributing increasingly to current knowledge of international communication have their sources in psychology and anthropology. These contributions may be related conveniently to the phenomena of the encoding and decoding of messages, referred to early in this discussion. When psychological and cultural considerations are taken into account in the study of international relations, they enrich the understanding of foreign policy and international politics; but they also tend to complicate matters and sometimes to confuse them. The introduction of "the human dimension in international relations" (Klineberg 1964) presents some problems in integrating new knowledge with old. It is the communication approach that appears to offer the best connecting link between psychocultural and political knowledge.

Political scientists have ordered their knowledge of international relations principally around the concept of power. Further, they have identified decision making as the most vital of the problems involved in the use of power. As the foregoing has indicated, communication research has concentrated on the study of the structures and processes of message exchange. At first sight, the political perspective and the communication perspective appear to belong to entirely different realms. This is not the case, however. Communication includes not only the study of psychological and cultural variables in information processes; it also includes branches of theory and research concerned with persuasion and influence and with the making of decisions under conditions of uncertainty. The latter concerns lie very close to the political scientists' preoccupations with power and political decision making. Thus, the possibility of connecting these two areas of interest and communication theory is of real significance. The following discussion is a sketch suggesting how the possible convergence of perspectives can be developed.

Conventional teachings of international politics hold that the participants in international affairs are guided in their talk and actions by the universal language of power politics. International actors may make errors and fall into misunderstandings, but these are the mistakes in the use of the calculus of power. The basic model of international politics is a distillation of centuries of historical experience, and it portrays a relatively small number of national states interacting as units according to national interests and under circumstances determined by the distribution of power among the units. This inherited model cannot be cast aside lightly, yet it has little room for the ideas and data of the human dimension that psychologists and anthropologists have cultivated. Factors of public opinion, the influence of personality variables, the differences in national character, the consequences of sheer ignorance about the world, and the dynamic interplay of conflicting beliefs and values among nations are squeezed into the model only with great difficulty. Thus, the accommodation of the human dimension would appear to require either the abandonment of the traditional model in favor of a new one or its expansion to encompass the additional interests. Let us see, tentatively, how the model might be enlarged.

Men act according to the information they have. As has been said many times, they act according to their perceptions of what is so. If the question of the differences in the availability of information is put aside, there remains the matter of what an individual does with the information that comes to him. Psychological theory and research have done much toward explaining the processing of information within human beings. Some messages reach the individual and are internalized because they are taken as significant or salient. Others may be noted casually, and still others are turned away and not internalized. The generalization is that men possess processing equipment to handle the receiving, selecting, categorizing, and storing of reports received about the world. This total resource has been called the "image" (Boulding 1956) or cognitive structure.

Two facts about the image are to be noted especially. Individuals act to keep a reasonably well-organized view of the world. The psychological theories of how this balance is maintained have been summarized conveniently by Maccoby and Maccoby (1961). One's cognitive organization must be understood as the product of personal experience, but its structure is also the reflection of upbringing and social training—the outcome of living in a particular cultural milieu. Osgood (1958) and Miller, Galanter, and Pribram (1960), among others, have extended the knowledge of the many intricacies in the workings of the image in human beings. How much of the individual's communication processing capability is shared among all men and how wide its variations are because of different upbringing and cultural conditioning are questions of interest to the students of international behavior. The answers are by no means clear at the present time. Cultural anthropologists have a strong opinion on the subject, however.

Cultural factors. The stock in trade of anthropology is the culture concept. The interrelated wholeness of a culture has been much emphasized (Benedict 1934). When most anthropologists think about international relations, their foremost thought is that international interactions involve people who carry different and distinctive cultural traits and patterns. It is small wonder that vigorous complaints have arisen from the anthropological quarter against the political analyses of international relations that disregard or slight the cultural factor. On the other hand, strong doubts have been expressed on the creditability of anthropologically oriented interpretations of American, German, Japanese, Russian, and other national cultures (Benedict 1946; Mead 1951; Hennessy 1962). Criticisms and countercriticisms notwithstanding, cross-cultural studies have been made on subjects more specific than whole national cultures. Investigations have been carried on of the experiences of foreign study (Selltiz et al. 1963); of modern acculturative situations (Lord 1958; Scotch 1961); and of specific linguistic, emotional, and gestural misperceptions and misunderstandings (LaBarre 1947; Haring 1951). Even some training on psychocultural situations has been introduced in education for foreign service. Hall (1959) has made available many fascinating examples of cultural influences on international communication and, in addition, has developed a conceptual scheme for studying cross-cultural phenomena. Enough is now known about the cultural factor that a place for it must be provided in a general model of international relations.

In the perspective of communication research, the actions of individuals and the influences of cultures have multifarious effects on the fidelity of the transmission of messages through the international system. What effects occur in the encoding and decoding of international information at the level of the individual? What happens in the processing as messages pass through one culture and enter another? These are, perhaps, the fundamental questions for which specific answers are needed from research on international communication. The human dimension of international relations finds its place as the coding process in a communication system. It remains now merely to indicate how else the concept of the international system as an elaborate communication network may enlarge conventional views of international politics.

Communication and international politics

The governments of sovereign states exert power to serve their national interests. This is the conventional statement. The relationships that arise from the pursuit of national interests have many properties and attributes. They may be extensive or slight, friendly or hostile, attentive or indifferent, peaceful or violent, stable or changing, and so on. However these different states of relationships are distinguished, they are recognized by the makers of foreign policy only from information that can be gathered about occurrences and events taking place in international relations. It follows that the central foreign-policy problem of a government is to decide, on the basis of the information at hand about the international environment, what to do either in making a demand on another government or in responding to a demand made by another government (Sprout & Sprout 1962, pp. 141–177).

The task of making decisions in foreign relations is never easy for at least three fundamental reasons: (1) there is never enough information to undergird a decision with complete certainty; (2) the outcome of the decision depends on the responding action of other governments; and (3) the outcome of one decision may impose the difficulty of making further decisions that were not anticipated at first. In brief, the source of danger is the uncertainty in the situation. To reduce uncertainty is to diminish the surprise factor in international relations. The better a decision maker becomes in deciding what to do—without being surprised by the result—the better are his chances of being able to advance the interests of his state.

Information theory (Cherry 1957; Pierce 1961; Garner 1962) was devised precisely for the systematic choosing of courses of action in the face of uncertainty. In order to use information theory, one needs to have stable sources of action (or of messages), an understanding of what *could* happen, and a reasonably extensive record of what has already happened. Foreign policy and international politics furnish data to these specifications. The data of international relations should prove to be amenable to analysis according to information theory.

All that must be done, then, to enlarge the conventional model of international relations is to regard national states as complex organizations that process incoming information through networks of communication and transmit abroad their reactions in the form of demands and responses. The national states are communication sources, and their demand and response actions generate the messages flowing between states. The units of international relations are the thousands of discrete messages that are exchanged. Only these few reconceptualizations are needed to modify the traditional model of power politics in international relations and to reorient understanding to the terms of reference of communication systems.

It becomes the task of the study of international relations in the communication perspective to trace the flows of communication; to determine the structure and content of these flows through the international system; to measure the intensity, volume, and variety in the messages; and to discover the methods best suited for using information, thus reducing uncertainty, in the making of decisions. The theory of power is translated into the theory of communicative influence (Dahl 1957; Singer 1963). Here are the ingredients for an expanded model of international relations. By bringing international communication into the mainstream of international studies, the researchers of international relations will advance the knowledge of their field and increase the possibilities of prediction and control in the international system.

CHARLES A. McCLELLAND

[See also FOREIGN POLICY; INTERNATIONAL POLITICS; INTERNATIONAL RELATIONS.]

BIBLIOGRAPHY

ALMOND, GABRIEL A. (1950) 1960 *The American People and Foreign Policy.* New York: Praeger.

ALMOND, GABRIEL A. 1954 *The Appeals of Communism.* Princeton Univ. Press.

BENEDICT, RUTH 1934 *Patterns of Culture.* Boston: Houghton Mifflin. → A paperback edition was published in 1961 by Houghton Mifflin.

BENEDICT, RUTH 1946 *The Chrysanthemum and the Sword: Patterns of Japanese Culture.* Boston: Houghton Mifflin.

BOULDING, KENNETH E. 1956 *The Image: Knowledge in Life and Society.* Ann Arbor: Univ. of Michigan Press.

BUCHANAN, WILLIAM; and CANTRIL, HADLEY 1953 *How Nations See Each Other: A Study in Public Opinion.* Urbana: Univ. of Illinois Press.

BUREAU OF SOCIAL SCIENCE RESEARCH, WASHINGTON, D.C. 1956 *International Communication and Political Opinion: A Guide to the Literature,* by Bruce L. Smith and Chitra M. Smith. Princeton Univ. Press.

CARTER, ROY E., JR. 1958 Newspaper "Gatekeepers" and the Sources of News. *Public Opinion Quarterly* 22: 133–144.

CHERRY, COLIN (1957) 1961 *On Human Communication: A Review, a Survey, and a Criticism.* New York: Wiley. → A paperback edition was published in 1963 by Wiley.

COHEN, BERNARD C. 1957 *The Political Process and Foreign Policy: The Making of a Japanese Peace Settlement.* Princeton Univ. Press.

COHEN, BERNARD C. 1963 *The Press and Foreign Policy.* Princeton Univ. Press.

CONFERENCE ON COMMUNICATION AND POLITICAL DEVELOPMENT, DOBBS FERRY, N.Y., *1961* 1963 *Communications and Political Development.* Edited by Lucian W. Pye. Princeton Univ. Press.

DAHL, ROBERT A. 1957 The Concept of Power. *Behavioral Science* 2:201–215.

DAUGHERTY, WILLIAM E.; and JANOWITZ, MORRIS 1958 *A Psychological Warfare Casebook.* Baltimore: Johns Hopkins Univ. Press.

DEUTSCH, KARL W. 1953 *Nationalism and Social Communication: An Inquiry Into the Foundations of Nationality.* Cambridge, Mass.: Massachusetts Institute of Technology.

DEUTSCH, KARL W. 1963 *The Nerves of Government: Models of Political Communication and Control.* New York: Free Press.

FREE, LLOYD A. 1959 *Six Allies and a Neutral: A Study of the International Outlooks of Political Leaders in the United States, Britain, France, West Germany, Italy, Japan, and India.* Glencoe, Ill.: Free Press.

GARNER, WENDELL R. 1962 *Uncertainty and Structure as Psychological Concepts.* New York: Wiley.

GEORGE, ALEXANDER L. 1959 *Propaganda Analysis: A Study of Inferences Made From Nazi Propaganda in World War II.* Evanston, Ill.: Row, Peterson.

GILLESPIE, JAMES M.; and ALLPORT, GORDON W. 1955 *Youth Outlook on the Future: A Cross-national Study.* Garden City, N.Y.: Doubleday.

HALL, EDWARD T. 1959 *The Silent Language.* Garden City, N.Y.: Doubleday. → A paperback edition was published in 1961 by Fawcett.

HARING, DOUGLAS G. 1951 Cultural Contexts of Thought and Communication. *Quarterly Journal of Speech* 37: 161–172.

HENNESSY, BERNARD C. 1962 Psycho–Cultural Studies of National Character: Relevances for International Relations. *Background: Journal of the International Studies Association* 6:27–49.

HERO, ALFRED O. 1959a *Americans in World Affairs.* Studies in Citizen Participation in International Relations, Vol. 1. Boston: World Peace Foundation.

HERO, ALFRED O. 1959b *Mass Media and World Affairs.* Studies in Citizen Participation in International Relations, Vol. 4. Boston: World Peace Foundation.

HERO, ALFRED O. 1960a *Opinion Leaders in American Communities.* Studies in Citizen Participation in International Relations, Vol. 6. Boston: World Peace Foundation.

HERO, ALFRED O. 1960b *Voluntary Organizations in World-affairs Communication.* Studies in Citizen Participation in International Relations, Vol. 5. Boston: World Peace Foundation.

HOLT, ROBERT T.; and VAN DE VELDE, ROBERT W. 1960 *Strategic Psychological Operations and American Foreign Policy.* Univ. of Chicago Press.

KATZ, ELIHU 1957 The Two-step Flow of Communication: An Up-to-date Report on an Hypothesis. *Public Opinion Quarterly* 21:61–78.

KATZ, ELIHU; and LAZARSFELD, PAUL F. 1955 *Personal Influence: The Part Played by People in the Flow of Mass Communications.* Glencoe, Ill.: Free Press. → A paperback edition was published in 1964 by Free Press.

KAYSER, JACQUES 1953 *One Week's News: Comparative Study of 17 Major Dailies for a Seven-day Period.* Paris: UNESCO.

KLINEBERG, OTTO 1964 *The Human Dimension in International Relations.* New York: Holt.

LABARRE, WESTON 1947 The Cultural Basis of Emotions and Gestures. *Journal of Personality* 16:49–68.

LASSWELL, HAROLD D. 1935 *World Politics and Personal Insecurity.* New York and London: McGraw-Hill.

LASSWELL, HAROLD D.; LERNER, D.; and ROTHWELL, C. E. 1952 *The Comparative Study of Elites: Introduction and Bibliography.* Stanford (Calif.) Univ. Press.

LERNER, DANIEL (editor) 1951 *Propaganda in War and Crisis: Materials for American Policy.* New York: Stewart.

LERNER, DANIEL 1958 *The Passing of Traditional Society: Modernizing the Middle East.* Glencoe, Ill.: Free Press.

LORD, EDITH 1958 The Impact of Education on Nonscientific Beliefs in Ethiopia. *Journal of Social Psychology* 47:339–353.

MACCOBY, NATHAN; and MACCOBY, ELEANOR E. 1961 Homeostatic Theory in Attitude Change. *Public Opinion Quarterly* 25:538–545.

MEAD, MARGARET 1951 *Soviet Attitudes Toward Authority: An Interdisciplinary Approach to Problems of Soviet Character.* New York: McGraw-Hill.

MILLER, GEORGE A.; GALANTER, E.; and PRIBRAM, K. H. 1960 *Plans and the Structure of Behavior.* New York: Holt.

NORTH, ROBERT C. et al. 1963 *Content Analysis: A Handbook With Applications for the Study of International Crisis.* Evanston, Ill.: Northwestern Univ. Press.

OSGOOD, CHARLES E. 1958 Behavior Theory and the Social Sciences. Pages 217–244 in Roland C. Young (editor), *Approaches to the Study of Politics.* Evanston, Ill.: Northwestern Univ. Press.

PIERCE, JOHN R. 1961 *Symbols, Signals, and Noise: The Nature and Process of Communication.* New York: Harper.

POOL, ITHIEL DE SOLA 1961 *Communication and Values in Relation to War and Peace.* Program of Research, No. 5. New York: Institute for International Order.

POOL, ITHIEL DE SOLA et al. 1952 *The "Prestige Papers": A Survey of Their Editorials.* Stanford (Calif.) Univ. Press.

ROSENAU, JAMES N. 1961 *Public Opinion and Foreign Policy: An Operational Formula.* New York: Random House.

ROSENAU, JAMES N. 1963 *National Leadership and Foreign Policy: A Case Study in the Mobilization of Public Support.* Princeton Univ. Press.

SCHRAMM, WILBUR L. 1959 *One Day in the World's Press: Fourteen Great Newspapers on a Day of Crisis, November 2, 1956.* Stanford (Calif.) Univ. Press.

SCOTCH, N. A. 1961 Magic, Sorcery, and Football Among Urban Zulu: A Case of Reinterpretation Under Acculturation. *Journal of Conflict Resolution* 5:70–74.

SELLTIZ, CLAIRE et al. 1963 *Attitudes and Social Relations of Foreign Students in the United States.* Minneapolis: Univ. of Minnesota Press.

SINGER, J. DAVID 1963 Inter-nation Influence: A Formal Model. *American Political Science Review* 57:420–430.

SMITH, BRUCE L. 1956 Trends in Research on International Communication and Opinion: 1945–55. *Public Opinion Quarterly* 20:182–195.

SNYDER, RICHARD C.; and PAIGE, GLENN D. 1958 The United States Decision to Resist Aggression in Korea: The Application of an Analytical Scheme. *Administrative Science Quarterly* 3:341–378.

SNYDER, RICHARD C. et al. (editors) 1962 *Foreign Policy Decision-making: An Approach to the Study of International Politics.* New York: Free Press.

SPANIER, JOHN W.; and NOGEE, JOSEPH L. 1962 *The Politics of Disarmament: A Study in Soviet–American Gamesmanship.* New York: Praeger.

SPROUT, HAROLD H.; and SPROUT, MARGARET 1962 *Foundations of International Politics.* Princeton, N.J.: Van Nostrand.

STAR, SHIRLEY A.; and HUGHES, HELEN MACGILL 1950 Report on an Educational Campaign: The Cincinnati Plan for the United Nations. *American Journal of Sociology* 55:389–400.

COMMUNISM

The articles under this heading deal with the political aspects of contemporary communism. For a detailed guide to related topics, see the articles listed under MARXISM.

I.   SOVIET COMMUNISM   *Merle Fainsod*
II. NATIONAL COMMUNISM   *Alexander Dallin*
III. THE INTERNATIONAL MOVEMENT   *Bernard S. Morris*
IV. THE INTERNATIONAL SYSTEM   *George Modelski*

I

SOVIET COMMUNISM

The origins and nature of Soviet communism are, and promise to remain, a subject of debate. Some scholars emphasize indigenous formative influences, stress factors of continuity with the Russian past, and tend to regard the Soviet political system as a modern form of traditional Russian despotism. Others view Bolshevism primarily as a Western heresy, whose roots can be traced to eighteenth-century French utopianism, Messianism, and Jacobinism but which, in a more immediate sense, was an offshoot of the activist, revolutionary ingredients in classical Marxism. Those who stress discontinuities with the Russian past argue that Russia in the late nineteenth and early twentieth century was embarked on a path of constitutional development, which the Bolshevik seizure of power aborted, and that in any case, Soviet totalitarianism, with its pretensions to all-encompassing control of society and world revolutionary objectives, must be sharply distinguished from tsarist authoritarianism, which functioned as a national state and operated a much more limited and inefficient control system.

As is not uncommon in scholarly polemics, there are elements of truth in all these contrasting interpretations, and no measuring rod exists to give precise value to their respective contributions. Soviet communism clearly owes much to its French revolutionary and Marxist forebears, but the way in which these borrowed ideas were adapted and transformed represented a response to the urgencies and peculiarities of the Russian environment.

Classical Marxism.   Classical Marxism may itself be viewed as a response to the dislocations and suffering of the working class in the early stages of the industrial revolution in Great Britain and western Europe. In the Marxian scheme the spread of capitalism and the intensification of working class misery were the necessary prelude to a socialist revolution; Marx's panorama of economic development clearly implied that the socialist revolution would arrive first in the most advanced industrial countries, where the proletariat or working class was expected to be most numerous, most highly organized, and ripe for the seizure of power.

Nineteenth-century Russia, with its overwhelmingly peasant population and low level of industrial development, hardly fit the specifications for a Marxist-type revolution. Indeed, through the 1880s the Russian revolutionary movement, which was dominated by the Narodniki, or Populists, looked to the peasant as the primary revolutionary force to overthrow the autocracy and dreamed of building socialism around the peasant commune, or *mir*. While Narodnik philosophers were familiar with the works of Marx and Engels and largely responsible for translating them into Russian, they regarded the evils of industrialization and proletarianization, which Marx and Engels described so graphically, as dangers to be avoided rather than stages to be traversed. Nor were Marx and Engels at first certain that Russia would have to recapitulate the economic development of the West. As late as 1882 they still thought that the *mir* might "serve as a starting-point for a communist course of development," but only "if the Russian revolution sounds the signal for a workers' revolution in the West, so that each becomes the complement of the other" (Engels [1890] 1963, pp. 264–265). By 1892, however, Engels had written off the *mir* as a Narodnik illusion; Russia seemed to him to be embarked on an irreversible capitalist course.

Russian Marxism.   Russian Marxism as an independent political movement originated in the split in 1879 of the Narodnik organization Zemlya i Volya (Land and Liberty). The seceders, who stood for propaganda and agitation as opposed to terrorism, established a rival organization, the Chernyi Peredel (Black Repartition), to propagate their doctrines. One of their leaders was Georgii Valentinovich Plekhanov, soon to be known as the father of Russian Marxism, but then still clinging to the Narodnik belief in the peasant as the driving force of revolution. The failure of the peasantry to respond either to agitation or terror and the rapid industrial development that was beginning to take place in the last decades of the nineteenth century impelled Plekhanov to re-examine his views and to turn to the new industrial working class—the proletariat, so-called—as the revolutionary hope of the future. The search for a new faith led him to Marxism. In 1883 Plekhanov, Paul Axelrod, Leo Deutsch, and Vera Zasulich, all of whom had been members of the Chernyi Peredel, joined in establishing the first important Russian Marxist organization, known as Osvobozhdenie Truda (Emancipation of Labor). By the 1890s the works of Marx and Engels were being widely and eagerly read by the more radically inclined students and intellectuals and propagated in workingmen's circles. One of the new converts was Vladimir Ilyich Ulyanov (Lenin), who was to change the face of world history.

The Russian Social Democratic Labor party, of which Lenin's Bolshevik faction was an offshoot, held its first congress in 1898 and its second in 1903. At the 1903 congress, divisions developed within the party. The split between "hards" and "softs" centered on the character of party organization. Lenin wanted a select, closed party of dedicated revolutionaries operating in strict subordination to the center and serving as a vanguard of leadership for the masses of workers who would follow the party without necessarily belonging to it. Martov (Iulii Osipovich Tsederbaum), leader of the "softs," pressed for a broad party open to anyone who believed in its program and was willing to work under its direction. At the 1903 congress, the views of Martov on party organization registered a temporary triumph. But in the election of officers at the end of the congress, Lenin's faction carried the majority and became known as Bolsheviks (in Russian, "majority men"). Lenin's opponents were dubbed Mensheviks ("minority men").

The differences between the two factions were not confined to organizational matters. A central issue that was to divide the party grew out of the problem of Russia's industrial backwardness and the political consequences to be drawn from it. How should Marxism, which provided a recipe for socialist revolution in the most advanced industrial countries, be applied in the Russian setting? The Mensheviks, who prided themselves on being orthodox Marxists, saw the arrival of socialism in Russia as the climax of a long process of industrial development. Impressed by the weakness of the Russian proletariat, they concluded that a socialist Russia was a matter of the distant future and that their first charge as good Marxists was to help the bourgeoisie discharge its historical responsibility to overthrow the autocracy. Meanwhile, they could only wait for the further growth of capitalism and the proletariat to establish the conditions for a successful socialist revolution.

At the opposite extreme from the Menshevik conception was the theory of "permanent revolution," developed by Parvus (Alexander Helphand) and adopted by Leon Trotsky during and after the 1905 revolution. For Parvus and Trotsky the industrial backwardness of Russia was a revolutionary asset rather than a liability. Because of the weakness of the Russian bourgeoisie and its dependence on the state, they looked to the proletariat to spearhead both a bourgeois and a socialist revolution. Once the proletariat had won power, its responsibility was to hold onto power and keep the revolution going "in permanence." The Russian revolution, Trotsky thought, would ignite a series of socialist revolutions in the West, which would in turn guarantee the success of the socialist revolution in Russia. Thus Trotsky's prescription for Russia's retarded economy was a new law of combined development. The two revolutions—bourgeois–democratic and proletarian–socialist—would be combined, or telescoped, into one. The working class would assert its hegemony from the outset and leap from industrial backwardness into socialism.

Leninism. Lenin's own views underwent an interesting transformation. He began by accepting the orthodox two-stage conception that Russia would have to pass through a bourgeois–democratic phase before it was ripe for a socialist revolution. But, unlike the Mensheviks, Lenin turned his back on the bourgeois liberals and looked to the peasantry as allies of the working class. Lenin's formula envisaged two tactical stages: first, "the revolutionary-democratic dictatorship of the proletariat and the peasantry" to complete the bourgeois–democratic revolution, and second, an alliance of the proletariat and the village poor to initiate the socialist revolution. Like Trotsky, Lenin came to believe that the two stages of the revolution could be telescoped into one; at the height of the 1905 revolution he pronounced, "We stand for uninterrupted revolution. We shall not stop half way." Despite many intervening conflicts, the bond with Trotsky was to be sealed by the events of 1917. The dialectic of backwardness was "resolved" by the Bolshevik seizure of power.

Out of that experience a new theory of revolution was to be developed with world-wide applications. The Leninist theory of revolution, as Stalin christened it, was a far cry from orthodox Marxism. Its prerequisites were no longer industrial development, a mass proletariat, or the completion of a bourgeois–democratic revolution. As Stalin summed it up, "The front of capital will be pierced where the chain of imperialism is weakest, . . . and it may turn out that the country which has started the revolution, . . . is less developed in a capitalist sense than other, more developed, countries, which have, however, remained within the framework of capitalism" (Stalin [1924] 1954, p. 37).

Thus Marx was "adapted" to the task of revolution making in the underdeveloped countries of the world. Industrial backwardness was transformed from obstacle to opportunity. The concept of the dictatorship of the proletariat shifted from a weapon of the majority into a tool of minorities. Consciousness triumphed over spontaneity, and the way was cleared for the organized and disciplined revolutionary elite capable of transmuting the grievances of a people into a new instrument of absolute power.

Early organizational development

"Give us an organisation of revolutionaries," said Lenin, "and we will overturn Russia" (Lenin [1902] 1961, vol. 5, p. 458). Lenin forged the instrument, but the prototypes of the professional revolutionary as the strategic lever of political upheaval were planted deep in Russian history and were nurtured by the conditions of the revolutionary struggle against the autocracy. It was against this background that the organizational concepts of Lenin took shape. By 1902, with the publication of *What Is to Be Done?* they were fully developed.

Four ideas stand out in this seminal source of Communist organizational doctrine. First, there was the fear of spontaneity, the notion that the working class could not be trusted to discover its own true interests and that, if left alone, it would follow the path of trade-union bargaining rather than commit itself to a revolutionary struggle for socialism. Second, there was the unquestioned assumption that the working class had to be guided and directed by a politically conscious revolutionary vanguard possessed of a superior knowledge of the laws of history. Third, there was the idea that this vanguard should consist of a small, carefully selected party of professional revolutionaries operating under highly centralized direction and discipline. Finally, there was the concept of political monopoly, that no other organizations should be permitted to compete with the party in obtaining access to the masses and that all mass organizations, such as trade unions, must be brought under the ideological influence and, if possible, the direct control of the party.

Lenin sought to put these ideas into effect in his struggle with the Mensheviks for ascendancy in the Russian Social Democratic Labor party. While a façade of surface unity was at first preserved, the factional strife became increasingly bitter, and finally in 1912 Lenin and his followers broke away, organized a "pure" Bolshevik central committee, and laid claim to the party title. The name "Communist" was not adopted until 1918, after victory was won, when the designation of the party was changed to Russian Communist party (Bolshevik) to distinguish it from the socialist or social-democratic parties of western Europe, whom the Bolsheviks charged with betrayal of the revolutionary cause during World War I.

The early organizational history of Bolshevism has more than historical interest. The experience of the formative years stamped the character and future development of the party. The elitism which was so deeply ingrained in Lenin, the theory of the party as a dedicated revolutionary order, the tradition of highly centralized leadership, the tightening regime of party discipline, the absolutism of the party line, the intolerance of disagreement and compromise, and the manipulatory attitude toward mass organization—all these patterns of behavior were to continue to shape the code by which the party lived and the way in which its institutional structure was organized.

The Bolshevik victory in November 1917 may fairly be described as one of the most remarkable triumphs of revolutionary engineering in human history. On the eve of the March revolution the total membership of the Bolshevik party was generously estimated at 23,600. In the short space of eight months, this small group was able to accumulate sufficient support to seize power in a nation of over 150,000,000 people. Russia, to be sure, was ripe for revolutionary action. The war, with its vast losses of men, territory, and resources, its revelations of incompetence and even degeneracy in the very highest circles, and the mounting war-weariness, hunger, and deprivation, induced a mood of desperation. The Bolsheviks alone among revolutionary parties were able to turn the resulting disorganization to their advantage. One major source of the strength of the Bolshevik party was its highly centralized organization, its activist disciplined membership, and the determination of its leader, Lenin, to seize power at the first opportune moment. Another source of strength was its success in exploiting all of the accumulated dissatisfactions in Russian society. The provisional government that replaced the tsar was weak, vacillating, and slow to respond to popular grievances. The Bolsheviks were willing to promise what the masses wanted—land to the peasants, bread to the hungry, and peace to the war-weary army. Finally, the Bolsheviks concentrated their efforts on building power where it would be strategically effective—among the sailors of the Baltic fleet, in the Petrograd garrison, and in the armed workers' Red Guard in the factories. The enemies of the Bolsheviks were far more numerous, but they were poorly organized, divided, and ineffective. As Lenin subsequently observed, "The Bolsheviks did have an overwhelming preponderance of force at the decisive moment in the decisive points" (Lenin [1919] 1932, vol. 29, p. 635). Relying on these tactical advantages, they succeeded in taking power.

The next problem was whether they could hold onto power in the face of the successive onslaughts of the Germans, the White armies, and the Allied intervention. The first decision of the Bolsheviks was to sue for peace with the Germans. The terms were harsh, but Lenin argued that there was no alternative except to bow. In the Treaty of Brest–Litovsk (March 1918) the Bolsheviks temporarily signed away to the Germans a third of their country and more than half of their industry. But the breathing space the treaty was designed to win never materialized. Although German pressure relaxed with the signing of the armistice in November 1918, the Bolsheviks had still to cope with the White armies, the Allied interventionist forces, and a war with Poland. After three years of civil war, the Whites were defeated, the Allies (the United States, Japan, France, and Great Britain) withdrew their forces, and the Bolsheviks survived.

Coincidentally with the civil war, the Bolsheviks proclaimed a state of siege, and all opposition parties were suppressed one by one. For a very brief period (from late December 1917 until March 1918), there were three Left Socialist Revolutionaries (who stood close to the Bolsheviks) in the Council of People's Commissars, the cabinet. But they left the government in protest against the Treaty of Brest–Litovsk and grain confiscations from the peasants, and the Soviet government reverted to its original exclusively communist composition, which it has since retained. Lenin at the time made no bones about the necessity for dictatorship and suppression of opposition groups. "There is no other way to Socialism," he insisted, "but the dictatorship of the proletariat. . . . Violence, when it is committed by the toiling and exploited masses, is the kind of violence of which we approve" (Lenin 1918, vol. 35, p. 265).

Since in Lenin's view it was the Communist party that was the sole custodian of the interests of the masses, the logic of his position led inexorably in the direction of the one-party state and the use of the Cheka (security police) to exterminate enemies of the regime. By abolishing freedom for opposition parties, the communists transformed the Soviets, the trade unions, and other forms of mass organization into transmission belts, as they came to be called, for carrying out the will of the monopoly party.

From the one-party state it was only a short step to the establishment of dictatorship within the party. This was uniquely Stalin's achievement. But Lenin had set the master precedent with his ultracentralist ideas on party organization. In attacking them as far back as 1904, Trotsky had prophetically observed that in Lenin's scheme the party takes the place of the working class; the party organization displaces the party; the central committee displaces the party organization; and finally, the "dictator" displaces the central committee (Trotsky 1904, p. 54).

The Stalinist era

It remained for Stalin to provide the final vindication of Trotsky's prophecy. In 1922 Stalin was appointed general secretary of the party, a post of key importance in controlling party patronage. His recommendations became increasingly decisive in appointments of regional and local party secretaries, who later returned to party congresses as voting delegates. When Lenin became ill in 1922–1923, the most prominent contender for the succession was Trotsky. But the man who commanded the party machine was Stalin. He joined with two other party leaders, Grigori E. Zinoviev and Lev B. Kamenev, who held strong positions in the party organization, and together they proved powerful

enough to shear Trotsky of a considerable degree of his authority. The *troika*, or triumvirate, that they established dominated the party Politburo after Lenin's death in 1924.

In that period Stalin was building up his personal machine and soon felt strong enough to dispense with the support of Zinoviev and Kamenev, who moved over in 1925 to join Trotsky in forming the so-called Left Opposition. In order to defeat them, Stalin allied himself with the right wing in the Politburo—Nikolai I. Bukharin, Mikhail P. Tomski, and Aleksei I. Rykov. Together, they crushed Trotsky and his new allies in 1926–1927. Not satisfied to share authority, Stalin then turned round in 1929 to rid himself of the right wing and ejected Bukharin, Tomski, and Rykov from leading positions in the party. Even though Stalin's position as the "supreme leader" of the party was now virtually unquestioned, he proceeded in the mid-1930s to carry through a series of bloody purges which left no corner of Soviet society untouched.

Stalin's drive to rid himself of all opposition was not confined to the Old Bolsheviks. Many of the most faithful of his erstwhile supporters were caught up in the fury of the purges. Perhaps the most dramatic and authoritative testimony on the damage the purges did to the top stratum of party leadership was provided by Khrushchev, when he revealed in his "secret" speech to the twentieth party congress in 1956 that "of the 139 members and candidates of the Party's Central Committee who were elected at the XVIIth Congress (1934), 98 persons, i.e., 70 per cent, were arrested and shot (mostly in 1937–1938) . . ." and that "of 1,966 delegates with either voting or advisory rights" at the same congress "1,108 persons were arrested on charges of anti-revolutionary crimes . . ." (Columbia University, Russian Institute 1956, pp. 22–23).

With the consolidation of Stalin's power, the figure of the infallible dictator emerged as the operative principle of Communist party leadership. His colleagues in the Politburo functioned as administrative henchmen and assistants on a high level; the central committee went into a shadowy eclipse; party congresses became rallies of the faithful; and the party apparatus operated as a subservient instrument of Stalin's will.

While the particular form of despotic rule that Stalin developed was no doubt peculiar to him and a reflection of his personality, the desperate desire of both Lenin and Stalin to overcome Russian backwardness reinforced reliance on authoritarian expedients. When the Bolsheviks seized power,

Russia was still a largely peasant country in the early stages of industrialization. Among Bolsheviks, consciousness of Russian backwardness was so strong that many feared it would be impossible to move forward to socialism, or even hold onto power, unless help was provided by successful proletarian revolutions in the advanced industrial nations of the West. When revolutionary aid from the West was not forthcoming, the Bolsheviks were thrown back on their own resources and faced with the task, as Lenin put it in 1921, of "adopting dictatorial methods to hasten the copying of Western culture," and of using "barbarous methods in combatting barbarism." Restated in non-Leninist terms, the historic burden that the communists assumed was that of modernizing an underdeveloped country by dictatorial and totalitarian means.

After the exhaustion of the civil war and the famine that accompanied and succeeded it, the communists were compelled to beat a retreat, to make concessions to the peasantry, and to permit a partial revival of private trade. During the years of the NEP—the New Economic Policy, which lasted from 1921 to 1928—prewar industry was rebuilt, but the regime encountered the greatest difficulty in accumulating the investment funds to finance a further expansion of the industrial sector. Agricultural output grew but so did peasant consumption, and efforts to increase the tax burden on the more well-to-do peasants met formidable resistance. The resulting stalemate was eventually resolved by forcing the peasants into collective farms, which operated essentially as collection agencies to extract grain from the peasantry at low prices. Thus a large part of the burden of accumulating an industrialization fund was transferred to the countryside.

Beginning in 1928 with the first five-year plan, Stalin launched Russia on a program of forced-draft industrialization. The decision carried with it a train of consequences: emphasis on heavy industry at the expense of light industry; the suppression of the claims of consumption; the "revolution from above," as Stalin termed it, by which the peasantry was brought to heel through collectivization; a new emphasis on technical education; a reorganization of the incentive system to reward those who contributed to industrial productivity; and finally, a strengthening of the coercive and totalitarian features of the regime to deal with the discontent that the new program generated.

Inherent in the industrialization drive was also a powerful nationalist, or patriotic, ingredient. As the prospects of world revolution dwindled in the 1920s, Russia, the home base of the revolution,

became the central preoccupation of the party leadership, and the need to strengthen its defenses and build up its power loomed as a more and more important task. In the process the legacy of Russian national interests became inextricably intertwined with broader Soviet goals and objectives. Industrial backwardness operated as a barrier both to the assertion of Russian national claims and to the realization of communist revolutionary hopes. To overcome this barrier was to ensure survival and to open the door to greatness. As Stalin put it in a speech to industrial managers in 1931: ". . . we are fifty or a hundred years behind the advanced countries. We must make good the distance in ten years. Either we do it, or they crush us" (Stalin [1931] 1954, p. 456). The speech was to prove prophetic. Exactly ten years later came the Nazi attack on the Soviet Union. Had it not been for the industrialization drive and the military power that it produced, it is doubtful whether the Soviet Union could have survived the onslaught.

The Stalinist years were a period of "practical tasks," rather than of great doctrinal ferment. The transformation of the Bolsheviks from a revolutionary into a governing party meant that Leninism (or Marxism–Leninism, as it came to be called) had become a state ideology. Its primary task was to explain, rationalize, and defend the decisions taken by the party leadership. Lenin himself in the prerevolutionary years had had little to say about how society would be organized under Bolshevik auspices, and after power was won, both Lenin and Stalin felt free to make practical adjustments within the framework of a general commitment to socialism.

Stalin's theoretical pronouncements, if they can be described as such, were essentially statements of operative ideology, which undertook to justify the policies he was pursuing. His theory of "building socialism in one country," which he developed in his polemic against Trotsky's doctrine of "permanent revolution," went beyond glossing over a disagreeable necessity to a positive affirmation of Russian strength and self-sufficiency. It laid the basis for his doctrine of Soviet patriotism, that strange amalgam of traditional nationalism and pride in Soviet achievements by which Stalin sought to unify the nation in the face of foreign dangers. His repudiation of egalitarianism and other "utopian" elements in the heritage of classical Marxism was closely geared to the requirements of productive efficiency as he understood them. His dialectical "discovery" that the state must grow stronger before it could wither away and his glorification of the state superstructure reflected the powerful role he assigned to the state apparatus in reshaping and directing Soviet society. His theory that the class enemy would become more desperate and dangerous as communism approached was nothing less than a justification of the great purges.

As Stalin neared the end of his days, his megalomania mounted. The controls that he exercised became increasingly rigid and stultifying. His totalitarian grip embraced every facet of Soviet life. Literature, drama, music, art, and every branch of learning were purged of any trace of independence and were forced to join in choruses of sycophantic adulation to the "supreme leader." The supercentralization on which Stalin insisted became increasingly anachronistic. It induced congestion at the center and paralysis below. Because authority was so concentrated in Stalin's person, in the last years of his life there was a perceptible decline in the influence of the party organization as such. The party apparatus was faced with increasing competition from an expanding government bureaucracy and an already inflated police apparatus. Meanwhile, Stalin stood at the apex of each hierarchy—party, government, and police—playing them off against one another, using their competition to reinforce his own authority, and relying on his system of calculated insecurity to keep them all submissive and responsive to his commands.

Stalin's legacy to his successors was replete with problems. His impressive achievements in forcing the pace of Soviet industrialization, building military power, and expanding his domain into eastern and central Europe were all purchased at a heavy price. Soviet agriculture remained backward and stagnant, and the food available to the Soviet public was monotonous, scarce, and high priced. Stalin's obsession with the development of heavy industry meant that light industry was ignored and underdeveloped, and shortages of consumer goods and housing were acute and widespread. The system of terror on which Stalin relied to protect his own security and to enforce his regime of deprivation and sacrifice had its debilitating effects. Frightened bureaucrats shrank from exercising initiative; there was a frozen and congealed quality about Soviet life which tended to rob it of all dynamism and revolutionary appeal.

The Khrushchev period

The death of Stalin marked the end of an era and opened the way to new policy initiatives and political and administrative arrangements better suited to the more mature stage of industrializa-

tion, which Stalin himself had done so much to create. Once the succession crisis had been resolved by Khrushchev's purge of his competitors, the outlines of a new model of Khrushchevian rule began to crystallize. It could best be described as a form of "enlightened," or rationalized, totalitarianism, which sought to eliminate or mollify the worst grievances of the Stalinist epoch and rationalize the system of administrative and economic controls, while preserving the substance of totalitarian power itself. Khrushchev's formula of governance relegated terror to a much less central position than it had occupied under Stalin, and the welfare reforms that he sponsored were designed to broaden popular support for the regime. But Khrushchev's vision of society remained total, and he saw nothing within it that could be permitted to remain free from the party's paternal guidance and control.

In contrast to Stalin, Khrushchev used the party as his primary instrument of rule. Within the party he sought to revive what he called Leninist norms—more active participation by the party rank and file in party discussions, encouragement of greater criticism from below, more frequent assemblages of party congresses, committees, and other important party organs, and greater emphasis on the recruitment of workers and collective farmers in order to strengthen the party's popular roots. But the revival of the forms of intraparty democracy did not extend to its essence. Khrushchev, like Stalin before him, jealously guarded his authority, and insisted that the party function as a monolith in executing his will. Party functionaries, nevertheless, flourished under Khrushchev. He depended heavily on them to strengthen his control of the armed forces and the police, to achieve centralized direction of industry and agriculture, and to provide the coordinating framework that held Soviet society together and forced it to march in step.

Khrushchev's use of the party apparatus as an integrating force was combined with a pragmatic willingness to experiment with forms of decentralized administration and new incentive systems where they promised more effective operational results. His recognition that the supercentralization of the Stalinist era was ill suited to the rational management of an increasingly complex economy drove him to shift the weight of supervisory authority much closer to the grass roots. Under Khrushchev the Soviet administrator was given more elbow room to exercise initiative and his conditions of work became more normalized, but he had still to adjust himself to goals and priorities that were centrally determined, and the ability to meet them remained the ultimate criterion of success.

Despite Khrushchev's repudiation of the Stalinist legacy of terror, the model which he held out for Soviet society was no Liberty Hall where individualism would run rampant. In his vision of Soviet society there was no place for the heretic, rebel, or skeptic. Even when communism was fully realized, he insisted, the Soviet Union would remain a highly organized, ordered, planned, and disciplined society in which the party would retain its leading role. The community for him was essentially a production enterprise where "each person must, like a bee in a hive, make his own contribution to increasing the material and spiritual wealth of society" (Khrushchev 1963*a*, p. 4, col. 1 ff.). For Khrushchev the key to mass freedom was the self-imposed discipline of willing workers, imbued with the love of work and profoundly believing in the cause to which they devoted their efforts.

What most sharply distinguished Khrushchev from Stalin was his apparently sincere faith that a society of the Soviet type could be governed without reliance on large-scale repression. The new "populism" that Khrushchev articulated was evident in his assiduous efforts to create an image of himself as a leader who was close to the people. In striking contrast to Stalin, who rarely ventured forth from the Kremlin, Khrushchev was the agitator par excellence, in constant motion, addressing meetings from one end of the country to the other, visiting collective farms and factories, speaking the language of the people, and reaching out for popular support. His efforts to mobilize the energies of the masses by providing for their more active participation in the tasks of communist construction reached out in many directions. It was manifest in his repeated calls for the recruitment of "leading" workers and collective farmers into the party, in his revival of comrades' courts to improve workers' discipline, in his use of peoples' guards (*druzhiny*) to help enforce public order, and in his reliance on neighborhood assemblies to mete out punishments to parasites and other social deviants. It was strikingly evident in a number of the theoretical formulations that he devised to signal the Soviet entry into the stage of building communism. Thus the theory of the dictatorship of the proletariat was replaced by the concept of an all-people's state, while the party of the proletariat became the party of the whole people. The 1961 party program promised that as the state withered away, agencies of public self-government would gradually replace state organs, and it pointed to already announced transfers of authority to trade unions, sports societies, the Komsomol, and Soviets as marking the pathway of future development.

While the party program spoke of wider mass participation in administrative functions, it also made clear that such participation would be subject to strong party guidance. No withering away of the party was contemplated in the communist stage; indeed the party program declared that it would become stronger than ever, performing the indispensable role of directing, guiding, and controlling all the activities of society, including "the organs of public self-government." Thus this effort to square the political circle by combining the appearance of popular control with the reality of party rule constituted still another in a long series of efforts to enlist mass energy and initiative in support of party-determined objectives.

As the Khrushchev era drew to a close, there were increasing signs that his popularity was waning. Under his aegis the Soviet Union continued for a time to make rapid industrial progress and score space triumphs, but there were also disturbing indications toward the end of his reign that the industrial growth rate was slowing and that agricultural output was declining. The promises of rapid improvement in living standards that he had made to his own people were belied by food shortages and an apparent inability to master the agricultural problem. Khrushchev's efforts to resolve intractable economic problems by periodic reorganizations of the state and party machinery only served to compound confusion. His unsuccessful efforts to dislodge the Western powers from West Berlin, the rebuff he received during the Cuban missile crisis, the increasing bitterness of the Sino–Soviet dispute, and declining Soviet influence in Eastern Europe and in the international communist movement contributed to undermining Khrushchev's prestige. Thus, his early accomplishments and bold destalinization initiatives tended to be taken for granted and forgotten, while he found himself increasingly measured by the expectations that he had aroused and failed to fulfill. In October 1964 his associates in the party presidium deposed him and instituted a new period of collective rule with its own short-term problem of maintaining a precarious power equilibrium and its longer-range challenge of coping with changes in Soviet society.

Trends in Soviet communism

Although any attempt to assess the direction of development of Soviet communism must necessarily be highly provisional, some trends can be identified that promise to leave their stamp on the future.

Industrialization. Perhaps the most important single development is the continuing transformation of the Soviet Union from a predominantly agrarian into a highly industrialized society. Industrialization has set new forces into motion. It has enhanced the importance of skilled labor at the expense of unskilled or semiskilled labor and has made necessary widespread literacy and a command of basic technical skills in the labor force. In bureaucratic terms, it has meant a vast expansion of managerial, engineering, technical, and scientific personnel and a recognition that they constitute an "industrializing elite" who must be appropriately rewarded for their crucial contribution to the industrialization process. It has required a heavy emphasis on scientific training and research and a recognition that the dynamic momentum of industrialization is intimately intertwined with and dependent on scientific creativity.

As the Soviet Union became a more and more highly industrialized society, dependent on its scientists, engineers, and managers to maintain its ongoing technological momentum, some redefinition of influence within the society appeared inevitable. The authority of scientific knowledge could not be denied without doing damage to the society's prospects. While this development did not necessarily challenge the party's formal monopoly of political power, it did mean that the party leadership had to come to terms with the scientific community and that party functionaries were being increasingly equipped with sufficient technical and scientific knowledge to exercise their controlling roles intelligently. It also opened up the prospect of gradual erosion, adaptation, and even outright rejection of ideological dogmas which operate as barriers to technical progress. A party that had embraced forced-draft industrialization as a key to its salvation promised to be transformed by the very burdens it had assumed.

Welfare totalitarianism. With advancing industrialization came other changes. The austere production ethic of the early stages of the industrialization process was increasingly challenged by a consumption ethic to which concessions had to be made. After decades of deprivation and sacrifice under Stalin, there was a widespread and insistent demand for improved incentives and more amenities. The spread of elementary and higher education stirred rising aspirations and presented the regime with new problems in adapting its system of controls to these expectations.

One of the keys to an understanding of the post-Stalinist era lies in the recognition that these aspirations could no longer be ignored. Unwilling as Khrushchev was to part with substantive authority, he did recognize that there were grievances to be remedied. His decision to mitigate Stalin's terror and provide greater welfare benefits for the Soviet people represented an effort to establish his regime on a more rational and popular basis. One of the questions still to be determined is whether this formula of "popular," or "welfare," totalitarianism, which epitomized the internal policies of the Khrushchevian period, will prove viable, whether the aspirations to which Khrushchev partially responded and which he helped activate will acquire a momentum of their own that will transform Soviet society in directions that his successors can neither fully anticipate nor control.

Peaceful coexistence. Equally indeterminate is the effect that relations with noncommunist states, as well as with other communist states, are likely to have on the development of Soviet communism. Unlike Stalin, Khrushchev operated under a compelling necessity to adjust the strategy and tactics of Soviet foreign policy to the realities of the thermonuclear age. These realities not only brought to the fore the common interests that he shared with Western leaders in avoiding mutual destruction; they also impelled him to seek out ways of advancing the communist cause that would minimize the risks of igniting a thermonuclear holocaust. They caused him to replace Lenin's doctrine of the inevitability of war between the Soviet Union and the so-called imperialist states with the new formula that such wars were not "fatalistically inevitable." They led him to reaffirm the theory of peaceful coexistence, even though peaceful coexistence as interpreted by Khrushchev did not imply a static acceptance of the existing correlation of forces between the camps of communism and capitalism, nor did it exclude Soviet aid to so-called national liberation movements. Despite these caveats, Khrushchev was not prepared to support a reckless and adventurous revolutionary strategy that would pose unacceptable risks of thermonuclear extinction. Charged with safeguarding Soviet interests and promoting the communist cause in a thermonuclear age, Khrushchev envisaged his main tasks as those of building up Soviet power, demonstrating the superiority of the Soviet system, and counting on the weaknesses and vulnerabilities of the noncommunist world to yield opportunities for communist advance within the framework of a nuclear stalemate.

Khrushchev's strategic posture reflected the relatively conservative interests of a mature communist power with a strong vested interest in preserving its hard-won industrial gains from total destruction. This strategy posited a prolonged, if perhaps uneasy, peace with the West, during which Soviet society would continue to evolve and develop without catastrophe. However pleasing this prospect might be from the Soviet point of view, it offered small comfort to the more militant elements in the international communist movement who saw their salvation in advancing the timetable of world communist triumph. It was particularly suspect to the Chinese communists, who believed that their own interests and ambitions were being sacrificed to promote Soviet development. It was against this background that the Sino–Soviet dispute intensified in bitterness, and separate eastern and western communist empires began to take form. The stage was also set for the emergence of communist forces that sought to escape the discipline of both. The world perspectives of Soviet communism promised to be increasingly restricted by two parameters: the strength of polycentric tendencies within the communist camp and the inhibitions that the thermonuclear strength of the West imposed on Soviet freedom to maneuver.

MERLE FAINSOD

BIBLIOGRAPHY

ARMSTRONG, JOHN A. 1961 *The Politics of Totalitarianism: The Communist Party of the Soviet Union From 1934 to the Present.* New York: Random House.

BRZEZINSKI, ZBIGNIEW; and HUNTINGTON, SAMUEL P. 1964 *Political Power: USA/USSR.* New York: Viking.

CARR, EDWARD H. 1951–1964 *History of Soviet Russia.* 7 vols. New York: Macmillan. → Volumes 1–3: *The Bolshevik Revolution: 1917–1923,* 1951–1953. Volume 4: *The Interregnum: 1923–1924,* 1954. Volumes 5–7: *Socialism in One Country: 1924–1925,* 1958–1964.

COLUMBIA UNIVERSITY, RUSSIAN INSTITUTE 1956 *The Anti-Stalin Campaign and International Communism: A Selection of Documents.* New York: Columbia Univ. Press.

CONQUEST, ROBERT 1961 *Power and Policy in the U.S.S.R.: The Study of Soviet Dynastics.* New York: St. Martins.

DANIELS, ROBERT V. (editor) 1960 *A Documentary History of Communism.* Edited, with an introduction, notes, and new translations. New York: Random House.

ENGELS, FRIEDRICH (1890) 1963 Preface to the German Edition of 1890. Pages 262–268 in Karl Marx and Friedrich Engels, *The Communist Manifesto.* Edited, with an introduction, explanatory notes and appendices by David Ryazanoff. New York: Russell.

FAINSOD, MERLE (1953) 1963 *How Russia Is Ruled.* Rev. ed. Russian Research Center Studies, No. 11. Cambridge, Mass.: Harvard Univ. Press.

FAINSOD, MERLE 1958 *Smolensk Under Soviet Rule.* Cambridge, Mass.: Harvard Univ. Press. → A paperback edition was published in 1963 by Random House.

FISCHER, LOUIS 1964 *The Life of Lenin.* New York: Harper.

HAZARD, JOHN N. (1957) 1964 *The Soviet System of Government.* 3d ed., rev. and enl. Univ. of Chicago Press.

History of the Communist Party of the Soviet Union. Edited by Andrew Rothstein (1959) 1960 Moscow: Foreign Languages Publishing House. → First published in Russian.

INKELES, ALEX; and BAUER, RAYMOND A. 1959 *The Soviet Citizen: Daily Life in a Totalitarian Society* . . . Russian Research Center Studies, No. 35. Cambridge, Mass.: Harvard Univ. Press.

KHRUSHCHEV, NIKITA S. 1963a Doklad (Speech). *Pravda* March 10:1–4. → Translation of extract in text provided by Merle Fainsod.

KHRUSHCHEV, NIKITA S. 1963b *Khrushchev Speaks: Selected Speeches, Articles and Press Conferences, 1949–1961.* Edited, with commentary, by Thomas P. Whitney. Ann Arbor: Univ. of Michigan Press.

KOMMUNISTICHESKAIA PARTIIA SOVETSKOGO SOIUZA [CPSU] 1962 *Soviet Communism: Programs and Rules, Official Texts of 1919, 1952, (1956), 1961.* Edited by Jan F. Triska. San Francisco: Chandler. → Contains documents first published in Russian.

LENIN, VLADIMIR I. (1902) 1961 What Is to Be Done? Volume 5, pages 347–529 in Vladimir I. Lenin, *Collected Works.* 4th ed. Moscow: Foreign Languages Publishing House. → First published as *Chto delat'?*

LENIN, VLADIMIR I. (1918) 1962 Doklad o deiatel'nosti soveta narodnykh komisarov (Report About the Activities of the Council of Peoples' Commissars). Volume 35, pages 261–279 in Vladimir I. Lenin, *Polnoe sobranie sochinenii* (Complete Works). Moscow: Gosudarstvennoe Izdatel'stvo Politicheskoi Literatury. → Translation of the extract in text provided by Merle Fainsod.

LENIN, VLADIMIR I. (1919) 1932 Vybory v uchreditel'noe sobranie i diktatura proletariata (Elections of the Constituent Assembly and Dictatorship of the Proletariat). Volume 29, pages 631–649 in Vladimir I. Lenin, *Sochineniia* (Works). 3d ed. Moscow: Partiinoe Izdatel'stvo. → Translation of extract in text provided by Merle Fainsod.

MEYER, ALFRED G. 1957 *Leninism.* Russian Research Center Studies, No. 26. Cambridge, Mass.: Harvard Univ. Press. → A paperback edition was published in 1962 by Praeger.

MOORE, BARRINGTON 1950 *Soviet Politics; The Dilemma of Power: The Role of Ideas in Social Change.* Russian Research Center Studies, No. 2. Cambridge, Mass.: Harvard Univ. Press.

PIPES, RICHARD (1954) 1964 *The Formation of the Soviet Union: Communism and Nationalism, 1917–1923.* Russian Research Center Studies, No. 13. Cambridge, Mass.: Harvard Univ. Press.

SCHAPIRO, LEONARD 1960 *The Communist Party of the Soviet Union.* New York: Random House.

STALIN, IOSIF (1924) 1954 The Foundations of Leninism. Pages 15–111 in Iosif Stalin, *Problems of Leninism.* Moscow: Foreign Languages Publishing House. → First published as "Ob osnovakh leninizma."

STALIN, IOSIF (1931) 1954 The Task of Business Executives. Pages 448–458 in Iosif Stalin, *Problems of Leninism.* Moscow: Foreign Languages Publishing House. → First published as "O zadachakh khoziaistvennikov"

TROTSKY, LEON 1904 *Nashi politicheskiia zadachi* (Our Political Tasks). Geneva: Rossiiskaia Sotsialdemokraticheskaia Rabochaia Partiia. → Translation of extract in text provided by Merle Fainsod.

TROTSKY, LEON (1931–1933) 1957 *The History of the*

Russian Revolution. Translated by Max Eastman. 3 vols. in 1. Ann Arbor: Univ. of Michigan Press. → Volume 1: *The Overthrow of Tsarism.* Volume 2: *The Attempted Counter-revolution.* Volume 3: *The Triumph of the Soviets.* → First published in Russian.

ULAM, ADAM B. 1960 *The Unfinished Revolution: An Essay on the Sources of Influence of Marxism and Communism.* New York: Random House.

ULAM, ADAM B. 1965 *The Bolsheviks.* New York: Macmillan.

WOLFE, BERTRAM D. (1948) 1964 *Three Who Made a Revolution: A Biographical History.* 4th rev. ed. New York: Dial Press.

II

NATIONAL COMMUNISM

The term "national communism" has been loosely used to describe certain modern political systems and ideologies. The term has been applied, for instance, to indigenous forms of communism, as represented by individual national parties in or out of power; to national variations of communism, representing adaptations of a single ideology to different national settings, with or without the assertion of national autonomy in policy determination; to defiance of supranational or foreign communist guidance on the part of a communist party or government; and to the upsurge of nationalist sentiments within a communist framework, whether directed against a communist or noncommunist external foe.

Despite this wide range of meanings and the lack of precise content and notwithstanding the absence of a systematic doctrine of national communism, two aspects appear to constitute the core of the term, as it is commonly used: (1) independence from outside control—notably, from the Soviet state and its ruling party; and (2) national distinctiveness of significant aspects of ideology, social institutions, or political strategy.

Historically, the primary content of national communism has been the effort to shake or reduce Soviet control, or hegemony, over other communist parties and states. With the increasing fragmentation of world communism, its various national units are bound to reflect the growing diversity of communism—as a political movement, as an ideology, and as a mode of political practice.

Historical development

National communism has arisen in situations where uncertainty has existed in regard to one or more of the following questions of communist theory and practice: (1) what is or should be the relation of class to nation and the relation of nationalism to internationalism? (2) is the belief in unilinear historical development and in "general laws" compatible with the support of "multiple paths" of revolutionary strategy and tactics? (3) are monolithic party unity and centralist discipline compatible with permissiveness regarding national diversities?

The early period.   Lenin accepted the Marxist view of nationalism and the nation-state as manifestations of the capitalist era, and he shared the Marxist belief in the future evanescence of national differences and antagonisms. But he came to recognize the revolutionary potential of national aspirations. Precisely this recognition has been at the root of the dual Soviet approach to nationalism—an effort to use it for their own ends but also a fear of being used by it; a vigorous endeavor to harness nationalism abroad against common foes (notably "imperialism") but also a firm though differentiated hostility to manifestations of nationalism as a divisive force within the Soviet Union and within the international communist movement.

The Leninist "concession" to national sentiment—a shrewd, tactical exception to the Bolshevik impulse toward centralization—aroused severe criticism from the extreme "left" even prior to the Russian Revolution. It equally failed to satisfy those non-Russian communists who, after the Soviet state was established, demanded greater self-determination or actual autonomy than Moscow permitted (e.g., parts of the Ukrainian and Georgian communist elites during the early years of Soviet rule: Pipes 1954). Their protests may be considered precursors of national communism.

The emergence of the Soviet Union as the sole communist state and of its party as the sole ruling one was bound to lead to a subordination of "proletarian internationalism" to Soviet state interests, as interpreted by the Soviet leaders. The stage for this development was set in Lenin's day with the "21 conditions" of the Comintern and the subsequent Bolshevization of the International. A variety of foreign communists protested, left, or were expelled, precisely because at some point they clashed with the Soviet striving for hegemony. Some went on to establish national communist groups or parties in their own countries (Borkenau 1938; Dallin 1962).

For the communist opponents, domestic and foreign, of Moscow's hegemonial tendencies and of Stalinism, national enmity was but one of many elements in their opposition, and usually a subordinate or even insignificant one. Then, as later, many of them had no opportunity to organize or express their hostility, because they lacked an autonomous power base. By the same token, the mere existence of nation-states and the establishment of communist parties within their boundaries were to provide a framework for the expression and organization of intracommunist opposition to Stalinism—regardless of the presence or intensity of specifically national ingredients.

The term "national communism" seems first to have appeared in connection with two phenomena which, unlike the above conflicts between national and communist impulses, stemmed from efforts to find a basis for joint action of communist and nationalist forces against a common foe. In the West this foe was the "Versailles system," and the endeavors were antiliberal, anti-British and anti-French. In Asia the foe was the colonial system, and the efforts were anti-imperialist.

In the confusion of German radical politics after 1918, some extremists of the left sought an alliance or an ideological amalgam with nationalist, right-wing extremists. At the same time, some militarists and nationalists, hardheaded or romantic, explored the possibilities of a national communist movement. While the label commonly attached to these explorations is "national Bolshevism," "national communism" was the name given in 1919 to a Hamburg group and also the title of a book (published in Munich in 1920) that characterized national communism as "Germany's bulwark against East and West." The notion of a united national communist party was discussed until 1933 —but without significant political results. The communists made no serious overtures to these groups (Schüddekopf 1960; Paetel 1965).

World War II and its aftermath.   World War II changed the nature of and the conditions for national communism. The dissolution of the Communist International in 1943, while a formality, made the communist parties in each country officially sovereign units, presumably free to interpret the doctrine and determine their own policies. War conditions also helped to crystallize national feelings (particularly under enemy occupation, e.g., in France, Yugoslavia, China). Hence, there ensued a series of partly opportunistic communist moves to identify their goals and values with national themes and purposes. Also, at the end of the war the foundations were laid for the establishment of communist regimes in some ten countries and thereby for the creation of a communist international system in eastern Europe and in east Asia.

Until 1947 Stalin gave evidence of approving of indigenous—i.e., national—variations in the states that had come under communist control. Largely because of their weak positions, communist leaders in eastern Europe felt compelled to stress national themes, and Moscow often made them "go slow" with radical reforms and deal gently with much-needed allies. These concessions were part of a "rightist" policy, which Moscow had always meant to be temporary and in fact substantially reversed in 1947 and 1948. The first years after the communist take-over likewise saw a substantial dose of what has been called "domesticism" (Brzezinski 1960). That is, priority was often given to domestic needs and interests by otherwise loyal pro-Moscow leaders who did not wish to sacrifice or jeopardize the broader needs and interests of world communism. On the whole, party leaders who had been put into power thanks to Soviet force and political pressure tended to follow Moscow's lead—as did the parties out of power.

Different conditions obtained in those few states where communists came to power substantially on their own: Yugoslavia, Albania, China, and at a later date North Vietnam and Cuba. Those regimes, however unpopular, had a broader, more truly national base of support than did communist regimes in the countries where the authority of local communist elites was established by the Soviet Union (Lowenthal 1964). Moreover, the local elites of such self-established regimes were conscious of their relatively autonomous position and were prepared to assert it. None of them initiated a break with the Soviet Union, but in the first dramatic contest of wills, Marshal Tito in 1948 responded to the Soviet challenge by defying requests that would have spelled increasing Soviet domination. While the dispute was not fundamentally due to Yugoslav nationalism—in fact, until 1948, the incorporation of Yugoslavia into an expanded Soviet Union was given serious thought—Tito was prepared to turn his proud patriotism against Moscow. As he wrote the Soviet leaders, no matter how much communists of other countries loved the Soviet Union, the land of socialism, they could in no case love their own country less (*Soviet–Yugoslav Dispute* 1948, p. 19).

After Stalin.   The general relaxation of controls at the center of Soviet power, which set in after Stalin's death in 1953, inevitably provided an opportunity for the assertion of greater authority and initiative by the other member states of the communist bloc. The following decade was to see a remarkable though uneven slipping of Soviet authority and control and, thus, a far-reaching assertion of national sovereignty by the various communist parties and regimes.

In the previous phase the official motif had been to make each communist country a little replica of the Soviet Union. Now the reaction against the centralism of the Stalinist era brought greater recognition of national diversities. Indeed, Moscow could scarcely deny its loyal allies and dependents in eastern Europe what it was prepared to grant renegade Yugoslavia. In the course of its reconciliation with Tito, the Soviet government in 1955 pledged to be guided on ideological, economic, and political questions by a policy of noninterference in internal affairs, saying that matters of internal organization and differences of social systems and of concrete forms of building socialism were exclusively the affairs of the individual countries. During the following 18 months other declarations went even further. But uncertainty about the limits of Soviet tolerance helped set the stage for the crises in Poland and Hungary in 1956. Here there were, for the first time, overt nationalist components in the outlook and motives of some of the protagonists.

The consolidation which followed proved to be temporary and largely formal. Soviet efforts to meet part way the anti-Soviet nationalism of foreign communists probably stimulated it even further. In effect, Moscow failed to provide a formula that could both satisfy the nationalist demands of the other communist regimes and assure its own continued control.

The weakening of Soviet authority among communist parties and states contributed to the eruption of the Sino–Soviet dispute, which in turn weakened Soviet prestige even more. The dispute bared the conflicting content of national interests, as interpreted by various communist elites, and it undermined confidence in the wisdom and leadership of both China and the Soviet Union. In over thirty countries communist parties split and rival organizations emerged, many of which turned against Soviet leadership and some against the Chinese as well. The Sino–Soviet rift dramatized the evanescence of the single, universal communist perspective: thereby it made each communist party "national." It provided opportunities for other states either to defy Soviet leadership and survive even when expelled from the fold (as in the case of Albania) or to tacitly and gradually pursue policies sharply at variance with those of other communist states without formal rupture or rebuke, as in the case of Rumania.

Rumania, in particular, provided evidence that a state at the borders of the Soviet Union and seemingly dependent on it could resist pressures for economic integration and coordination (Montias 1964), could undo a variety of measures that it considered cultural and political "Russification," and could have the central committee of its communist party resolve in 1964 that the sovereignty of the socialist state requires that it effectively and fully hold in its hands all the levers of economic and social life; that transmitting such levers to the competence of a superstate or extra-state bodies would make of sovereignty an idea without content; that there are not and cannot be unique patterns and recipes; and that no one can decide what is and what is not correct for other countries or parties.

Meanwhile, the cases of Kerala and Cuba had shown that communist movements could triumph without significant Soviet support and establish national communist regimes at a considerable distance from the Soviet bloc.

The national ingredient

The specific weight of national components in the national communist amalgam has been a source of recurring perplexity. There are no sure criteria or methods by which to assess them. The problem is further complicated by the confusion regarding the definition of "nationalism." It is important to note that the term "national" need not mean "nationalist" but may merely be descriptive of a nation-state serving as the vehicle of a political system. In common modern usage, "nationalism" is also taken to have an oppositional affective content, expressing an "anti" feeling—against a colonial power, against a rival nationalism, or against a supranational movement.

It is useful to distinguish between national factors antedating the communist experience and those identified with it. The earlier factors, which may re-emerge or reassert themselves under communist rule, include historical enmities (e.g., Polish–Russian, Russian–Chinese, Slavic–German), ethnic minority problems (e.g., in Czechoslovakia, China, Poland, Rumania), territorial conflicts and irredentism (e.g., Macedonia, the Soviet Maritime Territory, Bessarabia, Cieszyn, Trieste). Many of these factors have clearly reappeared and added to tensions (e.g., in the case of Rumania and Russia), but nowhere have they determined whether relations between two parties or states improve or worsen. Soviet relations with Hungary and Poland improved considerably after 1956 despite traditional enmity. Generally, traditional national conflicts appear to be vital only when they are exacerbated by fresh and more sensitive tensions (e.g., in the case of Yugoslavia and Albania).

As for the new elements introduced by the experience with communism, resentment of the Soviet treatment of foreign parties, especially during the Stalin era, was the obvious price Moscow had to pay for its various offenses to national pride, its economic exploitation, its clandestine surveillance, and its peremptory dictation of general domestic and foreign policy and even specific economic decisions in the satellite states.

In turn, the recognition of multiple "paths" in the pursuit of communism and the lessening of Soviet controls in the post-Stalin era stimulated the assertion of national consciousness and distinctiveness in these countries.

The shift of economic policy from making each communist state an autarkic replica of the Soviet model to (at least theoretically) a division of labor among the states involved implied a recognition of significant variations from country to country and approval of them by the Soviet Union.

Attempts at coordinating policies and ideological postures within the bloc have created new conflicts of interest, most visible in the economic sphere, where they have evoked a reassertion of national sovereignty in response to attempts at supranational integration or the national policies of other communist states (e.g., the relations of Rumania with Czechoslovakia and East Germany).

In the Stalin era there was little evidence of genuine nationalism among the ruling cadres of communist parties. The leadership in eastern Europe was, after all, overwhelmingly composed of Moscow-trained and Moscow-oriented "internationalists" dependent on Soviet power rather than responsive to popular will or sentiments. Significant exceptions to this pattern were those communist regimes which came to power substantially without foreign assistance, specifically Yugoslavia, China, and Albania.

By contrast, among the greater range of diverse communist types which have emerged, even in eastern Europe, since 1956, some may be considered not merely national in form but also nationalist in content. It has been observed that any regime, in order to remain in power, will sooner or later seek to identify itself with the defense of traditional interests and values of the country it claims to rule. Moreover, the gradual devolution of decision making from Moscow to the indigenous communist leadership prompted a "nativization" in each individual instance, including a greater sensitivity to national opinion and sentiment. Here was an opportunity to forge a unity of support on a broader, more truly national base than had previously been possible for communist regimes (e.g., in Poland, Hungary, Rumania). No doubt the result has been a growth of "true" nationalism among communist cadres (Shoup 1962).

At the same time, it is well to consider the deceptiveness of appearances with respect to nationalism. Much of "Titoist revisionism" is national only in the sense that it was introduced within the framework of the Yugoslav nation-state: it was not uniquely or specifically Yugoslav. The Soviet Union and other communist states did actually adopt a number of "Titoist" doctrines and policies at a later date. Similarly, all communist regimes and parties (e.g., China) have repeatedly shifted from "right" to "left" communism and back: neither posture can be considered distinctively national, although any specific decision to make such a shift may be determined by national considerations.

Asian communism. In the contest between communism and nationalism neither has swallowed the other. Modern nationalism has, even in the West, proved to be far more compatible with communism than had been surmised by either its friends or its enemies. There is evidence that communism has proved to have a particularly strong appeal for ethnic minorities suffering from national and socioeconomic discrimination. With due allowance for situational differences, this has been true both in eastern Europe (Burks 1961) and in Asia (Zagoria 1965).

It is commonly assumed that among the variants of modern communism a place of special importance is occupied by what may be called non-Western communism. One of its main characteristics is supposed to be the fusion of national and revolutionary objectives, since the communists themselves became the carriers of "national liberation." But the evidence suggests that this is not really a distinctively non-Western or Asian phenomenon.

Both in social composition—an intelligentsia leadership and a peasant mass—and in national appeal there are significant parallels between communist parties in eastern Europe and those in certain Middle Eastern, south Asian and Far Eastern countries. Compared with the "proletarian" mass parties of the West (such as the French or Italian), the "national-revolutionary" parties do, however, exhibit some distinguishing features. A number of them are characterized by a lack of discipline, ideological vagueness, espousal of voluntarism, and a proclivity for factionalism and "direct action."

While Asian communism may prominently feature an anti-Western animus combined with a commitment to modernization, it does not follow, as has been argued by some scholars, that the nationalist content has displaced the communist or that communism is merely a form of or a façade for nationalism (Kautsky 1962; Johnson 1962). While many of the non-Western parties have given prominent recognition to the national factor and made themselves spokesmen for the national cause, the specific models advocated and the strategies pursued by them have not necessarily been reflective of particularities in their national situation or heritage.

For a long time, the spokesmen for the priority (or even the propriety) of a distinctive anticolonial, non-Western model of communism were losers in the international movement. While some, like Sultangaliev, regarded industrial society itself as the enemy of the colonial peoples (Bennigsen 1960), others, like M. N. Roy in India and Tan Malaka in Java, ultimately broke with the Communist International and attempted to organize national communist movements of their own.

With the rise of Mao Tse-tung to the leadership of Chinese communism, the adaptation ("Sinification") of the common creed became more explicit and in turn was rapidly elevated into a model for other non-Western peoples to emulate in their struggle against "imperialism" (Schram 1963; Barnett 1963; Scalapino 1965). In other cases elements of Marxist–Leninist theory have been eclectically combined with national, tribal, or racial ideological ingredients into novel and not always viable amalgams, which have been labeled "syncreto-Marxism" (Feuer 1964).

All elements of the communist movement have recognized the growing potency of nationalism. The Soviet Union and the parties identified with its policies have aimed at alliances with national movements, hopeful of converting, subverting, or exploiting them on the road to power, without necessarily insisting on communist hegemony in the alliance. The Chinese communists developed at an early date a strategy of appropriating the nationalist content and subordinating the nationalist allies to themselves. In both instances there remain considerable uncertainties in the application of general strategic prescriptions. While the Soviet approach has permitted greater flexibility in communist alliance strategy, far greater successes have thus far been registered where the communists have themselves appropriated the national cause.

The substantive differences among the national components of international communism cannot even be adumbrated here: they range from explicit doctrinal and strategic variations to unarticulated divergencies in values and style. Suffice it to say that the extent or direction of a given party's "particularity" on one issue need not correspond to its position on any other issue. The categories of national differentiation do not coincide at all

with the classification according to degree of freedom from Soviet control (Skilling 1964, p. 36).

No single formula will account for the way in which various national communist parties have lined up on any particular issue. Some communist analysts have correctly identified certain factors without trying to assess their specific weight in individual instances: differences in "objective conditions" and historical and cultural traditions, in geographic situation and political circumstances, and in levels of socioeconomic development. Among additional factors, particularities in the history of a given communist party, its relations with Moscow, and the characteristics of its leadership should be listed. All in all, the divergent perception of national needs goes far toward explaining the outlooks and policies pursued by the individual parties.

Theory and ideology

Communist formulations regarding national communism, national "particularities," and "separate paths" in the pursuit of socialism and communism have invariably followed political zigzags. This has been as true of Soviet pronouncements as of those from Yugoslavia or China. While there has no doubt been a strong urge to find basic principles and consistent doctrinal formulas on these subjects, communist pronouncements have actually amounted to little more than post-factum legitimations of reality.

In the post-Stalin era, Soviet arguments have been consistent in rejecting the whole notion of national communism as nonsensical (for, by definition, communism must be internationalist) and in acknowledging that, while there are certain universal laws or "regularities" governing societal and political change, certain national particularities exist because of objective conditions in a given country. The limits of proper national distinctiveness, however, have remained appropriately vague and flexible. They do leave Moscow considerable discretion in determining what, in any given case, is to be deemed orthodox or deviant.

The most clear-cut Soviet generalization was formulated in terms of priorities. Soviet officials reportedly told Italian communists in 1957 that they condemned national communism, "not because it seeks out national particularities, but because it affirms on the theoretical level that national particularities are more important than general laws" (Kogan 1958, p. 662). In practice the situation has rarely been so clear-cut. Soviet writers have been quick to label national communism a major "weapon" of imperialism, an expression of petty-bourgeois narrowness or "bourgeois nationalism." Until 1961 it was considered a "rightist" phenomenon, i.e., a facet of revisionism. Since then, Soviet and pro-Soviet writers have argued that the Albanian and later the Chinese case have shown that a "nationalist" line can also be part of a militant, "pseudoleftist" communist posture (Moscow, Akademiia Obshchestvennykh Nauk 1960; Akademiia Nauk SSSR 1964).

Among non-Soviet communists, Yugoslav political scientists went furthest of all in systematizing their own views, but their theorizing, too, tended to follow political developments. From 1950 to 1952 they did explore similarities between Stalinism and fascism, the existence of "state capitalism" in the Soviet Union, and the persistence of the national problem even after the communists came to power. While the hostile analysis of Soviet conditions was soon toned down, the new program of the League of Yugoslav Communists developed a number of doctrinal pronouncements which were at variance with Moscow's views, e.g., that the uneven development of socialism and the wide diversity of its paths and forms produce a number of internal contradictions; that the state may turn into a factor of stagnation; that there is, in effect, no two-camp dichotomy in international affairs; and that as long as nations exist, communism must remain within the beneficent framework of a system of nation-states (Savez Komunista Jugoslavije 1958). The Yugoslav communists remained committed to proletarian internationalism—as they saw it—and continued to condemn national communism (Hoffman & Neal 1962).

Since 1956 the Italian communists have played a leading role in encouraging the autonomy of all communist parties. It is significant that in his last statement to the Soviet leadership, in 1964, Palmiro Togliatti chose to dwell on the revival of nationalism in the "bloc" as one of the forms of centrifugal tendencies there. He reiterated what Tito had stated earlier:

The national sentiment remains a permanent factor in the working class and socialist movement for a long period, also, after the conquest of power. Economic progress does not dispel this; it nurtures it. Thus in the socialist camp, too, one needs perhaps . . . to be on one's guard against the forced exterior uniformity and one must consider that the unity one seeks to establish and maintain must lie in the diversity and full autonomy of the individual countries. (Togliatti 1964, p. 80)

But it was not so much the verbal pronouncements that mattered, although even here subtle semantic nuances spelled significant political divergencies. Perhaps the one fraught with greatest potential for conflict was between those who seemed to accept national variations as a permanent fact, to which communism must adjust, and those who saw the nationalist gambit as a reluctant strategy, to be jettisoned when no longer needed. Echoes of both lines may still be heard.

To what extent is the Soviet experience mandatory or significant for other communist parties? Since 1954 Moscow has been inconsistent or vague on this matter, while the other parties have increasingly felt free to ignore the Soviet model in principle and in practice. In the early years after the Russian Revolution, those in the West who rejected it (e.g., Rosa Luxemburg, Paul Levi, and Hermann Remmele) found themselves in open conflict with Moscow; more recently, however, not only Yugoslav but also Italian, Polish, Swedish, and other communists have been able to assert, while remaining loyally on the Soviet side, that the Russian record, that of a lone socialist country, industrially backward, experiencing rapid modernization (as well as Stalinism) under special conditions, was too exceptional to constitute a model for other societies. The Chinese communists and their allies have likewise rejected the Soviet model of seizing and using power, claiming that it is irrelevant for the underdeveloped and non-Western parts of the world.

In summary, then, national communism must be considered a transitional phenomenon, not a stable sociopolitical system, because both the national and the communist elements in the twin formulas are susceptible to various meanings; because either may be real or a façade; and because either may prevail over the other. National communism emerged in the context of two broad processes: (1) the linkage of national and social revolutions; and (2) the disintegration of "monolithic" world communism, which precipitated in its wake an increasing variety of communist experience, ideology, doctrine, and conduct.

The content and nature of national communism have changed over time and have become more varied. Basically, the term "national communism" remains a misnomer, for it gives a single label to a variety of significantly diverse phenomena. But, however defined or delimited, national communism would appear to belie the conventional image of communism as a monolithic phenomenon, invariably possessed by universalist aspirations. Many, although not all, national communist states and parties are content to seek limited objectives, involving less than total control at home and limited ambitions abroad.

While by no means all national communism reflects true nationalism, nationalist feelings have also been growing in communist ranks. With the rise of a new generation of communist leaders everywhere, the future elites are more likely to find it important to respond to national sentiments than their elders did. The "nationalization" of communism may lend it greater appeal and authority; it has already, almost universally, freed the parties from some of the earlier odium of being "agents of a foreign power." But it also opens up the parties to gradual transformations. It would be foolish to predict whether, in the end, national communism will strengthen communism as a political force or help to destroy it.

ALEXANDER DALLIN

[*Directly related are the entries* NATION *and* NATIONALISM. *Other relevant material may be found in* CHINESE SOCIETY; ECONOMIC DATA; PLANNING, ECONOMIC; *and in the biography of* LUXEMBURG.]

BIBLIOGRAPHY

AKADEMIIA NAUK SSSR, INSTITUT MIROVOI EKONOMIKI I MEZHDUNARODNYKH OTNOSHENII (1964) 1965 *Mezhdunarodnoe revoliutsionnoe dvizhenie rabochego klassa* (The International Revolutionary Movement of the Working Class). 2d ed. Edited by Boris Ponomarev. Moscow: Izdatel'stvo Politicheskoi Literatury.

BARNETT, A. DOAK (editor) 1963 *Communist Strategies in Asia: A Comparative Analysis of Government and Parties.* New York: Praeger.

BENNIGSSEN, ALEXANDRE; and QUELQUEJAY, CHANTAL 1960 *Les mouvements nationaux chez les Musulmans de Russie.* Paris, École Pratique de Hautes Études, Section des Sciences Économiques et Sociales, Société et Idéologies, Série 2: Documents et témoignages, No. 3. Paris: Mouton.

BLACK, CYRIL E.; and THORNTON, THOMAS P. (editors) 1964 *Communism and Revolution: The Strategic Uses of Political Violence.* Princeton Univ. Press.

BOERSNER, DEMETRIO 1957 *The Bolsheviks and the National and Colonial Question: 1917–1928.* Geneva: Droz.

BORKENAU, FRANZ (1938) 1962 *World Communism: A History of the Communist International.* Ann Arbor: Univ. of Michigan Press. → First published as *The Communist International.*

BRZEZINSKI, ZBIGNIEW K. (1960) 1961 *The Soviet Bloc: Unity and Conflict.* Rev. ed. New York: Praeger.

BURKS, RICHARD V. 1961 *The Dynamics of Communism in Eastern Europe.* Princeton Univ. Press.

DALLIN, ALEXANDER 1962 The Use of International Movements. Pages 311–349 in Conference on a Century of Russian Foreign Policy, Yale University, 1961, *Russian Foreign Policy.* Edited by Ivo J. Lederer. New Haven: Yale Univ. Press.

FEUER, LEWIS S. 1964 Marxisms: How Many? *Problems of Communism* 13, no. 2:48–57.

HALPERIN, ERNST (1957) 1958 *The Triumphant Heretic: Tito's Struggle Against Stalin.* London: Heinemann. → First published as *Der siegreiche Ketzer: Titos Kampf gegen Stalin.*

HARRISON, SELIG S. 1960 *India: The Most Dangerous Decades.* Princeton Univ. Press.

HOFFMAN, GEORGE W.; and NEAL, FRED W. 1962 *Yugoslavia and the New Communism.* New York: Twentieth Century Fund.

JOHNSON, CHALMERS A. 1962 *Peasant Nationalism and Communist Power: The Emergence of Revolutionary China.* Stanford Univ. Press.

KAUTSKY, JOHN H. (editor) 1962 *Political Change in Underdeveloped Countries: Nationalism and Communism.* New York: Wiley.

KOGAN, NORMAN 1958 National Communism vs. the National Way to Communism: An Italian Interpretation. *Western Political Quarterly* 11:660–672.

LIU SHAO-CH'I (1948) 1952 *Internationalism and Nationalism.* 3d ed. Peking: Foreign Languages Press.

LOWENTHAL, RICHARD 1964 *World Communism: The Disintegration of a Secular Faith.* Oxford Univ. Press.

MONTIAS, JOHN M. 1964 Background and Origins of the Rumanian Dispute With Comecon. *Soviet Studies* 16:125–151.

MORRIS, BERNARD 1959 Soviet Policy Toward National Communism: The Limits of Diversity. *American Political Science Review* 53:128–137.

MOSCOW, AKADEMIIA OBSHCHESTVENNYKH NAUK 1960 *Obshchie zakonomernosti perekhoda k sotsializmu i osobennosti ikh proiavleniia v raznykh stranakh* (The General Laws of Transition to Socialism and the Particulars of Their Manifestation in Various Countries). Moscow: Izdatel'stvo Vysshei Partiinoi Shkoly.

NAGY, IMRE 1957 *On Communism: In Defense of the New Course.* New York: Praeger.

PAETEL, KARL O. 1965 *Versuchung oder Chance?* Göttingen (Germany): Musterschmidt.

PIPES, RICHARD (1954) 1964 *The Formation of the Soviet Union: Communism and Nationalism, 1917–1923.* Rev. ed. Russian Research Center Studies, No. 13. Cambridge, Mass.: Harvard Univ. Press.

PIPES, RICHARD 1963 Nationalism and Nationality. Pages 69–85 in Leonard B. Schapiro and Albert Boiter (editors), *The U.S.S.R. and the Future: An Analysis of the New Program of the CPSU.* New York: Praeger.

SAVEZ KOMUNISTA JUGOSLAVIJE, 7TH KONGRES, LJUBLJANA 1958 *Programme of the League of Yugoslav Communists.* Belgrade: Edition Jugoslavija.

SCALAPINO, ROBERT (editor) 1965 *The Communist Revolution in Asia: Tactics, Goals, and Achievements.* Englewood Cliffs, N.J.: Prentice-Hall.

SCHRAM, STUART R. 1963 *The Political Thought of Mao Tse-tung.* New York: Praeger.

SCHÜDDEKOPF, OTTO E. 1960 *Linke Leute von Rechts: Die nationalrevolutionären Minderheiten und der Kommunismus in der Weimarer Republik.* Stuttgart (Germany): Kohlhammer.

SHOUP, PAUL 1962 Communism, Nationalism and the Growth of the Communist Community of Nations After World War II. *American Political Science Review* 56:886–898.

SKILLING, H. GORDON 1964 *Communism, National and International: Eastern Europe After Stalin.* Univ. of Toronto Press.

The Soviet–Yugoslav Dispute: Text of the Published Correspondence. 1948 London: Royal Institute of International Affairs.

TOGLIATTI, PALMIRO 1964 Memorandum. Partito Comunista Italiano, *Foreign Bulletin of the Italian Communist Party* [1964] no. 5:67–80.

VRANICKI, PREDRAG 1961 *Historija marksizma.* Zagreb (Yugoslavia): "Naprijed."

ZAGORIA, DONALD S. 1965 Communism in Asia. *Commentary* 39, no. 2:53–58.

ZINNER, PAUL (editor) 1956 *National Communism and Popular Revolt in Eastern Europe: A Selection of Documents on Events in Poland and Hungary, February–November, 1956.* New York: Columbia Univ. Press.

III

THE INTERNATIONAL MOVEMENT

All political movements have been subject to change; the international communist movement is no exception. While the nature and thrust of world communism appeared unchanged and uncompromising in the light of hostile cold-war attitudes, its revolutionary ideology, strategic objectives, and organizational concepts have, nevertheless, not remained static. The debates in the international communist movement touched off by the Sino–Soviet dispute, which developed in the late 1950s, dramatically exposed the division over policy and orientation in the movement and marked a watershed in its history.

The emergence of change is often obscured by the tendency of language to lag behind deed. In political affairs deviation from some principle is customarily accompanied by reaffirmation of that very principle; in the communist world no leader is yet willing, explicitly, to acknowledge the attenuated revolutionary possibilities of the Communist parties or to cast doubt on the proposition that communism will replace capitalism. Like other political movements, however, communism has responded to changes in the environment and bowed to necessity. Beginning in 1918 with the goal of world revolution and with Soviet Russia as but one component of the international movement, international communism was turned inside out to become merely one of the instrumentalities of Soviet diplomacy, while Soviet Russia came to be regarded as the incarnation of the movement. In the post-1945 era, to an extent as yet unclear, this inverted relationship was again upset, altering the priority of loyalties and the structure and orientation of world communism.

International communism between the wars

Communism as an international movement, considered in organizational terms, is a product of Lenin's concept of party organization and the particular direction given the concept by Stalin's policies. Lenin's motives in creating a new organization were to pre-empt the mantle of international revolutionary Marxism before the European Social Democrats could re-establish their authority after World War I, and to create the instruments for a seizure of power, particularly in western Europe, to insure the survival of the Bolshevik revolution. The last point may strike the contemporary reader as incongruous, but the Bolshevik leaders of the time suffered a double insecurity. Having seized power in a backward country, they looked to revolution, notably in Germany, to provide the technical wherewithal for the transformation of their own society. They also feared, not wrongly, that in isolation Russia would be exposed to assault from the capitalist countries. Lenin therefore attempted to fashion a revolutionary international instrument modeled on his notion of the elitist party, ideologically pure, hierarchically organized, knit together into a single international party under strictest discipline, and dedicated to world revolution.

If the predisposition to conspiratorial Moscow-oriented organization was created by Lenin, the specific order of loyalties and behavior patterns was molded by Stalin. In Lenin's time—and perhaps till the end of the 1920s—the idea of the autonomous and fraternal character of the Communist parties still persisted, as did the preoccupation with internal, indigenous revolution. The failure of revolutionary attempts in Hungary, Germany, and, later, China and the general weakness of the Communist parties conditioned their acceptance of Soviet authority. In addition, the elimination of Trotsky, plus the successive purges of dissident elements, contributed to the weakening of the international revolutionary wing of the movement. In turn, Stalin exacted from the international movement precisely the same behavior he required internally, i.e., unquestioning obedience enforced by terror, purge, and intimidation. The role of the Communist parties was transformed, therefore, from one geared to their own requirements and prospects for revolution to one of supporting Soviet foreign and domestic policy. Whatever the line of Soviet policy, it was generalized for all parties and tactically adapted to the respective countries. Agility, flexibility, opportunism, and cynicism became hallmarks of communist political behavior. That the communist movement survived at all outside Russia is in the nature of a political miracle.

Nevertheless, if power is the criterion of success, communism as an international movement has vindicated Lenin's decision to break with the reformist Socialist (Second) International during World War I. While the parties of social democracy have been absorbed into the mainstream of Western industrial society, influencing it with ideas of social justice and often becoming indistinguishable from other political parties, international communism has become the most powerful international political movement of the modern world. From a haphazard union of left-wing groups and parties in 1919, it has become a movement that in 1964 could boast the allegiance of over 40 million Communists, united in some 90 parties, 12 of them holding the reins of state power (not including Cuba and Yugoslavia). For this, however, the movement has had to pay its own dialectical price; the very proliferation of communist states and important parties in Europe and Asia has introduced disintegrative tendencies into the movement whose outcome cannot yet be precisely foreseen. The international communist veneer has been pierced by the edge of national interest, which remains as much a feature of the communist as of the noncommunist world. The conflicting interests of the communist states have, in addition, created the necessary conditions for the emergence of the particularist interests of the Communist parties out of power and have been joined to the general trend away from Moscow domination and from centralization. These centrifugal forces spell the end of communism as an organized international movement in its Stalinist form.

The Third International. In its "ideal" Stalinist form, international communism was a global network of Communist parties bound by a common ideology, codified and interpreted by the Soviet center. "Proletarian internationalism" was the organizing principle of the movement, providing it with policy coordination and unity of action on the basis of unconditional support and subservience to the Soviet Union. Its structure and behavior patterns were shaped by the Communist (Third) International, or Comintern (1919–1943).

As its designation, the "Third International," suggests, the communist movement's antecedents were rooted in the earlier socialist movement, which had twice formed international organizations: the International Working Men's Association (1864–1876), subsequently referred to as the First International, and the Second (or Socialist) International (1889–1914).

Patterned on Lenin's organizational principles, the Comintern was a global extension of his concept of a Bolshevik party. Unlike the Second International, which was a loose federation of parties, the Comintern was specifically designed as an international Communist party in which each of the national parties constituted a section. Relations between the national units and headquarters were governed by the concept of "democratic centralism," adopted from the party usage that, in theory, provided for freedom of discussion and criticism (democratic) and absolute unity of action and purpose once decisions had been taken (centralism). By 1930, certainly, this pyramid of authority had been inverted; decisions were imposed on the parties by the Moscow center.

In sum, Russian domination of the Comintern, while not premeditated, became actual as a consequence of the success of the Russian Revolution—the only successful communist revolution between the wars. The organization, located perforce in Moscow, was dependent on the Russians for its staffing and financing. To paraphrase Trotsky's criticism of Lenin's concept of party organization, the organization of the Comintern took the place of the Comintern itself; the Soviet Communist party took the place of the organization; and finally the dictator took the place of the Soviet Communist party.

In its heyday, the Comintern developed an elaborate organizational network to bind the parties to it. Its executive committee played the role of an international staff translating the policies of the Soviet Politburo into programs for the international movement. The central committees of the national parties, in theory subordinate to their respective national congresses, were also subordinated to the executive committee, which was empowered to amend decisions of national congresses, pass on their programs, and expel individuals and, indeed, entire sections from the movement. Various Comintern "commissions" organized on a regional basis, supervised the activities of the parties, and such units as the International Liaison Department (OMS) were charged with the organization and operation of an international clandestine communications network, complete with undercover agents, facilities for forging documents, clandestine radio stations, etc. Supporting the Comintern were a number of special-purpose organizations or interest groups, such as the Youth International, some of which developed into "front" organizations to gain the support of those who did not wish to make the full commitment to communism. The executive committee itself, in expanded form, assumed the function of the world congresses, which met only twice after 1924 (in 1928 and 1935).

This complicated apparatus began to fall apart in the 1930s, first under the assault of the Nazis in Germany, where much of the plant and activity was centered, and then under the impact of Soviet collective-security policy, which required the Communist parties to cast off their conspiratorial and sectarian character in favor of cooperation with socialist and even bourgeois parties in antifascist fronts. By 1943, Stalin could abolish the Comintern as a gesture to his wartime allies without sacrificing anything of value. As for the Communist parties themselves, the calculation was that, schooled to loyalty over the years, they could be counted upon by Moscow without the insurance of formal organizational mechanisms.

Growth after World War II

World War II, however, decisively altered the shape of the international communist movement, changing its power structure and its operational mechanisms. Before the war, the movement had been essentially Western-oriented. It had looked for revolution in the advanced capitalist countries (except for abortive attempts in China in the 1920s), and whatever strength it had, had resided in the Western communist movements. With the breakdown of metropolitan control over the colonies during the war and their achievement of independence, Communist parties proliferated and grew throughout the world. The largest Communist party not in power developed in Indonesia, and influential parties appeared in Burma, India, Japan, the Philippines, Iraq, and Guatemala, in some cases backed up by guerrilla forces or significant labor movements. Soviet strategy was formulated and reformulated to meet the changed circumstances, playing now on the aspirations of the newly independent states and now on the potential of the local communist movements.

The seizure of power by the Chinese communists in 1949 and the establishment of the North Korean and North Vietnamese regimes transformed communism into an Asian power.

In eastern and central Europe communist revolutions were effected from outside and above. The Red Army and cadres loyal to Stalin imposed a revolution on those areas which the Allies had informally designated as part of the Soviet sphere of influence. Instead of the traditionally indirect exercise of power, organic control was introduced. Revolution by military conquest replaced the orthodox Marxian concept of indigenous proletarian revolution. This was the pattern for all countries except Albania and Yugoslavia, where the communists came to power more or less on their own, and Czechoslovakia, where a combination of political miscalculation on the part of the democrats, an aggressive policy pursued by the dominant Communist party, and a favorable international climate, resulted in a successful communist coup. By 1948, then, Poland, Hungary, Rumania, Bulgaria, Czechoslovakia, Albania, Yugoslavia, and East Germany had come under communist control.

In western Europe and, to some extent, in other parts of the West, the wartime alliance with the Soviet Union served to cover the Communist parties with a certain respectability and stimulate their growth. In France and Italy, where the communists had been active in the underground, parties of major importance emerged, claiming, in 1946, 850,000 and 2,300,000 members and polling 26 and 19 per cent of the popular vote respectively and dominating the trade-union movements of their countries. (In fact, with the inclusion of the Nenni socialists, who were then the communists' close allies, the Italian radical left polled 40 per cent.)

New circumstances did not, however, affect Stalin's method of dealing with these Communist parties; they were simply to be manipulated in support of Soviet policy. And, allowing for the expanded theater of Soviet operations in central and eastern Europe, Stalin's policy was again essentially isolationist, that is, focused on the area under his control. Priority of policy went to the rehabilitation of the Soviet Union, devastated by war, and consolidation of the central and eastern European states through social revolution under the aegis of a loyal Stalinist apparatus. The parties outside the communist-controlled orbit merely played a supporting role. In western Europe, they were used, not primarily to consolidate and increase their power, but to impede rehabilitation and rearmament. In Asia, they were employed in civil war and violence to weaken the rear, so to speak, of the western European countries and disrupt the transition of power to the nationalist regimes.

Strategy after World War II

The postwar strategy of the international communist movement falls into three slightly overlapping periods: the aggressive "forward" period associated with the Cominform; "peaceful coexistence," Stalin-style; and Khrushchev's era of "competitive coexistence," characterized by his emphasis on economic competition and the avoidance of war.

The "forward" period. The terms of reference for the communist movement during the first period were contained in the "two-camp" doctrine, which proclaimed a world divided between the Soviet Union, the communist countries and parties, and the national liberation movement, together with the scattered "peace" forces, on the one hand, and the "imperialist" United States and its allies, on the other. Strategically, the Communist parties were to disrupt the American policy of rehabilitating and rearming western Europe and to undermine the new nationalist regimes in Asia. Neither aspect of the strategy paid off: western Europe recovered phenomenally, while the Communist parties paid the price of opposition in decline of membership and influence. In Asia, where communist tactics took the form of civil war and violence, the revolts were broken or contained to the point where the Communist parties, beginning in 1950–1951, began to bid for a return to normal status.

The international organizational manifestation of the "forward" period was the Cominform, the Information Bureau of the Communist and Workers' Parties, established in September 1947. Composed of the Communist parties of the Soviet Union, Yugoslavia, Bulgaria, Hungary, Rumania, Poland, and Czechoslovakia (Albania, then a Yugoslav fief, was excluded), and the two mass parties of France and Italy, the Cominform was designed as an instrument of Soviet control to consolidate the new communist states and disrupt western Europe. As an organization of Communist parties, it bore little resemblance to the Comintern in membership or apparatus. If the Cominform had any potential for development as an effective communist international, it was nullified by the expulsion of Yugoslavia; that action, in effect, marked its demise. The visible evidence of the Cominform's existence was its weekly journal, *For a Lasting Peace, For a People's Democracy!* which purveyed the Soviet line to the international communist movement until the organization was dissolved on April 17, 1956.

Stalin's "peaceful coexistence." By 1950–1951, if not sooner, the "forward" policy had been played out. Tito had successfully defied Stalin. Western Europe was on the road to recovery and drawing together more closely in political and military agreement. The Communist parties had failed to undermine the governments of western Europe and, in their attempts to do so, had suffered losses in prestige, membership, and electoral support. In Asia, with the exception of Vietnam, violent tactics failed: the revolts in Indonesia, the Philippines, Burma, and Malaya were either crushed or contained; in India, limited guerrilla warfare was suppressed and contributed to the weakening of the Indian party's following. The fortunes of the Japanese Communist party, until 1950 quite promising, were reversed when it was forced into violent action, undoubtedly imposed on it to hamper logistical support for the American forces in Korea.

The failure of communist strategy was tacitly conceded in certain labyrinthine doctrinal pronouncements in connection with the nineteenth congress of the Communist party of the Soviet Union. The sharper edges were rubbed off the two-camp formula, and the Communist parties of western Europe were urged to adopt a more "national" position within their respective countries. Europe remained the chief geographical target of Soviet

diplomacy, and the broader tactical flexibility permitted the Communist parties was still couched in terms of a "united front from below" directed against American power on the Continent.

In Asia, the problem of the Communist parties under Stalin's broad direction was to reintegrate themselves into the normal political life of their respective countries. For the Philippine and Malayan parties, readjustment was painfully slow; in Burma, however, by 1956 the party had recouped to the point where the National United Front, a communist-dominated coalition, polled one-third of the popular vote. The Indian party's return to respectability was underscored by its electoral victory in Kerala, where it proceeded to organize the provincial government. The experience of the Indonesian party was unique. Although its revolt in Madiun in 1948 had been crushed, the party succeeded in rebuilding a substantial base of support to become the most powerful political organization within the country.

Khrushchev's "competitive coexistence." If Stalin's last move had been a relaxation of international policy, his successor, Nikita S. Khrushchev, steered the international communist movement on a new course whose direction came to be dictated more by events than by intention. Khrushchev's major pronouncements affecting the international movement were presented at the twentieth CPSU congress in February 1956. Surviving the vicissitudes of the ensuing years, they were reiterated at the party's 22d congress in October 1961, and incorporated into its new program: the "new communist manifesto." War between capitalist and communist states was officially proclaimed to be avoidable. Revising the Leninist doctrine on war, Khrushchev underwrote the orthodoxy of nonviolent communist activity as one of the "roads to power." Different roads to socialism were validated, bowing to the Yugoslavs, whom Khrushchev sought to bring back to the fold. This point, coupled with sanction for peaceful and parliamentary capture of power, gave the Communist parties a greater range of tactical flexibility. The denigration of Stalin, reiterated publicly at the 22d CPSU congress, reinforced the impression that the Communist parties were to be allowed their own choice of tactics.

Communist policy also experienced a dramatic shift in regard to the underdeveloped areas. Backed by personal diplomacy and relatively massive grants of aid and trade, the Soviet Union entered the former Western preserve as a new competitor. The newly independent countries and nationalist movements were accepted by and large as expressions of a progressive development deserving of communist support, whose aim was to insure, at the very least, anti-Western neutralism and, at best, ideological affinity. To complement Soviet diplomacy, the Communist parties, in their turn, gave open backing to nationalist leaders, such as Nehru, Sukarno, and Nasser. In the case of India, for example, the Communist party moved "right" through the political spectrum to support Nehru on all essential aspects of both his foreign and domestic policy. With the exception of certain countries closely linked to American security arrangements (e.g., Thailand), communist strategy in the underdeveloped areas became virtually a "united front from above."

The splintering of the communist movement

The shift in Soviet policy was the result of a number of factors. The death of Stalin in 1953 was the catalyst; the exercise of power and authority was totally invested in his person. Since succession of leadership and legitimization of authority had not been institutionalized in the Soviet system, Stalin's death opened the way to a scramble for power. Khrushchev was successful in neutralizing and eliminating his opponents partly because his bid for support capitalized on the revulsion against Stalinist practices. His turn in domestic policy was aimed at establishing a rule more responsive to the requirements of an advancing industrial society stripped of organized terror as "incentive" to performance and "normalized" in other respects as well.

Internationally, the Khrushchevite leadership came to terms with the realities of nuclear weapons systems and the resulting equilibrium of power between the United States and the Soviet Union by attempting to negotiate a *détente* with the United States. It also broke sharply with the Stalinist past in retooling its policy to win influence with the burgeoning nationalist regimes in the formerly Western-held colonial areas. The de-emphasis on violence as an instrument of policy and the endorsement of multiple roads to socialism in a bid to recapture Yugoslavia or to associate it more closely with world communism implied the tolerance of greater diversity and, with the attack on Stalin's method of rule, a greater degree of autonomy for the Communist parties. In effect, the shift was no less momentous than that of 1935, when the Comintern formally adopted a strategy of cooperation with leftist and bourgeois parties to support the Soviet policy of collective security against the fascist powers. Implicit in that strategy had been the more forthright identification of the Communist parties with the national interest of their countries and a wider measure of freedom in pursuit of allies. What was not at stake in 1935 was the authority of the Soviet leadership or the structure of the international movement.

The policy turn in 1956, however, took place in entirely different circumstances with regard to both the international environment and the structure of the communist movement itself. First and foremost, it did not reckon with the force of nationalism within the communist orbit and the aspiration for independent exercise of power by the leaders of the communist states. The successful Yugoslav resistance to Stalin's demands for complete subordination in 1948 foreshadowed the nationalist deviation. But the Yugoslav case was thought to be unique. Special circumstances—the indigenous conquest of power in a country not bordering on the Soviet Union—made the Yugoslav defection possible. In two other cases—China and Albania—such defection seemed theoretically possible, but was discounted by most Western observers on the grounds that these countries required economic support from, and protection by, the Soviet Union. Assertion of independence by the other communist countries was ruled out because of the Soviet military presence. Overlooked in this view were the operation of the irrational in politics and the subtle possibilities of extending the area of national decision making even within the framework of ultimate Soviet hegemony.

However that may be, the twentieth congress set off a sequence of events that almost led to the use of Soviet force to forestall the establishment of a more nationalist regime in Poland and did lead to its use in Hungary. These events underscored the intensity of anti-Soviet nationalism in eastern Europe and demonstrated to what extent the relationship between the east European communist states and the Soviet Union rested on sheer force. The challenge to Soviet authority spilled over the borders of eastern Europe, particularly to the Italian Communist party, whose leader, Palmiro Togliatti, questioned Khrushchev's analysis of Stalin's misdeeds, implying that something had gone basically wrong in the Soviet system as a whole. These events dramatized the urgency of finding a new organizing principle to preserve communism as a cohesive and united international movement. But the search for such a principle has been hopelessly complicated by China's bid for leadership in the international movement.

The Sino–Soviet controversy.   The Chinese communists never accepted Khrushchev's denigration of Stalin or his guidelines for world communism as expressed at the twentieth congress. Soviet solicitation of Chinese help in settling the disturbances in eastern Europe brought the Chinese into the process of decision making for the international movement at a crucial time. Chinese prestige reached a peak in November 1957, when the Chinese joined with the Russians in drafting a "declaration" of the twelve Communist parties (Yugoslavia declined); the declaration was designed to establish principles applicable to all countries developing a socialist society. With regard to the organization of the communist movement the declaration endorsed the dictum of proletarian internationalism, that is, loyalty to the Soviet Union. However, attempts at the November meeting to reestablish a formal international organization were rejected—the best illustration of weakening Soviet authority. A compromise was reached by designating bilateral exchanges and multilateral party meetings as the mechanism for ironing out differences and by launching a new international journal—*World Marxist Review: Problems of Peace and Socialism*, subsequently established in Prague under general Soviet editorship.

Containment of the centrifugal tendencies was of short duration, however; the deterioration of relations between the Soviet and Chinese communists split the international movement wide open. In retrospect it is ironic that it was the Chinese who insisted that the parties at the November meeting recognize the CPSU as the "head" of the communist camp. To the Chinese there was no contradiction between their willingness to exalt the CPSU as head of the movement and their proviso that policies prescribed for the movement meet with Chinese approval.

The Soviet–Chinese quarrel was compounded of differing national requirements and consequently differing views on international communist strategy. In most general terms, the Chinese have attacked the Soviet policy of peaceful coexistence geared to *détente* with the United States and the concomitant attenuation of uncompromising, revolutionary struggle by the Communist parties. The Chinese charge the Russians with subordinating the interests of the Communist parties and communist states, as well as those of the so-called national liberation movements in underdeveloped areas, to the Soviet policy of cooperation with the imperialists. The Chinese have been angered by the low level of economic assistance the Russians have provided them, by Soviet reneging on an agreement to help build China's nuclear capability, by the absence of strong support of their ambitions in Formosa, by Soviet criticism of their incursion

into India, and by other Soviet actions. They rejected Khrushchev's attacks on Stalin at the twentieth CPSU congress and again at the 22d congress as ill advised, his emphasis on peaceful transition to socialism as mistaken, his tolerance of revisionism of the Titoist variety as criminal, and his entire outlook as, in a word, disastrous to the communist movement.

The erosion of Soviet authority and control over the movement was dramatically revealed at the November 1960 meeting of 81 Communist parties in Moscow. Here the Russians attempted to call a halt to Chinese politicking against Khrushchev in the Communist parties and front organizations and to their support of Albania, which, suspicious of Khrushchev's *rapprochement* with Yugoslavia, had opted to defy Soviet policy. The Soviet attack took the form of a draft declaration binding the parties to accept the rule of democratic centralism—in this context, the majority opinion of Communist parties, which Khrushchev knew he could command. The declaration also explicitly banned "fractional" activity, that is, the Chinese attempt to win over parties or groups and individuals within parties. The Chinese refused to comply, stating that democratic centralism was a proper organizational principle *within* parties but not *between* them. The Chinese declaration of independence went beyond this by rejecting the time-honored custom of generalizing Soviet party statements for the communist movement. The Chinese insisted instead on the rule of unanimity in making international decisions, which implied their right to veto any decisions they found unpalatable. The final statement was a transparent compromise which left the question of authority open. So it remains.

The future of international communism

Unlike the Tito–Cominform split in 1948, the Soviet–Chinese split has resulted in the fractionalization of the international communist movement. Although the Yugoslav defection may be viewed historically as the harbinger of "polycentrism," or pluralization of the communist movement, that process was temporarily contained for a number of reasons. First of all, Stalin was in full command and did not hesitate to use purge and violence to prevent further eruptions. The communist states were too new and their leaders too insecure to challenge the Soviet leadership. Moreover, tension in world politics was at a high point and communist unity was an overriding concern. Finally, Yugoslavia did not have the magnetic attraction of China, a large country of potentially great power, with a special appeal for non-Europeans and for all those who were looking for a more dynamic policy.

Monolithism has succumbed to bicentricism. Nevertheless, the pattern of party alignments is still unclear. Those which have opted to support Peking, for instance, do not fall into a coherent pattern based on race, stage of political development, or type of leadership. However, a regional configuration does seem to be emerging; the communist states of North Korea and North Vietnam, together with the communist parties of Indonesia, Japan, Malaya, Burma, Thailand, and New Zealand, have backed Peking explicitly or, at the very least, implicitly by withholding support from Moscow on crucial issues. On the other hand, the Australian Communist party, whose problems do not differ significantly from those of the New Zealand party, has supported Moscow in spite of opposition from ranking leaders. The leadership of the Indian Communist party, also, has maintained traditional loyalties abetted by the Indian government, which imprisoned the pro-Peking radicals during the Sino–Indian border crisis. In addition, Peking has developed pockets of support throughout the world communist movement: dissident pro-Chinese groups came into existence rather early in Belgium, Brazil, Mexico, Peru, and Venezuela.

How far the fragmentation process will go is hard to say. Most of the Communist parties are observing their old habits of loyalty to Moscow. The dominant position in world communism is held by the Soviet Union, which, after all, is the traditional leader and a world power second only to the United States. Yet the Chinese defection appears, under present circumstances, permanent; Chinese inroads into Moscow's authority and control over the world movement are serious; and divisive forces in the movement seem to be growing stronger.

One of the by-products of the Sino–Soviet split has been the return of the movement to politics. Debate at the November 1960 meeting was wide open; parties have voted against Moscow or abstained; and individual communist leaders have taken it upon themselves to attempt to influence the decisions of the big parties. The Chinese communist lobby, by financial inducement, military support, propaganda, and cultivation of individual leaders, has contributed to a revival of independence within the movement. Rumania, for example, has capitalized on the situation by asserting its own national economic interests against Soviet-backed coordination of the Comecon countries. The Italian Communist party, sympathetic to Khrushchev's policy, has nevertheless used the controversy to further its own program of "structural reform," i.e., a policy of piecemeal socialism within the constitutional framework of Italian politics. To parties of some strength and influence within their respective countries, the circumstances offer considerable range and opportunity for improving their domestic fortunes without excessive interference from the center. For the smaller, more distant parties, whose existence depends on identification with a sharply defined revolutionary movement, there is little advantage to be gained from the disruption in the movement.

The coincidence of the erosion within the international communist movement and the emergence of radical nationalist movements in the underdeveloped areas suggests that a new dimension may be added to world communism. Symbolic testimony to this development was the presence of the ruling parties of Ghana, Guinea, and Mali as observers to the 22d congress. Leninist forms of organization and forced economic development seem to appeal to such parties, and though they may not favor integral association with the communist movement, they may nevertheless join in what might be called associative membership. Soviet–Chinese competition for their favor permits a looser arrangement than would have been possible at any time since 1928. Castro's position may be illustrative; since he declared himself a Marxist–Leninist and communist only after the Cuban revolution, his association with the international communist movement has been unique.

In sum, the Khrushchevian era in the Soviet Union represents a transition from Stalinism to a form of social organization whose features are still blurred. The international communist movement, changed in structure since the interwar period and beset by nationalist rivalries is similarly in a transitional phase. The vaunted unity of the communists, which, Stalin warned, should be safeguarded as the "apple of one's eye," has been shattered. What this will mean for the world at large still remains to be seen.

BERNARD S. MORRIS

BIBLIOGRAPHY

Indispensable for the history of the Communist International are the Comintern periodicals, Communist International *and* World News and Views, *published previously as* International Press Correspondence. *Selected documents on the Comintern appear in* Communist International 1956–1965. *International communist periodicals after World War II are* For a Lasting Peace, For a People's Democracy! (*Cominform journal, 1947–1956*) *and the current* World Marxist Review: Problems of Peace and Socialism. Peking Review *is a convenient source for documents on the Sino–Soviet dispute. The best single history of the Communist International is Borkenau 1938. The most substantial contemporary work on the early history of the Comintern is*

Carr 1951–1964. *A comprehensive survey of the communist movement with a useful bibliography is* Seton-Watson 1953. *Nollau 1959 contains an extensive description of the Comintern's organization. Information on international communism may be found in such regional surveys as* Schwartz 1951, Brimmel 1959, Laqueur 1956, Fischer 1948, *and* Draper 1960. *The leading book on the Sino–Soviet dispute is* Zagoria 1962. *Leading periodicals are* Survey: A Journal of Soviet and Eastern European Studies *and* Problems of Communism. *A comprehensive bibliography is* Hammond 1965.

BORKENAU, FRANZ (1938) 1962 *World Communism: A History of the Communist International.* Ann Arbor: Univ. of Michigan Press. → First published as *The Communist International.*

BRIMMEL, J. H. 1959 *Communism in South East Asia.* London and New York: Oxford Univ. Press.

CARR, EDWARD H. 1951–1964 *History of Soviet Russia.* 7 vols. New York: Macmillan. → See especially Volumes 1–3: *The Bolshevik Revolution, 1917–1923,* 1951–1953; and Volumes 5–7: *Socialism in One Country, 1924–1925,* 1958–1964.

Communist International. → Published simultaneously in Russian, French, English, and German from May 1919 to December 1940.

COMMUNIST INTERNATIONAL 1956–1965 *Communist International, 1919–1943: Documents.* 3 vols. Selected and edited by Jane Degras. London and New York: Oxford Univ. Press.

DRAPER, THEODORE 1960 *American Communism and Soviet Russia: The Formative Period.* New York: Viking.

FISCHER, RUTH 1948 *Stalin and German Communism: A Study of the Origins of the State Party.* Cambridge, Mass.: Harvard Univ. Press.

For a Lasting Peace, For a People's Democracy! → Published from November 1947 to April 1956.

HAMMOND, THOMAS T. (editor) 1965 *Soviet Foreign Relations and World Communism: A Selected Annotated Bibliography of 7,000 Books in 30 Languages.* Princeton Univ. Press.

LAQUEUR, WALTER Z. (1956) 1957 *Communism and Nationalism in the Middle East.* 2d ed. New York: Praeger.

NOLLAU, GÜNTHER (1959) 1961 *International Communism and World Revolution: History and Methods.* Translated by Victor Andersen. New York: Praeger. → First published as *Die Internationale: Wurzeln und Erscheinungsformen des proletarischen Internationalismus.*

Peking Review. → Published monthly since 1958.

Problems of Communism. → Published since 1952. Frequency varies.

SCHWARTZ, BENJAMIN I. 1951 *Chinese Communism and the Rise of Mao.* Cambridge, Mass.: Harvard Univ. Press.

SETON-WATSON, HUGH (1953) 1960 *From Lenin to Khrushchev.* 2d rev. & enl. ed. New York: Praeger.

Survey: A Journal of Soviet and Eastern European Studies (London). → Published monthly since 1956.

World Marxist Review: Problems of Peace and Socialism. → Published monthly since 1958.

World News and Views. → Published from 1921 to 1953. Until June 1938 published as *International Press Correspondence.*

ZAGORIA, DONALD S. 1962 *The Sino–Soviet Conflict, 1956–1961.* Princeton Univ. Press. → A paperback edition was published in 1964 by Atheneum.

IV

THE INTERNATIONAL SYSTEM

The contribution made by students of international relations to the understanding of communism as a world-wide political movement is reviewed in the present article. Communism has been seen alternately as a system of communist states (a "communist international system") and as a world system of political parties. These different approaches offer two perspectives and provide the first two sections of this article; the third and fourth sections discuss the main problems facing communism as a world system.

Marxist theory contains no permanent place for the role of the state and it therefore has no place for an organization of states; nor does Marxism recognize political autonomy as an explicit value; the concept of an international system and an international-relations approach are, therefore, basically alien to it. The primary units of analysis are class and the relations of production; the state is secondary, derivative, and liable to wither away. On the world scale, too, society is viewed first of all as a world market, while its political institutions, such as diplomacy, are seen as no more than a necessary evil. Contrasting with the underemphasis of politics is the consistent and strong awareness of the role of international class solidarities. Thus, the powers of the "capitalist world market" are to be defeated by the "international workers' movement" organized by communist parties. The several "internationals" have been the practical embodiment of this concern, but the literature of solidarity has been inspirational rather than analytical.

For a time, Soviet federalism was an implicit but not very influential model for relations between communist states (Goodman 1960). This might have served as the prototype of a world state, a possible world union of soviet socialist republics. But developments since World War II have brought about for the first time the simultaneous coexistence of a number of communist-ruled states, and, thus, the need has arisen for new conceptualizations. The concept now emplaced in Soviet ideology is that of a "world socialist system," defined in the 1961 program of the Communist party of the Soviet Union as "a social, economic and political community of free sovereign peoples pursuing the Socialist and Communist path, united by common interests and goals, and the close bonds of international Socialist solidarity." In a manner entailing some revision of classic theory, Kuusinen's text (1961, especially chapter 25) paints a picture of the "commonwealth of free and equal states" equally developed and freely associated in relationships unmarred by war, and it recalls Lenin's dictum that "national and state distinctions between peoples and countries would continue to exist for a very long time" (p. 769). However, the Chinese Communist party has neither accepted these pronouncements as authoritative nor clarified its own position on these points.

A system of states

The communist world appears above all as a system of states, possibly an international system in embryo. In 1947 the system could be said to have had about a half-dozen members; by 1965 membership had increased to 13 (the Soviet Union, Albania, Bulgaria, Czechoslovakia, East Germany, Hungary, Poland, Rumania, China, North Korea, North Vietnam, Mongolia, and Cuba). The principal international organizations of that system, the Warsaw Treaty Organization and the Council for Mutual Economic Assistance (CEMA), are both confined in membership to the European area (except that Mongolia belongs to CEMA).

For a time, students of politics characterized the system as primarily an expansive empire, an array of satellite governments dominated from one, and later possibly from two, centers. Others have seen it as a bloc of states assuming a place in a world system of bipolarity (Lasswell 1945; Kaplan 1957). It was then observed, however, that a potentially global political system might be developing whose constituent units nevertheless possessed a degree of independence. Modelski (1960) therefore described it as a partial international system that had the following attributes for becoming universal, while maintaining its essentially international character:

(1) *Aspiration to universality.* The ideologies of ruling communist states contain a claim to universal validity, and this is held to justify the principle of proletarian internationalism, according to which all communist parties have the obligation of mutual support in the "world proletarian struggle." Communism could, therefore, become a world-wide system of states controlled by communist parties. The constant reminder of this possibility is the existence, the world over, of close to one hundred communist parties on five continents, each upholding the principle of proletarian internationalism.

(2) *Segmentation of authority.* The international character of this potentially universal system is accounted for by the segmentation pattern obtaining among the political authorities within it (that is, the number and distribution of units within the system, their relative size and political potential). Especially since the establishment of the Chinese Peoples' Republic, the formerly preponderant influence of the Soviet Union has diminished and, if an elementary play-off mechanism is postulated, greater autonomy has in consequence accrued to other members of the system.

(3) *Separate identity.* Politically, communism is a system that is characteristically distinct and isolated. There are "boundaries" which separate communist from noncommunist states (an "iron curtain") and mechanisms which maintain this separateness, especially the solidarity of the movement and the distinctive political culture which it upholds.

(4) *Self-maintenance.* To persist through time, systems need structures to ensure their survival and operation. International systems require arrangements for performing functions of legitimate authority and for strengthening solidarity, maintaining culture and communications, and allocating resources. Modelski (1960) described the ways in which these functions are performed in the system of communist states, and he stressed the importance of arrangements for authority and leadership. Organizational devices, such as conferences of ruling parties and assemblies of both ruling and nonruling parties, have exploited the party channels but have not produced a framework of even mild formal authority such as is characteristic of modern international systems. Responsibility for initiating and pursuing policies aimed at the common interest still devolve upon individual authorities and, in particular, upon the most powerful parties and states. We now see that the leadership role held for many years by the Soviet party, the Soviet state, and, in effect, by Stalin has been implemented in a hegemonial manner and frequently without regard to the interests of other parties and governments. No accepted rules govern the succession to that role, and China's leaders as well as parties anxious for a more dispersed system of authority have contested the Soviet right to an exclusive occupancy of the leadership position. The achievement of modern structures of leadership—as well as the maintenance of solidarity—are among the most crucial problems of the system.

(5) *Conflict containment.* Despite the diverse causes for international conflict within the communist system, there has been considerable success, over a long period, in "containing" these conflicts within the system through the strength of solidarity. Communist states have hesitated to

call upon outsiders for aid in their intrasystem differences, and proletarian internationalism requires mutual support in case of conflict with the world outside. Failure to contain rather than failure to abolish conflict could become the most profound cause of change and, ultimately, transformation of the system.

Developments in the Sino–Soviet dispute have led observers to see the growth of semipermanent regional subsystems in Europe and in Asia, based on the Soviet Union and on China, respectively. In this context, the Council for Mutual Economic Assistance has attracted some attention, being seen as the counterpart of the European Common Market and having, like the latter, aroused the hostility of some of its members for being an instrument of excessive integration. But far from being subdivisions or regional sections of a world system, these new institutions are symptoms of declining solidarity and semipermanent alignments on intrasystem issues. They may be seen in the traditional light of spheres of influence of major organizing powers.

A system of parties

Communism may also be viewed as a world system of parties. This perspective is peculiarly congenial to political scientists, but it is one that students of world politics in particular must develop. The system of communist states cannot be properly understood without regard being paid to the structure of parties upon which it is built. Communist parties perform basic functions in the system of states: they facilitate communications and contact against the background of common culture, and they guard solidarity, legitimize the rule of governing parties, and serve as justification for claims to universality. The communist international system could not exist without the parties, but the parties could be, and have been, in existence on the world scene even before there was a system of communist states. That is why they deserve separate attention as an independent phenomenon of world politics.

The world system of communist parties has grown from 7 national parties with 400,000 members in 1917, to 56 parties and 4.2 million members in 1939, and to about 90 parties with more than 44 million members in 1964 (U.S. Department of State 1965).

Jan Triska (Triska et al. 1964, pp. 20–31) analyzed the data for 1963 with respect to nonruling parties. He found that most of these parties were small (34 out of 76 parties had less than 2,000 members). Most nonruling parties attract less than

0.1 per cent of their countries' population to membership. (The figures for ruling parties are, of course, considerably higher.) Electoral and comparative figures for the years 1953 to 1963 do not disclose any significant trends except an over-all rise in membership largely attributable to increases in world population as a whole.

The organization of the world system of communist parties has passed through a number of forms—the most important of them being the Comintern which lasted from 1919 to 1943 (Borkenau 1938; Nollau 1959). The Communist International was the most thoroughly international party known so far. It was world-wide and so highly centralized that its directing organs were empowered to issue binding orders to individual parties, officially known as mere "sections" of the Comintern. The ruling bodies of the organization initially reflected a variety of views from member parties, but within a few years the Soviet party assumed a position of absolute control. The Comintern of 1948 to 1955 (Brzezinski 1960), Europe-oriented and much weaker organizationally, was, again, merely one of the cloaks veiling Soviet control over eastern Europe. Since 1956 the organization of the party system has been a bone of contention, and efforts to re-create a centralized organization or even to institutionalize world-wide conferences have been handicapped not only by the memories of the Comintern but also by the accession to power of a number of parties each intent on preserving some autonomy and freedom to choose its own "road to socialism."

The Comintern can be categorized as an international pressure group on account of its international composition and world-wide sphere of action (Meynaud 1961); but communism as such does not seem to fit neatly into the "pressure group" category because of its primary character as a political movement, its diffuse objectives, and its revolutionary proclivities.

Propositions describing the behavior of communism as a world party system have been few, as most students adopt a single national party as a focus of analysis. Borkenau (1938, p. 413A) drew attention to a regular alternation between a "left" and a "right" tendency in communist policies and suggested some explanations, but swings have been much less marked since the dissolution of the Comintern and the declining centralization of the system. Nor is Soviet policy any longer a simple guide to the behavior of the communist system.

In modern world politics we can see the incipient growth of "parties" as a process similar to that suggested by Duverger for the national sphere

(1951). Such world "parties" are formed when delegates meet for international meetings and divide on contentious issues; they can be observed most clearly in international organizations. The "party" formed on such occasions by delegates of communist states may be seen as the reflection of a world system of communist parties. This "world communist party," is, in Duverger's terms, extra-parliamentary in origin and bears most of the characteristics attributed by him to national extra-parliamentary parties: greater centralization, reduced influence of parliamentary representatives, and lesser dependence upon the international political process.

Studies of voting and other political behavior at the United Nations (Hovet [1958] 1960, pp. 47–55; Dallin 1962, especially pp. 108–111) have shown that communist representatives caucus together, coordinate their behavior, and later vote and otherwise act in unison. They may therefore be regarded as forming a party whose potential "electorate" is world-wide.

Communism as a political party on the world stage should also be considered in relation to other parties on this stage. How extreme are its public views as compared with those of its rivals? In other words, is it an evolutionary or a revolutionary party? Does it promote a normal or a polarized international system? In origin communism was undoubtedly revolutionary in character, and its influence upon the structure of the international system has clearly been toward polarization. But other influences have been bearing upon it, and some evolutionary changes have apparently been at work, at least in the case of the Soviet Union; this at any rate is the burden of the Chinese complaint. It is hard to predict whether communism as a whole will maintain a revolutionary character or whether, like socialism half a century ago, it will separate into evolutionary and revolutionary wings.

Major problems

Solidarity.   A condition of the persistence of an international system is maintenance of solidarity within certain limits. We might postulate that if solidarity falls beneath a certain critical level, the system dissolves, and that if solidarity rises above a certain level, the international system becomes a supranational bloc.

In fact, little has been done to measure system solidarity or to establish appropriate indices; at most we can say that solidarity has been surprisingly strong in the past but that as the system grew, and as world society at large changed, this solidarity has declined. Another problem may have been created by the fact that communist leaders had aspired to a degree of solidarity higher than was compatible with the maintenance of an international system, being seemingly incapable of accepting the fact that monolithic styles of politics cannot (except at times of crisis) be reconciled with the universally strong demand for autonomy; they have been unable to accept the politics of what they still regard as "factionalism."

Solidarity may be maintained by an equitable distribution of benefits and resources. The feeling that the Soviet Union was inclined to appropriate an excessive share of such benefits and resources and was unwilling to redistribute them, through, for example, foreign aid, or in the form of military assistance, probably reduced solidarity and was conducive to "self-reliance" and, hence, to autonomy. For the Soviet Union, this might or might not have been an excessive price to pay. Solidarity may also be maintained through control of deviance by means of sanctions. Brzezinski (1962) has explored this problem by drawing on methods used by the Catholic church in the late sixteenth and seventeenth centuries to contain Jansenism and to manage disputes between religious orders. But this analysis posits the persistence of a "center" in one authority or location and reduces the problem of deviance to marginal proportions. A study of the schism between the Eastern Orthodox church and the church of Rome in the eleventh century might have been perhaps more useful, because control of deviance presents more serious problems in case of a major challenge: a bid for central authority.

Growth.   A revolutionary system must expand if it is to maintain its momentum, and the pressures on communism to maintain its growth remain strong.

Recent Soviet doctrine foresees both violent and nonviolent methods of "transition to socialism" (Black & Thornton 1964, pp. 417 ff.), but Soviet practice has in effect been a policy of seeking support of the "national democratic states" (now referred to as "revolutionary democracies") in the "third world," such as Algeria, Burma, Mali, the United Arab Republic, Ghana, and Guinea. Some degree of community of action, which also tends to fluctuate, has been achieved, but none of these states may be said to have become members of the system. Triska (Triska et al. 1964, pp. 32–37) has proposed indices for judging the degree of "affiliation"; they are trade, aid, and voting in the UN. These indices would have to be followed on a continuous basis, and they need to be refined, both to account for the influence of China and in the light of world-wide and comparative studies of cohesion and conflict.

Since 1960 the Chinese leadership has been on record as preferring the violent and revolutionary methods of promoting communism; despite caution in the execution of policy, it has advocated "wars of national liberation" even at the risk of an atomic conflict and has directed its appeal to the regimes in the new Afro–Asian nations. It remains to be seen whether this more extreme tendency will pervade the whole system or whether a separation might occur between a revolutionary and an evolutionary trend.

In their more optimistic moments, Soviet writers foresee a gradual yet irreversible growth of the system—through accretions mainly in the third world—as the result of a high rate of economic development in countries of the communist system. Looking some twenty years ahead, Strumilin (1961, pp. 390–391) wrote in terms of a shift of 30 per cent of the population of the "neutral" and 10 per cent of the population of the "imperialist" countries toward the "socialist" system, which latter system would by 1980 comprise 54 per cent of the world's population. Yet the possibility of contraction cannot be ignored. Yugoslavia was expelled from the communist system in 1948–1949, and in 1956 the government of Hungary was prepared to leave abruptly. Developments in Sino–Soviet relations may lead to drastic changes in the allegiance and viability of nonruling parties in particular. Indeed "reversibility" (that is, the possibility that accession may later be followed by withdrawal) could be the only condition which would make the entry of new members into the communist system acceptable to the noncommunist world.

Links to world society. International systems need to be related to the societies in which they function. In general terms the communist system might be described as one variant of the international systems of modern industrial world society (Modelski 1961, p. 141). But first a number of questions must be answered. How significant is this variant? How might the significance be measured? Is it a significant difference in structures of society or in the more restricted sphere of political organization? Is the difference so significant that communist states form in fact a separate world society? While its adherents claim that communism is a distinctive social system and while others voice impressionistic theories of convergence, there is little concrete research in this field.

Other problems relate to the interdependence of communist states as contrasted with their links to world society. Recent research shows that the extent to which trade takes place within the system varies from over 95 per cent for Albania to 50 to 65 per cent for Poland but that as of 1961–1962 all system-members, except Yugoslavia, conducted over 50 per cent of their trade within the system. As the foreign trade of communist countries is a government monopoly, these figures would seem to bear more directly upon the intensity of political relations than upon the existence of a rich pattern of social contact constituting an inclusive society. Data on social and cultural interaction are too sketchy to warrant any conclusions. But available information indicates the growth of separate European and Asian spheres and therefore again throws doubt upon the separateness of the communist system as a whole.

The distinctiveness and separateness of communist societies have of course a close bearing upon the degree of upheaval caused by a country's entry into or withdrawal from the system and, therefore, upon the revolutionary nature of such changes.

Future transformations

The communist international system is an interpretation of the international experience of communism. Implicit in it is the assertion that, given certain conditions, communist states would behave as though they formed a distinct system of independent yet solidary states—possibly the nucleus of a future international society. This concept fitted to a good degree the development of communism in the decade following the death of Stalin. Yet it might also be argued that this was an oversubtle interpretation of a transitional situation: the inevitable disintegration of the communist monolith and the gradual dissipation of revolutionary fervor. There might have been no more than a fleeting moment in which the emergence of a genuinely international communist system was a realistic possibility.

The argument that communism will not produce a genuinely international system is supported by what may be seen as a major cause of communist intrasystem difficulties: a doctrinal disdain for governmental and diplomatic forms of action and a contemptuous disregard for tried and tested methods of maintaining close relations in conditions of basic autonomy. Conceivably, a revolutionary nucleus cannot be held together with any but party–political links which ignore state institutions and the niceties of diplomatic behavior. But it is at least as conceivable that the communist international system poses the conditions which, if observed, would ensure the survival and possibly the expansion of such a system. We must leave this question unresolved. Even if the post-Stalin or post-Khrushchev communist system were to be essentially altered, the analysis of its experience would have served a more general purpose: it would have afforded an example of the operation and growth of extraparliamentary international systems that are built upon a revolutionary ideology and that have universal aspirations directed against an existing world society.

For the present let us consider the transformation possibilities confronting the communist international system, other than the possibility of universal extension. The possible transformations are (1) a monolithic bloc, (2) dissolution, and (3) entry into a "normal" world party system. A bloc would be likely to ensue if distinctiveness and separateness increased, authority structures became regularized and strengthened, economic integration advanced, the segmentation pattern was changed toward greater centralization, and conflict containment was improved. Dissolution would be the consequence of opposite trends, especially if distinctiveness declined and the structures of authority, solidarity, and culture lost power. If indices could be established for each of these characteristics, the transformation processes could be followed accurately.

The third possible transformation falls somewhere between the two other alternatives and is also distinct from the "revolutionary international system" concept discussed above. It would involve the development of at least part of the communist system into a looser yet still ideologically oriented association. If the revolutionary system were to mellow and shed some of its more extreme members, the remaining elements could find allies among noncommunist states by an appeal to Marxist ideas and by a policy of mutual support based on a modicum of organization. If a nonpolarized party system were to gain strength on a world scale—and such a trend is arguable on account of the growing complexity of global politics and the resulting need for greater regularity and predictability—a communist "party" could be one of its components. The need to exercise influence on the world stage through and with others makes it necessary for all governments to have associates. Communist participation might thus be acceptable as long as the aim is world influence and not absolute power or the overthrow of the world system.

GEORGE MODELSKI

[*See also* INTERNATIONAL ORGANIZATION; PARTIES, POLITICAL; SYSTEMS ANALYSIS, *article on* INTERNATIONAL SYSTEMS.]

BIBLIOGRAPHY

BLACK, CYRIL E.; and THORNTON, THOMAS P. (editors) 1964 *Communism and Revolution: The Strategic Uses of Political Violence.* Princeton Univ. Press.

BORKENAU, FRANZ (1938) 1962 *World Communism: A History of the Communist International.* Ann Arbor: Univ. of Michigan Press. → First published as *The Communist International.*

BRZEZINSKI, ZBIGNIEW K. (1960) 1961 *The Soviet Bloc: Unity and Conflict.* Rev. ed. New York: Praeger.

BRZEZINSKI, ZBIGNIEW K. 1961 Organization of the Communist Camp: Formal Institutional Aspects. *World Politics* 13:175–209.

BRZEZINSKI, ZBIGNIEW K. 1962 Deviation Control: A Study in the Dynamics of Doctrinal Conflict. *American Political Science Review* 56:5–22.

DALLIN, ALEXANDER 1962 *The Soviet Union at the United Nations.* New York: Praeger.

DUDINSKII, IL'IA V. 1961 *Mirovaia sistema sotsializma* (The World System of Socialism). Moscow: Izdatel'stvo Sotsial'no-ekonomicheskoi Literatury.

DUVERGER, MAURICE (1951) 1962 *Political Parties: Their Organization and Activity in the Modern State.* 2d English ed., rev. New York: Wiley; London: Methuen. → First published in French.

GOODMAN, ELLIOT (1960) 1961 *The Soviet Design for a World State.* New York: Columbia Univ. Press.

HOVET, THOMAS (1958) 1960 *Bloc Politics in the United Nations.* Cambridge, Mass.: Harvard Univ. Press.

KAPLAN, MORTON A. 1957 *System and Process in International Politics.* New York: Wiley.

KORBONSKI, ANDRZEJ 1964 COMECON. *International Conciliation* 549:1–62.

KUUSINEN, OTTO V. (editor) 1961 *Fundamentals of Marxism–Leninism.* Moscow: Foreign Languages Publishing House; London: Lawrence & Wishart.

LASSWELL, HAROLD D. 1945 *World Politics Faces Economics: With Special Reference to the Future of the United States and Russia.* New York: McGraw-Hill.

MEYNAUD, JEAN 1961 *Les groupes de pression internationaux.* Lausanne (Switzerland): Études de Science Politique.

MODELSKI, GEORGE A. 1960 *The Communist International System.* Princeton University, Center of International Studies, Research Monograph No. 9. Princeton Univ., Woodrow Wilson School of Public and International Affairs.

MODELSKI, GEORGE 1961 Agraria and Industria: Two Models of the International System. *World Politics* 14:118–143.

NOLLAU, GÜNTHER (1959) 1961 *International Communism and World Revolution: History and Methods.* New York: Praeger. → First published as *Die Internationale: Wurzeln und Erscheinungsformen des proletarischen Internationalismus.*

SPROUT, HAROLD H.; and SPROUT, MARGARET 1962 *Foundations of International Politics.* Princeton, N.J.: Van Nostrand.

STRUMILIN, STANISLAV G. 1961 *Problemy sotsializma i kommunizma v SSSR.* Moscow: Akademiia Nauk SSSR.

TRISKA, JAN et al. 1964 The World Communist System. Stanford Studies of the Communist System, Research Paper No. 1. Unpublished manuscript.

U.S. Department of State 1965 *World Strength of the Communist Party Organizations.* 17th Annual Report. Washington: Government Printing Office.

COMMUNISM, ECONOMIC ORGANIZATION OF

i. Overview   *Abram Bergson*
ii. Agriculture   *Joseph W. Willett*
iii. Public Finance   *Franklyn D. Holzman*
iv. International Trade   *A. Nove*

I
OVERVIEW

"Communism" is a term with various meanings. When we speak of a modern state as communist, however, we usually mean that political power there is concentrated in a single party, which is typically controlled from above through a bureaucratic structure and has gained, and ultimately maintains itself in, power by authoritarian means. Elections to public office, so far as they are held, are thus apt to have only a relatively formal character. Power was often seized initially, however, with appreciable popular support and the ruling party adheres to a social philosophy derived from Marx. The nature of this ideology is subject to continuing reinterpretation (and in a manner which would sometimes have surprised Marx), but access of the party to power has in fact been followed by extensive nationalization of private property, and much of the means of production, at least in the more strategic sectors, such as industry and transport, comes sooner or later to be publicly owned. The party also seeks to direct economic life generally.

These are cardinal features of the contemporary communist state, though persons considering themselves communists would no doubt find fault with this characterization. Curiously, in communist theory strict usage also dictates that a society that we would designate communist should be referred to otherwise. Depending chiefly on the degree of economic advance in it and the extent of socialization as measured by public and cooperative ownership, such a society is called either socialist or a people's democracy. As for the term "communism," this is reserved to describe a stage of social development which admittedly is yet to be achieved. This is the stage depicted long ago by Marx (Marx & Engels [1875–1891] 1938, p. 10), one which will be realized "after the enslaving subordination of individuals under division of labor, and therewith also the antithesis between mental and physical labor, has vanished; after labor from a mere means

of life has itself become the prime necessity of life; after the productive forces have also increased with the all-round development of the individual, and all the springs of cooperative wealth flow more abundantly." Only at this stage "can the narrow horizon of bourgeois right be fully left behind, and society inscribe on its banners: from each according to his ability, to each according to his needs." [*See* Marxism.] In this sense communism represents a form of utopia where there is free sharing of material goods. Such a society has also been called communist in the West, but our concern here is with the modern communist state and particularly with the organization of economic life in such a state.

The Soviet model

Communism first came to hold sway in a modern state in Russia after the revolution of November 1917. Moreover, other countries where this social system has since come to prevail have tended in economic affairs to emulate the U.S.S.R. They have also diverged from the Soviet model, sometimes radically, but the organization of economic life in the U.S.S.R. remains of particular interest.

Public ownership. In the U.S.S.R. public ownership of the means of production is indeed extensive. Such property was nationalized in a wholesale way shortly after the revolution, and public ownership has been extended even further since that time. Thus, a pervasive feature is the legally defined public enterprise (*predpriiatie*), which administers a publicly owned plant or other works in behalf of the government. Moreover, even where ownership is not public, the difference almost inevitably tends to be perfunctory. To a marked degree this is true even of the collective farm, which with its mixed public and cooperative ownership represents by far the chief departure from public ownership as such.

Ownership other than public, however, also exists in the nonfarm sector, on which attention is focused here, and is sometimes of some magnitude. Thus, the so-called consumers' cooperatives conducted 28.1 per cent of all retail trade in 1964. Familiar to all tourists to the U.S.S.R. is the collective-farm market, where the government allows the collective farm to sell surpluses which it does not distribute to its members and the members in turn to sell such as they wish of distributed supplies and of the produce from small household plots assigned them. The collective-farm market thus has much of the character of a peasant bazaar and represents another departure from public enterprise in retail trade. Housing is usually thought of as a consumer good rather than a means of production, but it should be observed that the government has also permitted extensive private ownership of such property.

Bureaucracy. Given public ownership of the means of production, economic life in a communist state might still be organized in various ways. The economic system of the U.S.S.R. has long been characterized by three other basic features. The first is the pervasive bureaucracy. Public enterprises are directed by an extraordinarily complex administrative apparatus beginning with the hierarchy of general organs of government conducting public affairs in all spheres: the Council of Ministers in Moscow, associated legislative and judicial organs of the all-union government, and corresponding bodies in 16 constituent republics and subordinate local administrations. In the administration of public enterprises in different economic sectors use has also been made of further complexes of specialized agencies. In industry, for example, authority over public enterprises has been vested at different times in such agencies as all-union and republican branch ministries and their subordinate departments and all-union, republican, and regional economic councils. Sometimes several enterprises are administered through a further agency, the firm.

The above are agencies through which general organs of government exercise operational control over public enterprises in different sectors. In the administration of such enterprises, use is also made of still other complexes of agencies of a more functional or staff nature, though inevitably these often have duties not very different from those of agencies exercising operational control. Among the more important bodies with such staff and functional responsibilities are the State Planning Committee of the U.S.S.R., or Gosplan, which, together with corresponding republican and local agencies, has major responsibilities for formulating and observing the fulfillment of economic plans; the Central Statistical Administration, which compiles and publishes statistical data; and the Ministry of Finance and the State Bank, which are concerned with money and finance.

While directing public enterprises in different sectors, general organs of government also oversee cooperative and in some degree even private economic activities. For this purpose, they rely on Gosplan and other agencies with functional and staff responsibilities in the public sector and sometimes, though not always, on those exercising operational control over the public sector. Consumers' cooperatives, however, are nominally administered by an apparatus of their own, at the apex of which is Tsentrosoiuz.

Planning. The second basic feature of the Soviet economic system is the all-embracing complex of plans which are intended to guide the economy. The most famous of these is the Five-Year Plan, the first of which went into effect in October 1928. But the Five-Year Plan is only one of a number of programs that the government has employed in directing economic affairs. From time to time it publishes plans of a very long-run sort, the most recent of these being the twenty-year program that avowedly is to establish "a material basis for communism" by 1980. Among plans of shorter duration, the last that was promulgated for a five-year interval was to have run from 1956 to 1960. This was superseded by the Seven-Year Plan, which was formulated for the years 1959 to 1965. Long-term plans are supposedly reflected in the plan drawn up for still another interval, the year. It is the latter plan that bears most immediately on current operations. For purposes of administration, however, the annual plan is further broken down into quarterly and, at least in some spheres, monthly installments.

Whatever the planning interval, ordinarily there is not one program but a complex of programs of varying scope and detail affecting operations at different bureaucratic levels. Thus, in industry there are programs for the U.S.S.R. as a whole, for different regions and branches. Finally, there is also a plan for each enterprise, that for the year being the *tekhpromfinplan*, or "technical–industrial–financial plan."

Monetary regimen. The third feature is perhaps not nearly as noteworthy as the first two, but it too is basic. This is the monetary regimen. Transfers of goods and services not only between households and enterprises but between one enterprise and another ordinarily take place at established money prices. The household, in other words, is paid money wages for its labor by the enterprise employing it, and the household in turn is charged money prices for the consumer goods supplied it, though some goods, chiefly education and health care, are by and large supplied the household without charge. Similarly, each enterprise pays other enterprises for goods it obtains from them and is paid, in turn, for goods it supplies. Within the enterprise, records are kept of costs and income, and it is considered not at all incongruous that in a communist state the resulting profit is also calculated.

Though they are largely supplied the household free of charge, education and health care generally are of such a nature that they might also have been made available at money prices. In addition to such "communal services," however, there are various "collective goods" (defense, internal security, etc.) which because of their nature must be made available to the community at large without direct charge. In the Soviet Union the government finances all such activities through various money taxes and other levies on both public and other enterprises and households. Of these, the chief levy by far is the notorious turnover tax (*nalog s oborota*). While imposed in different ways, this is in effect a sales tax. The government has also seen fit to finance other activities through its budget rather than through the monetary regimen. Principal among these is much of the new investment of public enterprises.

The monetary regimen described represents but a facet of a larger phenomenon, the system of *khozraschët*, or economic accounting. This system, other features of which will be discussed below, provides a basis for a distinction that otherwise might be difficult to make, that between economic agencies that may be viewed as institutions constituting the government as such and economic agencies acting on its behalf in the conduct of the public sector. Thus, under the *khozraschët* system the public enterprise usually is expected to finance out of its own revenue and hence without recourse to the government budget much or all of its current expenditures. Sometimes this has also been true of agencies immediately superior to the public enterprise, but generally such organizations have their current expenditures financed by appropriations from the government budget. As a rule, these budgetary organizations seem properly viewed as government institutions as such, while the former extrabudgetary organizations are seen as agencies acting on the government's behalf. In the U.S.S.R., extrabudgetary organizations are often referred to as being on *khozraschët*, or as *khozraschët* organizations.

How the system functions

Given the foregoing cardinal features, how does the system work and how well? The manner in which the economic system of the U.S.S.R. functions is a large, complex, and still often obscure theme. We can do little more than suggest the more significant patterns of operation that may be discerned.

Enterprise management. An outstanding feature of the economic system is the notable centralization of decision making, but authority is unavoidably dispersed in some degree. The economic plans become increasingly detailed as they descend the administrative ladder, but even the agency at the bottom, the public enterprise, must be allowed some discretion in their implementation.

Furthermore, contrary to a common supposition, the plans are not simply the creation of Gosplan, presented in final form for implementation to subordinate agencies exercising operational control. Nor, though this is somewhat nearer the mark, are the plans simply the creation of Gosplan with due regard to directives of the party leadership and the all-union Council of Ministers. Rather they are the product of an intricate administrative process in which not only Gosplan, the party leadership, and the all-union Council of Ministers but all subordinate agencies concerned participate. Targets formulated for each administrative level are subject to negotiation between those in posts of responsibility, their superiors, and, especially at higher levels, Gosplan. Sometimes administrators at one level take the initiative in proposing targets to superiors. It is also the task of administrators at any level to elaborate general directives into more detailed plans.

So far as decision making is decentralized, it must, of course, be subject to controls. Among these controls, first and foremost are the plans themselves. The annual plan particularly serves as a "success criterion" for managerial performance at all levels, and managerial personnel, by all accounts, act accordingly. Among the many targets in the plan, management has focused chiefly on that for total output, for apparently it has been especially in terms of performance in this respect that success has been judged. By fulfilling and overfulfilling the target for output, the manager of the enterprise and his chief assistants might earn sizable bonuses. Since 1959, however, priority has often been accorded another, related target, that for the reduction in costs per unit of output, and bonuses for management of the enterprise have been determined correspondingly.

Whether the concern has been with output or costs, managerial personnel understandably have sometimes been more interested in fulfilling than in overfulfilling the target, for with overfulfillment they may only be confronted with still higher targets in the future. Understandably, too, zeal in fulfillment of the plan does not carry over into its formulation. A recurring complaint in the U.S.S.R. concerns the "safety factor," which the management of the enterprise seek to establish for themselves by negotiating for low plan targets. The agency superior to the enterprise may try to counter this proclivity, but this agency too has reason to seek to establish a safety factor in negotiating with agencies at still higher levels.

As a plan target, total output usually must be calculated by the aggregation of a variety of products in terms of their prices, and such calculation must also underly that of the further target for the reduction in cost per unit of output. In seeking to fulfill the plan, therefore, enterprise management has had to consider the relative prices of different products, and, as will be discussed below, such prices have their limitations. Partly for this reason, as incessant complaints in the Soviet press testify, the resultant assortment is very often odd. Enterprises have reportedly produced, for example, an inordinate output of small-sized men's shoes relative to large-sized boys' shoes, of bandage cloth relative to shirt cloth, of large electric bulbs relative to small, and so on. Assortment of course is itself subject to plan targets, but managers apparently find it expedient to subordinate such targets in the interest of fulfilling that on total output or on cost per unit of output.

Quality too is a variable subject to controls, but these have been especially difficult to enforce. In the U.S.S.R. complaints about defective quality are hardly less numerous than those on violations of the assortment plan.

Reference has been primarily to the public sector and to industry, but working arrangements of a broadly similar sort usually prevail in the nonfarm sphere generally.

Coordination. At superior levels, especially in Gosplan, a cardinal concern must be with coordination. This is a task with many facets, of which one of the chief is industrial materials supply, the coordination of targets for industrial goods used as materials in industry. For important products of this sort, Gosplan applies its famous "method of balanced estimates." Essentially a balance is drawn up of supplies and requirements for each good. Supplies are calculated to reflect provisional targets for production on the part of supplying enterprises and for other availabilities. Requirements similarly are calculated to reflect provisional targets for production on the part of consuming enterprises and for other dispositions. Where supplies and requirements are found not to balance, the plan is suitably adjusted to remove the disparity. Such adjustments for any one product, of course, might necessitate further adjustments for others, and these might do so for still others. But adjustments apparently are imposed primarily where such secondary effects will be avoided: on supplies allotted to final uses, on production targets of sup-

plying enterprises without any accompanying change in material inputs, or on material inputs of consuming enterprises without any accompanying change in their production targets.

In the latter cases, the adjustments in effect entail changes in material input coefficients. Under *khozraschët* such coefficients are supposed to take into consideration the possibilities of economizing money costs through the substitution of one material for another, and so far as this is done in practice, the coefficients must depend on the relative prices charged for different goods. Yet prices of industrial materials tend to be fixed simply to cover average costs in a branch (including, under Soviet accounting practice, charges for labor, materials, and depreciation, but not for interest on fixed capital), together with a small "planned profit," and when once fixed are changed only infrequently. To some extent, however, such prices are varied in ways to restrict disparities in supplies and requirements. In effect, while coordination is achieved primarily by direct administrative controls, the task is sometimes eased by use of indirect market controls.

Unavoidably, however, market controls have a more important place in certain other spheres. The numerous and sometimes draconian restrictions which the government at different times has imposed on the workers' freedom of choice as to occupation and place of work make a story in themselves, but such of these as survived the war were very largely abandoned by 1956. Since then the worker has enjoyed substantial freedom in these choices, though there are still some impediments (for example, administrative assignment of college graduates to jobs during an initial three-year period). In order to recruit workers in required numbers in different occupations and branches, therefore, the government relies chiefly on a money wage system under which rates of pay are systematically differentiated between occupations, depending on such features as skill, complexity, and arduousness, and between branches, depending on their social importance. The worker, of course, also has much discretion over the effort he exerts in any pursuit. To control this aspect, the government makes extensive use of piecework (in 1961 about 60 per cent of the workers in industry were remunerated on this basis) and premium systems.

Similarly, in distributing among households goods for which money prices are charged, the government has relied on rationing during protracted intervals, but the last such period was brought to a close in December 1947. At that time the government re-established an open market where households could choose freely among different consumer goods, and such a market has prevailed ever since. At the same time the government relies on prices to limit consumer demand to available supplies. However, for various reasons the government has more often than not held prices below clearing levels. Hence, such familiar features exist in the U.S.S.R. as unavailability of supplies, queues, and the premiums over official prices prevailing in the collective farm market. In the collective farm market, prices are unregulated by the government and thus tend to be fully responsive to pressures of demand.

Technology and production capacity. In addition to coordination, superior agencies are largely responsible for the determination of technology, including the crucial aspect of capital intensity and of production capacity in different branches. Capital intensity has been settled on various bases and, for a long time, often without reference to any interest charge on capital. If by additional investment a given output could be produced at less cost, exclusive of interest, the investment supposedly was to be made, at least so far as the available supply of capital permitted. Recently, however, increased use has been made of an interest-like criterion, though under another name. Thus, for any two projects under consideration, a coefficient of capital effectiveness is calculated by comparing the difference in their respective capital requirements with the corresponding difference in current operating costs. The project requiring the greater volume of capital is chosen only if the coefficient of effectiveness exceeds some rate taken as a norm. While the reciprocal of the coefficient of effectiveness is referred to in the U.S.S.R. as a "period of recoupment," this differs from the payoff period familiar in Western business practice insofar as in the Soviet Union operating costs include depreciation expense.

The responsible authorities must somehow take into account also that, fixed in the manner described, prices of industrial materials in terms of which capital outlays and operating costs are calculated fail to reflect "scarcity values." This is also true of the prices of durable capital goods, which are fixed similarly. In addition to the coefficient of effectiveness, therefore, administrators have been told in a methodological handbook issued by the Academy of Sciences to consider pertinent "physical indicators, characterizing the productivity of labor . . . , expenditure of fuel, power, materials, utilization of equipment and productive space, applica-

tion of progressive construction designs, and so forth" (Bergson 1964, p. 263).

The principles applied in the determination of production capacity in different branches are not very clear. Among industrial branches producing substantially for household consumption, the responsible agencies apparently consider the divergence of prevailing retail prices from proportionality to average branch costs, though such a divergence may be viewed as "normal" (for example, for children's things prices are viewed as properly low). The degree to which supplies to households have fallen short of their demand at the prevailing prices is also considered. Recently, consideration has been given to "rational norms" of consumption for "healthy, culturally developed people," which have been worked out by the Nutrition Institute of the Academy of Medical Sciences and by other agencies.

The criteria used elsewhere must be similarly varied and often, too, not very incisive. Among basic industrial branches, for example, steel manifestly has long been an unquestioned favorite, but in November 1962 Khrushchev attacked Gosplan for allowing "steel blinkers" to blind it to economies that might be realized by use of competing materials, especially plastics, and apparently the latter products are now receiving more attention—though Khrushchev has been criticized in turn by his successors. There are reasons to think that at one time Gosplan also wore "coal blinkers," but for some years now the Russians have been shifting to the more extensive use of oil which their resource position permits.

Capital formation. Last but not least, the share of the community's total output that is allotted to capital formation is also determined by superior agencies. Indeed, the very highest authorities seek to reserve this matter almost exclusively for themselves, and on the whole probably succeed. A cardinal concern obviously has been to provide the wherewithal for rapid growth and in this way to permit realization of the Soviet imperative "to overtake and surpass" the advanced capitalist countries. Pursuit of this goal avowedly reflects various more basic concerns. Thus, according to its latest (October 1961) program, the party seeks in economic affairs "to develop the production of material goods for the highest satisfaction of all needs of Soviet man," "to win the economic competition with capitalism," and "to maintain the defenses of the country at a level allowing us to smash any aggressor" (Khrushchev 1961, p. 3).

How the party has weighed these diverse aims

in practice must be judged from facts such as the following: under the Five-Year Plans the Soviet economy has indeed grown rapidly, though, according to independent calculations, not so much as official claims suggest. During the period from 1928 to 1960 the gross national product of the U.S.S.R. grew at an estimated average rate of 4.5–6.3 per cent a year, or by 5.2–7.3 per cent if the entire growth is imputed to the 28 peacetime years. Of the total output measured in constant prices, the share devoted to investment rose over the same period from 12 per cent to perhaps 35 per cent, while that devoted to personal (as distinct from communal) consumption declined from 80 per cent to about 45 per cent. Though the share of consumption has thus fallen sharply, with output as a whole increasing as it has, the Soviet household has been able to realize a marked increase in standards. For the most part the increase has occurred only very recently, since the years under Stalin were years of denial. The average Russian in 1962 still enjoyed a per capita consumption of but $485 per year.

While seeking rapid growth, the U.S.S.R. has also sought to limit its dependence on foreign countries, particularly capitalist ones. Since Stalin this policy of autarky has been relaxed, but in 1962 exports still represented but 2.7 per cent of the national income. Hence, the U.S.S.R. must produce at home the great bulk of the capital goods required to realize the high rates of capital formation. Also production capacity must vary correspondingly as between consumer-goods and investment-goods branches. As the rate of investment has risen, therefore, the output of investment goods necessarily has increased more than that of consumer goods. In the U.S.S.R. this disparity of tempo has been described as an economic law. Often, however, the reference is actually to divisions within industrial output rather than within total output.

As the foregoing bare bones only begin to suggest, superior agencies in the U.S.S.R. bear onerous responsibilities. That the patterns described sometimes seem of a rather arbitrary sort must be read partly in this light. Indeed, as the activities of the superior agencies are examined more closely, arbitrariness only becomes the more manifest. In a modern, complex economy such as that of the Soviet Union, the responsibilities might have been onerous in any case, but they become the more so because of the pervasive limitations in money prices. Given these limitations, superior agencies must somehow digest and react to even more information than would confront them otherwise,

information not only of a summary, monetary sort but of a detailed physical sort. Alternatively they must risk miscalculation by relying on the former alone, and this too occurs.

Labor theory of value. In the economy generally, to what extent have operational patterns conformed to the labor theory of value? [See VALUE, LABOR THEORY OF.] In the U.S.S.R. the government has been held to be the master rather than the servant of "economic laws," and among the laws in question is Marx's "law of value." Yet the law has a place, though apparently now a diminishing one. Consider, for example, the practice of calculating costs without any allowance for interest on fixed capital and also the related practice of neglecting such a charge in the choice of technology, though here ideology seems by now to have been largely vanquished by scarcity. The labor theory is often not especially incisive regarding economic calculation, but it has tended to stand in the way of its more incisive competitor, marginal value theory as now understood in the West.

Comparative efficiency. In economics, how well an economic system works usually is taken to turn primarily on its efficiency, or the effectiveness with which available resources are used to produce wanted goods and services. The Soviet economic system manifestly must often leave something to be desired from this standpoint. This is true of the nonfarm sector, and needless to say, the performance is no better when agriculture, particularly that part under the notorious collective farm, is considered. But the chief rival system, Western private enterprise, has its limitations, too. These include, perhaps most notably, monopolistic business practices; trade union restrictions; distorting government measures, including farm controls, sales and income taxes, and tariffs; and cyclical and other extrafrictional unemployment. Which of the two systems is the more efficient?

In speculating about this complex question, we may consider, in addition to the sources of waste in the two systems, some related quantitative evidence: in 1960 the net national product of the U.S.S.R. per unit of factor inputs, including labor and reproducible capital, was less than one-half that of the United States. Depending on the method of measurement, the Soviet output per unit of factor inputs might be less than one-third that of the United States. Reference is to the net national product less certain items for which a satisfactory comparison of productivity is infeasible: personal services in education, health care, government administration and the like, and housing services. Correspondingly, the labor and capital employed in providing these services are omitted from factor inputs.

However, factor productivity and economic efficiency are not the same thing. Without any difference in economic efficiency, two economies might differ in factor productivity as calculated because of differences in labor skill, quality and quantity of farmland, and so on. Then, too, comparative data on factor productivity reflect the comparative volume of output but not how desirable it is in structure. The comparison of factor productivity has been held, however, to create a presumption that Soviet communism is less efficient than Western private enterprise, at least as the latter is experienced in the United States (Bergson 1964, pp. 340 ff.).

In the U.S.S.R., however, has not the cardinal concern been growth rather than efficiency? And from this standpoint is not the Soviet performance impressive after all? As we saw, the Soviet economy has grown rapidly under the Five-Year Plans. At least this was so until around 1958; since that year the tempo has fallen. But for the inefficiency, however, the government might have been able to invest and hence expand output still more, though the intense pursuit of growth no doubt has sometimes been itself a cause of inefficiency. Even from the government's standpoint, therefore, efficiency is the more basic standard. What goods are wanted and to what extent depends, of course, on the ends sought, and hence so must efficiency. But the Soviet economy must often fall short of its potential to produce goods of any sort that might be desired. Moreover, the ends sought in the U.S.S.R. are special, but not so much as is sometimes supposed. Thus, the government values investment goods highly, but obviously it also values consumer goods in some degree.

Rapid growth, of course, does not itself signify efficiency—though it is sometimes maintained that it does. Rather, growth in the U.S.S.R. has been induced by various factors different from, though not unrelated to, efficiency. The high tempo at most testifies not that efficiency is high but that it probably is rising from an initially low level. Among the chief growth-inducing factors are the high rate of investment, which has been the more potent because of the relatively limited capital stock initially available; the extraordinary opportunities to borrow Western technology, which have compounded still more the effect of the high rate of investment; and probably the opportunity to raise labor quality rapidly from an initially low level.

Is not the economic system, however, in the process of change? And are not new measures even now being introduced or considered that will raise its efficiency? The Soviet economic system has always been in flux, but lately it has been especially so. While we have sought to describe it as it has prevailed recently, interesting changes are in progress and further ones no doubt are in the offing. Among other things, in order to facilitate planning, the government is beginning to use mathematical techniques and electronic computers. Also, industrial enterprises are being given greater autonomy, with sales and profitability becoming major criteria of their success. The government is also reforming financial practices and industrial prices. But how such changes might affect efficiency is a question which must be left for the future to answer.

Income distribution. In addition to efficiency, how well an economic system works is usually judged in terms of the equity of income distribution. Here too the precise standard to be applied depends on the ends. Moreover, while the degree of inequality of incomes is of interest from the standpoint of almost any ends, this is a matter that is difficult to judge in the case of the U.S.S.R. because of the government's secrecy regarding earnings, especially of the more favored groups. As we have noted, however, wages are differentiated in a manner more or less similar to that obtaining under private enterprise. Sizable differences in earnings have been reported in many spheres. The inequality of incomes generally must be less than in, say, the United States, but at least if account is taken of taxes and perquisites, one wonders whether the difference is really very marked.

The merit of an economic system such as that of the U.S.S.R., where public ownership is predominant, has long been a subject of theoretic debate in economics. So far as we may judge from the Soviet experience to date, critics of this system would seem closer to the mark than proponents. As research proceeds, it may be hoped that we will gain further insight into this weighty theme.

The U.S.S.R. has served as a model in economic affairs for other communist countries, though they have sometimes diverged markedly from it. Among the more important of such countries, those in eastern Europe—with the exception of Yugoslavia—have economic systems that are broadly similar to that of the U.S.S.R. However, private enterprise in agriculture in the form of peasant farming is still predominant in Poland. This is also true in Yugoslavia, where, in addition, decision making is relatively decentralized. Correspondingly, there is greater reliance than in the U.S.S.R. on indirect market controls. Reforms entailing increased decentralization and reliance on markets are also being introduced elsewhere in eastern Europe and reportedly are to be especially sweeping in Czechoslovakia and Hungary. Despite doctrinal differences with the U.S.S.R., China continues to organize its economy in a manner often similar to that of the U.S.S.R., but the complex and rapidly shifting scene there defies easy summarization.

ABRAM BERGSON

[See also PLANNING, ECONOMIC, *article on* EASTERN EUROPE; ECONOMIC THOUGHT, *article on* SOCIALIST THOUGHT; ECONOMIC DATA, *article on* THE SOVIET UNION AND EASTERN EUROPE; *and the biography of* BARONE.]

BIBLIOGRAPHY

BERGSON, ABRAM 1961 *The Real National Income of Soviet Russia Since 1928.* Cambridge, Mass.: Harvard Univ. Press.

BERGSON, ABRAM 1964 *The Economics of Soviet Planning.* New Haven: Yale Univ. Press.

BERGSON, ABRAM; and KUZNETS, SIMON (editors) 1963 *Economic Trends in the Soviet Union.* Cambridge, Mass.: Harvard Univ. Press.

BERLINER, JOSEPH S. 1957 *Factory and Manager in the USSR.* Russian Research Center Studies, No. 27. Cambridge, Mass.: Harvard Univ. Press.

BORNSTEIN, MORRIS; and FUSFELD, DANIEL R. (editors) (1962) 1966 *The Soviet Economy: A Book of Readings.* Rev. ed. Homewood, Ill.: Irwin.

BROWN, EMILY CLARK 1966 *Soviet Trade Unions and Labor Relations.* Cambridge, Mass.: Harvard Univ. Press.

CAMPBELL, ROBERT W. (1960) 1966 *Soviet Economic Power: Its Organization, Growth and Challenge.* 2d ed. Boston: Houghton Mifflin.

CHAPMAN, JANET G. 1963 *Real Wages in Soviet Russia Since 1928.* Cambridge, Mass.: Harvard Univ. Press.

CLARK, M. GARDNER 1956 *The Economics of Soviet Steel.* Cambridge, Mass.: Harvard Univ. Press.

DOBB, MAURICE (1948) 1960 *Soviet Economic Development Since 1917.* 5th ed. London: Routledge.

ERLICH, ALEXANDER 1960 *The Soviet Industrialization Debate: 1924–1928.* Russian Research Center Studies, No. 41. Cambridge, Mass.: Harvard Univ. Press.

GERSCHENKRON, ALEXANDER 1962 *Economic Backwardness in Historical Perspective.* Cambridge, Mass.: Belknap.

GOLDMAN, MARSHALL I. 1963 *Soviet Marketing: Distribution in a Controlled Economy.* New York: Free Press.

GRANICK, DAVID 1954 *Management of the Industrial Firm in the USSR: A Study in Soviet Economic Planning.* New York: Columbia Univ. Press.

GROSSMAN, GREGORY (editor) 1960 *Value and Plan: Economic Calculation and Organization in Eastern Europe.* Berkeley: Univ. of California Press.

HAYEK, FRIEDRICH A. VON et al. 1935 *Collectivist Economic Planning: Critical Studies on the Possibilities of Socialism.* London: Routledge.

HOLZMAN, FRANKLYN D. (1962) 1963 *Readings on the Soviet Economy.* Chicago: Rand McNally.

HUNTER, HOLLAND 1957 *Soviet Transportation Policy.* Russian Research Center Studies, No. 28. Cambridge, Mass.: Harvard Univ. Press.

JASNY, NAUM 1961 *Soviet Industrialization: 1928–1952.* Univ. of Chicago Press.

KHRUSHCHEV, NIKITA S. 1961 O programme kommunisticheskoi partii Sovetskogo Soiuza (On the Program of the CPSU). *Pravda* October 19, p. 3, col. 3.

LIPPINCOTT, BENJAMIN E. (editor) (1938) 1952 *On the Economic Theory of Socialism.* Minneapolis: Univ. of Minnesota Press.

MARX, KARL; and ENGELS, FRIEDRICH (1875–1891) 1938 *Critique of the Gotha Programme.* New York: International Publishers. → Written by Marx in 1875 as "Randglossen zum Programm der deutschen Arbeiterpartei." First published with notes by Engels in 1891.

MOORSTEEN, RICHARD 1962 *Prices and Production of Machinery in the Soviet Union: 1928–1958.* Cambridge, Mass.: Harvard Univ. Press.

NOVE, ALEC (1961) 1966 *The Soviet Economy: An Introduction.* Rev. ed. New York: Praeger.

NUTTER, G. WARREN 1962 *Growth of Industrial Production in the Soviet Union.* National Bureau of Economic Research, General Series, No. 75. Princeton Univ. Press.

SCHWARTZ, HARRY (1950) 1960 *Russia's Soviet Economy.* 2d ed. Englewood Cliffs, N.J.: Prentice-Hall.

U.S. CONGRESS, JOINT ECONOMIC COMMITTEE 1962 *Dimensions of Soviet Economic Power.* 87th Congress, 2d Session. Washington: Government Printing Office.

U.S. CONGRESS, JOINT ECONOMIC COMMITTEE 1966 *New Directions in the Soviet Economy.* Parts I–IV. 89th Congress, 2d Session. Washington: Government Printing Office.

WILES, P. J. D. 1962 *The Political Economy of Communism.* Cambridge, Mass.: Harvard Univ. Press.

II

AGRICULTURE

Until very recently agriculture has nearly always been ranked toward the bottom in the ordering of priorities in communist economies. The leaders of communist states have generally decided that rapid economic growth and the development of economic power required a concentration of resources in industry, and especially in heavy industry. In pursuing their goal of rapid growth of heavy industry, they have demanded great sacrifices from their peoples and have tended to neglect the development of agriculture, which produces consumer goods and raw materials. Capital for the development of industry has been obtained from agriculture by confiscation of land and compulsory deliveries of farm products to the state, often at prices below cost. Exports of agricultural commodities have been used to pay for imports of industrial equipment. Investment and current inputs into agriculture have been severely restricted, and the movement of the better educated and more productive labor from the countryside into industry has been fostered.

In recent years, the communist leaders have made some revisions in their economic priorities. In the Soviet Union the stagnation of agriculture had become a threat to the future rate of industrial growth by the time of Stalin's death, and during the period 1954–1958 Khrushchev sought to achieve better balance between agriculture and industry. The proportion of total investment going to agriculture was increased, the prices the government paid farmers for their products were raised, and a number of changes in the organization of agriculture were made. Similar changes were reflected in the policies of the European satellites.

In the Soviet Union a large share of the increased resources devoted to agriculture during this period went into the expansion eastward into the new lands. These measures, together with good weather, brought about a substantial increase in Soviet agricultural output by 1958. However, since 1958 there has been little increase, and in 1961 and 1962 further reorganizations of the agricultural administrative apparatus were undertaken in an attempt to stimulate the lagging agricultural sector.

In Communist China a drastic drop in farm output after 1958 and the spectacular collapse of the "great leap forward" in 1960 brought about the adoption of more realistic measures, with a shift in priority from the development of heavy industry to the improvement of agriculture. Collectivization was relaxed, and measures were undertaken to provide greater incentives for farm production.

Domestic importance and foreign trade. Agriculture is a major sector of the economy in all countries under communist rule. In the Soviet Union agriculture uses about 45 per cent of the total labor force and in recent years has received about 15 per cent of the total investments, while producing about a fourth of the national income. In the European satellites the proportion of the labor force engaged in agriculture ranges from about 18 per cent in East Germany to over two-thirds in Rumania, while agriculture's contribution to the national income ranges from less than 10 per cent in Czechoslovakia to one-third in Bulgaria. In Communist China more than 80 per cent of the labor force is occupied in agriculture, which produces about 50 per cent of the national income. North Korea and North Vietnam are also primarily agricultural countries.

Farm products and products manufactured from raw materials produced by agriculture are important in the trade of the communist countries. In the period 1955–1961 agricultural commodities accounted for about 21 per cent of the Soviet Union's total exports and 25 per cent of its total imports. Grains and cotton have made up the bulk of the Soviet Union's exports of agricultural commodities. Although normally a large grain exporter during the postwar period, mainly to the European satellites, in 1963 the Soviet Union became a net importer of grain. This was a result of a very poor grain crop following several mediocre harvests, which probably had caused a decline in stocks of grain.

China has exported farm products and products manufactured from agricultural raw materials to pay for imports of machinery and heavy industrial equipment. Until the ideological break with the Soviet Union the trade of Communist China had been oriented mainly toward the Soviet bloc. However, the Soviet Union's imports of farm products from China declined 90 per cent between 1959 and 1961. Since 1960 China has been forced by serious food shortages to import large amounts of grain, mainly from Western countries.

Organization in the Soviet Union.   Between the revolution of 1917 and the year 1928 small-scale peasant farming predominated in the Soviet Union, with only a very small proportion of farm labor working on state and collective farms. In 1929 Stalin initiated mass collectivization of agriculture, which was carried through rapidly by various means of coercion, including mass deportation and heavy taxation. In the early 1930s the present forms of agricultural organization became dominant. The collectives were given a legal basis by the Collective-Farm Statute of 1935, which remained essentially unchanged until 1956.

Agriculture in the Soviet Union is made up mainly of the world's largest farms (the state farms and the collective farms) and some of the world's smallest agricultural enterprises (tiny private plots that belong for the most part to farm workers). There is a less important group of medium-sized farms owned by factories and other government organizations.

The collective farms, which occupy nationalized rent-free land, are nominal cooperatives with elected chairmen and management committees. However, the state and party exercise close control over the collectives, and party officials can readily determine the "election" of the chairman as well as reprimand or dismiss him (Nove 1961, p. 47).

The collective farm is the dominant form of agricultural unit in the Soviet Union. However, the proportion of the total sown area encompassed by collective farms declined from 84 per cent in 1953 to about 60 per cent in 1960 because of the conversion of collectives to state farms and to the predominance of state farms in the new lands to the east. As a result of the amalgamation into larger farms and the conversion to state farms the number of collective farms also declined, from more than 250,000 in 1950 to 53,400 in 1960. In 1960 the average collective farm encompassed nearly 6,800 sown acres and was worked by the labor from nearly 400 households.

The collective farmers are not paid wages as are workers in state-owned enterprises, but rather are residual claimants to the income of the collectives after the state's claims, production expenses, and investment needs have been met. The share which the collective farmer receives varies with the skill required in the work he performs. In recent years steps have been taken to distribute the collective farmers' share in quarterly or monthly payments rather than in a single annual payment.

Until 1958 most of the farm machinery used on the collectives was operated by state-owned Machine Tractor Stations (MTS), which supervised much of the collective farms' activities and performed machinery work on contract. The farms paid for the machinery services of the MTS with produce. In January 1958 it was decided to liquidate the MTS and sell their machinery to the collectives (the *kolkhoz*).

The state farm, or *sovkhoz*, which is considered in the Soviet Union to be ideologically the most desirable form of organization for agriculture, is becoming more important, accounting for a third of the total sown area in 1960. The state farms are owned by the state, and the farm workers are paid wages like factory workers. State farms tend to be more specialized than collective farms. They have a higher labor productivity, mainly because they have received most of the investment which the state has made in agriculture (Walters 1963, p. 8), have not been burdened with excess labor, and have offered higher incentives than have the collectives. The state farms are huge organizations, with an average in 1960 of nearly 22,500 sown acres and about 750 workers per farm.

The private plots which the farm workers are permitted to cultivate and the livestock which they own are remnants of legal private enterprise in the Soviet Union. The plots are considered to be ideologically undesirable but are tolerated for pragmatic reasons. Although they occupy only a little more than 3 per cent of the total sown area, they produce a significant share of the total output of some important items of food. The farmers and their families consume part of the produce from the plots, and the remainder, when sold—largely in free markets—contributes a significant share of the farmers' money income. The ideological unpalatability of the private plots and their competition for the labor time of the farmers have at times prompted the authorities to limit their operation through acreage restrictions, taxes, and other means.

Organization in eastern Europe. With the exception of Yugoslavia and Poland, the organization of agriculture in eastern Europe is generally patterned after that of the Soviet Union. In Yugoslavia and Poland, although collectivization of agriculture remains a long-run goal, 85 to 90 per cent of the farmland still is privately farmed. In the rest of eastern Europe a drive to complete the collectivization of agriculture, which had lagged in several countries, has been undertaken in recent years, and by 1962 the collectivized sector encompassed about 90 per cent or more of the arable land. Collectivization has been accomplished by the expropriation or purchase of privately owned land, taxes on private farmers, and a preferential policy toward the collectivized sector in the allocation of inputs and in the prices paid by the state for farm products (U.S. Department of Agriculture . . . 1964, p. 100).

Agriculture was socialized slowly in Poland, and despite great effort less than one-fourth of the total agricultural area was socialized by the middle of 1956. After the disturbances of October 1956, most of the collective farms were dissolved and the total area in state farms was reduced.

In Yugoslavia forced collectivization was abandoned in 1951. Most of the collective farms were disbanded by the end of 1953, and by 1962 the socialist sector occupied only 12 per cent of the arable land. Peasants' farms averaged less than 12 acres in size in 1962. They were limited by law to a maximum of 25 acres. Expansion of the socialized area in Yugoslavia is accomplished by means of the purchase of privately owned land by collective and state farms.

Organization in Communist China. The agricultural policy of China has been designed to increase agricultural output (both for export and for feeding the growing urban population) with minimum state investment, while maintaining central political control over the countryside. The Chinese communists have made strenuous efforts to achieve a breakthrough in agricultural as well as in industrial production. During the decade from 1950 to 1960 the leaders experimented with various combinations of centralized and decentralized control of the rural areas. China's problem was more difficult than that facing the Soviet Union before collectivization in that Chinese agriculture did not produce substantial surpluses which could readily be expropriated by the state.

By 1952 the landlord class was essentially eliminated and their land was distributed to poorer peasants. In 1954 and 1955 compulsory delivery quotas were established to provide the state with more farm products, and by the winter of 1955 the regime had decided on full collectivization.

In 1955 and 1956 private farmland was abolished and cooperatives were established with party cadres in charge. It was expected that the cadres would ensure the meeting of the state's needs for agricultural commodities, set aside larger shares for investment, and make effective use of seasonally unemployed labor in the construction of roads, irrigation works, and other projects. It was thought that collectivization would permit more rapid introduction of improved technology and more efficient use of the land (Perkins 1964, p. 219). Also, collectivization was desirable for political and ideological reasons.

Although regulations permitted the continuance of private plots, their size and the time available to work them were reduced, and the free market was closed. The output and availability of products from the private plots fell so drastically that the free market was soon reopened, however, and the size of private plots was increased. During 1957 some of the larger cooperatives were reduced in size and some authority was shifted to the subunits, the production brigades.

The net effects of the collectivization and centralization were unimpressive. In addition to the fostering of bureaucratic mismanagement, the incentives of the individual farmers to produce had been affected adversely.

In 1958 the regime embarked on the rapid establishment of the communes, a more radical form of organization of agriculture. Where the average cooperative had two hundred families, the typical commune had four thousand to five thousand. The communes took on additional functions, including responsibility for expansion of large-scale rural construction projects and control over local commercial, credit, and manufacturing establishments. Private plots and the free market were eliminated.

The communes were not subjected to effective financial or administrative restraints while the campaign atmosphere prevailed, and the pressure for spectacular results was such that ill-considered projects and procedures were widely adopted. Extreme demands were made on the farm people, and fantastic claims of success were made. Responsibility for the collection of statistics on agricultural production was given to the communes, and the statistics became extremely unreliable. The communes widened the distance between the workers' efforts and their rewards even further than did the cooperatives because wages were established on the basis of the income of the entire commune (Perkins 1964, p. 231).

Despite the shortcomings of the communes, the harvest of major crops in 1958, aided by excellent weather, was good. However, the regime later admitted that early claims of agricultural production were greatly exaggerated. The unusually good harvest of 1958 and the lack of reliable statistics made it difficult to ascertain the effects of the establishment of the communes, but by early 1959 the regime decided that output of the products formerly grown on the private plots had been seriously affected. The rural markets were reopened, but with tighter controls than formerly, and in 1960 private plots were restored.

The revolutionary development of the communes ended with the restoration in 1961 and 1962 of agricultural ownership and control to lower levels and with a decision to cut back on investment in heavy industry in favor of agriculture. Controls over production decisions and wage units were passed down to the subunits of the communes, until the rural institutions and levels of authority were essentially similar to those existing before the establishment of the communes. Although the communes remained as paper organizations, they had been stripped of their significant functions (Perkins 1964, p. 234).

Marketing and prices. In essence, communist economies are guided by central authorities toward centrally determined goals. However, managers of enterprises must necessarily have a degree of autonomy, especially in day-to-day operations. Although the managers are generally not free to react to prices to maximize profits, prices are expected to provide incentive and thus to assist in guiding the performance of the economy. But the function of prices is severely restricted, and, with the exception of limited free markets, prices are not free to respond quickly to supply and demand conditions.

The agricultural price systems of the communist countries are complex and have gone through numerous modifications. The analyst constructing even a simple index of output is forced to make a number of quite arbitrary choices of prices for weights. The economist attempting to evaluate the performance of communist economies must constantly keep in mind the limited functions of prices and the specific peculiarities of the price system relevant to the problem with which he is concerned. For agriculture, one peculiarity of the price system arises from the communists' refusal to permit land rent to perform its allocative function. There have at times been attempts to vary the requirements for compulsory deliveries to the state as a substitution for differenial rents, but these variations have been too crude to be effective. One of the effects of the elimination of rents is to penalize the farms with poorer land.

The use of a system of compulsory deliveries at very low prices and a system of multiple prices for the same product, with little logical relation between the prices of various products, greatly diminishes the value of prices as a measure of economic performance. The shortcomings of the agricultural price system have prevented the managers from developing useful cost-of-production estimates as guides for the allocation of resources. Since a large proportion of payments to collective farmers have been made by distributing commodities, it is extremely difficult, if not impossible, to measure labor costs. In addition, the costs of farm machinery and other inputs often have little relation to their value on the farm.

After a few years of free prices in the NEP (New Economic Policy) period, the Soviet Union established a system of compulsory deliveries of farm products to the state at very low prices, constituting in effect heavy taxes on the farm sector. Quantities over the compulsory quota were sold for higher prices. Prices paid by the state for most food commodities changed very little until 1953, although the prices of some industrial crops were raised during the period and were much more favorable to the farmers. During the period 1953–1955 the prices paid farmers were greatly increased, but the system of compulsory deliveries at low prices and over-quota sales at higher prices was continued. In addition, the farms paid the Machine Tractor Stations (MTS) in commodities for the performance of machinery operations.

In 1958, in connection with the abolition of the MTS, the entire agricultural price system in the Soviet Union was overhauled. The state now pays each farm a single price for each product, with regional variations in the prices. The regional variations in prices are intended to reflect, in part, differences in average production costs, and thus they are, to some degree, land-rent differentials. The tax element in the prices for a number of

products was reduced or eliminated, that is, there remained little difference between the price paid the farmers and the retail price, after deducting handling costs. However, grain and sugar beets were still purchased at below value prices. In 1962 and 1963 further increases were made in the prices of grain, potatoes, sugar beets, livestock products, and cotton.

The agricultural price system in eastern Europe has generally been patterned after that of the Soviet Union, although there are variations from country to country, and the Soviet Union's restructuring of farm prices in 1958 has not been copied uniformly. The state pays low prices, in many instances below cost, for compulsory deliveries of fixed quantities of agricultural products. The state also contracts with producers for the delivery of additional products at fixed, but sometimes higher, prices. After the compulsory quotas and contracted quantities are delivered, the producer sells his remaining available products to the state, at prices which are sometimes higher, or on the free market, at prices determined by supply and demand. In Yugoslavia compulsory deliveries of farm products to the state were abolished in 1953. Although the state and the purchasing agencies agree on the maximum prices which they will pay, the ceilings are sometimes ineffective when supplies are short (U.S. Department of Agriculture . . . 1964, p. 113).

In Communist China from 1950 to 1953 the state bought agricultural products from the peasants at centrally determined prices and collected an agricultural tax in kind, 90 per cent of which was paid in grain. Compulsory quotas were later introduced for most of the major crops. It was necessary to reduce quotas in 1956 in order to leave enough to the peasants for seed and feed as well as for their own consumption. In 1956 and 1957 the purchase prices were adjusted in an attempt to control the relative production of major crops, but the results were disappointing.

Because the cooperatives generally had to pay their own way they had a considerable incentive to adjust production in response to changes in purchase prices, although other factors often severely limited the adjustment. However, when the communes were established allocations were made directly to the communes from state budgetary funds and the credit available to agriculture was greatly expanded. The increased availability of funds, together with the campaign atmosphere of the commune drive, encouraged the local commune authorities to ignore economic criteria and concentrate on the production of a few key commodities emphasized by the campaign. For these and other reasons the production of subsidiary products fell sharply.

Trends in output. The collectivization drive in the Soviet Union started in 1928. The peasants resisted by slaughtering their livestock as well as in other ways, and, after adjustment for territorial changes, agricultural output exceeded the 1928 level in only two of the years between 1929 and 1951. In 1952 agricultural output was only six per cent greater than in 1928 on comparable territory.

After Stalin's death in 1953, concern over the impact of the stagnation in agriculture on future industrial growth stimulated a series of measures, including the development of the new lands and an expansion of the area planted to corn to support a desired expansion of the livestock industry. The expansion of acreage together with a good harvest of grain in the Ukraine in 1955 and a good harvest of wheat in the new lands in 1956 brought about substantially increased output. In 1958 excellent weather and increased output of livestock products resulted in the largest total agricultural production up to that time.

The seven-year plan, initiated in 1958, called for a 70 per cent increase in agricultural output by 1965, but the years after 1958 were disappointing, bringing little increase. The failure to increase production, while demand continued to rise, apparently caused a decline in grain stocks. Poor weather in 1962 and 1963, together with the perennial shortcomings of Soviet agriculture, caused agricultural output to fall sharply in 1963. Grains, especially wheat, were the hardest hit. The Soviet Union in the latter part of 1963 and the early part of 1964 contracted to buy more than 10 million tons of wheat and flour, mostly from Western countries. Though some of the imported grain was to be re-exported to eastern Europe, this trade situation was in sharp contrast to the 1959–1962 grain-exporting position when between 4.8 and 6 million tons were exported annually.

In East Germany and Czechoslovakia agricultural output had still not regained prewar levels by the early 1960s. However, output in the rest of the eastern European satellites was somewhat above the prewar level. Per capita agricultural output in all of east Europe other than the Soviet Union barely exceeded the prewar level in 1961 and 1962 and fell below it in the following two years.

Communist China apparently had a record harvest in 1958, although the early extravagant claims were later admitted by the regime to have been exaggerated. The authorities have released no official data on agricultural production since 1959, but production has apparently failed to keep pace with population growth. Mainland China has had chronic food shortages since 1960 and has been importing 5 to 6 million tons of grain annually.

Labor productivity. Although lack of information makes it impossible to calculate reliable measures of agricultural labor productivity for most communist countries, it is clear that the productivity is quite low. It has been estimated that before World War II the net agricultural production per person depending on agriculture was about 4.5 times as large in the United States as in the Soviet Union (Jasny 1949, p. 442). By the early 1960s this ratio of comparative labor productivity had widened to perhaps 7 or 9 to 1 (Walters 1963, pp. 4, 13). The Soviet Union's attempt to reduce the labor committed to agriculture has met with only moderate success. The number of people defined as the agricultural labor force declined slowly between 1940 and 1953 but rose for a period after 1953 in connection with settlement of the new lands. It has resumed its decline since then.

One of the reasons for the low labor productivity in Soviet agriculture as compared with the United States is the relative scarcity of capital. Although investment in agriculture has increased during the last decade, the stock of capital equipment has remained relatively small. For example, despite the fact that the Soviet Union has about 60 per cent more land in crops than does the United States, in 1962 Soviet agriculture had only one-fourth as many tractors, one-half as many grain combines, and slightly more than one-fourth as many trucks. Soviet agriculture is especially wasteful of labor in animal husbandry, in part because of poor management and labor-wasting practices and in part because of a lack of labor-saving equipment.

Although its labor force is very large, Soviet agriculture suffers from seasonal labor shortages. Especially during the harvest, peaks of demand for labor create shortages, and the Soviet press often stresses the need for young farmworkers, especially for skilled operators of equipment. A large part of the agricultural labor force consists of older persons and women with families—people who cannot readily be adapted to other kinds of work or transported to distant jobs.

The agricultural labor situation varies widely among the other east European countries. In East Germany the loss of agricultural labor to the cities and to West Germany has been at too great a rate to be adequately balanced by the increases in labor-saving machinery, although the number of tractors tripled between 1950 and 1961. The shortage of labor has been so great that members of the armed forces and urban workers have been required to help with the harvest.

In Czechoslovakia the agricultural labor force declined about one-third from 1950 to 1961, while agricultural output rose about 10 per cent. Agriculture occupied about 38 per cent of the total labor force in 1950 and 23 per cent in 1961.

In Rumania, up to the early 1960s, the agricultural labor force remained at about the level of 1938. However, during the harvest season it is necessary to obtain additional labor from factories, schools, and the armed services.

In Communist China the rural-to-urban shift in population has had little impact on the farm labor force, although between 1950 and 1956 the population of the cities rose by more than 30 million, or 55 per cent. After the collapse of the "great leap forward," the lack of jobs in the cities and the desperate need for food impelled the regime to institute a campaign to return people to the countryside.

In their pursuit of rapid industrialization, China's leaders attempted to make use of their relative abundance of rural labor by embarking on a campaign to establish large numbers of industrial enterprises in rural areas. The program was intended not only to make use of surplus rural labor but also to compel the people to work harder than ever before. The most spectacular enterprises in rural industrialization were the back-yard furnaces built during 1958–1959 to produce pig iron. But the demands of this program on the health and strength of the people were excessive, and most of the product was worthless. The program was largely abandoned in 1960.

Problems of analysis. The study of the economics of agriculture in communist countries is complicated by several serious difficulties [see ECONOMIC DATA]. There are large gaps in the available statistics, which often are of questionable reliability. The limited functions of prices or their function as taxing devices—as in obligatory deliveries at low prices—often results in their being of little use as criteria of economic rationality or performance or as weights for the construction of indexes. The ideologically determined refusal of the communists to charge explicit land rent complicates the analysis of most agricultural economic problems. Finally, because centralized decision making is dominant in communist countries and because the decision makers are often much more concerned with political rather than strictly economic goals, an economic analysis sometimes may be largely irrelevant or at least peripheral to the heart of the problem.

The interpretation of official data has always presented major difficulties for students of Soviet agriculture. A number of prominent statisticians were purged in the Soviet Union in the late 1920s, and agricultural statistics became largely subordinated to the goals of the central policy makers. From 1933 to 1953 the official statistics on agricultural output were generally seriously biased upward, being based on estimates of the crop in the field, which did not, as is normally done, take account of losses in harvesting. Indexes were customarily published without any indication of what prices were used as weights, thus making the indexes impossible to reconstruct and extremely difficult to evaluate. Important data often were not published at all. For example, although the publication of statistics on agricultural production increased somewhat after the death of Stalin in 1953, the statistics on the size of grain harvests continued to be restricted as a state secret until 1958. The official estimate of the disastrous grain harvest of 1963 has not been released to date.

Although the present official estimates of crop production in the Soviet Union apparently are intended to be in terms of "barn yields," there are serious questions as to the comparability and validity of some of the data. These questions arise in part from a lack of precise information about the procedure and concepts behind the statistics. Another reason for considerable skepticism about some of the statistics on the agricultural output of the Soviet Union in recent years is the amply reported incidence after 1957 of increased statistical malpractices at lower levels. Greed and the pressure of unfulfillable goals apparently motivated many officials to falsify production data reported to higher levels. Such practices are especially prevalent in the agricultural sector because it is impossible for central authorities to verify many of the statistics on agricultural production (Willett 1962, p. 97).

While the agricultural data for the other east European countries present problems similar to those of Soviet data, the data for Communist China are generally even less satisfactory in quality and much more limited in quantity. The problem of measuring the performance of Communist Chinese agriculture with any degree of precision is made impossible by the lack of reliable data, both for the communist and the precommunist period. In fact, none of the major statistical elements required for evaluation, such as population, food consumption, acreages, or yields, can be considered satisfactory. The data for the years before 1950 are meager and, especially the national aggregates, can be used only with major reservations. From October 1949, when the communist government was set up, through 1952 the agricultural-output statistics were produced by extremely unreliable procedures. Although the establishment of the State Statistical Bureau in 1952 probably brought about some improvement in procedures, the "great leap forward" of 1958 and the accompanying decentralization of statistical control caused a virtual breakdown of the state statistical system. The decentralized local operations produced highly exaggerated statistics on national agricultural production. Although the State Statistical Bureau's system was re-established in 1959 and 1960 and agricultural output surveys were introduced on a national scale in 1959, the operations of the system were placed under party committees at the local levels. The system was to operate under the "partisanship" principle, which required that the statistical work be programmed and developed to serve the political objectives of the party. There are no official data available on agricultural production since 1959.

JOSEPH W. WILLETT

[See also AGRICULTURE and ECONOMIC GROWTH.]

BIBLIOGRAPHY

CONFERENCE ON SOVIET AGRICULTURAL AND PEASANT AF-
   FAIRS, LAWRENCE, KANSAS, 1962   1963   Soviet Agri-
   cultural and Peasant Affairs. Edited by Roy D. Laird.
   Slavic Studies, No. 1. Lawrence: Univ. of Kansas
   Press.
JASNY, NAUM   1949   The Socialized Agriculture of the
   USSR: Plans and Performance. Stanford Univ. Press.
KARCZ, JERZY F.   1964   Quantitative Analysis of the Col-
   lective Farm Market. American Economic Review
   54:315–334.
LI, CHOH-MING   1962   The Statistical System of Commu-
   nist China. Berkeley: Univ. of California Press.
MITRANY, DAVID   1951   Marx Against the Peasant: A
   Study in Social Dogmatism. Chapel Hill: Univ. of
   North Carolina Press.
NOVE, ALEC   (1961) 1966   The Soviet Economy: An Intro-
   duction. Rev. ed. New York: Praeger.
PERKINS, DWIGHT H.   1964   Centralization and Decen-
   tralization in Mainland China's Agriculture, 1949–
   1962. Quarterly Journal of Economics 78:208–237.
U.S. DEPARTMENT OF AGRICULTURE, ECONOMIC RESEARCH
   SERVICE, REGIONAL ANALYSIS DIVISION   1964   Agri-
   cultural Policies of Foreign Governments, Including
   Trade Policies Affecting Agriculture, by Montel Ogdon
   et al. Agriculture Handbook No. 132. Washington:
   The Department.
VOLIN, LAZAR   1951   A Survey of Soviet Russian Agricul-
   ture. U.S. Dept. of Agriculture, Agriculture Monograph
   No. 5. Washington: Government Printing Office.
WALKER, KENNETH R.   1965   Planning in Chinese Agri-
   culture: Socialisation and the Private Sector, 1956–
   1962. Chicago: Aldine.
WALTERS, HARRY E.   1963   Agriculture in the United
   States and the Soviet Union. Washington: U.S. De-
   partment of Agriculture, Economic Research Service.
WILLETT, JOSEPH W.   1962   The Recent Record in Agri-
   cultural Production. Part 2, pages 91–113 in U.S.
Congress, Joint Economic Committee, Dimensions of
Soviet Economic Power: Hearings . . . . Washington:
Government Printing Office.

III
PUBLIC FINANCE

The fiscal systems of the communist countries are in some respects similar to those of comparable capitalist nations, while quite different in other respects. The similarities and differences stem largely from similarities and differences in economic and social institutions and in economic and political goals. The communist countries as a group, however, have many institutions and goals in common and have, therefore, very similar fiscal systems. These similarities are, furthermore, probably even greater than they would otherwise have been, because the budgets of the smaller communist nations were originally patterned after that of the Soviet Union. The discussion which follows will concentrate, therefore, on the Soviet budget as prototypical.

General characteristics. A major difference from the capitalist systems derives from the fact that the central governments of the communist nations are, relative to state and local governments, so much more powerful than the central governments of many Western nations. Furthermore, the governments of the communist nations use this power to centrally plan most of the economic activity which takes place within their borders. Correspondingly, the fiscal emphasis in these nations is also centralized. The Soviet state budget, which is ratified by the Supreme Soviet each year, is not just the budget of the "union," or central government, but rather represents a consolidation of the budgets of all political units in the Soviet Union: the union, republican, and numerous levels of local budgets. Whereas in the United States, for example, the federal, state, and local governments each operates its budget in substantial independence of one another, in the Soviet Union the consolidated over-all budget is the major instrument of central government policy.

The budgets of the communist nations tend to be larger and broader in coverage than those of capitalist nations. The Soviet budget is almost one-half as large as Soviet gross national product (GNP), or roughly double the proportion to GNP of the sum of U.S. budgets at all levels of government. This is explained by the fact that almost all investment, education, health, and research in the Soviet Union are controlled by the state and financed through the budget, whereas in capitalist nations a large part is privately controlled and financed. Furthermore, each of these activities involves a claim on national resources which is relatively larger in the Soviet Union than in most capitalist nations.

Because all industry in the Soviet Union is nationalized and its activity planned by the state, one might be led to assume, by analogy with capitalist practice, that the Soviet budget would be larger than it is. In capitalist countries, the gross receipts and expenditures of government enterprises (such as the post office) are often included in the budget. This was true also in the Soviet Union in the period of "war communism," from 1918 to 1920. Since then, however, most state enterprises have operated on an independent financial basis (a so-called *khozraschet* basis) in which they sell their products for money and use the resulting receipts to finance normal operating expenditures, neither the receipts nor expenditures ever appearing in the budget.

The nationalization of industry does change, in a fundamental way, the significance of taxes which are collected from industrial enterprises and which are of overwhelming importance in the communist countries. In capitalist nations, the fiscal process can be viewed as one in which the state divides the tax burden between households and private businesses (and their owners). Where industry is nationalized, taxes paid by state-owned enterprise cannot be viewed realistically as taxes on an independent sector. It appears most appropriate to view such taxes, when they are levied on enterprises producing consumers' goods, as sales taxes on the population, since their entire incidence is to raise the prices of such goods and to reduce the real purchasing power of household earnings. Taxes on capitalist enterprise are also partly on the consumer (to the extent that they are shifted) but fall on businesses (as legal entities) and their owners (a special class of households) as well. It is perhaps worth noting that Soviet economists do not view taxes paid by nationalized industry as taxes on the household at all but rather as a transfer to the state of surplus value created by rising industrial productivity.

One final important difference between the fiscal systems of planned and unplanned economies should be indicated. In the communist countries, the state economic plan sets forth the level and distribution of economic resources necessary for the fulfillment of national objectives. The financial plan, including the budgets, is a reflection of the economic plan and is designed to ensure that the economic plan is implemented without inflation or other undesirable consequences. Financial factors do not, however, in any substantial way constrain the operation of the plan. In capitalist countries, on the other hand, and particularly in peacetime, budgetary factors must be taken into account in the formation of economic policies. Insufficiency of funds, because it is not possible to increase either taxes or the public debt, is an important variable in the policy makers' considerations.

Budget revenues. Revenues of the consolidated state budget of the U.S.S.R. for the years 1955 and 1960 are presented in Table 1.

Table 1 — Revenues of the consolidated state budget of the U.S.S.R. (billions of post-1961 rubles[a])

	1955	1960
Indirect or commodity taxes	37.1	53.6
Turnover tax	24.2	31.3
Deductions from profits of state enterprises	10.3	18.6
Payroll tax	2.6	3.7
Direct or income taxes	4.8	5.6
Sales of state bonds to population	3.1	b
Other revenues[c]	11.4	17.9
Total revenues	56.4	77.1

a. In 1961 the Russians revalued the ruble to reduce all prices, wages, and other financial magnitudes to one-tenth their previous values. Following Soviet practice, these figures are presented in the new 1961 rubles.

b. Negligible.

c. Described in text.

The outstanding feature of the Soviet tax structure is the predominance of indirect or price-increasing taxes. These taxes amount to more than 60 per cent of the budget revenues of every eastern European nation.

The Soviet turnover tax has the impact of an excise or sales tax, as it applies at present only to consumers' goods (with a few minor exceptions like petroleum and petroleum products where the turnover tax substitutes for explicit rent payments). The tax is, however, usually levied at early stages in the production process of consumers' goods and is therefore largely hidden from the consumers' view. The rates are highly differentiated, ranging from 1 per cent of selling price on some commodities to as much as 90 per cent on others. Since 1955 the average rate of turnover tax in the Soviet Union has varied from 40 to 50 per cent of price. The turnover tax is the major source of budget revenue in every European communist country.

The deduction from profits is not a tax on state enterprise for reasons noted above. However, the deduction from profits, since it is part of profits over and above costs, adds to the price paid by the consumer. In this respect, it does not differ from the turnover tax and can properly be considered a tax on the household. Profits are used to make payments into the Directors' Fund (a profit-sharing incentive-type fund used for bonuses, workers' housing, and so forth) and to finance part of the investment in fixed and working capital planned for the enterprise. Any surplus of profits above these needs is *deducted* into the budget. In recent years, about two-thirds of total profits have been paid into the budget.

The payroll tax, or "social insurance markup" as it is called by the communist nations, is derived by adding to the cost of commodities some 5 to 10 per cent of the wage fund of each enterprise. The receipts from this tax are presumably earmarked for sickness and old-age insurance.

The current extensive use of these indirect taxes by communist nations is surprising in view of the fact that Marxist and early Soviet writings excoriated the use of such taxes as regressive, hence socially inequitable. The fact that such taxes are nevertheless relied upon attests to their superiority for the purpose of the planned economies. At least two important advantages of indirect taxes over direct taxes should be mentioned. First, the indirect taxes are cheaper to administer and more difficult for the population to evade. They are collected from thousands of enterprises rather than millions of households. This was particularly important in the early stages of development of these nations before the administrative apparatuses of the government were adequately developed and before literacy was widespread.

A second factor has to do with the so-called "money illusion" hypothesis which argues that workers are more conscious of the impact on their economic position of changes in wages than of the impact produced by changes in prices. A corollary to this is the hypothesis that workers are more sensitive to changes in direct taxes (take-home pay) than to changes in indirect taxes (reflected in higher prices). The money illusion, therefore, would cause an income tax of given size to have a greater negative impact on work incentives than an indirect tax of equal revenue. This is important for two related reasons. First, the communist nations, like Western nations, rely very heavily on differential wages to allocate labor. Second, as indicated above, the direct role of government in communist nations is so much greater than in capitalist nations that the rate of taxation is necessarily much higher. In the U.S.S.R., for example, taxes presently take about one-half of household income; in earlier years, taxes were even higher. If the

U.S.S.R. relied largely on income taxes to maintain monetary stability, and these taxes were progressive as income taxes almost always are, it seems clear that the monetary incentives created by the differential wage structure would be largely blunted —take-home pay would be substantially equalized. On the other hand, the indirect taxes probably have a much lesser disincentive effect. They are not progressive and are largely invisible.

Direct taxes on the population have never been very significant revenue earners and are, in fact, presently scheduled to be abolished in the U.S.S.R. gradually over the next few years. The major direct tax is the income tax on the urban population. At one time this tax was considered important as an instrument of class policy, in the sense that it was differentiated to discriminate very heavily against occupations the government wished to discourage. Thus, while workers and salaried employees paid a very low rate of tax, which progressed to a peak of only 13 per cent, doctors and lawyers with private practices, priests, artisans not belonging to cooperatives, and petty entrepreneurs paid at higher rates which reached peaks of from 55 to 65 per cent.

The rural counterpart to the income tax, a so-called agricultural tax, is levied on collective farmers. The tax is progressive, reaching a peak rate of 48 per cent. That its major purpose is to discourage collective farmers from spending too much time on their private plots of land at the expense of their work on the collective is suggested by the fact that income from working on the collective farm is exempted from the tax.

Until 1957 sales of so-called mass-subscription bonds to the population brought in almost as much revenue to the budget as did direct taxes. In fact, these bonds may well be considered to have been another form of direct levy on the population. Considerable social pressure was brought to bear on the population to subscribe from two to four weeks' wages a year, the appropriate amount being deducted, like the income tax, every month from wages at the place of work. Social pressure was necessary to get subscriptions because the standard of living was low, prices were rising rapidly (until 1948), the interest rate on bonds has been only 3 to 4 per cent in the postwar period, and the bonds were basically inconvertible until maturity. In later years, in an effort to increase the attractiveness of the bonds, bond holders did not receive interest as such, but instead, lotteries were held in which the few winners received all the interest in the form of large prizes. In 1957 sales of mass-subscription bonds were discontinued; at the same time, a moratorium on repayment of 20 to 25 years was declared. At present, small amounts of lottery bonds are sold annually on a purely voluntary basis. Until their discontinuation, the mass-subscription bonds were looked upon by the state as a regular source of revenue with none of the deficit-covering implications of government borrowing in the West.

The budget receives revenue from a number of other minor sources, many of which are unspecified. Profits taxes are levied on industrial and agricultural cooperatives (the collective farms). In 1960 receipts from these organizations amounted to 2 per cent of total revenue. Customs and other receipts from foreign trade operations are still another source of revenue. Other income sources are a fee for inheritance certificates (there is no explicit inheritance tax), sales of state property, fees for commercial forestry and fishing, income from revaluation of inventories, various small local fees and taxes, and gross receipts of organizations, like the post office, which are not on an independent financial basis.

No mention has been made, so far, of taxation in kind of agriculture, because it never *directly* provided the state with funds nor appeared explicitly in the budget. The tax in kind takes the form of compulsory deliveries of agricultural products by collective farmers and peasant farmers to government procurement agencies. These deliveries are based on units of tillable land and numbers of animals. While the farms and farmers are not uncompensated for their deliveries, until recently the prices paid by the state were usually far below costs of production. At the same time they were only a fraction of the retail price at which the state resold agricultural products to the urban population. The high retail price was achieved by superimposing a turnover tax on the procurement price plus costs of processing and distribution. The portion of the turnover tax collected by virtue of below-cost procurement price can be viewed as the monetary equivalent of the tax in kind on agriculture rather than as a sales tax on the urban household. In recent years the tax in kind equivalent of compulsory deliveries (now contractual deliveries) has been sharply reduced as a result of the much higher procurement prices which the state now pays for agricultural products.

Budget expenditures. Expenditures of the consolidated State Budget of the U.S.S.R for 1955 and 1960 are presented in Table 2. The largest item of budget expenditure is "Financing the national economy," to be expected where most economic activity is nationalized. The major expenditure (roughly half) in each of the listed subsectors is for invest-

Table 2 — Expenditures of the consolidated state budget of the U.S.S.R. (billions of post-1961 rubles)

	1955	1960
Financing the national economy	23.5	34.1
Industry and construction	11.0	15.6
State agriculture	5.1	4.4
Agricultural procurement	.8	.5
Trade (domestic and foreign)	1.1	3.6
Transportation and communications	2.0	2.8
Municipal economy and housing	.9	3.2
Other	2.6	4.0
Social—cultural measures	14.7	24.9
Education and science	6.9	10.3
Health and physical culture	3.1	4.8
Social welfare	4.7	9.8
Defense	10.7	9.3
Administration	1.3	1.1
Loan service	1.4	.7
Other	2.5	3.0
Total expenditures	54.1	73.1

ment in and repair of fixed capital. Other important expenditures are for the expansion of working capital, subsidies to cover losses, training of workers, experimentation and design, geological prospecting, and stockpiling of material reserves.

Expenditures for "Social–cultural measures" are next in importance to "Financing the national economy." Outlays for scientific research have risen rapidly in recent years and in 1960 amounted to almost one-third of the expenditures listed under "Education and science." "Social welfare" includes social security and insurance, aid to mothers, and other such transfer payments. These have been increasing rapidly of late as a result of the recent increase in size of pensions and because of the forthcoming extension of social security and insurance to the collective farm sector.

The "Defense" category is defined by Russian textbooks to include the expenditures of the Ministry of Defense for wages and material allowances of personnel, purchase of supplies and repair of combat equipment, support of military institutions and schools, military construction, and so forth. Presumably some of what might legitimately be considered part of the Soviet defense effort is not included in the explicit "Defense" item. For example, defense-connected research is probably financed under the science part of "Education and science," and it has been suggested that expenditures for atomic energy are included under "Financing the national economy." Finally, it is possible that some unspecified military expenditures are included in the "Other," or residual items, two of which appear in Table 2.

"Administration" includes, as in most countries, the support of the traditional political, judicial, and other such departments of the government. The final "Other" category is known to include internal security outlays, loan service, and some reserve funds.

The pattern of Soviet budget expenditures indicated above has been followed fairly closely by almost all the communist nations. There were some deviations, however. Almost all the nations devoted about 10 per cent more of their budgets to "Financing the national economy" and from 5 to 10 per cent less to "Defense" than the Soviet Union. An exception was Outer Mongolia, whose budget expenditures on the national economy amounted to only about one-third of the budget and whose defense expenditures were about as large a proportion as that of the Soviets. The importance of "Social–cultural measures" expenditures in the budget was relatively low in China (12 per cent) and Bulgaria (21 per cent) and relatively high in Czechoslovakia (39 per cent) and in the German Democratic Republic (38 per cent). As in the Soviet Union, "Defense" was much larger than "Administration" in Czechoslovakia, Rumania, Bulgaria, Albania, and China but much lower in Hungary and the German Democratic Republic. The significance of these comparisons is reduced to the extent that they may result in part from differences in expenditure classification.

Budgetary imbalance and monetary stability. Success or failure of the budgetary policies of the communist nations cannot be judged by observing the budget accounts in isolation. Although the budget is undoubtedly the most important financial institution, it is not the only one, and its policies must be viewed in the context of over-all financial policy. There seems little doubt that the budgets of the communist countries are designed to have a deflationary impact on the economy. With the exception of the years 1941–1943 for the Soviet Union, and 1950 and 1955–1956 for China, the budgets of the communist nations have returned surpluses for all years for which data are available. In part, these surpluses may be explained by the practice of including income from sales of government bonds as a regular item of budget revenue. However, as noted above, this is appropriate in circumstances where sales of bonds are compulsory, the bonds are not convertible until maturity and are not purchased by banks through printing of money.

Most of the communist nations have had strong inflationary pressures which, despite the existence of deflationary budgets, have not always been under control. This suggests that in the other financial institutions of the communist nations, offsetting inflationary policies have been pursued. The major culprit in the Soviet economy has been the Gosbank, or state bank. The state bank finances through short-term loans the expansion of the temporary working capital needs of state enterprises. One major source of its funds is the surplus deposited with it by the state budget. To the extent that short-term loans outstanding increase by more than the budget surplus, the state bank creates money (abstracting from other items in the bank balance sheet). If the amount of money created is large relative to the increase in output and if other (real) factors are conducive to inflation, then upward wage and price pressures tend to develop.

In recent years, the price levels of the communist nations have substantially stabilized relative to the earlier years. In the Soviet Union, two decades of inflation ended with the currency reform of 1947 and prices have been stable or declining ever since. One cause of this relative stability has to do with budgetary policy: it is the fact that the budget surplus has risen relative to the expansion of short-term bank credit. Second and third causes, perhaps as important, if not more so, are the facts that the Soviet government now has better direct control over rising wage levels than it had in the past and that the pressure on resources of overfull-employment planning has apparently been eased in the postwar period.

FRANKLYN D. HOLZMAN

[See also TAXATION.]

BIBLIOGRAPHY

DAVIES, ROBERT W. 1958 *The Development of the Soviet Budgetary System.* Cambridge Univ. Press.

ECKLUND, GEORGE N. 1966 *Financing the Chinese Government Budget.* Chicago: Aldine.

HOLZMAN, FRANKLYN D. 1953 The Soviet Budget: 1928–1952. *National Tax Journal* 6:226–249.

HOLZMAN, FRANKLYN D. 1955 *Soviet Taxation: The Fiscal and Monetary Problems of a Planned Economy.* Russian Research Center Studies, No. 16. Cambridge, Mass.: Harvard Univ. Press.

HOLZMAN, FRANKLYN D. 1957 The Tax System of Outer Mongolia, 1911–1955: A Brief History. *Journal of Asian Studies* 16:221–236.

HOLZMAN, FRANKLYN D. 1960 Soviet Inflationary Pressures, 1928–1957: Causes and Cures. *Quarterly Journal of Economics* 74:167–188.

KOMISSAROV, V. P.; and POPOV, A. N. 1960 *Den'gi, kredit, i finansy evropeiskikh stran narodnoi demokratii.* Moscow: Izdatel'stvo Sotsial'no-ekonomicheskoi Literatury.

KWANG, CHING-WEN 1963 The Budgetary System of the People's Republic of China: A Preliminary Survey. *Public Finance* 18:253–286.

PLOTNIKOV, K. N. (1953) 1959 *Gosudarstvennyi biudzhet S.S.S.R.* Moscow: Gosfinizdat.
SUCHKOV, A.; SVIDERSKII, IA.; and PAEVSKII, V. (1949) 1960 *Gosudarstvennye dokhody S.S.S.R.* Moscow: Gosfinizdat. → Suchkov was the sole author of the 1949 edition.

IV

INTERNATIONAL TRADE

Until communist regimes established themselves or were established in a number of countries in the aftermath of World War II, the Soviet Union was the only country claiming to be "socialist" (communist), and naturally, its trade was wholly with the "capitalist" world. However, the principles upon which it based its foreign trade and the organizational structure of its trade have changed little and have greatly influenced the procedures of other communist countries.

Historical development. After the seizure of power in 1917, the communist regime took all foreign economic transactions into its own hands, declaring a state monopoly of foreign trade. This principle meant at first simply that no private firm or individual could trade with foreign countries without specific authorization by state organs. It was a necessary reaction to the chaos of war and civil war, a means of preserving the pitifully small reserves of gold and foreign exchange and of combating black-marketeering and speculation. During the "war communism" period, from 1918 to 1921, the state nationalized all industry and trade, but there followed a period of relative economic liberalization, the New Economic Policy (NEP), during which some private industrial and internal trading activities were again allowed. However, foreign trade was deemed to be part of those "commanding heights" which it was essential to preserve in the hands of the communist state.

In 1920 a people's commissariat for foreign trade was created, and foreign trade deals were almost wholly the responsibility of this ministry and of the specialized trading departments which were created under it. It is true that so-called cooperatives were allowed to engage in trade and to maintain representatives in foreign countries (e.g., Amtorg in the United States and Arcos in Great Britain). However, these were mere devices to cope with such problems as nonrecognition of the Soviet government by the United States or prejudice against dealing with Soviet trade officials. It made no practical difference to the planning of foreign trade. Whenever possible the Soviet authorities established trade delegations with diplomatic status which were associated with Soviet embassies in foreign countries. These included representatives of the principal specialized trading departments most concerned in trade with that country.

This pattern has continued. The people's commissariat of trade, like other commissariats, was renamed "ministry" in 1946. There is such a ministry in each communist country; each has trading departments or corporations specializing in imports or exports (or both) of particular commodities, ship chartering, or other dealings abroad. With few exceptions this ministry and its organs exercise the monopoly of foreign trade as the sole intermediary between state enterprises and foreign countries. In other words, a doctrine which was designed to prevent private entrepreneurs or private traders from buying and selling abroad is now interpreted to mean something rather different: that state-salaried directors of domestic economic enterprises may not engage in deals with any foreign country, including, as we shall see, any communist country.

To explain why this has come about, let us return to the experience of the Soviet Union. By 1929, private enterprise in industry and trade had been virtually wiped out, and the Soviet Union was launched upon its industrialization and collectivization programs. There developed a planning system which, in essentials, survives to this day. All state enterprises are told by the planning organs what to produce, to whom to deliver and at what prices, and from whom to buy and at what prices. Material balances are drawn up of all principal commodities, both for the current year and for use in planning future growth. It is then determined whether, now or in the future, the country's needs for particular items can be met out of domestic production or whether imports are necessary. Similarly, material balances show export availabilities. Naturally, in the process of planning constant adjustments are made in the internal plans as well as in the foreign-trade plans. Sometimes domestic users have been deprived of much-needed commodities, which were then used to pay for urgent imports. A well-known example is the export of wheat to pay for capital equipment in the early 1930s, a time when many were hungry or even starving. This was a matter of political decision about priorities, which was reminiscent of trade planning in "capitalist" countries in wartime.

In such circumstances it is natural that all trade deals are centralized under a specialized ministry, which works closely with the planning organs. As will be shown this version of the principle of the "monopoly of foreign trade" leads to many practical

Table 1 — Growth of foreign trade and national income in the eastern European countries and the Soviet Union, 1960 to 1965

	VALUE IN 1962 (millions of current dollars[a])	PERCENTAGE INCREASE IN VALUE FROM CORRESPONDING PERIOD OF PREVIOUS YEAR					Planned annual rate to 1965[b]
		1960	1961	1962	First half 1963	1963 plan	
Albania							
Exports	c	42.8	c	c	c	26.4 ⎫	10.5–11.2
Imports	c	−4.9	−10.9	c	c	c ⎬	
National income	c	0.4	5.8	8	c	11.0	9.3
Bulgaria							
Exports	770	22.3	15.9	16.3	10	10.6	12.5
Imports	780	9.2	5.3	17.2	20	10.8	c
National income	c	7.0	2.8	6[d]	c	c	9.9
Czechoslovakia							
Exports	2,193	11.7	6.1	7.2	−1[e]	c	9.4
Imports	2,070	13.3	11.5	2.3	−8.4[e]	c	6.7
National income	c	8.2	6.4	0.5	c	1[f]	7.3
East Germany							
Exports	2,353	3.3	3.2	4.1	13	15	9.3
Imports	2,372	8.9	2.1	7.0	−6.5[e]	c	7.2
National income	c	4.6	3.7	4.2	c	2[d]	6.8
Hungary							
Exports	1,100	13.6	17.7	6.9	3.5	6	10.0
Imports	1,148	23.1	5.1	11.9	7.3	10[d]	5.9
National income	c	10.1	5.8	5.0	c	7–8	6.3
Poland							
Exports	1,646	15.7	13.4	9.5	1.5	6.0	9.2
Imports	1,886	5.3	12.8	11.8	4.8	3.2	4.9
National income	c	4.5	8.1	1½[h]	c	5	7.0
Rumania							
Exports	818	37.2	10.5	3.2	c	c ⎫	12.3
Imports	941	29.1	25.8	15.5	c	c ⎬	
National income	c	10.8	10.1	6.5	c	13[f]	9.3–10.3
Seven eastern European countries							
Exports	8,800[g]	12.8	9.0	7.0[g]	c	c ⎫	8½[h]
Imports	9,197[g]	12.1	8.8	9.1[g]	c	c ⎬	
National income	c	6.7[h]	6.3[h]	3½[h]	c	c	7½[h]
Soviet Union							
Exports	7,035	2.2	7.8	17.3 ⎫		c ⎫	6–10½[i]
Imports	6,450	11.0	3.5	10.7 ⎬	2	c ⎬	
National income	c	7.7	6.8	6.0	c	7	7.2–7.4
Eastern Europe and Soviet Union[g]							
Exports	15,915[g]	8.1	8.5	11.3[g]	c	c ⎫	9½[f]
Imports	15,647[g]	11.6	6.6	9.7[g]	c	c ⎬	
National income	c	7½[h]	6½[h]	5½[h]	c	c	7½[h]

a. Plan data for trade and all data for national income are at constant prices, except those for East Germany.

b. The periods covered are 1959–1965 for the Soviet Union and East Germany, 1960–1965 for Rumania, 1961–1965 for other countries. Some of these plans were in process of revision when table was constructed.

c. Not available.

d. Estimate by the Secretariat of the Economic Commission for Europe.

e. First quarter.

f. Approximate.

g. Excluding Albania.

h. National aggregates converted to a common basis of valuation by applying official exchange rates; they should be regarded as no more than indicators of the trend.

i. The lower figure was written into the plan as a target for trade with socialist countries. The higher figure represents an aspiration expressed by the Minister for Foreign Trade (*Pravda*, February 18, 1959).

Source: Adapted from Economic Bulletin for Europe, vol. 15, no. 1, p. 24.

difficulties. However, it is a logical and integral part of the system of internal planning established under Stalin, and it has not proved easy to reform the system after his death.

In the Stalin period Soviet trade policy was greatly influenced by the need to achieve self-sufficiency, especially in capital goods. This could be explained by military security considerations, especially in the 1930s. This tendency toward autarchy, which continued, though not to so marked an extent, into the postwar period, affects in varying degree all communist countries. It has two

Table 2 — External trade of six eastern European countries, by main regions, 1960 to 1962

	EXPORTS					IMPORTS				
	Value in 1962, millions of current dollars	Annual percentage increase			Percentage share 1962	Value in 1962, millions of current dollars	Annual percentage increase			Percentage share 1962
		1960	1961	1962			1960	1961	1962	
Bulgaria										
Total[a]	770	22.3	15.9	16.3	100.0	780	9.2	5.3	17.2	100.0
Soviet Union	387	18.5	9.6	15.0	50.3	440	16.0	7.0	23.6	56.3
Other eastern European countries	213	17.8	25.7	10.0	27.6	183	18.0	5.4	−1.4	23.4
Asian planned economies	5	8.9	5.7	−50[b]	0.7	6	6.2	46.2	−20.0[b]	0.8
Czechoslovakia										
Total	2,193	11.7	6.1	7.2	100.0	2,070	13.3	11.5	2.3	100.0
Soviet Union	828	12.1	8.3	16.1	37.7	781	5.4	4.1	19.1	37.7
Other eastern European countries	715	12.9	11.3	13.0	32.6	648	21.4	20.0	1.6	31.3
Asian planned economies	26	−1.6	−63.3	−46.6	1.2	45	−1.8	−47.4	−20.3	2.2
Western Europe	340	6.3	10.3	−5.2	15.5	359	21.1	8.0	−2.5	17.3
of which, EEC	(151)	(14.8)	(14.4)	(−1.8)	(6.9)	(157)	(18.1)	(17.8)	(−1.8)	(7.6)
Rest of the world	284	25.0	19.9	−2.9	13.0	237	16.7	48.1	−22.5	11.5
of which, less-developed regions[c]	(253)	(24.6)	(23.9)	(−2.8)	(11.6)	(202)	(13.5)	(44.5)	(−14.1)	(9.8)
Hungary										
Total[a]	1,100	13.6	17.7	6.9	100.0	1,148	23.1	5.1	11.9	100.0
Soviet Union	393	22.9	29.4	18.4	35.7	417	18.5	17.6	16.9	36.3
Other eastern European countries	368[b]	10.7	26.1	4.0[b]	33.4[b]	366[b]	26.1	−4.2	19.2[b]	31.9[b]
EEC	111	5.5	7.3	7.4	10.1	133	37.9	2.1	−1.1	11.6
Less-developed regions[c]	78	14.0	34.0	9.5	7.0	68	16.4	34.5	33.7	6.0
Poland										
Total	1,646	15.7	13.4	9.5	100.0	1,886	5.3	12.8	11.8	100.0
Soviet Union	569	24.7	24.3	17.2	34.5	578	2.9	5.3	18.0	30.6
Other eastern European countries	390	15.3	9.2	5.6	23.7	579	5.5	17.4	22.1	30.7
Asian planned economies	23	10.8	−41.6	−36.0	1.4	32	−12.1	−51.0	16.0	1.7
Western Europe	473	9.6	8.2	12.8	28.8	435	1.0	14.5	5.7	23.1
of which, EEC	(171)	(4.4)	(11.8)	(11.4)	(10.4)	(134)	(11.3)	(−9.0)	(−2.1)	(7.1)
Rest of the world	191	14.1	31.0	−1.4	11.6	262	27.4	34.9	−7.7	13.9
of which, less-developed regions[c]	(142)	(17.5)	(35.8)	(−7.1)	(8.6)	(129)	(40.4)	(4.4)	(13.6)	(6.8)
Rumania										
Total	819	37.2	10.5	3.2	100.0	941	29.1	25.8	15.5	100.0
Soviet Union	344	12.5	24.8	−2.2	42.0	371	13.3	12.4	24.1	39.4
Other eastern European countries	195	54.9	−10.9	15.0	23.8	233	28.3	21.2	10.5	24.7
Asian planned economies	11	18.6	−65.6	−29.1	1.3	15	−9.5	−11.6	−40.2	1.6
Western Europe	192	89.1	23.0	−2.7	23.4	262	95.4	56.6	12.0	27.9
of which, EEC	(126)	(87.0)	(22.0)	(9.8)	(15.4)	(157)	(119.0)	(30.3)	(28.5)	(16.7)
Rest of the world	77	48.1	43.3	29.4	9.5	60	27.4	53.3	32.2	6.4
of which, less-developed regions[c]	(72)	(49.7)	(31.3)	(33.5)	(8.8)	(52)	(4.6)	(75.8)	(33.7)	(5.5)
Soviet Union										
Total[d]	7,035	2.2	7.8	17.3	100.0	6,450	11.0	3.5	10.7	100.0
Other eastern European countries	3,971[e]	5.7	9.6	16.1[e]	56.5[e]	3,588[e]	11.9	8.7	17.0[e]	55.6[e]
Asian planned economies	495	−14.5	−40.0	−14.4	7.0	695	−17.6	−28.7	−2.7	10.8
Western Europe	1,078	10.8	2.1	8.8	15.3	1,143	27.4	−1.4	17.2	17.8
of which, EEC	(439)	(6.9)	(9.6)	(7.4)	(6.2)	(537)	(56.2)	(−0.8)	(17.0)	(8.3)
Rest of the world	1,491	4.3	98.6	47.8	21.2	1,024	46.1	31.6	−4.9	15.9
of which, less-developed regions[c]	(1,357)	(−5.2)	(115.6)	(56.7)	(19.3)	(817)	(29.5)	(37.8)	(−6.7)	(12.7)

a. Total is not sum of subitems, because of exclusion of the rest-of-the-world category.

b. Estimate by the Secretariat of the Economic Commission for Europe.

c. In general, "less-developed regions" includes all trade for which origin and destination are not specified. The spectacular rise in exports to that category in 1961 and 1962 was largely due to the inclusion of Cuba (e.g., Soviet exports to Cuba multiplied by four in 1961 alone).

d. Details may not add to total because of rounding.

e. Excluding Albania.

Source: Adapted from *Economic Bulletin for Europe*, vol. 15, no. 1, p. 25.

explanations. The first is fear that the foreign country may upset the plan by acting in some unpredictable way; thus a communist partner may alter its internal plan and cancel trade deals (this has happened several times) or a Western country may impose some unexpected embargo, or import duty, or add a desired item to a list of banned "strategic" goods. All this makes it seem easier to rely on supplies from within the country. Second, the same tendency is encouraged by the bureaucratic complexities encountered by attempts to import. These, in turn, are contributed to by the chronic and sometimes critical shortage of foreign exchange, which persistently plagues all communist countries.

After World War II trade between the Soviet-bloc countries grew rapidly, stimulated particularly by Western restrictions imposed at the time of the Korean War, but trade with China fell very sharply after 1960. After Stalin's death trade with most Western countries and also with the underdeveloped countries rose very fast from very low levels. An important exception is the United States, which, unlike its European allies, has continued a severely restrictive policy. Tables 1 and 2 show the pattern as it has developed.

Analysis of policies. In analyzing trade policies and problems, it is best to consider separately three kinds of transactions: those with the industrialized West, with underdeveloped countries, and with other communist states. While there are some questions common to them all, there are some peculiarities which it is necessary to dwell on. In addition it is important to bear in mind one further distinction, that between the U.S.S.R. and China on the one hand and the other communist countries on the other. The U.S.S.R. and China cover immense territories and are to a considerable extent self-sufficient. By this is not meant that foreign trade is unimportant. It is undeniably a source of essential materials, machinery, and know-how. However, the total volume of imports or exports represents a very small proportion of their gross national product, in the case of the U.S.S.R. about 3 per cent. Consequently, foreign trade is not among the most important factors governing growth, and domestic policy and economic organization are unlikely to be decisively influenced by foreign-trade considerations. For example, it is hardly likely that Soviet economic reforms would occur merely because the existing arrangements are inconvenient for foreign trade. By contrast, the smaller countries—notably Czechoslovakia, Poland, Hungary, East Germany, and increasingly also Rumania—depend greatly on foreign trade, which for them is *the* bottleneck in any plan of economic growth. Therefore the inconveniences of the "traditional" Soviet trading system matter very much more for them, and the pressures for change are greater.

Trade with Western industrialized countries. The U.S.S.R. and its allies buy machinery and equipment and also a number of minerals and semimanufactures from Western countries. In addi-

tion heavy imports of grain have been necessary, especially in years in which weather adversely affected the harvest. There is reluctance to spend scarce foreign exchange on manufactured consumer goods. Exports to Western countries have, of course, increased, but there have been serious problems in the way of finding more of the right goods to export. This has been partly a matter of availability of goods of the right type or quality but is also due to Western restrictions. These affect a wide range of agricultural products which these countries could export, as well as Soviet and Rumanian oil and many other products. Some of these restrictions are of a discriminatory character, that is, they apply only to goods from the Soviet bloc, and this is the subject of bitter complaint, understandably enough. Discrimination against trade with communist countries has been introduced on the following grounds. First, it was feared that the communist traders would resort to "dumping" and so disorganize the market. This fear does not, as a rule, go with the belief that the dumping and disorganization are intended. On the contrary, it is appreciated by most serious analysts that the Soviet, Czech, and other traders are under instructions to sell as dear as possible to maximize foreign currency earnings. However, they are also under instructions to *sell*, and, if faced with the need to cut prices, would undercut Western commercial competitors. A second reason for Western caution is fear of excessive dependence on supplies which might be cut off in the event of political trouble. This fear also affects, for equally valid reasons, the trading policies of communist countries. The canceling by the Germans, in 1963, of contracts for steel pipe, although this item was not on the list of strategically restricted Western exports, must have sharply reminded Soviet planners of this risk. A third cause of difficulty is the Western strategic list, which, though considerably pruned, still includes some items of no direct military significance which the Soviet bloc wishes to buy. Since the American interpretation of what is "strategic" is more stringent than western Europe's, snags arise when British or German chemical machinery happens to include some American-patented part or process. Fourth, discriminatory measures in Western countries are due to the belief that they are being discriminated against. Since state organs are the only buyers, it is open to the communist authorities, by unpublished interoffice memoranda, to tell their traders to buy in one market rather than another. The result is that Western negotiators press for quotas for their goods, especially "less essentials," in elaborate bilateral negotiations while imposing quotas on a range of "communist" goods of types which enter from elsewhere without quantitative restriction.

Trade with developing countries. Soviet-bloc trade with developing countries may be divided into two parts. The first, traditional in character, consists in the purchase of raw materials (e.g., rubber, cocoa, tin), often with sterling obtained from a favorable trade balance with Great Britain. The second, which became significant in and after 1956, is closely connected with aid programs and credits. Manufactures, and especially capital goods, are mainly involved, although the U.S.S.R. has also exported grain, timber, and oil to Egypt and a number of other countries. The credits are, as a rule, repayable in the goods normally exported by the recipient country, and so the Soviet bloc has been greatly increasing its imports of Egyptian cotton, Indian tea, and so on. The limiting factor on the expansion of this trade-with-aid has been, and is, the availability of resources within Soviet-bloc countries, which are heavily committed to these countries' own plans of economic growth. So far the bulk of trade-with-aid has been concentrated in a few countries. India, Indonesia, and Egypt have had the lion's share.

Trade within the Soviet bloc. In 1949 the Council for Mutual Economic Assistance (COMECON, or CMEA) was set up to coordinate the Soviet and European communist economies. China and other Asian countries sent observers, though since 1961 China and Albania have absented themselves, while Mongolia has become a member. COMECON virtually did nothing until 1955. Bilateral arrangements were the rule, with Soviet influence predominant. Unequal trade treaties were imposed, as may be surmised from the execution of officials in Bulgaria and Czechoslovakia on a charge of trying to strike too hard a bargain with the Soviet Union. Ex-enemy countries (Rumania, East Germany, Hungary) had to make large reparation deliveries. A number of joint companies were set up, under virtual Soviet control. After Stalin's death a gradual evolution began toward a less subordinate role of the Soviet Union's European allies. This process was greatly speeded up by the shock of the 1956 events in Poland and Hungary. Paradoxically, the period of direct political subordination to the U.S.S.R. was also one in which there was very little systematic effort at economic coordination. It was increasingly recognized that by failing to plan their investments and their trade so as to achieve rational economic specialization, the countries of the Soviet bloc, and particularly the smaller countries, were suffering unnecessary economic loss. There-

fore, questions of joint planning came to the fore, and COMECON began to be more active. Since 1956 a number of agreements have been concluded under the aegis of COMECON. These include specialization agreements, especially those covering some branches of the machinery and vehicles industries, some joint investment projects, an effort to standardize components and trade nomenclature, and arrangements for the joint use of railway wagons and for international electricity transmission lines and oil pipes. A COMECON bank came into existence in January 1964. The point was not lost on Khrushchev that the Common Market in western Europe showed that, contrary to doctrine, economic integration between capitalist states seemed to be advancing more rapidly than between socialist ones. Nonetheless there has still been relatively little joint planning, the COMECON organs have no executive authority, and actual trading arrangements remain almost wholly bilateral.

The special problems of trade between communist countries are the following: first, since in each country all major investment and resource allocation decisions are taken by the central planners, all matters relating to international specialization and therefore to trade become a matter for decision at the highest government and party levels. In the West most of the specialization is a consequence of a large number of decentralized arrangements between firms. This is impossible in the communist countries so long as their internal planning system is what it is. Effective joint planning under the circumstances requires a supranational authority which could oversee the requirements of the entire bloc and which could take appropriate and enforceable decisions. There is no such authority. In its absence the concentration of trading decisions in the hands of specialized trading organizations cuts off the enterprises from contacts with their markets and their customers and makes it difficult to study the requirements of users or to undertake market research.

Second, since prices in the various countries are fixed by government order and bear little relationship to relative scarcities or to need, they cannot be used as a guide as to whether anything should be imported or exported, nor as a basis of comparing costs. In practice the prices used in trade between Soviet-bloc countries are those of the capitalist world market (very roughly, since they are sometimes frozen for several years and seem on average to be rather higher than capitalist prices). These artificial foreign-trade prices have little or no connection with internal costs or with intrabloc exchange rates. This makes it difficult to find mutually acceptable objective criteria for specialization. The less-developed countries of the bloc, notably Rumania, have been strongly pressing their own ambitious industrialization plans, and it has proved virtually impossible to advance effective counter-arguments in the name of rational specialization.

Third, while it is realized that bilateralism causes economic loss, it has so far proved incurable. Trade negotiations have amounted to a kind of barter: each country exchanges with the other country goods worth the same amount, and the quantities in question are then incorporated in the plans and material balances of each country. Any considerable surplus convertible into a claim on a third country may not enable the holder of the surplus to convert it into the sort of goods that it wants, since there has been no provision in the plans of that third country to make these goods available. Theoretically it is possible to envisage multilateral barter, but in practice there has been very little of this. Since planning is essentially in terms of physical quantities, the multilateral facilities of the new COMECON bank are hardly relevant in this situation.

So long as each country continues to plan its own investments and resource allocation and so long as COMECON plays a purely advisory or consultative role, it is hard to see how the situation could improve. On political grounds the conversion of COMECON into a supranational organ is not practicable. The theoretical alternative solution would be to so decentralize the planning of each country that enterprises would be free to purchase their inputs from suppliers both within and outside the borders of the given country instead of having them allocated administratively. This may be the long-term solution but would plainly require some major changes in the internal arrangements of each country.

Meanwhile the volume of exchanges, bilateral it is true, between the communist countries in Europe has been steadily increasing. While the difficulties mentioned above are very real and are the cause of much worry to the planners of the countries concerned, one should recall the fact that the trade practices of many Western countries are far removed from the traditional principles of economic rationality and that developing countries such as India have been compelled to impose trade restrictions based on a political determination of priorities and not on a necessarily static analysis of comparative costs. Yet when all this has been allowed for, the special weaknesses of foreign trade of communist countries remain. Not the least of

them is the almost total failure to develop any theory of foreign trade or to devise a pricing policy or a method of assessing costs which could be followed in intercountry comparisons. It is not by any means always necessary to determine the pattern of trade by reference to such comparisons, but one should surely start by knowing these elementary economic facts of life.

A. Nove

[*See also* International trade controls, *article on* state trading.]

BIBLIOGRAPHY
Economic Bulletin for Europe. → Published since 1949 by the Economic Commission for Europe. See especially Volume 15, No. 1 and Volume 16, No. 2.
Kaser, Michael 1965 *COMECON: Integration Problems of the Planned Economies.* Oxford Univ. Press.
Nove, Alec; and Donnelly, Desmond 1960 *Trade With Communist Countries.* London: Hutchinson.
Pryor, Frederic L. 1963 *The Communist Foreign Trade System.* Cambridge, Mass.: M.I.T. Press.
U.S. Congress, Senate Committee on Foreign Relations 1964 *East/West Trade: A Compilation of Views of Businessmen, Bankers and Academic Experts* and *Statistical Appendix.* Washington: Government Printing Office.

COMMUNITY

The articles under this heading discuss three aspects of the community as a geographical and social unit. Other aspects of the community are discussed in many other articles in the encyclopedia. Major theoretical positions are reviewed in Community–society continua *and* Ecology, *article on* human ecology. *Communities of different sizes are described in* City; Neighborhood; Rural society; Village. *The major institutions that enable communities to function are described in* City, *article on* metropolitan government; Local finance; Local government; Local politics; Voluntary associations. *The fate of community in modern society is discussed in* Mass society. Planning, social, *article on* regional and urban planning, *and* Utopianism, *article on* the design of experimental communities, *describe sharply contrasting approaches to the problem of planning better communities. Loss or renunciation of community is described in* Homelessness. *Methods of research into community life are reviewed in* Anthropology, *article on* the anthropological study of modern society; Ethnography; Field work; Observation. *For material on social scientists who have particularly advanced the study of community, see the biographies of* BOOTH; BURGESS; GEDDES; PARK; REDFIELD; TOCQUEVILLE; TÖNNIES; WEBB, SIDNEY AND BEATRICE; WIRTH.

I. THE STUDY OF COMMUNITY
    POWER   *Nelson W. Polsby*
II. COMMUNITY DISORGANIZATION   *Jessie Bernard*
III. COMMUNITY DEVELOPMENT   *Irwin T. Sanders*

I

THE STUDY OF COMMUNITY POWER

Contemporary research on community power is distinguished by: (1) a concern with characterizing as a whole the political order of an entire community (generally an American local community); (2) radical disagreement on methods of going about this task; (3) both agreement and disagreement on specific findings; and (4) conflict over the proper interpretation of findings. At points of disagreement there has been a tendency for the literature to break roughly into two schools of thought—one based on a theory of social stratification, the other less systematically derived from theories of pluralist democracy. While contention between advocates of these schools has occupied much space in the literature, the problems, possibilities, and accomplishments of community power research neither begin nor end there.

There is a sense in which the beginnings of community power research are identical with the origins of Western thought, since the early speculations and investigations of Plato and Aristotle on the nature of man and his government referred to the polities and constitutions of Greek city-states (Friedrich 1959; Long 1962). The marked resurgence of interest in community power in recent years, however, has several distinctive features and immediate antecedents. Among sociologists, interest in American social problems created by industrialization, mass immigration, and urbanization reached a kind of crescendo in the late 1920s and during and after the great depression, notably under the leadership of Robert Park and W. I. Thomas at the University of Chicago. Investigations of Negro and Jewish ghettos by Zorbaugh (1929) and Wirth (1928), of the Polish immigrant by Thomas and Znaniecki (1918–1920), and of skid row bums, criminals, and prostitutes by others —while contributing significantly to the growth of sociological thinking—also reflected the policy-oriented, ameliorative interests of sociologists of this period. Later, the depression led sociologists to re-examine their equalitarian assumptions about American society and reactivated a long-dormant concern among them for theories of social strati-

fication. These theories had never gone out of fashion in Europe but had previously been thought to be of only limited applicability to the American experience. One illustration of a shift toward the use of stratification theory is contained in the contrast between the early classic study of *Middletown* (1929), by Robert S. Lynd and Helen M. Lynd, and its equally renowned successor, *Middletown in Transition* (1937), which emphasized community power much more than did the earlier book.

When American political science emerged as a formal discipline around the turn of the twentieth century, its members regarded the local community as a massive political problem requiring prescriptive rather than strictly descriptive activity. The adverse judgments on American city politics advanced by Bryce (1888), Ostrogorskii (1902), and others led to agitation for the professionalization of city management and to other suggestions for reform, but not to systematic attempts to comprehend local politics descriptively (see Sayre & Polsby 1965). In the 1920s and 1930s an energetic group of political scientists at Chicago, led by Charles E. Merriam, undertook to redress the balance; but most of their efforts were incorporated into ongoing research in political parties and voting behavior rather than into the field of local politics (see, for example, Merriam & Gosnell 1924; Key 1936).

World War II, with its large-scale displacement of academic talent into national and international arenas, no doubt served to delay further the discovery of local communities as suitable and attractive laboratories for the examination of traditional problems of empirical political theory. At any rate, it was not until the 1950s that this literature began to emerge in full flower, although its precursors and roots can be found in earlier writings.

Characterizing a whole community

Little attention has been devoted in contemporary community power research to the problem of defining a community—a question that has recently engaged, among others, students of international politics and organization (e.g., Deutsch 1953; Haas 1958; Russett 1963). For the most part, a conventional perspective has been adopted and a "community" has been defined as a population living within legally established city limits. Only rarely is the term used in this literature to describe a standard metropolitan area, marketing area, or some entity defined by functions other than political. The problem of setting boundaries on the community is, perhaps, ultimately insoluble except by arbitrary means, because it is freely conceded that *externally* made decisions may have a significant impact on the allocation of values and on important private and public decisions *within* the community, however defined. And it is the description of the shaping and sharing of these values and decisions that is the central concern of the community power literature.

Methods of research

A serious problem in characterizing the political order of a whole community concerns sampling procedures. Clearly not all decisions, or even a meaningful fraction of them, are normally studied in order to arrive at a description of power distribution within a particular community. The inevitable and necessary compromises that students have made have led to much disagreement on methods of research. To a certain extent each student of community power has had to fashion his own compromise with the fuzzy universe of decisions in the community in which he has worked— a compromise dictated in part by the time, help, and funds at his disposal, and in part by the theoretical presuppositions he has brought to the research.

"Total immersion." One method of study has consisted of what might be termed "total immersion" in the community by a researcher or research team for a lengthy period of time—sometimes as long as a year or more (see, for example, Lynd & Lynd 1929; 1937; Warner & Lunt 1941; Warner et al. 1949; Hollingshead 1949; Sayre & Kaufman 1960; Scoble 1961; Dahl 1961). The researcher thus has an opportunity to learn the perspectives of local residents, to identify issues and decisions they regard as significant, to absorb some of the history and background of the community, and to see its various groups and leaders in the round of daily life. More formal interviewing, participant observation, clipping of newspapers, and examinations of official records, census materials, and so on can also be employed during the period of residence. A variant of this is the method of gathering and generalizing from numerous case studies describing decision making in detail (see, e.g., Banfield 1961; Wildavsky 1964; *Decisions* 1961).

Clearly this method—insofar as it can be regarded as *a* method of research rather than as an eclectic combination of methods—is not open to much criticism. Most of the criticism of community power studies using this method has attacked the analysis of data and the appropriateness of conclusions drawn from the data, rather than the data-gathering methods of the studies.

"Reputational" studies. A drawback of the total immersion method of research is its expense in time and money. It also smacks to some of casual empiricism of a kind that renders either replication or comparative study difficult. And so it is not surprising that an attempt, however crude, to develop a more mechanical method of research in this field was warmly welcomed and quickly imitated. Such an attempt was made by Floyd Hunter (1953), who in a study of Atlanta, Georgia, introduced what later came to be called the "reputational" approach to discovering patterns of community power.

Although this method is not compactly described in the original study and modifications have been introduced by others (e.g., Miller 1958; D'Antonio et al. 1961; Klapp & Padgett 1960), we can present it in general outline. Briefly, the central goal of the method is to arrive at a list of people who can be called "top influentials" in the community. Often, lists of nominees are solicited from people who are presumed to be knowledgeable in various sectors of community life. These names are then winnowed (to 40 in Atlanta) by a panel of judges, so that only those on whom a number of people agree appear on the final list. Members of this list are customarily interviewed and asked such questions as: "If a project were before the community that required decision by a group of leaders—leaders that nearly everyone would accept—which ten on the list of 40 would you choose?" and "Who is the biggest man in town?" (Hunter 1953, pp. 61 ff., 268–271). Hunter's book consists largely of an account of his methods of identifying the top leaders, a discussion of their involvement in a few community decisions, and a demonstration that they were by and large well known to one another.

At first Hunter's book was favorably received, and a number of studies were planned and executed in other communities using this or a similar method (e.g., Form & Sauer 1960; Klapp & Padgett 1960; Hunter et al. 1956; D'Antonio & Erickson 1962; Pellegrin & Coates 1956; Schulze 1961; Thometz 1963). The reputational method has also been vigorously defended by admirers of its economy and compactness (Rossi 1960; Herson 1957; Ehrlich 1961; D'Antonio & Erickson 1962; and others). But it has also been attacked for a number of reasons.

Perhaps the most fundamental objection has been that the identification of presumed "influentials" is a very crude method of sampling the underlying shape of decision-making processes. Instead of focusing on how valued outcomes are distributed by those who actually distribute them in specific instances, it focuses on those who some people *say* distribute them under hypothetical circumstances. The identifiers, about whom we are told little in these studies, may be misguided, prejudiced, or ill-informed (Wolfinger 1960; LaPalombara 1964; Bauer et al. 1963). In fact, some people who have appeared on top leadership lists have been found not to belong there by criteria more closely tied to actual behavior; others not on the lists have been found to belong on them (Fanelli 1956; Scoble 1961; Wildavsky 1964; and others). Different decisions have been found to involve different influential people. In some issue areas there are persistent patterns of decision making; in others the patterns change rapidly. Critics charge that all these distinctions, crucial to an understanding of community power, are disregarded by the short cuts of the reputational method (see McKee 1953; Kaufman & Jones 1954; Dahl 1961; Scoble 1961; Polsby 1959; Wolfinger 1960; Polsby 1963).

Users of this method have often a priori picked among the alternatives posed by each of these distinctions. They have held, at least implicitly, that all those on the reputational list are the top leaders in the community (whether they actually are or not) by suggesting that there is a general top leadership group, influential in more than one issue area (whether it is or not) and persisting over time (whether it does or not). Even where researchers, conscious of latter-day criticisms, refrained from picking these particular alternatives a priori, the reputational method, because of its removal from real decision-making events, has rendered them no assistance in picking any other alternative. Thus, for example, attempts to demonstrate persistence of leadership groups by the reputational method fail because regardless of the similarities or differences in lists at times t_1 and t_2, the reputational method unaided fails to show the relations between the lists and actual behavior at either time (D'Antonio & Erickson 1962).

Attempts to improve the reputational method have concentrated mostly on reducing vagueness and ambiguity in questioning; thus, instead of a *hypothetical* "project," one or more *actual* projects or issue areas can be the subject of an interview (e.g., Thometz 1963). Instead of asking merely for a list of who might or should be involved in a decision, descriptions of specific events, actions, and reactions can be elicited. But there comes a point along this road at which the reputational method becomes indistinguishable from ordinary interviewing.

The central methodological issue is thus one of appropriateness. Are respondents being asked questions to which they can give answers capable of unambiguous interpretation? Are respondents able to give the best available testimony on the questions they are asked? Are they able to give competent testimony? Are their responses, if correctly interpreted, capable of answering underlying questions about community decision-making processes? If so, then the reputational method is clearly an appropriate tool of community power research. If not, as the weight of evidence and argument seems to suggest, then the method can be discarded.

Findings

The heated debate over the reputational method has obscured the fact that this method is not solely or even chiefly responsible for the promulgation of findings about the distribution of power in local communities that, on the basis of internal evidence, are quite likely incorrect.

Stratification theory. A number of studies— some reputational, some not—have set forth all or several of the following conclusions, which for several decades were widely accepted as scientifically established and accurate descriptions of American community politics: (1) the upper class rules; (2) political and civic leaders are subordinate to this class; (3) there is a single power elite dealing with a wide variety of community issues; (4) this upper-class power elite rules in its own interests; and (5) social conflict takes place chiefly between the upper and lower classes. A common thread running through these propositions is the dependency of political power on the class and status structure of the community; thus, for convenience, we may refer to these propositions as a "stratification theory" of community power.

Each of these findings has been questioned. In many instances the evidence supporting them has been weak, ambiguous, vague, or even contradictory. In some cases these propositions have not been tested directly or properly, and in others findings contrary to the propositions have been explained away unsuccessfully (see Polsby 1963). And so the extent to which any of the propositions actually holds and the circumstances in which one or more of them is applicable are now problematical.

"Pluralist" findings. Alternative findings, supported by a number of sources, can also be distilled from this literature. They include the apparent fact that participation in the making of most community decisions is concentrated in the hands of a few, but that different small groups normally make decisions on different community problems. Government officials are the most likely of all participants to overlap issue areas. Over time, the membership of decision-making groups appears to turn over at variable rates of speed.

These small groups have frequently been found to contain representatives of more than one interest; indeed, the finding is often made that participants in decision making disagree sharply among themselves. The powers of these groups also seem to be restricted in other ways—by expectations that they will not innovate, by threats that counterelites will "make an issue" and defeat them by enlarging the number of participants, and by the necessity to seek outside support to undertake nonroutine commitments. Finally, many members of these groups seem to be recruited by self-selection rather than co-optation, and many are answerable to the local electorate.

Valued outcomes are, in any event, only partially under the control of local participants in decision making. Decisions significant to local politics may be made outside the community—as, for example, the decision by a national corporation to move a plant in or out of a given locality—or outcomes may occur as a by-product of other activities, without explicit decisions being made by anyone. There is no sure connection between the intentions of community leaders and the actual distribution of values. Because of these and other considerations, knowing simply who gains and who loses in community politics is not sufficient to give a reliable picture of local decision-making processes.

Success in community politics evidently does not come automatically to possessors of great amounts of any one of the many possible resources available to actors in community life. Many resources in combination—time, knowledge, money, official position, energy, popularity, social status, and so on—must be applied with skill and diligence for actors to succeed in influencing decisions in desired directions. These resources must be disposable for political purposes, and it is helpful if they are convertible into other resources that may be in short supply. Skill and diligence in the application of resources to political ends are themselves often scarce. Successful actors in the community usually must also learn to choose goals that minimize costs to others in the system, that effect incremental rather than sweeping changes, and that distribute payoffs widely.

Findings such as these are often referred to as "pluralist" in character. They emphasize the diversity of decision-making processes and focus less on the social backgrounds and identities of participants and more on their actual roles and activities in local decision making. Whereas a stratification theory of community life by definition involves everyone in a hierarchical power relationship which can be ascertained by reference to his class and status position, the pluralist theory speaks more readily of "groups" whose size, cohesiveness, state of mobilization, range of interests, and durability are all subject to empirical examination.

Interpretations

Recent defenders of the stratification approach to the study of community power have been willing to concede that the original case for this approach rested on shaky empirical ground; yet, at the same time they have suggested that a full-blown pluralist theory accounting satisfactorily for all the facts has by no means emerged in the literature. They have also raised a number of specific points at which their interpretations of agreed-on facts diverge from pluralist interpretations. Of these, only three can be discussed here.

Middle-class leadership. Consider first the finding that leaders are drawn from a very small proportion of the total community and are much more likely to be middle class than lower class. To stratification analysts this suggests that there is an unspoken but very real "price of admission" to the political stratum, which can be paid in coin that is, for many participants, inherited and thus attributable to the stratification system of the community.

A pluralist response might be that nevertheless inherited membership in the middle class is probably not a necessary condition of participation. Participants may find it possible to enter the political stratum by other means. They may enter the middle class from below and acquire its values and social and economic resources by means other than inheritance. Or, while retaining low economic and social standing, they may become intensely involved in the disposition of a particular issue. Or they may come to community leadership through activity in a labor union, ethnic association, neighborhood group, or local party organization. The extent to which any of these routes to political participation is taken in a given community is, of course, always a matter to be determined by investigation.

Would it be proper to infer, then, that although membership in the middle class is not a necessary condition, it may be a sufficient condition for participation in decision making? Hardly. At most, only a small percentage of the middle class participates, and the rest do not.

In what circumstances are the class identities of decision makers crucial in determining the shaping and sharing of political outcomes? Certainly when local decision makers are faced with alternative courses that will distribute values differentially to the different classes, and also in all other instances where class membership is a meaningful determinant of political interests. Such circumstances must be assumed to exist in Middletown, where members of X family—identified as a major component of the upper class—were found to belong to both the Democratic and Republican parties. This report could be interpreted to mean that both parties were dominated by the cohesive, class-based interests of the X family (see Lynd & Lynd 1937, pp. 87, 91–93). However, an alternative interpretation might be that the X family was politically split (see Polsby 1960).

Pluralists often remark on conflict between decision makers and on the diversity of interests they represent. To them, an agreement between Walter Reuther and Henry Ford can be interpreted as something other than collusion between two relatively wealthy residents of the Detroit suburbs. In this case, as in many others, knowing the number of decision makers present and their class memberships would be less important to a pluralist than knowing what the subject of their discussion was and what interests were involved.

Inequality of influence.   Different constructions are also put on the palpable fact that equality of influence over decisions by all members of the community is nowhere approximated. Inequality in this sense is not a new discovery; the question is whether such inequality can somehow be reconciled with the democratic pretensions of American society. On the whole, stratification theorists have doubted that it can; pluralists have on the other hand called attention to the varieties of inequality, to the possibility that inequalities along various dimensions could be dispersed rather than cumulative, and to the ways in which dispersed inequalities lead to checks, balances, and standoffs in the political system, and consequently to bargaining and the spread of benefits.

The status quo.   Finally, there is disagreement among students of community power in their orientations toward the *status quo*. On the one hand, an ongoing political system can be regarded as a stacked deck of cards, in which some people are much better situated than others, with possible alternatives or correctives never brought into public discussion and never raised as issues. Thus aspects of social structure that are never controversial and hence never brought fully into focus

by the activity-oriented pluralist approach may exercise a profound influence on community decision making (see, in particular, Bachrach & Baratz 1962; Agger et al. 1964, e.g., p. 325). Insofar as pluralist researchers confine their attention to controversial, extraordinary, and highly conflictful events, this criticism has great merit. But when pluralists attempt to explain issue *areas* in which routine and structured decision making also takes place, they are less vulnerable to this charge.

When critics of the pluralist approach specify in some detail precisely which aspects—controversial or not—of the *status quo* must be investigated, and in the light of which unconsidered alternatives, then it is possible in particular cases to examine the justifications for describing local decision making in terms of alternatives suggested by outside observers rather than in terms of alternatives perceived and acted upon by local residents.

The *status quo* can be viewed as passively but powerfully restraining community residents from better possibilities and levying costs inequitably. But it can also be considered a synonym for the stability that is the *sine qua non* of organized society. Out of a universe of possibilities, and at undeniable but unavoidable costs, communities evolve habits and patterns of activity in response to a variety of internal and external pressures. The alternative to a deck stacked in *some* way, at persistent cost to somebody, is, in this conception, a kind of random world in which costs are levied unexpectedly and unpredictably. In situations of rapid flux and uncertainty, one may also suggest that the dependence of the many on the few for decision making is accentuated rather than diminished, and the forms of due process that are the bulwark of the rights of ordinary citizens in a democracy give way before the exigent demands of the powerful.

Obviously, not the mere fact of *status quo* but the undesirable aspects of *status quo* in particular communities give rise to the impulse to search for alternatives, even when local residents are not vocally among the search party. It is nevertheless a common mistake to view stability as uniquely costly in and of itself, when with equal cogency one can argue against change for the sake of change.

In any event, researchers interested in these problems should try to discover the consequences of change or of *status quo* empirically, rather than deducing them from a priori notions.

The major conflicts in this field over method and the interpretations of findings seem to have drawn scholarly attention and energy away from the discussion of local community politics. One result, perhaps, is that the literature of community power has as yet provided no firm basis for differentiating among communities by means of empirically verified propositions that state the varying conditions under which different findings hold. For it is manifestly the case that communities do differ in their politics and in other ways. Apparent as this is to the naked eye, the literature on community power has not yet effectively exposed and illuminated community differences as they affect local decision-making processes. The main contributions of this literature are to be found less in discussions of community politics than in discussions of the *study* of local politics as a problem in research methodology, philosophy of social science, and speculative social theory.

NELSON W. POLSBY

[*See also* LOCAL POLITICS; POWER.]

BIBLIOGRAPHY

AGGER, ROBERT E.; GOLDRICH, DANIEL; and SWANSON, BERT 1964 *The Rulers and the Ruled: Political Power and Impotence in American Communities.* New York: Wiley.

BACHRACH, PETER; and BARATZ, MORTON 1962 Two Faces of Power. *American Political Science Review* 56:947–952.

BANFIELD, EDWARD C. (1961) 1965 *Political Influence.* New York: Free Press.

BAUER, RAYMOND A.; POOL, ITHIEL DE SOLA; and DEXTER, L. A. 1963 *American Business and Public Policy: The Politics of Foreign Trade.* New York: Atherton.

BELL, WENDELL; HILL, RICHARD J.; and WRIGHT, CHARLES R. 1961 *Public Leadership: A Critical Review With Special Reference to Adult Education.* San Francisco: Chandler.

BRYCE, JAMES (1888) 1909 *The American Commonwealth.* 2 vols., 3d ed. New York and London: Macmillan. → An abridged edition was published in 1959 by Putnam.

COLEMAN, JAMES S. 1957 *Community Conflict.* A publication of the Bureau of Applied Social Research, Columbia University. Glencoe, Ill.: Free Press.

DAHL, ROBERT A. (1961) 1963 *Who Governs? Democracy and Power in an American City.* New Haven: Yale Univ. Press.

D'ANTONIO, WILLIAM V.; and ERICKSON, EUGENE C. 1962 Reputational Technique as a Measure of Community Power: An Evaluation Based on Comparative and Longitudinal Studies. *American Sociological Review* 27:362–376, 848–854.

D'ANTONIO, WILLIAM V. et al. 1961 Institutional and Occupational Representations in Eleven Community Influence Systems. *American Sociological Review* 26:440–446.

Decisions in Syracuse, by Roscoe C. Martin et al. Metropolitan Action Studies No. 1. 1961 Bloomington: Indiana Univ. Press.

DEUTSCH, KARL W. 1953 *Political Community at the International Level: Problems of Definition and Measurement.* Foreign Policy Analysis Series, No. 2. Princeton Univ. Press.

DRAKE, ST. CLAIR; and CAYTON, HORACE R. (1945) 1962 *Black Metropolis: A Study of Negro Life in a Northern City.* 2 vols., rev. & enl. ed. New York: Harcourt.

EHRLICH, HOWARD J. 1961 The Reputational Approach to the Study of Community Power. *American Sociological Review* 26:926–927.

FANELLI, A. ALEXANDER 1956 Typology of Community Leadership Based on Influence and Interaction Within the Leader Subsystem. *Social Forces* 34:332–338.

FORM, WILLIAM H.; and MILLER, DELBERT C. 1960 *Industry, Labor and Community.* New York: Harper.

FORM, WILLIAM H.; and SAUER, WARREN L. 1960 Organized Labor's Image of Community Power Structure. *Social Forces* 38:332–341.

FRIEDRICH, CARL J. 1959 The Concept of Community in the History of Political and Legal Philosophy. Pages 3–25 in Carl J. Friedrich (editor), *Community.* Nomos 2. New York: Liberal Arts Press.

HAAS, ERNST 1958 *The Uniting of Europe: Political, Social, and Economic Forces, 1950–1957.* Stanford Univ. Press.

HERSON, LAWRENCE J. R. 1957 The Lost World of Municipal Government. *American Political Science Review* 51:330–345, 783–784.

HERSON, LAWRENCE J. R. 1961 In the Footsteps of Community Power. *American Political Science Review* 55:817–830.

HOLLINGSHEAD, AUGUST DE B. (1949) 1959 *Elmtown's Youth: The Impact of Social Classes on Adolescents.* New York: Wiley.

HUNTER, FLOYD 1953 *Community Power Structure: A Study of Decision Makers.* Chapel Hill: Univ. of North Carolina Press. → A paperback edition was published in 1963 by Doubleday.

HUNTER, FLOYD; SCHAFFER, RUTH C.; and SHEPS, CECIL B. 1956 *Community Organization: Action and Inaction.* Chapel Hill: Univ. of North Carolina Press.

JENNINGS, M. KENT 1964 *Community Influentials: The Elites of Atlanta.* New York: Free Press.

KAUFMAN, HERBERT; and JONES, VICTOR 1954 Mystery of Power. *Public Administration Review* 14:205–212.

KEY, VALDIMER O. 1936 *The Techniques of Political Graft in the United States.* Univ. of Chicago Libraries.

KLAPP, ORIN E.; and PADGETT, L. VINCENT 1960 Power Structure and Decision-making in a Mexican Border City. *American Journal of Sociology* 65:400–406.

LAPALOMBARA, JOSEPH G. 1964 *Interest Groups in Italian Politics.* Princeton Univ. Press.

LONG, NORTON E. 1962 *The Polity.* Chicago: Rand McNally. → See especially pages 222–241 on "Aristotle and the Study of Local Government."

LYND, ROBERT S.; and LYND, HELEN M. (1929) 1930 *Middletown: A Study in Contemporary American Culture.* New York: Harcourt. → A paperback edition was published in 1959.

LYND, ROBERT S.; and LYND, HELEN M. 1937 *Middletown in Transition: A Study in Cultural Conflicts.* New York: Harcourt. → A paperback edition was published in 1963.

McKEE, JAMES B. 1953 Status and Power in the Industrial Community: A Comment on Drucker's Thesis. *American Journal of Sociology* 58:364–370.

MERRIAM, CHARLES E.; and GOSNELL, HAROLD F. 1924 *Non-voting: Causes and Methods of Control.* Univ. of Chicago Press.

MICHIGAN STATE UNIVERSITY OF AGRICULTURE AND APPLIED SCIENCE, INSTITUTE FOR COMMUNITY DEVELOP-

MENT AND SERVICES 1962 *Main Street Politics; Policy-making at the Local Level: A Survey of the Periodical Literature Since 1950.* Compiled by Charles Press. East Lansing, Mich.: The University.

MILLER, DELBERT C. 1958 Industry and Community Power Structure: A Comparative Study of an American and an English City. *American Sociological Review* 23:9–15.

OSTROGORSKII, MOISEI IA. 1902 *Democracy and the Organization of Political Parties.* 2 vols. London and New York: Macmillan. → An abridged edition was published in 1964 by Quadrangle Books.

PELLEGRIN, ROLAND J.; and COATES, CHARLES H. 1956 Absentee-owned Corporations and Community Power Structure. *American Journal of Sociology* 61:413–419.

POLSBY, NELSON W. 1959 The Sociology of Community Power: A Reassessment. *Social Forces* 37:232–236.

POLSBY, NELSON W. 1960 Power in Middletown: Fact and Value in Community Research. *Canadian Journal of Economics and Political Science* 26:592–603.

POLSBY, NELSON W. 1963 *Community Power and Political Theory.* Yale Studies in Political Science, Vol. 7. New Haven: Yale Univ. Press.

PRESTHUS, ROBERT V. 1964 *Men at the Top: A Study in Community Power.* New York: Oxford Univ. Press.

ROSSI, PETER H. 1960 Power and Community Structure. *Midwest Journal of Political Science* 4:390–401.

RUSSETT, BRUCE M. 1963 *Community and Contention: Britain and America in the Twentieth Century.* Cambridge, Mass.: M.I.T. Press.

SAYRE, WALLACE S.; and KAUFMAN, HERBERT 1960 *Governing New York City: Politics in the Metropolis.* New York: Russell Sage Foundation.

SAYRE, WALLACE S.; and POLSBY, NELSON W. 1965 American Political Science and the Study of Urbanization. Pages 115–156 in Philip M. Hauser and Leo F. Schnore (editors), *The Study of Urbanization.* New York: Wiley.

SCHULZE, ROBERT O. 1961 The Bifurcation of Power in a Satellite City. Pages 19–80 in Morris Janowitz (editor), *Community Political Systems.* New York: Free Press.

SCOBLE, HARRY M. 1961 Leadership Hierarchies and Political Issues in a New England Town. Pages 117–145 in Morris Janowitz (editor), *Community Political Systems.* New York: Free Press.

THOMAS, WILLIAM I.; and ZNANIECKI, FLORIAN (1918–1920) 1958 *The Polish Peasant in Europe and America.* 2 vols. 2d ed. New York: Dover.

THOMETZ, CAROL [ESTES] 1963 *The Decision-makers: The Power Structure of Dallas.* Dallas: Southern Methodist Univ. Press.

VIDICH, ARTHUR J.; and BENSMAN, JOSEPH 1958 *Small Town in Mass Society: Class, Power and Religion in a Rural Community.* Princeton Univ. Press.

WARNER, W. LLOYD et al. 1949 *Democracy in Jonesville: A Study in Quality and Inequality.* New York: Harper.

WARNER, W. LLOYD; and LUNT, PAUL S. 1941 *The Social Life of a Modern Community.* New Haven: Yale Univ. Press.

WILDAVSKY, AARON B. 1964 *Leadership in a Small Town.* Totowa, N.J.: Bedminster Press.

WIRTH, LOUIS 1928 *The Ghetto.* Univ. of Chicago Press. → A paperback edition was published in 1956.

WOLFINGER, RAYMOND E. 1960 Reputation and Reality in the Study of Community Power. *American Sociological Review* 25:636–644.

ZORBAUGH, HARVEY W. 1929 *Gold Coast and Slum: A Sociological Study of Chicago's Near North Side.* Univ. of Chicago Press.

II

COMMUNITY DISORGANIZATION

A community, in the sense in which the term will be used here, is a territorially bounded social system or set of interlocking or integrated functional subsystems (economic, political, religious, ethical, educational, legal, socializing, reproductive, etc.) serving a resident population, plus the material culture or physical plant through which the subsystems operate. The community concept does not include such characteristics as harmony, love, "we-feeling," or intimacy, which are sometimes nostalgically imputed to idealized preindustrial communities (Foster 1960–1961), but it does include a minimum of consensus. A normative structure is either inherited from the past or self-consciously instituted in each subsystem, and conformity to its demands is usually sufficient to guarantee that the above-mentioned functions will be performed.

Community disorganization may be defined as a state in which any one or more of the several subsystems, for whatever reason, fail to function at some specified expected level of effectiveness, or it may be defined as the processes that lead to such a state, or it may refer both to the processes and to the state. Failure of a subsystem may take the form of performance that is either better or worse than the expected one; the processes leading to such failure may be "natural" or purposive. Since community disorganization as a state may occur in a wide variety of subsystems and in a wide variety of circumstances and, as a process, may result from a wide variety of causes, it is not a unidimensional sociological phenomenon susceptible to simple theoretical conceptualization or definition.

The ideal-type of a community that is not disorganized would be one in which: (1) the physical plant is in good running order, capable of serving the needs of the people; (2) the people are in good physical and mental health, that is, able to perform at least at minimal levels of efficiency; (3) there is at least a tolerable fit between community needs ("functional requisites") and functional subsystems (institutions and groups) to serve them; (4) there is consensus with respect to norms, so that everyone knows what to expect of everyone else, and hence there is no confusion; and (5) these expectations are fulfilled. Change would not be precluded, but it would be change for which the community is prepared and change that is synchronous and compatible among all the subsystems. Change, in fact, may be in the direction of organizing rather than in the direction of disorganizing the community, as when a new traffic control system is introduced to overcome the disorganizing effect of traffic jams. Still, there is a nice theoretical question about just where to draw the line between organizing and disorganizing change.

Community disorganization as a state is not an all-or-nothing phenomenon; it is a matter of degree. It is currently believed that complete absence of any disorganization in a community is highly improbable. A certain amount of stress and strain (Moore 1963; Moore & Feldman 1960; 1962) or instability is seen as probably intrinsic in any social system. It may be taken for granted, therefore, that at least a certain degree of disorganization, however slight, is present in all communities. The extent may be wide, including the entire community system, or limited, affecting some parts more than others. Communities characterized by "organic" solidarity will be more susceptible to disorganization than those characterized by "mechanical" solidarity [see COMMUNITY–SOCIETY CONTINUA].

Community disorganization as a process may range in extent from a temporary tie-up in rush-hour traffic to a total collapse of all subsystems. It may be sudden and rapid, as in a cataclysmic "act of God," or slow and of long duration. It may be immediately and even spectacularly visible, or it may be almost imperceptible. There may even be controversy as to its very existence. (It has been asked, for example, whether the people of Rome ever knew that their empire was "falling.") Moreover, it may be reversible or irreversible, "natural" or purposive.

Community disorganization as a state. At what point in the process of community disorganization should we say that a community is in a state of disorganization? How much malfunctioning of any subsystem constitutes a state of community disorganization? Crisis disorganization, as in the case of a disaster, presents no problems of identification. But if a certain amount of nonconformity is endemic or chronic, in fact, intrinsic in the operation of communities, it is not at all clear at what point we should speak of a state of disorganization.

There is by no means always consensus among observers with respect to the existence, let alone the extent, of disorganization in any specific community. A classic example is the controversy among researchers with respect to family structure in the Caribbean. Some students view the family there as in a state of disorganization (Blake 1962; Goode

1960); others, however, view it as an institutionalized adaptation to a difficult set of circumstances (Rodman 1961). This difference of viewpoint illustrates a contrast between the sociological and the cultural conceptualization of disorganization. The anthropologist tends to underplay it; his emphasis is on the fact that if the community is surviving, the basic functions are at least being minimally performed. In the Caribbean, therefore, he does not see "friending" and "living" as nonconformity to community norms for marriage but rather as a cultural innovation for adapting to circumstances that make conformity to the community norms impossible [Rodman 1961; *see also* CARIBBEAN SOCIETY]. Similarly, one social anthropologist has detected a "culture of poverty," rather than a state of disorganization, in Mexican slum communities (Lewis 1959).

In answer, then, to the question raised above, all we can say is that there are no consensual standards that define the limits of community disorganization. For example, at one time and place, an economic subsystem is judged to be performing its function if it provides subsistence for everyone; at another, it is judged not to be performing its function if *anyone* is at a merely subsistence level. And such is the case for all of the subsystems.

Disorganizing processes

Competition and conflict. The subsystems in a community are not operated by self-programmed computers. They are operated by human beings who are socialized into subsystems and who come to identify with them. Thus, although they are all contributing to the "commonweal," they see themselves as competing and in conflict with one another. For example, the police system competes with the highway system for tax funds; the public school system competes with the private school system; and the public sector competes with the private sector for personnel and support. The conflict between political and economic institutions for power, classic in the nineteenth century, continues in the twentieth; even President Eisenhower, before he retired, warned against the encroachment of the military–industrial complex on political prerogatives.

But conflict between or among groups and subsystems, in and of itself, need not disorganize a community. Some kinds of conflict are highly institutionalized; that is, they are bound by consensual or legislated norms. Indeed, the philosophy of checks and balances in the United States constitution is itself an institutionalized form of conflict, as is the concept of a "loyal opposition" in the British constitution; so, too, is the system of parliamentary debate. The whole legal system also is designed to institutionalize conflict. The process of "countervailing power" in the economic sphere (Galbraith 1952) is another example. There is, in fact, one school of thought which holds that conflict in this institutionalized sense is an organizing rather than a disorganizing factor, a *sine qua non* of stability in our society; it is seen as a method for preventing too great a concentration of power in any one position, thus making for new equilibria to accommodate new statuses among the interest groups in the community. Since such conflict is institutionalized and provided for, either explicitly or implicitly, in the system itself, it does not disorganize the community; it is, rather, part of the organization of the system.

This does not mean that conflict cannot be a disorganizing process. Sometimes mass hysterias become hostile and lead to widespread violence, resulting in destruction of property and loss of life. If conflict takes the form of hatemongering, rabble-rousing, or *ressentiment,* it may disorganize the community by preventing the normal expectations of behavior. In the Middle East, street rioting has become a recognized technique of conflict that may be at least temporarily disorganizing. Rioting in some countries can be turned on and off almost at will by the dissident leadership (Rummel 1963).

Maximizing performance of function.   The division of labor implies common interests. It is thus clear that if any one subsystem *under*-performs its function, community disorganization may result. If the economic subsystem cannot produce and distribute goods and services, all the other subsystems are impeded in their functioning, and the total community system suffers some degree of disorganization; if the governing subsystem cannot preserve order, again, the other subsystems cannot perform their functions. These conclusions are obvious.

But precisely because it *is* part of a total system and not an isolated autonomous entity, the over-performance as well as the underperformance of a subsystem may also be disorganizing. Assigned a function to perform, a subsystem may do it so well that other subsystems suffer. Any one subsystem, performing at a high level and thus presumably contributing to the welfare of the total system, may by that very fact be interfering with the operation of some other subsystem performing a complementary function.

The economic subsystem, for example, has the function of creating and distributing goods and services. Institutional norms for achieving this goal are present, and conformity to them presumably leads to successful performance. Accordingly, such obstacles to successful performance as inefficiency, technical obsoleteness, and (if employers choose to define it as an obstacle) unionization, are regarded as contrary to the norms and tend to be suppressed whenever possible. The "natural" result of a high degree of conformity to the norms of the economic subsystem in its productive aspect, may, however, interfere with the adequate performance of its distributing function, resulting in widespread unemployment, or a high level of competitive stress and strain, demoralization, family trauma, and so on. In other words, the very norms of efficiency that maximize productivity may interfere with the distribution of the goods and services; the better the productive subsystem works, the worse other subsystems may work. Or, to take another example, the better the system of reproduction works for increasing the population, the worse the economic production system may work, as land becomes increasingly fragmented among heirs. If a school system attempts to make maximum use of its plant by sending children from crowded slum schools to uncrowded schools in better neighborhoods, families may withdraw their children from the better schools and parental interest in public schools may decline, to the detriment of the whole system. If the welfare and charitable agencies wish to maximize their services by assuring a decent level of living for their clients, unions may accuse them of disorganizing the labor market by subsidizing industry's low wages and weakening organized efforts to improve wages.

Overconformity.   Overconformity to community norms within any subsystem constitutes a disorganizing process that is analogous to overconformity to subsystem norms. The performance of community functions by any subsystem is usually mediated by way of institutionalized norms, and conformity to these norms presumably guarantees adequate performance of the functions by the subsystem. However, some community norms are, in effect, on a stand-by basis; they are not enforced most of the time but are there in case they are needed. It has been said, for example, that if every single norm were rigidly enforced, almost any system would collapse. For example, unwilling military conscripts report that resorting to punctilious conformity to every military norm serves admirably as a form of sabotage. It has been said that complete conformity to the political norms in the U.S.S.R. would bring the economic system to a halt and that only the presence of *blat* or fixing—itself illegal—keeps it performing at all (Crankshaw

1959). Complete and rigorous enforcement of all the laws, mores, conventions, and administrative rulings could throw a community into chaos. A large proportion of the population would end in jail; court dockets would run years behind schedule; and interpersonal ties would be shattered as the conventional white lies of the amenities that conflict with the mores were discarded.

The disorganizing effects of too-rigorous conformity to norms are counteracted by the emergence of informal, unarticulated, unofficial, crescive norms or understandings that optimize rather than maximize conformity to the formal, articulated, official norms. Only as much conformity as is needed is demanded; as much nonconformity is permitted as is needed to keep the community operating. There is, in effect, a new form of organization of nonconformity that performs a latent function. It constitutes "institutionalized evasion of the norms" (Merton [1949] 1957, pp. 318, 343–344; Bernard 1949).

A typology of disorganization processes

Community disorganization as a process may be classified according to any one of several criteria. For our purposes here, a simple twofold typology is used, namely, "natural" community disorganization and purposive or strategic community disorganization, each with several subtypes.

"Natural" processes. The term "natural" is placed in quotation marks because anything that human beings do is natural and the contrasting rubric, "purposive," refers to behavior as natural as any other. The term is used only for the sake of convenience.

"Natural" community disorganizing processes may be extrinsic or intrinsic in origin. There is little of theoretical interest in the state of community disorganization that results from the impact of outside forces. What theoretical interest there is lies in the effects, in tracing the process by which the impact finds its way through the system and in determining the relative susceptibility or resistance of the several subsystems to the impact of differing kinds of extrinsic forces (Coleman 1957). Is there a hierarchical order among the subsystems, some being more, some less, important for the total community system? The processes by which the impact of such extrinsic forces ramifies throughout the community will not be discussed here, except as the various subsystems constitute extrinsic influences on one another. [*See* DISASTERS.]

Intrinsic community disorganization as a process does present some interesting theoretical problems.

Is there, for example, anything inherent in the functioning of a community, even when protected from extrinsic influences, that leads to a state of disorganization? Are there, as Marx said of capitalism as a system, internal contradictions that make a state of disorganization inevitable? Or, conversely, if there were no extrinsic influences at work, would a community achieve a kind of "perpetual motion"?

Theoretical models. At least three theoretical models may be proposed to describe the "natural" processes of intrinsic community disorganization, namely, an escalation model, a deceleration model, and a stability or "natural limits" model.

The escalation model begins with the instituting of a subsystem in the community to perform a function perceived as needed. It may be, for example, a police system, a school system, or a traffic-control system. Although there are "bugs" in the system at first, those who instituted it hope that once it gets into operation they can be eliminated and the operation improved as it learns to dovetail its contributions into the over-all community system. If these hopes are justified, the end result will be a stable situation. But it is possible that the improved efficiency of the new subsystem may disorganize the over-all system, as noted above, by overperforming its function in terms of the expectations of other subsystems. The police find too many violators of the law; the schools find too many illiterate high-school students; and so on. This phenomenon is sometimes viewed in terms of the *unanticipated consequences* of purposive social action (Merton 1936); it is always disillusioning to reformers.

A second type of model, a deceleration one, is sometimes summarized in such aphorisms as "a new broom sweeps clean" or such mottoes as "turn the rascals out." It was more emphasized in the past than recently, under the rubric of "ossification" or "formalism" (Cooley 1909). In this model, the new subsystem operates very well at the beginning. But instead of improving with time, it deteriorates. In the process of "de-bugging" the system, new rules are established, and conformity to the rules becomes an end in itself. After the original goal for which the subsystem was instituted has been achieved or outlived, survival becomes an end in itself. The subsystem accumulates "dead wood" and red tape and finally spends all its time performing its own survival tasks rather than contributing to the total community system. Or a subsystem originally instituted to control another (e.g., a public utility regulating board) comes in time to identify with the subsystem it is supposed to regulate, so that its contribution to the total community system is subverted rather than implemented.

Finally, the stability or "natural limits" model posits an instituted system that escalates and decelerates in performance within certain limits. Early research on the business cycle, for example, viewed periodic stalling of the productive mechanism as part of the system, that is, as a necessary, normal, and even desirable correction. According to this view, there are built-in controls that stop the system if it is operating too fast and start it again when adjustment has been achieved. The automatic check might come from some other subsystem rather than from within the subsystem itself. As soon as the performance of any subsystem shows signs of adversely affecting the performance of other subsystems, an automatic set of checks goes into operation.

Purposive or strategic processes. Purposive community disorganization as a process may be viewed either as benign or as revolutionary and subversive. Benign community disorganization usually seeks reform rather than revolution, although sometimes, as in Gandhi's use of it, it is revolutionary in its effects. However, benign community disorganization is ordinarily nonviolent and sometimes ostensibly carried on with altruistic intentions (Sibley 1963). But if it does have to injure others, the theory is that the persons who start the disorganization must be willing to suffer also.

Destructive community disorganization that is strategic rather than irrational in character is often a technique for seizing political power. It is a recognized subversive technique in modern revolutionary movements, codified as the so-called "Phase One" of the revolutionary process in "wars of national liberation": "The greater part of any Phase One operation is covert and marked by a subtle, gradual deterioration of the existing sociopolitical system" (Pustay 1965, p. 59). Destruction of consensus or loyalty to a given status quo or set of incumbents is a major goal. All possible community conflicts are exploited to foment instability or to prevent stability in the system. The theory of community disorganization as subversion has been highly developed by communist leaders from Lenin (1905) to Mao Tsê-tung (1937).

The technique of community disorganization by an outside enemy is as old as war itself. It includes not only destruction of physical plant and people by violence but also the nonviolent destruction of morale. As the value of the physical plant increases, nonviolent techniques tend to be preferred in order to save the physical structure for the time when the community is taken over. In modern wars drug addiction, black marketing, counterfeit money, and alcohol have been used as subversive techniques to prevent the adequate functioning of the subsystems in the community and thus to weaken the ability to wage war.

Benign community disorganization—an attempt by those within the community to coerce or deter an opponent by nonviolent means—is fairly new, at least on any extensive scale. It did not develop until industrialization had transformed the mechanical solidarity of peasant society to an organic solidarity based on the division of labor. When, for example, families made their own candles, owned their own team of horses, and made their own bread, it was not possible to disorganize a community by threatening to turn off power, to go on strike, or to tie up traffic. Modern communities, highly specialized and functionally integrated, are peculiarly vulnerable to the use of strategic disorganization.

Early analyses of the strategic use of civil disobedience and nonviolence were in terms of ethical principles, as, for example, in the writings of Henry Thoreau and Theodore Parker. Marx and Engels saw, though they did not admit, that the division of labor, greatly elaborated with industrialization, made the class war a mixed-motive rather than a "zero-sum" game. Though the power struggle is a "zero-sum" game, the economic struggle is a mixed-motive game, since both parties have a common interest in not destroying the means of production, that is, the physical plant of the community. [*See* GAME THEORY, *article on* THEORETICAL ASPECTS.] Georges Sorel (1908) developed the concept of the proletarian general strike (as contrasted with the concept of the political general strike) to keep labor–capital cleavages alive and to serve as a strategic threat to those in power. Thus he sought to promulgate the idea of the transition to socialism as a catastrophe that the power elite would do anything to avoid. It was a myth that simultaneously organized the proletariat against the power elite and threatened the community with disorganization.

In the middle of the twentieth century, Negroes in American communities disorganized communities by civil disobedience, passive resistance, and demonstrations. Their purpose was not primarily to disorganize the community as an end in itself but rather to disorganize it just enough to call attention to the lack of consensus. Consensus implies "consent of the governed." It need not imply active or positive agreement or acceptance, but so long as people conform to any set of norms it will be assumed that these norms have their passive consent, if not their active approval. In order, therefore, to demonstrate the withdrawal of consent and the lack of consensus, there must be nonconformity. And this nonconformity must be conspicuous enough for the message to reach a wide audience. The target may be the political subsystem (with nonconformity taking the form of civil disobedience or passive resistance), the economic system (sabotage, slowdown, boycott, strike), the school system (boycott, picketing), or the system regulating race relations (sit-ins, marches, etc.). Whatever the target subsystem may be, the purpose of the disorganizing effort is to demonstrate that the consent of the governed is being withheld.

Those who use community disorganization as a process of communication have to walk a fine line between making the disorganization serious enough to get across their message but not serious enough to alienate a total community. Negro leaders in the 1960s developed a high degree of skill in locating strategic points where nonconformity would be conspicuously disorganizing but not too destructively so.

The "death" of communities

There is good archeological and historical evidence that communities "die," that is, pass from the historical scene altogether. But there is no evidence that "natural" disorganizing processes intrinsic to the operation of the community as a social system were the cause of their "death." Climatic change, exhaustion of natural resources, plagues, wars, technological change—these and a host of other explanations may be offered to explain the communities' demise.

On a macrosociological level, some of the best minds have for centuries grappled with explaining the fall of Rome, the breakup of the feudal communities, the disintegration of *anciens régimes*, the passing of colonial systems, and the demise of a host of other systems. Much of the work is descriptive; and although some attempts to explain and interpret have been made, there is little unanimity in the results. Carefully documented, microsociological (as distinguished from archeological) studies of the disappearance or decline of specific communities are rare, and those we have deal primarily with such extrinsic factors as the exhaustion of natural resources (Collins 1941; Schreiber & Schreiber 1955), technological change (Caudill 1963) or the impact of Western cultures on underdeveloped countries (Balandier 1955; Frazier 1955).

Is disorganization per se a threat to community survival? If it is almost universal, to some degree, among industrialized societies, then we must conclude that it is probably not fatal. However, there may be some level beyond which disorganization does become a threat to survival. Are there automatic corrections for disorganization when it reaches these limits? Are there determinable tolerance limits? If so, what are they? If not, *how* does disorganization endanger or threaten the survival of the community? Some processes of disorganization may be more lethal than others; some subsystems may be more critical than others in the lethal process, so that their malfunctioning is especially destructive; and some subsystems may be more susceptible to breakdown in the first place. As yet, we know little about these processes.

Any discussion of the "death" of communities should also take account of immigrant communities, which tend over time to disappear as distinct entities. In such communities boundary maintenance becomes difficult, and the subsystems suffer attrition or transformation, even if they do not actually disappear.

Since most sociological research is, of necessity, on surviving communities, in which some degree of disorganization is almost always present, we have no way of answering the question of the relationship between disorganization processes and the "death" of communities. We know that communities change, almost beyond recognition, but, in one form or other, they seem to survive. Disorganization, either as a state or as a process, does not appear to be lethal.

JESSIE BERNARD

[*Directly related are the entries* CONFLICT; DEVIANT BEHAVIOR; DISASTERS; SOCIAL CHANGE. *Other relevant material may be found in* INTERNAL WARFARE, *article on* GUERRILLA WARFARE; MENTAL HEALTH; NORMS, *article on* THE STUDY OF NORMS; *and in the biography of* SOREL.]

BIBLIOGRAPHY

BALANDIER, GEORGES 1955 Social Changes and Social Problems in Negro Africa. Pages 55–69 in Calvin W. Stillman, *Africa in the Modern World.* Univ. of Chicago Press.

BERNARD, JESSIE (1949) 1962 *American Community Behavior.* Rev. ed. New York: Holt. → See especially Part 7.

BLAKE, JUDITH 1962 *Family Structure in Jamaica: The Social Context of Reproduction.* New York: Free Press.

CAUDILL, HARRY M. 1963 *Night Comes to the Cumberlands: A Biography of a Depressed Area.* Boston: Little. → A paperback edition was published in 1964.

COLEMAN, JAMES S. 1957 *Community Conflict.* A publication of the Bureau of Applied Social Research, Columbia University. Glencoe, Ill.: Free Press.

COLLINS, HENRY HILL JR. 1941 *America's Own Refugees: Our 4,000,000 Homeless Migrants.* Princeton Univ. Press.

COOLEY, CHARLES H. (1909) 1956 *Social Organization: A Study of the Larger Mind.* In Charles H. Cooley, *Two Major Works: Social Organization* and *Human Nature and the Social Order.* Glencoe, Ill.: Free Press. → Each title reprinted with individual title page and pagination. Separate paperback editions were published in 1962 by Schocken.

CRANKSHAW, EDWARD (1959) 1963 *Khrushchev's Russia.* Harmondsworth (England): Penguin.

FOSTER, GEORGE M. 1960–1961 Interpersonal Relations in Peasant Society. *Human Organization* 19:174–178.

FRAZIER, E. FRANKLIN 1955 The Impact of Colonialism on African Social Forms and Personality. Pages 70–96 in Calvin W. Stillman, *Africa in the Modern World.* Univ. of Chicago Press.

GALBRAITH, JOHN K. (1952) 1956 *American Capitalism: The Concept of Countervailing Power.* 2d ed., rev. Boston: Houghton Mifflin.

GOODE, WILLIAM J. 1960 Illegitimacy in the Caribbean Social Structure. *American Sociological Review* 25:21–30.

LENIN, VLADIMIR I. (1905) 1962 Two Tactics of Social-democracy in the Democratic Revolution. Volume 9, pages 15–114 in Vladimir I. Lenin, *Collected Works.* Moscow: Foreign Languages Publishing House.

LEWIS, OSCAR 1959 *Five Families: Mexican Case Studies in the Culture of Poverty.* New York: Basic Books. → A paperback edition was published in 1962 by Science Editions.

MAO TSÊ-TUNG (1937) 1965 *On Guerrilla Warfare.* New York: Praeger. → First published as *Yu chi chan.*

MERTON, ROBERT K. 1936 The Unanticipated Consequences of Purposive Social Action. *American Sociological Review* 1:894–904.

MERTON, ROBERT K. (1949) 1957 *Social Theory and Social Structure.* Rev. & enl. ed. Glencoe, Ill.: Free Press.

MOORE, WILBERT E. 1963 *Social Change.* Englewood Cliffs, N.J.: Prentice-Hall.

MOORE, WILBERT E.; and FELDMAN, ARNOLD S. (editors) 1960 *Labor Commitment and Social Change in Developing Areas.* New York: Social Science Research Council.

MOORE, WILBERT E.; and FELDMAN, ARNOLD S. 1962 Society as a Tension-management System. Pages 93–105 in George W. Baker and Leonard S. Cottrell Jr. (editors), *Behavioral Science and Civil Defense.* National Research Council, Disaster Research Group, Disaster Study No. 16. Washington: National Academy of Sciences–National Research Council.

PUSTAY, JOHN S. 1965 *Counterinsurgency Warfare.* New York: Free Press.

RODMAN, HYMAN 1961 Marital Relationships in a Trinidad Village. *Marriage and Family Living* 23:166–170.

RUMMEL, RUDOLPH J. 1963 Dimensions of Conflict Behavior Within and Between Nations. *General Systems* 8:1–50.

SCHREIBER, HERMANN; and SCHREIBER, GEORG (1955) 1957 *Vanished Cities.* New York: Knopf. → First published as *Versunkene Städte: Ein Buch von Glanz und Untergang.*

SIBLEY, MULFORD Q. 1963 *The Quiet Battle: Writings on the Theory and Practice of Non-violent Resistance.* Garden City, N.Y.: Doubleday.

SOREL, GEORGES (1908) 1950 *Reflections on Violence.* Translated by T. E. Hulme and J. Roth, with an introduction by Edward A. Shils. Glencoe, Ill.: Free Press. → First published as *Réflexions sur la violence.* A paperback edition was published in 1961 by Collier.

III
COMMUNITY DEVELOPMENT

Community development embodies two major ideas. The first is that of conscious acceleration of economic, technological, and social change (development). The second, that of locality, refers to planned social change in a village, town, or city; it relates to projects that have obvious local significance and that can be initiated and carried out by local people. According to the widely accepted United Nations definitions, communities as units of action combine outside assistance with organized local self-determination and effort. They achieve goals that are both material (a new schoolhouse) and nonmaterial (literacy, lowered infant mortality).

The accent on development suggests that the emerging nations move through a series of stages on their way toward modernization. Leaders realize that to achieve economic goals more quickly, large numbers of people, especially in the rural areas, have to be mobilized. In the communist countries the collectivization of agriculture was the method chosen; in several noncommunist countries, such as India and the Philippines, community development or its equivalent is being used. Neither approach has proven a panacea, and each has had pronounced and often unanticipated social effects.

During the colonial period of many developing countries the central government concentrated upon communications and material resources, using the local settlements or groups of them for administration of justice and for tax purposes. Nevertheless, the colonial powers did initiate some activities resembling contemporary community development. In Africa there were the mass education programs in Kenya, Uganda, Gold Coast (now Ghana), *sociétés mutuelles de développement rural* and *sociétés indigènes de prévoyance* in French-administered areas, and *foyers sociaux* and cooperatives in Belgian-administered territories. In Asia the rural reconstruction in India in the 1930s and the rural development in Ceylon and mass education in Burma in the 1940s were programs that predated the current large-scale community development efforts throughout much of Asia today. The growing interest in community development in Latin America is relatively recent. In the Middle East, programs of rural reconstruction were carried out in the 1930s by the Near East Foundation, but the post-World War II pioneering efforts were with the rural social centers set up in the United Arab Republic (then Egypt) by the Ministry of Social Affairs.

The term community development now enjoys

wide usage in the West, even though community organization still best describes the mobilization of local resources for social welfare purposes. In 1948 the United Nations organization had one community development adviser in one country; in 1962 it had 47 such experts in 31 countries.

Intellectual and social origins

The mixed ancestry of community development gives a clue to the problems of defining the term. Social workers, adult educators, local government officials, economic planners, city planners, and agricultural extension workers consider their respective professional fields to have been forerunners of community development, a fact which supposedly gives them each the right to speak authoritatively about its content and methods.

In their descriptions of the current scene various writers not unexpectedly stress different themes. Arthur Dunham (1960) tends to view community development as organized efforts to improve the conditions of community life and the capacity for community integration and self-direction. Four basic elements ordinarily found are (1) a planned program; (2) encouragement of self-help; (3) technical assistance, which may include personnel, equipment, and supplies; and (4) integrating various specialties for the help of the community.

Governmental and national programs. T. R. Batten (1957) considers the field of community development "to include any action taken by any agency and primarily designed to benefit the community." He observes that one of the principal problems in using democratic methods in community development is that the central governments put pressure on village-level workers to achieve national goals within given time periods. As a result, the village workers attempt to speed up the programs with less democratic methods. When the program is highly formalized, as in many five-year plans, the focus sometimes tends to be upon the program rather than upon what is happening to the people involved in the program. The emphasis is upon accomplishing sets of activities in health, welfare, agriculture, industry, recreation, and the like that can be quantified and reported.

As these statements imply, many community development programs are national in scope and are geared to over-all governmental plans, be they three-year, five-year, or ten-year, for improving living and economic conditions. In this connection community development may be said to be a method through which national goals are to be achieved. The government of India (India 1958) has been quite specific in treating community development

as a method designed to initiate a process of transformation in the social and economic life of the Indian village. As a method it was supposed to do three things: achieve unity of thinking and action between all development agencies of government and between the official agency, the people's agency, and the people; transform the social and economic outlook of the people, chiefly through village organization; and conduct intensive area development based on a multipurpose approach. Recognition by the Indian government that agricultural development presented special problems too great to be borne by the Ministry of Community Development has led to abolition of this ministry. But there has been no decrease in the number of community development projects, and community development will no doubt continue to be regarded as the single most important method available to the government for coordinating social with economic planning.

Fredrick G. Friedmann, who has studied UNLA —the Association for the Fight Against Illiteracy— in southern Italy as a form of community development, observes that "many Western leaders interested in the subject look at community development as an attempt at extending, in the vein of the applied social sciences, proven techniques of 'handling' situations to the limited and relatively manageable proportions of a village community and at substituting 'projects' on a community level for large-scale government 'planning'" (1960, preface, p. xiv).

In the United Arab Republic "community development" refers to the organization of rural welfare. Unpublished research carried out during the early 1960s by Doreen Warriner in Egypt showed that "self-help" by rural communities and "participation" in solving community problems have been little more than government slogans, since the emphasis has not been upon setting up organizations *for* the rural community.

Programs based on local initiative. It must not be assumed that all community development programs are governmental in nature. In the United States, for example, the stress has been upon local initiative, usually sponsored by private groups or organizations (women's clubs, men's civic clubs, junior chambers of commerce, welfare councils), with only an occasional assist from some governmental agency. Thus, community development is viewed as a method of carrying out specific projects, each worthy in its own right, rather than as part of some detailed national plan or program. The nonmaterial benefits to the people are thought to be as valuable as the material goals achieved, since it is assumed that the more local residents are involved in planning and decision making, the more they will rely upon their own community resources and less upon the government. This reflects the strong individualistic and ameliorative strains in American culture as well as the value placed on local self-reliance and democratic participation. An OEEC (Organization for European Economic Cooperation) study team from Europe found one of the most surprising features of community development in the United States to be the importance of private efforts in community improvement and the small role played by local government officials in these matters (1960).

Various definitions incorporate this emphasis. J. D. Mezirow, for instance, has stated on several occasions that community development is an organized effort to make possible, through training and education, a wide range of individual participation in the democratic solution of community problems. Richard W. Poston (1958, p. 24) defines community development as "an organized body of knowledge which deals comprehensively with the community in its entirety, and with all of the various functions of community life as integrated parts of the whole." He suggests that "the ultimate goal of community development is to help evolve through a process of organized study, planning, and action a physical and social environment that is best suited to the maximum growth, development and happiness of human beings as individuals and as productive members of their society."

Lowry Nelson, Charles E. Ramsey, and Coolie Verner (1960) see community development as an "education-for-action process." It helps people achieve group goals democratically; the leader becomes an agent constructing learning experience rather than the proponent of a program for community improvement; primary importance is attached to the individual. Furthermore, it is problem-oriented at the community level; the means employed in the solution are more important than the solution itself; and it is one of several types of purposive change.

Noncoercion and the problem of incentives. The definitions just cited show that community development is noncoercive. Totalitarian regimes do not view it as politically realistic or as ideologically desirable, since community development stresses the voluntary rather than regimented participation of the individual. But for nontotalitarian regimes there are real dilemmas: How long can authorities desiring rapid social change wait for positive results from a slow educational process? Or in working out national economic and social plans, how much weight can they give to the pri-

orities of villagers throughout the land? To what extent can those sponsoring community development rely on local leaders to initiate projects in terms of the "felt needs" of their fellow citizens, or must this initiative come from outside professional workers who stimulate and help local people bring into being some form of local action? Although a community program is noncoercive it operates within certain social controls: pressure brought by neighbors upon a villager who fails to carry out his part of the program; positive incentives (e.g., in the form of wheat) provided to those working on community projects; or national recognition given to the community and its leaders for a well-conducted program.

Types of functionaries

Of course, the resolution of these dilemmas and the types of social control employed will depend upon the leaders of the program and their underlying assumptions. At least four types of functionaries are found in community development programs. First, local leaders are essential if there is to be genuine involvement of the people of the community. In some countries where community development is tied in with local government these leaders may be officials; elsewhere, they may be lay, voluntary leaders acting out of a spirit of public service. In developing countries great care is often taken to teach these leaders the importance of using democratic rather than authoritarian procedures in efforts to involve their fellow community members. Special courses, such as those in the American Farm School in Greece, are held for these leaders, because ultimate success depends upon them.

A second type of functionary is the community organizer, often called the village-level worker. He is the new element added by community development to earlier, traditional programs of rural change. He is trained in human-relations skills rather than in any subject-matter field, such as agriculture, health, or recreation. As a generalist, he is supposed to know how to relate these fields to the problem areas that the local people identify, but he does not claim high technical competence in them. By working with local leaders, he initiates, motivates, guides, and educates, supposedly taking into account the goals of the local people as well as the goals of the larger program that he is promoting. Once action has been decided upon by the community, the village-level worker becomes the expediter, the communication link, the one who marshals outside resources appropriate to the local needs at the time.

But he is relatively ineffective without a third type—the subject-matter specialist: agriculturist, sanitarian, literacy expert, and the like. Even before the village-level worker appeared on the scene after World War II, these specialists were trying to carry out changes in their special fields in rural areas. But they were doing it in a piecemeal fashion. One month a health worker would appear suggesting some line of action; later a livestock specialist would show up demanding vaccination for hog cholera. Under community development the local people are expected to prepare an over-all plan involving several of these fields, beginning with the project for which they have the greatest enthusiasm and sufficient means at their disposal. Thus, the subject-matter specialists, as in the case of some recent programs in the Philippines, are asked to go to a village as a team, not as competing professionals. A community development worker is also part of the team. Elsewhere, as in Ethiopia, the specialists may be assigned to community development authorities for full-time work under these authorities rather than as part of the old-line ministries to which they eventually expect to return. In most countries getting the specialists to work together effectively presents more of a problem than persuading the villagers to agree to a program of change.

This problem is related to the fourth functionary: the person responsible for keeping the administrative machinery of a national program in running order. In Venezuela, for instance, horizontal and vertical coordination is being achieved at the state level through "regional community development bodies." The larger the program, the greater the proportion of energy and money that goes into the mechanics of operation. Vast training programs, long hours (even years) of negotiation with other government agencies, detailed plans and budgets for three or five years are required. In addition, some officials must maintain a flow of technical materials (pesticides, schoolbooks, drugs, etc.) so that they are on hand for ready use when the local communities need them. One conclusion seems clear: unless the head of the government or some influential official with a charismatic, popular appeal makes community development a major concern, the bureaucratic pressures against its success on a national scale are so great that it is apt to bog down. But where people like Ramón Magsaysay in the Philippines or Jawaharlal Nehru in India have referred to it often in public and given it their full support, the program has enjoyed a measure of success.

Goals and achievements

In Asian countries, which for more than ten years have had the widest experience with community development, certain discernible trends are under way. First, the programs are stressing economic (including agricultural) goals more heavily than heretofore. Second, they are making greater use of local governments as the need for decentralization becomes more apparent. Third, the training of village-level workers is stressing the practical aspects (for instance, the actual grafting of fruit trees) as well as the theoretical aspects—a new educational departure for these countries. Fourth, new administrative arrangements are being devised to assure the coordination of subject-matter specialists in accomplishment of program aims. Undoubtedly, community development programs do give village people a feeling of political involvement which they would otherwise not have; they have substantial material accomplishments (roads, school buildings, new plant varieties, etc.) to their credit. But the biggest gain, perhaps, lies not at the village level but in the better understanding of village problems by higher government officials. The programs in Africa and Latin America are still too new to provide useful generalizations, except to indicate that they exhibit wide variety in organizational procedures and types of problems attacked. Land reform tends to be associated with community development more than it was in Asia. In the developed countries community development is increasingly being relied upon as a method for local improvements. Social workers, agricultural extension workers, public health educators are being trained in its techniques, and a few institutes have been set up to prepare specialists in community development as a special professional field.

The future of community development

Community development is still too young to justify any long-range predictions about its identity as a separate profession or its combination with some other field, such as public administration, agricultural extension, social work—to name but three.

Like any emerging profession, it has begun to develop its applied theory, set forth chiefly in the form of principles of action that should be followed for effective practice. Since community development is so new, each mature practitioner must perforce come out of some previously existing discipline or profession. This shows up in the lists of principles he sets down or passes on to his associates. Some stress the psychological overtones of motivation and group dynamics; others, the sociological caveats of recognizing social values and social structure; others, the administrative aspects of sound programming; and still others, the anthropological investment in cultural change, the educators' concern with learning, or the specialists' concern with appropriate technology.

There is not at the present time a body of tested theory on development. Nor do we know in any systematic way why some programs succeed, by the developers' standards, while other programs fail. To date, and this is a crucial test, existing training programs do not draw upon any identifiable community development theory as such but rely almost entirely upon social-science generalizations developed quite apart from community development activities.

IRWIN T. SANDERS

[See also AGRICULTURE, *article on* DEVELOPING COUNTRIES; FOREIGN AID; PLANNING, ECONOMIC, *article on* DEVELOPMENT PLANNING; PLANNING, SOCIAL.]

BIBLIOGRAPHY

The most comprehensive guide to community development literature is Sociological Abstracts . . . 1964; *a good shorter bibliography is* Dunham 1959. *Useful reviews of trends since World War II will be found in* Kaufman & Cole 1959; Lyfield & Schmidt 1959; Dunham 1960; *and* Sehnert 1961. *The leading journal in the field is the* International Review of Community Development; *also worth consulting is the* Community Development Review. *Much valuable information on community development in various parts of the world is continually being published by such organizations as the* U.S. Agency for International Development *and the* Economic and Social Council of the United Nations. *Reports of the proceedings of international conferences sponsored from time to time by the* U.S. Agency for International Development *(and by its predecessor, the* U.S. International Cooperation Administration) *often include interesting materials not available in any other form; some of these have been summarized in* Sociological Abstracts . . . 1964.

ALLEN, HAROLD B. 1953 *Rural Reconstruction in Action: Experience in the Near and Middle East.* Ithaca, N.Y.: Cornell Univ. Press.

BATTEN, THOMAS R. 1957 *Communities and Their Development.* Oxford Univ. Press.

BATTEN, THOMAS R. 1962 *Training for Community Development.* Oxford Univ. Press.

BRUYN, SEVERYN T. 1963 *Communities in Action: Pattern and Process.* New Haven: College and University Press. → See especially the Appendix entitled "The Community Movement in the United States," pages 161–184.

Community Development Review. → Published since 1956.

DUNHAM, ARTHUR 1959 Community Development in the United States of America: A Selective, Annotated Bibliography. *International Review of Community Development* 4:223–233.

DUNHAM, ARTHUR 1960 Community Development. Pages 178–186 in *Social Work Yearbook.* Edited by Russell

H. Kurtz. New York: National Association of Social Workers.

DU SAUTOY, PETER 1958 *Community Development in Ghana.* Oxford Univ. Press.

FOSTER, ELLERY 1953 Planning for Community Development Through Its People. *Human Organization* 12:5–9.

FRIEDMANN, FREDRICK G. 1960 *The Hoe and the Book: An Italian Experiment in Community Development.* Ithaca, N.Y.: Cornell Univ. Press.

GOODENOUGH, WARD H. 1963 *Cooperation in Change: An Anthropological Approach to Community Development.* New York: Russell Sage Foundation.

GREAT BRITAIN, COLONIAL OFFICE 1960 *Community Development.* A handbook prepared by a study conference on community development held at Hartwell House, Aylesbury, Buckinghamshire, September, 1957. London: H.M. Stationery Office.

INDIA, MINISTRY OF COMMUNITY DEVELOPMENT 1958 *Revision in the Programme of Community Development.* Madras (India): Controller of Stationery and Printing.

International Review of Community Development. → Published since 1958 under the auspices of the International Federation of Settlements and Neighbourhood Centers.

KAUFMAN, HAROLD F.; and COLE, LUCY W. 1959 Sociological and Social Psychological Research for Community Development. *International Review of Community Development* 4:193–211.

KELLY, ISABEL 1962/1963 Suggestions for the Training of Village-level Workers. *Human Organization* 21:241–245.

KING, CLARENCE 1958 *Working With People in Small Communities: Case Records of Community Development in Different Countries.* New York: Harper.

LYFIELD, WILLIAM G.; and SCHMIDT, WARREN H. 1959 Trends in Community Development: Some Results of a Survey. *International Review of Community Development* 4:33–40. → Focus is on the United States.

McCLUSKEY, HOWARD Y. 1960 Community Development. Pages 416–427 in *Handbook of Adult Education in the United States.* Edited by Malcolm S. Knowles. Chicago: Adult Education Association of the U.S.A.

MIAL, H. CURTIS 1958 Community Development: A Democratic Social Process. *Adult Leadership* 6:277–282.

MINICLIER, LOUIS M. 1962 Community Development in the World Today: Ten Years Progress. *Community Development Review* 7:69–74. → Sees rise of community development as a response to postwar social forces.

MOSHER, ARTHUR T. 1958 *Varieties of Extension Education in Community Development.* Comparative Extension Publication No. 2. Ithaca, N.Y.: Cornell Univ., New York State College of Agriculture, Rural Education Department.

NELSON, LOWRY; RAMSEY, CHARLES E.; and VERNER, COOLIE 1960 *Community Structure and Change.* New York: Macmillan.

ORGANIZATION FOR EUROPEAN ECONOMIC COOPERATION, EUROPEAN PRODUCTIVITY AGENCY 1960 *Community Development: Some Achievements in the United States and Europe.* EPA Project 387. Paris: The Agency.

POSTON, RICHARD W. 1958 Report of the Chairman, Division of Community Development. National University Extension Association, *Proceedings* 41:23–29.

PUSIC, E. 1960 Basic Principles of Community Development in Yugoslavia. *International Review of Community Development* 5:171–176.

RUOPP, PHILLIPS (editor) 1953 *Approaches to Community Development.* The Hague: Van Hoeve.

SANDERS, IRWIN T. 1964 Community Development Programs in Sociological Perspective. Pages 307–332 in James H. Copp (editor), *Our Changing Rural Society: Perspectives and Trends.* Ames: Iowa State Univ. Press.

SEHNERT, FRANK H. 1961 A Functional Framework for the Action Process in Community Development. Unpublished manuscript, Carbondale: Southern Illinois Univ., Department of Community Development.

SOCIOLOGICAL ABSTRACTS, INC., NEW YORK 1964 *Community Development Abstracts.* Washington: U.S. Agency for International Development, Office of Technical Cooperation and Research, Rural and Community Development. → Contains 1,108 abstracts summarizing most of the printed literature in the field for the last ten years.

UNITED NATIONS, BUREAU OF SOCIAL AFFAIRS 1955 *Social Progress Through Community Development.* New York: United Nations.

UNITED NATIONS, ECONOMIC AND SOCIAL COUNCIL 1953 *Programme of Concerted Practical Action in the Social Field of the United Nations and Specialized Agencies.* Document E/CN.5/291/Rev.1. New York: United Nations.

UNITED NATIONS, ECONOMIC AND SOCIAL COUNCIL 1957 *Twentieth Report of the Administrative Committee on Co-ordination to the Economic and Social Council.* Document E/2931, Official Records, 24th Session, Annexes, agenda item 4. New York: United Nations.

UNITED NATIONS, ECONOMIC AND SOCIAL COUNCIL, SOCIAL COMMISSION 1963 *Evaluation of Technical Assistance Activities in Rural Community Development Field.* Report by the Secretary-General. New York: United Nations.

WARREN, ROLAND L. 1963 *The Community in America.* Chicago: Rand McNally. → See especially pages 324–327 for useful distinctions between community development, community organization, and community planning.

COMMUNITY–SOCIETY CONTINUA

Since the emergence of the cities of antiquity, social philosophers have attempted to characterize and account for the contrast between tribal or rural life and the ways of city men. During the past century, the age-old contrast has been conceived in terms of pairs of societal types, such as rural–urban or primitive–civilized. The poles of such a pair are characterized by the opposite extremes of type-defining variables, such as the degree of importance of kinship or the extent of division of labor in a society. The range of variation of such characteristics creates a conceptual "con-tinuum" between the opposed polar types. Because the types can refer to either communities or societies, the term "community–society continua" is employed to cover these constructs.

Polar types are one kind of "ideal type." This term runs the risk of being misconstrued, for in this context "ideal" has no connotation of excellence. Here it means that the type is an "idea"—a mental construct. It is a concept derived from observable reality but not conforming to it in detail. Some aspects of that reality are selected and accentuated in defining the type, because of their apparent interdependence and theoretical importance. However, ideal types are not classifications. No actual society will conform completely to such a type. When used as a basis of comparison with life situations, however, the type suggests possible hypotheses and lines of investigation. Thus, ideal types are tools to be used in the analysis of empirical reality [*see* TYPOLOGIES].

Status and contract

Modern use of polar types in social science stems from the evolutionary concerns initiated by Charles Darwin's *Origin of Species* (1859) and Henry Maine's *Ancient Law* (1861). Maine's objective in this study was to discover how the institutions of his day had evolved from those of antiquity. In contrast to Johann Bachofen, John F. McLennan, and Lewis Morgan, who were his contemporaries, Maine avoided the pitfalls of flimsy historical reconstructions. He stated that much of the study could not have been undertaken had it not been for the long record of Roman law, linking evidence of remote antiquity to the rules and institutions of modern society. For lack of other evidence, he was forced to use Roman law as a "typical system." The propositions drawn from that law and other available evidence were held to be typical of the social changes experienced in the emergency of western European societies. The validity of most of Maine's interpretations rests not only upon the quality of his evidence but also upon the logic of the relationships which he discovered among the changes. The "typical" features of ancient and modern society, as he described them, have the elements of an ideal typology, although Maine did not represent them in any such terms.

On the basis of early writings of the Hindus, Hebrews, Greeks, and Romans, Maine concluded that primeval society was based on the patriarchal family, at least in those societies. There, the eldest ascendant male held absolute supremacy over the whole family, and the larger society consisted of an aggregation of such families. Maine then noted that the units of modern society were not families, but individuals. His study pursued the consequences of this difference through human history. Primitive law dealt with family groups as corporate entities defined by kinship. Crime, for instance, was a corporate act; land was jointly held; newcomers to such a system had to be incorporated into it through the creation of fictitious kinship.

As societies expanded, a new sort of definition of social membership emerged, informed by the principle of contiguity. Locality, rather than kinship, thus became the basis of state organization. As the powers and privileges once resident in the family shifted to the growing state, Maine argued, the nature of men's interrelations shifted from that of kin-based status to that of individually agreed-upon engagement or contract. Maine found vivid evidence of these changes in the decline of *patria potestas* (paternal authority), as dependents gradually achieved separate rights under the Roman state. Thus, Maine depicts an ideal-typical sort of change from society based on kinship, status, aggregations of families, and joint property rights to a kind of society based on territory, contract, and individual rights, including those to real property. These ideas had a wide influence on his contemporaries and on subsequent scholars.

Gemeinschaft and Gesellschaft

Ferdinand Tönnies was the first to make explicit the nature and use of ideal types, or "normal types," as he called them. Stimulated by Maine as well as by Marx and Hobbes, he developed two such types which gave their names to his book *Gemeinschaft und Gesellschaft* (1887). Tönnies' theory and typology rest on his view of the nature of human volition, of which he distinguished two types—*Wesenwille* ("natural will" or "essential will") and *Kürwille* ("rational will"). The former refers to volition that springs from an individual's temperament, character, and habits. With rational will, however, the distinction between means and ends becomes important, and volition is dominated by thinking.

Gemeinschaft cannot be accurately translated. It refers to the "community of feeling" (a kind of associative unity of ideas and emotions) that results from likeness and from shared life-experience. Natural will predominates in Gemeinschaft relationships, which are best illustrated by the links between mother and child, husband and wife, and brothers and sisters. Differences in power and authority do not in themselves destroy Gemeinschaft, which may characterize the relationship of a beneficent father to a dutiful child. Nor is Gemeinschaft limited to formal kinship, for neighborhood and collective proprietorship produce a similar unity, and friendship expresses a kind of Gemeinschaft that is tied to neither blood nor locality.

The predominance of rational will characterizes *Gesellschaft*. In Gesellschaft relationships, Tönnies says, "everybody is by himself and isolated, and there exists a condition of tension against all others . . . intrusions are regarded as hostile acts . . . nobody wants to grant and produce anything for another individual . . . all goods are conceived to be separate, as are their owners" (1887, p. 65 in 1963 paperback edition). In such a society, rational will operates in terms of the logic of the market place. Relationships are contractual; values are monetary. Profit is the sole end of trade, and one man's gain is another's loss. As the merchant tries to free himself from all relationships that might conflict with commerce, he becomes, as Adam Smith pointed out, an individual who is not bound to any particular country; indeed, every man becomes, in some measure, a merchant.

Since real social groups vary in the degree to which they resemble Gemeinschaft and Gesellschaft, the types provide a comparative basis for discovering order in that variation. Tönnies described one such application of the typology: "In the history of the great systems of culture," he wrote, "a period of Gesellschaft follows a period of Gemeinschaft" (Tönnies 1887, p. 231 in 1963 paperback edition). The latter period begins with social relations based on family life and on domestic economy; later, with the development of agriculture and rural village life, there is a shift to cooperative patterns based on locality. Then follows the growth of town life and the mental community of religious faith and artistry. The Gesellschaft period of history opens with the growth of city life based on trade and contractual relationships. Industrialization and the rational manipulation of capital and labor are accompanied by the growth of the state and of national life. Cosmopolitan life, toward which Tönnies thought society was moving, would be based on the ultimate expressions of rational will—science, informed public opinion, and control by "the republic of scholars."

Tönnies has been criticized for assigning the names of his ideal types to actual periods of history, for this makes it seem as though he is using them for simple classification. Actually, his discussion of this sequence stresses the *progressive shift* from a predominantly Gemeinschaft sort of society to one dominated by Gesellschaft. In later and little-known works, he used the typology to analyze other sorts of phenomena, such as morals and public opinion, but the types did not figure in his really empirical investigations.

The most specific attempt to operationalize the typology has been made by Charles Loomis and J. Allan Beegle (1950). They argue that Gemeinschaft and Gesellschaft have only limited scientific utility because they are "sponge" concepts, absorbing many vague meanings. To overcome this limitation, they break down the types into a dozen or so variables, largely derived from Talcott Parsons, Pitirim A. Sorokin, and Howard Becker and more or less directly related to Tönnies' typology. The methodology they have devised to illustrate the typology expresses each of these variables in terms of an 11-point linear scale extending between Gemeinschaft and Gesellschaft poles. Actual social systems, such as the Amish family, are then allocated to positions on these scales by averaging the scale assignments made by a panel of judges. When a number of such scales are juxtaposed, a "profile" of each social system can be created by drawing a line connecting its ratings on the various scales. Such profiles permit visual comparison of ratings of different aspects of the same system or of the same variable in different systems.

No claim was made that these ratings were based on anything more rigorous than the opinions of judges who had some personal experience with the social systems being judged. Nor was any theory tested by the procedure, although Loomis and McKinney (1956) have since used it to explore the nature of the difference between two Costa Rican communities selected to represent distinctive types of rural social organization in Latin America. In this investigation, only six scaled components of the ideal types were employed, including all of Parsons' "pattern variables."

Mechanical and organic solidarity

In his book *The Division of Labor in Society* (1893), Émile Durkheim examined the relationship between two facts that had already been noted by Auguste Comte and Herbert Spencer—that the division of labor in society was a source of social solidarity and that primitive society was relatively homogeneous in character. Noting the impossibility of observing social solidarity directly, Durkheim took variation in types of law as a symbol, or reflection, of types of solidarity. Maine afforded him the basis for further analysis in the observation that law in ancient societies was characteristically penal or criminal law, while civil law predominates in modern society. Durkheim called the first type of law "repressive" and identified it with *mechanical solidarity*, or social unity based on likeness. He held that the moral sentiments common to all members of a society constitute a "collective conscience"; criminal acts are those that violate the common conscience and call forth passionate reactions of vengeance. Violent punishment of the offender can expiate the act because the punishment protects the collective conscience of the society from further violation.

Durkheim pointed out that, from a logical point of view, the extreme case of an ideal-type society defined in terms of homogeneity would be an unorganized inchoate horde. In reality, however, although the mechanical solidarity of the most primitive known societies does indeed rest on homogeneity, these societies also show some differentiation into unspecialized aggregates such as clans. This simple repetition of segments caused Durkheim to suggest the term "segmental society" for this type. He recognized, however, that mechanical solidarity plays some role in all societies; as an index of its relative importance in a society, he took the proportion of law that was penal in character.

In contrast to repressive law, which deals with criminal acts against society, civil law deals with relationships between special parties in society. The sanctions of civil law involve restitution rather than punishment, and such "restitutive" law presupposes cooperation derived from the division of labor. The associated type of social solidarity is based on the interdependence of specialized parts; using the biological analogy, Durkheim called it *organic solidarity*. To the type of society it characterized he gave no specific name, although he referred to it as "occupationally organized."

Finally, Durkheim used the legal indices of solidarity to demonstrate that as one basis of solidarity develops the other regresses. It is always organic solidarity that wins out over the mechanical, he contended. The evolution of society can therefore be seen in terms of the passage from mechanical solidarity to organic solidarity, with "mechanical" or "organic" referring to the dominant type of solidary relationship at each evolutionary stage. Durkheim saw a connection between this evolutionary process and such factors as increasing population size and density, the growth of cities, and improvements in communication. In the increasing competition resulting from rising population density and increasing social interaction, he found the cause of the increase in division of labor.

Durkheim has been criticized by Robert K. Merton (1934) for his overemphasis on division of labor as the source of solidarity in modern society and his use of legal forms as indices of solidarity. In addition, anthropological research has shown that primitive law has important civil aspects that neither Maine nor Durkheim recognized. Despite such objections, Merton found the societal ideal types to be useful constructs.

The folk–urban continuum

Recognizing some commonalty among peoples possessing folklore, folk songs, and folkways, Robert Redfield sought other distinguishing features of the primitive and peasant peoples who constitute such "folk." On the basis of his study (1930) of the Mexican peasants of Tepoztlán, he concluded that they were like primitives in their self-sufficiency, nonliteracy, and the local, traditional, and sacred orientation of their lives. However, he also found that they were part of the modern urban world and were gradually being assimilated into it.

To pursue this process further, Redfield and two assistants studied a series of four communities in Yucatan: the modern capital city, a town, a village, and a tribal settlement of Indians. By comparing these communities in what had once been an entirely Mayan area, Redfield hoped to discover what was happening in the folk culture as it was being influenced by the modern city. In a more general sense, however, he was interested in the shift from the type of society represented by the more isolated village toward the type illustrated by the capital city.

In *The Folk Culture of Yucatan* (1941), Redfield stated that in drawing up his list of folk characteristics he had been influenced by Maine, Durkheim, and Tönnies. The list of characteristics continued to grow, but only five of them were explicitly studied in Yucatan. Evidence was sought to test the hypothesis that progressive loss of isolation, when associated with an increase in heterogeneity, produces social disorganization, secularization, and individualization. Intercommunity variation along these dimensions could be adequately assessed because of the original cultural homogeneity of the area. The total evidence, as well as the histories of individual communities, tended to confirm the hypothesis, but Redfield pointed out that it might not hold under all circumstances.

An opportunity to refine Redfield's hypothesis was presented when Sol Tax (1939) reported that in Guatemala, although Indian society was both small and homogeneous, it was also secularized and individualistic, with weak familial organization. This apparent conflict with the Yucatan findings now seems to have been due to the difficulty of defining the units of analysis. Actually, Tax had shown that although each Indian community was homogeneous, Guatemalan society as a whole was large and heterogeneous, with an indigenous commercialized economy based on agricultural and craft specialization among the Indian villages. Thus, the villages were removed from isolation by trade; and this loss of isolation, according to Redfield's hypothesis, would lead to the very characteristics observed by Tax. Where Tax and Redfield differed was on how marked such nonfolk characteristics were in Guatemala—which illustrates the difficulty of making such judgments without a clear basis of comparison. Nevertheless, the Guatemalan research highlights the fact that life can become less folklike and more urban as a result of participation in a highly commercial economy, even if that economy is not dependent upon modern cities.

Redfield never defined the urban type of society beyond indicating that it was characterized by the antitheses of the folk traits. The latter were set forth most explicitly in "The Folk Society" and summarized as follows.

Such a society is small, isolated, nonliterate, and homogeneous, with a strong sense of group solidarity. The ways of living are conventionalized into that coherent system which we call "a culture." Behavior is traditional, spontaneous, uncritical, and personal; there is no legislation or habit of experiment and reflection for intellectual ends. Kinship, its relationships and institutions, are the type categories of experience and the familial group is the unit of action. The sacred prevails over the secular; the economy is one of status rather than of the market. (Redfield 1947, p. 293)

The folk type has been criticized for its obvious lack of specificity and focus. This lack is really both a strength and a weakness. The advantage of the multiplicity of definitive traits lies in the variety of causal relationships that are suggested. The disadvantage lies in the lack of suggestion as to which traits should be considered as causes, which as effects, and under what circumstances. If we had the answer to all of these questions, however, there would be no need for the ideal types.

Further tests of the typology. Twenty years after Redfield studied Tepoztlán, Oscar Lewis conducted a restudy of the village. Some of his observations were sufficiently different from those of his predecessor to require explanation, and Lewis concluded his report (1951) with a detailed criticism of both the original study and the folk–urban continuum. The latter criticism was considered by Horace Miner (1952) in a general evaluation of the utility of the continuum. He concluded that Lewis' critique reflected a legitimate concern for detailed structural, psychological, and historical analysis, which differed from, but did not conflict with, Redfield's interest in developing general propositions based on formal concepts. Redfield himself concluded that the apparent substantive differences between the two reports were really differences in emphasis resulting from the subjective "hidden questions" with which he and Lewis had approached the community.

In the case of one of Miner's studies, *The Primitive City of Timbuctoo* (1953), emphasis was explicitly placed on the discovery of evidence of disorganization, secularization, and impersonalization. This was done to ascertain whether Redfield's "urban characteristics" would be found in a non-Western nonindustrial city. Timbuctoo was an African commercial center long before European contact, and it meets the requirements of Louis Wirth's minimal definition of the city as "a relatively large, dense, and permanent settlement of socially heterogeneous individuals" (1938, p. 8). Miner did find cheating, prostitution, usury, and theft in this city, but "urban" behavior was largely limited to commercial and other relations among the major ethnic elements of the population; *within* each of these groups, life was found to be remarkably folklike. Thus Timbuctoo, unlike Western cities, presented a mixture of folk and urban characteristics.

These observations were placed in a broader context by Gideon Sjoberg (1952; 1960), who recognized the similarly mixed character of all preindustrial cities. He also saw such cities and their associated peasant villages as the constituent parts of an ideal-typical "feudal society," which contrasted with both of Redfield's polar types. Sjoberg characterized feudal society as being static and having strongly sacred value orientations. Unlike the folk type, however, it is more heterogeneous and is commercially oriented. A primary element in this heterogeneity is the small, hereditary, urban elite, which controls the political, military, and religious institutions. These institutions, in turn, provide the principal links with the rural peasants. The elite incorporates a literate element of scholar-priests and is served by urban craftsmen, organized along guild lines. In commerce, standardization of weights, measures, and media of exchange are generally lacking, and *caveat emptor* is the rule. While cities and societies resembling these types have often been developmental stages in the cumulative process of urbanization, there is no implication that they are necessary stages in such development.

Social complexity. Of the many studies that have drawn stimulation from the folk–urban continuum, one other should be mentioned here because it employed an unusual analytic method. It also used cross-cultural data from the Human Relations Area Files. Linton Freeman and Robert Winch (1957) tested the single dimensionality of *social complexity*—a variable they found to be inherent in all of the continua discussed above. Various measures of complexity were applied to 48 societies and the resultant data subjected to Guttman scaling analysis; six of these variables scaled almost perfectly, indicating their unidimensionality.

Even more interesting were the hypotheses suggested by the scale relationships among the variables. For example, the appearance of a money economy seems to be the initial step toward the other forms of cultural complexity studied. On the other hand, written languages seem to appear at a much later stage, for they were found only in societies which also had complex systems of exchange, law, religion, education, and government.

Parsons' "pattern variables"

Four pattern variables constitute the basic components of Talcott Parsons' system of analysis of social action (1951, pp. 58–67; 1960). The variables are "ranges which, in their simplest form, can be defined as polar alternatives." In Parsonian analysis, the pattern variables figure as dichotomies: each expresses a "dilemma" of choice between two distinct alternatives that are faced by the "actor" in every social situation. The nature of the variables is suggested by the way each relates to the definition of behavioral expectations. *Affectivity* versus *affective neutrality* refers to whether immediate self-gratification or its deferment is expected. *Specificity* versus *diffuseness* is concerned with whether the scope of the relationship is seen as narrow, like that between a clerk and customer, or broad and inclusive, as between spouses. *Universalism* versus *particularism* has to do with whether action is governed in terms of generalized standards or in terms of a reference scheme peculiar to the actors in the relationship. Finally, the *quality* versus *performance* dichotomy (also called *ascription* versus *achievement*) is concerned with whether the characterization of each actor by the other is based on who or what the person is or on what he can do—for example, on whether he has royal blood (ascription), or on whether he is a college graduate (achievement).

Classification of societies. Parsons used combinations of two of these dichotomies—universalism–particularism and ascription–achievement—to define four principal types of society. He pointed out that all societies organized around kinship fall under the particularistic–ascriptive pattern. The general emphasis of the fourfold typology thus reflects the focus of the whole theoretical scheme on "variability among 'civilizations' rather than among primitive cultures." The scheme, therefore, has evolutionary implications, as it distinguishes three social structural "types which tend to emerge when major types of cultural development in the literate cultures have occurred" (Parsons 1951, p. 182). The emergent type characterized by the universalistic–achievement pattern is exemplified by the most industrialized societies. Division of labor in such societies emphasizes the specificity and affective neutrality of occupational roles, which contrast with the diffuse and affective character of kin roles in primitive societies.

If one disregards the two other possible types in favor of the universalistic–achievement pattern and the particularistic–ascriptive pattern, there is obviously a continuum between these ideal-typical poles. In empirical terms, one extreme characterizes all primitive societies and even feudal ones, while heavily industrialized societies resemble the other pole. There is a clear tendency for the four pattern variables to covary between these extremes, although all actual societies show mixtures of the two sets of characteristics. It is only the relative emphasis that differs. As Parsons says, these two clusters of pattern variables "very closely characterize what in much sociological literature have been thought of as polar types of institutional structure, the best known version of which perhaps has been the *Gemeinschaft–Gesellschaft* dichotomy of Tönnies" (Parsons et al. 1953, pp. 207–208).

Continua of economic development. It was Marion Levy who first used the pattern variables to define a continuum of economic development (1952). He suggested that societies could be placed on a scale of industrialization in terms of the efficiency of their use of energy and the sorts of energy employed. Furthermore, he contended that the social systems at the two extremes of such a scale differed with regard to certain basic qualities of social relationships—the degree to which they were based on nonrational traditionalism, whether they emphasized universalistic or particularistic criteria, and the degree to which they were functionally specific or diffuse. The economic systems of highly industrialized societies are more rational, universalistic, and functionally specific, and the problems of economic development can be seen in terms of the implied changes in these dimensions of nonindustrialized systems.

Bert Hoselitz (1953) followed this lead. Defining economic development in terms of per capita real income, he used Parsons' newly stated pattern variables in differentiating "underdeveloped" economic systems from "advanced" systems. With the exception of affectivity–neutrality, the other pattern variables seemed to Hoselitz to be related to degree of economic development. George A. Theodorson (1953) has pointed out, however, that affectivity is evident in the absenteeism and labor turnover in underdeveloped areas, where the workers are reluctant to accept the unfamiliar discipline of the factory. Theodorson's analysis also showed how the successful introduction of the factory system in nonindustrialized societies ultimately necessitated social changes which could be fruitfully conceptualized in terms of the pattern variables. He concluded that the pattern of universalism, achievement, specificity, and affective neutrality was inevitably linked to industrialization.

It will be recalled that Parsons delineated four societal types and that a continuum of economic development is achieved only by ignoring the universalism–ascription pattern that is evident in authoritarian collectivistic states, such as Nazi Germany, and the particularism–achievement pattern, such as that of imperial China. William Kolb (1954) brought these other alternatives into the discussion of industrialization and economic development. His focus was on the relation of cities to these processes, and his argument emphasized the danger of predicting the form of urban industrial development from the Western experience. He began by pointing out that population density and ethnic heterogeneity do not, in themselves, produce a universalism–achievement orientation. The need for government intervention in the industrialization effort of new nations lends itself to the universalistic–ascriptive orientation of authoritarianism. There is also the possibility that even with moderate development of emphasis on achievement and universalism in the industrial sector of life, other significant areas of life may remain under the older ascriptive–particularistic values. Reacting to these suggestions, McKimm Marriott (1954) expressed doubts concerning the feasibility of categorizing whole societies in terms of Parsons' variables; however, he ventured the opinion that urban India seems to live in terms of a particularism–achievement type of system of marked vitality.

At the North American Conference on the Social Implications of Industrialization and Technological Change in 1960, Hoselitz pointed out that the typologies of Tönnies and Redfield had been little used in studies of economic change. He contended that the Parsonian variables permitted sharper focus on the strategic mechanisms of change associated with industrialization. The conclusions of the conference *rapporteur général*, Wilbert Moore, can well stand as a final observation on this whole approach. Polar ideal types have heuristic value in the development of theory, he says, but "such modes of analysis present problems of operational identification in research, and of mensuration when mixed situations of empirical reality are approached" (1963, p. 361).

HORACE M. MINER

[*Directly related are the entries on* AGRICULTURE, *article on* SOCIAL ORGANIZATION; INDUSTRIALIZATION, *article on* SOCIAL ASPECTS. *Other relevant material may be found in* SYSTEMS ANALYSIS, *article on* SOCIAL SYSTEMS; VILLAGE; *and in the biographies of* DARWIN; DURKHEIM; MAINE; REDFIELD; TÖNNIES.]

BIBLIOGRAPHY

DARWIN, CHARLES (1859) 1964 *On the Origin of Species.* Cambridge, Mass.: Harvard Univ. Press. → A facsimile of the first edition.

DURKHEIM, ÉMILE (1893) 1960 *The Division of Labor in Society.* Glencoe, Ill.: Free Press. → First published as *De la division du travail social.*

FREEMAN, LINTON C.; and WINCH, ROBERT F. 1957 Social Complexity: An Empirical Test of a Typology of Societies. *American Journal of Sociology* 62:461–466.

HOSELITZ, BERT F. (1953) 1960 *Sociological Aspects of Economic Growth.* Glencoe, Ill.: Free Press. → See especially pages 23–51 on "Social Structure and Economic Growth," first published in 1953 in Volume 6 of *Economia internazionale.*

KOLB, WILLIAM L. 1954 The Structure and Functions of Cities. *Economic Development and Cultural Change* 3:30–46.

LEVY, MARION J. 1952 Some Sources of Vulnerability of the Structures of Relatively Nonindustrialized Societies to Those of Highly Industrialized Societies. Pages 113–125 in Bert F. Hoselitz (editor), *The Progress of Underdeveloped Areas.* Univ. of Chicago Press.

LEWIS, OSCAR 1951 *Life in a Mexican Village: Tepoztlán Restudied.* Urbana: Univ. of Illinois Press.

LOOMIS, CHARLES P.; and BEEGLE, J. ALLAN (1950) 1955 *Rural Social Systems: A Textbook in Rural Sociology and Anthropology.* Englewood Cliffs, N.J.: Prentice-Hall; London: Bailey & Swinfen.

LOOMIS, CHARLES P.; and McKINNEY, JOHN C. 1956 Systemic Differences Between Latin-American Communities of Family Farms and Large Estates. *American Journal of Sociology* 61:404–412.

MAINE, HENRY J. S. (1861) 1960 *Ancient Law: Its Connection With the Early History of Society, and Its Relations to Modern Ideas.* Rev. ed. New York: Dutton; London and Toronto: Dent. → A paperback edition was published in 1963 by Beacon.

MARRIOTT, McKIM 1954 Some Comments on William L. Kolb's "The Structure and Functions of Cities" in the Light of India's Urbanization. *Economic Development and Cultural Change* 3:50–52.

MERTON, ROBERT K. 1934 Durkheim's *Division of Labor in Society. American Journal of Sociology* 40:319–328.

MINER, HORACE M. 1952 The Folk–Urban Continuum. *American Sociological Review* 17:529–537.

MINER, HORACE M. (1953) 1965 *The Primitive City of Timbuctoo.* Rev. ed. Princeton Univ. Press. → A paperback edition was published in 1965 by Doubleday.

MOORE, WILBERT E. 1963 The Social Implications of Industrialization and Technological Change: Concluding Comments. Pages 360–368 in North American Conference on the Social Implications of Industrialization and Technological Change, Chicago, 1960, *Industrialization and Society.* Edited by Bert F. Hoselitz and Wilbert E. Moore. Paris: UNESCO.

PARSONS, TALCOTT 1951 *The Social System.* Glencoe, Ill.: Free Press.

PARSONS, TALCOTT 1960 Pattern Variables Revisited: A Response to Robert Dubin. *American Sociological Review* 25:467–483.

PARSONS, TALCOTT; BALES, R. F.; and SHILS, E. A. 1953 *Working Papers in the Theory of Action.* Glencoe, Ill.: Free Press.

REDFIELD, ROBERT 1930 *Tepoztlán, a Mexican Village: A Study of Folk Life.* Univ. of Chicago Press.

REDFIELD, ROBERT 1941 *The Folk Culture of Yucatan.* Univ. of Chicago Press.

REDFIELD, ROBERT 1947 The Folk Society. *American Journal of Sociology* 52:293–308.

SJOBERG, GIDEON 1952 Folk and "Feudal" Societies. *American Journal of Sociology* 58:231–239.

SJOBERG, GIDEON 1960 *The Preindustrial City: Past and Present.* Glencoe, Ill.: Free Press.

TAX, SOL 1939 Culture and Civilization in Guatemalan Societies. *Scientific Monthly* 48:463–467.

THEODORSON, GEORGE A. 1953 Acceptance of Industrialization and Its Attendant Consequences for the Social Patterns of Non-Western Societies. *American Sociological Review* 18:477–484.

TÖNNIES, FERDINAND (1887) 1957 *Community and Society (Gemeinschaft und Gesellschaft).* Translated and edited by Charles P. Loomis. East Lansing: Michigan State Univ. Press. → First published in German. A paperback edition was published in 1963 by Harper.

WIRTH, LOUIS 1938 Urbanism as a Way of Life. *American Journal of Sociology* 44:1–24.

COMMUTING

See TRANSPORTATION, *article on* COMMUTATION.

COMPARATIVE LAW

See *under* LAW *and under* LEGAL SYSTEMS; *see also* PUBLIC LAW.

COMPARATIVE METHOD

See ANTHROPOLOGY, *article on* THE COMPARATIVE METHOD IN ANTHROPOLOGY; PSYCHOLOGY, *article on* COMPARATIVE PSYCHOLOGY; SOCIAL INSTITUTIONS, *article on* COMPARATIVE STUDY.

COMPARATIVE POLITICS

See POLITICS, COMPARATIVE.

COMPARATIVE PSYCHOLOGY

See *under* PSYCHOLOGY.

COMPENSATION

See WAGES.

COMPETITION

Competition may be the spice of life, but in economics it has been more nearly the main dish. Competition has been a major force in the organization of production and the determination of prices and incomes: economic theory has accorded commensurate importance to the concept.

Competition enters all major areas of man's life and generally connotes rivalry between two or more men or groups for a given prize. Competition is often an end in itself. Sporting events are clear illustrations: we should be shocked if two teams called off the event or arranged a tie and divided the prize. Indeed, the prize is a minor goal in a true sporting event.

In economic life competition is not a goal: it is a means of organizing economic activity to achieve a goal. The economic role of competition is to discipline the various participants in economic life to provide their goods and services skillfully and cheaply.

Perfect competition

Market competition. When one asks (as Cournot was the first to do in a precise way in 1838) whether the competition of three merchants will serve better than two, or why two (or three) do not combine into a monopoly, the answers prove to be elusive. But one can partially evade such questions by posing a very extreme degree of competition, which the economist calls perfect competition.

A main requirement of perfect competition is that the largest firm in an industry make a trifling fraction of the industry's sales (or purchases) and therefore that there be many firms in the industry. No definite number has been found for the maximum share of one firm that is compatible with competition; presumably the permissible share can be larger the more elastic the industry demand and the easier the conditions of entry by new firms.

These many firms, no one or few of which account for an appreciable share of the industry's output, are assumed to act independently. This can be viewed as a second condition for perfect competition, or as an inevitable corollary of the large numbers in the absence of legal controls over the industry. For it is a fact that there are insuperable difficulties in organizing an effective combination of many persons when it is profitable for each person secretly to depart from the agreement, as is generally the case in economic life.

Such large numbers suggest what is true: that (perfect) economic competition is *impersonal*. In the economic race there are 1,000 or 100,000 runners, and each gets a prize proportional to his efforts. The fortunes of any one firm are independent of what happens to any other firm: one farmer is not benefited if his neighbor's crop is destroyed. The essence of perfect competition, therefore, is not strong rivalry but rather the utter dispersion of power to influence market behavior. The power, for example, to restrict quantities sold and raise prices is effectively annihilated when it is divided among a thousand men, just as a gallon of water is effectively annihilated if it is spread over a thousand acres.

A third condition of perfect competition is complete knowledge of offers to buy and sell by the participants in the market. This condition serves just the opposite purpose of the preceding condition. The assumption that traders act independently serves to keep them apart and, hence, numerous; the assumption that each seller knows what various buyers will pay, and vice versa, is necessary to keep the parties together—in the same market. If seller S and buyer B dealt only with one another in ignorance of all other traders, and similarly for every other pair of buyers and sellers, each transaction would represent an exchange under bilateral monopoly.

These conditions of perfect competition are enough to ensure that a single price will rule in a market (in fact, perfect knowledge is enough for this purpose) and that this price is affected only negligibly by the actions of any one or few buyers or sellers. (It is sometimes additionally assumed that the product of all sellers be homogeneous, but this can also be viewed as part of the definition of the market or industry.) The definition of perfect competition is therefore sometimes expressed in the equivalent form: the demand curve facing each seller is infinitely elastic; and the supply curve facing each buyer is infinitely elastic. (This definition also applies to the individual firm, which accordingly may be competitive even though the market in which it trades is not competitive.)

To these basic conditions of perfect competition —numerous traders on each side of the market, independence of action, and perfect knowledge— it is necessary to add *divisibility* of the commodity or service being traded. If the units are large, it is possible that minor discontinuities will emerge that allow some small market power to individuals. The point is sufficiently minor to be left to references (Edgeworth [1881] 1953, p. 46; Stigler 1957, pp. 8–9).

These conditions of perfect competition pertain to a single market, whether of shoes or bonds or carpenter's services. So far as the presence or absence of monopoly power is concerned, it is not necessary to look at any other market. For this reason these conditions pertain to what may be called *market* competition.

It is traditional, however, to enlarge the conditions of competition, so they will ensure an optimal allocation of resources, by specifying the nature of the movement of resources among markets and industries. This enlarged concept, which may be termed *industrial* competition, is our next subject.

Industrial competition. If a productive resource is to be utilized efficiently, it must be equally productive in all of its uses—clearly if its (marginal) product is less in one use than another, output is not being maximized. Hence, two additional conditions commonly have been made a part of perfect competition: resources are mobile among uses; and their owners are informed as to yields in these various uses.

A vast galaxy of private and public barriers to the mobility of resources has been erected in various times and places: boycotts, certificates of convenience and necessity, patent licenses, settlements laws, franchises, licensing of occupations. Such barriers are all actually or potentially incompatible with competition. But it is not necessary for competition that the movement of resources be free: the retraining of a worker, or the transportation of a tool, may be costly without interfering with competition. We must enlarge our earlier condition of full information to include knowledge of the yields on resources in alternative employments. From another viewpoint, we may say that ignorance is a barrier to profitable movement of resources.

If these conditions are fulfilled, the maximum possible output (measured by value) will be obtained from a productive resource. If this be true for each resource, the output of the economy is at a maximum. This famous theorem (labeled "on maximum satisfaction" by Walras and Marshall) is subject to a qualification, as all interesting propositions are: the *private* marginal product of a productive resource (the amount its owner receives and hence what governs its allocation) must equal the *social* marginal product (private marginal product plus or minus the effects on others). Of course, the maximum value output is dependent upon the distribution of income, which affects the demands for goods and hence their prices.

Time and competition. What we have termed industrial competition—competition including mobility of resources—obviously has an implicit time dimension. It takes time to move resources out of unprofitable fields, especially if the resources are specialized and durable, so that only through disentangling depreciation funds can the resources be withdrawn. It takes time, too, to construct a new factory or shop when one wishes to enter an industry. Comparable statements can be made about the geographical and occupational mobility of labor. Similarly, time is a factor in the completeness of knowledge. It takes time to learn which industries or jobs are most remunerative, or to learn the prices quoted by various sellers, or the quality of service and product; and one's knowledge is more complete and reliable, the more thorough the search for information and the larger the experience on which it is based.

Capital embodied in specialized and durable equipment will not be transferred to other uses in the short run except at extreme price differentials, even though in the long run the slightest differential in returns may be sufficient to move capital funds. Conversely, only under extreme incentives will new establishments be created virtually overnight, as we sometimes observe in wartime.

This fact that it is more expensive to do things very quickly than at a slower pace does not qualify the proposition that resources will tend to be put where they earn the most, but we are reminded of the implicit proviso: allowance must be made for the cost of moving the resources.

The differences in returns to a resource in various uses can be very great in the short run, but will decline in the long run to a minimum level set by the cost of the most efficient method of moving resources. There is implicit in economic literature the belief that these minimum costs of movement of resources are very small relative to their returns, so little imprecision arises from neglecting them entirely. This may be true but has not been demonstrated. The belief, nevertheless, led economists (for example, J. B. Clark) to postulate instantaneous and costless mobility as the pure case of perfect industrial competition. It seems preferable to say that minimum differentials in returns to resources are achieved only in the long run. Market competition is not so intimately related to time. One's information about price bids and offers improves somewhat as one searches the market more thoroughly—itself a time-consuming process—but the changing conditions of supply and demand lead to changes in prices that make the old information obsolete.

The theory of competitive prices

The competitive structure of industry leads to the establishment of competitive prices. Competitive prices are characterized by two main properties. The property of clearing markets is that of distributing existing supplies efficiently; the property of equalizing returns to resources is that of directing production efficiently.

The clearing of markets. A competitive price is one that is not perceptibly influenced by any one buyer or seller. When we say that such prices are fixed by "supply and demand" we mean that the ensemble of all buyers and sellers determines price.

Since every buyer can purchase all he wishes of the good or service at the market price, there are no queues or unsatisfied demands, given the price. Since every seller can sell all he wishes at this market price, there are no undisposable stocks, other than inventories that are voluntarily held for future periods. The competitive price, then, clears the market—it equates the quantities offered by sellers and sought by buyers.

Whenever we find a persistent queue among buyers, we know that the price is being held *below* the level that clears the market, which we naturally call the equilibrium price. For example, when housing is unavailable under rent controls, we know that rents are below the equilibrium level. Whenever we find stocks held by sellers to be in excess of inventory needs, we know price is *above* the equilibrium level. The vast stocks of agricultural products held by the U.S. government are evidence that the prices of these products (more precisely, the amounts the government will lend on the products) are above the equilibrium level.

The importance of prices that clear markets is that they put goods and services in the hands of the people who most urgently wish them. If a price is held too low, some buyers who set a lower value on the commodity will get it while others in the queue who set a higher value get none. If the price is set too high, goods that buyers would be glad to purchase at a lower price go unsold even though (if a minimum price is imposed on a competitive industry) sellers would prefer to sell at this lower price.

The equalization of returns. It is part of the definition of industrial competition that every resource in an industry earn as much as it would earn in other industries, but no more. The self-interest of the owners of productive resources (including, of course, that most important resource, the laborer) leads them to apply their resources where they yield the most and thus to enter unusually attractive fields and abandon unattractive fields.

This equalization of returns, however, can be shown to imply that the prices of goods and services equal their (marginal) costs of production.

The cost of a productive service to an industry is the amount that must be paid to attract it away from other uses—its foregone alternatives. (This most basic concept of cost is the essence of the alternative or opportunity cost theory.) If the amount the productive resource earns in an industry is in excess of this cost, clearly other units of the resource presently outside the industry could earn more if they entered. Conversely, if the productive resource is earning less than its cost or alternative product, it will leave the industry. Hence, if price exceeds cost, resources will flow into the industry and lower the price (and perhaps raise cost by raising the prices of the resources); if price is less than cost, resources will flow out and increase the price (and perhaps reduce cost).

The equality of the *marginal* products of a resource in all its uses is the condition for efficient production. The equality of *average* products has often been substituted, with a regrettable loss of logic: consider the catastrophic waste (of capital) in having equal output per worker in two industries when the capital equipment per worker is ten times as large in one industry as in the other. But if the *marginal product* of a resource is equal in its various uses, it follows that *marginal cost* must equal price. The resources necessary to produce one more unit of product A could produce an equal value of B, so the marginal cost of A—which is the foregone alternative of producing B—is equal to the value of A that it produces. Marginal cost, formally defined as an increment of cost divided by the increment of product associated with the increment of cost, and not the more easily measured average cost (total cost divided by output), is the economist's fundamental criterion of competitive price—and of optimum price.

Marshall's period analysis. The alternative uses open to a resource depend upon the time available for its redeployment (or more fundamentally, how much one is willing to spend on its movement). This principle, joined to an empirical observation that one can alter the rate of operation of a plant much sooner than one can build a new plant or wear out an existing one, provides the basis for the standard (Marshallian) theory of long-run and short-run competitive prices (Marshall 1890).

In the short run, defined as the period within which one cannot appreciably alter the number of plants (physical production units), the only method of varying output is to work a given plant more or less intensively. The so-called variable productive factors (labor, materials, fuel) are the only resources with effective alternative uses in this period and therefore the only services whose returns enter into marginal costs. The returns to the productive factors embodied in the plant are called quasi rents. So long as quasi rents are greater than zero it will be more profitable to operate a plant than to close it down.

The long run is defined as the period within which the entrepreneur can make any desired decision—including the decision to leave one industry and enter another. In this period all resources are variable in quantity, and therefore the returns to all factors enter into marginal cost.

The Marshallian apparatus permits very useful simplifications in price theory, but only if its underlying empirical assumption is fulfilled: the long-run adjustments of the firm are of negligible magnitude in the short run (and hence can be neglected), and the short-run adjustments do not appreciably affect the long-run costs. When these conditions are not met (they fail, for example, if discharge of workers in this period will lead to higher wage rates in the next period), the full analysis of the short run will still require explicit analysis of the long-run repercussions of the short-run decisions.

Alternative concepts

The austerity and abstractness of the concept of perfect competition have led many economists to seek a more "realistic" concept. This search has been reinforced by the need for a concept of competition usable in the enforcement of the U.S. antitrust statutes. A variety of concepts have accordingly been proposed, but because they were deliberately contrived to fit the infinitely varied circumstances of a vast economy they lack the analytical clarity of perfect competition.

Workable competition. The most popular of these variant concepts is that of J. M. Clark, which he labeled *workable competition* (1940). The philosophy of this concept is clear enough: actual industries will seldom have thousands of independent firms, and never will the entrepreneurs have complete knowledge. It is not useful to characterize all of these industries as imperfectly competitive, for some will be near-monopolies and others will have prices, outputs, and rates of progress that deviate in only minor respects from what perfectly competitive industries would experience. In particular, many industries do not depart sufficiently from perfect competition (which is, of course, unattainable) to create any need for antitrust actions or public regulation.

Workable competition has been a very popular concept since its formalization in 1940, but its serious ambiguity has not yet been reduced. How competitive an industry should be (using observable criteria we shall discuss below) to be workably competitive has never been settled. Indeed the criteria (prices, service, product innovation, rates of return) that deserve most weight in any application of the concept have not been agreed upon. Two competent persons who study a particular industry can disagree on its workable competitiveness, and there exists no analytical basis for eliminating the disagreement.

Monopolistic competition. The other leading concept, *monopolistic competition*, was formulated by E. H. Chamberlin (1933) and is directed to a different purpose. Chamberlin emphasized the diversity in the products of firms that are normally considered members of a single industry: they differ in details of quality, in repute, in locational convenience, in the religion of their producer, and a hundred other details that may influence their desirability to various buyers. He emphasized also the substitutability of products made by what are viewed as different industries: one may use aluminum or steel or wood to build a chair, and ostentatiously display one's wealth with jewels, servants, or trips abroad. Each firm, in this view, has some elements of uniqueness (monopoly power) and yet many rivals, and the admixture gives rise to the title of the concept. The theory of monopolistic competition has led to a much more thorough examination of the problems of defining commodities and industries. It has not been found useful in the analysis of concrete economic problems.

Competitive equilibrium. The lack of conscious coordination of the behavior of individuals in a competitive market has led many writers to assert the impossibility of any stable equilibrium. Some have denied that any order is observable: the Continental cartel literature usually uses the word "chaotic" as a prefix to competition, and most proposals for an "orderly" policy assume that a competitive system is disorderly. Others have found cumulative tendencies in competition: for example, W. T. Thornton said that "if a single employer succeed in screwing down wages . . . his fellow-employers may have no alternative but to follow suit" ([1869] 1870, p. 105). Sidney and Beatrice Webb elaborated this view into their famous theory of "higgling in the market" ([1897] 1920, part 3, chapter 2).

Modern economic analysis, on the other hand, makes competitive equilibrium the central part of the theory of prices and allocation of resources. The presence of order and continuity in markets composed of many independently acting buyers and sellers has been established beyond serious question, on both theoretical and empirical grounds.

The main stumbling block in the layman's acceptance of competitive equilibrium is the belief that many individuals acting independently will necessarily either undershoot or overshoot every appropriate change in output, prices, investment, and the like. If, for example, increasing demand calls for a 10 per cent increase in industry capacity, how can this precise total be achieved when a vast number of firms are individually and independently changing their plants in a hundred different proportions? In a sense this is a false question: no one can know that the following year's demand will be exactly 10 per cent larger, and neither a public body nor a private monopolist can guarantee to have the "right" amount of capacity the next year. But let us put this complication aside.

The answer, then, is that there is much information available to guide the decisions of the numerous independent firms. In part this is current information: every trade is abreast of the investment decisions of its various firms, of the developments in products and production methods, and so on. This information comes from salesmen, trade journals, customers and suppliers, and a host of other sources. The firm is guided also by past behavior in the industry: if previous increases of output were supplied in some part by new firms, this becomes a factor in current decisions.

Empirical evidence of competition

A variety of statistical tests of the existence of competition have been proposed at various times, and at least three deserve some attention.

The presence of numerous firms, none dominant in size, is directly observable and is usually described by a low *concentration ratio*. The main difficulty with this structural test of competition is that the maximum concentration compatible with competition has not been determined, so the test is clear only when concentration is low. The problem is complicated by the fact that we have had no theoretical guide in summarizing the frequency distribution of firm sizes, which can, of course, be done in many ways.

Since a single price will rule under perfect competition, *price homogeneity* has often been proposed as a test of competition. We have already remarked that perfect knowledge is enough to ensure a single price, whether the market is competitive or monopolistic. Indeed, in a market of numerous sellers and buyers it is improbable that all prices in a given short interval of time will be uniform. It is improbable for two reinforcing reasons: the transactions will seldom be in completely homogeneous goods (quantity discounts, promptness of payment, and a dozen other characteristics vary almost infinitely among transactions); and the cost of learn-

ing market prices, given numerous traders, is such that complete information is not worth it. As a result, strict uniformity of prices has properly been viewed by the courts as a phenomenon more suggestive of collusion than of competition.

A related evidence of competition is more powerful: the absence of systematic *price discrimination*. If sellers are persistently obtaining higher net receipts (which need not be the same as prices) from some buyers than from others, we may be confident that they are acting in concert—a truly independent firm would concentrate its sales on the buyers who yielded higher net receipts.

A fourth, and perhaps the most traditional, test of the absence of competition is a high rate of *return on investment*. It has lost much popularity because of the difficulty of measuring profitability (in particular, the valuation of durable assets can conceal monopoly profits or create fictitiously high rates of return) and because an absence of high profits is compatible with various cartel arrangements. Yet it is true that unusually high or low rates of return will not persist for long periods in a competitive industry. More specifically, a recent study suggests that in unconcentrated manufacturing industries the rates of return of one year will provide no useful clue to the rates earned, say, five years hence (Stigler 1963, chapter 3).

Public policies

Laws, both statutory and common, have sought to protect competition for centuries. The Statute of Monopolies, which was passed in 1623 to restrain the crown's use of grants of monopoly for revenue, was a famous example, as were the statutes (which Adam Smith compared in rationality to laws against witchcraft) against forestalling, engrossing, and regrating grain.

The Sherman Act of 1890 was pathbreaking, therefore, not in its prohibition of restraints of trade but in the implementation of this policy by an administrative force charged with ferreting out and prosecuting such acts. This most basic of all antimonopoly laws forbade not only conspiracies in restraint of trade but also attempts to monopolize—and in such broad terms as almost to defy conflicts of spirit and letter. Criminal penalties were supplemented by the incentive of triple damages to private parties who were injured by the forbidden acts.

The complaint that the Sherman Act came into force only after competitive markets had been destroyed (which was neither true nor wholly false), the belief that a group of specialists could deal with industrial problems more effectively than the judiciary, and the general impatience of reformers—

all combined to bring about in 1914 the Clayton Act, which prohibited a set of practices that (it was believed) often led to monopoly, and the act creating the Federal Trade Commission to enforce the Clayton Act. With amendments—the most important being the Robinson–Patman Act of 1936 and the Celler–Kefauver Merger Act of 1950—the legislative basis of U.S. policy had been developed. This policy includes certain discordant anticompetitive elements (the Robinson–Patman Act, with its goal of rigid uniformity of prices, and the legalization of resale price maintenance), as general policies have a habit of doing.

That this policy has contributed to the competitiveness of the U.S. economy is difficult to deny or to document. Yet international comparisons—in particular, of the same industry (often composed of the same firms) in Canada and the United States —suggest that the policy has had substantial effects. So, too, does the fact that the favorite practices of the formal cartel—a joint sales agency or division of customers—are quite uncommon in the United States.

The policy of restricting agreements among competitors (but not the policy of seeking to prevent monopolies) has spread to numerous other nations since its introduction in the United States. The most common form is to require registration of agreements among firms in an industry, and the subsequent approval or disapproval of the agreement by a specially constituted body. This is the practice of England, Germany, and several other nations, as well as of the European Common Market.

GEORGE J. STIGLER

[*See also* ANTITRUST LEGISLATION; CARTELS AND TRADE ASSOCIATIONS; INDUSTRIAL CONCENTRATION; MARKETS AND INDUSTRIES; MERGERS; MONOPOLY; OLIGOPOLY.]

BIBLIOGRAPHY

CHAMBERLIN, EDWARD H. (1933) 1956 *The Theory of Monopolistic Competition: A Re-orientation of the Theory of Value.* 7th ed. Harvard Economic Studies, Vol. 38. Cambridge, Mass.: Harvard Univ. Press.

CLARK, JOHN M. 1940 Toward a Concept of Workable Competition. *American Economic Review* 30:241–256.

EDGEWORTH, FRANCIS Y. (1881) 1953 *Mathematical Psychics: An Essay on the Application of Mathematics to the Moral Sciences.* New York: Kelley.

KNIGHT, FRANK H. (1921) 1933 *Risk, Uncertainty and Profit.* London School of Economics and Political Science Series of Reprints of Scarce Tracts in Economic and Political Science, No. 16. London School of Economics; New York: Kelley.

MARSHALL, ALFRED (1890) 1920 *Principles of Economics.* 8th ed. New York: Macmillan.

STIGLER, GEORGE J. 1957 Perfect Competition, Historically Contemplated. *Journal of Political Economy* 65: 1–17.

STIGLER, GEORGE J. 1963 *Capital and Rates of Return in Manufacturing Industries.* A study of the National Bureau of Economic Research. Princeton Univ. Press.

OTHER WORKS CITED

THORNTON, WILLIAM THOMAS (1869) 1870 *On Labour: Its Wrongful Claims and Rightful Dues.* 2d ed., rev. London: Macmillan.

WEBB, SIDNEY; and WEBB, BEATRICE (1897) 1920 *Industrial Democracy.* New ed. 2 vols. in one. London and New York: Longmans.

COMPONENTIAL ANALYSIS

Componential analysis is a method of describing the subject matter of a language. It aims at constructing verifiable models of how specific bodies of cultural (or ideational) content are coherently organized, insofar as such content is represented by words and expressions in a people's language. A method in both semantic and cultural description, componential analysis is perhaps best characterized as a method of ideography.

History. In *Coral Gardens and Their Magic* (1935), Malinowski demonstrated the immediate relevance of descriptive semantics for ethnography. But the application of rigorous method in this area began only after World War II, inspired by the methodology of structural linguistics and developed and utilized by anthropologists trained in this discipline (Goodenough 1957). Indeed, the term "componential analysis" is taken from linguistics, where it is used to refer to the criteria by which distinctive categories of sound in a language are distinguished and, subsequently, to refer to the analysis of semantic distinctions encountered in grammatical paradigms (Harris 1948).

The first ethnographic use of the method illustrated the categorization of kinship relations in Truk (Goodenough 1951). In 1955 Conklin published the conclusions of a similar analysis of Hanunóo color categories. Then Lounsbury (1956) and Goodenough (1956), working independently, simultaneously published extended statements of the method, again utilizing kinship materials. Since then several such kinship studies have been published (*see* Bibliography). Wallace and Atkins (1960) were concerned with how far the results of such analysis reflected the actual cognitive organization of phenomena in the minds of the people being studied. How ideational models constructed by componential analysis actually related to "psychological reality" became a subject of debate (Frake 1962; Burling 1964). A conference to discuss this and other matters relating to componential analysis was held in June 1964 under the sponsorship of the Wenner–Gren Foundation for Anthropological Research (Hammel 1965). Conklin (1962) observed that the method is applicable to the analysis and description of folk taxonomies generally and to a wide range of problems in lexicography and ethnography. Frake began to explore its use in the analysis of such aspects of culture as the classification and diagnosis of diseases (1960) and the organization of religious ideas (1964).

As of 1964, however, the clearest expositions of the method, of the theoretical issues it raises, and of its limitations by comparison with other methods for accomplishing similar descriptive objectives have been presented in connection with the analysis of kinship terminologies (Lounsbury 1964*a*; 1964*b*). Because kinship has been studied more intensively and extensively by anthropologists than any other single aspect of culture, it is one of the few cultural domains for which anthropologists are readily able to meet the data requirements of the method. Minimally adequate notations for recording the data are available, and there is a fairly well-developed metalanguage for talking about the properties of genealogical space. To go beyond kinship is to face the arduous but scientifically important task of developing suitable notations and metalanguages.

Specific aims of the method.   In the terminology of semiotics (Morris 1938), a linguistic expression designates a class of images or concepts, it denotes a specific image or subclass of images within the class on any one occasion of its use, and it signifies the criteria by which specific images or concepts are included or excluded from the class of images or concepts that the expression designates. Thus, what is signified are the definitive attributes of the class. An expression connotes other images or concepts that people associate with the expression's designatum but which are not themselves definitive attributes of the designated class. To say that the sky is cloudy is to designate a class or type of meteorological condition, to denote a specific image of such condition, to signify the definitive attributes of the class, and to connote such things as chill and rain. Componential analysis is concerned solely with the significational aspect of meaning. Thus, it differs sharply from most word-association approaches to semantics, which deal almost entirely with connotations (e.g., the "semantic differential" technique described in Osgood et al. 1957).

In its concern with signification and definitive attributes, componential analysis starts with extensional definitions (listings of denotata) and seeks to reduce them to intensional definitions. For example, an extensional definition of the English kinship term *uncle* would list such denotata after it as mother's brother, father's brother, mother's half-brother, father's half-brother, mother's sister's husband, mother's half-sister's husband, father's sister's husband, and father's half-sister's husband. An intensional definition might be as follows: An uncle is any kinsman by blood or marriage who is simultaneously (*a*) male, (*b*) two degrees of genealogical distance from ego, (*c*) not lineal, (*d*) in a senior generation, and (*e*) not connected by a marital tie in other than the senior generation of the relationship.

As this example shows, an intensional definition is conjunctive, seeking to reduce the disjunctive extensional definition to a unitary class described as a product of the combination of several definitive attributes. That these are definitive attributes in this case is evident from the fact that to vary any one of them results in the judgment that *uncle* is impermissible as a term of reference. *Aunt* becomes the appropriate term if we vary (*a*) sex; *great-uncle* if we vary (*b*); *grandfather* if we vary (*c*); *nephew* if we vary (*d*); and *wife's uncle* or *husband's uncle* if we vary (*e*). This, incidentally, illustrates a way in which the results of componential analysis are capable of verification.

General procedure in the method.   We arrive at definitive attributes by a combination of two operations: inspecting the set of a term's denotata for common attributes and contrasting the set of its denotata with the sets of denotata of other terms. The latter operation is the crucial one. It leads us, among other things, to recognize hierarchies of subject matter or of semantic domains.

To contrast the denotata of English *dog* and *mackerel* is to result in a bundle of discriminating features that also discriminate between *cat* and *pickerel*, *dog* and *pickerel*, and *cat* and *mackerel*. This provides a basis for distinguishing two semantic domains, the one to which *cat* and *dog* belong and the one to which *mackerel* and *pickerel* belong. That *mammal* and *fish* are cover terms designating these two domains shows us one kind of structural relationship between the significata of linguistic forms. The significatum of *dog* contains all the definitive attributes in the significatum of *mammal* plus some additional ones that discriminate its denotata from those of *cat, horse*, etc.

Hierarchical relationships among the significata of words and expressions seem obvious enough to speakers of English in an English example, but they appear to be characteristic of at least large portions of vocabulary in all languages. It is thus possible to sort vocabularies into distinct sets pertaining to different domains of experience. Componential analysis helps us to determine what "goes together" in unfamiliar languages so that we do not arbitrarily sort them on the basis of rough translations or glosses into the domains of English (or other language of description). In the language of Truk, *raaw* ("whale") belongs to the domain designated by the cover term *iik*, along with most things that we would subsume under the cover term *fish* in English. There seems to be no semantic domain in Trukese that corresponds to the domain designated by English *animal*.

Componential analysis has been directed primarily at systematically contrasting the sets of denotata of the several expressions within single domains or subdomains. Analysis has shown that the several expressions within a domain can be sorted into sets so that all the expressions in a set have mutually exclusive denotata at a given hierarchical level and differ from one another with respect to one or several dimensions of discrimination (such as the several dimensions used to discriminate *uncle* from *nephew*, *aunt*, etc., in the example given above). Such a set of expressions constitutes a terminological system. The method of *componential analysis* has been applied almost entirely to delimiting and depicting the ideational structure of terminological systems.

Illustration of the method—Moala kinship terminology. Moala is an island in Fiji whose social organization has been described by Sahlins (1962). His published data, which appear in Table 1, provide the material for analysis here. The definitions

Table 1 — Moala kinship data

KINTERM	EGO	ILLUSTRATIVE KINTYPES[a]
1. *tamaqu*	male or female	Fa, FaBr, Fa ♂ // Co, FaFa ♂ // CoSo, FaMo ♀ // CoSo, Mo ♀ // CoHu, MoMo ♀ // CoDaHu, Hu of any *tinaqu*, Mo ♂ XCo, WiMoBr, WiMo ♂ // Co
2. *tinaqu*	male or female	Mo, MoSi, Mo ♀ // Co, MoMo ♀ // CoDa, MoFa ♂ // CoDa, Fa ♀ XCo, Fa ♂ // CoWi, FaFa ♂ // CoSoWi, Wi of any *tamaqu*, HuFaSi, HuFa ♀ // Co
3. *luvequ*	male	Ch, BrCh, ♀ XCoCh, ♂ // CoCh, Ch of any ♂ Ch of any *tamaqu* or *tinaqu*, Fa ♀ // CoDaCh, Mo ♂ XCoSoCh,[b] WiSiCh, Wi ♀ // CoCh, BrWiSiCh, BrWi ♀ // CoCh
	female	Ch, SiCh, ♀ // CoCh, ♂ XCoCh, Ch of ♀ Ch of *tamaqu* or *tinaqu*, Mo ♀ // CoDaCh, Mo ♂ XCoDaCh, Fa ♀ XCoDaCh, Fa ♂ XCoSoCh, Fa ♀ // CoDaCh,[b] Fa ♀ // CoSoCh, HuBrCh, Hu ♂ // CoCh, SiHu ♂ // CoCh
4. *taciqu*	male	Br, ♂ // Co, Fa ♂ // CoSo, Mo ♀ // CoSo, all So of all *tamaqu* or *tinaqu*, all Fa of *luvequ*
	female	Si, ♀ // Co, Mo ♀ // CoDa, Mo ♂ XCoDa, Fa ♀ XCoDa, Da of *tinaqu* or *tamaqu*, Mo of *luvequ*
5. *wekaqu* or *ganequ*	male	Si, ♀ // Co, Mo ♀ // CoDa, Fa ♂ // CoDa, Fa ♀ XCoDa, all Da of *tamaqu* or *tinaqu*
	female	Br, ♂ // Co, Fa ♂ // CoSo, Fa ♀ XCoSo, Mo ♀ // CoSo, Mo ♂ XCoSo,[b] all So of *tamaqu* or *tinaqu*
6. *vugoqu*	male or female	MoBr, FaSi, Mo ♂ // Co, Fa ♀ // Co, Br of any *tinaqu*, Si of any *tamaqu*, ♂ XCo of any *tamaqu*, ♀ XCo of any *tinaqu*, Ch of any *wekaqu*, SoWi, DaHu, So of any *luvequ*
	male	SiCh, ♀ // CoCh
	female	BrCh, ♂ // CoCh
7. *tavalequ*	male	MoBrSo, FaSiSo, Mo ♂ // CoSo, ♂ // CoSo of any *tinaqu*, Fa ♀ // CoSo, ♀ // CoSo of any *tamaqu*, WiBr, Wi ♂ // Co, any *wekaqu* of Wi, SiHu, SiHuBr, SiHu ♂ // Co, any *taciqu* of SiHu
8. *dauvaqu*	female	MoBrDa, FaSiDa, Mo ♂ // CoDa, ♂ // CoDa of any *tinaqu*, Fa ♀ // CoDa, ♀ // CoDa of any *tamaqu*, HuSi, Hu ♀ // Co, any *wekaqu* of Hu, BrWi, BrWiSi, any *taciqu* of BrWi
9. *davolaqu* or *watiqu*	male	MoBrDa, FaSiDa, Wi, Mo ♂ // CoDa, ♂ // CoDa of any *tinaqu*, Fa ♀ // CoDa, ♀ // CoDa of any *tamaqu*, WiSi, Wi ♀ // Co, any *taciqu* of Wi, BrWi, BrWiSi, BrWi ♀ // Co, any *taciqu* of BrWi
	female	MoBrSo, FaSiSo, Hu, Mo ♂ // CoSo, ♂ // CoSo of any *tinaqu*, Fa ♀ // CoSo, ♀ // CoSo of any *tamaqu*, SiHu, HuBr, SiHuBr, SiHu ♂ // Co, Hu ♂ // Co, any *taciqu* of Hu or SiHu
10. *tukaqu*	male or female	FaFa, MoFa, Fa of any *tamaqu* or *tinaqu*, Fa of any relative of parents' generation
11. *tubuqu*	male or female	MoMo, FaMo, Mo of any *tamaqu* or *tinaqu*, Mo of any relative of parents' generation
12. *makabuqu*	male or female	SoCh, DaCh, BrChCh, SiChCh, Ch of any *luvequ*, Ch of any relative of ego's child's generation

a. Abbreviations used: Fa, father; Mo, mother; Br, brother; Si, sister; So, son; Da, daughter; Hu, husband; Wi, wife; Sp, spouse; Co, cousin; // Co, parallel cousin; XCo, cross cousin; and Ch, child.

b. Correction of error in source.

Source: Adapted from Sahlins 1962.

in Table 1 are extensional, listing after each term a number, but not all, of the conceivable kin relationships or kintypes that can be denoted by it. Any kin relationship, no matter how remote, can be denoted by one of the terms given. Because kinship terms are infinitely extendable to the kinsmen of kinsmen, it is not possible to exhaust the universe of kintypes that may be denoted by any one of them. Analysis must work with a sample of kintypes such as that provided in the data.

It seems evident from direct inspection of the data that 6 of the 12 kinship terms are used reciprocally, in the sense that if A is *taciqu* to B then B is *taciqu* to A. The remaining 6 terms fall into 2 reciprocating sets of 3 terms each: 1 and 2 reciprocate 3; and 10 and 11 reciprocate 12. This observation enables us to expand the data of analysis; e.g., we can assume that SiDaHu (man speaking) is a denotatum of 3 (*luvequ*) because the reciprocal WiMoBr is given as a denotatum of 1 (*tamaqu*).

Direct inspection of the data also allows us to conclude that the sets of denotata of the several terms are differentiated, among other things, according to

1. Degree of generation distance between ego and alter

    1.1 when ego and alter are in the same generation (including categorical terms 4, 5, 7, 8, 9),

    1.2 when ego and alter are one generation distant (including categorical terms 1, 2, 3, 6),

    1.3 when ego and alter are two generations distant (including categorical terms 10, 11, 12).

It is also evident that the difference between the denotata of term 4 and the denotata of term 5 and the difference between the denotata of terms 7 and 8 together and the denotata of term 9 are a matter of

2. Similarity of sex of alter and ego, with

    2.1 ego and alter of same sex (4, 7, 8),

    2.2 ego and alter of different sex (5, 9).

Furthermore, we readily observe that the difference between terms 1 and 2 and the difference between terms 7 and 8 are accounted for by

3. Sex of alter. Thus:

    3.1 alter male (1, 7),

    3.2 alter female (2, 8).

Finally, cursory inspection reveals that the difference between terms 1 and 2 and their reciprocal 3 and the difference between terms 10 and 11 and their reciprocal 12 are a matter of

4. Seniority of the alter's generation. Thus:

    4.1 alter's generation senior (1, 2, 10, 11),

    4.2 alter's generation junior (3, 12).

Leaving aside distinctions involving variables 2, 3, and 4 above, we show the distribution of terms according to variable 1 (degree of generation difference) in Table 2. What remains to be accounted for is the distinction between the reciprocal relationships involving terms 1, 2, and 3 and that involving term 6 and also the distinction between the reciprocal relationships involving terms 4 and 5 and those involving terms 7, 8, and 9.

Table 2 — Moala kinship terms by distance in generations

GENERATIONS DISTANT	KINSHIP TERMS	
Two	10, 11, 12	
One	1, 2, 3	6
Zero	4, 5	7, 8, 9

If Moala society were divided into two intermarrying patrilineal or matrilineal moieties, there would be no problem. All of these relationships would be readily distinguishable according to whether ego and alter were in the same or different moieties. But there are no moieties in Moala, and depending on how ego and alter choose to trace their relationship they may find themselves in a category covered by terms 1–5 or in a category covered by terms 6–9. Casual inspection of the data provided will not give us a clue as to what the discriminating factors are. But if we diagram every one of the denotata given—or that can be inferred by virtue of reciprocation—for terms 1, 2, 3, and 6, as briefly illustrated in tables 3, 4, and 5, patterns inherent in the data are much easier to discern.

In tables 3 and 4, every consanguineally related pair in the same generation in every chain of genealogical connection between ego and alter are (*a*) of the same sex, (*b*) of different sex an even num-

Table 3 — Structure of relationships denoted by 1 (tamaqu) and 3 (luvequ)*

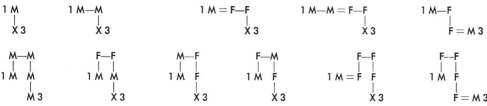

* M, male; F, female; X, person of either sex.

Table 4 — Structure of relationships denoted by 2 (tinaqu) and 3 (luvequ)*

```
  2 F              2 F—F            2 F = M—M         2 F—M            2 F—M
    |                  |                     |             |                |
   X 3              X 3                 X 3          M = F 3          F = M 3


       F—F              M—M              F—F              F—F
       | |              | |              | |              | |                      F—F
       F F              M M              M F              M M                      | |
       | |              | |              | |              | |                      F F
     2 F F            2 F F            2 F M          2 F = M M      2 F—F = M M
       |                |                |                |                |
      X 3              X 3              X 3              X 3              X 3
```

* M, male; F, female; X, person of either sex.

ber of times, or (*c*) of different sex an odd number of times when there is a marital tie in the most junior generation in the relationship. In Table 5 we find the complementary pattern exemplified. Every consanguineally related pair in the same generation in the chain of genealogical connection between ego and alter are (*a*) of different sex an odd number of times or (*b*) of different sex an even number of times (or not at all) when there is a marital tie in the most junior generation in the relationship.

This pattern also appears in the denotata of terms 4, 5, 7, 8, and 9, if we diagram them in a similar way. It is even more clearly evident that sex differences of consanguineal pairs in the same generation in the genealogical chain do not affect the most junior generation in the relationship, whereas the number of intervening marital ties count only if they occur in the most junior generation. Therefore, the discriminant variable may be described as

5. Number of sex differences among the consanguineally related pairs in the same generation in the genealogical chain between ego and alter, excluding the most junior generation in the relationship, and/or the number of marital ties in the genealogical chain that are in the most junior generation. This is represented as

    5.1, when the number of sex differences and/or marital ties is an even one (1, 2, 3, 4, 5),

    5.2, when the number of sex differences and/or marital ties is an odd one (6, 7, 8, 9).

The matrix of variables and kinship terms re-

sulting from this analysis is shown in Table 6. The variables by which the sets of denotata were discriminated have a definite structural relationship to one another. Variable 1 partitions the entire universe of kinship, being applicable to all of the terms, and is the only variable that is so applicable. The other variables subdivide the universe further. Thus the variables relate to one another as in a taxonomic hierarchy, but the terminology lacks cover terms for such implicit entities as "kinsman of my own generation."

Taxonomies and paradigms. The arrangement of variables in Table 6 reflects the hierarchical or implicit taxonomic structure. Since variable 1 (generation distance) ranks highest in the structure, it is in the extreme left-hand column. Variable 5 (odd or even number of sex differences and/or marital ties in the genealogical chain) is the next highest. Variables 2 and 4 are in complementary distribution in the matrix and occupy equivalent positions in the taxonomic structure. Variable 3 ranks lowest of all.

If all the variables applied equally to the discrimination of all terms, the arrangement of variables in columns in a matrix would be entirely optional. The matrix would have the structure of a paradigm instead of a taxonomy.

The kinship systems that have been analyzed so far produce matrices that are partially taxonomic and partially paradigmatic in structure. When several alternative models (involving a choice among several discriminant variables) can be constructed for a terminological system, they are usually alike

Table 5 — Structure of relationships denoted by 6 (vugoqu)*

```
   6 M—F           6 F—M           6 M            6 F            6 M = F—M        6 F = M—M
      |               |              |              |                |                |
     X 6             X 6          X = X 6        X = X 6           X 6            X = X 6


     M—M             F—F             M—M            F—F
     | |             | |             | |            | |
   6 M F           6 F F           6 F M          6 F M        6 M = F—F        6 F = M—F
     |               |               |              |              |                |
    X 6             X 6             X 6            X 6          X = X 6            X 6
```

* M, male; F, female; X, person of either sex.

in this respect. Most of them differ at the middle and lower levels of the taxonomic structure rather than at the higher levels. This has obvious significance for students of cognition, quite apart from the question of whether any particular model is the one from which the participants derive their "feel" of how things work.

Table 6

DISCRIMINANT VARIABLES					KINSHIP
1	*5*	*2*	*4*	*3*	TERMS
1.1	5.1	2.1	.	.	4. *taciqu*
1.1	5.1	2.2	.	.	5. *wekaqu* or *ganequ*
1.1	5.2	2.1	.	3.1	7. *tavalequ*
1.1	5.2	2.1	.	3.2	8. *dauvaqu*
1.1	5.2	2.2	.	.	9. *davolaqu* or *watiqu*
1.2	5.1	.	4.1	3.1	1. *tamaqu*
1.2	5.1	.	4.1	3.2	2. *tinaqu*
1.2	5.1	.	4.2	.	3. *luvequ*
1.2	5.2	.	.	.	6. *vugoqu*
1.3	.	.	4.1	3.1	10. *tukaqu*
1.3	.	.	4.1	3.2	11. *tubuqu*
1.3	.	.	4.2	.	12. *makabuqu*

Some terminological systems in the domain of kinship contain fifty or more terms and a dozen or more discriminant variables. Such systems produce large, complicated componential matrices. The procedural rules for grouping terms in rows and variables in columns in such matrices are an important feature of the method of analysis.

Componential analysis and anthropological theory. The Moala kinship terminology illustrates how componential analysis clarifies traditional problems in social anthropology. Anthropologists have regularly sought to explain kinship terminologies like the Moalan one—and there are a number of generally similar ones—in terms of a dual division of society into exogamous moieties or in terms of preferred or mandatory cross-cousin marriage. Moieties are entirely absent from Moalan society. Nor can cross-cousin marriage explain the terminology, for although one must marry a *davolaqu*, it is explicitly reported that by tracing different routes people can convert a *wekaqu* into a *davolaqu*. And they manage things so that they have many more *davolaqu* than *wekaqu*. Furthermore, marriage with a close *davolaqu*, a real cross-cousin, is prohibited. Neither moieties nor cross-cousin marriage can be said, therefore, to provide the criteria by which people sort one another into different kinds of kin. What maintains the terminological system conceptually is the simple odd–even pattern in variable 5. For it is not necessary to count the actual number of marriages or sex differences in the genealogical chain in distant relationships. If

A and B have a relative in common, they can immediately relate to one another by the rule that an even of my even or an odd of my odd is my even, while an even of my odd or an odd of my even is my odd. Aside from this, ego's and alter's sex and generation are the only things to take note of. This is but one example of how componential analysis calls into question some of the explanations of kinship terminology that have had wide currency among anthropologists (for another example, see Lounsbury 1964*b*).

Of perhaps greater theoretical interest is the attention componential analysis directs to the relationship between the ethnographer and what it is he seeks to describe. As advances are made in the rigor with which ethnographic data are analyzed and the coherency with which they are presented— a goal toward which componential analysis will have been, in retrospect, but one early step—cultural theory will of necessity be considerably transformed.

WARD H. GOODENOUGH

[*Directly related are the entries* COGNITIVE THEORY; KINSHIP; LINGUISTICS.]

BIBLIOGRAPHY

BURLING, ROBBINS 1964 Cognition and Componential Analysis. *American Anthropologist* New Series 66: 20–28.

CONANT, FRANCIS P. 1961 Jarawa Kin Systems of Reference and Address: A Componential Comparison. *Anthropological Linguistics* 3, no. 2:19–33.

CONKLIN, HAROLD C. 1955 Hanunóo Color Categories. *Southwestern Journal of Anthropology* 11:339–344.

CONKLIN, HAROLD C. 1962 Lexicographical Treatment of Folk Taxonomies. Pages 119–141 in Conference on Lexicography, Indiana University, 1960, *Problems in Lexicography: Report.* Bloomington: Indiana Univ., Research Center in Anthropology, Folklore, and Linguistics.

CONKLIN, HAROLD C. 1964 Ethnogenealogical Method. Pages 25–55 in Ward H. Goodenough (editor), *Explorations in Cultural Anthropology.* New York: McGraw-Hill.

FRAKE, CHARLES O. 1961 The Diagnosis of Disease Among the Subanun of Mindanao. *American Anthropologist* New Series 63:111–132.

FRAKE, CHARLES O. 1962 The Ethnographic Study of Cognitive Systems. Pages 72–85 in Anthropological Society of Washington, Washington, D.C., *Anthropology and Human Behavior.* Washington: The Society.

FRAKE, CHARLES O. 1964 A Structural Account of Subanun "Religious Behavior." Pages 111–129 in Ward H. Goodenough (editor), *Explorations in Cultural Anthropology.* New York: McGraw-Hill.

GOODENOUGH, WARD H. 1951 *Property, Kin, and Community on Truk.* Yale University Publications in Anthropology, No. 46. New Haven: Yale Univ. Press.

GOODENOUGH, WARD H. 1956 Componential Analysis and the Study of Meaning. *Language* 32:195–216.

GOODENOUGH, WARD H. 1957 Cultural Anthropology and

Linguistics. Pages 167–173 in Georgetown University, Washington, D.C., Institute of Languages and Linguistics, *Report of the Annual Round Table Meeting on Linguistics and Language Studies, Seventh.* Washington: Georgetown Univ. Press.

GOODENOUGH, WARD H. 1964 Componential Analysis of Könkämä Lapp Kinship Terminology. Pages 221–238 in Ward H. Goodenough (editor), *Explorations in Cultural Anthropology.* New York: McGraw-Hill.

HAMMEL, EUGENE A. 1965 Formal Semantic Analysis. *American Anthropologist* New Series 67, no. 5, part 2.

HARRIS, SELIG S. 1948 Componential Analysis of a Hebrew Paradigm. *Language* 24:87–91.

LOUNSBURY, FLOYD G. 1956 A Semantic Analysis of the Pawnee Kinship Usage. *Language* 32:158–194.

LOUNSBURY, FLOYD G. 1964a A Formal Account of the Crow- and Omaha-type Kinship Terminologies. Pages 351–393 in Ward H. Goodenough (editor), *Explorations in Cultural Anthropology.* New York: McGraw-Hill.

LOUNSBURY, FLOYD G. 1964b The Structural Analysis of Kinship Semantics. Pages 1073–1093 in International Congress of Linguistics, Ninth, Cambridge, Mass., 1962, *Proceedings.* The Hague: Mouton.

MALINOWSKI, BRONISLAW 1935 *Coral Gardens and Their Magic.* 2 vols. London: Allen & Unwin.

MORRIS, CHARLES W. (1938) 1955 Foundations of the Theory of Signs. Volume 1, pages 77–137 in *International Encyclopedia of Unified Science.* Univ. of Chicago Press.

OSGOOD, CHARLES E.; SUCI, G. J.; and TANNENBAUM, P. H. 1957 *The Measurement of Meaning.* Urbana: Univ. of Illinois Press.

POSPISIL, LEOPOLD 1964 Law and Societal Structure Among the Nunamiut Eskimo. Pages 395–431 in Ward H. Goodenough (editor), *Explorations in Cultural Anthropology.* New York: McGraw-Hill.

SAHLINS, MARSHALL D. 1962 *Moala: Culture and Nature on a Fijian Island.* Ann Arbor: Univ. of Michigan Press.

WALLACE, ANTHONY F. C.; and ATKINS, JOHN 1960 The Meaning of Kinship Terms. *American Anthropologist* New Series 62:58–80.

COMPULSIONS

See OBSESSIVE–COMPULSIVE DISORDERS.

COMPUTATION

In recent years there has occurred enormous technological development and widespread application of automatic information-handling techniques. These are relevant to three broad classes of tasks with which the scientist frequently finds himself faced: (*a*) *data processing*, the sorting and summarization of large files of information, usually representing the results of empirical observation; (*b*) *mathematical computation*, the derivation of numerical values associated with mathematically defined constructs (for example, matrix and differential equation systems); and (*c*) *simulation*, the generation of data supposed to represent the "behavior" of some temporal process (for example, a physical or economic system). Of course, a given task may have more than one of these components; the widely used technique of regression analysis, for example, may be thought of as consisting of a data-processing phase, for the selection and reduction of input data, followed by a computational phase, for the calculation of regression coefficients and related quantities.

Historically, various special-purpose mechanical aids have been used to facilitate operations in one or another of the areas cited. Most recently, the general-purpose automatic digital computer has been developed as an effective and flexible tool for handling all three types of application. Accordingly, after a brief survey of older methods, the main body of the present discussion will be concerned with this device.

Older methods

Methods for data processing are strongly conditioned by the characteristics of the medium in which the data are recorded. A file in which each data entry is recorded on a physically separate carrier, such as a card, has obvious manipulatory advantages. Thus traditional techniques for data processing have centered around the concept of a *unit record.* Various schemes for aiding the manual manipulation of files of cards have been devised; a useful one depends on notching the edges of cards in coded patterns to permit mechanization of selection and sorting. The most significant line of development here, however, has been that of the punched card system, in which special-purpose machines are used to perform sorting, collating, reproducing, and tabulating operations on decks of cards carrying information entirely in the form of coded patterns of punched holes. Such systems, the basic principles of which were developed by Herman Hollerith in the closing years of the last century, are in widespread use today. Their efficient use depends on the fact that file manipulation procedures can often be specified as a sequence of elementary operations repetitively performed. Processing of any complexity, however, may require many runs of the data cards through the same or different machines, and this is a factor that limits the magnitude of the tasks that can be attempted by the use of these techniques.

Mathematical computation can be mechanized in two basic ways, *digital* and *analog*. In digital computation numbers are represented and manipulated as symbolic entities; the abacus, in which the configuration of beads on a rod is taken as a coded representation of a decimal digit, is an elementary example of a computational aid based on the digital principle. In analog computation, by contrast, numbers are represented by the measure of physical aspects of some system; thus the slide rule, on which numerical magnitudes are marked off as lengths on a series of scales, is a basic example of a device for computing by the analog method.

The desk calculator is a special-purpose digital device that serves to mechanize the most onerous part of pencil-and-paper computing; since it performs only the fundamental arithmetic operations on numbers manually entered into its keyboard, however, elaborate computations still require a great deal of routine human labor. This sort of process can be mechanized one step further by incorporating elementary arithmetic capability into punched card equipment, but the inability of such machines to do more than a repetitive sequence of quite simple operations on a given run is still a limitation.

Manual analog methods include graphic techniques, such as the plotting of lines representing equations in order to determine their solution as an intersection point, and the use of nomograms, which may depend on predrawn forms suited to particular problems. In addition, a number of mechanical devices more advanced than the slide rule have been developed, such as the mechanical integrator. The evolutionary end product of this development is the modern analog computer, in which numerical magnitudes are represented as electrical voltages and circuit units interconnected by means of plug wires correspond to mathematical systems with various parameters. Analog techniques are subject to fundamental limitations regarding accuracy, since they depend on the precision with which physical quantities can be measured, and are restricted as to the types of problems that can be handled, since they must be capable of being formulated in physical terms.

Analog techniques also can be applied successfully in the area of simulation; in fact, here the distinction between mathematical computation and simulation becomes blurred. For, if an analog computer is set up to "solve" the differential equation that governs the behavior of a physical system through time, it can be thought of in a very real sense as a simulator of that system. This has led to the exploitation of such techniques in experimental work, where there is to be interaction, say, between an actual physical system and a simulated one.

Simulation by analog techniques is often useful but is limited; by contrast, any system with a mathematical description can be simulated by digital techniques. In fact, however, before the advent of the general-purpose computer, digital simulation of systems of any complexity was so inefficient as to be of little practical utility.

Further reading on the material of this section may be found in Brooks and Iverson (1963, pp. 52–144), Calingaert (1965, pp. 87–126), and Borko (1962, pp. 22–57).

General-purpose digital computer

The modern automatic digital computer, at the center of a system incorporating appropriate input, output, and auxiliary information storage devices, can be applied to data processing, mathematical computation, and simulation tasks in an integrated and flexible manner. This versatility is partly due to the physical speed and capacity made possible by contemporary technology, and partly due to a feature of the computer that was largely missing in earlier mechanisms—the internally stored program. Once a program or schedule of operations has been prepared, it can be introduced into the computer and used to control a long complicated sequence of steps, which are thus executed automatically at an extremely rapid rate without human intervention. The possibility of preparing programs of a general nature, which can then be tailored to particular cases by the specification of parameter values, and the fact that programs, once prepared, may be run by different users on different computers make the digital computer a tool of such power as to permit consideration of projects that would not formerly have been contemplated at all; this in turn often leads to the development of more advanced models and hence acts to influence the substance of the discipline to which the computer is applied. Thus, for example, the availability of programs incorporating provision for preliminary data editing, extensive computation of residuals, and graphic display of results has markedly influenced the manner in which statistical problems may be attacked.

This potential, however, is limited by the capacity of people to plan and implement effective programs; furthermore, the nature of computer operation is such as to make it most desirable for the user to have some comprehension of its inner workings rather than to depend completely on a professional programmer to interpret his needs. The following sections therefore contain a compact introduction to the subject, which, it is hoped, will at least enable the reader to become aware of some of the more obvious pitfalls that the computer user must anticipate.

Computer structure. In order to avoid too narrow a conception of function, it is appropriate to think of the general task for which an automatic digital computer is designed to be "symbol processing," rather than "computation" in the strictest (numerical) sense. The organization and operation of a computer may be basically described in terms of five functional units, as depicted schematically in the block diagram of Figure 1.

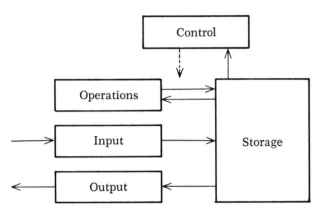

Figure 1 — Computer block diagram

The *storage* unit (usually picturesquely termed the "memory") acts as a repository for symbolic information and also as an intermediary for all interaction among other units. Internal processing of information is implemented by the transmission of symbolic operands from storage to the *operations* unit, where they are subjected to arithmetic or other transformations, the results of which are then transmitted back to storage. In order to set this process up initially an *input* unit is provided to introduce information from the external world into the storage unit, and in order that final results may be provided for the user there must also be an *output* unit for the opposite function.

Thus far, the functions described are roughly analogous to those performed by a man doing a hand calculation: he maintains a worksheet (storage) from which he derives numbers to be entered into the keyboard of his desk calculator (operations) and on which he copies the results; before the calculation proper starts some initial values may have to be entered (input), and when it is finished a separate sheet containing only the relevant results is prepared (output). The word "automatic" applied to a computer, however, implies mechanization not only of these physical processes but of the directing function supplied by the man, who causes a sequence of actions to be performed on the basis (presumably) of a predetermined schedule. In the computer the actuating function is performed by the *control* unit, and what dis-

tinguishes the computer from earlier devices is that the sequence of actions called for by this control can be in accordance with a pattern of arbitrary complexity, as specified by a symbolic *program* recorded in storage. Before processing can begin, therefore, a program must be introduced (via the input unit) into storage; the fact that the computer can be switched from one task to another by merely introducing a different program is what gives it its "general purpose" designation. Note also that the program, because it consists of symbolic information recorded in storage, can be altered by internal operations; this gives rise to powerful and flexible procedural techniques in which programs systematically modify themselves in order to achieve maximum processing efficiency.

Technological considerations dictate the use of bistable, or two-state, devices as the basic components of digital systems; this leads to the conception of all symbolic information ultimately coded in terms of just two symbols, the *bits* 0, 1. Particular patterns of several bits may then be interpreted as coded *characters* (letters, digits, etc.), which play the role of the elementary units of symbol processing. This notion is familiar from consideration of punched card or teletype tape codes, in which specified patterns of no-punch, punch represent characters drawn from a given set. In a computer, as in these contexts, the basic character set may include in addition to numeric digits the letters of the alphabet and selected special symbols such as mathematical signs and punctuation marks.

The unit of transmission of information within the computer may be the character, but on the more powerful computers efficiency dictates that characters be transmitted and operated upon in larger aggregates called for convenience *words*. Data-processing applications generally involve much manipulation of *alphanumeric* words, considered simply as arbitrary strings of characters; arithmetic operations, however, are meaningful only when applied to *numeric* words, which represent numbers in a more or less conventional manner. Finally, words formed according to a particular format are interpretable by the control unit as *instruction* words, and it is in terms of these that programs are specified for automatic execution.

Such special interpretations of computer words are applied only by the operations and control units; as far as storage goes, there is no distinction. Storage is organized into a series of subunits called *locations*, each of which is designated uniquely by an integer label, its *address*. The capacity of each addressed location is generally the same, being a character or a word of some standard length. Computer instructions are then typically designed to specify an operation to be performed and one or more storage addresses giving the locations at which operands are to be found or results stored.

Computers with storage capacities of the order of hundreds of thousands of characters and which carry out internal operations at the rate of hundreds of thousands a second have become available in the last few years, and in the more advanced systems both capacity and rate may effectively be in the millions. Although basic input/output operations (card or paper tape reading/punching, or printing) are generally much slower, delays can be reduced to a considerable extent by designing these units so that their operation can proceed concurrently with the main internal sequencing. Finally, the capabilities of the computer can be considerably enhanced by imbedding it in a system containing additional bulk storage (perhaps millions of characters stored in magnetic form on drums or disks) and intermediate input/output devices (magnetic tape units, for example), all communicating via the internal storage unit.

Further discussion may be found in Gregory and Van Horn ([1960] 1963, pp. 58–125), Green (1963, pp. 12–29), and Borko (1962, pp. 60–91).

Computer procedures. The popular conception of computer function seems to be that reflected in statements such as "Now they have a computer that can check everybody's tax return" or "Now they've come up with a computer that can simulate world politics." Although the area of intended application in the broad sense may influence design, as the previous discussion suggests, computers are not built to do specific tasks but are programmed to do them. This is important to the user because it shows the need for focusing attention not on computer availability but on program availability. And although the uninitiated but reasonably knowledgeable scientist may be aware of this fact, he often fails to anticipate the extent to which unqualified descriptions such as "regression analysis" fail to characterize a task definitively; details of matters such as input/output formats and computational methods are what determine whether or not a program is appropriate to the needs of a given user, and here information may be poorly communicated or not provided at all. Even worse, it may be erroneously communicated, partly due to lack of insight on the part of the program designer and partly because the tools for precise communication in the area of symbolic processing are as yet only imperfectly developed.

For these reasons it is desirable that the user have at least a rudimentary notion of the nature of computer instructions and programming techniques. This section and the one following outline briefly some of the concepts involved.

The first problem to be faced when planning to use a computer is that of precise specification of the task to be carried out, in a form sufficiently perspicuous so that the procedure can be communicated in human terms. Some form of *flow chart* can generally fulfill this function on several levels, from over-all to detailed. The basic idea here will be illustrated by an example.

Imagine that it is required to design an automatic procedure for computing the sample mean and standard deviation,

$$\bar{x} = \frac{1}{n} \sum_{i=1}^{n} x_i, \qquad s = \sqrt{\frac{1}{n-1} \sum_{i=1}^{n} (x_i - \bar{x})^2},$$

for several sets of x_i, not all of which necessarily contain the same number n of items (in all cases it must be that $n \geq 2$, however). If these are to be processed in a single input file (perhaps a deck of punched cards) some means must be provided for distinguishing the data sets from each other, and one practical way to do this is to suppose each file entry (card) contains two values x, m, the first of which is normally data (an x_i value) and the second of which is a "tag" to distinguish legitimate data items ($m = 0$) from "dummy" items used to signal the end of a data set ($m = 1$) or the end of the entire file ($m = 2$).

A complete flow chart for this task is given in Figure 2; it covers the repetitive reading of data sets and the computation and recording (for example, printing) of n, $\bar{x}$, and s for each. The flow chart is a formal specification of a procedure that is described as follows:

Initially, set the sum r and the index i to 0, in anticipation of a data run. Then read a pair of values x, m and test (in two steps) whether m is 0 or 1. If $m = 0$ add x to the sum r, and also increment the value i and enter x as x_i in a data list; then return to read the next entry. If $m = 1$ the data set is complete, and the current value of i is then n for the set and $\bar{x}$ is determined as r/n. Now compute a second sum p by adding values $(x_i - \bar{x})^2$ for $i = 1, 2, \cdots, n$; following this compute s as the square root of $q = p/(n-1)$ and record the values n, $\bar{x}$, s. Repeat this entire process until the test gives $m \neq 0$ and $m \neq 1$ (so presumably $m = 2$); this indicates that there are no more input files and the procedure is finished.

The stylized formalism of the flow chart employs mathematical notation of the conventional sort but also makes use of special symbols signifying procedural action. These are "←", meaning "set" (to a value); ":", meaning "compare" (for branching); and "___", meaning "execute" (a standard subprocedure). Thus "$r \leftarrow r + x$" means "set r to its former value plus x"; "$i:n$" means "compare i and n" (which causes the procedure to repeat as indicated if $i < n$ and go ahead if $i \geq n$); and "$\underline{\text{SQRT}}(s;q)$" means "execute a subprocedure $\underline{\text{SQRT}}(s;q)$" (which is designed to have the effect $s \leftarrow \sqrt{q}$).

The flow chart shows the structure of the computation in terms of procedural loops and re-entry

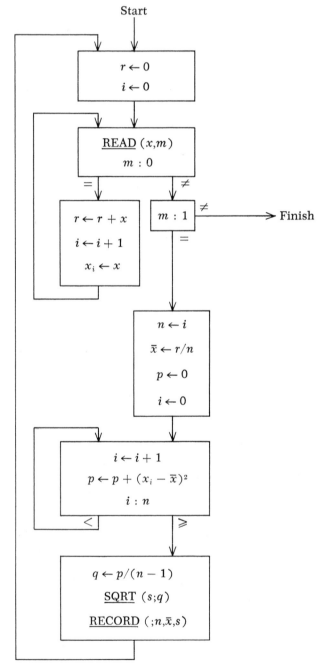

Figure 2 — Flow chart for mean and standard deviation calculations

points, without concern for details of printing formats, etc., which of course must be supplied if the procedure is to be actually carried out by computer. It is important to realize that these flow chart conventions are independent of the characteristics (and the idiosyncrasies) of any particular computer but that they do reflect general aspects of computer operation; thus both the notion that indices such as i can be manipulated independently in dealing with sets of values x_i and that parametrized subroutines such as $\text{SQRT}(\ ;\ )$ can be called upon and executed by a main program correspond to important features of actual computer operation.

The flow chart symbolism given here, for which detailed rules can be stated, is suitable primarily for expressing procedures of mathematical computation. The same basic idea, however, can be used to specify data-processing procedures; the main additional concept needed is a more versatile way of representing external files of given format and organization. Also, simulation and other internal processing applications that may involve nonnumeric elements can be handled by an extension of the flow charting technique.

Although no standardization of flow chart convention exists, and the choice depends to a certain extent on the application at hand, it nevertheless seems reasonable to ask that a flow chart represent an actual computer program accurately enough so that the filling in of details is routine and is unlikely to lead to serious discrepancies between what the user thought was to be done and what the programmer in fact specified was to be done.

For additional discussion of flow charting see Calingaert (1965, pp. 19–23).

Computer programs. To get some insight into the way in which a flow chart specification translates into a computer program, assume a computer with 1,000 storage locations $000, 001, \cdots, 999$, each of which holds a 12-character word interpretable as an alphanumeric datum, a number, or an instruction in the format "$\omega\alpha\beta\gamma$", where ω is a 3-character alphabetic operation code and each of α, β, γ is a 3-digit storage address.

Then the instruction

$$\text{ADD} \quad 500 \quad 501 \quad 500$$

might then have the significance "Add the contents of storage locations 500 and 501, and record the result in storage location 500." This would be appropriate only in case the 12-character words initially contained in storage locations 500 and 501 were in numeric format (say, 11 decimal digits preceded by algebraic sign), so that the addition operation has meaning. The execution of this instruction by the control unit results in the destruction of the original number in storage location 500, since it is replaced by the sum; the number in storage location 501, however, is not altered by the operation.

In order to be executed by the control unit, the ADD instruction itself must exist some place in storage, say at location 099; thus one must distinguish between the locations (here 500, 501) to which the instruction explicitly *refers* and the location (here 099) at which the instruction *resides*. Concern with the location of the instruction itself is necessary because of the sequential nature of computer operation; somehow there must be specified the order in which instructions are obtained and executed by the control unit, and the most straightforward way to do this is to design the computer so that instructions are executed in sequential order by resident address unless there is an explicit indication (in an instruction) to the contrary. To see the manner in which such an indication is typically set forth, consider a second hypothetical instruction

COM   500   550   099

which is to be given the interpretation "Compare the numbers in storage locations 500 and 550, and if the former is less than the latter, take the next instruction from storage location 099." This effects a "conditional jump" in the instruction sequence; if the stated condition is met, the next instruction executed is that residing in location 099, but otherwise it is the instruction whose address follows in sequence. If the COM instruction itself resides in location 100, then the pair of instructions introduced form a "program loop" schematized as follows:

(099)   ADD   500   501   500
(100)   COM   500   550   099.

The effect of this piece of program is to add the contents of 501 repeatedly to the contents of 500, which therefore acts as an "accumulator" for the sum; this addition process is continued (by virtue of the "jump back" to 099) until the accumulated sum exceeds the number residing in location 550, at which time the program proceeds in the normal sequence with the instruction following that numbered 100.

If one imagines that locations 500, 501, and 550 contain values, i, 1, and n, respectively, then the two-word loop is a computer implementation of the flow chart component shown in Figure 3 (which happens to perform a rather meaningless function

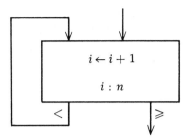

Figure 3 — Loop pattern

in itself but with appropriate instructions inserted between the ADD and COM becomes one of the loops of Figure 2). This would serve to suggest the manner in which flow charts may be translated into computer programs. Two important techniques in this connection, *indexing* of a set of values with a computed value (so as to be able to reference a general element x_i) and *linking* of subprocedures into a program (so as to be able to execute a subroutine such as SQRT and jump back to the main program at the proper point when finished) may be accomplished in a computer by programmed modification of instruction addresses.

Although the example illustrates some facets of computer control that are typical, the details of coding, format, etc. vary widely in practice. For example, it is common to have several different coding systems employed in the same computer for various purposes, perhaps a character code used for general alphanumeric information, a different code for number representation (often based on the binary radix 2 instead of the decimal radix 10), and a special format, not interpretable in either alphanumeric or pure numeric terms, for instructions. Also, the basic "three address" pattern of instructions given here is not typical; usually instructions are "one address" and require explicit recognition of registers for retaining intermediate results in the operations and other units. Thus on most computers the addition operation of the example requires three instructions: one that clears an accumulator register in the operations unit and records the contents of location 500 in it, one that adds the contents of 501 to this and retains the sum in the accumulator register, and one that records the contents of the accumulator in location 500. One or more special index registers are also customarily provided to facilitate indexing and linking operations.

Besides instructions for internal operations such as those described, the computer must have instructions for controlling the operation of input/output and other auxiliary devices with which it communicates; these would of course be used in procedures such as the READ and RECORD subroutines of the earlier example. The repertoire of a large computer may number instructions in the hundreds, many of these representing minor variants of each other to permit processing efficiency.

Two characteristic features of computer programs may be perceived from the discussion: a procedure is formulated for execution in terms of minutely small steps, and the symbolic representation of these steps is not conducive to quick apprehension of their effect in the aggregate. Not only does the preparation of a program for a given task require a great amount of routine labor, but the bookkeeping necessitated by the numerical addressing scheme tends to produce errors. Since computers are generally capable of performing routine tasks more reliably than humans, the question naturally arises of whether some of the burden of program preparation cannot be passed along to the very devices intended to execute the programs. This leads to the concept of program-preparation programs, which translate programs written in some language more or less "procedure-oriented" into direct computer code.

A basic example is the *assembly program*, which permits the programmer to write instructions in a form such as

$$\text{GO:} \quad \text{ADD, I, ONE, I}$$
$$\text{COM, I, N, GO.}$$

These instructions may be thought of as assembly language versions of those given earlier. GO is a label corresponding to the instruction address 099, and I, ONE, and N are labels corresponding to the data addresses 500, 501, and 550, respectively. The programmer writes in terms of such mnemonic labels, and the assembly program translates these symbolic instructions (made up of letters, commas, spaces, etc.) into corresponding direct computer instructions in appropriate format; generally, the programmer does not specify at all the actual numerical addresses that will be assigned to the various labels by the assembly program. There are also other features incorporated into assembly programs to simplify the specification of numeric constants, etc.

Assembly language makes a program more perspicuous but does not compress its level of detail. Higher order program-preparation programs exist for this purpose; for example, an *algebraic translator*, which permits specification of the computer action already discussed in a form such as

$$\text{GO:} \quad \text{I} = \text{I} + 1$$
$$\text{IF I} > \text{N, GO.}$$

This describes the procedure in terms much closer to a flow chart specification and also in general achieves an over-all symbolic compression. The program to translate such a language into computer code is correspondingly more complicated, however, and the resulting computer version may be considerably more inefficient than a program prepared directly in assembly language. There is an added disadvantage, which can only be appreciated through experience: the programmer is a level removed from the actual computer process, and this raises problems in the area of precise specification of computer procedures.

Further discussion of computer programming is given in Borko (1962, pp. 92–133), Green (1963, pp. 30–64, 75–99), and McCracken and Dorn (1964, pp. 1–42).

Program systems. From the previous section it may be seen that the user does not in general deal with the computer directly but through the mediation of some program system that provides for translation from procedure-oriented language into actual computer code. On the larger computers, where efficiency is at a premium, this function is expanded to include the batching of programs for sequential execution with a minimum of human intervention and the keeping of the computing log and accounting records. Such a system makes for highly efficient computer utilization but removes the user one level more from direct access to the computer; "debugging" under such circumstances, for example, requires a succession of runs, with the user progressively detecting and correcting the errors in his program.

This implies that in addition to a programming language the user must learn (or have access to someone who knows) the operating techniques associated with the particular computer installation with which he deals. The knowledge of what translators and diagnostic programs are available, and of details concerning the formats in which control information must be submitted with programs in order that they be usable, assumes a perhaps disproportionate but nevertheless critical importance. Although details vary widely from installation to installation, the type of support one may look for is indicated by the following categorization of "system routines":

loader—an elementary "job initiation" program that controls the reading of a program to be executed, perhaps supplying address modification based on the locations the program is to occupy in storage, etc.

assembler—a program that translates a program in assembly language (which may consist of several sections, each programmed using symbolic addresses and mnemonic operation codes) into a single coherent computer code (in a form that can be processed by a loader).

translator—(often called a "compiler") a program that translates a program in some algebraic or other problem-oriented language into some more elementary (perhaps assembly language) form.

monitor—a program that synchronizes translating, assembling, and loading functions and, further, has a certain batching, scheduling, and accounting capability permitting a whole set of jobs to be run with minimal human intervention.

multiprocessor—a supermonitor based on an ability to carry out several functions concurrently (for example, those of a central processor and several input/output devices) and dynamically schedule these for maximal efficiency.

The order of listing here corresponds to both historical evolution and increasing level of complexity; monitor and multiprocessing facilities, in particular, are appropriate only to the more powerful computer installations. At the time of this writing there is evolving an even more advanced program system concept, growing out of the idea of multiprocessing: an executive system that integrates one or more central processors, several auxiliary input/output processors, and a large number of remote user-operated consoles in a way so as to make efficient use of the centralized facilities but at the same time permit each user to interact directly, in an "on-line" fashion, with the computer complex. In order to achieve this, the system must be able to run programs piecemeal and respond, in what is to a human a short time, to a multiplicity of external demands. The requirements of this sort of "time-sharing" operation have led to radical new concepts in both the computer-design and programming areas.

Translators are generally identified by the problem-oriented language that they accept as input, such as Fortran, Algol (two general algebraic languages), Cobol (a standard file-processing language), Simscript (a simulation language), etc. A similar function is accomplished less efficiently but often more straightforwardly by an *interpreter* program, which both translates and executes simultaneously, thereby carrying out the whole computing task in one rather than several phases.

These system programs, along with various diagnostic programs for analyzing both computer operation and program operation, may be categorized as *service routines*; they serve the user by facilitating the execution of the particular procedure whose results he desires. This function may be contrasted with that of *standard routines* and *standard subroutines*, generally available on a "library" basis, which actually carry out all or a part of the desired task. One may anticipate the availability of subroutines for at least some of the following:

radix conversion—if the computer uses a number base other than 10, which is often the case. (This function will usually be incorporated at the assembly level.)

special arithmetic—"floating-point" (flexible scale) and "double-precision" (extended length) numeric manipulation if not directly available on the computer instruction level; also complex arithmetic, etc.

function evaluation—calculation of square root, exponential and logarithm, sine and cosine, etc. for arbitrary arguments. (A call for standard functions may be incorporated into translator specifications.)

polynomial and matrix operations—addition, multiplication by scalar, multiplication; evaluation, calculation of zeros (for polynomials); transposition, inversion, diagonalization (for matrices).

input/output editing—formating and sequencing card and paper tape reading and punching, magnetic tape, drum and disk file operations, printing and other forms of graphic display. (This function will sometimes be incorporated at the monitor level.)

By definition, a subroutine is supposed to serve as part of a larger program; its usefulness therefore depends not only on its conception with regard to generality and comprehensiveness but on its being accompanied by an appropriate set of specifications characterizing its action and the directions for "connecting" it into the program that uses it. Standard routines, by contrast, are programs for tasks that can be regarded as independent in their own right; the appropriate form of these depends very much on the applications environment. Programs for regression, factor analysis, linear programming calculations, and solution of differential equations are generally in this category, as well as those for standard file-processing operations such as sorting and input/output media conversion (card-to-tape, tape-to-card, etc.).

The importance to successful computer usage of a good available set of service routines, standard routines, and subroutines cannot be underestimated, and it is this that leads to "software" costs equaling or exceeding "hardware" costs for an installation, a fact often unanticipated by the administration that set up the budget. Some alleviation of the difficulty is provided by the existence of various "user organizations," generally associated with a particular class or type of computer, which maintain a pool of programs available to their members. These are only guaranteed up to minimum standards of documentation, however, and the problem of making effective use of work already done by others remains one of the most formidable and often exasperating problems facing the user who wishes to reap the benefits afforded by computers without investing the time to understand fully the device that he is entrusting with a major role in his research or operations.

The topics in this section are further developed in Borko (1962, pp. 140–170), Green (1963, pp. 65–74), and Gregory and Van Horn ([1960] 1963, pp. 439–478).

Error analysis

Although computer applications in general are subject to the problem that imperfect understanding of procedures by the user may lead to unsatisfactory results, computation related to familiar mathematical concepts is especially dangerous in this regard. This is because the user often starts out with some preconceptions based on his mathematical understanding and is thus likely to neglect or misjudge the effect of computational error, which may be considerable. It is customary to measure error in either absolute or relative units, depending on circumstances; thus if x is a computed value and it is assumed that it represents some "true" value x^T, then $\delta = x - x^T$, or possibly its magnitude $|\delta|$, is defined as the *absolute error* in x, and δ/x^T (which is approximated by δ/x) is defined as the *relative error*. Computational error may also be classified according to source as follows: *inherent error,* reflecting inaccuracies in initially given data; *generated error,* reflecting inaccuracies due to the necessity of rounding or otherwise truncating the numeric results of arithmetic operations; and *analytic error,* reflecting inaccuracies due to the use of a computing procedure that represents only an approximation to the theoretical result desired.

In the example of the mean and standard deviation calculation given earlier, one might wish to analyze the effect of inherent error in the input x values on the computed $\bar{x}$ and s values, that is, to analyze the manner in which errors δ_i attributed to the x_i induce errors $\delta_{\bar{x}}$ and δ_s in $\bar{x}$ and s, respectively. In the case of simple functions the effect can be estimated using the traditional techniques of calculus; in a calculation of complicated structure, however, it may be difficult even to get a feeling for the manner in which errors in input

values propagate. Of course, in this type of situation, inherent errors in the data may be just what the calculation itself is concerned with, and hence it might be more appropriate to consider the input values x as exact as far as the computation is concerned. Even then it would be important, however, to have some idea of the "sensitivity" of the computed results as a function of input; one might want to know, for example, that the closer to zero $\bar{x}$ gets, the more relative effect it will show from given relative changes in x values.

In any actual implementation of the procedure diagrammed in Figure 2 there will be generated error introduced at each arithmetic step, the exact nature of which depends on the rounding rules followed by the computer arithmetic unit, which are often obscure to one who communicates only via a procedure-oriented language. Furthermore, analytic error is necessarily introduced at the stage where the square root is called for, since functions such as this can be computed only approximately. The closeness of the approximation, and hence the level at which analytic error is introduced, depends on properties of the square root procedure, which also are frequently not very well documented for the user.

When it is considered that error effects of all three types may be interwoven in a calculation, and may propagate through all the calculational steps in a complicated manner, it is seen that the problem of error assessment is nontrivial. Furthermore, it is not generally taken into account how catastrophic relative error propagation effects can be; the subtraction of two numbers each with a relative error of order 10^{-8} which happen to have a relative difference of order 10^{-6} will yield a result with relative error of order 10^{-2}, and the arithmetic procedures used on most contemporary computers are such that this loss of significance is not brought to the user's attention unless special monitoring techniques are programmed into the calculation. And while it is generally true that both generated and analytic error can be minimized by computational techniques (carrying more precision and using more refined approximations), an assessment is required to know when such measures should be resorted to. Poor computational technique can magnify the effect of generated and analytic error unnecessarily; a typical case is use of the formula $\sum x_i^2 - n\bar{x}^2$ instead of $\sum (x_i - \bar{x})^2$ for calculating the standard deviation, since then the result tends to depend on subtraction of two large and nearly equal numbers. Finally, inherent error, as its name implies, is dependent only on the level of input error and the functional connection between input and output values, neither of which are subject to remedial action in the computational context. When small relative errors in input induce large relative errors in output, a process is said to be "ill-conditioned"; if this obtains, the most one can hope for is a means of detecting the situation.

The subject of error analysis, in its several facets, has been extensively studied; although no comprehensive set of directives can be given, the user will be well repaid for becoming familiar with at least some of the work already done in this area, as indicated in McCracken and Dorn (1964, pp. 43–64) and Hamming (1962, pp. 24–40).

ROBERT L. ASHENHURST

[*See also* SIMULATION.]

BIBLIOGRAPHY

BORKO, HAROLD (editor) 1962 *Computer Applications in the Behavioral Sciences.* Englewood Cliffs, N.J.: Prentice-Hall.

BROOKS, FREDERICK P. JR.; and IVERSON, KENNETH E. 1963 *Automatic Data Processing.* New York: Wiley.

CALINGAERT, PETER 1965 *Principles of Computation.* Reading, Mass.: Addison-Wesley.

GREEN, BERT F. JR. 1963 *Digital Computers in Research: An Introduction for Behavioral and Social Scientists.* New York: McGraw-Hill.

GREGORY, ROBERT H.; and VAN HORN, RICHARD L. (1960) 1963 *Automatic Data Processing Systems.* 2d ed. Belmont, Calif.: Wadsworth.

HAMMING, R. W. 1962 *Numerical Methods for Scientists and Engineers.* New York: McGraw-Hill.

McCRACKEN, DANIEL D.; and DORN, WILLIAM S. 1964 *Numerical Methods and* FORTRAN *Programming.* New York: Wiley.

YOUDEN, W. W. 1965 *Computer Literature Bibliography: 1946–1963.* National Bureau of Standards, Miscellaneous Publication No. 266. Washington: U.S. National Bureau of Standards.

COMPUTERS

See AUTOMATION; COMPUTATION; CYBERNETICS; INFORMATION STORAGE AND RETRIEVAL; OPERATIONS RESEARCH; SIMULATION; *and the biographies of* BABBAGE; VON NEUMANN; WIENER.

COMTE, AUGUSTE

Isidore Auguste Marie François Xavier Comte (1798–1857), French philosopher and sociologist, came from a Catholic and monarchical family in Montpellier. He abandoned the Catholic faith at the age of 13. In 1814 he entered the École Polytechnique in Paris. This school was then the center of political liberalism and of progressive thought in France; the mathematician Gaspard Monge had been one of its founders, and it remained committed to the development of mathematics and the sciences.

While it is clear that Comte soon shifted away from pure liberalism, close scrutiny is required to establish his position with respect to conservatism and liberalism. His early writings indicate that he had many ideas in common with the counterrevolutionary and conservative movements at the beginning of the nineteenth century; later, at the beginning of the fourth volume of his *Cours de philosophie positive* (1830–1842), he explicitly acknowledged this affinity, stating that he agreed in part with Joseph de Maistre's philosophy without, however, accepting his political views. Contrary to some views (Hayek 1952; Salomon 1955; Spaemann 1959), this does not mean that Comte can be identified with the counterrevolutionary thinkers of his time. Indeed, his attitude differed from that of the conservatives in the same way as did Saint-Simon's; both tried to repudiate the principles of the French Revolution without at the same time relinquishing its achievements. This twofold attitude, similar to that which Hegel had expressed somewhat earlier, is corroborated by Comte's position during the revolutions of 1830 and 1848 and by his humanitarian philosophy, which eventually became a religion of humanity: the worship of the *Grand Être.*

Comte's association with Saint-Simon, which began as early as 1817, is in itself further evidence that he does not belong with the conservatives. Despite Comte's later protestations that he did not owe anything to Saint-Simon, it is certain that he was deeply influenced by this remarkably brilliant and inspiring aristocrat who devoted himself to building a new society based on the principle that it is the working class which is, in the broadest sense, the class of "producers." Recent historical research (especially by Gouhier 1933–1941), has established that their collaboration during the period from 1817 to 1824 was much closer than Comte ever admitted. The change in Comte's personal feelings toward Saint-Simon can best be followed in his correspondence with his friend Valat (1870), which shows how much he was initially stimulated by Saint-Simon and how he later withdrew from the relationship.

Saint-Simon had recorded his essential ideas, before he ever met Comte, in the most coherent of his booklets, *Mémoire sur la science de l'homme* and *Travail sur la gravitation universelle,* both written in the year 1813. These contain the famous "law of three stages"; even though Saint-Simon was incapable of developing this idea into a comprehensive and consistent philosophy of history, as

Comte was to do in the *Cours*, the idea, nevertheless, was originally his. In general, Saint-Simon dissipated his ideas in innumerable letters, leaflets, prospectuses, and pamphlets, throwing out striking formulas and slogans rather than elaborating the ideas step by step. He was a great speaker, a vivid advocate of new conceptions, always an agitator rather than a philosopher or a disciplined scholar. Even though Comte's early work followed the same lines as Saint-Simon's, his mode of thinking was not only more consistent but also more profound.

An important similarity between Comte and Saint-Simon is their common negative attitude toward economic liberalism and their criticism of Adam Smith (Mauduit 1929). Here both came very near to Simonde de Sismondi and his *Nouveaux principes* of 1819 and sketched the first historical criticism of classical economics.

While the influence that Saint-Simon had on Comte should not be minimized, neither should the differences between them; these were differences not merely in style of thought but also in the substance of that thought. One such difference was revealed by Comte himself in his correspondence with Valat when he asserted that Saint-Simon's advocacy of political action before the scientific system of positivism had been sufficiently developed was putting the cart before the horse. Another and more subtle difference appeared when Comte, in an article published under Saint-Simon's name and in his journal, *Industrie*, called for the development of a secular system of morals and held that society is itself a system of "common moral ideas." This was nothing less than the discovery of the normative character of social behavior, that is, of a moral system inherent in social relations. Comte asserted the relativism of moral ideas—that they vary with different cultures and social systems—in opposition to the notion that norms are rooted either in divine revelation or in a general spiritual order, separate from social life and untouched by it. This clear-cut statement of what we now call cultural relativism aroused considerable turmoil among the subscribers of the journal, and in the next issue Saint-Simon formally promised that he would "return to his first manner" (Pereire 1912). Saint-Simon had never had any doubts about the origin of moral ideas and was, indeed, genuinely convinced that the traditional Christian norms could be adapted to the new conditions of industrialism by emphasizing the importance of philanthropy (*Nouveau christianisme* 1825). With respect to his conception of values, then, Comte was more radical than Saint-Simon.

This is not true of Comte's conception of the proper order of society. As has been judiciously stated by T. H. Huxley, Comte and positivism can be interpreted as "Catholicism minus Christianity," that is, as an all-embracing hierarchical system of society, based on secular values of a mystical, humanitarian kind. This, taken together with Comte's conception of the role of "consensus" in social processes, brings him nearer to the views of the conservative thinkers than to Saint-Simon's revolutionary demand that the producing class (the workers) be protected from exploitation by the idle or leisure class and that *la classe la plus nombreuse et la plus pauvre* be emancipated. With this demand Saint-Simon became a forerunner of Marx, whereas Comte remained a believer in the efficacy of a purely spiritual order, provided only that it is purged of theological and metaphysical ideas.

It has never been contested that Comte invented the term "sociology," which he first used in print in 1838, at the beginning of the fourth volume of his *Cours*. Earlier, in the general introduction to the first volume, he had used the term *physique sociale* just as Saint-Simon had used this term, interchangeably with such terms as *physiologie sociale* or *système de gravitation sociale*. A relatively casual reason for Comte's change of terminology was that the Belgian statistician Quetelet published his *Physique sociale* in 1835. There was also, however, a deeper reason: Having accepted for some years the teachings of the great French astronomer Laplace, with whose ideas he had become acquainted at the École Polytechnique, Comte began to reject the leadership of mathematics in the development of the social sciences. He replaced the methodology of the sciences with the historical approach, as developed in the *Cours*, and thus largely repudiated the education he had received at the École Polytechnique.

The development of sociology as a science occurs, according to Comte, within the framework of a general reorientation of human thought. According to the "law of three stages," that was expounded by Comte in the first two lectures of the *Cours* (after previous attempts in his early writings), every single branch of human knowledge has to pass through three different theoretical (or methodological) stages before it reaches maturity: the theological or fictitious; the metaphysical or abstract; and the scientific or positive stage. The function of the second stage is to act as an intermediary, since the first and the last stages are clearly so different in their general outlook that it is impossible to pass directly from the first to the third. In the third stage all phenomena are regarded as subject to invariable natural laws that can be investigated by observation and experimentation.

Comte began the second part of this new approach to human thought with the statement that the different sciences, because of the varying degree of complexity of their respective substances, reach the stage of maturity at different times, and he then proceeded to locate all the different sciences in terms of the stage of their development. The order followed in this encyclopedic system is the "natural" or logical order, beginning with the least complex or most general phenomena, which are also most remote from humanity, and ending with those more relevant to human beings as investigated by the social science. The order of the sciences is therefore astronomy, physics, chemistry, physiology, and, finally, social physics, or sociology. The science of mathematics is presented as an introduction to the encyclopedia and somewhat apart from this order; it is the most important of all the sciences in that it is the most general formal basis of both science and philosophy. The science of psychology does not appear in this enumeration. Comte was convinced that psychology as it existed in his time had not yet passed the metaphysical stage. There is evidence that he thought of psychology as an appendix to sociology, to be developed only *after* sociology had reached the positive stage.

Interesting as this "law" may initially appear, it is hardly more than a set of preliminary and formalistic categories and by no means constitutes the essence of Comte's thought. Indeed, this part of Comte's work has proved to be the least resistant to criticism. Comte's sociology was developed essentially as a scientific remedy for the long-lasting social, political, and cultural crisis in Europe. The 46th lesson of the *Cours* was devoted entirely to a sociological analysis of the contemporary crisis in France, which was the aftermath of the Revolution of 1789. What remained of the prerevolutionary system was being destroyed by the incessant and insoluble controversy between *ordre* and *progrès*. It was this "miserable oscillatory constitution of our social existence" that Comte sought to overcome by developing, with the help of scientific analysis, a third way that would eliminate the "intellectual anarchism" of his time. Since conservatism represented the party of *ordre*, and Jacobinism the party of *progrès*, Comte, following his own interpretation of history, divorced himself from both parties and tried to establish a third way, without succumbing to the eclecticism represented by Victor Cousin.

Comte's persistent ambivalence toward the French Revolution was already at the core of his thought while he was dominated by the ideas of Saint-Simon (see, for example, his essay of 1822, "Plan des travaux scientifiques nécessaires pour réor-

ganiser la société"). What was new in the *Cours* was his attempt to resolve it. It has been alleged that his panacea for the crisis of his time was a rational, scientific approach, based on observation and experimentation, and that this is what he meant by "positivism." But although there is evidence, especially if we limit ourselves to the consideration of the *Cours*, that this was an element in his thought, it was only one element, and perhaps not the most important one. Comte himself stated several times that empiricism per se is not equivalent to positivism (*Cours*, Lecture 58) and that positivism offers a synthesis of our knowledge, thereby producing a new system of thought and a new dimension of consciousness. This very significant view is made more explicit in *A Discourse on the Positive Spirit* (1844a), as well as in his *Appeal to Conservatives* (1855), where he dealt with the different meanings of the term "positivism."

As it was presented in the *Cours*, however, positivism was misunderstood by contemporary admirers and critics alike, the admirers seeing it as an unequivocal endorsement of the efficacy of science and the critics deploring it as "scientism." This misinterpretation has been given wide currency by the books on Comte by Littré (1863), Mill (1865), Ostwald (1914), and others. Having thus misconstrued the *Cours*, it became necessary for them to separate the Comte of the *Cours* from the Comte of such later writings as the *System of Positive Polity* (1851–1854), and the *Catechism of Positive Religion* (1852), since the *System* is permeated by reformist ideas and the *Catechism* by a new religion. The most common explanation of the "inconsistency" in his ideas stems from the vicissitudes of his personal life; since Comte had experienced one nervous breakdown in 1826 at the age of 28, the "change" in his outlook was attributed to the impact of another personal crisis, the dissolution of his relationship with Clotilde de Vaux in 1846 and her death in 1847. The alleged drastic shift from his positivistic and objective approach to a new "subjectivism" has been connected with this unhappy emotional experience.

The explanation would be plausible had the shift actually occurred. However, it is based on a completely distorted view of the *Cours* and of its general meaning, as can easily be demonstrated by noting Comte's repeated emphasis in that work on the necessity of an all-embracing moral and intellectual reform as the prerequisite of social reform. The last lectures of the *Cours* (56–60) are entirely devoted to a general appraisal of the achievements of science after the stage of positivism has been fully realized. Indeed, reformist intentions rather than rational analysis are so basic to his entire philosophy that he came very near to Marx's statement that "the philosophers have only interpreted the world in different ways, the point is to change it" (*Theses on Feuerbach* 1845). In fact, "praxis" was as important a goal to Comte as it was to Marx, the only difference between them being that Comte tried to combine this approach with the Cartesian heritage, whereas Marx, in his distrust of reason, destroyed the very foundation of philosophical rationalism and replaced it by revolutionary *action directe*.

As the British Neo-Hegelian philosopher Edward Caird (1885) rather early appreciated, Comte's humanism and the real meaning of his "subjective synthesis" is based on the fact that "nature becomes conscious of itself in man," so that, as Comte put it, "man sums up in himself all the laws of the world." Therefore, "to one who has understood the full meaning of the process, this 'subjective synthesis' will also be objective" (see also Marvin 1936). The different terms used to define the "metaphysical stage of history" produce similar evidence. This stage was also called by Comte the "negative stage," and its historical importance lies in the prevalence of criticism and destruction of the old conceptions of the world and of social life as well. Thus, the intellectual development of mankind had necessarily to pass through ages of anarchism and revolutionary restlessness, a true interregnum as Comte called it. The interregnum is characterized by "negative philosophy," which is the necessary forerunner and prerequisite for the establishment of "positive philosophy," or positivism, as Comte understood it, because a new order cannot be attained before the remains of the old system have been completely erased.

For an adequate understanding of Comte, one has to consider the whole of his intellectual career, integrating his early writings with the *Cours*, with the subsequent attempts at self-interpretation (1844a; 1848), with the *System*, and finally with his sketch of a humanitarian religion. This was his particular response to a general humanitarian trend in the philosophy, the art, and the literature of his time, which began with Honoré de Balzac and provisionally culminated in a system of humanitarian metaphysics as developed by Pierre Leroux, whose influence during the early 1840s in France was much more important than has been recognized so far (König 1931). Comte was neither a "mad" philosopher—Dumas (1905), Seillière (1924), Maurras (1905), Sokoloff (1961), all notwithstanding—nor a partisan of "pedantocracy." His main and vital interest was rather the systematization of the social background of human history into one body of knowledge, in preparation for a practical approach to social reform based on a lasting order, the theoretical and moral principles of which he saw in the development of a new science, sociology.

RENÉ KÖNIG

[*For the historical context of Comte's work, see* POSITIVISM; SOCIOLOGY, *article on* THE DEVELOPMENT OF SOCIOLOGICAL THOUGHT; *and the biographies of* LAPLACE *and* SAINT-SIMON. *For discussion of the subsequent development of his ideas, see the biographies of* BAGEHOT; BERNARD; DUGUIT; DURKHEIM; GIDDINGS; LE PLAY; MILL; SOROKIN; SPENCER; WARD, LESTER F.]

WORKS BY COMTE

(1819–1828) 1883 *Opuscules de philosophie sociale: 1819–1828.* Paris: Leroux.

(1822) 1883 *Plan des travaux scientifiques nécessaires pour réorganiser la société.* Pages 60–180 in Auguste Comte, *Opuscules de philosophie sociale: 1819–1828.* Paris: Leroux.

(1830–1842) 1877 *Cours de philosophie positive.* 6 vols., 4th ed. Paris: Baillière. → Volume 1: *Préliminaires généraux et philosophie mathématique.* Volume 2: *Philosophie astronomique et philosophie de la physique.* Volume 3: *Philosophie chimique et philosophie biologique.* Volumes 4–5: *Philosophie sociale.* Volume 6: *Complément de la philosophie sociale et conclusions générales.*

(1830–1842) 1896 *The Positive Philosophy of Auguste Comte.* Freely translated and condensed by Harriet Martineau, with an introduction by Frederic Harrison. 3 vols. London: Bell. → An abridged and simplified translation of *Cours de philosophie positive.*

(1844a) 1903 *A Discourse on the Positive Spirit.* London: Reeves. → First published in French as the preamble to *Traité philosophique d'astronomie populaire.*

1844b *Traité philosophique d'astronomie populaire.* Paris: Carilian-Goeury & Dalmont.

(1848) 1957 *A General View of Positivism.* New York: Speller. → First published as *Discours sur l'ensemble du positivisme.*

(1851–1854) 1875–1877 *System of Positive Polity.* 4 vols. London: Longmans. → First published in French.

(1852) 1891 *The Catechism of Positive Religion.* 3d ed. rev. & corr. London: Routledge. → First published in French.

(1855) 1889 *Appeal to Conservatives.* London: Trubner. → First published in French.

(1856) 1891 *Religion of Humanity: Subjective Synthesis, or Universal System of the Conceptions Adapted to the Normal State of Humanity.* London: Routledge. → First published as *Synthèse subjective: Ou système universel des conceptions propres à l'état normal de l'humanité.*

1870 *Lettres d'Auguste Comte à M. Valat: 1815–1844.* Paris: Dunod.

1877 *Lettres d'Auguste Comte à John Stuart Mill: 1841–1846.* Paris: Leroux.

(1884) 1910 *Confession and Testament of Auguste Comte and His Correspondence With Clotilde de Vaux.* Liverpool: Young. → First published in French.

1889a *Lettres d'Auguste Comte à Henry Edger et à M. John Metcalf.* Paris: Apostolat Positiviste.

1889b *Lettres d'Auguste Comte à Richard Congreve.* London: Church of Humanity.

1890 *Lettres d'Auguste Comte à Henry Dix Hutton.* Dublin: Ponsonby & Weldrick.

1903–1904 *Correspondance inédite d'Auguste Comte.* Paris: Société Positiviste.

1932 *Lettres inédites à C. de Blignières.* Paris: Vrin.

1939 *Nouvelles lettres inédites.* Paris: Société Positiviste.

WORKS ABOUT COMTE

ALENGRY, FRANCK 1900 *Essai historique et critique sur la sociologie chez Auguste Comte.* Paris: Alcan.

ARBOUSSE-BASTIDE, PAUL 1957 *La doctrine de l'éducation universelle dans la philosophie d'Auguste Comte: Principe d'unité systématique et fondement de l'organisation spirituelle du monde.* 2 vols. Paris: Presses Universitaires de France.

ARON, RAYMOND (1960) 1965 *Main Currents in Sociological Thought.* Volume 1: Montesquieu, Comte, Marx, Tocqueville: The Sociologists and the Revolution of 1848. New York: Basic Books. → First published in French.

BORCHERT, HEINRICH 1927 *Der Begriff des Kulturzeitalters bei Comte: Nach dem* Cours de philosophie positive *unter Mitberücksichtigung der Jugendschriften.* Halle (Germany): John.

BOYER DE SAINTE-SUZANNE, RAYMOND DE 1923 *Essai sur la pensée religieuse d'Auguste Comte.* Paris: Nourry.

CAIRD, EDWARD 1885 *The Social Philosophy and Religion of Comte.* New York: Macmillan.

CANTECOR, GEORGES (1904) 1930 *Comte.* New ed. Paris: Mellottée. → First published as *Le positivisme.*

CRESSON, ANDRÉ 1941 *Auguste Comte: Sa vie, son oeuvre, avec un exposé de sa philosophie.* Paris: Presses Universitaires de France.

DEFOURNY, MAURICE 1902 *La sociologie positiviste: Auguste Comte.* Paris: Alcan.

DE GRANGE, McQUILKIN (1923) 1930 *The Curve of Societal Movement: A Study of the Nature of Sociology in the Light of the Positive Politics of Auguste Comte.* Hanover, N.H. and Minneapolis, Minn.: Sociological Press. → First published in French.

DE GRANGE, McQUILKIN 1931 *The Method of Auguste Comte: Subordination of Imagination to Observation in the Social Sciences.* Pages 19–58 in Social Science Research Council, Committee on Scientific Methods in the Social Sciences, *Methods in Social Science: A Case Book.* Univ. of Chicago Press.

DELVOLVÉ, JEAN 1932 *Réflexions sur la pensée comtienne.* Paris: Alcan.

DEROISIN, HIPPOLYTE P. 1909 *Notes sur Auguste Comte: Par un de ses disciples.* Paris: Crès.

DUBUISSON, ALFRED 1910 *"Positivisme intégral," foi, morale, politique, d'après les dernières conceptions d'Auguste Comte.* Paris: Crès.

DUCASSÉ, PIERRE 1939 *Methode et intuition chez Auguste Comte.* Paris: Alcan.

DUMAS, GEORGES 1905 *Psychologie des deux messies positivistes: Saint-Simon et Auguste Comte.* Paris: Alcan.

DUPUY, PAUL 1911 *Le positivisme d'Auguste Comte.* Paris: Alcan.

DUSSAUZE, WALTER 1901 *Essai sur la religion d'après Auguste Comte.* Saint-Armand (France): Chambon.

GOUHIER, HENRI G. 1931 *La vie d'Auguste Comte.* Paris: Gallimard. → A bibliography appears on pages 289–300.

GOUHIER, HENRI G. 1933–1941 *La jeunesse d'Auguste Comte et la formation du positivisme.* 3 vols. Paris: Vrin. → A bibliography of the works of Comte appears in Volume 1, pages 294–301.

GRUBER, HERMANN 1889 *Auguste Comte, der Begründer des Positivismus: Sein Leben und seine Lehre.* Freiburg im Breisgau (Germany): Herder.

GUILMAIN, LÉON J. 1922 *La sociologie d'A. Comte: Ce qu'elle doit à la biologie du début du XIXᵉ siècle.* Algiers: Gaudet.

HARRIS, MARJORIE S. 1923 *The Positive Philosophy of Auguste Comte.* Hartford, Conn.: Case.

HAWKINS, RICHMOND L. 1936 *Auguste Comte and the United States: (1816–1853).* Cambridge, Mass.: Harvard Univ. Press.

LACROIX, JEAN 1956 *La sociologie d'Auguste Comte.* Paris: Presses Universitaires de France.

LÉVY-BRUHL, LUCIEN (1900) 1903 *The Philosophy of Auguste Comte.* New York: Putnam; London: Sonnenschein. → First published in French.

LEWES, GEORGE H. (1883) 1904 *Comte's Philosophy of the Sciences: Being an Exposition of the Principles of the* Cours de philosophie positive. London: Bell.

LITTRÉ, ÉMILE (1863) 1877 *Auguste Comte et la philosophie positive.* Paris: Bureau de "La philosophie positive."

LITTRÉ, ÉMILE 1866 *Auguste Comte et Stuart Mill.* Paris: Baillière.

LONCHAMPT, JOSEPH-VICTOR 1900 *Notice sur la vie et l'oeuvre d'Auguste Comte.* Paris: Fonds Typographique de l'Exécution Testamentaire d'Auguste Comte.

MACKINTOSH, ROBERT 1899 *From Comte to Benjamin Kidd: The Appeal to Biology or Evolution for Human Guidance.* New York and London: Macmillan.

MARCUSE, ALEXANDER 1932 *Die Geschichtsphilosophie Auguste Comtes.* Berlin and Stuttgart: Cotta.

MARÉCHAL, HENRI 1919 *Les conceptions économiques d'A. Comte.* Bar-sur-Seine (France): Saillard.

MARVIN, FRANCIS S. 1936 *Comte: The Founder of Sociology.* London: Chapman & Hall.

MAUDUIT, ROGER 1929 *Auguste Comte et la science économique.* Paris: Alcan.

MAURRAS, CHARLES (1905) 1925 *Auguste Comte.* Pages 89–127 in Charles Maurras, *Romantisme et révolution.* Paris: Nouvelle Librairie Nationale.

MEHLIS, GEORG 1909 *Die Geschichtsphilosophie Auguste Comtes kritisch dargestellt.* Leipzig: Eckardt.

MILHAUD, GASTON S. 1902 *Le positivisme et le progrès de l'esprit: Études critiques sur Auguste Comte.* Paris: Alcan.

MILL, JOHN STUART (1865) 1961 *Auguste Comte and Positivism.* Ann Arbor: Univ. of Michigan Press.

MILL, JOHN STUART 1899 *Lettres inédites de John Stuart Mill à Auguste Comte.* Published with the responses of Comte. Paris: Alcan.

MONTESQUIOU-FEZENSAC, LÉON 1907 *Le système politique d'Auguste Comte.* Paris: Nouvelle Librairie Nationale.

NEGT, OSKAR 1964 *Strukturbeziehungen zwischen den Gesellschaftslehren Comtes und Hegels.* Frankfurt am Main (Germany): Europäische Verlagsanstalt.

OSTWALD, WILHELM 1914 *Auguste Comte: Der Mann und sein Werk.* Leipzig: Verlag Unesma.

ROBERTY, EUGÈNE DE 1894 *Auguste Comte et Herbert Spencer: Contribution à l'histoire des idées philosophiques aux XIXᵉ siècle.* Paris: Alcan.

ROBINET, JEAN F. E. 1860 *Notice sur l'oeuvre et sur la vie d'Auguste Comte.* Paris: Dunod.

ROUVRE, CHARLES DE 1917 *L'amoureuse histoire d'Auguste Comte et de Clotilde de Vaux.* Paris: Calmann-Lévy.

ROUVRE, CHARLES DE 1928 *Auguste Comte et le catholicisme.* Paris: Rieder.

ROUX, ADRIEN 1920 *La pensée d'Auguste Comte: Le passé, le présent & l'avenir social.* Paris: Chiron.

SEILLIÈRE, ERNEST 1924 *Auguste Comte.* Paris: Alcan.

SOKOLOFF, BORIS 1961 *The "Mad" Philosopher Auguste Comte.* New York: Vantage.

STYLE, JANE M. 1928 *Auguste Comte: Thinker and Lover.* London: Paul.

UTA, MICHEL 1928a *La loi des trois états dans la philosophie d'Auguste Comte.* Paris: Alcan.

UTA, MICHEL 1928b *La théorie du savoir dans la philosophie d'Auguste Comte.* Paris: Alcan.

VARNEY, MECCA M. 1931 *L'influence des femmes sur Auguste Comte.* Paris: Presses Universitaires de France.

WAENTIG, HEINRICH 1894 *Auguste Comte und seine Bedeutung für die Entwicklung der Socialwissenschaft.* Leipzig: Duncker.

WATSON, JOHN 1895 *Comte, Mill and Spencer: An Outline of Philosophy.* New York: Macmillan.

WHITTAKER, THOMAS 1908 *Comte and Mill.* London: Constable.

SUPPLEMENTARY BIBLIOGRAPHY

BRIDGES, JOHN HENRY (1907) 1915 *Illustrations of Positivism: A Selection of Articles From the* Positivist Review *in Science, Philosophy, Religion and Politics.* Rev. & enl. ed. Chicago: Open Court.

DUCASSÉ, PIERRE 1939 *Essai sur les origines intuitives du positivisme.* Paris: Alcan.

DUCASSÉ, PIERRE 1940 *La méthode positive et l'intuition comtienne: Bibliographie.* Paris: Alcan.

HAWKINS, RICHMOND L. 1938 *Positivism in the United States: (1853–1861).* Cambridge, Mass.: Harvard Univ. Press.

HAYEK, FRIEDRICH A. VON 1952 *The Counter-revolution of Science: Studies on the Abuse of Reason.* Glencoe, Ill.: Free Press.

KÖNIG, RENÉ 1931 *Die naturalistische Ästhetik in Frankreich und ihre Auflösung: Ein Beitrag zur systemwissenschaftlichen Betrachtung der Künstlerästhetik.* Leipzig: Noske.

PEREIRE, ALFRED 1912 *Autour de Saint-Simon: Documents originaux.* Paris: Champion.

SALOMON, ALBERT 1955 *The Tyranny of Progress: Reflections on the Origins of Sociology.* New York: Noonday.

SPAEMANN, ROBERT 1959 *Der Ursprung der Soziologie aus dem Geist der Restauration.* Munich: Kosel.

CONCENTRATION CURVES

See GRAPHIC PRESENTATION; STATISTICS, DESCRIPTIVE, *article on* LOCATION AND DISPERSION; INDUSTRIAL CONCENTRATION.

CONCEPT FORMATION

Our world is filled with sets of objects, events, and ideas that share some common quality while differing in other characteristics. An organism that learns to respond to the common quality of a given set has learned a concept. The child, for example, learns the concept of *blueness* when he is able to select a *blue* balloon or a *blue* ball or a *blue* wagon from similar objects of different colors. When he makes this conceptual response, he is abstracting the *blueness* from other properties of the objects, like size, shape, or function. Similarly the child learns the concept of *triangle* when he distinguishes triangles of various shapes (right-angle, isosceles, scalene, equilateral, and obtuse) from other geometrical forms. Or he learns the concepts of *right* and *wrong* when he discriminates between socially approved and disapproved behavior.

In experimental psychology the field of concept formation has achieved neither the methodological nor the conceptual unity characterizing such areas as sensation, perception, learning, and motivation. Traditionally, psychologists have not looked upon conceptual behavior as reflecting any unique or fundamental psychological process. Instead the common view has largely been that conceptual behavior is a function of the interaction between basic psychological processes. As a result, psychologists have for the most part sought to extend theories from other areas (e.g., learning, perception) to conceptual behavior instead of formulating hypotheses concerned exclusively with the facts of concept formation.

Historical introduction. Experimental efforts to understand concepts were made initially by psychologists who by training or intellectual kinship were related to Wilhelm Wundt (1832–1920). For Wundt, introspection, the method of observing one's own conscious experience, was the primary method of the psychological laboratory. The goal in investigating concepts was, first, to identify their basic mental elements and, second, to discover the principles that govern their combination—a goal previously set in investigations of sensory and perceptual experience. As a step toward understanding the conscious correlates of a concept, Titchener described it as a "symbol which holds a large number of particular ideas together" ([1896] 1921, p. 312).

Although the goals of introspective psychology seemed clear, the results were not. Introspection, as a general method of psychology and as a specific technique for revealing the mysteries of thought, possessed severe limitations. Of paramount importance was its apparent unreliability. The content of the mind seemed to be influenced by how one was trained to observe it. Elements of consciousness observed in one laboratory could not be detected in another.

Introspective psychology was also handicapped by two related characteristics of phenomenal experience that apparently interfered with the analysis of the higher mental processes. First, mental experience seemed to be in a state of constant flux, incapable of being analyzed into static elements. William James, in his discussion of the conscious experiences associated with conceptual thinking (1892), recognized the inadequacy of formal introspection as a technique for describing subjective life. Second, introspective analysis of thought by H. J. Watt and N. Ach at Würzburg, Germany, sometimes revealed an extreme paucity of conscious experience and at other times, none at all.

Dissatisfaction with the introspective method encouraged some psychologists to propose a new approach to the science of psychology. Behaviorists argued that psychology would remain methodologically unreliable, and empirically restricted, if it persisted in identifying its subject matter as conscious experience. Instead, it was suggested, psychology should be conceived as the objective experimental science of behavior (Watson 1913).

Although the philosophical issues were more complicated than Watson understood, his vigorous and convincing arguments redirected experimental psychology in the United States from the study of consciousness to the study of behavior. The examination of the experiential correlates of concepts was discarded in favor of the objective investigation of their acquisition and utilization.

Hull (1920), in a doctoral thesis, illustrated how behavioristic methodology could be applied to the study of concepts. He trained college students to associate each of 36 Chinese characters with one of six sounds. These characters belonged to six different groups, each of which had a common part known as a radical. The appropriate sound (e.g., *oo yer*) was the same for all the characters having the same radical. The subjects were under the impression that their task was to memorize the response (the appropriate sound) to each stimulus (the Chinese character). After a subject was able to give the correct response for all 36 characters, he was tested with an entirely new set of characters that had the same radicals. Thus it was possible to discover whether the subject learned to respond to the common element (the radical) or whether he learned the appropriate response to each individual character. If he had learned to respond to the common element, he should now respond appropriately to all the new characters which had that common element. If, however, he had only learned to respond to the individual character, he would be unable to identify the new characters.

The results indicated that the subjects as a group behaved in a manner falling somewhere between the two extremes. On the very first trial 27 per cent of the responses were correct, indicating that the subjects had learned, to some extent, to respond conceptually, that is, to react to the common element characteristic of all the instances of that concept. It is interesting to note that Hull found the most effective method of teaching the six concepts was by presenting each series of characters with the common element in red, thus facilitating the discrimination between the essential cues.

Discrimination learning as a model. Hull's study set the course of research in conceptual behavior in the United States for decades to come. First, it offered an experimental method that could determine objectively the influence of numerous variables on concept formation. Second, the use of stimulus–response language in analyzing conceptual behavior was encouraged. The implication of this technical language system, a system that is widely used by neobehaviorists (the present-day descendants of Watson), is that there are at least three fundamental sets of variables in any psychological event: environmental (S), behavioral (R), and the association (–) between them. Within this language system a concept becomes "a common response to a set of dissimilar stimuli" (see T. S. Kendler 1961, p. 447). Finally, the results of Hull's study suggested that concept formation could be conceptualized as a case of discrimination learning based upon principles of conditioning. Pavlov explained the learning of a discrimination (conditioned differentiation) in terms of three fundamental principles: conditioning, stimulus generalization, extinction. When training a dog to discriminate between a white and a gray circle, it proved necessary not only to condition him to respond to the white circle but also to train him *not* to respond to the gray one. A dog who has been conditioned to salivate to a white circle will, without any additional training, salivate to similar stimuli, such as gray circles. Differential responses to gray and white circles can be learned only if the effects of stimulus generalization are neutralized. This can be done by extinguishing the generalized response to the gray circle, i.e., by not giving the dog food in the presence of the gray circle. Thus a discrimination can be established by the joint action of conditioning the response to the appropriate stimulus and extinguishing the generalized response to the inappropriate stimulus [see LEARNING, *article on* DISCRIMINATION LEARNING; *and the biography of* HULL].

This discrimination model, based upon the mechanisms of conditioning, generalization, and extinction, seemed to many psychologists obviously applicable to concept formation. The child who is learning the concept of red must not only acquire a common response to all red stimuli but must also extinguish the response to similar stimuli, such as orange objects.

The *S–R* discrimination model of concept formation instigated a wide variety of research studies, far too numerous to summarize here. Of the more systematic research programs some were primarily concerned with investigating the influence of a specific set of variables; others were more interested in analyzing the discrimination process underlying concept formation.

Order of difficulty. Heidbreder (1948) in a classic series of studies, with college students serving as subjects, investigated the order of difficulty of attaining different kinds of concepts: those representing objects (e.g., tree), form (e.g., circle), and number (e.g., five). Under varying conditions, the order of difficulty—concrete objects, form, and number—remained constant. This order was interpreted as being positively correlated with the "thing character," the concreteness, of the critical feature of the concept; a *tree* possesses more "thing character" than does a *circle*, which in turn is more concrete than *five* (see Vinacke 1952, chapter 7, for discussion of concrete–abstract dimension of conceptual behavior). The order of difficulty Heidbreder initially found was not, however, always replicated. By modifying the critical cues on which the concepts were based, the hierarchy of dominance could be changed. In another set of studies under somewhat different experimental conditions (e.g., Grant & Curran 1952), attaining concepts based on color proved to be more difficult than identifying either concepts of form or number. This simple ordering of difficulty again does not tell the whole story. With practice, concepts of number become relatively easy to learn. Also number concepts, once learned, tend to perseverate more than do concepts of form or color. The problem of the hierarchy of dominance of various concepts becomes even more complicated when the behavior of children is considered (see Russell 1956, chapter 8; Thompson [1952] 1962, chapter 9). Some data suggest that children under age three find form concepts easier to acquire than color concepts, but from three to five the relationship is reversed. Perhaps a fundamental order of difficulty will never be found, because the basic mechanisms responsible for concept formation will favor one order under one set of experimental conditions and an entirely different order under a different set of conditions.

Mediating processes. Rats have been reported capable of learning to choose a triangular form when paired with other forms despite variations in the size, shading, position, and amount of outline of the triangles. But is this "truly" conceptual behavior? Osgood believes not, since the rat probably does not understand the abstract concept of triangularity and therefore would not respond to "three dots in a triangular arrangement . . . or to three places on a map, a three cornered block . . ." (1953, p. 667). He suggests that there are two kinds of classificatory behavior. One kind occurs when an organism responds to a common specific element in different stimulus patterns (e.g., the specific Chinese radicals in Hull's study). The other kind of classificatory behavior, the "true" conceptual type, occurs when varying stimulus patterns, not necessarily containing any features in common, elicit a common mediating abstract response that serves as a cue for conceptual behavior. Although the qualification "not necessarily containing any features in common" can be a source of semantic confusion (see Kendler 1964, p. 219), Osgood's distinction directs attention to mediating processes that many investigators assume are of crucial importance to the discrimination mechanism underlying conceptual behavior. Experiments with simple concept-formation tasks with children of normal intelligence ranging from three to ten years of age (Kendler & Kendler 1962) suggest that the behavior of very young children is consistent with the principles of discrimination learning based on lower animals in that their responses are directly under the control of environmental stimuli. The behavior of older children, in contrast, is dependent upon responses, usually implicit, that intercede between the external stimulus and the overt response to provide stimulation that influences the course of overt behavior. As children grow older, the proportion of those who behave in a manner that reflects mediating processes increases in a stable fashion. The transition from behavior based on a direct connection between external stimulus and overt response to mediated behavior enables children to learn concepts more rapidly and utilize them under a wider range of conditions.

What are these mediational events underlying conceptual behavior and how can they be controlled? Instructing children to verbalize the relevant cues in a simple concept-learning task encourages mediational behavior. But whether these instructions to name provide the essential cue (e.g., the word "black") for conceptual behavior or instead direct attention to the essential cue (e.g., the stimulus black) or function in both ways simultaneously is not yet known.

Second signaling system. Closely related to the work of the American mediational theorists are the efforts of the Soviet psychologists who investigate what Pavlov described late in his career as the second signaling system. The first signaling system dealt with stimulation from the external world. But man, Pavlov noted, is a verbal organism that can produce words that can function as stimuli. Such stimuli, which constitute the second signal system, differ qualitatively from others because they can represent in an abstract manner the multitude of separate stimuli of the first signal system. According to Liublinskaya (1957) a word becomes a signal of the second signaling system only when it becomes a concept.

Natural development—Jean Piaget. There is practically no limit to the number of models of behavior that have been or can be used to investigate conceptual behavior. One of the distinguishing characteristics of both the S–R and the second signaling system orientations is the belief that classificatory behavior could, at least in large measure, be reduced to principles of behavior observed in conditioning. Other investigators of conceptual processes do not feel compelled to commit themselves to any psychological reductionism, while some actually oppose it. Jean Piaget has spent over forty years investigating the development of thought, or as he sometimes refers to it, "conceptual operations," in children. The fruit of his efforts, and those of his co-workers, is a theory that seeks to describe intellectual development from infancy to adolescence. The formulation is based on seminaturalistic observations of behavior of children in response to ingeniously designed problems and adroit questioning. In general the findings suggest to Piaget and his co-workers that intellectual development can be characterized as a series of stages in which each stage lays the foundation for the successor. The concepts Piaget deals with are quite different from those investigated by the S–R psychologists, who for the most part investigate nominal concepts, e.g., forms, shapes, vegetables. Piaget deals with concepts of relationships, such as those involved in logical operations, which have relevance for the way the child perceives and organizes his world. For example, in the first stage of intellectual development (from birth to two years of age) the child learns the concept of permanency of objects; a doll still exists after it is removed from the child's sight. In the second stage, which covers from two to seven years, the child can use language, and the internalization of actions becomes possible. Symbolic function appears, but there is an absence of both "reversible operations" and of the concepts of conservation of quantity, size, etc. (e.g., the child is apt to say that four checkers placed far apart are

more than four checkers placed close together). In the third stage (ages 7–11) the conceptual operations of the child include the ability to perform concrete operations that belong to the logic of classes and relations but do not take into account their combinatorial possibilities. The fourth stage (11–15), which leads to adult logic, is marked by the ability to reason by hypothesis. The logic is now concerned with propositions as well as objects. Movement from one stage to another is determined by a number of experiential and maturational variables, related to, but not exclusively determined by, age.

Piaget's impact on behavioristically oriented psychologists was initially not very great because of their strong methodological commitments to rigorous experimental procedures. In recent years, with an increase of interest in cognitive processes and the publication in English of a book (Flavell 1963) that attempts to both streamline and clarify Piaget's conceptions, a meeting of interests, if not of minds, has become more probable. Actually the interests of Piaget and the S–R psychologists supplement each other, the former being primarily concerned with changes that take place as children mature, while the latter are interested in discovering general principles of behavior that are applicable to all age groups [see DEVELOPMENTAL PSYCHOLOGY, *article on* A THEORY OF DEVELOPMENT].

Information and decision theories. There are psychologists whose orientations and conceptualizations are at odds with the neobehaviorists. Beginning with a disenchantment with the capability of a model of behavior based upon principles of conditioning and learning to represent the richness of true-life cognitive processes (e.g., Miller et al. 1960), these psychologists have turned to the recent developments of information theory, decision theory, and computers for both assistance and inspiration. Hovland (1952) offered a "communication analysis" of concept learning in which the information transmitted by specific instances of concepts could be measured. Such an analysis provided a frame of reference against which to evaluate the efficiency of the information-processing ability of human subjects. This communication-analysis orientation led to the planning of computer programs designed to simulate human behavior as well as experiments aimed at contributing information on which programs could be based. The task of simulating conceptual behavior has proved to be more difficult than initially anticipated (see Hunt 1962). Success will not be achieved by isolated demonstrations of the similarity between the behavior of computers and humans. What are needed, assuming that the primary interest is in the behavior of organisms and not the artificial intelligence of computers, are general principles that will generate programs capable of simulating human conceptual behavior exhibited in a wide variety of experimental studies. Hovland concluded that computers can function as potential aids in understanding concept formation by "sharpening our formulations concerning mental processes and phenomena," in encouraging "theories that have both descriptive and predictive power," and for coping with the complex problem of dealing with a multitude of interacting variables (Hovland 1960, pp. 691–692).

Bruner, Goodnow, and Austin (1956) approach the problem of concept attainment in a manner similar to the method of computer simulation of cognitive processes—but without the use of computers. Using the term "strategy"—borrowed from the mathematical theory of games and functioning like a computer program—they analyze the behavior of subjects categorizing a set of cards containing geometrical figures. In different experiments the subjects were instructed to form categories that were conjunctive, disjunctive, or relational. Interest was centered on the kind of strategies used to attain these concepts; a strategy being defined as "a pattern of decisions in the acquisition, retention, and utilization of information that serves to meet certain objectives . . ." (1956, p. 54). Their objectives were to maximize the information obtained from each instance, to reduce "cognitive strain," and to regulate the risk. The authors analyzed the results primarily in terms of four ideal strategies, and in terms of the advantages and disadvantages of each. Although the term "strategy" is rich in connotations, the questions of how they develop and influence behavior are far from clear. The value of the construct strategy would seem to depend on additional theoretical refinement and empirical data [see DECISION THEORY; INFORMATION THEORY].

In closing this article it may be appropriate to offer a brief summary of the crucial problems confronting investigators of concept formation. There is little doubt that the discrimination process is of primary importance in concept formation. The best method of teaching a concept would be to arrange the optimal conditions for discriminating between instances that belong to a concept and those that do not. Although such a principle would be generally accepted, there would be much disagreement about its specific interpretation. Whether optimal conditions for discrimination could be best ar-

ranged by reinforcing correct habits and not reinforcing incorrect ones, by encouraging suitable mediational responses, by training the organism to perceive crucial differences, by developing appropriate cognitive systems, or by some favorable combination of all of these factors—all these issues would be open to dispute. Basic to this disagreement are two related questions: Do these apparent differences always represent real differences? If so, does their resolution depend upon their being cast in precise mathematical language?

These theoretical issues are influencing specific experimental problems and shaping general research programs. A frank recognition among most investigators is that, to some extent, future theoretical progress must await advances in our understanding of the relationship between conceptual behavior and verbal and developmental processes as well as the design of new experimental techniques to tap the wide variety of concepts humans do learn and use.

HOWARD H. KENDLER AND
TRACY S. KENDLER

[*Directly related are the entries* REASONING AND LOGIC *and* THINKING.]

BIBLIOGRAPHY

BRUNER, JEROME S.; GOODNOW, J. J.; and AUSTIN, G. A. 1956 *A Study of Thinking.* New York: Wiley.

FLAVELL, JOHN H. 1963 *The Developmental Psychology of Jean Piaget.* Princeton, N.J.: Van Nostrand.

GRANT, DAVID A.; and CURRAN, JOAN F. 1952 Relative Difficulty of Number, Form, and Color Concepts of a Weigl-type Problem Using Unsystematic Number Cards. *Journal of Experimental Psychology* 43:408–413.

HEIDBREDER, EDNA 1948 The Attainment of Concepts: VI. Exploratory Experiments on Conceptualization at Perceptual Levels. *Journal of Psychology* 26:193–216.

HOVLAND, CARL I. 1952 A "Communication Analysis" of Concept Learning. *Psychological Review* 59:461–472.

HOVLAND, CARL I. 1960 Computer Simulation of Thinking. *American Psychologist* 15:687–693.

HULL, CLARK L. 1920 Quantitative Aspects of the Evolution of Concepts: An Experimental Study. *Psychological Monographs* 28, no. 1.

HUNT, EARL B. 1962 *Concept Learning: An Information Processing Problem.* New York: Wiley.

JAMES, WILLIAM (1892) 1948 *Psychology.* Cleveland, Ohio: World.

KENDLER, HOWARD H. 1964 The Concept of the Concept. Pages 211–236 in Symposium on the Psychology of Human Learning, University of Michigan, 1962, *Categories of Human Learning.* New York: Academic Press.

KENDLER, HOWARD H.; and KENDLER, TRACY S. 1962 Vertical and Horizontal Processes in Problem Solving. *Psychological Review* 69:1–16.

KENDLER, TRACY S. 1961 Concept Formation. *Annual Review of Psychology* 12:447–472.

LIUBLINSKAYA, A. A. 1957 The Development of Children's Speech and Thought. Pages 197–204 in Brian Simon (editor), *Psychology in the Soviet Union.* Stanford Univ. Press.

MILLER, GEORGE A.; GALANTER, E.; and PRIBRAM, K. H. 1960 *Plans and the Structure of Behavior.* New York: Holt.

OSGOOD, CHARLES E. (1953) 1959 *Method and Theory in Experimental Psychology.* New York: Oxford University Press.

RUSSELL, DAVID H. 1956 *Children's Thinking.* Boston: Ginn.

THOMPSON, GEORGE G. (1952) 1962 *Child Psychology.* Boston: Houghton Mifflin.

TITCHENER, EDWARD B. (1896) 1921 *An Outline of Psychology.* 3d ed. New York: Macmillan.

VINACKE, W. EDGAR 1952 *The Psychology of Thinking.* New York: McGraw-Hill.

WATSON, JOHN B. 1913 Psychology as a Behaviorist Views It. *Psychological Review* 20:158–177.

CONCEPTS AND INDICES
See SURVEY ANALYSIS.

CONCILIATION
See INTERNATIONAL CONFLICT RESOLUTION; LABOR RELATIONS; NEGOTIATION; RACE RELATIONS.

CONDILLAC, ÉTIENNE BONNOT DE

Étienne Bonnot de Condillac (1714–1780) was a philosopher of the Enlightenment, psychologist, economist, and educator; through his work he helped to bring about the dominance of the ideas of Locke and Newton over the philosophy of Descartes. Born at Grenoble into a well-to-do family with a legal background, he led the life of a man of letters from 1740 to 1758, enjoying the friendship or the acquaintance of France's leading philosophers and authors, among them Rousseau, Voltaire, Turgot, Diderot, d'Alembert, Morellet, Condorcet, Helvétius, Holbach, Grimm, Cabanis, Quesnay, Baudeau, Dupont de Nemours, Le Trosne, and Saint-Peravy. From 1758 to 1767 he served as tutor to the young grandson of Louis xv, the orphaned duke of Parma, for whom he prepared a series of works which reflect his educational theories; then he returned to Paris, only to retire in 1770 to a small property near Beaugency. There he remained, except for occasional visits to Paris, until his death, completing *La logique* ([1780] 1947–1951, vol. 2, pp. 369–416)—done at the request of the government of Poland for use in Palatinate schools—and other works. His reputation as a philosopher, together with his writings (renowned for precision, clarity, and simplicity), won him membership in the Royal Academy of Berlin in 1752 and in the French Academy in 1768.

Condillac's writings fall into three categories: the philosophical, the educational, and the economic. His systematization, exposition, and development of Locke's philosophy, together with his appreciation of Newton's empiricism, constitute four books, the most important of which, *Traité des sensations*, "no student of the history of philosophy can afford to neglect" ([1754] 1930, p. XV). In *Essai sur l'origine des connoissances humaines* ([1746] 1947–1951, vol. 1, pp. 1–118), he dealt with the origin of the faculties of mind and soul, the acquisition of knowledge, and the role of language in transforming sensation into reflection and in generating the highest operations found in thinking. In his *Traité des systèmes* ([1749] 1947–1951, vol. 1, pp. 119–217) he criticized in detail the doctrines of Descartes, Malebranche, Leibniz, and Spinoza, rejected recourse to fixed ideas and abstract principles, and urged reliance upon observation and experience. In his *Traité des sensations* Condillac made simple sensation the sole source of man's ideas and mental powers as well as of reflection and instinct or habit. He imagined a statue that has man's organic structure, whose sleeping senses are awakened one at a time, then in pairs, and finally all together. With one sense awakened, the statue can experience only the sensations of which that sense is capable; but although only touch can judge of externality, other senses can learn from touch how to judge external objects. The development of understanding, desires, passion, ideas, dreams, personality, and the faculties of the soul grows accordingly. Condillac explained the formation of general ideas, the genesis of attention, memory, judgment, reasoning, and various sensations as originating in the experience of pleasure or pain. To the *Traité des sensations* he appended a short *Dissertation sur la liberté* in which he showed that experience, cognition, and reflection lead man to apprehend the consequences of alternative courses of action and to choose the preferable course. In the *Traité des animaux* ([1755] 1947–1951, vol. 1, pp. 337–379) he criticized Buffon's animal psychology and his neglect of the role of language in the differentiation of man from animal.

Condillac's philosophy of education is represented mainly in his *Cours d'études* ([1775] 1947–1951, vol. 1, pp. 395–776; vol. 2, pp. 1–237), prepared for the duke of Parma but not published until 1775. In keeping with Condillac's earlier psychological theory that all knowledge arises from sensations, he supposed that the mind and its capacities develop best when a child's education proceeds by stages. The *Cours* consists of an introduction; sections dealing with grammar, the arts of writing, reasoning, and thinking; and extensive accounts of ancient and modern history, which also include treatments of philosophy, government, literature, and post-fifteenth-century scientific progress. Condillac also made use of *De l'étude de l'histoire*, a work prepared for him by his brother Gabriel Bonnot de Mably, a well-known author and expounder of collectivism. In *La logique* (1780) Condillac developed further his pedagogical views, explaining how "nature" teaches man to think and analyze, how ideas and faculties of the soul come into being, and how language develops and makes systematic analytical methods possible. In his incomplete and posthumous work, *La langue des calculs* ([1798] 1947–1951, vol. 2, pp. 417–529), having remarked the ambiguity and methodological inadequacy of verbal language as used in various sciences, Condillac noted the need in every science for exactitude similar to that found in mathematics and indicated how analogy might lead the student from the language and method of one science to the language and method of another.

Condillac's political economy is found almost entirely in *Le commerce et le gouvernement considérés relativement l'un à l'autre* ([1776] 1947–1951, vol. 2, pp. 239–367), only the second part of which conforms to the title. Therein he illustrated his opinion that economic science, while complicated and requiring (as does every science) a special language to convey its ideas, can be formulated in simple terms and yet serve analytical needs. He also showed how commerce can be constrained, as it was in France, and how, if it is free of all impediments, it fosters the growth and spread of wealth and prosperity.

Part 1 is concerned specifically with the dependence of occupations and classes upon one another, to the role of property and national and international markets, and to the beneficial organizing role of competition and the price system when not impaired by monopoly or other contrived barriers to commercial freedom—then price variation can keep the supply of each good in balance with the demand for it at "le vrai prix." Condillac's views reflect mainly those of Cantillon and some of those of Galiani, Verri, Turgot, and the physiocrats. He described value as depending upon utility and as varying inversely with supply, as does price; grain constitutes the best measure of value over time. While his comments on determinants of supply are scattered throughout his work, the gist of his argument seems to be that these determinants are reducible to terms of factor scarcity, cost of materials, and cost of labor (mainly subsistence).

Having rejected the nominalist theory of money and having shown how gold and silver became the dominant forms, he reasoned that their value depends upon their utility and scarcity, which, in turn, are conditioned by type of enterprise and access to credit, bills of exchange, and clearing arrangements. When unimpeded, gold or silver flows from places where its value is low to where its value is high, even as does grain, which, however, is less mobile; whence the supply of gold or grain comes into balance with demand, and "le vrai prix" tends to prevail. Condillac defended lending at interest, condemning its restriction, and noted that interest rates reflect the comparative abundance of borrowers and lenders and, in particular instances, degree of risk. He discussed the structure of demand and its determinants; the interaction of increasing wants and progress in the arts; the impact of changes in the composition of demand upon the employment of land and labor; population growth and concentration; class and occupational composition; and the adverse effects of some types of luxurious expenditure upon a nation's welfare and power. He did not appreciate the role of the division of labor, but he did identify the entrepreneurial role.

Condillac's psychological and epistemological theories exercised great influence in the eighteenth century and some influence in the early part of the nineteenth century. His views on pedagogy also seem to have exercised influence until the early nineteenth century; indeed, Joseph Neef's translation of *La logique* (see Condillac [1780] 1809) was used as a guide for education at Neef's school. Condillac's work on economics, however, exercised little influence. It appeared when Turgot and the physiocrats (with whose opinions his own were incorrectly identified) were in disfavor. Later, Condillac's economic ideas were overshadowed by the work of Adam Smith and J. B. Say—the latter dismissed Condillac's work as "ingenious trifling." Only in the later nineteenth century did the expounders of utility theory appreciate Condillac's merit as an economist.

JOSEPH J. SPENGLER

[*For the historical context of Condillac's work, see* ECONOMIC THOUGHT, *article on* PHYSIOCRATIC THOUGHT; LAISSEZ-FAIRE; *and the biographies of* CANTILLON; GALIANI; QUESNAY; TURGOT. *For discussion of the subsequent development of his ideas, see* DEMAND AND SUPPLY; UTILITY.]

WORKS BY CONDILLAC

(1746–1798) 1947–1951   *Oeuvres philosophique de Condillac.* Edited by Georges Le Roy. 3 vols. Corpus général des philosophes français, auteurs modernes, Vol. 33. Paris: Presses Universitaire de France.

(1754) 1930 *Condillac's Treatise on the Sensations.* Translated by Geraldine Carr. Los Angeles: Univ. of Southern California, School of Philosophy. → First published as *Traité des sensations.* The quotation in the text is from the translator's introduction.

(1780) 1809 *The Logic of Condillac.* Translated by Joseph Neef. Philadelphia: Privately published. → First published as *La logique, ou les premiers développements de l'art de penser.* The 1809 edition is a partial translation.

Lettres inédites à Gabriel Cramer. Edited by Georges Le Roy. Paris: Presses Universitaires de France, 1953.

Oeuvres de Condillac. 23 vols. Paris: Houel, 1798.

SUPPLEMENTARY BIBLIOGRAPHY

BAGUENAULT DE PUCHESSE, GUSTAVE 1910 *Condillac: Sa vie, sa philosophie, son influence.* Paris: Plon-Nourrit.

LEBEAU, AUGUSTE 1903 *Condillac économiste.* Paris: Guillaumin.

LE ROY, GEORGES 1937 *La psychologie de Condillac.* Paris: Boivin.

LE ROY, GEORGES 1947 Introduction à l'oeuvre philosophique de Condillac. Volume 1, pages vii–xxxv in Étienne Bonnet de Condillac, *Oeuvres philosophiques de Condillac.* Paris: Presses Universitaires de France.

MANN, JAMES L. 1903 *L'éducation selon la doctrine pédagogique de Condillac.* Grenoble (France): Allier.

MEOLI, UMBERTO 1961 *Il pensiero economico del Condillac.* Milan (Italy): Istituto Editoriale Cisalpino.

SALVUCCI, PASQUALE 1957 *Linguaggio e mondo umano in Condillac.* Urbino, Università Libera, Pubblicazioni, Serie di lettere e filosofia, Vol. 5. Urbino (Italy): Stabilimento Tipografico Edit. Urbinate.

CONDITIONING

See IMPRINTING; LEARNING; *and the biography of* PAVLOV.

CONDORCET

Marie Jean Antoine Nicolas Caritat, marquis de Condorcet (1743–1794), was a French mathematician, philosopher, and politician, the author of a philosophy of progress, of a program for educational reform, and one of the first to apply the calculus of probabilities to the analysis of voting and to social phenomena in general. He was among the most original thinkers of the revolutionary age.

Born at Ribemont in Picardy, Condorcet had a brilliant scholastic career with the Jesuits at Rheims and at the Collège de Navarre in Paris. He attracted the attention of such mathematicians as d'Alembert, Clairaut, Fontaine, and Lagrange, although his mathematical publications had no permanent importance. At the same time he attended the salon of Mlle. de Lespinasse, became a friend of Turgot's, and, with d'Alembert, made a pilgrimage in 1770 to Fernet to see Voltaire. He remained on excellent terms with Voltaire. He married Sophie de Grouchy in 1787; their salon at the Hôtel des Monnaies became one of the most brilliant in Paris.

Condorcet pursued three careers simultaneously and with varying success—an academic one, an administrative one, and a political one. As assistant to the secretary of the Académie des Sciences from 1769 on, he wrote a large number of *éloges* and recorded proceedings; he was elected a member of the Académie Française in 1782. As an administrator, he was appointed *inspecteur des monnaies* in 1774 and entrusted with various scientific missions by Turgot, then the minister of finance. Finally, in the context of politics, he drew up, in 1789, the petition of the nobility of Nantes (one of the *cahiers de doléances*). As a deputy to the Legislative Assembly, he was an active member of the Committee on Public Education. After being elected to the Convention, he was chosen to prepare the Girondist draft for the constitution, but although his proposals were almost always passed on the floor, they were very rarely put into effect. In 1793 he shared the fate of the Girondins: his arrest was ordered in July 1793, but he managed to remain hidden in Paris until March of the following year; then he was arrested, and he died under mysterious circumstances in the prison of Bourg la Reine.

An enlightened nobleman.   Prominent in scientific, political, and worldly circles, Condorcet is a typical example of the enlightened segment of the nobility that supported the Revolution. He was one of the first to be converted to the idea of republicanism. His ideology of social progress, his economic liberalism, and his faith in the omnipotence of rational knowledge allied him with the rising bourgeoisie rather than with his own class.

Condorcet might well be called the last of the Encyclopedists. He took an active part in the publication of the *Supplément à l'encyclopédie,* and more particularly in recasting its mathematical portion, the *Encyclopédie méthodique,* in 1784–1785. His curiosity was universal, and his most characteristic effort was his attempt to join and coordinate mathematics and philosophy and thus "satisfy two passions at once," as he wrote to Frederick the Great. He considered philosophy to include everything relating to the knowledge of man: "the metaphysical and social sciences, those that have man himself as their object . . ." (1847–1849, vol. 6, p. 494). His epistemological principles were borrowed from Condillac, but Condorcet differed greatly from Condillac in his conception of man's destiny and the fate of human societies.

Condorcet's best-known work, the *Sketch for a Historical Picture of the Progress of the Human Mind* (1795), was written while he was in hiding in Paris in 1793–1794. In it he presented a history of the errors and the advances of humanity, in order to predict, direct, and accelerate its forward march. In Condorcet's view, historical development coincides with the spread and triumph of the light of reason.

Condorcet believed that education, more than anything else, produced the triumph of the Enlightenment. He regarded inequality of education as one of the main sources of tyranny and advocated public education that would offer to all who might benefit from it the "aid hitherto confined to the children of the rich." Nonetheless, his interests remained those of the bourgeoisie and the enlightened nobility, and his educational recommendations consist, in effect, of two separate programs based on class distinctions; one is for the lower classes and is essentially technical; the other is for the ruling classes and develops the critical faculties of future citizens.

"Social mathematics." An essentially new feature of Condorcet's educational program was the importance he gave to science at every level of instruction, in particular to applied science. In addition, he believed that the social sciences should be taught in institutes and *lycées*. One of his central ideas is the importance to the progress of humanity of developing an "art of society" (*art social*).

In essence, Condorcet conceived of this *art social* as an "application of mathematics to the moral sciences," a discipline at once empirical and deductive, making use of genuine mathematical models of human phenomena. Condorcet was convinced that "the truths of the moral and political sciences can be as certain as those that make up the system of the physical sciences" (1785, p. 1). However, he believed that this certainty generally does not apply to causal relationships but to probable connections. The primary concern of what he called "social mathematics" is the application of the calculus of probability to the description and prediction of human phenomena.

This mathematics, as it emerges in Condorcet's published writings and unpublished manuscripts, comprises a statistical description of societies, an economic science (physiocratic in inspiration, but oriented toward the more recent idea of collective welfare), and a combinatory and probabilistic theory of intellectual operations.

This last theory appears in connection with the theory of voting, which is by far the best-developed part of social mathematics (1785). Voting was viewed by Condorcet as making manifest not so much a compromise among a number of conflicting forces as a *true* opinion. He assumed, therefore, that the question being voted on has a true solution that is independent of the wishes of those voting and that these voters express in their individual choices their greater or lesser understanding of that truth. The problem of structuring the process of voting is that of producing the maximum probability of a collective choice of the true solution; this may be done by varying the size of the voting body and the kind of majority required, as well as by considering the likelihood that each voter will make a correct decision. Condorcet was thus led to the construction of statistical models of voting bodies that permit the appraisal of the probability that collective decisions will correspond to the true answers to particular problems. This is, then, a real problem in operational research—how to establish voting procedures such that the chances of the emergence of correct decisions are maximized.

Since he conceived of voting as a collective search for the truth, Condorcet had to deal with the problem of defining precisely what a collective decision or judgment is. Given a series of dichotomous questions, the "yes" or "no" responses to them may be called "judgments"; how, then, may a single collective judgment or a coherent hierarchy of judgments be established on the basis of a set of individual judgments? Charles de Borda, 1733–1799, had shown that in the choice of the "best" among three candidates the one so designated by a simple majority might not be the same as the one arrived at when each is compared with the two others. Condorcet showed that such a weighing of preferences may reveal a circular order of preferences among the candidates— $A > B > C > A$—and, consequently, the possibility of an inconsistent collective choice even when individual choices are consistent. The mathematical apparatus available to Condorcet was too crude for him to obtain results that could be applied empirically, but he did open the way to a highly original and important social scientific conception.

Influence. The ideology of progress of Condorcet's *Esquisse* directly influenced Auguste Comte. His influence on the application of mathematics to human affairs can be found in such nineteenth-century works as those of Poisson and Cournot. The questions involved in the formation of a collective opinion have quite recently been taken up again by, among others, K. J. Arrow and G. Th. Guilbaud, although they have been reformulated in the light of welfare economics and the theory of games.

GILLES-GASTON GRANGER

[*For discussion of the subsequent development of Condorcet's ideas, see* Economic equilibrium; Game theory; Models, mathematical; *and the biographies of* Comte; Cournot; Poisson.]

WORKS BY CONDORCET

1785 *Essai sur l'application de l'analyse à la probabilité des décisions rendues à la pluralité des voix.* Paris: Imprimerie Royale.

(1795) 1955 *Sketch for a Historical Picture of the Progress of the Human Mind.* New York: Noonday. → First published as *Esquisse d'un tableau historique des progrès de l'esprit humain.*

1847–1849 *Oeuvres.* 12 vols. Edited by A. Condorcet O'Connor and M. F. Arago. Paris: Firmin-Didot.

WORKS ABOUT CONDORCET

Arago, François 1879 *Condorcet: A Biography.* Pages 180–235 in Smithsonian Institution, *Annual Report of the Board of Regents, 1878.* Washington: The Institution.

Cahen, Léon 1904 *Condorcet et la révolution française.* Paris: Alcan.

Granger, Gilles-Gaston 1956 *La mathématique sociale du marquis de Condorcet.* Paris: Presses Universitaires de France. → Contains a comprehensive bibliography of Condorcet's mathematical works.

Guilbaud, Georges Th. 1952 *La théorie de l'intérêt général. Économie appliquée* 4:501–584.

Todhunter, Isaac (1865) 1949 *A History of the Mathematical Theory of Probability From the Time of Pascal to That of Laplace.* New York: Chelsea.

CONFERENCES

A conference is a meeting of individuals called together to engage in discussion with the aim of accomplishing a limited task within a restricted period of time. Conferences are of special interest to the social sciences as a productive method of organizing research, including interdisciplinary research and research results; as a setting for transnational and international cooperation; as a formal means of validating social programs; as a method of inducing change in individuals; and as limited, observable group situations that are suitable for the study of group processes. The conference is also an area of action within which the interplay of theory, data gathering, and practice has been very productive. The increasingly widespread adoption of the conference form is creating a demand for a new set of professionals who are skilled in conference management.

Characteristics

The conference form may be modified in various ways. A conference may bring together three specialists for consultation. It may bring together all the personnel who have a permanent working relationship to one another in an ongoing organization, such as a psychiatric clinic, a government bureau, or an industry. It may bring together, periodically, individuals whose diverse professional interests overlap through their concern with a common problem. In its most expanded version, it may bring together thousands of delegates and observers, as, for example, in a White House conference or an international gathering of experts, to consider a wide range of problems in a very large field of interest. In its core form, however, a conference is a gathering that is small enough so that its members, meeting in one room, can take part in open-ended discussion.

Interchange at a conference is intended to be less formally structured than are the deliberations of a parliamentary body. At a very large conference that discharges such multiple functions as the discussion of substantive matters, the establishment of a new climate of opinion, the orientation of its members to a new viewpoint, the validation of a proposed program, or the preparation of a set of resolutions and recommendations, several types of sessions are held. There are plenary sessions, in which the entire body participates and formal parliamentary procedures are followed. There are also smaller sessions, designated as discussion groups, working groups, panels, "buzz" sessions, and so on, the organization of which is intended to encourage a more informal and active interchange among the participants. Ideally, the arrangement of a small conference is such that all its members sit facing one another around a table, and their interchange is mediated but not dominated by a chairman.

Conferences in their many different forms draw on the pattern that is characteristic of group deliberations for special or periodic purposes at all levels of social complexity. In its more familiar modern versions, however, the conference is a Euro–American invention, the development of which has been vastly accelerated both by the need for and by the possibilities of rapid communication in the twentieth century. Although large conferences, governmental and nongovernmental, rely particularly heavily on traditional western European parliamentary procedures, the format and style of the modern conference have other derivations as well. One important source is the format of the scientific meeting, as exemplified by the meetings of the Royal Society of London, at which substantive matters are presented to a group of peers; another is the format of the ecclesiastical councils, called together to issue validating pronouncements on matters of moment. Modern conference form and style also have been influenced by the long tradition of intellectual controversy within eastern European Judaism; by the procedures through which humble people, meeting together, have attempted to arrive at consensus; and by the procedures of the Quaker business meeting, with its emphasis on a search for "the sense of the meeting." Residues of these and other historical forms still may be discerned in contemporary conference organization.

A conference is formal in certain well-defined respects. It must have a scheduled beginning and end, identifiable sessions, and a designated membership. Its subject matter is specified. The conference plan must include, as a final step, a projected outcome, whether this takes the form of a report, a set of recommendations or resolutions, a pronouncement about some program, or the formulation of new insights.

Modern conference methods have developed in response to the need for forms that will permit a group to transcend, through face-to-face discussion, various barriers to good communication. Today, communication may be greatly hindered by the divisions that result from bureaucratic arrangements or the compartmentalization of specialized subject matter. It may be reduced to insignificance by difficulties arising from differences in nationality, status, race, caste, class, or ideology. Especially in new fields, where the quantity of information and the lag in publication make it difficult for research workers and practitioners to keep abreast of developments, the conference provides means for the rapid dissemination of new knowledge. But the conference group atmosphere also may be used to thaw stereotyped antagonisms, an aim that may conflict with other conference goals.

The small substantive conference, specifically, has made one unique contribution to intradisciplinary, interdisciplinary, domestic, and transnational communication. It is simultaneity of participation. In place of the older linear system of publication, written rejoinder, and written rebuttal, there is immediacy of challenge, correction, and redefinition in the actual presence of all the participants to a discussion. Moreover, everyone present, whether or not he speaks, takes part in the conference process. Intrinsic to this type of conference is a form of communication that is not one-to-one but many-to-many, visible, audible, and sensible to all those sitting around a table. Each member, not only as he speaks but also as he remains silent or moves restlessly, is part of what is happening. And in their subsequent work, individual members draw on the whole, not merely on the conclusions or even the transcribed proceedings. Participation in a small substantive conference resembles the apprenticeship learning experience gained by work in a laboratory under a great experimentalist or in the atelier of a great painter. In its purest form, such a conference is self-contained; its members are not required, for example, to meet the demands made on committees with definite purposes to serve. At its best, it is the source of new ideas that otherwise would have developed only much later or, sometimes, not at all.

The conference as a research procedure

In the 1930s, the interdisciplinary conference became part of the newer paraphernalia of research procedures in the social sciences and the life sciences. Its precursor, the interdisciplinary team in the child development clinic, was designed to coordinate action among cooperating disciplines, i.e., medicine, psychiatry, psychology, and social work. Similarly, the interdisciplinary conference was deliberately designed to introduce cross-disciplinary correctives into the thinking of compartmentalized and isolated disciplines. The Josiah Macy, Jr. Foundation conferences, beginning in 1936 (Josiah Macy, Jr. Foundation 1955), are an outstanding example of this development.

More recently, since the mid-1940s, a related type of conference, more focused and more immediately utilitarian in its aims, has become an integral part of research procedures. Conferences of this kind may be convened to generate research plans, elaborate upon earlier plans, evaluate progress, introduce new ideas into an ongoing research program, or present and evaluate research results. With various modifications, they are modeled on the "Macy conference" style. That is, they are characterized by free, informal interchange and by rapid cross communication from many to many; eliminating the transitions and explanatory steps essential to written communication, they can make use of shortcuts possible only in face-to-face situations. Conferences so organized will inevitably occupy an increasingly large segment of the time of applied social scientists as they deal with problems that require a multidisciplinary approach.

In an academic seminar in which the primary emphasis is on intellectual interchange or teaching, the material is to a certain extent incidental (Tannenbaum 1965). In contrast, the research conference is substantively concerned with the data of a research project. Shared data may be used, much as psychiatrists use case materials, as the medium of communication to carry preliminary and as yet unclarified and sometimes ambiguous formulations. Today, a large and complex research program may include within a common framework a cluster of small research groups whose membership is interlocking. Here the research conference, drawing on the work of all the groups, speeds up the development of fruitful hypotheses (Mead & Métraux 1953). The research conference also has been used to prepare materials for final publication through a series of preliminary conference sessions with various groups of specialists (Hoagland & Burhoe 1961; Luszki 1958; Mandelbaum et al. 1963; Roe & Simpson 1958). This format combines the symposium and the conference method. In still another format, prepared papers, distributed in advance to the participants, are designed primarily as a stimulant to informal interchange within a multidisciplinary group. The published symposia of the Conference on Science, Philosophy and Religion, which pioneered in the development of this conference style, only formally reflect the interchange of the discussions (Conference on Science, Philosophy and Religion . . . 1941–1943; subsequent volumes in this series).

Initiating social change

Conferences have become a recognized method of launching a new program, validating a new approach, or establishing a climate of opinion within which action, often a new type of action, can be taken. Most new programs undertaken in the United States, the United Kingdom, or internationally are inaugurated by conferences of representative and significant people who set the stamp of approval on a program's aims and procedures. A conference of this kind is essentially a sanctioning device. Subsequently, other conferences may be convened to reaffirm a program's aims or to redirect it toward new goals. The White House conferences on children, held decennially, and conferences on world mental health (International Preparatory Commission . . . 1948; World Federation for Mental Health 1961) are examples of the validating and renewal types of conference. The sanctioning and stimulating roles of the conference may be amplified by setting topics several years in advance and, by this means, focusing research attention on a coordinated set of problems. Conferences of this general type may also be specifically designed to prevent the premature organization of an action program.

Methods derived from group dynamics and group psychotherapy have been used in conference settings; here individuals may undergo a personality transformation somewhat analogous to a personal conversion. This method may be very effective in reorienting members of an ongoing organization when, for example, a bureaucratic institution is being transformed from an authoritarian to a democratic, or from a centralized to a decentralized, structure (Lewin 1935–1946; Lippitt 1949; Bradford et al. 1964).

The conference as the focus of research. Since the 1920s there has been a steady growth of interest in the scientific study of small groups, group processes, the management of group situations, and the design of experimental groups for research purposes. This field, as it has developed, represents a fusion, on the one hand, of the procedures of social work, psychotherapy, progressive education, and industrial relations, and, on the other hand, of allied interests within social psychology, sociology, and anthropology. Under the leadership of Elton Mayo, important work originated at the Harvard Graduate School of Business Administration. In the same period, Moreno developed methods for the sociometric analysis of group structure and for the simulation of group situations through sociodrama. Under the leadership of Kurt Lewin research was carried out on group dynamics and group decision, and techniques were developed for experimental studies of group structure and innovation (Bavelas 1951; U.S. Office of Naval Research 1951; Gyr 1951). Others concentrated on problems of group structure and interaction. One outcome of this research has been the expansion of interest in group processes in the policy sciences and among those concerned with public opinion formation.

Parallel work on small groups, carried out in England, has been strongly influenced by an interest in the therapeutic situation. Research there has centered particularly in the group associated with the Tavistock Clinic and the Tavistock Institute of Human Relations.

The conference as a social unit has provided a ready-made focus of attention for research workers concerned with problems of group process. The fact that investigations, whether intradisciplinary or interdisciplinary, have tended to be carried on by groups of research workers has had important consequences for the development of conference procedures. Social scientists interested in the study of groups formed a number of small societies, among them the Society for the Psychological Study of Social Issues, the Society for Applied Anthropology, and the American Sociometric Association. As meetings of these societies made extensive use of the conference form, the special sophistication of those actively engaged in research on groups was fed back into ongoing thinking about conferences. Modern recording techniques, such as stenotyping and tape recording, which facilitated the study of conferences, gradually became standard equipment, and verbatim transcripts became available not only for conference analysis but also for future conference planning. A further step was taken when the conferences that were convened to plan, coordinate, or evaluate the research on small groups also were subjected to the scrutiny of those whose observational and experimental work was concentrated on problems of group interaction.

Throughout its development, the scientific study of group processes has been characterized by the most intense, continuous interplay of theory, data gathering, and practice. The methodology of this interplay is intrinsic to theories of the relevance of research to social action that developed in the late 1930s and early 1940s. Equally important, however, has been the double position of those involved in investigations, both as research workers studying group processes and as participants in situations on which such research was being carried out. [*See* Groups; Interaction.]

In the 1950s, a further development took place as new disciplines concerned with the analysis of nonverbal behavior entered the field. Although the published output of those engaged in research in kinesics, proxemics, paralinguistics, and metalinguistics is not as yet large (Indiana University . . . 1964), these several new approaches hold great promise for a further clarification of the communication process as it evolves in the setting of a conference. [*See* Kinesics.] In the same period, a growing interest in ethology among students of human social behavior also has stimulated attention to nonverbal elements in communication. In addition, the development of photographic techniques for the visual recording of interaction promises to add still another dimension to the analysis of the communication process.

In the late 1940s several large-scale studies of the conference form were inaugurated. Some of these failed in their purpose, as no adequate solution had then been found for the problem of the relationship between the detached observer of a conference and its deeply involved, committed membership. Since the conference form had become part of the regular procedures of organizations having a professional interest in the conference process, it seemed reasonable to build research plans around their meetings. However, when these conferences have been used for purposes of impartial objective research, the professional participants sometimes have rebelled against serving, simultaneously, as the subjects of observation. Their objections, which have seriously impeded research that might otherwise have been productive, have stemmed from the failure—perhaps on both sides—to grasp one essential characteristic of every successful conference, namely, the complete temporary commitment of every participant to the shared purposes of the group as a whole. In a situation in which the observer can share in this commitment to content and can channel his observations in such a way that they facilitate the work of the conference, his insights are welcomed. In contrast, where his role is so defined that he must stand aside, taking notes that will be useful only in some context external to the purposes of the conference, his very presence is resented. This requirement of involvement has a corollary. A natural history method of recording and the use of artifacts intrinsic to the conference procedure, such as preconference letters, drafts of formulations prepared within the conference, and the conference transcript, are appropriate for conference research, but instruments developed for other purposes, for example, the questionnaires and self-evaluation forms used in measuring changes of attitude, are often completely inappropriate. One example of a conference that successfully combined the application of research with self-observation was the Eastbourne conference, which had the assigned task of organizing international conference procedures (Capes 1960).

Conference management as a profession. Conference management is developing as a profession whose major focus may be problems of organization, the guidance of the group process, transcription, editing and publication, or some combination of these. Today, large organizations and institutions are likely to employ specialists in all these branches of conference management.

The demand for specialists is related to, and has expanded with, the development of conference technology, particularly that aspect of it concerned with interpretation (Glen 1954). While conference management skills must still be acquired through informal apprenticeship learning, a more identifiable career specialization is likely to emerge as the number of international conferences, for which very special skills are required, continues to increase. Concurrently, it may be expected that high-level skills in conference communication, earlier the subject of intense research, will be more widely diffused among social scientists and the scientific community as a whole.

Margaret Mead

[*Other relevant material may be found in* Communication; Diffusion, *article on* interpersonal influence; Groups; Interaction; Kinesics; Science, *article on* scientific communication.]

BIBLIOGRAPHY

ARGYRIS, CHRIS; and TAYLOR, GRAHAM 1951 The Member-centered Conference as a Research Method. II. *Human Organization* 10:22–27.

BALES, ROBERT F. 1950 *Interaction Process Analysis: A Method for the Study of Small Groups.* Cambridge, Mass.: Addison-Wesley.

BALES, ROBERT F. 1954 In Conference. *Harvard Business Review* 32:44–50.

BAVELAS, ALEX 1951 Communication Patterns in Task-oriented Groups. *Journal of the Acoustical Society of America* 22:725–730.

BAVELAS, ALEX 1959 Group Size, Interaction, and Structural Environment. Pages 133–179 in Conference on Group Processes, Fourth, *Group Processes: Transactions.* Edited by Bertram Schaffner. New York: Macy Foundation.

BEAL, GEORGE M.; BOHLEN, JOE M.; and RAUDABAUGH, J. NEIL 1962 *Leadership and Dynamic Group Action.* Ames: Iowa State Univ. Press.

BRADFORD, LELAND P.; GIBB, JACK R.; and BENNE, KENNETH D. (editors) 1964 *T-group Theory and Laboratory Method: Innovation in Re-education.* New York: Wiley.

CAPES, MARY (editor) 1960 *Communication or Conflict: Conferences; Their Nature, Dynamics, and Planning.* New York: Association Press.

CARTWRIGHT, DORWIN C. 1953 The Strategy of Research on International Conferences. *International Social Science Bulletin* 5:278–286.

COHEN, JOHN 1952 Some Working Hypotheses and Provisional Conclusions in the Study of Committees and Conferences. *Occupational Psychology* (London) 26:70–77.

COLLINS, BARRY E.; and GUETZKOW, HAROLD 1964 *A Social Psychology of Group Processes for Decision-making.* New York: Wiley.

CONFERENCE ON GROUP PROCESSES 1955–1960 *Group Processes: Transactions* [of the First–Fifth Conferences]. Edited by Bertram Schaffner. New York: Macy Foundation.

CONFERENCE ON SCIENCE, PHILOSOPHY AND RELIGION IN THEIR RELATION TO THE DEMOCRATIC WAY OF LIFE 1941–1943 *Science, Philosophy and Religion.* 3 vols. New York: The Conference. → Titles of the fourth, and subsequent, symposia vary.

DENNETT, RAYMOND; and JOHNSON, JOSEPH E. (editors) 1951 *Negotiating With the Russians.* Boston: World Peace Foundation.

FOX, WILLIAM M. 1957 Group Reaction to Two Types of Conference Leadership. *Human Relations* 10:279–289.

GLEN, EDMUND S. 1954 Semantic Difficulties in International Communication. *ETC* 11:163–180.

GYR, JOHN 1951 Analysis of Committee Member Behavior in Four Cultures. *Human Relations* 4:193–202.

HOAGLAND, HUDSON; and BURHOE, RALPH W. (editors) (1961) 1962 *Evolution and Man's Progress.* New York: Columbia Univ. Press. → First published in Volume 90 of *Dædalus.*

INDIANA UNIVERSITY, CONFERENCE ON PARALINGUISTICS AND KINESICS, BLOOMINGTON, *1962* 1964 *Approaches to Semiotics: Cultural Anthropology, Education, Linguistics, Psychiatry, Psychology.* Edited by Thomas A. Sebeok et al. Janua Linguarum, Series Maior, No. 15. The Hague: Mouton.

INTERNATIONAL PREPARATORY COMMISSION FOR THE INTERNATIONAL CONGRESS ON MENTAL HEALTH 1948 *Mental Health and World Citizenship: A Statement Prepared for the International Congress on Mental Health, London, 1948.* New York: Distributed by the National Committee for Mental Hygiene, Division of World Affairs.

JOSIAH MACY, JR. FOUNDATION, NEW YORK 1955 *The Josiah Macy, Jr. Foundation, 1930–1955: A Review of Activities.* New York: The Foundation.

KRAPF, E. E. 1952 Thoughts on the Specific Functions of Our International Congresses and Annual Meetings. World Federation for Mental Health, *Bulletin* 4:57–59.

KRIESBERG, MARTIN; and GUETZKOW, HAROLD 1950 The Use of Conferences in the Administrative Process. *Public Administration Review* 10:93–98.

LEWIN, KURT (1935–1946) 1948 *Resolving Social Conflicts: Selected Papers on Group Dynamics.* New York: Harper.

LINE, WILLIAM 1953 A Functional Approach to the Study of International Conferences. *International Social Science Bulletin* 5:300–311.

LIPPITT, RONALD 1949 *Training in Community Relations: A Research Exploration Toward New Group Skills.* New York: Harper.

LUSZKI, MARGARET B. 1958 *Interdisciplinary Team Research: Methods and Problems.* New York Univ. Press.

MANDELBAUM, DAVID G.; LASKER, GABRIEL W.; and ALBERT, ETHEL M. (editors) 1963 *The Teaching of Anthropology.* American Anthropological Association, Memoir No. 94. Berkeley: Univ. of California Press.

MARQUIS, D. G.; GUETZKOW, HAROLD; and HEYNS, R. W. 1951 A Social Psychological Study of the Decision-making Conference. Pages 55–67 in U.S. Office of Naval Research, *Groups, Leadership, and Men: Research in Human Relations.* Pittsburgh: Carnegie Press.

MEAD, MARGARET 1958 A Meta Conference: Eastbourne, 1956. *ETC* 15:148–151.

MEAD, MARGARET 1964 *Continuities in Cultural Evolution.* New Haven: Yale Univ. Press.

MEAD, MARGARET; and MÉTRAUX, RHODA (editors) 1953 *The Study of Culture at a Distance.* Univ. of Chicago Press.

MYRDAL, GUNNAR 1952 Psychological Impediments to Effective International Cooperation. *Journal of Social Issues* Supplement Series, No. 6.

ROE, ANNE; and SIMPSON, GEORGE G. (editors) 1958 *Behavior and Evolution.* New Haven: Yale Univ. Press.

RUESCH, JURGEN; and BATESON, GREGORY 1951 *Communication, the Social Matrix of Psychiatry.* New York: Norton.

SCELLE, GEORGES 1953 The Evolution of International Conferences. *International Social Science Bulletin* 5:241–257.

SHARP, WALTER R. 1953 A Check List of Subjects for Systematic Study of International Conferences. *International Social Science Bulletin* 5:311–339.

Suggestions on the Organizing of International Conferences. 1952 Council for International Organizations for Medical Sciences, *Bulletin* 3, nos. 3–4.

TANNENBAUM, FRANK (editor) 1965 *A Community of Scholars: The University Seminars at Columbia.* New York: Praeger.

TANNER, JAMES M.; and INHELDER, BARBEL (editors) 1956–1960 *Discussions on Child Development: A Consideration of the Biological, Psychological and Cultural Approaches to the Understanding of Human Development and Behaviour.* New York: International

Universities Press. → Consists of the proceedings of the first four meetings of the World Health Organization Study Group on the Psychobiological Development of the Child, held in 1953–1956.

UNITED NATIONS EDUCATIONAL, SCIENTIFIC AND CULTURAL ORGANIZATION 1952 *Meeting of Experts on the Technique of International Conferences, UNESCO House, 22–24 October, 1951: Final Report.* UNESCO/SS/5. Paris: UNESCO.

U.S. OFFICE OF NAVAL RESEARCH 1951 *Groups, Leadership and Men: Research in Human Relations.* Edited by Harold Guetzkow. Pittsburgh: Carnegie Press.

WHITMAN, ROY M. 1956 The Rating and Group Dynamics of the Psychiatric Staff Conference. *Psychiatry* 19: 333–340.

WORLD FEDERATION FOR MENTAL HEALTH 1961 *Mental Health in International Perspective: A Review Made in 1961 by an International and Interprofessional Study Group.* New York: The Federation.

CONFIDENCE INTERVALS AND REGIONS
See under ESTIMATION.

CONFLICT

I. PSYCHOLOGICAL ASPECTS   Edward J. Murray
II. POLITICAL ASPECTS   Robert C. North
III. SOCIAL ASPECTS   Lewis A. Coser
IV. ANTHROPOLOGICAL ASPECTS   Laura Nader

I
PSYCHOLOGICAL ASPECTS

Conflict refers to a situation in which a person is motivated to engage in two or more mutually exclusive activities. In a monogamous society a man cannot marry two women at the same time, no matter how attractive they are to him. A businessman may be faced with the choice of hiring a lazy relative or an efficient stranger for an important position. The soldier in combat may be torn between the desire to run away and the fear of losing face with his comrades. Incompatible responses cannot occur simultaneously.

Conflict may occur on many different levels. On the overt behavioral level, a tribesman may be motivated both to approach and to avoid the taboo object. On the verbal level, a person may want to speak the truth but fear to offend. On the symbolic level, ideas may clash and produce cognitive dissonance. On the emotional level, the visceral responses involved in fear and digestion are incompatible. Motives are important in conflict, and for this reason the term motivational conflict is often used. However, there is nothing basically incompatible about motives as such. Sigmund Freud suggested that opposite instincts exist side by side in the unconscious, with no disharmony. Conflict occurs only when the overt, verbal, symbolic, or emotional responses required to fulfill one motive are incompatible with those required to fulfill another.

Social existence involves a great many conflicts. The prediction and explanation of social behavior require more than knowing that a person has learned to make a certain response at a given time and place when properly motivated. The situation frequently involves other motives that produce incompatible response tendencies. The individual in society, subject to the pressures of the many groups to which he belongs and the demands of the many roles he must play, often experiences personal conflict. The entire process of the socialization of the child has been viewed as a conflict between the individual and society. Freud has gone so far as to say that civilization itself is a product of the clash between the incompatible demands of biological urges and social conformity.

The concept of conflict is particularly significant in the areas of personal adjustment and mental disorder. Freud maintained that no neurosis exists without a conflict. Clinical studies suggest that psychological conflicts are of central importance not only in neuroses but also in psychosomatic disease, sexual deviation, and functional psychosis. Furthermore, psychological conflicts appear to contribute to various forms of social pathology, such as marital, educational, and vocational failure; delinquency, crime, and prostitution; and alcoholism and drug addiction. Laboratory animals with experimentally induced conflicts may exhibit such maladaptive behavior as response fixation, tantrums, and catatoniclike posturing. They may also develop gastrointestinal ulcers, acquire a taste for alcoholic beverages, or become viciously aggressive.

The psychoanalytic contribution. The first important use of the concept of psychological conflict was by Joseph Breuer and Sigmund Freud in their work on hysterical neuroses (see Freud 1893–1895). These authors explained hysterical symptoms as the consequence of a conflict between incompatible ideas. For example, Anna O. was a sensitive young girl much devoted to tending her dying father. Her ideas of devotion to her father were shaken by the eruption of a wish for him to die quickly and end his suffering. The disturbing thoughts were repressed, and a series of crippling hysterical symptoms developed.

In his subsequent development of psychoanalytic theory, Freud placed a great deal of emphasis on a conflict between sexual and self-preservative instincts. Later, he phrased this as a conflict between libidinal wishes and ego anxiety. In order for a neurosis to develop, however, the libidinal wish must be repressed by anxiety. The unconscious libidinal urge then seeks an indirect outlet through such things as dreams, slips of the tongue, or neurotic symptoms. A neurotic symptom is a compromise between the repressed libidinal wish and the inhibiting anxiety. Personality development may be viewed as a series of conflict resolutions. The most adaptive method of conflict resolution is sublimation, by which the libidinal urge is discharged in socially useful activities, such as science, art, and work.

The relationship between internal and external sources of conflict is of some theoretical significance. While Freud speaks of the clash between the individual and society, he also says that a neurotic conflict must involve an internal source of inhibition. Thus, a prisoner who is denied a sexual outlet may be frustrated and rebellious but not neurotic. On the other hand, a person whose own guilt feelings deny him a sexual outlet may indeed become neurotic. The guilt feelings derive from society, of course, but have become internalized. It might be best to reserve the term "frustration" for the external blocking of a motive and the term "conflict" for internal blocking. In both cases, the blocking can increase *tension* in the individual.

Much of the controversy in psychoanalytic theory has centered on the motives that enter into neurotic conflict. Alfred Adler suggested as critical in neurosis the will to power and Carl Jung the inability to achieve self-realization. Freud, at a later stage, added an aggressive motive in the form of the death instinct. Many contemporary psychoanalysts emphasize conflicts involving achievement, affiliation, and dependency motives. Nevertheless, the basic Freudian idea of a conflict between some motivated response and anxiety as crucial in neurosis has gained widespread acceptance.

The psychoanalytic ego theorists have challenged the Freudian concept of personality developments resulting primarily from conflict resolution. On the basis of direct observation of children, they have concluded that whole areas of development are conflict-free, particularly those that are ego functions, such as language, physical mastery, and curiosity. Thus, social interests in science, art, and work may be independent of libidinal development. Civilization may be more than a product of conflict.

Finally, the culturally oriented psychoanalytic theorists, such as Karen Horney, Erich Fromm, and Harry Stack Sullivan, have seriously challenged the Freudian concept of conflict between biological instincts and socially derived inhibitions. Karen Horney, for example, suggests that the developing personality is concerned only with security. In a threatening social environment, certain coping mechanisms become exaggerated and may come into conflict. For example, the neurotic person may vacillate between hostility and helplessness. Thus, the conflict is between coping mechanisms, and both arms of the conflict are motivated by insecurity deriving from society.

Lewin's taxonomy of conflict.   Kurt Lewin made a comprehensive analysis of personality in terms of field theory (see Lewin 1926–1933). The behavior of the individual was seen as determined by a field of psychological forces. These forces were dependent, in part, on the positive and negative valences attached to various goals in the situation. Conflict was thought to arise when the forces relevant to two or more goals were of equal strength [*see* FIELD THEORY *and the biography of* LEWIN].

Lewin distinguished between three types of conflict: (1) where a person is between two goals of positive valence; (2) where a person faces a goal with both positive and negative valence; and (3) where a person is between two goals of negative valence. These types of conflict have become known as approach–approach, approach–avoidance, and avoidance–avoidance, respectively. A fourth type has been added, double approach–avoidance conflict.

The approach–approach type of conflict is perhaps the simplest. For example, a child may be required to choose between two equally attractive desserts, a situation reminiscent of the donkey who starved to death when placed equidistant between two bales of hay. In fact, however, experimental studies with both human and animal subjects show that this type of conflict is resolved easily and rapidly. The equilibrium is not stable so that any slight movement toward one of the positive goals results in increasing the positive valence of that goal and in rapidly increasing momentum toward that goal.

The approach–avoidance type of conflict, on the other hand, is quite stable. The approach and avoidance tendencies are pitted against one another so that an approach movement results in an increase in the negative valence and in a compensatory avoidance movement, and vice versa. The experimental studies show that approach–avoidance conflict results in a great deal of vacillating behavior. Lewin gives the example of a child required to perform some unpleasant task in order to get a reward. In addition to vacillation, the child may deal with the situation by minimal task performance, abandoning the reward, or attempting some detour.

The avoidance–avoidance type of conflict can be illustrated by the child who is required to perform an unpleasant task under threat of punishment. The child's first tendency is to avoid both alternatives and leave the situation. However, if the child is forced to remain in the situation, Lewin suggests he may withdraw into himself or engage in an emotional outburst. The experimental studies show that avoidance–avoidance conflicts are resolved very slowly and with great difficulty. Frequently, the subject simply freezes or blocks or makes a response that keeps him equidistant from both alternatives.

The double approach–avoidance type of conflict is seen in the situation in which there are two goals with approach and avoidance tendencies toward each. This type of conflict also seems to produce a great deal of blocking. Double approach–avoidance conflict is an important paradigm when one or more of the components are hidden or unconscious. For example, a man deciding between two attractive women appears to be in an easily resolved approach–approach conflict. Instead, he may be unable to make up his mind because he unconsciously fears both women. Thus, he is really in a double approach–avoidance conflict.

Miller's approach–avoidance model.   The most influential contemporary theory of conflict is that proposed by Neal E. Miller. Miller concentrated on approach–avoidance conflict on the assumption that this type was of most significance in psychopathology and social behavior. Miller's strategy was to establish a theoretical model of conflict on the basis of carefully controlled laboratory experiments with animal subjects and then to extend these principles to complex human behavior.

The model of conflict developed by Miller is a special application of more general principles of learning, specifically the stimulus–response learning theory of Clark Hull. Approach and avoidance tendencies are conceived of as motivated responses whose strength is a function of the stimulus situation and its relation to past learning, the motivation of the subject, the incentive value of the goal, and the number of times the response in question has been reinforced. In a situation in which there are two incompatible responses conflicting with each other, the stronger response will tend to occur.

Miller's analysis of conflict also rests on another important learning principle—the goal gradient. A white rat in a simple runway will tend to run faster the closer he gets to the end containing a goal object, such as food. In other words, the ap-

proach tendency gets stronger the nearer the animal is to the positive goal. It has also been shown that the further away an animal gets from a noxious stimulus, such as an electric shock, the slower he runs. Therefore, there appears to be a gradient with respect to the tendency to avoid a negative goal. Miller also made the crucial observation that the avoidance tendency fell off more rapidly with distance from the goal than did the approach tendency. Chiefly on the basis of the observation that the avoidance gradient is steeper than the approach gradient, Miller constructed his theory of conflict.

Miller's model is shown graphically in Figure 1. The distance from a goal that is both desired and feared is shown on the abscissa while the strength of the tendency either to approach or to avoid is shown on the ordinate. Both gradients fall off in response strength as distance from the goal increases, but the avoidance tendency drops off more rapidly. The approach–avoidance gradients are represented most simply as straight lines, but Miller emphasizes that curves of many shapes could satisfy the requirements of the theory.

The particular situation shown in Figure 1 involves an intersection of the approach and avoidance gradients. The intersection is called the conflict point. To the right of the conflict point the net difference between the strengths of the response tendencies is in favor of approach, while to the left of the conflict point avoidance predominates. Therefore, a subject at some distance from a desired and feared goal should approach part way until the conflict point and then stop. A subject finding himself at the goal should retreat to the conflict point and stop.

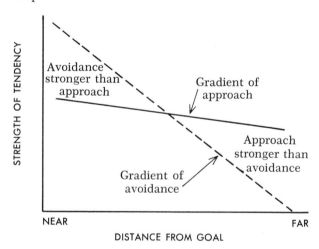

Figure 1 — A simple approach–avoidance conflict

Source: Neal E. Miller—"Experimental Studies of Conflict" in PERSONALITY AND THE BEHAVIOR DISORDERS, edited by J. McV. Hunt, Copyright 1944 The Ronald Press Company, New York.

The above basic prediction about conflict behavior has been confirmed in numerous laboratory experiments with animal and human subjects. In a classic series of experiments, the response tendency was measured by the strength with which a white rat would pull against a temporary restraint either to get to a food goal or to get away from an electric shock in a straight alley runway. The strength-of-pull measure reflected the greater steepness of the avoidance gradient. Other animals trained both to approach and to avoid the goal were observed to go part way down the alley and stop. Actually, they did not stop abruptly at the conflict point but advanced and retreated alternately in a highly tentative manner. This behavior—reminiscent of the vacillation of human subjects in an approach–avoidance situation—has been called conflict oscillation. It has been suggested that conflict itself is aversive and increases tension level above and beyond a summation of the usual motives involved.

The real power of the theory is, however, that varying outcomes of conflict situations can be predicted on the basis of knowledge about the factors assumed to influence the strength of the competing response tendencies and their effect on approach and avoidance gradients. The evidence shows that gradients are influenced by motivation as well as the number and size of reinforcements. Figure 2 shows the effects of increasing the strength of the approach tendency. As the approach tendency is increased the entire gradient is raised and the intersection point with the avoidance gradient is much closer to the goal. Therefore, a subject should approach much closer to the goal but at the same time would experience much greater fear at point A than at point B in Figure 2. Conversely, lowering the avoidance gradient should also enable the subject to advance closer to the goal but with considerably less increase in fear.

The avoidance gradient can be lowered by reducing fear with such drugs as alcohol, sodium amytal, and chlorpromazine. However, caution should be used in drawing therapeutic implications from these studies because there is some question whether the conflict resolution will continue once the drug is withdrawn. The simplest way of eliminating these experimentally induced conflicts is to allow the process of fear extinction to take place. Other methods include feeding the animal so as to evoke an emotional response incompatible with fear, gradually bringing the fear stimulus closer, and changing the stimulus conditions. [*For discussion of treating humans, see* MENTAL DISORDERS, TREATMENT OF, *article on* BEHAVIOR THERAPY.]

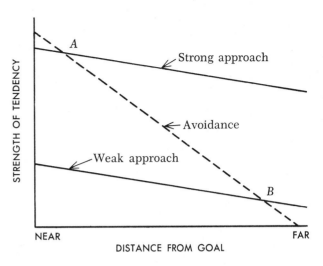

Figure 2 — The effects of varying strength of approach

Source: Neal E. Miller—"Experimental Studies of Conflict" in PERSONALITY AND THE BEHAVIOR DISORDERS, edited by J. McV. Hunt, Copyright 1944 The Ronald Press Company, New York.

An unresolved problem in connection with Miller's model concerns the exact shape of the approach and avoidance gradients. The most recent evidence suggests that the curves are ogival or S-shaped. However, the shape of the curve depends on the discriminability of cues along the path to the goal, the level of illumination, the species involved, and other factors.

A more critical problem has to do with the relative steepness of approach and avoidance gradients. Miller postulated that the avoidance gradient is steeper because it is based on the learned motive of fear, which varies greatly with external stimulus conditions, while the approach tendency is based on hunger, which is more dependent on the subject's internal cues and less influenced by external cues. While there is some evidence for this, other studies show that a learned approach tendency may conflict with a learned avoidance tendency, although both should be steep and possibly parallel. However, it may be that learning has more complex effects on the steepness of a gradient than has been assumed. For example, fear and guilt are both learned, but they may have gradients of differing steepness because fear is more dependent on external cues than is guilt. Internal, cue-producing responses, such as thoughts and verbal labels, would be expected to have a great effect on the shape, slope, and height of approach and avoidance gradients in most social situations.

Extension to displacement. The dimension of nearness may be viewed as a special case of stimulus generalization. Therefore, the model should be applicable to other situations involving the generalization of approach and avoidance gradients. This would include generalization from one goal object to another along a dimension of object similarity.

Miller saw a connection between goal object generalization and the psychoanalytic concept of *displacement*. For example, an individual who feels hostile toward his father might dream about a policeman, since dreaming about his father directly would produce anxiety. It has been shown that children whose parents severely punish aggression in the home are more aggressive outside the home. The scapegoat theory of ethnic prejudice is based on the idea of displacement and may be extended to situations involving aggression to outgroups.

The same graphic model used for conflict may be extended to displacement, with the exception that the dimension along the abscissa is one of stimulus similarity instead of spatial distance. Miller also assumes that the point of maximal displacement will not be at the intersection of the gradients, as in conflict, but to the right, where the net difference between the two response strengths is maximal in favor of approach.

Several studies have supported this extension of the theory. In one, two rats were placed in a cage and taught to attack each other in order to turn off an electric shock. During this time they showed no tendency to strike a plastic doll in the cage with them. Later, when the rats were placed in the cage one at a time and the shock turned on, each attacked the plastic doll. In this study, the learned aggression toward the partner rat was prevented by his absence and the aggression was displaced toward the previously ignored doll.

There are a number of situations in which conflict and displacement might operate simultaneously. Murray and Berkun (1955) attempted to account for this by developing a three-dimensional model combining Miller's theories of conflict and displacement. In this model, the ordinate still represented strength of response. The two other orthogonal dimensions were nearness to a goal and degree of similarity of various goals to the original goal. The approach and avoidance gradients were joined to produce intersecting approach and avoidance planes.

The Murray–Berkun model was tested in an apparatus consisting of wide white, medium width gray, and narrow black alleys adjacent to one another. In one alley (for example, wide white) the animals were trained first to approach for food and then to avoid a shock on the food tray. The alleys were connected by small windows so the animals could move from one to the other. After the conflict was established in the original alley, but not

before, the animals moved into the intermediate gray alley and approached closer to the goal, then entered the most dissimilar alley (for example, narrow black) and advanced all the way to the goal, as predicted by the model.

The main results of the Murray–Berkun study have been confirmed by other investigators, but some controversy has developed over the dimension of similarity to the original goal. Some results suggest that simple distance may play a role, but other results suggest that stimulus similarity is still operating. The color of the alleys may be less important than the width. Furthermore, olfactory cues may be important.

Projective techniques. The conflict and displacement theories have also been extended, by Seymour Epstein (1962) and his associates, to the area of projective techniques. Projective pictures and word association stimuli can be arranged in sequence according to their relevance to a motive, such as sex. It is found, frequently, that the motivation appears more openly on the pictures of low relevance. This can be explained as a displacement effect by assuming that the test responses are determined by intersecting approach and avoidance gradients. Epstein and his associates have also developed a three-dimensional model, similar to the Murray–Berkun one, in which a sequence of projective test stimuli form one dimension and time another. This model accounts for such findings as a parachutist's anxiety toward association words of less and less relevance to parachuting as the time for the jump draws nearer.

Personality, psychotherapy, and culture

In their learning analysis of neurosis and psychotherapy, John Dollard and Neal E. Miller (1950) have made extensive use of the conflict model. These theorists have reinterpreted many of the psychoanalytic observations on psychosexual development in terms of conflicts learned in childhood. Punitive parental training methods can establish conflicts in the areas of weaning, cleanliness, sexual behavior, and aggression. More subtle conflicts between social motives can be learned at later stages of development.

Dollard and Miller agree with Freud that neurosis requires that the conflict be at least partly repressed. Repression involves the inhibition of thoughts, feelings, and behavior and may be viewed as the result of an approach–avoidance conflict. The emergence of thoughts of a sexual nature may be likened to an approach response, and the stopping of these thoughts is similar to avoidance behavior. A sexually arousing situation increases the approach tendency and may also increase anxiety. Thus, the person may become anxious without knowing why.

Various neurotic symptoms may be viewed as responses reinforced by anxiety reduction. A phobia represents an avoidance response to an anxiety-arousing stimulus and may also involve displacement. Conversion symptoms often serve an avoidance function. Obsessional thinking may function to block out anxiety-arousing thoughts. However, since the approach tendency is still operating, the neurotic symptoms are rarely effective and the person keeps finding himself driven back into the conflict situation. Therefore, the person shows oscillating, inconsistent, and maladaptive behavior.

Psychotherapy is viewed by Dollard and Miller as a way of reducing conflict and eliminating repression. The permissive, nonpunitive attitude of the therapist constitutes a new set of learning conditions. Anxiety can gradually be extinguished, and the need for repression is thereby reduced. The patient can discuss his fears and motives. Of great importance in therapy is the transference relationship, or the generalization or displacement to the therapist of the conflict originally learned in the family situation. As repressions and symptoms drop out, the person can use his higher mental processes to solve his problems in his social behavior outside of the therapy situation.

An example of the more detailed use of the conflict model is Dollard and Miller's explanation of the negative therapeutic effect. It often happens in psychotherapy that, following a period of progress in which the patient gains some understanding, he suddenly becomes more anxious and symptomatic. This could happen if the therapeutic progress resulted in the lowering of an avoidance gradient. With the lowering of the avoidance gradient the patient might advance in thought or behavior closer to the goal but then would reach a new conflict point involving an increase in anxiety. Thus, therapeutic progress may have the paradoxical effect of making things worse for a time.

The theories of conflict and displacement have been applied to a broader class of cultural phenomena by several social scientists. For example, in a cross-cultural study of primitive societies, John Whiting and Irvin Child (1953) have related a number of socialization variables to religious beliefs concerning illness. They found that fear of others was related to socialization anxiety about aggression. However, the actual objects of aggression—ghosts of relatives or animal spirits—were more difficult to predict. By assuming that these aggression objects lie along a continuum of simi-

larity to parental socialization agents and by applying a modification of Miller's displacement theory, they were able to account for different patterns of aggression. When aggression anxiety is low, aggression is displaced more toward ghosts of relatives than of animal spirits; but, when aggression anxiety is high, aggression is displaced toward both ghosts of relatives and of animal spirits.

The application of the theories of conflict and displacement to problems of complex human behavior has been promising, but a great deal more research needs to be done. A major technical problem has to do with the scaling of important social dimensions along which generalization may take place. A related problem is the role of symbolic processes, language, and socially learned discriminations in conflict and displacement phenomena. Finally, more research is needed on the basic mechanisms involved, such as the determinants of the shape of the gradients, particularly with human subjects in a wide variety of social situations.

EDWARD J. MURRAY

[See also AGGRESSION, article on PSYCHOLOGICAL ASPECTS; PHOBIAS.]

BIBLIOGRAPHY

DOLLARD, JOHN; and MILLER, NEAL E. 1950 *Personality and Psychotherapy: An Analysis in Terms of Learning, Thinking, and Culture.* New York: McGraw-Hill. → A paperback edition was published in 1965.

EPSTEIN, SEYMOUR 1962 The Measurement of Drive and Conflict in Humans: Theory and Experiment. Volume 10, pages 127–209 in *Nebraska Symposium on Motivation.* Edited by Marshall R. Jones. Lincoln: Univ. of Nebraska Press.

FREUD, SIGMUND (1893–1895) 1955 *The Standard Edition of the Complete Psychological Works of Sigmund Freud.* Volume 2: Studies on Hysteria, by Josef Breuer and Sigmund Freud. London: Hogarth. → First published in German.

KOCH, SIGMUND (editor) 1959 *Psychology: A Study of a Science.* Volume 2. New York: McGraw-Hill.

LEWIN, KURT (1926–1933) 1935 *A Dynamic Theory of Personality: Selected Papers.* New York: McGraw-Hill.

LURIIA, ALEKSANDR R. 1932 *The Nature of Human Conflicts: Or, Emotion, Conflict and Will, an Objective Study of Disorganization and Control of Human Behaviour.* New York: Liveright.

MILLER, NEAL E. 1944 Experimental Studies of Conflict. Volume 1, pages 431–465 in Joseph McV. Hunt (editor), *Personality and the Behavior Disorders: A Handbook Based on Experimental and Clinical Research.* New York: Ronald.

MILLER, NEAL E. 1959 Liberalization of Basic S–R Concepts: Extensions to Conflict Behavior, Motivation and Social Learning. Volume 2, pages 196–292 in Sigmund Koch (editor), *Psychology: A Study of a Science.* New York: McGraw-Hill.

MURRAY, EDWARD J.; and BERKUN, MITCHELL M. 1955 Displacement as a Function of Conflict. *Journal of Abnormal and Social Psychology* 51:47–56.

WHITING, JOHN W. M.; and CHILD, IRVIN L. 1953 *Child Training and Personality: A Cross-cultural Study.* New Haven: Yale Univ. Press. → A paperback edition was published in 1962.

YATES, AUBREY J. 1962 *Frustration and Conflict.* London: Methuen; New York: Wiley.

II

POLITICAL ASPECTS

In the nineteenth century, Marx and Engels analyzed class conflict and the social Darwinists examined conflict among societies. But Marxism developed essentially as a doctrine of reform and revolution, while social Darwinism failed to progress beyond oversimplified concepts like "absolute hatred," "survival of the fittest," and "the conquest state." The first sociologist to focus on conflict as a process both internal and external to the individual and also to the group was Georg Simmel, whose ideas have been critically restated by Lewis A. Coser (1956). Most sociologists lost interest in conflict, however, and became increasingly engrossed with patterns and processes of social integration. It is only in recent years, and especially with the threat of nuclear holocaust, that social scientists have focused serious attention upon problems of conflict.

Conflict and integration

It now seems evident that all human relations may be viewed as interlaced by two closely related processes—the conflictual and the integrative. To one degree or another, these two kinds of interaction appear as soon as, and as long as, two or more individuals are in contact. They disappear only when the parties withdraw and the relationship is completely broken.

Whenever two or more individuals or groups come into contact with each other, they may choose to make their relationship primarily conflictual or primarily integrative (i.e., cooperative, supportive, agreed upon). If the initial relationship is primarily conflictual, there will nevertheless emerge at least a few minimal strands of understanding and reciprocity—rules of combat, or perhaps only an agreement to disagree. If, on the other hand, the initial relationship is primarily integrative, it is certain that conflict will develop—if for no other reason than through the demands of the association itself as they compete with the preferences of individuals and component groups.

Some degree of community, organization, or integration is inherent in the concept of conflict. If the parties in question were not in the same place at the same time, or performing two incompatible functions at the same time, or cooperating to inflict reciprocal injury, there would be no conflict (Bernard 1957*b*, p. 112). Almost any aspect of conflict, however destructive, requires interaction between the antagonists, considerable communication, and the establishment and maintenance of many reciprocal ties and subtle understandings. Conflict thus functions as a binding element between parties who may previously have had no contact at all (Coser 1956, p. 121).

On the other hand, conflict may result in the disruption or destruction of all or certain of the bonds of unity that may previously have existed between the disputants.

Conflicts take place between individuals, between individuals and organizations or groups, between distinct organizations or groups, between an organization and one or more of its components, or between component parts of a single organization or group. A conflict emerges whenever two or more persons (or groups) seek to possess the same object, occupy the same space or the same exclusive position, play incompatible roles, maintain incompatible goals, or undertake mutually incompatible means for achieving their purposes.

Inner conflict

The type of conflict discussed above—essentially social conflict—should be distinguished from the inner conflict or quandary that emerges when incompatible or mutually exclusive values present themselves in the form of an actual or potential choice or decision (Bernard 1957*b*, p. 113). Thus, an individual finds himself unable to make a decision because he is being pushed or pulled in opposite directions. (The same holds true for a group.) He wants to be in two places at the same time or to perform two mutually exclusive functions at the same time. Like the proverbial ass between two equally attractive bales of hay, he finds himself immobilized by the choice confronting him (Boulding 1957, p. 132). Or perhaps he finds himself equally immobilized in trying to decide upon the "lesser of two evils."

In the individual human being the distinction between the inner conflict and the outer, or social, conflict seems relatively clear: the former involves a confrontation by the individual of a difficult choice between incompatible values, whereas the latter is concerned with an incompatibility between that individual and another individual or group. Yet the inner conflict can be viewed also as a conflict between internal components of the individual: Her heart said Yes, but her common sense said No.

When groups and organizations are considered,

the inner conflicts of a given unit are undoubtedly social conflicts (conflicts between antagonistic actors) when viewed on one system level; but they are also sometimes analogous to the inner conflicts *or quandaries of the individual*, when viewed on another level. Among groups and organizations, then, the dialogues, debates, and struggles associated with decision making may be considered on one system level as social conflicts between individual parties; or they may be treated under certain circumstances as quandaries—conflicts internal to the organism—from the perspective of another level in the systems hierarchy. A group can be immobilized either because all the members are caught between opposing repulsions or attractions or because one component of the group is attracted (or repelled) in one direction, the other component in another direction. Thus, the distinction between the quandary and the so-called social, or external, conflict is frequently a matter of system perspective, which must be determined by requirements of the problem, the method of analysis, and the theory of the investigator (Lewin 1935–1946).

An actor who has the capacity for absorbing or destroying another actor may be viewed as dominant. An actor who cannot be absorbed by another actor or destroyed as an independent decision maker is sovereign or unconditionally viable. Conversely, the actor who survives only through the sufferance of another, dominant, party is said to be conditionally viable.

In circumstances where both actors are unconditionally sovereign or viable, or where it does not pay the dominant party to extinguish the other—to secure conditional viability—we have what Strausz-Hupé has called "protracted conflict" (1959). Here the problem is how to control the conflict, i.e., how to maintain limits, rather than to resolve it (Boulding 1962, p. 59).

Each actor or system (individual, group, organization, nation-state, and so forth) may be viewed as responding to various stimuli, including projections of his or its own needs, desires, and expectations. Or, one may equally postulate that each system possesses as an inherent part of its structure a "view of the universe" or an "image" that includes some notion or "plan" of its role and purpose (Boulding 1957, pp. 125–126; also Miller et al. 1960). Within the first view, each choice-point offers alternatives to which some combination of perceived rewards and penalties is attached. In connection with the second view, behavior or action may be seen as the carrying out of a process that moves the system toward the most highly valued part of the total image.

In any case, as the actor system carries out its means–end process, a certain number of links (choices or potential choices) will "snag" or "collide" with the links of other actors. Conflict generally emerges whenever at least one party perceives that one (or more) of his goals, or purposes, or preferences, or means for achieving a goal or preference is being threatened or hindered by the intentions or activities of one or more other parties. The parties may be seeking to move or expand into the same field or physical space, or, more abstractly, into the same field of influence or behavior (Boulding 1957, p. 124).

Perhaps the most important class of conflict processes is the reaction process in which a movement on the part of one actor "so changes the field of the other that it forces a movement of this party, which in turn changes the field of the first, forcing another move of the second, and so on" (Boulding 1962, p. 25). Party A perceives—rightly or wrongly—that he is being threatened or injured by party B. Taking what he considers to be defensive action, A behaves in a way that B perceives as injurious or threatening. When B responds "defensively," A, perceiving now that his initial observations and fears have been validated, increases his activities, and thus the conflict spirals.

As the reciprocal threats and injuries rise, the parties may find no alternative other than to fight it out until one has reduced the other to submission. On the other hand, at some point the penalties associated with an added increment of hostility may appear too great to one or both parties, and the conflict may decelerate. In due course, however, the anxieties, fears, and discomforts associated with their basic relationship are likely to become unbearable again, and the spiraling will resume. Essentially, the cold war is such a conflict in that it vacillates between a plateau of minimal, day-to-day conflict and occasional peaks where the hostile interchange stops just short of large-scale violence.

The initial perception of threat or injury may or may not be accurate or justified. Many conflicts arise from what parties *think* may happen—from their anxieties, prejudices, fears, and uncertainties —rather than from any phenomenon that is actually threatening.

Competition

Conversely, even where actors are aware of incompatibility, there may be no actual conflict if there is no strong desire on the part of at least one party to carry out the means—or achieve the ends —which are, or appear to be, incompatible (Boulding 1962, p. 5). Whether competitive situations become conflictual may depend, then, upon whether the incompatibility is perceived and also upon whether the issues involved are considered important by the parties.

Conflict suggests a special situation of competition in which both actors are aware of the incompatibility of potential future positions and in which each is strongly impelled to occupy a position incompatible with the perceived interests of the other.

Whenever two or more systems come into contact, they may choose either a "conflict set," where an action will benefit one actor at the expense of another; or a "trading set" of means and ends, where movements benefiting both parties are feasible (Boulding 1957, p. 131).

Yet conflict is inherent in the trading set: each party is likely to seek a maximum advantage that cannot be achieved without reducing the advantage of the other party. A satisfactory trade can be achieved only if both parties, tacitly or otherwise, observe certain rules and limitations.

Superordinate goals.   A special type of competition evolves when an otherwise conflictual struggle is consciously joined by two or more parties in the interest of some more important, mutually supportive, promotively interdependent goal: two traders decide to "dicker"; two friends meet for tennis; two teams play a violent, but carefully regulated, game of football; or two neighborly merchants try to outdo each other in the same line, but on the assumption that each will prosper (Levinger 1957, p. 337). In each case, neither side is seeking to destroy the other nor to inflict more than the limited amount of injury that has been more or less agreed upon and stipulated by the rules of their competitive game. Two or more parties in conflict may be drawn into a cooperative relationship through their perception of an overriding, superordinate goal (see Oklahoma, University of . . . 1961).

In any one of these "institutionalized" arrangements, the parties accept, consciously or unconsciously, a contract or compact—elaborate arrangements or rules of the game for achieving their common purposes (fixing and enforcing boundaries, deciding on possession of the ball, identifying violations, enforcing penalties, and so forth).

The consensus may include not only rules but also rules for formulating rules; and it may designate roles—messengers, referees, judges—to help in deciding the issue or to enforce the agreed-upon stipulations. The "game" is likely to provide for assignments of function, special prerogatives, limitations of power, and so forth.

A procedure for resolving conflicts can be honored by usage and thus gain status of custom. Or, when established or recognized and enforced by recognized authority, such a procedure takes force as law. A large part of both custom and law functions to resolve conflicts, or to prevent them, or to confine them within designated limits.

In analyzing relationships between individuals or groups, we are not concerned, then, whether the relationship contains conflict; we assume that it does. The question is, How do they handle their conflicts—by unconfined violence and destruction and without institutional restraint, or by some regulated means within an agreed-upon framework? Have the two parties achieved sufficient integration to channel their conflicts within tolerable limits, and how is the basic contract or integration maintained? Most organizations, including political organizations on all system levels, may be viewed in these terms.

State A and state B, each seeking possession of an island, may thus be in conflict. To resolve the issue one state may withdraw its claim; or the two states may divide the island by mutual agreement; or they may both decide to fight for it. If state A withdraws without consultation or communication with state B, the conflict has been eliminated, but there is no integration—no agreement—between the two parties.

If both sides agree to fight, the two states, while still in conflict over possession of the island, are not in conflict over the means of resolution. Thus, the conflict continues, but an element of integration has emerged to the extent that the parties have agreed upon the method for deciding the issue. Later, if both sides tire of combat, they may agree upon an equal-sided armistice for achieving resolution by nonviolent and noncoercive means. On the other hand, if the armistice is unequal and it is clear that one side is coercing the other, then the agreement, although integrative, has been shaped by threat of superior force.

Integrative instruments

Integrative arrangements between parties can be reached in a number of ways. They can be entered into consciously and voluntarily. They can be imposed by one party upon another. They can be "grown into," more or less unconsciously, through habit and custom. They can be inherited, and individuals can be—and, if we refer to states, normally are—born into them.

If, in the course of a conflict situation, one side uses force and the other submits, the assumption is that the submitting side has "agreed" and that the consequence is an integrative but essentially violent and coercive relationship. On the other hand, if one party uses force and the other refuses to submit but eschews force and turns to some method of passive resistance, then there is a highly disintegrative double conflict involving both incompatible purposes and incompatible rules of warfare. A contract, then, may be essentially violent and coercive or nonviolent and voluntary in nature.

Separate parties with a common enemy can arrange an integrative compact against the outside threat. A prolonged conflict with the British crown had much to do with the unification of the thirteen colonies under the Articles of Confederation, at first, and later under the constitution.

The American Civil War illustrates a somewhat different process. Here there was no common enemy. The contestants were at war against each other, and yet, in the long run, the conflict had a unifying consequence. The pre-existing ties between North and South, severely challenged prior to the war, were slowly and painfully repaired and *greatly strengthened* during the decades following the war. Many deep incompatibilities remained, but the conflicts were contained below the level of major violence.

Depending on the system level, the means, or instrument, of a compact may take the form of a marriage or other contract, articles of incorporation or confederation, a treaty, an elaborate constitution, and so forth. The instrument need not be written, however, or even explicit: two Indian tribes may smoke a pipe of peace; or the slave—whether through love, or fear, or constraint—may "agree" to the slavery "contract," honoring the arrangement by choosing not to escape. In its implications, then, an integrative arrangement may take any form, from the wholly consensual, to the minimally consensual; from the nonviolent, noncoercive, to the overwhelmingly violent and coercive.

An integrative instrument can be wrung from a conqueror or ruler by a group of his subjects whose capability has increased sufficiently. In the later Middle Ages, European towns achieved their charters largely in this way. Such an instrument may increase the cohesion of the group at the expense of its relationship with the ruler or grantor, or, as has happened over the course of history in England, the instrument may have the effect of strengthening bonds between the parties—the king, the parliament, the church, the people. In either case, however, the conclusion of the instrument signals a change in the relative capabilities of the parties.

How is the degree of integration determined? Clearly, it is revealed through the *kind* of function controlled by the contract rather than the mere number of functions, the power of the contract to implement these kinds of functions, and the time span of its effectiveness.

A given category of integrative means may include a single action taken to resolve a conflict at a particular time, and also a procedure or set of procedures designated for the resolution of issues relating to a problem over time. If two parties decide that a conflict over fish caught in disputed waters shall be resolved in a single instance by an even division of the catch, this means falls in the single-action category. If the parties decide, on the other hand, that all fish caught in these same disputed waters will be divided in this fashion for the rest of the season, or over a period of five years, or in perpetuity, then the procedural "over-time" category is appropriate. Treaties and similar agreements over time are designated in this way.

Two distinct units signing a fisheries treaty have not integrated significantly. At the point when they agree to merge such functions as defense, taxation, legislation, and the enforcement of laws, however, the parties have gone a long way toward extinguishing their separate personalities and giving rise to a new state entity. When the populations of the two primary components transfer their loyalties to the new unit, when they internalize its symbols, when those who do not belong are viewed as "foreigners," "outsiders," and even enemies, then the integration may be considered virtually complete (Deutsch et al. 1957, pp. 5–6). Herein lies the difference between a simple treaty and a federative instrument or a constitution.

Constitutions as integrative instruments. Treaties respect and preserve the distinct identities of the individual parties, whereas a constitution joins separate contracting entities into a single unit of a new order. (Some so-called constitutions are programs rather than contracts. In such cases, there is a compact somewhere inherent, but it may be tacit rather than explicit, or it may reside in some document carrying a different label.) Historically, many constitutions have developed from treaties.

It often happened that a state enlarged its territory by conquest of adjoining peoples or acquired colonies across seas or at other great distance from the homeland. Not infrequently, the populace of the central unit enjoyed nationality and rights of citizenship, whereas the conquered people were forced into a tributary or dependent or colonial status. The Roman Empire extended its jurisdiction over much of Europe and into Africa and Asia Minor somewhat in this fashion. This far-flung integration "dis-integrated" with the Christian era, but a millennium later a number of European nation-states began reaching around the globe in a not dissimilar pattern.

Through a royal charter, the British East India Company, like overseers of a private estate, ruled over many differing peoples of India. By making treaties with native princes, moreover, the company extended its own jurisdiction—and in the long run, British sovereignty—over large reaches of further territory.

Other European chartered companies—the Dutch East India Company, the Hudson's Bay Company, the Plymouth Company, the London Company, and others—played similar roles over much of the earth. In America the companies concluded solemn compacts with the Indians, and in Africa they followed the same pattern with native chiefs.

The charter of the British East India Company became the model for the Massachusetts Bay Colony charter, from which, in turn, a direct lineage can be traced to the constitution of the United States. Thus, the same kind of integrative instrument gave form, in the one instance, to British imperial control over India and, in the other instance, to unification of the thirteen colonies into the United States of America.

Not all colonial powers expanded through written compacts, of course, although the compulsion to sign a treaty, even with the most impotent up-river chieftain, was surprisingly widespread. In any case, the relationships that were established, whether unwritten or formalized on paper and whether reached by free consent or the imposition of superior strength, were essentially contractual, or became so by observance, custom, and usage. Thus the great empires spread.

An integrative means category may be no more than a rule for resolving a common conflict of the road: [We agree that] *the first vehicle to enter an intersection shall have the right of way.* A more comprehensive set is likely to combine a number of related rules into a code, for example, all rules for avoiding or resolving conflicts on the streets and highways. A still more comprehensive level will be characterized by means categories that specify by what methods the various rules are to be enforced (powers) and by whom (roles). Such an instrument combines within itself a complicated means–end hierarchy, a role structure, a pattern of communications channels, and a wide range of procedures for avoiding, containing, and resolving highway conflicts.

By a particular law, then, we mean a rule of behavior established by recognized authority to prescribe regulations or govern interactions, transactions, conflicts, and other human relationships. Any law can be viewed as a generalized integrative instrument to which the authorities who enact and enforce it and the individuals and groups who are subject to it are all parties, although they may not be equal before it. The function of a given law is usually to prevent conflict, to resolve conflict, or to constrain conflict within agreed-upon limits.

A law always presupposes the existence of a "superior" compact, agreement, constitution, or other integrative relationship from which the law derives its authority and to which the law is tributary. A treaty bridges two integrated, but more or less independent, units. Treaties, indeed, belong to the same order of integrative instrument as do constitutions, that is, they provide the primary ties between parties from which further arrangements are derived and to which they are tributary.

A law and its "superior" constitution or other integrative instrument can both be viewed as links in a means–end chain. One function of the courts is to decide precedence when laws are themselves in conflict. It should be clear, then, that the relative order of links in a means–end chain—the whole problem, indeed, of what is a means, what is an end, and which links are superior and which are tributary—depends upon the chosen perspective, the unit that is chosen to be viewed as the behaving and value-invoking system. Inevitably, there will be conflicts of interest between actors on different levels.

From the organizational, legal, or state viewpoint, the single law is a means toward supporting and maintaining the constitution, which, in turn, is a means toward the achievement of security, justice, and other goals of the total system.

The individual citizen, by contrast, may understandably view the constitution as a means toward enforcement of the law for the protection of his personal interests and the achievement of his individual purposes. This view, an essentially Western democratic concept, goes a long way (although not in any sense the whole way) toward subordinating the state means–end structure to the order of a subset in the means–end hierarchy of the individual. In practice, however, the individual, even in a democratic state, stands alone if he pushes his own interests too far at the expense of the fundamental integration and the society it represents.

Durability of integrative instruments. Are there methods whereby the probable durability of an integrative instrument can be assessed?

A party that is dominant and enjoys unconditional viability under an integrative arrangement will tend to perpetuate the relationship. On the other hand, a conditionally viable party to the contract will not have much choice other than to accede, unless he perceives a possibility for increasing his own viability.

Reduced to simplest terms, the durability of a given compact or other integrative relationship will depend upon two main variables: (1) the relative capability of each party, that is, his power or relative capacity for inflicting his will; and (2) the amount of dissatisfaction evoked, or penalty demanded, by the relationship among the participating parties.

The durability of an integrative relationship will depend also upon the precedents, that is, upon whether or not previous agreements have worked to the satisfaction of the parties and have been generally long lasting.

Against this background, it is possible, by arranging the capability and satisfaction–dissatisfaction (also utility–cost, or reward–penalty) variables in different combinations, to suggest a number of hypotheses.

If parties A and B are about equally strong and equally dissatisfied with their contract relationship, but if both also feel that the additional cost of breaking it would be undesirably high, then we may postulate that the treaty's durability will be long but its effectiveness will be low. Neither party will wish to abrogate the compact, and neither will hesitate to interpret its provisions broadly or even to disregard them when there is not much danger of detection or reprisal. The levels of conflict and tension within the relationship will be high.

In another circumstance, A may be powerful and consider his relationship with B satisfactory, whereas B is deeply dissatisfied (*but weak*). In this pattern, we might expect high durability and, in view of B's low capacity, a considerable measure of effectiveness. A, in short, will be in a position to dominate B and enforce B's strict adherence to the agreement. The relationship will be characterized by numerous petty conflicts, a submerged pattern of potential conflicts, and considerable tension.

Over time, B's stored dissatisfaction may amount to a deep and growing sense of frustration. If, then, B's capability should begin to rise for any reason, there is a strong possibility of his striking against A even before his strength is greater than or even equal to A's. His perceptions of dissatisfaction will be so high, in short, that he will strike for the reward of ending the relationship—even at considerable risk. The possibilities of this outcome may be enhanced, moreover, because the weak and frustrated party with increasing strength will tend to overestimate his ability to punish his offending partner in the relationship.

On the other hand, if we assume that B's capability will remain low and that his dissatisfaction will diminish with time, it seems reasonable to predict his gradual acceptance—as custom or law or simply as "the way things are"—of the once irritating relationship. Various institutions for handling conflict will become increasingly accepted. This, indeed, is how time frequently functions on the side of the invader by gradually resolving or subordinating a wide range of conflicts separating him from the vanquished.

We have postulated that the durability of a given compact or other integrative instrument will depend upon the capabilities of each party to the relationship and the amount of satisfaction or dissatisfaction that the various parties derive from it. The durability of a complex organization—a city-state, nation-state, or empire—will depend upon similar variables except that there may be more issues involved, and the "parties" to the relationship are likely to consist of a ruling elite, on the one hand, and a body of subjects, citizens, or rank and file on the other.

The willingness of any participant to contribute freely to the state will depend upon the satisfactions that he perceives accruing to him from the association.

All states use some degree of force in order to endow their laws with authority and in order to control criminal elements. The difference between a state that relies primarily upon consent for its cohesion and management of conflict and one that depends upon coercion lies, first of all, in whether the force that is used has been agreed upon by the majority of the people and is exercised for designated purposes and within sanctioned limits; and, second, whether dissident minorities within the state are afforded certain minimal protection. Unless this protection is available, a majority can coerce and tyrannize a minority even though the officers of the state are applying force by virtue of legal mandate.

ROBERT C. NORTH

[*Other relevant material may be found under* INTERNATIONAL RELATIONS; PEACE; POLITICAL BEHAVIOR; WAR.]

BIBLIOGRAPHY

BAGEHOT, WALTER (1872) 1956 *Physics and Politics: Or, Thoughts on the Application of the Principles of "Natural Selection" and "Inheritance" to Political Society.* Boston: Beacon.

BERNARD, JESSIE 1950 Where is the Modern Sociology of Conflict? *American Journal of Sociology* 56:11–16.

BERNARD, JESSIE 1957a The Sociological Study of Conflict. Pages 33–117 in International Sociological Association, *The Nature of Conflict: Studies on the Sociological Aspects of International Tensions.* UNESCO, Tensions and Technology Series. Paris: UNESCO.

BERNARD, JESSIE 1957b Parties and Issues in Conflict. *Journal of Conflict Resolution.* 1:111–121.

BOULDING, KENNETH E. 1957 Organization and Conflict. *Journal of Conflict Resolution* 1:122–134.

BOULDING, KENNETH E. 1962 *Conflict and Defense: A General Theory.* A publication of the Center for Research in Conflict Resolution at the University of Michigan. New York: Harper.

COLEMAN, JAMES S. 1957 *Community Conflict.* A publication of the Bureau of Applied Social Research, Columbia University. Glencoe, Ill.: Free Press.

COSER, LEWIS A. 1956 *The Functions of Social Conflict.* Glencoe, Ill:. Free Press.

DAHRENDORF, RALF (1957) 1959 *Class and Class Conflict in Industrial Society.* Rev. & enl. ed. Stanford (Calif.) Univ. Press. → First published in German as *Soziale Klassen und Klassen-Konflikt in der industriellen Gesellschaft.*

DEUTSCH, KARL W. et al. 1957 *Political Community and the North Atlantic Area: International Organization in the Light of Historical Experience.* Princeton Univ. Press.

FOLLETT, MARY P. (1924) 1951 *Creative Experience.* Gloucester, Mass.: Peter Smith.

GUMPLOWICZ, LUDWIG 1883 *Der Rassenkampf: Soziologische Untersuchungen.* Innsbruck (Austria): Verlag der Wagner'schen Universitäts Buchhandlung. → Also published in 1893 in French as *La lutte des races: Recherches sociologiques.*

LEVINGER, GEORGE 1957 Kurt Lewin's Approach to Conflict and Its Resolution: A Review With Some Extensions. *Journal of Conflict Resolution* 1:327–339.

LEWIN, KURT (1935–1946) 1948 *Resolving Social Conflicts: Selected Papers on Group Dynamics.* New York: Harper.

MILLER, GEORGE A.; GALANTER, E.; and PRIBRAM, K. H. 1960 *Plans and the Structure of Behavior.* New York: Holt.

OKLAHOMA, UNIVERSITY OF, INSTITUTE OF GROUP RELATIONS 1961 *Intergroup Conflict and Cooperation: The Robbers Cave Experiment,* by Muzafer Sherif et al. Norman, Okla.: University Book Exchange.

OPPENHEIMER, FRANZ (1907) 1914 *The State: Its History and Development Viewed Sociologically.* Indianapolis, Ind.: Bobbs-Merrill. → First published in German.

PARK, ROBERT; and BURGESS, ERNEST W. (1921) 1929 *Introduction to the Science of Sociology.* 2d ed. Univ. of Chicago Press.

SIMMEL, GEORG (1908) 1955 *Conflict; The Web of Group Affiliations.* Glencoe, Ill.: Free Press. → These essays were first published under the titles "Der Streit" and "Die Kreuzung sozialer Kreise" in Simmel's *Soziologie.*

STRAUSZ-HUPÉ, ROBERT et al. 1959 *Protracted Conflict.* New York: Harper. → A paperback edition was published in 1963.

WARD, LESTER F. (1903) 1925 *Pure Sociology: A Treatise on the Origin and Spontaneous Development of Society.* 2d ed. New York and London: Macmillan.

WRIGHT, QUINCY (1942) 1944 *A Study of War.* 2 vols. Univ. of Chicago Press.

III
SOCIAL ASPECTS

Social conflict may be defined as a struggle over values or claims to status, power, and scarce resources, in which the aims of the conflicting parties are not only to gain the desired values but also to neutralize, injure, or eliminate their rivals. Such conflicts may take place between individuals, between collectivities, or between individuals and collectivities. Intergroup as well as intragroup conflicts are perennial features of social life.

Conflict is an important element of social interaction. Far from being always a "negative" factor that "tears apart," social conflict may contribute in many ways to the maintenance of groups and collectivities as well as to the cementing of interpersonal relations.

Nineteenth-century sociology paid much attention to social conflict. In all social thought derived from Hegel, particularly in Marxian thought, conflict is the key explanatory variable. The same is the case with social thinkers directly or indirectly inspired by social Darwinism, such as Herbert Spencer, Gustav Ratzenhofer, Ludwig Gumplowicz, and William Graham Sumner. The struggle for power and influence is one of the themes of Pareto's theories, as well as those of Mosca, Michels, and Sorel. Similarly, in the classical tradition in German sociology, from Tönnies to Simmel and Weber, conflict was considered a major social phenomenon. Weber, for example, insisted that "conflict cannot be excluded from social life . . . 'Peace' is nothing more than a change in the form of the conflict or in the antagonists or in the objects of the conflict, or finally in the chances of selection" ([1904–1917] 1949, pp. 26–27). Simmel, to whom we owe a classical analysis of various forms of conflict, insisted that "conflict is a form of sociation" and that "a certain amount of discord, inner divergence and outer controversy, is organically tied up with the very elements that ultimately hold the group together" ([1908] 1955, pp. 17–18). Similarly, the fathers of American sociology saw in conflict an inherent and ineradicable component of social structures. Most of them agreed with Robert Park that "only where there is conflict is behavior conscious and self-conscious; only here are the conditions for rational conduct" (1924, p. 578).

In a more recent period, the functions of conflict and the study of conflict phenomena were neglected by American sociologists. If conflict was discussed at all, attention was paid mainly to its dissociative aspects. The stress on the need for common values and harmony led a number of social theorists, from Lloyd Warner to Talcott Parsons, to consider conflict a kind of sickness of the body social. Within the last decade, however, a number of theorists opposing the prevailing harmony model have endeavored, partly under the influence of Marx and Simmel, to develop a conflict model of society. The works of Jessie Bernard (1957), Lewis Coser (1956), Ralf Dahrendorf (1957), and Max Gluckman (1956) illustrate this approach.

The objective bases of conflict

The objective bases of social conflict must be sharply separated from subjective elements. Failure to do so results in excessively psychologistic explanations, which cannot do justice to the structure of conflict or to the situations that give rise to it. Such objective bases for contentions vary widely. Conflicts may break out over the distribution of a great variety of scarce values and goods, such as income, status, power, dominion over territory, or ecological position. Such occasions for conflict behavior need to be analyzed separately from dispositions and attitudes such as hostility, aggressiveness, *ressentiment,* hatred, and the like. In certain types of conflicts, such as modern management–labor conflicts, the antagonists may harbor only a minimum of hostile emotions toward each other. Conflicts and hostile sentiments, although often associated, are, in fact, different phenomena.

The distinction between realistic and nonrealistic conflict has proved valuable in analysis. Realistic conflict arises when men clash in the pursuit of claims and the expectation of gain. It is viewed by the participants as a means toward the achievement of specific goals, a means that might be abandoned if other means appear to be more effective. On the other hand, nonrealistic conflict, arising from aggressive impulses that seek expression no matter what the object, allows no functional alternative of means, since it is not aimed at the attainment of a concrete result but at the expression of aggressive impulses. Scapegoating provides an example; the object of attack is secondary to the dispositional need for attack. Thus, in nonrealistic conflict there are functional alternatives for the target, in contrast to realistic conflict in which there are functional alternatives to the means used. In concrete empirical cases, it is likely, of course, that mixtures between the pure types of realistic and nonrealistic conflict will be found to be present.

Hostile attitudes do not necessarily result in conflict; nor need we expect that objective discrepancies in power, status, income, and the like will necessarily lead to the outbreak of conflict, although they can be conceived as potential sources of conflict. Here, as elsewhere, the way men define a situation, rather than the objective features of the situation, must be the focus of analysis. Potential claimants for greater income, status, deference, or power may be deterred from conflict because of fear of consequences or because they consider existing discrepancies in the distribution of valued objects to be legitimate.

The structural impact of conflict

The impact of conflict on social structures varies according to the type of such structures. In loosely structured groups and in open, pluralistic societies, conflict that aims at a resolution of tension between antagonists is likely to have stabilizing functions. If the direct expression of rival claims is permitted, such conflicts may serve to eliminate the causes for dissociation and to re-establish unity. In such flexible structures, multiple affiliations of individuals make them participate in a variety of group conflicts so that those who are antagonists in one conflict are allies in another. Thus, multiple conflicts, although varying in intensity, are likely to crisscross one another and thereby prevent cleavages along one axis. The pluralism of associations in such types of societies leads to a plurality of fronts of conflict, and the intensity of any one of these conflicts is likely to be relatively low. Segmental participation in a multiplicity of conflicts constitutes a balancing mechanism within the structure. In this way, conflicts may be said to sew pluralistic society together.

In rigid social structures and in closed groups, on the other hand, the impact of conflict is likely to be quite different. The closer the group, the more intense are conflicts likely to be, that is, the more highly involved the parties. Such groups tend to inhibit the open acting out of hostility since they fear its disruptive effect. Closed groups tend to absorb the total personality of their members; they are jealous of members' affiliation with other groups and desire to monopolize their loyalty. The resultant deep involvement of the members and the intimate association among them is likely to lead to a great deal of hostility and ambivalence, a hostility, however, to which the group denies legitimate outlets. Hence, if conflicts break out in groups that have tried to prevent them, they are likely to be peculiarly intense. This is so because, first, the personality absorption in such groups tends to favor the mobilization of all psychic energies in the conduct of the struggle, and, second, because these conflicts now are not likely to remain limited to the issues at hand but to revive all those grievances that were denied expression previously. All the previously latent causes for conflict are now superimposed upon one another.

A similar situation prevails in large social structures that are organized in unitary and rigid patterns. Here also, conflict, if it occurs at all, is likely to be intense. The lack of multiplicity of crisscrossing associations and multiple allegiances between members is likely to have as a consequence the superimposition of the various latent sources of conflicts. In such structure, a basic division of society into two large hostile classes or groups (the situation envisaged by Marx) becomes a strong probability.

While closeness of association and structural rigidity tend to lead to high intensity of conflict, they do not necessarily lead to a high degree of violence of conflict. Violence, as distinct from intensity, refers to the choice of means for carrying out the conflict rather than to the degree of involvement of the participants. Intensity and violence may vary independently of each other. The more integrated into the society or group are the parties to the conflict, the less likely will the conflict between them be violent. The greater the degree of integration, the higher the likelihood that the conflicting parties will choose weapons that will not permanently menace their common bonds. Violent class struggles or class wars are likely to give way to less militant means, such as institutionalized strikes or regularized contests, in those societies that permit the integration of lower classes or ethnic and other minorities into the social order.

Ideology and conflict

Conflicts are likely to be more intense, and more violent as well, to the degree that the contenders are collectivity-oriented rather than self-oriented and hence consider that their struggle is waged for the sake of superindividual ends. Ideological struggles that transcend the merely individual ones allow the participants a "good conscience" in the choice of their means of struggle. Hence, individuals who see themselves acting as representatives of a cause, fighting not for self but only for the ideals of a collectivity they represent, tend to be more radical and merciless than those who fight for personal advantage. The ideological end may justify the means in the eyes of the participants and lead them to consider justifiable, in public

ideological contention, means that they might reject in private conflict.

This order of phenomena highlights the importance of intellectuals, that is, the makers and shapers of ideologies in society. Intellectuals who transform conflicts of interests into conflicts of ideas help provide public justification of conflicts and hence to make them more intense. Conflicts may involve the pursuit of personal interests by private individuals or they may arise from the pursuit of the interests of various types of collectivities. Intellectuals, when they function as "ideologists," tend to strip such conflicts of their merely personal or merely interested aspects and to transform them into struggles over eternal truths. They thereby deepen and intensify them. Yet, lest the social role of intellectuals be overrated, it needs to be stressed that they can effectively function as "ideological agents" only in structures that favor the growth of ideologies. In pluralistic societies, crisscrossed by manifold conflicts upon a variety of axes, the role of ideologists is likely to be much less pronounced and their influence considerably reduced; they are likely to assume more important roles in those structures in which the superimposition of conflicts upon one axis favors the emergence of unified ideological fronts.

When manifold conflicts are superimposed upon each other, many and variegated interests can be fused by the adherence to a common ideology.

Conflict, consensus, and social change

The distinction between conflicts that exceed the limits imposed by societal consensus and those taking place within the basic consensus has informed political thought ever since Aristotle. Conflicts that do not attack the basic consensus and are in effect waged upon the very ground of consensus are likely to lead to adjustments between the various parties and hence to contribute to a closer integration of the society. In contrast, conflicts that attack basic assumptions of collective existence dissociate and split the society into warring camps.

Loosely structured groups and open pluralistic societies, by allowing conflicts to be fought out among a variety of contenders and on a variety of fronts, institute safeguards against types of conflict that might endanger basic consensus. They minimize the danger of divergences touching upon central consensual values. However, in rigid groups or societies the chances are high that if conflict occurs despite the effort to repress it, it will reach down to the basic layers of consensus. For example, if major strata of a society's population are permanently excluded from participation in the society's benefits, they will tend to reject the very assumptions upon which the society is built, and, if the systems of legitimation no longer fully operate, they will attempt to attack the social order through revolutionary violence. On the other hand, where no stratum of the population considers itself totally excluded from society's benefits, although all may still engage in multifarious struggles to increase their respective shares of income, wealth, power, or prestige, conflicts will tend to be waged within the limits of a consensus.

Each society contains some elements of strain and potential conflict. Analysis of social change needs to focus attention on these elements, since they provide the dynamics of change. Elements that evade and resist the patterned structure of norms and the habitual balance of power and interests may be considered harbingers of the emergence of new and alternative patterns emerging from an existing structure. Conflict prevents the ossification of social systems by exerting pressures for innovation and creativity; it prevents habitual accommodations from freezing into rigid molds and hence progressively impoverishing the ability to react creatively to novel circumstances. The clash of values and interests, the tension between what is and what some groups or individuals feel ought to be, the conflict between vested interest groups and new strata demanding their share of wealth, power, and status are all productive of social vitality.

Social change can be analyzed only in relation to specified structures. This is why it is necessary to distinguish between changes that take place *within* particular structures and changes that lead to the decay of old structures and the emergence of new ones. We may talk of a change *of* a social system as distinct from changes *within* a social system when all major structural relations, basic institutions, and prevailing value systems have been drastically altered. This theoretical distinction needs to be made, even though it is recognized that the concrete changes *of* a system may be the consequence of previous changes *within* the system.

Whether conflicts within a society will lead to adjustments between existing institutions or to systemic changes of the institutions depends on the degree of flexibility of the social structure. Flexible systems allow progressive rearrangements in their structures in tune with the outcome of various types of group conflict within them. Rigid societies, refusing to make such adjustments and allowing

the accumulation of unresolved latent conflicts, are likely to maximize the chances of violent outbreaks attacking the consensual structure and leading to changes *of* social systems.

Ingroup and outgroup

Sumner's dictum that the distinction between the ingroup (ourselves) and the outgroup (everybody else) is established in, and through, conflict has found general acceptance. One of the prime mechanisms for the strengthening of group bonds and for the emergence of new groups has always been the creation or strengthening among group members of a sense of common values, interests, and purposes, all leading to a mobilization of the group's energies against outsiders. The distinction between "us" and "them," perhaps the most fundamental social distinction, is established and periodically reaffirmed in social conflict between insiders and outsiders, between friends and enemies. In homogeneous societies, in which individuals participate in only small numbers of social circles, this distinction is likely to be so encompassing that it allows only minimal relations between the members of all but a few social circles. However, in heterogeneous societies, that is, in societies in which individuals are likely to participate in a great number of social circles in which there will be high degrees of overlapping memberships in a variety of associations and groupings, this sense of exclusiveness will be successfully minimized. In such societies, with their varieties of functionally specific and nongeneralized conflict, men who will be friends in one relationship might well be enemies in another; conflicts with some lead to new alliances with others. If everyone is somebody's ally in some respects and his opponent in many others, such conflicts will draw all into a multifarious and varied group life in which the very crisscrossing of allegiances among men segmentally involved on a variety of fronts prevents exclusiveness and withdrawal.

Peace and feuding, conflict and order, are correlative. Both the cementing and the breaking of the cake of custom constitute part of the dialectic of social life. One is hence ill-advised to distinguish sharply a sociology of order from a sociology of conflict, or a harmony model of society from a conflict model. Such attempts can only result in artificial distinctions. The analysis of social conflicts brings to awareness aspects of social reality that may be obscured if analytical attention focuses too exclusively on phenomena of social order; but an exclusive attention to conflict phenomena may obscure the central importance of social order and needs to be corrected by a correlative concern with the ordered aspects of social life. We deal here not with distinct realities but only with differing aspects of the same reality, so that exclusive emphasis on one or the other is likely to lead the analyst astray. Perhaps we need return now to Charles Horton Cooley's statement: "The more one thinks of it the more he will see that conflict and co-operation are not separable things, but phases of one process which always involves something of both" (1918, p. 39).

LEWIS A. COSER

[Relevant material may be found under PEACE; SOCIOLOGY, article on THE DEVELOPMENT OF SOCIOLOGICAL THOUGHT.]

BIBLIOGRAPHY

The major works of most of the classical social theorists contain references to, and discussions of, social conflict. The work of Karl Marx and Georg Simmel has been of special fruitfulness for subsequent theorizing. Marx's analysis is dispersed throughout most of his works. Simmel's major contribution is Conflict; The Web of Group Affiliations 1908. For more recent work in the area, consult the analytical summary in Mack & Snyder 1957.

BERNARD, JESSIE 1957 The Sociological Study of Conflict. Pages 33–117 in International Sociological Association, The Nature of Conflict: Studies on the Sociological Aspects of International Tensions. UNESCO, Tensions and Technology Series. Paris: UNESCO. → Contains a comprehensive bibliography.

BOULDING, KENNETH E. 1962 Conflict and Defense: A General Theory. A publication of the Center for Research in Conflict Resolution at the University of Michigan. New York: Harper.

COOLEY, CHARLES H. 1918 Social Process. New York: Scribner.

COSER, LEWIS A. 1956 The Functions of Social Conflict. Glencoe, Ill.: Free Press.

DAHRENDORF, RALF (1957) 1959 Class and Class Conflict in Industrial Society. Rev. & enl. ed. Stanford (Calif.) Univ. Press → First published in German as Soziale Klassen und Klassen-Konflikt in der industriellen Gesellschaft.

DAHRENDORF, RALF 1962 Gesellschaft und Freiheit: Zur soziologischen Analyse der Gegenwart. Munich: Piper. → This work incorporates a series of papers previously published in English.

GLUCKMAN, MAX 1956 Custom and Conflict in Africa. Oxford: Blackwell; Glencoe, Ill.: Free Press.

MACK, RAYMOND W.; and SNYDER, RICHARD S. 1957 The Analysis of Social Conflict: Toward an Overview and Synthesis. Journal of Conflict Resolution 1:212–248.

PARK, ROBERT E.; and BURGESS, ERNEST 1924 Introduction to the Science of Society. Univ. of Chicago Press.

SIMMEL, GEORG (1908) 1955 Conflict; The Web of Group Affiliations. Glencoe, Ill.: Free Press. → These essays originally appeared as "Der Streit" and "Die Kreuzung sozialer Kreise" in Georg Simmel's Soziologie, published by Duncker and Humblot, Berlin.

WEBER, MAX (1904–1917) 1949 Max Weber on the Methodology of the Social Sciences. Translated and edited by Edward A. Shils and H. A. Finch. Glencoe, Ill.: Free Press.

IV
ANTHROPOLOGICAL ASPECTS

Conflict results from competition between at least two parties. A party may be a person, a family, a lineage, or a whole community; or it may be a class of ideas, a political organization, a tribe, or a religion. Conflict is occasioned by incompatible desires or aims and by its duration may be distinguished from strife or angry disputes arising from momentary aggravations. It is safe to assume that some of the causes of conflict are to be found in the aggressive behavior that is almost universal among the vertebrates and is presumably adaptive in a broad range of environments. The function of much conflict appears to be the control of food and reproduction through the control of territory and the maintenance of well-organized dominance hierarchies that serve to reduce the amount of fighting in a group (Ciba Foundation 1966).

Field studies of nonhuman primates reveal that relations between different species of mammals are usually peaceful or neutral; between groups of the same species, reactions range from avoidance to agonistic display and even to violence. Conflict between individuals within the local group occurs far more frequently than intergroup or interspecies conflict. One kind of behavior that appears to be limited to primates is the use of objects in agonistic display. This use of objects has not yet been observed in other animal orders.

The evolutionary frame of reference of most primate studies leads to consideration of conflict and aggression as part of the species-specific pattern of adaptive behavior. Since this aggression is the result of the long-term evolution of the species, it is functionally adaptive in the present only if the conditions of the present are the same as those under which the behavior evolved. Today man's way of life is radically different from that of the past. Yet we still inherit the biology of aggression that was adaptive in times past. In nonhuman primates, evolution has progressed slowly enough to maintain the balance between species-specific biological behavior patterns and social behavior.

We cannot ignore man's biological heritage as a framework within which culture is elaborated and developed. We must not, on the other hand, ignore the fact that man did develop culture and the ability to manipulate symbols. As a result, the evolution of human behavior needs to be explained by the processes of cultural selection as well as of biological selection. The study of conflict may be further clarified if conflict is not equated with aggressive behavior, since it is not a type of behavior but, rather, a situation resulting from incompatible interests or values. The anthropologist studies conflict as a multidimensional social process that operates in many different contexts and results in a variety of consequences. The simplest as well as the most elaborate display of conflict behavior is defined by its function, by the part it plays within a system of human activities, and by the ideas and values attached to it.

Although theoretical attention to social and cultural conflict is relatively new in anthropology, ethnographers have long been recording instances of conflict occurring under a variety of guises. Such diverse phenomena as witchcraft practices, feuds, factionalism, warfare, competitive games, contradictory values, and discord between spouses have been viewed as conflict or as the potential means for displacing conflict from one level of social grouping to another. Anthropological studies of feuds, warfare, and witchcraft have frequently concerned themselves with institutionalized or socially regulated conflict involving groups. Conflict not formalized by institutional means has been described by ethnographers as part of the case material of primitive legal systems or in terms of acculturation pressures.

The major theories of conflict, primarily influenced by the structural–functional theory of social organization and only indirectly by the psychoanalytic theory of personality, have assumed conflict to be a valid generic term for such diverse phenomena as those mentioned above; this is in part because all these conflict situations involve opposition over scarce goods and resources, either in a literal or in a figurative sense.

Some recent theoretical studies emphasize the associative aspects of conflict; others approach conflict from the viewpoint of contradictions in systems of values. Anthropologists have also attempted to use theories of frustration–aggression displacement in studies of intergroup conflict and have applied psychoanalytic concepts such as identification and status envy in interpreting frequency of intragroup aggression.

The structural–functional approach to the study of conflict or aggression emphasizes the social structural sources of conflict, the functions of conflict at various structural levels, the mechanisms for resolution or control of conflict, and the various behavioral means for communicating conflict.

While anthropologists insist that conflict is in great part a cultural product, they are also cognizant of the biological and social aspects of conflict among nonhuman primates. Although there may be discontinuities in the phenomena under observation as they pertain to nonhuman species and as they pertain to human beings, field studies of primates may be useful in constructing an evolutionary view of social and cultural conflict that will help the anthropologist to determine the universal aspects of human conflict.

The functions of conflict

Equilibrium model. Confusion of the concepts of equilibrium, integration, and stability has led to ambiguity in the study of conflict. Conflict is discord; its opposite is harmony—which for many implies integration. Integration and conflict have often been discussed as opposites, and indeed conflict has been equated with anomie—deviant, abnormal behavior which impedes the successful integration of society. Integration and related terms frequently have been used with strong value connotations, especially when changes resulting from acculturative pressures are described. Cultural integration refers to coherence among cultural elements and some degree of integration is, of course, characteristic of all societies. The absence of conflict and the presence of cooperation and coordinated action are sometimes used as indexes of integration or societal stability. Conflict is more readily observable than is integration. As a result, much of anthropological discussion of integration or stability is implicit rather than explicit, as is illustrated both by the configurational view, which employs a psychological approach to cultural integration, and by the functional view, which attempts to study the interrelations of various institutions of a culture. The configurationalists are particularly interested in discovering the themes or values that hold a culture together and distinguish it from others, and they refer to consistent, harmonious, balanced cultures as "genuine" rather than "spurious." There has been a marked trend, however, to consider conflict and change as inevitable and essential aspects of the social process; this has led some to criticize the equilibrium model characterized by the functionalists, referred to by Dahrendorf as utopian. The functionalists' stress on common values and equilibrium may have stemmed from a concern with normative behavior and the study of those societies not undergoing rapid change.

In recognizing conflict as an inevitable consequence of the operation of a social system, several anthropologists have raised an interesting question:

Given the proposition that conflicts are both disruptive and inevitable, how can a social system persist as a going concern? Gluckman (1956) takes the position that conflict need not disrupt a social system, that, indeed, it may contribute toward the maintenance of society. He points out that struggles between the Zulu princes of South Africa for the throne occur within a continuing social system. In this example the society directs and controls the quarrels through conflicts of allegiance so that, despite rebellion among the Zulu, for example, the same social system is re-established. Multiplicity of conflicts within a social system creates a division of society into a series of opposed groups with cross-cutting membership. The degree to which conflict is regulated can vary, but the dysfunctional aspects of conflict always tend to be minimized by the channeling of behavior along controllable lines. In a Welsh village, conflicts within the social system may be institutionalized in the activities of its football clubs, carnival associations, and brass bands, whereas among the Zulu and Swazi of South Africa the fundamental conflicts of the social system are acted out in the rituals of rebellion. Social cohesion, then, is found in the conflicts between differing allegiances or in the displacement of conflict onto institutionalized forms of entertainment.

In certain African stateless societies organized on the lineage principle, stability was maintained by virtue of segmental opposition; equilibrium was achieved by a balanced opposition between territorial segments of the same order. Ethnographic study of the Iroquois and the Zuni in America and of the Tonga and the Nuer in Africa has led to an alternative suggestion, namely, that stability is the indirect result of the presence within each local group of people of a diverse set of ties cross-linking them with other groups.

The stress–strain theory. While still dealing with intragroup dissension, the stress–strain theory contrasts with the previous theories in holding that group solidarity is reduced under certain conditions of external stress, and, in fact, is maladaptive. Factionalism is likely to appear when there are strains within the social structure and when certain kinds of external stresses occur. Navajo witchcraft is described by Kluckhohn (1944), who suggests that belief in and practice of witchcraft permit the expression of direct and displaced aggression in situations of stress which, prior to the presence of U.S. authority, might have been expressed in warfare. Acculturation pressures, domination by an alien social system that overrides traditional patterns of authority, and a combination of environmental and economic threats accentuated by the impact of a dominant culture may also strain weak points in the social structure. Siegel and Beals (1960) attempt to isolate types of conflict, each having its own particular explanation. *Pervasive factionalism,* which occurs between unorganized and transient groupings, is distinguished from *schismatic conflicts,* which lead to the dissolution of subgroups of the larger society. Institutionalized conflicts are permanently or periodically resolved; examples of this are found in political party behavior, sport teams, dual organizations, and intermarrying kin groups. Relevant to the question of how conflict may produce instability are observations made among the Soga of west Africa. Fallers (1957) describes the strain and instability produced by a society structured both by corporate lineages and by the state; in this example there is a conflict of roles that results when incompatible institutions apply to the same persons. Conflicts which cannot be resolved within the existing social system eventually produce changes in the social structure.

The literature allows us to distinguish more generally between "elastic" and "rigid" social systems. An elastic social system tolerates open and direct expression of conflict and allows for organizational adjustment; within an elastic system there will be institutionalized arrangements for the expression of conflict, such as duels, feuds, joking relations, and witchcraft. In such societies conflict may serve to stabilize and integrate. Rigid societies have a tendency to suppress conflict, since they have less tolerance for it. In rigid societies, the acting out of pent-up conflict may cause changes in the social structure. The degree of tolerance of conflict varies and quite clearly affects the function of conflict.

The occurrence of conflict

Conflict occurs in all human societies but varies in degree and form of expression. In some societies verbal rather than physical aggression is more frequent, while in other societies more passive forms of expression may predominate. Some peoples inhibit aggression within the local community, only to wage war with surrounding groups. Some social anthropologists have suggested that environmental factors, such as ecology, demography, and economy, affect cross-cultural variations in social conflict. For example, warfare may be related to the level of economic development and population density. Archeological evidence indicates that warfare was unknown in Europe and the Orient until the late Neolithic period. Organized warfare was unknown in aboriginal Australia. Groups like the

Pueblo Indians of the southwest United States rarely engaged in offensive warfare. It appears that competition between groups seeking to exploit the same territory or resource leads to conflict.

Demographic factors. Density of population, which seems to be associated with greater individual restraint and inhibition, may be a factor in the elaboration of verbal aggression or witchcraft practices. For example, LeVine (1961) suggests that among the Gusii of Africa, proximity of co-wives is responsible for the great number of witchcraft accusations. Observations and experiments on nonhuman animals support the conclusion that density of population seems to increase in-group aggression, which takes such forms as homicide and assault. Human beings sometimes invent institutions that provide a sort of safety valve whereby aggression generated in the in-group may be drained off internally instead of being translated into out-group hostility and warfare. Thus it is possible that some form of dual organization (such as the widespread phenomenon of twofold factional divisions) may be an instance of a socially invented safety valve. Greater population density may also call for more centralized and elaborated adjudication procedures which, in theory at least, may curb the degree of violent conflict. However, although environmental factors may have specific influence, they cannot provide a general explanation of intergroup or intragroup variations. Variation is not explained by any general theory of conflict. Rather, anthropologists are exploring a number of hypotheses that rest upon systemic factors focusing on one of several structural levels—intrafamily, intracommunity, intercommunity.

Conflict within the family. Gluckman (1956), in his attempt to relate estrangement in the family to the type of extended kinship system, postulated that the structure or type of descent system is a major determinant of the frequency of divorce. He suggests that divorce is rare among societies with extreme patriliny and frequent in matrilineal societies; bilateral societies would be expected to fall between the highest and the lowest rate. He distinguishes a fundamental conflict between rights centered in a woman as a wife and rights centered in her as a child-bearer, arguing that it is the rights in woman as child-bearer which establish firm husband–wife relations. In a matrilineal society these two rights are separated, for the wife's descent group maintains rights in the woman as child-bearer. Where the woman bears children for her own blood kin, her wifely bond is weak and divorce is frequent. In patrilineal societies, however, the woman's kin transfer to the husband their

rights in her both as wife and as child-bearer. Where the woman bears children for her husband's group, her wifely bond is strong. Fallers (1957) later observed that the Soga of east Africa were patrilineal in descent but not characterized by stable marriage, as Gluckman would have predicted. This led Fallers to reformulate the original hypothesis, pointing out that the crucial variable in patrilineal systems is the degree to which the woman is socially absorbed into her husband's patrilineage. Where a woman is not absorbed into her husband's lineage, patriliny tends to divide marriages by dividing the loyalties of the spouses.

While the single major factor, descent, and its concomitant features may be useful in explaining marital conflict when comparing societies as wholes, it does not predict what correlates are relevant to the relative incidence of marital conflict within a society. Political and economic relations established by marriage may be powerful determinants, and Cohen (1961), in his description of variations in marital conflict within a single society, the Kanuri of northeastern Nigeria, suggests that conflicting allegiances may be only a part of the picture. He argues that economic relations between husband and wife maintain or disrupt marriage relations. Dependency of men on female services seems to undermine the expected husband–wife authority relation, and where men among the Kanuri are dependent on women, the divorce rate is high.

Intergroup conflict. The analysis of conflicting loyalties has also been used in explaining intergroup conflict. Both Colson (1953) and Gluckman (1956) argue that in stateless segmentary societies, peace may be achieved through divided loyalties. Gluckman notes that among the Nuer of east Africa the vengeance group is sufficiently scattered so that when an intergroup killing occurs, retaliation may force a person into a position of having to fight with his neighbors against his kinsmen or of being treated as an enemy by his neighbors. In this untenable situation an attempt may be made to mitigate conflict through compensation rather than blood vengeance. Evans-Pritchard's earlier analysis of the Nuer (1940) emphasized the balance of power through segmental opposition, rather than cross-cutting ties, as the chief deterrent to intergroup violence.

Murphy (1957) explored the problem of cross-cutting group loyalties and their effect on intergroup hostility and intragroup cohesiveness among the Mundurucu of the Brazilian rain forest. It has often been noted by social scientists that severe inhibition of aggression within a society encourages the channeling of aggression through external out-lets such as warfare; it has also been noted that a threat coming from outside the group causes inter-nal solidarity. In the case of the Mundurucu, war-fare was not inspired by desire for material gain but, rather, served to release tensions built up by a society rigid in its inhibition of violence. There was a contradiction between the norms of behavior applicable to members of the in-group on the one hand and to members of the out-group on the other. Murphy links the form of residence with out-group aggression: matrilocal societies, characterized by multiple and conflicting loyalties of males sepa-rated at marriage from consanguineal kinsmen, must repress overt aggression in order to ensure cohesion. Hostilities that are built into the structure of such societies must be expressed by displaced aggression or unrealistic conflict if the societies are to continue to exist. The assumption is that there is aggression which must be repressed and that it is likely to find an outlet by displacement onto an outside group. Murphy believes that such societies are less likely to exhibit internecine violence than are patrilocal societies, in which men tied through descent continue living together after marriage.

Thoden van Velzen and van Wetering (1960) tested the hypothesis associating matrilocality with the absence of in-group violence by comparing 50 unstratified societies divided between matrilocal and patrilocal. They confirmed the correlation of matrilocality with intrasocietal peace, but their ex-planation is a significant departure from that of conflicting loyalties. They see most matrilocal so-cieties as lacking power groups—that is, groups which resort to aggression when the interests of one of the members are threatened. According to their view, aggression develops as a result of patri-local structures; it does not develop in matrilocal so-cieties, so that there is no need for them to repress aggression, as Murphy suggests. These approaches are not concerned with psychoanalytic assumptions concerning intersocietal aggression or with explain-ing warfare; they do attempt to explain why some stateless, unstratified societies are more peaceful than others.

Recent studies which combine demographic with psychological explanations suggest that there are a type of culture and a type of social structure which produce an adolescent and adult personality predisposed to behave at times in a violent and aggressive fashion. Beatrice Whiting (1965) in-vestigated the frequency of assault and homicide in six societies. She considers their higher fre-quencies in two of the six societies in the light of the concept of "protest masculinity," the status envy hypothesis of identification, and the preva-lence of female-based households.

Briefly, the status envy theory states that an in-dividual identifies with the person who seems most important to him, the person who is perceived as controlling those resources which he wants. If dur-ing the first two or three years of life a child is constantly with his mother and sees and is handled by his father infrequently, he will identify strongly with his mother, not with his father. In short, if he is a boy, he will have cross-sex identification. If, later in life, he is involved in a world obviously dominated by men, he will be thrown into conflict and will develop a strong need to reject his earlier underlying female identification. This identity con-flict may lead to an overdetermined attempt to prove his masculinity, manifested by a preoccupa-tion with physical strength and athletic prowess, or attempts to demonstrate daring and valor, or behavior which is violent and aggressive, i.e., pro-test masculinity.

Conflict resolution and prevention

An understanding of the ways in which conflict is resolved is particularly relevant to an under-standing of the functions of conflict and its ex-pression. LeVine (1961) distinguishes five forms of conflict-indicating behavior: physical aggres-sion, public verbal dispute, covert verbal aggres-sion, breach of expectation, and avoidance. All of these forms may be found within the same culture: for example, Zapotec women rarely make use of physical aggression; Zapotec men rarely employ forms of verbal aggression. It is important to note, however, that those behaviors which proceed from and are indicative of conflict may also operate to resolve the conflict. If avoidance or physical ag-gression does not successfully resolve a conflict, the use of a third party to achieve settlement by arbitration, mediation, compromise, or adjudica-tion is likely. Certain institutionalized forms of resolution, such as councils, courts, go-betweens, or "crossers," perform these functions. Anthropolo-gists have made significant note of the fact that the resolution and control of conflict need not necessarily be identified with specialized political offices. There are viable, stable societies which lack central government and specialized political roles but which nonetheless have available other means of resolving and regulating conflict. In such state-less societies a variety of institutions and person-nel, such as diviner and shaman, may function as agents of conflict resolution. Among the Bedouin, institutions such as the feud function to punish serious transgressions and act as a brake to prevent aggression, for feuds are dreaded. Among the Dobu, sorcery is a socialized ritual that operates as the medium for a nonviolent adjustment of opposing interests. The style of conflict resolution derives from a society's structural principles of human association.

The conditions which define the presence and use of specific controlling procedures are various. Greater density of population and the dissolution of family authority and power that accompanies the development of a centralized state system may strengthen adjudication procedures in place of mediation or arbitration. In general, the procedural aspects of legal organization are more developed as political organization becomes more specialized, but other factors, such as the allocation of authority, are also relevant. For example, for the resolution of marital conflict, the differential use of the court systems available to each of two Mexican villages is closely correlated with the degree of authority allocated respectively to the family and to the court systems (Nader & Metzger 1963). Indeed, the development of courts or councils may be inhibited by the dual organization structure of a community.

A more comprehensive approach to the occurrence, function, control, and resolution of conflict may be achieved by examining the life cycles of particular conflicts. The processes through which a conflict may pass may be found to be inherent in the type of conflict. Various mechanisms are employed within the same society to heal breaches of peace. These actions may range from informal arbitration to formal legal machinery or to the performance of public ritual. Mystical beliefs and ritual action, rather than judicial machinery, are particularly effective in dealing with disturbances arising from processes inherent in the life cycle of a group.

Laura Nader

[See also Feud; Integration; Political anthropology; Social structure; War. *Directly related are the entries* Myth and symbol; Social behavior, animal; Social control.]

BIBLIOGRAPHY

Campbell, Donald T.; and LeVine, Robert A. 1965 Propositions About Ethnocentrism From Social Science Theories. Unpublished manuscript.

Ciba Foundation 1966 *Conflict in Society.* Edited by Anthony de Reuck and Julie Knight. London: Church-ill; Boston: Little. → See especially the article by Sherwood L. Washburn, "Conflict in Primate Society."

Cohen, Ronald 1961 Marriage Instability Among the Kanuri of Northern Nigeria. *American Anthropologist* New Series 63:1231–1249.

Colson, Elizabeth 1953 Social Control and Vengeance in Plateau Tonga Society. *Africa* 23:199–211.

Coser, Lewis A. 1956 *The Functions of Social Conflict.* Glencoe, Ill.: Free Press.

Dahrendorf, Ralf (1957) 1959 *Class and Class Conflict in Industrial Society.* Rev. & enl. ed. Stanford Univ. Press. → First published as *Soziale Klassen und Klassen-Konflikt in der industriellen Gesellschaft.*

Dahrendorf, Ralf 1962 *Gesellschaft und Freiheit: Zur soziologischen Analyse der Gegenwart.* Munich: Piper.

Evans-Pritchard, E. E. (1940) 1963 *The Nuer: A Description of the Modes of Livelihood and Political Institutions of a Nilotic People.* Oxford: Clarendon.

Fallers, Lloyd A. 1956 *Bantu Bureaucracy: A Study of Integration and Conflict in the Political Institutions of an East African People.* Cambridge: Heffer.

Fallers, Lloyd A. 1957 Some Determinants of Marriage Stability in Busoga. *Africa* 27:106–123.

Fortune, Reo F. (1932) 1963 *Sorcerers of Dobu: The Social Anthropology of the Dobu Islanders of the Western Pacific.* Rev. ed. London: Routledge.

Gluckman, Max (1956) 1959 *Custom and Conflict in Africa.* Glencoe, Ill.: Free Press.

Kluckhohn, Clyde 1944 *Navaho Witchcraft.* Cambridge, Mass.: Peabody Museum.

Leach, Edmund R. 1954 *Political Systems of Highland Burma: A Study of Kachin Social Structure.* A publication of the London School of Economics and Political Science. London School of Economics and Political Science; Cambridge, Mass.: Harvard Univ. Press.

LeVine, Robert A. 1961 Anthropology and the Study of Conflict: An Introduction. *Journal of Conflict Resolution* 5:3–15.

McNeil, Elton B. (editor) 1965 *The Nature of Human Conflict.* Englewood Cliffs, N.J.: Prentice-Hall. → See especially "The Sociology of Human Conflict," by Robert C. Angell.

Marx, Karl (1844–1875) 1964 *Selected Writings in Sociology and Social Philosophy.* 2d ed. Edited by T. B. Bottomore and M. Rubel with a foreword by Erich Fromm. New York: McGraw-Hill.

Murphy, Robert F. 1957 Intergroup Hostility and Social Cohesion. *American Anthropologist* New Series 59:1018–1035.

Nader, Laura; and Metzger, Duane 1963 Conflict Resolution in Two Mexican Communities. *American Anthropologist* New Series 65:584–592.

Rapoport, Anatol 1965 Is Warmaking a Characteristic of Human Beings or of Cultures? [A review of *The Natural History of Aggression.*] *Scientific American* 213, no. 4:115–118. → This is an excellent review of the problems encountered in generalizing the findings on aggression from animals to man.

Siegel, Bernard J.; and Beals, Alan R. 1960 Pervasive Factionalism. *American Anthropologist* New Series 62:394–417.

Simmel, Georg (1908) 1955 *Conflict; The Web of Group Affiliations.* Glencoe, Ill.: Free Press. → These essays appeared originally as "Der Streit" and "Die Kreuzung sozialer Kreise" in Georg Simmel's *Soziologie,* published by Duncker and Humblot.

THODEN VAN VELZEN, H. U. E.; and VAN WETERING, W.
    1960 Residence, Power Groups, and Intra-societal
    Aggression: An Inquiry Into the Conditions Leading
    to Peacefulness Within Non-stratified Societies. *International Archives of Ethnography* 49:169–200.

WHITING, BEATRICE B. 1965 Sex Identity and Physical
    Violence: A Comparative Study. *American Anthropologist* Special Publication 67, no. 6, part 2:123–140. →
    This contains a short review of the literature on cross-
    sex identification.

CONFLICT OF INTEREST

How can there be assurance that a government official, businessman, or professional person will properly perform his duty to the public, to his employer, or to his client when that duty affects his own private economic interests? In its narrowest sense, this is the key question of conflict of interest. The question rapidly broadens when the range of primary interests attached to duty are considered in relation to the dazzling variety of property and other interests potentially in conflict. In modern industrial society, where services abound, where government and business intersect in countless ways, the nature of conflicting interests is most complex. Government employees retain private economic interests that may be benefited by official actions. Officers of one corporation may own stock of another, whose value may be affected by actions of the first.

An ethical crisis in the public life of the United States after World War II was expressed in concern over conflicts of interest for upper-echelon civil servants. The matter was isolated and widely recognized as a moral and legal issue about 1950, and has been pondered and studied ever since. Conflict-of-interest legislation and regulations eventually were adopted for the United States government and a number of states and municipalities and by governments of other nations. Every sign suggests that this movement of concern and control will become more widespread in the world and will apply beyond the executive branch of government.

Since its control involves *preventive law*, conflict of interest must be distinguished from other kinds of criminal behavior, such as theft or bribery. A government official may be found guilty of bribery if he agrees to act in response to money or favors. The first general federal bribery statute in the United States, dating from 1853, declares that a payment to influence official action is a clear abuse and declares it a criminal act. By contrast, the term "conflict of interest" implies the need for preventive action to mark the kinds of situations individuals should avoid. "Regulation of conflicts of

interest seeks to prevent situations of temptations from arising" (Association of the Bar . . . 1960, pp. 3–4). It is regulation of potential harm, of evil before it occurs. The added subtlety of preventive law gives the control of conflicts of interest unusual delicacy.

In the nineteenth century, if an official resolved a clash between his personal advantage and public duty in favor of personal advantage, it was called corruption. But since then "corruption" has come to be associated with only the most odious and obvious forms of venality and self-service, and the term "conflict of interests" was coined to cover less blatant cases. The leading study on the subject limited itself to two interests: ". . . one is the interest of the government official (and of the public) in the proper administration of his office; the other is the official's interest in his private economic affairs. A conflict of interest exists whenever these two interests clash, or appear to clash" (Association of the Bar . . . 1960, p. 3). The present article, accepting this usage, will review the significant recent developments in the framing of a system of relevant, up-to-date restraints against conflicts of interest in federal service in the United States. These limitations are being widely copied or adapted in other countries and by state and local governments in the United States. After surveying conflicts of interests in government service, this article will touch on other arenas in which such problems are now identified.

The legal profession, far more than any other professional group or social-science discipline, has scrutinized the problem of government officials' conflicts of interest. Leaders of the bar, as well as their clients in business and in other professions, have long counted public service as part of a viable career. Conscientious effort to disentangle public duty from private opportunity could not always shield such men from criticism. After World War II, American law on the subject of conflict of interest was so antiquated that little protection was afforded either the public or the large numbers of people entering and leaving public service, and many individuals were discouraged from taking jobs in the federal government. This was the chief impetus that led the New York City Bar Association to form, in 1956, a special committee, which has developed a corpus of knowledge on the subject (Association of the Bar . . . 1960, pp. vii–xii; Perkins 1963, p. 1114; Manning 1964).

Several other factors have been behind a trend toward deepening attention to conflicts of interest in the public service: (1) the growing reliance of government on the skills of individuals in private life, notably in the fields of science and technology; (2) the mobility of individuals in industry, business, and the professions, in and out of government employment; (3) the intricacy and extent of government regulatory, promotional, and financially supportive programs affecting private sectors of the economy; (4) the expansion in peacetime of government as a customer of business; (5) growing stock ownership among individuals, who have a resulting stake in the private economy (Perkins 1963, p. 1114); (6) the emergence of government during the past decade as a major source of wealth. "The Wealth of more and more Americans depends upon a relationship to government. Increasingly, Americans live on government largess . . ." (Reich 1964, p. 733). These accelerating changes have multiplied the number of potential conflicts of interests. The newness of these situations has led to subtleties difficult to understand, explain, or curb.

Legal analysis has succeeded in isolating some of the peculiar problems of conflict of interest in modern society. Some relevant skills in coping with the issue were noted by the *Harvard Law Review* in this way: ". . . behavior profitable but in itself innocent may be outlawed because it tempts abuse of power or allows misuse of information and advantages gained through government service. The resulting tension taxes the lawyer's faculty for inference drawing, for weighing competing interests, and for ingenuity in framing legal solutions" ("With the Editors . . ." 1963, p. vii). Lawyers have analyzed the aims of the conflict-of-interest statutes of the past and willingly specified the ethical norms upon which new rules of law should be based. Five principles have been established as fundamental to prudent conflict-of-interest regulations at the federal level in the United States (Perkins 1963, pp. 1118–1122).

The first moral imperative to be protected by conflict-of-interest rules is that against self-dealing. A public official may not participate in government action where that specific action might significantly affect his private economic interests.

A second principle, less distinct than the concept of self-dealing, stops a public official from accepting transfers of economic value from private sources. It is believed that gifts should be barred, even though bribery is absent, on the assumption that a danger of subservience remains present. A government official acting in his official capacity must be free of the relationship created when an individual accepts gifts and other valuable transfers from private sources (Perkins 1963, pp. 1119–1120).

Third, a public official should not ordinarily be allowed to drop his official role to help private individuals or organizations in their dealings with the government. This is an especially forceful conflict-of-interest principle when compensation is received for the assistance.

Fourth, the same principle also applies to a former public official in connection with his past official responsibilities. This principle is usually cushioned by a limitation of time, although objection has been made that any definite limit, say two years, is both artificial and ineffective. Nevertheless, the principle remains that a former official should not be able to trade against the government with influence gained from past association or friendship in his official capacity (Perkins 1963, pp. 1120–1121).

The fifth conflict-of-interest principle holds that a public official should not be allowed to use for private gain confidential information acquired in his official capacity. There may be no specific injury to the government, but it is argued that a wrong occurs in the private use of information that belongs to the public (Perkins 1963, pp. 1121–1122).

In 1962, following several years of study, education, and agitation, the federal code and regulations governing conflicts of interest were overhauled to express these principles better. The new act applies to all officers and employees "in the executive, legislative, or judicial branch of the Government, or in any agency of the United States" (Public Law 87-849, 76 Stat. 1121). Conflict-of-interest principles are applied to all forms of modern decisions: ". . . any proceeding, application, request for a ruling or other determination, contract, claim, controversy, charge, accusation, arrest, or other particular matter in which the United States is a party or has a direct and substantial interest." The official is culpable if he "participates personally and substantially" in any of these transactions "through decision, approval, disapproval, recommendation, the rendering of advice, investigation, or otherwise." The 1962 act thus embodies a creative effort to make the chief conflict-of-interest principles applicable to today's circumstances.

Criminal sanctions imposed by statute play a limited role in protecting conflict-of-interest principles. Bayless Manning has named many other means of conflict-of-interest regulation in the federal government:

The Senate, in its conduct of confirmation proceedings, has frequently imposed special conflict of interest standards not found in the statutes. Congress may also bring strong pressures to bear through its investigatory process. Many relationships that might be legally acceptable, and not considered morally reprehensible conflicts of interest, may be politically very sensitive and politically unacceptable. And, finally, many agencies of the government have developed their own operating rules and their own internal regulations for dealing with the problem of ethics as it affects their own operations. No one called upon to consider a question of conflict of interest in the federal service will have done his job unless he has weighed and investigated, in addition to the statutes in the field, the applicable administrative regulations, likely Congressional response, and the general political environment. (Manning 1964, pp. 10–11)

The American press almost daily reports incidents that bring wide public disapproval but where neither the statutes nor informal sanctions have been effective in preventing a conflict of interest in the federal service. Resignations occur, but public criticism is not always effective. This becomes comprehensible when it is recognized that the goal of avoiding corruption is balanced against other, competing goals, particularly employee recruitment and morale. This is a typical statement of the view: "In drafting a conflict-of-interests statute it is easy to become overzealous and to forget the impact which a broad restriction may have. A well-drawn statute should prohibit conflicts of interests which are most damaging to the standards of good government and yet not prohibit so much that competent people will be discouraged from serving" (Harvard Student Legislative Research Bureau 1964, p. 69).

This view has been carried further by some critics of conflict-of-interest regulation. In particular, a proposal to establish a commission on ethics in government was criticized as irrelevant to the problem, which is seen fundamentally as a question of the status of the government employee in the community (Davis 1954, p. 915). Thurman Arnold said this: "Ethics in any group arise out of a sense of tradition and pride in his particular calling. Humiliate that group. Subject them to constant restriction and supervision. Refuse to trust them in any of their activities in or out of Government and you destroy any possibility of an effective ethical code" (U.S. Congress . . . 1951, p. 372).

Altogether, several criticisms may be made of the approach to conflict of interest of the Bar Association, the 1962 act, and the federal regulations. The code-of-ethics approach has been mentioned. Another view is that in a democratic society all government employees should be required to disclose their personal assets and economic interests

to the public or to Congress (Ross D. Davis in Chicago, University of . . . 1961, pp. 83–84). More often this suggestion is applied only to elected officials, on grounds that voters are the appropriate judges of improper conflicts of interests. But such publicity would unduly violate the private affairs of all the employees. Such a requirement for elected officials is more pertinent, but whether voters function effectively as judges of impropriety is open to question.

Another view is that the kinds of conflicts of interest described here are only a small part of the pressure and cross fire public officials feel. Against this, a concept of the "public interest" is put forward as the value to be served, and words like "neutral," "objective," and "disinterested" describe the desired stance. Davis remarked that "in an ideal state the only influence brought to bear upon a public official should of course be his enlightened consideration of the public interest as defined by law" (Chicago, University of . . . 1961, p. 81). Yet the acceptance of interest groups at all levels and branches of government as legitimate registers considerable faith in the capacity of public officials to be disinterested. Of course, gross forms of pressure have been banned, and disclosure of lobbying and campaign expenses is required. The Bar Association report (Association of the Bar . . . 1961, pp. 20–22) distinguishes conflicts of policy from the problem of personal conflicts of interest. The view is that when an organization seeks to persuade, even though the persuasiveness is backed by reprisal, the acts are political. Accordingly, conflicts of policy are altogether proper and desirable.

Actually, the Bar Association approach recognizes that public officials cannot put aside longtime associations. The legal realists of a past generation saw that emotional nuances and environmental conditioning inevitably affect the approach men take to the decisions they face. Of course, values such as affection or rectitude color official decisions. Indeed, nepotism is banned in government and other institutions, as a kind of conflict of interest. But the outlook of officials cannot and should not be neutralized or sterilized, and the conflict-of-interest laws can never control more than a small part of the total possible relationships that bear on those who make decisions. From the standpoint of the individual, conflicts of interest, under this usage, are a small part of political and personal ethics; from the standpoint of public affairs, they are a part of corruption and of the factors entering into the formation of public policy.

Setting tolerable limits to conflicts of interest also

troubles many nongovernmental institutions. Corporation officials may have conflicting economic interests with competing companies. Law firms and advertising agencies may have client relationships that impinge on other loyalties. Philanthropic foundations and universities encounter conflicts of interest. Accountants, physicians, scientists, and athletes are among those whose conflicts have been reported.

Every group develops informal and unwritten codes of conduct, and it is only after a violation of such a standard that discussion begins to shape more precise rules. Then problems essentially like those in government come to the surface. Consider this definition of the attributes of conflicts in a corporation: "A conflict of interest exists where an employee has a private financial interest or other relationship outside the company that has the *potentiality* of being antagonistic to the best interests of the company, even though it may result in no financial loss to the company and irrespective of the motives of the individual concerned" (Adam 1963, pp. 12–13). The discovery and isolation of employee relationships that could bring potential harm raise delicate questions of supervision. These questions are so difficult that most private organizations continue to cope with them through informal methods rather than by formal rules and procedures.

Social scientists have yet to make studies designed to answer a number of key assumptions of popular writers on the subject. Is morale insurance against corruption? How may concepts such as morale and corruption best be defined and measured? Are salary and tenure protection against employee conflicts of interest? To the extent that conflicts of interest can be distinguished from bribery and from conflicts of policy, what circumstances nourish them? The effectiveness of statutory and other regulatory controls also needs to be measured. The effect of conflict-of-interest restrictions on the recruitment of public officials and on the entry of persons into particular businesses should also be ascertained with exactitude. Such knowledge is needed to understand the subject, and it will also be pertinent to future efforts to delineate and regulate conflicts of interest.

If the factors giving rise to these problems have universality, then developed societies are no more conflict-of-interest prone than developing ones. (This is another area where research is much needed.) Yet if the subject is not limited either to economic conflicts or to the public sector, conflicts of interest appear to be inevitable by-products of complex societies, of the development of sophisticated relationships among business, professional, and governmental institutions.

CLEMENT E. VOSE

[*See also* CIVIL SERVICE; CROSS PRESSURE; LOBBYING; OFFICE, MISUSE OF; POLITICAL FINANCING.]

BIBLIOGRAPHY

ADAM, PAUL J. 1963 What Is a Conflict of Interest? Management Dilemma. *Challenge* 11:11–14.

APPLEBY, PAUL H. 1952 *Morality and Administration in Democratic Government.* Baton Rouge: Louisiana State Univ. Press.

ASSOCIATION OF THE BAR OF THE CITY OF NEW YORK, SPECIAL COMMITTEE ON THE FEDERAL CONFLICT OF INTEREST LAWS 1960 *Conflict of Interest and Federal Service.* Cambridge, Mass.: Harvard Univ. Press.

CALIFORNIA, UNIVERSITY OF, BUREAU OF PUBLIC ADMINISTRATION 1961 *Conflict of Interest in the Federal Government: A Bibliography.* Compiled by Dorothy Campbell Tompkins. Berkeley: Univ. of California Press.

CHICAGO, UNIVERSITY OF, LAW SCHOOL 1961 *Conference on Conflict of Interest, February 20, 1961.* Chicago: The School.

Conflict of Interests: State Government Employees. 1961 *Virginia Law Review* 47:1034–1076.

Conflicts of Interest of State Legislators. 1963 *Harvard Law Review* 76:1209–1232.

Congress Amends Conflict-of-interest Laws. 1962 *Congressional Quarterly Almanac* 18:385–389.

DAVIS, ROSS D. 1954 The Federal Conflict of Interest Laws. *Columbia Law Review* 54:893–915.

GRAHAM, GEORGE A. 1952 *Morality in American Politics.* New York: Random House.

HARVARD STUDENT LEGISLATIVE RESEARCH BUREAU 1964 A Conflict-of-interest Act. *Harvard Journal on Legislation* 1:68–85.

LASSWELL, HAROLD D. 1930 Bribery. Volume 2, pages 690–692 in *Encyclopaedia of the Social Sciences.* New York: Macmillan.

MCELWAIN, EDWIN; and VORENBERG, JAMES 1952 The Federal Conflict of Interest Statutes. *Harvard Law Review* 65:955–983.

MANNING, BAYLESS 1964 *Federal Conflict of Interest Law.* Cambridge, Mass.: Harvard Univ. Press.

NOEL-BAKER, FRANCIS 1961/1962 "The Grey Zone": The Problem of Business Affiliations of Members of Parliament. *Parliamentary Affairs* 15:87–93.

ODEGARD, PETER H. 1931 Corruption, Political: United States. Volume 4, pages 452–455 in *Encyclopaedia of the Social Sciences.* New York: Macmillan.

PERKINS, ROSWELL B. 1963 The New Federal Conflict-of-interest Law. *Harvard Law Review* 76:1113–1169.

REICH, CHARLES A. 1964 The New Property. *Yale Law Journal* 73:733–787.

SENTURIA, JOSEPH J. 1931 Corruption, Political: General. Volume 4, pages 448–452 in *Encyclopaedia of the Social Sciences.* New York: Macmillan.

Unchanging Rules in Changing Times: The Canons of Ethics and Intra-firm Conflicts of Interest. 1964 *Yale Law Journal* 73:1058–1079.

U.S. CONGRESS, SENATE, COMMITTEE ON LABOR AND PUBLIC WELFARE 1951 *Establishment of a Commission on Ethics in Government: Hearings Before a Subcom-*

mittee to Study Senate Concurrent Resolution 21 of the Committee on Labor and Public Welfare. 82d Congress, 1st Session. Washington: Government Printing Office.

WILSON, H. HUBERT 1951 *Congress: Corruption and Compromise.* New York: Rinehart.

With the Editors . . . . 1963 *Harvard Law Review* 76, no. 6:vii.

CONFLICT OF LAWS

Conflict of laws, a subject also known as private international law, arises from the universal acknowledgment that not every human transaction can be, or ought to be, governed by local law. The affairs of men are often conducted in such a way that a legal dispute contains a foreign element, and the conflict of laws is the systematic study of how national courts, in fact and in theory, take account of such foreign elements.

Scope and character

The main emphasis in the conflict of laws has generally been upon the rules used to select foreign law, these rules being called *choice-of-law rules.* It is also common to include in the subject matter of the conflict of laws various related matters pertaining to the jurisdiction of courts and to the degree of respect due foreign judgments, but in the main the classical problems in the field have been created by legal transactions in which the private law of more than one legal unit is potentially applicable and a choice must be made between the competing claims. For centuries judges and scholars have been baffled in their search for acceptable procedures and for the criteria with which to conduct the search itself.

There is a traditional distinction between public and private international law related mainly to whether the participants involved in legal controversy are governments or individuals. In this vein, public international law is defined as the corpus of rules binding governments in their relations with one another and the processes available for implementing these rules; private international law is considered as the law applied by domestic courts whenever a foreign element is relevant to the resolution of a legal controversy. Many specialists in this latter field of law object to the label private international law, suggesting that the law applied by domestic courts—even if it leads to the application of foreign law—is a field of national law. Such a view is especially prevalent in the United States, accounting, in part, for the currency of the term "conflict of laws" to describe the subject, although its use also reflects the emphasis among American scholars, perhaps to an excessive degree, upon the conflict of laws as it has evolved from interstate (intranational) transactions. In Europe, even in federal states, the subject, in contrast, is dominated by its international aspects, that is, by the study of the rules and processes by which the courts in one country give effect to the law of a foreign country or show respect for a judgment already reached by a foreign court.

A concrete indication of the character of the subject can be given by way of an oversimplified example of a legal situation calling for the application of choice-of-law rules. A Dutch sailor employed on an American ship is injured in the course of work by allegedly faulty equipment while the ship is at anchor in a Japanese port. He sues for recovery in a Dutch court and seeks application of the American law on the subject because it leads to the largest recovery with the smallest burden of proof. The American shipowner, as defendant, contends that the negligence of the seaman was the cause of the accident and argues for the application of Japanese law, which, we shall assume, is least favorable to any recovery in these circumstances and least generous in its award of damages if some recovery is allowed. Which legal system and what legal rules would be chosen by a Dutch court as providing the governing law? Would the same governing law be chosen for this kind of case by a court in the United States, the Netherlands, and Japan? Why is it so difficult to obtain uniform treatment of choice-of-law questions? Is uniform treatment necessarily desirable? What approaches dominate the analysis of choice-of-law problems in the contemporary literature? It is with questions of this sort that the field of the conflict of laws is principally concerned.

The character of the solution given to problems of the choice of law has an intense practical relevance to the lives of people. Increasingly, it is impossible to confine human happenings to a single jurisdiction. Whether in matters of personal status arising from marriage, divorce, birth, and death or in such typical commercial phenomena as the regulation of anticompetitive business practices, expropriations of alien property, and the sale of goods, there is an increasing multinational complexity that in the event of controversy may make the choice of applicable law at once crucial and far from self-evident.

Of course, the practical interest in the conflict of laws emerges as a consequence of the fact that the substantive laws of states are diverse, inconsistent, and, occasionally, contradictory. Obviously, if all substantive law were the same, it would make little difference which system of law was selected to govern a controversy. But, in a world of diverse national, cultural, and ideological perspectives, there has never been a prospect of such substantive uniformity. Widespread attention has, therefore, been given throughout the history of international relations to the method and rationale used by various courts to select the proper system of law governing controversies. It appears, at least superficially, that all states have a strong, common, and mutual interest in the adoption of uniform choice-of-law rules. For unlike the substantive rules to which they refer, choice-of-law rules appear to seek nothing more than the ordering of relations in a fair and convenient fashion and do not seem to express any commitment to policies or values of a particular state. Despite this appearance of neutrality, however, efforts over several centuries to advance the acceptance of uniform choice-of-law rules have yielded few encouraging or tangible results.

The study of conflict of laws has been developed by lawyers and has traditionally been neglected by social scientists. This neglect can be explained, in part, by the fact that so many of the typical problems in the conflict of laws are either highly technical (for example, dealing with the devolution of property located abroad) or too humdrum (for example, concerning the status of a foreign mail-order divorce) to be either accessible or interesting to those who lack formal legal training. Even lawyers find the subject unusually complex, since it presupposes a familiarity both with the law governing a wide body of substantive problems (for example, how does the treatment of the foreign element vary when one is dealing with matters of personal status, inheritance, torts, contracts, real and personal property, etc.?) and with the laws and decisions operative in a number of foreign states with different legal systems.

Despite these obstacles, there are strong reasons why social scientists should have at least some awareness of the major trends of thought evolving in the conflict of laws. For one thing, the conflict of laws is a precursor by many centuries of the current interest in the study of conflict resolution. A vast literature has developed a whole range of techniques to adjust the conflicting requirements of local law and foreign law, and debate continues on the character of justice in the face of such conflicts.

Furthermore, the approach taken to the conflict of laws in different subject-matter areas might provide students of comparative social and political systems with an interesting insight into such concerns as the hierarchy of social values and governmental policies prevailing in different national societies. For certainly the refusal to defer to foreign law in some areas suggests the importance accorded domestic policy. The approach used to solve internal choice-of-law problems in federal states without much experience in international affairs (for example, Nigeria, Malaysia) may also be a useful way for those studying world order to gauge the acceptance of supranational sources of legal authority.

The revived interest of political scientists in the study of the role of norms in world politics clearly makes the conflict of laws relevant, for the same endeavor is at the center of both subjects: to find a just and efficient way to allocate legal authority among the actors in a multiunit social system. The conflict of laws offers the inquirer not only a parallel setting in which to study the efforts to introduce order into a social system that lacks centralized institutions, but it also provides a setting that tends to be less inflamed by political passions and therefore more susceptible to systematic analysis, concerned as it mainly is with interpersonal as distinct from intergovernmental legal disputes.

Interstate and international conflicts. It is important to distinguish the study of interstate from international conflict of laws. Rules to resolve interstate conflicts generally arise in a federal social structure which shares a traditional language and possesses an overriding organic law (constitution) and central legal institutions of interpretation and enforcement. These institutions are available to resolve serious conflicts that arise at the unit level and to set normative limits upon the discretion of a state to adopt "eccentric" or excessively egocentric rules of conflict of law. For example, the United States constitution imposes obligations on each state to give "full Faith and Credit . . . to the public Acts, Records, and judicial Proceedings of every other state" (Art. IV, 1); to respect "the privileges and immunities of citizens of the United States" and to grant every person "within its jurisdiction the equal protection of the laws" (XIVth Amendment, §1). Although the U.S. Supreme Court has acknowledged a considerable discretion at the unit level that allows the states to adopt diverse rules for dealing with foreign facts, there exists a higher law that remains potentially available to impart unity and coherence.

In contrast, the international system is relatively decentralized, lacks an organic law, and possesses only very weak institutions for the adjustment of disputes at the internation level. In addition, the differences in ideology, stages of economic development, domestic politics, and attitudes toward individual and governmental liability from nation to nation are generally much greater than are the differences among the units in a federal state. Whereas the interstate conflict of law can depend upon the resources of the national government to promote the realization of a fair and reasonable system, the international regime for the conflict of laws is dependent to a far greater degree upon the highly decentralized ordering techniques of reciprocity, self-help, and self-restraint in order to bring a fair system of conflict of laws into being. Public international law does not exercise any very widely accepted "constitutional" function at the present time in the stabilization of private international law. It does not provide a set of limits upon national discretion that might be invoked in diplomatic negotiation or when appearing before a "higher" tribunal, for instance, the International Court of Justice at The Hague. (A regional form of legal integration, intermediate between the centralization of a federal state and the decentralization of international society, exists, especially in Europe and somewhat in Latin America, and may soon develop to the point where it will warrant separate attention.)

The distinction between the operation of choice-of-law rules in a centralized (interstate) and in a decentralized (international) multiunit social system has many unexplored consequences. One of the most important is the difficulty of supplying juridically convincing reasons why the courts of one state should apply the law of another under certain specified circumstances. True, this is part of the wider need in international law to demonstrate how legal obligations can be binding on the national level in the absence of any supranational source of law other than agreement among states or customary usage. However, in the area of the conflict of laws neither treaty nor custom provide any generally acceptable guidelines, and with the virtual disappearance of natural-law thinking the traditional mode of explaining the basis of legal obligation is no longer very persuasive. These circumstances have prompted most commentators in recent times to regard the subject of the conflict of laws as a part of national law.

This position is reinforced by the virtually universal refusal of courts to apply the public law of foreign states to such matters as crime, taxation, or the regulation of business activities. The refusal stems primarily from a territorial notion of national sovereignty in which the public law of the sovereign reigns supreme within the boundaries of the state but nowhere else. The result of this refusal to apply foreign public law is to deny jurisdiction rather than to apply local law, except in the area of crime, where an elaborate system of extradition agreements operates as a partial substitute for the direct application of foreign criminal law.

Historical development

The systematic exposition of the conflict of laws rested originally upon the assumption of a supranationally ordained system obligatory upon judges at the unit level. The objective of the system was to assure uniformity of result in a legal dispute regardless of where the legal action was instituted. Naturally, such an objective could be realized, given the diversity of substantive law, only if a uniform system of either substantive or choice-of-law rules could be established.

The dominant idea in the Roman legal system was that Romans were everywhere to be governed by the Roman law and that foreigners were to be governed by the *jus gentium*, the law of the peoples, a "superlaw" of substantive rights and duties that was assumed to be universally applicable. Thus there was no occasion to apply foreign law and no need for a system of conflict of laws. The city-states of Italy legislated on matters not covered by Roman law, and it was out of the conflict between these legislative acts (*statua*) that a need for some approach to selecting the governing *statute* was initially felt. The need was acknowledged, in part, because of the regularity with which commercial intercourse among the city-states occurred. The technique evolved by the great Roman glossators Bartolus and Baldus to resolve the problem was to classify every *statute* as either real (for example, land rights), or personal (for example, status of person), or mixed. Elsewhere in medieval Europe somewhat different approaches to the resolution of conflict-of-law situations developed, the character of solution depending above all on the insularity of the social order and upon its prevailing political ideology, especially concerning the proper relationship between the domestic society, its members, and foreign societies.

Territoriality. In France the feudal system in force gave great weight to the *coutumes* and to residues of earlier tribal law. The resolution of conflicts depended on whether the issue had a territorial cause of action, and came under local law, or a transitory locus to which foreign law could properly be applied. This notion of giving primacy to the customs of each place prepared the intellectual climate for an era of territorial law, which gradually displaced the earlier acquiescence to the universal claims of Roman law. The growth of territoriality was abetted by the rise of the ideology of national sovereignty, the loss of the authority of the Roman church as a unifying influence, and the gradual decline of natural law as the basis of legal obligation. These nationalizing tendencies came to intellectual fruition in the seventeenth century when Johannes Voet (1698–1704) and Ulrich Huber (1689), scholars from the Dutch provinces, fully rationalized the primacy of the territorial lawgiver by discarding any pretense of a supranational basis for deference to foreign law. To the extent that such deference was accorded, they explained it on the basis of comity, a concept that Joseph Story later carried forward in a treatise that exercised a formative influence upon the Anglo–American development of the conflict of laws (1834). England's system of common law, as the law of the realm, did not give rise to internal conflicts, and external conflict situations were so infrequent that no real approach to the conflict of laws developed.

Nationality. The waves of nationalism occasioned by the French Revolution and later by the unification of Italy influenced the growth of conflict of laws, especially in those parts of the world where the continental European influence prevailed. Stress was put upon nationality, at the expense of territoriality, as the dominant connecting factor. An individual was first and foremost a Frenchman or an Italian, recipient of rights and responsible for duties under a particular national law, and only very secondarily subject to the law of the place where he happened to be. In contrast, doctrine in the common-law countries came increasingly to stress territoriality as the key variable: events were subjected to a particular law in terms of where the acts took place or where the property was located, and only a very secondary stress was given to the nationality of the actors in the process of selecting the governing legal system.

As a consequence of this division between conflicts based on the primacy of nationality and conflicts based on the primacy of territoriality it is difficult, if not impossible, to unify the conflict of laws by means of the voluntary agreement of nations through treaty. There has been some success on a regional basis on the Continent, where there is general agreement on the proper basis for solving choice-of-law issues. Several European treaties operate partly to codify and harmonize different national practices and partly to obtain uniform treatment of certain troublesome details, especially in highly technical areas, for example, the interpretation of multilateral shipping documents.

Basic problems of conflict of laws

Despite the supranational origins of the conflict of law, first in the *jus gentium* of Roman times and later in the natural-law basis of all law, the subject has been increasingly regarded as a part of national law. This nationalization results from the diversity of national practice and doctrine, the absence of any accepted supranational doctrine of obligation, and the general dominance of positivistic thinking that requires evidence of state consent as a prerequisite to the existence of binding rules of international law. (To be valid, according to the positivists, the law must be posited by an authorized lawgiver, and those authorized in international society are the states themselves. Furthermore, their acceptance of legal obligation must be indicated either explicitly, as in treaty law, or tacitly, as in customary law.)

At the same time, however, it is widely accepted that a stable and just system of conflict of law plays a critical role in international life.

This dilemma is clearly manifest in the work of Martin Wolff, who vigorously asserts the national character of the conflict of laws: "Today undoubtedly Private International Law is national Law. There exists an English private international law as distinct from a French, a German, an Italian, private international law. The rules on the conflict of laws . . . differ nearly as much from each other as do those on internal (municipal) law" (Wolff [1945] 1950, p. 11). Despite the vigor of this statement Wolff, along with all but the most nationalistic of writers, is at pains to point out that justice requires that each state consider the merits of the claims put forth by potentially applicable legal systems relative to the expectations of the parties, the stability of transnational social and economic intercourse, and the realization of the legitimate interests of foreign states. Wolff puts this international aspect as follows: "Private International Law is not itself international, but it should certainly be drawn up in an international frame of mind." One of the real jurisprudential challenges of today is to devise a satisfactory juridical account of an "international frame of mind" (*ibid.*, p. 16).

Comity. If international law does not compel deference by a domestic court to foreign law, then it is difficult to generate a satisfactory legal basis for such deference. The problem of finding a basis is artificial to some extent, being one of the many unfortunate by-products of dichotomizing national and international law. Given the almost universal adherence to this dichotomy, however, scholars have been eager to rest the conflict of laws on some extranational legal foundation that stops short of claiming legal compulsion. The most influential of these attempts has undoubtedly been associated with the concept of comity, the traditional means by which Anglo–American courts acknowledge the policy of deference to foreign law in domestic courts and, thereby, fulfill the injunction to manifest an international frame of mind.

Comity is supposed to express the reality of a practice that is habitual and yet not clearly or formally required as a matter of legal duty. That is, a court refusing to apply foreign law would not be violating any legal duty and no foreign state would have a legal basis for complaint. However, it is so widely recognized as desirable to apply foreign law with a certain consistency that a need arises to fit the practice into a description of the workings of the legal system. It has, at the same time, become commonplace for jurists to criticize this reliance upon the idea of comity because of its ambiguity and vagueness. Since it provides guidance for neither courts nor private parties in specific cases, and since it seems to identify the process of adjudication with some type of "international etiquette," comity makes the whole subject of the conflict of laws appear to rest upon a system of obligation no more substantial than the practice of international politeness.

In response, writers have tended in recent decades to abandon comity as the explanation for the application of foreign law, either affirming the completely national character of the conflict of law or searching for some substitute to express its international aspect. One of the most persuasive efforts to evolve a substitute for comity is found in the work of Myres McDougal and Nicholas deB. Katzenbach. These writers approach the problems of conflicts as but a special case of the more general task in international society to divide up the competence to apply law among the territorial sovereigns that constitute international society. They argue for a form of legal order that can successfully emerge in a highly decentralized multiunit social system by being truly responsive to the demands of the units. The implication of this orientation is to urge upon domestic courts the legal duty to defer to foreign law whenever, in terms of protecting and realizing mutual freedom for national societies, it is appropriate. As Katzenbach puts it: "So long as formal authority is organized and administered territorially, there is a mutual and reciprocal interest—a 'sense of the inconveniences which would otherwise result'—in extending areas of tolerance" (1956, p. 1131). McDougal identifies law with the reasonable expectations of those participating in international life, suggesting, in contradistinction to the traditional nationalization of the conflict of laws, that it is a matter of international law to defer in appropriate circumstances to foreign law (McDougal & Feliciano 1961).

This sociopolitical approach to the study of law in international affairs eliminates such dichotomies as those between private and public international law and even calls into question the mainstay of traditional analysis—namely, the distinction between national and international law. Although this work seems certain to attract the interest of social scientists, it is regarded with great suspicion by most international lawyers, especially those in Europe, and it has not yet been properly applied to the subject matter of the conflict of laws. Instead, most theoretical attention is still focused on the problem of finding general criteria for the solution of conflict problems.

The search for general criteria.   There is wide disagreement, especially in the United States, as to whether the search for general criteria is worthwhile and, if it is, what form it should take.

The critics.   Albert Ehrenzweig, the author of the leading contemporary treatise in English on the conflict of laws (1962), takes the position that the whole search for general rules for the solution of conflict-of-laws problems in unsettled areas of the law has proceeded on the wrong basis. Ehrenzweig contends that all a priori approaches are bound to be deceptive because courts in practice will not be bound by overly abstract and mechanistic rules of reference that direct them to apply a certain legal system for a given class of cases (for example, the law of the place of making for contracts, the law of the place of injury for torts, and the law of the situs for real property), but will use manipulative devices to promote the just outcome of particular disputes or to give preference to local as against foreign interests. The real indicators of how a conflict problem will be solved, then, arise not from the doctrinal language used by a court to explain its decision but from the awareness of the sense of justice or bias that underlies the doctrinal explanation. Ehrenzweig thus sets for himself the very ambitious task of finding "true rules"—the living law, as distinct from the enunciated law—and asserts that only by this search can the pattern of judicial decision be made intelligible and predictable standards of result be obtained. The most fundamental rule Ehrenzweig finds is that a court will tend to apply its own law to a controversy in those situations in which it is one of several plausibly applicable laws. Thus all instances of deference to foreign law are derogations from this underlying "true rule." Ehrenzweig's approach is based both on a critique of judicial practice (cutting through the technical or legalistic explanation to the real one) and upon an acceptance of its authoritative status (the role of a scholar is not to supply higher criteria but to analyze judicial practice so as to discover the operative criteria).

What for Ehrenzweig is a matter of pervasive methodology becomes for Brainerd Currie a matter of pervasive ideology (Currie 1963). Currie is less interested in what courts do than in developing an approach leading to what they should do, although his jurisprudential strategy is to proceed by way of very close analyses of particular cases. He believes, to overstate it some, that a court should always apply local law when the forum has a governmental interest in the outcome of the controversy and that foreign law is appropriately applied only when the forum is disinterested in the outcome. In this regard he opposes the recent tendency of courts to balance the interests of various potentially applicable legal systems and to choose the law of that legal system which has the greatest interest in the particular case. Such balancing is for Currie inappropriately undertaken by courts and is more properly a matter for legislative determination.

Currie and Ehrenzweig repudiate the traditional search in the conflict of laws for allocation criteria posited in advance, and both affirm the fundamental governance of controversies by local law. In consequence they renounce the ideal of uniformity of result. Currie not only denies the duty to defer to foreign law but also argues that courts should not defer except when they affirm both jurisdiction and disinterest. In the rare cases that satisfy these two conditions the courts cannot reach a proper decision and might just as well apply local law, or flip a coin, or dismiss the cases.

The balancers.   A less extreme approach, but one that very likely accords more closely with what judges think they should be doing and seems to have the strongest following in the United States, is best exemplified by the work of Willis Reese and Elliot Cheatham (Reese 1963; Cheatham 1960; Cheatham & Reese 1952) and by the tentative drafts of a second restatement of the conflict of laws under the influential auspices of the American Law Institute (1953–1965). These authors share with Currie and Ehrenzweig a distrust of the traditional stress on general solutions to conflicts problems, but they also argue for an intermediate approach whereby policy factors are grouped in any particular case so as to identify the legal system with the dominant interest in the outcome and to choose the legal result most in accord with substantial justice. Ehrenzweig, a harsh critic of this enterprise, contends that it produces vague formulas and keeps alive, despite denials, the tradition of discerning a priori forum-selecting choice-of-law rules. Reese and Cheatham defend their balancing approach on the grounds that both practice and doctrine confirm this type of analysis and that recent landmark decisions in the conflict of laws exhibit the tendency to search for criteria by which to select the most interested forum and by this means to reach the most just result.

We find, then, that the very character of the conflict of laws, its methodology, and its governing ideology have been seriously questioned in recent years. There exists no scholarly or judicial consensus on choice-of-law rules. In particular, the traditional ideals of seeking uniformity of result and of establishing equality between domestic and foreign laws have come in for heavy criticism on the grounds that such ideals are unrealistic and inappropriate, since domestic courts actually do and, in fact, should accord preference to domestic law in a situation where it is one of the applicable legal systems.

Operational problems.   No less serious than the theoretical problems are the dilemmas facing the practitioners of private international law. Judges in courts are confronted by the operational necessity of choosing the legal system that shall govern most justly a particular controversy and of giving a satisfactory explanation of their solution on a particular occasion. Scholars through the centuries have sought to find a general solution that combines just choice-of-law rules with the universality of their acceptance. The overriding objectives are to get the just decision and to be assured that there will not be one just decision in Japan, another in Holland, and a third in the United States.

There is, unfortunately, no broad consensus as to the form a general solution should take. The problem of legal systems using nationality as the criterion versus those using territoriality has already been mentioned. (If a Frenchman lives in Brazil, is his estate properly governed by French or Brazilian law?) Furthermore, courts are less inclined to follow the dogmatic solutions proposed by scholars than to seek to do substantial justice to the parties in dispute. Therefore, a court will tend to manipulate the criteria governing the choice of laws to fulfill its view of what justice demands. A good illustration is the basic idea that a court will always apply domestic *procedure* even if it defers to foreign *substance*. This allows it to characterize as "procedure" any device that will produce the desired result.

The promise of conflict of laws

Despite the critiques of the subject, the dominant trend continues to be the pursuit of uniformity and equality, especially if the emphasis is put upon the international as distinct from the interstate aspect of the conflict of laws. The challenge today is to find an acceptable supranational basis for promoting these ideals in a divided world composed of states with different economic, cultural, and political outlooks. This challenge cannot be met by a new global ideology but rather by a series of more modest and concrete undertakings. One of the more promising research developments consists of the comparative-law efforts to take specific inventory of the differences in both substantive standards and in choice-of-law rules and to examine the prospects for their harmonization by unilateral or multilateral action.

A sociological extension of this inquiry would be to take stock of the diverse social interests that account for differences in the conflict of laws from one national system to another and to work toward a set of solutions on the basis of mutual interests. This type of inquiry has been undertaken by Kenneth S. Carlston (1962). It draws heavily upon functional sociology, especially organization theory and systems theory. Its persuasiveness also depends on the acceptance of a new image of global unity, eloquently summarized by C. Wilfred Jenks (1958) as "the common law of mankind," in which the nation-state is supplanted to some extent in legal consciousness by new forms of social and political order that take greater account of both international institutions and of individuals in specifying the link between law and human welfare in transnational phenomena. As might be expected, it is the powerful states that seem most reluctant to participate in this new attempt to supranationalize the conflict of laws. Such states as the Soviet Union, the United States, China, and France oppose most efforts to diminish sovereign prerogatives for the sake of an operative global system.

In conclusion, the stability and fairness of international legal undertakings seem to depend upon the strengthening of this renewed attempt to supranationalize the conflict of laws. As a result of the increasing interdependence of human activity there is a growing need for predictable outcomes in legal disputes. These outcomes should have a more substantial base than the national affiliation of the forum. Given the diversity of contemporary international society it is not realistic to seek this end by reconciling national policies so as to create a single substantive law. There is more reason for hope if the ancient quest for order amid diversity is pursued through a uniform approach to the allocation of legal competence among the national units that compose the global system. One illuminating context within which this allocation can be studied and realized is the application of choice-of-law rules by domestic courts.

RICHARD A. FALK

[See also INTERNATIONAL CONFLICT RESOLUTION; INTERNATIONAL LAW. Other relevant material may be found under CONFLICT; INTERNATIONAL RELATIONS; LAW.]

BIBLIOGRAPHY

AMERICAN LAW INSTITUTE 1953–1965 Restatement of the Law Second: Conflict of Laws. Tentative Draft Nos. 1–13. Philadelphia: The Institute.

ASSOCIATION OF AMERICAN LAW SCHOOLS, COMMITTEE ON SELECTED ARTICLES ON CONFLICT OF LAWS 1956 Selected Readings on Conflict of Laws . . . St. Paul, Minn.: West.

BATIFFOL, HENRI (1949) 1959 Traité élémentaire de droit international privé. 3d ed. Paris: Librairie Générale de Droit et de Jurisprudence.

BEALE, JOSEPH H. 1935 A Treatise on the Conflict of Laws. 3 vols. New York: Baker.

CARLSTON, KENNETH S. 1962 Law and Organization in World Society. Urbana: Univ. of Illinois Press.

CAVERS, DAVID F. 1933 A Critique of the Choice-of-law Problem. Harvard Law Review 47:173–208.

CAVERS, DAVID F. 1950 The Two "Local Law" Theories. Harvard Law Review 63:822–832.

CHEATHAM, ELLIOTT E. 1960 Problems and Methods in the Conflict of Laws. The Hague, Academy of International Law, Recueil des cours 99:233–355.

CHEATHAM, ELLIOTT E.; and REESE, WILLIS L. M. 1952 Choice of the Applicable Law. Columbia Law Review 52:959–982.

CHESHIRE, GEOFFREY C. (1935) 1965 Private International Law. 7th ed. London: Butterworth.

COOK, WALTER W. 1942 The Logical and Legal Bases of the Conflict of Laws. Harvard Studies in the Conflict of Laws, No. 5. Cambridge, Mass.: Harvard Univ. Press.

CURRIE, BRAINERD 1963 Selected Essays on the Conflict of Laws. Durham, N.C.: Duke Univ. Press.

EHRENZWEIG, ALBERT A. 1962 A Treatise on the Conflict of Laws. St. Paul, Minn.: West. → The first part is a revised edition of a work first published in 1959 as Conflict of Law.

HUBER, ULRICH (1689) 1937 De conflictu legum. Pages 64–78 in British Yearbook of International Law: 1937. Oxford Univ. Press. → Text in English and Latin.

JENKS, C. WILFRED 1958 The Common Law of Mankind. New York: Praeger.

JESSUP, PHILIP C. 1956 Transnational Law. New Haven: Yale Univ. Press.

KATZENBACH, NICHOLAS deB. 1956 Conflicts on an Unruly Horse: Reciprocal Claims and Tolerances in Interstate and International Law. Yale Law Journal 65:1087–1157.

KEGEL, GERHARD (1960) 1964 Internationales Privatrecht: Ein Studienbuch. 2d ed., rev. Munich: Beck.

LORENZEN, ERNEST G. (1910–1945) 1947 Selected Articles on the Conflict of Laws. New Haven: Yale Univ. Press.

McDOUGAL, MYRES S.; and FELICIANO, FLORENTINO P. 1961 Law and Minimum World Public Order: The

Legal Regulation of International Coercion. New Haven: Yale Univ. Press.

MORELLI, GAETANO (1946) 1962 *Elementi di diritto internazionale privato italiano.* 7th ed. Naples (Italy): Jovene.

NIBOYET, JEAN P. 1938–1949 *Traité de droit international privé français.* 6 vols. Paris: Sirey.

NUSSBAUM, ARTHUR 1943 *Principles of Private International Law.* New York: Oxford Univ. Press.

RABEL, ERNST 1945–1958 *The Conflict of Laws: A Comparative Study.* 4 vols. Ann Arbor: Univ. of Michigan Press. → A second edition is in progress.

REESE, WILLIS L. M. 1963 Conflict of Laws and the Restatement Second. *Law and Contemporary Problems* 28:679–699.

SAVIGNY, FRIEDRICH K. VON (1849) 1880 *Private International Law and the Retrospective Operation of Statutes: A Treatise on the Conflict of Laws . . .* 2d ed. Edinburgh: Clark. → First published in German.

STORY, JOSEPH (1834) 1883 *Commentaries on the Conflict of Laws, Foreign and Domestic in Regard to Contracts, Rights, and Remedies, and Especially in Regard to Marriages, Divorces, Wills, Successions, and Judgements.* 8th ed. Boston: Little.

Symposium on New Trends in the Conflict of Laws. 1963 *Law and Contemporary Problems* 28:673–869.

VOET, JOHANNES (1698–1704) 1955–1958 *The Selective Voet: Being the Commentary on the Pandects.* 8 vols. Translated with explanatory notes by Percival Gane. Durban (Union of South Africa): Butterworth. → First published in Latin. Includes a supplement by Johannes van der Linden.

WENGLER, WILHELM 1961 The General Principles of Private International Law. The Hague, Academy of International Law, *Recueil des cours* 104:273–469.

WESTLAKE, JOHN (1858) 1925 *A Treatise on Private International Law, With Principal Reference to Its Practice in England.* 7th. ed. London: Sweet & Maxwell.

WOLFF, MARTIN (1945) 1950 *Private International Law.* 2d ed. Oxford: Clarendon.

WORTLEY, B. A. 1954 The Interaction of Public and Private International Law Today. The Hague, Academy of International Law, *Recueil des cours* 85:239–342.

CONFLICT RESOLUTION

See CONFLICT; COOPERATION; GAME THEORY; INTERNATIONAL CONFLICT RESOLUTION; NEGOTIATION; PEACE.

CONFORMITY

Every aggregation is necessarily characterized by some degree of uniformity. This is true of any set of objects, events, ideas, or organisms, be they members of these sets by virtue of natural determinants or by virtue of our own conceptions, however arbitrary. Sugar and alcohol are members of such a set because they are both carbohydrates. But my pencil, my headache, and the spelling mistake I made three years ago in a letter to my wife are also members of a set; they share at least one thing in common: they all belong to me.

In human and animal aggregations some uniformities are genetically determined, as is the case with various morphological attributes of the species, while some evolve and are maintained by means of a social process. Often, socially evolved and maintained uniformities (i.e., social norms) redefine and channel biological uniformities. Sexuality, eating, nursing, elimination, etc., are behaviors which have in one way or another been subjected to normative controls in every society. The regulation of these biologically significant functions may be very pervasive or quite superficial. In all societies there are norms about when, what, how much, and in what manner one should eat. But similar regulations have not evolved with respect to sneezing. It is probably the case that those biological functions that are important to the survival of society are subject to pervasive normative regulation of their behavioral manifestations. Because sexuality is a significant factor in the survival and welfare of a society as a unit, sexual functions are jealously regulated by normative pressures. However, another biological function, breathing—absolutely necessary for the individual's own survival but insignificant for the society—is not subject to normative regulation. Perhaps if air were less abundant and, like food, posed problems of distribution, breathing too would be normatively regulated. As a matter of fact, breathing does become subject to rather strict normative controls on submarines in emergencies.

Although not all social uniformities revolve around the expression of biological functions, it has generally been recognized that normative regulation is imposed upon behavior (*a*) that is not under complete control of biological factors and (*b*) whose nonsocial (i.e., psychological or biological) determinants might lead to instrumental behavior that is socially undesirable or harmful.

The behavioral processes that establish and maintain social uniformities are subsumed under the concept of *conformity*. We shall speak of *conformity* when the behavior of an individual is under the control of a group norm. A group (social) norm, as was already noted, is a uniformity of behavior among the members of a given group that is not the result of a physiological or biological uniformity among them.

Sherif's classic study

While theoretical work on conformity dates from the earliest social philosophers, the experimental study of conformity is a more recent development. In 1935 Muzafer Sherif brought the process of conformity into the laboratory for the first time and subjected it to systematic observation. He utilized the autokinetic phenomenon, which is a perceptual distortion occurring when individuals view a stationary pinpoint of light in a completely dark room. Normally, the light appears to move about three or four inches. The illusion of movement is enhanced when the individual does not know the distance between himself and the light and when he expects that the light will move. But even when he is told that the light is stationary, the illusion of movement is rather compelling.

Sherif's pioneering experiment consisted in the collection of judgments about the apparent movement of the pinpoint of light from individuals tested alone and in groups of two and three. Each subject made one such judgment on each of four consecutive days, and 100 trials were given each day. Two conditions were examined, and in both the subjects were required on each trial to announce aloud how many inches they thought the light had moved. In both conditions, too, one day was devoted to testing the subjects one at a time, and three days to testing them in groups of two and three. The conditions differed only with respect to the position of the "isolated" block of trials in the experimental sequence. In one condition the sequence began with subjects making 100 judgments in isolation and continued with 300 group judgments. In the other condition the block of 100 isolated judgments followed three blocks in which judgments were made in groups. Sherif's results were unequivocal: (a) when individual judgments were made prior to the group experience, relatively high variability was observed between judgments made by different subjects; (b) when subjects made judgments in groups of two and three, variability between their judgments disappeared, regardless of whether these judgments were made with or without prior individual experience; (c) when individual judgments followed group judgments, they were characterized by greater uniformity than when they preceded them. The group situation is sufficient to produce a uniformity among individual judgments, and the uniformity resulting in this way maintains a measure of stability even after the group members have been separated from one another. More recent work shows that norms reached in this manner are maintained for a period of more than one year (Rohrer et al. 1954).

Sherif's experiment stimulated a vast amount of research concentrating on three classes of problems that roughly correspond to the essential features of his experimental design. Sherif made observations of (a) an individual (b) engaging in an activity (c) in the presence of a group also engaged in that activity. Research questions investigated in the field of conformity were generally formulated in terms of these three features. First, what sort of individuals are susceptible to group influence? How does the individual's past experience influence the likelihood of his yielding to group consensus? Second, what sort of behavior or judgment is easy and what sort difficult to manipulate by means of group consensus? How stable are these effects? Third, what characteristics of the group are related to the influence it can exert over individual behavior? Are some types of groups better able to influence a given individual than others? Is complete uniformity in the group a necessary condition for a successful influence upon its members? More complex questions revolve around the interaction of these classes of variables. Are individuals who are susceptible to group influence in one situation also susceptible to it in other situations? Are they susceptible equally for all sorts of behavior and to all sorts of groups? Are there, in other words, personality predispositions on the basis of which tendency to conform can be predicted? Research in the area of conformity focused on the above three classes of factors and on the interaction among these factors as they affect the likelihood and degree of yielding to a group consensus. It should be noted that in all experiments situations are examined in which, for obvious reasons, the group attempts to influence the individual to behave in ways in which he would not normally behave. The measure of influence accomplished by the group consensus depends therefore on the comparison of the individual's likelihood of behaving in a given manner when the group influence is absent with that likelihood when the group influence is present. This review of problems in conformity research will be divided into three classes of interests: those concerned with the task and behavior under control of the group, those concerned with the individual characteristics of the conformer, and those concerned with the nature of the group responsible for the changes in the individual's behavior or judgment or opinion.

Task variables

In Sherif's experiment conformity occurred when individuals, confronted with an ambiguous stimulus, made judgments about it in the presence of one another. It was possible, however, that the autokinetic situation, because of its *ambiguity*, did not involve conformity as it occurs in vivo. The judgments of each individual in the group were based on two sources of information: (a) the announced estimates of his partners and (b) his own very vague and unstable impression of the autokinetic movement. Clearly, from the subject's point of view, the second source of information had questionable reliability. There were no solid grounds for depending on what one thought one saw in this situation. It was, therefore, tempting for the subject to simply rely on the judgments of the other group members. The most important contribution to furthering the understanding of the conformity process along these lines was made by Solomon Asch (1952; 1956). The basic question that Asch raised was whether results like those of Sherif's would be obtained from judgment tasks that were considerably clearer and easier. Would the individual yield to a consensus among a group of peers even when it was perfectly obvious to him that the consensus was wrong?

The experimental design employed by Asch involved two important modifications of Sherif's technique. First, nonambiguous stimuli were used: his subjects were asked to estimate the length of a line by matching it with one of three comparison lines. The standard stimulus and the comparison stimuli were always presented under optimal viewing conditions. Also, the comparison stimuli always included a line identical in length and all other respects to the standard line. The differences among the lengths of the comparison lines were so large that an individual making these psychophysical judgments by himself could easily achieve 90 per cent accuracy.

Second, instead of utilizing *ad hoc* groups, Asch employed trained confederates who were previously instructed about what estimate to make on each trial. Normally, the experimental situation in Asch's experiment consisted of 12 trials; on each trial the confederates, one at a time, would announce their estimates before the subject announced his. On seven of these trials the confederates would unanimously select the wrong comparison line. Sometimes their choice would differ from the correct one by as much as 70 per cent. This procedure removed the reciprocal and mutual aspect from the influence process present in Sherif's experiment, thus rendering the analysis of conformity pressures more manageable.

Asch's experimental paradigm became the standard one in subsequent conformity research. It unveiled the opposing forces involved in the conformity process and allowed their systematic manipulation. The force of the individual's own conviction could be manipulated by varying the difficulty of the psychophysical estimates he was asked to make. The force of conformity pressures exerted upon him could be manipulated by the size of the false majority, by how expert or confident

they were made to appear, by the subject's dependence upon them for various gratifications, etc.

Asch's experiments gave a strong impetus to conformity research partly because of their provocative results and partly because his experimental design brought into focus many new problems that until then had not been well formulated. In one of his first experiments individuals judging the length of lines in the absence of a false majority attained about 93 per cent accuracy. But subjects who were exposed to the prior judgments of the experimenter's confederates reached only 67 per cent accuracy—a drop of 26 per cent. The difference between the accuracy levels of judgments made independently and those made in the presence of a false majority has generally been taken as the measure of conformity.

It was Asch's original suspicion that Sherif's results were obtained mainly because of the ambiguous stimuli he used. Asch thought that individuals would exercise greater independence of judgment when given a more definite, clearer, and easier task. As we noted above, however, Asch's first experiment shattered these expectations. Even under optimal conditions his subjects yielded to the false majority 26 per cent of the time. In further work Asch reduced task difficulty even further. On several critical trials the judgments of the false majority were quite obviously false. For instance, on one of the trials the three comparison lines were three, ten, and two inches long. The standard line was ten inches long, but the experimenter's confederates unanimously chose the three-inch line as the "correct" match. On another trial the line chosen by them differed from the standard stimulus by four inches. In experiments of this sort the judgments are quite easy to make, and subjects working in isolation reached 98 per cent accuracy. But even with judgments extremely easy to make, there was as much as 26 per cent yielding, that is, subjects responding in the presence of a false majority reached only 62 per cent accuracy.

It is generally found that the yielding is not completely eliminated by decreasing task difficulty (Blake, Helson, & Mouton 1957), but the degree of yielding can be somewhat reduced by such a decrease (e.g., Coleman et al. 1958). We shall return to the problem of task difficulty when we consider the effect of certainty on yielding to a false majority.

While most experimental work in conformity has concentrated on perceptual or psychophysical responses of the sort used by Sherif and Asch, there are a few experimental studies to show that similar effects are obtained with other forms of behavior.

For instance, Blake, Rosenbaum, and Duryea (1955) report that contributions to a fund for a gift for a departing secretary followed patterns similar to those obtained by Asch. When presented with a list on which the gifts of others were marked, the individuals who were asked to make a contribution tended to match their gifts to those already listed. Thus, subjects who were given a list with gifts averaging 25 cents pledged an average of 28.5 cents. Those who were presented with a list averaging 75 cents pledged to contribute an average of 63.5 cents. But subjects asked to contribute a sum of money without being exposed to a pre-arranged list averaged 75 cents.

Blake, Mouton, and Hain (1956) solicited students at the University of Texas to sign a petition requesting ". . . University officials [to] place lights on Littlefield Fountain to add to the beauty of the memorial." In two conditions an experimenter's confederate was invited to sign the petition in the presence of the subject. In one of these the confederate responded by saying, "Sure, I'll sign," adding his signature to the petition. In another he said, "No, I'd rather not," and walked away. In a third condition subjects were asked to sign the petition in the absence of a confederate. When confronted with a positive action of a confederate, 89 per cent of those asked signed the petition. In the absence of a confederate, 58 per cent of the subjects complied with the request. However, when confronted with a refusal of the confederate, only 29 per cent signed the petition.

In a similar attempt Rosenbaum (1956) invited students studying in the library to volunteer for a psychological experiment. In two conditions the subject was asked only after the experimenter addressed his confederate, who either accepted or rejected the request. In a third condition no confederates were present. With a positive response of the confederate, 67 per cent of those asked volunteered for the "psychological experiment." In the absence of a confederate, 41 per cent volunteered, but with a negative response of the confederate, only 38 per cent of those asked volunteered.

An interesting variation of such experiments was introduced by dealing with *violations* of existing rules or customs. Thus, Freed and others (1955) affixed a "no admittance" sign to the main classroom building at the University of Texas. As in previous experiments, a confederate made either a positive or a negative response or no confederates were present. Thus, in one condition a confederate read the sign and entered the building. In another he read the sign and walked away. Given a model who himself conformed to the rule, 30 per cent of the subjects entered the building. In the absence of a confederate, 60 per cent of those observed violated the sign. But when preceded by a confederate who violated the sign, 90 per cent were observed entering the building.

Individual variables

Asch's dramatic findings and the findings of those who further pursued his pioneering work clearly demonstrated the powerful influence a group can exert on an individual. But these studies also showed that conformity did not occur in all trials, nor did all individuals yield to the false majority. The question immediately arose whether individuals who maintained independence of judgments in the face of a strong, albeit false, majority did so because of an underlying personality trait. Is the tendency to conform a stable personality characteristic of the individual? Can this characteristic be identified on the basis of other knowledge about him?

Consistency of conforming. Evidence indicates that tendency to conform is indeed a stable individual characteristic showing up consistently in different situations. For instance, Ferguson (1944) studied responses to different attitude scales (religion, humanitarianism, nationalism). After having answered the attitude questionnaires, the subjects were informed about the responses to these questions made by a reputed majority. The attitude questionnaires were again given to the subjects. The results showed that individuals who shifted their attitudes on one scale also shifted attitudes toward the reputed majority on other scales.

Using various tasks (i.e., recall of nonsense words, recall of entire paragraphs, the embedded-figures test, and Asch's line-judgment test), Rosner (1957) found clear evidence of consistency of the yielding response. His findings indicate that within a single task and within a single experimental session the individuals who yield to the majority on early trials are also likely to yield on later trials. Second, individuals who yield in performing the given task during one experimental session tend to yield on that task in a repeated administration at a later date. His results also showed consistency among the various tasks: those subjects who yield to the false majority on one task also yield on others.

Skill and confidence. The experiments reviewed above, in which judgment difficulty was manipulated, reflect in part the operation of task variables and in part individual difference factors. Tasks are never *intrinsically* easy or difficult. They are so only in relation to the individuals who work on them. The clarity and difficulty of judgments reflect at the same time a property of the task and a characteristic of the individual engaged in it. The subjective aspect of task difficulty is the individual's skill at that task, and the subjective aspect of ambiguity of judgments is his certainty or confidence. Various experiments have tried to show that task difficulty or ambiguity of the judged stimuli are not in themselves able to enhance conformity. Rather, the significant variables were found to be the subject's task skill and his confidence (e.g., Coleman et al. 1958).

Individual difference factors that are related to task skill and certainty of judgment seem to show a similar pattern of results. Thus, for instance, Tuddenham (1961) found that children tend to conform more readily than adults, girls more than boys, and women more than men. Tuddenham (1959) reported that intelligence and conformity are negatively related. Appley and Moeller (1963) found a sizable correlation between conformity and the Edwards abasement scale, which in large measure reflects the person's lack of self-confidence. Crowne and Liverant (1963) reported that conformers tend to have low expectations of success in judgmental tasks. When the prior judgment experiences of the individual are generally successful (i.e., accurate) and when he is aware of his accuracy, his tendency to conform to a false group consensus is reduced in later trials (e.g., Hollander 1964).

Strength of commitment. When pressures are exerted by a group on the individual in an attempt to change his attitudes or opinions, the relative success of the group depends, in large measure, on how strongly the individual is committed to his point of view. Conformity to a false majority is considerably reduced when it involves fairly stable values (e.g., Gerard 1953). But even when we deal with a strong commitment, some measure of conformity is observed.

Dependency. Among the personality variables found to be significantly related to conformity, dependency is perhaps the most outstanding. Various scales exist to differentiate between individuals in terms of whether they tend to depend on others for the gratification of various needs, for gaining understanding about the things and events around them, for learning if they behave appropriately or are considered worthwhile human beings. We would naturally suppose that a dependent individual would be more prone to conform than one who can function independently and who does not need

to rely on others in judging his own actions. This conjecture is borne out by substantial research evidence. It was already noted that children tend to conform more readily than adults and that females conform more readily than males. And it is generally found that children are more dependent than adults and females more dependent than males. Kagan and Mussen (1956) have shown that subjects who tend to respond to the Thematic Apperception Test cards in terms of dependency themes conform consistently more than others. Strickland and Crowne (1962), on the other hand, found that conformity is intimately associated with the individual's need for social approval. Because schizophrenics are less responsive to the social environment and consequently less psychologically dependent upon it, one would expect them to conform less than normal subjects. This hypothesis was tested but was not substantiated by Schooler and Spohn (1960). Interestingly, they found that the mental patients tended to respond neither in terms of the false consensus nor in terms of the correct stimulus match, but often chose the third alternative, i.e., a wrong response not supported by the false majority. It would seem that the schizophrenic is unresponsive not only to the social environment but to the physical one as well.

Authoritarianism. The picture of the conformist as a dependent, submissive person with little confidence in his own ability leads one immediately to suspect that he is also quite sensitive to his relationships with authority figures. A considerable literature exists to show some not entirely clear relationship between authoritarianism, as measured by the *F* scale, and the tendency to conform (e.g., Steiner & Johnson 1963). Mussen and Kagan (1958) reported that the conformist tends to perceive his parents as harsh, rejecting, restrictive, and punitive figures. These authors suggested that the tendency to conform might be acquired in early childhood. Their hypothesis was based on an earlier work by Hoffman (1953), who pointed out that some forms of conformity are motivated by guilt caused by the person's hostile feelings toward figures of authority and in particular toward his parents.

Affiliation and achievement. Dependency is a personality disposition related to the affiliative strivings of the individual. Independence, on the other hand, is related to his achievement strivings. Numerous studies have shown that need for affiliation and need for achievement fairly reliably predict a tendency to conform, the first predicting an increase, the second a decrease in conformity (e.g., DiVesta & Cox 1960; Samelson 1958; Zajonc

& Wahi 1961). Often, however, these predictions have been complicated by an interaction between the two needs and by an interaction of these needs with birth order (e.g., Samelson 1958).

Evaluation. On the whole, research that concentrated upon the discovery of a unitary personality predisposition to conform was less than fully successful, and some of the research quoted above was not always borne out by follow-up studies (e.g., Steiner & Johnson 1963). The most reliable finding in this field has been that females tend to conform more than males. Other results have enjoyed considerably less frequent confirmation.

Group factors

One of the important factors that enhance the individual's resistance to group pressure is his confidence. We noted above that experimental manipulations that tend to increase his feelings of confidence (such as prior experience of success) result in an attenuated conformity response. But in a typical conformity experiment, before making his own judgments, the subject is confronted with the responses of a group of people. This response is often at odds with what he perceives. Clearly, the characteristics of the group, its size, its unanimity, its reputed expertness in the task, are factors diminishing the individual's confidence in his own judgments.

Size and perceived accuracy of majority. Early work by Asch (1952) has shown that the conformity effect is almost completely eliminated when the subject's judgments are preceded by the judgment of only one confederate. Asch reports that the subject's confidence in his own judgments is maintained when contradicted by only one person. There is, however, a dramatic increase in conformity when the subject's response is preceded by those of two other "judges," and still a further increase when preceded by three. Thereafter an increase in the size of the group has little further effect. These findings have been in large part substantiated (e.g., Rosenberg 1961).

Stimulus ambiguity has its subjective counterpart in the individual's self-confidence. But in the conformity situation the individual's confidence in his own judgments is always relative to what he perceives the accuracy of the group to be. If he perceives that others are more accurate, he will be more likely to agree with them in the case of conflict between stimulus information and group consensus (e.g., Deutsch & Gerard 1955).

Consensus and divergence. Yielding to a false majority is reduced somewhat when the majority includes an individual making a correct judgment.

Asch (1952) found that not only did the extent of conformity decrease when a "partner" was added to the group of confederates but that the subjects felt considerably less tense during the experimental situation—a condition almost universally observed in conformity experiments with a unanimous group.

The amount of divergence between what the subject thinks is the "correct" response and the group response is a significant factor in maintaining the individual's confidence in his own judgments. Most findings in this area agree that as this divergence departs from zero, conformity increases. (At zero divergence, of course, the degree of conformity cannot be evaluated.) Conformity reaches a maximum at a moderately small extent of divergence, depending largely on the task, and with a further increase in divergence conformity falls off (e.g., Blake, Helson, & Mouton 1957; Whittaker 1964). There is at least one study, however, in which no effects of divergence on conformity were found (Birney & Houston 1961).

Attraction and status. The relationship between the group constituting the false majority and the conformist has been investigated from various points of view. The two main foci of interest among these studies have been the attractiveness of the group and the status of its members. In general, the findings indicate that conformity increases with the individual's attraction to the group (e.g., Thibaut & Strickland 1956). Bovard (1953), however, found no relationship between conformity to a group norm and the attraction of the members for one another. On the other hand, Kiesler (1963) reports a curvilinear relationship between attraction to the group and conformity, with maximum conformity obtaining at moderate levels of attraction. Status of the group, too, was found to enhance conformity. In particular, a difference in status between the group and the conformist seems to have pronounced effects on the likelihood of conformity (e.g., Raven & French 1958). It is interesting to note in passing, however, that the status of the conformist itself does not bear a simple relationship to yielding. Harvey and Consalvi (1960), working with delinquent cliques, found that the second-ranking member is more likely to conform to a false consensus among the members of his clique than is either the first-ranking or the last-ranking member.

Private and public situations. The operation of group factors upon conformity is well illustrated in numerous studies that compare responses made under public and private conditions. Two important findings emerge when individuals, confronted by a false majority, are observed making their judgments privately, convinced that these will never be known by the group. The first of these is that, in comparison with the public situation, conformity decreases (e.g., Deutsch & Gerard 1955; Thibaut & Strickland 1956). The second and more important finding is that conformity to a false majority is not completely eliminated even when the judgments are made privately, secretly, and anonymously. Since the group is a significant source of rewards and punishments for the individual, the difference between conformity under public and private conditions depends to some extent on what consequences the individual expects from the group as a result of his nonconformity. Dittes and Kelley (1956) have shown that individuals who were not fully accepted by the group but who perceived their chances of becoming full-fledged group members to be high conformed to the false majority regardless of whether they were asked to make a public or only a private commitment. Individuals who thought that their chances of being fully accepted by the group were low and who, as a matter of fact, feared rejection from the group showed conformity only in public. The false majority had little influence on their private opinions. These results have been further corroborated in a field setting (Menzel 1957).

While research results on conformity are not always perfectly reliable, a good deal of information has been gathered in this field since the pioneering studies of Sherif and Asch. These results, which show that even under completely private conditions the individual is likely to surrender, at least in part, to the pressures of a group making an obviously wrong judgment, clearly demonstrate the degree to which groups may control individual behavior and perception. The experiments on conformity, moreover, do not deal simply with trivial responses and psychologically trivial forces having little significance for behavior outside of the psychological laboratory. From the point of view of the subject, the experimental conformity situation is quite real and quite serious. His involvement in it and its impact have been demonstrated by physiological activity symptomatic of stress arising during the confrontation of the individual with a false consensus (e.g., Back et al. 1963) and declining as a result of his agreement with the group (Lawson & Stagner 1957).

ROBERT B. ZAJONC

[Directly related are the entries COHESION, SOCIAL; IMITATION; SUGGESTION. Other relevant material may be found in GROUPS, article on GROUP FORMA-TION; REFERENCE GROUPS; SOCIAL CONTROL; SOCIALIZATION; and in the biographies of LE BON and TARDE.]

BIBLIOGRAPHY

APPLEY, MORTIMER H.; and MOELLER, GEORGE 1963 Conforming Behavior and Personality Variables in College Women. Journal of Abnormal and Social Psychology 66:284–290.

ASCH, SOLOMON E. (1952) 1959 Social Psychology. Englewood Cliffs, N.J.: Prentice-Hall.

ASCH, SOLOMON E. 1956 Studies of Independence and Conformity. I. A Minority of One Against a Unanimous Majority. Psychological Monographs: General and Applied 70, no. 9, whole no. 416.

BACK, KURT W. et al. 1963 An Interpretation of Experimental Conformity Through Physiological Measures. Behavioral Science 8:34–40.

BIRNEY, ROBERT C.; and HOUSTON, JOHN P. 1961 The Effects of Creativity, Norm Distance, and Instructions on Social Influence. Journal of Personality 29:294–302.

BLAKE, ROBERT R.; HELSON, HARRY; and MOUTON, JANE S. 1957 The Generality of Conformity Behavior as a Function of Factual Anchorage, Difficulty of Task, and Amount of Social Pressure. Journal of Personality 25:294–305.

BLAKE, ROBERT R.; MOUTON, JANE S.; and HAIN, JACK D. 1956 Social Forces in Petition-signing. Southwestern Social Science Quarterly 36:385–390.

BLAKE, ROBERT R.; ROSENBAUM, MILTON; and DURYEA, RICHARD 1955 Gift-giving as a Function of Group Standards. Human Relations 8:61–73.

BOVARD, EVERETT W. 1953 Conformity to Social Norms and Attraction to the Group. Science New Series 118:598–599.

COLEMAN, JANET F.; BLAKE, ROBERT R.; and MOUTON, JANE S. 1958 Task Difficulty and Conformity Pressures. Journal of Abnormal and Social Psychology 57:120–122.

CROWNE, DOUGLAS P.; and LIVERANT, SHEPHARD 1963 Conformity Under Varying Conditions of Personal Commitment. Journal of Abnormal and Social Psychology 66:547–555.

DEUTSCH, MORTON; and GERARD, HAROLD B. 1955 A Study of Normative and Informational Social Influences Upon Individual Judgment. Journal of Abnormal and Social Psychology 51:629–636.

DITTES, JAMES E.; and KELLEY, HAROLD H. 1956 Effects of Different Conditions of Acceptance Upon Conformity to Group Norms. Journal of Abnormal and Social Psychology 53:100–107.

DiVESTA, FRANCIS J.; and COX, LANDON 1960 Some Dispositional Correlates of Conformity Behavior. Journal of Social Psychology 52:259–268.

FERGUSON, LEONARD W. 1944 An Analysis of the Generality of Suggestibility to Group Opinion. Character and Personality 12:237–243.

FESTINGER, LEON; SCHACHTER, STANLEY; and BACK, KURT (1950) 1963 Social Pressures in Informal Groups: A Study of Human Factors in Housing. Stanford (Calif.) Univ. Press.

FREED, A. M. et al. 1955 Stimulus and Background Factors in Sign Violation. Journal of Personality 23:499.

GERARD, HAROLD B. 1953 The Effect of Different Dimensions of Disagreement on the Communication Process in Small Groups. Human Relations 6:249–271.

HARVEY, O. J.; and CONSALVI, CONRAD 1960 Status and

Conformity to Pressures in Informal Groups. *Journal of Abnormal and Social Psychology* 60:182–187.

HOFFMAN, MARTIN L. 1953 Some Psychodynamic Factors in Compulsive Conformity. *Journal of Abnormal and Social Psychology* 48:383–393.

HOLLANDER, EDWIN P. 1964 *Leaders, Groups, and Influence.* New York: Oxford Univ. Press.

KAGAN, JEROME; and MUSSEN, PAUL H. 1956 Dependency Themes on the TAT and Group Conformity. *Journal of Consulting Psychology* 20:29–32.

KIESLER, CHARLES A. 1963 Attraction to the Group and Conformity to Group Norms. *Journal of Personality* 31:559–569.

LAWSON, EDWIN D.; and STAGNER, ROSS 1957 Group Pressure, Attitude Change, and Autonomic Involvement. *Journal of Social Psychology* 45:299–312.

MENZEL, HERBERT 1957 Public and Private Conformity Under Different Conditions of Acceptance in the Group. *Journal of Abnormal and Social Psychology* 55:398–402.

MUSSEN, PAUL H.; and KAGAN, JEROME 1958 Group Conformity and Perceptions of Parents. *Child Development* 29:57–60.

NEWCOMB, THEODORE M. (1943) 1957 *Personality and Social Change: Attitude Formation in a Student Community.* New York: Dryden.

RAVEN, BERTRAM H.; and FRENCH, JOHN R. P. JR. 1958 Group Support, Legitimate Power, and Social Influence. *Journal of Personality* 26:400–409.

ROHRER, J. H. et al. 1954 The Stability of Autokinetic Judgments. *Journal of Abnormal and Social Psychology* 49:595–597.

ROSENBAUM, MILTON E. 1956 The Effect of Stimulus and Background Factors on the Volunteering Response. *Journal of Abnormal and Social Psychology* 53:118–121.

ROSENBERG, LEON A. 1961 Group Size, Prior Experience, and Conformity. *Journal of Abnormal and Social Psychology* 63:436–437.

ROSNER, STANLEY 1957 Consistency in Response to Group Pressures. *Journal of Abnormal and Social Psychology* 55:145–146.

SAMELSON, F. 1958 The Relation of Achievement and Affiliation Motives to Conforming Behavior in Two Conditions of Conflict With a Majority. Pages 421–433 in John W. Atkinson (editor), *Motives in Fantasy, Action, and Society: A Method of Assessment and Study.* Princeton, N.J.: Van Nostrand.

SCHOOLER, CARMI; and SPOHN, HERBERT E. 1960 The Susceptibility of Chronic Schizophrenics to Social Influence in the Formation of Perceptual Judgments. *Journal of Abnormal and Social Psychology* 61:348–354.

SHERIF, MUZAFER 1935 A Study of Some Social Factors in Perception. *Archives of Psychology* 27, no. 187.

SHERIF, MUZAFER (1936) 1965 *The Psychology of Social Norms.* New York: Octagon.

STEINER, IVAN D.; and JOHNSON, HOMER H. 1963 Authoritarianism and Conformity. *Sociometry* 26:21–34.

STRICKLAND, BONNIE R.; and CROWNE, DOUGLAS P. 1962 Conformity Under Conditions of Simulated Group Pressure as a Function of the Need for Social Approval. *Journal of Social Psychology* 58:171–181.

SYMPOSIUM ON CONFORMITY AND DEVIATION, LOUISIANA STATE UNIVERSITY, *1960* 1961 *Conformity and Deviation.* Edited by Irwin A. Berg and Bernard M. Bass. New York: Harper.

THIBAUT, JOHN W.; and STRICKLAND, LLOYD H. 1956 Psychological Set and Social Conformity. *Journal of Personality* 25:115–129.

TUDDENHAM, READ D. 1959 Correlates of Yielding to a Distorted Group Norm. *Journal of Personality* 27:272–284.

TUDDENHAM, READ D. 1961 The Influence of a Distorted Group Norm Upon Judgments of Adults and Children. *Journal of Psychology* 52:231–239.

WHITTAKER, JAMES O. 1964 Parameters of Social Influence in the Autokinetic Situation. *Sociometry* 27:88–95.

ZAJONC, ROBERT B.; and WAHI, N. KISHOR 1961 Conformity and Need-achievement Under Cross-cultural Norm Conflict. *Human Relations* 14:241–250.

CONFUCIANISM
See BUDDHISM; CHINESE POLITICAL THOUGHT.

CONGESTION
See QUEUES.

CONSANGUINITY
See KINSHIP.

CONSENSUS

I. THE CONCEPT OF CONSENSUS   *Edward Shils*
II. THE STUDY OF CONSENSUS   *Lewis Lipsitz*

I
THE CONCEPT OF CONSENSUS

Consensus is a particular state of the belief system of a society. It exists when a large proportion of the adult members of a society, more particularly a large proportion of those concerned with decisions regarding the allocations of authority, status, rights, wealth and income, and other important and scarce values about which conflict might occur, are in approximate agreement in their beliefs about what decisions should be made and have some feeling of unity with each other and with the society as a whole. Consensus may also exist between individuals in primordial or personal face-to-face relationships as in a family or in friendship; it may exist within a charismatic corporate body like a church or sect or within a society. Here we shall be considering only the consensual state of a society, that is, "macrosocial" consensus. (Dissensus exists in situations where potentially divergent "interests" confront each other and consensus is absent.)

Three elements crucial to the functioning of consensus are (1) common acceptance of laws, rules, and norms, (2) attachment to the institutions which promulgate and apply the laws and rules, and (3) a widespread sense of identity or unity, which discloses to individuals who experience it, those features in respect to which they are identical and therefore equal. The sense of identity diminishes the significance of the differences on which dissensus and hostile sentiments would otherwise focus. Although these elements may vary independently, the strength of any one of them helps to strengthen the others.

The pattern of consensual belief. Consensus refers to distributions of scarce values among individuals who are in face-to-face interaction and who are competing for these values. Between workers and supervisors and among workers on a shop floor, among members of different political parties, or members of different factions within a political party, consensus operates to restrict the extension of dissensus and to limit conflict with regard to the allocation of valued objects. In these face-to-face situations the consensus is ordinarily, although not always, a "derivative" of beliefs which have a wider range of reference. The adjudication of conflicts with immediate superiors, colleagues, or political rivals is often a specific product of norms or maxims which have a more general and a wider relevance. (The same applies to dissensus.) Relatively few persons are in face-to-face interaction with those who are remote from them in such society-wide distributions as income, power, and deference, but it is to these larger distributions that attention is given, and it is about them that "serious" beliefs are held. Individuals are capable of perceiving the approximate dimensions of these larger distributions and of passing judgment on their rightfulness; indeed, the greatest importance is attributed to these distributions. Human beings are capable of rendering judgments about situations in which they do not actually participate, and many are strongly inclined to do so. Intellectual and moral sensibility impel them to judge the quality of their society and to formulate the attitude they should take toward it and toward the larger distributions which determine it. The fact that beliefs about such distributions are beliefs about power—a fact which draws attention to itself and which urgently demands judgment—makes macrosocial distributions into objects of vital beliefs.

The beliefs with respect to which consensus may exist include both cognitive propositions and moral standards about the justice or injustice of the distribution of roles, facilities, and rewards and about the worth of the institutions of authority and order by which these distributions are brought about, maintained, and changed. These beliefs usually concern the rightness and the qualifications of those in authority to exercise it and of those re-

ceiving different amounts of the valued objects to receive what they do. These beliefs also concern the legitimacy of the institutions through which the bearers of authority and the recipients of the different shares are selected. In a condition of macrosocial consensus, the most important beliefs relate to the sense of unity which extends from those who possess it, whatever their own position, to strata of the population very differently situated in the distributions of rewards and very different in their share in the exercise of authority. Macrosocial consensus by definition does not include such beliefs as those which refer to the right order of personal relationships, the proper objects of aesthetic experience and judgment, the origin and structure of the cosmos, and the nature and powers of divinity. (It is of course quite likely that where consensus exists with respect to such beliefs, the macrosocial consensus in which we are interested is more probable and more enduring.)

Until the emergence of the modern liberal state with a plurality of religions, diverse political parties, and institutions for the conduct and control of class and other sectional conflicts, rulers tended to believe that consensus in religious beliefs was a necessary condition of the consensus required for social order. In the nineteenth century this view ceased to be regarded as valid. Yet it is quite possible that consensus of beliefs apart from those about the justice or injustice of the distribution of scarce and desired objects helps to create and maintain the vague sense of unity which is an essential part of consensus. There is perhaps a deeper truth hidden in the quip which asserted that England was a "country of a hundred religions and one sauce." The approximate uniformity of standards of taste might have contributed to the sense of unity which enabled a macrosocial consensus to function despite the divisions concerning questions of theology and ecclesiastical organization [*see* LEGITIMACY].

Abstract or general ethical and political beliefs ("principles") can enter into consensus insofar as they affect agreement or disagreement on particular issues of legitimacy, distribution, selection, and so on. A situation in which general principles, ratiocinatively or affectively arrived at, explicitly and visibly determine particular orientations is by no means impossible. Still, it is relatively rare in any society, and only rigorous ideologists insist on a very close dependence of particular decisions on the explicit principles which are part of an explicit and systematic belief system.

Human beings assess the actions and orientations of other persons in general categories, and their assessments give some direction to their particular and immediate response to these persons. General ethical standards, vague notions of the right ordering of life, and conceptions of the virtues which entitle men to power, deference, and other rewards and facilities can have some influence on concrete responses to particular issues; insofar as they are consensually shared, such general orientations may be said to constitute part of the consensus.

The beliefs which enter into consensus are not clearly articulated or systematically ordered. They are expressed sometimes in maxims and sometimes in ambiguous terms like "fairness." They are often formulated negatively, repudiating particular situations but not indicating what is positively right. Even the corpus of law, which is the most articulated precipitate of consensus, is full of gaps and is rarely very coherent in a logical sense; what is more, the specific imperatives and prohibitions contained in law are far more differentiated than the beliefs actually formulated or articulated by those who share in consensus. In societies with written constitutions, the body of beliefs and rules and images contained therein has some correspondence with the prevailing consensus, but the correspondence is only approximate and uneven.

Dissensual patterns of belief are often more explicit and systematic than are the consensual patterns which affirm the existing central institutional system. The more dissensual it is, the greater the likelihood of explicitness and systematic coherence in a pattern of belief. Accordingly, consensual belief patterns tend to be more pluralistic in the sense that they espouse a number of beliefs which are not wholly consistent with each other and which are able to coexist quite easily as long as no one of them is carried out in full. Thus, in contemporary Western liberal societies both equality and liberty are believed to be very important, but neither is pressed to complete fulfillment. They remain vague indicators of a direction or tendency rather than specific imperatives. A greater monism is generally but not always characteristic of dissensual patterns of belief. There probably is a positive correlation between monism in the pattern of belief and the degree of dissensuality vis-à-vis the prevailing patterns of belief.

The beliefs which enter into consensus (or dissensus) vary in the intensity with which they are adhered to even within a single pattern of belief; some component beliefs might be very stringently insisted upon, others less so. Correspondingly, within a given society some of the adherents of a given pattern of belief might have a high average level of intensity of adherence, others might have a lower average level. The adherents of a dissensual (internally consensual) pattern of belief will usually have a higher average level of intensity of adherence than the adherents of a consensual pattern.

Consensual patterns of belief tend to be affirmative about the distribution of authority, the legitimacy of its results, and the mechanisms and standards by which it is effected. There is nothing in the definition of consensus that requires this to be so, and there might indeed be occasions when the prevailing system of authority becomes the object of a widely shared negative consensus. This would be a situation in which the paradox of a dissensual consensus is realized. But that would be the exception. Insofar as a dominant consensus exists in a society, it usually more or less affirms the existing system of authoritative institutions and the distributions associated with them because authority, when it is effective, tends to establish its own legitimacy. The coercive powers of authority also help it to call forth a conformity which justifies itself by an acknowledgment of the legitimacy of the powerful. Perhaps even more important is the close affinity of outlook of the central cultural system with the central institutional system, and this, through teaching and exemplification, tends to diffuse itself into the outlook and the programs of large parts of the society.

The empirical analysis of the pattern of consensus confronts the same difficulties as the empirical analysis of beliefs actually held by individuals. Because of vagueness, ambiguity, unsystematic character, and variations in level of abstraction, actually held beliefs are difficult to describe, and there is a tendency on the part of sociological and anthropological analysts to systematize, clarify, and specify actually held beliefs to a point which makes the holder of such beliefs appear to be a systematic philosopher. Premises are rendered explicit and particular judgments are generalized; as a result of this process, beliefs which are not knowingly held are imputed by the analysts, who thus distort the nature of consensus and the mechanisms through which it operates.

The social structure of consensus. In no society, however consensual, is the consensus ever universally shared. Nor does it depend upon universal participation to be effective. Those adults who do share it, do so with very different degrees of intensity or concern. Of course no adult member of society is outside the system of allocation of scarce roles, facilities, and rewards, and as a result no adult, unless he is utterly—indeed almost catatonically—apathetic, can entirely avoid rendering judgments at least about that sector of the distribution which he perceives immediately around him. Moreover, the judgments which he renders are related in a determinate way to those current in the culture of his society. Yet his interest in the larger distribution and the problems of legitimacy associated with it might be very faint and infrequent.

Since one of the most important foci of consensus is the system of allocation of the whole society, those persons who do not concern themselves much or intensely with the total allocation may be said to be somewhat marginal in the structure of consensus. Even where they share general beliefs, about what is "fair," for instance, the fact that they apply these beliefs only or primarily to their immediate environment and not to the larger society means that they do not participate in the consensus to the same extent and in the same way as those who apply the consensually shared norms more intensely and frequently to the macrosocial system of allocation.

In societies which are relatively unintegrated and where centrally made decisions therefore impinge only very intermittently and marginally on certain sectors of the society (e.g., isolated villages which do not participate in a national economy), the members of those sectors might be entirely outside the structure of consensus. But in modern societies, where government plays such a large part in influencing allocations and where country-wide communication and transportation systems bring at least some features of the central institutional system into the field of attention of even the uneducated and apathetic, complete abstention from the structure of consensus (or dissensus) is very rare.

On some issues and on some occasions most of the adult population is consensual, but even within such general consensus there are many individual differences. Apart from differences in intensity among those who share in any particular belief in a consensus, there are differences in the number or proportion of beliefs adhered to. Every consensus is constituted by a plurality of beliefs, such as beliefs about the right principles of remuneration, the proper shape of particular distributions (equality and inequality), the prerogatives of property ownership, the propriety of incumbency by certain individuals and classes of individuals in certain positions on particular distributions, and the value of the total national community. Within the "public" of a consensus, some sectors might be attached intensely to all the beliefs, others intensely only to some of them and faintly to others, and some might

be attached only to a very few and repudiate most others. A common acceptance of certain of the beliefs might bind the entire "public" into a partial consensus; just how partial it is depends on the extent to which other beliefs are repudiated and various contrary ones espoused by the various subsectors of that public. For example, nearly everyone in a given country might accept the legitimacy of the electoral system and of the authorities selected through it, and they might also accept a particular unequal distribution of income; but they might disagree sharply about the distribution of deference, and about the capacity of particular incumbents of authoritative roles to act beneficially on behalf of the society as a whole.

Consensus exists in a complex interplay with dissensus. Dissensus is the state of disagreement of beliefs about allocative decisions and results. Those who are dissensual with respect to a particular feature of an allocative system or process might be consensual with respect to other features or about the general properties of the system. Thus the dimensions or boundaries of the structure of consensus are variable within a given society, not only over a longer trend but from situation and problem to situation and problem.

Party politics in modern societies are organized efforts to shift the boundaries of the partial dissensus within the framework of a partial consensus. But alongside these deliberate efforts to change the structure of consensus, there is a continual shifting of boundaries among partially dissensual groups. Beliefs about which there was once disagreement (e.g., concerning the right of the unemployed to public assistance) become consensual, while previously consensual beliefs, such as those concerning the right of the inheritance of property, become partially dissensual. These historical shifts in the structure of consensus arise in part from the struggles of the proponents of the partially dissensual programs, in part from demographic and technological changes, which are accompanied by changes in occupational structure, and in part from the unfolding of the dynamic potentialities of various patterns of belief.

The variations in the "public" of consensus (i.e., in the size of the population participating in it) testify also to the simultaneous coherence and incoherence of the patterns of belief which individuals bring into consensus. If each individual had a perfectly systematized pattern of belief, those who disagreed with him on one particular belief would disagree with him on all others. On the other hand, if this pattern of belief were totally incoherent, there would be no stability in the "publics" formed by the consensus around particular beliefs. Agreement on one issue would not entail any probability of agreement on any other. Yet, as we know, every consensual pattern of belief is borne in the first instance by a persisting "public" of adherents who gather around them, on particular issues and clusters of issues, extended and somewhat fluctuating "publics." Some who are consensual on most issues are dissensual on a few; others who are dissensual on most issues are consensual on a few. From this determinateness of pattern an approximate stability of the "publics" is borne.

The function of consensus. Consensus maintains public order, that is, it reduces the probability of the use of violence in the resolution of disagreements; it increases the amount of cooperation which is not impelled by fear of the coercive power of the stronger party. It does so by (1) the reduction of the probability of disagreements, (2) the restriction of the intensity of affect and strength of motivation with which disagreements are conducted and the softening of the rigidity of the attachment to the objectives about which the disagreements exist, and (3) the fostering of a readiness to accept peaceful modes of adjudicating disagreements among those who have a sense of mutual affinity or identity.

There is no natural harmony of interest among men in society. Men are diverse in their propensities, and the material and symbolic objects which they seek are scarce in relation to the demand for them. Their "interests" are in conflict. Furthermore, a society—particularly a large-scale society—differentiated by generations, by occupations, by status and culture, will naturally tend toward a differentiation in beliefs regarding the rightness of the actions of authority and the justice of the existing social order [see CONFLICT]. Where it exists, consensus is a counterforce against the fulfillment of the divisive potentialities of these divergent "interests" and beliefs. Consensus facilitates collaboration: it reinforces the cooperation which arises from coincidences of interest, limits the range of the divergence of interests by defining ends in a way which renders them more compatible, and circumscribes the actions injurious to cooperation which might arise from the divergent interests.

To be effective consensus depends particularly on those persons scattered throughout the society in many classes, regions, and occupations who have a fairly continuous concern with (1) the macrosocial distribution of roles, facilities, and rewards, (2) the particular decisions taken in the center of the society inasmuch as they affect these distributions or are affected by them, and (3) the

institutions in which these decisions are taken or which influence the distributions. The concern may take the form of institutionalized participation in the decisions bearing on these three aspects of distributive events, or it may take the form of attitudinal involvement which affects action. The concerned are elites who, on behalf of the strata and collectivities generated by the distributions or on behalf of some ideal arrangement, take it upon themselves or are institutionally entitled to pass judgment and to attempt to influence opinion and decision. Their agreement or disagreement on particular issues can promote harmony or conflict in the working of institutions and in the relationships of strata and collectivities. [See ELITES.]

Public order and effective cooperation among the diverse parts of the society do not, however, require complete and continuous consensus even among the elites. What is important for the maintenance of order is that their disagreements about particular issues should exist within a consensual matrix. This consensual matrix is maintained largely by the sense of oneness with each other and with the whole society; this sense of oneness manifests itself in a sense of affinity even with persons with whom there might be many particular disagreements. Coalitions of interests, the boundaries of which cut across each other, keep the sense of oneness from disintegrating. (Cleavages formed by the coincidence of boundaries of interest coalitions, on the other hand, do serious damage to the sense of oneness.) The power to coerce is another important element in maintaining order in society, but it never operates alone for any length of time. Without a strong consensual reinforcement, coercion could in itself never be effective. It is a supplement to consensus, not a mutually exclusive alternative.

The formation and change of consensus. The family which inducts the newly born organism into society is the first instigator of consensus. Within the family the child acquires generalized and affirmative attitudes toward authority, which are the preconditions of a subsequent assimilation into a consensus based on authoritative institutions at the center of society. In school the child acquires some of the culture of the larger society, some knowledge and appreciation of its heroes, great events, and territorial scope; he forms an image of the society. From childhood on, great collective rituals repeatedly renew the sense of unity with the larger society, and recurrent interaction with like-minded persons maintains and reinforces the disposition to attribute validity to those who speak and act through and for the central institutional system and those who speak on behalf of the central cultural system. As a result, a substantial proportion of the indigenous population grows into a consensual culture which accepts the rightness and justice of existing distributions, the norms for judging them, and the institutions for maintaining and changing them [see SOCIALIZATION].

But the consensus never includes all the population. Some families and sectors of the population —classes and ethnic groups—are at the margins of the dominant consensus or even outside it. Some people even reject the pattern of the beliefs which inform the dominant consensus as far-reachingly as is possible under the pressures of authority and the permeative influence of the central cultural system. Every large society has a dissensual as well as a consensual culture, which is sustained by religious traditions and regional and class cultures as well as by recurrently renewed ethical and metaphysical criticism of the prevailing system of authority and the allocations of which the incumbents of authoritative and elite roles are the beneficiaries. Those who experience pain from the existing distributions of income, power, and status, although often sharing much of the consensual pattern of belief, also have contrary inclinations. A society which inflicts the distress of a sense of exclusion and inferiority cannot wholly succeed in assimilating into its affirmative consensus those whom it wounds.

The numerous particular situations of conflicts of interest and of norms of what is fair and just constitute the occasions for repeated rearrangements and regroupings of those who are consensual and those who are dissensual. The boundaries shift and shade off from the one zone into the other. At times the consensus might be very inclusive and at others it might lose some or much of its following.

The strength of the central institutional system and the deep penetration of the central cultural system result, however, in a considerable tenacity of the beliefs that make up the consensus. But the beliefs themselves undergo gradual changes. Indeed, the traditional character of most of the consensual beliefs renders such changes feasible, and this too helps to maintain the consensus. The ambiguity which is inherent in traditionally transmitted beliefs fosters flexibility and permits continuity in the face of changing circumstances. Moderate changes in the structure and in the incumbents of the various positions in the distributions of power, income, and status can be borne without a serious diminution in adherence to the main beliefs in a prevailing consensus. If the losers by these allocative changes are not too drastically

affected, their participation in the consensus will not be greatly affected. Much depends on the continued strength of the central institutions. If these continue to maintain the appearance of effectiveness, dissensual tendencies will be held in check. Strong attachment to the society as a whole, aided by the apparent effectiveness of authority, inhibits dissensual tendencies. Beliefs about "luck" and a belief that results are indicative of qualifications render losses even more bearable.

When, however, drastic changes occur, the consensus is likely to be weakened by a deeper and more comprehensive withdrawal of those who are severely hurt by the changes. The diverse potentialities of interpretation which every consensus contains tends, under these circumstances, to be subjected to constructions which run in opposed directions, and reconciliation becomes more difficult. It is also likely that large and rapid increments in the quantity of rewards received will disrupt the participation of the *gainers* in the hitherto dominant consensus. Such increments often raise the level of aspiration well beyond the limits permitted by the beliefs of the traditionally established consensus.

Changes in technology disclose new possibilities of changing the share in valued objects possessed by various strata of the population. Those who perceive these possibilities and who, by virtue of their control over resources, are in a position to enhance their share will usually seek to do so. If they are prevented from doing so by the fixity of attachment of the incumbent elites to the existing distributions and by the rigidity of the patterns of belief of those elites about the rightness of the existing distributions, a new focus of dissensual beliefs will be formed. Technological innovations also engender new occupations with new occupational cultures. These new cultures might contain beliefs which cannot always or easily be accommodated within the existing consensus, and this too leads to new foci of dissensual beliefs.

Yet, despite the strains to which it is constantly subjected, the consensus of a society has much adaptability and considerable powers of endurance. Even in periods of acute civil disorder, when the previously legitimated authority has been expelled or has shown its weakness, the consensus is not entirely in dissolution. Society can never dissolve into a Hobbesian state of nature. Even though it has ceased to bind the warring groups, the sections of the population which are not intensely involved in the conflict might be quite consensual in their orientations toward each other or, at least, much more so than the groups which are violently in conflict with each other. The disruption of society in situations of acute civil disorder consists of the active contention of violently dissensual elites for the machinery and symbols of authority and the control of the system of distribution. The persistence of the more consensual sections of the population in the beliefs they have hitherto held fosters the re-establishment of a substantial measure of consensus when the crisis passes. Even the two warring parties usually contend against each other on behalf of divergent interpretations of a commonly shared constellation of beliefs. It is only that the sense of unity, of attachment to the whole society, which is an essential constituent of consensus, has been so violently ruptured that the affinity of substantive beliefs retains no restraining power.

Once civil order is restored, consensus gradually becomes re-established. It will not be exactly the same consensual pattern of belief that existed previously. The newly established elite, legitimated by effective incumbency, will both deliberately and unwittingly infiltrate some of its own beliefs into the previously operative consensus. However, the members of the new elite will, in their turn, become assimilated into the basic consensual pattern which is held by those they rule and which they too shared before coming to power.

EDWARD SHILS

[*See also* AUTHORITY; CONFLICT; COOPERATION; DEMOCRACY; EQUALITY; IDEOLOGY; NORMS; VALUES. *Other relevant material may be found under* LAW.]

BIBLIOGRAPHY

ABRAMS, MARK 1964 Party Politics After the End of Ideology. Pages 56–63 in Erik Allardt and Yrjö Littunen (editors), *Cleavages, Ideologies and Party Systems: Contributions to Comparative Political Sociology.* Helsinki: Westermarck Society.

LIPSET, SEYMOUR M. 1964 Political Cleavages in "Developed" and "Emerging" Politics. Pages 21–55 in Erik Allardt and Yrjö Littunen (editors), *Cleavages, Ideologies and Party Systems: Contributions to Comparative Political Sociology.* Helsinki: Westermarck Society.

LOCKWOOD, DAVID 1964 Social Integration and System Integration. Pages 244–257 in George K. Zollschan and Walter Hirsch (editors), *Explorations in Social Change.* Boston: Houghton Mifflin.

MCCLOSKY, HERBERT 1964 Consensus and Ideology in American Politics. *American Political Science Review* 58:361–382.

PLAMENATZ, JOHN; GRIFFITH, ERNEST S.; and PENNOCK, J. ROLAND 1956 Cultural Prerequisites to a Successfully Functioning Democracy: A Symposium. *American Political Science Review* 50:101–137. → See especially pages 115–127, by John Plamenatz.

PROTHRO, JAMES W.; and GRIGG, C. W. 1960 Fundamental Principles of Democracy: Bases of Agreement and Disagreement. *Journal of Politics* 22:276–294.

SHILS, EDWARD 1961 Centre and Periphery. Pages 117–130 in *The Logic of Personal Knowledge: Essays Presented to Michael Polanyi.* London: Routledge; New York: Free Press.

TOCQUEVILLE, ALEXIS DE (1835) 1945 *Democracy in America.* 2 vols. New York: Knopf. → First published in French. Paperback editions were published in 1961 by Vintage and by Schocken.

TÖNNIES, FERDINAND (1887) 1957 *Community and Society (Gemeinschaft und Gesellschaft).* Translated and edited by Charles P. Loomis. East Lansing: Michigan State Univ. Press. → First published in German. A paperback edition was published in 1963 by Harper.

TÖNNIES, FERDINAND (1909) 1961 *Custom: An Essay on Social Codes.* New York: Free Press. → First published in German.

II
THE STUDY OF CONSENSUS

Political consensus involves kinds of agreements that are politically relevant. Students of this subject have been concerned largely with questions of the stability of regimes, particularly democratic regimes.

Four uses of the idea of consensus have been developed by writers interested primarily in the viability of democratic political processes. One conception has seen consensus as agreement on the "fundamentals" of democratic government. There is marked divergence, however, on the questions of what it means to agree on fundamentals and just how significant such agreement is (Griffith et al. 1956). Others have argued that the consensus necessary in a democracy is chiefly a matter of habitual patterns of behavior which are more important than conscious agreement on democratic principles (Prothro & Grigg 1960). A third position has emphasized the question of the acceptability of governmental policy to significant social groups. In this view, consensus on emotion-laden issues such as those embodied in the welfare state can have decisive influence on the stability of the political system (Lipset 1964). A fourth view of consensus in the democratic context has defined consensus as existing where all structurally important social groups contain adherents of major political parties. This view of consensus sees it as the outcome of "cross-cutting cleavages" which ensure that social divisions and political conflicts do not reinforce one another too thoroughly. Here consensus is the opposite of acute conflict and is hypothesized as leading to political tolerance and a low-tension politics (Parsons 1959). It should be clear that these four conceptualizations of politically relevant consensus are not mutually exclusive but in some cases complement each other, while in others they conflict.

Two other views of consensus, although also

related to the problems of democracy, have been developed and employed in different political contexts as well. The first of these is consensus as legitimacy: approval of the existing government and/or its directives. Understood in this sense, consensus is seen to be one of the key elements in governmental stability. Others have discussed consensus in terms of the basic moral and social perspectives that underlie political life. This has been a matter of deep concern to students of developing nations. In this view, the problem of creating consensus is closely related to questions of political socialization, ideology, political myths and rituals, modernization, and personality structure.

Each of these concepts of politically relevant consensus deals with a form of *agreement*. Although this notion of agreement appears to be the core of the idea of consensus, such a conclusion hardly begins to clarify the important problems. Of acute concern, and the object of most controversy among students of consensus, are the questions of how various kinds of agreement or lack of agreement are related to political stability, democracy, and the limitation of conflict.

Consensus and political philosophy. Preoccupation with problems of social cohesion and legitimacy was characteristic of political philosophy from its beginnings. Plato and Aristotle explored questions of political consensus. Both, for example, emphasized the significance of appropriate political socialization through education if the polity was to be stable. Several of the books of Aristotle's *Politics* are concerned with problems of political viability and revolution and deal extensively with governmental legitimacy.

Concern with political cohesion has been a recurrent one in the modern period. Contract theorists such as Locke, Hobbes, Rousseau, and Paine emphasized the need for a rational, conscious creation of political consensus and employed the idea of the "contract" as the basis of legitimate authority. The utilitarians, and to a certain extent John Stuart Mill, provided an "interest" justification of government. In their view, a secular consensus should be based on a recognition that government should serve the interests of the greatest number.

Political theorists of a more conservative or aristocratic hue have been profoundly concerned with consensus as a problem. Burke, for example, feared the spread of the ideology of the French Revolution because, in his view, it called into question the legitimacy of all forms of government. He championed political ritualism, a hierarchical social order, and close church–state relations as impor-

tant sustainers of consensus about governmental legitimacy. De Tocqueville emphasized the peculiar problems of consensus in a democratic polity and argued for the increased significance of religion as a binding force in direct proportion to the growth of political liberty. Concern continues with the significance of ritualism and religiosity in creating consensus. Several authors have emphasized the role of political holidays and ceremonies in producing a sense of national unity.

Nationalism has been discussed as a semi-religious unifying motif in Western nations (Key 1961, p. 43). It has also been argued that the American president and the British monarch inspire a semireligious attachment which serves as a primordial unifying bond in the political system. Similar hypotheses have been offered with regard to the role of nationalist ideologies and nationalist leaders in developing nations (Apter 1963).

Modernization and political consensus. There is agreement that modernization processes generally involve acute crises of political consensus.

Western societies. Lipset (1960, pp. 76–97) has discussed this process as it occurred in Western societies in terms of three basic crises of legitimacy: first, the crisis involving church–state relations; second, the crisis involving the entry of the working class into politics; and third, the crisis surrounding questions of redistribution of wealth. He argues that governmental legitimacy can be undermined by these crises in various ways. For one, the entry of the working class into the political arena can be delayed too long, thus making for a revolutionary ideology in that class. Second, crises can accumulate through the inability to solve any one of them. In such a case, as in France, cleavages are intensified and governmental stability fundamentally endangered. Finally, too radical a change in the political system, again as in France, can alienate the more conservative groups, thus undermining the conditions for mutual tolerance.

Lipset concludes (1964) that the wide acceptance of a secularized welfare state marks the ends of these crises of consensus. Post-World War II developments, especially economic growth, settled the intense political conflicts of previous western European politics. The older, largely nineteenth-century ideologies are outmoded. A new ideology, named "conservative socialism" by Lipset, has gained acceptance among major social groups and the major political parties. Political conflict, then, has lost its intensity and no longer revolves around what are felt to be fundamental differences of view. Europe is described as coming to resemble America in its politics, in that political parties offer similar programs and a large middle class plays a crucial moderating role. Many have seriously questioned this view. LaPalombara (1966a; 1966b), for example, has raised important methodological issues and also has challenged the substance of the argument as it applies to Italian politics.

Lane (1962) has explored this new "ideology" as it appears among upper-working-class and lower-middle-class Americans. His data are drawn from intensive interviews of 15 men. He maintains that the strata these individuals represent are largely satisfied with the existing political system, as well as with the present patterns of social stratification. Their political attitudes are characterized by pragmatic responses, an absence of moral perspectives on current issues, and the lack of a distinct ideological identity. Lane argues that these individuals identify with various social groups and therefore their ideology, such as it is, is diffuse and tolerant. His findings support those of survey research concerning the attitudes of Americans toward the political parties and their candidates. It is unclear whether this "nonideology" is a distinctly contemporary phenomenon in America or is merely the modern version of older aspects of American politics. It is also unclear whether the "ideology" Lane has uncovered is confined to a particular geographic section of the United States and to a particular stratum of the population.

Developing nations. Political consensus expressed in terms of governmental stability is regarded as a fundamental problem in developing nations. Many maintain that discontinuous social change, creating sharp imbalances between expectations and opportunities, makes political stability a rare and yet overwhelmingly necessary commodity. This gap between expectations and opportunities is conceptualized variously as a result of excessively rapid urbanization, the absence of employment for highly trained personnel, or the spread of ideas of equality and economic development.

One problem of modernization involves the gap between mass and elite. This gap prevents effective communication in both directions and therefore blocks the development of a national normative culture and national identity, as well as preventing widespread needs and demands from becoming known to the elite with sufficient speed (Binder 1964).

Intense conflict and the absence of consensus on the ends and means of political life are also characteristic of developing states. Students of many countries have observed the severity of political party conflict involving groups with sharply different world views, which often takes on some of the aspects of warfare. In these cases, the stakes involved in politics are perceived as being so high that no political group is willing to concede defeat voluntarily. The norms of tolerance cannot develop and governmental legitimacy is constantly threatened. Democratic politics may be able to develop only where political activists do not feel the stakes of competition are too high. We know little, however, about the circumstances in which such perceptions change, and this knowledge is critical to the problems of developing nations.

Consensus and "fundamentals" of democracy. Scholars have maintained that agreement on certain fundamentals is a prerequisite of democracy. These fundamentals have been variously seen as the belief in human equality, the belief in the superiority of democracy, the belief in tolerance for dissenting views, and the belief in majority rule. Recent empirical examinations of the actual state of agreement on such matters in the United States has led to a more complex picture of the relationship between consensus on fundamentals and democratic practices.

Prothro and Grigg (1960), using 90 per cent agreement as a measure of consensus, found it to exist on matters of majority rule and minority rights in two American cities, as long as statements were phrased in very abstract terms. When statements were made more specific, however, consensus broke down. Agreement appeared to be especially fragile when communists and Negroes were involved in the specific statements. The authors found that higher education and higher social status were related to greater agreement on the worth of majority rule and minority rights. They concluded that democracy can exist without consensus because many of the undemocratic are apathetic, and because agreement on specific policies sustains unity despite lack of consensus on fundamentals.

McClosky (1964), building on earlier work, found important differences in support of democratic norms between party activists and the general electorate. Party activists were more likely to support majority rule and minority rights and to believe in governmental fairness. But even among activists disagreement was widespread, and there was frequently failure to achieve consensus on specifics. (McClosky defined consensus as 75 per cent agreement.) Consensus was highest among both activists and electorate on abstract statements concerning freedom of speech and of dissent. Consensus was weakest on questions of political, social, and economic equality. McClosky noted the usefulness of apathy when many do not share democratic norms, although he maintained that this condition has its dangers. In particular he stressed that many may mistakenly support undemocratic organizations and practices while thinking that they are defending freedom. In general, he argued, consensus is not necessarily a condition of political stability. When conditions are stable, consensus may be unnecessary. Only in time of social disorganization is consensus important as a stabilizing force. Finally, he argued that the conditions which enhance consensus on democratic norms are becoming more widespread in the United States: education, urbanization, social mobility, proliferation of the mass media, expansion of the middle class, reduced size and isolation of rural groups, declining number of groups living on substandard incomes, and more complete integration of minority groups into social and cultural life.

Consensus and political symbols.   The role of national holidays, ceremonies, and rituals in creating or sustaining consensus has been little explored. It remains questionable that such events facilitate consensus. Arguments concerning the supposed integrative role of the British coronation ceremony have been effectively challenged (Shils & Young 1953; Birnbaum 1955). Contrary hypotheses also exist. It has been observed, for example, that the creed of Americanism and the ceremonies that accompany it have sometimes served as a focal point of conflict (Key 1961, p. 43). A fervent belief in this creed has often been associated with persecution of those groups regarded as foreigners or aliens. At present, one cannot be certain about the function of any particular political ritual without knowing the social circumstances in which it is enacted.

It is fairly clear, however, that myths and symbols can play a role in diminishing conflict in specific policy areas (Edelman 1960). Consumer groups, typically poorly organized, often achieve symbolic victories through the passage of regulatory legislation covering a particular area of the economy. Producer groups, more involved in the details of policy making, can often shape the substance of this regulation in a direction congenial to them. If the public is unaware of this change in the original intentions of the legislation, it assumes that these intentions are being carried out. In such a case, the general public believes policy is made in its favor, while those being regulated are also content with the arrangements, and a rather strange consensus may be said to exist. One must, however, ponder the consequences of such a consensus for the real content of political democracy.

Problems and research needs.   The empirical and speculative work concerning consensus on fundamentals in the United States is open to serious question on several points (Willhoite 1963).

Measuring democracy.   Some researchers seem to have assumed that the United States is in fact a democracy. This assumption has confused the picture of the relationship between consensus and democracy. For example, when Prothro and Grigg discovered that consensus is weakest on questions involving Negroes and communists, they went on to conclude that democracy can exist without consensus. But if, in fact, American democratic practices are least adequate where Negroes and communists are concerned, then lack of consensus appears to be far more significant. In order to relate attitudinal consensus to democratic practices, one needs to measure not only the degree of consensus but also the degree of democracy. This has not yet been done. Therefore one must retain an open mind on the question of the exact connections between these two variables.

Negative consensus.   A different line of attack flows from the analysis of negative consensus. Many authors have pointed out the significance of a consensus on behavior that will *not* be allowed. This matter has been of particular interest to students of international relations who have concentrated on the problem of "encapsulating" conflict (Etzioni 1964). The shared fear of war has been cited as a major factor in keeping conflict under control. Likewise, negative consensus may play a role in domestic politics. For example, the tacit agreement, perhaps conscious, *not* to raise certain sorts of issues is of great importance in facilitating peaceful adjustment of disputes. If this is the case, then negative consensus may take the place in domestic politics once credited to a positive consensus on democratic norms. The gains of the civil rights movement in America have flowed, in part, from a negative consensus among whites on the need to avoid violence. Given such a consensus, certain Negro demands have had to be met (Killian & Grigg 1964). This interpretation runs counter to the assertion that the civil rights movement has been successful because equality is a significant tenet in the American creed. The hypothesis is that negative consensus operates in place of positive belief. These conflicting interpretations are in need of further investigation.

Consensus, cooperation, and stability.   The conviction that consensus, in any sense, is necessary for political life has been vigorously challenged. In many cases social cooperation and political cohesion may not depend upon consensus. Further, conflict as well as consensus can lead to social integration and successful problem solving.

There is no direct relation between consensus and political equilibrium or integration. Consensus can retard political and social adaptation as well as facilitate it. For example, as Van den Berghe has pointed out (1963), consensus on such norms as extreme competition, individualistic laissez-faire, treachery, and witchcraft does not necessarily aid social solidarity. Moreover, consensus *within* groups can hinder consensus *among* groups.

Consensus is not identical with cooperation, and the latter can exist without the former. Many factors besides consensus may contribute to cooperative behavior. Williams (1964, p. 383) has observed that such factors include mutual advantage, power, technical capacities for communication, and social mechanisms for settling conflicts. The precise role of consensus in political stabilization clearly remains a matter of dispute.

Problems of creating consensus.   How is consensus created, and how is it changed? Under what circumstances, for example, do previously outlawed forms of conflict become legitimate or acceptable? Such changes have taken place in the domestic politics of many countries, involving, for example, issues raised by political pamphleteering, strikes, and mass demonstrations. In these cases, more democratic norms have been achieved primarily through serious social conflict. It is clear, therefore, that the identification of democracy with government by consensus can make sense only in that ideal case in which a perfect democracy has already been created.

Under what circumstances will governmental initiative be successful in altering a previously existing consensus? Research into American race relations has demonstrated that attitudes adapt over time to overt behavior, but clearly such adaptation has limits and preconditions. Related to this question is the problem of determining under what circumstances governmental legitimacy itself is undermined, particularly in relation to the government's ability to cope with social change.

On the policy-making level, democracy has often been described as politics involving bargaining among political leaders through which a consensus is created. There has been little systematic study, however, of this consensus-creating process. Finally, a critical problem for students of international behavior is consensus creation concerning the limitation of conflict. Osgood (1962) has described the general principles of a process of tension reduction based on the building of trust through graduated reciprocal initiatives by the

parties to the conflict. Fisher (1964) has advocated the "fractionation" of conflict, that is, the breaking down of complex, emotion-laden disputes into smaller parts which may prove easier to compromise (see also Etzioni 1964). The difficulties faced in achieving a negative consensus on conflict are clear, but these highly suggestive strategies may help to overcome some of them.

LEWIS LIPSITZ

[*See also* DEMOCRACY; MAJORITY RULE; MODERNIZATION; SOCIALIZATION. *Other relevant material may be found in* POLITICAL SOCIOLOGY; PUBLIC OPINION; SOCIAL CONTRACT; *and in the biographies of* BURKE; HOBBES; LOCKE; MILL; PAINE; ROUSSEAU; TOCQUEVILLE.]

BIBLIOGRAPHY

APTER, DAVID E. 1963 Political Religion in the New Nations. Pages 57–104 in Chicago, University of, Committee for the Comparative Study of New Nations, *Old Societies and New States: The Quest for Modernity in Asia and Africa.* Edited by Clifford Geertz. New York: Free Press.

BINDER, LEONARD 1964 National Integration and Political Development. *American Political Science Review* 58:622–631.

BIRNBAUM, NORMAN 1955 Monarchs and Sociologists. *Sociological Review* 3:5–23.

DAHL, ROBERT A. (1961) 1963 *Who Governs? Democracy and Power in an American City.* New Haven: Yale Univ. Press.

EDELMAN, MURRAY 1960 Symbols and Political Quiescence. *American Political Science Review* 54:695–704.

ETZIONI, AMITAI 1962 *The Hard Way to Peace: A New Strategy.* New York: Collier.

ETZIONI, AMITAI 1964 On Self-encapsulating Conflicts. *Journal of Conflict Resolution* 8:242–255.

FISHER, ROGER D. 1964 Fractionating Conflict. Pages 91–109 in Roger D. Fisher (editor), *International Conflict and Behavioral Science: The Craigville Papers.* New York: Basic Books.

GRIFFITH, E. S.; PLAMENATZ, J.; and PENNOCK, J. R. 1956 Cultural Prerequisites to a Successfully Functioning Democracy: A Symposium. *American Political Science Review* 50:101–137.

HOROWITZ, IRVING L. 1962 Consensus, Conflict and Cooperation: A Sociological Inventory. *Social Forces* 41:177–188.

KEY, VALDIMER O. 1961 *Public Opinion and American Democracy.* New York: Knopf.

KILLIAN, LEWIS M.; and GRIGG, CHARLES 1964 *Racial Crisis in America.* Englewood Cliffs, N.J.: Prentice-Hall.

LANE, ROBERT E. 1962 *Political Ideology: Why the American Common Man Believes What He Does.* New York: Free Press.

LAPALOMBARA, JOSEPH 1966a Decline of Ideology: A Dissent and an Interpretation. *American Political Science Review* 60:5–16.

LAPALOMBARA, JOSEPH 1966b A Reply to "Some Further Comments on 'The End of Ideology.'" *American Political Science Review* 60:110–111.

LERNER, DANIEL 1958 *The Passing of Traditional Society: Modernizing the Middle East.* Glencoe, Ill.: Free Press.

LIPSET, SEYMOUR M. (1959) 1962   *Political Sociology.* Pages 81–114 in American Sociological Society, *Sociology Today: Problems and Prospects.* Edited by Robert K. Merton, Leonard Broom, and Leonard S. Cottrell, Jr. New York: Basic Books.

LIPSET, SEYMOUR M. 1960   *Political Man: The Social Bases of Politics.* Garden City, N.Y.: Doubleday.

LIPSET, SEYMOUR M. 1964   The Changing Class Structure and Contemporary European Politics. *Dædalus* 93:277–303.

LIPSET, SEYMOUR M. 1966   Some Further Comments on "The End of Ideology." *American Political Science Review* 60:17–18.

McCLOSKY, HERBERT 1964   Consensus and Ideology in American Politics. *American Political Science Review* 58:361–382.

OSGOOD, CHARLES E. 1962   *An Alternative to War or Surrender.* Urbana: Univ. of Illinois Press.

PARSONS, TALCOTT 1959   Voting and the Equilibrium of the American Political System. Pages 80–120 in Eugene Burdick and Arthur J. Brodbeck (editors), *American Voting Behavior.* Glencoe, Ill.: Free Press.

PROTHRO, JAMES W.; and GRIGG, C. W. 1960   Fundamental Principles of Democracy: Bases of Agreement and Disagreement. *Journal of Politics* 22:276–294.

SHILS, EDWARD; and YOUNG, MICHAEL 1953   The Meaning of the Coronation. *Sociological Review* 1:63–81.

TOCQUEVILLE, ALEXIS DE (1835) 1945   *Democracy in America.* 2 vols. New York: Knopf. → First published in French. A paperback edition was published in 1961 by Vintage and by Schocken. See especially Volume 1.

VAN DEN BERGHE, PIERRE L. 1963   Dialectic and Functionalism: Toward a Theoretical Synthesis. *American Sociological Review* 28:695–705.

WILLHOITE, FRED H. 1963   Political Order and Consensus. *Western Political Quarterly* 16:294–304.

WILLIAMS, ROBIN M. JR. 1964   *Strangers Next Door: Ethnic Relations in American Communities.* Englewood Cliffs, N.J.: Prentice-Hall.

CONSERVATION

I. POLITICAL AND SOCIAL ASPECTS   *Arthur Maass*
II. ECONOMIC ASPECTS   *Anthony Scott*

I
POLITICAL AND SOCIAL ASPECTS

Whatever else it may mean, "conservation" when used in relation to natural resources is a virtuous, a worthy word. Just men do not oppose conservation. As U.S. President William Howard Taft complained in 1910, "The subject of Conservation is rather abstruse, but there are a great many people in favor of Conservation, no matter what it means."

In the United States, where this good word has been used most, it has been called to the support of many policies and programs that on their face do not seem terribly consistent. If there is any regularity among them, it is that the policies and programs have demanded reform, based on certain scientific, democratic, and moral objectives.

When "conservation" came to be used in the United States, at the beginning of the twentieth century, it was associated principally with new federal programs for forestry; for regulating the use of western public lands to protect, in addition to timber, the livestock ranges, outstanding scenic and recreational sites, and wildlife habitats; and for developing water resources for irrigation of western deserts and navigation of eastern rivers.

A half century later, in the 1960s, "conservation" was being used to describe and support government programs relating to cities. The "new conservation," as spokesmen for President John F. Kennedy's New Frontier and President Lyndon B. Johnson's Great Society have called it, is concerned with the quality of the urban environment—with programs to acquire and protect open land in metropolitan areas and to prevent ugliness and the pollution of the environment. Between 1900 and 1960 the nation's population and its social problems and government programs had shifted from being dominantly rural to being dominantly urban; the use of "conservation" to describe problems and programs followed the same course.

Furthermore, "conservation" had been used in the intervening years with reference to pressing needs of the moment. The great depression of the 1930s and the cold war of the 1950s are examples. Most of the conservation programs of the New Deal were undertaken to pull the nation out of a deep depression and to redistribute income to disadvantaged groups. The Central Valley project, Bonneville Dam, and many other resource-development projects were begun with funds appropriated to stimulate the economy by emergency public works. Payments to farmers for soil-building practices were basically supplements to their low incomes. The public lands were improved by unemployed urban youth recruited into the Civilian Conservation Corps.

In the 1950s conservation was linked to plans and programs to insure the adequacy of raw materials to meet the needs of the free world. The report of the President's Materials Policy Commission, which articulated this approach, was concerned with how to "avert or overcome materials shortages which threaten the long-run economic growth and security of the United States and other free nations" (U.S. President's Materials . . . 1952, vol. 1, p. 2). The public policies recommended by the Materials Commission were radically different in kind from those that had been associated with conservation in earlier years, among them policies for influencing the rates of technological development in American industry and for guaranteeing private American investments for the processing of materials in foreign countries.

Notwithstanding the number of policies and programs that have been called conservation, certain types of objectives have recurred sufficiently frequently to give some loose form to the concept. The first of these is scientific method.

Scientific method as an objective

Science and technology have played so dominant a role in conservation policies and programs that the scientific method has been used not only as an analytical technique for solving resource problems but as an objective of public policy as well. The authority of science has been used regularly to justify conservation programs. Supporters of conservation have understood the public decision-making process to be the somewhat automatic one of collecting scientific data and applying scientific principles to them. Thus, for example, a physical *inventory* is made of the forest resource; *scientific principles* of forestry are applied to the data thus collected; and there results a *public policy* of prescribed cutting *practices* on timber lands. The word "planning" has often been used to describe this process.

Alongside the great reliance on science and technology for solving problems, conservation programs have normally included general and specific proposals for the support and promotion of science, technology, and data collection on their own accounts—to add to knowledge.

The conservation movement of the 1900s was above all a scientific movement, and its role in history arises from the implications of science and technology for modern society (Hays 1959, p. 2). The leaders of the movement came from such fields as forestry, hydrology, geology, anthropology, and civil engineering—several of which had come to be recognized as professions, with societies and standards, only in the last part of the nineteenth century. A central theme of the movement was support for scientific data collection by such agencies as the then recently established U.S. Geological Survey and for scientific research by the new Forest Experiment Stations and the Agricultural Experiment Stations.

The conservation programs of the New Deal were also scientifically oriented. The high-level National Resources Planning Board served several purposes during its ten-year lifetime, which began in 1933; but the one for which it was created initially, and which remained a central purpose, was to guarantee that public projects undertaken with emergency and other public-works funds were planned by technicians in accordance with scientific principles.

In the report of the Materials Commission, which dominated thought on conservation in the 1950s, more pages are devoted to technology and its promise than to any other subject. Although the commission found that "the Government, up from almost nothing since the beginning of the century, is now the great force behind scientific and technical research in this country," it concluded that the effort was not sufficient and recommended more funds for basic research on materials and more government planning and coordination of materials technology (U.S. President's Materials . . . 1952, vol. 1, pp. 144–145).

The "new conservation" of the 1960s, with its focus on beauty and quality of the environment, continues to emphasize science and technology. However, the classes of expert skills called upon to develop the technical principles to be applied are broader. Thus, the conservationist today may be a lawyer working on scenic easements, a land planner, or an architect.

Scientific elitism.   The central role of science in conservation programs has meant a central role in decision making for experts and, concomitantly, a reduced role for lay judgment. And since the conservation scientists have been largely in government service, there has developed a scientific elitism that emphasizes government regulation, by the experts, of private interests; and executive, or expert, power at the expense of legislative, or lay, power.

As for the distribution of power within government, scientific elitism has led to the belief that the experts of the executive branch are better equipped than the laymen of the Congress to make decisions relating to conservation, because these are considered to be basically technical in nature. Foresters should determine the allowable annual timber cut; engineers should study the feasibility of river-development projects; agronomists should determine which ranges to keep open for grazing; soil scientists, which lands to retire from agriculture; planning technicians should select the public-works projects to be built. Furthermore, conflicts among competing resource users should be dealt with by experts and not by the political processes that involve the legislature. Land-management experts should resolve land-use differences between forestry, livestock, wildlife, irrigation, and settler groups. Water-resource experts should adjust power, navigation, flood-control, recreation, and upstream–downstream interests to promote the best multipurpose development of river basins.

Legislators, being poorly prepared in matters technical, fall easy prey to special interests that have no concern for scientific truth. Members of Congress, therefore, when they have tried to reconcile conflicting groups, have worked a positively bad influence on conservation programs.

As a consequence of this scientific elitism, proponents of conservation programs have held, first, that the legislature should grant the executive the very broadest discretion to deal with problems, and, second, that executive officers have an inherent discretionary power and responsibility to do everything for the public good—as they interpret it—that is not prohibited by law. Thus, executives who are technically competent should be encouraged to do everything that the law will let them do, not merely what the law directs them to do. This latter doctrine, as far-reaching a statement of the public servant's discretion as is to be found in the literature of American government, was set forth by Pinchot and practiced by him and his professional colleagues in the U.S. Forest Service (Pinchot 1947, chapter 12). A similar doctrine was expounded by Pinchot's superior, Theodore Roosevelt, and came to be known as the "stewardship theory" of presidential power. Roosevelt said: "I declined to adopt the view that what was imperatively necessary for the Nation could not be done by the President unless he could find some specific authorization to do it. My belief was that it was not only his right but his duty to do anything that the needs of the Nation demanded unless such was forbidden by the Constitution or by the laws" (Roosevelt [1913] 1946, p. 357). Of course, it was one thing, and at that, quite controversial, for Roosevelt to claim such broad authority for the president, deriving it from the inherent constitutional powers of that office; it was quite another for Pinchot to claim it for forestry and other conservation technicians.

The claims for broad bureaucratic discretion in conservation programs were more regular and explicit early in the century than they have been since. Nonetheless, this feature of scientific elitism has continued to apply to programs called conservation. Thus, in the 1960s a major controversy developed over the Wilderness Bill, the executive departments holding that their technicians should be authorized to designate, subject to presidential approval, which public lands should be set aside for wilderness, excluding thereby all other resource users; laymen legislators holding that such designations should be authorized by the Congress, with full opportunity for legislative hearings.

Finally, scientific elitism has helped to pin a bad reputation on the nation's legislature—that of proponent of special interests and opponent of scientific method.

Physical versus economic objectives. The emphasis on natural science in conservation programs has led to analyses of problems and statements of goals in physical rather than economic terms. The barrels of oil in the ground and the number of barrels pumped out each year; the timber inventory and the board feet of lumber cut each year; the inches of topsoil on the land and the tons of it that annually wash down the Mississippi River —these have been considered the relevant data. They have led to simple conclusions: We are in danger of running out of oil; the topsoil will be entirely gone in another x years—unless vigorous government conservation programs are activated. The responsive government programs have included most physical solutions—contour plowing and the construction of dams are examples—to satisfy goals that, also, have been put in physical measures. "To each acre according to its needs and capabilities," was the motto of the soil-conservation program; and proponents of the federal reclamation program in California have sought, as their goal, to ensure that not a drop of fresh water is wasted from the rivers to the sea.

The close association of conservation in the 1930s with efforts to redistribute national income to disadvantaged groups raised obstacles for those who analyzed resource problems in physical terms. Nonetheless, the limitations of a heavy reliance on physical data for identifying and solving conservation problems were not exposed systematically until the 1950s, in the report of the Materials Commission. According to this report, the traditional view of conservation had perpetuated two fallacies. First, it regarded the resource base as a fixed inventory that, when used up, would leave society with no means of survival. Second, it equated physical waste and economic waste—it encouraged the feeling that it is wasteful to use materials in ways that make them disappear. This attitude, said the commission, can lead to devoting a dollar's worth of work to "save" a few cents' worth of paper and old string. In its own analysis, the commission estimated the resource requirements of the United States and the rest of the free world and devoted special attention to those resources that would not be forthcoming in sufficient quantity to meet future needs except at significantly higher relative prices. In other words, the commission attempted to foresee potential price rises and to plan in advance to forestall them or adjust to them by various types of measures.

Recently scholars have developed new techniques for combining the physical and economic analyses of complex resource systems (McKean 1958; Maass et al. 1962). The production function for a resource, representing relations between physical factors, and its benefit function, representing relations between economic factors, are believed to be so closely interrelated that they should be developed and analyzed synchronously. The methods of operations research and systems analysis make this possible [see OPERATIONS RESEARCH; PLANNING, SOCIAL, *article on* RESOURCE PLANNING].

Scientific research and action programs. Principles derived from the natural sciences have been developed for the conservation of each resource— forests, ranges, soil, wildlife—and one principle, that of ecological balance, or nature's balance, for the several resources in combination. This latter principle states that under natural conditions the resources of a region tend to be in balance and to remain relatively stable over long periods of time. Thus, under natural conditions the soil, cover, and moisture supply of a watershed are believed to be in balance, in the sense that plant growth is adjusted to the amount and distribution of rainfall, and stream channels to the runoff they must carry. Even under natural conditions this balance is not static. It is influenced by long-term natural processes, such as climatic forces, and by natural catastrophes. The principle of ecological balance holds that the long-term processes are virtually imperceptible to man and that the natural catastrophes are infrequent, their effects usually confined to small areas that heal rapidly.

Man, however, interferes with nature's balance in a destructive way, according to the ecological theory that has been popular with supporters of conservation programs (Frank & Netboy 1950). He tends to set in motion forces that seriously and sometimes permanently disrupt the ecological balance. For example, his livestock may overgraze a watershed. The plants lose their vigor—that is, their ability to produce new leaves and roots and to deposit litter that covers and nourishes the soil. The carpet of litter not only wears thin but is destroyed by exposure to the elements and to animal hoofs. In time the soil loses its virility, including its capacity to absorb water and to resist forces of destructive erosion. Concomitantly, the flow and quality of water deteriorate.

The public-policy consequences of the principle of ecological balance are clear: control man's activities so that he cannot permanently or seriously disrupt nature's balance. A great many conservation programs have been based on this scientific principle. Furthermore, the principle provides its own criterion for evaluating the condition of the resources of a region: measure it against what were believed to be the natural conditions prior to man's settlement.

In response to this theory, certain scientists, frequently men who have not been associated with conservation programs, have argued that man is only the most recent and most complex of nature's creatures; that he and his activities are a part of, not apart from, nature's balance (Tansley 1939; Firey 1960). Conservation ecologists have replied that man is unique; that he is endowed with capacities not found in other animals or found there only in concentrations so weak as to make a qualitative difference. These capacities are, of course, consciousness, intellect, and conscience.

Quite separate from this continuing and, in part, philosophical debate, recent scientific studies have challenged the principle of natural ecological balance and, therefore, the scientific bases of many public programs. Raup (1964) and his colleagues at the Harvard Forest have demonstrated that natural catastrophes have such persistent and serious effects on natural environment that stable natural equilibriums may be infrequent. On certain slopes of the forest over 50 per cent of the trees are growing on blowdown stumps that were razed by numerous hurricanes. Malin (1956) has described the influences that kept the Great Plains grasslands in a disturbed state for countless years before the coming of the fur traders and settlers. His studies make an impressive case against the theory of nature's balance and the doctrine that man, primarily, destroyed this. Scientists like these have modified their search for ecological balance, with its resulting emphasis on "Do Not Disturb"— on protection. They have instead focused their studies on adaptation, with its resulting emphasis on a dynamic and flexible system of controls and de-emphasis of the destructive character of human occupance. Yet the traditional association of many conservation programs with ecological balance is so strong that supporters of these programs tend to disregard or disagree with any contrary or even partially nonsupporting scientific theories.

Conservation programs have been devised and then supported on the "authoritative base of science," but when this scientific base or any part of it is challenged by new findings, supporters of the program, both in and out of government, are ambivalent. Their dedication to science leads them to promote the type of research that can turn up new and contrary results. But the fact that their public, and most often their legislative, support is based on a previously proclaimed scientific authority makes them hesitant to give currency to these new findings.

Another illustration of this is the U.S. Forest Service and fire (Schiff 1962). When the service began its program for ridding the nation's forests of what was then considered to be their greatest scourge, the doctrine that trees and fires don't mix was generally believed to be a scientific truth. Public and legislative support for the now familiar Smoky Bear program was built largely on this truth. In the mid-1920s, however, Professor H. H. Chapman, the noted Yale forester, confirmed a new truth, which had been suggested previously by other forest scientists; namely, that fire is essential for the reproduction of longleaf and loblolly pine in the southeastern United States. Without fire to burn off the brush growth and ground litter, pine seedlings are unable to survive. If the Forest Service had been fully successful in its fire-protection program in the southeast, it would have eliminated these valuable species.

For over six years the Forest Service refused to investigate or check the new findings, though Chapman insisted they should. When Forest Service scientists did conduct investigations at their Southern Experiment Station, these confirmed the case for burning; but the service then refused to release the results.

Finally, in 1939, after the incessant insistence of Chapman, the service published their scientific findings; but not until after World War II did they make any effort to inform the public that controlled burning was in some situations desirable and in others essential. Throughout this period of about twenty years, the Forest Service supported publicly the original scientific doctrine that forests and fire should never mix. The leaders of the agency feared that to modify or contradict this in any way might lead the public to be less vigilant and cause the federal and state legislatures to be less sympathetic to providing the means for preventing forest fires throughout the nation.

The Forest Service and other conservation agencies are not the only government organizations that have encountered problems in accommodating both scientific research and action programs. The general problem, a fascinating one in bureaucracy and organization, is beyond the scope of this article. At the same time, because of their very heavy reliance on scientific method as an objective, conservation agencies have suffered the problem in an aggravated form.

American conservation programs, with the possible exception of those based on the analysis of the 1952 Materials Commission, have been reform programs. Like other American reform programs of the twentieth century, but much more so, conservation programs have relied on the authority of science. Faith in science has had a high standing among the beliefs and commitments of the American people. Science has come to stand for material well-being, soundness, objectivity, and truth. A society with a proper respect for science and technology can enjoy the liberties of a free people. Much the same can be said of democracy, as an objective of American reform programs in general and of conservation programs in particular.

Democracy as an objective

For the American people, democracy has been not only their form of government but a faith, an ideal, an objective, "our form of patriotism" (Waldo 1948, pp. 12–13). Every individual is important; every man should be master of his own destiny; all men are endowed with rights that should not be violated; the privacy of individuals should be free from unwarranted intrusion—these are the first tenets of the American democratic faith, and they have been associated directly with conservation programs. "Rugged individualism" is a phrase common to conservation literature from the beginning of the century until today, and a highly evocative phrase this has been—whether it calls to mind Theodore Roosevelt on horseback or today's heavily knapsacked citizen on foot, solitary in his enjoyment of nature's wilderness. Conservation begins with the American people, who have been nurtured on "a fierce sense of individualism," and it "rests in the people's hands," according to the school text published by the American Association of School Administrators and written by its Commission on Conservation (1964).

Conservation programs, again apart from those inspired by the Materials Commission, have typically defended this rugged individual, "the little man," against monopolies and concentrated wealth, special interest and special privilege. Big business and financial power have been identified with the wasters of resources and the destroyers of beauty.

The conservation movement of the early twentieth century was in part a reaction against the influence of private corporations, which had been growing rapidly since the Civil War. Unless the corporations were controlled, said the supporters of conservation-reform programs, the basic resources of the nation would come to be concentrated in the hands of a few, and these few would use up the nation's wealth wastefully and profligately, for quick private profit, with no concern for the long-range benefit of the people. Furthermore, the organization of industry into combinations threatened the independent, self-made man with a faceless, ugly, and largely urban materialism. In recent years, as conservation has been used more and more in relation to urban problems, the real estate interests, the large industrial polluters of the environment, the billboard lobby, and others have been added to the oil trust, the lumber lobby, the power interests, and the cattle barons as enemies of the common man—selfish despoilers of his heritage.

There runs through all conservation literature the notion of a common, or public, good that differs from the self-interest, the "selfishness," of private operators, especially those with great financial power. To define and enforce this common good, governmental action and public education are needed. Thus, alongside the basic belief in rugged individualism, there has developed a strong commitment to positive government as a means of effecting the common good. In fact, this pro-government attitude has been a principal characteristic of conservation programs, joining the emphasis on science. At the turn of the century, such an attitude represented a drastic departure from then dominant values with respect to the role of government in society (Wengert 1962), and ever since, demands for governmental action to support conservation have been more far-reaching than those for action to support most other domestic policies.

Commitments to rugged individualism on the one hand and to positive government on the other are presumably harmonized in a commitment to democratic institutions, and the literature on conservation programs is sprinkled with references to faith in democracy and to consent of the governed. But when the investigator looks carefully, he finds that supporters of conservation programs have in fact had little confidence in democratic institutions. They have considered popularly elected assemblies to be agents of special interests; they have opposed advisory committees in connection with administration of the national forests. Their confidence has rested with the technicians of the executive, who are qualified both to define the common good in relation to the subject at hand and to enforce government action to realize it. The common good, thus, is equated with scientific elitism.

At the same time, conservation men have sought direct popular support for their government programs through public education and public information. As a result of the sustained effort of government conservation agencies and their allies outside government, conservation is a subject taught today in thousands of public schools all over the country. The curriculum emphasizes the scientific principles of conservation; in the classroom and in the woods children are taught ecology, soil classification, game management, etc.

The government conservation agencies have also depended heavily on adult education to gain support for, and cooperation with, their programs to reduce forest fires, to promote soil-erosion control and other agricultural practices, to preserve scenic areas, etc.

If the supporters of conservation programs, while claiming democracy as an objective, have shown little confidence in democratic institutions, they have, through their outstanding efforts in public education, shown confidence in the common man. But one could argue that this has been more to gain public support for programs based on the scientists' definitions of the common good than to encourage popular participation in defining this goal.

The commitment to positive government has led, as might be expected, to the organization of a large number of special-interest groups and to an intense form of interest-group activity in conservation programs (Wengert 1955). Since the conservation technicians are concerned to see that the general interest, rather than special interests, prevails and since the general interest, for them, is the result of the application of scientific principles, they are ever on guard against the influence of these groups. This is in part why they have opposed advisory committees that represent one or more classes of users of the public lands, and why they have been suspicious of popularly elected assemblies, which are susceptible to the influence of special interests.

Big and little operators.   From the beginning, but especially since World War II, the "little-man" component of the democratic objective of conservation programs has meant contradictions in these programs; for the big operators, even or especially the very big ones, frequently practice better "conservation" than the little ones.

Take forestry, for example. In a massive inventory report entitled *Timber Resources for America's Future* (U.S. Forest Service 1958), the Forest Service reported that "the forest condition is best" on public forest lands and on those owned by forest industries such as Weyerhaeuser. "There is little distinction," said the service, "between the productivity of recently cut lands in public ownership as contrasted to those owned by forest industry." The real contrast in quality of forest practices is between the public and forest-industry ownerships on the one hand and the small private holding on the other: "There is conclusive evidence that the condition of recently cut lands is poorest on the farm and 'other' [meaning 'small'] private ownerships" (*ibid.*, p. 106).

Reduction in numbers of livestock on public ranges that are overgrazed is another example. Government range supervisors assert that it is easier to effect this conservation measure if the range is used by a few permittees, each with a large number of livestock, than by a large number of permittees, each grazing relatively few head. This is because the large operators, with their commensurately large private holdings, can absorb a cut of 10 or 20 per cent in public range use; whereas a similar cut for small permittees might force them into economic ruin. Thus, the small man presents the conservation problem.

Morality as an objective

In addition to commitments to science and government, conservation programs have had a strong moral commitment or objective. Historians (Hofstadter 1955) have shown that reform programs in America—prohibition, civic improvement, or conservation—have often been a product of the "Protestant mind." Reformers have both found their arguments in and made their appeals to the traditional biases of American Protestants: individualism; a tendency to see every issue as a moral issue; an emphasis on man's and society's guilt for abusing God's gifts and on the need for missionary work to repair this. Conservation reformers, in particular, have inherited the moral traditions of rural evangelical Protestantism, even though today they use them in connection with urban problems. The present condition of our natural resources, as revealed by scientific inventories, "constitutes the gravest indictment that has ever been returned against a civilized people," said a conservation magazine in 1909; and pronouncements concerning today's conservation problems frequently are similar in tone and appeal.

What precisely have been man's and society's sins? Of what are we guilty? First, of interfering with nature's balance. The scientific principle of ecology is supported by and gives support to religious beliefs. All things owe their gift of life to God, and nature's balance is God-given. At the same time, man is outside nature's balance because of his unique endowments, endowments that give him the power to transgress the balance (i.e., in-

tellect) and that make his transgressions sinful (i.e., conscience). These transgressions should be controlled, for man is in the relationship of steward to the resources that surround him. Man "has been made responsible for something that belongs to God. The good steward acknowledges this responsibility as a trust. . . . The orderly conservation and development of natural resources is man's recognition of his responsibility under God to protect and use wisely His precious gifts" (National Association of Soil Conservation Districts 1962, inside front and back covers).

One sin is, then, to destroy nature's balance. A second one is to waste, and a third is to use our natural resources for private benefit rather than for common good. The importance of the sin of wastefulness in the American ethos is well known. It has led us, as the Materials Commission said, to saving old string. "In the orderly world of our Creator," warns a recent conservation pamphlet, "there are penalties for extravagance."

"Our resources are God-given heritages that belong no more to the present generation than to generations that are to come." This is a common concern in conservation literature, and it is usually accompanied by the idea that single-minded pursuit of present profit in the development of resources may not protect the interests of unborn children. Supporters of conservation programs, in other words, have had little confidence that the discount rate of the private competitive market will account for legitimate long-run interests. Since those who develop resources for private benefit can thus fly in the face of the common good, they can act immorally.

This third sin is especially likely to occur where monopolies, trusts, and conspiracies in restraint of trade are present in industrial organization. The supporters of conservation almost invariably find that such private combinations are operating against their programs, so they are typically engaged in battle against immoral conspiracies. Since Americans have a propensity to believe in conspiratorial theories of history, a propensity derived in part from their Protestant ethic (Hofstadter 1955), the battles of conservation have been popular engagements.

The political and social consequences of the moral objective of conservation programs generally have reinforced the consequences of the scientific and democratic objectives. The cases for positive government and for executive power have been enhanced; both are needed to combat evil, as well as to promote science and democracy. Reinforced with a sense of moral righteousness, the supporters of conservation programs have considered those who disagree with them to be not merely misinformed or wrongheaded but wicked and possibly vicious. The conservation men are ever fighting for their programs in a milieu of recurrent crises. See the remarkably readable works of Pinchot (1947) and Ickes (1934) and the exquisitely written and influential commentaries of DeVoto (1955) for examples.

As in the cases of science and democracy, recent findings have questioned some of the bases for the moral content of conservation programs. But the moral component is so ingrained that the findings have frequently been challenged or ignored. Thus, Malin's and Raup's researches have questioned the evilness of man's encroachments on nature's balance. The Materials Commission has redefined waste in a way that makes the concept more difficult to relate to sin. And the good conservation practices of large industrial resource users, as compared with the poor performance of small operators, tend to blunt the charges of immorality made against corporations and combines.

Conclusion on American conservation

This article has sought to explain the social and political aspects of conservation programs, not to evaluate them. Because of the difficulties of explaining frequent contradictions in these programs, however, the reader may have gained an erroneous impression that the writer's purpose was to evaluate and even to condemn. The contradictions are present because conservation has been used in relation to so many different programs and because the unifying theme, insofar as there is one, is simply that these have been programs for reform, based on certain attitudes toward science, democracy, and morality.

Without trying to evaluate the substantive achievements of individual conservation programs —for example, forests protected from fire, topsoil protected from wind and water erosion, income redistributed to tenant farmers, highways protected from billboards—we can point to some meritorious consequences of scientific elitism and the acceptance of positive government. These factors undermined the Spencerian view, prevalent at the turn of the century, that government could not perform effectively. Insofar as conservation agencies were involved, the executive branch of the government was radically reformed, and these agencies—the Forest Service and the Geological Survey are examples—continued, for almost half a century, to be models of what a professionally competent and efficient bureaucracy should be. They developed

professional standards and loyalty to professional ideals; they introduced personnel programs emphasizing the selection of officials through competitive examinations, professional training, and career planning; they enjoyed stability of leadership; they established close relations for research and recruitment with the nation's leading universities; they pioneered new methods of program planning. Scientific elitism and the acceptance of positive government put a new and handsome face on the executive; but not so meritoriously, they have helped to blacken the eyes of the legislature and have contributed little to reforming it.

Finally, for general evaluation, the highly charged moral battle against evil that has characterized conservation programs has probably been good catharsis for the American people. A balanced opinion on this requires a general view of American social, economic, and political history that is beyond the scope of this article.

Now that conservation has come to be associated with urban as well as rural problems, it will be interesting to observe whether this unique combination of science, democracy, and morality, with its resulting emphasis on positive government and on scientific elitism, will accomplish similar results for the government's urban functions.

Conservation outside the United States

Research to date has not shown that similar objectives have been combined to produce similar reform programs outside the United States. To be sure, all nations have some government programs like the conservation programs of the United States. In many cases these foreign programs were adopted long before their American counterparts. The scientific principle of sustained-yield forestry was brought to the United States from Germany, and the idea of protecting and conserving forests for national self-sufficiency and national survival was practiced in Napoleonic France. In other cases United States programs, e.g., those of the Tennessee Valley Authority (TVA), have been models for foreign activity. In fact, TVA, meaning multipurpose water development, is now a universal concept.

In some countries these programs have not been called conservation at all, and in others, where the word is used, it has been in a different context. Thus, for example, the forestry activities of the French in north Africa were not called conservation, whereas similar British activities in India were described as "forest conservancy." The Indian government, however, in its five-year development plans, no longer uses "conservation" with reference to timber programs, reserving the word for nature, wildlife, and soils; and the British at home have always used the word as do the Indians today. In any case, outside the United States conservation has not meant programs of reform involving a combination of scientific elitism, a positive attitude toward government, and a religious commitment. Neither western European nor developing nations have needed a reform rationale to justify the power of government to act in forestry and related natural-resource areas.

The United Nations and its specialized agencies pursue many programs for resources and related activities that superficially are similar to United States conservation programs; yet the United Nations activities are not typically called conservation, nor do they, in fact, combine the several elements that have given character to the United States programs. The student who seeks references to the international programs in the indexes of United Nations publications should look under such entries as "economic development," "technical assistance," "land reform," "natural resources," "arid zones"; for he will find few or no references under the heading "conservation."

In 1949 the United Nations did sponsor the Scientific Conference on the Conservation and Utilization of Resources, but its subsequent conferences on the same and similar subjects have been given titles that emphasize, instead of conservation, the application of science and technology to various resources for the purpose of economic development. Julian Huxley's UNESCO report on the conservation of wildlife in central and east Africa (1961)—with its insistence that "the world is ecologically out of joint," that man has destroyed nature's balance for shortsighted economic advantage, that African and world opinion must be aroused through popular education to protect Africa's wildlife and its habitats from exploitation by Africans—approaches the United States model that we have elaborated, but this report is atypical in the vast documentation of the United Nations.

ARTHUR MAASS

[*See also* PLANNING, SOCIAL, *article on* RESOURCE PLANNING. *Other relevant material may be found in* ECOLOGY; LANDSCAPE; SCIENCE, *article on* SCIENCE-GOVERNMENT RELATIONS.]

BIBLIOGRAPHY

AMERICAN ASSOCIATION OF SCHOOL ADMINISTRATORS 1964 *Conservation: In the People's Hands.* Washington: The Association.

DEVOTO, BERNARD A. 1955 *The Easy Chair.* Boston: Houghton Mifflin.

FIREY, WALTER I. 1960 *Man, Mind and Land: A Theory of Resource Use.* Glencoe, Ill.: Free Press.

FRANK, BERNARD; and NETBOY, ANTHONY 1950 *Water, Land and People.* New York: Knopf.

HAYS, SAMUEL P. 1959 *Conservation and the Gospel of Efficiency.* Cambridge, Mass.: Harvard Univ. Press.

HOFSTADTER, RICHARD 1955 *The Age of Reform: From Bryan to F.D.R.* New York: Knopf. → A paperback edition was published in 1961 by Vintage.

HUXLEY, JULIAN S. 1961 *The Conservation of Wild Life and Natural Habitats in Central and East Africa: Report on a Mission Accomplished for UNESCO, July–September, 1960.* Paris: UNESCO.

ICKES, HAROLD L. 1934 *The New Democracy.* New York: Norton.

MAASS, ARTHUR et al. 1962 *Design of Water-resource Systems: New Techniques for Relating Economic Objectives, Engineering Analysis, and Governmental Planning.* Cambridge, Mass.: Harvard Univ. Press.

MCKEAN, ROLAND N. 1958 *Efficiency in Government Through Systems Analysis, With Emphasis on Water Resources Development.* New York: Wiley.

MALIN, JAMES C. 1956 *The Grassland of North America: Prolegomena to Its History, With Addenda.* Lawrence, Kan.: Malin.

NATIONAL ASSOCIATION OF SOIL CONSERVATION DISTRICTS 1962 *The Stream of Life.* League City, Tex.: The Association.

PINCHOT, GIFFORD 1947 *Breaking New Ground.* New York: Harcourt.

RAUP, HUGH M. 1964 Some Problems in Ecological Theory and Their Relation to Conservation. *Journal of Ecology* 52 (Supplement):19–28.

ROOSEVELT, THEODORE (1913) 1946 *An Autobiography.* New York: Scribner.

SCHIFF, ASHLEY L. 1962 *Fire and Water: Scientific Heresy and the Forest Service.* Cambridge, Mass.: Harvard Univ. Press.

TANSLEY, ARTHUR G. 1939 *The British Islands and Their Vegetation.* Cambridge Univ. Press.

U.S. FOREST SERVICE 1958 *Timber Resources for America's Future.* Washington: Government Printing Office.

U.S. PRESIDENT'S MATERIALS POLICY COMMISSION 1952 *Resources for Freedom.* 5 vols. Washington: Government Printing Office.

WALDO, DWIGHT 1948 *The Administrative State: A Study of the Political Theory of American Public Administration.* New York: Ronald Press.

WENGERT, NORMAN I. 1955 *Natural Resources and the Political Struggle.* Garden City, N.Y.: Doubleday.

WENGERT, NORMAN I. 1962 The Ideological Basis of Conservation and Natural-resources Policies and Programs. American Academy of Political and Social Science, *Annals* 344:65–75.

II

ECONOMIC ASPECTS

The economist concerns himself with the allocation of scarce inputs among different uses and over time. The conservationist's mission is narrower: ignoring the scarcity of labor and capital, he sets standards for the use of land or natural resources. Originally the conservation movement considered chiefly the allocation of natural products over time; later, their allocation among competing uses (the "multiple-use" approach); most recently, in the adaptation of benefit–cost analysis, the allocation of capital to the development or preservation of nature.

Thus, the gulf between conservation and economics has narrowed. But there is still a special conservationist approach: nature must be protected from man's ruthlessness, wastefulness, and ignorance, both because mankind jeopardizes its own present and future gain from the natural endowment and environment and because the preservation of nature is a good thing in itself. The liberally trained economist, distrustful of such absolute value judgments, has also been disturbed by the imprecise and demagogic use of such phrases as "natural heritage," "waste," "wise use," "debt to the future," and "greatest good of the greatest number for the longest period of time." Consequently, after a brief examination of the writings of the nineteenth-century economists on similar topics, this article will attempt to distinguish and interpret the economic problems embedded in the writings of the conservationists.

At least three important classical economists anticipated the conservation movement's writings about the uses of natural resources, although only Malthus is acknowledged by the conservationists to have done so, and then only in connection with population growth. But Malthus is actually the least significant of the three in the economic analysis of the conservation question.

Malthus (1798), in his basic model, for example, envisaged ever-increasing food production (at an "arithmetic" rate), a possibility denied by the pessimistic conservationists. Furthermore, Malthus' commentators asserted that he had understated the ability of improved technology to obtain adequate produce from the earth. Both he and his critics, therefore, ignored the possibility of depletion. [*See* MALTHUS.]

Ricardo (1817), on the other hand, taught that man must extend production to ever less fertile lands until society's growth would be stopped in an equilibrium of human and natural fertility characterized by low standards of living and high land values. Furthermore, in some inconclusive passages on minerals, Ricardo showed himself aware of the possibility of complete depletion. Indeed, Goundrey (1960), has argued that the conservationist literature approximates a layman's discussion of the Ricardian stationary state. [*See* RICARDO.]

For fifty years following Malthus and Ricardo, economists accepted this view of the relation of man to his resources [*see* RENT]. Although this analysis was couched in the sweeping dynamics of the early classicists, it actually did not deal with rates of growth or depletion, a neglect remedied by Jevons in *The Coal Question* (1865). This vigorous work, a model of research, forecast the Ricardian decline of both British mining and the industrial might dependent upon it. Jevons then posed the question, Should exhaustion be delayed by conserving coal for the future? His answer was not explicit, but his approach was clear:

The alternatives before us are simple. . . . If we lavishly and boldly push forward in the creation of our riches, both material and intellectual, it is hard to over-estimate the pitch of beneficial influence to which we may attain in the present. *But the maintenance of such a position is physically impossible. We have to make the momentous choice between brief but true greatness and longer continued mediocrity.* ([1865] 1906, pp. 459–460; italics in the original)

Jevons had already considered substitutes for coal but concluded that their possible appearance would not contribute to Britain's "superiority." In the above quotation he summarized two important principles: first, that natural resources can be transformed into man-made riches, including intellectual capital, that might be of greater future value to all mankind than a stock of coal; second, that the *rate* of growth itself and the "fabric of varied interests" connected with change should be encouraged, rather than a high or a sustained *level* of output. This fine study is still a source of inspiration to economists pondering the terms of trade between present and future production.

Like Malthus and Ricardo, Jevons alarmed his contemporaries, his ideas leading, for example, to statistical examinations of Britain's wealth and to political debates on her liabilities—the public debt. [*See* JEVONS.]

Conservation goals. But economists had little impact on the conservation movement, which instead developed certain unique social principles [*see* CONSERVATION, *article on* POLITICAL AND SOCIAL ASPECTS]. These principles were applied in the advocacy of a set of policies about resource use that could be traced back through European economic history to suggest that conservation had long been inherent in enlightened official action. Four distinct policies, in fact, were frequently cited as anticipations of what was to become the conservation movement.

Preservation of wildlife and forests. The first of the four policies was the preservation of wildlife and forests. Feudal Europe had set aside "forests," or hunting preserves, for the monarch and had guarded them against farming and urban encroachment by stern laws, savagely enforced. The result was that by the nineteenth century many of these large areas were still wooded and comparatively undeveloped, some being used for timber, others as parks and game preserves. Although the undemocratic reasons for creating these reservations and the bloodthirsty enforcement of encroachment laws were sometimes glossed over, the fact that these areas existed, had survived commercial opportunities, were often highly valued by the public, and were well managed by the state was frequently cited by conservationists. These reserves were undoubtedly an important model for the national and state parks and forests set up in the United States and in some of the British countries. Also an important forerunner of the nature sanctuaries that public and private agencies have recently promoted, they can be said, in retrospect, to have inspired what has probably been the most successful aspect of conservation policy: the setting aside of natural areas as a source both of productive resources, chiefly timber and fish, and consumption resources for the leisure and recreation of an increasingly urban and educated public.

Access to natural resources.   The second policy goal was the achievement of a widespread ownership of and access to natural resources. Conservationists pointed out that in feudal times the supposedly absolute rights of the monarch over resources were actually limited by his duties to his tenants and by the fact that he was forced to delegate land management to those who were using the land. This system, it was argued, had eventually degenerated and succumbed to the age of liberalism, when land was enclosed by capitalists and accumulated into large holdings; the countryside was heavily depopulated; and resource wealth was "seized," "grabbed," and "wasted." The conservationist reaction to this trend was widespread.

In Scandinavia, for example, especially in Sweden, the liberal policy of alienating royal land to timber and iron companies was suddenly reversed; the remaining area was set up as government forest, managed by public enterprise. In other parts of Europe too, as the great American conservationist Pinchot noted during his period of training in France, the government had resolved to hold forests "for the people." In many newly settled countries, large landholdings were disfavored, and it became official policy to encourage homesteads instead of ranches and plantations. Similarly, the American alienation of mineral and water rights was organized so as to maximize the access of small operators to these resources. Thus, both in the United States and elsewhere, the conservationist had goals in common with latter-day physiocrats, single taxers, socialists, muckrakers, and trust busters: the prevention of resource accumulation by a small number of "land capitalists," and the widespread distribution of land ownership or of rental income.

Prevention of depletion.   The second goal, of course, was frequently in conflict with a third policy: the prevention of rapid depletion and eventual disappearance of resources. This third policy has been called "conservation proper": a program of state action or intervention to change modes or rates of use of natural resources. Both casual observation and economic analysis strongly suggested that "waste," erosion, and overrapid mining and logging were most common where holdings were small or where users had an incomplete title to the land. "Democratization," as it is called in the preceding article, was frequently antipathetic to long-term conservation.

For conservationists, however, the pressing task was not the reconciliation of their objectives but the demonstration of the imminence of resource depletion. This was no small task. At first they had no evidence to offer except the logical proposition that because production was continuing and increasing, reserves must be declining—a proposition that was applied indiscriminately to reserves of timber, coal, oil, helium, whales, groundfish, salmon, and gold. When scientific inventories and geologic surveys eventually became available, near the end of the nineteenth century, they did seem to indicate increasing scarcity, although they also imposed a certain discipline on conservation orators. Among the facts stressed was a decline in the number of large trees in the annual cut and a decrease in the size of fish being caught. It was shown, too, that petroleum reserves amounted to less than twenty years' production and that the delta of the Mississippi was apparently building up, through upstream soil erosion, at an alarming rate.

In the present century, however, the revision and perfection of these inventories has weakened the impetus of the conservation movement. In the first place, improved knowledge of animal and forest science has shown that population dynamics and ecology, rather than static inventories, are required for an understanding of future yields from the so-called renewable resources, so that attention has become focused on the many problems of management, rather than on the unique goal of hoarding. In the second place, it was realized that inventories have an economic dimension: the estimate of "ore" and "commercial" timber reserves available depends upon prices and costs, as modified by ever-changing technologies. Thus, not only did increasing resource scarcity become difficult to demonstrate, but also the essential unity that a feared generalized depletion of all resources had imposed on the movement was lost. From the technical point of view, the United Nations Scientific Conference on the Conservation and Utilization of Resources (UNSCCUR) meeting in 1949 showed the impossibility of taking a global view of natural resource inventories, so complex were the uncertainties and the interconnections between resource industries (United Nations . . . 1953). And from the policy point of view, the United States President's Materials Policy Commission report (1952), subsequent European energy studies (Organization for European Economic Cooperation 1960), and the mammoth investigations by the staff of the Resources for the Future foundation (1963) utilized an economic approach to the problem of possible scarcities that left little room for the conservation faith.

Management of common-property resources. The conservation movement was also influenced, although to a minor degree, by the problems of common-property resources—those in which private investment aimed at changing the form, scale, or management of a resource would be unprofitable because the investor cannot be sure he will harvest the returns. Much of the literature on this subject was bequeathed by the eighteenth-century and nineteenth-century writers on the European common pastures and woods to those who later observed the low yields and unprofitable investment in oil fields, ocean fisheries, and certain water resources, where unrestrained private utilization caused external diseconomies of production. In addition, when the resources were capable of producing recreation benefits, there were external diseconomies of consumption. [*See* EXTERNAL ECONOMIES AND DISECONOMIES.] Thus, when the conservationists turned to the prevention of depletion and the advocacy of "prudent use" of oil fields and water bodies, they found there was no single, responsible owner or manager.

Eventually it was left to the technologists and scientists to define some conservation ideal for such resources. Petroleum engineers invented the concept of "maximum efficient rate" of production, designed to recover a high percentage of the underground crude. And fisheries biologists designed fishing regulations that would achieve a fish stock's "maximum sustained catch." Both these concepts implied regulation of the users of common-property resources, and holding to the prescribed rates was designated "conservation." But the technical complexities of these subjects and the limited number of persons interested in them have left them somewhat outside the wider conservation movement.

The conservation movement. The four subjects —preservation of wildlife, redistribution of landed wealth, prevention of depletion, and prudent use of common property—became the basic precepts of the conservation movement. Upon them was based a structure of thought that, as formulated by scientists, attempted to show the loss to mankind from continued misuse and abuse; as formulated by more extreme and romantic writers, it attempted to find villains and scapegoats among those who "exploited" the natural heritage. While the former group projected nineteenth-century trends into the future, predicting shortages, low living standards, and high costs, the latter group attacked the farmers who used bad agricultural practices, the insatiable hunters and fishermen, and above all, the large mining and logging companies who, negligently or malevolently, despoiled the earth.

The scientists' work has led them into many byways. As they have learned more about new techniques of exploration, production, and concentration, the oversimplified conservation ideals have been abandoned. National and international multiresource conferences, such as the UNSCCUR meeting mentioned above, have been highly interesting but have failed to reveal the common aims and problems proclaimed in the 1900s. The more sophisticated contemporary discussions of water recycling, desalinization, and purification, of mineral development, forest genetics, fisheries' biology and oceanography, game behavior, and population dynamics, have, instead, revealed a multitude of social science problems concerning the re-education and adjustment of producers and consumers to new practices, costs, and opportunities.

Further, there is nowadays no single "economics of conservation"; many methods of analysis, from the use of econometrics in demand and production studies through regional input–output studies to decision theory in the business firm, are now relevant. In what follows, therefore, we must confine the discussion to the economic analysis of the older conservation assertions, particularly to the claim that the market mechanism is powerless to deal with imminent depletion and shortage.

Economic analysis of conservation

At any given time, there exists for each resource what Ciriacy-Wantrup (1952) has called its "state of conservation," the expected temporal distribution of use rates. A conservation policy, therefore, is one that would induce those who manage resources to change this state so that more use will take place at a later date.

How does the original degree of conservation

come about? The economic forces at work can best be understood by studying the behavior of the firm making planning and production decisions. The firm is deterred from postponing *all* use of its resources by the discount on future net revenues. A profit of $1 postponed one year is worth $1/(1 + i)$, where i is the rate of interest relevant to the firm's lendings and borrowings. This expression is less than $1 and diminishes exponentially with the number of years the profit on resource use is delayed. Consequently, there is an incentive to reap the harvest of its durable and its growing assets as soon as possible. The rate of interest, i, here stands for all the forces of time preference, shortsightedness, and liquidity preference that the conservationist believes are leading to early depletion and future shortages.

But if the firm advances the dates of use of its resources, its output per day must then increase. This increased rate will be possible only at higher unit costs, so the profit per unit will be smaller and the incentive to early depletion will be counterbalanced.

The precise nature of such increasing costs has been debated by economists since Ricardo wrote his chapter "On the Rent of Mines" ([1817] 1962, pp. 46–47). It is now agreed that three types of increasing costs may be distinguished. *In the short run,* a resource operation with a given plant, transportation, and underground or surface layout will experience ordinary diminishing returns. *In the long run,* however, these facilities and layouts are flexible; the question now becomes whether the "law of diminishing returns" applies. Marshall's assertion that it did not led to a controversy with Taussig, Wicksell, and Cassell. Today it is agreed that higher costs associated with ores located farther away from the plant are irrelevant to the discussion of the costs of alternative *rates* of output, indicating only that costs will be higher in later periods than in early periods or that more elaborate workings will become necessary. They do not indicate that the curve of costs must, in the long run, rise with higher rates of output per year or per shift. In general, it would appear that the economic debate about proportionality and returns to scale applies as well to resource operations as to other businesses, with the added element of the limited space within which commercially attractive materials are to be found. This factor of limited space would appear to be an additional reason for expecting the long-run cost curve to be U-shaped.

Amortization of fixed capital is a third source of rising costs. Except in extremely large sites, the life of a resource operation is shorter than the durability of the fixed capital needed to work it. Apart, therefore, from those items of capital that can be moved to new workings, the equipment costs must be amortized over the number of units of material to be removed. Consequently, higher rates of extraction can be accomplished only by higher fixed costs per unit.

The firm may encounter any or all of these sources of increasing costs and so be deterred from attempting an immediate exhaustion of raw materials. In addition, it must contemplate the expected course of future prices for its product.

In the typical situation deplored by the conservationists, mineral extraction is proceeding, reserves are shrinking, mines are closing, and metal prices are gradually rising. Under such circumstances the firm has an additional incentive to lengthen the state of conservation. Future use will be expected to receive higher market prices and unit profits than current use. It will pay the firm to adjust its production plan in favor of output in later periods. This incentive will be presented to all firms, so the evil day of future scarcity, dreaded by the conservationist, is postponed by today's planning for higher future profits.

Thus, the firm must balance present profits, future profits, and the rate of interest. Discounted profits become an opportunity cost, or more precisely a *user cost*, of present production. (User cost is the present worth of the profit that could be earned on an extra unit if its extraction were postponed to the best future date.) Present operations should therefore be expanded until marginal current profits equal marginal user costs, in order to maximize the present value of the natural resource enterprise.

In a perfectly competitive commercial economy, it could be said that the firm that only maximizes current profits is acting on the expectation that future prices and profits will be very poor. Assuming that the firm's foresight is not only normal but is sharpened by the opportunity to gain from accurate perception of future markets, society can have no complaint about such a firm's state of conservation. On the contrary, such present-worth maximizing firms will produce an optimum degree of conservation. This is why the academic economist rejects the conservationist's contention of the probability of a future starved of natural resources.

But the conservationist can rightly point to the many assumptions underlying this economic model. If, for example, the firm (like many small miners, farmers, and loggers) discounts the future at a rate higher than that used in the rest of the economy, user costs will be too small to prevent present extraction of material that competitive forces would have awarded to the future. Or if the firm is irrational, unthinking about its own best interests, future consumers may lose. Such market imperfections are the first of three important justifications for conservation policies.

Market imperfections. The presence of market imperfections in the capital market, the labor market, or the final-product market can weaken the economists' case that present-worth maximization by individual sellers will ensure an optimum state of conservation. Ciriacy-Wantrup (1952), Gordon (1958), and Scott (1955) investigate the consequences of such imperfections and weigh the arguments for remedial policies, such as regulation, subsidies, public ownership, and so forth. It is usually held that an imperfect land market—that is, a common-property situation—presents the best prima-facie case for interference in the interest of conservation.

Other imperfections may also be serious. But conservation action is not justified by a few firms having a strong time preference, extreme illiquidity, or lethargic indifference to their own gain. For the too rapid production of a few firms will be counterbalanced by compensatory action of the other firms in their industry. The relatively high rates of . output of the "imperfect" firms will raise market supplies and so depress prices; the depressed prices will discourage production by other firms and also discourage the opening of new operations. The competitive interperiod allocation of total supplies will be restored. Only if such a large fraction of total stocks is dumped on the market that the remaining producers have insufficient reserves to restore the intertemporal balance will conservation intervention be justified. Hence, the mere citing of imperfections in some portions of the market does not in itself justify conservation policies. The market must be overwhelmingly imperfect.

A better case for conservation intervention can be made if the owner has been placed in a situation where he cannot gain by delaying sale of his stocks until the future period comes. At least five types of circumstance may be responsible. First, governments may, by tax-free inducements to new resource firms, make it less profitable to extend production much beyond the duration of the tax holiday. Second, government purchase, stabilization, or stock-piling schemes may create an incentive to take early advantage of supported prices. (In this circumstance, however, conservation objectives may be achieved by the stock-piling, even though it is done away from the original site.) Third, as discussed above, users of common-property resources are incapable of taking advantage of future markets and must extract as much as is profitable today. They may, however, "unitize" the management

of the resource in order to gain from the process outlined earlier; or they may encourage the government to intervene to slow down present extraction; or, finally, they may individually produce in the present for their own inventory (because of the high costs of storage off the site, this is rarely an important alternative). Fourth, future values may be so enveloped in uncertainty that firms may individually opt for present profits. Fifth, future values may be in different uses than present values and may be unmarketable. That is, they may be the source of external economies to other producers (in controlling floods or erosion) or "intangible" services (of scenery or recreation) to consumers.

All of these circumstances are common in the resource industries, and many have been dealt with by special government institutions, such as those mentioned in the last section of this article. While it is true, as suggested earlier, that small resource owners are sometimes irrational and do not know their own best interest, investigation often shows that nonconservation behavior can be explained satisfactorily by one or more of the five circumstances above.

A less clear-cut situation exists when the value of production to some portion of society, such as the inhabitants of a province or country, is greater than the market value. Thus, a unit of timber output postponed may prevent a town from degenerating into a "ghost town." Forest and oil conservation may well prolong the industrial importance of communities and nations that might otherwise suffer from the migration of labor and capital to locations where their incomes and productivity would be higher. Such cases are complicated, and it does not follow that anyone's interest is actually served by postponing the day of final exhaustion and closing down. There are indeed many direct and indirect subsidies for production from dwindling reserves, to support otherwise stranded communities. But such subsidies are hotly debated. Even if they are justified, it does not follow that it would have been better to reduce the early rates of extraction of such deposits than to subsidize them later.

But the strongest case for conservation ultimately depends upon opposing views of responsibility to the future and opposing views of the future situation. It is true that there are many externalities, but taken together they are insufficient to motivate the conservation movement. Let us take up these two matters one at a time.

Responsibility to the future. The preceding account of the theory of use has shown that the future is not ignored by resource firms. The future is provided with such raw materials as are justified by the owner's cost of holding wealth (the rate of interest). Although monetary fluctuations and changes in desire for liquidity may change the rate of interest from period to period, it is here a rough indicator of both the rate of return on other types of capital investment and the desire of present generations to save. It is this connection between saving and the state of conservation that has led many writers to conclude that the heart of the conservation problem is in the conflict between present and future (Gray 1913). Clearly, a lower rate of interest would reduce a firm's tendency to discount user costs and to divert consumption of a raw material from the near future to the more remote future.

In general equilibrium this diversion, however, might not occur for all resources. If, for example, savers became more willing to provide for the future, the supply of savings would increase (and interest rates fall) not only for resource owners but also for all potential borrowers. As the amount borrowed for private and social capital formation rose, the current demand for raw materials for these investment goods would expand; meanwhile, the demand for raw materials specifically needed for consumer goods would fall. It is quite possible that some index of demand for all natural resource raw materials would rise, not fall. Without knowledge of the elasticities of substitution between resource-based inputs and other inputs, it is, of course, impossible to predict what the outcome would be. Unless substitute inputs are generally adopted, however, the demand for resource-based raw materials by makers of both capital and consumer goods should be about the same as with the former, higher rate of interest. If the resource industries supply this unchanged demand as before, then the change in the interest rate has had no effect. If they do so at higher prices, the final outcome may be that although the money rate of interest has fallen, the real (Wicksellian) rate has returned to its previous level.

A third outcome is that the lower rate might induce resource owners to reject permanently some of the current demand and hold their resources longer. This possibility might emerge if it is expected that all (present and) future prices for raw materials will be higher, but the discount rate remains lower, than before the change in rate. This third outcome, similar to the effect described by the Austrian economists as "lengthening the period of investment," is the only one of the three possibilities favorable to general conservation of stock, or durable resources.

Which of the three possible outcomes will materialize depends on the new general equilibrium following a change in the propensity to save, which new equilibrium may take many years to emerge. The raw materials demand from other types of new investment may develop rapidly or slowly; and the contraction of consumer goods requirements may also depend upon the durability of the consumer goods in question. Thereafter there will be a response lag as the resource industries, especially those producing renewable resources, make and remake decisions about investment in extractive and regenerative activities. In other words, a simple change in the rate of interest will produce a new degree of conservation only after a long adjustment period, during which resources may be depleted more or less rapidly than before the change and more or less rapidly than after the final equilibrium is reached.

Another difficulty about applying the interest rate concept is that although many writers concede a lower rate of interest will lengthen the period of investment, such theories do not offer predictions of which types of investment will actually increase in "duration." The general lengthening may be accomplished by the shortening of some types and the lengthening of others (Hayek 1941).

It is, of course, impossible to dispense with the rate of interest in resource calculations. Some guide is needed by which today's managers can spread possible output over a stated period of years. Otherwise they would have no measure of the amount of stock resources to be taken out of possible future use for present consumption. Graaff has described decision making about intertemporal allocation as planning to bequeath a certain "terminal capital" at a certain date; of the problems beyond this date, man takes no heed. This approach has proved to be a useful approximation in recent papers on welfare economics and growth, but its value for reasoning about resource allocation is limited. The planning horizon recedes as we approach it, so that some discounting is still required, with perhaps a sudden discontinuity at a certain point in the stream of future revenues and costs.

Predicting the needs of the future.   If some discount must be used and if society is to depend upon commercial estimates of future prices to indicate future needs, can we be sure that these needs are being correctly estimated? It is clear that many owners are not foresighted, but in view of the many government studies now available, it is hard to believe that the information is now any worse than the rest of the information by which persons and governments govern their behavior.

The real difficulty about these predictions is the certainty that requirements are going to change. The dynamism of the world economy means that once-essential materials may become mere chunks of matter, of low economic value. Not only do fashions change (e.g., from cotton to man-made fibers), but new techniques change entirely the type of process responsible for providing a certain part of the consumer budget (e.g., from mail carried by coal-powered railroad to telephone and television), and these changes are apparently accelerating. Hence, producers are feeling less confident that their resource will have a future market.

Furthermore, there is increasing evidence that expected future scarcity brings about its own solution—through "self-generating technical change," as Barnett and Morse (1963) have called it. An anticonservation view is now plausible: that mankind can invent itself out of any shortage. Barnett and Morse feel that the only difficulty here is that increasing recourse to substitutes and increasing shortage of space may lead to some general deterioration in the "quality of life."

Hence, estimates of future scarcity not only are uncertain but also are probably overstated. The resource owner can be forgiven if he decides that it is not worthwhile arranging to have supplies available for some remote posterity. Such uncertainty is now likely to provide a large discount, additional to the interest rate, in computing user costs of current production and depletion.

Conservationists have disputed this conclusion on two grounds. The first is that energy sources are likely to become an ultimate bottleneck. Fossil fuels and falling water are known to be limited; tidal energy may be expensive to harness; we might soon have to depend upon sunlight and other solar radiations. This argument has been recently weakened by the discovery of the practicability of nuclear power sources. In any case, it is not at all clear what should be done, in a large way, to delay the time when lack of energy might become a seriously limiting factor to production or growth.

The other ground for conservation action, based on uncertainty about technical progress, has been formulated by Ciriacy-Wantrup. Confining himself to renewable or flow resources (soil, water, plants, and animals), he argues that society should not gamble on the possibility that changes in technology, tastes, and institutions will be favorable. He advocates, instead, that the level of such resources should be kept above a "critical zone," below which any decline is irreversible. It should be the business of society to keep a stock of timber, soil, plants, fish, and wildlife available, which can be expanded to fill an "immoderate" need if such should arise. This view is close to that of the ecologists, who advocate keeping the relationship of various living species to each other and to their habitat (swamps, rivers and lakes, wilderness, desert, and so forth) more or less intact. In effect, Ciriacy-Wantrup claims that the maintenance of this "safe minimum standard" is a fairly inexpensive insurance policy against the possibility that unpredictable changes may put a high value on living forms and water and soil complexes after they have become irrecoverable.

Conclusion—the role of economics. It will be seen that the economists' analysis of the conservation question depends heavily upon the theory of capital, which (as in welfare economics, macroeconomics, and growth theory) is probably the least-rewarding branch of economic theory in terms of useful generalizations about the real world. The objective fears of conservationists, under particular circumstances, could be realized; their assertions about subjective benefits and costs are more questionable but have indicated fields for valuable analysis, so far mostly ignored by economics. What economics has done up to now is to show the variety of problems and objectives implicit in the conservation question; to attack the notion that all resource problems are susceptible to a common analysis or policy; to stress the scarcity of labor and capital, as well as that of natural resources; and to undertake the detailed description and analysis of land and raw material situations.

Such applied research began early in the nineteenth century, in forest economics, an ingenious combination of population theory and actuarial finance most fully developed in Germany and Scandinavia. The objectives, such as maximum sustained yield, were more technocratic than economic, but the methodology is easily adapted to other ends. Agricultural economics, too, got off to an early start and was well equipped to analyze soil exhaustion and conflicting land use from both institutional and marginalist points of view.

The economics of mining, petroleum, fisheries, water-supply, and recreational land operations, however, were largely ignored by economists until the late 1930s. Most progress in these fields was made in peripheral studies of market organization, labor conditions, taxation, or public utility pricing, and most of these had little impact on resource policy or business practice. Indeed, today's specialists in conservation economics frequently find that the best pioneering contributions have been made by geologists, engineers, biologists, and administrators.

From the marriage of such "engineering economics" with orthodox welfare economics have emerged the variants of benefit–cost analysis, a technique of decision making first applied in Europe and the United States to the evaluation of water-resource projects [see WATER RESOURCES; WELFARE ECONOMICS]. It has been generalized to deal not only with fixed investments but also with conflicting uses of land resources. It is discussed more fully in another article [see INVESTMENT, *article on* THE INVESTMENT DECISION]. All that needs to be said here is that it makes possible the full and systematic study of any investment which claims to increase income or stability or fulfill other objectives. Variants of this approach, designed especially to deal with uncertainty, the discovery of new resources, intangible services, and opportunity costs, have been worked out in many countries. In view of the numerous distortions interfering with the optimum use of actual resources (such as the market imperfections previously discussed), it is a particularly useful substitute for market forces in government decision making about the form and rate of resource exploitation.

Conservation institutions

The state of conservation of any particular natural resource is not alone the outcome of a variety of personal and economic determinants, such as the intelligence, education, taste, and means of the owners and managers. In addition, special pressures are brought to bear by taxes and tax rebates, subsidies, licenses and regulations, tariffs, quotas, labor laws, safety rules, and zoning statutes. These institutional arrangements temper and divert the forces of the market for each raw material and resource location. In some countries public ownership and the force of custom and habit are so overwhelming that the price mechanism works only slowly and spasmodically. In others, markets for the resource site, for shares in ownership, for capital, labor, and the final product, are so well developed that criticism of the state of conservation is implicitly criticism of the open-market system itself.

In all countries, however, a variety of special institutional arrangements have been made to modify the private regime of resource exploitation and renewal. Some of these supplement market mechanisms by providing information, education, or special assistance where these seem to be lacking. For example, many countries have systems of farm credit, which have, as one of their purposes, the supplementing of poorly organized private systems of farm, livestock, and crop loans.

Similarly, many countries maintain some kind of geologic survey, which performs for the mining industry as a whole a basic research function similar to the basic research carried on by the government for agriculture and by the universities for industry.

A number of other such public institutions, important but auxiliary to the basic market mechanism, might be identified. In the following paragraphs, however, it is intended to mention some institutions that go further and that compensate for the absence of a market or replace it. In addition, there are institutions concerned with common-property resources that basically compensate for the absence of sole ownership.

International institutions. From the administrative point of view, the most interesting international institutions are those concerned with resources that are open to several nations, either because they are in the high seas or in other areas outside national jurisdiction (Antarctica or outer space) or because the resource moves from country to country (fish, migratory birds, international rivers and air).

In the absence of specific treaties, customary international law governs the conditions of use of these resources. Usually the effect is that there is little restriction on the resource's use. Thus, in the absence of specific agreements, high-seas fisheries, migrating birds and animals, rivers and air flowing across boundaries, may usually be exploited much as the nationals of each country wish, subject only to their domestic laws. And since the country has no power to regulate the actions of other countries' nationals, there is little to be gained by making restrictions.

For that reason, there have long been agreements whereby certain countries were given rights or sole rights to certain fisheries or bodies of water, although the older of these agreements rarely called for regulation to protect fish or animal population. Since 1900, however, a variety of conservation treaties have dealt with fisheries in waters used by two countries, fish migrating between two countries' seas, and high-seas fish populations. The first important example was the 1911 fur seal convention between Great Britain (for Canada), Japan, Russia, and the United States. Since then, fisheries treaties governing research, catching, and improvement have been made for whales, Pacific tuna, and Pacific salmon and halibut, and agreements have been made regarding North Sea and Baltic Sea trawling, and the northwest Atlantic fisheries. The general effect of such treaties is to leave fishing open to the members but to restrict the time, place, or technique of fishing in such a way as to increase the sustained yield. This is certainly a gain, in that more fish are available for consumers. However, the regulations have been criticized because they aggravate the overemployment and overinvestment that are already inherent in the utilization of common-property resources. First, by raising the potential catch without limiting the entry of vessels, they draw still more vessels into the fishery (Christy & Scott 1965). Second, the method of protecting the fish stock (for example, the prohibition of modern methods or the setting up of closed seasons) frequently creates idle capacity or requires expensive off-season storage facilities. Recent studies of the operations of the Pacific halibut convention have demonstrated that the industry is by no means healthy, although the treaty is frequently and correctly cited as a striking success in the management of wildlife, in that it has produced or maintained large catches compared with what would have been the case in the absence of international agreement.

In this connection, it should be noted that the UN Geneva meetings on the law of the sea, in 1958, succeeded in introducing two conventions, one on high-seas fisheries and the other on the mineral resources of the continental shelf. Probably on the way to becoming accepted international law, these conventions should increase the possibility of bringing marine resources under economic management.

There are a number of international river agreements, negotiated between the riparian states. Among them are agreements on the Indus, the Rhine, the Danube, the Rio Grande, the St. Lawrence, and the Columbia. All permit more valuable development than would have been possible had the signatories confined their activities to their own waters. Few, however, have gone so far as to encourage the full utilization of the river without regard to the boundary.

Some action has also been taken to protect migratory wildlife. Eleven European states interested in bird protection signed a convention for this purpose in 1902, and Canada and the United States agreed on joint action in 1916. International action has also produced the 1936 convention on the protection of African flora and fauna and the 1954 convention on the prevention of pollution of the sea by oil. Such conventions are interesting because they seek "nonmarket" objectives: they have been supported mainly by sportsmen, on the one hand, and by amateur and scientific ornithologists, on the other. The great destructiveness of modern hunting methods makes it possible to annihilate certain species entirely (an outcome that is much less likely in most fisheries), so these treaties should indeed be classified as preserving certain resources "for future generations."

National institutions. The conservation of resources within each country is implemented by a rich complex of specialized institutions. This is particularly so for common-property resources, which would otherwise be overexploited, depleted, and perhaps destroyed. Almost all countries now have fisheries' regulations, applicable within their territorial and inland waters. Some of these regulations are explicitly to protect the exploiting rights of certain communities or tribes or the owners of certain outmoded kinds of equipment. But others exist to protect fish stocks by regulating time, place, and method of catching. Usually, however, permission to fish is free or cheaply obtained, so that conservation (actually, management) of the fish stock may be achieved while labor and capital are, as already indicated, economically underemployed.

Similarly, pressure of oil and gas in petroleum fields and levels of water tables in aquifers may be regulated to prevent destructive loss from competitive exploitation. Prorationing of oil fields is a well-known technique. But spacing by unitization is rare in North America. It is more common in other countries, where concessions are given for management of, and investment by firms and syndicates in, entire fields. Conservation of the resource may, therefore, be achieved, but at the opportunity cost of a substantial waste of labor and capital.

In the same context, the special tax treatment for petroleum and mineral exploration and development should be noted. Generally based on the "unusual degree of risk" in exploration ventures, these amount to an amelioration of income tax by depletion allowances and the "expensing" of prospecting costs against other income. It is, however, hotly disputed whether this undoubted risk is a sufficient reason for special treatment; in addition, it would, in general, seem to be an anticonservation treatment because it leads to more rapid exploration, production, and depletion than would otherwise be the case.

Another device is the export control board. This has occasionally been used in time of national emergency to prevent the export of scarce raw materials and is, in that restricted sense, a conservation institution. Canada's National Energy Board, however, has powers to prevent the export of fuels or electricity until it is satisfied that Canada's future needs have been covered. A Norwegian policy respecting the export of electricity has somewhat the same effect. This type of policy is often indistinguishable from that of forbidding the export of certain raw materials in order to encourage further processing by home industries. It is, therefore, frequently a type of industrial protection, akin to the tariff.

Forests and forestry are also the business of a large group of special institutions. On the one hand, as has been noted, many forests are publicly owned and come under management rules that, if anything, exaggerate future needs. Not only have some governments invested more than private owners in land acquisition away from agriculture and in the planting to forest of such lands, they also tend to grow plantations to ages ("rotations") that aim at maximizing the physical volume of wood produced rather than its maximum present value. Many European countries, especially in Scandinavia, now obtain a large proportion of their wood from public lands (which are frequently in regions that were not wanted for any other purpose and remained, by default, in public ownership). The tropical countries, also, own most of their own timber resources. In addition, logging and processing lumber, on some, at least, of these lands, tends to be a nationalized industry, although in the United States and Canada it is common to have short-tenure loggers or logging contractors undertake the harvesting.

On the other hand, there is an increasing tendency for private forests to be regulated by government, in the interest of ensuring reforestation and fuller utilization. The economic value of regulation by law is uncertain, but such regulation may be defended as a means of drawing to the attention of small owners the profitability of more intensive forest management; the burden of compliance with the law is frequently very small.

This legalistic approach is usually supported by a system of property taxation applicable only to forest lands, which reduces the incentive created by value-based taxes to cut while trees are still small. In addition, there are special income tax and inheritance tax arrangements available that reinterpret the usual tax distinctions between income and wealth, to deal with the fact that a growing forest is both a capital good and a crop. Scandinavian taxation is most elaborate in these respects, but attention should also be drawn to the capital gains status of forests in American federal taxation and to the reliefs for forests provided under the British death duties. Most important, however, is the administration of these laws and taxes, which has an educative effect similar to that of farm-extension work.

Conservationists, often biologists, have long been concerned about recreation, but the study of park and recreational-site planning in general is just commencing. As explained at the outset of this article, most public lands and parks "survived" the nineteenth-century period of liberal land alienation into private use. In most countries these parks today—in a period of increased population, higher incomes, and increased leisure—are intensively used by the general public and are imaginatively managed by conscientious park services. But because their services are given freely, there is no market profit reaped; access is unrationed; parks are congested; and a "problem" has emerged. There is a clear public desire for more facilities, but governments have been slow to respond. Economic analysis of land-acquisition policies is just commencing, and conflicting users of land close to centers of populations have not been slow to dispute the establishment of public parks, nature conservancies, camp grounds, green belts, playing fields, and so forth. A few private substitutes have appeared, charging for their services, but the problem of land allocation between recreation and market uses is largely neglected by the social sciences, although it should be amenable to techniques now used in the economics of education.

Finally, we may refer to the preservation of sport fish and wildlife. As has been mentioned, international agreements exist that have some effect on the preservation of some species. But for the most part, protection is achieved by the domestic control of hunting and, to a lesser extent, of habitat.

In general, rights to hunt and fish are conveyed by licenses or permits, it being an offense to hunt without one. In addition, certain species are protected absolutely in certain seasons or places or up to a certain quota. Usually permits are free or cost only a nominal amount, although permits for the hunting of big game (especially by foreigners) may be sold close to what the market will bear. Sometimes hunting or fishing rights are attached to the land or water, are owned privately, and may be leased or sold. Such private rights produce revenues that can be used to conserve the resource, and these revenues also ration the demand.

But "public" hunting is not usually rationed in this way. Enforcement of prohibitions against an extensive activity that takes place in open country is, of course, very expensive and in some countries has been quite ineffective. Elsewhere, a trio of problems prevents a sophisticated conservation regime: the problem of acquiring or protecting habitats from other land uses; the problem of learning the needs of the various species inhabiting the environment; and the problem of arranging an understandable set of regulations, permits, and prices that will encourage the harvesting of surplus stocks of some species while protecting the diminishing stocks of others. In the long run, there is the additional danger that a really effective management system will lead to the virtual domestication of the conserved species, thus negating much of the ethical and recreational value claimed for the preservation of wildlife.

ANTHONY SCOTT

BIBLIOGRAPHY

BARNETT, HAROLD J.; and MORSE, CHANDLER 1963 *Scarcity and Growth: The Economics of Natural Resource Availability.* Baltimore: Johns Hopkins Press.

CHRISTY, FRANCIS T. JR.; and SCOTT, ANTHONY 1956 *The Common Wealth in Ocean Fisheries: Some Problems of Growth and Economic Allocation.* Baltimore: Johns Hopkins Press.

CIRIACY-WANTRUP, SIEGFRIED VON (1952) 1963 *Resource Conservation: Economics and Policies.* Rev. ed. Berkeley: Univ. of California, Division of Agricultural Sciences, Agricultural Experimental Station.

GORDON, H. SCOTT 1958 Economics and the Conservation Question. *Journal of Law and Economics* 1:110–121.

GOUNDREY, G. K. 1960 Economics and Conservation. *Canadian Journal of Economics and Political Science* 26:318–325.

GRAY, L. C. 1913 Economic Possibilities of Conservation. *Quarterly Journal of Economics* 27:497–519.

HAYEK, FRIEDRICH A. VON (1941) 1950 *The Pure Theory of Capital.* London: Routledge; Univ. of Chicago Press.

INTERNATIONAL ECONOMIC ASSOCIATION 1957 *The Economics of Fisheries: Proceedings of a Round Table . . . .* Edited by Ralph Turvey and Jack Wiseman. Rome: Food and Agriculture Organization.

JEVONS, W. STANLEY (1865) 1906 *The Coal Question: An Inquiry Concerning the Progress of the Nation, and the Probable Exhaustion of Our Coal-mines.* 3d ed., rev. London and New York: Macmillan.

MALTHUS, THOMAS R. (1798) 1958 *An Essay on Population.* 2 vols. New York: Dutton.

ORGANIZATION FOR EUROPEAN ECONOMIC COOPERATION, ENERGY ADVISORY COMMISSION 1960 *Towards a New Energy Pattern in Europe: Report.* Paris: The Organization.

RESOURCES FOR THE FUTURE 1963 *Resources in America's Future: Patterns of Requirements and Availabilities, 1960–2000,* by Hans H. Landsberg, Leonard L. Fischman, and Joseph L. Fisher. Baltimore: Johns Hopkins Press.

RICARDO, DAVID (1817) 1962 *Principles of Political Economy and Taxation.* London: Dent; New York: Dutton. → A paperback edition was published in 1963 by Irwin.

SCOTT, ANTHONY 1955 *Natural Resources: The Economics of Conservation.* Univ. of Toronto Press.

SEMINAR ON THE DEVELOPMENT AND ADMINISTRATION OF THE INTERNATIONAL RIVER BASIN, VANCOUVER, *1961* 1963 *The International River Basin: Proceedings of a Seminar. . . .* Edited by J. D. Chapman. Vancouver: Univ. of British Columbia, Publications Centre.

UNITED NATIONS SCIENTIFIC CONFERENCE ON THE CONSERVATION AND UTILIZATION OF RESOURCES, LAKE SUCCESS, N.Y., *1949* 1953 *Proceedings.* 7 vols and 1-vol. index. New York: United Nations.

U.S. PRESIDENT'S MATERIALS POLICY COMMISSION 1952 *Resources for Freedom.* 5 vols. Washington: Government Printing Office. → Commonly known as the Paley report.

CONSERVATISM

"Conservatism" is a word whose usefulness is matched only by its capacity to confuse, distort, and irritate. Since the patterns of thought and action it denotes are real and enduring, and since no substitute seems likely to be generally accepted, "conservatism" will doubtless have a long life as a handy, if dangerous, tool of social science. Scholars who use it lie under a severe obligation to be as exact as they can ever be in the handling of words that are encrusted with tradition and saturated with emotion. In particular, they must recognize, and thus distinguish among, the uses of this word that have become fairly standard in the years since World War II. There are, it would appear, four such uses.

Temperamental conservatism. Conservatism, by one definition, is both the "natural" and the culture-determined disposition to resist dislocating changes in a customary pattern of living and working. It describes, crudely and yet effectively, a temperament or psychological stance, a cluster of traits that are on daily display by most men in all societies. The important elements in the conservative temperament would appear to be habit (what William James called "the enormous fly-wheel of society, and its most precious conservative agent"), inertia (a force that often seems to be as powerful in the social world as in the physical), fear (especially fear of the unexpected, the irregular, and the uncomfortable), and emulation (a product of both fear of alienation from the group and a craving for its approval).

All these traits of character flourish with particular vigor among some of the most unfortunate, insecure, and expendable groups in society. One may speak with propriety, if also with pity, of the conservatism of the poor, the conservatism of the aged, and the conservatism of the ignorant. At the same time, one must assign a high value to the conservative temperament in the pattern of social survival and even of social progress. A community made up entirely of men engaged in the quest for security and order would be dreary, decayed, and perhaps even cruel, but a community that counted no such men would be a scene of anarchy. Neither the division of labor nor the maintenance of law and order, neither the gathering of knowledge nor the transmission of experience from generation to generation would be possible if the conservative temperament, especially as it is transformed into the imperatives of organization, were not an active force in the lives of men.

Situational conservatism. Conservatism, by a second definition, related to the first, is an attitude of opposition to disruptive change in the social, economic, legal, religious, political, or cultural order. It describes, somewhat less crudely and somewhat more effectively, a pattern of social behavior, a cluster of principles and prejudices that are on daily display by many men in all developed societies. The distinguishing mark of this conservatism, as indeed it is of any brand of conservatism, is the fear of change, which becomes transformed in the political arena into the fear of radicalism—in this instance, the radicalism of men who propose to "make the world over," or at least to "improve" it at the expense of old values, institutions, and patterns of living. Situational conservatism is not confined to the well-placed and well-to-do. Persons at all levels of being and possessing may lament change in the *status quo*. For reasons that range from the intuitive to the pragmatic by way of the traditional, many men in developed societies can be counted upon to express a highly personal sense of satisfaction and identity with the established order. One happy home of situational conservatism is the upper reaches of society; another is the land. Where these two shaping forces come together, as in the situation of an English duke, the result can often be a caricature of conservatism.

Somewhat unfortunately for the reputation of both temperamental and situational conservatism among social scientists, as well as for the reputation of social science among political conservatives, several studies of political behavior have tended, despite repeated disclaimers of ill intent, to equate conservatism with authoritarianism, obscurantism, racism, fascism, alienation, maladjustment, and "the closed mind." Some social scientists have elected to probe the dark frontier between politics and personality by constructing a spectrum that runs from an extreme labeled "conservatism" to an extreme labeled "liberalism," and then, by eliciting and tabulating responses to questions designed to reveal attitudes toward controversial social and personal problems, to place the persons questioned —be they workers in Detroit or criminals in San Francisco or citizens chosen at random in Liverpool—along the scale. It is revealing that "liberal" responses to the questions of even the most fairminded students of political behavior are almost always given "plus" values in the resulting tables and scales, while "conservative" responses are tagged with the ever so slightly tainted "minus" sign.

The prototype of such studies was carried through by T. W. Adorno and his associates and was published as *The Authoritarian Personality* (1950). The question may well be raised whether this kind of study has not done damage to the image of conservatism and rendered the word itself suspect among many social scientists who hitherto found it useful and not at all pejorative in content. In any case, much careful research must be done before political and philosophical conservatism can be linked causally with the unpleasant aspects of temperamental and situational conservatism that are assumed to form this polar phenomenon known as "the closed mind."

Political conservatism. If we bring together in imagination a goodly number of conservatives of temperament and situation, then thrust them into the hurly-burly of active politics, we move naturally toward a third definition of conservatism that is roughly synonymous with the worn but still convenient label "the Right." Most persons who talk of conservatism mean political conservatism, that is to say, the aspirations and activities—most of them defensive rather than creative—of parties and movements that celebrate inherited patterns of morality and tested institutions, that are skeptical about the efficacy of popular government, that can be counted upon to oppose both the reforming plans of the moderate Left and the deranging schemes of the extreme Left, and that draw their heaviest support from men who have a substantial material and psychological stake in the established order.

Political conservatism is a phenomenon which, if we stretch the definition beyond the boundaries of common sense, is a universal of organized society. One may find, if one seeks them intensively enough, political conservatives in every country and culture. One may even say that since conservatism is essentially the defense of a going society, the leaders of the Soviet Union are conservatives. This, however, is to ignore both the history and logic of this phenomenon, which comes fully to life—as does its great partner and adversary, liberalism—in the civilized political and cultural struggles of the open, ordered, constitutional society. The Tories of Great Britain, the Republicans of the United States, the Gaullists of France, and the Christian Democrats of a half-dozen European countries are conservative parties in the most meaningful sense, the Liberal Democrats of Japan and the Swatantra party of India in a rather less meaningful sense, the Communist party of the Soviet Union in no sense at all except the arbitrary or whimsical. The political situation in which they lived and wrought made it fully possible for Herbert Hoover, Stanley Baldwin, Dwight D. Eisenhower, Konrad Adenauer, Sir Winston Churchill, and Charles de Gaulle to act as conservative statesmen, but we would not easily find counterparts of such men in most parts of Asia and Africa.

A distinction should be made, although it is often impossible to maintain in politics, between the two classic political positions of the Right: conservatism and reaction. Reaction is the position of men who sigh for the past more intensively than they celebrate the present and who feel that a retreat back into it is worth trying. While the conservative, a man essentially at rest, may indulge from time to time in reveries of 1945 or 1928 or 1896 or even 1788, he is generally well adjusted, psychologically as well as programmatically, to "a world he never made."

The reactionary (or, as some might prefer, the restorationist), a man in motion, refuses to acknowledge that whatever has been settled must henceforth be considered good or at least tolerable, and he seems willing to erase some laws, scrap some institutions, even amend his nation's constitution, so that he can roll back the social process to the time at which his countrymen first went foolishly astray. The restorationist should not be confused with the violent reactionary, who, like the violent revolutionary, seems ready to shed blood and to subvert all order in pursuit of his immediate ends.

There is, it can be seen, an essential relationship—or perhaps nonrelationship—between conservatism and revolution. The historic mission of political conservatism in the West has been not to defeat but to forestall revolutions, not to crush but to anticipate them. Conservatism in a truly revolutionary situation is a politics of delusion; a society that bursts into revolution will not be able to smother it by conservative means. The conservative is above all a man of order, and a shattered society has no place for him. To speak of conservatism in France in 1792 or Russia in 1917 or Cuba in 1962 is to speak of political arts that no man could have practiced. The explosion of a genuine social revolution is rather certain evidence that political conservatism has never flourished in a community or, if it has flourished as an important movement, has failed in its mission.

Political conservatism is a posture, whether adopted by individuals, classes, or parties, that is increasingly difficult to maintain in the twentieth century. In many parts of the world—for example, in totalitarian countries like the Soviet Union and Hungary, unstable countries like Colombia and Peru, and only half-formed countries like some of the new states of Africa and Asia—genuine conservatism as a political force can hardly be said to exist, and persons who might make excellent conservatives in more ordered societies must choose between the nihilism of "standing pat," the frustration of trying to recreate a dead past (which may never have existed in the first place), or the cryptoradicalism of riding the tiger of revolution. Even in those parts of the world in which the politics of tradition, wealth, and aristocracy has been a historic force—for example, in Great Britain, the United States, Canada, France, Japan, and the Scandinavian countries—conservatives are sorely tried by the pressure of events over which neither they nor, as it often seems, any men seem to exercise effective control.

The political conservative is almost always the prisoner of the social process as it is embodied in the traditions and institutions of his country, and thus the foil of those men who, knowingly or unknowingly, keep the process in motion. They act; he only reacts—except on those rare occasions when he can emulate Benjamin Disraeli and "steal the Whigs' clothes." If they act as liberals, if the social process moves steadily but not explosively, his reactions can take the form of conservatism. But if they act as radicals, if the process begins to speed up sharply, his reactions must aim beyond mere preservation and at restoration. If, as now seems to be the case all over the world, the pace of history gets out of control, the conservative can no longer fall back on the simple, instinctive acts of conservation. He, like the liberal, must reason and discriminate; he, like the radical, may have to plan and gamble. The "conservative as reformer," the right-wing politician who tries to outpromise liberals in the area of welfare legislation, is an uncomfortable man. The "conservative as revolutionary," the traditionalist who acts "radically" to preserve the crumbling values and institutions of his community, is no conservative at all. Small wonder that many conservatives in Western countries have turned away from politics to fight the good fight of tradition in such areas as art, criticism, and education.

In no country in the world is the dilemma of the true conservative, the man who wants to be neither a reactionary nor a pseudoliberal, more poignant than in the United States. For many reasons—the suddenness with which both democracy and industrialism came to stay as the American way of life, the absence of such comforting relics of a more ordered age as an established church or a monarchy, the crushing of self-conscious aristocracy by the forces of an upstart plutocracy, the feebleness of political and theoretical radicalism (to which men of status and substance could react creatively)—conservatism has never flourished in America as successfully as it has in Great Britain. Now that the kind of social change resulting from automation and the reach for space has become the style of the American way of life, the true agents of change—the business and managerial classes—are proving conclusively that sponsorship of social revolution and opposition to political reform can go hand in hand. The dilemma of the American conservative will never be more dramatically demonstrated than it was in the career of Henry Ford—in his personal habits and opinions the most conservative of men, in his influence upon America one of the most marvelous agents of profound and protracted social change the world has ever known.

Conservatism as philosophy. Beyond the conservatisms of mood and deed, yet almost always relating directly back to them, is the conservatism of thought. As a philosophy dedicated to the defense of an established order, and also to the leadership of certain groups or classes within the order, conservatism is an important intellectual force in most countries of the West. In the years since World War II, a season of disillusionment over the broken promises of the once-ascendant liberal tradition, conservative and pseudoconservative thinkers have been more active than at any period in the past two centuries.

Wherever it is an intellectual force, conservatism has earned its measure of respect and influence the hard way. Unlike the radical or liberal, the genuine conservative engages reluctantly in political speculation. The most famous conservative statesman of the twentieth century, Sir Winston Churchill, steadfastly refused, for all his literary skills, to reflect upon and write down the principles that animated his career. The mere intention to spin out a theory of conservatism is somehow an unconservative impulse, and the pursuit of this intention carries a person dangerously far from that simple social piety, that hesitation about poking a finger into the "cake of custom," that is the essence of the conservative point of view. There would seem to be a few grains of truth in the observation of many critics that a conservatism in search of clear-cut principles is a conservatism already in retreat.

Whether it is, in fact, in retreat or on the attack in the realm of politics, conservatism is flourishing in the realm of ideas, and one must recognize the existence of a core of principles that is the common property of the moderate Right wherever it flourishes as a legitimate force. These, it would seem, are the persistent themes of the philosophers of modern conservatism:

The existence of a universal moral order sanctioned and supported by organized religion.

The obstinately imperfect nature of men, in which unreason and sinfulness lurk always behind the curtain of civilized behavior.

The natural inequality of men in most qualities of mind, body, and character.

The necessity of social classes and orders, and the consequent folly of attempts at leveling by force of law.

The primary role of private property in the pursuit of personal liberty and defense of the social order.

The uncertainty of progress, and the recognition that prescription is the chief method of such progress as a society may achieve.

The need for a ruling and serving aristocracy.

The limited reach of human reason, and the consequent importance of traditions, institutions, symbols, rituals, and even prejudices.

The fallibility and potential tyranny of majority rule, and the consequent desirability of diffusing, limiting, and balancing political power.

One could go further with this catalogue, for example, by taking note of the conservative preference for liberty over equality, the conservative insistence that education must discipline before it can liberate, the conservative delight in such phrases as "the tragedy of history" and "the inadequacy of politics," and the conservative celebration of the prudent man and the ordered society; but the principles listed would seem to be the essence of self-conscious conservatism in the twentieth century.

Two points should be noted about the list. First, it is a series of abstractions, and since conservatives express a horror of abstract thinking each of these ideas must be referred back to a particular society and tradition. Second, in the special case of the United States, society is confidently progressive and the dominant tradition happily democratic, indeed liberal. As a result, the philosophy of conservatism in modern America is a jumble of crosscutting answers to the persistent questions of political theory, especially the question of where the line is to be drawn between the rights of the individual and the demands of the community. Deep inside the shell of his half-Jeffersonian, half-

Hamiltonian ideology, however, the American conservative nurses principles and prejudices that are closely related to those of conservatives in other, less self-consciously democratic countries.

The conservatism of Burke. These considerations lead to a discussion of the most famous brand of philosophical conservatism, the school of political thought identified with Edmund Burke. This conservatism sprang to life in the turmoil of the 1780s and was especially a reaction to the excesses of the French Revolution. Although men as separated in time and purpose as Aristotle, Cicero, St. Augustine, St. Thomas Aquinas, Richard Hooker, and John Locke had created essentially conservative systems of political thought, Burke's *Reflections on the Revolution in France* (1790) is properly considered the purest source of consciously conservative principles. Other important events in the birth of this conservatism were the industrial revolution, which made change rather than stability the style of the social process, and the Enlightenment, which put reason in place of tradition as the surest guide to human conduct. The result was the emergence of a political faith that celebrated the beauties of stability and tradition.

The conservatism of Burke has been and remains a Western phenomenon, a philosophy peculiar to the Atlantic community and some of its extensions throughout the world. Indeed, although it has loyal adherents in many countries, this conservatism has held continuous sway as a major political and intellectual force only in Great Britain. It has not flourished as it might have in France or Germany or Italy because, among other reasons, there has not been sufficient agreement among the men of the Right as to what institutions and values they want to conserve. It does not flourish as it once did in the United States because, among other reasons, democracy and industrialism have swept so much more powerfully, abruptly, and successfully over the American scene than they have over any other country of the West. While John Adams could be a conservative in the style of Burke and serve as president of the United States, his real and spiritual descendants—Henry Adams, Brooks Adams, Irving Babbitt, Ralph Adams Cram, Paul Elmer More, and, more recently, Russell Kirk—have been cast, as Kirk himself has admitted ruefully, in "the role of Don Quixote."

At its present stage of development, this conservatism is prepared to defend most of the values and institutions of the West. The conservatism of Burke, as it is proclaimed in the writings of his political and intellectual heirs, is full of doubts about the goodness and equality of men, the pos-

sibilities of progress, and the wisdom of the majority—that is to say, about the democratic dogma —but it has long since accepted constitutional democracy as the only viable alternative to the totalitarianisms of Right and Left. The Burkean conservative has learned to suppress his persistent antidemocratic urges and to give new definitions, and thus a new influence, to such cherished concepts as tradition, order, and aristocracy. It must be remembered that he draws his inspiration from the Whiggish Burke, not from the reactionary Joseph de Maistre; his concern is ordered liberty, not order pure, simple, and at any cost. If he is a democrat by chance rather than choice and is gripped by a mood of pessimism rather than optimism about the prospects of democracy, he is nonetheless a democrat.

Whether as a pattern of personal behavior, a cluster of social attitudes and prejudices, a force in the realm of politics, or an enveloping way of life and thought, whether as a phenomenon to be found on display by individuals, classes, interests, sections, parties, or even entire nations, conservatism bids well to be a major force in the latter part of the twentieth century. Even as great winds of social change sweep across the world and make it more difficult for men to think and act as conservatives, the desire to discipline change, if no longer to arrest it, becomes, paradoxically, an ever more powerful urge. If conservatives can no longer afford to repeat after Lord Falkland that "when it is not necessary to change, it is necessary not to change" (White [1950] 1957, p. 127), or after Samuel Johnson that "most schemes of political improvement are very laughable things" (Rossiter 1962, p. 51), they can at least insist, in the admonishing words of Disraeli, that those men who would pile change upon change and reform upon reform be properly deferential to "the manners, the customs, the laws, the traditions of the people" (White [1950] 1957, p. 127). It is their task to prove to an always doubting world that conservatism is an essential part of any pattern of ordered liberty.

CLINTON ROSSITER

[*See also* LIBERALISM; PERSONALITY, POLITICAL; RADICALISM; *and the biography of* BURKE.]

BIBLIOGRAPHY

For an introduction to conservatism as a behavioral phenomenon, see the many references in Bassett 1952. *Also consult* Adorno et al. 1950, *in conjunction with* Christie & Jahoda 1954; McClosky 1958, *with attention to the comments of* Kendall 1958 *and* Frisch 1958; *and* Rokeach 1960. *For histories of conservatism as a political and cultural phenomenon, see* Kirk 1953; Auerbach 1959; Graubard 1961; *and* Viereck 1956.

For modern classics of philosophical conservatism, see Eliot 1939; Oakeshott 1962; Strauss 1953; Lippmann 1955; *and* Ortega y Gasset 1930.

For sympathetic modern expressions of the conservatism of Burke, see Kirk 1956; Viereck 1949; White 1950; Cecil 1912; *and* Hogg 1947.

For general studies of conservatism and social science, see Nisbet 1952; Huntington 1957; Mannheim 1953; *and* Rossiter 1962. *The last has an extensive bibliography on pages 310–327.*

ADORNO, T. W. et al. 1950 *The Authoritarian Personality.* American Jewish Committee, Social Studies Series, No. 3. New York: Harper.

AUERBACH, MORTON 1959 *The Conservative Illusion.* New York: Columbia Univ. Press.

BASSETT, T. D. SEYMOUR (bibliographer) 1952 Radicalism and Conservatism. Pages 368–375 in Donald D. Egbert and Stow Persons (editors), *Socialism and American Life.* Volume 2: Bibliography; Descriptive and Critical. Princeton Studies in American Civilization, No. 4. Princeton Univ. Press.

BURKE, EDMUND (1790) 1955 *Reflections on the Revolution in France.* New York: Liberal Arts.

CECIL, HUGH R. H. 1912 *Conservatism.* London: Williams & Norgate.

CHRISTIE, RICHARD; and JAHODA, MARIE (editors) 1954 *Studies in the Scope and Method of* The Authoritarian Personality. Glencoe, Ill.: Free Press.

ELIOT, T. S. (1939) 1940 *The Idea of a Christian Society.* New York: Harcourt.

FRISCH, MORTON J. 1958 On McClosky's "Conservatism and Personality." *American Political Science Review* 52:1108–1111.

GRAUBARD, STEPHEN R. 1961 *Burke, Disraeli and Churchill: The Politics of Perseverance.* Cambridge, Mass.: Harvard Univ. Press.

HOGG, QUINTIN M. (LORD HAILSHAM) 1947 *The Case for Conservatism.* London: Penguin.

HUNTINGTON, SAMUEL P. 1957 Conservatism as Ideology. *American Political Science Review* 51:454–473.

KENDALL, WILLMOORE 1958 Comment on McClosky's "Conservatism and Personality." *American Political Science Review* 52:506–510.

KIRK, RUSSELL (1953) 1960 *The Conservative Mind: From Burke to Eliot.* 3d ed. Chicago: Regnery. → First published under the title *The Conservative Mind: From Burke to Santayana.*

KIRK, RUSSELL 1956 *Beyond the Dreams of Avarice: Essays of a Social Critic.* Chicago: Regnery.

LIPPMANN, WALTER 1955 *Essays in the Public Philosophy.* Boston: Little.

McCLOSKY, HERBERT 1958 Conservatism and Personality. *American Political Science Review* 52:27–45.

MANNHEIM, KARL (1922–1940) 1953 *Essays on Sociology and Social Psychology.* Edited by Paul Kecskemeti. London: Routledge.

NISBET, ROBERT A. 1952 Conservatism and Sociology. *American Journal of Sociology* 58:167–175.

OAKESHOTT, MICHAEL 1962 *Rationalism in Politics and Other Essays.* New York: Basic Books.

ORTEGA Y GASSET, JOSÉ (1930) 1961 *The Revolt of the Masses.* London: Allen & Unwin. → First published as *La rebelión de las masas.*

ROKEACH, MILTON 1960 *The Open and Closed Mind: Investigations Into the Nature of Belief Systems and Personality Systems.* New York: Basic Books.

ROSSITER, CLINTON 1962 *Conservatism in America: The Thankless Persuasion.* 2d ed., rev. New York: Knopf. → The first edition was published in 1955.

STRAUSS, LEO 1953 *Natural Right and History.* Univ. of Chicago Press.

VIERECK, PETER 1949 *Conservatism Revisited: Revolt Against Revolt.* New York: Scribner.

VIERECK, PETER 1956 *Conservatism From John Adams to Churchill.* Princeton, N.J.: Van Nostrand.

WHITE, REGINALD J. (editor) (1950) 1957 *The Conservative Tradition.* New York Univ. Press.

CONSTANCY, PERCEPTUAL
See under PERCEPTION.

CONSTITUENCY
See APPORTIONMENT; ELECTIONS; REPRESENTATION.

CONSTITUTIONAL LAW

The articles under this heading deal with the major substantive concerns of American constitutional law. For broader aspects of these topics see JUDICIAL PROCESS; JUDICIARY; PUBLIC LAW. *A guide to related articles appears under* LAW.

I. INTRODUCTION	C. Herman Pritchett
II. DISTRIBUTION OF POWERS	John P. Roche
III. CIVIL LIBERTIES	Robert G. McCloskey
IV. CIVIL RIGHTS	Milton R. Konvitz

I
INTRODUCTION

Constitutional law is law derived from, related to, or interpretive of a constitution. The term may in fact be used synonymously with constitution, since the function of a constitution is to provide the basic law for a governmental regime. But it is more common, at least in governments with written constitutions, for the term constitution to refer to the actual text of the basic document, while constitutional law connotes the constitution as interpreted and applied by the organs of government and as elaborated and rationalized by scholarly commentators.

Every regime must have an organizational framework, an agreed division of responsibilities among public instrumentalities, and a system of definitions of individual rights and status in the community. In a traditional society these arrangements and understandings are established by custom, but in more modern societies they are subject, through a process of conscious choice, to determination or revision by the policy-making institutions of government. These determinations have, since the adoption of the American and French constitutions toward the close of the eighteenth century, generally been codified in a comprehensive written document that has status superior to ordinary statute law and that can be amended only by a special legislative procedure.

In England, however, it has proved possible to proceed on into the twentieth century without any systematic codification of the rules of the political system. Constitutional law in England consequently cannot be clearly distinguished from other public law, since it has no superior legal authority; and any constitutional practice, even the most fundamental, can be overridden or revised by act of Parliament. A treatise on English constitutional law is simply a treatment of all the written and unwritten law generally considered essential to the operation of the governmental system.

Where, as is now generally the case, a written constitutional instrument is in existence, constitutional law is a formal category of law defined by the scope and provisions of the document. Any matter covered in the constitution, even arrangements of slight general importance, takes on the stature of constitutional law. Conversely, matters not covered in the constitution, no matter how important—such as political parties not being included in the U.S. constitution—are not subjects of constitutional law.

Responsibility for interpretation

Where a written constitution provides the foundation for a political regime, the principles of constitutional law for that regime are derived by interpretation of the language of the document; these interpretations are then applied in making governmental decisions and settling constitutional controversies. Some constitutional language is so specific that little interpretation is required, as, for example, the provision that the U.S. president "shall hold his office during the term of four years." But most constitutional language leaves room for varying views as to its meaning, and such provisions as "due process of law" or "freedom of speech" or "unreasonable searches and seizures" can never be applied without making a choice among alternative interpretations.

Whose responsibility is it to interpret a written constitution and authoritatively to declare constitutional law? An important part of this function falls to the executive branch, which must inevitably and continually interpret the constitution in making decisions on the use of executive power. In 1841 a U.S. president died in office for the first time. The language of the constitution left it unclear whether it was the "office," or only the "powers

and duties" of the office which devolved on the vice-president. This important constitutional question had to be determined by the then vice-president, John Tyler, who, after some initial hesitation, decided that he was actually president and not simply vice-president acting as president. This view was quickly accepted as the constitutional law on presidential succession.

Congress also must continuously construe the constitution as a guide to action. For example, the constitution authorizes the president to make treaties, "by and with the advice and consent of the Senate." George Washington assumed that this provision meant that he should sit down with the senators and get their advice on treaties while they were being negotiated, but when he went to the Senate for this purpose, the senators preferred not to discuss the matter in his presence and voted to refer it to a committee. Washington had no choice but to withdraw, yielding to the Senate's interpretation of "advice and consent," and no subsequent president has ever sought to repeat this tactic.

These two instances indicate how it is possible for the executive and the legislature to make binding interpretations of their own respective powers under a constitution. In fact, it was argued by many during the early years of the American republic that each branch of government should be the authoritative interpreter of all those provisions dealing with its own status and powers. However, this tripartite theory of constitutional interpretation was strongly challenged by Justice Marshall in the 1803 case of *Marbury* v. *Madison* (1 Cranch 137), where he asserted the primacy of judicial interpretation of the constitution.

In the Marbury case the Supreme Court declined to enforce a statute duly enacted by Congress because, as Marshall interpreted the act, it was contrary to the constitution. The judicial power to declare acts of Congress unconstitutional is not explicitly stated in the constitution, and the argument as to whether the drafters intended the Court to have such power has never been entirely settled. Some of the major battles of American politics have resulted from legislative or executive resistance to the Court's interpretations, and notable efforts have been made to deny the supremacy of judicial views on constitutional interpretation. Both Andrew Jackson in his veto of the Bank Bill in 1832 and Abraham Lincoln in his first inaugural address took this position.

In spite of such opposition, the Supreme Court's qualifications to act as pre-eminent interpreter of the constitution have been generally accepted. The Court has minimized resistance to its role by adopting rules of self-restraint, which keep it from passing on certain constitutional questions of a "political" nature, and has generally been deferential toward the constitutional interpretations by the president and Congress. It has seldom asserted a constitutional position that challenged a dominant popular opinion, although there have been such "self-inflicted wounds" as the Dred Scott decision in 1857 and the invalidation of the income tax in 1895.

During the twentieth century the Court's most serious miscalculations on constitutional issues came in 1935 and 1936, when it declared a number of New Deal statutes unconstitutional. President Roosevelt was unable to get through Congress legislation authorizing him to appoint additional justices who would support the New Deal; but in 1937 the Court itself reversed its position, thus terminating the dispute. Two decades later the Court's constitutional views again became the center of controversy, primarily on the issue of racial segregation in the public schools, but also on certain national security issues in 1957, on legislative apportionment in 1962, and on the problem of religion in the public schools in 1962 and 1963.

The enormous prestige of the United States Supreme Court has helped to popularize judicial review of legislation and judicial supremacy in constitutional interpretation. Prior to World War II it was primarily in federal systems within the British Commonwealth—notably Canada and Australia—that courts with constitutional responsibilities somewhat comparable to the U.S. Supreme Court were found. However, following World War II constitutional courts were established in West Germany, Italy, India, and elsewhere.

Principles of interpretation

Wherever the process of constitutional interpretation goes on, it must be guided by some more or less articulate theory about the extraction of meaning from constitutional language. The interpreter cannot merely insist that the constitution means whatever he wants it to mean, or at least he cannot admit such an approach to the interpretative process. For the essence of constitutional purpose is to establish a degree of certainty, to impose limitations that will affect all alike, and to give effect to rules that are external to the value system of the interpreter. Various approaches to the establishment of stable constitutional meanings have been proposed.

First, it may be contended that the constitution should mean what its framers meant it to mean. In the United States it is a rare constitutional debate in which someone does not appeal to "the intention of the framers." Thus, when the question is raised whether reciting prayers in public schools is an "establishment of religion," it will be argued by some that this depends upon what the members of the first Congress meant by this phrase when they were drafting the first amendment. In the case of some provisions, the purpose of the drafters may seem reasonably clear from the language of the document or the historical data. But generally this is not true. Constitutional language is always the product of group effort and compromise and may be deliberately chosen to bridge over differences of opinion. The intentions involved are the intentions of many individuals who participated to a greater or lesser degree and at various stages in the process of constitutional draftsmanship and subsequent ratification. The proceedings of the Constitutional Convention are known largely through the incomplete notes taken by James Madison. Some of the men who participated in drafting the constitution were in wide disagreement about its intention within a few years.

Because individual and group intentions are difficult to determine, a second theory of constitutional interpretation proposes concentration on word meanings. As Justice Oliver Wendell Holmes put it, "We ask, not what this man meant, but what those words would mean in the mouth of a normal speaker of English, using them in the circumstances in which they were used" ([1885–1918] 1952, p. 204). This method employs somewhat narrower lexicographic skills as compared with the social historicism on which the first method relies. It is more rigorously confined by the document itself and more closely related to the processes by which the written instruments of private law are construed.

An alternative to these two basically historical methods of determining constitutional meaning is the approach of logical analysis, which was heavily used by Chief Justice Marshall in his great decisions. In *Marbury* v. *Madison*, for example, Marshall cites no judicial decisions to support his arguments and, although referring to "original intention," makes no effort to quote contemporaneous evidence or opinion. His argument is primarily an exercise in logic. "It seems only necessary to recognize certain principles," he says, "supposed to have been long and well established, to decide [the case]." The major principle is that the constitution is the supreme law of the land. The Supreme Court has taken an oath to uphold the constitution. The conclusion logically follows that when an act of Congress conflicts with the superior law, the Supreme Court cannot enforce it, but must declare it null and void.

This position has been so long accepted that the

logic supporting it may seem unassailable. But it is equally logical to argue that the constitution is the supreme law of the land, and since the president has taken an oath to support the constitution he cannot enforce a Supreme Court decision that conflicts with the constitution, but must declare it null and void. The problem is simply not one to which logic can guarantee a correct answer. The limitations on the contribution of logic can be made clearer by stating a part of Marshall's argument as a syllogism.

Major premise: A law repugnant to the constitution is void.

Minor premise: This law is repugnant to the constitution.

Conclusion: This law is void.

Assuming the validity of the major premise, the soundness of the conclusion depends upon whether the minor premise is factually true. But logic cannot tell us whether a particular law is repugnant to the constitution. That is a matter of informed opinion and judgment. Justice Holmes, in one of his most famous passages from *The Common Law* ([1881] 1963, p. 5) disparaged the logical approach: "The life of the law has not been logic: it has been experience. The felt necessities of the time, the prevalent moral and political theories, intuitions of public policy, avowed or unconscious, even the prejudices which judges share with their fellow-men, have had a good deal more to do than the syllogism in determining the rules by which men should be governed."

It seems clear that no one rule of constitutional interpretation can be asserted to be the proper or sole approach to constitutional understanding. A constitution is more a political than a legal document. Consequently, all of the factors that go into the formation of divergent political preferences will also be operative in the minds of constitutional interpreters, be they executives, legislators, or judges. How a constitution will be read depends in large part upon the men who are doing the reading and how the world looks to them. The constitutional system is not separate from the political system, but a necessary part of it, performing the vital function of giving order and structure to the processes of policy formation. Holmes put the conception of a "living" constitution into eloquent language when he wrote:

. . . when we are dealing with words that also are a constituent act, like the Constitution of the United States, we must realize that they have called into life a being the development of which could not have been foreseen completely by the most gifted of its begetters.

It was enough for them to realize or to hope that they had created an organism; it has taken a century and has cost their successors much sweat and blood to prove that they created a nation. The case before us must be considered in the light of our whole experience and not merely in that of what was said a hundred years ago. (*Missouri* v. *Holland*, 252 U.S. 416, 1920)

Stability and change

The central problem in the development of a system of constitutional law is, as Holmes suggests, to recognize the need for adapting and changing to meet new circumstances, while preserving the basic values of the constitutional system. In a world growing constantly more crowded and complex with new ideas, new technical developments, new ways of living, new standards of social responsibility, and new world crises, the pressure on constitutional rules established to meet the different conditions of an earlier day will inevitably force their revision or abandonment.

The most obvious method of adapting constitutional law to changed conditions is to replace the old constitution with a new one. When an existing political system is overthrown, the new holders of power customarily seek to organize and legitimize their regime by the adoption of a new constitution. It is an index to the political instability of France that it has had 15 constitutions since the Revolution. American states also adopt new constitutions often, but not because of political upheaval. State constitutions tend to be very long and detailed, regulating the minutiae of the state and local governmental system, and can become obsolete quite rapidly. Periodically, therefore, states find it more expedient to draft a new constitution than to attempt to patch up the old one.

More commonly, the process of constitutional adaptation is achieved by amendment, interpretation, and custom. The drafters of the U.S. constitution were the first to recognize the need for making provision within the document itself for its own revision. The presence of the amending clause was one of the factors that led Thomas Jefferson, originally inclined to oppose the constitution, to decide in its favor.

The method of amending the constitution is usually more difficult than the passage of normal legislation, although this is not true in some countries, such as New Zealand and the Republic of South Africa. The arrangements for amending the U.S. constitution, requiring approval by two-thirds of each house of Congress and three-fourths of the states, have on occasion been criticized as too difficult. Following the Civil War amendments (thirteenth, fourteenth, and fifteenth), there was a period of more than forty years during which the constitution appeared unamendable, in spite of strong pressure for revision to meet the problems of a rapidly expanding economy. But between 1913 and 1933 six amendments were added to the constitution, and the experience with the eighteenth (prohibition) amendment showed that it was even possible for a small but dedicated pressure group to exploit the amending machinery.

Article 89 of the French constitution provides for amendment of the constitution by vote of parliament. In 1962, however, President de Gaulle ignored this method and submitted to a popular referendum an amendment providing for election of the president by popular vote instead of by limited suffrage. In Australia proposed amendments, after passage by each house of Parliament, must be approved by a popular referendum throughout Australia and also by a majority vote in four of the six states. The Canadian constitution (British North America Act of 1867) contains no provision for its own amendment; consequently, constitutional change has required recourse to the original source of the constitution, the British Parliament.

The amending power has been less important in the development of the U.S. constitution than has the previously discussed process of interpretation. The document, drafted in 1787, could scarcely have met the needs of a world power in the twentieth century unless it had been construed with some flexibility. It was one of John Marshall's greatest achievements that he saw the need for a broad construction of the constitution. "We must never forget, that it is a constitution we are expounding," he said, one that is "intended to endure for ages to come, and consequently, to be adapted to the various crises of human affairs" (*McCulloch* v. *Maryland*, 4 Wheaton 316, 1819).

Revising a constitution by interpretation does create both theoretical and practical problems. Justice Frankfurter once suggested that "nothing new can be put into the Constitution except through the amendatory process. Nothing old can be taken out without the same process" (*Ullmann* v. *United States*, 350 U.S. 422, 1956). It must be presumed that he was using this rather extreme method of warning that if a constitution is to fulfill its function of acting as a stabilizing and controlling influence in a political system, the interpretations given to it must be maintained with some measure of continuity, and the agencies that interpret and apply the constitution must feel under some compulsion to accept the views announced by their predecessors.

Regard for precedent is, of course, one of the foundation stones of legal systems generally, applicable in both constitutional and statutory interpretation. However, the principle of *stare decisis*, necessary as it is in the settlement of normal legal controversies, presents unusual difficulties when applied to constitutional meanings. If a constitutional interpretation, once announced, can be modified only by constitutional amendment, an impossible burden is thrown on the amending machinery. The U.S. Supreme Court has, therefore, on occasion overruled its earlier decisions. One of the most noteworthy instances of the overruling of a prior constitutional position occurred in 1954 in *Brown* v. *Board of Education* (347 U.S. 483). In an 1896 decision the Supreme Court had held that segregated facilities for Negroes were not a violation of the equal protection clause of the fourteenth amendment, provided they were the "equal" of the facilities provided for white persons. But when the Court had to decide in 1954 whether racial segregation was permissible in the public schools, it held unanimously that "we cannot turn the clock back . . . to 1896. . . . We must consider public education in the light of its full development and its present place in American life throughout the Nation." Such consideration convinced the Court that the rule of "separate but equal" was no longer compatible with the concept of equal protection under the laws, and consequently it was abandoned.

The study of constitutional law

Traditionally, students of constitutional law have concerned themselves with collecting and analyzing constitutional interpretations and organizing and rationalizing them into a coherent system. Some constitutional commentators gain such prestige by the force of their reasoning that they themselves become authoritative sources of constitutional law. Thomas Cooley's *A Treatise on Constitutional Limitations* (1868), which appeared in the same year the fourteenth amendment was adopted, so effectively argued for the doctrine of implied constitutional limitation on the powers of American states that it was a powerful force toward the stricter judicial review of state legislative action that characterized the latter part of the nineteenth century.

In the twentieth century the general constitutional commentary has tended to give way to treatises on the constitutional status of particular institutions, such as Corwin's *The President: Office and Powers* (1940) or Jennings' *Parliament* (1940). There have also been frequent analyses of the application and interpretation of specific constitutional provisions, such as Chafee's study of the first amendment in *Free Speech in the United States* (1941). Constitutional law has been taught in U.S. colleges and law schools almost entirely by use of Supreme Court decisions collected in casebooks, reflecting the degree to which constitutional interpretation is monopolized by the courts.

Behavioral trends in the social sciences have had a significant impact on the study of constitutional law. As early as 1913, Charles Beard argued that economic advantage had motivated the framers of the constitution. Later, prominent political scientists such as Corwin and Robert Cushman, biographers of Supreme Court justices such as Swisher (1930) and Mason (1956), and the school of legal realists headed by Jerome Frank (1930) all emphasized the influence of judicial personality on constitutional interpretation. Finally, in the 1950s, judicial behavior, particularly the decision making of the Supreme Court, began to be subjected to study through a whole armory of sociological and psychological tools, including voting bloc analysis, small group theory, Guttman scaling, vector analysis, and game theory (Schubert 1963).

C. HERMAN PRITCHETT

[*See also* PRESIDENTIAL GOVERNMENT.]

BIBLIOGRAPHY

ANSON, WILLIAM R. (1886–1892) 1922–1935 *The Law and Custom of the Constitution.* 2 vols., 5th ed. Oxford: Clarendon. → Volume 1: *Parliament.* Volume 2: *The Crown.*

BEARD, CHARLES A. (1913) 1961 *An Economic Interpretation of the Constitution of the United States.* New York: Macmillan.

CHAFEE, ZECHARIAH, JR. 1941 *Free Speech in the United States.* Cambridge, Mass.: Harvard Univ. Press. → Supersedes Chafee's *Freedom of Speech,* 1920.

COOLEY, THOMAS M. (1868) 1927 *A Treatise on Constitutional Limitations Which Rest Upon the Legislative Power of the States of the American Union.* 2 vols., 8th ed. Boston: Little.

CORWIN, EDWARD S. (1928–1929) 1959 *The "Higher Law" Background of American Constitutional Law.* Ithaca, N.Y.: Cornell Univ. Press. → First published in the *Harvard Law Review.*

CORWIN, EDWARD S. (1940) 1957 *The President: Office and Powers.* 4th rev. ed. New York Univ. Press.

DICEY, ALBERT V. (1885) 1961 *Introduction to the Study of the Law of the Constitution.* 10th ed. With an Introduction by E. C. S. Wade. London: Macmillan; New York: St. Martins. → First published as *Lectures Introductory to the Study of the Law of the Constitution.*

DOUGLAS, WILLIAM O. 1956 *We the Judges: Studies in American and Indian Constitutional Law From Marshall to Mukherjea.* New York: Doubleday.

FRANK, JEROME (1930) 1949 *Law and the Modern Mind.* New York: Coward-McCann.

FREUND, PAUL A. 1961 *The Supreme Court of the United States: Its Business, Purposes, and Performance.* Cleveland: World.

HOLMES, OLIVER WENDELL (1881) 1963 *The Common Law.* Cambridge, Mass.: Harvard Univ. Press.

HOLMES, OLIVER WENDELL (1885–1918) 1952 *Collected Legal Papers.* Edited by Harold J. Laski. New York: Smith.

JENNINGS, WILLIAM IVOR (1940) 1957 *Parliament.* 2d ed. Cambridge Univ. Press.

MCWHINNEY, EDWARD (1956) 1960 *Judicial Review in the English-speaking World.* 2d ed. Univ. of Toronto Press.

MASON, ALPHEUS T. 1956 *Harlan Fiske Stone: Pillar of the Law.* New York: Viking.

MURPHY, WALTER F. 1962 *Congress and the Court: A Case Study in the American Political Process.* Univ. of Chicago Press.

PRITCHETT, C. HERMAN (1948) 1963 *The Roosevelt Court: A Study in Judicial Politics and Values, 1937–1947.* New York: Octagon Books.

PRITCHETT, C. HERMAN 1959 *The American Constitution.* New York: McGraw-Hill.

SCHUBERT, GLENDON (editor) 1963 *Judicial Decisionmaking.* International Yearbook of Political Behavior Research, Vol. 4. New York: Free Press.

SCHUBERT, GLENDON (editor) 1964 *Judicial Behavior: A Reader in Theory and Research.* Chicago: Rand McNally.

STORY, JOSEPH (1833) 1891 *Commentaries on the Constitution of the United States.* 2 vols., 5th ed. Boston: Little.

SWISHER, CARL B. (1930) 1963 *Stephen J. Field: Craftsman of the Law.* Hamden, Conn.: Shoe String Press.

WARREN, CHARLES (1923) 1937 *The Supreme Court in United States History.* 2 vols., rev. ed. Boston: Little.

II

DISTRIBUTION OF POWERS

From the beginnings of political speculation, much time and theoretical effort have been assigned to the demarcation and definition of jurisdictions between competing elites within various societies. While the bases of jurisdiction have shifted over the centuries, one can hear in contemporary Israel echoes of Old Testament disputes between kings and prophets, and in contemporary America the rhetoric of states' rights has archetypal resemblances to the polemical literature of the early modern struggle between royal centralists and feudal autonomists. And although the external form of modern disputes is radically different from earlier jurisdictional disputes, the key issue has not altered in two thousand years, namely, where does the final jurisdiction to define jurisdictions rest?

This issue has always been, and remains today, the crux of the matter; in the vocabulary of modern politics it is known, of course, as the question of sovereignty. Even the most ultramontane pope never denied the existence of the *imperium,* the emperor's sector of jurisdiction. Nor did the most ambitious of the Holy Roman emperors ever assert that the *sacerdotium,* the ecclesiastical jurisdiction, was nonexistent. But a struggle raged for centuries that, although seemingly centered on the scope of the respective jurisdictions, was in fact directed to the antecedent problem of ultimate determination of the appropriate forum for settlement of jurisdictional disputes. Archbishop Thomas à Becket's argument in his confrontation with Henry II in 1164 over the question of the criminous clerk (Pollock & Maitland [1895] 1952, vol. 1, pp. 447–457) was thus at base analogous to the logic of the Virginia and Kentucky resolutions of 1798–1799; like the archbishop, Thomas Jefferson and James Madison denied their opponents the right to define their own jurisdictions.

Every political community larger than the Greek *polis* has been faced with the problem of distributing power, at least in functional terms. Subgovernments—provinces, exarchates, shires, communes, etc.—have been established for purposes of administrative convenience. Other varieties of subgovernment have originated from more complex origins, for example, Huguenot autonomy in France as a consequence of the Edict of Nantes, Scottish privileges under the Act of Union with England, Turkish communal rights as stipulated in the Cypriot constitution. In this context, what problems arise do so as a result of ambiguity in the relationship of the peripheral units to the center. When sovereignty, i.e., the final power to define jurisdictions, clearly resides in the center, we have what is commonly called a "unitary" system. In France, for example, the authority of *départements, arrondissements,* and *communes*—the units of subgovernment—is clearly subject to determination by the central government. This does not prevent occasional conflicts: communist-dominated *communes* from time to time invoked the wrath of the minister of the interior by banning hydrogen bombs from their territory, passing resolutions against the Algerian war, or renaming streets after communist heroes, but the results contributed more in the way of publicity than jurisprudence. The offending local council, in such instances, is simply dissolved by order of the central government.

At the other end of the spectrum we find the confederation, which is characterized by the fact that the powers of the central government are subject to definition by the peripheral units. A classic instance of this type of government was the United States under the Articles of Confederation; a modern example is Switzerland, where residual power still—in theory if not always in practice—rests with the component cantons.

Between these two polar positions can be found a huge variety of intermediate forms of which the most significant for our purpose is American federalism. For almost two centuries political theorists have been attempting to define "federalism," and have had uniformly disastrous results because in analytical terms federalism is an institutionalized technique of question begging. It is, to put the matter differently, an effort to exorcise sovereignty from the political sector. Since definition is therefore understandably elusive, we shall have to settle for a description drawn from K. C. Wheare, which suggests that federalism is a system in which two levels of government operate within the same geographical limits and neither has the power to destroy the other. [*See* FEDERALISM.]

However, before turning to a historical examination of the distribution of powers between the American national government and the states, it would be advantageous to define the other major dimension of the distribution of power: the relationship of various agencies of government to one another—or, in the American context, the issue of the separation of powers within the national government. Again, the problem is one that has been canvassed since the time of Aristotle (*Politics* 1298a40), although the form that the "separation of powers" took among political theorists through the eighteenth century was almost totally irrelevant to the American innovation. From Polybius and Cicero through Montesquieu, the "separation of powers" involved the allocation of governmental functions to orders of the realm or to estates, with the ideal result of a mixed government or "polity." Thus, Thomas Aquinas (*Summa theologica* Quaestio CV), discussing the "right ordering of power in a principality," argued that the best form of constitution incorporated a "judicious admixture of the kingdom . . . of aristocracy . . . and of democracy."

This was the essence of medieval constitutionalism—the conciliar movement, indeed, attempted with ephemeral success symbolized in the *Frequens* decree, issued in 1417 by the Council of Constance, to apply this formula to the government of the church—and it provided the foundation for Montesquieu's famous chapter in *The Spirit of the Laws* (1748): "On the Constitution of England." To state the point differently, the tripartite division of the United States constitution was not intended to balance the authority of the "one, the few, and the many"; it was a functional differentiation between governmental organs. John Locke's notion of the "separation of powers" was founded on another premise, but one equally irrelevant to

American constitutional law. It is true that Locke identified a threefold division of powers ("The Second Treatise of Government" 1690), but he never asserted the equivalence of his three branches: his "executive" was a thoroughly dependent figure (§152) and, so far as domestic jurisdiction was concerned, was little more than an agent of the "supreme" legislative power (§149). And his third division, the "federative," was indeed given wide authority and prerogative—but only for the purpose of conducting foreign relations (§147). The judiciary was attached to the executive.

What then are the origins of the American doctrine of the "separation of powers"? What did this doctrine involve in practice? By what means and to what degree has it been incorporated in American constitutional law? These are the issues that will concern us in the last section of this analysis. First, however, we shall examine the division of powers in the American federal system, that is, the relationship between the national government and the states.

The division of powers

The American federal system has been widely acclaimed as a great, even original, contribution to political science, and it has provided the model for many subsequent governments. Federalism has always appealed to spokesmen for vested minority interests—whether religious, ethnic, or economic—who are seeking institutional guarantees against the power of a majority (Riker 1964). Nowhere has the connection between the integrity of the peripheral jurisdiction, i.e., the states, and the privileges and property of a national minority—slaveholders—been expressed more cogently than in John C. Calhoun's *A Disquisition on Government* (1851). Today we can discern variations on the Calhoun theme in the rhetoric of the Cypriot Turks, the French Canadians, the Ceylonese Tamils, the Fijis (outnumbered on their ancestral islands by Indians), the Nigerian Yoruba—to name only a few instances.

The theory that underpins this adulation is that federalism provides a viable framework for the reconciliation of majority power and minority rights. In terms of the distribution of power, the model rests on two assumptions: first, the central government has a plenary jurisdiction over certain sectors of policy making; second, certain other sectors of decision making are reserved in equally plenary fashion to the peripheral units (states, provinces, ethnic or religious communities). Obviously, such a system requires a written constitution, and for our purposes it is irrelevant whether

residual power remains with the peripheral units (for example, U.S. constitution, article x of the bill of rights) or the center (for example, Canada under the provisions of the British North America Act of 1867).

In principle, then, an impenetrable wall is built between the jurisdiction of the center and the jurisdiction of the peripheral units. The nation as a whole exercises the necessary sovereignty to hold its place in the international community, while within the society the rights of minorities are protected from "nationalization." The character of the minorities may vary widely; in the United States—as in Australia—geographical prescription served as the justification for the establishment of the peripheral units: the previously self-governing units were integrated as the operating components of federalism. In Canada and the Union of South Africa, geography mixed with ethnic considerations (the French in Quebec, the Afrikaners in the Transvaal and Orange River Colony) supplied the rationale.

It has been suggested (McLaughlin 1932) that when the framers of the United States constitution met in Philadelphia in 1787, they found the theoretical and practical arguments for federalism overwhelming, largely as an outgrowth of their colonial experience. In their struggle with the British over the status of the colonies, American spokesmen developed a wide-ranging theory of American rights. However, it is hard to assert that the colonial experience provided a formula for the new federal experiment; on the contrary, it supplied full support for precisely the form of association that the Constitutional Convention destroyed: the Articles of Confederation. The essence of the colonial position vis-à-vis the British was that the Americans had the right to define the jurisdiction of king and parliament, i.e., the peripheral units defined the authority of the center, the very principle that later was incorporated into the Articles of Confederation. Curiously, then, when the framers set to work to limit the authority of the states (and the caprice of "Rogues Island"), the arguments they utilized were drawn from the British, not the American, arsenal. They were in search of sovereignty in the classic Hobbesian sense, and, with few exceptions, took a dim theoretical view of states' rights.

This may seem to be an eccentric interpretation, flying as it does in the face of conventional wisdom. However, it has the great merit of being solidly grounded on the proceedings in the Constitutional Convention (Roche [1952–1963] 1964, pp. 91–126), rather than on the a posteriori theoretical patina supplied by *The Federalist*. The views of "Publius" on the high merits of the constitution were analogous to a man's eulogies of a wife he had secretly been forced to marry: both James Madison and Alexander Hamilton had supported the establishment of a unitary system at the convention, but debates were secret and no significant record was published until after Madison's death in 1836. What had occurred at the convention was that a strong unitary system—the "Randolph Plan," prepared by Madison—which put the states completely at the mercy of the nation, was modified into what later became known as federalism. The latter was an improvisation that only subsequently was promoted into a political theory. In practical terms, it was a compromise between the unitary convictions of the delegates and their sense of political reality; the leading opponents of the Randolph Plan endorsed its goals but argued that it would be an act of political suicide to return to their constituent states with such a radical innovation. Thus the scope of national power over the peripheral units was cut down, the sectors of national jurisdiction stipulated, and the states given equal representation in the Senate. In the course of ratification, proponents of the new government were forced to promise a bill of rights as a further safeguard to the jurisdiction of the states.

When the constitution went into operation and the newly elected officials assembled in New York, there was nothing particularly lucid about federalism. The constitution was a model of studied ambiguity at certain key points, reflecting its authors' pragmatic notion that the best way to deal with sticky problems was to turn them over to the future unclarified. The institutions of the new republic were provided for, but even here a conflict in the convention had resulted in a semantic compromise: Congress was given the power to establish an independent federal judiciary (below the Supreme Court, which was explicitly created) but left with discretion to utilize inferior state judicial machinery for national purposes if it so chose. Yet the distribution of power within the national government was a model of clarity when compared with the relationship between the latter and the states.

An early dictionary, which Sir Ernest Barker was fond of quoting, defined a cello as a big violin and a violin as a small cello. The relationship between national and state powers under the constitution was a similar exercise in logical circularity. In the body of that document there was no discussion whatever of the distribution of power

between the center and the peripheral units; state objections led to the addition of the ninth and tenth amendments in 1791, but these did little more than restate the central ambiguity. Article IX announced that "the enumeration in the Constitution, of certain rights, shall not be construed to deny or disparage others retained by the people." Article X provided that "the powers not delegated to the United States by the Constitution, nor prohibited by it to the States, are reserved to the States respectively, or to the people."

In other words, the ninth and tenth amendments, like the constitution itself, ignored the crucial institutional question: How, and by whom, were jurisdictional conflicts between states and nation to be resolved? What was to be the truth-finding mechanism in this open-ended situation? The immediate answer is the United States Supreme Court, and although there is no direct evidence that the framers intended the Court to exercise this supervision over the distribution of powers (there was no recorded discussion of the problem in the Constitutional Convention), circumstantial evidence supports this contention. The Supreme Court's power to review both acts of Congress and state legislation was probably taken for granted; indeed, the notion of a written constitution containing limitations on states and nation carried with it a need for machinery of enforcement, and the Supreme Court seems to have been assigned this task *sub silentio*.

The constitution was hardly ten years old before the question of states' rights shook the new republic to its foundations. In a desperate effort to hold their slipping popularity, the Federalists, marshaled by Alexander Hamilton, attempted in 1798–1799 to cripple the Jeffersonians by national legislation, primarily in the Sedition Act of 1798, which was designed to muzzle the Jeffersonian press. The Jeffersonians lost the battle in Congress and then appealed to the courts to declare the Sedition Act unconstitutional as an intrusion on states' rights. The litigation never reached the Supreme Court, but at the circuit level the act was sustained as a legitimate exercise of congressional power. At this point, Jefferson and Madison realized that the rules had to be changed, that it was improper for an agency of the general government to have the right to assess the national jurisdiction, that, in Locke's phrase, "no one should be a judge in his own cause." The result was the Virginia and Kentucky resolutions of 1798–1799, the former prepared by Madison, the latter secretly drafted by Vice-president Jefferson, which attempted to reopen the whole issue of distribution of powers. These resolutions have served ever since as the intellectual fountainhead for states' rights formulations.

Jefferson put the question concisely:

. . . the several States composing the United States of America, are not united on the principle of unlimited submission to their general government; but that by compact . . . they constituted a general government for special purposes, delegated to that government certain definite powers, reserving each State to itself, the residuary mass of right to their own self-government; and that whensoever the general government assumes undelegated powers, its acts are unauthoritative, void, and of no force: . . . That the government created by this compact was not made the exclusive or final judge of the extent of the powers delegated to itself; . . . but that as in all other cases of compact among parties having no common Judge, *each party has an equal right to judge for itself, as well of infractions as of the mode and measure of redress.* (Kentucky resolutions, Nov. 16, 1798)

Thus began the states' rights tradition. In characteristic American fashion, it was an *ad hoc* response to political peril by the losing faction in national politics; Jefferson and Madison took a very dim view indeed of the logic of the Virginia and Kentucky resolutions when the latter were employed against the embargo of 1807 by Federalist state governments in New England (Levy 1963, pp. 93–141). Moreover, in a paradoxical fashion, Jefferson and Madison were engaged in precisely the behavior they were criticizing: their concept of "compact" made the states the final judges of the extent of the powers of the general government, i.e., made the states judges in "their own cause." Each side engaged in *petitio principii* by silently incorporating their conclusions in their premises: on the one hand, the centralist view was founded on the assumption that the national government was founded by "the people"; on the other, the states' rights position rested on the notion that the states as integral units of sovereignty had made a "compact." And history was ransacked by all hands to "prove" the validity of the respective cases —with what a historian must report as inconclusive results.

But the problems of Jefferson and Madison fade into insignificance when compared with the definitional crisis that precipitated the Civil War. This is not the place to examine the constitutional turmoil over slavery except to note that the crucial question was not juridical, but moral, and was thus insoluble by legal mechanisms. If one took for granted that a Negro slave was "property," then the injunction of the fifth amendment that no person "shall be deprived of life, liberty, or property, with-

out due process of law" stood as a massive barrier against national regulation of the South's "peculiar institution." If, in contrast, one assumed that a Negro slave was a "person," then slavery constituted an unconstitutional limitation on his life and liberty. *Pace* Chief Justice Taney's efforts in *Dred Scott* v. *Sanford* (60 U.S. 393, 1857), one does not settle this order of problem in a court of law.

The Union victory in the Civil War gave the compact theory its *coup de grâce*, and in *State of Texas* v. *White* (74 U.S. 700, 1869), the Supreme Court gave ideological approval to the work of Lincoln's armies. In constitutional terms, however, states' rights lived on and was from time to time extracted from the museum of antiquities as a device for limiting federal legislation deemed "radical" by a majority of the Supreme Court (see Corwin 1936; 1938; 1941). It is reasonable to argue that in the 1960s states' rights constituted no meaningful legal barrier to the exercise of national authority, and that the federal government operating in a national economy could reach any objective it wished through the exercise of the commerce power, the taxing power, or—as in the Civil Rights Act of 1964—a combination of the commerce power and the long-ignored jurisdiction provided by the fourteenth amendment.

Yet, curiously, to say this is not to assert that the United States has achieved a unitary form of government. Indeed, in net terms the substantive power of the states today is greater than it has ever been. What has occurred is a remarkable *de facto* distribution of power between states and nation (sometimes called "cooperative federalism"), in which the state governments exercise enormous autonomy. For many areas of public policy, for example, education, public welfare, urban renewal, road construction, federal funds are extensively provided to supplement local resources. In these areas the states are, in effect, "sovereign," provided they do not push their autonomy too hard or attempt to assert a theoretical basis for their jurisdiction. However, if state officials try to assert final power through gerrymanders, discriminatory practices in race relations, taxation of interstate commerce, the Supreme Court tends to reaffirm the principle of national supremacy. Moreover, since the states are the effective units of political party organization they often provide political obstacles to centralization that are far more effective than their constitutional position might indicate.

In short, the United States in a highly nontheoretical fashion has developed a relationship between the center and the peripheral units built around the operating principles of *de jure* national supremacy and *de facto* local autonomy. Most of the time this relationship works extremely well on the basis of a political consensus not to clarify issues of sovereignty but, rather, to get on with the business of governance.

The separation of powers

The doctrine of the separation of powers has occupied a distinguished position in the history of American constitutionalism. In its classic formulation the doctrine had two operating principles. The first was set forth by John Adams in article xxx of the Massachusetts constitution of 1780: "In the government of this commonwealth, the legislative department shall never exercise the executive and judicial powers, or either of them: the executive shall never exercise the legislative and judicial powers, or either of them: the judicial shall never exercise the legislative and executive powers, or either of them: to the end it may be a government of laws and not of men." The second, drawn from a maxim attributed to Bracton, announced that *delegata potestas non potest delegari*, that delegated powers could not be further delegated, for example, that authority delegated to Congress by article I of the constitution could not be passed on by the legislature to the president.

The difficulty with this doctrine, however, is that from the outset it was honored more in the breach than in the observance. The constitution of Massachusetts, which contained Adams' absolute interdict, also gave the governor a veto over legislation that could be overridden only by a two-thirds vote of the General Court. In other words, the governor of Massachusetts exercised immense "legislative" power. Elsewhere in the same document there was a provision that a number of "executive" officers (by our definition) would be "chosen annually by joint ballot of the senators and representatives in one room." All judicial appointments had to be approved by the Council, which was a curious hybrid of executive, legislative, and judicial powers chosen by joint ballot of the two houses. In sum, the Massachusetts paradigm of the separation of powers on close examination is a shambles of interlocking powers and overlapping jurisdictions.

Yet, if we examine Adams' handiwork rather than his rhetoric, we discover a principle of separation founded on the proposition that the executive, legislative, and judicial *institutions* should have autonomous constituencies. The governor was to be elected annually by the people as a whole; the legislature by geographical subdivisions of the commonwealth; and the judiciary was to hold tenure for life on good behavior. Adams was not, in other words, interested in separating powers in terms of their substantive content (executive, judicial, legislative) but divided authority among discrete agencies (governor, General Court, judiciary, Council), each of which exercised judicial, executive, and legislative jurisdictions. Conflict among these quasi-autonomous power centers, he believed, would prevent the growth of any centralized autocracy. The separation of powers, then, rested on political physics, not metaphysics.

The original Madison draft of the constitution, which served as the basis for discussion and modification at the convention, contained no trace of the separation of powers. All power was vested in a supreme legislature; the upper house was picked by the lower house; the president and judges were selected by both houses. Gradually over the summer of 1787 this centralist model was weakened, over the militant objections of Madison, Hamilton, and James Wilson, and in an *ad hoc* fashion the "separation of powers" (like "federalism") emerged from the compromises. Later, in the 47th *Federalist*, Madison observed that "the accumulation of all powers legislative, executive and judiciary in the same hands, . . . may justly be pronounced the very definition of tyranny" (Hamilton et al. [1788] 1961, p. 324). Later in the same essay he adopted John Adams' operational model, noting that the separation of powers did not mean that the "departments ought to have no *partial agency* in, or no *controul* over the acts of each other. [Montesquieu's] meaning, . . . can amount to no more than this, that where the *whole* power of one department is exercised by the same hands which possess the *whole* power of another department, the fundamental principles of a free constitution, are subverted" (*ibid.*, pp. 325–326).

Historically speaking, the doctrine of the separation of powers entered American constitutionalism as a fairly simple and matter-of-fact division of the agencies of the national government rather than as a subtle effort to differentiate powers in terms of their innate characteristics. The president exercised judicial power (pardons) and legislative power (the veto); the legislature undertook executive functions (approval of appointments, treaties) and judicial functions (amnesties); and the courts to a lesser degree dabbled in executive and legislative activities. Moreover, there is no empirical evidence to suggest that the maxim about delegated power not being subject to further delegation had any standing: the statutes of the first 20 years of the republic are full of laws delegating national authority to state institutions; state courts, for instance, were given the power to naturalize aliens and to handle a number of offenses against the laws of the United States.

There were a number of disputes in the early nineteenth century that touched marginally on the doctrine of the separation of powers. President Jackson, for example, justified his employment of the veto on policy grounds (his predecessors had felt that the veto should be reserved for legislation the chief executive believed to be unconstitutional) by asserting the full autonomy of the presidency. And, of course, a similar concept of institutional independence underlay Chief Justice Marshall's exercise of judicial review over acts of Congress. But a careful search of the precedents suggests that the separation of powers, although it occupied an honored position in the polemical literature, was not articulated as a serious principle of constitutional interpretation until the 1850s, when Justice Benjamin Curtis invoked it in two leading decisions.

Denying the practice of 60 years, Curtis asserted in *Cooley* v. *Board of Wardens of Port of Philadelphia* (53 U.S. 299, 1851) that "if the States were divested of the power to legislate on [interstate and foreign commerce] by the grant of the commercial power to Congress. . . Congress cannot regrant, or in any manner reconvey to the States that power." Suddenly *delegata potestas non potest delegari* attained constitutional status—and by ipse dixit: Curtis did not linger to justify his pronouncement. Nor did the justice stipulate the precise constitutional foundation for his views. Further reflection presumably indicated to him that a violation of the separation of powers fell afoul of the due-process clause of the fifth amendment; at least this was the thrust of his presentation in *Murray's Lessee et al.* v. *Hoboken Land and Improvement Co.* (59 U.S. 272, 1855). Ignoring Adams' model, Curtis attempted to define the separation of powers in terms of substance; embarking on an elaborate gloss on the *nature* of judicial authority, he rejected the time-honored operational definition of judicial power as that power exercised by judges.

It would be pointless to catalogue the subsequent instances where the separation of powers turned up as a *ratio decidendi* in Supreme Court litigation. What is important is to note that this doctrine became a major theoretical roadblock to the development of administrative law, regulatory commissions, and delegations of emergency authority to the president. The nub of the argument was that Congress could not delegate "legislative" or "ju-

dicial" power to administrative officers (whether located in the executive branch or in the so-called independent regulatory commissions)—a contention which, if accepted by the Court, would have destroyed the whole regulatory apparatus that developed in the wake of the industrial revolution and the growth of a national economy. An agency such as the Interstate Commerce Commission, for example, clearly fuses executive, legislative, and judicial power: it administers, it makes rules, and it engages in enforcement.

The Supreme Court, however, was seldom prepared to fortify this high ground. Instead, the justices devised various escape mechanisms from the logical chains of separation doctrine: on one hand, they found that the powers exercised by administrative bodies were not legislative and judicial, but "quasi-legislative" and "quasi-judicial" (see *Rathbun* v. *United States*, 295 U.S. 602, 1935); on the other, they held that when Congress delegated authority to various administrative instruments, this did not constitute delegation of "legislative power" if meticulous standards of administration were specified (see *J. W. Hampton Co.* v. *U.S.*, 276 U.S. 394, 1928)—it was merely an implementation of legislative power (Cushman 1941). Indeed, in 1934 the leading authority on the question, Edward S. Corwin, declared the doctrine of the separation of powers moribund (1934, p. 145).

Ironically, in 1935 the corpse arose from its bed and provided the Supreme Court with the basis for striking down the Oil Code promulgated under the National Industrial Recovery Act (*Panama Refining Co.* v. *Ryan*, 293 U.S. 539, 1934) and for several other subsequent judicial forays against the evils of the New Deal. But later decisions by the "Roosevelt Court," notably that reached in *U.S.* v. *Rock Royal Co-operative, Inc.* (307 U.S. 533, 1939), seem to have put this tumultuous spirit finally to rest. The closest the Supreme Court came to a separation-of-powers ruling in the years since 1941 was in *Sweezy* v. *New Hampshire* (354 U.S. 234, 1957), when Chief Justice Warren, while denying the applicability of the separation of powers, seemed to suggest that New Hampshire had violated due process of law by delegating to its attorney general plenary authority to act as a subcommittee of the state legislature.

To conclude, the separation of powers is thus back where it began in 1789 as an abstract affirmation of the independent constitutional existence of the president, the Congress, and the Supreme Court. And the notion that delegated power cannot be further delegated has been demolished by constitutional logic drawn from John Marshall: that congressional power where it exists is plenary, and that plenary jurisdiction includes the power to give power away. Limits on delegation do exist, but they are political, not constitutional, in character (Roche [1952–1963] 1964, pp. 127–161).

JOHN P. ROCHE

[*Directly related are the entries* FEDERALISM; PRESIDENTIAL GOVERNMENT. *Other relevant material may be found in* CENTRALIZATION AND DECENTRALIZATION; DELEGATION OF POWERS.]

BIBLIOGRAPHY

AMERICAN ASSEMBLY 1955 *The Forty-eight States: Their Tasks as Policy Makers and Administrators.* New York: Columbia Univ., School of Business.

BOWIE, ROBERT R.; and FRIEDRICH, CARL J. (editors) 1954 *Studies in Federalism.* Boston: Little.

CALHOUN, JOHN C. (1851) 1953 *A Disquisition on Government, and Selections From the Discourse.* New York: Liberal Arts Press. → Published posthumously.

CARPENTER, WILLIAM S. 1928 Separation of Powers in the Eighteenth Century. *American Political Science Review* 22:32–44.

CORWIN, EDWARD S. 1934 *The Twilight of the Supreme Court: A History of Our Constitutional Theory.* New Haven: Yale Univ. Press.

CORWIN, EDWARD S. (1936) 1962 *The Commerce Power Versus States Rights.* Gloucester, Mass.: Peter Smith.

CORWIN, EDWARD S. (1938) 1957 *Court Over Constitution: A Study of Judicial Review as an Instrument of Popular Government.* Gloucester, Mass.: Peter Smith.

CORWIN, EDWARD S. (1941) 1946 *Constitutional Revolution, Ltd.* Claremont, Calif.: Pomona College.

CUSHMAN, ROBERT E. 1941 *The Independent Regulatory Commissions.* New York: Oxford Univ. Press.

HAMILTON, ALEXANDER; MADISON, JAMES; and JAY, JOHN (1788) 1961 *The Federalist.* Edited with introduction and notes by Jacob E. Cooke. Middletown, Conn.: Wesleyan Univ. Press.

LEVY, LEONARD W. 1963 *Jefferson and Civil Liberties: The Darker Side.* Cambridge, Mass.: Harvard Univ. Press.

LOCKE, JOHN (1690) 1964 The Second Treatise of Government: An Essay Concerning the True Original, Extent, and End of Civil Government. Pages 283–446 in John Locke, *Two Treatises of Government.* Cambridge Univ. Press.

MCLAUGHLIN, ANDREW C. 1932 *Foundations of American Constitutionalism.* New York Univ. Press. → A paperback edition was published in 1961 by Fawcett.

MACMAHON, ARTHUR W. (editor) (1955) 1962 *Federalism: Mature and Emergent.* New York: Russell.

MCWHINNEY, EDWARD 1962 *Comparative Federalism: States' Rights and National Power.* Univ. of Toronto Press.

MONTESQUIEU, CHARLES L. (1748) 1962 *The Spirit of the Laws.* 2 vols. New York: Hafner. → First published in French.

POLLOCK, FREDERICK; and MAITLAND, FREDERIC W. (1895) 1952 *The History of English Law Before the Time of Edward I.* 2 vols., 2d ed. Boston: Little.

RIKER, WILLIAM H. 1964 *Federalism: Origin, Operation, Significance.* Boston: Little.

ROCHE, JOHN P. (1952–1963) 1964 *Shadow and Substance: Essays on the Theory and Structure of Politics.* New York: Macmillan.

SHARP, MALCOLM P. 1935 The Classical American Doctrine of "the Separation of Powers." *University of Chicago Law Review* 2:385–436.

WHEARE, KENNETH C. (1946) 1964 *Federal Government.* 4th ed. New York: Oxford Univ. Press.

WRIGHT, BENJAMIN F. 1933 Origins of the Separation of Powers in America. *Economica* 13:169–185.

III
CIVIL LIBERTIES

"Civil liberties," as commonly used, is not a technical, precise term but a loose one denoting the personal rights and freedoms that are—or ought to be—respected by government. The phrase is not quite so broad as "liberty." It does not apply to the freedom of Robinson Crusoe on his island, where there was no government; it does not embrace those areas of private option where the law can play no part, as when a man freely chooses to be a fool, or a gentleman, or a knave; nor can the term be used very meaningfully in connection with such a concept as the "right of revolution," which is by nature a nonlegal privilege. But in its broadest usage the term is applicable to all those many claims of right that involve an actual or potential legal nexus between the individual and government. However, lately, especially in the United States, there has been some tendency to single out "civil rights" (the protection of minorities) as a separate category and to use "civil liberties" to describe all other claims of personal right. The distinction is not entirely stable, but it has the merit of subdividing an almost impossibly multifarious subject, and in the discussion that follows "civil liberties" is used in this somewhat narrower sense.

Even within these defined limitations the subject is very extensive, and further problems of definition and classification remain. It is evident that civil liberty can be thought of either negatively, as the individual's right *not* to have something done *to* him, or positively, as his right to have something done *for* him—for example, as the right against state interference with the publication of a political pamphlet or as the right to be provided with the facilities for publishing it. The negative category is the traditional one, and it will command the lion's share of attention in this article. But the truism that underlies the idea of positive liberty should not be overlooked: the freedom to read is meaningless if no books are available. Negative liberties can themselves be further subdivided into rights against interference by government and rights against interference by private individuals or groups. Again the former category is the more traditional, but again the less orthodox view merits a word by way of emphasis. In order to be really free to speak, a street-corner orator may need not only the assurance that the police will leave him alone but also the assurance that they will protect him from the angry reactions of his audience, that the state will "hinder hindrances" to his freedom (see Table 1).

Rights against government are sometimes still further divided into three types: political rights (those bearing on the political process, such as the right to vote or to engage in political controversy), economic rights (such as entrepreneurial freedom or the right to practice a profession), and private rights (which is a catch-all term meant to cover all rights that are neither political nor economic). Obviously these are imperfect categories, since they are not always mutually exclusive (is freedom of artistic expression a private right, or can it be said to bear indirectly on the political process?), but they do represent distinctions that have been drawn in practice and in the literature, and they have, therefore, a loose pragmatic value.

Finally, each of these three classes of rights against government subsumes two kinds of rights, the "substantive" and the "procedural." The sub-

stantive civil liberties are those regarded, in some degree, as ends in themselves; procedural rights are those having to do with the way in which government must proceed in dealing with substantive liberties.

Rise of the modern concept

Some concept of civil liberty can be traced far back into European history. Athenians of the age of Pericles gloried in their freedom of discussion and in their right to participate in public decisions. In the Middle Ages the feudal order rested heavily on the idea of legal rights that even the greatest lord was bound to respect, always in theory and often in fact. The barons who wrung the Magna Charta from King John were not, as they saw it, claiming new privileges but demanding that traditional immunities be reconfirmed. Nevertheless, the modern concept, although related to these older forms, is different enough to be regarded as a new species. In the Greek city-state freedom was a matter not so much of private right as of public good: the individual's liberty was instrumental to and defined by the welfare of the city. And in both the Greek and the medieval understanding men held their rights by virtue of their status rather than by virtue of their manhood. The freedom of

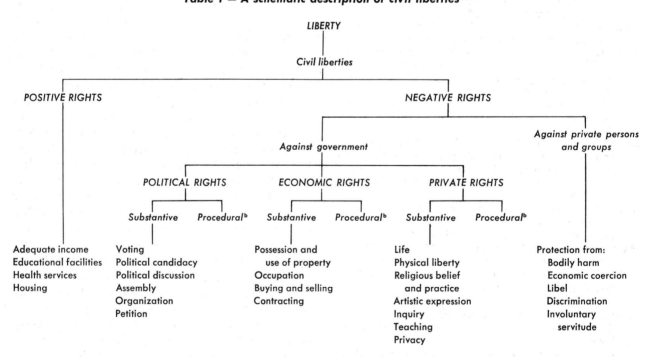

Table 1 — A schematic description of civil liberties[a]

a. The enumeration of specific rights and liberties in this table is meant to be suggestive, rather than exhaustive.

b. The same procedural rights apply generally to the three categories of substantive rights: security against arbitrary administrative action (e.g., illegal detention, coerced confession, unreasonable search and seizure, confiscation of property), security against unfair trial procedures (e.g., inadequate notice and hearing, denial of counsel, compulsory self-incrimination, double jeopardy, cruel and unusual punishment), and security against vague statutory prohibitions, ex post facto laws, and bills of attainder.

the Greek citizen did not extend to noncitizens, and the feudal vassal enjoyed the rights associated with his rank and order and was obliged, of course, to perform reciprocal duties. The dominant modern idea acknowledges a realm of personal value that is a good in itself, quite apart from the welfare of the community, and with some exceptions it assumes that rights accrue to men because they are men and not because of their status or their performance.

This idea, indeed, also finds some antecedents in premodern times; it smacks of the viewpoint that penetrated Roman law by way of the Stoics and Cicero. But in modern history the idea was given a new and irresistible thrust by the Reformation, which fostered a belief in individualism, and by the rise of capitalism, which provided that belief with the indispensable support of the nascent bourgeoisie. At various times since the seventeenth century, historical forces have emphasized one or another of the classes of civil liberties described in the opening paragraphs above. At first the main thrust was for freedom from the private power of the nobles and others who monopolized trade and restrained its development; this antifeudal movement supported a strengthened monarchy and a unified nation-state. Then, as the stronger monarch himself became a threat, the partisans of freedom sought to curb the state authority he embodied, first by demanding that his agents, judicial and administrative, respect certain procedural limitations when enforcing his will, then by claiming political rights that challenged his monopoly of state powers. The latter movement gathered force in the seventeenth and eighteenth centuries and reached a climax in the American and French revolutions. Its full implications have not been realized even to the present day, but under its impetus governmental power in western Europe and in North America tended gradually to devolve from the monarch to an oligarchy and finally to the majority of the populace. As this development proceeded it became apparent that political rights, although vital, were not enough: the majority, like the monarch, might use state power for good or ill. One result of this realization was a re-emphasis of substantive rights, a re-emphasis that began in the nineteenth century with an increased demand for economic freedom and shifted in the twentieth century to a new concern for other rights against government. This shift was accelerated by the spectacle of the "totalitarian" systems that arose in Europe after World War I. Another result was the development of the concept of positive liberty— "freedom for" rather than "freedom from"—which

in some modern systems is regarded as a supplement to, and in others as a substitute for, the negative view of civil liberty.

Problems of conflicting liberties

Although, as has been said, different concepts of civil liberty have been emphasized at different times in the Western world, in general the development has also been cumulative—that is, the shift to a new emphasis has seldom led to an explicit repudiation of the old. The result is that most modern states at least profess to respect nearly the whole vast and sometimes bewildering congeries of civil liberties that has been described. Evidently this profession creates problems, not the least of which arises from the fact that these heterogeneous liberties may conflict with one another. If government undertakes to ensure positive rights—for example, the right to an adequately paid job—it must assume broad authority to control the economic order, and a government thus endowed with powers may use them to encroach not only on economic liberty but on liberty in general. In the communist world this dilemma has been more or less frankly resolved by the subordination of even such rights as free speech and fair trial to the cause of "strengthening the socialist system." In the West peoples have tried, with varying success, both to enjoy the "welfare state" and to maintain private and political freedom, although the range of economic freedom from public control has certainly contracted since the heyday of laissez-faire ideology in the nineteenth century. There is an old and still controversial question whether other rights can survive in a state where economic rights have been thus demoted. So far the evidence suggests a very tentative "yes." In the United States, for example, the increase in government economic control since 1930 has been accompanied by a growing (although still inadequate) concern for other personal freedoms. But a different answer might have seemed justified in the 1930s, when the twin phenomena of economic depression and fascism dominated the world landscape, and history has perhaps not yet provided enough data so that the book can be closed on this issue.

However, even if the problem of economic liberty is defined away or bypassed, potential conflict between other civil liberties remains a difficulty. The right to comment on public affairs is no doubt essential in any free society, yet if the comment concerns a pending court case, it may impair the right to fair trial, which is equally essential. The religious zealot must be allowed to urge his views, but he may in doing so encroach on the right of others to be let alone, the "right to privacy." Most discussion of such perplexities has so far been limited to ritualistic advocacy of "freedom" or "order," categories of little analytic value in this context. There is need for more treatments that recognize and cope with both horns of the dilemma.

Much the same thing can be said about the overarching problem of drawing the line between personal rights and public authority in concrete instances. Because they were struggling against an outright state policy of repression, the historic spokesmen of freedom usually employed the language of exhortation: their declarations took the form of general and often absolutist propositions. Opposition to them, on the other hand, was equally unqualified: liberty was "license," which in turn was defined as anything the governors wished to proscribe. Such polarization was inevitable in a predominantly authoritarian system, and exhortation will always have its uses. But in states whose governments are committed to recognizing a range of legitimate civil liberty (and this is true today in most states in the noncommunist world), these uses are limited. The problem in such polities is to develop a just and workable reconciliation of two acknowledged goods—personal rights and community need. Hortatory, absolutist generalizations on either side can carry only part of the way to the problem's solution. Indeed, if depended on too much, they may hamper the solution by obscuring the fact that such a solution exists, that both the claims of the individual and the claims of authority must usually be weighed in the scales.

It is arguable that certain personal rights ought to be absolutely immune from state transgression: the "right to believe" has sometimes been so regarded; some procedural immunities, such as the right against forced confession, may fall in the same category. But all legal systems have recognized that at some point most freedoms may be restricted; the difficulty is where and how to set that point so as to admit valid community claims and yet ensure the maximum of personal liberty. The general principle is that government should inhibit freedom only as much as it has to in order to serve important community needs, and various attempts have been made to formulate a rule or a test that would implement this premise. The "clear and present danger" concept (that speech can be restricted only when it threatens an immediate and serious evil) represents one such attempt; the "balancing test" (that speech can be restricted when the state interest in suppression outweighs the private interest in freedom) represents an-

other. But insofar as these "rules" are not merely tautological, they are shorthand phrases for a large number of alternatives that must be considered before a reasonable conclusion is reached—for example, the distinctions between "advocacy" and "incitement," between "prior restraint" and "subsequent punishment," between "state convenience" and "state necessity." It would be desirable to analyze these alternatives in terms of the issues posed by the conflict between various exertions of state power and various kinds of liberty (e.g., an outright prohibition of free speech may raise questions different from those raised by an ordinance that only regulates the time, place, and manner of such speech; freedom of religious utterance and freedom of political advocacy may stand on different grounds).

Although conceptual treatments of the kind discussed above would be useful, they would leave unanswered other very important questions that should not be overlooked. Even if analysis can provide formulas for the reasonable protection of civil liberties, there remain the issues of what conditions are most likely to secure that protection in practice and, more specifically, what constitutional arrangements are most useful in this regard.

Conditions for protection of civil liberties

The first question is really an aspect of a much broader one—what conditions make for a "democratic" or "competitive" political system—and this is an issue too large and complex to be adequately treated here. However, a few contingent suggestions can be ventured. As might be expected, economic abundance in a given society seems to enhance the likelihood that civil freedom will be tolerated: broadly speaking, the more highly developed the country, the less the chance of arbitrary, authoritarian government. Yet this correlation may not be entirely dependable: it has been argued that in the early stages of economic progress a country may be more, rather than less, prone to generate the tensions that lead to authoritarianism. Education is another factor that appears to produce a national milieu favorable to civil liberties. Indeed, studies have found that even within nations the most educated tend to be the most favorable to "democratic values." But it has been contended that the first steps toward widespread literacy may turn a nation in quite the opposite direction, and the case of Nazi Germany demonstrates that even a high educational level is not enough. Habit and custom also play a part: a well-established tradition of libertarianism tends to perpetuate itself. It has been urged that "pluralism" with respect to economic and social interests conduces to a free polity; certainly a nation sharply divided into two camps (e.g., the rich and the poor) is not likely to be a free one. Scholars have also from time to time argued that such factors as "national character" and "consensus on fundamentals" are determinative, but empirical study so far has not fully confirmed these insights. Finally, it is worth noting that certain political characteristics may affect the matter. Heavy involvement in politics of the military or of religious groups is often unfavorable to civil freedom; a one-party state need not be tyrannical, but it is likely to be. With the proliferation of new nations in modern times, political scientists are finding examples of an almost endless variety of objective circumstances, and further progress can be expected toward systematic understanding of the environmental prerequisites for civil liberty.

Constitutional guarantees

The emergence of new nations should shed brighter light on the constitutional arrangements for civil liberties. The past offers several prescriptions, but two stand out: the British system of parliamentary supremacy, in which civil liberties are preserved by the tradition of governmental self-restraint, and the American system, with a written bill of rights interpreted and enforced by judicial review. The difference is not so sharp as this bare description suggests—in practice Parliament also feels committed to historic written documents, such as the Act of Settlement, and custom plays a part in determining the actual constitutional structure in the United States—but a difference it is nonetheless. In spite of Britain's impressive success in maintaining civil liberties, the device of a written, nominally binding bill of rights has been adopted very widely by modern nations (Israel and some of the states of the British Commonwealth are among the exceptions), and debates on this matter seem rather academic. But questions remain about the content and character of such a statement. What kinds of rights should be included? Should the declaration list "positive rights," such as the right to employment, which was formally secured by Germany's Weimar constitution and by the Soviet constitution of 1936? Should it include guarantees of rights against private action, such as the right against "abuse of economic power," which is specified in the constitution of modern West Germany? The difficulty is that such rights are not self-executing; they de-

pend on the willingness of the government to take the positive steps that are necessary to make them real—e.g., to stimulate the economy, or to adopt adequate regulatory measures. It has been argued that such guarantees are useful as statements of aspiration and as admonitions to the governors. Contrariwise, it has been suggested that being legally unenforceable, such merely moral prescriptions may cheapen the whole concept of rights in the minds of both governors and governed.

Even if the bill of rights takes the traditional form of negative restrictions on government, should these restrictions be expressed in general terms ("due process of law," "freedom of religion") or should they be spelled out in detail? Should the rights be stated as absolutes ("Congress shall make no law . . . abridging the freedom of speech") or in qualified terms (as in the Nigerian provision that rights may be limited in ways that are reasonably justified in a democratic society)? Should the declaration list all negative rights that seem important (the Weimar constitution protected motherhood and forbade public instruction that hurt the feelings of nonconformist pupils); if not, which rights do merit explicit statement? Common sense and past experience suggest tentative answers to such questions; further observation and future experience should bring more enlightenment.

Finally, supposing a nation's cultural and political environment makes civil liberty plausible and the nature and content of the bill of rights has been determined, how can those rights be best enforced? Probably the primary, and surely an indispensable, agency is an independent judiciary. It is hard to see how civil liberty can be more than an empty promise unless there are courts free to handle claims between persons and to check the arbitrary acts of administrative officials. Whether the judiciary should also be granted the power to enforce the bill of rights against the legislature itself—that is, whether it should exercise the power of judicial review—is an important question discussed elsewhere [see JUDICIAL PROCESS, *article on* JUDICIAL REVIEW]. A few decades ago many scholars, even in the United States, were skeptical of judicial review, which they felt had been used by the Supreme Court to restrain economic reform rather than to protect the rights of man. Since then that court and, to a lesser extent, the judiciaries of some American states have done more to defend civil liberties than any other agency of American government, and the attitude of scholars has changed accordingly. During the same period there has been a tendency, although not an overwhelming one, for other countries (e.g., the German Federal Republic, Italy, India) to adopt judicial review in some form, and as history proceeds there will be a growing body of evidence on the relation between civil liberties and this once uniquely American institution.

ROBERT G. MCCLOSKEY

[*See also* CIVIL DISOBEDIENCE; DEMOCRACY; EQUALITY; FREEDOM; HUMAN RIGHTS.]

BIBLIOGRAPHY

CHAFEE, ZECHARIAH JR. 1941 *Free Speech in the United States.* Cambridge, Mass.: Harvard Univ. Press. → Supersedes Chafee's *Freedom of Speech,* 1920.

COMMAGER, HENRY STEELE et al. 1951 *Civil Liberties Under Attack.* Philadelphia: Univ. of Pennsylvania Press.

CORWIN, EDWARD S. 1948 *Liberty Against Government: The Rise, Flowering and Decline of a Famous Juridical Concept.* Baton Rouge: Louisiana State Univ. Press.

CUSHMAN, ROBERT E. 1956 *Civil Liberties in the United States: A Guide to Current Problems and Experience.* Cornell Studies in Civil Liberty. Ithaca, N.Y.: Cornell Univ. Press.

EMERSON, THOMAS I.; and HABER, DAVID (1952) 1958 *Political and Civil Rights in the United States: A Collection of Legal and Related Materials.* 2d ed., 2 vols. Buffalo, N.Y.: Dennis.

FELLMAN, DAVID 1958 *The Defendant's Rights.* New York: Holt.

HOBHOUSE, LEONARD T. 1911 *Social Evolution and Political Theory.* New York: Columbia Univ. Press.

KAUPER, PAUL G. 1962 *Civil Liberties and the Constitution.* Ann Arbor: Univ. of Michigan Press.

MEIKLEJOHN, ALEXANDER 1960 *Political Freedom: The Constitutional Powers of the People.* New York: Harper.

ROCHE, JOHN P. 1963 *The Quest for the Dream: The Development of Civil Rights and Human Relations in Modern America.* New York: Macmillan.

SCHUMPETER, JOSEPH A. (1942) 1950 *Capitalism, Socialism, and Democracy.* 3d ed. New York: Harper; London: Allen & Unwin. → A paperback edition was published by Harper in 1962.

STOUFFER, SAMUEL A. (1955) 1963 *Communism, Conformity, and Civil Liberties: A Cross-section of the Nation Speaks Its Mind.* Gloucester, Mass.: Smith.

IV
CIVIL RIGHTS

Although the terms "civil rights" and "civil liberties" are often used interchangeably, when they are differentiated the latter generally denotes the rights of *individuals,* while the former refers to the constitutional and legal status and treatment of *minority groups* that are marked off from the majority by race, religion, or national origin. The following illustration will show the difference. In the United States since the end of slavery, there has never been any question about the Negro's equal rights to freedom of religion or freedom of the press—basic *civil liberties*; at the same time, he could be treated as a member of his race, and not as an individual, with respect to the schools he could attend and the public facilities he could enjoy—basic *civil rights*. The distinction between the person as an individual and the person as a member of a group has its roots in history, morality, and social psychology. Reinhold Niebuhr noted that

It may be possible, though it is never easy, to establish just relations between individuals within a group purely by moral and rational suasion and accommodation. In inter-group relations this is practically an impossibility. The relations between groups must therefore always be predominantly political rather than ethical, that is, they will be determined by the proportion of power which each group possesses at least as much as by any rational and moral appraisal of the comparative needs and claims of each group. (1932, pp. xxii–xxiii)

While individual and group rights are to be differentiated, it is probably true that there is no chance for the emergence of the latter if the former are denied, so that the struggle for civil liberties must first be won and the fundamental human rights vindicated and secured before minority rights will be recognized. The struggle for civil rights cannot be conducted for those who are yet denied basic human rights.

In the broad sweep of history—though no doubt there have been numerous exceptions—the relations of a dominant majority toward a weak minority group, or of the conqueror toward the defeated enemy, first took the form of total annihilation or of cannibalism; then the form of slavery or total subjection; then the milder yet still severe form of assignment to an inferior caste; then cooperation and equality. Yet in modern times all forms have coexisted: in Nazi Germany the Jewish people were exterminated, in India the Untouchables still suffer because of the caste system, and in the United States the Negroes are moving into full equality. Even in the ancient world, while Aristotle was teaching that non-Hellenic peoples were fit only for slavery, his former pupil, Alexander of Macedon, acted on the principle that Greeks and Persians, victors and vanquished, could associate on the basis of equality and fraternity.

On one hand, one finds everywhere and at all times fear and hatred of the foreigner, the stranger, the man of different color or tongue or beliefs; on the other hand, there is evidence of an effort of the human consciousness to be aware of the universal in all men, of a common bond and a common destiny. "The universal in its true and inclusive sense is a thought," Hegel said, "that it has cost thousands of years to bring to human consciousness, and that received its full recognition only through the aid of Christianity. The Greeks knew neither God nor man in their true universality" ([1817] 1841, p. 321). This is too sweeping a judgment, for Stoicism of the Hellenistic age taught the ideal of the cosmopolis, or world state, in which all men, Greek and barbarian, urban and rural, would enjoy equality; but it is true that the ideals of the Fatherhood of God and the brotherhood of men found their clearest expression in the Hebrew prophets and Christian teachings. In time, Stoic and Biblical ideals became fused in various schools of natural law that dominated political thought in the West down to the nineteenth century. Thus, denial of equality to minority groups could and was challenged in the name of religion or political theory or philosophy. In modern times the denial of equality to religious, racial, and ethnic minorities also assumed ideological and even religious formulations in theories of racial inferiority and in various political ideologies; but with respect to all such formulations, Arnold Toynbee's judgment seems appropriate: "The present vogue of racialism in the West," he wrote, "however, has really little to do with current scientific hypotheses. A prejudice so strong as this cannot be accounted for by a cause so rational" (1934).

Until World War I one could hardly speak of a struggle for civil rights; one could see only a record of oppressions and persecutions of minority groups. But then came an awakening of nationalism, and, at least in Europe, oppressed nations became independent, and minority religious and ethnic groups within nations were guaranteed their collective rights by constitutions and international treaties. Although these guarantees generally proved ineffective, they were significant for recognizing the moral claims of minorities.

The claims became universal and reached a climax at the end of World War II. First the Indian subcontinent won freedom in 1947, then Indonesia, then in 1957 the Gold Coast (Ghana), in Africa. In 1945, when the United Nations was organized, the white race of Europe and North America dominated the world. The UN Charter was signed by fifty nations. By the 1960s the UN had over 100 members, more than thirty of them new African nations; and the white race had begun to recognize its own minority status. Almost throughout the world there was violence. However, whereas in former centuries what was obvious was the oppressive measures imposed upon minorities by the dominant group, now one saw minority groups resort to violence against what they considered

to be oppressive majorities: for example, Turks against Greeks in Cyprus; Kurds against Arabs in Iraq; Negroes against East Indians in British Guiana; Muslims against Hindus in India; and Hindus against Muslims in Pakistan. In some countries, as in Belgium and India, there were struggles over language rights. No minority group was willing to remain in a position of relative inferiority and subjection. In some instances the struggle for civil rights was against a dominant minority, as by Buddhists against Roman Catholics in South Vietnam or by the nine million African Negroes against the three million whites in the Republic of South Africa. Sometimes the struggle for civil rights, as on behalf of the three million Jews in the Soviet Union, was conducted by concerned persons living outside the area (the Jews of Israel and of the West). The pattern, when viewed ecumenically, is extremely complex.

Apart from national emancipation after World War I and the winning of independence by the peoples of Asia and Africa after World War II, the most dramatic developments in the struggle for civil rights have been in India, the United States, and in international organizations. These will be reviewed briefly.

India.   More than fifty million Indians were deemed to be Untouchables by birth and were prevented by custom and law from social and religious contact with other Hindus. For decades Mohandas K. Gandhi had led a nonviolent struggle for their equality. When India became a member of the (British) Commonwealth of Nations and adopted a constitution in 1949, the Untouchables won official political, economic, and social equality. This equality affected their status as well as their competitive opportunity, thus striking at the roots of the caste idea of "outcastes." In guaranteeing the right of equality, the constitution states that the state shall not discriminate against any citizen on account of caste; that no citizen shall, on the ground of caste, be subject to restriction in access to or use of shops, restaurants, public wells, and tanks; and that the practice of untouchability is forbidden. The constitution also guarantees the practice of any calling without restriction and provides that the state shall promote "with special care" the educational and economic interests of "the weaker sections of the people" and shall protect them "from social injustice and all forms of exploitation." The law grants former Untouchables preferential treatment by the government in jobs and offices and reserves for them educational and professional opportunities.

The struggle for equality has been helped not

only by law but also by certain material forces, notably expanding urbanism and industrialism and the growth of transport and communications.

However, factors have developed that tend to perpetuate, and even to strengthen, the caste organization of Indian society: all castes, high and low, have become corporate political bodies that court favor and power, so that elections are fought on caste lines, party tickets tend to be formed on the same bases, and recruitment and promotions reflect caste consciousness. Caste associations have grown in number and strength. At the National Integration Conference in 1961, President Radhakrishnan stated that although caste is ceasing to be a social evil, it has become a political and administrative evil. Caste loyalties are utilized for the purpose of winning elections or getting people into jobs, for exercising some kind of favoritism or nepotism. It is doubtful, however, that untouchability is no longer a "social evil," for the vast majority of the caste, illiterate and economically weak, submit silently to continued discriminations; and in a country where there is substantial unemployment, it is natural that members of the most depressed classes should suffer continued discrimination rather than run the risk of losing their jobs through retaliation and intensified prejudice. In any case, India demonstrates the difficulties involved in establishing civil rights in traditional societies.

United States. The first civil rights challenge in the United States was presented by the Indians. As the white man pushed westward, he demanded more and more of the Indians' land. Congress in 1830 enacted the Indian Removal Act, which was based on the assumption that segregation would end the conflict between the races, as land would be provided for the Indians in western territory and the whites would occupy all of the eastern lands. Coupled with land hunger was the policy of putting Indian cultures and tribal organizations into the "melting pot," where they would be destroyed, and of converting Indians from hunters and fishermen into farmers and cattlemen. Cultural, social, and economic assimilation would, at the same time, make available much of the "surplus" Indian lands, which consisted of 150 million acres in 1873. The policy was expressed in the General Allotment Act of 1887, called the Dawes Act, under which it was possible to individualize the Indian landholdings and to permit Indians to dispose of the land as they wished. Citizenship could be acquired by Indians as they left their tribes and chose to live among the civilized people. By 1933, two-thirds of the lands held by the Indians in 1887 had been lost.

An act of 1924 gave citizenship to all Indians, but as late as 1956 there were states that denied them the franchise. Other discriminatory practices, some of them required by law or regulation, were prohibited by a 1934 statute. In the same year Congress enacted the Indian Reorganization Act, the most comprehensive law since 1887. Under its terms, Indian landholdings were increased and land conservation measures were introduced; the organization of Indian tribes was reinvigorated, and tribal customs and laws were given dignity and power; liberal credit policies were established to aid the tribes and individual Indians. The law encouraged respect for Indian cultural life and institutions, especially Indian arts and crafts (under an act of 1935).

Government policy in the 1950s reversed the trends and reverted to pre-1934 positions; in 1961, however, there was again a fundamental change in course when the federal government apparently returned to the Indian policies of the Franklin D. Roosevelt and Truman administrations. Federal policy thus fluctuates between a desire not to recognize the Indians as in any way differentiated from the rest of the population, and thus not entitled to any special claims or rights, and a desire to afford them an opportunity to develop their own styles of life and to protect them against greed and prejudice. Thus, there is a conflict between total assimilation and cultural pluralism. While the Indian encounters varying degrees of prejudice and discrimination in many parts of the country, his friends continue to debate his future between the poles of integration and disintegration of Indian life and culture.

The Negro presented problems of a different complexity and order, for after emancipation he had to bear the memory, habits, and history of slavery; he had no indigenous culture and tribal life that he wanted to preserve; he could never claim that he once owned all the land. His skin was darker, he originally came from another continent, and he could be counted in the millions; and there were no large reservations where he could make his home—he had to live in close proximity to those who had been his masters.

At the end of the Civil War and after adoption of the thirteenth amendment, which outlawed slavery and peonage, Congress proceeded to ensure equality for the four million freedmen by providing for their "personal liberty, personal security," and their "free enjoyment" of "immunities and rights." "Civil rights" began with passage on April 9, 1866, of "An Act to Protect All Persons in the United States in Their Civil Rights, and Furnish the Means of Their Vindication." Since the act's constitutionality was doubted, two months later Congress passed the fourteenth amendment, which was ratified in 1868. Under its terms, Negroes became citizens of the United States and of the states wherein they resided; the amendment provided, too, that no state shall deprive any person of his life, liberty, or property without due process of law nor deny to any person the equal protection of the laws. The fifteenth amendment, ratified in 1870, provided that the right to vote shall not be denied or abridged by the United States or by any state on account of race, color, or previous condition of servitude.

To implement these constitutional provisions, Congress, until the end of Reconstruction in 1877, enacted a series of civil rights acts. The most important of them was the Civil Rights Act of 1875, which prohibited racial discrimination in inns, public conveyances, theaters, and other places of public amusement. From the debates on this act in Congress, it is clear that its purpose was to wipe out all the incidents and badges of slavery. In 1883 the Supreme Court held the act unconstitutional on the ground that the statute prohibited racial discrimination by *private individuals*, while the fourteenth amendment authorized congressional action only to enforce prohibitions on *state action*. Then in 1896 the Supreme Court, in *Plessy* v. *Ferguson*, upheld as constitutional state laws that required racial segregation in public conveyances, on the theory that "separate but equal" facilities were not a denial of equality. This decision was interpreted as extending the cloak of constitutionality to racial segregation in schools, all public buildings and institutions, restaurants, theaters, and all other public accommodations, publicly or privately operated. Racial segregation was the pattern in 17 southern and border states and in the District of Columbia.

The "separate but equal" rule was flagrantly flouted—separation was enforced, but equality was not provided. The schools and other facilities afforded Negroes were patently, and often grossly, inferior; for example, for 1951 the expenditure per pupil in average daily attendance for nine segregated states was $136.73 for white and $74.67 for Negro; and the average salary per member of staff was similarly disproportionate. In 1938, in a case brought by a Negro who sought admission to the law school of the state University of Missouri, and in 1950, in cases involving a Negro student of law at the University of Texas and a Negro graduate student in education at the University of Oklahoma, the Supreme Court questioned the way the "separate but equal" rule was operating and raised serious doubt whether this rule could be used at all in graduate and professional studies without denying the Negroes' constitutional right to equal protection under the fourteenth amendment. In the field of interstate transportation, also, in cases decided in 1946 and 1950, the Supreme Court considerably weakened the constitutional underpinnings of racial segregation. The deathblow to *de jure* racial segregation came in 1954, in *Brown* v. *Board of Education of Topeka* (347 U.S. 483), in which the Court unanimously upheld the contention of the National Association for the Advancement of Colored People (NAACP) that segregated public schools are not "equal" and cannot be made "equal." In subsequent cases the Court outlawed segregation in state colleges and universities, transportation, parks, municipal golf courses, public beaches, and wherever the state participated in a property's maintenance.

Compliance with the mandate to desegregate public facilities was resisted in the 17 affected states, especially with respect to public schools, and particularly in Mississippi and Alabama. Under the banner of "states' rights," all sorts of devices were resorted to by segregationists to nullify the orders of the federal courts; and the segregation forces attempted to paralyze the NAACP so that it might not continue its legal defense operations in the south.

In 1955 and 1956, under the leadership of Martin Luther King, Jr., a Negro minister, the Negroes of Montgomery, Alabama, engaged in a boycott of the segregated buses in that city. King was a follower of Gandhi and Thoreau in his philosophy of nonviolent resistance to immoral or unconstitutional laws and customs. Three years later, under NAACP leadership, Negro high-school students in Oklahoma City, Oklahoma, launched a sit-in demonstration at lunch counters in chain stores to win nonsegregated service. At Greensboro, North Carolina, in 1960 several Negro college students staged a sit-in at a lunch counter, spontaneously and without organizational support. These instances served as a pattern for what soon became a widespread movement throughout the southern and the border states against segregation in privately owned places of public accommodation. In many cities the sit-in demonstrations were successful; but everywhere in the affected states and cities there was massive resistance, and white extremists often resorted to violence and even murder. The situation was aggravated by attempts made by Negro organizations to induce Negroes to register as voters in places where they were systematically kept off the suffrage rolls.

When it became apparent that the situation had become intolerable, President John F. Kennedy submitted to Congress a comprehensive civil rights bill to outlaw racial segregation in places of public accommodation, to eliminate discrimination in employment, to assure free suffrage to the Negro, and to end discriminatory practices in housing. The bill was based on the assumption that the Supreme Court would overrule or circumvent its decision in the so-called Civil Rights Cases of 1883, just as it had overruled *Plessy* v. *Ferguson* (1896) in 1954. Congress (following a filibuster in the Senate) passed the bill on July 2, 1964, and it was immediately signed by President Lyndon B. Johnson. Although Congress had passed civil rights acts in 1957 and 1960, the act of 1964 was the first really significant civil rights breakthrough in Congress since the end of Reconstruction in 1877.

The new federal law was not as necessary in the north as in the south. In 1865 Massachusetts enacted the first state law in the country banning racial discrimination in places of public accommodation. By 1900 there were similar statutes in 18 states; by 1960 there were 24. In 1945 New York became the first state to enact a fair employment practice act; by 1960 there were similar laws in 17 states. There was a network of related laws dealing with discrimination in housing and in education. The statutes barred discrimination on account of religion or national origin as well as on account of race or color. Yet the combination of criminal, civil, and administrative remedies provided by this complex of laws did not prevent the rise and spread of *de facto* racial segregation, especially in the northern urban centers, where Negro ghettos came into being and were enlarged by the Negro migrations from the south. In these ghettos the schools were almost exclusively Negro; the rate of unemployment was substantially higher than it was for white workers; the housing was substandard or constituted a slum area that was a breeding place for crime, delinquency, drug addiction—evils that in turn fostered unemployment, apathy, frustration. Under these circumstances, enactment of the Civil Rights Act of 1964 did not bring to the Negroes of Harlem and other slum centers in the north promise of a new day, and in the summer of that year there were outbursts of violence in the Negro ghettos in Manhattan, Brooklyn, and Rochester, New York; Jersey City, New Jersey; and elsewhere.

These outbreaks of anger against the evils of *de facto* segregation precipitated two reactions: on the one hand, a white "backlash" against civil rights; on the other hand, a more widespread recognition of the fact that the movement for civil rights must be intimately linked with policies of full employment, greatly improved educational facilities

and techniques for all economically underprivileged children, urban redevelopment that would provide better housing and neighborhoods for lower-income groups, and, in general, policies that would cope with the social, economic, and cultural aspects of the modern megalopolis. The Economic Opportunity Act of 1964 and the creation, in 1965, of the Department of Housing and Urban Development, headed by the first Negro in the cabinet, were in part responses to civil rights challenges. The Voting Rights Act of 1965 was a major step toward implementing the fifteenth amendment and promised greater political power for the large masses of Negroes in the southern states.

International arena. The ideas of human dignity, equality, and fundamental human rights are deeply rooted. Numerous passages in the Old Testament command nations not to oppress the alien and the stranger and to protect the poor, the orphan, and the widow. At the same time, the pages of history record "man's inhumanity to man" that has made "countless thousands mourn." The struggle for equality has been aided by the revolution in travel and communication, and in technology generally, so that men see themselves as being interdependent more than they had ever been before. For example, Negroes in the United States know that the African peoples have won their independence and that their representatives have places of equal dignity and rights in international organizations and meetings; and this phenomenon has brought moral strength to U.S. Negroes, so that they demand, and struggle for, their rights as Americans and as members of the human family.

Lord Acton, in an address in 1877, stated that the "most certain test by which we judge whether a country is really free is the amount of security enjoyed by minorities" ([1861–1910] 1948, p. 33). It was not until the twentieth century that official agencies for judgment came into being. Following World War I, as we have noted, there was an attempt to protect some national minorities by treaties; the mandates system under the League of Nations should also be noted in this connection. But the international, programmatic promotion of minority protection and human rights in general was undertaken only after World War II. Articles 1 and 55 of the Charter of the United Nations were designed to promote and encourage respect for human rights and fundamental freedoms for all, without distinction as to race, sex, or religion. UN bodies that work toward this end are the Third Committee of the General Assembly, the Economic and Social Council, the Human Rights Commission, the Commission on the Status of Women, and the Sub-Commission on Prevention of Discrimination and Protection of Minorities.

In 1948 the United Nations General Assembly adopted the Universal Declaration of Human Rights as a statement of principles to be implemented by subsequent conventions that would be binding on ratifying member states. In December 1965 the Assembly approved the convention on the elimination of all forms of racial discrimination. An important feature of the convention was the provision that allowed ratifying nations to bind themselves to permit individuals or groups to charge their governments with violations.

Other international organizations that are concerned with these matters are UNESCO, the International Labour Organisation, the European Commission on Human Rights and the European Court of Human Rights, and the Inter-American Commission on Human Rights. Mention may also be made of the International Commission of Jurists and the International League for the Rights of Man.

While the European Convention on Human Rights has established compulsory machinery, the Commission and the Court, for dealing with cases involving violations of human rights, and the International Labour Organisation has established effective machinery for investigation and reports respecting certain areas of human rights, other agencies normally rely on implementation through reporting systems.

The chief utility of the agencies has been to expose to general view the facts of human rights violations and to win support for the claim that there is a universal law of humanity, under which individuals and groups (religious, racial, cultural, and national) should somehow be protected against attempts to destroy (genocide), discriminate against, or humiliate them. What Walter Bagehot called "government by discussion" (1872, chapter 5) has not come into existence in the international field; yet the open and vigorous discussion of human rights in governmental and nongovernmental agencies has done much to make meaningful the preamble to the UN Charter, which proclaims the determination of the nations "to reaffirm faith in fundamental human rights, in the dignity and worth of the human person, in the equal rights of men and women and of nations large and small. . . ."

Thus, a denial of civil rights—whether it takes place in Birmingham, Alabama, or in Birmingham, England, or in the U.S.S.R., or in South Africa, or in Bechuanaland, or in Algeria—is no longer a parochial domestic question, but has become a matter of universal concern, a concern that implies the belief (as stated by Pope John XXIII in *Pacem in terris* 1963) that human society is founded on the principle that every human being is a person, that his nature is endowed with intelligence and free will, that he has rights that flow directly from his very nature, and that these rights are universal, inviolable, and are such that they cannot in any way be surrendered.

MILTON R. KONVITZ

[*See also* ASSIMILATION; HUMAN RIGHTS; MINORITIES; RACE; RACE RELATIONS; SEGREGATION.]

BIBLIOGRAPHY

ACTON, JOHN E. D. (1861–1910) 1948 *Essays on Freedom and Power.* Boston: Beacon. → A paperback edition was published in 1955 by Noonday.

BAGEHOT, WALTER (1872) 1956 *Physics and Politics: Or, Thoughts on the Application of the Principles of "Natural Selection" and "Inheritance" to Political Society.* Boston: Beacon.

BALDRY, H. C. 1965 *The Unity of Mankind in Greek Thought.* Cambridge Univ. Press.

BARRON, MILTON L. (editor) 1957 *American Minorities: A Textbook of Readings in Intergroup Relations.* New York: Knopf.

BROOKS, ALEXANDER D. 1962 *Civil Rights and Civil Liberties in the United States: An Annotated Bibliography.* New York: Civil Liberties Educational Foundation.

CHIEF MINISTERS' CONFERENCE ON NATIONAL INTEGRATION, DELHI 1961 *National Integration: Decisions Taken by the Chief Ministers' Conference.* New Delhi: Directorate of Advertising and Visual Publicity.

COLLIER, JOHN 1947 *The Indians of the Americas.* New York: Norton. → An abridged paperback edition was published in 1953 by New American Library.

EPSTEIN, BENJAMIN R.; and FOSTER, ARNOLD 1962 *"Some of My Best Friends . . . ."* New York: Farrar, Straus.

FRANKLIN, JOHN H. (1947) 1956 *From Slavery to Freedom: A History of American Negroes.* 2d ed., rev. & enl. New York: Knopf.

GLAZER, NATHAN; and MOYNIHAN, DANIEL P. 1963 *Beyond the Melting Pot: The Negroes, Puerto Ricans, Jews, Italians, and the Irish of New York City.* Cambridge: M.I.T. Press.

GORDON, MILTON M. 1964 *Assimilation in American Life: The Role of Race, Religion, and National Origin.* New York: Oxford Univ. Press.

GOSSETT, THOMAS F. 1963 *Race: The History of an Idea in America.* Dallas, Texas: Southern Methodist Univ. Press.

GREENBERG, JACK 1959 *Race Relations and American Law.* New York: Columbia Univ. Press.

GRIMES, ALAN P. 1964 *Equality in America: Religion, Race, and the Urban Majority.* New York: Oxford Univ. Press.

GUMPLOWICZ, LUDWIG 1883 *Der Rassenkampf: Sociologische Untersuchungen.* Innsbruck (Austria): Verlag der Wagner'schen Universitäts Buchhandlung. → Also published in 1893 in French as *La lutte des races; Recherches sociologiques.*

HANDLIN, OSCAR 1957 *Race and Nationality in American Life.* Boston: Little.

HANDLIN, OSCAR 1959 *The Newcomers: Negroes and Puerto Ricans in a Changing Metropolis.* Cambridge, Mass.: Harvard Univ. Press.

HANDLIN, OSCAR 1964 *Fire-bell in the Night: The Crisis in Civil Rights.* Boston: Little.

HARRIS, ROBERT J. 1960 *The Quest for Equality: The Constitution, Congress, and the Supreme Court.* Baton Rouge: Louisiana State Univ. Press.

HEGEL, GEORG W. F. (1817) 1841 *Werke.* Volume 6: Encyklopädie der philosophischen Wissenschaften im Grundrisse. 2d ed. Berlin: Duncker. → Translation of extract in text provided by Milton R. Konvitz.

KALLEN, HORACE M. 1924 *Culture and Democracy in the United States: Studies in the Group Psychology of the American Peoples.* New York: Liveright.

KONVITZ, MILTON R. 1946 *The Alien and the Asiatic in American Law.* Ithaca, N.Y.: Cornell Univ. Press.

KONVITZ, MILTON R. 1947 *The Constitution and Civil Rights.* New York: Columbia Univ. Press.

KONVITZ, MILTON R. 1953 *Civil Rights in Immigration.* Ithaca, N.Y.: Cornell Univ. Press.

KONVITZ, MILTON R. (editor) (1954) 1965 *Bill of Rights Reader.* 3d ed. Ithaca, N.Y.: Cornell Univ. Press.

KONVITZ, MILTON R. 1961 *A Century of Civil Rights.* New York: Columbia Univ. Press.

KONVITZ, MILTON R. 1966 *Expanding Liberty: Freedom's Gains in Postwar America.* New York: Viking.

MONTAGU, ASHLEY (1951) 1952 *Statement on Race: An Extended Discussion in Plain Language of the UNESCO Statement by Experts on Race Problems.* 2d ed. New York: Schuman.

MOSKOWITZ, MOSES (1958) 1959 *Human Rights and World Order: The Struggle for Human Rights in the United Nations.* Dobbs Ferry, N.Y.: Oceana; London: Stevens.

MYRDAL, GUNNAR (1944) 1962 *An American Dilemma: The Negro Problem and Modern Democracy.* New York: Harper. → A paperback edition was published in 1964 by McGraw-Hill.

NIEBUHR, REINHOLD 1932 *Moral Man and Immoral Society: A Study in Ethics and Politics.* New York and London: Scribner. → A paperback edition was published in 1960.

ROBINSON, JACOB 1946 *Human Rights and Fundamental Freedoms in the Charter of the United Nations: A Commentary.* New York: Institute of Jewish Affairs.

ROSE, ARNOLD M. (editor) 1951 *Race Prejudice and Discrimination: Readings in Intergroup Relations in the United States.* New York: Knopf.

ROSE, ARNOLD M.; and ROSE, CAROLINE 1948 *America Divided: Minority Group Relations in the United States.* New York: Knopf.

SILBERMAN, CHARLES E. 1964 *Crisis in Black and White.* New York: Random House.

STAMPP, KENNETH M. 1956 *The Peculiar Institution: Slavery in the Ante-bellum South.* New York: Knopf.

TANNENBAUM, FRANK 1947 *Slave and Citizen: The Negro in the Americas.* New York: Knopf. → A paperback edition was published in 1963 by Random House.

TOYNBEE, ARNOLD J. 1934 *A Study of History.* Volume 1: Introduction: The Geneses of Civilizations. Oxford Univ. Press.

UNITED NATIONS CHARTER 1945 *Charter of the United Nations and Statute of the International Court of Justice.* New York: United Nations.

U.S. COMMISSION ON CIVIL RIGHTS 1959 [and subsequent years] *Report.* Washington: Government Printing Office.

U.S. PRESIDENT'S COMMITTEE ON CIVIL RIGHTS 1947 *To Secure These Rights.* Washington: Government Printing Office.

WESTIN, ALAN F. (editor) 1964 *Freedom Now! The Civil-rights Struggle in America.* New York: Basic Books.

WOODWARD, COMER V. 1955 *The Strange Career of Jim Crow.* New York: Oxford Univ. Press. → A revised edition was published in paperback in 1957.

Yearbook of the European Convention on Human Rights. → Published since 1955/1957.

Yearbook on Human Rights. → Published by the United Nations since 1946.

CONSTITUTIONAL PSYCHOLOGY

See under PSYCHOLOGY.

CONSTITUTIONS AND CONSTITUTIONALISM

Constitutionalism in its distinctive sense is a modern phenomenon which can be defined only by facing the complexities of defining a constitution. From Aristotle to the present day, many such definitions have been offered, and some of these will be discussed below in connection with the history of constitutionalism.

At the outset, however, the eighteenth-century and nineteenth-century concept of a constitution as a formal written document ought to be discarded. All such documents are subject to a steady evolution; and the living constitution, like all living law, is something transcending such formal enactment as well as preceding it. Furthermore, a constitution such as that of Britain or Israel is just as much "written" as the American or French constitution, that is to say, embodied in written documents of all kinds even though not codified and assembled in a single document. Although outmoded, this documentarian, or code, concept of a constitution played a significant role in the heyday of constitution-making after the French Revolution—as it does, in fact, even today in many of the emergent nations.

In addition to this documentarian concept, one finds several broad philosophical and legal concepts of constitutions which have been important, even though they lack the distinctiveness of the modern Western conception. Aristotle in a sense set the stage for the equivocation which has characterized the basic term throughout its history. When speaking of the *politeia*, he employed the term to refer both to a distinctive political order, the so-called mixed constitution of the "polity," and to political order or regime in general. In other words, every regime, even a tyranny, was said to have its constitution or *politeia*.

Related to this Aristotelian notion is the more modern idea of a constitution as the organization of a government, its offices, and the relation of the offices. A variant is the conception which considers the actual power relations the "living" constitution (McBain 1927; Sternberger 1956). This, too, is a term that might be (and has been) applied to an absolute monarchy or a totalitarian dictatorship as readily as to a political order such as the United States or Great Britain.

Similar to these two conceptions, although distinct from them, is the notion that the constitution is the "basic law" in the sense of incorporating the basic legal rules and conceptions of a given community; it, too, would apply to an absolute monarchy or dictatorship as readily as to any other regime. In contemporary juristic works, however, a constitution is more commonly defined as a decision concerning the organization of government (Kägi 1945; Schmitt 1928), as a legal system of integration (Smend 1928), or as the basic norm (Kelsen 1945). Kelsen would trace any constitution to the one from which it is derived. "The document which embodies the first constitution is a real constitution, a binding norm, only on the condition that the basic norm is presupposed to be valid," he wrote (1945, p. 115), after having pointed out that "the validity of this first constitution is the last presupposition, the final postulate, upon which the validity of all the norms of our legal order depends" (1945, p. 115). These and similar definitions clearly embody a genetic theory of law; they all derive from a positivist notion of law, according to which law has its origin in the power (usually seen as force) of a government. Still different are those definitions, embodying morphological theories, which describe a constitution in such terms as a system of divided powers (Lowenstein 1957), as a mixture of monarchy, aristocracy, and democracy, and similar indications of the pattern or design of a government. Definitions of this kind are usually given in more concrete terms and refer to a particular pattern or design, making it at times a paradigm or norm for all. Not only in popular parlance but also in advanced juristic thought do we find such statements. A sophisticated variant of morphological theorizing is represented by propositions alleging that the constitution, usually a particular one, is merely a *symbol* or a *myth*.

None of these generalized concepts of a constitution—whether philosophical, political, or legal (juristic)—are capable of providing the underpinning for the distinctive notion of constitution-

alism as a kind of political order which contrasts sharply with nonconstitutional systems, such as a totalitarian dictatorship. In order to develop such a concept, a constitution must be defined in a way that indicates the features which make it contrast with other kinds of political order. These features come into view when we ask: What is the political function of a constitution? If that question is asked, the constitution is seen as a process by which certain political objectives are realized. What are these objectives?

The first and foremost objective is that of protecting the individual member of the political community against interference in his personal sphere of genuine autonomy. It is his *self* that each man presumably wishes to have safeguarded. The roots of this concern with the self are predominantly Judaic and Christian, although it must be recognized that self-concern is not completely lacking in Islam, Hinduism, Buddhism, and Confucianism. Such a self is first of all defined by a convictional core which is seen as "inviolable," if the self is to be maintained in its uniqueness and independence. It is seen as possessing the right (or freedom) of religion. Beyond this core, the individual's sphere is variable; constitutionalism has stressed different rights at different times, and the content of such rights has undergone significant changes. The seventeenth and eighteenth centuries liked to talk about such rights as "natural" and by that adjective to suggest that they inhere in human nature and hence are unalterable. Nowadays the term "human" rights is preferred, because comparative historical observation has shown that these rights are subject to differentiation in time and place and that their real significance must be seen in terms of a minimum sufficient to protect the individual's convictional core.

The basic objective of protecting the individual member of the political community is reinforced and institutionally safeguarded by the division of political power, both functionally and spatially. Such division may therefore be considered the second objective of a constitution. Typically, the "separation of powers" serves as the functional division, while federalism serves as the spatial. Both require a constitution for their effective operation. They operate as restraints on governmental power. In this perspective, then, a constitutional government is one in which effective restraints divide political power, or, to put it negatively, prevent the concentration of such power. Thus, constitutionalism is both the practice of politics according to "rules of the game," which insure effective restraints upon governmental and other political action, and the theory—explanatory and justificatory—of this practice.

Historical development

Modern Western constitutionalism, with its emphasis upon the individual's rights, is not the only form in which constitutionalism, defined as a system of restraints upon governmental action, has historically been practiced. Not to go too far afield, the historical discussion will be limited here to Greek, Roman, and medieval constitutionalism, before turning to the history of English, French, and American constitutionalism. For Greek and Roman, as well as medieval, constitutional ideas have been so important in shaping modern constitutionalism that they greatly help us to understand it. At the same time, the failure to distinguish them clearly from modern constitutionalism has been the source of many confusions and misunderstandings.

Greek constitutionalism (as well as Roman) was largely practice, rather than theory, although Aristotle's doctrine of the *politeia* in the specific sense of the model regime constituted a significant first theory. Before we turn to it, Plato may be said to have pointed the way by making *nomos* the criterion by which to distinguish good from bad regimes. For the *nomos*, while not oriented toward the individual, embodied the prevalent communal notions about what is right and just, and provided a standard that transcended the particular system of rule. Plato was convinced, however, that the observance of *nomos* could be insured only by concentrating power in the hands of the wise. In his later years, especially in the *Laws*, he was inclined to concede that much of the *nomos* might be spelled out in *nomoi* that were observed by all. However, the mode of finding these *nomoi*—by means of a *nomothetes*, or legislator—as well as their ultimate enforcement through the Nocturnal Council, shows him to have retained his ultimate confidence in the wise man rather than in the safeguarding constitution—as do both Confucianism and Hinduism [see PLATO]. Aristotle, preoccupied with the general happiness, advanced further toward institutional safeguards. His notion of a mixed constitution which would be a mean between monarchy, aristocracy, and democracy was philosophically related to his preference for *mesotes*, the middle road, the mean between extremes. Historically, it constituted a rationalization of political practice in a number of Greek *poleis*, if we are to credit the few hints that survive [see ARISTOTLE].

Both the Aristotelian argument in favor of a mixed constitution and the corresponding practices in a *polis*, such as those which Solon sought to establish at Athens, rested upon a value preference very different from that of modern constitutionalism. The stress was upon stability and strength. Such was also the core objective of Roman constitutionalism. Slowly evolved over the centuries, the Roman constitution was a wonder of complicated and interrelated restraints. All the different offices, from that of the consuls down to those of the minor functionaries, were subject to carefully elaborated rules embodied in law supported by powerful religious beliefs. Polybius provided a celebrated analysis of this constitutional order, as it presumably worked around 200 B.C.; and Cicero, in the *Republic* and the *Laws*, added further touches of insight and rationale. What Polybius marveled at, however, was not how it protected the individual but how it provided the strength which made Rome great by giving the Roman political community a measure of internal stability and providing a balance of the different classes. It was this strength and stability which later inspired Machiavelli, Harrington, and Montesquieu. The problem which they and many others contemplated at length, and which each solved in terms of his own political convictions, was the problem of how this strong and stable system came to decline and eventually to be replaced by monarchical absolutism. John Dickinson added his own interpretation in *Death of a Republic* (1963), making an analogy between the process and the modern rise of totalitarian dictatorship. Like Montesquieu and others, he interpreted Roman constitutionalism in the perspective of contemporary problems of constitutionalism. The problem is basically simpler; Roman constitutionalism provided strength and stability for a city-state. It was unsuited to the larger territorial power which Rome became as the result of this strength and stability. Rome's decline was inherent in its rise—a built-in dialectic often observed in nature. As McIlwain has insisted, there can be no doubt that the theory of the Roman constitution was that "the people and the people alone are the source of all law" (1940, p. 48). This means, of course, that for an understanding of Roman constitutionalism a grasp of the nature of *lex* is vital. The distinction between private and public law is essential and is "a distinction that lies to this day behind the whole history of our legal safeguards of the rights of the individual against encroachment of government" (McIlwain 1940, p. 48). The Roman notion that law is the common solemn promise of the public became a vital ingredient of Western constitutionalism. Without such a concept of law, constitutionalism's political function as a system of restraints is greatly weakened.

Medieval constitutionalism built on the basis

thus laid. It sprang from the medieval idea that all legitimate government is government according to law. But that law was held to be largely in existence and merely in need of being made "public," although the idea of legislation was never entirely lost. How could it be to men who read the Old Testament and the corpus juris, which are filled with evidence of legislation as a matter of historical fact? But all this law was already at hand, as was the customary law by which men lived in their particular national communities. Medieval constitutionalism arose, as did Greek and Roman constitutionalism, from the struggle of an aristocracy seeking to restrain a monarchical ruler who threatened to become a tyrant. In this struggle, constitutionalism became associated with the church, which in some places and at certain times even played a leading role. The share of the bishops in the fighting preceding the issuance of Magna Charta certainly was considerable. King John's attempts to deal with this ecclesiastical opposition by enlisting the support of the pope miscarried; he misunderstood the position of the church. Vitally interested in the restraining of governments, and anxious to retain control over certain fields of law, such as family law, the church developed the doctrine of natural law as it had come down from the Stoics, more especially Cicero, and had been incorporated in the imperial code, the Corpus Juris Civilis. To determine whether particular laws were in keeping with the natural law—for only then could they be considered fully just laws—the church felt it ought to participate in the making of such laws as well as in the interpretation of established law and custom. In the Roman law, a *constitutio* was a law established by the emperor; in the medieval world, such collective bodies as the "king in parliament" were seen as the successors to the emperor. *Legem constituere* meant to establish the law by formal enactment. Ecclesiastics ought to participate—and fairly generally did participate—in this process. For example, the Golden Bull, which regulated the election of the Holy Roman emperor, was a *constitutio* in this classical sense. The archbishops of Cologne, Mainz, and Trier participated and were made electors under this "constitutional" charter. For many medieval thinkers, jurists, and philosophers, no distinct constitutional problem existed apart from the general proposition that all government should be according to and under the law. Had not the great Aquinas treated of government just incidentally within the context of a discussion of law and justice as part of the *Summa theologica*? [*See* AQUINAS.]

In England, Bracton is perhaps most representa-

tive of this medieval stress on law and the legal restraints on government. But a more distinctive sense of the contrast between English and Continental practice is found in John Fortescue, who made the distinction between a *regimen regale* and a *regimen regale et politicum* the keynote of his discussion of English government. Here the word *politicum* appeared as representative of the Aristotelian *politeia* in its differentiating sense of a model government of mixed and restrained powers. As authority Fortescue cited Aquinas, thereby incidentally suggesting what has often since been overlooked or even denied, namely, that the great Scholastic was a constitutionalist. In the *Summa* he clearly states that a mixed government is the best (II, 1, 94, 4 and II, 1, 105, 1); similar statements can be found elsewhere. This view is in accord with the later part of *De regimine principum*, in which Ptolemy of Lucca elaborated the views of his master, albeit with some liberty. For both Aquinas and Fortescue, it was crucial that a government be subject to legal restraints; government was best when instituted by law. From here the road leads to English seventeenth-century constitutionalism, but before this development is traced, it is necessary to sketch the constitutionalism embodied in conciliarism.

Conciliarism is, in a sense, the application of medieval constitutionalism to the church itself. The ecclesiastical insistence upon the need for subjecting all authority to legal restraints was claimed to apply to the church. Effective participation of the lower ecclesiastical orders and even of the laity was demanded in the councils which were called upon to formulate the law. In this discussion, the constitutional aspect became increasingly explicit. From William of Ockham to Nicholas of Cusa, the idea of consent as a vital ingredient of law gained ground, and the question of how to organize the expression of such consent was faced. Church councils appeared in analogy to feudal representative assemblies, such as the English Parliament, and their traditional participation in establishing the law was claimed to be applicable to the government of the church.

Even though the conciliar movement failed, there can be little doubt that it spread some of the key ideas of constitutionalism. Thus reinforced, constitutionalism might have triumphed throughout Europe in a broader secular form, had it not been thwarted by the countervailing arguments arising from religious dissension and civil war. For against these divisive tendencies, the ineluctable demand arose for a concentration of power in the hands of a ruler—the famous doctrine of sovereignty as first enunciated by Jean Bodin [*see*

BODIN]. Although this doctrine was perfected and radicalized by Thomas Hobbes, England's insularity made the demand seem less urgent [see HOBBES]. The constitutionalist position had in the meantime been maintained in spite of Tudor "absolutism" and was developed in the sixteenth century by Sir Thomas Smith and Richard Hooker. In his *De republica Anglorum* (1583), Smith stressed the representative function of the "king in parliament" and delineated in functional terms the emergent notion of a mixed government through a separation of powers. Richard Hooker, in his celebrated *Laws of Ecclesiastical Polity* (1593–1597), developed a careful elaboration of Aquinas' philosophy of law and the need for general consent, if it is to hold. But the consensus in terms of which both Smith and Hooker wrote and argued gradually declined, and the more poignant issues of modern constitutionalism presented themselves in the course of the revolution and its aftermath which filled much of the seventeenth century.

Probably the most significant and certainly the most lasting legal contribution to the modernization of medieval constitutionalism was made by Edward Coke. With all the skill of a great lawyer and an extraordinary capacity for historical learning, combined with a striking lack of historical sense, he brought medieval precedent to bear upon the issues arising between the king and Parliament or, more realistically, between Puritans and Anglicans, between old wealth and new wealth, between landed property and trading interests. Coke, more than any other man, made Magna Charta the battle cry of those who insisted on man's rights [see COKE]. The Petition of Rights of 1628, while the first major official declaration of such rights, was still preoccupied with the rights of Englishmen, as prescriptively recognized since Magna Charta. As the revolutionary movement gained momentum after the calling of the Long Parliament in 1640, the historic and legal guarantees were reinforced by the idea that these rights derive from the very essence of man's nature. And while the Petition of Rights had been concerned with property rights, the right to a man's freedom of conscience—the right, that is, of freely confessing one's religious conviction—moved into the foreground. It was at the heart of Oliver Cromwell's outlook and was given eloquent expression in John Milton's *Areopagitica* (1644). The so-called Agreement of the People proposed by Cromwell's more radical following was the first of a series of attempts toward effectively institutionalizing these rights through the protection of a constitutional system. In a number of epoch-making statements,

Cromwell proclaimed the idea that in any constitution there is "somewhat fundamental" which ought not to be subject to change by Parliament. Since Parliament insisted on violating such restraints upon its own exercise of power, Cromwell eventually had to rule arbitrarily, a *dictateur malgré lui*.

Cromwell's desperate efforts were accompanied by two striking theoretical efforts, each reflecting, in a sense, one horn of his dilemma. Thomas Hobbes, the philosopher, rejecting outright the idea of constitutionalism, pleaded in his *Leviathan* (1651) for a radical concentration of powers in the hands of the sovereign. Opposing him, James Harrington, the political theorist, in his *Oceana* (1656) recognized that the hoary doctrine of a mixed constitution implied a separation of the powers of governing and that a "government of laws and not of men" can be achieved only if those governing are "constrained to shake off this or that inclination." According to him, there are two everrecurring orders, the "natural aristocracy" and the common people. They must concur in making laws, and together constitute the legislative power. A third power, the magistracy, must execute the laws. The balance between these three bodies is achieved in a constitution, and a commonwealth consists of "the senate proposing, the people resolving, and the magistracy executing." It is evident that Harrington's generalization was based upon Roman and English experience [see HARRINGTON].

Soon after Cromwell's death, English sentiment swung back to its traditional constitution and in the course of the Restoration recaptured a measure of that consensus upon which it had rested. When James II threatened to disrupt this consensus, it powerfully reasserted itself in the so-called Glorious Revolution, a smoothly efficient *coup d'état* that replaced one king with another and reaffirmed the basic rights in a traditional declaration, the bill of rights, in 1689. John Locke was, of course, the theorist of these events, who skillfully summed up and generalized English constitutional thought. His *Two Treatises of Government* (1690), although they antedate the Glorious Revolution by nearly a decade, have long and rightly been taken to be a justification of this proceeding; for, especially in the second treatise, Locke plainly asserts a people's right to give itself its own constitution [see LOCKE]. This right, although first stated by John Milton, was part of a congeries of rights that Locke held to be natural and universal, and epitomized in the formula of the rights of life, liberty, and property. Property was, of course, dear to the rising bourgeoisie; but in Locke's understanding, it still was very broadly construed to mean virtually the entire personal sphere of what is a man's own. It was the firm belief of Locke and succeeding generations that no government which failed to recognize these rights could possibly be considered legitimate, because no one could be held to have surrendered what "he has no power to part with." Hence, the "freedom" to choose a form of government really excluded the right to choose a nonconstitutional government. Constitutional government was a government in which the crucial power to make laws was divided between king, Lords, and Commons, while the other two powers, the executive and federative, distinguished by Locke from the legislative one, were attributed to the king along with his share of the legislative power. Only in the Act of Settlement in 1701 was the independence of the judiciary recognized, thus laying the basis for Montesquieu's interpretation of the separation of powers in more strictly functional terms.

In a celebrated chapter of *The Spirit of Laws* (1748) Montesquieu undertook to restate the doctrine of restraints in more nearly systematic and "logical" terms than Locke's tradition-derived view had offered. His formulation of the doctrine, distinguishing the legislative, executive, and judicial functions and attributing each to a separate individual or group, achieved universal acclaim, was institutionalized in the American and French revolutions, and became the basis of nineteenth-century constitution making. These three functions still revolved around the idea of law: the law-making function was contrasted with the law-administering (executive) and the law-interpreting (judicial) functions [see MONTESQUIEU]. Although he called these three functions "powers," Montesquieu pointed out that the judicial power was "in a sense nil" (*dans une façon nul*)—that is, no power at all. By this curious phrase, Montesquieu did not, of course, wish to suggest that the judiciary had no function but, rather, that this function depended for its implementation upon sanctions which ultimately required force. (It was precisely this "impotence" of the judicial power which recommended it to the American constitution makers as the "guardian" of the constitution.) The French revolutionary movement, which far transcended the governmental and constitutional sphere, did not stop to consider such niceties. Bent upon achieving the millennium, the successive constitutions were increasingly inspired by Rousseau's radicalism, which would "force men to be free" [see ROUSSEAU]. Between the Declaration of the Rights of Man and Citizen, issued in 1789, and the dictatorship of Napoleon, the French ranged

through all the phases of revolutionary violence; and the truly constitutional beginnings, inspired by Montesquieu and Mirabeau, soon yielded to a concentration of powers in support of a program of social transformation and renewal carried out with religious zeal. Even so, the French more fully grasped the key notion of a constituent power than had previously been the case.

Very different and sharply contrasting was the evolution of constitutional thought in America. Starting from English precedent and utilizing the experience derived from colonial charters, the fathers of American constitutionalism were anything but revolutionary in outlook. Washington, Adams, Jefferson, Hamilton, and Madison—to mention only the most illustrious names—were all men who believed in order as well as progress. To them, the position which independence had occasioned required orderly resolution without delay. The two successive constitutions which they helped fashion were both inspired by the ideas of Locke and Montesquieu and of the entire constitutionalist tradition which they represented and embodied. But such inspiration as the American constitutionalists received was tempered by their knowledge that concrete and unprecedented problems were facing them. As a result, they discovered a number of highly significant institutional solutions which past constitutionalism had failed to resolve, notably federalism, judicial review of legislation, and the process of constitutional amendment. This achievement was theoretically reinforced by its skillful defense in *The Federalist*, in which Hamilton, with the help of Madison and Jay, expounded the doctrine of modern constitutionalism in such elaboration that it could become the basis of nineteenth-century constitution making. Along with the ideological stimulation of the French revolutions —for the great revolution of 1789 was followed by a series of *coup d'état*-like revolutions in 1833, 1848, 1851, and 1871—the American Revolution seemed to prove that a community's political order may be rationally constituted and that an act of political decision making can organize the government and make it legitimate.

In spite of lingering doubts which the notion of organic growth instilled in the minds of the more conservative elements, European nations undertook the task of constitution making. Belgium, the Netherlands, the Scandinavian kingdoms, the several German kingdoms, Switzerland, Spain, Austria-Hungary, and Italy all fashioned constitutions in the image of those of Britain and the United States. Constitutionalism became the battle cry of all progressive forces; and broadly based popular movements, such as that of German unification, were conceived in terms of making a constitution. The unsuccessful attempt, in 1848, to achieve such a constitutional order on a broadly representative and liberal basis was, to be sure, replaced by an authoritarian solution in the *Reich* of Bismarck's creation; but even then a constitution crowned the newly won unity.

Indeed, many monarchical rulers sought added legitimacy during the post-1848 period by "giving a constitution" to their people. Such royal constitution making regarded the constitution as a grant from the "sovereign" and hence as an alternative to the democratic legitimacy of a popularly elected constituent assembly. While imperfect as a realization of constitution making, it was nonetheless a step in the direction of establishing restraint on government, through autolimitation. That it constituted progress may readily be surmised, if one considers the possibility of a totalitarian regime today believing itself to be bound by the "constitution" it has established, instead of treating it merely as a façade. Monarchical constitutionalism was, in the sense of autolimitation, government according to law. As the democratic forces gained ascendancy in the course of the nineteenth century, such monarchical constitution making became outmoded. It lacked the legitimacy of a constitution based upon popular approval. In Switzerland and other countries, democratically based procedures, similar to those used in the United States, were generally adopted.

Making constitutions of this democratic kind generally calls for a representative constituent assembly in which the constitution is debated and eventually adopted. The work of such an assembly may be reinforced by submitting the constitution to popular referendum, but such plebiscites are of doubtful value. Rejections have been few, the most striking recent instance being that of the first postwar constitution, submitted to the French electorate in April 1946. In the case of federal systems, there is also likely to be some procedure for securing the assent of a majority of the member units, through either legislative action or referenda. As constitutional experience has accumulated, the role of "experts" has become more and more important. Indeed, preparatory commissions have often been established to draft a constitutional proposal, as was done in the case of Puerto Rico in 1952 and the several German *Länder* under American occupation in 1946. Experts, whether jurists or political scientists, can be most effectively employed at this formative stage of constitution making. The problem confronting the modern constitution maker is

that of fitting past experience with constitutional government to the particular circumstances of time and place. In the emergent nations, this task often involves complicated problems of cultural adaptation. But such adaptations apart, there is the more general problem of determining the components of a model constitution. Within a particular cultural context, such models have been laid out for municipalities and states in the United States. Whether it is possible to formulate a broadly conceived common denominator of universal validity is an open question.

Contemporary problems

It remains to delineate briefly some aspects of contemporary constitutionalism in Europe, the emergent nations, and the Soviet sphere. Since the second world war, constitutionalism in Europe has served the goal of giving expression to what have been called the "negative revolutions" in France, Italy, and Germany. By these revolutions a defunct and generally rejected totalitarian fascist past has been negated and replaced by a more or less conventional constitutional order. The constitutions of the Fourth Republic, of the Italian Republic, and of the Federal Republic of Germany closely resemble the orders which existed prior to the seizure of power by Mussolini, Hitler, and the Pétain–Laval group. There were and are significant differences, of course: the Fourth Republic attempted the federalization of France's colonial empire; Italy abolished the monarchy; and the Federal Republic is still only a torso, although it is stabilizing its executive and moving toward a two-party system. Moreover, the Fourth Republic has yielded to the Fifth, which is characterized by a vigorous presidential system with little more than the trappings of parliamentarism remaining. At the same time, its colonial empire has all but vanished. Both changes together constitute a more radical and revolutionary transformation than has occurred in either Italy or Germany. The constitution under which they have occurred did not envisage them, even though it has permitted them. It has proved a feeble restraint upon de Gaulle's determination to govern the country as he sees fit. While the Italian and German constitutions have more nearly achieved the functional purpose of restraint, they, too, have been bent and twisted in various ways. Thus all three constitutions serve to illustrate the weakening of constitutionalism in Europe. This decline is not to be wondered at when one observes the lack of interest in and support for constitutionalism among the citizenry.

Beyond the national borders, constitutionalism

has played a certain role in the broad movement for the unification of Europe. Within the European movement, there has been considerable discussion about the most suitable constitution, with federalism and parliamentarism as the key issues. Beyond the initial Council of Europe, the Community of the Six emerged. A draft constitution for this political community was fashioned by a constituent assembly, the Assemblée Ad Hoc, in 1952/1953; quite a few other drafts have been put forward by organizations and individuals. A radical group of European federalists has pleaded for a popularly elected constituent assembly—so far without any significant result. In the meantime the unification has gone forward slowly within the context of cultural and economic life, sanctioned by international treaties and enforced by international institutions. Even a European bill of rights has been agreed upon (within the broader and looser framework of the Council of Europe), and its enforcement machinery has been ratified by a number of states. The role of constitutionalism in all these developments has been limited. To some extent, the lingering conviction of its importance has actually been a hindrance rather than a help to progress, because of its tendency to formalize and institutionalize before the underlying political and social realities justify such actions.

Although constitutionalism is apparently weakening in its heartland, it has been a factor of considerable importance in the emergent nations. To most of them, the fashioning of a constitution for their political order has been significant as a symbol of their newly won freedom. Some of the constitutions are of extraordinary complexity and formal sophistication, notably that of India. Here the task of organizing a whole culture of continental dimensions presented problems never before solved by Western constitutionalism. Working with European and American precedents, India had to add totally new provisions. It is, however, widely felt that the Indian constitution does not really express political reality—a criticism which could, of course, also be applied to most other constitutional systems. Only those parts of politics which can be expressed in legal rules can be reflected in a constitution. Behind the formal organization, an informal one will always operate. It is an essential part of the living constitution, which could not function without it. Insight into this aspect of constitutionalism has often led and continues to lead to a cynicism which looks upon a constitution as merely a façade behind which the true reality of the political order is hidden. Such arguments usually overlook some of the most obvious counter-

arguments. Terms of office, modes of election, territorial divisions, and many other provisions in modern constitutions are descriptive of at least part of the political reality. Clearly they do not exhaust that description and may not even mention certain important political institutions—for example, parties. In many of the emergent nations constitutionalism cannot fulfill even this more modest function, and does not restrain the government because it is not the expression of a firm belief in the importance of doing so. More especially, bills of rights remain empty paper declarations because the ruling party or clique readily identifies itself and its power with the public interest. This tendency is enhanced by the practice in totalitarian communist states.

Within the Soviet sphere, and more particularly in the Soviet Union itself, the constitutions are largely façades. The purely formal character of such documents as the successive constitutions of the Soviet Union is revealed by the fact that they do not evolve. They remain what they are, on paper, until one day they are completely altered by the effective rulers of the dominant party. They embody essentially what the regime wishes the world outside and its own people to believe about the political order. They therefore invariably contain extended bills of rights devoid of all enforcement machinery or possibility of implementation. The bill of rights is seen as a declaration of principle, and its function was summed up in 1962 by the Soviet scholar A. I. Lepyoshkin as follows: ". . . every constitution . . . is a result of changes in the balance of class forces; it expresses the will and interest of the classes in power, guarantees the principles of such social and state order as is advantageous for and agreeable with the interests of these classes. . . . The Soviet constitution embodies the principles of socialist democracy, it is a genuinely democratic constitution." Surprisingly enough, Lepyoshkin did not hesitate to claim that the Soviet constitution "serves as the most important instrument of safeguarding the rights and interests of the Soviet citizens from any encroachment. . . ." No details were furnished, however, as to how such a constitution actually safeguards these rights; it might conceivably be "the most" important instrument without being an important one, since no other instruments exist.

The broad tradition of constitutionalism has in this century been projected onto the world plane. The Covenant of the League of Nations and the Charter of the United Nations are both embodiments of this international constitutionalism. Quite in keeping with the constitutionalist tradition, a

Universal Declaration of Human Rights was adopted after vigorous debate by the United Nations in December 1948; but no enforcement machinery has been set up, except for the weak supervisory machinery provided for dependent territories. Indeed, it is very doubtful that any such enforcement could at present be implemented. International constitutionalism is not a mere façade; but the very fact of the participation of totalitarian regimes makes it inevitable that this constitutionalism partakes to some extent of the character of totalitarian constitutionalism. That such constitutionalism is imperfect, that it does not restrain the governments operating under it to any significant degree, is obvious. That it may nevertheless become the basis for gradual implementation, and thus the starting point for the achievement of genuine constitutionalism, is the hope of many. Such hope may find some confirmation in the past history of constitutionalism.

CARL J. FRIEDRICH

[*See also* CONSTITUTIONAL LAW; DEMOCRACY. *Other relevant material may be found in* CRISIS GOVERNMENT; DELEGATION OF POWERS; ELECTIONS; FEDERALISM; MODERNIZATION; PARLIAMENTARY GOVERNMENT; PRESIDENTIAL GOVERNMENT; REPRESENTATION; *and in the biographies of* BAGEHOT; BEARD; DICEY; HARRINGTON.]

BIBLIOGRAPHY

Classical statements on constitutions and constitutionalism can be found in Aristotle's Politics; *Cicero's* Republic; *Thomas Aquinas'* Summa theologica 1265–1273; *Marsilius of Padua's* Defensor pacis 1324; *John Fortescue's* The Governance of England 1471; *Thomas Smith's* De republica Anglorum 1583; *Richard Hooker's* Laws of Ecclesiastical Polity 1593–1597; *John Milton's* Areopagitica 1644; *Thomas Hobbes's* Leviathan 1651; *John Harrington's* Oceana 1656; *John Locke's* Two Treatises of Government 1690; *Montesquieu's* The Spirit of Laws 1748; *Rousseau's* The Social Contract 1762; The Federalist 1787–1788; *Edmund Burke's* Reflections on the French Revolution 1790; *Immanuel Kant's* Rechtslehre 1797; *Benjamin Constant's* Cours de politique constitutionnelle 1818–1820; *Georg Hegel's* The Philosophy of Right 1821; *and John Stuart Mill's* Considerations on Representative Government 1861. *For contemporary treatments see the works listed below.*

BEARD, CHARLES A. 1943 *The Republic: Conversations on Fundamentals.* New York: Viking.
BRYCE, JAMES 1905 *Constitutions.* New York: Oxford Univ. Press.
BURDEAU, GEORGES 1959 *Droit constitutionnel et institutions politiques.* 8th ed. Paris: Librairie Générale de Droit et de Jurisprudence.
DICKINSON, JOHN 1963 *Death of a Republic: Politics and Political Thought at Rome 59–44 B.C.* Edited by George Lee Haskins. New York: Macmillan.
ESMEIN, ADHÉMAR (1896) 1927–1928 *Éléments de droit constitutionnel français et comparé.* 8th ed. 2 vols. Paris: Sirey.
FRIEDRICH, CARL J. (1937) 1950 *Constitutional Government and Democracy: Theory and Practice in Europe and America.* Rev. ed. Boston: Ginn. → Originally published as *Constitutional Government and Politics: Nature and Development.*
FRIEDRICH, CARL J. 1957 *Constitutional Reason of State: The Survival of the Constitutional Order.* Providence, R.I.: Brown Univ. Press.
KÄGI, WERNER 1945 *Die Verfassung als rechtliche Grundordnung des Staates: Untersuchungen über die Entwicklungstendenzen im modernen Verfassungsrecht.* Zurich: Polygraphischer Verlag.
KELSEN, HANS (1945) 1961 *General Theory of Law and State.* 20th Century Legal Philosophy Series, Vol. 1. New York: Russell & Russell. → First published in German.
LOEWENSTEIN, KARL 1957 *Political Power and the Governmental Process.* Univ. of Chicago Press.
McBAIN, HOWARD LEE 1927 *The Living Constitution: A Consideration of the Realities and Legends of Our Fundamental Law.* New York: Workers Education Bureau.
McILWAIN, CHARLES H. (1917–1937) 1939 *Constitutionalism and the Changing World.* Cambridge Univ. Press; New York: Macmillan.
McILWAIN, CHARLES H. (1940) 1947 *Constitutionalism, Ancient and Modern.* Rev. ed. Ithaca, N.Y.: Cornell Univ. Press. → A paperback edition was published in 1958.
POCOCK, JOHN G. A. 1957 *The Ancient Constitution and the Feudal Law: A Study of English Historical Thought in the 17th Century.* Cambridge Univ. Press.
SCHINDLER, DIETRICH 1932 *Verfassungsrecht und soziale Struktur.* Zurich: Schulthess.
SCHMITT, CARL 1928 *Verfassungslehre.* Munich: Duncker & Humblot.
SMEND, RUDOLF 1928 *Verfassung und Verfassungsrecht.* Munich: Duncker & Humblot.
STERNBERGER, ADOLF 1956 *Lebende Verfassung: Studien über Koalition und Opposition.* Meisenheim (Germany): Hain.
STUBBS, WILLIAM 1874–1878 *The Constitutional History of England, in Its Origins and Development.* 3 vols. Oxford: Clarendon.
WHEARE, KENNETH C. 1951 *Modern Constitutions.* Oxford Univ. Press.
WORMUTH, FRANCIS D. 1949 *The Origins of Modern Constitutionalism.* New York: Harper.

CONSTRUCTION
See HOUSING.

CONSUMER CHOICE
See UTILITY.

CONSUMER CREDIT
See INSTALLMENT CREDIT.

CONSUMER SOVEREIGNTY

"Consumer sovereignty" is one of those concepts that flourish and are widely influential long before they are explicitly recognized and named. (Their belated recognition is often concomitant with their decline.) Much of the substance of consumer sovereignty is implied in Adam Smith. The focus of subsequent classical economics on cost of production as the basic determinant of market decisions temporarily sidetracked this emphasis. It returned more strongly with the Austrian school of Wieser and Menger, and in the work of Jevons, Pareto, Marshall, Pigou, and Wicksell. In 1936 W. H. Hutt in *Economists and the Public* coined the term to refer to a common fundamental presupposition in all these works.

Consumer sovereignty has been used in both a descriptive and a normative form. In the first form, the term simply means that all economic processes are ultimately focused toward satisfying the wants of the final consumer. Production, exchange, and distribution are all means; consumption is the end. Moreover, in a free market system, market performance is in fact responsive to the specific wants of the consumers within the system. The question of *how* responsive leads to the normative form. As a normative principle, consumer sovereignty asserts that the performance of any economy ought to be evaluated in terms of how well it fulfills the wants of its consumers. Performance will be affected by the structural characteristics of the economy, by public policy, by behavior of participants that is not uniquely determined by structure and public policy, and by certain external circumstances. Our discussion will center on the normative form of the concept, since this will automatically illuminate both forms.

Association with a free market economy. Consumer sovereignty has been frequently associated closely—but misleadingly—with a free market economy. Since it can help to isolate the boundaries of the principle, we shall examine the alleged association. It comprises the following four steps:

(1) *Knowledge of consumer wants.* No one knows what a consumer wants as well as he does himself. Consequently, his wants will be best reflected in his market demand for commodities.

(2) *Expression of wants.* Consumer demand is best expressed in terms of actual choices made by consumers in the market—in terms of market transactions—since, being rational, consumers will adequately inform themselves of how best to realize their wants in the presence of given opportunities.

(3) *Responsiveness of production to wants.* Free enterprise, directed by the profit motive and intense competition in all markets, brings about the best possible adaptation of resources to meet consumer market demands, given the available resources and state of technology. "Best" is defined as a set of outcomes such that, whichever one of these obtains, no feasible alteration can bring about an alternative outcome in which any individual is made better off without at least one individual being made worse off.

(4) *Laissez-faire.* So long as the conditions for a free competitive market system obtain, a laissez-faire public policy will lead to a maximum degree of consumer sovereignty.

The emphases in this version are on individualism, on free competitive markets, and on laissez-faire. "Wants" are the wants of individual consumers; individual consumers know their own wants; they are self-motivated to become informed about the real alternatives available to them; and competition both protects them against exploitation and guarantees appropriate responsiveness in the use of resources to meet their expressed wants. Thus, governmental interference is at best superfluous and, more likely, destructive of consumer sovereignty. Finally, the very criterion by which the appropriateness of market response is evaluated is one that refuses to sacrifice any one consumer's well-being to that of others.

This version of the principle has sometimes been advanced as its true, or official, version. This is incorrect. The position just described is not in fact simply an interpretation of consumer sovereignty. It is a complex of at least three distinct normative principles: consumer sovereignty, freedom of choice, and Pareto optimality. Freedom of choice asserts that every economic unit should be permitted to make and implement all decisions bearing upon its own welfare. Pareto optimality asserts that when comparing any pair of social outcomes, one state can be declared superior to the other state if, *and only if*, at least one individual is better off and no individual worse off in the first state than in the second state.

Relation to freedom of choice. Comparing consumer sovereignty with freedom of choice, the first refers to the ends of economic activity and the second to the means by which these or other ends can be attained. Concretely, freedom of choice refers to the administrative procedure of allowing economic units to use their own property to make whatever voluntary trades they wish in the market (Lange 1938; Bergson 1948). While an administrative procedure—a means—can become valued as an end in itself, this is not the same end as envisaged under consumer sovereignty. Either of these principles can be supported without the other. We may have a system adhering to consumer sovereignty without freedom of choice where a central authority uses nonmarket means to discover what consumers' commodity preferences are (for example, by questionnaires, votes, or psychological projective tests) and then channels resources to meet them. Freedom of choice can be supported without consumer sovereignty where a central authority itself decides what the basic goals should be, independently of what it thinks consumers want, then employs resources to produce in accordance with its own goals, but allows the output to be distributed by means of market choices on the part of consumers, setting prices so that all markets clear. As another example of this last, consumers might be permitted to trade in free, perfectly responsive markets, yet, in a sense to be examined below, might not really know what they truly want and as a result make deluded choices.

The relationship can be more complicated, so that, despite appearances, one principle may be present without the other. In purchasing medical services from a physician, the patient seems to be sacrificing his sovereignty, since the doctor makes all decisions of importance about treatment. Yet, in effect, the patient delegates the doctor to decide for him: the goal of treatment is the patient's best interests. On the other hand, a television viewer may believe that he votes for programming because he is free to choose what to watch; yet the sponsor's programming decisions are responses to viewers' purchases of his product, not necessarily to their viewing decisions. It is only a precarious and variable association between viewing programs and being responsive to the sponsor's commercials—at least insofar as any such association is believed by the sponsor to exist—that preserves the viewer's illusion of influencing program content. His influence is actually far less direct and decisive than he may believe.

Notwithstanding these examples showing the logical independence of consumer sovereignty from freedom of choice, there is, of course, a strong empirical affinity between them. The individual consumer's wants can, in a wide variety of situations, be accurately reflected in his overt choices. Moreover, the alternative of indirect nonmarket inquiry is considerably more expensive for discovering wants that can be so reflected. Thus, as an empirical generalization, to satisfy freedom of choice in the context of responsive markets is also to satisfy consumer sovereignty to a first approximation; further, to want to satisfy consumer sovereignty is to be willing to see freedom of choice satisfied to a first approximation as well. In practical circumstances these first approximations may actually involve considerable and important divergences from the respective principles. We shall consider this below.

Relation to Pareto optimality.   The relationship between consumer sovereignty and Pareto optimality is significant just because it is not as close as is sometimes thought. It is sometimes believed that the former implies the latter. This is incorrect. What does consumer sovereignty imply about the relative evaluation of alternative outcomes? The problem is that different individuals have different wants (expressed as implicit preferences). Any pair of outcomes is therefore likely to affect different individuals differently, so that in the preponderant number of cases some individuals will be better off with one alternative, while others are better off with the other. The principle of consumer sovereignty would seem to imply that an improvement in any individual's position, all others remaining the same, represents a net social improvement. It has, for example, been used this way in Arrow's influential work in welfare economics (1951) and in the resultant literature. (For a bibliography, see Rothenberg 1961.) But it has nothing specific to say about aggregating some individuals' gains against others' losses. It neither specifies a particular method of aggregation, nor precludes the possibility of such specification. Thus, while it is not inferable from it, it is also not inconsistent with consumer sovereignty to judge that a social change that makes 100 million people significantly better off ("significantly," in terms of their own well-being), while making one person slightly worse off ("slightly," in terms of his well-being), represents social improvement. To do so formally would simply require supplementing consumer sovereignty with a particular normative criterion from which this assertion *is* inferable.

On the other hand, Pareto optimality, while going at least as far as consumer sovereignty, goes beyond this and *forecloses* the meaningfulness of any such aggregation, where contrary changes occur for different persons. It *is* inconsistent with Pareto optimality to hold that a social improvement occurred where ten million gained while one person lost. Thus, consumer sovereignty is a less complete criterion than Pareto optimality for judging aggregate social changes. On the other hand, it is also less restrictive because, needing to be supplemented by additional normative criteria, it can be adjoined to any of a number of different criteria. Pareto optimality represents only one such possible combination—consistent with, but not exhaustive of, consumer sovereignty. It is neither the exclusive, nor even the most appropriate, combination, remembering our example of near, but not complete, unanimity improvement. The whole family of normative criteria with the property that non-contrary improvements to any individual register as social improvements qualify as potential supplements, regardless of how variously they formulate interpersonal comparisons of welfare change.

The distinctiveness of the three principles signifies that consumer sovereignty, while not inconsistent with, is not uniquely to be associated with, an individualistic, laissez-faire, free market orientation. A proper appreciation of its scope therefore requires deeper examination of the concept itself.

The aggregation problem.   Assuming that consumer wants are to be fulfilled, there are two major problems to be considered in giving this operational significance. The first we have already touched on. How does one evaluate the extent to which different situations fulfill wants, when "wants" refers to the typically heterogeneous collection of a whole population? Assuming scarcity to be a universal condition, an economy can meet consumer wants only by compromising between the consumers' ends and the particular constraints imposed by the resources and state of technology available. Each pair of alternative compromises will typically have disparate effects on different members of the population. A complete criterion for comparing degree of fulfillment must make provision for aggregating gains and losses across individuals. Consumer sovereignty does not itself do this; it must be supplemented by additional normative assumptions. Such supplementation is by no means easy. Indeed, the search for a highly consensual formulation has monopolized much of the attention of welfare economics in the past twenty years (Kaldor 1939; Hicks 1939; Bergson 1938; Samuelson 1947, chapter 8; Arrow 1951; Boulding 1952; Rothenberg 1961). The upshot is that a supplemented consumer sovereignty criterion can take many forms. Its character will depend greatly on the specific supplementation. No particular supplementation has succeeded in commanding a consensus among economists.

The identification problem

The problem of aggregating wants assumes at best that each of the elements to be aggregated is the appropriate one. Such an assumption begs a critical question. Does consumer sovereignty contain clear guidelines for identifying the relevant individual ends to be fulfilled?

A reasonable model of consumer wants may be as follows. Consumers have directional strivings known as wants. These are operationally reflected in preferences toward different commodities. These preferences can be elicited by a variety of means, the most common being simply to observe actual market choices (under freedom of choice). The translation of wants into market choices involves an intermediate step of becoming informed about alternative trading opportunities. For our present purposes, the information involved concerns the prices and qualities of the respective commodities.

Applied to a model like this, the spirit of consumer sovereignty begs for consideration of two major types of qualifications on elicited preferences. One type concerns the concordance between choice and underlying wants—supportive qualifications. The other concerns qualifications designed to "correct" attitudes lying below the level of choice, on grounds of a deeper contradiction among wants—corrective qualifications. There exists a midregion where the two types are difficult, if not impossible, to distinguish.

Supportive qualifications.   Suppose individual consumers know ultimately what kinds of commodities they want. Given the constraint of purchasing power, the factor that mediates between this knowledge and the satisfaction of their wants is the availability of information about the specific commodity opportunities open to them. In the naive form of the consumer sovereignty principle, which combines freedom of choice and is popularly reflected in the motto *Caveat emptor* ("Let the buyer beware"), this information is largely integrated within the principle itself. Information is itself a scarce commodity, in that scarce resources (e.g., time and effort) must be expended to obtain it. Thus, it is not rational for a consumer to seek exhaustive information about every commodity he consumes. He will, if left to his own devices, choose just that amount of information which the particularity of each commodity and the cost of information together warrant. More information will be sought for commodities where information makes a big difference than where it does not, more where its acquisition cost is low than where it is high. Thus, the consumer will allocate his limited budget on an optimal combination not only of commodities but of information as well. The buyer must be responsible for decisions about information—that is, he must "beware"—just as he must be responsible for decisions about other commodities.

This version of the principle depends for its persuasiveness on low acquisition costs for "adequate" information, a high degree of market competitiveness, and only slight damage to be suffered by consumers for making an erroneous choice. If the consumer needs to know only very little, if competition in the market is so great that inferior brands will be quickly submerged by superior alternatives, and if an occasional error by him on the way to becoming experienced does not do great harm, then each consumer can be counted on to adjust efficiently to a long-run equilibrium without requiring any outside aid or interference on his behalf.

Unfortunately, the real world of choice for the consumer violates these conditions in important ways. The massive differentiation of products and the profuse flow of extremely complicated new commodities resulting from innovation have immeasurably increased the amount and subtlety (and thus the cost) of information needed by the consumer. Moreover, they have done so in commodities that matter greatly to the consumer—foods, drugs, and durables. There are a number of important markets where consumer ignorance is substantial and persistent. One manifestation of such ignorance is the magnitude and persistence of fraud. In markets where frequent repeat sales are not important, competitive forces may actually engender depreciation, rather than appreciation, of quality. Finally, there are many instances where *single* transactions have substantial, even vital, impact on the consumer, either in terms of his wealth or health or perhaps even his life itself. Purchase of a house, of ownership in a corporation, of a dangerous surgical operation, are examples. In these cases, errors on the way to informedness may be disastrous.

Under these circumstances, the individual consumer may either rationally or inadvertently remain very poorly informed; thus, the risk that his choices will lead to very unfortunate surprises is substantial. One may seriously question whether in such circumstances the consumer's externally unencumbered choices are really accurately directed toward fulfilling his wants.

The scope of consumer sovereignty therefore makes the degree of informedness a relevant qualification of free choice. It is an ambiguous qualification, however. How much informedness is enough? There is ample room for divergent views within the context of fulfillment of wants. Consideration of this qualification in practical affairs has had two major effects. First, it has rationalized direct government intervention in the market to regulate, control, and forbid certain production and marketing practices. Second, it has led the government to require specific levels of private information disclosure and to disseminate information on its own. Both effects will be discussed below.

In sum, actual market choices may reflect varying degrees of uninformedness. Application of the criterion of consumer sovereignty requires evaluating such choices in terms of their appositeness to underlying wants. These judgments, and any public intervention in the market taken to increase informedness, are to be interpreted as qualifications designed to improve the congruence between choices and the underlying wants that engender them: they support, rather than compete with, the satisfaction of these wants.

Corrective qualifications. Another set of qualifications that is integral to consumer sovereignty is aimed not at correcting means to consumer-recognized ends but at the ends themselves. There are two forms of such corrective qualifications: the first is intrapersonal, the second interpersonal.

Intrapersonal. The basic argument is that some individuals do not know what they truly want. Consumers have a hierarchy, rather than simply a collection, of wants. Just as some commodities are improper means for achieving certain ends, so some more proximate ends are less important than, and are inefficiently addressed to attaining, more ultimate ends.

Thus, children are deemed not really "to know what is good for them"—what they "really" want. An "improved" set of ends is externally substituted for their own perceived ends, whether in the form of actual interference with their choices or simply in how close an outsider judges their choices to reflect their "best interests." Much the same procedure is involved with respect to the psychotic and even the neurotic. In these latter categories it is not immaturity but internal conflict of goals or impaired introspection that makes a "corrective" qualification of free choice consistent with consumer sovereignty.

The category can be extended. Drug addicts are deemed not to be able to act in their own best interests. They may know in some sense that their overriding want is inconsistent with the fundamental pattern of their system of ends, yet be unable to control themselves. The same type of conflict may well exist in less dramatic form in many normal persons, in whom no physical addiction is present. The discipline of psychotherapy is substantially grounded on the assumption that conscious and unconscious conflicts of ends are pervasive. Thus, the degree to which given choices fulfill the "real" wants or interests of the choosers is clearly a question of some profundity—a question open to a whole spectrum of interpretations consistent with the emphasis of consumer sovereignty.

One final extremity of this category can be mentioned. An influential position in behavioristic ethics holds that all humans are subject to important uniformities in basic needs. Codes of social norms come into being as formulas by which individuals can efficiently realize these needs in a social setting. Thus, behavior that violates these codes—"immoral" behavior—really represents "unwise" behavior, behavior that is poorly aimed to meet the actor's own abiding ends. While the source of the adverse judgment seems to come from outside the individual and be at odds with him, the logic of the approach stresses that the ends, in terms of which the judgment is made, are the individual's own.

Thus, immaturity, internal conflict, and even "immorality" provide criteria that can be used in evaluating the accuracy of free choice. Each of these dimensions provides grounds for asserting that a given actor may not know what he truly wants.

The set of intrapersonal corrective qualifications has an important similarity to the previous set of supportive qualifications. Both involve individual responses to new information. It is not only decisions about means that are affected by new information; ends are affected as well. Accumulating experience with commodities influences specific and even general preferences: it influences wants. The three grounds for corrective criteria—immaturity, internal conflict, and immorality—are all subject to the accumulating experience of the individual, the first almost by definition. Thus, the problem of "incorrect ends" is partly a problem of uninformedness. A distinction remains, however, in that uninformedness about means enables us to specify far more accurately both the relevant missing information and the effect on choice of supplying it. We know far less about dependably inducing desired changes in values.

The practical difficulty of distinguishing between the learning components of means and ends is suggested by a brief look at advertising. Existing ostensibly to inform, advertising in fact attempts to persuade as well. The dividing line between the two is almost nonexistent. How, for example, is one to interpret the sheer repetition of advertising content, or simply of brand name, except as persuasion? The implications of advertising for consumer sovereignty are serious and perplexing. Do buyer responses to advertising represent a correction of means or of ends? In other words, when there is a divergence between the arrow and the target, does advertising have the pure information-feedback effect of getting the arrow to move or the persuasive effect of getting the target to move? Insofar

as it is the latter, and the latter is a significant and pervasive impact, the whole force of the doctrine of consumer sovereignty (especially when joined to freedom of choice) diminishes appreciably. If wants are mercurial, trivial, easily manipulable from without, there ceases to be much justification in orienting the whole engine of production and distribution to their precise satisfaction. Resources might then more efficiently be used to produce what can be produced cheaply and then to persuade consumers that this is exactly what they want.

Interpersonal. An individual's choices may be "wrong" from the point of view of consumer sovereignty, not because they reflect ignorance about means or confusion about ends, but because they have effects that diminish the possibility that other individuals will be able to satisfy their wants. The actions of one individual sometimes spill over to affect other individuals directly, not simply through influencing relative prices on the market. These are so-called external effects. External effects can be adverse or favorable, and both directions raise the possibility of pertinent qualifications on free choice. Actions with adverse reverberations need discouraging; those with favorable reverberations deserve encouraging. Thus, from the point of view of consumer sovereignty—involving consideration of the wants of the entire population—if a certain individual can serve himself equally well by actions A, B, or C, but A has adverse effects on others, B is neutral toward others, and C enhances goal-fulfillment by others, then both A *and* B are wrong, and only C is the right choice.

Most decisions have spillover effects, but they are generally minor. The issue of corrective qualification is involved only when the external component of the decision is major, as for example, the planting of ragweed, the failure to dispose of garbage, the failure to treat or isolate a contagious disease, the reckless use of an automobile, the use of a ladder to commit burglary, or the use of a gun to hunt the neighbor's children. Nontrivial favorable spillovers are involved in the development of a beautiful garden, the immunization against contagious disease, or the shoveling of snow from the sidewalk in front of one's house. Somewhat more complex cases concern drug addiction, education, and medical care. We have already suggested an intrapersonal qualification for drug addiction. In addition, it often leads to "antisocial" consequences: decreasing the productivity of the afflicted person and therefore of the total resource stock available to the population, increasing crime and "pushing," adding to the burden of governmental welfare services by requiring care for the person's family. Education has opposite effects of the same sort: it enhances the individual's productivity and therefore the community's total effective resource stock, and it decreases the probability of antisocial behavior and the burdening of the government's welfare load. Medical care decreases direct contagion externalities. It also has a positive effect on human productivity and on independence from government.

In principle, interpersonal corrective qualifications are very difficult to handle, because they force one to confront the problem of interpersonal comparisons of worthwhileness—comparing the gain to some and the loss to others of particular actions having spillover effects. Thus, they are embedded in the very same morass of controversy that we discussed in connection with a criterion of aggregate want satisfaction. In practice, fortunately, the problem has been kept within manageable bounds. For the most part, only actions with substantial aversive spillover effects have been considered. The interpersonal comparison problem is thereby more straightforwardly resolvable on ethical grounds, rather than in terms of any nice balancing of effects under the principle of consumer sovereignty. The ethical principle involved is simply that an individual ought to be prevented from harming others. The exercise of freedom does not consist in allowing anyone to abridge the freedom of others. Thus, we shall see in the next section that this type of qualification has been socially interpreted for the most part as calling for a set of injunctions against harmful acts.

To conclude this section, consumer sovereignty must be spelled out in order to have practical relevance. Externally unencumbered consumer choices do not invariably constitute accurate evidence about the wants they ostensibly serve. Such choices may be critically uninformed about alternative opportunities; they may stem from internal goal conflicts; or, while accurately designed to satisfy the wants of their agent, they may adversely affect the want satisfaction of other consumers. These factors must be considered in judging the degree of want satisfaction that inheres in different social situations and, thus, in judging the consistency of different public policies with consumer sovereignty.

It is one thing to indicate that these factors must be considered; it is quite another to delineate exactly how they should be considered. How much information is necessary for specific choices; how much is inadequate? How does one discover a consumer's—*every* consumer's—true underlying wants? How does one trace the spillover effects of

different actions? It is fortunately beyond the scope of this article to try to answer. But it is instructive of the content of consumer sovereignty to indicate briefly how a relatively free market society like the United States has attempted to spell out these qualifications in public policy.

Institutional qualifications

Dedicated to free markets, to freedom of choice, and to consumer sovereignty simultaneously, American public policy can be interpreted as showing a consensual belief in the respects to which the first two must be compromised in order to be consistent with the third. Clearly, not all public interventions in the market have been motivated by an attempt to improve the degree of consumer sovereignty, but a surprising number fit into the classification of qualifications given above. We shall indicate some of the ways that the American public has been willing to compromise the working of free markets.

Supportive policies. In general, *Caveat emptor* has been the dominant policy, but with a series of exceptions that have become more important only in recent years. Traditionally the consumer was protected at law, only *after the fact*, by the common law of fraud, warranty, and negligence. (Much of the material in this section is from Wilcox [1955] 1960, chapters 8, 12.) This essentially meant that consumers could sue for damages actually suffered if due to misrepresentation or negligence. But even early practice recognized an exception. Some transactions could cause massive irreversible damage to life and health. If, in addition, the consumer was technically incapable of judging in advance the quality of the commodity to be obtained, then he needed *advance* protection. Medical services were clearly a case in point. The solution hit upon was legal licensing, by which acceptable quality standards are guaranteed to the consumer in advance by the conditions that practitioners must meet in order to be granted a license to practice.

Licensing spread to many services that involve personal health and safety, such as nursing, pharmacy, and dentistry. But it also spread considerably beyond, to occupations only remotely, if at all, resembling these. Examples are dry cleaning, barbering, and photography. Since licensing is a method of legally limiting supply, it represents a profitable collusive agreement for insiders and, thus, attractive public policy for them. It is interesting that in some cases of licensing that are inappropriate from the present point of view the same language of public health and safety is nonetheless used to justify its legal status as under the appropriate cases.

The same advance protection was not given consumers for tangible commodities until the federal Pure Food and Drug Act of 1906 and its subsequent amendments. Food and drugs qualify as potential factors in one-shot massive or irreversible damage to life and health. Adulteration and use of toxic ingredients are prohibited. In more recent legislation, the burden of proof of nontoxicity is largely shifted from government to the producer, especially with respect to drugs, and must be satisfied *before* the commodity can be marketed. Informational requirements are also imposed on sellers of these commodities, in the form of honest and complete labeling. Subsequent legislation, involving the Federal Trade Commission, extends informational constraints to advertising. Thus, for a particular subset of commodities uniquely "affected with the public interest," the seller is legally required to furnish certain information, and this, as well as information voluntarily advanced, must not be misleading.

Informational constraints have been imposed on other commodities quite remote from this concept of "public interest." Compulsory labeling exists for commodities made of wool, for example. As with licensing, many of these represent regulations in the interest of collusive competitive advantage for producers, rather than consumer-oriented support. There is a general constraint against misrepresentation in advertising, but this too seems to stem from, and be largely administered in the context of, protection of producer rather than of direct consumer interests. This has focused largely on the protection of sellers from unfair methods of competition.

There is a further class of informational constraints, which is in the spirit of consumer sovereignty. It is in the area of financial securities transactions. Here too the justification for intervention seems to be the possibility of massive single transaction damage; but here the damage is to the wealth position of transactors, rather than to life and health. Elaborate requirements for full and honest disclosure by sellers, as well as behavioral regulations on brokers and organized exchanges themselves, are imposed to prevent fraud.

Supportive qualifications have thus tended to be concentrated on commodities where single transactions could produce important harm to life, health, or wealth. No serious attempt is made to expand information available to consumers on consumption generally. (I neglect specific free information programs by the federal government for child care, agricultural and homemaking techniques, and other miscellany.) A minor attempt is made to control the substance of advertising excess (misrepresentation), but not the deeper problems involved in pervasive persuasion.

This pattern of intervention is not hard to understand. In fact, most public intervention arose not out of theoretical analyses of subtle consumer suboptimization but as a response to concrete national traumas—dramatic scandals concerning damage from specific foods and drugs, scandals concerning massive fraud and irregularity in financial markets, etc. Thus, laissez-faire was cast aside not on theoretical grounds but on the evidence of acute malfunctioning of markets.

Corrective policies.   The most widespread form of government intervention against free choice is in the regulation of antisocial externalities. The almost uniform definition of aggression against person or property as crime, and hence illegal, is obvious. But the consensus extends to less obvious forms as well. Thus, government enforces quarantine regulations and sanitary codes for dwellings; it imposes compulsory smallpox immunization; it outlaws transactions in narcotics. At a third level, taxation is sometimes employed with sumptuary goals, for example, the high excises on liquor. (This should not be thought to apply to special excises generally. Gasoline taxes, for example, are typically justified on a modified benefit argument: they are designed to pay for roads and other motorist benefits.)

Desirable externalities receive government attention as well. The public school system, free medical care for the poor, public housing, social welfare services, and many others can be understood as subsidization of forms of consumption that are believed to have substantial desirable spillover effects. Since most of these represent rectification of dismal alternatives, they can also be seen as measures to prevent certain adverse spillover effects. The difference between the treatment of positive and negative spillovers is that for the latter, injunction generally suffices (plus the deterrent effect of possible punishment), whereas for the former, actual subsidization of consumption is necessary.

Two types of regulation that are on the borderline are censorship and the regulation of "immorality" (in a broad sense, including divorce law and "blue laws"). The illegality of homosexuality and fornication, for example, is sometimes justified in terms of preventing the spread of practices that could undermine fundamental institutions of the society, such as the family. Sometimes, however, it is justified as protecting possible participants from corruption—an example of intrapersonal correction. Similarly, censorship is sometimes justified on the grounds that exposure to censorable materials may provoke crimes of violence. Sometimes it too receives its major justification as protection of the individual from himself.

These borderline cases are significant. Government in the United States undertakes almost no intervention based on intrapersonal correction. This sphere has been left to private responsibility, and governmental concern has typically been treated as unwarranted invasion. One would therefore predict that cases partaking of intrapersonal correction would be controversial. This is exactly so of censorship and immorality regulations. There exists no real consensus supporting them: divorce laws are widely assailed in reputable quarters; blue laws are kept on the books only if they are not seriously enforced; the illegality of sexual "immoralities" is highly controversial; every act of censorship is protested by important segments of the population; and even the illegality of narcotics transactions (insofar as it is designed to protect an addict from himself) is responsibly controversial. One might imagine that heavy taxation of tobacco represented an exception. This is not so. Ironically, the sumptuary background of tobacco taxation stems from the notion that it is a quasi-luxury item. It is taxed as an example of pleasurable, not deleterious, consumption.

A major public action that seems on the surface to fit this category is the government's massive intervention in the market during national emergencies, resulting in price control, rationing, and direct control over the allocation of resources. This would appear to constitute a radical abrogation of consumer sovereignty. In a deeper sense, however, it is not so. It is fruitful to consider the situation as one in which everyone's basic interests in the maintenance of the social pattern require a coordinated mobilization of resources. No one individual or small group can achieve such coordination. Government, as the instrumentality of consensual wants, is required to bring it about. It acts as the agent of each consumer, just as we noted the physician does in the individual case. If the political system is truly representative, the government's coordinative acts can be considered consistent with consumer sovereignty. Thus, this case does not involve any new qualifications on individual choice.

It simply represents an unusual instrumentality through which individual choices are realized. A number of other general governmental activities can be similarly interpreted.

In sum, abrogation of free choice for corrective reasons essentially leaves the individual's perception of his own ends sacrosanct; it is only where individual choices have important spillover effects that government intervenes, and here preponderantly to prevent aversive spillovers. The few cases where government seems to be legislating private norms for individuals are cases in which some spillover elements are present as well, and these cases are highly controversial.

Consumer sovereignty, insisting on the want-fulfillment of the ultimate consumer population as the proper end of economic activity, is an influential but ambiguous and incomplete normative principle. It is often incorrectly limited to a version that strongly supports laissez-faire in a free enterprise economy. That version represents a particular composite of one interpretation of consumer sovereignty with other value judgments. Consumer sovereignty can be interpreted in many ways and be joined to many distinctive normative packages (for example, to the goals of a socialist economy), no one of which has earned the consensual support of economists as the authoritative package.

Analysis of the principle itself indicates that neither the wants that are the presumed goals of economic activity nor their reflection in the concrete choices of individuals are unproblematic. The degree of informedness about alternatives, the coherence of the whole structure of individual wants, and the significance of spillover effects on others are all variables relevant to the interpretation of the principle. Moreover, its persuasiveness depends strongly on the stability of wants and on the depth at which they are integrated within the personality of each individual. Extreme suggestibility and volatility of wants seriously undermine the principle's force.

In the American version of a free enterprise society there appears to be a consensus that consumers should be given public protection in the form of regulations about quality and information when making what are potentially momentous market decisions. Public intervention should also be invoked to prevent private actions that have deleterious effects on others. There is no consensus that public power should be used to protect individuals from their own confusions about means and ends. In this interpretation of consumer sovereignty the individual is still free to be his own worst enemy—or his own best friend. The range between them still allows life to be a great adventure.

JEROME ROTHENBERG

[*See also* ADVERTISING, *article on* ECONOMIC ASPECTS; CONSUMERS, *article on* CONSUMER BEHAVIOR; LICENSING, OCCUPATIONAL; WELFARE ECONOMICS.]

BIBLIOGRAPHY

ARROW, KENNETH J. (1951) 1963 *Social Choice and Individual Values.* 2d ed. New York: Wiley.

BERGSON, ABRAM 1938 A Reformulation of Certain Aspects of Welfare Economics. *Quarterly Journal of Economics* 52:310–334.

BERGSON, ABRAM (1948) 1954 Socialist Economics. Volume 1, pages 412–448 in Howard S. Ellis (editor), *A Survey of Contemporary Economics.* Homewood, Ill.: Irwin.

BOULDING, KENNETH E. (1952) 1958 Welfare Economics. Volume 2, pages 1–38 in Bernard F. Haley (editor), *A Survey of Contemporary Economics.* Homewood, Ill.: Irwin.

COCHRANE, WILLARD W.; and BELL, CAROLYN S. 1956 *The Economics of Consumption: Economics of Decision Making in the Household.* New York: McGraw-Hill.

GORDON, LELAND J. (1939) 1961 *Economics for Consumers.* 4th ed. New York: American Book.

HICKS, JOHN R. 1939 The Foundations of Welfare Economics. *Economic Journal* 49:696–712.

KALDOR, NICHOLAS 1939 Welfare Propositions of Economics and Inter-personal Comparisons of Utility. *Economic Journal* 49:549–552.

LANGE, OSKAR (1938) 1952 On the Economic Theory of Socialism. Pages 55–143 in Benjamin E. Lippincott (editor), *On the Economic Theory of Socialism.* Volume 2: Government Control of the Economic Order. Minneapolis: Univ. of Minnesota Press.

ROTHENBERG, JEROME 1961 *The Measurement of Social Welfare.* Englewood Cliffs, N.J.: Prentice-Hall.

SAMUELSON, PAUL A. (1947) 1958 *Foundations of Economic Analysis.* Harvard Economic Studies, Vol. 80. Cambridge, Mass.: Harvard Univ. Press.

WILCOX, CLAIR (1955) 1960 *Public Policies Toward Business.* Rev. ed. Homewood, Ill.: Irwin.

CONSUMERS

I. CONSUMPTION LEVELS
    AND STANDARDS   *Margaret G. Reid*
II. CONSUMER ASSETS   *Robert Ferber*
III. CONSUMER BEHAVIOR   *Herbert E. Krugman*

I
CONSUMPTION LEVELS AND STANDARDS

Consumption is defined as the use of goods and services. Differences in consumption among individuals at a given time and between points in time are called differences in consumption *levels.* Consumption *standards* are goals to be striven for,

maintained, or regained. These standards influence the ways in which families spend their income, that is, consumption *patterns.* Standards also can cause feelings of discontent that may result in action when consumption is below the standard—when, for example, people consider that the dwelling they occupy is overcrowded, the food they eat is inadequate, or the quality of schooling available for their children is poor. Consumption standards are part of a larger set of standards pertaining to work, leisure, social relationships, and living in general. Consumption is influenced by standards and by income, and income in turn is influenced by standards of living insofar as standards affect incentives (Davis 1945; Pipping 1953).

The goals of life are many, so that choices must be made among them. These choices are influenced by the hierarchy of preferences expressed in the standard of living and by the costs of the things desired. The availability of resources of several types acts as a constraint on total achievement. Earning additional income, obtaining more unpaid services from family members, and making wiser choices among products are all important paths to higher consumption. A consumption standard that is low relative to current money income tends to weaken the motives to earn and to economize in the use of income.

Consumption is overt behavior, and standards are among the forces shaping it. Consumption data, therefore, indirectly provide some information about standards; the strength of preferences is implied by what is chosen. Attempts have also been made to gauge more directly the intensity of desire for things not currently being consumed. The notions of "poverty," "comfort," and "affluence" are found to be related to earlier experiences, especially to recent changes. However, our knowledge of standards comes largely from observing behavior under varying conditions.

Differences within and among countries. About a century ago Engel formulated a very important law of consumption, namely, that as total consumption increases, the percentage of expenditures going to food tends to decrease (Stigler 1954). This percentage is referred to here as the food rate. Historically, Engel's law seems to apply even though many changes have accompanied the increase in total consumption. For example, in the United States the food rate of urban families of two or more persons whose head was a wage earner or clerical worker was 41 per cent in 1888–1891 (Williams 1958); 38 per cent in 1918–1919 (U.S. Bureau of Labor Statistics 1924); and 35 per cent in 1934–1936 (U.S. Bureau of Labor Statistics 1941). For all urban consumer units of two or more persons the food rate was 24 per cent in 1960–1961 (U.S. Bureau of Labor Statistics 1964). Changes in prices as well as in incomes may have had an effect on this rate. The Consumer Price Index shows that between 1913 and 1957 rents in large cities increased 77 per cent and food prices increased 187 per cent (U.S. Bureau of the Census 1960).

Relationships between the food rate and income similar to those indicated by the secular change in the food rate of urban families in the United States are apparent in comparisons among countries that obviously differ in real income as well as in other ways (Bennett 1951; Williams 1958). For example, in 1962 the food rate of countries ranged from 51 and 50 per cent for Ghana and Ceylon to 22 and 21 per cent for Canada and the United States, respectively (United Nations 1964). It seems probable that among countries the food rate is a suitable proxy for total consumption: the lower this rate, the higher is total consumption.

The food rate is correlated with a number of conditions closely related to total consumption. Among 24 countries investigated around 1960, the coefficient of correlation between the food rate and the infant mortality rate was approximately 0.74. At the same time among 23 countries the coefficient of correlation between the food rate and the percentage of households with 1.5 or more persons per room was 0.86. Similar relationships have been observed among states and cities of the United States (U.S. Bureau of Labor Statistics 1964; U.S. Bureau of the Census 1963; 1964).

Expenditures as measures of consumption. Expenditures may be viewed as numbers of units of consumer goods and services multiplied by their prices. The prices of products of specified quality differ from time to time and place to place, and differences in expenditures may therefore not represent differences in consumption. Many countries have developed price indexes that permit at least crude intertemporal comparison of real consumption, that is, of the quantity of consumer products measured in dollars of constant purchasing power. Differences in expenditures among places within countries may also reflect differences in prices as well as in the quantity of products purchased. Food prices probably vary with the distance between consumers and primary producers; in other words, they are a function of the regional specialization of agriculture. The price of residential housing probably increases with urban congestion. The costs of services are much influenced by the availability

of job opportunities outside the service industries and hence tend to be positively correlated with local incomes. Little progress has so far been made in providing interplace indexes of consumer prices (Brady & Hurwitz 1957). If consumer prices are correlated with regional and local income, as seems probable, then the variation in expenditures among the consumers of a country overstates the variation in consumption.

Expenditure data seldom distinguish precisely between consumption expenditure and outlays made to provide income. With the growth of cities and suburbs and the increased mobility of the labor force, job expenses have increased. In the United States from 1940 to 1963 the share of transportation in total expenditure increased from 9.7 to 12.6 per cent (U.S. Bureau of the Census 1964). Some of this increase was caused by the greater distances traveled to work and thus represents an increase in the cost of production rather than an increase in the consumption of transportation service for personal or recreational purposes. There are still few estimates of job expenses, and even these are limited in their coverage (Holmes 1962). It seems reasonable to expect that such expenses tend to increase with earnings.

The boundaries between consumption and savings are also blurred. Expenditures for term life insurance are often classified as savings, although outlays for other forms of current insurance against risk are not. Capital investments in owner-occupied housing are classified as savings, whereas the purchase of an automobile is not. The purchase of land to establish a son in farming is counted as savings, but expenditures for the professional education of a son are not, although both are investments designed to augment future income.

Expenditure data understate consumption if some products or services consumed are excluded. Among the items usually not represented in survey data are (a) products withheld from sale by producers for their own use, such as food and fuel produced and used by the same farm families; (b) the services of owner-occupied housing in excess of current expenditures for them; (c) the services of the stock of consumer durables, such as automobiles and household equipment, in excess of expenditure for its maintenance; (d) nonmarket services used, such as those of family members; and (e) products or services provided from public funds.

Income in kind. Consumer products used but not purchased are commonly referred to as income in kind. Some income in kind, notably items (a) and (b) above, are included in national estimates of personal consumption expenditures and occasionally in survey data. The other types of income in kind are seldom if ever included in data on personal consumption. Many types of income in kind are negatively correlated with the money income of consumers, and their omission therefore tends to increase the inequality of consumption as it is inferred from expenditures.

Investment in owner-occupied housing is an important source of income in kind. At about 1950 in the United States such income was approximately $6 for every $100 of expenditures of nonfarm consumers. Income in kind from this source tends to increase with the age of the head of the consumer unit, since older heads are more likely to have full equity in their homes (U.S. Bureau of Labor Statistics 1964; Reid 1962; U.S. Bureau of the Census 1963). In addition, it tends to increase with average lifetime income, and in this respect differs from many other types of income in kind.

The omission of income in kind results in considerable understatement of the consumption of farm families. For example, the income in kind of farm families, largely in the form of food and housing, in a low-income area of the United States during 1957 was $52 for every $100 of expenditures (Pennock 1964). In 1955, despite a general decline in subsistence farming, food produced on the farm and valued at the prices that would have been paid had it been purchased accounted for about 40 per cent of the food consumption of all farm households (U.S. Agricultural . . . 1956–1961).

Current expenditure overstates consumption when a stock of consumer durables is being increased. A stock of consumer capital, such as furniture, equipment, an automobile, and clothing, is a source of income in kind. The time of purchase of these products tends to differ with the age of the family head. In the United States in 1960–1961, expenditures for furnishings, equipment, and transportation were 25 per cent of consumption expenditures for consumer units whose head was under 25 years of age and 11 per cent for those whose head was 75 years of age or more (U.S. Bureau of Labor Statistics 1964). This difference reflects different stages in the cycle of building up consumer capital and allowing it to depreciate, as well as some differences in income and consumption.

Expenditure data do not include the value of services to the household by its own members. There has been a downward trend in the percentage of households with a full-time homemaker. Consequently, time series of expenditure data are likely to overstate the increase in consumption. In addition, consumption seems likely to exceed expenditure by larger amounts where there is a full-time rather than a part-time homemaker (Clark 1958; Holmes 1962; Rowntree & Lavers 1951). Since earning by wives tends to increase with family income, the higher the family income, the less important, in general, are the unpaid services supplementing expenditure.

Consumption wholly or partly financed by public funds has become an increasing proportion of total consumption. In the United States public expenditure for health, education, recreation, food, and housing was $7 per $100 of personal expenditure in 1950 and $9 in 1962. Public expenditure differs by type of product. During 1962 private expenditure for education and related research in the United States was $1.46 per $100 of total private expenditure. When public expenditure for education is included, this relation increases to $7.50. However, private expenditure for medical care was $6.20 per $100 of total private expenditure, and when public expenditure for "health and medical services" is included, this relation increases only to $7.63 (Social Security Bulletin . . . 1961; U.S. Bureau of the Census 1964).

Publicly provided products or services available only to low-income families, such as public housing, subsidized food, medical care, and legal services, tend to decrease the inequality of consumer real incomes. This also occurs if the product publicly provided is one much used by low-income families or if its quality is too poor to be acceptable to high-income consumers. In some communities of the United States expenditures for tuition in private high schools increase markedly with income, although publicly financed high school education is available without charge to all persons. Public financing of colleges probably benefits families of moderate to high incomes more than those of low incomes; this is probably also true of subsidies to encourage owner occupancy of housing. The extent to which the inequality of real income is affected by public financing of consumption is almost a virgin field of inquiry (Peacock 1954).

Expenditure patterns. Three sets of conditions cause consumption to differ among families: needs and preferences for various consumer products, the resources available, and the cost of things desired. Each of these sets includes a vast array of factors. Intercorrelations among them and incomplete information about them have been formidable obstacles to obtaining definitive estimates of the effect of any one factor. A large stock of survey data describes expenditure in relation to income, the size and composition of consumer units, the occupation of the household head, tenure of dwelling, place of residence, and other conditions. The effect of any one factor, such as prices, income, or the age of the head, appears to differ among sets of data (Friedman 1957; Houthakker 1957; Reid 1962; Reid & Dunsing 1956). Understanding the cause of such differences among survey findings is essential to knowledge of the structure of consumption, and inquiry along many lines is under way.

Engel curves and permanent income theory. The allocation of increased income between expenditure and saving and among the various types of products has important implications for economic development. Engel curves describe the average expenditures of consumers by income levels. The ratio of the rate of increase in expenditure to the rate of increase in income is called the coefficient of income elasticity of expenditures. It is common to describe as necessities products with an income elasticity of less than 1.0 and as luxuries those with an income elasticity greater than 1.0. In comparing the Engel curves of broad consumption categories such as food, clothing, housing, and transportation this distinction has little merit, since income elasticities as great as 1.0 are seldom observed. Each of these categories includes some necessities and some luxuries.

As the stock of survey data has grown, it has become obvious that the slopes of Engel curves differ from group to group and time to time. Such differences have been observed for total expenditures (Friedman 1957; Houthakker 1957) and for food and housing (Reid 1962; Reid & Dunsing 1956). The permanent income theory of consumption has done much to rationalize these differences. It views annual incomes as having two components, one positive component representing expected income and a second, which may be negative or positive, representing deviations from this expected income. These deviations are referred to as transitory income [see CONSUMPTION FUNCTION]. The theory postulates that consumption is highly correlated with expected income but not with transitory income. Although the theory is by no means fully tested, there seems to be no doubt that it explains much of the variation in Engel curves for a single type of product and that transitory income is more highly correlated with expenditures for durable goods than with expenditures for housing and food.

The mixture of transitory and expected income represented by income distributions is not constant. With the decrease in the proportion of consumer units whose head is self-employed (a group for which transitory income is common) and with the increase in income made available through transfer payments during periods of unemployment, sickness, and disability, the relative size of the transitory component of consumer income seems likely to decrease. Such a decrease will tend to increase the slope of Engel curves. On the other hand, an increase in the progressive taxation of incomes, which makes the normal income of consumer units less unequal, is likely to increase the proportion of the income variation that represents transitory income. This will tend to reduce the slope of Engel curves.

Engel curves are useful chiefly for indicating the short-run response to changes in income. They do not describe the differences in consumption between the rich and the poor or the effect on consumption of secular changes in real income. Observations describing the average consumption and income of subsets of consumers by the occupation of the head have considerable merit for this purpose. The designing of consumer surveys suitable for testing the effect on consumption of differences in permanent, or normal, income is still in a preliminary stage.

Role of assets. The growth of data on assets has lagged behind that of data on expenditures and income. A comprehensive survey of the assets of consumer units in the United States was made for 1962 (Survey of the Financial . . . 1964). Marked increases in the value of assets were reported with increases in the age of the head of consumer units and with increases in income. Even so, units with incomes under $3,000 had a mean net worth of about $9,000. This figure reflects in part a concentration at incomes under $3,000 of consumer units with an elderly head. Short-run declines in income also result in some large holdings of assets being reported among units with low current incomes. Better data on assets will aid greatly in explaining the deficit spending observed at low annual incomes.

Role of time. The role of time in decisions concerning earning and consumption is receiving increasing attention (Clark 1958; Kriazhev & Markovich 1959; Scientific Conference . . . 1962; Moscow 1959–1962). Time must be allocated among earnings to provide current income, formal training to provide future income, unpaid productive services to supplement expenditure, and leisure or consumption activities as such. Mincer (1963), in his consideration of the gainful employment of women, notes that the time costs incurred by individuals in earning their money income must be considered if the effects of money income and prices of products on consumption are not to be misunderstood. Income foregone while attending college is widely recognized as a cost of college education. Becker (1965) extends the consideration of time cost to the purchase of consumer products in general and to use of leisure time. For example, the cost of attending the theater includes the time entailed as well as the price of tickets and of transportation. The cost of commuting to work involves time as well as money. In this frame of reference leisure is assessed in terms of consumption foregone because of reduced income.

Household composition. The economic aspects of household membership are also receiving considerable attention (Brady 1958). The rise in real income and the growth of programs providing retirement income have been accompanied by a reduction in the number of three-generation households. At what income does preference for separate households offset the economies of scale of households of three generations? How does this undoubling change the correlations between income and household size and composition, and hence the observed expenditure–income patterns? It seems likely, for example, that undoubling increases the proportion of low-income consumer units that have an elderly head.

Expenditure data tell us a great deal about consumption. Their usefulness for this purpose would be increased if allowance were more fully made for differences in the cost of living due to interspatial differences in prices and in climate, for job expenses, and for income in kind. Without such allowance, the measurement of consumption is still in a very elementary stage.

Consumer budgets. Budgeting by consumers for the most part appears to be very informal. What are commonly referred to as consumer budgets are plans prepared by specialists used for consumer education and for the administration of public programs. Among the best known consumer budgets are the low-cost and moderate-cost food plans of the U.S. Department of Agriculture (Cofer et al. 1962) and the City Worker's Budget of the U.S. Department of Labor (Lamale & Stotz 1960). These budgets combine data on the purchases of consumers as reported in occasional surveys with the recommendations of specialists as to physical and social needs. For example, the recommended dietary allowance of the Food and Nutrition Board (Cofer et al. 1962) are intended to represent physical needs, and the standard that there be at least one room per person in the family is intended to represent social needs. Budgets are developed for consumer units of specified size and composition, and scales have also been developed that permit an adjustment in the cost of the budget to the size of the consumer unit.

The recommendations of specialists involve arbitrary judgments, as does the use of data on purchases. The low-cost food plan of the U.S. Department of Agriculture tends to represent the dollar value of the food consumption of families at the first quartile of the income distribution of the group referred to in preparing the plan; the moderate-cost plan tends to represent that of families at the median income. A new national survey is followed by a revision of the food plans with purchase patterns reflecting a new income distribution. Hence, secular change in the food plans tends to approximate secular change in the expenditure for food at the first quartile and the median of the income distributions, when account is taken of the size and composition of consumer units. A lag exists between the consumption represented by the food plans and that of families surveyed because the collection, tabulation, and analysis of the data are time consuming.

The City Worker's Budget purports to represent a modest but adequate level of consumption. It is less explicitly related to a particular position in the income distribution than are the food plans discussed above. The recommendations of many sets of specialists are utilized. When purchase data from surveys are used, they tend to represent the expenditure of median-income families with a husband, a wife who is not in the labor force, and two children living at home. The mean City Worker's Budget for 20 large cities for the autumn of 1959 was $6,083. The median income in 1959 for urban families with a husband who worked and a wife who did not was $6,283 (U.S. Bureau of the Census 1961–). Thus it seems reasonable to conclude that the City Worker's Budget in 1959 tended to approximate the consumption of median-income families. Successive revisions of this budget have brought it to higher levels. For 20 large cities the mean budget for 1959 exceeded the mean budget for 1947 by 88 per cent. Over the same period national per capita personal income increased only 65 per cent. The "modest but adequate" City Worker's Budget has at times been interpreted as a minimum budget. In such terms, about half of the population is below the minimum, and the secular rise in the budget makes any change in this proportion unlikely.

Inequality and poverty. In the antipoverty program launched by the federal government of the United States in 1964, an annual money income of $3,000 was used as a dividing point between poverty and not-poverty (U.S. President 1964).

According to this definition, a startling amount of poverty was found to exist in the midst of general affluence. The use of an annual income of $3,000 as the test of poverty has been much debated. What the criterion should be is not an issue that scientific procedure can resolve. It is, however, obvious that a yardstick of this type, with certain modifications, can serve useful purposes. For example, it can be used to determine what progress has been made in reducing the frequency of income that is low in relation to need.

In 1961 urban consumer units with a money income of $3,000 had a per capita income of $1,224 (U.S. Bureau of Labor Statistics 1964). Thirteen per cent of the urban population was in consumer units with incomes of less than $3,000. A per capita income of $1,224 in 1961 had the same purchasing power as $984 in 1950, and 24 per cent of the urban population of 1950 was in consumer units with incomes below this level (*Study of Consumer Expenditures . . . 1957*). An income of $1,224 in 1961 had the same purchasing power as $602 in 1941, and 40 per cent of the urban population of 1941 was in consumer units with incomes below this level (Hanson 1945). These changes imply a secular decline of more than one per cent a year in the percentage of the urban population receiving purchasing power of less than 1,224 1960 dollars per capita.

After a study in Great Britain of the income of wage earners and families receiving assistance in 1936 and 1953, Schulz concluded that "poverty, in the sense in which the term was understood before the war, has been abolished for the families of the type considered" (1955, p. 232). Rowntree identified five comparable consumption standards for 1936 and 1950, and for the city of York, England, found 18 per cent of the population in the two lowest classes in 1936 and 2 per cent in 1950 (Rowntree & Lavers 1951).

A yardstick of poverty can also be used to discover the people who are most likely to be poor and the conditions that contribute to their poverty. To be suitable for this purpose a yardstick must represent the same level of consumption wherever it is applied. To consider only money income is to ignore income in kind and important interspatial differences in prices and other conditions that affect the cost of living, such as climate. How the size and composition of consumer units affect needs is also ignored when a single yardstick is used for all units. However, many descriptions of "who are the poor" have taken into account variation in need that depends on the number of persons per consumer unit. The other shortcomings of the single money measure of poverty have tended to be neglected. As a result, descriptions of poverty in the United States have tended to overstate the frequency of low consumption in farm and other rural populations and in warmer regions where the cost of shelter is low; they have tended to understate the frequency of poverty in large cities where the costs of housing and of transportation to work are high.

Relative as well as absolute poverty is a matter of considerable importance. [*See* INCOME DISTRIBUTION, *article on* SIZE.] Data on the size distribution of money income have been the most important basis for estimates of the degree of inequality. For industrialized countries, a secular decrease in inequality is indicated (Kuznets 1965). However, the biases of money income as an index of consumption and the failure to consider the changing membership of consumer units greatly limit the reliability of such estimates. These biases have not been constant through time and differ greatly among populations. The limiting conditions include income taxes, job expenses, correlations between current income and prices, income in kind, the characteristics of consumer units, and the extent to which income distributions represent transitory conditions. Systematic exploration of many of these biases has yet to be undertaken.

Data available leave no doubt that the inequality of expenditures is appreciably less than the inequality of money incomes (Snyder 1960). When urban consumer units of two or more persons are ranked by 1961 income, those in the lowest fifth of the income distribution are found to have received 6.9 per cent of the money income and 7.6 per cent of the disposable income and to have made 9.5 per cent of all consumer expenditures. Measurement in terms of the number of persons in the consumer units further reduces the apparent inequality of consumption. The lowest fifth of the urban population (ranked by the income of consumer units) received 8.8 per cent of the money income and 9.6 per cent of the disposable income and made 11.9 per cent of all consumer expenditures. So far expenditure data have been little used to provide insights into the inequality of consumption and of normal income.

Viewed historically, scientific discoveries and new technology stand out as the main factors bringing about changes in consumption. They have resulted in new products, greater efficiency of production, higher real income, and changes in the relative cost of various products. During much of the twentieth century the tempo of change has been very rapid—within a few decades transforming rural, rather static, societies into urban, highly dynamic societies. In general, current changes sustain an expectation of further increases in consumption, year-by-year improvement in old products, and a continuing flow of new products.

Changes in the structure of market economies, in the relation of private to public economies, and in the welfare objective of societies create a need for increased knowledge of consumption and of the forces shaping it and for a greater understanding of its implications for social goals. Considerable progress has been made in measuring the total output of consumer products of the market economy. Only moderate advances have been made in understanding the response to changes in costs as reflected in money outlays, in consumer or home production, and in the use of the products of the public economy. Nor has much progress been made in measuring changes in the inequality of consumption.

MARGARET G. REID

[See also the biography of ENGEL.]

BIBLIOGRAPHY

BECKER, GARY 1965 A Theory of the Allocation of Time. *Economic Journal* 75:493–517.

BENNETT, MERRILL K. 1951 International Disparities in Consumption Levels. *American Economic Review* 41:632–649.

BRADY, DOROTHY S. 1958 Individual Incomes and the Structure of Consumer Units. *American Economic Review* 48, no. 2:269–278.

BRADY, DOROTHY S.; and HURWITZ, ABNER 1957 Measuring Comparative Purchasing Power. Conference on Research in Income and Wealth, *Studies in Income and Wealth* 20:301–347.

CLARK, COLIN 1958 The Economics of House-work. Oxford University Institute of Statistics, *Bulletin* 20:205–211.

COFER, ELOISE; GROSSMAN, EVELYN; and CLARK, FAITH 1962 *Family Food Plans and Food Costs: For Nutritionists and Other Leaders Who Develop or Use Food Plans.* U.S. Department of Agriculture, Home Economics Research Report No. 20. Washington: Government Printing Office.

DAVIS, JOSEPH S. 1945 Standards and Content of Living. *American Economic Review* 35:1–15.

FRIEDMAN, MILTON 1957 *A Theory of the Consumption Function.* National Bureau of Economic Research, General Series, No. 63. Princeton Univ. Press.

HANSON, ALICE C. 1945 *Family Spending and Saving in Wartime.* U.S. Department of Labor, Bulletin No. 822. Washington: Government Printing Office.

HOLMES, EMMA G. 1962 *Job-related Expenditures and Management Practices of Gainfully Employed Wives in Four Georgia Cities.* U.S. Department of Agriculture, Home Economics Research Report No. 15. Washington: Government Printing Office.

HOUTHAKKER, HENDRIK S. 1957 An International Comparison of Household Expenditure Patterns, Commemorating the Centenary of Engel's Law. *Econometrica* 25:532–551.

KRIAZHEV, V.; and MARKOVICH, M. 1959 The Time Budget and Measures to Improve the Living Conditions of the Working People. *Problems of Economics* [1959] no. 8:49–53.

KUZNETS, SIMON 1965 *Economic Growth and Structure.* New York: Norton.

LAMALE, HELEN H.; and STOTZ, MARGARET S. 1960 The Interim City Worker's Family Budget. U.S. Bureau of Labor Statistics, *Monthly Labor Review* 83:785–808.

MINCER, JACOB 1963 Market Prices, Opportunity Costs and Income Effects. Pages 67–82 in *Measurement in Economics: Studies in Mathematical Economics and Econometrics in Memory of Yehuda Grunfeld.* Stanford Univ. Press.

MOSCOW, NAUCHNO-ISSLEDOVATEL'SKII INSTITUT TRUDA 1959–1962 *Metodologicheskie voprosy izucheniia urovnia zhizni trudiashchikhsia* (Methodological Problems in the Study of the Standard of Living of Workers). 2 vols. Moscow: Izdatel'stvo Social'no-ekonomicheskoi Literatury.

PEACOCK, ALAN T. 1954 *Income Redistribution and Social Policy: A Set of Studies.* London: Cape.

PENNOCK, J. L. 1964 *Rural Family Spending and Consumption in a Low-income Area in Kentucky.* U.S. Department of Agriculture, Home Economics Research Report No. 26. Washington: Government Printing Office.

PIPPING, HUGO E. 1953 *Standard of Living: The Concept and Its Place in Economics.* Societas Scientiarum Fennica, Commentationes humanarum litterarum, 18, No. 4. Helsingfors (Finland): Societas Scientiarum Fennica.

REID, MARGARET G. 1962 *Housing and Income.* Univ. of Chicago Press.

REID, MARGARET G.; and DUNSING, MARILYN 1956 Effect of Variability of Incomes on Level of Income–Expenditure Curves of Farm Families. *Review of Economics and Statistics* 38:90–95.

ROWNTREE, BENJAMIN S.; and LAVERS, G. R. 1951 *Poverty and the Welfare State: A Third Social Survey of York Dealing Only With Economic Questions.* London: Longmans.

SCHULZ, T. 1955 The Means of Subsistence: Income From Earnings and From Assistance, 1935–1953. Oxford University Institute of Statistics, *Bulletin* 17:215–238.

SCIENTIFIC CONFERENCE ON STATISTICAL PROBLEMS, BUDAPEST, *1961* 1962 *The Standard of Living: Some Problems of Analysis and of International Comparison.* Edited by M. Mod et al. Budapest: Akademiai Kiadó.

SNYDER, ELEANOR M. 1960 Low Income in Urban Areas. *American Economic Review* 50, no. 2:243–250.

Social Security Bulletin: Annual Statistical Supplement, 1961. → Published since 1956.

STIGLER, GEORGE J. 1954 The Early History of Empirical Studies of Consumer Behavior. *Journal of Political Economy* 62:95–113.

Study of Consumer Expenditures, Incomes, and Savings; Statistical Tables: Urban U.S.–1950. Vol. 18. 1957 Philadelphia: Univ. of Pennsylvania. → Tables tabulated by the Bureau of Labor Statistics for the Wharton School of Finance and Commerce, University of Pennsylvania.

Survey of the Financial Characteristics of Consumers. 1964 [U.S.] Board of Governors of the Federal Reserve System, *Federal Reserve Bulletin* 50:285–293.

UNITED NATIONS, STATISTICAL OFFICE 1964 *Statistical Yearbook, 1963.* New York: United Nations. → Published since 1948.

U.S. Agricultural Research Service, Household Economics Research Branch 1956–1961 *Household Food Consumption Survey, 1955: Report.* 16 pts. Washington: U.S. Department of Agriculture.

U.S. Bureau of Labor Statistics 1924 *Cost of Living in the United States.* Bulletin No. 357. Washington: Government Printing Office.

U.S. Bureau of Labor Statistics 1941 *Money Disbursements of Wage Earners and Clerical Workers: 1934–1936: Summary Volume.* Bulletin No. 638. Washington: Government Printing Office.

U.S. Bureau of Labor Statistics 1964 *Consumer Expenditures and Income: Urban United States 1960–61.* BLS Report 237. Washington: Government Printing Office.

U.S. Bureau of the Census 1960 *Historical Statistics of the United States; Colonial Times to 1957: A Statistical Abstract Supplement.* Washington: Government Printing Office.

U.S. Bureau of the Census 1961— *U.S. Census of Population: 1960.* Washington: Government Printing Office.

U.S. Bureau of the Census 1963 *U.S. Census of Housing: 1960.* Volume 1, Part 1: United States Summary. HC[1]–1. Washington: Government Printing Office.

U.S. Bureau of the Census 1964 *Statistical Abstract of the United States.* Washington: Government Printing Office. → Published since 1878.

U.S. President 1964 *Economic Report of the President.* Washington: Government Printing Office. → Published since 1947.

Williams, Faith M. 1958 International Comparisons of Patterns of Family Consumption. Pages 270–307 in Lincoln H. Clark (editor), *Consumer Behavior: Research on Consumer Reactions.* New York: Harper.

Williams, Faith M.; and Zimmerman, Carle C. 1935 *Studies of Family Living in the United States and Other Countries: An Analysis of Material and Method.* U.S. Department of Agriculture, Miscellaneous Publication No. 223. Washington: Government Printing Office.

II

CONSUMER ASSETS

In a general sense, consumer assets encompass all tangible goods or intangibles which consumers own or on which they have claims. This includes not only household goods but also most of the assets of business corporations and of government, as evidenced by consumer holdings of stocks and bonds.

It is customary to classify consumer assets in various ways, roughly analogous to the definition of national wealth [see NATIONAL WEALTH]. Perhaps the most frequently encountered of such classifications are the following.

Tangibles vs. financial. Tangibles include all material possessions owned directly by the consumer, e.g., household goods, cars, homes, jewelry, and ownership of a farm. Intangibles, or financial assets, include cash and claims on money or goods, such as checking and savings accounts, common and preferred stock, bonds, cash value of life insurance, mortgages held on property of others, and loans to others.

Financial assets may be subdivided into fixed-dollar and variable-dollar holdings. The former represent assets for which the consumer has a claim on a fixed number of dollars, such as cash, a checking account, or a mortgage. In contrast, variable-dollar holdings are those for which the return is dependent on the price level or on other economic conditions. Thus, the current value of 100 shares of common stock originally purchased at $25 per share will depend on the performance of the company since that time, and may be substantially more or less than $2,500. Other examples of variable-dollar holdings include debentures and the variable annuity.

Liquid vs. nonliquid. Liquid assets are those which are immediately convertible into cash, into a fixed number of dollars. Hence, a liquid asset is a fixed-dollar asset, but not all fixed-dollar assets are liquid assets. For example, U.S. government Series E bonds are fixed-dollar assets, immediately convertible, and therefore liquid assets. Series H bonds, however, which are also fixed-dollar assets, are not immediately convertible into cash and are therefore nonliquid assets. The principal forms of liquid assets in the United States, other than money itself, are savings accounts and U.S. government Series E bonds.

Gross vs. net. The total wealth of the consumer, without deduction for debts or liabilities, is known as his gross, or total, assets. Deducting his debts, or liabilities, from this total yields net assets. The gross assets of a consumer are equal to his net assets only if he possesses no debts.

Holdings of consumer assets. Accurate estimates of consumer assets, or wealth, are as yet obtainable only for national totals and only for certain aggregates and certain countries. The reason is that, with a few exceptions, such data can be obtained only from consumers, and consumers are notoriously unreliable reporters on such subjects. Financial holdings tend to be understated and distorted in various ways. Nonfinancial holdings, such as the value of one's appliances or of clothing, cannot be estimated with much reliability because of the difficulty of ascertaining such holdings and because of the very poor basis for estimating the resale value of such goods. The estimation of consumer financial holdings from institutional records is usually hardly feasible either, partly because of the difficulty of collating holdings in different institutions for the same consumer unit and partly because few institutions distinguish between consumer holdings and holdings of businesses or of institutions.

The latter problem makes it difficult to estimate even aggregates of consumer assets from institutional data.

For these reasons, the consumer asset, or wealth, estimates that have been made should be treated as rough approximations and not as exact figures. For the United States, estimates of total household wealth have been made as part of the national wealth estimates of Raymond Goldsmith. These estimates are discussed and presented for the end of 1958 in the article NATIONAL WEALTH. As shown in Table 1 of that article, household net wealth at that time in the United States amounted to just under $1.5 billion, or over 60 per cent of the national total. Roughly three-fifths of this household wealth was in financial form, with the rest in physical assets.

Detailed estimates of the aggregate financial wealth of individuals are published by the U.S. Securities and Exchange Commission, based on data obtained from financial institutions, and are shown in Table 1 for selected years between 1950 and 1964. These data include not only consumers but also nonprofit institutions, and encompass such peripheral items as private insurance and pension reserves. Therefore, not all of these holdings can be attributed to consumers or to households. Nevertheless, these data suggest that the great bulk of consumer financial wealth is in the form of preferred and common stock, insurance, and savings deposits of one form or another. The table also brings out the dramatic increase in the post-World War II period in mortgage and consumer debt, on the liability side, and in equities and savings shares (mostly in savings and loan associations), on the assets side.

Another source of estimates of the financial wealth of consumers is sample surveys of saving or of components of wealth made periodically by governmental and other agencies. The annual *Survey of Consumer Finances* of the University of Michigan Survey Research Center provides information on the liquid asset holdings of U.S. consumers as well as on ownership of homes, cars, and selected durable goods and on different types of consumer debt. The most comprehensive study of this nature so far is the "Survey of Financial Characteristics of Consumers" conducted for the Federal

Table 1 — Financial assets and liabilities of individuals, United States, selected years (in billions of dollars as of end of year)ᵃ

	1950	1955	1960	1964
Financial assets:				
Currency and deposits	130	154	181	243
Currency and demand deposits	(73)	(80)	(80)	(97)
Time and savings deposits	(57)	(75)	(101)	(146)
Savings shares	15	34	66	109
Securities	b	397	505	730
U.S. savings bonds	50	(50)	(46)	(49)
Other U.S. governmentᶜ	18	(20)	(27)	(29)
State and local government	13	(23)	(31)	(36)
Corporate and otherᵈ	b	(304)	(401)	(615)
Bonds and notes	b	(21)	(22)	(22)
Investment company shares	b	(12)	(23)	(39)
Other preferred and common shares	b	(271)	(357)	(554)
Private insurance and pension reserves	68	106	152	206
Insurance reserves	(57)	(77)	(96)	(118)
Insured pension reserves	(6)	(11)	(19)	(25)
Noninsured pension reserves	(6)	(18)	(37)	(63)
Government insurance and pension reserves	40	57	71	84
Total assets	b	749	975	1,372
Liabilities:				
Mortgage debt	38	78	130	187
Consumer debt	18	34	51	70
Securities loans	3	5	5	8
Total liabilities	58	117	185	265
Net equity (assets — liabilities)	b	632	790	1,107

a. Includes Alaska and Hawaii.
b. Not available.
c. Beginning 1955, includes nonguaranteed federal agency issues. In 1950, such issues were included with corporate and other bonds.
d. Rough estimates of market value.

Source: U.S. Securities and Exchange Commission, *Annual Report.*

Reserve Board by the U.S. Bureau of the Census in the spring and summer of 1963 (Projector 1964). This study sought to obtain from a national sample of roughly 3,600 families information on ownership of liquid assets, common and preferred stock, marketable bonds, life insurance, annuities and investment in retirement plans, the value of ownership of a business (both farm and nonfarm), ownership of homes and automobiles, and ownership of different forms of debt. Reinterviews with this sample were conducted in 1964.

The survey-based estimates of consumer financial wealth tend to complement the aggregative estimates, because only the survey data provide extensive information on the extent to which asset holdings are distributed among different types of consumer units. These and other data indicate that consumer wealth is highly concentrated [*see* NATIONAL WEALTH, *article on* DISTRIBUTION]. Some idea of the extent to which wealth is concentrated among consumer units is given by Table 2.

Table 2 — *Estimated distribution of U.S. families in 1963 by net worth and the average net worth of the members of each group*

Net worth (in dollars)	Per cent of families[a]	Average net worth (in dollars)
Negative	8	−538
0–999	17	302
1,000–4,999	17	2,809
5,000–9,999	14	7,305
10,000–24,999	24	16,281
25,000–49,999	11	35,309
50,000–99,999	5	67,042
100,000–199,999	1	129,958
200,000–499,999	1	293,655
500,000 and over	b	1,176,281

a. Per cents do not add to 100 because of rounding.
b. Less than half of one per cent.

Source: Projector 1964, pp. 289–293.

As a rule, net worth, as well as total assets, tend to be higher for older families, for families with above-average incomes and savings rates, and for the self-employed.

Perhaps equally striking is the extent to which average holdings of different types of assets vary by family characteristics, as is shown in Table 3. Lower-income families have most of their assets in tangible goods or liquid form (mostly checking and savings accounts); this is much more so than the table indicates because most widely owned durable goods are not included. At higher income levels, and also among older people, holdings tend to be concentrated increasingly in a business and in investment assets (primarily common and preferred stock). Particularly noteworthy is the fact

that among the wealthiest families in the United States in 1962—the fraction of 1 per cent having a net worth of $500,000 or more—over 90 per cent of these assets were in variable-dollar form (mostly a business, stocks, and marketable bonds), and only a very small fraction was in liquid assets or in other fixed-dollar investments.

These data have to be treated as approximations only, because consumer financial survey data are subject to substantial biases. These biases may not only lead to substantial underestimates of the aggregative value of consumer financial holdings but may also distort the pattern of these holdings. In particular, tendencies exist for small holdings to be overstated, for large holdings to be understated, and for the degree of understatement to increase with the sensitivity of the respondent about the asset.

Consumer durables. Much less is known about consumer holdings of durable, or tangible, goods than of intangibles because of the many problems involved in locating and valuing such goods. For the United States, the Goldsmith estimates indicate that roughly a fourth of consumer wealth is in land and housing, and about 10 per cent is in other consumer durables.

Only for the two most expensive such goods—houses and automobiles—are many data available. The Federal Reserve survey data cited earlier indicate that at the beginning of 1963 roughly three-fifths of all U.S. families owned the house in which they lived. Summary data on the characteristics of these homes are shown in Table 4, relating to one-family homes with Federal Housing Authority insured mortgages. The table shows how the value of these homes rose between 1950 and 1964 and suggests that further increases are in store because of the higher costs and values in 1964 of new homes than of existing homes. The table also illustrates the relative growth during this period of mortgages in relation to home values and of land in relation to building costs.

Automobiles were owned by nearly four-fifths of all U.S. families in 1965, as shown in Table 5. Nearly a fourth of the families owned two or more automobiles. The table also brings out the fact that just under a third of all cars in 1965 were eight years old or more and slightly more than another third were less than four years old, and that most cars, especially new ones, have been purchased through the use of credit.

Extensive data on the value and characteristics of other durable goods owned by U.S. consumers, as well as of houses and cars, were obtained as part of the 1950 and 1960–1961 Consumer Ex-

Table 3 — Average family holdings of specific types of net worth, in dollars, by selected characteristics, December 31, 1962[a]

GROUP CHARACTERISTIC	TOTAL NET WORTH	TANGIBLE ASSETS					LIQUID AND INVESTMENT ASSETS						MISCELLANEOUS ASSETS	LESS: PERSONAL DEBT (excludes auto)
		All	Own home	Automobile	BUSINESS, PROFESSION (farm and nonfarm)	LIFE INSURANCE, ANNUITIES, RETIREMENT PLANS	All	Liquid assets	Investment assets All	Stocks	Marketable bonds	Other		
All families	22,588	6,612	5,975	637	3,913	1,376	9,642	2,579	7,063	4,072	456	2,535	1,528	483
Size of net worth:														
Negative	−538	121	37	84	92	67	82	64	18	7	1	10	3	903
0–999	302	214	72	141	30	124	108	98	11	1	2	8	13	186
1,000–4,999	2,809	1,706	1,284	422	127	563	731	631	100	46	4	50	76	394
5,000–9,999	7,305	4,536	3,996	540	404	927	1,665	1,268	397	150	8	240	197	374
10,000–24,999	16,281	9,422	8,634	789	1,656	1,511	3,980	2,266	1,715	567	8	1,140	241	529
25,000–49,999	35,309	14,956	13,721	1,236	5,283	2,625	11,874	5,961	5,914	2,132	272	3,510	795	225
50,000–99,999	67,042	15,748	14,429	1,319	15,701	4,342	30,560	9,512	21,048	9,659	461	10,928	1,181	490
100,000–199,999	129,958	26,960	25,215	1,745	22,484	5,312	73,068	14,454	58,614	38,301	2,202	18,111	3,795	1,662
200,000–499,999	293,655	27,209	24,691	2,519	65,832	8,803	182,006	19,151	162,855	105,160	4,249	53,445	11,464	1,659
500,000 and over	1,176,281	54,006	51,452	2,554	248,811	18,677	590,160	40,973	549,187	363,208	79,023	106,956	273,272	8,646
1962 income:														
0–2,999	8,875	3,901	3,752	149	1,418	190	3,458	1,330	2,128	1,480	201	448	113	205
3,000–4,999	10,914	3,956	3,544	412	1,902	635	4,663	1,738	2,925	818	19	2,088	137	378
5,000–7,499	15,112	5,615	4,973	643	2,050	1,135	5,426	1,716	3,710	2,365	18	1,326	1,339	453
7,500–9,999	21,243	8,367	7,499	868	2,577	1,879	7,500	2,722	4,779	1,476	44	3,258	1,632	712
10,000–14,999	30,389	10,873	9,527	1,346	5,174	2,975	11,202	4,233	6,969	3,761	316	2,893	749	584
15,000–24,999	74,329	17,004	15,188	1,816	9,088	5,196	39,880	9,241	30,638	18,733	1,445	10,460	3,664	502
25,000–49,999	267,996	35,090	32,215	2,875	66,144	10,819	111,761	19,098	92,663	58,111	4,742	29,810	48,736	4,553
50,000–99,999	789,582	48,764	45,961	2,803	251,977	19,559	387,573	41,845	345,728	204,665	71,971	69,092	86,313	4,604
100,000 and over	1,554,152	89,645	85,634	4,011	288,915	32,309	1,058,672	54,426	1,004,246	758,253	121,985	124,008	96,879	12,268
Age of family head:														
Under 25	762	544	248	297	36	125	381	256	125	44	b	81	169	493
25–34	7,661	2,798	2,300	498	1,014	678	1,566	647	915	515	29	375	2,098	492
35–44	19,442	5,952	5,244	708	3,939	1,496	6,061	1,556	4,505	2,356	195	1,953	2,541	546
45–54	25,459	8,557	7,645	912	5,776	2,241	8,144	2,563	5,581	2,834	272	2,475	1,472	730
55–64	34,781	9,206	8,465	741	6,275	1,789	16,647	4,117	12,530	7,542	695	4,293	1,220	356
65 and over	30,718	7,846	7,474	372	3,267	873	18,452	4,670	13,782	8,349	1,234	4,198	535	256
Employment—housing status:														
Nonfarm homeowner	31,478	10,996	10,148	848	4,441	1,827	12,778	3,301	9,477	5,453	565	3,459	2,013	576
Self-employed	96,385	17,695	16,403	1,292	34,367	3,883	37,148	6,710	30,438	14,388	2,642	13,408	4,646	1,355
Employed by others	22,026	9,902	8,974	928	702	1,884	8,067	2,388	5,678	3,586	195	1,897	2,010	539
Retired	29,752	11,287	10,952	335	748	603	16,991	5,023	11,969	7,361	678	3,930	421	299
Nonfarm renter	8,092	383	48	335	1,167	753	5,239	1,586	3,654	2,411	303	940	903	354
Self-employed	73,691	1,297	415	882	25,815	2,298	23,890	4,754	19,136	11,270	5,865	2,001	23,819	3,428
Employed by others	5,268	395	28	367	420	803	3,813	1,244	2,569	1,600	90	879	150	312
Retired	10,827	161	75	85	73	212	10,183	3,212	6,970	5,312	82	1,576	212	13
Farm operator	43,973	6,182	5,501	681	25,767	1,278	10,138	2,309	7,829	1,354	535	5,940	1,095	486
Region:														
Northeast	23,980	7,141	6,611	530	3,026	1,708	10,833	3,400	7,434	5,581	682	1,171	1,783	512
North Central	23,632	7,454	6,728	726	4,954	1,312	9,153	2,626	6,527	3,006	335	3,186	1,245	486
South	18,318	5,168	4,571	597	3,409	1,128	8,112	1,915	6,197	3,258	513	2,426	929	429
West	26,192	6,941	6,219	723	4,423	1,408	11,300	2,415	8,885	4,949	212	3,725	2,647	529

a. Note: All data are preliminary and are subject to revision. Details may not add to totals because of rounding.
b. No cases reported.

Source: Projector 1964, p. 293.

Table 4 — Median cost and value of new and existing one-family homes in the United States with Federal Housing Authority insured mortgages, selected years (in dollars)

	NEW HOMES				EXISTING HOMES			
	1950	1960	1962	1964	1950	1960	1962	1964
Estimated value	8,286	14,607	15,151	16,063	8,865	13,043	14,082	14,614
Mortgage amount	7,101	13,569	14,195	15,118	6,801	11,978	13,100	13,725
Ratio: Mortgage to value	88.0	93.5	94.4	94.5	77.8	92.6	94.4	94.8
Price of site	*	2,404	2,649	2,990	*	2,285	2,653	2,824
Ratio: Site to value	*	16.1	17.0	17.9	*	16.8	18.1	18.7

* Not available.

Source: U.S. Housing and Home Finance Agency 1964.

penditures Studies of the Bureau of Labor Statistics. More recent estimates of the frequency of ownership of different appliances are shown for the U.S. in Table 6 for 1963. It is interesting to note that by that year only one appliance (electric refrigerators) was owned more widely than television sets.

Assets and consumer behavior. A number of studies have been made of the factors that influence consumers to hold particular combinations of assets, some dealing with financial assets and others with durable goods. Still other studies have sought to ascertain the effect of asset holdings on consumer spending and saving.

Influencing factors. Reasons for consumer holding of financial assets have been discussed in the theoretical literature for some time (for example, Keynes 1936, chapter 16; Katona 1951, pp. 98–107). However, relatively few empirical studies have been made on this subject, to a large extent, no doubt, because of lack of data. The findings of the principal such studies may be summarized, briefly, as follows:

(1) The composition of consumer portfolios is influenced by numerous social, economic, and environmental variables (Watts & Tobin 1960). In particular, holding other variables constant in each case:

(*a*) Financial assets rise in importance and the value of durables declines as a percent of the total as household income rises.

Table 5 — U.S. automobile ownership, age, and financing: selected years[a]

	Unit	1950	1955	1960	1961	1962	1963	1964	1965
Total number of families in U.S.	millions	45.2	49.3	53.4	54.2	54.9	56.5	56.8	58.4
Total owning automobiles	per cent	59	70	77	76	74	80	78	79
Owning 1 automobile	per cent	52	60	62	58	57	58	56	55
Owning 2 or more automobiles	per cent	7	10	15	18	17	22	22	24
Automobiles owned, by age:									
Less than 2 years old	per cent	17	12	14	13	12	13	13	16
2 and 3 years old	per cent	19	22	20	17	21	18	20	21
4, 5, 6, and 7 years old	per cent	6	43	41	42	38	36	33	33
8 years old and over	per cent	58	23	25	28	29	33	34	30
Total automobiles purchased	millions	b	13.6	14.3	16.4	15.6	18.9	17.3	18.3
New car	millions	b	4.4	5.2	5.4	4.6	5.9	6.0	7.2
Average price paid	dollars	b	2,730	3,140	3,010	2,830	2,990	3,130	3,140
Used car	millions	b	9.2	9.1	11.0	11.0	13.0	11.3	11.1
Average price paid	dollars	b	780	980	800	800	840	920	920
Method of financing purchases:[c]									
All passenger cars:									
Full cash (including trade-in allowance)	per cent	51	37	38	47	43	45	47	48
Installment credit and other borrowing	per cent	49	61	61	52	56	55	53	52
New passenger cars:									
Full cash (including trade-in allowance)	per cent	56	38	33	39	37	38	39	40
Installment credit and other borrowing	per cent	44	61	66	61	62	61	60	60
Used passenger cars:									
Full cash (including trade-in allowance)	per cent	47	37	41	52	44	48	51	53
Installment credit and other borrowing	per cent	53	62	57	47	53	50	44	44

a. Excludes Alaska and Hawaii.
b. Not available.
c. Percentages may add to less than 100 per cent because of not ascertained cases.

Source: Survey of Consumer Finances.

Table 6 — *Number and per cent of U.S. households with specified household appliances, 1963*[a]

	HOUSEHOLDS[b]	
	Number, in thousands	Per cent
Major appliances:		
Air conditioner:		
Room unit	7,240	13.2
Central	962	1.8
Clothes dryer:		
Electric	8,210	14.9
Gas	3,523	6.4
Combination washer–dryer	1,119	2.0
Dishwasher	3,920	7.1
Freezer	11,197	20.3
Garbage disposer	4,789	8.7
Range, electric	19,047	34.6
Range, gas	33,914	61.6
Refrigerator, electric	53,063	96.4
Refrigerator, gas	1,313	2.4
Sewing machine, electric	25,408	46.2
Television:		
Black and white	50,001	90.8
Color	915	1.7
Washing machine:		
Automatic	26,194	47.6
Wringer	14,535	26.4
Vacuum cleaner	39,803	72.3
Small electrical appliances:		
Blanket	13,758	25.0
Blender	4,484	8.2
Broom, upright	1,045	1.9
Can opener	5,973	10.9
Coffeemaker, automatic	27,165	49.4
Clock (excluding radio)	34,968	63.5
Floor polisher	5,076	9.2
Frying pan	21,673	39.4
Hair dryer (hat box)	8,719	15.8
Mixer	35,781	65.0
Phonograph:		
Portable	11,576	21.0
Other	15,524	28.2
Radio (including clock)	26,665	48.4
Radio, pocket/purse	15,089	27.4
Radio, other portable	21,247	38.6
Shaver	24,705	44.9
Steam iron	35,754	65.0
Toaster	42,356	76.9

a. Excludes Alaska and Hawaii.
b. Total number of households = 55,050,000.

Source: Look Magazine 1963.

(*b*) Financial assets rise in importance and debt declines with increased education of the household head.

(*c*) Older households have fewer holdings in durables and less debt.

(*d*) Larger households tend to have more of their holdings in durables and fewer in liquid assets.

(*e*) Pronounced, though erratic, differences in asset holdings exist by occupation, by region, and by city size.

(2) Holdings of variable-dollar assets are also influenced by numerous factors, principally age, home ownership, total assets, and occupation (Claycamp 1963).

(3) Holdings of liquid assets are influenced primarily by total wealth rather than by income (Lydall 1958; Claycamp 1963; Butters et al. 1953). Liquid assets as a proportion of total assets tend to decline as the amount of wealth rises. Liquid assets in relation to income tend to rise with age, to fall as the size of the consumer unit rises, and to be higher for those with permanently depressed incomes (Guthrie 1960).

(4) Holdings of specific assets such as life insurance and common stock are also influenced by a large number of different variables, though income and occupation emerge frequently as dominant factors. Of particular interest is the finding that price expectations and attitudinal variables are related to ownership of common stock (Kreinin 1957; 1959; Kreinin et al. 1961).

Factors influencing the ownership of durable goods have been studied largely in terms of the purchase of such goods, but also in terms of the acquisition patterns of such goods. Thus, attempts have been made to derive so-called saturation curves, showing how ownership of particular goods spreads through a population. Such information has been used as a basis for forecasting durable goods purchases as well as for general analytical purposes (Brown, Buck, & Pyatt 1965; Pyatt 1964). Various sociological studies have explored the role of the innovator in durable goods purchases and the manner in which ownership of a good spreads through a population. These studies bring out the importance of the group, and of group leaders, in influencing such purchases (Bourne 1957; Katz & Lazarsfeld 1955; Whyte 1954). These innovators appear to be scattered through the population but, judging by one such study, are generally found among younger, better-educated people as well as among those who already own similar products and are financially optimistic (Mueller 1958).

Other studies have shown that many factors enter into the durable goods purchase decision, some economic, some sociological, and some psychological. The socioeconomic factors include income, income change, assets, age, family size, and occupation (Ferber 1955; Crockett & Friend 1960; Morgan 1958). The life cycle of the family has been found to be particularly relevant (*Consumer Behavior* 1955), with purchases increasing and accumulating as a family begins to raise children, and then declining as the children grow up and leave home. These studies also suggest that although many durable goods purchases are planned and carefully thought out in advance, many others are made almost on the spur of the moment (Ferber 1955; Juster 1964; Katona & Mueller 1954). Social psychologists have attempted to explain this decision process in terms of accumulation of desires for and against making a particular purchase (Bilkey 1957) and in terms of the interplay of different motivations and status intensities (Clawson 1961).

Effects of ownership. Increasing attention has been focused in recent years on the role of assets in determining consumer spending and saving behavior as well as on the factors influencing asset holdings. In the former connection, assets serve as the bridge for reconciling the cross-section tendency for saving to rise with income and the rising levels of income with the virtual constancy in the United States of the aggregate proportion of income saved over time. Assets play a central role in the so-called "permanent income" hypothesis of Milton Friedman and in the life-cycle hypothesis of Franco Modigliani and his associates; in each case, anticipated expenditure or saving is geared to a long-run perspective of the resources available to the consumer [*see* CONSUMPTION FUNCTION].

In a more pragmatic vein, the accumulation of assets seems to lead not to saturation but to the desire for still more assets, a phenomenon which appears to be characteristic of both tangibles and of financial assets (Katona 1964; 1965). Particularly evident is the tendency for those saving through pension funds to save at least as much in other forms as do those not in pension funds, though one may question which is cause and which is effect. At the same time, it is also clear that holdings of some assets influence holdings of others —that consumers try to "balance" their asset holdings (Watts & Tobin 1960)—and that to a large extent purchases of durable goods serve as substitutes for financial saving (Klein 1955; Maynes 1959; Friend & Jones 1960).

ROBERT FERBER

[*See also* NATIONAL WEALTH.]

BIBLIOGRAPHY

ANDO, ALBERT K.; and MODIGLIANI, FRANCO 1963 The "Life Cycle" Hypothesis of Saving: Aggregate Implications and Tests. *American Economic Review* 53:55–84. → Includes a bibliography on pages 82–84.

BILKEY, W. J. 1957 Consistency Test of Psychic Tension Ratings Involved in Consumer Purchasing Behavior. *Journal of Social Psychology* 45:81–91.

BOURNE, FRANCIS S. (1957) 1961 Group Influences in Marketing and Public Relations. Pages 207–257 in Rensis Likert and Samuel P. Hayes (editors), *Some Applications of Behavioral Research*. Paris: UNESCO.

BROWN, D. A.; BUCK, S. F.; and PYATT, F. G. 1965 Improving the Sales Forecast for Consumer Durables. *Journal of Marketing Research* 2:229–234.

BUTTERS, JOHN K. et al. 1953 *Effects of Taxation: Investments by Individuals*. Boston: Harvard Univ., Graduate School of Business, Division of Research.

CLAWSON, C. JOSEPH 1961 Family Composition, Motivation, and Buying Decisions. Pages 200–217 in *Consumer Behavior*. Volume 4: Household Decision-making. Edited by Nelson N. Foote. New York Univ. Press.

CLAYCAMP, HENRY J. JR. 1963 *The Composition of Consumer Savings Portfolios*. Studies in Consumer Savings, No. 3. Urbana: Univ. of Illinois, Bureau of Economic and Business Research.

Consumer Behavior. Volume 2: The Life Cycle and Consumer Behavior. Edited by Lincoln Clark. 1955 New York Univ. Press.

CROCKETT, JEAN; and FRIEND, IRWIN 1960 A Complete Set of Consumer Demand Relationships. Volume 1, pages 1–92 in Conference on Consumption and Saving, University of Pennsylvania, 1959, *Proceedings*. Edited by Irwin Friend and Robert Jones. Philadelphia: Univ. of Pennsylvania Press.

FALK PROJECT FOR ECONOMIC RESEARCH IN ISRAEL 1961 *Survey of Family Savings 1957/1958 and 1958/1959*. Jerusalem (Israel): The Project.

FERBER, ROBERT 1955 *Factors Influencing Durable Goods Purchases*. Urbana: Univ. of Illinois, Bureau of Economic and Business Research.

FERBER, ROBERT 1962 Research on Household Behavior. *American Economic Review* 52:19–63.

FRIEDMAN, MILTON 1957 *A Theory of the Consumption Function*. National Bureau of Economic Research, General Series, No. 63. Princeton Univ. Press.

FRIEND, IRWIN; and JONES, ROBERT 1960 The Concept of Saving. Volume 2, pages 336–359 in Conference on Consumption and Saving, University of Pennsylvania, 1959, *Proceedings*. Edited by Irwin Friend and Robert Jones. Philadelphia: Univ. of Pennsylvania Press.

FRIEND, IRWIN; and NATRELLA, VITO 1954 *Individuals' Saving: Volume and Composition*. New York: Wiley.

FRIEND, IRWIN; and SCHOR, STANLEY 1959 Who Saves? *Review of Economics and Statistics* 41:213–248.

GOLDSMITH, RAYMOND W. 1955–1956 *A Study of Saving in the United States*. 3 vols. Princeton Univ. Press. → Volume 1: *Introduction; Tables of Annual Estimates of Saving, 1897–1949*. Volume 2: *Nature and Derivation of Annual Estimates of Saving, 1897–1949*. Volume 3: *Special Studies*. See especially Volume 3.

GOLDSMITH, RAYMOND W. 1962 *The National Wealth of the United States in the Post War Period*. National Bureau of Economic Research Studies in Capital Formation and Financing, Vol. 10. Princeton Univ. Press.

GOLDSMITH, RAYMOND W.; and SAUNDERS, CHRISTOPHER (editors) 1960 *The Measurement of National Wealth*. Income and Wealth Series, No. 8. Chicago: Quadrangle.

GUTHRIE, HAROLD W. 1960 Consumers' Propensities to Hold Liquid Assets. *Journal of the American Statistical Association* 55:469–490.

HILL, T. P. 1955 Incomes, Savings and Net Worth: The Savings Survey of 1952–1954. Oxford University Institute of Statistics, *Bulletin* 17:129–172.

JUSTER, FRANCIS T. 1964 *Anticipations and Purchases: An Analysis of Consumer Behavior*. Princeton Univ. Press.

KATONA, GEORGE 1951 *Psychological Analysis of Economic Behavior.* New York: McGraw-Hill. → A paperback edition was published in 1963.

KATONA, GEORGE 1964 *The Mass Consumption Society.* New York: McGraw-Hill.

KATONA, GEORGE 1965 *Private Pensions and Individual Saving.* Ann Arbor: Univ. of Michigan, Institute for Social Research, Survey Research Center.

KATONA, GEORGE; and MUELLER, EVA 1954 A Study of Purchase Decisions. Pages 30–87 in *Consumer Behavior.* Volume 1: The Dynamics of Consumer Reaction. Edited by Lincoln Clark. New York Univ. Press.

KATZ, ELIHU; and LAZARSFELD, PAUL F. 1955 *Personal Influence: The Part Played by People in the Flow of Mass Communications.* Glencoe, Ill.: Free Press. → A paperback edition was published in 1964.

KEYNES, JOHN MAYNARD 1936 *The General Theory of Employment, Interest and Money.* London: Macmillan. → A paperback edition was published in 1965 by Harcourt.

KLEIN, L. R. 1955 Major Consumer Expenditures and Ownership of Durable Goods. Oxford University Institute of Statistics, *Bulletin* 17:387–414.

KREININ, MORDECHAI E. 1959 Factors Associated With Stock Ownership. *Review of Economics and Statistics* 41:12–23.

KREININ, MORDECHAI E. 1961 Analysis of Liquid Asset Ownership. *Review of Economics and Statistics* 43:76–80.

KREININ, MORDECHAI E.; LANSING, J. B.; and MORGAN, J. N. 1957 Analysis of Life Insurance Premiums. *Review of Economics and Statistics* 39:46–54.

LOOK MAGAZINE 1963 *National Appliance Survey, 1963.* 2 vols. New York: Cowles Magazine and Broadcasting, Inc. → Volume 1: *Major Household Appliances.* Volume 2: *Portable Household Appliances.*

LYDALL, HAROLD F. 1958 Income, Assets, and the Demand for Money. *Review of Economics and Statistics* 40:1–14.

MAYNES, E. SCOTT 1959 The Relationship Between Tangible Investment and Consumer Saving. *Review of Economics and Statistics* 41:287–294.

MORGAN, JAMES 1958 Consumer Investment Expenditures. *American Economic Review* 48:874–902.

MUELLER, EVA 1958 The Desire for Innovations in Household Goods. Pages 13–37 in *Consumer Behavior.* Volume 3: Research on Consumer Reactions. Edited by Lincoln Clark. New York: Harper.

PROJECTOR, DOROTHY S. 1964 Survey of Financial Characteristics of Consumers. *Federal Reserve Bulletin* 50:285–293.

PYATT, F. GRAHAM 1964 *Priority Patterns and the Demand for Household Durable Goods.* Cambridge Univ. Press.

Survey of Consumer Finances. → Published since 1946 in the *Federal Reserve Bulletin.*

U.S. BUREAU OF THE CENSUS *Statistical Abstract of the United States.* → Published since 1878.

U.S. HOUSING AND HOME FINANCE AGENCY *Annual Report.* → Published since 1947.

U.S. SECURITIES AND EXCHANGE COMMISSION *Annual Report.* → Published since 1934/1935.

U.S. SECURITIES AND EXCHANGE COMMISSION *Statistical Bulletin.* → Published since 1942.

WATTS, HAROLD W.; and TOBIN, JAMES 1960 Consumer Expenditures and the Capital Account. Volume 2, pages 1–48 in Conference on Consumption and Saving, University of Pennsylvania, 1959, *Proceedings.* Edited by Irwin Friend and Robert Jones. Philadelphia: Univ. of Pennsylvania Press.

WHYTE, WILLIAM H. JR. (1954) 1955 The Web of Word of Mouth. Pages 113–122 in *Consumer Behavior.* Volume 2: The Life Cycle and Consumer Behavior. Edited by Lincoln Clark. New York Univ. Press.

III
CONSUMER BEHAVIOR

In recent decades large masses of consumers in the Western world have moved into relatively affluent and secure positions. Their increased purchasing power has given them the opportunity to embroider upon basic needs with a sense of individual taste and creativity, as they search for a style of life rather than for security. Style of life, in this case, refers to the conscious and carefully developed sets or patterns of individual preferences in personal consumer behavior. Increases in disposable income and leisure time have permitted types of personal explorations that have made possible the rise of huge new industries devoted to cultural, recreational, and sports products. At the same time political ideologies based on conflict between the economic classes have all but disappeared (Bell 1959), and minority groups are looked at with almost as much interest in their innovations in consumption (for example, how they dress and play) as in their political views (Kluckhohn 1958). Because the potential variation in consumer behavior is now quite suddenly at a level far over and above that which was once economically dictated, the consumer's search for a personalized style of life becomes mankind's first large-scale nongovernmental, spontaneous, and awkward groping with the problem of economic freedom. The idea of this type of freedom has been appreciated in many lands, even in politically unfree lands where affluence and security do not exist. While it is too early to say what political consequences may emanate from the new consumer ideal, the apparently vast possibilities open to consumer exploration now demand the serious attention of the social sciences in a way that they did not before.

Some social scientists who might otherwise be interested in studying the consumer have been held back by the "silly" effects of initial affluence, an affluence which may permit such strange imbalances in family spending patterns as "living on beans" in order to afford a Cadillac. Yet in more mature forms affluence permits wiser shopping, for example, the ability to shop at a greater number of supermarkets to take advantage of price cuts and sales without the hindrance of a slavish single-store "loyalty" (Tate 1961), the opportunity generally to obtain better and fairer prices (Caplovitz 1963), and a lesser susceptibility to advertising (Smith 1965). The same selection factors apply to style of life. Here, too, early exploration may produce bizarre or "silly" effects and combinations, but ultimately, with experience, comes more mature behavior.

Other social scientists who would seriously study the consumer have been held back by a distaste for what seemed to be tendencies toward local conformity in style, not realizing, for example, that the ability to flock together into homogeneous and "conforming" communities may itself be an expression of economic freedom. Furthermore, as changes in style are required by further changes in the cycle of family development, these same consumers flock easily and freely into other but different types of again homogeneous communities. That certain types of life style are now made more visible by the greater freedom for similar people to congregate may suggest an appearance of strong group conformity that persists even in the face of the individual consumer's easy, though less noticed, ability to shift from one style to another.

It is not enough to say that people have more time and more choice. The striking thing is that they are tending not to buy more and more goods as a form of conspicuous consumption, but to buy time to experiment more with their choices. The most conspicuous form of time consumption is the vacation trip. At the same time employees seem eager to receive leisure hours as a substitute for wage dollars. They bid against their employers for their own time, and their time budgets are becoming more important and more worthy of study than their money budgets [*see* WAGES].

While these tendencies have appeared primarily in those areas of Western affluence which initially made the new consumer innovation possible, their study is also of importance to the less affluent lands of the East. That consumer freedom happened first in the "rich" West does not make it irrelevant to the East. Hopefully, the spirit of that freedom may be built into economic advances in the East and still newer and equally stimulating styles of life may emerge to compete creatively with those of the West. If anticipated, it may not be necessary to attain Western levels of affluence before the equivalent ideas take hold. For example, it may be possible during the stage of first or early affluence to leapfrog, or at least to inhibit, the consumer tendencies to spend more in terms of class and status considerations and to arrive more quickly at a point

where spending reflects the greater freedom of individual style. In the West, it has happened without forethought or warning and even while some poverty remains. The release from serious economic anxiety has permitted many consumers, although not swamped with wealth, to look around for the first time with a sense of real choice about how they might spend their time, what kind of life they would make for themselves, and what kind of people they might be.

Conceptions of the consumer. Professional or official definitions of the study of consumer behavior are somewhat less focused. For example, the division of consumer psychology of the American Psychological Association defines its purpose as the study of human behavior as it relates to the consumption of goods and the uses and acceptance of services. The definition is broad enough to serve as well for a sociological or anthropological association. This breadth may reflect the newness of the concern with professional study of the consumer. That is, behavioral scientists, especially psychologists, have entered into the study of matters related to commerce and industry only in this century, a century which has seen the economy of the United States move from an orientation based primarily on production to one that is based as well on sales and distribution, and finally, and still in the process, to one that is also concerned with consumer needs.

In between the two world wars there developed what might be called the older orientation to consumer psychology, one that was based primarily on an identification with the businessman, the seller of goods and services. With this identification came early emphasis on sales research and studies of advertising effectiveness. To be sure, the latter coincided well with the psychologist's special ability to conduct experimental research on the learning of information, and, by so doing, an enormous research literature developed in advertising psychology (Lucas & Britt 1950). Nevertheless, the new definition of consumer psychology is based not so much on an identification with the manufacturer (as is common in industrial psychology), not so much on an identification with the salesman (as is common in advertising psychology), but more on an identification with the changing consumer himself.

As the consumer begins to innovate in life style, a change is also taking place in how he is viewed by social scientists. The old way was to view him, even define him, predominantly through the eyes of economics. The term "consumer" was not then a social science term, but a focus for concern over efficiency and for a harmonious balance of forces in the free market place. In response to the new affluence the old way of thinking was reflected in a swing from concern with alleged consumer wastefulness to concern with advertising's alleged overpersuasiveness. However, once Packard (1957) and similarly inclined critics had clearly and widely raised the alarm that consumers were being made to buy more than they actually needed, the older type of thinking had to be abandoned as a serious approach, that is, it had no further comments to make or questions to ask about what was happening to consumers as people.

While proponents of the older view may acknowledge that the purchase of household appliances saves the time and attention of family members for performance of higher level activities and that consumers spend more on such living aids as they become more affluent, it comes as something of a surprise for them to discover that the proportion of consumer incomes which is spent after taxes, at least in the United States and except for a post-World War buying spree, has remained relatively constant at 92 to 94 per cent (White 1961). Great changes in consumer behavior have occurred, therefore, during a period when, strictly speaking, changes in economic behavior did not. The more serious concern, then, of the social sciences is to chart the social consequences of consumer access to these new living aids and resources.

Theories of consumer behavior. Ordinarily, when an area of human behavior is marked off for study by social scientists, one may expect much employment of comparative or experimental analyses to uncover and identify regularities in behavior within the area. These then provide a basis for understanding, as well as for testing the understanding. The tests usually are set up in the form of prediction studies. This testing is efficiently accelerated by a clear outline and definition of the area to be studied. One of the functions of theory is to pose a persistent set of questions and thereby to define what is considered important. However, there is not now a general theory of consumer behavior, although Katona (1951) has developed a theory of the role of consumer expectations or confidence upon the levels of spending and saving in the economy. A general theory of consumer behavior has probably not existed since Veblen examined the psychological pressures of social class for their impact on the efficiency of human consumption of goods and resources. From Veblen to Packard, a half century saw no marked change in this eco-

nomic–psychological approach, except that Packard identifies the cause of consumer inefficiencies not so much in social class pressures per se but in their exploitation and manipulation by advertising and business interests. Both Veblen and Packard are essentially social critics using psychological insights to advance a theory which is basically economic, wherein utility and efficiency are defined as the important qualities.

Any theory based on economics might have deserved to be considered quite seriously in a day when economic indicators were the best predictors of human behavior. Today, this is less so. Income is no longer the best predictor of consumer purchasing; for example, a time series correlation between the data of 17 University of Michigan consumer surveys from 1952 to 1960 and the level of national expenditures for durable goods showed that estimates based on both recent disposable income and *attitudes* approximate future durable goods expenditures much more closely than the estimates based on disposable income alone. An analysis of variance indicated that consumer demand was more a function of willingness to buy than of ability to buy. In effect, Katona (1960) has turned the tables on economics by showing how consumer attitudes of optimism or pessimism initiate changes in economic indicators. The causal flow has been somewhat reversed, therefore, first in observation and then in theoretical formulations. If this is so, if economic predictors are no longer all powerful, what new indicators should we be looking at more closely?

Predictors of consumer behavior. Perhaps stages in the family life cycle are the best predictors of consumer behavior (Clark & Foote 1955–1961). Is the family a childless couple? Is there a young baby in the family? Have the children grown and left? [See LIFE CYCLE.]

In addition there are the many household buying decisions made within one particular stage of the cycle. What predictors seem to work here for the shorter run? One set seems to involve the career roles brought into the marital relationship by the two partners. This is partially a matter of relative buying influence within the pair, as affected by such simple considerations as whether or not the wife earns income outside the home. More important however is the matter of what particular occupations and specific career commitments may be brought together within the pair. Every occupation, especially if it has the lifelong involvement of a career, sets forth certain style of life requirements based on where the work is performed, the standards for success, who are the co-workers (clients, colleagues, supervisors), etc. Next to family cycle it is probably industry itself which has the most pervasive, though less direct, influence on style of life. It is important to note, however, that in this sense occupation and profession are not economic but social variables, involving different types of networks of interpersonal relationships much more than different levels of income.

Family and jobs make good starting places for understanding consumers as whole people. Strangely, industry does not yet seek this whole view but tends to spend vast sums on the study of particular consumer functions (for example, food preparation) and closely related products. Yet some sociologists have looked at the new consumer life styles, have asked what products consumers are buying, and have come up with a whole view of the consumer which has relevance to all industry. Riesman and Roseborough (1955), for example, have said that today's young people learn to want a recognizable complex of goods and services which they call "the standard package." This may include a college education, car, gadget-equipped home, and annual travel vacations as base elements. The package may come in a series of standard through de luxe grades, and with the aid of credit progress through those grades can be made easy. Such a view does not, as some have inferred, suggest increased conformity, for obtaining the elements of the package is intimately related to the acquisition of mobility and freedom, that is, greater job choice, reduction of household chores, and increased facilities for and use of transportation. It would seem, however, that as something like a standard package becomes universally wanted, especially for the freedom that is seen in it, then deprivation becomes less tolerable for those without jobs and/or education. On the level of individual protest it may lead to delinquency and crime, but on the level of mass protest it may lead to an insistence on educational and job rights for underprivileged or minority groups. Thus do matters of consumer style shade over into social and political issues.

The matter of social issues raises questions of intensity and amount. For example, to what extent are consumers motivated by the standard package? And how de luxe or how large may this package become? At present we can only cite Chinoy's (1955) study of the American automobile worker, which concludes that satisfactions are reported in terms of a small package of independence represented in home and car ownership, with aspirations for further advancement focused on the children

and their chances for social mobility through education. While this modest version of the dream may apply only to industrial workers, the emphasis is more on having some of the good things of life and the time to use them and less on the ideologically distant goals. While it is true that in the United States a blue-collar majority is giving way rapidly to a "middle-class" white-collar majority, a similar evaluation has not yet been made for the latter group. This latter group, of course, is exposed to a different side of American industry and is more likely to work in office buildings than in factories. The standards for home ownership and decor of this group may therefore be different and possibly higher than that of the blue-collar group.

The question of what kind of houses people want and what they want in them is a good over-all way of assessing the consumer market. For example, the number of new homes for which construction has started each year is the best single indication of whether or not it will be a good year for business. The question of what kinds and numbers of homes to build, and where to build them, becomes a critical determiner of both national economic well-being and of the consumer's physical environment, complete with built-in limitations and opportunities for style development. Thus, the home architects, the appliance designers, the federal housing laws, and the bank credit policies all have significant effects on the potentialities of this environment.

It should also be noted that new houses reflect consumer demand and initiative, or put another way, consumer investment. As Katona (1960) emphasizes, the growth and expansion of the economy are dependent on consumer investment as well as business investment, and these are equally important forces in the extent to which they can stimulate or retard the economy.

Research approaches. With the consumer now seen as so "powerful," it is to be expected that attempts to study him have become intensified. One reviewer (Halbert 1965) has identified six different general approaches:

(1) General studies of consumer behavior: the role of consumers and consumption, consumer spending as investments, consumption in economic development.

(2) Income studies: changes in income distribution, credit, and expenditures by various classes. This category accounts for a large part of past studies.

(3) Population studies: population trends and shifts, life-cycle influences, various demographic classifications.

(4) Life-style factors: studies of factors influencing styles of living, such as purchases, status symbols, social class, images, needs, leisure, convenience. This area is receiving increasing emphasis.

(5) Consumers as decision makers: studies of who makes what decisions, what decisions are planned, who is influential in various situations, the household as a decision unit.

(6) Specific purchase and consumption studies: studies of purchases and determinants of purchases for specific products such as coffee, cleansers, gasoline.

The first three of these approaches are dependent upon availability and analysis of mass data. While the federal and state governments have long made such data available, it is only recently that correspondingly massive tools of analysis have become available (for example, the computer). This means that research in these areas was until recently primarily reportorial. With so much detailed data to comprehend it was all that scholars could do to keep up with descriptive identifications of major historical trends. The computer brings a new type of inquiry to such data—an inquiry that seeks to build dynamic theory and is not daunted by complexities in the manipulation of data. One may expect therefore to hear more in future years, from investigators with a primarily methodological orientation, about the *science* of retailing, of marketing, and of other fields.

The fourth and fifth approaches seem to represent more clearly the opening up of consumer study to sociologists and psychologists. Traditionally, the former have studied the ills of society, such as divorce and unemployment. Psychologists, too, have been involved, if not with society's ills, then with the emotionally ill. However, as the current generation of social scientists has put behind it depression and World War II, and has also participated in the new affluence, there has gradually developed a new curiosity about the nature of the normal personality, a shift away from concern with irrational processes to rational thought, and an interest in theories about how various everyday decisions are made.

All of these areas of research involve a move away from descriptive or reportorial research to inquiry guided by the use of theory and undertaken for the purpose of further theory development. This means that the study of the consumer has now finally linked up with the main body of the behavioral sciences.

As for the consumer himself, we may expect further inroads on his ancient image of himself as a person in want and as one who is preoccupied with the allocation of scarce means to satisfy basic needs. Foote (1963) proposes that as the proportion of household expenditures devoted to food continues to fall, today's somewhat obese consumer may well develop wants that do not require production or consumption, such as stimulating conversation or the creation of music. The constraint on wants such as these will not be income but learning ability. In short, consumers may yet outgrow consumption.

Herbert E. Krugman

[*See also* Advertising, *article on* advertising research; Market research, *article on* consumer research. *Other relevant material may be found in* Conformity; Identity, psychosocial; Leisure.]

BIBLIOGRAPHY

Bell, Daniel 1959 *The End of Ideology.* Glencoe, Ill.: Free Press. → A paperback edition was published in 1961 by Collier.

Caplovitz, David 1963 *The Poor Pay More: Consumer Practices of Low-income Families.* New York: Free Press.

Chinoy, Ely 1955 *Automobile Workers and the American Dream.* Garden City, N.Y.: Doubleday.

Clark, Lincoln H.; and Foote, Nelson N. (editors) 1955–1961 *Consumer Behavior.* 4 vols. New York Univ. Press. → Volume 1: *The Dynamics of Consumer Reaction,* 1955. Volume 2: *The Life Cycle and Consumer Behavior,* 1955. Volume 3: *Research on Consumer Reactions,* 1958. Volume 4: *Household Decision-making,* 1961.

Foote, Nelson N. 1963 The Image of the Consumer in the Year 2000. Pages 13–18 in *Boston Conference on Distribution, Thirty-fifth Annual, 1963.* Chestnut Hill, Mass.: Boston College.

Halbert, Michael 1965 *The Meaning and Sources of Marketing Theory.* New York: McGraw-Hill.

Katona, George 1951 *Psychological Analysis of Economic Behavior.* New York: McGraw-Hill.

Katona, George 1960 *The Powerful Consumer: Psychological Studies of the American Economy.* New York: McGraw-Hill.

Kluckhohn, C. 1958 Have There Been Discernible Shifts in American Values During the Past Generation? Pages 145–217 in Elting E. Morison (editor), *The American Style: Essays in Value and Performance.* A Report on the Dedham Conference of May 23–27, 1957. New York: Harper. → See especially page 197.

Lucas, Darrell B.; and Britt, Steuart H. 1950 *Advertising Psychology and Research: An Introductory Book.* New York: McGraw-Hill.

Packard, Vance O. 1957 *The Hidden Persuaders.* New York: McKay. → A paperback edition was published in 1958 by Pocket Books.

Riesman, David; and Roseborough, Howard 1955 Careers and Consumer Behavior. Pages 1–18 in Lincoln H. Clark and Nelson N. Foote (editors), *Consumer Behavior.* Volume 2: *The Life Cycle and Consumer Behavior.* New York Univ. Press.

SMITH, STEWART A. 1965 Criteria for Media Comparisons: A Critique. *Journal of Marketing Research* 4: 364–369.

TATE, RUSSELL S. 1961 The Supermarket Battle for Store Loyalty. *Journal of Marketing* 25:8–13.

WHITE, WINSTON 1961 *Beyond Conformity.* New York: Free Press. → See especially Chapter 8.

CONSUMER'S SURPLUS

Consumer's surplus denotes the difference between the maximum amount of money a consumer would be willing to pay for a product or service and the amount he actually pays. The term was first introduced into economics by Alfred Marshall in his *Principles of Economics*, but the first person to enunciate the idea in a precise way appears to have been Jules Dupuit, a French engineer, in a paper published in 1844. Rudolf Auspitz and Richard Lieben (who knew of Dupuit's work but not Marshall's) gave an account of consumer's surplus in 1889 in their book *Untersuchungen über die Theorie des Preises* ("Investigations on the Theory of Price"); but their work was neglected, and it was Dupuit, and above all Marshall, who influenced modern economists.

The importance of consumer's surplus is that it provides a monetary measure of the benefit that a consumer derives from the supply of a product given the terms on which it is made available. It seems therefore to offer the possibility of assessing the net effect on welfare of policies that alter the terms on which different products are supplied. Economists have used the concept to argue that some systems of taxation are worse than others because they lead to a greater loss of consumer's surplus. It has also been proposed that in decreasing cost industries in which consumers' expenditures for a product would not cover total costs— if the product were sold on the market at a uniform price or, in most modern formulations, at a price equal to marginal cost—the state should make possible production of the product by means of a subsidy when the gain in consumer's surplus would justify this. In effect, what consumers *would be willing to pay* but do not (or, more exactly, the state's estimate of this) should be treated as an auxiliary factor in addition to *what they do pay*, in determining production, because it indicates as much as what they do pay the worth of the product to them.

Recent work, particularly that of J. R. Hicks, to be discussed below, not only has thrown much light on the meaning of the concept of consumer's surplus but has also revealed more clearly than before the ambiguities and complexities involved in its definition and measurement. It cannot be said that a consensus has yet emerged in the economics profession concerning the validity and usefulness of the concept of consumer's surplus.

Jules Dupuit. Dupuit was concerned with a double question: how to measure the utility derived from a public works (such as a bridge) in order to decide whether it ought to be constructed and how the charges should be set for the services it provides. Dupuit explained his general approach in his 1844 paper "On the Measurement of the Utility of Public Works." He elaborated his views on pricing in a paper published in 1849, "On Tolls and Transport Charges."

Dupuit argued that the amount of money paid by consumers for a product was not an accurate measure of the utility derived from its consumption. It was what a person would be willing to sacrifice to obtain a product that indicated what the product was *really* worth to him. More concretely, it was the maximum amount of money that a consumer would be willing to pay that measured its absolute utility or, as it has been commonly termed by later economists, its "total utility." The difference between the maximum a consumer would pay and what he actually paid (what is now called consumer's surplus), Dupuit termed "relative utility."

Dupuit pointed out that the absolute utility derived from any given quantity of a product would differ among consumers; and, consequently, if it were made available to all consumers at a uniform price the relative utility (consumer's surplus) for that given quantity would also differ. Furthermore, for any one consumer, the absolute utility derived from an additional quantity of the product, and consequently the maximum he would pay for it, would vary with the amount of the product that he was already consuming. Dupuit took as an example the demand for water. A fall in price would open up more uses in which the monetary value of the absolute utility of a unit of water exceeded the price, and the amount demanded would therefore expand. The difference between the sum of the maximum amounts of money a consumer would pay for the various units used for these different purposes and the amount actually spent (the price multiplied by the total number of units consumed) is his consumer's surplus.

On the basis of his analysis, Dupuit argued that in deciding whether to construct a public works it is the monetary value of the absolute utility that ought to be compared with cost. He advocated recouping this cost by a system of discriminating prices in which the price charged to different groups of consumers varied with the maximum that each group would pay (the greater the value of the absolute utility the greater the charge). It should be noted that Dupuit did not advocate a free service when marginal cost was zero. He left this question open. He pointed out that if he were to consider whether a toll should be established or not he "would have had to examine by what new tax or what increase in taxation tolls could be replaced and what would be the effects of these taxes" [*see* DUPUIT].

Alfred Marshall. Alfred Marshall's treatment of consumer's surplus is, in essentials, similar to that of Dupuit although it shows a greater awareness of the underlying difficulties. But Marshall's practice of indicating, but at the same time glossing over, these difficulties made his exposition less clear than that of Dupuit, and there has been much discussion about what Marshall meant by his various statements, questions that probably can never be resolved beyond all doubt. Marshall's analysis seems to have been developed without knowledge of Dupuit's work. His views on consumer's surplus were first published in the privately printed *Pure Theory of Domestic Values* (1879) as well as in a more extended form in the first edition of his *Principles of Economics* (1890).

Marshall pointed out that when a consumer purchases something he is normally better off, that is, he derives a "surplus of satisfaction." The economic measure of this surplus satisfaction is consumer's surplus, which Marshall defined as the "excess of the price which he would be willing to pay rather than go without the thing, over that which he actually does pay" ([1890] 1961, vol. 1, p. 124). Marshall explained his meaning by examining the demand for tea. Suppose a consumer would just be induced to buy one pound per annum if the price were 20 shillings per pound but that if the price fell to 14 shillings per pound that he would just be induced to buy a second pound. Then, according to Marshall, the consumer would be willing to pay 34 shillings for two pounds per annum (20 shillings for the first pound plus 14 shillings for the second). But if the price were 14 shillings per pound, he would pay 28 shillings for the two pounds and thus would obtain a consumer's surplus of 6 shillings. Marshall put this argument in diagrammatic form, as had Dupuit before him (see Figure 1). If the price were *OC*, the quantity demanded would be *OH*. The maximum amount of money that the consumer would be willing to pay for the quantity *OH* is represented by the area *OHAD*. At price *OC*, the amount of money that the

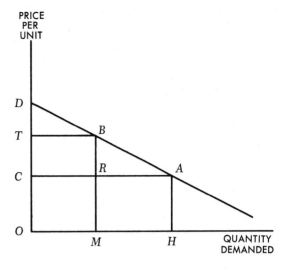

PRICE PER UNIT

QUANTITY DEMANDED

Figure 1

consumer would actually pay is represented by the area *OHAC*. Consumer's surplus is represented by the triangular area *CAD*. Marshall confined his analysis to cases in which expenditure on the product represented a small part of the consumer's total expenditure. The purpose of this restriction appears to have been to ensure that the amount that a consumer would pay for additional units was not affected by the amount that he had paid for the units already demanded. Marshall's failure to deal explicitly with how he would handle the question if this restriction were removed undoubtedly contributed to a feeling that consumer's surplus was a concept of limited usefulness.

In applying his concept to actual problems, Marshall himself was suitably, and characteristically, cautious. He warned against using the loss or gain of consumer's surplus in situations in which different income groups were affected differently. He emphasized that consumer's surplus was a "rough economic measure" and suggested that the calculation should be confined to relatively small changes around the customary price, particularly when dealing with necessaries. Marshall seems originally to have had high hopes of being able to make statistical estimates of consumer's surplus, and in one case he actually made such an estimate: the loss of consumer's surplus due to the British Post Office's not allowing cheap local postal rates. But gradually Marshall became aware of the problems posed by complementarity and substitution and he became disillusioned about the possibility of making such statistical estimates, although he never revised the rather optimistic remarks included in the *Principles*.

Marshall illustrated the use of consumer's surplus by means of examples taken from the field of taxation. If, to refer back to the diagram, a tax of *CT* per unit is placed on the product and this results in a rise in price of the same amount (from *OC* to *OT*) and a reduction in the amount demanded (from *OH* to *OM*) the amount that the consumer would pay in taxes is the sum represented by the area *CRBT*. But the consumer is not only worse off because he has suffered a reduction in the amount available for spending represented by the area *CRBT*. The consumer would cease to demand the quantity *MH* for which he would have been willing to pay the sum of money represented by the area *MHAB*. He would gain the sum of money represented by the area *MHAR* (the money he previously spent to secure *MH*). The money gained would be less than the value to him of the product lost. Consequently, in addition to the loss suffered as a result of paying over a certain amount in taxes, there would be a loss of consumer's surplus represented by the area *RAB*. Marshall suggested that a government, having to obtain a given sum by taxation, should choose objects of taxation with a view to minimizing the loss of consumer's surplus.

Marshall's most celebrated application of the concept of consumer's surplus was his suggestion that it might be advantageous to tax industries subject to diminishing returns (in which, owing to a fall in the supply price due to the *decrease* in output, the loss of consumer's surplus could well be less than the proceeds of the tax) and to subsidize industries subject to increasing returns (in which, owing to the reduction in supply price brought about by the *increase* in output, the gain in consumer's surplus could well exceed the amount of the bounty). Thus the combination of tax and bounty might, on balance, lead to a net gain for consumers. The proposal to make price equal to marginal cost in industries in which average cost is greater than marginal cost—the amount by which consumer expenditures fall short of total costs being made up by a government subsidy (which has had the support of many modern economists)—may be regarded as a variant of the Marshallian suggestion.

Although Marshall originated the term consumer's surplus and although it did appear in the first edition of the *Principles*, the term that Marshall normally used until the fourth edition, in 1898, was "consumer's rent." In view of this, it is hardly surprising to find that Marshall also introduced into economics the analogous concept of "producer's surplus," the difference between the amount of money a producer receives for a product and the minimum for which he would be willing to supply it. It corresponds to one of the meanings of the term "rent" [*see* RENT]. Perhaps because the problems associated with producer's surplus are more commonly considered under the heading of rent, the separate discussion of producer's surplus has been less extensive than that of consumer's surplus. It has, however, been argued that in computing the gain from the supply of a product it is necessary to include not only the consumer's but also the producer's surplus since it is the minimum for which a producer would be willing to supply a product that represents the value of what is lost through the diversion of factors to produce it. However, a diversion of factors on any considerable scale is likely to lead to a loss of consumer's surplus elsewhere and this also needs to be taken into account. The proper although in practice extremely difficult procedure, if the additional output is to be valued including consumer's surplus, would seem to be to compare this with the value of the output lost through the diversion of the factors, including in this case the loss of consumer's surplus.

Recent developments. Marshall's analysis gained many adherents; but some economists remained unconvinced. J. S. Nicholson expressed skepticism (1894) and was answered by F. Y. Edgeworth (1894); Edwin Cannan (1924) was also skeptical and was answered by D. H. Macgregor (1924) and A. L. Bowley (1924). Doubts persisted. In recent times J. R. Hicks has attempted to rehabilitate the concept of consumer's surplus. In *Value and Capital* (1939), he suggested that the way to measure consumer's surplus was to discover the reduction in income that would just offset the gain brought about by a fall in price, thus leaving the consumer no better off than before. Such a definition was not subject to the Marshallian restriction that expenditure on this item be a small proportion of the total. The marginal utility of money need not be constant and it could therefore be applied to products that took an appreciable part of consumer expenditures. A. M. Henderson (1941) argued, however, that what was described by Hicks's new definition was not the Marshallian consumer's surplus, which could be regarded as the amount a consumer would pay for the opportunity of buying at the existing price the amount he was in fact buying (the alternative being to give up consuming the product entirely). Hicks's consumer's surplus was the amount a consumer would pay for the opportunity of buying at the existing price whatever quantity he wished. Since Hicks allowed the consumer to do something that according to Henderson was ruled out by the Marshallian definition (it allowed him to adjust his consumption as the amount he had available for spending was reduced), it was to be expected that the monetary value of Hicks's consumer's surplus would, in general, be greater. Henderson also showed that the monetary value of the consumer's surplus derived from a given change in price would differ according to whether the higher or the lower price was taken as the starting point. Hicks accepted Henderson's analysis and elaborated on it in subsequent articles and in *A Revision of Demand Theory* (1956). Four measures of consumer's surplus were derived, depending on whether the consumer is assumed to pay to obtain or be paid to forgo the opportunity under consideration and on whether the opportunity is one in which the consumer is or is not able to adapt his consumption to take account of the payment made or received. Hicks pointed out, however, that in the cases in which Marshall made use of consumer's surplus—those in which the marginal utility of money could be assumed to remain constant—all four measures had the same value.

While Hicks's analysis clarified the problems that arise when an attempt is made to measure consumer's surplus, the formidable nature of these problems and particularly the existence of different (but equally valid) measures of consumer's surplus understandably have strengthened the tendency to regard consumer's surplus as a concept of limited usefulness. A. P. Lerner (1963) has argued that such an attitude is unwarranted, maintaining that there is no need for a consumer's surplus that assumes that the consumer is not allowed to adjust his demand to the price, a category that, according to Lerner, arose as a result of too literal a reading of Marshall. Only one consumer's surplus is needed: "the tax or the subsidy that would have the same effect on real income if it took the place of the price change considered." He argued that consumer's surplus could help in the analysis of such problems as taxation, trade restrictions, and monopoly—the kinds of problems, in fact, for which Dupuit and Marshall devised the concept. There is no question that many economists have found the concept of consumer's surplus useful in their thinking on such questions. But until satisfactory methods have been devised to estimate in practice the gains and losses of consumer's surplus resulting from any given change in policy, other economists are likely to continue to regard the concept of consumer's surplus as, in Little's words (1950), "a theoretical toy."

R. H. COASE

[*See also the biography of* AUSPITZ AND LIEBEN.]

BIBLIOGRAPHY

AUSPITZ, RUDOLF; and LIEBEN, RICHARD 1889 *Untersuchungen über die Theorie des Preises.* Leipzig: Duncker & Humblot. → Published in French in 1914.

BOWLEY, A. L. 1924 Does Mathematical Analysis Explain? A Note on Consumer's Surplus. *Economica* 4:135–139.

CANNAN, EDWIN 1924 "Total Utility" and "Consumer's Surplus." *Economica* 4:21–26.

DUPUIT, JULES (1844) 1952 On the Measurement of the Utility of Public Works. *International Economic Papers* 2:83–110. → First published in French.

DUPUIT, JULES (1844–1854) 1933 *De l'utilité et de sa mesure: Écrits choisis et republiés par Mario de Bernardi.* Turin (Italy): La Riforma Sociale.

DUPUIT, JULES (1849) 1962 On Tolls and Transport Charges. *International Economic Papers* 11:7–31. → First published in French.

EDGEWORTH, F. Y. 1894 Professor J. S. Nicholson on "Consumer's Rent." *Economic Journal* 4:151–158. → For further comments see pages 347–348.

HENDERSON, A. M. 1941 Consumer's Surplus and the Compensating Variation. *Review of Economic Studies* 8, no. 2:117–121.

HICKS, JOHN R. (1939) 1946 *Value and Capital: An Inquiry Into Some Fundamental Principles of Economic Theory.* 2d ed. Oxford: Clarendon.

HICKS, JOHN R. 1941 The Rehabilitation of Consumers' Surplus. *Review of Economic Studies* 8, no. 2:108–116.

HICKS, JOHN R. 1943 The Four Consumer's Surpluses. *Review of Economic Studies* 11, no. 1:31–41.

HICKS, JOHN R. 1946 The Generalised Theory of Consumer's Surplus. *Review of Economic Studies* 13, no. 2:68:74.

HICKS, JOHN R. (1956) 1959 *A Revision of Demand Theory.* 2d ed. Oxford: Clarendon.

HOUGHTON, R. W. 1958 A Note on the Early History of Consumer's Surplus. *Economica* New Series 25, no. 97:49–57. → An account in English of Auspitz and Lieben's views on consumer's surplus.

KNIGHT, FRANK H. 1944 Realism and Relevance in the Theory of Demand. *Journal of Political Economy* 52, no. 4:289–318.

LERNER, ABBA P. 1963 Consumer's Surplus and Micro–Macro. *Journal of Political Economy* 71:76–81.

LITTLE, IAN M. D. (1950) 1957 *A Critique of Welfare Economics.* 2d ed. Oxford: Clarendon. → See especially pages 166–184 on "Indivisibilities and Consumers' Surplus."

MACGREGOR, D. H. 1924 Consumer's Surplus: A Reply. *Economica* 4:131–134.

MARSHALL, ALFRED (1879) 1949 *The Pure Theory of Foreign Trade* and *The Pure Theory of Domestic Values.* Series of Reprints of Scarce Tracts in Economic and Political Science, No. 1. London School of Economics and Political Science.

MARSHALL, ALFRED (1890) 1961 *Principles of Economics.* 2 vols., 9th ed. New York and London: Macmillan. → A variorum edition. The eighth edition is preferable for normal use.

MISHAN, E. J. (1960) 1964 A Survey of Welfare Economics: 1939–1959. Pages 3–97 in E. J. Mishan, *Welfare Economics: Five Introductory Essays.* New York: Random House. → First published in Volume 70 of the *Economic Journal.* Section 4 discusses consumer's surplus.

NICHOLSON, JOSEPH S. (1893) 1902 *Principles of Political Economy.* Vol. 1, 2d ed. London: Black.

NICHOLSON, JOSEPH S. 1894 The Measurement of Utility by Money. *Economic Journal* 4:342–47.

PATINKIN, DON 1963 Demand Curves and Consumer's Surplus. Pages 83–112 in *Measurement in Economics: Studies in Mathematical Economics and Econometrics in Memory of Yehuda Grunfeld.* Stanford Univ. Press.

CONSUMPTION FUNCTION

Economists have long been interested in the factors determining how a society divides its income proportionally between consumption and saving. In the past thirty years theoretical and empirical investigation of these factors has been focused by the concept of the *consumption function*—a list of the variables that influence consumption, together with the direction and magnitude of their effects. *Income* itself is, of course, high on any such list; and much of recent investigation has concerned the nature, reliability, and measurement of the dependence of consumption on income.

Since *saving* is by definition the difference, positive or negative, between *income* and *consumption*, whatever relationships are summarized in a consumption function can be summarized equally well in a saving function. It is a matter of indifference whether attention is directed to the determinants of consumption or to the determinants of saving; the results of one approach can always be translated into the other. For example, the proposition that U.S. households in the aggregate spend for consumption 95 per cent of their income after taxes can also be stated by saying that they save 5 per cent of the income at their disposition. In either form, incidentally, the statement is no better than a good first approximation.

Why have economists been interested in the division of social income between consumption and saving? There are two main reasons.

The first principal reason is the importance of saving for accumulation of the wealth of nations and for growth in their capacity to produce goods and services. Broadly speaking, consumption uses productive resources in the present, while saving enlarges the resources available for production and consumption in the future—by increasing stocks of finished goods or materials, productive plant and equipment, and net claims on foreign countries.

In practice it is difficult to measure these concepts of social accounting—net national product or income, consumption, saving, and wealth—in ways that correspond to the fundamental distinction between provision for the present and provision for the future. Very likely, saving, as measured in our national accounts, understates our society's provision for the future. One problem is to measure the value of the services rendered by existing stocks of producers' and consumers' durable goods, and to allow for their depreciation and obsolescence. This is difficult enough for business plant and equipment. Housing is the only consumers' durable asset for which such accounts are estimated; for other consumers' durable goods, consumption is simply equated to new purchases. And no attempt is made in many national accounts (including those of the United States) to estimate the accumulation of real wealth by governments, even before allowance for depreciation.

An even greater practical and conceptual problem, which has attracted considerable research interest recently, is to identify and to measure the saving embodied in human beings in the form of increased education, new skills, and greater capacities. The national accounts do not now count any educational outlays as saving or associate with them any increase in national wealth [*see* CAPITAL, HUMAN].

In spite of these and other difficulties, there can be no doubt of the importance for economic growth of the processes of individual and social decision that determine the share of saving, as conventionally measured, in net national product. This has been underscored in recent years by the shortages of capital confronting the less developed countries.

The second principal reason for concern with the consumption function is an outgrowth of the depression of the 1930s and of the revolutions in economic thought and policy to which it led. An economy will not produce at the rate that its manpower and capital resources permit unless total effective demand for goods and services suffices to purchase its capacity, or "full employment," output. If private consumption demand falls short of capacity output, the difference must be made up by nonconsumption spending, that is, private investment at home or abroad and government expenditure. If these sources of demand do not absorb the saving that the economy would perform at full employment, then output, employment, and the use of industrial capacity will all fall short of their full employment levels. The national propensity to save will not be realized in additions to national wealth but wasted in unemployment and idle capacity.

The observation that saving is not always an unmixed blessing has a long history, associated with "underconsumption" explanations of the business cycle. But it received its most sophisticated, convincing, and influential expression in J. M. Keynes's *General Theory of Employment, Interest and Money* (1936). Keynes emphasized that consumption is on the whole a predictable and reliable component of aggregate demand. He saw investment spending, in contrast, as inherently volatile and unstable. And in the periodic failure to use the potential saving of the economy he found the main reason for the repeated lapses of capitalist economies into recession and depression. He feared, further, a chronic tendency in wealthy countries for full employment saving to outrun investment, leading in the absence of corrective policies to chronic unemployment.

The same theoretical apparatus can be applied to the opposite problem, excess demand and inflation, although this was not the economic disease originally at the center of Keynes's attention. Inflation occurs when nonconsumption spending, by governments or private enterprises, more than fills the gap between full employment output and the consumption expenditure that it normally induces.

In recent decades Keynes's theory has been the major impetus to research on the consumption function. This theoretical impetus was reinforced by the simultaneous development of national accounts providing the statistical raw material for empirical research on the subject. Note that the Keynesian motivation for understanding the social choice between consumption and saving does not require, to the same degree as the growth motivation first mentioned, close identification of consumption with the present and saving with the future. What is more important for Keynes's purpose is identification of consumption with the predictable, and investment with the volatile, elements of nation expenditure.

Keynes's "propensity to consume"

Keynes's consumption function is a simple relationship between national consumption—and accordingly national saving—on the one hand, and national income on the other. He called this relationship "the propensity to consume" and derived certain conclusions as to its form from what he asserted to be a "psychological law"—that the community will divide an increase in income in some regular proportion between an increase in consumption and an increase in saving. That is, both the "marginal propensity to consume" (mpc) and the "marginal propensity to save" (mps) are between zero and one. (By definition the two marginal propensities sum to one.) This is all his theory required, but Keynes went further and speculated

that the "average propensity to consume" (apc), the share of national income consumed, would be found to decline with increases in total income. This decline could reflect either or both of the following: (a) the mpc falls with income; (b) a certain component of consumption expenditure is independent of income. This means that the apc will be lower for higher incomes even if the mpc is constant, as is illustrated in Figure 1. Evidently Keynes believed in both.

Figure 1 displays a Keynesian consumption function and in the lower panel the corresponding saving function. Net national income, Y, is measured along the horizontal axes. The vertical axis represents consumption, C, in the upper panel and saving, S, in the lower. The 45° line from the conventional origin in the upper panel is a reference line, showing how much consumption would be if it were always exactly equal to income. The other line,

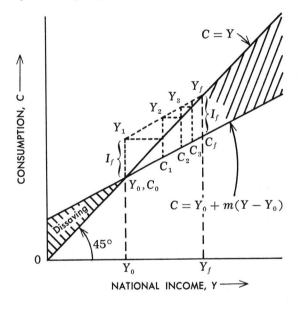

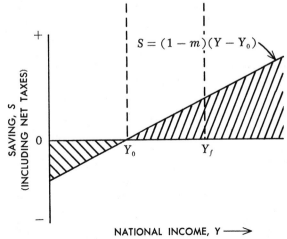

Figure 1 — The Keynesian consumption function

more gently sloped, is the consumption function. It shows that below a break-even level of national income, Y_0, the nation will wish to consume more than its income, drawing on past savings. Above Y_0, however, consumption falls short of income, by an increasing margin. The *mpc* is the slope of this line, m, positive but less than one. Given a one-dollar increase in income, the community will increase its consumption by $m and increase its saving, or diminish its dissaving, by $(1 - m)$. In the diagram the *mpc* is constant; a diminishing *mpc* would be pictured by a consumption function curving away from the 45° reference line, and by an upward-curving saving function. But even along the linear consumption function in Figure 1, the *apc* declines with income. Below Y_0 the ratio of consumption to income, C/Y, exceeds one; at Y_0 it is exactly one; above Y_0 it is below one.

The multiplier. The use that Keynes made of the consumption function in explaining unemployment can also be indicated in Figure 1. Net national product or income, Y, is three things at once: (*a*) The sum of the incomes earned for productive services (wages and salaries, interest, rents, profits), plus taxes paid by businesses prior to the payment or calculation of these factor incomes. (National accounting practice distinguishes *net national product* and *national income* by deducting these "indirect business taxes" from *net national product* in order to arrive at *national income*. This means that *net national product* measures the market value of net output, at prices that include these taxes, whereas *national income* values production at prices corresponding to the income payments to productive factors. This distinction is not made in this article; the two terms are used interchangeably to refer to the market value of net output.) (*b*) The total market value of goods and services produced. (*c*) Total purchases of goods and services, the sum of consumption expenditure, private investment, and government purchases. To sustain any given level of production and income, say Y_f, total spending must add up to Y_f. Since consumption spending will amount only to C_f, nonconsumption spending must make up the difference. If Y_f represents the full employment potential of the economy, failure of nonconsumption spending to reach I_f would mean failure of production and income to attain Y_f. The result would be unemployment and excess capacity. (Likewise, should nonconsumption spending exceed I_f, total demand would tend to exceed Y_f, causing inflation.)

Further, the consumption function enabled Keynes to say by how much national income would fall short for a given shortfall in nonconsumption expenditure. A difference of a dollar in nonconsumption expenditure means a difference of more than a dollar in national income. The *multiplier*, which expresses this relationship, depends on the *mpc*. In Figure 1, for example, if nonconsumption spending is equal to zero instead of to I_f, income will be at the break-even level, Y_0, instead of at Y_f. The difference in income, $Y_f - Y_0$, is $1/(1 - m)$ times the difference in nonconsumption spending I_f. The multiplier is $1/(1 - m)$. Thus, if the national *mpc* is $\frac{3}{4}$, the multiplier is 4; if the *mpc* is $\frac{2}{3}$, the multiplier is 3; and so on.

The multiplier is a measure of the response of total production, income, and employment to changes in nonconsumption spending, whether these changes reflect natural volatility of private investment or conscious policy in public expenditure. It was in the latter context that the concept of the multiplier was first advanced, by Kahn (1931), as a means of estimating the response of employment to public works expenditure during the depression.

The dynamics of the multiplier can be exhibited by assuming, along with Kahn and many other writers, a lag in the adjustment of consumption to income. Suppose nonconsumption spending was initially zero and income and consumption were in equilibrium at $C_0 = Y_0$. Now nonconsumption spending rises to I_f and stays there. Initially, income and production rise by a like amount, that is, to $Y_1 = C_0 + I_f$. But then consumption adjusts to Y_1 along the consumption function and rises to C_1. This raises income to $Y_2 = C_1 + I_f$. The process converges to income Y_f, where the consumption function indicates consumption of C_f, leaving just enough room for the new level of nonconsumption spending I_f.

For an example with numerical concreteness, take $m = \frac{3}{5}$ and suppose the sustained increase ΔI in nonconsumption spending to be 10. Then the process is as presented in Table 1, where ΔY, ΔI, and ΔC are the increases in these variables over their *initial* levels.

Table 1

"Round"	ΔI	$\Delta C = \frac{3}{5} \Delta Y_{-1}$	$\Delta Y = \Delta I + \Delta C$
0	0	0	0
1	10	0	10
2	10	6	16
3	10	9.6	19.6
4	10	11.76	21.76
5	10	13.06	23.06
6	10	13.83	23.83
7	10	14.30	24.30
⋮	⋮	⋮	⋮
∞	10	15	25

The dynamic formulation serves to make two points. First, stability requires that the national *mpc* be smaller than one. Otherwise the multiplier process would never converge. An initial stimulus would keep spending and income rising indefinitely. (It is a mistake, therefore, to conclude from the formula, multiplier = $1/(1-m)$, that the multiplier is negative if *m* exceeds one. Rather the whole multiplier concept is inapplicable in that case.) Second, assuming the *mpc* to lie in the normal stable range, as Keynes assumed, a one-shot injection of investment or government expenditure cannot lift income more than temporarily. A sustained higher level of income requires a sustained higher level of nonconsumption spending. Multiplier theory offers no comfort for "pump primers." A temporary stimulus can work only if there are some unstable elements in national spending that can be set into sustained motion by an initial surge in economic activity. According to Keynes, consumption is not an unstable element of this kind.

Price and population adjustments. The consumption–income relation is intended to link *real per capita* magnitudes, measured in constant prices. An increase in national income in Figure 1, for example, represents an increase in production and purchasing power rather than an increase in the prices at which production is valued. The community cannot be expected to react to a doubling of money income in the same way when it reflects a doubling of prices and wages (with real output constant) as when it reflects a doubling of output (with prices constant). Creating a new franc by deleting two zeros from the old one should not change anyone's basic behavior. Of course, actual price movements are not so uniform, universal, and neutral as de Gaulle's decimal reform. Consequently both the level of prices and their rate of change may affect the relation between real consumption and real income; some of these possible effects will be mentioned below.

For somewhat similar reasons, the variables in the consumption function must also be corrected for changes in population. The logic of the argument that the average propensity to consume is lower when society is better off implies that an increase in real national income accompanied by an equal proportionate rise in population would leave the average propensity to consume unchanged. Consequently the variables in Figure 1 should be regarded as per capita measures. (The theoretically appropriate correction for population change is somewhat more complicated. Presumably persons of different age, sex, and family status have different consumption requirements and

should receive different weights, as in the "equivalent adult" procedures used in studies of food consumption.)

However, this gross correction for population change is not the end of the story, any more than simple "deflation" for price changes disposes entirely of price effects. As noted below, both price and population changes play important roles in recent theories of the consumption function.

The reliability of the multiplier. Although the propensity to consume and the multiplier have become standard items in the tool kits of economists, these concepts have not gone unchallenged. When quarterly income and consumption data became available in the United States after World War II, they showed erratic fluctuations in the response of consumption to quarter-to-quarter changes in income. And at times, notably during the Korean War, there have been wide swings in the propensity to consume. Some critics have questioned the view that consumption is a particularly stable or predictable element in national expenditure, that consumers respond passively to shocks originating in business investment and government expenditure. In their view the multiplier is not a reliable tool of analysis and prediction, certainly not one that can be applied mechanically. It should be noted that the multiplier multiplies error as well as truth in translating fluctuations of nonconsumption expenditure into predicted changes in national product.

In a series of statistical studies, Friedman and Meiselman (1963) have argued that multiplier analysis performs less well in explaining fluctuations of national product than an alternative model of equal simplicity relating national product to the quantity of money. In a different vein, Katona (1960) has contended that consumers in a modern rich society possess sufficient discretion and autonomy to originate, not just respond to, fluctuations in over-all economic activity. Consequently he has pioneered in conducting surveys of consumer intentions and attitudes, which can be used to improve the short-run forecasts of consumer behavior made from conventional economic variables (see Katona & Mueller 1953; 1956). The record suggests that these surveys contain useful forecasting information, at least for the short-run timing of the durable goods component of consumer expenditures. [See SURVEY ANALYSIS, *article on* APPLICATIONS IN ECONOMICS.]

A doubt of somewhat different import concerns a possible ambiguity in the direction of causal influence between income and consumption. Keynes and virtually all subsequent writers on the consumption function take income to be the determining variable and consumption to be the determined variable. The income of an individual or household or corporation is assumed to be outside its own control, at least in the short run. It is a datum, determined by market forces, constraining consumption and saving decisions. But there are many opportunities in an advanced economy for households to adjust their incomes, by working more or less, or by movement of wives and other secondary earners in or out of the labor force. A study by Rosett (1958), for example, shows the influence of the financial position of the household on the labor force participation of wives. It is possible that many households adjust their incomes to their consumption standards, rather than vice versa. An analogous opportunity is presumably available to some corporations; that is, if they are in need of profits to pay dividends or to make investments, they can take steps to increase them.

National versus household propensities. Keynes was concerned with the propensity to consume of a whole society, the relation of its consumption to its net national product. The difference between these magnitudes takes various forms: household saving, the retained earnings of enterprises, the receipts of governments. Accordingly, the national consumption function reflects a variety of social institutions and patterns of behavior—a mixture of family, business, and political habits and decisions. If it is based on any psychological law, the law must be founded in social psychology rather than in the psychology of individual consumers and savers.

Personal saving proper is defined as the difference between private consumption and *personal disposable income*—the income that individuals and households have wholly free disposition of. This differs from net national product by the sum of (*a*) taxes and other government receipts, net of government "transfer payments," which are in the nature of negative taxes (pensions, benefits, subsidies, etc., for which no current productive services are rendered), and (*b*) the net earnings, after taxes, retained by corporations. The national *mpc* depends not only on the response of consumers to an increase in disposable income, but also on the response of personal disposable income to an increase in net national product. The latter response, in turn, reflects (*a*) the sensitivity of government tax receipts (net of transfer payments)—state and local as well as federal—to increases in national product and (*b*) the share of corporate profits after taxes in such increases in national product, together with the "propensity" of

corporate directors to retain these earnings rather than to disburse them as dividends. In the analytical framework of Keynes's *General Theory*, a change in any of this complex of relationships would shift the consumption function, changing its level and perhaps its slope and shape. For example, tax rate reductions, increases in public welfare payments, increases in corporate dividends, reductions in the share of profits in national product would all raise the national propensity to consume. This could happen even though the thriftiness of households, as measured by their propensity to consume from disposable income, remained unchanged.

The practical quantitative importance of this observation can be illustrated from recent experience in the United States. In the short run at least, both the *apc* and *mpc* from disposable income appear to be between .92 and .96. But the *apc* with respect to net national product is about .70 and the *mpc* about .55. Thus the gap between disposable income and net national product accounts for the major part of the gap between consumption and net national product.

Of course, not all the difference between net national product and private consumption is saving in the sense of augmenting national wealth and future consumption possibilities. On the expenditure side, the counterpart of this gap includes government purchases of goods and services as well as net private investment. Some government expenditure is investment in the future, and some is collective consumption. Unfortunately, our present government accounting techniques do not permit a useful quantitative classification. But, as observed above, this failure is not crucial for the purposes for which Keynes designed the consumption function.

Subsequent theoretical and empirical investigation has not followed Keynes in postulating a single stable relationship linking consumption to national product. Instead "the consumption function" has come to have a narrower meaning: the relationship of consumption to disposable income and other variables. The linkages between disposable income and national product have been set to one side for independent investigation. Despite the fact that they are of greater quantitative importance than household saving proper, less theoretical and statistical effort has been expended on them (see, however, Ruggles & Ruggles 1949).

Although this division of labor is probably an advance over Keynes's global approach, the propensity to save from disposable income is surely not entirely independent of corporate saving or of certain tax payments. Retained earnings do not enter disposable income, but they are reflected in the value of corporate stocks and thus in the wealth of households and individuals. Accumulation of wealth by this route may substitute for personal saving; evidence that wealth affects the household propensity to save is noted below. Tax payments connected with social security programs are excluded from both disposable income and personal saving, even though private withholdings from wages and salaries for similar purposes are counted as both income and saving. One may suspect that socialization of saving for retirement, medical emergencies, and unemployment would lower the apparent propensity to save from personal disposable income. But it is hard to support this suspicion empirically.

What follows will concern the consumption function in the narrower sense, the division of disposable income between consumption and personal saving.

The postwar reappraisal

The Keynesian consumption function, typified in Figure 1, fits admirably two kinds of empirical data. First, economy-wide time series of consumption and income for the period between the two world wars lie along a function of the Keynesian type; there are even observations of negative private saving in the depths of the great depression. Second, any cross-section survey of household budgets appears to confirm the "psychological law" at a microeconomic level. When households are classified into income brackets, and the average consumption for a bracket is plotted against income, the scatter of points traces out a path (Engel curve) like the consumption function of Figure 1. Dissaving in low brackets gives way to positive saving at higher levels. Indeed some survey evidence suggests that the *mpc* falls in high brackets.

After World War II, however, several pieces of evidence combined to cast doubt on the Keynesian consumption function. The reappraisal that followed led to new theories and deeper empirical investigation of the determinants of household consumption.

First, extrapolations of statistical consumption functions based on prewar United States data to potential postwar income levels greatly underestimated the postwar propensity to consume. These extrapolations led some analysts to pessimistic views of postwar economic prospects in the United States, which were in the event quite unjustified. These extrapolations were based either on interwar time series or on Engel curves relating household consumption and income in prewar budget studies of 1935–1936.

The Keynesian propensity to consume is primarily a tool for the short run, for analysis of the determination of income and employment during a business cycle or a period of underemployment. The failure of the postwar forecasts did not impair its usefulness for this primary purpose. Moreover, Keynes certainly did not exclude shifts in the consumption function, and no doubt he himself would have understood the significance of the artificial shortages of consumers' goods and the abnormal accumulations of liquid savings that a great war leaves in its aftermath. At the same time, many of his obiter dicta suggest that he expected rich capitalist societies to face in the long run a chronic and increasing excess of potential saving at full employment. Experience since the war, persisting beyond its immediate legacy of backlogs and liquidity, compels a considerable modification of this expectation.

Second, just as the interwar Keynesian consumption function forecasts too much saving after World War II, it "backcasts" too little saving before World War I. Indeed it would not indicate any positive saving until about 1908, when per capita income reached the break-even point observed during the depression. One does not require data to know that U.S. economic growth in the nineteenth century and the early twentieth century was not generated from dissaving. But a statistical study by Kuznets (1946) provided the data, showing that the share of capital formation in U.S. output, averaged for overlapping decades, has been roughly constant since the Civil War. Moreover, Brady and Friedman (1947) took the trouble to look at earlier household budget studies, going as far back as 1901. They found that while any one survey indicates the same kind of Keynesian consumption–income relationship observed in the 1935–1936 study, the relationship shifts upward in successive surveys. A family with, say, an income of $3,000, corrected for price changes, will in general be observed to save much less in 1918 than in 1901, still less in 1935, and, as it has later turned out, less in 1950 than in 1935 or 1941. This finding, of course, undermines the simple use of the Engel curve of a cross-section survey for prediction or aggregation. The hypothesis that Brady and Friedman offered to explain the finding anticipates that of Duesenberry, which will be discussed below.

Recognition of these facts led a number of investigators to formulate and test hypotheses that would explain them—broadly speaking, hypotheses that would reconcile the short-run, or cyclical, success of the Keynesian consumption function with its long-run, or secular, failure. Indeed in the early 1940s Samuelson (1943) proposed a "ratchet" model: Consumption grows in the long run roughly in proportion to income; but during cyclical interruptions of long-run growth, consumers defend living standards already attained, and consequently consumption follows a flatter (lower *mpc*) Keynesian path. In independent but similar contributions, Duesenberry (1948) and Modigliani (1949) formalized the ratchet idea and tested it statistically, making the *apc* depend inversely on the ratio between current income and previous peak income.

These formulations do the trick in a statistical sense. They do it by eliminating absolute real income from the determination of the long-run average propensity to consume, which becomes a constant. Why should this be so?

Relative income. Duesenberry (1949) offered one explanation, his "relative income" hypothesis. Consumer utility depends, he reasoned, not on absolute amounts of consumption but on the relation of these amounts to the consumption of others with whom the consumer feels in social competition or under pressure to conform. This hypothesis has obvious support in many findings of modern sociology and psychology, and in some older ideas of Veblen. Duesenberry's hypothesis rationalizes the Brady–Friedman findings, in much the same way they themselves suggest. The pattern of any one cross section reflects the fact that the consumption leaders, in the upper ranks of the income distribution, can "afford" high propensities to save, while the followers in the lower ranks respond to social pressures by high propensities to consume. A general increase in absolute incomes, leaving the relative income distribution unchanged, will leave unchanged both these social pressures and the responses to them in terms of shares of income consumed. Most of the differences between successive budget surveys disappear when consumption ratios are plotted not against absolute incomes but against relative income positions. The broad conclusion is that while substantial changes over time in the inequality of incomes might alter the aggregate consumption ratio—contrary to the usual view, equalization would tend to increase the saving ratio—sheer growth in per capita income will not.

Permanent and lifetime income. In independently developed formulations, Friedman (1957) and Modigliani and Brumberg (1954) offered alternative explanations of the same phenomena. Students of household consumption behavior have long observed that incomes other than current in-

comes affect current consumption. Consumers suffering income declines resist departures from their previous consumption standards; and those enjoying income gains generally consume less than other households who long ago achieved the same income level. Similarly, the investigations of Katona and his colleagues (Katona & Mueller 1953; 1956) at the Survey Research Center at the University of Michigan indicate that optimistic expectations of future incomes encourage current consumption, while pessimistic expectations have the reverse effect.

According to Friedman's "permanent income hypothesis," the consumption of a household is proportional to its *permanent income*, that is, the average income it expects to earn over its planning horizon. Friedman is not definite about either the factor of proportionality—which might vary with the household's stage in the life cycle, its wealth, the interest rate, and other variables—or about the length of the planning horizon. On these matters the *lifetime income* hypothesis of Modigliani is much more explicit, as will be seen below. In any case, Friedman employs his hypothesis to explain both the evidence of cross-section budget surveys and the ratchet effect observed in aggregate time series.

In budget surveys the low-income brackets are bound to be abnormally loaded with families temporarily below their permanent incomes, while the high brackets naturally have more than their share of families temporarily above their permanent status. This is the reason that the low brackets in any cross section exhibit a higher propensity to consume, relative to measured current incomes, than the high brackets—even though the propensity to consume from permanent incomes, unobserved, may be the same for all groups. When the households of a cross section are classified, not by current incomes but by other observed attributes—occupation, educational attainment, residence, age—better correlated with permanent income status, the scatter of points relating average consumption to average income gives a better approximation of the long-run consumption function. It starts from the origin—after all, groups with low permanent income status cannot do much dissaving—and shows a higher marginal propensity to consume than the usual Engel curve (see Watts 1958). Whether this *mpc* is a constant or diminishing function of income is, however, an open empirical question.

As for the ratchet effect, many households are below their permanent incomes in recessions and depressions; therefore their consumption is high relative to their current incomes. Like the "previous peak" hypotheses discussed above, this explanation is more satisfactory for recessions clearly believed to be temporary than for prolonged depression periods like the 1930s when the memory of the preceding peak grows faint.

The Modigliani–Brumberg model is in the same spirit, but by being bolder in its assumptions it is more specific in its conclusions. In its most stark formulation, the planning horizon of the individual consumer is his whole lifetime. And the factor of proportionality between consumption and permanent income is simply one. Individuals are assumed to plan no net lifetime saving; they transfer to their heirs no more and no less than they inherited. Subject to this constraint, they try to spread their lifetime consumable resources evenly over their lives. In particular, they seek to accumulate enough savings during their earning years to maintain the same consumption standard during their years of retirement. The division of life between work and retirement is taken, somewhat implausibly, as an institutional fact, a constant independent of national and individual incomes. The model has several interesting implications:

(a) In a society with stationary population and income, aggregate net personal saving would be zero. The dissaving of the retired would exactly offset the saving of the workers, whose only purpose in saving is to provide for their own future retirement.

(b) In a society with growing population or growing per capita income or both, aggregate net personal saving will be positive. Indeed, the higher these rates of growth, the higher will be the ratio of saving to aggregate income. For in a growing economy, the retired of the future always exceed—in number or in lifetime income, or in both—the retired of the present. Consequently the saving necessary to provide for future retirements always exceeds the dissaving of the currently retired. (See Modigliani & Ando 1963 for precise calculations.)

(c) Changes in this year's income affect this year's consumption only to the extent that current consumption benefits, equally with consumption in all future years, from a general recalculation of lifetime consumable resources. This effect will not be large unless current income changes are regarded as permanent. This is the counterpart of Friedman's more extreme contention that all temporary income gains will be saved and none consumed, and symmetrically that temporary income losses will be wholly offset by dissaving.

This implication of the two models has attracted widespread attention and controversy. One reason

is that it casts doubt on the efficacy of temporary changes in tax rates or income transfers as measures of economic stabilization. Some caution is required in drawing this inference from the permanent income or lifetime income hypotheses. Strictly speaking, these theories concern consumption rather than expenditures on consumers' goods, for example, the use of an automobile rather than its purchase. It may be that temporary windfalls are used to purchase durables but do not appreciably increase their use; the purchaser uses the newer product with the same intensity. But from the standpoint of economic stabilization, the stimulus of such expenditure is equally good whether it is properly classified as saving or as consumption. The pure theories assume, moreover, that there are no obstacles in financial markets to borrowing against expected future incomes. In actual fact many households are at the limits of their lines of credit and are therefore prevented from adjusting current consumption fully to their permanent incomes. Temporary windfalls may increase their consumption expenditures simply by adding to their liquid resources.

Empirical measurement of the *mpc* from temporary income has not been conclusive. But Bodkin (1959) observed that the households of veterans who received unexpected national service life insurance dividends during the 1950 budget survey spent significantly more than households similar to them in income and in other respects. Using different methods and data, Watts (1958) estimated the *mpc* from temporary income to be significantly positive, although perhaps only half of the *mpc* from permanent income. Watts's results also indicated that household reaction to temporary income changes may not be symmetrical for positive and negative changes.

(d) An individual whose life proceeds according to plan will gradually build up his wealth, so that at any age his wealth plus his remaining expected earnings during working years just suffice to maintain his consumption throughout his lifetime, including his years of retirement. To every age there corresponds a normal ratio of wealth to income. But unexpected income changes, consumption emergencies, or capital gains and losses on past savings may cause an individual's wealth to deviate from its normal relation to income. A high wealth–income ratio permits the individual to consume more, both now and in retirement, while a low wealth–income ratio requires him to consume a lower fraction of his current income in order to provide for undiminished consumption in retirement. Extended to the whole population, this argument suggests that the aggregate saving ratio depends inversely on the wealth–income ratio. Along with the effects of growth rates mentioned in *b*, this is the major aggregate implication of the lifetime income hypothesis.

Wealth and the propensity to consume. The importance of wealth in the consumption function had been urged by several earlier writers. They based their view on more general considerations than those involved in the Modigliani–Brumberg model. In particular, saving may be motivated by the desire to make bequests or other transfers of wealth to the next generation, as well as by the need to even out consumption over the savers' lifetimes. The adequacy of wealth to meet a bequest target—which may itself be a function of lifetime income, of course—will then be one of the determinants of current saving and consumption.

Pigou (1947) emphasized the wealth effect in the course of an abstract theoretical attack on the whole structure of Keynes's *General Theory*. Keynes had contended that in certain circumstances no amount of wage and price deflation could restore aggregate real demand to full employment levels. Pigou pointed out that the real value of private wealth can be indefinitely increased by price deflation. The reason is that deflation would increase the purchasing power of gold, government-issued currency, and interest-bearing government debt, all of which are fixed in money value. As the owners of these assets become saturated with real wealth, their propensity to consume is bound to increase. Via what has come to be known as the "Pigou effect," the absolute price level, because of its effect on the real value of private wealth, has a bearing on the propensity to consume.

Quite apart from the theoretical context of Pigou's argument, a general wealth effect is an alternative explanation of some of the same phenomena explained by the other hypotheses under review. Over the long run disposable income and private wealth tend to grow in step, with wealth five to six times income. Recent empirical calculations (Modigliani & Ando 1963) suggest a marginal propensity to consume from income of .5 to .7 and from wealth of .05 to .07. When income and wealth grow in step, estimates in these ranges explain how consumption can consistently take about 90 per cent of increases in disposable income. But the apparent *mpc* from income can be quite different when cyclical fluctuations break the normal long-run linkage of wealth and income. Assuming that the real value of wealth fluctuates less than real income, consumption will appear less sensitive to income in the short run than in the long run.

At the level of individual households in budget surveys, the dissaving recorded for the lower brackets is of course supported by past savings. As pointed out by Tobin (1951), differences in the wealth available to households at a given real income can help to explain the differences observed in different surveys in their propensities to save or to dissave. This explanation is not inconsistent with those by which Duesenberry, Friedman, and Modigliani explain the same phenomenon.

Sometimes the wealth effect on saving and consumption has been attributed to a particular kind of wealth, liquid asset holdings, rather than to total net worth. In principle net worth is the relevant variable. This is the constraint that the past and the market impose on consumers, a constraint that they can change only slowly and to which they must meanwhile adjust. In contrast, many households can, within wide limits, decide for themselves at each moment of time how much of their wealth they wish to hold in liquid form; and they can implement such decisions very quickly by purchases or sales of other assets and debts. But for many households below the top brackets, liquid assets (bank deposits, savings accounts, savings bonds) are virtually the only assets held; their total serves as a good proxy for total wealth. In other cases, the remaining constituents of net worth are not easily convertible into current purchasing power—home real estate, consumers' durable goods, pension rights. Consumption functions fitted to survey data indicate a positive effect of liquid asset holdings on consumption, especially for households suffering income reverses (see Michigan, University of . . . 1954).

Income and wealth distribution. Aggregate consumption can be affected not only by changes in aggregate income and wealth but also by changes in the distribution of a given aggregate income or wealth. However, these distributional effects are commonly exaggerated by observers who are struck by the wide discrepancies in average propensities to consume among different economic and social groups. Redistribution will affect total consumption only to the extent that the *marginal* propensities of the affected groups differ. And these appear to differ much less than average propensities. Nevertheless, the prevailing evidence is that certain redistributions of income and wealth would increase saving; for example, from low or middle to top income brackets, from employees to self-employed, from urban residents to farm operators.

It is necessary to beware of another frequently heard argument, namely that reduction in taxes levied on individuals with high saving propensities, in particular those in the upper brackets of income and wealth, will by itself increase saving. This increase in disposable income will doubtless increase *personal* saving and probably by more than would equal tax reductions benefiting others. But it will increase consumption too. By raising disposable income relative to net national product, it raises the propensity to consume with respect to national product and leaves less room in the economy for nonconsumption expenditures.

The hypothesis that "capitalists" save while "workers" spend has a long history, and it has recently been revived in connection with certain analyses of economic growth and development. Kaldor (1955–1956) has gone so far as to build a theory of the functional distribution of income on the differences between capitalists and workers in their marginal propensities to save. Houthakker, who has conducted some pioneering studies of intercountry differences in saving propensities, finds (1957) that the saving ratio appears to be higher in countries where the property share of income is higher. This statistical result can, however, be alternatively rationalized.

This hypothesis may be more relevant to underdeveloped economies with a well-defined division of the population between high-income property owners and low-income workers than to advanced economies like the United States, where ownership of property is widely diffused and some *rentiers* are poor while some "workers" are rich. But if "capitalists" are identified with corporations and their saving with retained corporate earnings, the proposition has some applicability to the United States.

The importance of the distribution of income has also been stressed in the analysis of "forced saving" during inflation. If wages lag behind prices and the marginal propensity to consume from profits is less than from wages, the process of inflation suppresses some demand for consumption goods, which would occur if prices were stable. The same effect can occur without a change in income distribution if consumers are slow to adjust their money expenditures to rising prices and money incomes.

The rate of interest. Prior to Keynes the economic variable that economists usually stressed in analyzing the choice between consumption and saving was the interest rate. The classic exposition of the theoretical relation of saving decisions to the rate of interest is Fisher's (1930). Conard (1959) provides a good review of doctrine on this subject. An increase in the rate of return on saving was expected to tip the balance of choice in favor of the future. But it was recognized that for many positive savers, an increase in interest rates means an over-all increase in consumable resources, from which current as well as future consumption might benefit.

Whether because of this real ambiguity or because of the narrow range of variation of observed interest rates, econometricians have not been able to detect significant interest rate effects on saving. Perhaps these effects would be more evident if it were possible to relate net saving not merely to rates paid on savings accounts and bonds, but to the effective rates at which consumers can borrow and the rates of return on business capital, corporate equities, houses, other real estate, and consumer durables. These assets, after all, absorb the bulk of national saving; but their returns are difficult to measure. The positive correlation internationally between saving and the property share of income cited above could be interpreted to mean that saving is higher in those countries where its yield is greater.

Other variables. Observed differences among households in consumption and saving behavior are, of course, attributable to a long list of differences in their circumstances, habits, and preferences. Some of these are, like income and wealth, variables whose influence is the major interest of economists. Others are, like demographic characteristics, variables that can differ widely among households even though their distribution over the population changes only very slowly. It is nonetheless important to measure their effects, if only to disentangle them from the measurement of the influence of variables more important in economic fluctuations and economic policy. Considerable statistical effort has been devoted to the "life cycle" variables—age, marital status, family size and composition—and other demographic characteristics, such as educational attainment, occupation, race, and geographical location (see, for example, Michigan, University of . . . 1954; Lydall 1955).

A set of variables of a different nature are the "psychological" ones—attitudes, intentions, expectations, personality attributes—which Katona and his associates seek to measure. Unlike demographic variables, the distribution of some of these psychological variables in the population may change radically in the short run, in ways that can be ascertained in our present state of knowledge only by new surveys. If household surveys are to contribute further to our understanding of the propensity to consume and make possible more powerful tests of competing theories, they will have to take a longer perspective. To measure the effects of past and expected levels of income and wealth and of retirement and bequest objectives, it is necessary to observe not only the current status of households but their lifetime histories, plans, and aspirations.

JAMES TOBIN

[*See also* INCOME AND EMPLOYMENT THEORY.]

BIBLIOGRAPHY

ACKLEY, GARDNER 1951 The Wealth–Saving Relationship. *Journal of Political Economy* 59:154–161.

ARENA, JOHN J. 1963 The Wealth Effect and Consumption: A Statistical Inquiry. *Yale Economic Essays* 3:251–303.

BODKIN, RONALD 1959 Windfall Income and Consumption. *American Economic Review* 49:602–614.

BRADY, DOROTHY S.; and FRIEDMAN, ROSE D. 1947 Savings and the Income Distribution. Volume 10, pages 247–265 in Conference on Research in Income and Wealth, *Studies in Income and Wealth.* New York: National Bureau of Economic Research.

BURNS, ARTHUR F. 1954 *The Frontiers of Economic Knowledge: Essays.* Princeton Univ. Press.

CONARD, JOSEPH W. 1959 *An Introduction to the Theory of Interest.* Berkeley: Univ. of California Press.

CORNFIELD, JEROME; EVANS, W. DUANE; and HOFFENBERG, MARVIN 1947 Full Employment Patterns, 1950. *Monthly Labor Review* 64:163–190, 420–432.

DUESENBERRY, JAMES S. 1948 Income–Consumption Relations and Their Implications. Pages 54–81 in *Income, Employment and Public Policy: Essays in Honor of Alvin H. Hansen.* New York: Norton.

DUESENBERRY, JAMES S. 1949 *Income, Saving and the Theory of Consumer Behavior.* Harvard Economic Studies, Vol. 87. Cambridge, Mass.: Harvard Univ. Press.

FARRELL, MICHAEL J. 1959 The New Theories of the Consumption Function. *Economic Journal* 69:678–696.

FISHER, IRVING (1930) 1961 *The Theory of Interest.* New York: Kelley. → Revision of the author's *The Rate of Interest,* 1907.

FRIEDMAN, MILTON 1957 *A Theory of the Consumption Function.* National Bureau of Economic Research, General Series, No. 63. Princeton Univ. Press.

FRIEDMAN, MILTON; and MEISELMAN, DAVID 1963 The Relative Stability of Monetary Velocity and the Investment Multiplier in the United States, 1897–1958. Pages 165–268 in *Stabilization Policies,* by E. Cary Brown et al. Englewood Cliffs, N.J.: Prentice-Hall.

HOUTHAKKER, HENDRIK S. 1957 An International Comparison of Household Expenditure Patterns, Commemorating the Centenary of Engel's Law. *Econometrica* 25:532–551.

KAHN, RICHARD F. 1931 The Relation of Home Investment to Unemployment. *Economic Journal* 41:173–198.

KALDOR, NICHOLAS 1955–1956 Alternative Theories of Distribution. *Review of Economic Studies* 23:83–100.

KATONA, GEORGE 1960 *The Powerful Consumer: Psychological Studies of the American Economy.* New York: McGraw-Hill.

KATONA, GEORGE; and MUELLER, EVA 1953 *Consumer Attitudes and Demand, 1950–1952.* A Survey Research Center Publication. Ann Arbor: Univ. of Michigan.

KATONA, GEORGE; and MUELLER, EVA 1956 *Consumer Expectations 1953–1956.* Survey Research Center Publication No. 16. Ann Arbor: Univ. of Michigan Press.

KEYNES, JOHN MAYNARD 1936 *The General Theory of Employment, Interest and Money.* London: Macmillan. → A paperback edition was published in 1965 by Harcourt.

KEYNES, JOHN MAYNARD 1940 *How to Pay for the War: A Radical Plan for the Chancellor of the Exchequer.* New York: Harcourt; London: Macmillan.

KOOPMANS, TJALLING 1942 The Dynamics of Inflation. *Review of Economics and Statistics* 24:53–65.

KUZNETS, SIMON 1946 *National Product Since 1869.* New York: National Bureau of Economic Research.

KUZNETS, SIMON 1953 *Shares of Upper Income Groups in Income and Savings.* Publication No. 55. New York: National Bureau of Economic Research.

LINTNER, JOHN 1953 The Determinants of Corporate Savings. Pages 230–258 in Walter W. Heller, Francis M. Boddy, and Carl L. Nelson (editors), *Savings in the Modern Economy.* Minneapolis: Univ. of Minnesota Press. → Includes four pages of comments.

LIVINGSTON, S. MORRIS 1945 Forecasting Postwar Demand. *Econometrica* 13:15–24.

LUBELL, HAROLD 1947 Effects of Redistribution of Income on Consumers' Expenditures. *American Economic Review* 37:157–170, 930.

LYDALL, HAROLD 1955 The Life Cycle in Income, Saving, and Asset Ownership. *Econometrica* 23:131–150.

MACK, RUTH P. 1948 The Direction of Change in Income and the Consumption Function. *Review of Economics and Statistics* 30:239–258.

MICHIGAN, UNIVERSITY OF, SURVEY RESEARCH CENTER 1954 *Contributions of Survey Methods to Economics.* Edited by Lawrence R. Klein. New York: Columbia Univ. Press.

MODIGLIANI, FRANCO 1949 Fluctuations in the Saving–Income Ratio: A Problem in Economic Forecasting. Volume 11, pages 371–443 in Conference on Research in Income and Wealth, *Studies in Income and Wealth.* New York: National Bureau of Economic Research.

MODIGLIANI, FRANCO; and ANDO, ALBERT 1963 The Life Cycle Hypothesis of Saving: Aggregate Implications and Tests. *American Economic Review* 53:55–84.

MODIGLIANI, FRANCO; and BRUMBERG, RICHARD 1954 Utility Analysis and the Consumption Function: An Interpretation of Cross Section Data. Pages 388–436 in Kenneth K. Kurihara (editor), *Post Keynesian Economics.* New Brunswick, N.J.: Rutgers Univ. Press.

PIGOU, A. C. 1947 Economic Progress in a Stable Environment. *Economica* New Series 14:180–188.

ROSETT, RICHARD N. 1958 Working Wives: An Economic Study. Pages 51–99 in Thomas F. Dernburg et al., *Studies in Household Economic Behavior.* Yale Studies in Economics, Vol. 9. New Haven: Yale Univ. Press.

RUGGLES, RICHARD; and RUGGLES, NANCY (1949)1956 *National Income Accounts and Income Analysis.* 2d ed. New York: McGraw-Hill. → First published as *Introduction to National Income and Income Analysis.*

SAMUELSON, PAUL A. 1943 Full Employment After the War. Pages 27–53 in Seymour E. Harris (editor), *Postwar Economic Problems.* New York and London: McGraw-Hill.

SMITHIES, ARTHUR 1943 The Behavior of Money National Income Under Inflationary Conditions. *Quarterly Journal of Economics* 57:113–128.

SMITHIES, ARTHUR 1945 Forecasting Postwar Demand. *Econometrica* 13:1–14.

TOBIN, JAMES 1951 Relative Income, Absolute Income, and Saving. Pages 135–156 in *Money, Trade, and Economic Growth: Essays in Honor of John Williams.* New York: Macmillan.

WATTS, HAROLD W. 1958 Long-run Income Expectations and Consumer Saving. Pages 101–144 in Thomas F. Dernburg et al., *Studies in Household Economic Behavior.* Yale Studies in Economics, Vol. 9. New Haven: Yale Univ. Press.

CONTAINMENT

Containment has been the primary strategy of the United States in its conduct of foreign policy in the postwar era.

The term defines the objective: to "contain" communism within the spheres of influence which it controlled effectively in 1947. It was then that American leaders first fully perceived the extent to which communist expansionism threatened the security and freedom of the noncommunist world.

In the opinion of some observers, the concept of containment has guided the foreign policies of the Soviet Union and the Western powers, although the ground rules have differed for each side. For the West, containment of communism signified a *status quo* policy which did not envisage any attempt to regain any territory absorbed by the Sino–Soviet bloc. The communist powers, however, while insisting on the inviolability of their domain behind the iron and bamboo curtains, considered the lands within the West's defense perimeter fair game for aggression—if not by direct military means, then by indirect methods hardly less effective (Strausz-Hupé et al. 1959; Stillman & Pfaff 1961).

Evolution. The United States policy of containment evolved during that unhappy period, from about 1945 to 1947, when the United States was forced by ineluctable realities to reassess Soviet intentions. Repeated shocks were necessary in order to impress the hard fact of Soviet hostility upon the American consciousness, so long conditioned during the war years to regard the U.S.S.R. as a gallant ally. As the implications of Soviet dominion over eastern Europe began to dawn on Western leaders, their resistance to further Soviet encroachment began to stiffen. When Soviet troops failed to evacuate Iran by the established deadline in March 1946, American and British pressure was brought to bear, forcing their withdrawal. That same month, Winston Churchill helped to arouse Americans to the growing communist threat with his famous "iron curtain" speech at Fulton, Missouri.

The communist-inspired civil war which erupted in Greece that fall hastened the formation in the United States of a wide consensus on policies designed to halt communist aggression. In March 1947, Britain asked the United States government to take over the support she had been providing to Greece and Turkey. President Truman and his advisors responded with a proposal to Congress to provide substantial aid to these two countries. The policy outlined by the president, which became known as the Truman Doctrine, promised American aid to any country whose freedom and independence were threatened by external aggression. The Truman Doctrine proved to be the inspiration for the American concept of containment. From it issued the Marshall Plan, NATO, Point Four, and other programs and alliances designed to build up the economic, political, and military strength of the "free world."

The containment policy, with its rationale and its objectives, was articulated most clearly by George F. Kennan (1947), a career diplomat, who organized and served as the first head of the Policy Planning Staff of the Department of State, created in 1947. He specified that "the main element of any U.S. policy toward the Soviet Union must be that of a long-term, patient but firm and vigilant containment of Russian expansive tendencies" (1951, p. 119). The communist threat, Kennan maintained, "can be contained by the adroit and vigilant application of counter-force at a series of constantly shifting geographical and political points, corresponding to the shifts and maneuvers of Soviet policy . . ." (1951, p. 120).

Kennan developed his thesis, in somewhat general terms, from an analysis of Soviet ideology and society. It was his contention that if the West could successfully block the communists' "unceasing constant pressure" toward world dominion for a period of time—perhaps 10 to 15 years—the resulting frustration would so heighten the internal strains of Soviet society that the Kremlin regime would collapse or, at the least, seek a realistic accommodation with the West.

The policy of containment has been executed by a variety of means. One of the chief architects of the policy, Dean G. Acheson, who served as undersecretary of state during the crucial spring of 1947 and later succeeded George C. Marshall as secretary of state, saw the problem as primarily one of converting situations of weakness in the free world into "situations of strength." This meant, first of all, the building of military strength but, in addition, "the buttressing of all the other forms of power—

economic, political, social, and moral—and the utmost resolution and unity among the free nations of the world" (Acheson 1950, p. 965). Embracing a policy of containment, the United States clearly repudiated such alternative policies as isolationism, appeasement, and preventive war.

The principal tools which the United States has employed to carry out its policy have been economic assistance and a system of military alliances. Perhaps the most important objective of the United States' alliance diplomacy has been to secure overseas bases along the perimeter of Sino–Soviet bloc territory in return for military assistance and mutual security pacts.

Critique. The critics of the containment policy have found it wanting on several accounts. Perhaps the least serious of the charges leveled against it has been the argument that American resources are not equal to the task of policing the entire frontier of the communist empire. Defenders of containment counter with the assertion that in time our European allies, whom we assisted in regaining economic strength, will help shoulder a larger portion of the burden.

More telling has been the contention that the supporters of containment as the most rational and only possible policy of the United States toward the Soviet Union have failed to take into account the transformation in Soviet society which has occurred since Kennan published his celebrated analysis in 1947. Soviet economy and technology have outpaced rates of growth predicted 15 years ago. Furthermore, the Soviet Union has thus far overcome the difficulty of the transfer of supreme power, a hurdle which many Western Kremlinologists thought Soviet leadership could not surmount.

A corollary to the criticism that containment has been too inflexible is the charge that the policy has been, from the beginning, wholly unsuitable for application in Asia. Those who hold this view are willing to concede that the strategy of containment has been reasonably successful in Europe, where the crisis was of long standing, where the remedies were fairly obvious, and where a shared cultural heritage facilitated political and military cooperation. As these critics see it, the mistake was in attempting to extend the European formula to other areas of the world where similar conditions did not exist.

The sharpest critics of containment have been those who felt that the policy was too passive, too static, too apt to concede victory to the enemy by default. This school of thought contends that the free world, simply by maintaining the *status quo*,

leaves the communist camp free to consolidate its gains. Thus, the hope for a break-up or a mellowing of the Soviet regime in some far-distant future is considered both erroneous and dangerous. According to this view, by accepting the communist ground rules, which forbid waging the cold war on any territory already under Sino–Soviet control, the West commits a folly that is all the more unpardonable because it is, besides being dangerous, exceedingly costly.

Despite such adverse criticisms, nearly all Americans conversant with international affairs are willing to concede that containment has achieved some success in imposing on the Soviet Union, in Kennan's words, "a far greater degree of moderation and circumspection." In fact, even the severest critics of the policy of containment agree that it provides the basis upon which must rest any future foreign policy adopted by the United States. To be sure, the United States must "contain" before it can assume the initiative. Generally, those who believe that containment can be no more than a stopgap argue that it should be superseded by a more positive policy. Such a policy should place greater emphasis on political realities, especially the need for the political reformation of the western alliance; persist in the maintenance of military defense; and, in addition, concentrate greater efforts on the nonmilitary aspects of the conflict; i.e., means must be found to carry the contest beyond the bounds of the free world and to exploit the divergencies and vulnerabilities of the communist camp itself.

History has yet to render a final verdict on the success or failure of containment. Given the existing political and intellectual climate of the United States in 1946–1947, it seems reasonable to assert that containment was probably the one and only effective foreign policy that did not exceed the physical and psychological capabilities of the United States at that time. How the American people can put to best use the experience derived from containment in order to develop a foreign policy adequate for the world of today—this is a matter which still demands their and their leaders' most thoughtful attention.

ROBERT STRAUSZ-HUPÉ AND
DAVID EDWIN LEBBY

[*See also* DISENGAGEMENT; FOREIGN POLICY; STRATEGY; *and the guide under* INTERNATIONAL RELATIONS.]

BIBLIOGRAPHY

ACHESON, DEAN G. 1950 The Strategy of Freedom. U.S. Department of State, *Bulletin* 23:962–967. → An address to the National Council of Churches of Christ in the United States. Also available as U.S. Department of State Publication No. 4034.

ARON, RAYMOND 1962 Reflections on American Diplomacy. *Dædalus* 91:717–732.

ARON, RAYMOND 1965 Has Russia Lost Her Grip on Europe? (Russian and United States Influences Compared.) *Réalités* (English edition) [1965] October: 17–19.

DONNELLY, DESMOND 1965 *Struggle for the World: The Cold War, 1917–1965.* New York: St. Martins.

GRAEBNER, NORMAN A. 1962 *Cold War Diplomacy: American Foreign Policy, 1945–1960.* Princeton, N.J.: Van Nostrand.

KENNAN, GEORGE F. 1947 The Sources of Soviet Conduct. *Foreign Affairs* 25:566–582. → Published under the pseudonym X.

KENNAN, GEORGE F. 1951 *American Diplomacy, 1900–1950.* Univ. of Chicago Press.

SPANIER, JOHN W. (1960) 1965 *American Foreign Policy Since World War II.* 2d rev. ed. New York: Praeger.

STILLMAN, EDMUND O.; and PFAFF, WILLIAM 1961 *The New Politics: America and the End of the Postwar World.* New York: Coward.

STRAUSZ-HUPÉ, ROBERT et al. 1959 *Protracted Conflict.* New York: Harper. → A paperback edition was published in 1963.

CONTENT ANALYSIS

Content analysis is used in the social sciences as one means of studying communication—its nature, its underlying meanings, its dynamic processes, and the people who are engaged in talking, writing, or conveying meaning to one another. Although not a research method *sui generis*, content analysis is roughly distinguishable from other methods by two characteristics. First, its data—in contrast to ethnographic reports, for example, or census enumerations—are the verbal or other symbols which make up the content of communications (letters, books, sermons, conversations, television programs, therapeutic sessions, paintings, and the like). Second, its procedures differ in emphasis from those of the historian or literary critic: they aim to be exact and repeatable, to minimize any vagueness or bias resulting from the judgments of a single investigator. Thus, each content analysis employs an explicit, organized plan for assembling the data, classifying or quantifying them to measure the concepts under study, examining their patterns and interrelationships, and interpreting the findings.

Within these broad limits the techniques of content analysis are diverse, and the objectives range from mapping propaganda campaigns, for example, to explaining international conflict and integration; from abstracting the ideas and beliefs expressed in folklore or movies of a given period to

tracing the epochal alternations in societal values over many centuries; from charting the interaction between patient and therapist to assessing the psychological states of great men in the past.

No general theory of communication is yet in common use among the several social sciences to guide these varied analyses. Implicit in each investigation is a special conceptual model, or set of ideas and assumptions, about the nature of the particular communication process under study. To test this conceptual model or to add new ideas to it, the researcher uses the concrete data of communication. In the empirical phase of the research he is led by his model to select particular communications and to search for order among them by adapting certain conventional procedures of sampling, measurement, and analysis. In the interpretative phase, in comparing his findings with his initial conceptions, so as to understand their broader significance, he encounters certain special problems and possibilities.

Historical background

The use of content analysis in the social sciences today—its methods and its problems of interpretation—has been affected both by related developments in other fields and by historical demands for certain practical applications. Early in the twentieth century students of journalism began to count the newspaper linage devoted to foreign affairs or to sports, comparing one newspaper with another, for example, and later comparing newspaper content with the content of other media. In literary criticism such devices as type of rhyme or ratio of adjectives to verbs were tabulated, as a means of differentiating the styles of writers or of literary periods or to settle disputes about authorship or the chronology of an author's work. Meanwhile, educators were constructing formulas for the readability of printed materials, utilizing proportions of easy and hard words, length of sentences, and the like.

During the 1930s certain applications of such techniques began to be made in the social sciences. Sorokin's monumental study of social and cultural changes in western Europe over the entire course of history rests in part upon an analysis of works of art, music, literature, and philosophy according to their central meanings (1937–1941). Lasswell developed a scheme for categorizing the content of patients' responses in psychiatric interviews as *pro-self, anti-self, pro-other,* or *anti-other,* and for counting the frequency with which such categories occurred (1938). Lasswell also, with a number of associates, pioneered the application of content analysis to the study of public opinion and propaganda, an effort immensely stimulated by the demands of the United States government during World War II. Mass communication was conceptualized, within a political framework, as "who says what to whom, how, with what effect," and large-scale analyses were made, for example, of the frequency with which key symbols (democracy, communism, England, Hitler) were given indulgent, deprecatory, or neutral presentation (e.g., Lasswell & Leites 1949). These wartime efforts encouraged content analyses in other areas—focused on the intentions of particular communicators, the kinds of material brought to the attention of particular audiences, or the cultural values underlying the communicator's assessment of what the audience wants.

When Berelson (1952) made his critical survey of the applications of content analysis methods, he found several books and articles reporting the use of various techniques, e.g., techniques of sampling the content of newspapers by successively selecting specific newspapers, issues, and relevant content within each issue; techniques of categorizing and counting key words, themes, or whole documents; techniques of increasing the reliability of classifying and counting. To guide the application of such techniques, however, Berelson found only one conceptual model in widespread use: the Lasswellian model of the purposive one-way communication intended to influence a mass audience on controversial public issues (Berelson 1952, p. 57 and *passim*). Thus, broader scientific utilization of the available techniques waited upon a growing interdisciplinary understanding of the many-faceted communication process and upon the closer fitting of techniques to theory.

Examples of uses of content analysis

Important developments in the application of content analysis to social science models may be illustrated by a few examples from the profuse literature of the 1950s and 1960s (see also Work Conference on Content Analysis 1959).

Interaction process. Bales and his associates have developed one of several procedures for analyzing the content of communication observed in small groups (e.g., Bales 1952). Observers sitting behind a one-way screen categorize each of the remarks and gestures (acts) directed by each group member to other members as the group attempts to solve an assigned problem. Bales's standard set of 12 categories (shows solidarity, shows tension release, agrees, gives suggestions, etc.) indexes cer-

tain sociological properties of the interaction of a group: positive or negative direction, instrumental or expressive character, and the focus on such system problems as control, tension management, or integration. Thus categorized, data from many groups are used (with the aid of statistical devices and mathematical models) to describe the group process—the patterning of content, phasing over time, group structure. From these descriptions inferences are drawn about the underlying nature of this process. For example, the findings may show that typically a group leader emerges who both initiates and receives more communications than any other member; or that the process of problem solving goes through phases emphasizing, first, orientation; then, evaluation; and, finally, control [*see* INTERACTION, *article on* INTERACTION PROCESS ANALYSIS].

Studies of therapy. Such analyses of the content of interaction, made at the time of observation or, later, through recordings or transcripts, are also applied to the therapeutic process in social work, counseling, and psychiatry (e.g., the review by Auld & Murray 1955). Category systems based on psychological theories of behavior combined with principles of client-centered therapy are used to trace the interview process, the client–therapist relationship, changes in predominant content over time, or differences between types of treatments. Standard measures employed in content analysis of psychotherapy include Bales's categories (1952) and the Discomfort–Relief Quotient (D.R.Q.), developed by John Dollard and O. H. Mowrer (see, e.g., Auld & Murray 1955, pp. 379–380) to show the ratio between the client's discomfort responses (reflecting tension, unhappiness, pain) and his relief responses (reflecting satisfaction, comfort, enjoyment). In Japan (Shiso . . . 1959) content analysis has been applied to the exchanges of letters published in life-counseling columns of newspapers and magazines. [*See* MENTAL DISORDERS, TREATMENT OF, *article on* CLIENT-CENTERED COUNSELING.]

Psychological state of the communicator. Analysis of an individual's communications as an index of his underlying motives is exemplified in a study of suicide letters by Osgood and Walker (1959). Within the framework of stimulus–response theory these researchers formulated a number of predictions about the structure and content of suicide letters in contrast to ordinary letters and to simulated suicide notes: the letters of *bona fide* suicides are characterized, for example, by greater stereotypy; more evidences of conflict; more constructions of the demand, command, and request type that express needs of the speaker and require some reaction from another person to satisfy these needs.

To test these predictions, the researchers use 16 different measures—some already standard and some specially designed—for the analysis and comparison of the letters. As measures of the stereotypy of each letter, for instance, they divide the number of different words by the total words, count repetitions of phrases, or take the ratio of nouns and verbs to the number of adjectives and adverbs. To measure conflict, they determine the degree to which assertions are qualified, the number of syntactical constructions expressing ambivalence (such as "but," "if," "however"), or the extent to which both positive and negative assertions are combined in the same letter. They also employ Osgood's evaluative assertion analysis, a standard procedure that isolates from their context all terms by which the communicator evaluates an object, rates these terms as favorable or unfavorable, and then combines these ratings to index the communicator's over-all attitude toward the object (see, e.g., Work Conference on Content Analysis 1959, pp. 41–54). Comparisons of such measures for suicide letters and ordinary letters support the researchers' hypotheses in most instances, although the results for suicide versus simulated suicide notes are less clear.

Historical personalities. In similar fashion, content analysis seems potentially useful to the historian or biographer who is seeking to understand the personalities of great men through their writings and speeches. For solving questions about authorship of documents, rigorous procedures have been developed (as in the study of the disputed *Federalist* papers: Mosteller & Wallace 1964). For examining motives, attitudes, and psychological states of historical persons, however, content analysis of their communications has been less widely used, despite suggestive studies of Goebbel's diary or the autobiography of Richard Wright (see Garraty in Work Conference on Content Analysis 1959, pp. 171–187).

Culture and society. In their study of popular religion, Schneider and Dornbusch (1958) illustrate the use of content analysis to reflect, not the psychological states of single persons, but the values of an entire society. These researchers selected 46 representative works of American inspirational literature, published over an 80-year period, choosing best sellers to assure that the books were read. They classified each, paragraph by paragraph, according to its main themes ("religion brings physical health," "happiness can be expected by

most men") and then ascertained what proportion of the total paragraphs is devoted to each theme. In their report they described the changes in these themes within the wider context of historical trends in American religion and culture and used a sociological model to interpret the functions of popular religion in society.

A considerable tradition of such analyses rests on the assumption that cultural values which have been institutionalized in certain segments of the society are represented in the communications of individuals from these segments. Some analyses stress the social determinants of the ideas or values expressed in folklore and sermons, for example; some emphasize the cultural determinants of such expressions. Thus, public communications of American business leaders are taken to reflect their business creed; Brazil's riddles and myths, to reflect the didactic aspects of its religion; Japan's popular songs, to reflect the loneliness and helplessness of its postwar era (Shiso . . . 1959, p. 122).

Empirical methods

Content analyses are conducted by selecting and adapting certain empirical procedures used in social science generally: typically, the methods of using available data (although new materials for special objectives may occasionally be acquired by questioning or observing) and the methods of measurement combined with sampling and statistical analysis.

Use of available data. Most commonly, the content analyst chooses from the vast store of communications already available in libraries, clinics, archives, records, and family attics. Thus, he must know how to utilize the benefits of available data, while avoiding their pitfalls.

Advantages. Several advantages accrue to the student of communication who decides to use materials that already exist rather than to elicit new ones. (1) Time, labor, and expense can often be saved when the researcher can go directly to the heart of his analysis, bypassing preliminary field work, experimentation, or commissioning of documents. (2) When massive data are required, beyond the scope of a single new study, existing content materials frequently afford wide ranges of potentially relevant variables and of refinement in the measurement of each variable. (3) Most important, the available data afford the only means of studying certain kinds of communication problems. Past events cannot be observed directly by the researcher, nor can events beyond the recollection of respondents living today be reached through questioning. Thus, the analysis of historical situations or of long-term trends—the important study of social change—depends upon the prior existence of relevant materials. Similarly, study of cross-cultural communications from remote places (e.g., of world-wide tastes in movies or folklore or of similarities and differences in attention to major political symbols in different countries) may require materials that cannot be elicited by the researcher directly. Communication contents in technical fields that are beyond the competence of the researcher may have been originally assembled in usable form by an expert such as a psychiatrist, a social worker, or an ethnographer. Sometimes, as in letters or diaries, existing materials may provide deep insights into intimate feelings or personal relationships; and sometimes, as in Sorokin's analysis, they may widen the investigator's focus to include macroscopic social or cultural systems.

Pitfalls. Against such impressive assets must be set certain basic problems to be overcome in the utilization of data not originally assembled for the present purposes. (1) The materials are often incomplete. The content analyst must attempt to discover any absences of letters from a file of correspondence or of speeches from a set, which may mean that the data lack representativeness. (2) The data may lack reliability or validity. An isolated record of a historical event, for example, cannot be checked through comparison of different accounts or through direct observation or questioning by the researcher. Clues to validity can often be obtained, however, by comparing two sets of data believed to reflect the same concept, as does Sorokin (1937–1941) when he shows the parallelism between trends in scientific discoveries and the trends in empirical thought derived from content analysis. (3) Data from differing sociotemporal contexts may not be directly comparable, as sources of information may themselves change over time or from one country to another, or the same categories may take on different meanings. This difficulty requires careful documentation and the search for linguistic equivalences. (4) Finally, the data that come to the researcher in a form he does not fully understand may not fit his definitions of the concepts under scrutiny. Unlike the researcher who handles data he himself has collected, he is often unfamiliar with the circumstances under which the communications originally took place. Yet the content of a diary may depend upon whether it was written for public or private consumption, and the answer to an open question may be affected by interviewer bias. Here the important caveat is to attempt to reconstruct the process by which the data were produced, spelling out and, insofar as possible, offsetting any limitations and biases and recasting the data in a form suitable for the new problem.

Although the researcher may on occasion have to reject given data because he cannot adequately assess their limitations or find suitable means of compensating for them, the great variety of available data which may in some sense be classified as communications constitutes a highly valuable resource for the further application of content analysis.

Use of measurement. The content analyst makes use of his data to measure his concepts, rather than to describe them in discursive language. His data consist of certain concrete communications of certain concrete individuals (the *cases*). His conceptual model contains corresponding definitions of particular types of orientations, actions, or characteristics (the *properties*) of particular types of persons or collectivities. What he does, in effect, is to treat the sense data (the written or spoken words, the gestures or pictures which he observes as manifestations or *indicants* of these properties (the ideas which he holds in his mind). Measurement is defined here, then, as the classification of cases (persons, groups) in terms of a given property, according to some rules for selecting and combining appropriate communications data as indicants.

Composite measures. The measurement rules followed in content analysis vary in detail with the study; but in general they are characterized by a two-stage procedure that results in a composite, rather than a simple, measure. The researcher does not simply classify (code) each case as a whole. Rather, he breaks down the total communication into a set of constituent units (e.g., words, assertions, articles, books); he first codes each of these content units separately, and then he recombines the coded units to provide the composite measure. Bales, for example, in classifying his cases (groups) according to various dimensions of interaction, might well have observed an entire small-group session and then assigned over-all ratings (simple measures) to indicate the extent to which, for example, solidarity was expressed or tension-management activities had occurred. Instead, he broke down the property (interaction) into small content units (acts), categorized the behavior act by act, and then counted the number of acts in each category. This composite measure gives a group profile —a distribution of the total number of acts among code categories—by which groups are classified according to the extent to which members show agreement, engage in tension-management activities, and so on.

Coding. At the first stage the coding process involves a measuring instrument for assigning to each content unit certain code designations that indicate how much of (or which attributes of) the property it possesses. This instrument consists of (1) a *code*, or set of code designations. Made up of numerals, symbols, or names of categories, the code lists all the categories marked off on each dimension of each property. (Properties are conceived of as having one or more main dimensions, or aspects; for multidimensional measures, the measures of single dimensions—whether simple or composite—must ultimately be combined to reflect the property as a whole.) The instrument further contains (2) *coding instructions*, which, on the one hand, define each dimension and its categories in terms of the conceptual model and, on the other hand, specify the kinds of data to be taken as indicants under each category. The coding instrument for a particular study is sometimes taken from an existing body of theory (such as Riesman's "inner-direction" versus "other-direction"); it may be a standard code developed by other researchers (such as the D.R.Q. or the verb–adjective ratio); or it may be developed from the empirical data of the study.

Combining. At the second stage—combining the content units to refer to the communication as a whole—the content analyst may simply count the number of units in each category (e.g., to show the number of favorable and unfavorable assertions or to arrive at the mean percentage of paragraphs devoted to dogma in a sample of religious books). Such *frequency counts* of similar units have the effect of weighting the category to show how predominant or pervasive that category is within the communication as a whole. Sometimes the units are given equal weight (e.g., Bales 1952); or different weights may be assigned, e.g., for different degrees of attitude intensity, as assessed by judges, or for differing degrees of impact upon an audience; Sorokin (1937–1941) weighted the influence of great thinkers according to the number of special monographs devoted to each.

Alternatively, the content analyst may adapt various available procedures to uncover the empirical *patterning* among different types of units, to show how specific acts, attitudes, or characteristics may fit together within a single communication process. For instance, factor analysis may be used to isolate broad dimensions (as of mental health attitudes expressed in mass media or of sensationalism in the handling of news), or Guttman scaling may be used to uncover cumulative patterns (as of the various duties and functions assigned in state laws to boards of education). Such procedures have the virtue of containing built-in tests of the correspondence between the researcher's conception of the property and the rules that he follows in making his measurements. These tests obviate the necessity of relying entirely upon the investigator's arbitrary judgment for the combining and weighting of indicants.

Such patterning is further disclosed, of course, when the investigator, having completed his measurement of single properties, proceeds to examine the positive or negative correlations between properties. References to the devil and to writing may be found to go together in certain folk tales; or a psychotherapy patient may tend to dissociate his thoughts of mother from his thoughts of homosexuality (e.g., Osgood's contingency analysis in Work Conference in Content Analysis 1959, pp. 54–78). Some content analysts apply statistical tests to estimate the likelihood that such correlations are due entirely to chance, although there are often problems of appropriateness of the particular tests (as when the several communications of selected individuals may not meet the assumptions of statistical independence).

Utility of composite measurement. The characteristic two-stage measurement procedure of first coding and then combining content units often enhances the precision possible in simple over-all measurement, while intercoder reliability is reportedly high. Coding rules can be defined more specifically and coding decisions made more easily for a small content unit than for an entire communication (see Schneider & Dornbusch 1958, pp. 165–169, for a comparison of global ratings of entire books with paragraph-by-paragraph ratings of the same books). Although the detailed procedure is typically more time consuming and laborious, computer programs will without doubt be increasingly used to expedite a number of these operations (e.g., the General Inquirer system for content analysis, Stone et al. 1962). Mathematically, the composite measure is quantitative, a characteristic which often facilitates its use in relation to other measures. Even though each act or unit of meaning may be coded on a nominal scale (described in words as favorable or unfavorable, showing or not showing solidarity, etc.) at the first stage of the procedure, at the second stage, when all these codes are combined, the resultant measure consists of numbers or proportions (of remarks that are favorable or of group activities that show solidarity). Such numerical data are used to classify the individuals or groups along scales that are at least at the ordinal level.

Nevertheless, the quantitative, precise appearance of many composite measures used in content analysis may be deceptive. Without a clear correspondence between measurement operations and the communication process, serious problems of interpretation arise.

Sampling. Just as content analysis requires measurement, it also requires rigorous procedures for sampling. The procedures generally employed by social scientists refer to the selection of both the concrete cases to be studied (the communicating persons or groups) and the communications to be used as indicants. Some content analyses deal with only a single case (e.g., Wilson as a single historical figure or western Europe as a single society). When many cases are studied, so as to separate common properties from those peculiar to exceptional cases, samples are often chosen by standard probability procedures that aim to represent the conceptual universe through the sample selected. A second important aim is to select a sample of cases that will facilitate the analysis—as Osgood chooses samples for comparative analysis of ordinary persons and suicides.

Similar sampling procedures are applied to the determination of which communications will be examined, since it is by no means always necessary to analyze all the writings of a given man, all the meetings of a given group, or all the propaganda of a given country. Selections are often made by stratifying or classifying the major items, such as books, prayers, pictographs, records of single meetings, paragraphs, and then taking a probability sample from each stratum.

Interpretations

Just as each piece of content analysis uses certain empirical methods to arrive at its findings, it also employs procedures for interpreting the scientific and theoretical significance of the findings by comparing them with the conceptual model. The methods for arriving at such interpretations have been less clearly codified than the empirical methods —many of which have been taken over wholesale from other applications—and there is much discussion and some confusion about the kinds of inferences which are appropriate or valid. Nevertheless, the accumulating body of interpretations derived is now beginning to explain the relationships between communicators, recipients, and the patterned content of the communications themselves. These interpretations shed light on historical changes and dynamic processes of communicative

interaction. They often go behind the meanings of the language to the underlying social structure of the group or the psychological state of the individual. Content analysis may show, for example, that—quite apart from the content of communication—in a task group a leader tends to emerge who initiates and receives about half the communication. Or such nonlexical aspects of speech as stuttering or hesitation may reveal the anxiety of a patient in an interview.

Exploration. The content analyst whose main objective is exploratory makes his interpretations by working primarily from data to model, adding new ideas to his theories *after* he has completed the empirical phase of the research. Here the special character of the composite measurement procedure can be a notable asset. The careful handling of details and the search for patterning among them often serves to clarify the concepts with which the inquiry began, and to uncover latent relationships and processes not immediately apparent to an investigator. Thus, the sociologist can reveal the balance between instrumental communications, through which a group may pursue its goals but which place strains upon its members, and expressive communications, which ease such strains and tend to re-establish the equilibrium (Bales 1952). Or the historian, through composite measures based on subject matter and key words in the clauses of the Grand Remonstrance, enacted by the British Parliament in the seventeenth century, can expose its character as a propaganda vehicle rather than a constitutionally important document (Knight 1960). In such exploration the methods of interpretation, though rarely explicit, require creative effort —a jump from evidence to ideas, a sensitivity to potential linkages between empirical clues and existing theory and knowledge.

Inadequate use of theory. The fruitless character of content analysis without careful reference to adequate theory is, unfortunately, all too often overlooked. Complex techniques of measurement and analysis may be applied blindly, without questioning their theoretical relevance. Content may be arbitrarily broken down into units that distort messages by wrenching them from their setting. One-to-one inferences may be drawn, from content descriptions to states of the communicator or his social system, without recognition or assessment of the isomorphism implied (as discussed in George 1959). Little consideration may be paid to the meaning of a particular frequency count, as this might refer to the intensity of an individual's attitude or to the consensus with which several individuals hold the same attitude or to the calculated impact of repetition upon an audience. Yet such oversights in connecting techniques with theory can yield meaningless—even misleading—results.

Hypothesis testing. Errors of sheer empiricism are less likely when the researcher, instead of exploring, can use content analysis to test hypotheses. This is often feasible when the conceptual model is highly enough developed to suggest an interpretation *in advance* of the content analysis (e.g., Osgood & Walker 1959). In hypothesis testing the researcher cannot avoid an explication of the presumed relationship between theory and operations. Here he uses logical or mathematical reasoning to specify what the expected findings would be if the assumptions of the model were in accord with the facts. Again, of course, any evidence derived from testing the model can only be as good as the model itself; the importance of the evidence is bounded by the imagination and the theoretical grasp with which the research begins.

Supporting analyses. Just as the model of communication includes not only the message unit but also underlying attitudes, behavior patterns, values, and social structures, so content analysis alone cannot provide a full understanding of communication. However ideally executed and interpreted and however widely replicated, the approach must often be supplemented by other approaches, which focus more widely upon the several aspects of the communication process. Thus, precise estimates of the intended meaning of a communication depend on knowledge of the situational and behavioral context (George 1959); the content of therapy cannot be assessed without an outside measure of the recovery of the patient; the interpretation of a suicide letter requires the identification of the writer as actually suicidal or not; the presumed appeals of propaganda or advertising must be checked against the responses of the audience. The very ability of the language to communicate must often be tested —for instance, by Taylor's "cloze" procedure, in which sample recipients are given a message in mutilated form and asked how far they can reconstruct it (see Work Conference on Content Analysis 1959, pp. 78–88).

A full understanding of communication will rest ultimately, of course, upon accumulation of ideas and facts from many related studies. Among these, the findings of content analysis can make a special contribution because of their objectivity. The content analysis of letters by Osgood and Walker, for example, is more open to evaluation and replication by other scholars than the less systematic handling of Polish peasant correspondence by Thomas and Znaniecki; the content analysis by Schneider and Dornbusch is more open than Max Weber's insightful construction of ideal types from the writings of a Benjamin Franklin or a Jonathan Edwards.

MATILDA WHITE RILEY AND CLARICE S. STOLL

[*Other relevant material may be found in* FACTOR ANALYSIS *and* SCALING.]

BIBLIOGRAPHY

AULD, FRANK JR.; and MURRAY, EDWARD J. 1955 Content Analysis Studies of Psychotherapy. *Psychological Bulletin* 52:377–395.

BALES, ROBERT F. (1952) 1963 Some Uniformities of Behavior in Small Social Systems. Pages 98–111 in Matilda White Riley, *Sociological Research.* New York: Harcourt.

BERELSON, BERNARD 1952 *Content Analysis in Communication Research.* Glencoe, Ill.: Free Press.

GEORGE, ALEXANDER L. 1959 *Propaganda Analysis: A Study of Inferences Made From Nazi Propaganda in World War II.* Evanston, Ill.: Row, Peterson.

KNIGHT, OLIVER 1960 The Grand Remonstrance. *Public Opinion Quarterly* 24:77–84.

LASSWELL, HAROLD D. 1938 A Provisional Classification of Symbol Data. *Psychiatry* 1:197–204.

LASSWELL, HAROLD D.; and LEITES, NATHAN 1949 *Language of Politics: Studies in Quantitative Semantics.* New York: Stewart.

MOSTELLER, FREDERICK; and WALLACE, DAVID L. 1964 *Inference and Disputed Authorship:* The Federalist. Reading, Mass.: Addison-Wesley.

OSGOOD, CHARLES E.; and WALKER, EVELYN G. 1959 Motivation and Language Behavior: A Content Analysis of Suicide Notes. *Journal of Abnormal and Social Psychology* 59:58–67.

SCHNEIDER, LOUIS; and DORNBUSCH, SANFORD M. 1958 *Popular Religion: Inspirational Books in America.* Univ. of Chicago Press.

SHISO NO KAGAKU KENKYŪKAI 1959 *Japanese Popular Culture: Studies in Mass Communication and Cultural Change Made at the Institute of Science of Thought, Japan.* Edited and translated by Hidetoshi Kato. Rutland, Vt.: Tuttle.

SOROKIN, PITIRIM A. (1937–1941) 1962 *Social and Cultural Dynamics.* 4 vols. Englewood Cliffs, N.J.: Bedminster Press. → Volume 1: *Fluctuation of Forms of Art.* Volume 2: *Fluctuation of Systems of Truth, Ethics, and Law.* Volume 3: *Fluctuation of Social Relationships, War, and Revolution.* Volume 4: *Basic Problems, Principles, and Methods.* See especially Volume 1 and Volume 2.

STONE, PHILIP J. et al. 1962 The General Inquirer: A Computer System for Content Analysis and Retrieval Based on the Sentence as a Unit of Information. *Behavioral Science* 7:484–498.

WORK CONFERENCE ON CONTENT ANALYSIS, MONTICELLO, ILL., *1955* 1959 *Trends in Content Analysis: Papers.* Edited by Ithiel de Sola Pool. Urbana: Univ. of Illinois Press.

CONTINGENCY TABLES

See COUNTED DATA; STATISTICS, DESCRIPTIVE, *article on* ASSOCIATION; SURVEY ANALYSIS.

CONTINUOUS DISTRIBUTIONS

See under DISTRIBUTIONS, STATISTICAL.

CONTRACEPTION

See FERTILITY CONTROL.

CONTROL CHARTS

See QUALITY CONTROL, STATISTICAL, *article on* PROCESS CONTROL.

COOLEY, CHARLES H.

Charles Horton Cooley (1864–1929), American sociologist, was born in Ann Arbor, Michigan, and spent almost his entire life there. His father, Thomas McIntyre Cooley, was the first dean of the University of Michigan Law School, a justice of the Michigan Supreme Court, first chairman of the Interstate Commerce Commission, and the author of several famous legal treatises. The younger Cooley, who was delicate in health and painfully shy, early discovered the joys of reading. From the age of 18 until the end of his life he kept a journal in which he set down his ambitions and cares, his reactions to the books he read, his comments on the world around him, and the first intimations of ideas that he later developed in his sociological works. This journal was the source of the *pensées* that make up his last book, *Life and the Student* (1927).

Emerson, Goethe, and Thoreau were among Cooley's early mentors. From Emerson he drew moral inspiration and a love for democracy, from Goethe the notion that one's life should be a work of art, and from Thoreau a taste for the simple life and the willingness to be a nonconformist.

Cooley's interest in sociology was first aroused by reading Spencer, but he soon concluded that Spencer's thought was too full of mechanistic analogies to be of much value. Albert Schäffle's *Bau und Leben des socialen Körpers* he found more satisfactory, although still too analogical. He read other early sociologists—Comte, Gumplowicz, Maine, Lewis Henry Morgan, Tarde—without enthusiasm. Tocqueville he found stimulating, but he did not share the view that democracy tends, by reducing everyone to the same level, to hinder distinctive achievement. Cooley met both Ward and Giddings early in his career and was grateful for their encouragement.

It was, however, to three men outside the field of sociology that he felt his greatest scientific debt. Foremost among these was Darwin, whose combination of patient empirical study and imaginative theoretical speculation Cooley greatly admired. Later in his life he was to regret that although he might claim to have accomplished something on the theoretical side, he had never matched it with the painstaking empirical work exemplified by Darwin's. To Darwin, perhaps more than to anyone else, he owed his appreciation of the interrelatedness of the elements of life and his conviction that parts are never separable from wholes.

James Bryce was another scholar Cooley revered. His careful analysis of American democracy and his belief in its strength appealed both to the sociologist and the optimist in Cooley. Finally, deeply impressed by William James's *Principles of Psychology*, he sought to emulate James's willingness to look at every new event without preconceptions, and he accepted James's belief that nature progresses through a trial-and-error process. He also greatly admired the beauty of James's literary style.

Cooley did not decide to devote himself to sociology until he was 28. He had prepared himself at the University of Michigan to be an engineer, and he worked briefly as a draftsman. But his heart was not in this work, and he accepted an opportunity to go to Washington, D.C., in preparation for graduate work in political economy. There he collected and analyzed statistics on street railways for the Bureau of the Census—his first research undertaking. Returning to the University of Michigan in 1890, he became an instructor while still a graduate student in economics. He had already begun to read Spencer and to become interested in sociology. It was arranged for him to take a minor in the subject for his doctorate (the examination was to be set by Giddings). He was awarded his PH.D. in 1894 and taught his first course in sociology that fall. His thesis, "The Theory of Transportation" (1894), is a pioneering study in human ecology, still highly regarded. But he had already begun to be dissatisfied with analyzing the external, ecological features of society and decided to attempt instead to search out the underlying sociopsychological facts. One of the works that stimulated him to turn his energies in this direction was James Mark Baldwin's *Social and Ethical Interpretations in Mental Development*.

There are two principal themes in Cooley's great trilogy, *Human Nature and the Social Order* (1902), *Social Organization* (1909), and *Social Process* (1918). One is his organic view of society; the other is the central role he gave to mind.

Society as an organism. Cooley was fully aware of the pitfalls in the analogy between society and the biological organism. By the organic view he meant merely that the student of society must avoid all particularistic theories. He must realize that neither the individual nor the group is basic, that both are aspects of the same whole. Different aspects of life are systematically related, so that an economic interpretation of history is no more plausible than a religious one. All elements of life interact with one another. For a particular purpose one can concentrate on the study of a single institution, but one must view it in the context of the whole and never forget that the special approach is just a convenience. Other starting points are equally valid; the ideal would be to take a number of standpoints until a rounded view is obtained.

Cooley called the dynamic aspect of the organic view the "tentative process." By this he meant that all forms of social life—whether persons, small groups, role-constituted institutions like schools, or abstract institutions like languages—are constantly growing and changing, attempting to push out into new territory. This thrusting forward, however, is a selective process. Some attempts succeed, some fail: the test is a pragmatic one. Those that are adapted to the surrounding situation survive because they "work." This is as true of conscious try-outs—for example, applications for jobs—as it is of unconscious processes by which a language evolves. Cooley saw this tentative process as one of continual organization and reorganization, since the various elements are always developing new relations to one another as they move forward.

Consistent with this position, Cooley emphasized the dialectic or dramatic aspect of social life. He saw the thrust and counterthrust of forces in any social whole as being like the "conversations" among the various sections of a symphony orchestra.

Although Cooley did not use the term "functionalism," his view is suggestive of it. If "to work" is to survive, then all existing culture traits and institutions must be functional.

Primacy of mind. The second principal theme in Cooley's work is that the essence of social life is its mental character. Mind is all-pervasive; it is the medium in which thought develops and through which it is communicated. Human action, so far as it is superior to the action of animals, flows from mind. Thus, there is a sort of universal stuff, mind, that becomes nucleated and organized at particular points—persons, groups, institutions, publics. The history of a language and the history of a human being are equally instances of mind in process.

Cooley was not merely saying that the mind of the child is developed socially, which is universally acknowledged, but something much more radical—that the theater of all interaction is the mind. Persons and groups exist for each other only as they are conceived in the mind, and thus their interaction takes place only within the mind. This extremely mentalistic view undoubtedly sprang from Cooley's own inclination toward introspective analysis. He sought to encompass society in his own mind, believed that others did the same, and made this activity a scientific principle.

It would be a mistake to suppose that Cooley's mentalistic emphasis is an emphasis on rationality. He believed that the child learns such sentiments as justice and kindness by experiencing them in his relations with others, by the same kind of intercourse through which thought is learned. The basic process in learning sentiments is what he called sympathy and what we would now call empathy. Since sentiments are symbolized in the process of learning, they can, like thought, be communicated.

In *Human Nature and the Social Order*, Cooley concentrated on the person and the subtleties of his relations with others. A central concept is the self, which to Cooley is composed of whatever the person appropriates from the general flow of life, in contrast to that which belongs to others. The self can be discovered by examining the referents of the word "I." Although the physical body is included among them (except in the case of ascetic extremists), it is only a minor part of the self because men cherish their values, ideas, achievements, and possessions more than they do their bodies. Cooley worked out his conception of the self by studying the social development of his own children. Perhaps the best piece of empirical research he did was a verification (1908) of the hypotheses set forth earlier in the 1902 chapter, "The Meaning of 'I.'"

To Cooley the sense of self arises partly from experience, as in the child's competitive appropriation of toys, but also from imagining others' conceptions of oneself. A person tends to accept the view of himself held by those whom he admires. In a brilliant analysis of various phases of the self he drew upon the works of Shakespeare, Goethe, Montaigne, Meredith, Stevenson, Thoreau, Thomas Aquinas, Disraeli, Pascal, Lecky, and George Eliot to discuss such matters as vanity, pride, humility, self-respect, withdrawal, and self-transformation. Although he did not use the term "reference group," he clearly used the idea of reference persons in his treatment of emulation and fame and the idea of reference groups in his discussion of the need for setting of standards in society.

Conscience, for Cooley, was the expression of a mature participation in social life. "To violate conscience is to act under the control of an incomplete and fragmentary state of mind; and so to become less of a person, to begin to disintegrate and go to pieces" ([1902] 1956, p. 329). What is right is not necessarily what is altruistic, since one individual may be able to make a greater contribution with a scarce resource than another. Conscience is strongly affected by group norms and by ideal persons, but in the end the person has to synthesize all these influences and thus develop his conscience. In discussing morally deviant conduct, Cooley pointed out that the organic view diffuses responsibility but by no means exonerates the actor.

Conception of social structure. In *Social Organization* Cooley shifted the focus from the person to the social structure, but he did not abandon the mental emphasis. Society is a mental complex; it is tied together by communication. For Cooley the social mind is molded in the intimacy of the primary group—the family, the children's play group, the neighborhood or local community. Experience in the primary group underlies both the development of the person and the development of the larger organization of society. From this experience the person receives his fundamental orientation to life, and the society receives its model for integrated living.

Cooley did not define his concept of human nature until he discussed primary groups, although he had used the term in the title of his previous book. By human nature he did not mean original biological nature but that nature which everywhere and always develops in the intimate contact with others that is characteristic of primary groups. Beneath cultural differences there is a common core of experience in primary groups which is so similar around the world that it produces a common human nature.

The connection between primary groups and the wider society is made through what Cooley called primary ideals. He believed that life in the primary group tends to be satisfying and that it generates an ideal of moral community. For analytical purposes this ideal can be broken up into loyalty, truth, service, and kindness, but actually it is the broad notion of living in a moral whole that is idealized. Indeed, *Social Organization* can perhaps best be seen as an attempt to analyze the difficulties in and opportunities for achieving some kind of moral wholeness in a complex industrialized society.

For Cooley, a truly democratic society—one in which the self-expression of all leads to the decisions in accordance with which controls are exercised—is an embodiment of primary ideals. He conceived of public opinion not as the aggregated individual judgments of a majority of the people but as the crystallized judgment of all persons, whether they are in the majority or in a minority. "It is not at all necessary that there should be agreement; the essential thing is a certain ripeness and stability of thought resulting from attention and discussion" ([1909] 1956, p. 122). Thus, public opinion is a stage in a process. The masses contribute to it sentiment and general tendency; the leaders, the formulation of alternatives for policy. Public opinion can judge only broad questions of change and readjustment; the details of public business must generally be handled by specialists. But Cooley realized that democracy will not work unless there is a latent moral unity—a tradition of justice, freedom, and humanity—beneath the differing class views expressed in public opinion.

Since Cooley saw wealth as generalized power, he tended to see social classes as economically based. He discriminated, however, between a caste system and a system of open classes. The caste system tends to be fostered by cultural and racial differences in the population, by the absence of social change, and by a low level of education and enlightenment. Because a democracy enlists the energies of all and educates its citizens, an open-class system is suitable to it. To the degree that public opinion operates successfully, hostile feeling between classes is kept in check.

Consistent with his general view of social organizations, Cooley defined an institution as "a definite phase of the public mind"; it is the organization of human thought around a certain task. The state, for example, represents the practical working out of men's ideas in the field of government. A social structure is developed within which individuals participate, but they participate with only a specialized part of themselves. An institution represents the accumulation of human experience, but it does not have the wholeness and humanness of the person. Institutions all too readily become formalized, since formalism represents the line of least resistance for the participants. If formalism goes so far that participants lose all interest, it may result in decay and disorganization; or a reform movement may successfully spur reorganization.

Cooley's ideas about institutions may be illustrated by his discussion of pecuniary valuation in *Social Process*. He demonstrated that economic value is not merely the result of free market choices of autonomous individuals; it also results from a special structure of thought and action that has to be studied in its own right if current values are to be understood. Thus, each rising generation is conditioned to want certain things and not others—breakfast cereals, perhaps, but not bird's-nest soup. Further, those of great wealth have a disproportionate amount of influence in setting standards of taste because they consume more goods and services. In addition, in the great corporate structures of our day the salaries of high officials are not set by a market mechanism; hence, these officials determine their own value. In short, economic institutions, like all others, are not merely the result of great impersonal forces but are in part the result of a special stream of thought and practice. When an institution becomes too divergent from the general norms of the society, critics, inspired by human values, lodge protests and attempt to initiate reform.

Social philosophy. Cooley mixed his aspirations for democracy with his sociological analysis. He defined success as self-development in social service; he had great confidence in the moral integrity of the common man; and he thought that there is a natural affinity between democracy and art, that communication fosters humanitarianism, and that there is an onward and upward tendency to life. Behind his sociology, and combined with it, was a social philosophy. He believed that as communication improved life was organized humanely in wider and wider circles. As a result, national democracies were already in being, and some sort of democratic world order was bound to come.

Although Cooley did not regard himself as more than incidentally a social critic, his views on the world around him are clear in his work. He applauded differentiation as the main guarantee of democracy, and at the same time he was an enemy of particularism either in thought or in the guise of simplistic reforms. Provided that the system is an open one, he believed in altering it through gradual, not revolutionary, change. Although he found much that was crude and selfish in the capitalism of his day and much that was admirable in socialism (especially its humane spirit), he was in no sense a radical. He believed too strongly in a ramified tentative process to favor monolithic organization and too strongly in the need of guidance and control to embrace anarchism.

Assessment of Cooley.   It is not accurate to label Cooley an "armchair" sociologist. It is true that he drew much from the great observers of life, such as Goethe and Bryce, that he did little systematic research, and that his students were not trained to become conventional researchers. But he did have an empirical bent. In his essay "Genius, Fame and the Comparison of Races" (1897), he marshaled both historical and contemporary evidence to refute those portions of Galton's *Hereditary Genius* that belittle the influence of social factors in producing great men. He also used empirical materials closer at hand. Among the important sources of his knowledge were self-analysis, the study of his children, novels about contemporary life, and the autobiographies that he encouraged students to write.

Again, Cooley was not a systematic theorist. His organic view postulates so seamless a web of social life that no emphasis on structure is made. Rather than constructing a general scheme and then successively dealing with each of its features, he preferred to dip into life at the points where he had a flash of insight, let his thought mature, express it beautifully and illustrate it convincingly, and then pass on to something else. He left it to the reader to fashion a general scheme.

Cooley was distrustful of reliance upon mensuration in sociology. He did not believe that units for measuring the subtleties of relation and process in social wholes had been devised. "The Roots of Social Knowledge" (1926) is a plea for using one's own experience as a means of interpreting the experience of those under study. Statistics are only as good as their basic units of measurement and are therefore of secondary importance in sociological research. Only mind can predict what mind will do. Since Cooley's day sociologists have tried to overcome the obstacles he saw by asking open-ended questions and coding the answers afterward and by social experiments in the laboratory, which include the simulation of lifelike situations. They have also greatly increased the use of his favored method, participant observation.

Throughout his career, Cooley lived a quiet, uncomplicated life. Reading, writing, and teaching were his daily round. Personal conflict was distasteful to him, and he had no fondness for administration. During his lifetime sociology at the University of Michigan remained under the wing of the economics department.

Soon after Cooley's death, George Herbert Mead (1930) wrote an appreciative critique of his work. In it, however, he disagreed with Cooley's view that the differentiation of self and other takes place wholly within mind. Whereas Cooley saw communication arising within mind, Mead saw mind arising in communication; he held that communication begins in gestures and preverbal sounds, to which words are gradually added to create mind. He also pointed out that it is very difficult to give adequate recognition to the nonmental side of the person and the technological side of the society if one views society as wholly mental. He admitted that the immediate process of most adult interaction is mental but not that mind is the ultimate social reality.

A second but more limited criticism was made by another admirer of Cooley, L. L. Bernard (1936). He doubted the validity of Cooley's belief that the larger relations of society could and should be controlled by the "extension of primary ideals." He took the position that the problems of large-scale organization are so different from the problems of primary groups that special ideals (which he called derivative) would have to develop from the broader context to control social processes at this level.

A third criticism was leveled by both Jandy (1942) and Rieff (see Cooley 1902, "Introduction" to the 1964 edition). Although laudatory on many points, they took Cooley to task for his excessive optimism—for believing that American society was what he wanted it to be. They charged him with ignoring the deep schisms that are glossed over by the organic view, for believing that the majority of men are unselfish and capable of ascetic motivation, and for seeing modern communication as a means of humanizing urban life.

Perhaps these and other criticisms might be summed up by saying that Cooley's society, which he offered as the real world, is in fact a selective model, an ideal type. In it the mental aspect of life is salient, and within this aspect connection and balance are emphasized. The significance of crude power is not appreciated, since it is neither a mental phenomenon nor a reciprocal one. And Cooley did not deal adequately with social structure: there are no sharp edges in the mind, only the flow of messages through more and less permeable filters.

Despite these deficiencies, Cooley's work stands as a monumental achievement. Indeed, his ideas seem so simple and so true that the reader may not appreciate their originality. His empirical work on the sense of self, for instance, was ground breaking. With his conception of primary groups he crystallized prior thought and added to it the significant idea that human nature is developed in such groups. His organic view of public opinion was a fresh insight, and his treatment of public will foreshadowed information theory and cybernetics. He anticipated Durkheim in his understanding of the role of festivals in revitalizing the spirit of large groups. His analysis of pecuniary valuation was a significant contribution to institutional economics. His treatment of social classes in *Social Organization* was vastly superior to anything in the American sociological literature that preceded it. Cooley did not create a system of sociology, but he greatly enriched the discipline in many areas.

ROBERT COOLEY ANGELL

[*For the historical context of Cooley's work, see* INTERACTION, *article on* SOCIAL INTERACTION; *and the biographies of* BALDWIN; BRYCE; DARWIN; GIDDINGS; JAMES; SPENCER. *For discussion of the subsequent development of his ideas, see* CREATIVITY, *article on* SOCIAL ASPECTS; GROUPS, *article on* THE STUDY OF GROUPS; REFERENCE GROUPS; TRANSPORTATION, *article on* SOCIAL ASPECTS; *and the biographies of* BERNARD; MEAD; ROSS; THOMAS; WALLER.]

WORKS BY COOLEY

(1894) 1930   The Theory of Transportation. Pages 15–118 in Charles H. Cooley, *Sociological Theory and Social Research, Being the Selected Papers of Charles Horton Cooley*. With an introduction and notes by Robert Cooley Angell. New York: Holt.

(1894–1929) 1930   *Sociological Theory and Social Research, Being the Selected Papers of Charles Horton Cooley*. With an introduction and notes by Robert Cooley Angell. New York: Holt.

(1897) 1930   Genius, Fame and the Comparison of Races. Pages 119–159 in Charles H. Cooley, *Sociological Theory and Social Research, Being the Selected Papers of Charles Horton Cooley*. With an introduction and notes by Robert Cooley Angell. New York: Holt.

(1902) 1956   *Human Nature and the Social Order*. Rev. ed. In Charles H. Cooley, *Two Major Works*: Social Organization *and* Human Nature and the Social Order. Glencoe, Ill.: Free Press. → Each title reprinted with individual title page and pagination. A separate paperback edition of *Human Nature* was published in 1964 by Schocken; see especially the "Introduction" by Philip Rieff.

(1908) 1930   A Study of the Early Use of Self-words by a Child. Pages 227–247 in Charles H. Cooley, *Sociological Theory and Social Research, Being the Selected Papers of Charles Horton Cooley*. With an introduction and notes by Robert Cooley Angell. New York: Holt.

(1909) 1956   *Social Organization: A Study of the Larger Mind*. In Charles H. Cooley, *Two Major Works*: Social Organization *and* Human Nature and the Social Order. Glencoe, Ill.: Free Press. → Each title reprinted with individual title page and pagination. A separate paperback edition of *Social Organization* was published in 1962 by Schocken.

(1918) 1966   *Social Process*. Carbondale: Southern Illinois Univ. Press.

(1926) 1930   The Roots of Social Knowledge. Pages 287–309 in Charles H. Cooley, *Sociological Theory and Social Research, Being the Selected Papers of Charles Horton Cooley*. With an introduction and notes by Robert Cooley Angell. New York: Holt.

1927   *Life and the Student: Roadside Notes on Human Nature, Society, and Letters*. New York: Knopf.

SUPPLEMENTARY BIBLIOGRAPHY

ANGELL, ROBERT C. 1930   Cooley's Heritage to Social Research. *Social Forces* 8:340–347.

ANGELL, ROBERT C. 1956   Introduction. In Charles H. Cooley, *Two Major Works*: Social Organization *and* Human Nature and the Social Order. Glencoe, Ill.: Free Press.

BERNARD, LUTHER L. 1936 The Conflict Between Primary Group Attitudes and Derivative Group Ideals in Modern Society. *American Journal of Sociology* 41: 611–623.

GUTMAN, ROBERT 1958 Cooley: A Perspective. *American Sociological Review* 23:251–256.

HAMILTON, WALTON H. 1929 Charles Horton Cooley. *Social Forces* 8:183–187.

JANDY, EDWARD C. 1942 *Charles Horton Cooley: His Life and His Social Theory.* New York: Dryden.

MEAD, GEORGE H. 1930 Cooley's Contribution to American Social Thought. *American Journal of Sociology* 35:693–706.

WOOD, ARTHUR E. 1930 Charles Horton Cooley: An Appreciation. *American Journal of Sociology* 35:707–717.

COOPER, JOHN M.

John Montgomery Cooper (1881–1949) was an American ethnologist, ethnographer, and priest who also made important contributions to the fields of education and social welfare.

Although his father's family was Quaker, his mother was of French Catholic stock, and at an early age Cooper felt the desire to enter the priesthood. His academic work at St. Charles College near Baltimore, Maryland, was followed by six years of study in Rome and travel on the Continent. At the American College in Rome he received a PH.D. in 1902 and a degree of doctor of sacred theology in 1905, the year in which he was ordained. On returning to the United States, he was appointed to St. Matthew's church in Washington, D.C.

In 1909 Cooper became associated with the Catholic University of America as part-time instructor in religious education and was soon relieved of parish duties. In 1923 he became an associate professor in the department of sociology and a full professor in 1928. When the department of anthropology was established in 1934, he became its chairman, a position he filled until his death.

From 1917 to 1925 Cooper's attention was turned to subjects broadly sociological in nature. Practically all his writings concerned group work, social hygiene, and related topics. His association with the National Catholic Welfare Council, 1918–1920, brought him to international prominence as a leader in social group work. His last contribution to applied sociology was his book *Children's Institutions* (1931a).

Although subsequently he made original contributions to several fields of anthropology, such as linguistics (1945), and to the psychiatric approach to certain ethnographic phenomena (1934), Cooper was primarily an ethnologist. His vacation trips to northern Canada led to an interest in American Indians, which was encouraged by John Reed Swanton and Frederick W. Hodge, ethnologists at the Smithsonian Institution. His first notable contribution to ethnology, which preceded his sociological work, was his *Analytical and Critical Bibliography of the Tribes of Tierra del Fuego* (1917). This study revealed in high measure the qualities that marked all of his work—craftsmanship, lucidity of expression, and critical judgment. His recurrent visits to the Algonquian-speaking Indians of northeastern Canada and the Great Plains resulted in many papers on various aspects of their culture —material, social, and magico–religious. His last full-length monograph, the second part of *The Gros Ventres of Montana* (1957), on religion and ritual, was published posthumously.

As a theorist Cooper was particularly intrigued with questions of distribution and historical reconstruction. His paper on the areal and temporal distribution of culture in South America (1942) inspired the over-all arrangement of the *Handbook of South American Indians* (Steward 1946–1959). To this large compendium he contributed ten articles, all of which exhibit his complete mastery of the often widely scattered sources. In his *Temporal Sequence and the Marginal Cultures* (1941) he presented evidence for the hypothesis that the nonliterate peoples of the ethnographic present represent "tarriers" with relatively unchanged cultures from prehistoric times, and he worked out several canons to be applied in historical reconstruction. One of these canons is as follows:

(a) Where a given cultural phenomenon is consistently found among present-day marginal peoples it was probably present in early prehistoric human culture as such. (b) The probability of such early prehistoric presence is augmented where the factors underlying the given phenomenon can be assumed on probable grounds to have been continuously operative among the cultural ancestors of the present-day marginals and to have been operative in early prehistoric times. (Cooper 1941, p. 64)

Cooper was aware that the applicability of his canons was distinctly limited. "As is obvious they cannot yield a total all-embracing reconstruction of prehistoric culture . . ." (1941, p. 66). Exhibiting proper scientific caution, he drew conclusions when the evidence warranted but never subscribed to what he considered the overbroad generalizations of the Viennese Kulturkreis theory, which claimed by means of "the culture-history method" to be able to reconstruct original primeval human culture.

Lowie (1949, p. 291) stated that Cooper's

essay "Andamanese–Semang–Eta Cultural Relations" (1940), "which presents a powerful argument for the pristine unity of the Asiatic Pygmies," was possibly "the most superb example of what sound judgment coupled with control of the material can accomplish." His interpretative paper "The Relations Between Religion and Morality" (1931*b*) was selected for inclusion in *The Golden Age of American Anthropology*. In this paper Cooper called attention to a certain fundamental order and uniformity underlying the extremely varied moral standards that prevail among the nonliterate peoples of the world and showed that while among some of the marginal peoples religious sanctions are clearly operative, among a good number of them social sanctions alone back up the moral code. He concluded therefore that neither the classical theory, which maintained an early dissociation of religion and morality, nor the theory holding that in earlier times both duties to God and to neighbor were looked upon as the will of God can be maintained in the light of the anthropological evidence.

In addition to his purely academic activities Cooper evidenced extraordinary organizing skill. He was largely responsible for founding the Catholic Anthropological Conference in 1926. He initiated and edited several valuable publications, including the periodical *Primitive Man* (title changed to *Anthropological Quarterly* in 1953). He never shirked professional responsibility and participated actively in numerous organizations. His religious beliefs and his priestly vocation completely penetrated his life. He never felt that they interfered in any way with his scientific attitude as an anthropologist.

REGINA FLANNERY

WORKS BY COOPER

1917 *Analytical and Critical Bibliography of the Tribes of Tierra del Fuego and Adjacent Territory*. U.S. Bureau of American Ethnology, Bulletin No. 63. Washington: Government Printing Office.

1931*a* *Children's Institutions: A Study of Programs and Policies in Catholic Children's Institutions in the United States*. Philadelphia: Dolphin.

(1931*b*) 1960 The Relations Between Religion and Morality in Primitive Culture. Pages 560–572 in Margaret Mead and Ruth L. Bunzel (editors), *The Golden Age of American Anthropology*. New York: Braziller.

1934 Mental Disease Situations in Certain Cultures: A New Field for Research. *Journal of Abnormal and Social Psychology* 24:10–17.

1940 Andamanese–Semang–Eta Cultural Relations. *Primitive Man* 13:29–47.

1941 *Temporal Sequence and the Marginal Cultures*. Anthropological Series, No. 10. Washington: Catholic University of America.

1942 Areal and Temporal Aspects of Aboriginal South American Culture. *Primitive Man* 15:1–38.

1945 Tête-de-Boule Cree. *International Journal of American Linguistics* 11:36–44.

1957 *The Gros Ventres of Montana*. Part 2: Religion and Ritual. Edited by Regina Flannery. Anthropological Series, No. 16. Washington: Catholic University of America.

SUPPLEMENTARY BIBLIOGRAPHY

Bibliography of John Montgomery Cooper. 1950 *Primitive Man* 23:66–84.

FURFEY, PAUL H. 1950 John Montgomery Cooper: 1881–1949. *Primitive Man* 23:49–65.

LOWIE, ROBERT H. 1949 John Montgomery Cooper: 1881–1949. *Boletín bibliográfico de antropología americana* 12, part 2: 289–292.

MÉTRAUX, ALFRED 1950 The Contribution of the Rev. Father Cooper to South American Ethnography. *Primitive Man* 23:39–48. → This number contains a comprehensive bibliography of Cooper's works.

STEWARD, JULIAN H. (editor) (1946–1959) 1963 *Handbook of South American Indians*. 7 vols. U.S. Bureau of American Ethnology, Bulletin No. 153. New York: Cooper Square.

TIBESAR, LEOPOLD H. 1950 Doctor Cooper Initiates the Catholic Anthropological Conference. *Primitive Man* 23:35–38.

COOPERATION

Cooperation is joint or collaborative behavior that is directed toward some goal and in which there is common interest or hope of reward. Cooperation may be voluntary or involuntary, direct or indirect, formal or informal, but always there is a combination of efforts toward a specific end in which all the participants have a stake, real or imagined. At its higher intellectual levels cooperation involves reciprocity of intent as well as jointness of behavior, and it may even become an end in itself. There is no limit to the potential range for cooperation; it is to be found in groups as small as the dyad and as large as leagues of sovereign states.

It is possible to regard cooperation as an ethical norm, as a social process, or as an institutional structure. In ethics and religion, cooperation has been among the most honored of values throughout human history. Indeed, some philosophers and religious teachers have made cooperation synonymous with the whole fabric of morality. Cooperation is stressed in all of the major religions and moral systems of the world. It is at the very heart of Hinduism and Confucianism and has a hallowed place even in such relatively individualistic religions as Christianity.

Considered as a *process*, cooperation is central

to the formation of types and to changes in types. Studies by modern naturalists have shown this to be as true in the plant and animal world as in the human–cultural. Closely related to competition, as will be emphasized below, cooperative behavior is one of the central mechanisms of the evolutionary process; it is to be observed in conditions leading to change as well as to stability.

As a *social structure*, cooperation is manifest in countless organizations created expressly by man for the purpose of joint behavior toward a given goal. Such structures range in size from primitive hunting groups to modern insurance companies and in kind from criminal conspiracies, at one extreme, to the World Health Organization, at the other. They are as often religious, political, and cultural in character as they are economic. Only the fact that the modern renewal of interest in cooperation as a process and structure occurred in the nineteenth century, a century overwhelmingly preoccupied by the impact of laissez-faire capitalism on the social order, can account for the distressing tendency among social scientists even today to conceive of cooperation and competition as processes primarily economic in significance.

Types of cooperation

Five types of cooperation may usefully be distinguished: *automatic*, *traditional*, *contractual*, *directed*, and *spontaneous*. Each can be found in all spheres of human society—political, religious, economic, cultural—and while it is important to distinguish the types from one another, it is equally important to emphasize that rarely, if ever, does any one of them exist in isolation.

Automatic. Automatic cooperation refers to the varied types of impersonal coordination, jointness of behavior, and mutuality of interest that arise directly from *ecological position*. Within this type fall most of the instances of cooperation stressed by naturalists (see, for example, Allee 1938). Such cooperation in the plant and animal world is almost largely sexual or commensal in nature, although among the higher orders it is related to security. It is commonly instinctual in basis. Despite traditional emphasis on the struggle for existence, observable patterns of plant and animal order would be incomprehensible apart from the premise of vital cooperative processes.

Automatic cooperation is also observable in the human world. To the eye of the social ecologist, human populations, both urban and rural, appear as directed in considerable part by processes that are unplanned and usually unnoticed by participants. Among these processes is cooperation: jointness of behavior toward a common end that arises solely from the fact of strategic location in the larger ecological pattern. Unplanned cooperation between two groups (whether national, economic, religious, or racial) may exist simply by virtue of an independently perceived threat to the security of each; such cooperation may be stimulated by action or threat of action by an outside group, but it is predicated upon a pre-existing compatibility of norms and aspirations. Defense by each group of its own position (normative or spatial) can, without any conscious effort, produce a considerable degree of cooperation that can only be called automatic. Automatic cooperation is a cardinal feature of the complex relations among the primary, secondary, and tertiary orders of the modern economy, and it is no less a feature of relations among ethnic and religious groups and of sovereign states.

Traditional. Cooperation of the traditional type is regulated neither by instinct, volition, nor simple location, but rather by traditional social norms. Prime examples are the joint family of India, the Chinese clan, the village community of Asia and medieval Europe, and craft and merchant guilds the world over in ancient and medieval times. The Hindu family, "joint in food, worship, and estate," is based upon the inviolable morality of mutual aid among the generations and branches, however remote in space or time; the family in perpetuity is conceived as a cooperative relationship among the dead, the living, and the unborn. Similarly, in the agricultural village community, which is one of the most universal of institutions, such matters as the planting, cultivation, and harvesting of crops are dealt with cooperatively by the villagers. In the medieval guild, prices, techniques of craftsmanship, and standards of work were all established cooperatively by the guild masters, and direct competition was forbidden. In all such instances, cooperation—however it may have been started in the first place—is one of the mores, as binding upon the participants as any other part of morality.

Contractual. In modern industrial society cooperation is more likely to be contractual than traditional in character. Terms of cooperation are specific and conditional upon the will of the participants or governed by legal sanctions, and they are precise both in terms of length of cooperation and of what is specifically required by the relationship. Contractual cooperation commonly increases sharply in historical periods during which the close ties of the traditional community are supplanted by the more individualistic and utilitarian ties of an open society. Contractual cooperation is one of the most basic patterns of contemporary Western society. The whole vast array of consumer and producer cooperatives, credit unions, cooperative apartment houses, profit-sharing plans, and the like make plain how dependent contemporary capitalism is on this type of cooperation. It is sometimes thought that informal contractual cooperation tends to wane in mass society, but the profusion of baby-sitting and car pools suggests that contractual cooperation at the grass roots is far from moribund.

Directed. Military organization is probably the oldest and most universal form of directed cooperation, but, in the modern world, the large-scale business enterprise, labor union, school system, and even religious and recreational organizations could hardly survive without the form of cooperation that arises from command or direction. The source of cooperation here is only incidentally or derivatively a common recognition of goal or a clear norm. It would be difficult to find a more dramatic instance of directed cooperation than in the great atomic bomb project of World War II; tens of thousands of persons, at all levels of skill and responsibility, cooperated under remote direction in the making of a product known to but the tiniest handful of top leaders in the project. Such an instance, although dramatic, is far from unique in the contemporary age. What Max Weber called "rationalization" is a process in modern society that has had the effect of converting a great deal of human cooperation into the directed type. It is inconceivable that complex, large-scale organizations could operate today without directed cooperation, and we are witnessing an ever increasing amount of this type of cooperation as a result of the intricate and far-reaching operations of data-processing and computer systems.

Spontaneous. Spontaneous cooperation is the oldest, most natural, and widespread form of cooperation. Unprescribed by tradition, contract, or command, it is situational in character and practically constitutes the essence of relationships within the family, neighborhood, play group, and other close, personal forms of association. Everything we know about this type of cooperation suggests that it is most common when there is a prior basis of amity. Thus, irrespective of the type of tasks assigned, spontaneous cooperation is least likely when friendly acquaintance has not had an opportunity to arise. This type of cooperation is by no means absent from even the most regimented of organizations. In army, corporation, or government, types of spontaneous cooperation arise, given propitious conditions that may support (or negate) the planned, directed type; as every military observer has emphasized, spontaneous cooperation is the ultimate requisite of victory in battle. No matter what the sphere of activity, not even the most rationally and meticulously planned operation will altogether obviate spontaneous cooperation among participants.

History of the concept

In one form or another, speculative or reflective interest in cooperation is as old as human thought. Some of the most ancient proverbs and legends embody man's realization not only of the importance but also of the elements of cooperation. From Confucius, Lao-tzu, and Gautama in the Far East, as from the prophets of the Old Testament, the centrality of the ethic and psychology of cooperation may easily be inferred. For both Plato and Aristotle, cooperation was the keystone of the good state, and what Aristotle called *stasis*, or political factionalism, was the infallible sign of civic degeneration. In the writings of the Christian fathers, the imperative of cooperation was based in part on their organismic image of the world and society, but also on the remembered reality of early Christian cooperative communities—often, indeed, communistic—and on the kinds of brotherhood and interest associations that flourished throughout the Middle Ages. The theme of cooperation was a powerful one in medieval religious thought, and a great deal of modern thought on cooperation is but a secularization of this theme.

From a sociological point of view early modern theories of society may be seen as falling within either a cooperation or conflict orientation. On the one hand, there were those who, like Thomas Hobbes (1588–1679), saw the natural state of man as characterized by conflict and war of all against all, with the life of man left "solitary, poor, nasty, brutish, and short"; the absolute state was seen as man's only refuge from this conflict. There were others, however, like the great Johannes Althusius (1557–1638), who believed that amity and cooperation were basic in the human species and that the social ties of family, community, and association had long preceded the rise of the state. Down through the nineteenth century, conflict theories of society vied with those based upon cooperation; Ludwig Gumplowicz (1838–1909) was perhaps the most notable exponent of the former.

Nineteenth-century thought. The nineteenth century witnessed a major renewal of interest in the ethic and nature of cooperation. This renewal must be seen as a profoundly important reaction against three major tendencies of the age. The first, hedonistic utilitarianism, declared all human behavior to be the product of self-interest and to be governed solely by drives leading to the maximization of pleasure and minimization of pain. Similarly, classical economic theory made the units of society discrete, self-interested individuals, united chiefly by ties of impersonal competition. Finally, the doctrine of natural selection affirmed the primacy, and even the exclusiveness, of competition and conflict in the whole evolutionary process. The term "social Darwinism" was used to cover views that insisted that only through competition and struggle could society progress, although Darwin himself had reservations about this, especially as applied to human society.

The rise of the theory of cooperation is to be seen in an attack on all three of these propositions, which by mid-century had become significant in European thought. In the writings of the historical jurists Henry S. Maine, Otto von Gierke, and Léon Duguit, the ethnologists Lewis Henry Morgan and George Laurence Gomme, and the political philosophers Francis H. Bradley and Thomas H. Green, a very different view of man and society emerged: one in which the social group, not the individual, was the element of society and man was understood in terms of his interactive ties with others rather than through instinct forces presumed to be resident within the solitary individual.

The rise of systematic sociology played a major role in disabusing men's minds of the priority of economic values and of the universality of competition. What began in a quasi-utopian and even apocalyptic context in the work of August Comte and Charles Fourier became, by the latter part of the century, an ever more rigorous scientific demonstration of the irreducibility of the social bond, including cooperation, into presocial individual "atoms." Durkheim's great work emphasized not only the long history of cooperation that was embodied in what he called "mechanical solidarity" but also the more ecological type of cooperation reflected by the restitutive sanctions of modern "organic solidarity." He was also keenly concerned with the needs of modern society with respect to the creation of large-scale cooperative occupational associations, which, he thought, would rescue worker and citizen from the *anomie* and isolation of modern urban and industrial life.

Undoubtedly the most influential single work specifically directed to cooperation was *Mutual Aid: A Factor of Evolution* (1890–1896), by P'etr Kropotkin, the founder of anarchism. Written with extraordinary insight and based upon a vast knowledge, this book quickly achieved the status of a classic. Kropotkin addressed himself critically to the doctrines of natural selection and competitive individualism, and his book is filled with numerous instances of behavior in both the animal and human worlds that is based upon cooperation rather than conflict and struggle. It gives examples of mutual aid at all stages of evolution: in the ecological relationships of plants, the behavior of subhuman species, and in such universal human institutions as the commune, the village community, the guild, the cooperative, and the trade union.

In terms of direct human action, as well as theory, cooperation was a significant force in the nineteenth century. There were the great consumer cooperatives, of which the Rochdale Equitable Pioneers' Society in England was perhaps the best known, although it was far from exceptional in either size or influence. Consumer cooperatives, both rural and urban, were founded in Europe and the United States; producer cooperatives also arose, although these were fewer and had their chief impact on the utopian movement. Literally hundreds of colonies were founded on the principle of producer, as well as consumer, cooperation. Although most of these were defunct by the end of the century, they were an important part of the life of that period. Furthermore, there was a profusion of mutual-aid societies and self-help and friendly associations, which dealt cooperatively with such matters as education, life insurance, and burial expenses. In sum, despite the common conception of the nineteenth century as wholly individualistic and competitive, we have to conclude that cooperation, both in thought and practical affairs, was an important aspect of this period.

Contemporary research

Since the nineteenth century the behavioral sciences have steadily expanded the investigation of the processes of cooperation and their varied contexts. In reference to the schema of types of cooperation described above, it can be said with only a few reservations that the earliest *scientific* investigations were studies of the first three types. Interest in *automatic* cooperation was manifest early in the century in the works of the human ecologists who followed Robert E. Park and the Chicago school. *Traditional* cooperation among preliterate and folk peoples was studied by ethnologists and in agricultural areas by rural sociologists. Types of *contractual* cooperation and the social norms underlying them constituted the subject matter of some of the works of Roscoe Pound and other legal sociologists.

More recent have been the studies of *directed* and *spontaneous* cooperation. The field of industrial relations, which burgeoned as an academic discipline in the United States during the 1940s, contains most of the research of the former type; specifically, studies of patterns of cooperation in industry and bureaucracy followed the style of the earlier and justly heralded work of Elton Mayo, Fritz Roethlisberger, and their colleagues (see Roethlisberger & Dickson 1939). Until the 1950s virtually all study of *spontaneous* cooperation was in the field of child psychology or psychology of learning, with small schoolchildren the inevitable subjects.

Two areas of research have cut across those listed above and appear to be the most relevant to present and emerging tendencies: research in *social interaction* and *comparative-historical* research. Studies of interaction are undoubtedly the most valuable and suggestive investigations of cooperation to be found anywhere at the present time in the behavioral sciences: investigations that seek the molecular or microcosmic elements of the process, its sources of motivation, and the effects upon it of changes in the quality and intensity of interaction. It is unfortunate that progress in microsocial analyses of cooperation is not matched by that in studies of the macrosocial: that is, the actual structures through which the process of cooperation has revealed itself in such diversity throughout the ages and in all cultures. This imbalance, it is worth noting, has its parallel in the biological sciences, where interest in microevolution has virtually displaced older but still needed inquiries into macroevolution.

Studies of social interaction.   Two recent studies best portray the kind of analysis of cooperation that occurs in the field of social-interaction research. The first is Morton Deutsch's notable study (1953) of the effects of cooperation and competition upon group process. Fifty college men from an introductory psychology course were given personality tests, and on the basis of the results they were divided into ten groups of five men each; the groups were matched according to their members' range of ability and personality. On the basis of a further test involving a problem in human relations, the ten groups were divided into two sets of five groups, with each set containing the same number of high-scoring and low-scoring individuals. All of the groups within the two sets, meeting each week, received a logical puzzle and a problem in human relations to work on. One of the sets was given "competitive treatment," and the other set received "cooperative treatment." In the former set, each student was made to understand that his grade would depend strictly upon how well he did as an individual in solving the given problems; in

the latter, each student's personal grade was made contingent on how well the group as a whole did in meeting the problems. Differences in both group and individual results between the two sets of groups were carefully noted by trained observers, and questionnaires about results, spaced a week apart, were given to the students themselves.

Given the difference in rewards promised to the participants in each set, there is nothing surprising in the finding that there was a manifestly greater cooperativeness and sense of group cohesion in the one set and a greater degree of competitive individualism in the other; the same is true of the differences in the degree of friendliness within groups of the two sets. However, there were more striking conclusions. The cooperative groups met the puzzle problem more efficiently and contributed in more detail to the analysis of the human-relations problem, although not necessarily with more insight. Within the cooperative groups there was more differentiation of individual function, that is, more division of labor; in the competitive groups, on the other hand, duplication of effort was considerable, for all were equally on their own to do all that was required. Communication was smoother in the cooperative group; there was, however, as much interaction in the competitive group, a condition resulting from the fact that merely in order to demonstrate individual ability on the human-relations problem, spirited contribution to a discussion was mandatory. Despite the contrasting environments of the two sets of groups, no significant differences were discernible in the amount of psychology learned by individuals in the two sets. Such are a few of the conclusions; obviously they say nothing, nor are they intended to, about the ultimate values of competition and cooperation in a society, for such values are related to the entire normative order [*see* GROUPS, *article on* GROUP BEHAVIOR].

The Robbers Cave experiment.   The second social-interaction study is that of Muzafer Sherif and his associates (see Oklahoma, University of . . . 1961). The setting was a summer camp, and the subjects were twenty boys of homogeneous background. The boys were divided into two groups, and the first stage of the experiment consisted of welding each of the groups into a unity. This was done by separating the groups and ensuring that each group had experiences of a kind that would bind its members into prideful unity. The second stage of the experiment was designed to intensify group cohesiveness by putting the two groups into situations where sharp competition would develop: athletic contests, raids on each other's camp areas, slogans of hostile character. The result was a rising tension between the two groups, combined with strong "we group" loyalties in each. In the third stage of the experiment, an effort was made to heal the breach between the two groups. First, they were brought together in a series of purely passive encounters, such as eating or watching a movie together; however, competitive friction only increased. Then, in the final and crucial stage of the experiment, members of the two groups were brought together for the performance of tasks that clearly required cooperation between the two groups for successful completion: repairing a damaged water tank, fund raising, and so on. The changes were quite striking. Whereas near-hostility had been the relation between the groups by the end of the third stage, in the final stage a majority of cross-group judgments by members were favorable, and the number of friendships went up correspondingly. Such experiments as Sherif's and Deutsch's give microcosmic sanction to what (in military combat or professional sports, for example) has long been clear: that the most effective way of reducing intergroup tensions lies in mobilizing individuals into activities where cooperation is absolutely vital to success—where, in short, it is functional.

The comparative-historical approach. The value of social-interaction studies would be greatly enhanced if their results could be placed against studies that deal, not with contrived or experimental situations, but rather with actual, institutionalized groups in all ages and cultures. Unfortunately, the comparative-historical approach to cooperation is not well developed in terms of methodology, nor is it represented by a significant number of studies. Kropotkin's great work at the beginning of the century pointed to some of the social structures (guilds, cooperatives, and similar associations) through which human cooperation has been carried on historically, and he offered many valuable insights into their functioning and context. His objective, however, was more moral than scientific. A few followers of the French sociologist Frédéric Le Play, most notably Patrick Geddes and his students, in England, also did some work in the field. One should also note the too little known field studies of Demetrius Gusti (1941) in Rumania, whose investigations of rural villages included informal systems of cooperation among villages as well as internal patterns. In India the early work of Radhakamal Mukerjee (1923) and his students gave much attention to processes of cooperation through which interfamily and intervillage projects were carried on in such areas as irrigation.

In the United States it is chiefly in the works of the earlier rural sociologists that any attention to cooperation is to be found in significant degree. Scattered throughout historiography and ethnology, there are, of course, specific references to the various cooperative enterprises that have marked man's struggle for existence. But nowhere have these been brought together, and nowhere has a systematic, scientific effort been made to deal with cooperation as a cultural and historical force. Margaret Mead, in her notable work *Cooperation and Competition Among Primitive Peoples* (1937), showed what could be done among preliterate peoples, but few have chosen to follow. In a remarkable monograph Mark A. May and Leonard W. Doob (1937) made a distinguished effort to summarize existing knowledge on the subject and to arrive at central principles. This work provided an analysis of experimental approaches to cooperation and competition as well as an evaluation of existing anthropological and sociological studies; and it covered a wide range of types of cooperation in military organizations, utopian communities, and varied clubs, associations, and economic enterprises. However, what was chiefly lacking in this pioneering work was a sense of history.

Nothing of comparable stature has been done since May and Doob's contribution. Given the seemingly assured place of cooperation as the subject of social-interaction studies, it may therefore be said without reservation that the most urgent sphere of research in the future must be the comparative-historical. Types of cooperation drawn from all ages and social orders must be distinguished, their structures and internal processes analyzed, their relations to the surrounding scene investigated, and their impact upon members assessed. Moreover, such studies should be coordinated with inquiries into the dynamics of social development. One of the major aspects of the rise of new nations is the impact—often dislocative—of the emerging administrative structures of national authority upon cooperative systems that have been in existence for centuries.

Cooperation and competition

Although cooperation is commonly contrasted with competition (a process in which efforts toward a common objective are separate and in rivalry with one another), it must be emphasized that the two rarely, if ever, occur separately. Indeed, each may have a contributory relation to the other. Competition requires at least the degree of prior cooperation that is necessary for the setting of rules and imposing of sanctions without which competition would dissolve into open war. Conversely, it is doubtful that cooperation would be the major force it is were it not for pressures of competition that spur some to cooperate with others as a means of enhancing their effectiveness in the struggle for existence. In any event, a purely cooperative or purely competitive relationship would be hard to imagine.

In each of the types of cooperation outlined above—ranging from the automatic to the spontaneous—elements of competition are to be found side by side with, indeed often embedded in, those of cooperation. However dependent two orders or types may be upon one another in natural or human ecology, competition is always a latent possibility. Within traditional cooperation, role rivalries are legion; contractual cooperation draws its very efficacy from the fact that it represents legally specifiable surcease from normal competition; within directed (and especially bureaucratic) cooperation, competition of roles and strata goes on constantly. Even in the most elemental, spontaneous types of cooperation—that of the small, conjugal family, for instance—there cannot help but be competition between members: between parents for affection of children, between children for rewards from parents. The same is true in the largest of political and economic systems. Capitalism, commonly thought of as competitive, would founder if it were not for vast systems of economic and legal cooperation within it that help give it direction and stability; and, at the opposite extreme, all that we have learned of socialism in practice indicates that competition can be a powerful force in bringing the various sectors of society to desired levels of performance.

ROBERT A. NISBET

[See also COOPERATIVES; ECOLOGY; INDUSTRIAL RELATIONS, *article on* HUMAN RELATIONS; INTEGRATION; SOCIOMETRY; *and biographies of* DURKHEIM; GEDDES; KROPOTKIN; LE PLAY; PARK; TOCQUEVILLE.]

BIBLIOGRAPHY

ALLEE, WARDER C. (1938) 1951 *Cooperation Among Animals, With Human Implications.* Rev. & enl. ed. New York: Schuman. → First published as *The Social Life of Animals.* A paperback edition was published in 1958 by Beacon.

BAKKE, EDWARD W. 1950 *Bonds of Organization: An Appraisal of Corporate Human Relations.* New York: Harper.

BLAU, PETER M. 1956 *Bureaucracy in Modern Society.* New York: Random House.

DEUTSCH, MORTON (1953) 1960 The Effects of Cooperation and Competition Upon Group Process. Pages 414–448 in Dorwin Cartwright and Alvin Zander (editors), *Group Dynamics: Research and Theory.*

2d ed. Evanston, Ill.: Row, Peterson. → Condensed from two articles that appeared in *Human Relations* in 1949.

GUSTI, DEMETRIUS 1941 *La science de la réalité sociale: Introduction à un système de sociologie d'éthique et de politique.* Paris: Alcan.

HARE, A. PAUL; BORGATTA, E. F.; and BALES, R. F. (1955) 1964 *Small Groups: Studies in Social Interaction.* 2d ed. New York: Knopf.

HOMANS, GEORGE C. 1961 *Social Behavior: Its Elementary Forms.* New York: Harcourt. → See pages 130–138 for an evaluation of Deutsch 1953.

KROPOTKIN, P'ETR (1890–1896) 1955 *Mutual Aid: A Factor of Evolution.* Boston: Extending Horizons. → Thomas Huxley's "The Struggle for Existence" is included in this book.

MAY, MARK A.; and DOOB, LEONARD W. 1937 *Competition and Cooperation: A Report.* Bulletin No. 25. New York: Social Science Research Council.

MEAD, MARGARET (editor) 1937 *Cooperation and Competition Among Primitive Peoples.* New York: McGraw-Hill. → A paperback edition was published in 1961 by Beacon.

MUKERJEE, RADHAKAMAL 1923 *Democracies of the East: A Study in Comparative Politics.* London: King.

MUKERJEE, RADHAKAMAL 1964 *The Destiny of Civilization.* New York: Asia Publishing House.

OKLAHOMA, UNIVERSITY OF, INSTITUTE OF GROUP RELATIONS 1961 *Intergroup Conflict and Cooperation: The Robbers Cave Experiment,* by Muzafer Sherif et al. Norman, Okla.: University Book Exchange.

ROETHLISBERGER, FRITZ J.; and DICKSON, WILLIAM J. (1939) 1961 *Management and the Worker: An Account of a Research Program Conducted by the Western Electric Company, Hawthorne Works, Chicago.* Cambridge, Mass.: Harvard Univ. Press. → A paperback edition was published in 1964 by Wiley.

COOPERATIVES

The beginnings of the cooperative movement are usually associated with the name of Robert Owen. The real association lies, however, more in Owen's ultimate ideals than in his immediate plan of organization. Owen's central plan was for a self-supporting community, such as Fourier's *phalanstère,* where producers and consumers were one and the same people, not for an organization either of producers or of consumers. In contrast to some utopians, however, Owen knew by practical experience the consequences of the industrial revolution for working-class producers and consumers, and he urged production, by voluntary associations, for the use of consumers and not for profit. Although he regarded them as mere steppingstones to his communities, Owen approved of the few short-lived cooperatives that existed prior to the foundation of the Rochdale society, which is still alive today. These societies claimed his authority for their activities and were, together with the Rochdale pioneers, composed mostly of his adherents. Owen appears to have been the first (Digby 1948, p. 15) to apply the term "cooperative" to these activities. So Owen may be accepted as the father of the cooperative movement, if not of its precise type of organization.

The characteristic trait of the cooperative as a form of organization of economic activity is the absence of any special capital-providing class. In producer cooperatives, the workers put up the capital; in consumer cooperatives it is the consumers. Apart from farm marketing cooperatives, producer cooperatives have not proved successful unless some outside individuals or some outside organization, such as a consumer cooperative, helps substantially in providing capital and in supervising production. In practice, workers in industry have been found to be too unwilling, or else unable, to put up and risk the amount of capital required for modern equipment. They have not always been the best judges of an efficient manager, and in spite of enthusiasm and high morale, they often have not exercised sufficient discipline over their own operations.

Consumer cooperatives have, on the other hand, proved very successful in many countries, notably Great Britain and Sweden. British cooperative organization will, in the following paragraphs, be taken as the prototype. Like other cooperatives, the consumer societies rely on no special capitalist class. In addition they have certain particular economic and organizational characteristics.

British cooperatives

The main economic characteristic of the British consumer cooperative is the payment (after provision for depreciation and a fixed interest on a limited amount of the shares held by consumer members) of a dividend on member purchases. Its main organizational characteristic is control by the consumer in place of the nonexistent capitalist. All consumers, even members who have paid only a small deposit on their shares, have the right to vote at the quarterly or half-yearly meeting. One man, one vote is the rule. The members vote for a management committee, or board of directors, which is usually unpaid. This committee appoints the paid manager and, usually meeting every week, exercises general supervision over the conduct of business. In form, the organization is thus extremely democratic. The existence of a number of autonomous retail societies of widely varying size is a further manifestation of democracy. The complete independence of the locally organized societies distinguishes the cooperatives in free enterprise and mixed economies from the communist cooperatives, which are not covered in this article.

Organization and growth. In Great Britain the retail societies formally control the two wholesale societies, English and Scottish, each of which conducts large-scale production. In appointing the wholesale societies' full-time directors, one society, one vote is not the principle, however; voting is weighted according to the value of the goods that the retail society has bought from the wholesaler.

For purposes other than trading, such as settlement of disputes or legal and financial advice, the British retail societies have formed the Cooperative Union. The final authority of the union is the annual congress, to which societies send a number of delegates roughly proportionate to their membership and which, in its discussion of policy, has been described as the focus of cooperative democracy. Most societies are affiliated with the Cooperative party, which, in 1964, had 19 members in Parliament—normally voting with the Labour party.

The opportunities for democratic control offered by cooperative constitutions are, however, not fully exercised, particularly as societies grow larger. Only a minute fraction of the members attend their retail society meetings. An inquiry in 1955 (Ostergaard 1963) revealed that only 0.5 per cent attend business meetings and only 1.65 per cent vote for the management committee. If the actual informal practice of consumer cooperatives is less democratic than its formal constitution presupposes, it is, however, more democratic in worker participation. In theory, the position of the labor employed is no different from that in capitalist enterprises. But when few consumers attend meetings, a small group of members, who are also employees, can elect workers or committeemen favorable to the workers' interests. About one-third of the places on the committees of the larger societies are now occupied by cooperative employees or former employees (Ostergaard 1963, p. 60). Democracy is also manifest in the emphasis on education in cooperative principles, particularly at the Cooperative College, in the many publications discussing all aspects of cooperatives, and in the organization of local discussion groups such as the "women's guilds."

The growth of the British consumer cooperatives is usually traced from 1844, when the Rochdale pioneers adopted the principle of dividend on purchase. During the next half century, the development was rapid, aided by the Industrial and Provident Societies Act of 1852. This act allowed the privileges of incorporation to cooperative societies, provided no individual member held more than

£200 in shares. The limit is now £1,000. When the act was amended in 1862 to permit one society to hold unlimited shares in another society, the retail societies founded the two wholesale societies. By 1900, these wholesale societies had over 12,000 workers engaged in production. Roughly the same number were employed in production by the larger retail societies together with the local federations of societies.

British consumer cooperatives continued to develop well into the twentieth century. Between 1901 and 1931, membership in the retail societies rose from 1.75 million to 6.5 million. During the same period, the total value of sales of both the retail and the wholesale societies quadrupled, while the retail price of food rose by only one and a half. By 1931, the English wholesale society owned 171 factories, employing 40,000, and the Scottish society had 56, employing 9,000. Both societies singly, or jointly, produced a wide range of goods, conducted integrated warehousing, provided shipping and business services (such as building the retail societies' premises), were involved in banking and insurance, and even owned tea and other plantations abroad.

Throughout the history of the consumer cooperatives in Great Britain, success has been greatest in Scotland and in the North. In 1939, for instance, annual cooperative retail trade per head of population was £8.8 in Scotland, £7.2 in the North, and £6.4 in the Midlands, as against £4.5 and £4.0 in the southwest and south, and this in spite of the much higher per capita income in the London area of the south.

The causes of this cooperative success must be sought in the emergence, which occurred first in Great Britain (particularly in Scotland and northern England), of an industrial and mining wage-earning proletariat. This group was cut off, in contrast to the village community, from the middle classes and developed a strong sense of class solidarity. The more intensive development of cooperation in the North, away from the "squirearchy," is some indication of this. Until the Education Act of 1902, education in England beyond the age of 13 was a rarity for working-class children, and, in the absence of opportunities for moving up any education ladder, potential leaders were lost to their class.

The British cooperatives were in fact firmly based on the same class solidarity as the British trade unions and the political labor movement. And the membership of the cooperatives had the same cautious, solid financial approach. To this fundamental condition of success of the cooperatives—

their solidarity in two senses of the word—must be added two specific economic "techniques," the attraction of the dividend on purchase and the branch store.

The first British Census of Distribution, taken in 1950, showed that retailing as a whole was operated by 403,839 organizations with 528,450 establishments, an average of 1.3 stores per organization. Among retail cooperative societies, however, some 1,000 organizations owned 27,263 establishments, an average of 27.3 stores per society.

The efficiency of the multiple stores is attested to by the present rapid increase in their sales, to be indicated shortly. The British cooperatives were first in this field, and for a considerable period they were without large rivals.

Recent stagnation. At first sight the continued progress of the British cooperative societies seems to be indicated by the further rise in their membership from 6.5 million in 1931 to almost 11 million in 1952, and almost 13 million in 1962. But sales per member have fallen, and total sales have, since 1950, remained fairly constant in volume with a definite fall relative to the sales of the multiple (chain) stores.

The British Board of Trade now publishes an index number of the value of retail sales of cooperative and other forms of retail organization. Taking sales in 1950 as 100, the cooperative index was 176 in 1962. But although higher than the corresponding general department store index of 160 and the index of 165 for independent retailers, it was much lower than the index of 239 for multiple stores and indeed lower than the general retailing index of 181 for all organizations.

A part of this relative decline is due to the relative decline in population and income of the regions where cooperation was most successful—Scotland and the North. But several more general causes are at work, and to predict the future of consumer cooperatives in Great Britain and, as we shall see, in other countries too, an analysis of these causes is essential.

Fortunately analysis can be firmly based on two very detailed inquiries into the British consumer cooperatives, which, while sponsored by the cooperatives themselves and so allowed full access to their records, were conducted by independent authorities. The first inquiry, an "examination" by Sir Alexander Carr-Saunders, Professor Robert Peers, and the author (1938), dealt with all the activities of the movement. The second inquiry was by the Co-operative Independent Commission (1958), which had Hugh Gaitskell as chairman, and which had terms of reference limited to "a survey of cooperative production and marketing." These two inquiries will be referred to as the 1938 examination and the Gaitskell report.

Up to 1938, consumer cooperatives were almost unreservedly praised by English economists. Professor Alfred Marshall served for a year as president of the Cooperative Congress, and Sidney and Beatrice Webb were enthusiastic (1921). The 1938 examination, however, was critical in several respects and foretold possible stagnation, while the Gaitskell report had to take account of some actual stagnation and foretold possible decline. Both reports tried to analyze stagnation and possible decline in terms of the cooperatives' own (1) financing, (2) management, and (3) local organization. A further internal factor (4) may be the weak incentive for growth. Both reports also stressed the external factor (5) of changes in the society that the cooperatives are trying to serve.

(1) Compared to large-scale capitalist trading, the cooperatives' investment in both fixed capital and research is low. This is partly due to fear of financial insecurity expressed, as the 1938 examination says, in such slogans as "no speculation with depositors funds" and "owe no man anything" (1938, p. 456). In consequence, the cooperatives have invested heavily in supposedly safe liquid funds, such as long-term government stock. Low fixed investment is also due to the high rates of dividend on purchases. In 1935 societies with 80 per cent of the retail trade paid dividends of between one shilling and two shillings on the pound, that is, 5 per cent to 12.5 per cent on turnover. This range is higher than the average capitalist dividends on sales turnover and meant less of the surplus was available for development.

(2) The cooperatives do not secure managers of the necessary ability and enterprise for growth under competition. This is due partly to the low scale of salaries they offer compared to their capitalist competitors and partly to the bias toward appointing persons from within the movement. The independent small retail entrepreneur was not particularly efficient, but the large British capitalist retail firms now displacing him are increasingly recruiting university graduates as future managers, while the British cooperatives still consider it undemocratic to recruit even grammar school graduates over the heads of those working their way up after leaving school at the minimum age. This view of democracy is becoming more and more damaging to efficiency because so many more university places are now available to the more intelligent children of the working class in England. Those now without degrees are likely to be unintelligent.

This was not necesarily so previous to the Education Act of 1902 but has become particularly so since the act of 1944, which increased so greatly the number of "free places" in secondary schools.

The quality of management depends not only on the principles of appointment but also on those of discharge. The British working-class tradition, reacting against ruthless capitalist practice, seldom allows the removal of cooperative managers or indeed the unseating of elected directors, however inefficient they may prove to be. "In some societies," to quote from the 1938 examination (Carr-Saunders et al., p. 87), "it seems to be assumed that the only cause which can lead to a member leaving the committee is death." Once the managers are appointed, their actions are likely to be cramped by the elected directors, who tend, because of the principle of no unseating, to be old. This cramping varies from society to society, according to the personalities of the directors, but will probably be greatest wherever the directors are paid and are on on the job full-time, as are the wholesale societies' directors.

(3) A criticism in the Gaitskell report concerned the uneconomically small scale of the nonfood sales, which is a result of the strictly local organization and control of retail societies not specializing in particular trades. The Gaitskell commission advocated (1958, p. 252) a national retail development society which would, among other activities, set up chains of specialized shops, notably in clothing and footwear, "in which the advantages of multiple shop organization are well-proved and in which local societies restricted by boundary agreements are in no position ever to attain to these advantages."

(4) Looking into deeper economic causes of the relative cooperative stagnation, it is possible that the incentives to growth are weak. When income and prestige are in the form of a profit on capital, a strong motive exists to use that capital to capacity and to spread the overhead over the maximum possible output. But if income and prestige are in the form of a margin or dividend on sales, the motive is to cut costs per unit of output (even, possibly, by doing less business) so as to increase that margin. Empirical evidence to sustain this hypothesis can be found in the comparatively low distributive costs of cooperative retailing shown in the British Census of Distribution.

Cooperative shops achieve this low cost by trying to spread the load of shoppers. Some societies even avoid heavy peak loads by closing shops on Saturday afternoons, when the load would be greatest! By this means, the cooperative shops need not keep so large a sales staff; and sales staff, not capital overhead, is the heaviest item of cost in retailing. Since market prices are charged, this policy achieves a high margin of profit on the goods actually sold, but it does not stimulate growth as directly as does the increasing of profit on capital by the sale of more and more goods.

(5) With the distinct rise in the standard of living since World War II and the wider variety of goods demanded by the working class, the cooperatives have met much enterprising competition.

In the food trades, capitalist multiple stores have paid increasing attention to the tastes of consumers. When the cooperatives were first founded, the cheap shops where the working class traded offered foodstuffs of inferior quality. The cooperatives, accordingly, stressed the "purity" of the foods they sold and produced—often to the neglect of their taste. Indeed, the 1938 inquiry organized tasting panels for identically priced foodstuffs, the makers of which could not be identified, and found a preference even among cooperative society members for a majority of capitalist food products.

Engel's law, moreover, has operated to make expenditure on foods a lower proportion of the working-class budget. The cooperatives, with their concentration on foods, do not seem to have risen to the occasion. While the British Census of Distribution for 1961 gives 14.8 per cent as the cooperatives' share of the total food trade (including as high or higher a percentage for the simpler wants, for example, around 35 per cent for milk), the cooperative share of the total dry goods trade is only 5.8 per cent (including 4.3 per cent of apparel and 4.5 per cent of furniture).

The pattern outside Great Britain

In countries other than Great Britain, consumer cooperatives started later and, judging by the percentage of membership to total population, still lag behind. In 1961, these percentages were Great Britain 24.7, Finland 23.0, Sweden 16.0, Switzerland 14.2, and Denmark 12.8. Lower down the percentage scale were France 7.1, Australia and Austria 5.8, Canada 4.7, West Germany 4.6, Italy 3.9, Argentina 1.8, and the United States 0.8. Underdeveloped countries—except Israel 6.9, Burma 3.2, Ceylon 3.0, Mauritius 2.2, and Pakistan 1.6 —all have a cooperative membership to total population below 0.7 per cent, in spite of government encouragement in many of them (Statistical Statement No. 1 in International Co-operative Alliance 1963).

In total value of cooperative retail trade, Great Britain again comes first with about four times that of Finland or of Sweden, which have the next highest trade. But if the trade per head of population is used as an index, Finland ranks first, Switzerland second, and Great Britain is bracketed third with Sweden. The most striking impression in reviewing the activities and structure of consumer cooperatives throughout the world is the similarity of the pattern of organization and achievement (although deviations appear here and there):

(1) The local retail society is the original and basic unit; federations of retail societies, and wholesale societies controlled by retail societies, follow later and undertake production. The Swedish wholesale cooperative, the Kooperativa Förbandet, which was founded in 1899, has gone further in production activity than the two British wholesale societies. Its products form a higher proportion of the sales of the retail societies, and by price reductions it has successfully fought monopolies or near-monopolies in such products as electric lamps, detergents, and rubber overshoes.

(2) The wide variation in the size of the retail societies is pervasive. The largest own a great number of branch stores and undertake production for local consumption, such as baking. The smaller societies are being amalgamated and, with the enlargement in size, difficulties are encountered in maintaining a real democracy. In Sweden, members of large societies meet by districts to elect a local committee for the supervision of shops in that district. Delegates from the local committees form the general meeting of the society.

(3) Some income is spent on education and propaganda. Journals are published and discussion groups organized. Economic activities are not confined to distribution and production but have spread into insurance and banking, on which the French societies concentrate. But the main activity remains the sale of foodstuffs and household consumables, particularly the more standard goods such as milk, margarine, flour, and bread.

(4) The proportion of cooperative society membership to the total population is increasing, but the sales per member are diminishing. The rates of dividend on purchase are becoming lower, and although a rapid growth in business occurred at first, an approach to a ceiling of 12 per cent to 15 per cent of national sales is indicated in most countries. Finland, however, has broken through this ceiling.

Comparing the relative strength of consumer cooperation in different countries, the greatest contrast is seen to occur between the old (European) developed countries where cooperatives are strong and the underdeveloped and the new developed countries, such as the United States, Canada, and Australia, where cooperatives are weak. Weakness in the underdeveloped countries is due to the consumer's lack of spendable income. A high proportion of the population is engaged in agriculture, and most of that proportion are subsistence farmers with no cash income to spend.

The weakness of consumer cooperation in the new developed countries has no such simple explanation. It is partly due to the higher standard of living, which has, as we have seen, checked cooperative progress in Great Britain, checking food consumption relative to other consumption. It is also partly due to the relative absence of the class solidarity so characteristic of nineteenth-century Great Britain. Indeed, the few consumer cooperatives that exist in the United States are largely found on university campuses, not in industrial sections. Cooperative weakness may also, perhaps, be due to the greater efficiency of capitalist retail management. Certainly the specialized chain store that has proved so successful was introduced into America under capitalist, not cooperative, auspices.

As among the old developed countries, in all of which class solidarity counts, the more classless ones, such as the Scandinavian countries and Switzerland, have an advantage because the class outlook does not preclude educated management and risk taking. In proportion to total population, Germany and Italy have a smaller number of cooperative members because of Nazi and fascist suppression in the 1930s.

Farmers' purchasing cooperatives

The cooperatives that have been discussed so far were formed by final, "household" consumers to provide for their own consumption. An important branch of the consumer cooperative movement, however, is engaged in the purchase of materials and supplies consumed in further production. In contrast to the cooperatives of producers formed to market their products, these purchasing associations are, logically, consumer cooperatives. They answer the same need for good quality commodities at reasonable prices. This need arises particularly among producers who operate on a small scale and are unable independently to buy in sufficient bulk to realize large-scale economies. Cooperatives have thus been organized among the small traders and craft industries in Germany and among fishermen, particularly in Spain (Digby 1948, pp. 76–77, 126–127). But farmers are the outstanding example of such small-scale producers, and cooperation has become firmly established in supplying requirements for agricultural production.

These requirements include not only materials such as feedstuffs for livestock and seed and fertilizer but also petroleum products for operating tractors, electrical power equipment, and various farm implements. To this list, facilities for insurance and credit might also be added.

The use of cooperatives for obtaining these supplies varies among countries, largely because of different economic and technological circumstances. The cooperative provision of the mainly imported feedstuffs is important in Great Britain, and the provision of electrical power is important in the rural areas of the United States. The methods of organization also vary from country to country. In Great Britain, large purchases are made from the powerful consumers' wholesale societies already mentioned. In Sweden and Norway, the supply associations have their own wholesale organizations. Sometimes, as in Denmark, the cooperatives' supply organizations specialize in one commodity, such as feeds or fertilizers; sometimes, as in Finland, the organization does a general trade, both in farmers' supplies and household goods.

Beyond the main function of these various institutions—the function of supplying "reliable goods at reasonable prices"—Margaret Digby points out (1948, p. 95) that the farmers' societies "raise the standard of farming by keeping in touch, in a way which is sometimes impossible for the individual farmer, with developments in agricultural science and technology, and transmitting them to him by means of the improved seeds, chemicals and implements which it is able to put at his disposal."

In the underdeveloped countries where primitive small-scale agriculture is the rule, supply societies should thus play a large role and are, in fact, substantially helping development. However, because of the almost universal shortage of enterprise and saving and the rate of population increase in these countries, considerable government subsidies have been required in order for the cooperatives to provide land, capital, organizers, and expert technicians adequate for economic growth.

P. SARGANT FLORENCE

[See also AGRICULTURE, article on MARKETING; CREDIT. Other relevant material may be found in the biography of OWEN.]

BIBLIOGRAPHY

BAILEY, JACK 1955 *The British Co-operative Movement.* London: Hutchinson's University Library.

CARR-SAUNDERS, ALEXANDER M.; FLORENCE, P. S.; and PEERS, R. 1938 *Consumers' Co-operation in Great Britain: An Examination of the British Co-operative Movement.* London: Allen & Unwin.

CO-OPERATIVE INDEPENDENT COMMISSION (GREAT BRITAIN) 1958 *Report.* Manchester Co-operative Union. → Known as the Gaitskell Commission report.

DIGBY, MARGARET 1948 *The World Co-operative Movement.* London: Hutchinson's University Library.

FAY, CHARLES R. (1908) 1948 *Co-operation at Home and Abroad: A Description and Analysis.* 2 vols. New ed. New York and London: Staples.

HOUGH, JOHN A. 1945 Cooperative Retailing: 1914–1945. Unpublished manuscript, International Co-operative Alliance (London).

INTERNATIONAL CO-OPERATIVE ALLIANCE 1963 Reports and Statistics. Unpublished reports of the Alliance (London).

OSTERGAARD, GEOFFREY 1963 Democratic Control in British Retail Co-operatives. *Applied Economic Papers* (Hyderabad, India) 3:55–65.

STEPHENSON, THOMAS E. 1963 *Management in Co-operative Societies.* London: Heinemann.

WEBB, SIDNEY; and WEBB, BEATRICE 1921 *The Consumers' Co-operative Movement.* London and New York: Longmans.

WOOLF, LEONARD 1918 *Co-operation and the Future of Industry.* London: Allen & Unwin.

CORPORATION

The corporation, the central economic institution of modern society, is, in its most general definition, an association of individuals united for a common purpose and acting in a common name. With this definition, it is an institution of unknown antiquity. Certainly corporations organized for business and other purposes were well known to the Romans, but there is evidence that such institutions, intermediate between the individual and the state, are much older than this. Other characteristics that particularize the corporation as we know it have been present or absent throughout history, depending on the purposes of the association, the character of institutional innovation, and the permissiveness of the state.

Early history

The law is prone to emphasize that the corporation is a body chartered or recognized by the state; that it is a formal agreement, in the nature of a contract, among people joined in a common purpose; that it can hold property, contract, and sue and be sued in a common name; and that it has a length of life not subject to the lives of its members. These formal attributes, however, tend to compress the corporation as a historical and developing institution into too narrow a mold. Roman corporations were not chartered by the state before the third century A.D., and in seventeenth-century England there were many associations doing business on a joint-stock basis that were not chartered by either Crown or Parliament. Indeed, alarm at the activities of these unchartered associations was an important reason for the Bubble Act of 1720.

The significance of the agreement of the several hundred thousand stockholders of a large American corporation and the commonness of their purpose is a matter of some doubt. The holding of property, contracting, and suing in a common name are highly significant attributes of the business corporation; but they may have little importance to an association incorporated for the improvement of the breed of Airedales. Even a life beyond the lives of its members is not a necessary attribute of the corporation as a historical entity.

Likewise, most of the elements that are emphasized as essential attributes of the modern business corporation are the product of social invention and have not been characteristic of business corporations from their beginning. Roman business corporations traded on a joint stock; but prior to the development of double-entry bookkeeping in the Italian city-states, the distinction between common and individual stocks tended to be somewhat fuzzy. The early English overseas trading companies also traded on a joint stock, but normally the capital was redistributed to the stockholders at the expiration of a voyage and reconstituted only for the next. The Dutch East India Company, founded in 1602, is supposed to be the first corporation established with a permanent capital stock. The practice of issuing transferable shares developed on the Continent and was brought to England in the sixteenth century. It was, and still is, the Continental practice to issue bearer shares, a device that has not been used in Anglo-Saxon jurisdictions. Limitation of the liability of stockholders for the debts of the corporation, characteristic of most modern business corporations, is a privilege that, on occasion, has been granted or withheld. In England it was not generally made available until 1855.

The delegation of authority to manage the corporation's daily affairs to a board of directors has developed slowly. This delegation is of no—or little —importance to the small, privately owned corporation and, in the large corporation, it has been subject to limitations that have varied considerably among countries and over time. The proliferation of participation rights in capital and income represented by different classes of securities is largely the product of American railway finance in the nineteenth century. And the various devices for assuring and perpetuating minority ownership or management control, such as voting trusts, non-voting and multiple-voting stock, pyramiding via the holding company, and use of the proxy, are largely the invention of our own epoch.

In other words, the corporation is an evolving entity, and the end of its evolution is by no means in sight. There is every reason to believe that the business corporation a century hence will be a rather different institution from the one we now behold. The relations between the corporation and the state, between management and the various participants in capital and income, and between the corporation and its suppliers, customers, and labor force are in process of change.

If we consider the long sweep of corporate history, it is useful to distinguish the typical forms and uses of the corporation before and after the industrial revolution. Although the corporation was early put to business use, in the early period it was established predominantly for other purposes. Universities, monasteries, guilds, bishoprics, boroughs, were familiar types of corporations. Typically, the emphasis was on association for a common purpose rather than for utilization of a common stock of capital. The incorporators were a group of men related to each other by the place where they lived and the things they did. In the period since the industrial revolution, the business corporation has become the overwhelmingly important form. The emphasis has come to be placed on the management of a stock of capital rather than on the cooperation of a group of individuals. In the words of one observer, the "associative elements have been refined out" of the corporation, and in law it has become the expression "of a complicated relationship between men and things."

In England the corporation was known as early as the Norman period; and from the fourteenth century on, incorporation by the Crown of boroughs, guilds, and ecclesiastical bodies was used as both an administrative device and a method of extending royal power against the baronage. Insofar as business activities were involved, the emphasis was not on a common stock, but rather on the regulation of the affairs of a group of craftsmen or tradesmen, each operating with his own capital. To this end the incorporated guilds developed effective internal legislative, judicial, and executive instrumentalities. More often than not, a functional or territorial monopoly was claimed for its membership.

The use of the corporation as both a business device and an arm of the state is clearly evidenced in the operations of the large overseas trading and colonizing companies of the sixteenth and seventeenth centuries. The British East India Company, the Levant Company, and others were as much governments as they were business enterprises. The American colonies were established by char-

tered corporations that governed as well as traded in their respective areas. Here again a grant of monopoly privileges was a common feature of incorporation. The colonists had every reason, from their experience, to associate monopoly with incorporation; and this view continued to influence American attitudes toward the corporation until well into the nineteenth century.

This customary relation between monopoly privilege and incorporation contributed in a major way to making the right of incorporation one of the issues in the struggle between Crown and Parliament in the seventeenth century. Parliament first sought the right to confirm such grants and later the independent power to grant charters. During the eighteenth century, corporations were chartered by both the Crown and Parliament; this issue was not finally settled until the enactment of general incorporation laws in the nineteenth century.

If we consider the transition from the older business or nonbusiness corporation to the modern, predominantly business corporation to be principally a shift from the emphasis on association, with all the problems of governance of men in association for a common purpose, to an emphasis on the administration of a joint stock of capital for profit, it is probable that the British joint-stock company is the closest forerunner of the modern business corporation. Before the industrial revolution, the sole proprietorship and partnership were overwhelmingly the most important types of business organization, both in numbers and in assets owned and controlled. But the seventeenth century witnessed an increasing number of business associations, both incorporated and unincorporated, trading on a common stock and acting in a common name. Participation in a joint stock recommended itself particularly as a device for spreading the risk in hazardous overseas trading operations. Before the end of the seventeenth century, many joint-stock companies had been formed in England for domestic operations as well.

Early in the eighteenth century, in both England and France, the formation of such companies assumed boom proportions. The two companies that achieved particular prominence in the ensuing debacle, the South Sea Company in England and John Law's Compagnie de la Louisiane ou d'Occident in France, were both chartered—the South Sea Company in 1711 and John Law's company in 1717. But in England, at least, many of the joint-stock companies that fell into disrepute were not chartered. The Bubble Act of 1720 struck directly at these unchartered companies, but its effects seriously inhibited the formation of chartered companies as well. This piece of legislation described itself as "An Act to Restrain the Extravagant and Unwarrantable Practice of Raising Money by Voluntary Subscriptions for Carrying on Projects Dangerous to the Trade and Subjects of this Kingdom." It prohibited:

the acting or presuming to act as a corporate Body or Bodies, the raising or pretending to raise transferable Stock or Stocks, the transferring or pretending to transfer or assign any Share or Shares in Such Stock or Stocks without Legal Authority either by Act of Parliament or by any charter from the Crown to warrant such acting as a Body Corporate. . . . (quoted in Davis [1905] 1961, pp. iii–iv)

Although the Bubble Act left the door open for duly chartered corporations, very few business corporations were in fact chartered. During the eighteenth century the corporation was in eclipse. It was not that businessmen ceased to understand the merits of the corporation as a business form. Applications for the privilege of incorporation during the eighteenth century continued to stress the advantages of the holding of property in a common name; the legal right to contract, sue, and be sued; the effective delegation of power to a directorate; life extending beyond the lives of members; and limited liability. But the sentiments aroused by the crash of 1720 were deep and long-lasting. Adam Smith, writing on the eve of the industrial revolution, expressed these sentiments firmly. In his view, the joint-stock company, without monopoly privileges, was likely to be a successful enterprise only in conducting such routine operations as banking and insurance, or the management of canals and urban water systems.

Such enterprises usually required more capital than could be provided by a sole proprietor or a partnership. With the advent of the industrial revolution, the number of business opportunities that could be effectively exploited only by sizable amounts of capital increased rapidly. The joint-stock company was frequently the most effective way of assembling the required quantities of capital, and the management of such companies rather quickly demonstrated that the effectiveness of this type of business enterprise was not, in fact, limited to routine operations. With the industrial revolution the business corporation came into its own. Its subsequent development falls roughly into two periods. The first saw the spread of free incorporation under permissive general laws. The second has witnessed the growth of the large, multiplant corporation, frequently through the amalgamation of small local and regional concerns.

Nineteenth-century growth

France took the leadership in liberalizing corporation laws. The Code de Commerce of 1807 recognized three classes of business associations, of which one—the *société anonyme*—was the business corporation with transferable shares. The formation of such companies required special government authorization until the law of 1867, which permitted corporations to be formed on the basis of public registration. In England the Bubble Act was repealed in 1825, but incorporation continued to be permitted only by special grant until 1844. Limited liability was not granted as a matter of course until 1855. In Germany freedom of incorporation was not established until 1870.

The terms used to characterize the business corporation in different countries emphasize different aspects of the institution. The German *Gesellschaft mit beschränkter Haftung* stresses limited liability. The French *société anonyme* suggests the juristic as against the real person—a "person" whose life is independent of the lives of the incorporators. The British "limited joint-stock company" emphasizes the common capital, with participating rights and limited obligations. The American "corporation" refers back to the older meaning of an association of individuals united for a common purpose.

In the American colonies the only business corporations important enough to justify the investment in royal charters were the colonies themselves. And the extension to the colonies of the principles of the Bubble Act in 1741 effectively precluded the formation of unincorporated joint-stock companies. Thus, the United States came into being with a population highly suspicious of the business corporation as an instrument of royal prerogative and royal favor. It was not long, however, before the business corporation was domesticated to the American environment. The state legislatures, conceived as heirs to the sovereign power, took it upon themselves to grant charters, and a sizable number of businesses were incorporated before the constitution was ratified. Despite the fact that a power of the federal government to incorporate was deliberately omitted from the constitution, Congress chartered a corporation as early as 1791; the Supreme Court, in *McCulloch* v. *Maryland*, ratified this use of power. Federal incorporation, however, has been relatively rare; and corporate policy very early in the nineteenth century became a prerogative of the several states.

Some 335 businesses had been incorporated in the United States by 1800, mainly banks, insurance companies, and canal, turnpike, and bridge companies. Although special charters were required, these were readily granted for almost any business purpose; in 1811 New York enacted the first law permitting extensive self-incorporation. This act covered the principal areas of domestic manufacture and permitted the self-incorporation of companies with an authorized capital of less than $100,000. Larger companies required special charters, and such charters continued to be sought even by a number of small companies. The Connecticut Act of 1837 was still more general, and before the beginning of the Civil War a dozen states had enacted general incorporation laws. Most of these states, however, still left the way open for special charters. In fact, the general laws tended to be relatively restrictive and limited to smaller companies. Larger companies frequently attained a substantially greater freedom of action by special legislative enactment.

Competition among the states for the business of incorporating led, after the Civil War, to a rather rapid relaxation of legislatively imposed limitations. This movement was favored by a business environment in which incorporation came to be regarded as a "right" rather than a "privilege"; a "right" that was conceived to be an essential element of the doctrine of individual liberty. The New Jersey Act of 1875, which was highly permissive, was perhaps the first of the modern incorporation laws; it was followed over the next two decades by similar laws in other states. This process led to a substantially more lax regulation of business corporations than characterized the company law of most European countries.

The modern corporation

The large majority of business corporations formed in any economically advanced country are hardly to be distinguished from other types of business organization. They normally enjoy limited liability and a different tax status, but in essential respects function like other small firms. Economic theory has tended to see entrepreneurial activity as unaffected by the particular organizational form with which it happens to be clothed. But while the small, private corporation may be economically— and in other respects—undistinguishable from other types of firms, this is clearly not true of the large, quasi-public corporation. The large firm, because of its capital requirements, is almost inevitably a corporation; most of the problems commonly associated with corporate activity are problems of size and dispersion of ownership. The

small, private corporation and the large, quasi-public corporation as legal persons may be equal in the eyes of the law, but they are so in no other respect.

The business area in which capital requirements first demanded the large corporate organization was railway transportation. Since individual fortunes were quite inadequate to meet these financial requirements, means were sought to enlist the savings of both public bodies and small private contributors. American railways were typically undercapitalized, and, in search of funds to meet underestimated financial requirements, a long series of financial instruments was devised. Preferred stock was issued first in 1830, when the Baltimore and Ohio ran out of funds and appealed to the Maryland legislature. The state sought to protect itself by asserting a first claim on earnings. Early preferred stock was cumulative, participating, voting, and temporary. All these characteristics were later varied and combined in different relationships. Debt financing was typical from the beginning of the railway era; and a wide variety of forms, sound and unsound, was evolved during the century. This variety of financing techniques developed by the railways became available to the growing industrial corporations after the Civil War. Still, as late as 1900, three-quarters of the corporations whose securities were listed on the New York Stock Exchange were railways.

The wide variety of financial instruments in common use created a similar variety in the participation rights of various types of security holders to capital and earnings. In theory, participants, at least in equity, were all bound together in a common interest and all working toward a common end. In fact, their interests and purposes tended to differ substantially. With this proliferation of securities, management acquired powers to apportion earnings and assets among various participants that were in addition to and distinctly different from older powers to manage the enterprise. Corporate law has slowly taken cognizance of this difference and, to prevent or limit the possibilities of exploitation inherent in the ability to influence participation rights in earnings and assets, has been developing the doctrine that all such powers have been granted only in trust, to be used equitably among the participants.

The great merger movement of 1897–1903 created in the industrial area corporations of a size that had formerly been by and large limited to the field of railway transportation. It was during this period that the big "twos," "threes," and "fours" characteristic of so many American industries were largely established. These large manufacturing and mining corporations, together with the older railway enterprises and the rapidly growing corporations in the newer utilities, were organizations substantially different from private businesses incorporated for tax reasons or to secure the advantages of limited liability. Their market position, absolute size, and internal organization created a set of problems essentially unknown to the world of the early nineteenth-century, family-type corporation. [See MERGERS.]

Typically, these large corporations possess assets of $250 million or more, employ 5,000 or more workers, count their stockholders in thousands or hundreds of thousands, account for a relatively large share of output in their respective industries, and operate establishments in a number of different locations. A relatively small number of such corporations account for a large percentage of the economic activity in manufacturing, transportation and utilities, mining, banking and insurance, and in certain branches of commerce. A recent compilation of corporate income tax returns revealed 525,000 active nonfinancial corporations in the United States with assets of $413,000 million. The 202 largest of these, all with assets of $250 million or more, owned 40 per cent of total corporate assets.

This is not a recent development in the United States, nor is it limited to the United States. Although the evidence is far from complete, it suggests no significant increase during the last four or five decades in the share of business activity (by various measures) accounted for by the largest corporations in the areas of manufacturing, mining, and public utilities. Such increase in concentration as has occurred in the economy as a whole during this period is mainly to be attributed to the decline in the relative importance of agriculture, a typically small-enterprise sector. And with the relative growth of service industries, it is possible that concentration in the economy as a whole may even decrease. Recent studies in Canada, Britain, and western Europe suggest a degree of concentration that, by certain measures, is higher than in the United States. The large corporations in the United States are much larger than elsewhere, but so also is the economy.

Nevertheless, the facts indicate a situation in which a few very large corporations account for a high percentage of business activity in a number of important sectors. And there is, moreover, a high correlation between absolute size and relative size within the different sectors and the industries constituting the manufacturing sector. The "twos," "threes," and "fours" in most industries tend also to be very large corporations. It is the relation between relative and absolute size that occasions most of the concern for what is commonly called "the problem of the large corporation." [See ECONOMIES OF SCALE; INDUSTRIAL CONCENTRATION.]

The controversy

A high degree of concentration in a particular industry, i.e., a measure of relative size, is commonly supposed to indicate a substantial degree of monopoly power. The difficulties, however, of assessing the "degree of monopoly" are so formidable that it is doubtful whether this is a useful concept. An industry, however defined, inevitably differs so substantially from a market, within which it is appropriate to discuss the relations of monopoly and competition, that the one substitutes only very imperfectly for the other. Products of one industry compete with products from another, and firms in one industry are sheltered by transport costs from the competition of other firms in the same industry. It may be possible through the study of the structure of particular industries and of the behavior of firms within this structure to come to a more or less objective judgment that the area of choice or scope of decision making of large firms is significantly greater than that of small firms or of firms whose behavior is compatible with the competitive model, but this is about as far as agreement among different students of the problem can be pushed. [See the articles MARKETS AND INDUSTRIES; MONOPOLY.]

The area of choice or scope of action open to the large corporation has a good deal to do with the significance of the "corporate problem." If large corporations were as circumscribed in their behavior as firms operating within the context of the competitive model, most of the aspects of this problem, as elaborated in the literature of the subject, would tend to disappear. In an atomistically competitive environment, firms—whether incorporated or not—have no alternative but to buy and sell at established market prices; and a failure to maximize profits is tantamount to a failure of the firm. Under these circumstances, the legal characteristics or the internal organization of the firm is irrelevant to its behavior. Economic analysis has, in fact, tended to neglect questions of internal organization and to assume that entrepreneurial behavior is unaffected by the absolute size of firms. There is reason to believe that the

95 per cent of American corporations employing fewer than 20 workers do indeed behave much as do small proprietorships and partnerships. Insofar, however, as large corporations are able to escape from competitive market restraints, they command an area of decision making within which behavior may be significantly affected by absolute size and the character of their internal organization. [*See* COMPETITION.]

The aspects of size and internal organization most often stressed in the literature on the large corporation are the separation of ownership from control, the growth of a managerial class with motivations allegedly different from those of the classical nineteenth-century entrepreneur, and a changing relationship of the corporation to government and to the local community. The separation of ownership from control is alleged to be producing, on the one hand, a change in the meaning and significance to be attached to private property and, on the other, a group of manager–controllers no longer owing exclusive responsibility to owners but also to other groups, such as suppliers, workers, and customers, who are attached in one way or another to the corporation. The management groups in large corporations are said to be self-selected and their activities to have the customary bureaucratic characteristics: hierarchical organization, professionalization of function, formality of recruitment and promotion procedures, and a proliferation of written rules, orders, and record keeping. The changing relation of the large corporation to government is described by some as an increasing vulnerability of size to public opinion and governmental action or threats of action, and by others as increasing opportunity for manipulation of public policies by large business as a "system of power." The changing relation to the local community is supposedly the product of multiestablishment corporations whose local installations are run by hired managers with only tenuous roots in the community. Obviously, some of these assertions are more speculative than others.

Separation of ownership and control. An increasing separation of ownership from control of the large corporation was clearly portrayed in the classic study of Berle and Means, *The Modern Corporation and Private Property* (1932). Nothing has appeared since then to deny this thesis, and much to confirm it. Very few among the largest corporations in the United States could be correctly described as majority-controlled. A larger number are controlled by discernible minority interests but, under the influence of estate duties, this group is declining relatively. A still larger number can only be described as management-controlled, and this number is increasing. The dominant influence at work, of course, is the increasing percentage of equity holdings in the hands of those concerned with returns rather than control. Management control has been assisted by such devices as voting trusts, nonvoting and multiple-voting stock, and pyramiding; but the trend to management control would exist without these devices. Nor has the securities legislation of the 1930s in the United States, which sought to support "shareholders' democracy" by regulating the system of proxy voting, had significant effect on this trend.

Much less clear, however, are the effects, if any, on the controllers and on the owners of the separation of ownership from control. Wide dispersion of shareholdings has accentuated certain characteristics of corporate ownership that have been there from the beginning. The shareholder of today has typically become a *rentier* concerned only with dividends and capital gains, but this is implicit in an organization that puts many capitals together to form a joint stock. In Berle's words, "The capital is there, and so is capitalism. The waning factor is the capitalist" (1954, p. 39). The capitalist as owner–manager of a local grist mill or corner garage is indeed hard to discover in the owner of 100 shares of Standard Oil. Eighteenth-century justifications of private property become somewhat obsolete in this context. But whether the stock-and-bond owner of the twentieth century is any less devoted to the institution of private property than the "full-blooded capitalist" of the nineteenth century is not obvious.

Nor is it clear to what extent the separation of ownership from control has affected the behavior of the firm. Managements of large firms typically and increasingly recruit their own replacements, taking account frequently of the interests of large lenders, investors, and possibly suppliers and customers; but without consulting the amorphous mass that represents majority stockholdings. This procedure of self-recruitment and self-replacement of management, together with a certain vagueness as to whom management owes responsibility, does raise questions concerning the "legitimacy" of managerial power. But it does not follow that this power, whether legitimate or not, is used very differently than it would be if it were in the hands of owners. There is considerable evidence that, with respect to policies affecting dividends, retention of earnings, and relative reliance on outside financing, separation of ownership from control has not had much influence. In other areas the supposed influence is rather speculative. Furthermore, there are influences other than the separation of ownership from control that impinge on the behavior of the large corporation.

Role of size. Absolute size, particularly if measured in terms of numbers of employees, regardless of the location of ultimate control, creates a managerial problem for which bureaucracy is the only answer. Major decisions tend to be group decisions in which the divergent interests of separate functional or area divisions of the corporation are represented by established suborganizations with procedures and expectations of their own. Authority that would be centralized in a small firm is delegated, but within the limits necessary to the maintenance of cohesion in the organization as a unit. The major as well as the minor decision makers are hired employees whose principal remuneration is by salary and whose expectation of economic improvement is through advancement in the hierarchy.

Insofar as absolute size is correlated with size in relation to the markets in which the corporation purchases inputs and disposes of output, the possibility exists of escape from the profit-maximizing behavior necessary to the continued existence of the competitive form. This is true whether the corporation is owner-controlled or management-controlled. But whether a management-controlled firm is more prone to take one or another course of action alternative to profit maximization than an owner-controlled firm is not clear.

The large corporation is likely to be confronted, on both the buying side and the selling side of the market, with units that are also large and well organized. In the capital market it confronts large banks, insurance companies, and other institutional investors well able to look after their own interests as capital suppliers. In the labor market it typically deals with large trade unions. The distribution of its product is frequently through dealers who are well organized and often protected by antidiscriminatory legislation. Finally, the large corporation acts within a political and social environment in which its size and conspicuousness make it a legitimate object of political inquiry and of public interest.

The large corporation is, then, typically management controlled; it is bureaucratically organized; it is usually able to escape to some degree from the competitive restraints that would compel action within a narrow range of alternatives; it is frequently confronted on the buying and selling sides

of the market with large and well-organized units or groups; and it operates in a political and social environment in which its size makes it conspicuous. How these various characteristics act and react on each other and what influence, in concert, they have on the behavior of the large corporation is a subject on which there exists a large body of literature but little hard evidence. There does seem, however, to be substantial agreement that the "managerial capitalism" of the twentieth century is a different entity from the "classical capitalism" of the nineteenth and that the emergence of the large, multiproduct corporation, with widely dispersed shareholding, lies at the heart of the difference.

Profit maximization. There is strong emphasis in the literature of managerial capitalism on the proposition that profit maximization, as it was understood in the nineteenth-century context, does not now govern the behavior of the large corporation. By some this is interpreted to mean that long-run considerations rather than considerations of immediate gain are determining. Some hold that there are groups in addition to the owners whose interests are considered in the distribution of the gross proceeds of the corporation. Still others maintain that in a management-controlled corporation there are managerial preferences, running counter to profit maximization and concerned with the security and continued growth of the firm, that significantly influence corporate behavior. It must be said that whether corporations do or do not maximize long-run profits is not a proposition subject to statistical demonstration. Profit maximization can be precisely defined only in a static context with known cost and revenue functions. Any demonstration that corporations do not follow profit-maximizing procedures must produce weighty evidence of behavior clearly incompatible with any plausible concept of profit maximization.

That large corporations shape their price, output, and other policies with a relatively long time horizon in view does not require demonstration. But such behavior is not limited to large firms, nor is it dependent on particular forms of business organization. It is, rather, technologically determined and is dependent on the length of life of various inputs and on the possibility of cultivating persistent customer attachment.

Assertions that management is no longer exclusively responsible to ownership but owes obligations to labor, suppliers, customers, and others abound in writing on corporate management. But a distinction must be drawn between changes in the environment external to the corporation, to which management may react in ways that are compatible with sensible conceptions of profit maximization, and internal changes in corporate organization, creating obligations to interests other than ownership and incompatible with any principle of profit maximization. The twentieth-century corporation confronts an external politico–economic environment substantially different from that of its nineteenth-century counterpart. It would be strange if profit-maximizing behavior did not adapt itself to this environment. Increased emphasis on institutional advertising, expenditures devoted to improving the "corporate image," grants for university scholarships, contributions to local community chests, the lending of executive personnel to various types of government service, are all evidence of an adaptive reaction to the changed environment within which the corporation operates; but they are not necessarily evidence of departure from profit maximizing.

Somewhat more persuasive is the argument that, in managerially controlled corporations in which the principal decision makers are not profit receivers, managerial preferences are likely to run counter to sensible interpretations of profit maximization. The obligations that management recognizes are not so much to various interest groups as to itself. Management compensation tends to be highly correlated with the size of the firm. So likewise are power, prestige, and status. It is suggested, therefore, that management's concern is centrally with the growth of the enterprise at rates and in ways that do not endanger the continued viability of the firm or the position of the existing officeholders. This may or may not be compatible with a sensible interpretation of profit maximization. There is a certain plausibiilty to, and some evidence for, this proposition. It would be rather strange if the relaxation from immediate competitive pressures attendant on relative size, the administrative changes attendant on absolute size, and the expansion of managerial control had not had some significant influence on managerial preferences. Nevertheless, it must be said that these suggestions have not as yet been shaped into a clear and persuasive account of managerial motivation and behavior.

EDWARD S. MASON

BIBLIOGRAPHY

ANSHEN, MELVIN L.; and BACH, G. L. (editors) 1960 *Management and Corporations, 1985.* New York: McGraw-Hill.

BARNARD, CHESTER I. (1938) 1962 *The Functions of the Executive.* Cambridge, Mass.: Harvard Univ. Press.

BAUMOL, WILLIAM J. 1959 *Business Behavior, Value and Growth.* New York: Macmillan.

BERLE, ADOLF A. JR. 1954 *The Twentieth Century Capitalist Revolution.* New York: Harcourt.

BERLE, ADOLF A. JR.; and MEANS, G. C. 1932 *The Modern Corporation and Private Property.* Chicago: Commerce Clearing House.

COHN, GEORG 1921 *Die Aktiengesellschaft.* Edited by Frederick Fick and Richard Zehntbauer. Zurich: Füssli. → Published posthumously.

DAVIS, JOHN P. (1905) 1961 *Corporations: A Study of the Origin and Development of Great Business Combinations and Their Relation to the Authority of the State.* 2 vols. New York: Putnam.

DAVIS, JOSEPH S. 1917 *Essays in the Earlier History of American Corporations.* 2 vols. Harvard Economic Studies, Vol. 16. Cambridge, Mass.: Harvard Univ. Press.

DODD, E. MERRICK JR. 1954 *American Business Corporations Until 1860: With Special Reference to Massachusetts.* Cambridge, Mass.: Harvard Univ. Press.

DODD, E. MERRICK JR.; and BAKER, R. J. (1940) 1951 *Cases and Materials on Corporations.* 2d ed. New York: Foundation Press. → First published as Volume 1 of the authors' *Cases on Business Associations: Corporations.*

DRUCKER, PETER F. 1946 *Concept of the Corporation.* New York: Day.

DU BOIS, ARMAND B. 1938 *The English Business Company After the Bubble Act, 1720–1800.* New York: Commonwealth Fund; Oxford Univ. Press.

FLORENCE, P. SARGANT 1953 *The Logic of British and American Industry: A Realistic Analysis of Economic Structure and Government.* London: Routledge.

GORDON, ROBERT A. 1945 *Business Leadership in the Large Corporation.* Washington: Brookings Institution. → A paperback edition was published in 1961 by the Univ. of California Press.

GOSSETT, WILLIAM T. 1957 *Corporate Citizenship.* Lexington, Va.: Washington and Lee Univ.

HUNT, BISHOP C. 1936 *The Development of the Business Corporation in England; 1800–1867.* Harvard Economic Studies, Vol. 52. Cambridge, Mass.: Harvard Univ. Press.

KAYSEN, CARL 1957 The Social Significance of the Modern Corporation. *American Economic Review, Papers and Proceedings* 47:311–319.

MARRIS, ROBIN L. 1963 A Model of the Managerial Enterprise. *Quarterly Journal of Economics* 77:185–209.

MASON, EDWARD S. 1958 The Apologetics of "Managerialism." *Journal of Business* 31:1–11.

MASON, EDWARD S. (editor) 1960 *The Corporation in Modern Society.* Cambridge, Mass.: Harvard Univ. Press.

PENROSE, EDITH T. 1959 *The Theory of the Growth of the Firm.* New York: Wiley.

RADIN, MAX 1910 *Legislation of the Greeks and Romans on Corporations.* New York: Tuttle.

ROUSSEAU, RODOLPHE (1878) 1912 *Des sociétés commerciales françaises et étrangères.* 2 vols. 4th ed., rev. & enl. Paris: A. Rousseau.

SCOTT, WILLIAM R. 1912 *The Constitution and Finance of English, Scottish and Irish Joint-stock Companies to 1720.* 3 vols. New York and London: Macmillan.

WARNER, W. LLOYD 1962 *The Corporation in the Emergent American Society.* New York: Harper.

CORPORATISM
See FASCISM.

CORRECTIONAL INSTITUTIONS
See PENOLOGY *and the biographies of* BECCARIA *and* BENTHAM.

CORRELATION
See under MULTIVARIATE ANALYSIS; *see also* STATISTICS, DESCRIPTIVE, *article on* ASSOCIATION.

COST

In economics, the cost of an event is the highest-valued opportunity necessarily forsaken. The usefulness of the concept of cost is a logical implication of choice among available options. Only if no alternatives were possible or if amounts of all resources were available beyond everyone's desires, so that all goods were free, would the concepts of cost and of choice be irrelevant. If choices are made on anything other than a random, purposeless basis, a criterion of choice is implied. Whatever the criterion, the chosen option will involve a loss of the highest-valued forsaken option. This implies that only if one chooses actions so as to maximize the value realized will cost be covered.

Failure to appreciate the purpose of the concept of cost can lead to confusing the concept of cost with the undesirable attributes of some event. For example, when one builds a swimming pool, the toil and trouble of digging it and the nuisance of noisy, disobedient neighborhood children and uninvited guests who use it are undesirable attributes of the pool. They are not the costs of creating and having a pool. This distinction between (*a*) undesirable attributes inherent in some event and (*b*) the highest-valued forsaken option necessary to realize that event is fundamental, for only the latter is cost as the term is used in economics.

We can illustrate. The construction and possession of the pool involve an amalgam of undesirable and desirable attributes. But if, in some sense, the desirable exceed the undesirable, it does not follow that one would choose to have the pool. One might choose something else instead, say having an extra car, and that too would involve desirable and undesirable attributes. The decision maker must choose among events that are amalgams of "goods and bads." He cannot choose all events whose desirable features more than offset their undesirable ones, given the limited resources at his disposal. A comparison among all the *available* options (each consisting of an amalgam of good and bad) yields for each option a rank-indicating measure of value. The cost of one amalgam is the best of the forsaken amalgams. It is not necessary that for each event the good and bad attributes be separated and that there be assigned a measure of the undesirable attributes and also a measure of the desirable. Such a procedure would indicate only that many events are desirable on net, and a criterion of choice among these would still be needed.

We can illustrate with the person deciding whether or not to have a swimming pool. He determines that the "good" consequences of a pool are worth what we shall call "100 units," while the "bad" are equivalent to the loss of "70 units." The best alternative to having a pool is, let us say, to take action "A," with "good" attributes valued at 50 and "bads" valued at a loss of 10. The pool has a net value of 30, while event A is worth 40. The cost of the pool is 40 (not 70), while the cost of A is 30 (not 10). What is lost if the pool is selected is the 40 units of value otherwise available by opting for A.

The temptation to think that because events are *valued* by comparing the good attributes with the bad, cost must be the bad attributes is encouraged by business usage. Businessmen weigh revenues (as good consequences) against expenses or costs. Considering these costs as the bad attributes overlooks the distinction between *valuation* and *costing*. The *value* of a given event is obtained by weighing its good and bad consequences against each other—if one wants to think in terms of good and bad rather than less or more desirable—but the *cost* of that event is still not revealed. The highest-valued forsaken option must still be ascertained in order to determine the cost. Even in the businessman's calculation, what his cost really measures, as shown below, is not the bad consequences of an action but the highest-valued forsaken opportunity.

It is sometimes fallaciously thought that if building a pool involved even more pain or other undesirable consequences, its costs surely must be higher. But the costs of the pool are not higher unless the best alternative is affected. More pain in building a pool may or may not affect my alternative opportunities. If an extra hour of work is involved, then my alternatives are changed because I lose another hour of other desirable uses. The definition of cost does not deny that the pain and time and trouble of producing some event are influential in the measure of cost. But it does show that these aspects enter into costs only by affecting the value of the best forsaken opportunities.

This can be seen more clearly if we consider the

following situation in which the alternatives are not affected. Suppose that in building the pool, the pain to be suffered during a given time was to be more intense—but not longer-lived. In this case, the increase in intensity of pain (assuming that recovery is immediate upon the cessation of the work) does not affect the alternative opportunities. These stay the same. What this more intense pain does is *reduce the value of the pool, not raise its cost.*

Another example of an increase in undesirable attribute that does not increase costs is one that increases that attribute uniformly for *all* opportunities. In this case, the feature cannot be avoided no matter what one does. A uniform reduction in the value of all options reflects the lower level of "utility" now generally available. One could even call this effect a *decrease* in costs—since the best-valued options are now lower valued. The costs are lower because the values are lower, for that is what cost reflects.

Clarification of the logical role of the concept of cost in order to explicate clearly the distinction between the two ideas—the value of forsaken alternatives and the so-called undesirable attributes —was begun by the Austrian school of economics in the nineteenth century and was further developed by Frank Knight (1924). [See ECONOMIC THOUGHT.]

Money costs in a society.   The preceding is relatively unambiguous for choices or selections of options in a one-person world. But in a society, selection among options involves not only different options for the same person but also different options available to different people. Therefore an interpersonal value measure is necessary. A society in which choices are made in accord with a single dictator's preferences resembles the one-person world. In a pluralistic (individualist) society, an interpersonal value measure can be based on interpersonal exchange rates. Voluntary market exchanges among individuals reveal the highest values of available options and, hence, their costs in terms of values of forsaken options. These market prices, to which all people can adjust their choices, provide a common measure of the value of increments of one event relative to others.

For example, a market exchange rate of 1 Coca-Cola for 2 ounces of chocolate indicates the relative value of each. The optional event—having 1 more Coke—is compared with the option of having 2 more ounces of chocolate. In an open market— one in which all people have access to all goods— the exchange rate, or price, of Cokes must at least equal the highest-valued alternatives to 1 more Coke. If the price does not equal the highest-valued alternative, those who value a Coke at more than the market exchange price will prefer, and will be able, to enter the market and offer more for a Coke. And this will raise the exchange rate to at least the highest-valued alternative. Rather than expressing the values of alternatives to 1 Coke in terms of the amounts of chocolate, beer, or other individual goods that are as much desired as 1 Coke, convenience dictates agreement on a common measure of value. Since almost all formal contractual exchanges are conducted with the medium of money, all exchange rates typically are measured in units of money—as so many dollars or cents per Coke. The use of money prices does not mean that money is all that counts, or that people love money. It means simply that money is the medium of exchange and therefore is the convenient denominator of interpersonal exchange values of events or options.

In sum, because goods are substitutable sources of utility, and because substitution is facilitated by exchange via money, it is possible to measure the value of a forsaken option in money terms. When goods can be obtained not only by interpersonal trade but also by production, at the "cost" of other things that could have been produced, the costs incurred in production choices will be related to the market prices of interpersonal exchanges if producers have access to markets in which to offer their products.

Market prices and cost.   The preceding discussion implies that cost in an exchange economy is based on market-revealed values. If some productive resources are used in ways that yield less than their highest achievable alternative, or "opportunity," values, these uses will not cover cost. The incentive to increase one's wealth induces shifts of resources to their higher-valued use until their cost is at least matched by the value of their currently yielded product. As the output of the service now being produced at a higher rate increases, the value of additional increments will fall until there is no further shifting of resources from other uses. By drawing resources from lower-valued to higher-valued uses, the value of a producible good or service influences the allocation of resources and so the rate of output of the good or service itself.

This adjustment or reallocation of resources among various uses is often expressed less rigorously. For example: (*a*) "Lower cost resources are shifted to their higher valued uses." (*b*) "If costs of production are less than potential values of output, low cost resources will be shifted to increasing the output of the higher priced goods, thus inducing a lower price of that good, until ultimately no disparity exists between costs and values of output." Both of these formulations, while explaining the shift in resource uses, are misleading in that they refer to "lower-cost" resources. The resources are not really lower-cost; rather, they are being used in lower-valued uses. It is only the lower value of their use that makes them appear to be lower-valued or lower-cost resources. Strictly speaking, the cost of the use of any resource is never less than the highest-valued opportunity for its use; it is always equal to the amount bid by the most optimistic (highest) bidders in the market for that resource.

No matter how any particular set of resources is used, the cost of their use will be the same—only the realized value of the output, or event yielded, will be affected. If resources are used in less than their most valuable ways, their cost will not be covered, and the difference will be an economic loss. This suggests the query, Is it possible for resources to yield a value in excess of their cost? The answer is "Yes," in the sense that the current market values do not reflect the future value of the resources—which depends upon unforeseen events or actions. For example, if the use of a resource is changed so as to expose a preferred result to the market, the market value of the resource will be raised. This increase in value of the resource above the former market value is initially a profit. With the unforeseen revaluation, however, costs will be revised upward. In effect, profits are capitalized by the market into costs of subsequent use of the resources.

We may digress to note that we can now interpret the principles underlying the categories "demand" and "supply" as applied to factors affecting price, allocation, and value. *Demand* reflects the value of different amounts of available resources in a particular class of use, say to produce A, while *supply* represents the value of the resources in all *other* potential uses. The demand function indicates a negative relationship between the rate at which good A is made available and the value of another unit of availability of A; the supply function indicates an increasing value of all *other* opportunities of use as more and more of them are forsaken in order to increase the amount of resources devoted to the production of A. If another unit of A has a value greater than the highest value of other necessarily forsaken options (costs on the supply function), the output of A will increase, thereby lowering its unit value and increasing the "costs" (value in *other* uses only) until the two are brought to equality.

The meaning of costs in the demand for and

supply of A refers to the value in the *second* or next best use—not in the over-all best use. As long as the value of resources in other uses is lower than in the production of good A, more resources will be shifted to A until the value of another unit of A falls to a level that is no greater than that of its component resources in the *next* best other use. At this point the transfer of resources stops and the rate of output of A will not increase further. But this supply schedule reflects costs *only* in the *other* uses; it does not reflect cost of resources in the sense of *best* opportunities for use over *all* opportunities, including A. The demand-and-supply classification is satisfactory for investigating factors that affect the output of particular goods relative to other goods, but it is not a satisfactory analytical classification for understanding the meaning of the cost concept in its wider range of application and function.

When are costs incurred?   Forsaken alternatives to a current choice are not necessarily composed only of present events. A decision to build a pool can involve a commitment to a sacrifice of future events. In general, a sacrifice of present consumption is valued more highly than the sacrifice of an equivalent future good is valued *now*. The relationship between the present value of two events, identical except in their time of availability, defines a rate of interest. [*See* INTEREST.] A rate of interest of 10 per cent per year means that a unit of good A, which would be worth $1.00 if available now, will, if it is available only a year hence, have a value *now* (referring to the time of valuation, not to the time of availability) of $.909. It follows that if an event A involves the sacrifice *both* of an alternative good available and worth $1.00 now and of a good available in one year and worth $1.00 at *that* time (but only $.909 now), the present-value cost of the compound event A is $1.909—the sum of the *present* value of the present item ($1.00) plus the *present* value ($.909) of the future item. The cost of event A is therefore the present value of the implied chain of sacrificed options, whether they are realizable now or later.

From this it is tempting to try to draw distinctions such as the following: The present event A involves costs that, although incurred now, are not experienced now. That this distinction is not meaningful can be seen by carefully considering the meaning of incurring a cost. The individual incurs a cost by choosing event A in the sense that his choice makes unavoidable the loss of some otherwise available alternatives. Even if these alternatives were otherwise realizable only far in the future, the cost is incurred now if the present choice of the event *A* eliminates these future possibilities. The cost is incurred now in the sense that the current choice of the event has meant the irretrievable loss of certain alternatives.

Although the cost is incurred now, the consumption loss can be in the future. For example, a person who buys a car now incurs a cost, but by borrowing he can shift the reduction in consumption to the future. There is no necessity for the reduced consumption to be simultaneous with the incurring of the cost. This is especially true for an individual; borrowing from other people will permit him to transfer the consumption loss to any time he wishes within the limits of the borrowing and repayment schedules available to him.

The cost of a *decision* to perform some event is not always the same as the cost of the *event*. For example, if I decide to build a swimming pool that will cost $3,000, does my making a commitment to build a pool involve the entire cost? Not if I can change my mind tomorrow. Thus, the cost of the *contracting* for a swimming pool may be only $500, in that if subsequently I change my mind, I lose only $500. If, then, the cost of the current commitment to build a pool is $500, when are the remaining $2,500 of costs incurred? They are incurred as work progresses and the successive options are irretrievably lost. In sum, the cost of the decision *and the completion* of a swimming pool is $3,000. At any moment the whole $3,000 cost may not have been incurred, and has not been incurred to the extent that one can still avoid the loss of the subsequent options included in the $3,000 that would have been lost had the work progressed to completion. What is emphasized in this paragraph is the need to avoid ambiguity in the meaning of the *events* being costed—e.g., the decision is one event and the execution of the project may be a series of subsequent events. Exactly to what event the costs apply should be made unambiguous.

Examples of measures of cost.   Principles underlying the measurement of cost as defined above are simple and will now be illustrated, but it must be emphasized that in actual practice the measurement is very imprecise in that it involves estimates of uncertain future events. We shall consider first the cost of *purchasing* (obtaining and retaining ownership of) a car, and then the cost of *using* the car. Its purchase price is $3,000. If we retain the car until it becomes worthless (and if we incur no other costs), the cost of ownership for the indefinite future is $3,000. Assume that we could sell the car immediately for $2,500. At the moment of purchase, then, we have incurred a cost of $500, the cost of acquiring ownership. If we

retain the car, we will gradually incur the remaining $2,500 of cost; however, since we can always sell the car, the cost of ownership up to any moment is not the $2,500 but only that portion which cannot be recovered by resale. If a month later we can sell the car for $2,300, the cost of acquiring and retaining ownership for one month is $500 plus $200.

Suppose now we plan to keep the car for two years and then sell it (without using it in the meantime) for $2,000. Of course, $2,000 two years hence does not have the same value as $2,000 now. At a 10 per cent rate of interest the present value of $2,000 deferred two years is $1,652. The present-capital-value measure of the cost of owning a car for two years is equal to the purchase price minus the present value of the resale price two years hence: $3,000 − $1,652 = $1,348. The decrease in the value of the car from the $3,000 purchase price to the $2,000 resale value is called *depreciation* (for expository simplicity we ignore maintenance expenditures, which are assumed to be optimal). If the reduction were greater than expected, the excess would be called *obsolescence*.

Table 1

	Beginning of year 1	Beginning of year 2	End of year 2
Purchase price	$3,000	$ —	$ —
Taxes and insurance	150	150	—
Resale value	(2,500)	(2,200)	−2,000
	$3,150	$ 150	−$2,000
10% present-value factor	(1.00)	(.909)	(.826)

Present-value cost: $1,634.35 = $3,150.00 + $136.35 − $1,652.00

Ownership of a car usually involves more than the costs of acquisition of ownership, even though the car is never to be driven. For example, there are the costs of taxes and insurance. If these total $150 yearly, to be paid at the beginning of each year, the cost of ownership for two years is reckoned as shown in Table 1.

The cost of obtaining and retaining (insured) possession for two years is $1,634.35. By rearranging the data we can express this cost as the sum of depreciation (purchase price minus resale price, adjusted to present value) plus the other ownership costs (taxes and insurance), as in Table 2.

Operating the car will involve more costs and a lower resale value, $1,700 rather than $2,000. Suppose outlays for gasoline, maintenance, and such amount to $500 in the first year and $400 in the second year. (Let these outlays be payable at the end of each year.) The costs of ownership and operation are now $2,667.05, compared with the cost of $1,634.35 for ownership only (see Table 3).

Table 2

Purchase price	$3,000	
Resale value	−1,652	(present value of $2,000 deferred two years)
Depreciation	$1,348	
Taxes and insurance	150	(first year)
Taxes and insurance	136.35	(present value of second year's payment)
Present-value cost	$1,634.35	

Events are rarely indivisible; instead, the magnitude of the event can be varied. Thus, in the automobile example, we could consider a set of alternative output programs, e.g., running the car zero miles in two years, one mile in two years, two miles in two years, etc., up to, say, 20,000 miles in two years. Suppose that for each of these we can determine the costs. The differences in costs between adjacent alternative programs is the incremental or marginal cost for the mileage increment. That is, the difference in cost between two-year programs of 19,999 miles and 20,000 miles is called the marginal cost of a mile of travel at 20,000 miles: it is the increment in cost for a 20,000-mile program over the cost for a 19,999-mile program. If we computed the cost for one mile of distance, for two miles, etc., up to 20,000 miles, we could compute a series of marginal costs at, or associated with, one mile more than no miles, one mile more than one mile, one more than two, etc. The sum of all these (including the cost of zero miles with two-year ownership) will total to the cost of ownership *and* 20,000 miles of travel. The concept of marginal cost is relevant for deciding among available programs because it tells by how much the cost of one program differs from that of adjacent available programs.

In the comparison of mileage programs we do not mean that one performs the program of, say, 10,000 miles of travel and then, *after* completing that program, asks how much one more mile would cost. Instead, initially one considers the cost of a proposed 10,000-mile program and the cost of a proposed 10,001-mile program. The difference in cost between the proposed programs is the mar-

ginal cost. (To run one more mile as the result of a last-minute decision may involve a higher extra cost than if one had planned for that extra mile from the beginning. In the extreme situation one might have to buy another car in which to do it.)

For any event there are two associated concepts of cost—total and marginal (the latter referring to a comparison between one particular event and another differing by one unit in some dimension of the event). For every alterable dimension there is a marginal cost of increments in that dimension. Two important dimensions in most output programs are the *rate* or speed of output and the total *volume* to be produced. We shall confine our subsequent discussion to changes in these rate and volume dimensions.

The present-capital-value measure of total (or of marginal) cost can be converted into a variety of other equivalent measures for expressing that cost. For example, the present capital value can be re-expressed as a *future* capital value with the future value measure (t units of time in the future) in the ratio $(1 + i)^t$ to the present value, where i is the rate of interest. Alternatively, the present capital value can be converted to a *rate* of costs over some interval. For example, a present-capital-value cost of $1,000 is, at 10 per cent per year, equivalent to a perpetual rate of cost of $100 per year, or to a rate of $263 per year for 5 years.

If the event being costed consists of a group or collection of homogeneous units, e.g., the production of pianos, or the production of miles of service from a car, or the production of bushels of wheat, the cost can be prorated or expressed as an average cost per unit of each item. In the automobile example, the event consisted of owning and driving a car 20,000 miles in two years, the cost of which was $2,667.05. This can be expressed as $2,667.05/20,000 = 13.3$ cents per mile of distance. This is the prorated amount that, if received *now* for each future mile of service, will enable the receipts to cover the cost.

Sometimes the rate at which revenues must be received in order to cover costs is measured not by dividing the capital-value measure of costs by the total volume of output, but instead by dividing an annual rate of costs by an annual rate of performance or output. For example, the present-value measure of cost in the above illustration was $2,667 (for a two-year program of 20,000 miles of travel at the rate of 10,000 miles per year). The $2,667 present value can be re-expressed as an equivalent-valued continuous-flow annuity for two

Table 3

	Beginning of year 1	Beginning of year 2	End of year 2
Purchase price	$3,000	$ —	$ —
Taxes and insurance	150	150	—
Gas, oil, and maintenance	—	500	400
Resale value	—	—	−1,700
	$3,150	$650	−$1,300
10% present-value factor	(1.00)	(.909)	(.826)

Present-value cost: $2,667.05 = $3,150.00 + $590.85 − $1,073.80

years, at 10 per cent per year compounded continuously. This steady-flow or rate measure is $1,479 per year for two years (and since there are 8,760 hours in a year, this is equivalent to $1,479 per year/8,760 hours per year = 16.9 cents per hour). The speed of service, at the rate of 10,000 miles per year for two years, is equivalent to 10,000 miles per year/8,760 hours per year = 1.14 miles per hour. If we divide one annual (or hourly) rate of costs by the other annual (or hourly) rate of service (i.e., $1,479 per year/10,000 miles per year, or 16.9 cents per hour/1.14 miles per hour), we get 14.8 cents per mile. Therefore, if costs are to be covered by revenues received concurrently with the service performed, the receipts must be 14.8 cents per mile of distance. (This differs from the earlier cost measure of 13.3 cents per mile paid at the beginning of the entire two-year program because the 14.8 cents is paid later and includes interest on the *average* delay.)

Extreme care must be taken to ensure that rates are divided by rates or that present-capital-value measures are divided by volume measures of the output. Confusion will result if rate (flow) measures of output are divided into capital-value (stock) measures of cost. That would yield cost per unit of speed of output (e.g., miles per year), not per unit of output (e.g., miles). Since outputs are usually sold or priced in units of output or volume, rather than in units of speed of service, it is more useful to consider the covering of costs by receipts per unit of volume of output rather than per unit of speed or of rate of production.

Fixed and variable costs. The preceding discussion distinguished among events being costed according to whether they involved (*a*) the ownership of some good, (*b*) the operation of that good to produce some service, or (*c*) a unit expansion of the event, giving a marginal cost. For some purposes a classification of costs may be useful. It may be relevant to know, for a chosen output program, what costs have been incurred even if we were, at some subsequent moment, to abandon the program. As was seen in the automobile example, at the moment of purchase we have incurred some loss of resale value, e.g., $3,000 − $2,500 = $500. That "cost" is "sunk" or "historical." Once we purchase the car, it cannot be escaped. It should play no role (except as a help in forecasting costs of similar future events) in any subsequent decision, for regardless of what we do, that historical "cost" has been incurred, and is inescapable and unaffected. For any ensuing decision only the escapable, or "variable," costs are relevant.

Having separated sunk or historical "costs" (which really are no longer costs) from future costs, we can proceed to classify future costs into invariant and variable costs. Suppose a person can choose among a *restricted* set of output programs but that associated with all those options there is a common set of activities or inputs, the cost of which is therefore common to each option in the subset. The cost of these common activities is sometimes called a "fixed" cost. Regardless of which option in the subset he chooses, he cannot avoid those "fixed" costs. But since the real range of options is greater, he really *can* escape that "fixed" cost by choosing an option outside that subset. Therefore that "fixed" cost is not a "sunk" cost. Fixed cost is a useful concept, for example, in situations in which there can be delegation of authority to choose within some subset. So long as the selection is to be made within that subset, only the costs other than the "fixed" costs are relevant. But for the larger range of options, the "fixed" costs are not "fixed" and are relevant for comparing options. To avoid the impression that "fixed" costs are fixed upon a person as an inescapable loss, it seems appropriate to use the name "invariant" rather than "fixed," but this is not yet a generally accepted terminology. (Fixed or invariant costs would be "sunk" if and only if the subset was in fact the entire set of possible options, for then regardless of what one did, one could not avoid the sacrifice of those alternatives.)

Law of costs. So far, we have classified costs according to differences in the event being costed, and also in terms of various ways of expressing the costs of a specified event or output program. The question to which we turn now is whether there are any laws or general propositions that relate the magnitude of costs to the characteristics of output programs. But first it is pertinent to identify the relevant characteristics or dimensions of an output or production program. As suggested earlier, the total volume and the rate or speed of production are two important dimensions of such a program. A third is the timing of the output. We may denote these three variables as follows: V is the volume of output, $v(t)$ is the rate of output at moment t, T_0 is the present moment, and T_m is the terminal moment. An increase in $v(t)$ will either increase V or, for fixed V, will decrease T_m (move is closer to T_0). Let C denote the capital-value measure of cost of the entire program. Several laws can now be stated in terms of these symbols.

(1) It is a well-recognized and validated law that cost is larger the larger V is (whether V is

increased by increasing $v(t)$ or by increasing T_m). Simply put, a bigger output costs more than a smaller one. Symbolically this means $\partial C/\partial V$ is positive, even for fixed or unchanged $v(t)$. The expression $\partial C/\partial V$ is called the marginal cost with respect to volume.

(2) Another proposition is that $\partial C/\partial V$ is smaller (but always positive) the larger V is (again with the rate of production held constant and with the increased V being obtained by increasing T_m). In symbols, $\partial^2 C/\partial V^2$ is negative. This effect is sometimes referred to as the lower costs effect of mass or large-volume production. A larger output can always be produced by replicating the technique for a smaller output. However, sometimes a larger output can be produced at lower cost through the use of different techniques (e.g., metal dies instead of sand casting for forming metal), but this cheaper method cannot be subdivided proportionately for smaller volume. It follows that larger volume will at most involve proportional increases in total cost (by replication of the cheapest methods for small volumes) and may permit utilization of lower-cost methods. Learning and improvement in methods with a larger volume of output are also predictable. Both effects, substitution of cheaper methods for larger volume and learning, contribute to the decrease in increments of total cost for increments in volume.

The two laws relating costs to volume of output imply that (3) the average cost per unit of volume of output decreases, the larger the volume —a widely recognized phenomenon. This lower unit cost with larger volume is manifested in the extensive standardization of products, in contrast with the less common individually styled, custom-built goods, which would be preferable if the costs were no higher. This lower cost with larger volume (along with the gains from specialization in production resulting from the greater heterogeneity of productive resources) is one reason why larger markets and population areas permit lower costs per unit.

(4) A law relating cost to the *rate* (not volume) of output is that the cost, C, is a positive function of $v(t)$ for any given V; that is, $\partial C/\partial v$ is positive. The more rapidly a volume of output is produced, the higher its cost.

(5) Another, possibly less general, law is that the marginal cost with respect to rate, $\partial C/\partial v$, while always positive, increases for larger v (that is, $\partial^2 C/\partial v^2$ is positive). This law is possibly less general because the evidence is contradictory for "very low" rates of output, at which it is sometimes claimed that increases in the rate might lead to decreasing increases in total cost. Nevertheless, a general and universally valid law is that for every volume of output there exists an output rate beyond which the marginal cost with respect to rate always increases. This is commonly called the law of increasing marginal costs and reflects the well-known law of diminishing marginal returns with respect to rate of output. If expressed in terms of average costs per unit of *volume* of output, the effect of higher rates of production of *that* volume is persistently to raise the average cost—after a possible initial fall in average cost for very low output rates.

(6) Instead of increasing the rate at which some constant volume is produced, output programs can be different in that both the rate *and* the volume are proportionally larger over a specified interval of time. Joint proportional increases in both the rate and the volume (over the given interval of production) will of course raise total costs. The effect on the cost per unit of product is not predictable except for "high" rates of output. Unlike proposition (3), concerning per-unit cost, proposition (6) involves an increase in the rate of output as well as in the volume. These two work in opposite directions on the per-unit cost, with the higher rate increasing unit costs while the larger volume decreases them. The rate effect ultimately will dominate as programs with higher rates are considered. For production programs arrayed according to the rate and volume of output (both varying strictly in proportion to each other) it follows that the average cost per unit of volume of output can be decreasing for small outputs. But as larger outputs are considered, the average cost will, beyond some output rate, begin to rise persistently and with increasing rapidity until a limiting rate of production is realized—at which all the resources of the world are devoted to this one program over that given time interval.

Short-run and long-run costs. We are now in position to examine another classification—short-run and long-run. Although it is common to see references to the short-run and long-run costs of some production program, there is in fact only *one* cost for any program. The short-run–long-run cost distinction rests on two concepts that are sometimes confounded with each other. A short-run cost is sometimes used to refer to a short, as contrasted with a long, program of production. At other times it is used to refer to the cost of doing something more quickly rather than less quickly. Yet in each case the shorter output and the quicker output both involve higher per-unit costs than do the longer output and the later output. Sometimes the higher per-unit short-run cost (no matter in which of the two different senses) is attributed to an alleged fixity in some of the productive units. In fact, of course, no producer is stuck with literally fixed inputs (except in the sense that momentarily it is hardly possible to increase anything). What is true is that it is more expensive to vary some inputs in any given interval than to vary others. That differential cost of adjusting various inputs is often oversimplified into an extreme bipolar classification of fixed and variable inputs.

The purpose of the long-run–short-run distinction is to note the differences in cost between *different* output programs, those achieved in the more immediate future in contrast with those undertaken later, when one can get the advantage of less expensive, less hasty adjustments. For example, if the demand for some good increases, producers will be able to respond immediately, but at a higher cost than for less hasty revisions of output. Although the "same" good is being produced (except, of course, for the important difference in the time of its availability), the cost is lower for the later output. To trace the impact of a demand change on output and prices, one will want to recognize the difference in the output and price with the passage of time. Instead of tracing out a continuous history or sequence of subsequent developments, it is convenient to divide the history arbitrarily into two episodes: the relatively immediate response (the short-run) and the limiting ultimate response (the long-run). The difference between these two "runs" indicates the path and direction of effects subsequent to the initial event.

While the long-run–short-run distinction serves as a convenient two-stage analysis of a sequence of effects, obviously there are as many "runs" as one wishes to consider. However, in analyzing total effects, three states or runs are usually considered: the "market period" (referring to that period of adjustment in prices which occurs before there is any change in output), and the aforementioned short-run and long-run, during both of which output is changed.

Joint products and unallocable costs. Suppose that an output program yields several joint products, e.g., wool, meat, and leather from sheep; or gasoline and kerosene from crude oil; or heat and light from electrical energy; or passenger-miles and freight-miles from an airline. What is the cost of each of the joint products? Depending upon which one is called the residual, or by-product, a different allocation of costs can be obtained. By calling meat the "basic" product and attaching most of the costs to it, the costs of wool can be made

small, and conversely. It is tempting to jump to the conclusion that something must be wrong with the concept of cost or with the economic system if such indefiniteness can result. After all, if costs cannot be uniquely allocated, how can one tell what prices are right? How can one tell on which of the joint products he is making a profit? If costs cannot be assigned, how can one tell which to produce or what prices to charge? In fact, however, the presence of cost that cannot be allocated uniquely among the joint products does not upset anything or prevent unique prices.

If we recall the purpose of the cost concept— that of enabling choices among alternatives according to some criterion of preference—we see that what is required is a way of assessing the consequences of *changes* in the output. If the airline program is revised to transport more passengers and less freight, or revised so as to transport more passengers with the same amount of freight, what happens to costs? Comparing the costs of alternative programs gives marginal costs, which with the marginal value of the revised output give a basis for a decision. There is no possibility and no necessity for allocating costs into uniquely identifiable parts for each product in order to determine what to produce and what prices to ask. The prices set will be those which allocate the amount produced among the competing claimants and yield a maximum wealth to the producer of the joint products. His power to maximize his wealth will of course depend upon competitors' access to the market. The function of inducing output does not require an assignment of portions of total cost to each of the joint outputs. What *is* necessary is a comparison of the total cost of the set of joint products with its value. If the market value of the *set* does not cover the cost, in an open market, the loss of wealth will induce reduced production (of some or all the joint outputs) and higher prices, until the value of the set of joint products covers the costs. (If joint products can be produced only in fixed combinations, then not even marginal costs of each output can be ascertained; nevertheless, everything said in the preceding two sentences is still valid and applicable.)

Private and social allocations of costs. Throughout the preceding discussion the costs of a choice were assumed to be borne by the chooser; none of the forsaken options are forsaken by anyone else. If Smith builds a swimming pool, the forsaken options—the costs—are all borne by him. The options open to the rest of the community or to any of its members are in no way reduced. So we assumed. If, however, Smith builds a pool and in doing so creates a "nuisance" for his neighbor, Jones, Smith has taken away Jones's peace and quiet. If Smith's pool overflows and harmfully floods Cohen's land, Cohen has had options removed from his range of choice. Being less careful and thereby letting water run over into a neighbor's land, or having a more riotous time and disturbing the peace, is less costly for Smith if he does not incur the costs of being more careful in watching the water level or in soundproofing his play area.

The situation is similar to that of the factory owner who "dumps" smoke, waste, smells, noises, and night lights on other people's land. By doing so he keeps his land in better condition and avoids the costs of filtering his smoke, collecting and disposing of his own garbage, etc. He makes others bear some of the costs, instead of bearing them himself. His actions involve a sacrifice of alternative uses of goods, which sacrifice, instead of being borne by the decision maker, is in part borne by or imposed on other people.

"Property rights are not private" is another way to express this situation. The use of "one's" resources is not subject solely to the owner's voluntary control, but is in fact and *de jure* controllable in part by other people. This ability to "use" other people's resources for one's benefit, and thereby remove their options, enables one to make other people bear part of the costs of one's decisions. The costs are divided between the decision maker and outsiders. This division or separation is called a divergence between private and social costs—where social costs are treated as the whole of costs as defined in the earlier portions of this discussion, with private costs being the portion of those costs borne by the decision maker or owner of the resources directly concerned. Social and private costs are not two different costs—they are merely classifications according to the bearer of the cost. If there is no divergence, so that all social costs are private costs, then all the costs of use are borne by the person choosing or authorizing the choice of action. The divergence between private and social costs is also characterized as the presence of "external" costs. [*See* EXTERNAL ECONOMIES AND DISECONOMIES.]

Parallel reasoning is relevant on the side of benefits. The *value* of a resource in *this* use may be incompletely revealed or have incomplete influence on decisions if that value is dispersed so that only a part of it accrues to the decision maker. This is a divergence between private and social value in *this* use. If the value measure assigned to any particular potential use by the chooser is less than the total value in that use, then there will be a divergence between his private valuation and the social valuation. In this case, values of some uses of resources are not as fully revealed and available as inducements to the competing resource users as are the values of other uses. As a result, the values of some uses will be understated, which encourages more of other kinds of use by leading to an underestimation of their cost. Thus the analysis of external versus private or of social versus private values or costs is an essential part of the analysis of the meaning and role of costs.

But whatever they are called, such effects are commonplace and well-nigh universal. For example, every voluntary act of exchange involves a choice of use of resources that benefits the other party as well as oneself. However, the external effect is "internalized" as an inducement on the acting agents. If you give me "that," I will do, or give you, "this"; and what you give me reflects the gains you will get from what I do. The external effects of my actions are made internal or effective by your ability to offer me a gain reflecting the value to you. The external costs of my acts are internalized or made effective in controlling my behavior by laws prohibiting my imposing any such costs on you unless I pay you an acceptable amount for the right to do so. Our laws of property and the right to engage in exchange help to make private costs also contain the social costs, and to make private gain reflect social gains. In other words, external effects are usually internalized.

In every society the extent of a divergence between private and social costs (or the presence of external effects) for some resource use depends upon the technological facts *and* upon the legal structure of property rights. The costs of defining, policing, and enforcing various types of property rights vary. Private property rights, defined as those in which external physical effects are not permissible, may be too expensive to enforce with respect to some effects. But if there is a cheap way to internalize external effects or to make the private costs equal the social costs, then the use of resources will respond more fully to the cost or values of use. If there were some cheap means of excluding other people from enjoyment of some use I may make of my resources, then I could charge them for the availability of that enjoyment and thereby make that value of use effective in my decision as to how to use resources. This is a means of internalizing external effects or of making external effects "inducive" with respect to my choices about resource uses.

Often the costs that must be borne in order to

internalize external effects exceed the value of those external effects but may nevertheless be worth incurring if they involve associated revenues and a more profitable, larger enterprise. For example, a golf course provides benefits to neighboring landowners. A golf course builder could buy enough land to build a course and to build homes on the surrounding property, thus internalizing the higher value from proximity to the golf course. Another example is that of the apartment building in which the rental includes the cost of maintenance of common gardens and recreation areas, rather than having each tenant maintain his own area. The purchase of cemetery lots includes a payment for upkeep of the whole cemetery. By such devices, neighborhood effects are made the owners' effects.

Another important means of internalizing or making external effects "inducing-effects" is the development corporation, which enables a larger venture to be undertaken so that more of the benefited resource owners can be included in the unit of ownership that provides the benefits. If all the land of a suburban shopping center is owned by one enterprise, there can be more complete response to the total value of the shopping center, which includes values external to the component units resulting from their proximity. Similarly, department stores with several departments in one building are a means of "internalizing" values or of making private and social effects converge. Signal decoders and wire transmission systems for television, fences around athletic pavilions to keep out nonpaying spectators, and walls around theaters are examples of devices (not costless) for internalizing and increasing the value of the service to those who provide it, and so are "inducive" to that resource use.

In other cases the value of complete suppression of external effects may be less than the cost. For example, automobile exhaust suppressors and smoke filters are not universally required. As a result, those who create smoke and smog thrust part of the costs of their actions on other people. An especially instructive example is provided by the problem of noisy airplanes. If an airport owner had to compensate the nearby landowners for the noise made by the airplanes using his airport, the landowners would in effect be selling rights to that particular use of their land, and the airport owner could in turn charge the airplane owners. Instead, one of the following solutions is usually adopted: (1) There is no compensation for the noise. (2) The planes are prohibited. (3) The neighboring land is bought up and people are prohibited from living there—even though many would prefer to

do so, *if* they could buy the land at a low enough price to reflect the value of the lost quiet. These extreme policies are sometimes explained by an incorrect presumption that it is impossible or undesirable to buy the rights to "dump" noise on neighboring land; in fact, they are used because neighboring landowners do not have a legally recognized right to the undisturbed use of their land.

As the preceding remarks have indicated, often our *legal structure* of property rights is such that decisions are made in which only part of the costs are operative in affecting the choice. This may be a result of a deliberate attempt to attenuate the role of costs in decision making or, because of technological features, it may be the result of the difficulty (cost) of defining, policing, and enforcing rights to resources in such a way that private and social costs do not diverge much. Laws may be what they are because those most influential in affecting them may want resources to be used with less regard to the exchange-value measure of costs. It may be thought that the values the people of the society would express in the way they would use resources are inappropriate or improper and therefore should not be so influential in affecting resource allocations. If so, choices about uses of resources should be insulated from those alternative use values (i.e., costs). This can be achieved by suppressing a market place in which market prices would reveal alternative use values, or it can be achieved by not sanctioning private property rights, so that no one can negotiate an exchange that would reveal alternative use values (that is, resources would not be "owned," in the sense of being salable).

Policing and enforcing of property rights is not performed exclusively by the government. In many cases other forms of control are effective. Etiquette and socially accepted codes act as determiners of rights. These institutions serve, in part, to restrict the extent to which a person can impose the costs of his choices on others. That is, they are often means of inducing behavior of a type that would occur if resources involved were "privately" owned and exchangeable. Custom and etiquette, along with property rules, affect the degree of concentration of costs on decision makers.

External value effects and costs.   Still another source of confusion is the confounding of the external *price* effects of some event with its costs. Cost has been defined as the highest-valued option necessarily sacrificed consequent to action *A*. Suppose that I open a restaurant near yours, and by virtue of my superior cooking talents attract customers away from you, with a consequent loss of wealth by you of, say, $50,000. So far as *you* are concerned, my effect on you is as bad as if I had burned your uninsured $50,000 building for the joy and excitement this afforded me. From an analytical point of view, the *former* loss of $50,000 of value is not a cost, whereas the destruction of the building would have been a cost. Why the difference? Simply that opening a restaurant does not necessarily involve a sacrifice to society at large, while the destruction of the building does. My superior cooking skills do not involve a sacrifice of $50,000 of alternatively valuable output, whereas my enjoying the fire would. My superior cooking may impose a *loss of wealth* on you because I outcompete you in providing services to third parties. But the $50,000 loss to you is more than matched by the gain in the value of service to the third parties who were formerly your customers but who have shifted to me, and by the increase in my own wealth. No formerly available options are forsaken by society as a whole. Everything that could be done before I opened my restaurant still can be done. That $50,000 is not a sacrificed opportunity—instead, it is a measure of a *transfer of wealth* from you to two other parties, me and the customers. The distinction between the transfer of rights to uses of resources and the costs of use of goods should be kept clear. For example, when I open a new restaurant service, and the public offers less for your goods and more for mine, they are telling you that the exchange rights formerly attached to your goods—their market value—is being transferred by them to my goods.

The transfer of rights of choice of use and the revision of exchange values consequent to changes in offers by competitors, or consequent to changes in tastes by customers, do not reduce the total set of alternative use options. The transfer changes the person authorized to control the decision as to use. When my superior culinary talents reduce the exchange value of your services (without affecting their physical attributes in any way) and so reduce your wealth, society could in principle take away some of my gains and those of my customers (who gain by accepting my offers rather than yours) and fully reimburse you, while still leaving me and the customers better off than before I entered the market. Such compensation is not possible for true costs.

The person who loses wealth either via transfer of goods or the reduction of their exchange value is suffering a real loss of wealth, but not a cost. That loss is different in principle, in kind, and in fact from a cost. From the private point of view both sources of loss of wealth are "bad" for him.

Both are losses of opportunities to *him*, though only a cost is a loss to the *community as a whole*. What he loses in the pure price revaluation case, someone else gains.

There are many examples of the use of public policy to reduce such transfers. Taxes have been imposed on innovations or on new products in order to reimburse owners of resources formerly used to produce the displaced products. Sometimes laws are passed prohibiting new, cheaper devices, in order to preserve the marketable wealth of users of older, more costly methods. Sometimes general taxes are imposed to aid those whose wealth is reduced by new methods, e.g., government financing of retraining of displaced workers and low-interest loans to business firms in distressed areas. Taxes on innovations make the innovators count the taxes as part of their costs. The "costs" of innovation are thereby biased upward, with a resultant attenuation of the incentive to introduce new methods or products that would produce a larger total wealth.

Although wealth transfers via market revaluations are not costs, they may influence behavior. For example, if such market revisions of wealth are (somehow) deemed undesirable, steps can be taken to restrain people from taking actions that revise the distribution of wealth, or steps can be taken to redistribute the wealth again so as to restore the *status quo ante* wealth for each individual. Social policy (laws of property) may be evolved to insulate decisions from these effects or, conversely, to make them more sensitive. But in neither case are these market-price side effects on wealth components of costs.

We conclude by returning to the initial theme. The costs of some event are the highest-valued options necessarily forsaken. We have seen that he who is to forsake those options and he who makes the decision about the chosen option may or may not be the same person. Furthermore, the privately borne costs may be less or greater than the true costs, depending upon laws and upon the structure of property rights.

ARMEN A. ALCHIAN

BIBLIOGRAPHY

BÖHM-BAWERK, EUGEN VON (1884–1912) 1959 *Capital and Interest.* 3 vols. South Holland, Ill.: Libertarian. → First published in German. See especially Volume 2, pages 248–256, "The Law of Costs," and Volume 3, pages 97–115, "On the Value of Producers' Goods and the Relationship Between Value and Costs."

CLARK, JOHN MAURICE (1923) 1962 *Studies in the Economics of Overhead Costs.* Univ. of Chicago Press.

COASE, R. H. 1960 The Problem of Social Cost. *Journal of Law and Economics* 3:1–44.

Demsetz, Harold 1964 The Exchange and Enforcement of Property Rights. *Journal of Law and Economics* 7:11–26.

Knight, Frank H. 1924 Some Fallacies in the Interpretation of Social Cost. *Quarterly Journal of Economics* 38:582–606.

Stigler, George J. (1942) 1960 *The Theory of Price.* Rev. ed. New York: Macmillan. → First published as *The Theory of Competitive Price.*

Viner, Jacob 1931*a* Cost. Volume 4, pages 466–475 in *Encyclopaedia of the Social Sciences.* New York: Macmillan.

Viner, Jacob (1931*b*) 1952 Cost Curves and Supply Curves. Pages 198–232 in American Economic Association, *Readings in Price Theory.* Homewood, Ill.: Irwin.

COST ANALYSIS

See Production and cost analysis.

COST OF LIVING

See Index numbers.

COUNSELING PSYCHOLOGY

Counseling psychology, a specialty within the area broadly designated as applied psychology, is not primarily an entitative science but draws heavily upon the basic and applied fields of psychology and upon other behavioral sciences for its foundations (Berdie 1959). It uses concepts, tools, and techniques that are also used by other specialty groups—notably industrial and personnel, clinical, and school psychology. It is, however, most appropriately viewed as the application of psychological and behavioral science knowledge in the form of a unique personal service furnished by professional practitioners with special qualifications. As such a specialty the most important characteristic of counseling psychology is its focus on the decisions and plans that individuals must make in order to play productive roles in their social environments. It is irrelevant whether the person receiving professional assistance is sick or well, normal or abnormal, handicapped or whole—that is to say he is a *client* and not a *patient.* In counseling psychology the emphasis is on further development as an individual; its concern is the identification and enhancement of possibilities and potentialities (American Psychological Association 1961).

Other important defining characteristics of counseling psychology include the following: (*a*) a primary focus on normal people; (*b*) service that is available throughout the life span; (*c*) emphasis on the individual's strengths and assets; (*d*) emphasis on cognitive elements, especially where choice

and decision are involved, with rationality and reason stressed; (*e*) the dealing with personality difficulties in the context of the total goals, plans, and roles of the individual; (*f*) the giving of full consideration to situational and environmental factors, with emphasis on the utilization of environmental resources and on environmental modification where judged necessary.

Basically, counseling psychology is concerned with the choices, decisions, and plans that *every* individual must make, as contrasted, for example, with clinical psychology, which is largely concerned with the problems and difficulties that *some* individuals face (Sundberg & Tyler 1962). This distinction is demonstrated by the historic and continuing emphasis on *vocational* counseling as a major element in establishing the unique identity of counseling psychology (Brayfield 1963).

Historical background. Counseling psychology (it came to be so designated in the early 1950s) evolved historically under a variety of influences. The first, vocational guidance, began in this century under the auspices of social welfare agencies and took shape around 1909 with the writings of Frank Parsons (1909), who described vocational guidance as a process of vocational orientation, individual analysis, and counseling; primary focus was upon the collection and dissemination of occupational information in the absence of useful methods of individual appraisal and theories and techniques of interviewing (Brewer 1942).

At about the same time the scientific study of individual differences, sparked by James McKeen Cattell, and the development of psychometric devices got under way. Psychometric efforts yielded useful measures of individual differences in occupationally significant aptitudes and interests by the middle 1920s. In the early 1930s large-scale programs of vocational guidance—as developed by Donald G. Paterson (see Paterson & Darley 1936) for the Minnesota Employment Stabilization Institute and at the Adjustment Service in New York—demonstrated the practicality of professional counseling based on the available psychological knowledge. During this period the student counseling program established at the University of Minnesota—under the leadership of Paterson, Edmund G. Williamson, and later John G. Darley—set a pattern which has been widely emulated in colleges and universities (Williamson & Darley 1937).

In the 1940s, personality and learning theories and the increasing interest of psychologists in psychotherapy and practice, particularly under the influence of Carl R. Rogers (1942), helped shape the course of counseling psychology. Psychodynamic interpretations of behavior and an accompanying concern with psychopathology contributed to the emerging specialty.

New elements were introduced in the early 1950s, when the ideas and findings of developmental and social psychology were recognized as directly relevant to counseling. The psychology of careers, as formulated by Donald E. Super (1957), took on a new dimension when viewed in this context. Gradually this approach has been extended by Milton E. Hahn (1963) and others to include the major events of the entire life span—including the formation of a family, participation in community and leisure-time activities, adaptation to cultural changes, and retirement.

Psychological foundations. The most important foundations for counseling psychology, as it has evolved under these influences, are found in differential psychology and psychometric theory; basic processes of learning, perception, motivation, and emotion; personality theory and dynamics; developmental psychology; and in social psychology along with selected aspects of economics, sociology, and anthropology. The selective emphasis and organization of concepts and materials from these areas is the distinctive contribution of counseling psychology as a substantive field of knowledge (Pepinsky & Pepinsky 1954).

Although counseling psychologists draw upon a wide range of psychological and behavioral science literature, one mark of the development of the field is the publication of the *Journal of Counseling Psychology*, which began in 1954.

Counseling is best understood as a *process* including assessment and counseling per se. *Assessment* includes the systematic collection, organization, and interpretation of information about a person and his situation. *Counseling* is the process in which a professionally trained person and his client relate the materials brought to light by the assessment process to the choices and decisions confronting the client in his formation of goals and life plans, in essence providing a learning and problem-solving setting for the client in which the crucial element is the relationship established between counselor and client. This constructive relationship is characterized by such words as friendly, accepting, sincere, and confidential as viewed by the client. The establishment of such a relationship constitutes a real test of counseling skill; it provides the psychological environment in which the special knowledge and understanding of the counselor can best be utilized by the client in making the choices and decisions that will give full play to his potentialities (Tyler 1953).

Although face-to-face counseling with individuals is the heart of counseling psychology, the counseling psychologist also plays an active role in exploring and coordinating community resources such as placement, habilitative and social services, and educational opportunities in order to provide a comprehensive and effective service for his clients. Increasingly the counseling psychologist is in demand as a consultant to local and state agencies and institutions concerned with human welfare and effectiveness.

Training and qualifications. It is customary to define the counseling psychologist as a person who has completed training in psychology, with a concentration in counseling psychology, at the level of the doctor of philosophy degree. Recommended standards for training psychologists at the doctoral level were published by the Division of Counseling and Guidance (now Division of Counseling Psychology) of the American Psychological Association in 1952 (1952*a*). Additional reports from the same source have made recommendations for practicum training and internships (American Psychological Association 1952*b*; 1960). In 1964 the division published the report of a conference on professional preparation of counseling psychologists, which made recommendations for further improvements in training (Conference on the Professional Preparation of Counseling Psychologists 1964).

In the United States approximately 48 universities offer graduate training at the doctoral level in what is essentially counseling psychology. Of these programs approximately half have met the standards required for accreditation by the Education and Training Board of the American Psychological Association (1958). Although some individual changes have occurred, there has been little growth in approved programs since the first listing in 1955, which included 23 departments. Approved programs vary in their administrative sponsorship and essential nature: about one-third are in departments of psychology and are undifferentiated from the clinical psychology program; about one-third are in psychology departments but differentiated from clinical psychology; and the remainder are jointly administered by a department of psychology and either a department of education or of educational psychology.

The most distinctive recognition of qualifications and competence which can be accorded a counseling psychologist is the diplomate status conferred by the American Board of Examiners in Professional Psychology (1953). These diplomates number slightly in excess of 250.

In 1965, 1,500 was a reasonable estimate of the number of doctoral-level counseling psychologists employed in the United States. Although counseling psychologists work in a variety of settings, approximately 60 per cent of them are found in colleges and universities, where they are engaged in counseling, teaching, research, and administration. About 10 per cent, the next largest group, are employed by the Veterans Administration. Smaller proportions are found in community counseling agencies, public schools, business and industry, city, state, and federal agencies including rehabilitation services, and private practice.

Although the number of counseling psychologists is limited—and only 40 to 50 are produced annually—counseling psychology has an extensive and important impact on the general field of counseling. The major share of direct counseling in public schools, rehabilitation agencies, state employment services, and community agencies is offered by nonpsychologists (Brayfield 1961). A substantial share of their formal preparation, however, is based on materials developed or made readily available by counseling psychologists who provide the research undergirdings of practice, the intellectual leadership, and frequently the supervision and administration of counseling services. The outlook for nondoctoral counselors is the requirement of two full years of graduate training that will provide substantial amounts and kinds of instruction in psychology (Wrenn 1962).

The major locus of counseling psychology is in the United States, particularly with respect to the numbers of practitioners. However, there has been increasing interest in the field in other countries. Great Britain has produced a considerable amount of relevant research, especially in the field of vocational guidance. French psychologists have made contributions in recent years, and there are important developments in India and Japan.

Arthur H. Brayfield

[*Directly related are the entries* Clinical psychology; Educational psychology; Industrial relations, *article on* industrial and business psychology; Mental disorders, treatment of; Vocational rehabilitation. *Other relevant material may be found in* Interviewing; Occupations and careers; Personality measurement.]

BIBLIOGRAPHY

American Board of Examiners in Professional Psychology 1953 *The Certification of Advanced Specialists in Professional Psychology.* Washington: American Psychological Association.

American Psychological Association, Division of Counseling and Guidance, Committee on Counselor Training 1952a Recommended Standards for Training Counseling Psychologists at the Doctorate Level. *American Psychologist* 7:175–181.

American Psychological Association, Division of Counseling and Guidance, Committee on Counselor Training 1952b The Practicum Training of Counseling Psychologists. *American Psychologist* 7: 182–188.

American Psychological Association, Division of Counseling Psychology, Committee on Current Status 1961 The Current Status of Counseling Psychology. Unpublished manuscript.

American Psychological Association, Division of Counseling Psychology, Committee on Internship Standards 1960 Recommended Standards for Internships in Counseling Psychology. Unpublished manuscript.

American Psychological Association, Education and Training Board 1958 Criteria for Evaluating Training Programs in Clinical or in Counseling Psychology. *American Psychologist* 2:59–60.

Berdie, Ralph F. 1959 Counseling. *Annual Review of Psychology* 10:345–370.

Brayfield, Arthur H. 1961 Vocational Counseling Today. Pages 22–58 in E. G. Williamson (editor), *Vocational Counseling: A Reappraisal in Honor of Donald G. Paterson.* Minnesota Studies in Student Personnel Work, No. 11. Minneapolis: Univ. of Minnesota Press.

Brayfield, Arthur H. 1963 Counseling Psychology. *Annual Review of Psychology* 14:319–350.

Brewer, John M. 1942 *History of Vocational Guidance.* New York: Harper.

Conference on the Professional Preparation of Counseling Psychologists, Columbia University 1964 *The Professional Preparation of Counseling Psychologists: Report of the 1964 Greystone Conference.* New York: Columbia Univ., Teachers College, Bureau of Publications.

Hahn, Milton E. 1963 *Psychoevaluation: Adaptation–Distribution–Adjustment.* New York: McGraw-Hill.

Parsons, Frank 1909 *Choosing a Vocation.* Boston: Houghton Mifflin.

Paterson, Donald G.; and Darley, John G. 1936 *Men, Women and Jobs: A Study in Human Engineering.* Minneapolis: Univ. of Minnesota Press.

Pepinsky, Harold B.; and Pepinsky, Pauline N. 1954 *Counseling: Theory and Practice.* New York: Ronald Press.

Rogers, Carl R. 1942 *Counseling and Psychotherapy.* Boston: Houghton Mifflin.

Sundberg, Norman D.; and Tyler, Leona E. 1962 *Clinical Psychology.* New York: Appleton.

Super, Donald E. 1957 *The Psychology of Careers.* New York: Harper.

Tyler, Leona E. (1953) 1961 *The Work of the Counselor.* 2d ed. New York: Appleton.

Williamson, Edmund G.; and Darley, John G. 1937 *Student Personnel Work.* New York: McGraw-Hill.

Wrenn, Charles G. 1962 *The Counselor in a Changing World.* Washington: American Personnel and Guidance Association.

COUNTED DATA

Counted data subject to sampling variability arise in demographic sampling, in survey research, in learning experiments, and in almost every other branch of social science. The counted data may relate to a relatively simple investigation, for example, estimating sex ratio at birth in some specified human population, or to a complex problem, investigating the interaction among qualitative responses of animals to stimuli in a physiological experiment. Further, a counted data approach is sometimes useful even when the actual data are inherently not counted; for example, a classical approach to so-called goodness of fit uses the counts of numbers of continuous observations in cells or intervals. Again, some nonparametric tests are based on a related device. [*See* GOODNESS OF FIT; NONPARAMETRIC STATISTICS.]

Investigations leading to counted data are often described by giving percentages of individuals falling in the various categories. It is essential that the total numbers of individuals also be reported; otherwise reliability and sampling error cannot be estimated.

The structure of this article is as follows. First, simple procedures relating to one or two sample percentages are considered. These procedures exemplify the basic chi-square approach; they may be regarded as methods for treating particular contingency tables in a way falling in the domain of the basic chi-square theorem. Second, special aspects of contingency tables are considered in some detail: power, single degrees of freedom, ordered alternatives, dependent samples, measures of association, multidimensional contingency tables. Under the last topic is considered the important topic of three-factor interactions. Third, some alternatives to chi-square are briefly mentioned.

Binomial model

Consider an experiment in which animals of a group are independently subjected to a stimulus. Assume two, and only two, responses are possible (A and $\bar{A}$). Of 20 animals exposed independently to the stimulus, responses of type A are exhibited by 16. Such a count, or the corresponding percentage, 80 per cent, may be the basis of an estimate of the probability of an A response in all animals of this kind; or it may be the basis of a test of the hypothesis that responses A and $\bar{A}$ are equally likely. The evaluation of either this estimate or the test is dependent upon the assumptions underlying the data collection.

One of the basic models associated with such experiments is the binomial. The binomial model is associated with a series of independent trials in each of which an event A may or may not occur and for which it is assumed that the probability of occurrence of A, denoted p, is constant from trial to trial. If the number of occurrences of A among n such trials is v, then v/n is the maximum likeli-

hood and also the minimum variance unbiased estimator of p. [*For further discussion of the binomial distribution, see* DISTRIBUTIONS, STATISTICAL, *article on* SPECIAL DISCRETE DISTRIBUTIONS.]

Additional insight as to the reliability of the estimator is obtained from a confidence interval for p. Tables and graphs have been prepared to provide such confidence intervals for appropriate levels of confidence. The best known of these is the graph, by Clopper and Pearson (1934). This graph or the tables that have been computed for the same purpose (for example, Owen 1962) determine so-called central confidence limits; that is, the intervals that are "false," in the sense that they do not include the true parameter value, are equally divided between those that are too low and those that are too high. [*See* ESTIMATION, *article on* CONFIDENCE INTERVALS AND REGIONS.]

Confidence intervals may also be used to test a null hypothesis that p has the value p_0. If p_0 is not included in the $1 - \alpha$ level confidence interval, then the null hypothesis $p = p_0$ is rejected at level α.

Equivalently, a direct test may be made of this hypothesis by utilizing the extensive tables of the binomial distribution. Two of the best known are those of Harvard University (1955) and the U.S. National Bureau of Standards (1950).

More usually both confidence intervals and test procedures are based upon an approximation to the distribution, that is, on the fact that $(v - np) \cdot [np(1 - p)]^{-\frac{1}{2}}$ has a limiting standard normal distribution. [*See* DISTRIBUTIONS, STATISTICAL, *article on* APPROXIMATIONS TO DISTRIBUTIONS.]

Denote by $Z_{1-\alpha}$ the $100(1 - \alpha)$ percentile of the standard normal distribution. The null hypothesis $p = p_0$ tested against the alternative $p \neq p_0$ is rejected at level α on the basis of an observation of v successes in n trials if

$$|v - np_0| - \tfrac{1}{2} > Z_{1-\frac{1}{2}\alpha}[np_0(1 - p_0)]^{\frac{1}{2}};$$

in case the alternatives of interest are limited to one side of p_0, say $p > p_0$, the test procedure at level α is to reject H_0 if

$$v - np_0 - \tfrac{1}{2} > Z_{1-\alpha}[np_0(1 - p_0)]^{\frac{1}{2}}.$$

The subtracted $\frac{1}{2}$ is the so-called continuity correction—useful when a discrete distribution is being approximated by a continuous one.

Thus, in the experiment described above, the experimenter might be testing whether the choice is made at random between A and $\bar{A}$ against the possibility that A is the preferred response. This is a test of the hypothesis $p = \frac{1}{2}$ against the alternative $p > \frac{1}{2}$. Corresponding to the conventional 5 per cent significance level, $Z_{0.95} = 1.64$; then if

$v = 16$ (16 A responses are observed), the hypothesis is rejected at the 5 per cent level since

$$16 - 10 - \tfrac{1}{2} > 1.64 \,[(20)(\tfrac{1}{2})(\tfrac{1}{2})]^{\frac{1}{2}}.$$

The normal approximation to the binomial is thought to be quite satisfactory if $np_0(1 - p_0)$ is 5 or more. However, for many practical situations the normal approximation provides an adequate test (in the sense that the type I error is sufficiently close to the specified level) for values of $np_0(1 - p_0)$ well below the bound of 5 mentioned above.

The simplest confidence limits for p based on the normal approximation are

$$\frac{v}{n} \pm Z_{1-\frac{1}{2}\alpha} \sqrt{\frac{1}{n} \frac{v}{n} \left(1 - \frac{v}{n}\right)}.$$

The binomial model requires independence of the successive trials. Much sampling, especially of human populations, is, however, done without replacement so that successive observations are in fact dependent and the correct model is not the binomial but the hypergeometric. In sampling theory this is taken into account by the finite population correction, which modifies the variance. Thus, where the binomial variance is $np(1 - p)$, the hypergeometric variance for a sample of size n from a population of size N is $np(1 - p)(1 - n/N)$. If n is a small fraction of N, the finite population correction is negligible; thus, the binomial model is often used as an acceptable approximation.

Chi-square tests

For one or two proportions. The statistic $(|v - np_0| - \tfrac{1}{2})[np_0(1 - p_0)]^{-\frac{1}{2}}$, which for sufficiently large n may be used to test the hypothesis $p = p_0$ against $p \neq p_0$, yields, when squared, an equivalent test procedure based on the chi-square distribution with one degree of freedom; this follows from the fact that the square of a standard normal variable has a chi-square distribution with one degree of freedom. [See DISTRIBUTIONS, STATISTICAL, *article on* SPECIAL CONTINUOUS DISTRIBUTIONS.]

Following recent practice, "X^2" is written for the test statistic, and the symbol "χ^2" is reserved for the distributional form.

$$\begin{aligned}
X^2 &= \frac{(|v - np_0| - \tfrac{1}{2})^2}{np_0(1 - p_0)} \\
&= \frac{(|v - np_0| - \tfrac{1}{2})^2}{np_0} + \frac{(|n - v - n(1 - p_0)| - \tfrac{1}{2})^2}{n(1 - p_0)}.
\end{aligned}$$

This algebraic identity shows that the statistic X^2 may be written (neglecting the continuity correction term, $\tfrac{1}{2}$) as (observed $-$ expected)^2/expected,

summed over the two categories A and $\bar{A}$. Such a measure of deviation of observations from their expected values under a null hypothesis is of wide application.

For example, consider the counts of individuals with characteristic A that occur in two independent random samples and suppose that the null hypothesis at test is that the probability of occurrence of A is the same in both populations; call the common (but unspecified) probability p. The observations may be tabulated as in Table 1.

Table 1 — Observations in two samples

		NUMBERS OF OBSERVED		
		A's	$\bar{A}$'s	Totals
SAMPLE	1	v_{11}	v_{12}	n_1
	2	v_{21}	v_{22}	n_2
Totals		$v_{.1}$	$v_{.2}$	n

If p were known, then under the null hypothesis the expectation of the number of A's in sample 1 would be $n_1 p$ and in sample 2 the expectation would be $n_2 p$, where p is the probability of occurrence of A. Since p is unknown, however, it must be estimated from the data [*see* ESTIMATION, *article on* POINT ESTIMATION].

If the hypothesis were true, the two samples could be pooled and the usual (minimum variance unbiased) estimator of p would be $v_{.1}/n$. With this estimator the estimated expected number of A's in sample 1 is $n_1(v_{.1}/n)$ and in sample 2 is $n_2(v_{.1}/n)$. Similarly the estimated expected numbers of $\bar{A}$'s are $n_1(v_{.2}/n)$ and $n_2(v_{.2}/n)$ in the two samples. These estimated expectations are tabulated in Table 2.

Table 2 — Estimated expected number of observations in two samples

		ESTIMATED EXPECTATIONS FOR NUMBER OF OBSERVED	
		A's	$\bar{A}$'s
SAMPLE	1	$n_1\left(\dfrac{v_{.1}}{n}\right)$	$n_1\left(\dfrac{v_{.2}}{n}\right)$
	2	$n_2\left(\dfrac{v_{.1}}{n}\right)$	$n_2\left(\dfrac{v_{.2}}{n}\right)$

An expression similar to X^2 can be calculated for each sample where now, however, p_0 is replaced by the estimator $v_{.1}/n$. These expressions are

$$\frac{[|v_{11} - n_1(v_{.1}/n)| - \tfrac{1}{2}]^2}{n_1(v_{.1}/n)(1 - v_{.1}/n)}$$

and

$$\frac{[|v_{21} - n_2(v_{.1}/n)| - \tfrac{1}{2}]^2}{n_2(v_{.1}/n)(1 - v_{.1}/n)}.$$

Since the estimator of p will tend to be close to the true value for large sample sizes, it is intuitive to conjecture that each of these are squares of normal variables (at least approximately for large samples). The sum does have a limiting chi-square distribution but with one degree of freedom, not two. The "loss" of the degree of freedom comes from estimating the unknown parameter, p. The test statistic, which more formally written is

$$X^2 = \sum_{i=1}^{2} \sum_{j=1}^{2} \frac{(|v_{ij} - n_i v_{\cdot j}/n| - \frac{1}{2})^2}{n_i v_{\cdot j}/n},$$

may be simplified to

$$\frac{n(|v_{11}v_{22} - v_{12}v_{21}| - n/2)^2}{n_1 n_2 v_{\cdot 1} v_{\cdot 2}}.$$

If $|v_{11}v_{22} - v_{12}v_{21}|$ is less than or equal to $n/2$, the correction term is inappropriate and possibly misleading. In practice this problem rarely arises.

Basic chi-square theorem.   The above chi-square test statistics for one or two proportions may, as was seen, be written as sums of terms whose numerators are squared deviations of the observed counts from those "expected" under the null hypothesis. (*Expected* is placed in quotation marks to emphasize that the "expectations" are often estimated expectations obtained via estimation of unknown parameters.) The denominators may be regarded as weights to standardize the ratios. This pattern may be widely extended.

For example, consider a questionnaire with respondents placing themselves in five categories: strongly favor, mildly favor, neutral, mildly oppose, strongly oppose. The n independent responses might furnish data for a test of the hypothesis that each of the responses is equally likely. If the probabilities of the five responses are denoted p_1 through p_5 this null hypothesis specifies $p_1 = p_2 = p_3 = p_4 = p_5 = \frac{1}{5}$ and under the null hypothesis the expected number of responses in each category is $n/5$. The appropriate weights in the denominator of the chi-square test statistic are suggested by the expanded form of X^2 given above; each term (observed − expected)^2 is divided by its expected value. Thus in this example,

$$X^2 = \sum_{j=1}^{5} \frac{(v_j - n/5)^2}{n/5}.$$

That these weights lead to the usual kind of null distribution can be shown by considering the multinomial distribution, the extension of the binomial distribution to a series of independent trials with several outcomes rather than just two. If the null hypothesis is true, this X^2 has approximately a chi-square distribution with four degrees of freedom.

More generally, suppose that on each of n inde-

pendent trials of an experiment exactly one of the events $E_1, \cdots, E_J$ occurs. Let p_j, depending in a given way (under the null hypothesis under test) on unknown parameters $\theta_1, \cdots, \theta_m$, be the probability that E_j occurs and suppose there are asymptotically efficient estimators of the θ's, from which are obtained asymptotically efficient estimators of the p_j, denoted $\hat{p}_j$; thus $n\hat{p}_j$ estimates the expected frequency of occurrence of E_j under the null hypothesis. Let the random variable v_j be the number of times E_j actually occurs in the n trials. Then

$$X^2 = \sum_{j=1}^{J} \frac{(v_j - n\hat{p}_j)^2}{n\hat{p}_j}$$

has, under the null hypothesis for large n and under mathematical regularity conditions, approximately the chi-square distribution with $J - m - 1$ degrees of freedom. When the null hypothesis is false, X^2 tends to be larger on the average than when it is true, so that a right-hand tail critical region is appropriate, that is, the null hypothesis is rejected for large values of X^2.

Note that the above "chi-square" statistic is of form

$$\text{Sum} \left[\frac{(\text{observed number} - \text{``expected'' number})^2}{\text{``expected'' number}} \right].$$

(The quotation marks around *expected* indicate that this is actually an asymptotically efficient *estimator* of the expectation under the null hypothesis.)

The above development can readily be extended to I independent sequences of trials, with n_i trials in the ith sequence, p_{ij} denoting the probability under the null hypothesis of event j for sequence i, and v_{ij} denoting the number of times E_j occurs in sequence i. As before,

$$X^2 = \sum_{i=1}^{I} \sum_{j=1}^{J} \frac{(v_{ij} - n_i \hat{p}_{ij})^2}{n_i \hat{p}_{ij}}$$

is, for large n_i, approximately chi-square with $I(J - 1) - m$ degrees of freedom, under the null hypothesis, and with appropriate regularity conditions. Note that when $I = 1$, $J - m - 1$ degrees of freedom are obtained, as before.

The primary problem in such tests is the derivation of asymptotically efficient estimators. For example, such estimators may be maximum likelihood estimators or minimum chi-square estimators. The latter are the θ's that minimize X^2, the test statistic, subject to whatever functional restraints are imposed upon the p_{ij}'s. Neyman (1949) has given a method of determining modified minimum chi-square estimators, a method that reduces to solving only linear equations, as many as there are unknown parameters to estimate. A review of the methods of generating such minimum chi-square estimators for this model, and for a more general one, is given by Ferguson (1958).

It is easily seen that the comparison of two percentages is a special case of the general theorem. Here $I = J = 2$ and the null hypothesis can be put in the form $p_{11} = p_{12} = \theta$; $p_{21} = p_{22} = 1 - \theta$. Here p_{11} is the probability of A occurring on a trial in the first series, p_{12} is the probability of A occurring on a trial in the second series; p_{21}, p_{22} are defined similarly with respect to $\bar{A}$. The maximum likelihood estimator of θ is $v_{\cdot 1}/n$ and the degrees of freedom are seen to be one from insertion in the general formula.

Proofs of the basic chi-square theorem and statements of the mathematical regularity conditions may be found in Cramér (1946) or Neyman (1949).

Power of the chi-square test. The chi-square test is extensively used as an omnibus test without particular alternatives in view. Frequently such applications are almost useless in the sense that their sensitivity (that is, power) is very low. It is therefore important not only to make such tests but also to specify the alternatives of interest and to determine the power, that is, the probability that the null hypothesis is rejected when in fact such alternatives are true. A fairly complete theory of the power of chi-square tests has been given recently by Mitra (1958) and Diamond (1963).

Because chi-square tests are based upon a limiting distribution theorem it is necessary to express the alternative in a special form, depending on the sample size, n, in order to obtain meaningful results. Consider first the case where $I = 1$ and the null hypothesis completely specifies the p_j^0 as numerical constants. (In the questionnaire experiment above, since there are five responses the null hypothesis that the responses are equally likely specifies $p_j^0 = \frac{1}{5}$.) Write an alternative p_j^A in the form

$$p_j^A = p_j^0 + \frac{C_j}{\sqrt{n}}, \qquad \text{where } \sum_{j=1}^{J} C_j = 0.$$

If in fact $p_j = p_j^A$ then the test statistic X^2 has a limiting *noncentral* chi-square distribution with noncentrality parameter

$$\lambda = \sum_{j=1}^{J} C_j^2 / p_j^0$$

and with $J - 1$ degrees of freedom [*see* DISTRIBUTIONS, STATISTICAL, *article on* SPECIAL CONTINUOUS DISTRIBUTIONS].

The λ required to obtain a specified probability of rejection of an alternative p_i^A for tests at signifi-

cance levels 0.01 and 0.05 has been tabulated; such a table is given, for example, by Owen (1962, pp. 61–62). These tables are useful not only in calculating the power function but also in specifying sample size in advance. For the example where there are five responses and the null hypothesis is $p_1^0 = p_2^0 = p_3^0 = p_4^0 = p_5^0 = 0.20$, consider the alternative $p_1^A = p_2^A = p_3^A = p_4^A = 0.15$, $p_5^A = 0.40$. Then $C_j = \sqrt{n}\,(0.05)$, $j = 1, \cdots, 4$; $C_5 = -\sqrt{n}\,(0.20)$, so that $\lambda = n(.25)$. To achieve a probability of 0.80 of rejecting the null hypothesis for this alternative, it is found from the tables that λ must be 11.94 (four degrees of freedom and 0.05 significance level). This requires a sample size of 11.94/.25 or, to the nearest whole number, 48.

For the comparison of two samples, a similar power theory is available. Consider two sequences of n_i trials each of which results in an outcome $E_1, E_2, \cdots, E_J$. Here p_{ij} $(i = 1, 2, j = 1, \cdots, J)$ is the probability of outcome j on sequence i and the null hypothesis of homogeneity is $p_{11} = p_{21}$, $p_{12} = p_{22}$, $\cdots$, $p_{1J} = p_{2J}$. Now consider a sequence of alternatives $p_{ij}^A(n)$ which for some p_j $(j = 1, 2, \cdots, J)$ satisfy the equations $p_{ij}^A(n) = p_j + C_{ij}/\sqrt{n}$, where $n = n_1 + n_2$ and $\sum_j C_{1j} = \sum_j C_{2j} = 0$. Then, for the sequence of alternatives, X^2 has, in the limit as $n \to \infty$, a noncentral chi-square distribution with $J - 1$ degrees of freedom and noncentrality parameter λ, where

$$\lambda = \frac{n_1 n_2}{n^2} \sum_{j=1}^{J} \frac{(C_{1j} - C_{2j})^2}{p_j}.$$

In actual practice, when the statistician considers a specified alternative for finite n, p_j is not uniquely defined; it is convenient to define $p_j = \frac{1}{2}[p_{1j}^A(n) + p_{2j}^A(n)]$ but whether other choices of p_j might improve the goodness of the asymptotic approximation to the actual power appears not to have been investigated. For the case $J = 2$, and with $n_1 = n_2$, a nomogram is available showing the sample size required to obtain a specified level of power for one-sided hypotheses, that is, for comparison of an experimental and a standard group (Columbia University 1947, chapter 7). In the general case the formulation of λ is more difficult.

Contingency tables. In the example of comparing two percentages, the observations were conveniently set out in a 2×2 array. Similarly, in the more general comparative experiment (the power of which was just discussed), it would be convenient to set out the observations in a $2 \times J$ array. These are special cases of *contingency tables*, which, in general, have r rows and c columns; counted data that may be so represented arise, for example, in many experiments and surveys.

Such arrays or contingency tables may arise in at least three different situations, which may be illustrated by specific examples:

(1) Double polytomy: A sample of n voters is taken from an electoral list and each voter is classified into one of r party affiliations $P_1, \cdots, P_r$ and into one of c educational levels $E_1 \cdots, E_c$. Denote by p_{ij} the probability that a voter belongs to party i and educational level j, so that $\sum_i \sum_j p_{ij} = 1$. The usual null hypothesis of interest is that the classifications are independent, that is,

$$p_{ij} = p_i. \, p._j ,$$

where $p_i.$ = probability a voter is in party i (regardless of educational level) and $p._j$ = probability a voter is in educational level j, again regardless of the other classification variable (that is, $p_i. = \sum_j p_{ij}$ and $p._j = \sum_i p_{ij}$). In this case both the vertical and horizontal marginal totals of the $r \times c$ sample array are random.

(2) Comparative trials: Consider instead of a single sample from the general electoral roll, r samples of sizes n_i from the r different party rolls. The voters in each sample are classified as to educational level (levels $E_1, \cdots, E_c$). Denote as before by p_{ij} the probability that a voter drawn from party i belongs to educational level j (so that $\sum_j p_{ij} = 1$). The hypothesis of homogeneity specifies that $p_{1j} = p_{2j} = \cdots = p_{rj}$ for each j. In this case the row totals are fixed $(n_1, \cdots, n_r)$, while the column totals are random. Into this category falls the two-sample experiment discussed earlier; in that case $r = 2$.

(3) Independence trials (fixed marginal totals): Consider a group of n manufactured articles, of which fixed proportions are in each of the quality categories $C_1, \cdots, C_c$. The articles have been divided into r groups of fixed size $n_1, \cdots, n_r$ for further processing or for shipment to customers. The question arises whether the partitioning into the r groups can reasonably be considered to have been done randomly, that is, independently of how the articles fall into the quality categories. Since the number of articles in each of the categories $C_1, \cdots, C_c$ as well as the $n_1, \cdots, n_r$ are fixed, both marginal totals are fixed in this situation.

For these three cases let v_{ij} denote the number of individuals falling into row i, column j, and denote by $v_i.$ and $v._j$ the row and column totals, whether fixed or random. While different probability models are associated with the three cases, the approximate or large sample chi-square test is identical. The test statistic is

$$X^2 = \sum_{i=1}^{r} \sum_{j=1}^{c} \frac{[v_{ij} - (v_i. v._j)/n]^2}{(v_i. v._j)/n},$$

which has, if the null hypothesis is true, an approximate chi-square distribution with $(r-1) \cdot (c-1)$ degrees of freedom.

For the comparative trials case, this is an extension of the comparison of two percentages. The maximum likelihood estimator of the common value of $p_{1j}, p_{2j}, \cdots, p_{rj}$ is $v._j/n$ under the null hypothesis. The comparative trials model consists of r sequences of trials, each of which may result in one of c events; $c - 1$ parameters are estimated. Because $\sum_{j=1}^{c} p_{ij} = 1$, as soon as $c - 1$ of the probabilities are estimated the final one is determined. Hence the degrees of freedom are $r(c-1) - (c-1) = (r-1)(c-1)$.

In the double polytomy case there are $(r-1) + (c-1)$ independent parameters to be estimated under the null hypothesis: $p_1., p_2., \cdots, p_{r-1}., p._1, p._2, \cdots, p._{c-1}$, since again the restrictions $\sum_i p_i. = \sum_j p._j = 1$ provide the last two needed values. The maximum likelihood estimators of the $p_i.$ are the $v_i./n$ and of the $p._j$ are the $v._j/n$, so that the estimated expected values are $n(v_i./n)(v._j/n)$ or $v_i. v._j/n$. The degrees of freedom in this case are $(rc - 1) - (r-1) - (c-1)$ or $(r-1)(c-1)$, since there is only one sequence of trials with rc outcomes.

Like all chi-square tests, these are based upon asymptotic distribution theory and are satisfactory in practice for "large" sample sizes. A number of rules of thumb have been established in regard to the acceptable lower limit of sample size so that the actual type I error, or probability of rejecting the null hypothesis when true, does not depart too far from the prescribed significance level. For a careful discussion of this problem, and of procedures to adopt when the samples are too small, see Cochran (1952; 1954).

2×2 tables. The special case of contingency tables with $r = c = 2$ has been extensively studied, and the so-called Fisher exact test is available. Given $v_1., v_2., v._1, v._2$, under any of the null hypotheses, v_{11} has a specific hypergeometric distribution; hence probabilities of deviations as numerically large as, or larger than, the observed deviation can be calculated and a test can be made. The application of the test is now greatly facilitated by use of tables by Finney et al. (1963). For the comparative trials model and the double dichotomy model this exact test is a conditional test, given the marginal counts.

While the hypotheses associated with the three different models in $r \times c$ tables, in general, and 2×2 tables, in particular, can be tested by the same chi-square procedure, the power of the test varies according to the model. For the 2×2 case, approximations and tables have been given for each of the three models. The most recent of these are by Bennett and Hsu (1960) for comparative and independence trials and Harkness and Katz (1964) for the double dichotomy model. Earlier approximations are discussed and compared by these authors.

Single degrees of freedom. The statistic X^2 used to test the several null hypotheses possible for $r \times c$ contingency tables can be partitioned into $(r-1)(c-1)$ uncorrelated X^2 terms, each of which has a limiting chi-square distribution with one degree of freedom when the null hypothesis is true.

Planned comparisons. Planned subcomparisons, however, can be treated most easily by forming new contingency tables and calculating the approximate X^2 statistic. For example, in the comparison of three experimental learning methods with a standard method the observations might be recorded for each pupil as successful or unsuccessful and tabulated in a 4×2 table. These are four comparative trials; and X^2, the statistic to test homogeneity, has, under the null hypothesis, an approximate chi-square distribution with three degrees of freedom.

In this situation, two subcomparisons might be indicated: the standard method versus the combined experimental groups and in the experimental groups among themselves. Tables 3a and 3b show the two new contingency tables. The X^2 statistics calculated from these two subtables may be used to make the indicated secondary tests. The two X^2 values (with one and two degrees of freedom respectively) will not sum to the X^2 calculated for the whole 4×2 array. Short-cut formulas for a partition that is additive and references to other papers on this subject are given by Kimball (1954).

Table 3a — Comparison between standard method and combined experimental methods

	Successful	Unsuccessful
Standard (method 1)	v_{11}	v_{12}
Experimental methods combined	$v_{21} + v_{31} + v_{41}$	$v_{22} + v_{32} + v_{42}$

Table 3b — Comparison among experimental methods

	Successful	Unsuccessful
Experimental (method 2)	v_{21}	v_{22}
Experimental (method 3)	v_{31}	v_{32}
Experimental (method 4)	v_{41}	v_{42}

Unplanned comparisons. As in the analysis of variance of linear models, distinction should be made between such planned comparisons and unplanned comparisons. Goodman (1964a) has given a procedure to find confidence intervals for a family of "contrasts" among multinomial probabilities for the $r \times c$ contingency table in the com-

parative-trials model. A "contrast" is any linear function of the probabilities p_{ij}, with coefficients summing to zero, that is,

$$\sum_{i=1}^{r} \sum_{j=1}^{c} b_{ij} p_{ij}, \qquad \sum_{i=1}^{r} b_{ij} = 0 \text{ for each } j.$$

[See LINEAR HYPOTHESES, *article on* MULTIPLE COMPARISONS.]

Thus in the comparison of teaching methods experiment referred to above, where p_{i1} is the probability of a pupil being successful when taught by method i, the unplanned comparisons or contrasts might be $p_{21} - p_{31}$, $p_{21} - p_{41}$, $p_{31} - p_{41}$. These represent pairwise comparisons of the three experimental methods.

Denote a contrast by θ; an estimator of p_{ij} is $\hat{p}_{ij} = v_{ij}/v_i$. and an estimator of θ is

$$\hat{\theta} = \sum_{i=1}^{r} \sum_{j=1}^{c} b_{ij} \hat{p}_{ij}.$$

An estimator of the variance of $\hat{\theta}$ is

$$S^2(\hat{\theta}) = \sum_{i=1}^{r} \left\{ \left(v_i^{-1} \left[\sum_{j=1}^{c} b_{ij}^2 \hat{p}_{ij} - \left(\sum_{j=1}^{c} b_{ij} \hat{p}_{ij} \right)^2 \right] \right) \right\}.$$

The large-sample joint confidence intervals for θ with confidence coefficient $1 - \alpha$ have the form $\hat{\theta} - S(\hat{\theta})L$, $\hat{\theta} + S(\hat{\theta})L$, where L is the square root of the upper $100(1-\alpha)$th percentage point of the chi-square distribution with $(r-1)(c-1)$ degrees of freedom. An experiment in which one or more of the totality of all such possible intervals fail to include the true θ may be called a violation. The probability of such a violation is α.

If instead of all contrasts, only a few, say G, are of interest, then L in the last formula may be replaced by $Z_{1-\alpha/2G}$ (the $100 [1-\alpha/2G]$ percentile of the standard normal distribution), which often will be smaller than L and hence yield shorter confidence intervals while the probability of a violation is still less than or at most equal to α.

Comparative trials; ordered alternatives. In the comparative trials model, with $r \times 2$ contingency tables, frequently the only alternative of interest is an ordered set of p_{i1}'s. For example in a 2×2 comparative trial involving a control and a test group, the question may be to decide whether the groups are the same or whether the test group yields "better" results than the control group. In the 2×2 case, this situation is handled simply by working with the signed square root of X^2, which has a standard normal distribution if the null hypothesis is true. A one-sided alternative is then treated in the same manner as a test for a percentage referred to earlier.

For the more general $r \times 2$ table, the most complete treatment is that of Bartholomew (1959); his test, however, requires special tables. If the experimenter believes that the p_{i1} have a functional relationship to a known associated variable, x_i, then a specific test can be derived from the basic theorem. Such a test would be a particular example of a planned comparison. Many authors have given short-cut formulas and worked out examples of this type of problem (cf. Cochran 1954; Armitage 1955).

Comparative trials; dependent samples. A sample is taken of n voters who have voted in the last two national elections for one of the major parties. Denote the parties by L and C, and suppose that in the sample 45 per cent voted L in the first election and 55 per cent voted L in the second. Does this indicate a significant change in voter behavior in the subpopulation of which this is a sample? To make such a comparison in matched or dependent samples, it is necessary to obtain information on the actual changes in party preference [see PANEL STUDIES]. These can be read from a 2×2 table such as Table 4.

Table 4 — Voter preference in two elections

		ELECTION 1	
		L	C
ELECTION 2	L	v_{11}	v_{12}
	C	v_{21}	v_{22}

Such a 2×2 table with random marginals appears to fall into the double-dichotomy model, but the hypothesis of independence is not of interest here. The changes are indicated by the off-diagonal elements v_{12}, v_{21}, and the hypothesis of no net change is equivalent to the hypothesis that, given $v_{12} + v_{21}$, v_{12} is binomially distributed with probability $\frac{1}{2}$. Thus, the test of comparison of two percentages in identical or matched samples reduces to the test for a percentage. If the normal approximation is adequate, the square of the normal deviate, with the continuity correction, is

$$X^2 = \frac{(|v_{12} - v_{21}| - 1)^2}{v_{12} + v_{21}},$$

which has a limiting chi-square distribution with one degree of freedom under the null hypothesis that the probabilities are the same in the two matched groups. Cochran (1950) has extended this test to the $r \times c$ case. The test described above does not at all depend on v_{11} and v_{22}, but of course these quantities would enter into procedures pointed toward issues other than testing the null hypothesis of no net change.

Chi-square tests of goodness of fit. Chi-square tests have been used extensively to test whether sample observations might have arisen from a population with a specified form, such as binomial, Poisson, or normal. Such chi-square tests are again special cases of the general theory outlined above, although there are many other types of tests for goodness of fit [see GOODNESS OF FIT].

There are some special problems in connection with some nonstandard chi-square tests of goodness of fit for the binomial and Poisson distributions. The standard chi-square test of goodness of fit for these two discrete distributions requires (in most cases) estimation of the mean. The sample mean is an efficient estimator of the population mean; it appears to make little difference whether the sample mean is computed from the raw or grouped data.

There is evidence that two simpler tests are more powerful, at least for some alternatives, for testing whether a set of counts does come from one of the distributions. These test statistics are the so-called indices of dispersion, studied by Lexis and Bortkiewicz, which in fact compare two estimators of the variance—the usual sample estimator and the estimator derivable from the fact that for these distributions the variance is a function of the mean. Alternatively they may be viewed as chi-square tests, conditional on the total count and placed in the framework of the basic theorem. Thus if the observations are $v_1, \cdots, v_n$, which according to the null hypothesis come from a Poisson distribution, the appropriate index of dispersion test statistic is

$$X^2 = \frac{\sum_{i=1}^{n} (v_i - \bar{v})^2}{\bar{v}},$$

where $\bar{v}$ is the sample mean of the v_i. For large n and if the null hypothesis is true, X^2 is approximately distributed as chi-square with $n - 1$ degrees of freedom [see BORTKIEWICZ; LEXIS].

The corresponding test for the binomial can be expressed similarly, but it is also useful to set out the n observations in a $2 \times c$ contingency table such as Table 5.

Table 5 — Arrangement of data to test for binomial

	Sample 1	Sample 2	...	Sample c
Successes	x_1	x_2	...	x_c
Failures	$n_1 - x_1$	$n_2 - x_2$	...	$n_c - x_c$
Total	n_1	n_2	...	n_c

The variance test is equivalent to the chi-square test of homogeneity in this $2 \times c$ array, which has, of course, $c - 1$ degrees of freedom.

Whereas in general the chi-square test is a one-tailed test, that is, the null hypothesis is rejected for large values of the statistics, the dispersion tests are often two-tailed tests, not necessarily with equal probability in the tails. The reason for this is that a too small value of X^2 reflects a pattern that is *more* regular than that expected by chance, and such patterns may correspond to important alternatives to the null hypothesis of homogeneous randomness.

Contingency table association measures. If in the double-dichotomy model the hypothesis of independence is rejected, it is logical to seek a measure of association between the classifications. Distinction must be made between purely descriptive measures and sampling estimators of such measures. [*See* STATISTICS, DESCRIPTIVE, *article on* ASSOCIATION.]

A large number of such measures have been presented, usually related to the X^2 statistic used to test the null hypothesis of independence. Goodman and Kruskal (1954–1963) have emphasized the need to choose measures of association that have contextual meaning in the light of some probability model with predictive or explanatory value. They distinguish between two cases—no ordering among the categories and directed ordering among them.

Multidimensional contingency tables. The analysis of data that have been categorized into three or more classifications involves not only a considerable increase in the variety of possibilities but also introduces some new conceptual problems. The basic test of mutual independence is, however, a straightforward extension of the two-dimensional one and a simple application of the main theorem. The test will be discussed for three classifications.

This is a test of the hypothesis that p_{ijk}, the probability of an observation falling in row i, column j, and layer k, can be factored into $p_i.. p_{.j.} p_{..k}$. Under this null hypothesis the estimated expected value in cell ijk is $n^{-2}(v_i..)(v_{.j.})(v_{..k})$, where the dots indicate summation over the corresponding subscripts of the observed counts, v_{ijk}. The X^2 statistic has the usual form, sum of (observed − expected)^2/expected, and has $rcl - r - c - l + 2$ degrees of freedom if there are r rows, c columns, and l layers.

Tests for partial independence, for example that $p_{ijk} = (p_i..)(p_{.jk})$, or for homogeneity (between layers, for example) may be derived similarly. New concepts and new tests are introduced by the idea of *interaction* between the different classifications.

In linear models, interactions are measures of nonadditivity of the effects due to different classifications. With contingency models several definitions of interaction have been given; the present treatment follows Goodman (1964b). Consider, for example, samples drawn from rural and urban populations and classified by sex and age, with age treated dichotomously (see Table 6).

Table 6 — Classification of rural and urban samples by sex and age

	URBAN			RURAL		
	Young	Old	Totals	Young	Old	Totals
Male	20	14	34	34	11	45
Female	42	24	66	36	19	55
Totals	62	38	100	70	30	100

For the urban group there is a sex ratio 20/42 among the "young" and 14/24 among the "old." The ratio of these may be regarded as a measure of the interaction of age and sex in the urban population. Similarly the same ratio of sex ratios is a measure of the interaction in the rural population. These are, of course, sample values; and the population interactions must be defined in terms of the probabilities p_{ijk}. It is useful to define

$$\Delta_k = \frac{p_{11k}}{p_{21k}} \Big/ \frac{p_{12k}}{p_{22k}}$$

and to write the three-factor no interaction hypothesis as $\Delta_1 = \Delta_2$ for this $2 \times 2 \times 2$ contingency table. The maximum likelihood estimator of Δ_k is $d_k = v_{11k}v_{22k}/v_{12k}v_{21k}$, and its variance can be estimated consistently by $s_k^2 = d_k^2 u_k$ where $u_k = \sum_i \sum_j v_{ijk}^{-1}$. A simple statistic to test the hypothesis $\Delta_1 = \Delta_2$ is $X^2 = (d_1 - d_2)^2/(s_1^2 + s_2^2)$, which, if the null hypothesis is true, has a large sample chi-square distribution with one degree of freedom.

For the data given $d_1 = 0.816$, $d_2 = 1.631$, $s_1^2 = 0.125$, $s_2^2 = 0.534$, and $X^2 = 1.01$ so that the three-factor no interaction hypothesis is not rejected at the usual significance levels. Goodman has extended this test in an obvious way to the $2 \times 2 \times l$ contingency table. Here the test statistic is

$$X^2 = \sum_{k=1}^{l} \frac{(d_k - \bar{d})^2}{s_k^2}, \qquad \text{where } \bar{d} = \frac{\sum_{k=1}^{l} d_k / s_k^2}{\sum_{k=1}^{l} s_k^2},$$

which has $l - 1$ degrees of freedom. The extension to $r \times c \times l$ tables is based on logarithms of frequencies rather than the actual frequencies. Goodman also provides confidence intervals for the interactions Δ_k and indicates a number of equivalent tests. A bibliography of the very extensive literature on this topic is given in this paper.

Alternatives to chi-square

While the chi-square tests are classical for the analysis of counted data, with the original simple tests going back to Karl Pearson, they are not the likelihood ratio tests. The latter are based upon statistics of the form

$$\sum_{j=1}^{J} v_j \log \frac{v_j}{np_j} = \sum_{j=1}^{J} v_j \log [1 + (v_j - np_j)/np_j]$$

in the general case with one sequence of trials. It is easy to show, by expanding minus twice the logarithm of the likelihood ratio statistic in a power series, that its leading term is X^2, and that further terms are of a smaller order than the leading term so that the tests are equivalent in the limit. However, they are not equivalent for small samples.

Another test for contingency tables (comparative trials model) is that of C. A. B. Smith (1951). Further work appears to be necessary before any of these alternatives is accepted as preferable to the chi-square tests. The most widely used alternative analysis is that indicated in the next section.

ANOVA of transformed counted data. Contingency tables have an obvious analogy to similar arrays of measured data that are often treated by analysis of variance techniques (ANOVA). The analysis of variance models are more satisfactory if the data are such that (1) effects are additive, (2) error variability is constant, (3) the error distribution is symmetrical and nearly normal, and (4) the errors are statistically independent. [*See* LINEAR HYPOTHESES, *article on* ANALYSIS OF VARIANCE.]

Counted data that arise from a binomial or multinomial model fail most obviously on the second property since the variances of such data vary with the mean. However, some function or transformation of the observations may have approximately constant variance. Transformations that have been derived for counted data to make variances nearly constant have been found empirically often to improve the degree of approximation to which properties (1) and (3) hold also. These transformations include: (*a*) Arc sine transformation for proportions

$$y = \text{arc sin } \sqrt{v/n}\,,$$

which is applicable to dichotomous data with an equal number of trials in each sequence. If the number of trials (n_i) varies from sequence to sequence the problem is more complicated (see Cochran 1943). (*b*) Square root transformation: $y = \sqrt{v + 1}$ for Poisson data. (*c*) Logarithmic transformation: $y = \log (v + 1)$ for data such that the standard deviation is proportional to the mean. Use of the arc sine transformation, and subsequent analysis, is facilitated by the use of binomial probability paper; graphic techniques are simple and usually adequate. The basic reference for such procedures is Mosteller and Tukey (1949).

Refinements of these transformations and discussion of the choice of transformations is given a thorough treatment by Tukey (1957). If a suitable transformation has been made, the whole battery of tests that have been developed in analysis of variance (including covariance techniques) is applicable. Estimation problems may be more subtle; in some situations estimates may be given in the transformed variable but in others it may be desirable to transform back to the original variable. [*See* STATISTICAL ANALYSIS, SPECIAL PROBLEMS OF, *article on* TRANSFORMATIONS OF DATA.]

Precautions in the analysis of counted data

The transformations discussed above were derived to apply to data that conform to such models as the binomial or Poisson and that could be analyzed by chi-square methods. However, counted data often arise from models that do not conform to the basic assumption; in particular independence may be lacking, so that the chi-square tests are not valid. Such data are often transformed and treated by analysis of variance procedures; the justification for this is largely empirical. Examples of situations where this is necessary are experimental responses of animals in a group where dependence may be present, eye estimates of the numbers in a group of people, and comparisons of proportions in heterogeneous and unequal-sized groups. In such situations care is necessary that the proper transformation is selected to achieve the properties listed above and in the interpretation of the results of the analysis.

The lack of independence and the presence of extraneous sources of variation are frequent sources of error in the analysis of counted data because the chi-square tests are invalidated by such factors. A discussion of these errors and others is found in Lewis and Burke (1949). The two careful expository papers by Cochran (1952; 1954) represent an excellent source of further reading on this topic. See also the monograph by Maxwell (1961).

DOUGLAS G. CHAPMAN

[*See also* QUANTAL RESPONSE.]

BIBLIOGRAPHY

ARMITAGE, P. 1955 Tests for Linear Trends in Proportions and Frequencies. *Biometrics* 11:375–386.

BARTHOLOMEW, D. J. 1959 A Test of Homogeneity for Ordered Alternatives. Parts 1–2. *Biometrika* 46:36–48, 328–335.

BENNETT, B. M.; and HSU, P. 1960 On the Power Function of the Exact Test for the 2 × 2 Contingency Table. *Biometrika* 47:393–398.

CLOPPER, C. J.; and PEARSON, E. S. 1934 The Use of Confidence or Fiducial Limits Illustrated in the Case of the Binomial. *Biometrika* 26:404–413.

COCHRAN, WILLIAM G. 1943 Analysis of Variance for Percentages Based on Unequal Numbers. *Journal of the American Statistical Association* 38:287–301.

COCHRAN, WILLIAM G. 1950 The Comparison of Percentages in Matched Samples. *Biometrika* 37:256–266.

COCHRAN, WILLIAM G. 1952 The χ^2 Test of Goodness of Fit. *Annals of Mathematical Statistics* 23:315–345.

COCHRAN, WILLIAM G. 1954 Some Methods for Strengthening the Common χ^2 Tests. *Biometrics* 10:417–451.

COLUMBIA UNIVERSITY, STATISTICAL RESEARCH GROUP 1947 *Techniques of Statistical Analysis for Scientific and Industrial Research and Production and Management Engineering.* Edited by Churchill Eisenhart, Millard W. Hastay, and W. Allen Wallis. New York: McGraw-Hill.

CRAMÉR, H. 1946 *Mathematical Methods of Statistics.* Princeton Univ. Press. → See especially Chapter 30.

DIAMOND, EARL L. 1963 The Limiting Power of Categorical Data Chi-square Tests Analogous to Normal Analysis of Variance. *Annals of Mathematical Statistics* 34:1432–1441.

FERGUSON, THOMAS S. 1958 A Method of Generating Best Asymptotically Normal Estimates With Application to the Estimation of Bacterial Densities. *Annals of Mathematical Statistics* 29:1046–1062.

FINNEY, DAVID J. et al. 1963 *Tables for Testing Significance in a 2×2 Contingency Table.* Cambridge Univ. Press.

GOODMAN, LEO A. 1964a Simultaneous Confidence Intervals for Contrasts Among Multinomial Population. *Annals of Mathematical Statistics* 35:716–725.

GOODMAN, LEO A. 1964b Simple Methods for Analyzing Three-factor Interaction in Contingency Tables. *Journal of the American Statistical Association* 59:319–352.

GOODMAN, LEO A.; and KRUSKAL, WILLIAM H. 1954–1963 Measures of Association for Cross-classifications. Parts 1–3. *Journal of the American Statistical Association* 49:732–764; 54:123–163; 58:310–364.

HARKNESS, W. L.; and KATZ, LEO 1964 Comparison of the Power Functions for the Test of Independence in 2×2 Contingency Tables. *Annals of Mathematical Statistics* 35:1115–1127.

HARVARD UNIVERSITY, COMPUTATION LABORATORY 1955 *Tables of the Cumulative Binomial Probability Distribution.* Cambridge, Mass.: Harvard Univ. Press.

KIMBALL, A. W. 1954 Short Cut Formulas for the Exact Partition of χ^2 in Contingency Tables. *Biometrics* 10:452–458.

LEWIS, D.; and BURKE, C. J. 1949 The Use and Misuse of the Chi-square Test. *Psychological Bulletin* 46:433–489. → Discussion of the article may be found in subsequent issues of this bulletin: 47:331–337, 338–340, 341–346, 347–355; 48:81–82.

MAXWELL, ALBERT E. 1961 *Analyzing Qualitative Data.* New York: Wiley.

MITRA, SUJIT KUMAR 1958 On the Limiting Power Function of the Frequency Chi-square Test. *Annals of Mathematical Statistics* 29:1221–1233.

MOSTELLER, FREDERICK; and TUKEY, JOHN W. 1949 The Uses and Usefulness of Binomial Probability Paper. *Journal of the American Statistical Association* 44:174–212.

NEYMAN, JERZY 1949 Contribution to the Theory of the χ^2 Test. Pages 239–273 in Berkeley Symposium on Mathematical Statistics and Probability, *Proceedings.* Edited by Jerzy Neyman. Berkeley: Univ. of California Press.

OWEN, DONALD B. 1962 *Handbook of Statistical Tables.* Reading, Mass.: Addison-Wesley. A list of addenda and errata is available from the author.

SMITH, C. A. B 1951 A Test for Heterogeneity of Proportions. *Annals of Eugenics* 16:15–25.

TUKEY, JOHN W. 1957 On the Comparative Anatomy of Transformations. *Annals of Mathematical Statistics* 28:602–632.

U.S. NATIONAL BUREAU OF STANDARDS 1950 *Tables of the Binomial Probability Distribution.* Applied Mathematics Series, No. 6. Washington: Government Printing Office.

COURNOT, ANTOINE AUGUSTIN

Antoine Augustin Cournot (1801–1877), French mathematician, economist, and philosopher, was born at Gray (Haute-Saône), the son of a notary. He came from a family of farmers who had lived in Franche-Comté since at least the middle of the sixteenth century. Until age 15, Cournot attended the *collège* at Gray; then, for the next four years, he read a great deal on his own, especially works by scientists and philosophers, such as Laplace and Leibniz. After preparing at Besançon, Cournot was admitted in 1821 to the scientific section of the École Normale Supérieure, in Paris. The school was closed by the reactionary regime the following year, but Cournot stayed in Paris and in 1823 received the licentiate in sciences. He attended sessions at the Académie des Sciences and associated with the principal scholars of the day; it was through one of them that he met Proudhon. In October 1823, Cournot entered the household of Marshal Gouvion Saint-Cyr in the double capacity of literary adviser to the marshal, who wanted to complete some unfinished manuscripts, and tutor to the marshal's son.

Cournot spent ten years with the marshal, all the while continuing his scientific studies. In 1829 he received a doctorate in science, writing a main thesis in mechanics and a supplementary one in astronomy. He also studied law. A series of articles that he published on scientific questions attracted the attention of the great mathematician Poisson, who was then professor at the École Polytechnique and later at the University of Paris. Poisson was then in charge of the instruction in mathematics throughout France and arranged Cournot's appointment to the chair of mathematical analysis in the faculty of sciences at Lyon. Cournot taught for only one year, however; subsequently, most of his life was spent in university administration, in which he was very successful. He became, successively, rector of the Académie de Grenoble in 1835, inspector general of the University of Dijon, and rector of the Académie de Dijon from 1854 to 1862. Cournot then accepted no further public positions and returned to Paris, where he died just as he was about to apply for membership in the Institut de France. Toward the end of his life he was nearly blind.

Cournot's administrative work left him ample time for a great deal of scientific writing. Unfortunately, his books suffer from a lack of the stimulation that contact with an audience gives to teachers. Ten of his works appeared between 1838 and 1877. These books have three major themes: (1) algebra, infinitesimal analysis, and calculus of probabilities; (2) the theory of wealth; and (3) the philosophy of science, the philosophy of history, and even general philosophy. These themes were interdependent in Cournot's work, and although the economic side will be stressed here, the profound unity of his thought must be remembered. Cournot started with mathematics, was then attracted to economics, and ended with a general interpretation of the world that was infused with his profound understanding of probabilities. It is the concept of probability that integrates the three parts of his work.

Cournot's rather melancholic and solitary temperament considerably delayed the influence he was ultimately to have. Modest and self-effacing, he did nothing to make his books attractive. They tend to be austere, crowded with facts and proofs. Even the titles he chose reflect his modesty: *Researches*, *Essay*, and *Considerations*. It is not surprising, then, that he is less well known in the field of probability than Laplace and Poisson, less appreciated among economists than Bastiat, Say, or Proudhon (to mention only French economists), and less quoted in philosophy than Comte or Spencer. And yet Cournot, having the rare knowledge required to use the language of all of these authors, combined many of their qualities and made a quasi-prophetic synthesis of their ideas.

Mathematics and probability theory. Cournot's mathematical works, econometrics aside, appeared between 1840 and 1850. In his *Exposition de la théorie des chances et des probabilités* (1843), he put forward a definition of statistics as that science which deals with collecting and coordinating numerous facts of every kind, in such a way as to obtain numerical relationships that are markedly independent of the anomalies of chance, and that manifest the existence of uniformly operating causes whose effects have been confounded, however, with other, accidental effects.

Cournot, living in the first half of the nineteenth century, stood at the crossroads of two ways of mathematical endeavor: the one originated with Pascal and Fermat and led to the work of Jacques Bernoulli, Gauss, Laplace, and Poisson on the doctrine of chances; the other, renouncing the mathematical study of chance and uncertainty, focused on the mathematics of rigorous determinations by algorithms that admit no margin of uncertainty—as if science were perfectly deterministic. This concept that the perfect is the determined was to play a major role in the development of the early science of economics, as one can see from the still current term "perfect competition." Cournot foresaw that science could not be intrinsically and definitively tied to such determinism. He believed that a science of margins and chances is not only viable but perhaps better suited to the needs of economics than a science of absolute, exact equilibria. Nonetheless, Cournot is often regarded as having introduced into economic theory the use of deterministic mathematics.

Economics. Cournot wrote three works in economics, in 1838, 1863, and 1877; thus, his career began and ended with writings on economics. When *Recherches sur les principes mathématiques de la théorie des richesses* (1838a) first appeared, it was such a fiasco that Cournot remained silent on the subject of economics for 25 years. He then wrote *Principes de la théorie des richesses* (1863), putting into "literary" language what he had previously said in the language of mathematics. Despite the concessions Cournot made in the form of presentation, the *Principes* was no better received than the *Recherches*; indeed, if Cournot had produced only his nonmathematical work, he would never have been recognized as anything but a minor figure.

Strictly speaking, to be sure, Cournot was not the first to have used mathematical language to express economic problems. There was Nicolas Canard, in France, whom Cournot did quote, but Canard did not have Cournot's scope and erudition. Great erudition is needed to combine economics and mathematics, and if mathematical economics has had its setbacks, the reason is that it has not always been guided by such clear minds as Cournot's.

Cournot's great merit is that, without saying so explicitly, he was the first to construct a true theory of prices and markets. Chapter 4 of *Recherches*, entitled "Of the Law of Demand," is the first model of its kind. Cournot was interested exclusively in the demand that is followed by an actual sale and that is, therefore, observable and measurable. He is recognized for having revealed the concept of function and for having made available to economists the immensely useful language of functional concepts. Sales are, in general, a decreasing function of price. This function is continuous, at least when the number of consumers is not limited.

Moreover, the sales function is not purely abstract; it may be constructed on the basis of mean annually observed data. And since it is not merely an a priori function but an empirical, experimental one, Cournot may be considered to have made the initial step in developing econometrics.

In this econometric mode of analysis, a related idea is that of imperfection, hence of uncertainty and, in turn, of chance in measurement. Here again, Cournot's knowledge of probabilities saved him from incorrectly associating mathematics with the idea of rigorous precision. He asserted that even if the object of numerical calculation "were unattainable, it would be nevertheless not improper to introduce the unknown law of demand into the analytical combinations, by means of an indeterminate symbol; for it is well known that one of the most important functions of analysis consists precisely in assigning determinate relations between quantities to which numerical values and even algebraic forms are absolutely unassignable" ([1838a] 1960, p. 48). We must give up trying to grasp what cannot be grasped rigorously. It is for this reason, perhaps, that we must reason mathematically ". . . by showing what determinate relations exist between unknown quantities, analysis reduces these unknown quantities to the smallest possible number, and guides the observer to the best observations for discovering their values. It reduces and coordinates statistical documents; and it diminishes the labour of statisticians . . ." (*ibid.*, pp. 48–49).

Cournot's first construction is worked out in this spirit: it consists in drawing up, within suitable limits, tables of correspondence between the values of the demand, $D = f(p)$, and the price, p. In a second stage, the function $pf(p)$, the total value of the amount sold, is considered. This becomes the crux of the theory of markets. Long before Alfred Marshall, Cournot presented a theory of elasticity: depending on whether $\Delta D/\Delta p < D/p$ or $\Delta D/\Delta p > D/p$, the price increase will make the product $pf(p)$ larger or smaller. Hence commercial statistics should begin by dividing merchandise into two categories, depending on whether their current prices are lower or higher than the value making $pf(p)$ a maximum. In this formulation, Cournot was truly a great innovator.

Instead of attacking the general price equilibrium directly, as Léon Walras and Vilfredo Pareto were later to do, Cournot proceeded by gradual steps. He started with monopoly, then considered competition limited to a few participants, and in the end took up the case of indefinite or unlimited competition, using the intercommunication of markets to complete his theory. This procedure has been criticized, for economists in the classical tradition follow the inverse procedure, starting with unlimited competition or, as they call it, perfect competition and ending up with monopoly. However, Cournot's point of view has again been adopted in the modern theory of games and of the rational search for decisions. Although his theory of duopoly was criticized in 1883 by the mathematician Joseph Bertrand, the theory of bilateral monopoly was later to be erected on a similar base. The model with two parties was changed to a three-sided model (triopoly), and as the number of parties increased, the system was called oligopoly, pliopoly, and finally polypoly; the larger the number, the more closely the model approached that of classical competition. Today, makers of models no longer believe that there is an irreducible difference between models with many elements and those with few, but instead they relate the theory of markets to the general theory of economic interaction; hence their work is in the tradition of Cournot's model, at first so poorly understood. There is still much to be learned from this 1838 model. Although Cournot has been rehabilitated, his contribution to economics has not been exhausted.

Philosophy. In Cournot's philosophical works there emerge a philosophy of order and one of history. Cournot firmly maintained that, appearances to the contrary, chance does not imply disorder. By virtue of the theory of probabilities it is possible to see regularities: it is, as it were, the point of intersection of multiple independent causal series. And it permits the joining of the sciences with philosophy. The meaning of history, for all its incoherence, and the meaning of the future, for all its unpredictability, are profoundly related. To discover the course of ideas and events is the function of knowledge and the vocation of the human mind.

Cournot was a pioneer. He did nothing to court his contemporaries, and they, in turn, not only failed to appreciate him but ignored him. By a fitting reversal, his triumph came 80 years after his death. The most advanced of the econometric school recognize him as their ancestor. The theory of probabilities, whose full import Cournot realized, is a vital component of the structure of recent science. The problems that did not interest the men of his time are those that guide the building of tomorrow's world; Cournot had anticipated the concern with predictions and decisions that now preoccupies economists.

HENRI GUITTON

[*For the historical context of Cournot's work, see biographies of the* BERNOULLI FAMILY; GAUSS; LAPLACE;

POISSON. *For discussion of the subsequent development of his ideas, see* DEMAND AND SUPPLY; OLIGOPOLY; PROBABILITY.]

WORKS BY COURNOT

1829 *Mémoire sur le mouvement d'un corps rigide soutenu par un plan fixe.* Paris: Hachette.

(1838a) 1960 *Researches Into the Mathematical Principles of the Theory of Wealth.* New York: Kelley. → First published in French.

1838b *Mémoire sur les applications du calcul des chances à la statistique judiciaire. Journal de mathématiques pures et appliquées* 3:257–334. → This is an early example of work on what is now called "latent structure."

(1841) 1857 *Traité élémentaire de la théorie des fonctions et du calcul infinitésimal.* 2d ed. Paris: Hachette.

1843 *Exposition de la théorie des chances et des probabilités.* Paris: Hachette.

1847 *De l'origine et des limites de la correspondance entre l'algèbre et la géométrie.* Paris: Hachette.

(1851) 1956 *An Essay on the Foundations of Our Knowledge.* New York: Liberal Arts Press. → First published in French.

(1861) 1911 *Traité de l'enchaînement des idées fondamentales dans les sciences et dans l'histoire.* New ed. Paris: Hachette.

1863 *Principes de la théorie des richesses.* Paris: Hachette.

(1872) 1934 *Considérations sur la marche des idées et des évènements dans les temps modernes.* 2 vols. Paris: Boivin.

(1875) 1923 *Matérialisme, vitalisme, rationalisme: Études des données de la science en philosophie.* Paris: Hachette.

1877 *Revue sommaire des doctrines économiques.* Paris: Hachette.

1913 *Souvenirs (1760–1860).* With an introduction by E. P. Bottinelli. Paris: Hachette. → Published posthumously.

SUPPLEMENTARY BIBLIOGRAPHY

[A. A. Cournot.] 1905 *Revue de métaphysique et de morale* 13:291–343. → The entire issue is devoted to Cournot.

BERTRAND, J. 1883 [Book Reviews of] *Théories mathématiques de la richesse sociale,* par Léon Walras; *Recherches sur les principes mathématiques de la théorie de la richesse,* par Augustin Cournot. *Journal des savants* [1883]:499–508.

BOMPAIRE, FRANÇOIS 1931 *Du principe de liberté économique dans l'oeuvre de Cournot et dans celle de l'école de Lausanne (Walras, Pareto).* Paris: Sirey.

BOTTINELLI, E. P. 1913 *A. Cournot: Métaphysicien de la connaissance.* Paris: Hachette.

EDGEWORTH, F. Y. (1894) 1963 Antoine Augustin Cournot. Volume 1, pages 445–447 in Robert H. I. Palgrave, *Palgrave's Dictionary of Political Economy.* New York: Kelley.

LIEFMANN-KIEL, ELISABETH 1937 Die wissenschaftliche Methode und das Gesamtwerk Cournots. *Archiv für mathematische Wirtschafts- und Sozialforschung* 3: 238–251.

LOISEAU, GEORGES 1913 *Les doctrines économiques de Cournot.* Paris: Rousseau.

MENTRÉ, FRANÇOIS 1908 *Cournot et la renaissance du probabilisme au XIXᵉ siècle.* Paris: Rivière.

MENTRÉ, FRANÇOIS 1927 *Pour qu'on lise Cournot.* Paris: Beauchesne.

MILHAUD, GASTON S. (1902–1911) 1927 *Études sur Cournot.* Paris: Vrin.

ROY, RENÉ 1933 Cournot et l'école mathématique. *Econometrica* 1:13–22.

SEGOND, J. 1911 *Cournot et la psychologie vitaliste.* Paris: Alcan.

COURTS

See ADJUDICATION; JUDICIAL PROCESS; JUDICIARY.

COURTS MARTIAL

See MILITARY LAW.

CRAFTS

The term "craft" derives from the Anglo-Saxon *cræft,* meaning "strength, skill, or cunning," in contrast to "art," which usually implies an intention of producing beauty or pleasure. Contemporary scholars often consider "arts and crafts" together because of the difficulties in so many societies of differentiating the aesthetic from the strictly utilitarian. Anthropologists prefer to use "technology" to refer to the processes of manufacture and "material culture" for the artifacts themselves. Since crafts include all activities that produce or modify objects by manual means, with or without the use of mechanical aids, such as looms or potters' wheels, the range of study is very broad. There is an equally wide range of social forms within which the craftsmen operate.

In a second sense, "craft" is synonymous with "guild," commonly used as a term of class ascription and role delineation in contemporary sociology, and is applied to occupational associations. Within this meaning the status of craftsmen differs by culture, epoch, and craft.

History of the study of technology

It was the change in the role of the craftsman that first drew the attention of scholars to the importance of studying the history of technology. When it became apparent in the middle of the nineteenth century that the impact of the industrial revolution was causing rapid degeneration in traditional peasant crafts, European folklorist–ethnographers set themselves to recording and collecting as much as possible before the crafts became extinct. As these collections grew, the study of technology grew with them and raised some of the basic questions with which the infant science of anthropology was to be concerned. The exhaustive collections of European museums, often made under the impetus of chauvinistic nationalism, tempted some scholars to postulate a number of diffusion theories of differing degrees of sophistication and other scholars to devote their careers to the refutation of these theories. The product of these controversies has been of infinite value to the social sciences.

European students of local arts and crafts have made superbly documented analyses of the diffusion of particular objects, styles, and techniques, such as de Rohan-Csermak's study (1963) of the spread of sturgeon hooks across Eurasia, and most European countries now boast folk museums or reconstructed villages where peasant crafts are produced, displayed, and sold. Folk craftsmen, along with folk musicians, dancers, and other artists, are subsidized by the national governments to discourage crass commercialization and to ensure the continuity of tradition. In many countries, such as Sweden, Denmark, Mexico, and Japan, folk craft products have been adapted to the world market to such an extent that they have become a valuable asset in economic development and national prestige.

However, American scholars view much of this European research as both questionable and beside the point. On the basis of the work of Sapir (1916, pp. 5–25), Dixon (1928, pp. 145–146), and others, they tend to feel that far-reaching historical reconstructions on the basis of distribution studies of artifacts are unwarranted, and they are particularly cynical if the result happens to support a nationalistic claim. Only very limited and tentative historical inferences are allowable from the study of artifacts, and then only in a restricted area whose historical unity can be assumed, or where the artifacts are used to corroborate and illustrate historical documentation. Archeology, which might be defined as the study of the more durable arts and crafts of past societies, provides a model. In spite of extreme care in distribution study and typing of artifacts, archeologists reach only very tentative conclusions and are loath to attempt the outlining of even a small segment of protohistory.

Thus, in their zeal to understand more fully the relationships between art and culture, American scholars eschew historical reconstruction based on techniques for chipping flint or the distribution of beads. Instead, such monographs as Bunzel's *The Pueblo Potter* (1929), O'Neale's *Yurok–Karok Basket Weavers* (1932), and Adair's *The Navajo and Pueblo Silversmiths* (1944) analyze the integration of craft activities with the structure of living societies, the economic base of the crafts, their social functions, the roles of the craftsmen, and the value systems that may be expressed through them;

these monographs are, accordingly, as pertinent to art historians, aestheticians, and psychologists as to anthropologists. But even when the art is moribund or the culture extinct, intensive study of museum specimens can yield useful insight into the nature of style and the processes of creativity. In this way, Olbrechts (1946) was able to postulate the so-called Master of Buli as the creator of the long-faced Luba sculptural style, and Proskouriakoff (1950), through analysis of significant stylistic details on dated Maya stelae, was able to give provisional dates for the great mass of undated Maya sculpture. The inconclusive results of studies in measurement, such as Reichard's *Melanesian Design* (1933), or in typology, such as Schweeger-Hefel's *Holzplastik in Afrika* (1960), suggest the need for more sophisticated statistical and computer analyses of dimension, proportion, and the frequency of particular stylistic characteristics in objects from a given area, the ultimate goal being the mathematical quantification of each style. Research projects by Yehudi Cohen and Alvin Wolfe, as yet unpublished, are hopeful attempts to correlate particular styles or forms of art with types of social organization. Where the arts and crafts are still practiced in reasonably traditional ways, it would be possible to study the aesthetic value systems of the craftsmen and their audiences and thus help answer the ancient questions about the existence of an absolute criterion of art above culture, epoch, and individual.

The social organization of crafts

Craft organization by sex. In most human societies throughout history, the crafts have been organized primarily on the basis of the sexual division of labor, with all the men of an ethnic group learning with varying degrees of skill all of the "masculine" crafts, and all the women learning a separate set of "feminine" crafts. Although it would seem logical for women to make clothing and utensils for food processing, and for men to provide shelter, transport, weapons, and hunting and fishing equipment, actually there is no clear consensus as to which sex should practice which particular crafts. Women are the weavers in the American southwest, but men are in Africa. Men of the Northwest Coast Indians design the Chilkat blankets by making drawings on boards, but women do the actual twining process. Men are the potters in Europe, India, and central Africa, but women are in west Africa and the Americas. Bark cloth is made by men in Africa, but by women in southeast Asia. Baskets made for the home are usually the domain of women, but men may make baskets for sale or barter. In spite of its obviously arbitrary nature, the division of craft labor by sex is usually considered a "law of nature," the breaking of which brings serious consequences. Many nonliterate societies provide the role of the *berdache,* or transvestite, for men who are not necessarily homosexuals but who choose to practice, and often excel women in, the feminine crafts. Even in Western culture, where industrialization has blurred the sexual division of labor, female welders, engineers, or surgeons face as much opposition as male nurses or secretaries, although there is no innate supracultural reason why they cannot perform the required services as well as, or in some cases better than, the opposite sex, to whom the role is usually assigned.

Craft organization by family. A second basic structuring device for crafts is the family unit. This device occurs in fairly complex societies and is seen in its most extreme form in Indian occupational castes. Here all the men of a family practice the same craft, the techniques of which are handed down from father to son. Ideally at least, every son follows the same craft as his ancestors and marries the daughter of a member of the same caste. Wherever appropriate, the women also practice the craft or help in the preparation of raw materials. Such endogamous occupational castes as *sonār* (goldsmiths), *lohār* (blacksmiths), *kumhār* (potters), and *camār* (leatherworkers) prove quite stable even when technological change or emigration requires radical modification of their occupational activities to keep their product marketable. Many occupational castes have subcastes, each endogamous, which specialize in particular designs or types of the caste product. Although castes effectively minimize competition, they are all interdependent economically because they need one another's products.

In many other societies castelike family organization exists among craftsmen. The Senufo and Bambara of west Africa, for instance, group all artisans together in a single endogamous kin unit, whether they be male blacksmiths, jewelers, wood or stone carvers, or female potters. They usually live apart in their own villages or in compounds at the edge of towns. Even though they obtain most of their livelihood from farming, as do other Senufo, they have a separate initiation system and are both feared and disdained because of the magical associations of their callings. In central Africa those who know the secret of smelting iron from local ore are also considered magicians but are often of chiefly status and are accorded great admiration, rather than fear.

In many other cultures, such as traditional Japan, China, Dahomey, and Polynesia, the right to practice a particular craft was hereditary, and these craft families often served as courtiers who supported the political authority by providing suitably elegant objects for the king and his court. In contemporary Euro-American culture one may find families who have practiced a particular and often highly specialized craft for many generations and often in many countries. Examples are the Dolmetsch family, makers of recorders and other archaic instruments, the Zildjian family, who alone possess the formula for making the finest cymbals, and, in the humbler crafts, Swiss woodcarvers and watchmakers, Belgian lacemakers, and Irish and Scottish tweed weavers.

Craft organization by village. Since nearly all crafts require particular materials for their manufacture, craftsmen try to settle as near as possible to their source of supply or, alternatively, to their markets. In this way, an area possessing an outcropping of fine pottery clay will often develop one or more villages of potters. In such a situation, it is not difficult to see how potters originally of different origins could combine forces to regulate prices, standardize designs or specializations, minimize competition, and ultimately to intermarry and form a complex kin unit. Within such a craft village, the family organization is likely to approximate a caste; indeed, in India many craft villages are inhabited by a single occupational caste. Even where there is no limitation on marriage, the common economic and technological interests of the young people tend to draw them together socially.

Just as with interdependent castes, craft villages and families also are complementary. For instance, craft villages in Melanesia trade extensively with one another, often in connection with ceremonial exchanges. The need for one another's exclusive products is so great that trade is often carried on through neutrals during periods of war. In the Nilgiri hills of south India, three non-Hindu tribes have a similar symbiotic relationship, the Toda providing clarified butter (*ghī*) for food and ritual purposes, the Kota cultivating grain, and the Badaga serving as craftsmen, merchants, and musicians.

Mexican popular arts, probably the richest and most varied being produced today, come from family groups in Mexico City or from small craft villages. In the Lake Pátzcuaro district of Michoacán, for instance, Uruapan produces fine lacquer work; Paracho, musical instruments, toys, and lathe-turned wooden objects; Santa Clara del Cobre, hammered copper utensils and fringed black serapes; Apatzingán (until recently), leather-covered *equipale* furniture; Patamban, Capula, and

Tzintzuntzan, three or more distinctive pottery wares; Erongarícuaro, woven *cambaya* cotton textiles and embroideries; and Pátzcuaro itself, *rebozo*, reed mats, and silver jewelry. Even in pre-Columbian times the Tarascan Indians of Michoacán had a high degree of craft specialization, including lapidaries, stonemasons, woodcarvers, paper and feather workers, weavers of cotton textiles, matmakers, lacquer makers, drum makers, and makers of bows and arrows. Today the products not consumed locally are sold in nearby Morelia, and a few reach international markets. Similar conglomerates exist around Guadalajara, Toluca, Puebla, Oaxaca, and other Mexican cities, and there are many isolated craft-producing areas, such as Santa María del Río for silk *rebozo* and Saltillo for serapes.

Part-time professionals. In most societies there is no economic surplus to support full-time craftsmen, so that all practitioners of crafts, even those recognized as consummate experts, must make their livings largely through agriculture. As an example, the Chokwe of Angola and the Congo (Leopoldville) teach all boys to carve *mahamba* figures for hunting magic and *jinga* charms for female fertility in the course of the *mukanda* initiation rites. Except for a few special cases, no full-time artists exist, but a number of skilled carvers have so impressed their individual styles on the community that their work can be recognized far and wide, and young men pay for the privilege of being apprenticed to them. Yet such a master carver (*songi*) works his farm and hunts at the end of the rainy season. The few masks, figures, or stools he might be commissioned to make in the course of a year would bring him only a small amount in cash or livestock to supplement his regular income from the sale of peanuts, manioc, or other crops. The paucity of output helps explain why each piece is stylistically unique and why traditional carvers employed full time as producers or teachers turn out only repetitive and stereotypic work. Such part-time experts also supervise the making of masks and paraphernalia for the elaborate socioreligious rites, for instance, of the west African Dogon (Griaule 1938) and the Melanesian Orokaiva (Williams 1940).

Development of craft associations

In all their variety of style and technique, most crafts can be shown to have been invented at least twice (in the Old World and in the New World) and probably many more times in the hundreds of centuries man has had at his disposal, and they do not seem to follow a strongly evolutionary pattern of development. On the contrary, the elegantly idealized animals of the Magdalenian cave painters were drawn virtually with the same methods, tools, and materials as are found in a contemporary art studio. By 1500 B.C. craftsmen in Egypt and the Near East, using almost all the techniques now known to us, were able to turn out work comparable to the finest of any other epoch. Five hundred years earlier in Sumeria, craft guilds were formed to protect full-time craftsmen working in the royal courts and developing urban centers. Craft associations with such features as the apprenticeship system, standardization of production, and a division between utilitarian and luxury goods existed in most classical cultures. But for a long period after the fall of the Roman Empire, craftsmen could safely earn their livings only as retainers of an isolated and virtually self-sufficient baronial manor. Because a weaver, armorer, or saddler could produce more than even a populous manor could consume, full-time craftsmen in late medieval times began to move into towns, where they could offer their services to more numerous and richer clients.

Town craftsmen accepted commissions to be carried out to the taste of the purchaser, and often with materials provided by him. Craftsmen also discovered that they could profitably produce objects in advance for sale to all. In this situation the craftsmen were no longer working for wages as in the manor, but had become merchants buying and selling raw materials and finished products in their own right for profit. In such politically independent commercial centers as Milan, Florence, Barcelona, Bruges, and Ghent, merchant guilds were established primarily to create a legal monopoly on the sale of local products within the town under municipal authority. The merchants in return could promise a "fair" fixed price for products of each quality and could effectively prohibit any attempts by their members to corner the market in these goods. Guild rules were strictly enforced, and expulsion meant that the merchant could no longer do business in that city. Membership became so desirable that it could be attained only by purchase or inheritance, not unlike a seat on a contemporary stock exchange. A further important function of merchant guilds was the lending of money to members at equitable rates. In time the wealthier merchants began to purchase for export some or all of the output of other craftsmen at less than retail prices. This wholesale trade proved so profitable that merchants soon set up central craft workshops employing craftsmen full-time, foreshadowing the factory.

By the fourteenth century the merchant guilds had become too cumbersome for efficiency and broke down into smaller units limited to the practitioners of a single specialized craft within a city. These craft guilds, or "companies," besides protecting their members from competition, ensured fair wages and fair prices, forbade night work, inspected workrooms, and protected the apprentices and journeymen. The considerable revenues received by the craft guilds were expended on public works, such as bridges and roads, religious processions, public festivals, and charity and occasionally were used for political purposes. The guilds, often run by powerful family dynasties, resisted both technical innovation and the growth of trade as destructive of their monopoly. By the end of the seventeenth century the improvement of transportation made possible a greater exchange of goods, and the power of the guilds was gradually broken by the spread of laissez-faire economic policies. Craft guilds were legally abolished in England in 1835, but some continue to have ritual functions. Among the contemporary Yoruba of southwestern Nigeria, new guilds are being organized for recently introduced crafts, and their pattern of development parallels that of European guilds.

Outside the secular urban setting of guilds, full-time professional craftsmen are often organized by means of socioreligious brotherhoods. In India painters who were also Buddhist monks spent centuries decorating their cave retreats with gigantic murals, while medieval Christian monks in Europe lavished comparable time, effort, and taste on the illumination of sacred manuscripts. Female artists have been organized into similar associations, the incomparable textiles of the Incas of Peru having been produced by the *acllacuna*, women trained from childhood as weavers of ritual and burial robes.

One characteristic distinguishes craft production in most cultures and epochs—a single individual carries on all the processes of production, from the gathering of the raw material to the finishing of the article. But when craftsmen are brought together in a central workshop, it soon becomes apparent that some excel in one process and some in another. When each step in the production of a craft is carried out by a specialist who does nothing else, the result need not be inartistic even though standardized. Chinese porcelains pass through at least twenty hands in the process of production, and Japanese blockprints are turned out by a series of experts, each of whom carries out only one step. Although many crafts are now produced by production-line methods for the market, a surprising number of craftsmen have resisted specialization of technique and standardization of product, preferring aesthetic satisfaction to greater efficiency and profit.

DANIEL J. CROWLEY

[*Directly related are the entries* GILDS; PRIMITIVE ART.]

BIBLIOGRAPHY

ADAIR, JOHN 1944 *The Navajo and Pueblo Silversmiths.* Norman: Univ. of Oklahoma Press.

BUNZEL, RUTH L. 1929 *The Pueblo Potter: A Study of Creative Imagination in Primitive Art.* New York: Columbia Univ. Press.

DIXON, ROLAND B. 1928 *The Building of Cultures.* New York: Scribner.

FOSTER, GEORGE M. 1948 *Empire's Children: The People of Tzintzuntzan.* Institute of Social Anthropology, Publication No. 6. Washington: Smithsonian Institution.

GOLDWATER, ROBERT J. 1964 *Senufo Sculpture From West Africa.* New York: Museum of Primitive Art.

GRIAULE, MARCEL 1938 *Masques dogons.* Paris: Institut d'Ethnologie.

HERSKOVITS, MELVILLE J. (1940) 1952 *Economic Anthropology: A Study in Comparative Economics.* 2d ed., rev. & enl. New York: Knopf. → First published as *The Economic Life of Primitive Peoples.*

LLOYD, PETER 1953 Craft Organization in Yoruba Towns. *Africa* 23:30–44.

OLBRECHTS, FRANS M. (1946) 1959 *Les arts plastiques du Congo Belge.* Brussels: Erasme. → First published as *Plastiek van Kongo.*

O'NEALE, LILA M. 1932 *Yurok–Karok Basket Weavers.* University of California Publications in American Archaeology and Ethnology, Vol. 32, No. 1. Berkeley: Univ. of California Press.

PROSKOURIAKOFF, TATIANA A. 1950 *A Study of Classic Maya Sculpture.* Washington: Carnegie Institution.

REICHARD, GLADYS A. 1933 *Melanesian Design: A Study of Style in Wood and Tortoiseshell Carving.* Columbia University Contributions to Anthropology, Vol. 18. New York: Columbia Univ. Press.

ROHAN-CSERMAK, GÉZA DE 1963 *Sturgeon Hooks of Eurasia.* Viking Fund Publications in Anthropology, No. 35. New York: Wenner-Gren Foundation for Anthropological Research.

SAPIR, EDWARD 1916 *Time Perspective in Aboriginal American Culture: A Study in Method.* Canada, Geological, Survey Memoir 90, Anthropological Series, No. 13. Ottawa: Government Printing Bureau.

[SCHMIDT, JAMES N.] 1959 *In Mexico: Where to Look, How to Buy Mexican Popular Arts and Crafts,* by James Norman [pseud.]. New York: Morrow.

SCHWEEGER, ANNMARIE (HEFEL) 1960 *Holzplastik in Afrika: Gestaltungsprinzipien.* Vienna: Braumüller.

WILLIAMS, FRANCIS EDGAR 1940 *Drama of Orokolo: The Social and Ceremonial Life of the Elema.* Oxford: Clarendon.

CREATIVITY

I.	PSYCHOLOGICAL ASPECTS	*Donald W. MacKinnon*
II.	SOCIAL ASPECTS	*J. M. B. Edwards*
III.	GENIUS AND ABILITY	*Robert E. L. Faris*

I
PSYCHOLOGICAL ASPECTS

Creativity, although currently much emphasized in psychological research, has been one of the most neglected topics in the history of psychology. The neglect of so complex a phenomenon as creativity by a psychology newly born in 1879 with Wilhelm Wundt's founding of the first psychological laboratory at Leipzig is understandable. In its attempts to cut its affiliation with its parent discipline, philosophy, and to establish itself as an empirical and experimental science, psychology turned its attention to the simpler aspects of consciousness and behavior, e.g., simple sensory, perceptual, and motor responses, for the study of which manageable techniques were available. In the second decade of the twentieth century, when behaviorism became the dominant emphasis in American psychology, the climate was even less congenial to such global and complex topics as that of creativity. Before creativity could become a conceivable concern of psychologists, the discipline itself had to change.

Several events brought about that change: the demonstration by the gestalt psychologists, most notably Max Wertheimer and Kurt Lewin, that complex processes of thought and action could be brought into the laboratory and submitted to experimental manipulation and measurement; the introduction of the topic of personality into academic psychology, especially by Gordon W. Allport and Henry A. Murray; the demonstration by Murray and his colleagues of the possibility of gaining an understanding of personality through the use of a multiplicity of assessment techniques; the development of a cognitive psychology, particularly by the gestalt psychologists and Edward C. Tolman; the reintroduction into psychology of the concepts of self (George H. Mead) and ego (Allport), and the development of an ego psychology; the development of interest in and techniques for the assessment of the effective functioning of man (the United States Army Air Corps selection program, under the guidance of John C. Flanagan and J. P. Guilford, and the Office of Strategic Services assessment program, under the leadership of Murray); and Guilford's presidential address to the American Psychological Association, entitled "Creativity" (1950).

What is creativity? In spite of the enormous amount of psychological research on creativity in recent years, there is today, as in the past, little conceptual agreement as to what creativity is. It is perhaps most often conceived to be the ability to bring something new into existence, yet others think of creativity not as an ability but rather as the psychological process or processes by which novel and valuable products are created. For others creativity is not the process but the product. Rather than attempt a complete listing of all the proposed meanings of creativity, it will suffice to indicate that definitions of the term range in scope and complexity from simple problem solving to the actualization of self.

Instead of seeking to choose from among this plethora of definitions, it might be argued, as it has been in the case of mental health, that creativity is not a theoretical construct at all but a general rubric, under which fall a variety of evaluative concerns. Such will be the orientation of the present treatment of creativity, and there are four major psychological aspects of creativity upon which attention will be focused: (1) the creative product; (2) the creative process; (3) the creative person; and (4) the creative situation. Each of these can be formulated as a question to which empirical research, if it has not already done so, can provide some answers: (1) what are creative products, and by what qualities are they identified? (2) what is the nature of the creative process, and what are the qualities and kinds of psychological processes that lead to the production of new creations? (3) what are the distinguishing traits and characteristics of the creative person? (4) what are the characteristics of the creative situation, the life circumstance, the social, cultural, and work milieu, that facilitate and encourage the appearance of creative thought and action?

The creative product

Anything that is experienced or made by man, for example, an idea, a response, a performance, a work of art, a scientific theory, a building, etc., may be a creative product. But of these, only a subclass that meets, at least to some degree, certain specified requirements or criteria will qualify as creative products.

To state that the first requirement of a creative product is simply that it be something novel or original is not sufficient; for one must next ask, novel or original within what range of experience or frame of reference—that of an individual, of a group, or of mankind? Much of a young child's experience and many of his ideas will be new to him and in that sense creative for him; but if these experiences and ideas are ones that practically every child encounters in the course of growing up, they are not creative products for the society in which the child lives. Similarly, a man may think a thought new to him, yet it may be one of the most common thoughts in the whole world. Thus, the creativeness of a product, when judged in terms of its novelty, originality, or statistical infrequence, is always relative to a given population of products. The most creative products are those that are novel or original in the experience of an entire civilization or of all mankind.

Mere novelty or originality of a product is, however, not alone sufficient to justify its designation as creative. There is the second requirement that it be adaptive to reality. It must, in other words, serve to solve a problem, fit the requirements of a given situation, accomplish some recognizable goal. Artistic creation, no less than scientific creation, involves the solving of a problem: e.g., in painting, to find a more appropriate expression of one's own experience; in dancing, to convey more adequately a particular mood or theme, etc.

But all solutions to problems are not equally good, even though they all may be equally correct or right. Thus, there enters a third requirement that a creative product must meet, although this requirement, like all the others, can be fulfilled to varying degrees. A response or product, if it is a truly creative one, meets the demand that the answer it provides be an aesthetically pleasing one. It is not sufficient that a solution is offered; it must also be, in the mathematician's term, elegant. A product that meets this criterion is at one and the same time simple and complex, its apparent simplicity masking great complexity and its complexity hiding a simplicity that binds many complex elements into a single whole.

The truly creative product meets a fourth criterion, namely, that it in turn creates new conditions of human existence. In order to do this, it must transcend or transform the generally accepted experience of man by introducing new principles that defy tradition and radically change man's view of things. Examples of creative products that have in their time transcended and transformed the then existing constraints of reality are the heliocentric theory of Copernicus, Darwin's theory of evolution, and Freud's theory of psychoanalysis.

The fifth requirement of a creative product is that the insightful solution that underlies it be realized and that it be evaluated and elaborated, developed to the full, and communicated to others. In other words, the creative product must be produced.

In one sense much is known about creative products, since they are the manifest and tangible expressions or resultants of creative activity. A thorough examination of these should permit inferences to be drawn concerning the nature of the creative process, and it is only through the existence of these products that creative persons can be distinguished from their noncreative peers and from those others whose creative potential has not yet found expression. Yet, curiously, although the problem of the criteria is basic to any study of creativity, no fully adequate and systematic study of the distinguishing marks of creative products has been made.

All too often investigators have settled for obviously crude and fallible criteria, e.g., performance on so-called tests of creativity, self-reports of subjects on their creative interests and achievements, and over-all ratings of the creativity of products, rather than struggle with the more difficult task of developing better-differentiated criteria. In each field of creative endeavor there are several dimensions peculiar to the product of the field to which the five criteria listed above may be applied. For example, in determining the creativeness of architectural designs, one could seek to determine the degree to which they satisfy the five criteria of originality, adaptiveness, elegance, transcendence, and realization in meeting the several traditionally recognized demands of architecture, namely, firmness (technological requirements), commodity (planning requirements), and delight (aesthetic requirements). A similar extension of the criteria of creativity could be undertaken in all fields of endeavor.

The creative process

Stages described autobiographically. The largest literature on the nature of the creative process is found in the writings of highly creative persons who, fascinated by their extraordinary creative experiences, have sought to describe them for others. There is remarkable agreement among those who have enjoyed the peak experience of high creativity, as well as among psychologists who have made systematic analyses of the introspective and retrospective reports of highly creative persons, as to how, in the main, the process is to be described. Both types of studies have observed distinguishable stages, or phases, of creativity. To be sure, different terms have been used by different writers to describe the same phases, and there has been some variation in the number of stages that have been noted. It has even been argued that the differentiated phases should be thought of, not as stages at all, but rather as aspects of the creative process, since they blend together and do not always occur in the order of their usual listing. Yet despite these disagreements, the following generalized description has emerged.

The first phase of the creative process involves a period of preparation, during which one acquires the skills and techniques and the elements of experience that make it possible for one to pose a problem to oneself. In one sense the individual's life history up to the moment of posing a problem constitutes the first, protracted phase of the creative process. Some have asserted, however, that only the acquisition of those skills and techniques and elements of experience that are directly relevant to the solution of the problem constitute the preparatory phase and that such purposeful and directed acquisition of knowledge occurs only after one has already posed a problem to oneself; consequently, they have argued that the creative process always starts with the recognition of a problem.

There is general agreement, however, that there follows next a period of concentrated attention in an attempt to solve the problem. This may involve a relatively brief period of time, during which attention is focused solely upon the problem until it is solved; but perhaps more often, and especially when the highest levels of creativity are ultimately reached, there is a blocking of one's efforts to solve the problem and the experiencing of so much frustration, tension, and discomfort that one is led, out of sheer self-protection, to the third phase, a period of withdrawal from the problem, a psychological "going out of the field," a period of renunciation of the problem or recession from it. Following this phase, which is usually referred to as a period of incubation and which may be of quite variable length, there is the fourth, brief phase, a moment or period of insight, accompanied by exhilaration, glow, and elation at the moment of insight. The fifth and final phase is a period of verification, evaluation, elaboration, realization, and communication of the insight that has been experienced. These phases may be telescoped into a very brief period of time, as in musical improvisation, or may involve a considerable span of years, as was required for Einstein's creation of the theory of relativity.

Factor analysis and qualities of thinking. Although a gross analysis of the creative process reveals the phases just described, a more searching analysis indicates that the creative process is a complex set of cognitive and motivational processes, involving perceiving, remembering, thinking, imagining, deciding, etc. As more is learned about these processes, the more fully will the creative process itself be understood. Indeed, it was Guilford's approach to the study of creativity and his attempt to conceptualize the intellectual processes that enter into it that led to his construction of a new model of intellect, for he soon realized that the intelligence tests developed prior to 1950 had almost entirely ignored the crucial variables of creative thinking. Consequently, he set about to construct a battery of tests hypothesized to measure these relevant but previously neglected variables. From the factor analysis of the correlated test scores of large samples of persons have emerged what Guilford believes to be the primary intellective factors that account for individual differences in creativity: associational fluency, ideational fluency, originality, adaptive flexibility, spontaneous flexibility, redefinition, and sensitivity to problems.

Out of this work there has developed a now widely recognized distinction between *convergent thinking*, which places a premium on analysis and reasoning, measured by the traditional tests of intelligence, and *divergent thinking*, which places a premium on richness and novelty of ideas, for the measurement of which the new tests of creativity have been developed. After a short period in which creativity was assumed by some enthusiasts for the new testing to be solely the result of divergent thinking, there is now general recognition that both divergent thinking and convergent thinking are required in all creative thought, although their relative proportions will vary widely from one creative task to another.

Other methods. In addition to the introspective autobiographical and factor-analytic approaches to the study of creativity, three other methods of study are frequently employed. One seeks to elicit and study creative performance under standard conditions of observation, e.g., a person is assigned a specific task, such as writing a poem, etc., under controlled conditions and within certain time limits. Another method, preferred by the experimental psychologist, seeks to test particular hypotheses about details of the creative process, e.g., comparing the relative speeds with which the insightful solution to an assigned problem is achieved under varied conditions of initial information, instructions to the subject, level of motivation, etc. A fifth method, of more recent origin and radically different from the others, seeks insight into the creative process by attempting to simulate creative problem solving and thinking on high-speed electronic computers.

Enhancement and inhibition of creativity. From the use of these several methods, information is being gained concerning, on the one hand, those factors that further the creative process and, on the other hand, those factors that block it. Among cognitive factors that have been shown to hinder creative thought are failure to perceive and define a problem correctly; too much, as well as too little, information; and the embeddedness of required elements in a functional context that makes it difficult or impossible to perceive their relevance to the solution, i.e., functional fixedness; rigid persistence of a misleading set; the formulation of inappropriate and rigid categories and schemata of information; an excessively analytical attitude; premature closure of cognitive processes, etc. Among motivational factors known to inhibit creative performance may be noted too much motivation (leading to incapacitating anxiety); too little motivation; a preponderance of extrinsic motivation (interest in external rewards) over intrinsic motivation (interest in a problem for its own sake); and a host of inhibiting fears, such as the fear of making a mistake, the fear of social disapproval, the fear of separateness and nonconformity, the fear of one's images and impulses and of one's own unconscious processes, etc. The obverse of these factors, both intellective and motivational, has been shown to facilitate creative thought and action.

The creative person

The determination of the characteristics of creative persons requires first that such individuals be accurately identified and the level of their creativeness measured. This is the troublesome problem of criteria, which is seldom if ever ideally solved in the study of the creative person. Far too often subjects' performance on so-called tests of creativity have been taken as indicating the level of their creativeness, despite the fact that it has not yet been clearly demonstrated that, either singly or in combination, an individual's scores on the presumed factor-pure tests of creative thinking yield a valid measure of his performance in actual creative work. When, on the other hand, creative persons are identified and the level of their creativeness is judged on the basis of their known products, such judgments, even when made by experts, are to some unknown degree contaminated and confounded by factors such as the subject's social prestige and reputation. When, in a third type of study, the criterion of a person's creativeness is taken to be the degree of his self-actualization or the extent to which he is a fully functioning individual, the criterion is even more vague and suspect.

Despite these unresolved methodological difficul-

ties, there is an impressive congruence of findings from quite varied studies concerning the characteristics of the creative person. Those researches that have contributed most significantly to the picture of the creative person have relied on the opinion of experts who have identified members of a single profession whose creativeness, judged on the basis of their tangible creative products, has ranged from relatively low to extremely high. Such researches have involved intensive psychological assessment of the nominated subjects.

Relation to intelligence. The creative person appears to be intelligent, yet there is a far from perfect correlation between intelligence as measured by intelligence tests and creativity. In several professional groups, e.g., architects and research scientists, the correlation is essentially zero. The relationship in these instances is doubtless to some degree attenuated, because of a restriction in range of both creativity and intelligence. The general conclusion with respect to intelligence and creativity is that a certain degree of intelligence is required if one is to be creative, but beyond that point being more or less intelligent does not determine the level of a person's creativeness; and the level of intelligence required for creativity, which varies from field to field, is sometimes surprisingly low. What is more important than the level of intelligence as measured by an intelligence test is the effectiveness with which the creative person uses whatever intelligence he has.

In addition to general intelligence, special skills and abilities appropriate to a person's field of creative endeavor are clearly necessary for the achievement of high levels of creative performance.

Psychological health and cognitive styles. As to the relationship between a person's creativeness and his psychological health—a relationship widely studied and widely disputed—the situation is again not a simple one. There is no doubt that some quite disturbed persons have been highly creative; yet there is no doubt, also, that many persons of apparent good health, both physical and psychological, have shown unusual creativeness. Perhaps the more general picture, and one that reconciles the opposites of well-being and pathology, is one in which there is a good deal of psychic turbulence and at the same time adequate ego control. In several studies, creative persons have earned, on the average, scores some five to ten points above the standard score mean of 50 on the clinical scales of an inventory that measures tendencies toward the major psychiatric disturbances. The meaning of such elevated scores, as well as the self-reports of creative subjects in psychiatric interviews, are less suggestive of psychopathology than of good intellect, complexity and richness of personality, general lack of defensiveness, and candor in self-description—in other words, an openness to experience and especially to experience of one's inner life. Most typically, one finds evidence of psychopathology in test profiles of creative subjects, but at the same time there is evidence of superior mechanisms of control.

One of the prominent characteristics of the test performance of male creative groups is a tendency to score high on scales that measure femininity. This finding could be easily misunderstood. The proper interpretation is this: creative men reveal an openness to their feelings and emotions, a sensitive intellect, and an understanding self-awareness, and their wide-ranging interests include many that in Western culture are thought of as feminine. They give fuller expression to the feminine side of their nature than do their less creative peers. In the language of Jungian psychology, creative males are not so completely identified with their masculine *persona* roles as to blind themselves to or deny expression to the more feminine traits of the *anima* [see ANALYTICAL PSYCHOLOGY; *and the biography of* JUNG].

The perceptiveness of the creative person and his openness to richness and complexity are revealed also in his preference for perceptual complexity. As between perceiving and judging, they are on the side of perception—open to and receptive of experience. They are challenged by disordered multiplicity and by the unfinished, which arouses in them an urge, indeed a need, to achieve the most difficult and far-ranging ordering of the richness they are willing to experience.

The creative person is not only open to experience; he is intuitive about it. In perceiving, one may emphasize sense perception, focusing upon what is yielded by the senses, things as they are, the facts; and in the extreme, one can remain stuck there, bound to the stimulus, the presented material, or the situation. Or one may, in any perception, be intuitive about and responsive to its deeper meanings, its implications, and its possibilities, immediately grasping the real, as well as the symbolic, bridges between what is and what can be. Creative persons show a marked preference for intuitive perception.

With their awareness of inner life and their interest in the symbolic equivalents of experience, it is not surprising that highly creative persons are more often introvert than extravert, though there

is no evidence that introverts as such are more creative than extraverts.

Relation to interests and values. Studies of the interests of creative persons have been remarkably consistent in revealing them to have interests similar to those of certain vocational groups and unlike those of others. If one focuses, not upon the specific interests that are shown, but upon what they reveal about those who hold them, it may be said that creative persons are inclined to be relatively uninterested in small details or in facts for their own sake and more concerned with their meanings and implications, cognitively flexible, verbally skillful, interested in communicating with others, and relatively disinterested in policing either their own impulses and images or those of others.

As with interests, so in the realm of values, creative persons show a preference different from that of their less creative colleagues. Of the six values conceptualized by the philosopher Eduard Spranger—the theoretical, economic, aesthetic, social, political, and religious—creative persons strongly value the theoretical and the aesthetic. For them it is not sufficient that problems be solved; there is the further requirement that the solutions be elegant. They seek both truth and beauty.

Although highly creative persons are characteristically independent in thought and action and are nonconformists in their ideas, they are not deliberately nonconforming. Often, in fact, they are quite conventional in matters and actions that are not central to their areas of creative endeavor.

General profile and summary. If a general picture of the productively creative person were to be drawn, it would read as follows:

He is dominant, possessed of those qualities and attributes which underlie and lead to achievement of personal status; poised, spontaneous, and self-confident in social interaction, although not of an especially sociable or participative temperament; intelligent, outspoken, sharp-witted, demanding, aggressive, and self-centered; persuasive and verbally fluent, self-confident and self-assured; and relatively uninhibited in expressing his worries and complaints.

He is comparatively free from conventional restraints and inhibitions, not preoccupied with the impression he makes on others, and thus, he is capable of great independence and autonomy and is relatively ready to recognize and admit self-views that are unusual and unconventional.

He is strongly motivated to achieve in situations in which independence in thought and action is called for, but unlike his less creative peers, he is not inclined to strive for achievement in settings where conforming behavior is expected or required. In efficiency and steadiness of intellectual effort, however, he does not differ from his fellow workers.

Finally, he is definitely more psychologically minded, more flexible, and possessed of more femininity of interests than less creative persons.

This is the generality. What needs to be equally emphasized is that there is no single mold into which all who are creative will fit. The full and complete picturing of the creative person will require many images.

The problem of the identification of the creative person by means of assessment techniques is still largely unsolved. Many personality correlates of creativity, both intellective and nonintellective, have been reported in the literature and summarized above. Which of them, individually or in combination with others, will most accurately identify creative persons or persons with creative potential in any given profession or field of endeavor is today not known. That is an empirical problem that seems much less difficult of solution today than it did in the past, but it is one that must be solved separately for each professional group. There is no general solution, to be applied to all professions, because of the enormous differences between them. A core of techniques and a basic methodology for the identification of creativity are now available. What is needed are the energy and ingenuity to modify and extend them in the study of creativity, and of the creative person, in all fields of endeavor.

The creative situation

To speak of a creative situation is to imply that creativity is not a fixed trait of personality but something that changes over time, waxing and waning, being facilitated by some life circumstances and situations and inhibited by others. While such an assertion would be accepted by almost everyone, much less agreement can be found for statements that specify the types of situation or life circumstance that facilitate or inhibit creativity. Such disagreement merely underscores the continuing need, despite a considerable body of research findings, for studies to determine what kinds of situations contribute most significantly to the encouragement of what kinds of creativity in what types of person. The problem almost certainly has to be phrased in this manner, for it is unlikely that all persons will find the same situation equally conducive to creative effort.

Questions concerning the facilitating or inhibiting effect of environment on creativity can be directed both to the historical past and to the contemporaneous present of the individual.

Life history. Looking first at life-history data, the widest variety of early circumstances and family situations has been reported for persons of high creativeness. Despite this diversity, there are, however, several themes to be noted. For example, so recurrent is the theme of remembered unhappiness in childhood that one is led to speculate about its role in fostering creative potential. In the absence of a sensitive awareness of one's own experience and that of the world around one, without considerable development of and attention to one's inner life, and lacking an interest in ideational, imaginal, and symbolic processes, one can hardly be expected to exhibit highly creative responses. Something less than complete satisfaction with oneself and one's situation in childhood, if not a prerequisite for the development of a rich inner life and concern for things of the mind and spirit, may nevertheless play an important contributory role.

In a nationwide study of creativity in architects, a number of events and circumstances have been discovered in the life histories of the more creative subjects that appear to have fostered their creative potential and independent spirit and to have provided the opportunity, if not the necessity, for their developing the secure sense of personal autonomy and zestful commitment to their profession that so markedly characterize the creative person (Mac-Kinnon 1962).

These factors may be briefly summarized as follows: an extraordinary respect by the parent for the child and an early granting to him of unusual freedom in exploring his universe and in making his own decisions; an expectation that the child would act independently but reasonably and responsibly; a lack of intense closeness between parent and child, so that neither overdependence was fostered nor a feeling of rejection experienced, in other words, the sort of interpersonal relationship between parent and child that had a liberating effect upon the child; a plentiful supply in the child's extended social environment of models for identification and the promotion of ego ideals; the presence within the family of clear standards of conduct and ideas as to what was right and wrong, but at the same time an expectation, if not requirement, of active exploration and internalization of a framework of personal conduct; an emphasis upon the development of an individual ethical code; the experience of frequent moving, within single communities or from community to community or from country to country, which provided an enrichment of experience, both cultural and personal, but which at the same time contributed to experiences of aloneness, shyness, isolation, and solitariness during childhood and adolescence; the possession of skills and abilities that, although encouraged and rewarded, were nevertheless allowed to develop at their own pace; and finally the absence of pressures on the child to establish prematurely his professional identity.

This particular set of early circumstances and interpersonal experiences, although observed in one study, takes on added significance because of its congruence with the set of life-history factors that Otto Rank thought so conducive to man's winning his own individuality and the realization of his creative potential; with those interactions between the child and the significant others in the environment that Erik Erikson described as so crucial to the fullest development of ego; and with those experiences that, in Robert W. White's theory, sustain and nurture the fullest development of competence.

It remains something of a moot question whether creative thought and action are most stimulated by solitariness and separateness—the individual working alone—or by interaction with others in group activity. There is mounting evidence that here again individual differences play an important role.

Implications for education.   To many, the implications of the observed characteristics of highly creative persons for the training or nurturing of creativity seem rather clear. In contrast to earlier emphases in education, there is today a tendency to stress freedom and autonomy for the child, a substitution of self-discipline for discipline imposed from outside, an openness to all ideas and a deferment of judgment in choosing from among them, the adoption of a more playful attitude toward study, engagement in imaginative play, the nurturing of a feeling for analogies, similes, and metaphors, a searching for common principles in terms of which quite different domains of knowledge can be related, etc. It has yet to be demonstrated, however, that these new emphases do indeed foster more creativeness than did earlier forms of education, which stressed rote learning, repeated drill of material, precise memorization, orderly habits of study, strict discipline, etc. It may well be that here, as in so many other domains of creative performance, some reconciliation of these opposites (and the resultant tension that experi-ence of the opposites produces) will turn out to be most nurturing of creative potential.

DONALD W. MACKINNON

[*Other relevant material may be found in* AESTHETICS; FANTASY; PROBLEM SOLVING; STIMULATION DRIVES; *and the articles listed under* ART.]

BIBLIOGRAPHY

BARRON, FRANK X. 1963 *Creativity and Psychological Health: Origins of Personal Vitality and Creative Freedom.* Princeton, N.J.: Van Nostrand.

BERGSON, HENRI (1907) 1944 *Creative Evolution.* New York: Modern Library. → First published in French.

BRUNER, JEROME S. (1960) 1965 *The Process of Education.* Cambridge, Mass.: Harvard Univ. Press.

ERIKSON, ERIK H. (1950) 1964 *Childhood and Society.* 2d ed., rev. & enl. New York: Norton.

GARDNER, JOHN W. 1964 *Self-renewal: The Individual and the Innovative Society.* New York: Harper.

GHISELIN, BREWSTER (editor) 1952 *The Creative Process: A Symposium.* Berkeley: Univ. of California Press. → A paperback edition was published in 1963 by Mentor.

GORDON, WILLIAM J. J. 1961 *Synectics: The Development of Creative Capacity.* New York: Harper.

GUILFORD, J. P. 1950 Creativity. *American Psychologist* 5:444–454.

HADAMARD, JACQUES S. (1945) 1954 *An Essay on the Psychology of Invention in the Mathematical Field.* New York: Dover.

KOESTLER, ARTHUR 1964 *The Act of Creation.* New York: Macmillan.

KNOWLSON, THOMAS S. (1917) 1918 *Originality: A Popular Study of the Creative Mind.* Philadelphia: Lippincott.

KRIS, ERNST 1944 Art and Regression. New York Academy of Sciences, *Transactions* 6:236–250.

KRIS, ERNST 1952 *Psychoanalytic Explorations in Art.* New York: International Universities Press.

KUBIE, LAWRENCE S. 1958 *Neurotic Distortion of the Creative Process.* Lawrence: Univ. of Kansas Press.

MCKELLAR, PETER 1957 *Imagination and Thinking: A Psychological Analysis.* London: Cohen & West; New York: Basic Books.

MACKINNON, DONALD W. 1962 The Personality Correlates of Creativity: A Study of American Architects. Pages 11–39 in International Association of Applied Psychology, 14th Congress, Copenhagen, 1961, *Proceedings.* Volume 2: Personality Research. Copenhagen: Munksgaard.

MACKINNON, DONALD W. 1965 Personality and the Realization of Creative Potential. *American Psychologist* 20:273–281.

MARITAIN, JACQUES 1953 *Creative Intuition in Art and Poetry.* New York: Pantheon. → Paperback editions were published in 1955 by Meridian and in 1961 by World.

MEDNICK, SARNOFF A. 1962 The Associative Basis of the Creative Process. *Psychological Review* 69:220–232.

PARNES, SIDNEY J.; and HARDING, HAROLD F. (editors) 1962 *A Source Book for Creative Thinking.* New York: Scribner.

POINCARÉ, HENRI (1908) 1952 *Science and Method.* New York: Dover. → First published in French.

RANK, OTTO (1929–1931) 1945 *Will Therapy* and *Truth and Reality*. New York: Knopf. → The first work in this book is a translation of the second and third volumes of *Technik der Psychoanalyse*. The second work was first published as *Wahrheit und Wirklichkeit: Entwurf einer Philosophie des Seelischen*.

RESEARCH CONFERENCE ON THE IDENTIFICATION OF CREATIVE SCIENTIFIC TALENT 1963 *Scientific Creativity: Its Recognition and Development*. New York: Wiley.

USHER, ABBOTT P. (1929) 1954 *A History of Mechanical Inventions*. Rev. ed. Cambridge, Mass.: Harvard Univ. Press. → A paperback edition was published in 1959 by Beacon.

WERTHEIMER, MAX (1945) 1961 *Productive Thinking*. Enl. ed., edited by Michael Wertheimer. London: Tavistock.

WHITE, ROBERT W. 1960 Competence and the Psychosexual Stages of Development. Volume 8, pages 97–141 in Marshall R. Jones (editor), *Nebraska Symposium on Motivation*. Lincoln: Univ. of Nebraska Press.

II
SOCIAL ASPECTS

Creativity is a concept that emerged during the Renaissance and was first given formal expression by the philosophers of the Enlightenment; its original use was as a term in the "great analogy" (Nahm [1956] 1965, chapter 2) between the divine creator of the natural world and the artist with his power to create, as Sir Philip Sidney put it, "forms such as never were in Nature" ([1595] 1895, p. 25). Modern associations of the concept are nearly all psychological: creativity is often held to consist in personal attributes such as spontaneity, originality, sincerity, high intelligence, or some combination of these or of similar qualities. It would seem, then, that the sociology of creativity (however creativity may be defined) should consist in the study of those social conditions which either favor or impede the appearance of creative individuals.

But there is another sense altogether in which it is possible to speak of creativity as having social aspects. Civilizations, social institutions, formal organizations, and small groups can all be called creative, and this may imply much more than that they include creative individuals. One possible implication is that there is something about the way in which a social unit is organized without which none of its members would have become creative. Another is that the members of a social unit may in some sense work together to produce collective achievements that reflect creative qualities of the group as a whole.

Creativity can also be seen as an attribute of objects. Indeed, the terms "creative product" and "creative object" have by now become standard in the psychological literature on creativity (see, for instance, Bruner 1962, p. 8; Roe 1963, p. 155) and can be used to denote whatever is counted as evidence for the existence of individual creativity. It is here that a basic difference becomes apparent between the psychological and sociological approaches to creativity. Understandably, much of the psychological research has been concerned with measuring creative potential rather than creative achievement; the focus of interest has been on the internal psychological processes that issue in the finished creative object, with the general assumption that, once the object has seen the light, the creative process is complete. It is admitted that various social factors may facilitate or retard the process, but they are not generally thought of as part of it. Psychological study of creative actions of course involves more extensive consideration of social factors, but such study is usually carried out in a context other than that of creativity (see, however, Fiedler 1964).

But sociological theories, whether they are developed by professional sociologists or by historians and other authors with an interest in the quality of human achievement, also tend to give an incomplete account of the creative process. Many authors have remarked on the way in which the creative object seems to live a life independent of its creator, in the sense that the social mechanisms by which it is distributed, or the amount and type of attention paid to it, seem to be matters that are mostly beyond his control (see, for example, Rank 1932, p. 215; Valéry [1940] 1952, pp. 94–96). But historical studies of such processes are usually confined to the level of particular social institutions, such as literature or the fine arts, at particular periods and do not make structural comparisons between institutions.

However, there is a growing realization that practitioners of the various social sciences who have studied creativity may have been talking not about different sets of problems but about the same problems from different points of view (see the discussion in Mooney [1957] 1962). Moreover, a distinctively social conception of the creative process is slowly gaining recognition. Thus Rogers has defined the creative process as *"the emergence in action of a novel relational product, growing out of the uniqueness of the individual on the one hand, and the materials, events, people, or circumstances of his life on the other"* ([1954] 1962, p. 65). In similar fashion Guérard has argued that "the word Art applies at the same time to the creative urge, to the process through which that urge is manifested, to the material result of the process, to the appreciation of the result. These are different phases or aspects of the same reality" ([1936] 1963, p. xxvii). The key notion in both of these definitions is that of the interrelatedness of the different phases through which the creative object passes in the course of becoming part of a culture. In short, and leaving on one side for the moment the question of how to establish criteria of creativity, the creative process in its social aspect is the process by which creative objects are produced and *then* become cultural objects (for a discussion of the "process versus product" issue by psychologists, see Utah Creativity Research Conference 1964, pp. 112–121).

But creative objects are not merely cultural objects, nor are they usually created with the whole culture in mind. To produce a work of art or science, for instance, is primarily to make a claim on the attention of other artists or scientists. The artist may desire self-expression but, as a Marxist sociologist has expressed it, this "is really self-socialisation, the casting of . . . private experience in such a form that it will be incorporated in the social world of art and appear as an art-work" (Sprigg [1937] 1963, p. 202). The *creative* work of art or science does not only claim to be incorporated into the institution appropriate to it; it also claims to modify or even subvert the collective ideology of the institution in some important respect. It is the fact that the claim is made good that enables us to identify the work as creative. In order to reach this conclusion it is not necessary to make assumptions about the intentions of creative individuals, but only to note that the objects produced by such individuals do in fact exert a fruitful influence on other members of the same institution. A creative object, then, is a successful demonstration that the sum of established institutional values does not exhaust the range of possible institutional values. It is through the incorporation of creative objects that institutions are saved from eternal elaboration of what is already known or believed.

The creative process

Person-oriented approaches, which focus on the psychological processes that issue in creation, can be contrasted with object-oriented approaches, which are more concerned with what is created. Many of the early person-oriented studies of creativity foundered because they treated established fame as if it were an infallible index of creative achievement. Such studies therefore became involved not only with the vastly complicated problem of estimating the degree of fame a creative individual enjoyed at any particular time but also with the fluctuations to which fame is subjected by changes in taste or interest. But if an object-oriented approach is adopted, considerations of personal fame and reputation become secondary; the main problem is to determine which scientific, artistic, or other objects had effects of an order that distinguished them from the common run of cultural objects. This is not to equate creativity with extent of influence, but it is to equate it with a certain type of influence on a certain institution during a specifiable period. The length of the period need not depend on anything but the purpose of the study.

Social institutions. A cultural system can be divided into as many parts or subsystems as suit the purpose of an inquiry, but the principal subdivisions are generally conceived in terms of the mutually irreducible classes of values that are generated in the pursuit of major human interests. The organized cultivation of a distinctive class of values in pursuit of a major human interest will here be designated as a social institution. This view of social institutions is quite close to that adopted by the Whites in their study of the nineteenth-century French art world (White & White 1965, p. 2). However, it differs somewhat from the traditional view in American sociology, which has tended to follow W. I. Thomas in regarding institutions as the systems formed by the "more or less explicit and formal *rules* of behavior by which the group tends to maintain, regulate, and make more general and more frequent the corresponding type of actions among its members" (Thomas, *Social Behavior and Personality*, p. 52). By contrast, the present definition emphasizes the ultimate values, whether religious, artistic, scientific, or political, that rules of behavior are designed to preserve.

It is generally realized that the social structure of a society may affect the creativity of its institutions. Most writing in this area has focused on the problem of cultural integration and disintegration. Some authors have argued that a high degree of cultural integration is necessary for creativity to reach its greatest heights in any institution, but they fail to explain why all institutions are not equally creative, even in societies that they regard as highly integrated. Other authors, pointing to the greater efficiency achieved through an increasing division of labor both within and between institutions, have seemed to support the opposite point of view, though they have not been able to demonstrate that a high degree of institutional autonomy is inconsistent with a high degree of social integration. A very few authors have confined themselves to demonstrating that creativity in one institution can have indirect effects on creativity in another. More often, comparison between creative achievement in different institutional spheres has taken the form of seeking to explain one type of achievement in terms of another, as when an outburst of artistic creativity is said to have been caused by a particular state of the economic system. But in any case it is clear that social institutions are interconnected as well as distinct, and there is a strong assumption, though little systematic evidence, that the type and degree of creativity that they display is somehow related to their mode of interconnection [see INTEGRATION, *article on* CULTURAL INTEGRATION].

Social institutions vary not only in autonomy and distinctiveness but also in structural complexity, which usually increases with size. But the major institutional functions remain the same in spite of these changes. Thus creative objects cannot become cultural objects unless they are *appraised* by members of an appropriate institution, nor can they be offered for appraisal unless they find an appropriate institutional *outlet*. The process of appraisal, which is essentially collective, is the means by which the institution asserts its claim to a distinctive interest in the cultivation of those values which are its *raison d'être*. Appraisal is therefore a matter of deciding, for instance, not only how good a work of art is (a question that, in any case, is never finally settled) but first and foremost of deciding whether it is a work of art at all. If the work is never displayed for appraisal through a recognized outlet—that is, if it is never published, exhibited, or at the very least brought to the attention of someone whose influence on the process of appraisal makes him a kind of living outlet—then, from an institutional point of view, it does not yet exist as a work of art.

The nature of an institution's outlets is sometimes determined largely by its appraisal system, though under open market conditions the relationship is often reversed. The form taken by outlets is also shaped by technology, including marketing techniques, which tends, as it grows ever more complex, to create multiple outlets for ever new classes of consumers. But the intimate connection between outlets and appraisal persists in spite of technological change, though various new types of appraisal may arise to match the new types of outlet. Indeed, if the volume of products is very great, release of a product through a certain type of outlet may largely supplant appraisal as the means by which products are, so to speak, stamped with the required institutional marks of identification.

An apparent difference between art and science in this respect has often been noted (see, for instance, Kuhn 1962, p. 163): an artist is thought to produce for a public that does not consist only of other artists, while a scientist's work is appraised only by his professional colleagues. But whether or not one perceives a real structural difference here depends on where one draws the boundaries of art and science as institutions. If the full range of scientific products is considered, from high-level theories to minor technological innovations, it immediately becomes obvious that, like artistic products, they are submitted through different kinds of outlets for different kinds of appraisal.

Creative ideologies

Creative objects affect institutional ideology because they are themselves ideological creations. It is convenient to call the particular constellation of values expressed by a creative object its "creative ideology," since in this way the elements common to several apparently divergent traditions of thought about creativity can be brought together under one head.

Personal and collective ideologies. The notion of artistic creation as essentially a process of conflict between personal and collective ideologies was first developed by Rank, who defined the artist as someone who "constructively applies his will-power in the service of *ideological* creation" (1932, p. 159). Rank draws attention to the institutional base of the art form or style by calling it "the ideology of the art" (*ibid.*, p. 112; compare p. 186), and he further distinguishes between this and the "something personal" of the artist, on the one hand, and the "general ideology of the culture," on the other (*ibid.*; compare chapter 4, *passim*). Thus art, for Rank, is neither mere self-expression, since it must make use of forms that are collective in origin, nor simply an expression of collective ideology, since artistic creation fulfills purely personal needs for the artist (for a similar view, see Hauser [1958] 1963, p. 407). In fact, the more creative the artist, the more his personal needs will conflict with the needs of the collectivity. Rank therefore reverses the Freudian theory of creativity. The artist does not create because he is neurotically maladjusted to society; rather, he lives in a state of necessary conflict with society because he is creative (Rank 1932, p. 169). Rank's views have not been generally adopted by psychoanalysts, although the bulk of empirical psychological evidence would appear to support him (see, for instance, Barron 1963). Nor has it been pointed out that Rank's emphasis on the difference between the neurotic and the creative personality is remarkably similar to W. I. Thomas' distinction between the "Bohemian" and the "creative individual" (Thomas, *Social Behavior and Personality*, p. 159). But Thomas' approach to the problem of creativity was essentially person-oriented. Rank, on the other hand, went far beyond both the person-oriented and the object-oriented approaches to the creative process by including in his schema not only the artist's own conception of his role (*ibid.*, p. 202) and the social basis of artistic creation (p. 207) but also the use to which society puts the creative object. "The artist in himself provides in his work the raw material the community uses in the creation of biographies and fame as an expression of its own eternalization" (p. 221).

Internal and external ideologies. The ideological content of a creative object can also be analyzed into those value elements which pertain only to the institutions for which the object has been created and those which pertain to other institutions or, it may be, to no institution at all. The former elements constitute the object's *internal* ideology (as we speak of something as being of "purely artistic" or "purely scientific" interest), and the latter its *external* ideology (as, for instance, the glorification of aristocratic ideals in a portrait or the religious world view implicit in a system of astronomy).

The extent to which art seems more capable than science of serving external ideologies—what might be called its apparent ideological penetrability—has been pointed out so often that some authors maintain that science as such has no ideological penetrability at all. Nor is it generally admitted that scientists are in any sense engaged in the production and elaboration of ideologies. This is probably because, with reference to science, ideology is considered only in an external sense. But the concept of *paradigm*, as developed by Kuhn (1962) in his study of scientific revolutions, has a distinct affinity with the concept of internal creative ideology. A paradigm is a body of scientific achievement that is "sufficiently unprecedented to attract an enduring group of adherents away from competing modes of scientific activity . . . [and] sufficiently open-ended to leave all sorts of problems for the redefined group of practitioners to resolve." In this way it provides "models from which spring particular coherent traditions of scientific research" (Kuhn 1962, p. 10). Clearly, the same kind of service is performed for art by those artists who, whether singly or in a group, introduce a major new idiom or style that serves for any considerable length of time to define the range of artistic problems worth exploring. A scientific paradigm such as Newton's laws of motion and gravi-

tation (Kuhn 1962, pp. 39–40) can certainly be compared, in terms of its long-lasting influence and eventual replacement by other models, with a "musical paradigm" such as the major scale (Allen [1939] 1962, p. 192). Artistic and scientific paradigms are creative objects par excellence, since they institute the guiding principles that make many other discoveries possible. Such paradigms are almost never the unaided work of one individual, and it is this collective origin of theirs that makes them highly appropriate units of study for the sociology of creativity. In this respect they can be compared with what Ogburn called "basic inventions" ([1950] 1964, p. 23), though Ogburn's preoccupation with the larger social effects of applied science and technology seems to have kept him from exploring the effects of discoveries in pure science upon the structure of science itself (see especially Ogburn 1942, pp. 235–236).

Creativity and ideological succession

The most striking fact about creative ideologies is that all of them are sooner or later subject to change. Here, this phenomenon will be called *ideological succession*. Any theory of creativity, regardless of the social level to which it is intended to apply, can be classified according to the kinds of assumptions that its author makes about the dynamics of ideological succession. Four major types of theory can be distinguished in this field: organicist, dialectical, societal, and factorial.

Organicist theories. At the societal level, the most celebrated attempt in modern times at an organicist account of ideological succession is that of Oswald Spengler, whose historical pessimism in his *Decline of the West*, published 1919–1922, owed more to Nietzsche than to Darwin. The most impressive application of biological evolutionism to the problem of creativity was Francis Galton's *Hereditary Genius*, published in 1869, in which it was demonstrated empirically that certain families consistently produced more men of distinction than could be accounted for by chance (a point on which Galton has never been refuted). From these findings Galton inferred not only that distinction in any field is the result of superior genetic endowment but also, as a kind of sociological extension of Darwin's principle of natural selection, that genetic superiority inevitably overcame social obstacles to achievement.

All such theories and approaches had in common a tendency to reduce creativity to a merely descriptive category with no independent causal role in the process of ideological succession. Regardless of the adequacy or inadequacy of the data on which they are based, organicist theories lack any real explanatory power because, although they assume that some periods of civilizations (or some races, nations, or families) are more creative than others, they have nothing to say about the dynamics of ideological succession except that efflorescence is inevitably followed by decline (or, in the case of Galton, will be followed by decline if nature is left to pursue its course).

Dialectical theories. Theories of creativity based on dialectical reasoning claim, like organicist theories, both to explain what has happened and to predict what will happen. In order to sustain this claim, they are forced to conceive the dynamics of ideological succession in terms of a fixed superstructure that determines once and for all the possible range of basic ideological forms. Creative ideologies as they actually occur and succeed one another are held to be composed of elements attributable to one or another of these basic forms, either singly or in combination. The forms are eternal opposites but may interact in the temporal sphere to produce unique combinations.

If the number of basic ideological forms is limited, it follows that any concrete ideology at a particular moment of its existence is closer to one basic form than it is to the others. The implication is usually that the more closely the ideology exemplifies some basic form, the more creative it is, though a position of equilibrium between two or more opposing forms is sometimes regarded as the most creative state of all. At any rate, dialectical theories of ideological succession tend to be prejudiced in favor of historical periods when some clearly identifiable style or set of values seems to have dominated a whole culture in such a way as to give it—at least in the eyes of the historian— a certain coherence and internal consistency.

Such periods of cultural integration are supposed to have been far more productive of outstanding creative achievements than the more confused periods of transition from one state of cultural integration to the next. Creative people born during periods of transition can hope to do little more than hasten the destruction of outworn ideologies and lay the foundations of the new. In this way, dialectical theorists seem to assign a somewhat more autonomous role to creative individuals. But this concession is an illusory one, since the dialectical theory itself becomes the only criterion of what is to count as creative. Thus, for the revolutionary Marxist only what is "progressive"—i.e., consistent with the Marxist interpretation of history—can be truly creative, though some

of the more aesthetically-minded Marxists try to avoid the absurdities inherent in this doctrine by claiming that a bourgeois writer, for instance, can be "progressive" if his work mirrors the supposed decadence of capitalist society (Fischer [1959] 1963, chapter 3).

Some dialectical theories, however, contain valuable sociological elements, since they treat ideological succession not only in terms of the effects of one ideology on another but also in terms of the ideology's structural base in the social system. Thus Sorokin, in his *Social and Cultural Dynamics*, published in 1937–1941, emphasizes that what at the cultural level appears as an abstract configuration of the ideological supersystem is, when viewed at the individual level, a matter of voluntary human allegiance to certain concrete institutional structures. According to Sorokin, transfer of allegiance from one basic form to another is possible because cultural integration is never absolute; values derived from other basic forms are always present in a subordinate cultural role. In short, Sorokin recognizes that a certain pluralism of values may exist in any social institution and that if this pluralism is not preserved as a basis for ideological succession, the culture will not be able to make the transition from one basic form to another and so will become "petrified, and uncreative" (Sorokin [1941] 1957, p. 25).

Dialectical theories of internal ideological succession at a purely institutional level are clearly of sociological interest only when they are related to accounts of institutional organization and structure. They are, moreover, extremely difficult to construct, because of the conceptual problems involved in setting up a set of categories that between them exhaust the known range of specialized ideological possibilities. The outstanding example of such a dialectic is Wölfflin's theory of stylistic development in European painting during the sixteenth and seventeenth centuries (Wölfflin [1915] 1956; for extensive comment, see Antoni [1940] 1959, chapter 6; Hauser [1958] 1963, pp. 139– 149).

Societal theories. The revolution in social thought that took place during the period 1890– 1910 was especially notable for its emphasis on society as a unique kind of entity that could not be reduced to a combination of other kinds of entities [*see* SOCIETY]. The societal approach had little use for organicist or dialectical theories, since they seemed to ignore such distinctively social processes as symbolic interaction, cultural accumulation, and socialization. Thus Cooley (1897) and many others (see Ogburn [1950] 1964, pp. 19–20) rejected Galton's geneticism on the grounds that it was far more plausible to assume a constant and uniform amount of creative potential in all societies and to attribute differences in creative achievement to manifest differences in social conditions, such as literacy. This environmentalist position appeared to have been confirmed beyond all reasonable doubt by studies showing that identical twins, when reared in different settings, developed differences that could not, it was thought, be accounted for in terms of heredity (Newman et al. 1937). Thus the famous controversy about the importance of "nature," or genetic endowment, as compared with "nurture," or socialization, was not so much settled as abandoned. The social Darwinist model of creative achievement as a product of natural selection gave way to a model of creative potential as a kind of subterranean resource that had only to be "tapped" by the provision of educational opportunities in order to become creative achievement. This model, reinforced by popularized Freudian notions of creativity as an attribute of the unconscious, still underlies much of American educational theory and practice.

Cultural base as creative agent. Another key assumption of the societal approach was that, although the historical process is not just a succession of unique events, it does not evolve in any predetermined direction. This was a natural result of the vast increase, by the end of the nineteenth century, in the stock of historical knowledge, which now revealed processes that seemed too complex to fit into any deterministic theory. One such process was cultural diffusion, which for the first time began to be studied on a scientific basis [see DIFFUSION]. Discovery of the great variety of influences that went into the making of any advanced culture, and of the capacity of some cultures to absorb influences from almost any source while others succumbed to alien penetration, destroyed the heroic image of culture as something created locally by a few outstanding individuals and replaced it with that of the common social heritage or "cultural base" (Ogburn [1950] 1964, pp. 24–25), which set the conditions for individual achievement.

This increase in historical and anthropological knowledge was paralleled by an increase in biographical knowledge of creative individuals; it became clear how much these individuals owed their pre-eminence to the peculiar historical circumstances into which they had been born. Study of the diffusion of ideas from one creative individual

to another led to a search for more general societal mechanisms of cultural interchange and ideological succession. Thus it was pointed out that major discontinuities in ideological succession—the decisive "breaks" in the history of ideas—could be analyzed in terms of generational series [see GENERATIONS]. Most generational studies have been person-oriented and have hardly advanced beyond the descriptive level. They do not attempt to explain what general social or psychological mechanisms could make one rising generation differ so much from another in its ability to free itself of its predecessors' ideas. One such mechanism was, however, proposed by W. I. Thomas, who argued that social change proceeds through a series of situations that disturb habitual ways of thought. These situations, which Thomas called "crises," are perceived and reacted to in different ways by different members of the population affected, but only the creative individuals in that population are fully able to discriminate between situations in such a way as to surmount habit and adjust themselves to radically new social demands (Thomas, *Social Behavior and Personality*, p. 169, note 29; *ibid.*, pp. 218–220). This theory of Thomas' deserves more attention than it has received in recent years; certainly, the ability to deal constructively with changing circumstances is one aspect of creativity, and the empirical research that now exists on the diffusion of innovations might well be re-examined in this light [see DIFFUSION, *article on* INTERPERSONAL INFLUENCE].

The city as creative setting. The theory of the city (for which see Martindale 1958) has also shed some light on the mechanisms of ideological succession. The city is often held to constitute a uniquely *creative setting;* thus Weber declared: "The city and it alone has brought forth the phenomena of the history of art. . . . So also the city produced science in the modern sense" ([1919–1920] 1961, p. 234).

The model underlying the city theory of ideological succession is one of a multiple stimulus proceeding from a central and cumulative cultural base that is open to all the available influences of cultural diffusion. Proponents of this theory are therefore inclined to equate creativity with rapid growth in complexity, which they see as a necessarily cumulative process taking place at ecologically determined central locations. This viewpoint is partly the result of an emphasis on particular organizational outlets and on the physical properties of the cultural base—properties that are coming to seem far less relevant now that modern techniques of mass reproduction and communication can diffuse knowledge of creative objects at low cost, regardless of distance.

Institutional creativity. The new emphasis on the variable properties of social systems and their elements resulted in a view of social systems and subsystems as creative agents. Those systematic properties which enabled the system or subsystem to vary adaptively in structure and type of output were assumed to be the same that caused creativity to emerge at the individual level. Durkheim's theory of the collective origin of all values and concepts finally caused him to adopt a view of society itself as supremely creative ([1912] 1961, pp. 482–496). At the institutional level, Durkheim helped to direct a far more widely diffused preoccupation among social scientists with the processes of education and socialization. Since it was evident that, even if society was in some sense a creative agent, the more specialized creative ideologies were not uniformly diffused throughout society, sociological interest in creativity began to focus on the ways in which these ideologies had been institutionalized for cultivation by creative elites. As the division of labor increased, it seemed as if creative activity necessarily became professional activity. At the same time the influence of Marxist sociology led to an awareness of ideological vested interests that might stand in the way of creativity, not only because of their possibly uncreative character but also because they tended to recruit institutional members mainly from the upper and middle classes. Some theorists—not all of them Marxists —began to maintain that the more organized the cultivation of creative ideologies, the more ideological succession was likely to be a product of conflict between organized ideological interests.

Deviance and marginality. A variation on the theme of ideological conflict that has played a large part in the psychological study of creativity is that ideological succession is brought about by individuals who have deviant personality characteristics, since only such individuals could be motivated to overthrow received ideas. The sociological equivalent of this is the theory of marginality, which holds that "marginal men"—that is, individuals who are marginally located in the social structure —will, because they have been imperfectly socialized into the dominant value system (and therefore have no vested interest in maintaining it), have a greater potential for creative achievement than those who are more centrally located. The achievements of minority group members, especially Jews, have often been cited as evidence in support of this hypothesis (see, for instance, Veblen 1919).

But such arguments tend to overlook the discrepancy between societal values and the values in terms of which creative achievement is appraised by experts. It is probably true in all complex societies that entry to fields where distinction is based *entirely* on achievement is less restricted than entry into other fields where financial success is more easily come by (compare Toynbee [1934*b*] 1962, vol. 2, pp. 209, 217–220). Nevertheless, the theory of the marginal man has some value in the study of creativity because it raises the question of whether the *experience* of marginality, however acquired, may help to strengthen those faculties of detachment and self-reliance which some psychologists believe to characterize creative individuals (see, for instance, Henle 1962, pp. 45–46; Crutchfield 1962, p. 139). There is no good evidence that socialization into a marginal status, or voluntary adoption of such status, is necessarily favorable to creativity. On the contrary, everything we know of minority group psychology and of the psychology of deviance suggests that, for most people, marginality tends to produce feelings of insecurity and even self-hatred that are more likely to find an outlet in compulsive overconformity than in creative achievement. But it does seem likely that the creative person—for reasons that are not yet understood—is an exception to this pattern, in the sense that he is able to turn his marginal status, whether sought or unsought, to good advantage. Biographies of creative individuals suggest that marginality is usually a temporary episode in a creative career and that when it is sought out and cultivated (as Rilke, for instance, sought out the absolute solitude of the Château de Muzot), this is done with a very definite purpose. From a sociological point of view, the striking fact about such careers is the ability of creative individuals to alternate periods of disaffiliation and solitude with periods in which a variety of social roles are sustained with great effectiveness.

Factorial theories. The virtue of the societal approach to creativity was that, in spite of its failure to produce definitive results, it succeeded in demonstrating that collectivities can plausibly be regarded as creative agents and that their creative properties can be analyzed in structural terms. The ambivalence of this approach with regard to the autonomy of the creative individual can be traced to a far more general ambivalence in sociological thought with regard to the relation of the individual and society. In contrast, there is a large class of theories that succeed in evading this problem because they treat creativity as a purely individual property and regard creative achievement as a type of individual response to various social pressures. The sociological problem of creativity, in terms of this approach, is to establish correlations between the distribution of creative individuals or objects and the presence or absence of one or (more usually) a number of social factors. It therefore seems appropriate to call this the *factorial approach.*

Factorial studies of creativity are rarely concerned with explicating structural relations between the social factors that are held to stimulate creative achievement, and still less with constructing models of the creative process that would relate social factors to psychological ones. They do not attempt to explain why a creative response should have taken a particular form, or whether it need have occurred when it did. Because of these and other omissions, many factorial studies are open to the charge of determinism, since they tend to ignore the voluntary element in creative efforts, as well as the extent to which the creative individual defines problems for himself or chooses to deal with certain problems rather than others. Factorial theories also tend to play down the existence of conflict between institutional values. In this sense such theories often seem, as Kuhn points out, to "write history backward" (1962, p. 137).

Toynbee's theories of creativity

Toynbee's important historical treatment of creativity has often been criticized by social scientists on the grounds that it overemphasizes the "great man" at the expense of social factors. But this is to ignore Toynbee's conception of society as a complex of institutions (vol. 1, pp. 454–455) and his carefully stated view on the relationship between the individual and society (vol. 3, pp. 223, 230). The difference between Toynbee's approach and that of most contemporary American sociologists is that he judges the influence of institutions on creativity to be mainly negative (see especially vol. 4, pp. 133–245, 303–423). In this he can be compared with Thomas, who thought that the control exercised by the group over the individual "tends to destroy much more than to construct . . ." (Thomas, *Social Behavior and Personality*, pp. 164–165). But Toynbee also regards the communication of creative experience and the display of creative products as essential parts of the creative process (vol. 1, p. 454, note 3; compare vol. 3, pp. 235–236). His main contention is that the process also requires a withdrawal of potentially creative persons and minorities from these institutions into a socially marginal position where they are set free to carry out the creative work. The final stage in

the process is reached only *after* the creative person or minority has returned to society in order to gain acceptance for a creative product (vol. 3, pp. 248–263, 366–377).

This model of withdrawal and return is also applied to whole nations and civilizations as creative agents, and it is here that Toynbee's theory of creativity exhibits both dialectical and organicist features. It is organicist insofar as civilizations are conceived as entities that undergo the natural processes of birth, growth, and decay; it is dialectical insofar as these processes are conceived as necessarily determined by cycles of creative withdrawal and return (see, for instance, vol. 4, p. 125). Loss of command over the environment, whether physical or human, is explicitly ruled out as a cause of decadence; for Toynbee, it is merely a symptom (vol. 4, pp. 39–119). Yet Toynbee never goes as far as attributing creative primacy to the social structure or to any of its elements; structural arrangements as such originate nothing (vol. 3, p. 230). This is because, in Toynbee's basic model of society, a clear line is drawn between those who lead—the creative minority—and those who are led. Loss of creative power by the leaders is equivalent to loss of influence and cannot be replaced by the use of force; once the majority have withdrawn their assent to the leaders' values, they have in effect seceded from society, which then progressively disintegrates (vol. 1, pp. 187–188; compare vol. 4, pp. 5–6). From such a situation a new society can arise only through emergence of a new creative minority.

Need, demand, and support

Most societal and factorial theories of creativity assume that potentially creative individuals are stimulated to creative achievement by some combination of social need, social demand, and social or economic support. But the relative importance assigned to each of these factors varies greatly, as does the social level at which they are held to operate.

Demand and need in Toynbee's theory. Toynbee explains the birth of civilization in terms of creative societal response to unusually severe environmental challenge (vol. 2, p. 18; see also vol. 2, *passim*). But he does not pay much attention to the way in which a society sets about recognizing its needs, or to the possibility that its perception of need—that is, the nature of its societal demands —may not accurately reflect the true state of affairs. On the other hand, it is clear that fulfillment of need sufficient to ensure a society's survival is only part of what Toynbee means by creativity at this level. Similarly, his application of the term "response" to creative individuals and minorities often implies that they succeeded in doing far more than was required by the situation that "challenged" them.

Ogburn's theory of invention. Ogburn differs greatly from Toynbee, first, in viewing creative potential simply as the upper end of the normal distribution of mental ability and, second, in adopting a conception of culture that makes the creative individual not so much a leader as a "medium in social change" (Ogburn [1926] 1964, p. 43; compare [1950] 1964, p. 22, note 4).

Ogburn's overriding preoccupation with technological invention, and his commitment to a cumulative model of scientific development, gave rise to certain anomalies in his treatment of creativity that he recognized but was unable to resolve. Other social institutions did not appear to evolve in the same way or at the same rate as science, and this made it difficult to apply the theory of cultural accumulation to whole cultures, at least when dealing with complex societies. Moreover, different societies clearly evolved at different rates—a fact that Ogburn could not explain in terms of the accumulation of purely internal cultural materials, once he assumed that all races had the same creative potential and that cultural accumulation was the prime creative force.

The social processes adduced by Ogburn in order to remove these difficulties have an adventitious character. Cultural evolution is said to be explicable in terms of four factors—invention, accumulation, diffusion, and adjustment—of which invention is the "central" factor, while the others "all lead to further invention, but they do more. Each is a significant and special process, irrespective of its stimulation of new inventions" (Ogburn [1950] 1964, p. 23, note 6). In dealing with concrete examples, Ogburn tends to play these different factors off against each other rather than to analyze the way in which they are interrelated. For example, he states that the "inventional process" consists in the "operation of three factors: mental ability, demand, and . . . the 'cultural base.'" But then he admits the existence of a class of inventions that "are made accidentally while working on something else; for these, demand did not direct the invention. Such are many discoveries in pure science. The use of an invention, however, implies a demand" (Ogburn [1950] 1964, pp. 23–24). In other words, the absence, in a given type of situation, of one of Ogburn's factors does not lead him to question his general model of invention but merely to change the topic. Elsewhere, Ogburn explains the fact that "significant invention" is not usually accompanied by change in all other parts of society by adducing his celebrated theory of cultural lag, which is based on the hypothesis that all societies seek through invention to regain the equilibrium that invention has upset (*ibid.*, p. 30; compare Ogburn 1957). But by Ogburn's own admission his theory of cultural evolution does not accord at all with his conception of artistic creativity ([1936] 1964, pp. 56–57)—though it is hard to believe, on this evidence, that he ever gave any serious attention to the history of art.

Demand and institutional appraisal. Both Toynbee and Ogburn tend to overlook the relationship between social demand and institutional processes such as appraisal. Thus the phenomenon of neglected genius—a central problem for the sociology of creativity—cannot be explained wholly or even mainly in terms of lack of demand, as it would have to be under Ogburn's theory, nor yet as a deficiency of qualities making for successful leadership, as Toynbee would probably argue. Both of these factors are certainly capable of overshadowing creative achievement, but it must be very seldom that they obscure it altogether. A far more likely explanation in many cases is that, because of a breakdown in the system of appraisal (which may be associated with a sudden upsurge of new creative ideologies after a period of stagnation, or with the emergence of a new kind of audience for creative products) there is as yet no outlet for a certain type of creative object in those social areas where a demand for it exists. In any case, it is certain that different types of appraisal are linked with different types of demand and that appraisal systems are highly complex structural entities which are rarely examined as such.

Thus, for the creative individual, the existence of a stratified social demand mediated by a sophisticated appraisal system is likely to intensify the conflict between the claims of creative achievement and those of public recognition—or, as Rank put it, the antagonism between success and fame (1932, chapter 6). Little systematic work has been done on any of these questions, but notice should be taken of Kuhn's suggestion (1962, p. 69) that the breakdown of established paradigms, as evidenced by their increasing failure to solve the problems they themselves generate, may have a greater effect on the emergence of scientific creativity than the more generalized social pressures that preoccupied theorists such as Toynbee and Ogburn.

Support. Social demand for creative products is so often measured in terms of economic support for their creators that these two factors have become inextricably confused. Yet it is clear that although they are for the most part closely associated, at least in capitalist societies with a high degree of literacy, they may vary independently. Thus, American concert and opera audiences, possibly from a historically conditioned sense of cultural inferiority, have always preferred European to American composers, even when the latter were of outstanding merit. This has not deterred the Ford Foundation from subsidizing American opera on a lavish scale (Rockefeller Brothers Fund 1965, pp. 29–31). Nevertheless, there is no regular audience for native contemporary opera in the United States, and American composers would probably cease to write operas were it not for foundation support. The reverse situation—a widespread demand that goes unfulfilled for lack of support—is probably quite rare in American society but can be inferred to exist in the Soviet Union, for instance, where the prerevolutionary classics of Russian literature are bought and read in huge numbers, while the output of contemporary Soviet writers seems quite insufficient to match this evident demand for serious reading matter (Friedberg 1962, chapters 6 and 7).

But economic support for cultural activities and products is not the same thing as economic support for creativity, nor is it possible to prove, simply from inspection of the amount a society spends on art museums, symphony orchestras, libraries, and the like, that the arts of that society are in either a creative or an uncreative state. This is the most damaging criticism that can be made of otherwise useful studies, such as that of Toffler (1964). One distinction that would go far to clear up this and many other confusions about the relation of creativity to support is that between economic and social support. The fact that few women have distinguished themselves in science or in most of the arts except acting and musical performance is clear evidence of the lack of social support for women to compete in these fields. There are also obvious differences in the nature of the social support meted out to the same pursuits in different cultures. For instance, the amount of social support for the creative scientist in the United States differs markedly from that for the creative artist—a fact that reflects the naively utilitarian conception of science that predominates in American society. In the Soviet Union, on the other hand, it is the official theory of art that is naively utilitarian, and the artist who succeeds in accommodating himself to this credo enjoys the kind of prestige that, in the United States, is more often accorded to scien-

tists. Such differences in the ideological basis of economic support undoubtedly affect creativity, but they have yet to be systematically investigated.

Patronage systems. Most writers on creativity who consider patronage treat it as synonymous with economic support. Patrons are usually classified according to their social status—for instance, aristocratic, as opposed to bourgeois—and frequent attempts have been made to relate the rise of this or that creative ideology to the growing economic prosperity of a social class (see, for instance, Hauser [1951] 1957–1958, vol. 2, pp. 26–52). Such analyses assume that the form taken by a creative product is determined largely by the tastes or demands of those who pay for it.

But even if we grant the assumption that some kinds of patronage are especially favorable to creativity, it is by no means clear what these are. For instance, Italian art patrons during the age of the baroque could hardly have been more generous or more tolerant, yet the achievements of Italian painting during that period were disappointing when compared with developments in other parts of Europe, in spite of the superior Italian "cultural base" for the fine arts. It has been suggested that one reason for this decline in creativity may have been the extreme tolerance of the patrons: "Unorthodoxy was killed with kindness" (Haskell 1963, p. 385). On the other hand, major creative ideologies have been propagated successfully under systems of patronage that, by all common-sense criteria, would seem to have been peculiarly unfavorable: one has only to remember William Hazlitt's embittered description of the social conditions that attended the birth of the English romantic movement ([1825] 1948, pp. 737–738).

None of the standard explanations of these anomalies are very satisfactory. The usual thesis is that to maximize social and economic support for any institution is to maximize its opportunities for creative development. But there is always the risk that hypertrophy of an institution may generate a flood of mediocrities and a corresponding dilution of basic institutional values (see, for instance, Butler [1962] 1963, pp. 21–22; White & White 1965, pp. 2, 44–54). A more systematic approach to the problem would be to study patronage systems as institutionalized patterns of support in which the social status of patrons and the amount of their financial outlays would be only two of the many elements to be considered. The essential features of this approach are already present in Haskell's analysis of seventeenth-century art patronage (Haskell 1963, chapter 1). It is clear from Haskell's account that many different types of patronage, serving many different needs, can coexist within the same system. What differentiated this system from the one that eventually replaced it was not so much the social status of its patrons as the set of values, shared by artists and patrons alike, relating to the nature of art as an institution. From a sociological point of view, it is this homogeneity of values that should probably be singled out when comparing baroque patronage with, for instance, the art market of the late nineteenth century. Clearly, a patronage system in which painters and patrons have different conceptions of art *as an institution* is likely to need entrepreneurs who will mediate between supply and demand. The forms taken by the mechanisms of display and appraisal are also likely to be different.

But these and similar hypotheses cannot be investigated systematically in the absence of a historically sound typology of patronage systems. Four such types can be readily identified: the *personalized* system described by Haskell, in which there is a clear distinction between patronage for public and private purposes, though in either case the patron is the direct employer of the artist or scientist; the *academy* system, which is essentially a system of ideological control based on official patronage and is the system preferred by authoritarian and communist regimes; the *open market* system, of which American show business is perhaps the purest form; and the *subvention* system, in which a variety of patrons, both public and private, underwrite the cost of cultural activities that would otherwise cease for lack of demand.

All of these systems—and probably others, too— may coexist in the same society. Thus a society's art may be supported by an open market system and its science by an academy system. There may also be more than one system of support for a single institution, as when art is supported by both the personalized and the open market systems. Under these conditions, the creative individual may have a choice of patronage systems, any one of which will impose a definite type of demand. It may be difficult for him to serve more than one of these systems once he has made his initial choice. But these and related problems in the sociology of creativity have as yet scarcely been identified, let alone discussed.

Empirical studies

Most empirical studies of creativity are person-oriented. The samples on which they are based fall into two main categories: those in which the individuals studied have been selected on the basis of acknowledged creative achievement at some arbitrarily defined level and those in which an entire population has been sampled and classified, usually on the basis of projective psychological tests (though ratings by peers or supervisors are often collected as well), into "creative" and "uncreative" groups. Samples based on achievement criteria have often been institutional in scope; for instance, the entire population of "creative" American scientists is continually being studied (Roe 1963). A few attempts, of which Galton's is still the best-known, have been made to study the characteristics of creative individuals at different historical periods on a national basis (*Genetic Studies of Genius*, vol. 2, 1926; White 1931). Studies using psychological measures have usually been conducted at the level of formal organizations and of the organized work groups that they contain (for a brief review, see Hughes 1963; for some of the current research, see Utah Creativity Research Conference 1964, parts IV and V; Fiedler 1964).

Few of the psychological studies examine their subjects over any considerable period of time: the outstanding exception is the work of Terman and his associates, who drew a sample of over 1,400 school children with IQs of 140 or more and successfully conducted follow-up studies over a period of 25 years (see, for instance, *Genetic Studies of Genius*, vol. 4, 1947). Studies using projective tests are occasionally made of mature creative individuals selected on the basis of acknowledged achievement in the arts or sciences (a good example is Barron 1963, chapter 19); such individuals are never identified, and it is therefore impossible to make an independent appraisal of their creative ideologies. The most interesting achievement of the psychological studies so far has been the differentiation of intelligence from creative potential (Getzels & Jackson 1962), and there are many indications that these two factors, though associated, may vary independently within a certain range (Meer & Stein 1955). Studies and autobiographies of creative individuals have, of course, been analyzed by social scientists, but Rank's devastating criticism of the psychological approach to biographical material is still valid (1932, p. 150; compare pp. 129–130, 143–144).

A complete list of studies that fall into the categories outlined above would include nearly all the social science literature ostensibly concerned with creativity. But this list would omit most of the studies that have relevance for the sociological approach to the topic. Unfortunately, there is as yet no agreement on the nature of this relevance, though it has been clear to sociologists for some time that it exists. In my opinion, one of the main obstacles to the inauguration of a sociology of creativity is the assumption that all studies of creativity must be person-oriented. But the study of creativity need not be confined to the individual level. Many empirical studies of social movements, formal organizations, and small groups deal with creative actions and products, even though they may not use the word "creativity." Findings at these different levels could be compared with respect to their definitions of the creative object; the amount of attention they pay to institutional values, creative ideologies, and outlets for creative products; and the ways in which they describe the basic mechanisms of ideological succession, display, appraisal, and support. But if a mature sociology of creativity is ever to emerge, far more empirical studies will have to be undertaken at the institutional and societal levels.

Societies. Social systems are usually conceived as having various kinds of outputs. Within this frame of reference any attempt to explain creativity at the societal level must be concerned with the quality of such outputs. But there is no agreement about what they are and considerable confusion about what they might be. Some studies treat the output of a single institution, such as art, as if it were a societal output and then relate variations in the quality of this output to different states of the social system. Thus Kavolis has made use of the phase–cycle theory of Parsons and Bales in order to argue that a society's artistic creativity is likely to increase when social conditions are such as to "increase the social utility of art as a symbolic facility for reintegration, without necessarily destroying or massively diverting the resources needed for artistic creation" (1966, p. 215). This theory is held to be supported by Sorokin's data on the rate of internal disorders in various countries. But even if it is granted that the social function of art is social integration, there remains the question of how institutional values are related to societal needs. Highly specialized creative ideologies such as artistic styles are clearly not generated by the social system acting as a whole, nor does an upsurge of creativity in a single institution constitute evidence that the entire social system is in a creative state. It might be possible to measure the outputs of different institutions on the same scale, but this would only obscure the question of how the institutions were related to each other. It may be that a truly creative state of society would be one in which the different institutions stand in relations of reciprocity and mutual support. In this case, the output of the creative social system would be, presumably, the civic morality that made such relations possible. Conversely, an uncreative social system would be one characterized by chronic and acute disharmony between its institutions (compare Toynbee [1939] 1962, p. 133). This hypothesis attributes creativity to social integration, not cultural integration, since if each institution had as much creative autonomy as was consistent with civic morality, considerable heterogeneity of cultural forms and styles would result.

Another topic on which more empirical research is needed is the relationship between creativity and national character. Although the notion of national character, generally accepted in David Hume's day (see Toynbee, vol. 1, p. 470), has now fallen into discredit as a tool of social science, it still appears to have some use in literary and art criticism. For instance, Nikolaus Pevsner (1956) has argued that the English national character, as revealed in English art and architecture, has undergone a series of radical changes: opposing stylistic traits such as "moderation" and "fantasy," which derive from the English social heritage, appear in different combinations at different periods without ceasing to reflect certain dominant formal qualities. What is impressive about Pevsner's method of analysis, which owes much to Wölfflin, is the way in which he links aspects of internal ideology (that is, purely formal properties such as emphasis on verticals, and disembodiment) with aspects of external ideology (that is, with values such as conservatism, which derive from institutions other than art). Since Pevsner associates creativity in the arts with intensity and even fanaticism, he concludes that the diminishing frequency of these two qualities in English art since the Reformation shows that England is no longer a "visual nation," and he attributes this decline in artistic creativity to the growth of reason and tolerance in English political institutions ([1956] 1964, p. 206). Whatever one may think of such daring analogies between internal and external ideological succession, the facts on either side of the analogy are clear enough, and the problem of connecting them more systematically than Pevsner has done is a genuine one for sociology [see STYLE].

Institutions. The importance of institutional values for the study of creativity has already been emphasized. There is no lack of relevant literature here; rather, there is a need for the development of formal categories in terms of which the internal dynamics of ideological succession can be systematically described. The greatest progress in this area so far has been made by those art historians who have followed the example of Wölfflin, but without his bent for dialectics.

A far more neglected area is institutional structure. The concept of institutional structure should (but usually does not) include not only the means by which an institution deals with recruitment, socialization, and ideological succession but also such aspects of its relations with the larger society as its sources of support (both social and economic), its outlets, and its provisions for display and appraisal. One of the very few sociological attempts at meeting all these requirements is a study by White and White (1965) of institutional change in the French art world during the nineteenth century. In this study the dimensions of painting as an institution are systematically mapped out in terms of such parameters as the total number of painters and the rate at which they produced paintings. The object-oriented ideology and centralized formal structure of the academic appraisal system are seen as contributing to the academy's eventual loss of control over institutional values (White & White 1965, pp. 88–89, 100) and thus to the successful emergence of impressionism as a creative ideology. But the study does not deal with the internal ideology of impressionism except insofar as it brought a new importance to the previously minor genre of landscape painting. Impressionism, however, represented a far more drastic revolution in pictorial values, and it is possible that too much stress on institutional continuity may serve to obscure this.

In contrast, Kuhn (1962) stresses the discontinuity that accompanies radical change in the realm of scientific values. The introduction of a new paradigm—presumably the most creative feat a scientist or group of scientists can accomplish—is essentially a noncumulative episode in the history of science and represents such a sharp break with the established scientific world view that it can gain acceptance only after science has entered a period of acknowledged crisis. Thus the creative genius of a Galileo consists in the introduction of an entirely new mode of interpretation that, because it enlarges the whole field of scientific perception, cannot be described in terms of a single discovery or invention—rather, it is a "scientific revolution" (Kuhn 1962, pp. 118–122). But, as Kuhn has emphasized, it is "normal science" that makes scientific revolutions possible, since only to those who have mastered a particular scientific tradition does it become evident that the tradition has been exhausted ([1959] 1963, pp. 349–350).

These considerations suggest that neither personality factors nor basic abilities have any part to play in the higher forms of creative scientific achievement unless they are associated with thorough socialization into a firmly established tradition. Thus, for Kuhn the most important precondition of scientific creativity is an institutionalized

consensus. Again, there are obvious parallels with the history of art. For instance, White and White have pointed out that the impressionist rejection of tradition was made more meaningful by the existence of a firmly established tradition to reject (1965, pp. 160–161); similarly, Shils (1964, p. 356) has pointed out that the function of an avant-garde in any institution is to reinterpret tradition. But if the history of art is to be systematically compared with the history of science, it will be necessary to give an account of artistic creativity in terms of problem solving and to distinguish between the different kinds of artistic problems as they are seen from the artist's point of view, just as Kuhn has examined creativity in science from the scientist's point of view. The creative object in art and science is essentially a solution to a series of problems; accordingly, the sociological researcher will always fail to understand why or in what respects an object should be considered creative unless he also understands what these problems are and how they relate to each other. From an object-oriented point of view, both art and science present themselves as hierarchically ordered complexes of problems—some basic, some less basic, and some quite trivial. Since creativity occurs at all these levels, the task of appraising creative objects for sociological purposes is not so much one of ranking them according to degree of creativity as of assigning to each object its appropriate place in the total hierarchy of problems and solutions to problems. To say that one creative object is more or less creative than another is to imply that it solves problems of a higher or a lower order. How this order is to be conceived is a question that can be decided only with reference to the values which constitute the internal ideology of the institution in question.

Other problem areas that still await investigation at the institutional level are the relation between ideological succession and patterns of support, the effects of technology upon institutional outlets, and the systematic comparison of patronage systems.

Study of creativity at the societal and institutional levels has traditionally been a historical enterprise. But it is one thing to evaluate a dead civilization and quite another to diagnose the state of an ongoing civilization of which no one knows the outcome. Thus Toynbee's theories, when applied to the contemporary United States (Toynbee 1964), issue in conclusions that are suggestive but that could be substantiated only by sociological analysis of data that are not likely to be available for many years to come. A more sophisticated account of obstacles to creativity in modern industrialized society is that of Murphy (1958), who offers hope that the rigidity of the cultural base can be counterbalanced by deeper understanding of human potentialities. This raises a question that has escaped most historians, Toynbee included: What will be the social effects of the increasing psychological knowledge of creativity? Historical research has no answers to this question because no civilization but the present one has had the opportunity to develop such knowledge. Intelligence and aptitude tests are now so widely used that they obviously meet a permanent demand in modern society. If a similar demand for creativity tests should ever make itself felt, the structure of society, especially its present highly inefficient mechanisms for ideological succession, might be permanently changed.

J. M. B. EDWARDS

[*Directly related are the entries* CULTURE; FILM; FINE ARTS; LEADERSHIP; LITERATURE; SCIENCE. *Other relevant material may be found in* CITY, *article on* FORMS AND FUNCTIONS; COMMUNICATION, MASS, *article on* AUDIENCES; GROUPS, *article on* GROUP BEHAVIOR; ORGANIZATIONS, *article on* EFFECTIVENESS AND PLANNING OF CHANGE; *and in the biographies of* BUBER; COOLEY; DURKHEIM; FREUD; GALTON; KROEBER; OGBURN; RANK; SOROKIN; TERMAN; THOMAS; WEBER, MAX.]

BIBLIOGRAPHY

ALLEN, WARREN D. (1939) 1962 *Philosophies of Music History: A Study of General Histories of Music, 1600–1960.* New York: Dover. → Revised and updated edition of a work first published in 1939.

ANTONI, CARLO (1940) 1959 *From History to Sociology: The Transition in German Historical Thinking.* Detroit, Mich.: Wayne State Univ. Press. → First published as *Dallo storicismo alla sociologia.*

BARRON, FRANK X. 1963 *Creativity and Psychological Health: Origins of Personal Vitality and Creative Freedom.* Princeton, N.J.: Van Nostrand.

BRUNER, JEROME S. 1962 The Conditions of Creativity. Pages 1–30 in Howard E. Gruber et al. (editors), *Contemporary Approaches to Creative Thinking.* New York: Atherton.

BUTLER, REGINALD C. (1962) 1963 *Creative Development.* New York: Horizon Press. → Based on lectures given at the Slade School, University College, London.

COLER, MYRON A. (editor) 1963 *Essays on Creativity in the Sciences.* New York Univ. Press.

COOLEY, CHARLES H. (1897) 1930 Genius, Fame and the Comparison of Races. Pages 119–159 in Charles H. Cooley, *Sociological Theory and Social Research, Being the Selected Papers of Charles Horton Cooley.* With an introduction and notes by Robert Cooley Angell. New York: Holt. → First published in Volume 9 of the *Annals* of the American Academy of Political and Social Science.

CRUTCHFIELD, RICHARD S. 1962 Conformity and Creative Thinking. Pages 120–140 in Howard E. Gruber

et al. (editors), *Contemporary Approaches to Creative Thinking.* New York: Atherton.

DURKHEIM, ÉMILE (1912) 1961 *The Elementary Forms of the Religious Life.* New York: Collier. → First published as *Les formes élémentaires de la vie religieuse, le système totémique en Australie.*

FIEDLER, FRED E. 1964 A Contingency Model of Leadership Effectiveness. Volume 1, pages 149–190 in *Advances in Experimental Social Psychology.* New York: Academic Press.

FISCHER, ERNST (1959) 1963 *The Necessity of Art: A Marxist Approach.* London and Baltimore: Penguin. → First published in East Germany as *Von der Notwendigkeit der Kunst.* A work much inferior to Sprigg 1937 but worth reading as representative of the "soft" line in communist aesthetics.

FRIEDBERG, MAURICE 1962 *Russian Classics in Soviet Jackets.* New York: Columbia Univ. Press. → A well-documented study of Soviet publishing.

Genetic Studies of Genius. Volume 2: The Early Mental Traits of Three Hundred Geniuses, by Catharine M. Cox et al. 1926 Stanford Univ. Press.

Genetic Studies of Genius. Volume 4: The Gifted Child Grows Up: Twenty-five Years' Follow-up of a Superior Group, by Lewis M. Terman et al. 1947 Stanford Univ. Press.

GETZELS, JACOB W.; and JACKSON, PHILIP W. 1962 *Creativity and Intelligence: Explorations With Gifted Students.* New York: Wiley.

GUÉRARD, ALBERT L. (1936) 1963 *Art for Art's Sake.* New York: Schocken.

HASKELL, FRANCIS 1963 *Patrons and Painters: A Study in the Relations Between Italian Art and Society in the Age of the Baroque.* New York: Knopf; London: Chatto & Windus.

HAUSER, ARNOLD (1951) 1957–1958 *The Social History of Art.* 4 vols. New York: Vintage. → First published in German.

HAUSER, ARNOLD (1958) 1963 *The Philosophy of Art History.* Cleveland and New York: World. → First published as *Philosophie der Kunstgeschichte.*

HAZLITT, WILLIAM (1825) 1948 Mr. Coleridge. Pages 725–738 in William Hazlitt, *Selected Essays of William Hazlitt: 1778–1830.* Edited by Geoffrey Keynes. London: Nonesuch. → Originally published in his *The Spirit of the Age.*

HENLE, MARY 1962 The Birth and Death of Ideas. Pages 31–62 in Howard E. Gruber et al. (editors), *Contemporary Approaches to Creative Thinking.* New York: Atherton.

HUGHES, HAROLD K. 1963 Individual and Group Creativity in Science. Pages 93–109 in Myron A. Coler (editor), *Essays in Creativity in the Sciences.* New York Univ. Press.

KAVOLIS, VYTAUTAS M. 1966 Community Dynamics and Artistic Creativity. *American Sociological Review* 31:208–217.

KUHN, THOMAS S. (1959) 1963 The Essential Tension: Tradition and Innovation in Scientific Research. Pages 341–354 in Research Conference on the Identification of Creative Scientific Talent, *Scientific Creativity: Its Recognition and Development.* Edited by Calvin W. Taylor and Frank Barron. New York: Wiley. → A paper given at the 1959 Utah Conference on the Identification of Creative Scientific Talent.

KUHN, THOMAS S. 1962 *The Structure of Scientific Revolutions.* Univ. of Chicago Press. → A paperback edition was published in 1964.

MARTINDALE, DON (1958) 1962 Prefatory Remarks: The Theory of the City. Pages 9–67 in Max Weber, *The City*. New York: Collier.

MEER, BERNARD; and STEIN, MORRIS I. 1955 Measures of Intelligence and Creativity. *Journal of Psychology* 39:117–126.

MOONEY, ROSS L. (1957) 1962 A Conceptual Model for Integrating Four Approaches to the Identification of Creative Talent. Pages 73–84 in Sidney J. Parnes and Harold F. Harding (editors), *A Source Book for Creative Thinking*. New York: Scribner. → A paper given at the Research Conference on the Identification of Creative Scientific Talent in Utah in 1957; the published version includes the discussion that followed the paper.

MURPHY, GARDNER 1958 *Human Potentialities*. New York: Basic Books.

NAHM, MILTON C. (1956) 1965 *Genius and Creativity: An Essay in the History of Ideas*. New York: Harper. → First published as *The Artist as Creator*.

NEWMAN, HORATIO H.; FREEMAN, FRANK N.; and HOLZINGER, KARL J. 1937 *Twins: A Study of Heredity and Environment*. Univ. of Chicago Press.

OGBURN, WILLIAM F. (1926) 1964 The Great Man Versus Social Forces. Pages 33–43 in William F. Ogburn, *William F. Ogburn on Culture and Social Change: Selected Papers*. Edited by Otis Dudley Duncan. Univ. of Chicago Press. → First published in Volume 5 of *Social Forces*.

OGBURN, WILLIAM F. (1936) 1964 Stationary and Changing Societies. Pages 44–61 in William F. Ogburn, *William F. Ogburn on Culture and Social Change: Selected Papers*. Edited by Otis Dudley Duncan. Univ. of Chicago Press. → First published in Volume 42 of the *American Journal of Sociology*.

OGBURN, WILLIAM F. 1942 Inventions, Population, and History. Pages 232–245 in Percy Long (editor), *Studies in the History of Culture*. Menasha (Wis.): Banta.

OGBURN, WILLIAM F. (1950) 1964 Social Evolution Reconsidered. Pages 17–32 in William F. Ogburn, *William F. Ogburn on Culture and Social Change: Selected Papers*. Edited by Otis Dudley Duncan. Univ. of Chicago Press. → First published as a supplementary chapter to the 1950 edition of Ogburn's *Social Change With Respect to Culture and Original Nature* (1922).

OGBURN, WILLIAM F. (1957) 1964 Cultural Lag as Theory. Pages 86–95 in William F. Ogburn, *William F. Ogburn on Culture and Social Change: Selected Papers*. Edited by Otis Dudley Duncan. Univ. of Chicago Press. → First published in Volume 41 of *Sociology and Social Research*.

PEVSNER, NIKOLAUS (1956) 1964 *The Englishness of English Art*. Baltimore and London: Penguin.

RANK, OTTO (1909–1932) 1959 *The Myth of the Birth of the Hero and Other Writings*. Edited by Philip Freund. New York: Vintage. → Contains only the three opening and three closing chapters of *Art and Artist*, slightly less than half the original. However, it is the only English-language version in print.

RANK, OTTO 1932 *Art and Artist: Creative Urge and Personality Development*. Translated by Charles F. Atkinson. New York: Knopf. → Pages cited in the text are from the selections reprinted in Rank 1909–1932.

RESEARCH CONFERENCE ON THE IDENTIFICATION OF CREATIVE SCIENTIFIC TALENT 1963 *Scientific Creativity: Its Recognition and Development*. Edited by Calvin W. Taylor and Frank Barron. New York: Wiley. → A selection made from papers delivered at the first three Utah Conferences on the Identification of Creative Scientific Talent, held in 1955, 1957, and 1959 and supported by the National Science Foundation.

ROCKEFELLER BROTHERS FUND 1965 *The Performing Arts: Problems and Prospects; Rockefeller Panel Report on the Future of Theatre, Dance, Music in America*. New York: McGraw-Hill.

ROE, ANNE 1963 Psychological Approaches to Creativity in Science. Pages 153–182 in Myron A. Coler (editor), *Essays on Creativity in the Sciences*. New York Univ. Press. → A very useful review of the field by a leading contributor to it.

ROGERS, CARL R. (1954) 1962 Toward a Theory of Creativity. Pages 63–72 in Sidney J. Parnes and Harold F. Harding (editors), *A Source Book for Creative Thinking*. New York: Scribner. → First published in Volume 11 of *ETC: A Review of General Semantics*.

SHILS, EDWARD 1964 The High Culture of the Age. Pages 317–362 in Robert N. Wilson (editor), *The Arts in Society*. Englewood Cliffs, N.J.: Prentice-Hall.

SIDNEY, PHILIP (1595) 1895 *Apologie for Poetrie*. Westminster (England): Constable.

SOROKIN, PITIRIM A. (1941) 1957 *The Crisis of Our Age: The Social and Cultural Outlook*. New York: Dutton. → A readable summary, with some of the original tables, of the conclusions reached in the same author's *Social and Cultural Dynamics*.

[SPRIGG, CHRISTOPHER] (1937) 1963 *Illusion and Reality*, by Christopher Caudwell [pseud.]. New York: International Publishers. → A brilliant Marxist treatise on the sociology of poetry. The author, an English communist, was killed in 1937 at the age of 29 while fighting for the Republicans in the Spanish Civil War.

STEIN, MORRIS I.; and HEINZE, SHIRLEY J. 1960 *Creativity and the Individual: Summaries of Selected Literature in Psychology and Psychiatry*. New York: Free Press. → A well-designed collection of abstracts. However, the entries on empirical studies are more lucid than the ones on conceptual and theoretical studies, and the abstract of Rank's *Art and Artist* is misleading and inaccurate.

THOMAS, W. I. 1951 *Social Behavior and Personality: Contributions of W. I. Thomas to Theory and Social Research*. Edited by Edmund H. Volkart. New York: Social Science Research Council. → A posthumously published selection of readings, with a good commentary.

TOFFLER, ALVIN 1964 *The Culture Consumers: Art and Affluence in America*. London: St. Martins. → A paperback edition was published in 1965 by Penguin. A carefully researched but somewhat overstated attack on the critics of mass culture.

TOYNBEE, ARNOLD J. (1934a) 1962 *A Study of History*. Volume 1: The Geneses of Civilizations, Part 1. Oxford Univ. Press.

TOYNBEE, ARNOLD J. (1934b) 1962 *A Study of History*. Volume 2: The Geneses of Civilizations, Part 2. Oxford Univ. Press.

TOYNBEE, ARNOLD J. (1934c) 1962 *A Study of History*. Volume 3: The Growths of Civilizations. Oxford Univ. Press.

TOYNBEE, ARNOLD J. (1939) 1962 *A Study of History*. Volume 4: The Breakdowns of Civilizations. Oxford Univ. Press.

TOYNBEE, ARNOLD J. 1964 Is America Neglecting Her

Creative Minority? Pages 3–9 in Utah Creativity Research Conference, *Widening Horizons in Creativity.* Edited by Calvin W. Taylor. New York: Wiley.

UTAH CREATIVITY RESEARCH CONFERENCE 1964 *Widening Horizons in Creativity.* Proceedings of the Fifth Conference, edited by Calvin W. Taylor. New York: Wiley.

VALÉRY, PAUL (1940) 1952 The Course in Poetics: First Lesson. Pages 92–106 in Brewster Ghiselin (editor), *The Creative Process.* New York: Mentor. → First published in French. This translation is a revision of one first published in Volume 5 of the *Southern Review* in 1940.

VEBLEN, THORSTEIN (1919) 1948 The Intellectual Preeminence of Jews in Modern Europe. Pages 467–479 in Thorstein Veblen, *The Portable Veblen.* Edited with an introduction by Max Lerner. New York: Viking.

WEBER, MAX (1919–1920) 1961 *General Economic History.* Translated by Frank H. Knight. New York: Collier. → Contains lectures delivered in 1919–1920.

WEBER, MAX (1921) 1962 *The City.* Translated and edited by Don Martindale and Gertrud Neuwirth. New York: Collier. → First published as *Die Stadt.*

WHITE, HARRISON C.; and WHITE, CYNTHIA A. 1965 *Canvases and Careers: Institutional Change in the French Painting World.* New York: Wiley.

WHITE, RALPH K. 1931 The Versatility of Genius. *Journal of Social Psychology* 2:460–489.

WÖLFFLIN, HEINRICH (1915) 1956 *Principles of Art History: The Problem of the Development of Style in Later Art.* New York: Dover. → This English translation is from the seventh (1929) German edition.

III
GENIUS AND ABILITY

In a popular nineteenth-century conception, geniuses were innately gifted men who somehow made history. The "great-man" theory, as argued by Carlyle and supported by Galton, Lombroso, and others, may be stated in the following simplified form: Fame is a consequence of genius and can seldom be achieved without it, and genius as a rule achieves fame, almost regardless of any environmental and social conditions. Furthermore, men gifted with high abilities overcome virtually all obstacles, but men having social advantages and lacking in high abilities cannot rise to eminence. All truly great achievements, in this view, are made by the few eminent men of high ability.

Although some sociologists were briefly influenced by the above view, the main trend of sociological thinking ran steadily in a contrary direction. C. H. Cooley (1897) published a lengthy and effective challenge to the great-man theory, based on his examination of lists of distinguished European men to see if any had risen to eminence despite the total lack of educational advantages. He found no case in which there was not at least some formal childhood education. Illiteracy, at least, he concluded, would constitute a sufficient barrier to eminence for persons of any degree of innate ability.

Galton (1869) had accounted for exceptional flowerings of culture, such as that of Athens between 530 B.C. and 430 B.C., in terms of abrupt genetic improvement following unplanned selection of superior types of immigrants. Cooley (1897) explained the same phenomenon in sociological rather than biological terms. The operating factors included the accumulation of traditions of technical skills that developed atmospheres encouraging valued types of achievement and linked these activities to other dominant motivating enthusiasms, such as political and religious interests. Cooley did not hold innate differences to be irrelevant, but he did contend that both ability and favorable conditions were essential to the flowering of human achievement. For the most part the subsequent sociological tradition has developed in this direction of thinking.

Genius as a sociological concept

The concept of genius is not widely used in contemporary sociological writings, perhaps because of an aversion to popular usage, in which the term implies an exaggeration of the abilities and powers of men of achievement so that they appear to possess hereditary equipment of an order entirely apart from that of the rest of the population. The modest, but essentially correct, self-deprecation by persons commonly reputed to be geniuses is widely overlooked or dismissed as only a display of good manners.

Sociological attention to the subjects of creation and social change has increasingly tended to be fixed mainly on broad social processes. The responsibility of research into the nature and importance of individual abilities is nowadays, for the most part, left to the psychologists. Even from the early days of their discipline, however, sociological scholars have warned against giving undue weight to the importance of the abilities of individual persons as a factor bearing on the course of history.

However, direct attention to the evaluation of mental achievements of specific persons is not entirely lacking in sociology. In many cases of persons nominated by popular acclaim or by judgment of historians as true geniuses, it is difficult or impossible to separate the contribution of mental ability from that of other personal qualities and from factors external to the persons, including good luck. There is no justification, for example, for the sometimes attractive inference that a victorious military leader has, solely by the fact of his triumph, qualified himself as a genius; the mental powers of Caesar, Napoleon, or Grant cannot be usefully estimated from the materials of history. The same methodological difficulty applies to the assessment of the intelligence, ex officio, of heads of governments, leaders of movements, and spectacularly successful criminals.

Popular lists of geniuses are heavily contaminated by the arbitrary standards of popular or critical approbation. Thus Rembrandt was widely held to be a great artist during the age when his work was in vogue and was later dismissed by some critics as a hack painter. Longfellow seemed to be a greater poet in the nineteenth century than in the twentieth. Whatever one's view of aesthetic values, it is clear that the future standing of contemporary artists of renown cannot be known in their own time; and this is an undeniable handicap to empirical research.

The search for unmistakable instances of genius, in the more narrow sense of extraordinary and effective mental ability, has led to the examination of the mental operations of creative mathematicians, research scientists, and prolific inventors. The results of such inquiries support the theory that the admired feats of such persons do not rest on exceptional native ability or on special talents not possessed by the rest of the population, but can be attributed to a variety of factors such as effective training or experience, possession of symbolic tools that facilitate mental operations, exceptionally strong motivation, and sometimes the good luck of being at the right time and place for an important advancement of knowledge to be made (Faris 1940).

Types of ability. Psychologists have shown that tests of ability can usefully be divided into separate factors, and it is now generally conceded that ability is not a single entity but that there are various kinds, each valuable in a different way (Goslin 1963; see also Gruber et al. 1962). Ability for routine research and invention, effective judgment and wisdom, strong administrative and leadership qualities, various performing skills, and general creativity—all have seemed to be distinguishable; and expanding attention has recently been turned to the development of separate measures for the various types.

Of these, the concept of creativity has in recent times aroused a particularly strong research interest, in the wake of a realization that the conventional tests of mental ability have failed to identify a type of person who seems to be able to make distinctly original contributions to knowledge or the arts, even though he does not achieve a score at the top IQ level. Attempts have been made to identify such creativity in schoolchildren and to account for its occurrence (Getzels & Jackson 1962). No clear pattern has emerged so far, however, and it is possible that an abundance of ideas and an indifference to conventionality are the principal qualities that are assumed to forecast a capacity for making original and valuable contributions. Correlations among tests designed to reveal creativity are for the most part low and, in general, scarcely higher than the correlation of the creativity test scores with IQ.

Adults who have actually made original contributions in their professional fields have also been studied in order to find out the nature and sources of their creativity (MacKinnon 1962). Direct and intensive examination of a large number of specially selected writers, architects, mathematicians, and research workers in science and engineering failed to discover a clear and uniform pattern of anything that could be unambiguously labeled "creativity." Compared to a more representative sample of professionals in their fields, however, the persons judged to be creative were in general more open to experience, were independent rather than either conformist or nonconformist, tended toward introversion without restraints or inhibition, and were relatively rich in range of thoughts. But there were differences among the creative persons by profession: writers, for example, scored high on verbal intelligence measures, and architects high on spatial intelligence.

The concept of creativity thus remains elusive. It may turn out that a variety of factors, rather than a unitary talent, will account for the observed achievements of valuable originality.

Ability and achievement

A contribution to the evaluation of the factor of genius was made by William F. Ogburn in his studies of the role of invention in social change (1922). He found that no inventor develops a complex device in its entirety; an invention is always made by a series of small steps, and the various steps in each machine are made by a number of different inventors. It is, therefore, a scientific error to designate, as so many uninformed persons have done, Fulton, Edison, and Marconi as the inventors of the steamship, electric light, and radio, respectively. Each of these men contributed only a small part of the series of innovative ideas required for the above inventions. In the case of the electric light, for example, it was already well known that current passing through a wire could cause it to glow and emit light. Enclosure of the source of light in a glass container was already a feature of the arc light. Edison's achievement, admittedly worthy of appreciation, required not so much an exceptional amount of mental ability but rather an unusual degree of optimism, coupled with a persistence in finding the right materials. In fact, his "invention" was achieved far more by trial and error than by abstract mental effort.

Ogburn further found that when the cultural base of existing knowledge is ready, so that only one small additional step is needed to develop an important invention, more than one inventor is likely to take that step independently and at about the same time. Convincing evidence for this assertion is provided in an extensive list of simultaneous inventions (Ogburn 1922, pp. 90–102). It seems probable that similar conclusions apply to scientists, artists, and innovators of all kinds. The progress of civilization does not rest solely on the extraordinary contributions of a gifted few but more importantly on the uncounted achievements of persons whose abilities exhibit almost the entire range of human possibilities.

Civilization, and social organization, furthermore, may be seen not only as a result of human abilities but also as a cause of them. The limits of human potentiality for mental achievement cannot be measured at present; there are no tests that succeed in measuring the utmost mental capacities of a person, only tests that estimate crudely what he has already achieved. Some contemporary judgments hold that most, if not all, persons are in fact capable of far greater mental performance than they ever actually reach (Bruner 1960; Faris 1940).

Social development of ability. Human powers rest not only on the physiological equipment of the nervous system and supporting mechanisms (Brain 1961) but also, and to a large extent, on the way in which they become organized in experience. Two persons starting with equally efficient brain mechanisms may become greatly unequal in mental performance if their life experiences differ importantly in the various aspects that influence mental organization.

The components of mental ability contributed by experience are not completely known, partly because the search for them has been delayed by the long-prevailing assumption that innate differences were of greater significance. It now seems fairly well established, however, that through both formal education and unique individual experience, the latter sometimes accidental in character, persons may acquire mental tools that contribute efficiency to their accomplishments by simplifying the operations, in a manner analogous to the simplification of arithmetic computations through the use of tables of logarithms.

Mental calculators, whose feats have appeared spectacularly superior to normal performances, achieve their results by the use of mental equipment known to be obtainable through training. All such prodigies have exceptional memory for digits, but previously "untalented" persons have been trained to equal the experts in this respect. Much of mental calculation is simplified by the use of tables and other arrangements of numbers held in the memory. A contemporary prodigious calculator, for example, able to multiply two 10-digit numbers in a little over a minute and six pairs of 3-digit numbers in nine seconds, is aided by his memory of multiplication tables up to 100 times 100 and by tables of logarithms to 14 decimal places up to the number 150. Specific devices vary, but all mental calculators reported in the literature make effective use of such memorized aids (Faris 1940). It is highly likely that equally prodigious mental feats in many other fields are simplified by such acquired mental structures. Chess, for example, is perceived by a master player in coordinated image patterns of a different order from those of a beginner, so that an extremely complex series of thoughts by the beginner may be handled by the expert through use of a single organized concept.

It also seems probable that man's most important acquired mental tool is language itself, and differential mastery of language may be the greatest contributor to ability variation in the general population. Size of vocabulary surely contributes to thinking powers, as does orderliness and consistency of language use. Special languages support special abilities, in fields as separate as art, music, and mathematics and science. An important part of the widely known correlation of abilities of parents and their children is a consequence of differential linguistic heritages within families.

It has also long been recognized that variations in amount of reading correlate with school achievement and mental-test scores. The speed with which a person reads has been found to be related to the amount of reading he does, and speed is readily improved by training. It is also virtually certain that most of the population reads far below its potential with respect to both speed and quantity. Contemporary Western culture contains various factors operating in both directions to influence this variable in the population—from schools that train persons to read to diverting and distracting amusements that cut into the time they might have spent in reading [see COMMUNICATION, MASS, *article on* AUDIENCES].

Ability and motivation.   Formal education, however, provides only part of the actual differentiation of ability in a population. A variable of possibly equal importance is *level of aspiration,* on which recent research is tending to place ever-increasing emphasis. Opportunities to learn appear to be mainly wasted on persons with low motivation, and almost all instances of exceptional mental achievement are performed by persons whose aspirations are of obsessional strength.

Contemporary research indicates that aspiration levels are affected by the general atmosphere of a residential community, by peer groups, and by family traditions and interaction. It may also be suggested that among the various ways in which family interaction contributes to the mental development of children are the degree of richness and warmth of relation between parents and children, variations in clarity and orderliness of communication within the family, how much a child is encouraged to take the initiative in talking and relating his experiences, the development of early familiarity and ease in handling quantities and measurements, acquisition of advance motivation for reading and school learning, the creation of a broad appetite for orientation to the world and a hunger for knowledge of all kinds, a delight in novel thoughts, the development of a sense of confidence that answers to questions are not too hard to find, and a prejudice against persons and influences that would tend to distract from intellectual concerns.

The supply of ability

To the extent that achieved ability is determined by experience, the general intellectual power of a society is improvable by conscious design. Research in methods of making formal education more effective, plus research in ways of improving informal influences on ability, promise to give a society the power "to lift itself by its bootstraps." As new levels of collective ability are achieved, the natural tendencies of cultural life would tend to maintain the new level, barring the occurrence of disorganizing influences.

The spread of formal education in the United States, especially at the college level, has been very rapid in recent years and gives promise of much more to come. Indeed, the country seems to be in process of upgrading ability levels throughout the population—a process that is likely to continue for half a century or more.

At the lower levels of education, the rate of illiteracy has declined in recent decades, so that the small number of illiterates remaining are mainly in the older age groups. The average number of years of schooling is steadily increasing, and there has been a long and accelerating rise in the proportion of the population graduating from high schools and colleges and earning graduate degrees. The effects of such increases cannot be fully experienced for at least half a century, since a permanent increase in the proportion of young persons graduating from colleges at the age of 21, for example, must automatically continue to enrich the intellectual level of the population as this generation ages all the way to the retirement stage of life, replacing year by year, all through the process, the older and less educated generations.

Improving formal education.   An additional possibility of improvement lies in the enrichment of the educational process at all grade levels. Efforts are being made to speed the learning processes of preschool children as well as children at all other educational levels. Mathematical subjects formerly thought suitable only for college students are being taught in high schools, and a number of concepts once thought too difficult are now successfully taught in the lower grades. Similar enrichment is being tried in science, social studies, languages, and literature. Colleges and universities are also in a constant process of improvement through new instructional methods, teaching machines, honors courses, and other efforts. It appears likely that graduate education is also becoming ever more efficient, not only with the progress of knowledge but also with the availability of technical means, including computers, that reduce energy-consuming and drudgery operations.

There is no precise way to measure the consequences of such improvements in educational procedures, nor any realistic means of estimating future gains. There is reason, however, to suppose that the possibilities are of important magnitude. It has been found in a contemporary inquiry (Bray 1954) that among children having the advantage of "excellent cultural opportunities," about 25 per cent have IQ's of 125 or more—the level presumed to be adequate for earning a PH.D. Since only about 6 per cent of children in the general population achieve so high an IQ, it appears likely that an extension of similar cultural opportunities to all could quadruple the proportion of those with PH.D. ability in the population. Since improvements in quality of education may, in turn, create future cultural opportunities superior to those of the present, even further advance in the ability level would appear to be possible.

American society and human resources.   Present trends toward mechanization and more elaborate organization of the economic and political order reveal the critical importance of effecting such increases in the ability levels in the population. During the early 1960s in the United States, a gap between the needed and the existing capacities of the population was indicated by the rate of unemployment among persons of low educational level and by an acute shortage of persons with high technical skills. In a situation of intense political and economic competition among large industrialized nations, it is conceivable that progress in the sociology of ability could become a major factor in determining the outcome of the contest. Knowledge, skills, and capacity for invention have sometimes been collectively called "human capital," and some economists have suggested that it may become a more important factor in economic growth than "tangible capital." Some areas of the world are relatively undeveloped, even though rich in natural resources, because of severe lack of such "human capital." More significant, however, is the principle that great wealth of human capital would tend to give any nation relative independence of limiting environmental conditions.

ROBERT E. L. FARIS

[*See also* ACHIEVEMENT MOTIVATION; ACHIEVEMENT TESTING; CAPITAL, HUMAN; EDUCATION; INTELLIGENCE AND INTELLIGENCE TESTING; *and the biographies of* COOLEY; GALTON; OGBURN.]

BIBLIOGRAPHY

BRAIN, WALTER R. 1961 *Some Reflections on Genius, and Other Essays.* New York: Lippincott.
BRAY, DOUGLAS W. 1954 *Issues in the Study of Talent.* New York: King's Crown Press.
BRUNER, JEROME S. (1960) 1965 *The Process of Education.* Cambridge, Mass.: Harvard Univ. Press.
COOLEY, CHARLES H. (1897) 1930 Genius, Fame and the Comparison of Races. Pages 119–159 in Charles H. Cooley, *Sociological Theory and Social Research, Being the Selected Papers of Charles Horton Cooley.* With an introduction and notes by Robert Cooley Angell. New York: Holt.
FARIS, ROBERT E. L. 1940 Sociological Causes of Genius. *American Sociological Review.* 5:689–699.
GALTON, FRANCIS (1869) 1952 *Hereditary Genius: An Inquiry Into Its Laws and Consequences.* New York: Horizon Press. → A paperback edition was published in 1962 by World.
GETZELS, JACOB W.; and JACKSON, PHILIP W. 1962 *Creativity and Intelligence: Explorations With Gifted Students.* New York: Wiley.
GOSLIN, DAVID A. 1963 *The Search for Ability: Standardized Testing in Social Perspective.* New York: Russell Sage Foundation.
GRUBER, HOWARD E. et al. (editors) 1962 *Contemporary Approaches to Creative Thinking.* New York: Atherton.
MACKINNON, DONALD 1962 What Makes a Person Creative? *Saturday Review* 45:15–17, 69.
OGBURN, WILLIAM F. (1922) 1964 *Social Change With Respect to Culture and Original Nature.* Gloucester, Mass.: Smith.

CREDIT

For consumer credit, see INSTALLMENT CREDIT. *For a broad treatment of credit, see* BANKING; FINANCIAL INTERMEDIARIES.

I. GOVERNMENT CREDIT   Raymond J. Saulnier
II. AGRICULTURAL CREDIT   Harold G. Halcrow

I
GOVERNMENT CREDIT

Programs under which public credit is extended to individuals, private businesses, cooperatives, and public agencies have grown in most countries in such variety and to such size that they must now be regarded as a major activity of government. Their variety in the United States is such that virtually every type of program may be found. Because of this fact and because information on U.S. programs is more extensive than that on programs in other countries, government credit programs may best be illustrated by arrangements found in the United States.

Classification. U.S. credit programs may be classified on several bases, of which the first is according to the *sector of the economy served.* These are (*i*) agriculture, which is perhaps the progenitor of most government credit programs; (*ii*) housing; and (*iii*) business, including foreign trade and regional or area development.

Second, government credit agencies and programs may be grouped according to the *methods they employ* to achieve their purposes. There is, first, the *direct extension of credit,* in which funds are made available directly to the borrower. Along with other agencies, the Small Business Administration and the Farmers Home Administration have such programs, the former extending intermediate-term credit directly to qualifying small businesses, the latter extending long-term mortgage loans to help farmers acquire farm ownership or improve farms already owned. Next are the methods of *loan insurance and loan guarantees,* in which credit is extended by a private lender under full or partial government protection against loss. Loan insurance is illustrated by the Federal Housing Administration programs under which private financing institutions may, at a fee which is intended to underwrite losses and to make the program self-supporting, obtain full insurance on qualifying residential mortgage loans (on single or multiunit structures) in which they have invested their own funds. Loan guarantees are illustrated by the Veterans Administration program under which qualifying loans made by private lending institutions to veterans to help them buy homes or acquire small businesses are guaranteed against loss up to a stated maximum amount without fee and without the use of a reserve for meeting losses. Under both of these programs the lenders are closely limited as to the interest rates and other contract terms on which loans may be made. A variant of loan insurance is the *deferred participation arrangement* under which a credit agency agrees at the option of an original, private lender to take up all or part of a loan. Because the option can be exercised when a loan is approaching or is in default, it is in effect a guarantee against loss.

A third type of public credit program is the *secondary market operation*, which is illustrated in the United States by the Federal National Mortgage Association. In this case, the agency stands ready to purchase specified types of financial assets (in the case of FNMA, only mortgages) from lending agencies or other investors who wish to sell them. The purpose is to provide a liquid and orderly market, which at times can be a function of crucial importance.

A fourth method, which has a supporting effect resembling the secondary market approach, is illustrated by functions served by the Federal Home Loan Bank System through its 11 regional banks and by the Federal Reserve System through its 12 regional banks. The former supplies short-term credit to member institutions, mainly member savings and loan associations in the Home Loan Bank System, to meet temporarily heavy mortgage loan demands; the latter lends exclusively to member commercial banks in the Federal Reserve System to meet temporary reserve deficiencies that arise as a result of their lending and investing operations. [*For other functions of the Federal Reserve System, see* BANKING, CENTRAL.]

Fifth and finally, there are programs under which direct subsidies are made in lieu of the extension of credit, although these cannot perhaps be regarded strictly as credit programs. An illustration in the United States is the program under which the Public Housing Administration commits itself to make annual payments over periods up to forty years to local public housing authorities to make up any deficiency there may be between the cost of servicing obligations issued at the local level to finance public housing and the amount of cash available for this purpose that remains from rental income after meeting other operating costs. This has the legal standing of a guarantee by the federal government of local public housing authority bonds.

There is one respect in which U.S. government credit programs differ from those found in a number of other countries: apart from the now virtu-

ally abandoned postal savings system and the essentially war-emergency-type government savings bonds, there never has been any determined effort in the United States to collect savings through a public agency, and there never has been any mechanism at all for channeling such funds as were collected to nongovernment users through a government credit agency. In many other countries, on the other hand, the collection of savings is a major activity of government, and savings so collected are in many cases channeled, at least in part, directly to nongovernment purposes, most often to the financing of home purchases. This difference reflects the fact that the United States is amply supplied with mutual or stock savings institutions, whereas nongovernment savings-assembling facilities are inadequate in many countries or absent altogether.

Government credit agencies may be grouped also according to their *form of organization and financing*, that is, whether they are (*i*) wholly public; (*ii*) quasi-public joint ventures using a combination of public and private funds; or (*iii*) agencies having a relationship with government, such as tax exemption or guaranteed access to financial help if needed, that justifies their being regarded as federally sponsored. The Federal Intermediate Credit Banks, which still utilize some federal funds along with funds obtained in the open market by sale of Intermediate Credit Bank obligations and funds that must be subscribed by its borrowers as a condition of obtaining credit, are an example of the quasi-public type. The Intermediate Credit Banks operate through local "production credit associations" to provide medium-term financing for farmers. The Federal Land Banks, on the other hand, which provide long-term farm financing through local "national farm loan associations," used federal capital at their inception and for many years thereafter but now have retired all of this and rely exclusively on open-market borrowings and obligatory borrower subscriptions of capital. However, because Federal Land Banks are still supervised by the Farm Credit Administration which is an integral part of the Department of Agriculture, and because they enjoy certain cost-reducing privileges not available to private lending institutions, they still must be considered as federally sponsored agencies.

A fourth basis for classifying government credit programs is found in the *reasons that have led to their establishment*. In the United States, many programs have been launched because it was felt that private financial institutions were not providing credit in adequate amounts or at rates of inter-

Table 1 — U.S. government credit programs in fiscal year 1966 (millions of dollars)

	AMOUNT OF LOANS ESTIMATED TO BE OUTSTANDING, END OF FISCAL YEAR 1966		LOAN FUNDS ESTIMATED TO BE DISBURSED DURING FISCAL YEAR 1966
	Direct loans	Guaranteed or insured loans	
Office of Economic Opportunity	52	—	37
Department of Agriculture:			
Commodity Credit Corporation	1,524	835	2,297
Rural Electrification Administration	4,270	—	365
Farmers Home Administration	2,019	1,343	1,036
Department of Commerce:			
Area Development Administration	202	5	73
Maritime Administration	86	560	0
Department of Defense:			
Defense production guarantees	21	55	7
Military assistance credits	132	126	94
Department of Health, Education and Welfare:			
Office of Education	772	100	221
Public Health Service	43	10	25
Department of Interior: Reclamation loans	108	—	18
Department of State:			
Loans to United Nations	119	—	0
Agency for International Development	10,650	565	1,816
Treasury Department:			
Loans to District of Columbia	192	—	42
Foreign loans	3,658	—	0
Housing and Home Finance Agency:			
Community Facilities Administration	2,673	—	434
Urban Renewal Administration	231	1,856	266
Federal National Mortgage Association	1,574	1,555	283
Federal Housing Administration	555	52,762	194
Public Housing Administration	47	5,641	394
Veterans Administration	649	29,700	466
Export–Import Bank of Washington	1,826	3,642	601
Interstate Commerce Commission	15	208	*
Small Business Administration	923	122	366
Total (including small amounts and agencies not listed)	32,743	99,123	9,035

* Not available.

Source: Taken from U.S. Bureau of the Budget 1965, pp. 408, 410.

est and other contract conditions thought to be "reasonable." It perhaps goes without saying that what is adequate and reasonable are debatable questions. In any case, a "gap" theory has been basic to the establishment of financing agencies for agriculture, for which private credit is often more costly than for industrial and commercial borrowers. It is typical also that credit facilities are less available to small business than to large companies, and a "gap" theory has been important here also. Where credit programs are set up on this basis, it is frequently required that the borrower, in order to qualify for assistance, show he has tried and failed to obtain credit from private sources.

A related reason for setting up a public credit program is that the government wishes to provide assistance to what it regards as an especially im-

portant activity and one which it believes cannot obtain credit in the open market at sufficiently low interest cost. This is illustrated in the United States by the Rural Electrification Administration, which was set up to make low-interest long-term loans to cooperatively owned light and power companies. Further examples are found in FNMA's "special assistance" programs, under which the agency purchases at par mortgages which would sell at a discount in the open market because of the relatively low contractual interest rates they typically carry. Among types of mortgages so favored are those issued to finance college housing, nursing homes, housing projects for older people, cooperatively owned housing projects, housing for medium-income groups (especially when located in urban-renewal areas), and the like. The now inactive V-loan program, under which U.S.-guaranteed loans were made during World War II to defense contractors, is a further illustration.

In some cases, however, the special assistance feature is such a prominent element in the program that the activity lacks what may be regarded as a true credit quality. Thus, loans made to farmers by the Commodity Credit Corporation against price-supported commodities are used only as a substitute for a price or income support that could be supplied by other methods. In this case, the price-support purpose is so prominent that the activity hardly qualifies as a credit program. [*See* AGRICULTURE, *article on* PRICE AND INCOME POLICIES.]

Two other purposes for founding government credit agencies may be mentioned: (*i*) to offset recessionary tendencies in the economy and (*ii*) to upgrade standards of private lending practices. The Federal Housing Administration illustrates both of these. FHA was established in the early 1930s to promote home construction and home improvement, primarily as an anti-recession measure. But it has also sought to upgrade lending practices by offering insurance only on mortgages that meet certain standards of credit quality and only on properties constructed to meet specified physical standards.

As would be expected, there has usually been a mixture of reasons behind the establishment of specific programs, and credit agencies frequently follow more than one general approach (that is, direct loans or loan insurance) in seeking to achieve their purpose. Thus, it is difficult to classify them by either of these criteria. Broadly speaking, however, they limit their activities to a particular sector of the economy—agriculture, housing, or business—and accordingly are most often classified in this manner.

Scope and size of U.S. programs. The scope and size of U.S. credit programs may be seen in Table 1. In addition there are the "quasi-public" credit programs presented in Table 2.

Relative importance of U.S. programs. The relative importance of government credit programs in the financial system of the United States is not easy to measure, but it may be noted that it was estimated by the federal government that as of the end of June 1964 its outstanding direct loans to domestic private borrowers amounted to 2 per cent of the then estimated U.S. private debt of $778,000 million. At the same time, private loans wholly or partly guaranteed by federal agencies constituted close to 10 per cent of total private debt. The percentages would be much higher, of course, if comparisons were made with privately supplied credit

Table 2 — Quasi-public U.S. credit programs in fiscal year 1966 (in millions of dollars)

	AMOUNT OF LOANS ESTIMATED TO BE OUTSTANDING, END OF FISCAL YEAR 1966
Farm Credit Administration:	
Banks for Cooperatives	887
Federal Intermediate Credit Banks	2,990
Federal Land Banks	4,371
Federal Home Loan Bank Board:	
Federal Home Loan Banks	4,600
Housing and Home Finance Administration:	
Federal National Mortgage Association	
(Secondary market operations trust fund)	2,233
Veterans Administration:	
National Service life insurance fund	573
U.S. government life insurance fund	84

Source: U.S. Bureau of the Budget 1965, p. 414.

of a type comparing closely with credits supplied or insured by the several federal programs.

The importance of government credit programs is suggested also by their relative weight in the federal budget, although this is not readily seen in the United States because of the way credit programs appear in budget accounts. In the U.S. budget, repayments of loans are netted against disbursements of loan funds, with only the difference, which can be a minus quantity, counted as an administrative budget expenditure. However, in the fiscal year 1965 disbursements under direct loan programs (thus excluding loan insurance and guarantee programs) were close to 10 per cent of net administrative budget expenditures.

Sales by government agencies of accumulated loans and investments further complicate measurement of the budgetary and economic impact of federal credit programs. As indicated in Table 1, the federal government estimated it would hold something over $30,000 million of loans at the end of fiscal year 1966. At the same time, it planned to sell something over $3,000 million of loans during that fiscal year. Since sales of loans are counted as a repayment, they tend to shrink budgetary deficits or expand budgetary surpluses. And if there is a deficit in the budget, by shrinking this below what it would otherwise be, the credit programs appear to reduce the direct burden which federal finances place on capital markets. But the sale of loans is also a burden on the capital market, so that the total market effect must be regarded as the amount of reported deficit plus sales of loan assets.

Credit programs in other countries than U.S. Government credit institutions similar in point of function and method of operation to those found in the United States are present in virtually all countries of the world. Major reliance tends to be placed, however, on direct lending programs. To cite examples in the field of agriculture: Britain has its Agricultural Mortgage Corporation; Ireland has its Agricultural Corporation of Eire (for general agricultural financing and for financing cooperatives) and has departments for rural credits and for mortgage banking in the Commonwealth Bank of Ireland; South Africa supplies similar services through the Land and Agricultural Bank of South Africa, established in 1912; Egypt has its Crédit Agricole d'Égypte, established in 1930; and India has its government-sponsored financing cooperatives.

It would be a mistake, however, to conclude that public institutions are in all cases the major or even a principal source of rural and agricultural credits. Thus, the All-India Rural Credits Survey showed that in 1960 only 7 per cent of all borrowings came from government cooperatives and commercial banks, whereas 70 per cent came from local lenders (mainly individuals) and 23 per cent from relatives, traders, and other private agencies. In Denmark, to cite the case of a capital-intensive agriculture in a developed economy, only about 8 per cent of funds used in agriculture in 1954 came directly from government sources. In the more developed economies, greater emphasis is usually placed on loan insurance or guarantees than on direct extension of credit.

The picture is somewhat different with regard to the financing of residential construction. It has been estimated that more than half of new residential construction carried out in recent years in western Europe received some form of government assistance, ranging to as much as 98 per cent in the Netherlands. At least the nucleus of a national home and construction finance corporation exists in practically every Asian country (for example, Pakistan has its Building Finance Corporation; Ceylon its House Loan Board; Burma its Town and Country Development Board; Japan its House Loan Corporation, etc.). In some cases these are allied to, or are departments of, government agencies that collect savings through a widespread system of branches. Naturally, the use of such agencies is especially extensive where interest rates and equity requirements in home financing are high and credit availability is limited, reflecting a shortage of savings.

Finally, there has been an extensive development recently of government agencies devoted primarily to financing production facilities and infrastructure under national development plans. In industrialized countries these agencies are designed primarily to assist small business or business in areas affected by abnormally high levels of unemployment. In less developed countries, "development companies," as these agencies are frequently termed, have a broader function, reflecting a more general lack of credit facilities. Among these are the Istituto Mobiliere Italiano (IMI); ETIBANK in Turkey; the Corporación de Fomento de la Producción in Chile; and the Pakistan Industrial Credit and Investment Corporation (PICIC), to name a few. Private capital plays a role in many of these, but some represent entirely public efforts to channel resources into development projects. [*See* CAPITAL, SOCIAL OVERHEAD; DEVELOPMENT BANKS.]

Policy questions. There are a number of important policy questions involved in government credit programs which cannot be examined here. Among these are the following:

What are the relative advantages of direct lending, insurance, and guarantee of privately extended credits as ways of achieving program purposes?

On what interest rate and other loan contract terms should government credit programs be extended? On what terms should private credits be insured or guaranteed?

What standards and policies should be followed in the relationship between private and public credit programs?

Under what conditions should government credit programs be self-supporting?

How should these programs be coordinated with general monetary and fiscal policies for promoting the economy's growth and stability?

RAYMOND J. SAULNIER

BIBLIOGRAPHY

BELSHAW, HORACE 1959 *Agricultural Credit in Economically Underdeveloped Countries.* FAO Agricultural Studies, No. 46. Rome: Food and Agriculture Organization of the United Nations.

DIAMOND, WILLIAM 1965 Development Finance Companies. *Fund and Bank Review: Finance and Development* 2:97–102.

Federal Credit Agencies: A Series of Research Studies Prepared for the Commission on Money and Credit. Prepared by F. Break et al. 1963 Englewood Cliffs, N.J.: Prentice-Hall.

Federal Credit Programs: A Series of Research Studies Prepared for the Commission on Money and Credit. Prepared by Stewart Johnson et al. 1963 Englewood Cliffs, N.J.: Prentice-Hall.

FOOD AND AGRICULTURE ORGANIZATION 1964 *New Approach to Agricultural Credit.* Rome: The Organization.

SAULNIER, RAYMOND J.; HALCROW, HAROLD G.; AND JACOBY, NEIL H. 1958 *Federal Lending and Loan Insurance.* A study by the National Bureau of Economic Research, New York. Princeton Univ. Press.

UNITED NATIONS, ECONOMIC COMMISSION FOR EUROPE 1961 *European Housing Trends and Policies, in 1960.* Geneva: United Nations.

UNITED NATIONS, ECONOMIC COMMISSION FOR EUROPE 1962 *Report of the Seminar on Housing Surveys and Programmes, With Particular Reference to Problems in the Developing Countries . . .* Geneva: United Nations.

U.S. BUREAU OF THE BUDGET 1965 *Budget of United States Government, Fiscal Year 1966.* Washington: Government Printing Office. → Includes an appendix on federal credit programs.

II

AGRICULTURAL CREDIT

Agricultural credit is the term applied to funds borrowed by individuals, farm businesses, and others for use in producing, storing, processing, and marketing crops and livestock products. Modern farming requires increasingly large amounts of capital, and credit is one way of supplying this capital. Usually the borrowers are farmers, but they can also be other agricultural producers, such as ranchers in the western United States, graziers in Australia, cooperative farming associations, farm partnerships, and corporations. Sometimes the term includes funds extended to agricultural marketing firms and to those supplying services to agriculture, such as machinery, equipment, feed, fertilizer, and seed companies.

Those supplying agricultural credit include individuals, commercial and savings banks, cooperative lending associations, government and government-sponsored credit agencies, life insurance companies, mortgage and loan associations, farm service companies, and agricultural marketing associations, including cooperatives. In general, both commercial credit institutions and government-sponsored programs are most active where industrial economies are advanced and agriculture is highly commercialized. Direct government aid programs usually originate for specific purposes, such as aid to low-income groups, reclamation and development, permanent improvements, or help in case of disaster.

In contrast, where economies are not highly developed, a noninstitutionalized type of lending by merchants, local moneylenders, and landlords tends to predominate. Although in recent years governments have sometimes assisted by lending directly for specific purposes, in most underdeveloped economies agricultural credit is not efficiently organized, resulting in an almost static condition in agriculture. As a consequence, during the past quarter century the gap in per capita food production between the highly commercialized and the underdeveloped nations has widened considerably. In many instances, there has been no net increase in land productivity, income, or net assets. Under most conditions soil productivity remains low, risks are great, interest rates are excessive, income is low, and farmers remain poor indefinitely. Either the farmer is deeply in debt or he works for others as a tenant or hired hand.

In most underdeveloped countries, where the problem is broad, the solution may require land reform and other drastic changes in the social and economic order. Nevertheless, agricultural credit can help provide conditions under which crop yields can be increased and farmers can get a larger net return from the sale of farm products. The small size of many farms adds to the per unit cost of obtaining credit and creates a problem for farmer and banker alike. Agricultural credit is not the sole means of providing needed increases in food production, but it is an important element.

The importance of credit cannot be judged in isolation or by its amount. Land may be leased or rented as an alternative to ownership financed through credit. In commercialized agriculture the total debt may be only a small fraction of the resources used in agriculture. In the mid-1960s in the United States, for example, agricultural debt, or the aggregate of agricultural credit outstanding, was only one-seventh of total assets. Yet the fact is that agriculture has made great progress through expanded use of credit, which has served as a catalyst in resource development.

Types and sources of credit. If use of credit in agriculture is to be effective, it must be adapted to the peculiar needs of farming. In commercial enterprises, some loans must be made for longer periods than usual, and the repayment schedule must be flexible enough to allow for variations and uncertainties in farm income. Generally three types of credit are required: short-term financing to cover operating and family living costs between cropping seasons; intermediate-term credit to finance machinery, livestock, and improvements; and long-term credit for land and major improvements.

The need for short-term credit arises from the fact that, except on well-diversified farms that sell crops or livestock throughout the year, farm income fluctuates from season to season, and swings in prices or crop conditions sometimes cause additional variation in income. This uncertainty, combined with the typically small amount of reserve or working capital held by farmers, creates a demand for short-term credit. Such credit is used to pay family living expenses and to buy goods and materials used in production, such as feed, fertilizer, seed, and tractor fuel.

The demand for intermediate-term credit, covering one to five years, arises from the need to finance farm improvements and to buy equipment. Modern farming requires substantial amounts of capital for these purposes, often running into tens of thousands of dollars for a single family-type farm.

Long-term credit, extending over six years or more, is used to finance or refinance the purchase of farm real-estate, to construct farm buildings, and to make major improvements. Long-term credit often extends over 20 or 25 years and, in some countries, 50 to 75 years. Mortgage security is usually required. In recent years amortization systems have permitted repayment of loans in regular annual, semiannual, quarterly, or monthly installments.

In almost every country the first steps in developing an agricultural credit system have been taken by individuals and other private lenders. In many countries, cooperatives and credit unions designed to provide credit on more favorable terms have followed. Government has entered the field, either as a direct lender or as a sponsor of cooperative credit agencies, to provide more adequate sources of credit and to standardize the terms under which credit is extended. In many advanced economies, credit cooperatives and government-sponsored agencies provide more varied and complete services to agriculture than are available to any other sector. Government-sponsored agencies have played a more significant role in agriculture than in any other major segment of the economy. Thus, credit systems range from private through completely cooperative forms to government lending and loan insurance, with several systems often operating concurrently.

Government-sponsored cooperative systems. Credit cooperatives are usually sponsored by government through laws and administrations established for their operation. Usually government funds are appropriated to purchase capital stock and to cover some of the costs of administration. Once established, the government-sponsored agency tends to become self-supporting, and at least part, if not all, of the funds advanced by the government are usually repaid. Management may be directed in part by government officials. Boards of directors for cooperatively organized banks and loan associations are usually named by member borrowers and stockholders.

In most countries of western Europe, local cooperative societies belong to regional and state organizations that are part of a national system. Extension of credit is subject to national regulation, but management decisions are in the hands of local officers responsible to the members. Usually the local societies are small, serving a village or a single community. Credit operations are sometimes combined with such cooperative activities as purchasing, processing, marketing, and other services.

Other sources of credit supplement the government-sponsored cooperative agencies. For example, Belgium, Sweden, Italy, the Netherlands, Switzerland, Denmark, and West Germany each have a system of savings banks that loan to farmers. In some instances obligations are guaranteed by local government units.

Government-managed systems. In a number of countries agricultural credit agencies are associated with the government through a system of central management. Sometimes the agency depends on the government for financing; in other cases a cooperative program is maintained and the government role is restricted to management. France, Italy, Japan, and Turkey provide examples of government-managed credit systems.

In France, the Caisses de Crédit Agricole Mutuel are government-managed cooperative societies that lend about three-fifths of the credit extended to agriculture. The organization includes La Caisse Nationale de Crédit Agricole, which enjoys financial autonomy and is administered by a plenary commission or board; the Caisses Régionales, which are private lending organizations serving a region; and the Caisses Locales, which are subordinate to the Caisses Régionales and lend to local areas or communities. La Caisse Nationale is a public body that coordinates and controls the Caisses Régionales and helps them by making advances on loans that they cannot provide from their own resources. The Caisses Régionales in turn help the Caisses Locales and serve as correspondent banks on large loans. Both the regional and the local banks are cooperatives with generally limited liability.

Italy has a central farm-credit organization run by the state. There are also local lending institutions—savings banks, credit banks, people's cooperative banks, rural and artisan banks, and agricultural syndicates. Special regional or interregional institutes (sometimes with local correspondents), under control of the state, coordinate and direct agricultural credit in each region. Above the regional institutes is the national central authority, the Consorzio Nationale per il Credito Agraria, which, along with the regional institutes, operates throughout Italy, making farm improvement loans that are subsidized in part by the Ministry of Agriculture and Forestry. Farm operating loans, usually short-term, are made by the local banks and rural cooperative banks.

Japan has a cooperative agricultural credit structure and an agricultural, forestry, and fisheries finance corporation. The corporation is an independent government institution entirely capitalized by the government, existing for the purpose of extending long-term, low-interest loans to farmers, forestry men, and fishermen and their associations, where other credit is difficult to obtain. The corporation has no local representatives but operates through the branches of the Central Cooperative Bank for Agriculture and Forestry, the prefectural credit federations, and local commercial banks. The Japanese cooperative system includes village cooperative unions, a federation grouping by districts, and the Central Cooperative Bank. This bank is organized as a cooperative society with limited liability and with an administrative council, largely responsible to the government, which appoints the president, vice-president, 19 governors, and three monitors. The affiliated cooperatives have a council of delegates elected by holders of the bank stock.

Turkey finances about three-fourths of the loans made to farmers through an agricultural bank, a government-owned institution with branches and agencies serving all rural areas. Cooperatives, the second most important source of credit, borrow from the bank to finance their operations.

Direct government systems. In many underdeveloped countries and in some countries where commercial banks or cooperative lending associations have been slow to develop, the government has established a direct system of lending to farmers and others in agriculture. Direct lending through state-controlled credit agencies is also sometimes undertaken for special purposes, such as development of new lands, promotion of a particular kind of agriculture, expansion of output of certain commodities, aid to farmers suffering from adverse weather or low prices, and help to particular classes of the farm population who are unable to obtain credit from other sources. Although some financing may be available from private sources, government has provided credit in many of these cases to supplement these sources and to provide a larger aggregate supply, generally at reduced cost, to borrowers. Many nations with highly developed economies and well-developed cooperative credit systems, such as the United States and some of the western European countries, have also created government agencies for direct lending for one or more of these purposes. More illustrations are found throughout Latin America, Canada, and the Near East.

The United States example. The United States offers the best example of an agricultural credit system in which nearly every known method of credit is utilized. Although both government-spon-

sored agencies and direct lending are important, major reliance is on credit supplied by private sources. Of the total farm mortgage debt of $21,213 million reported and estimated to be outstanding on January 1, 1966, about 40 per cent was held by individuals and private businesses, 23 per cent by life insurance companies, 20 per cent by federal land banks, 14 per cent by commercial and savings banks, and 3 per cent by the Farmers Home Administration. On the same date non-real-estate credit, including both short-term and intermediate-term, totaled $18,913 million. Of this amount, about 41 per cent was held by commercial banks and about 14 per cent by production-credit associations and federal intermediate credit banks. Farmers Home Administration direct loans were about 4 per cent of the total. The balance, or 41 per cent, was an estimate of loans and credits extended by dealers, merchants, finance companies, individuals, and others. Not included in the above were loans of the banks for cooperatives ($1,055 million) and of the Rural Electrification Administration ($3,044 million).

Federal credit services to agriculture, which compete directly with commercial banks, insurance companies, and other private lenders, including individuals, are more varied and complete than in any other sector of the economy. Mortgage loans and short-term production credit for farmers are supplied through two separate systems of cooperatively organized district banks and local lending associations. These are grouped with the banks for cooperatives under the Farm Credit Administration to form a complete system of farm credit in which the government-sponsored agencies help to coordinate activities of local cooperative lending associations.

The cooperative farm-credit system. For many years prior to the close of the nineteenth century and in the early part of the twentieth, United States farmers had agitated for a system that would provide agricultural credit on more favorable terms and more reliably than was then provided by private lenders. In many parts of the country interest rates were high, varying from 6 or 7 per cent up to 11 or 12 per cent per year. Also, long-term loans were unusual, and farmers had to depend on the willingness and ability of lenders to renew their notes. Uncertainties in the banking system in respect to renewal added to their difficulty.

In 1916, after several years of study, the U.S. Congress passed the Federal Farm Loan Act, creating two kinds of banks: a system of joint-stock land banks, which were privately incorporated and financed, and federal land banks, whose original capital was furnished mostly by the federal government and which were made subject to close government direction and supervision. The joint-stock land banks flourished for a short time, but widespread defaults on their loans caused them to be placed in liquidation in 1933. Twelve federal land banks, one in each of the Federal Reserve districts of the United States, became the foundation for the cooperative long-term farm-mortgage system.

In the postwar agricultural depression of the 1920s, it became evident that farmers also desired a more uniform system of short-term credit. The Agricultural Credits Act of 1923 established 12 intermediate credit banks. The $60 million of original capital, $5 million for each bank, was subscribed by the government and is still in use. The initial purpose was to liberalize short-term farm-production credit by making loans to commercial banks, agricultural credit corporations, and other agencies lending to farmers. This purpose was largely unfulfilled until 1933, when Congress provided for a nationwide system of cooperative production-credit associations to make loans directly to farmers.

The third major part of the cooperative farm-credit system is the banks for cooperatives. There are 13 banks, one in each of the Federal Reserve districts and a Central Bank for Cooperatives in Washington.

The service and experience of the farm credit system can be grouped roughly into three periods, 1917 to 1932, 1932 to 1940, and 1941 to date. During the first period the activity of the federal land banks was limited to serving a minor part of the total farm-mortgage market. By the end of 1932 farm-mortgage holdings of the federal land banks totaled only $1,147 million, scarcely more than one-eighth of the total farm mortgages outstanding, and the joint-stock land banks, already in financial trouble, held less than half as much. The intermediate credit banks were not a significant factor, with less than $80 million loans outstanding. Neither of these banking systems was playing a major role in agricultural credit. As they were then capitalized and organized, they were not strong enough to do so.

As a means of combating depression and aiding agriculture, Congress in 1932 appropriated $125 million capital for the federal land banks and in 1933 about $189 million as a subscription to paid-in surplus to enable the land banks to make extensions and deferments of defaulted farm loans. Appraisal and lending standards were made more liberal and flexible. The federal land banks, lending through local cooperative associations, greatly increased their activities, especially from 1933

through 1936. By the end of 1940 the federal land banks and the Federal Farm Mortgage Corporation, which was affiliated with the banks, held more than 40 per cent of the total farm mortgages outstanding.

The importance of federal farm credit during the 1930s can scarcely be overemphasized. In deep depression it was used to stabilize the farm real-estate market and to liquidate loans of lenders, who were often in distress. It provided financing for farmers who otherwise could not have survived financially. Interest rates on land-bank loans were kept relatively low, about 4 to 4½ per cent per year.

From 1941 onward the federal land banks played a more passive role in the farm-mortgage market, dropping by the end of World War II to about one-fourth of total farm-mortgage debt outstanding and by 1954 to less than one-fifth, at which point the shares of the market tended to stabilize.

The experience of major groups of farm-mortgage lenders is remarkably similar, on the average, over the years since the beginning of the farm credit system. During the 1920s life insurance companies and commercial banks suffered heavy defaults and delinquencies. Until the end of the 1920s the land banks had a very small number of their mortgages delinquent, but by 1932 about half of them were delinquent or extended. The 1930s were a time of heavy delinquency for all bankers. Foreclosures and bankruptcies would have been much more numerous had not the federal government expanded farm-mortgage lending. Since 1940 almost all lenders have had very low losses on farm-mortgage loans, as rising real-estate values have consistently allowed those who were in financial difficulty to liquidate through sale of their property.

Non-real-estate lending of the farm credit system grew slowly during the 1930s but has shown a strong and steady growth since that time. Production-credit associations (PCA's) make production loans for periods of thirty days to five years, with interest rates generally around 5 to 6½ per cent. The system is a government-sponsored cooperative, with stock in local associations held by member-borrowers, who are required to invest 5 per cent of a loan in capital stock. The PCA's provide services comparable to those of commercial banks, and their rates and loss experience have been about the same over similar periods as those of commercial banks.

Banks for cooperatives, created in 1933, make loans to eligible farmer cooperatives engaged in marketing agricultural products, purchasing farm supplies, and furnishing farm business services. Facility loans for constructing and acquiring buildings and equipment are secured by first mortgages and are limited to 60 per cent of the value of the property and a twenty-year term. Commodity loans are secured by first liens on storable commodities, warehouse receipts, and other title documents representing agricultural products and supplies. Operating loans are made for short periods and may or may not be secured. The banks for cooperatives, like other agricultural lenders, suffered losses during the 1930s; since then, however, they have had few losses, and cumulative profit has easily covered the cost of government capital originally invested.

Farmers Home Administration. Direct government lending to agriculture in the United States has in recent years been confined largely to the Farmers Home Administration. In 1918 and for many years afterward, the Congress appropriated money to aid financially distressed farmers who had experienced drought or other natural disaster and who were too poor to obtain credit from other sources. In 1935 establishment of the Resettlement Administration combined in one agency various loan and aid programs for relief of low-income farm families. In 1937 this program was transferred, under the name of the Farm Security Administration, to the Department of Agriculture. In 1946 the Farmers Home Administration was established to combine all programs of emergency loans for operation and production, loans to disaster areas, and crop, drought relief, and seed loans.

Real-estate loans made by the Farmers Home Administration include farm ownership loans, rural housing loans, and small amounts in soil and water conservation loans. The organization also insures loans made by other bankers for farm ownership. A new rural housing program was begun in 1949. Since about 1961 the amount of loans made for rural housing has greatly exceeded the amount made for farm ownership and about equals the amount of farm ownership loans insured.

Non-real-estate loans are made chiefly for operating purposes, are generally shorter in term than the others, and tend to be concentrated in areas where economic conditions are unfavorable.

The experience of the U.S. government in direct lending varies from high losses on emergency disaster-type loans to results in real-estate lending much the same as those of commercial lenders. At present the major net expense is administrative costs, which have in recent years run $15 to $20 million a year. Losses during the 1930s were much higher. Results indicate that even the direct government farm-mortgage lending that involves some degree of emergency can be successful if loans are based on the potential earning capacity of the farm property.

Rural Electrification Administration. The Rural Electrification Administration (REA) was established in 1935 to provide credit to cooperative associations and others engaged in the generation and distribution of electric power. The policy of the federal government has been to provide loan funds to the REA at relatively low cost. From 1935 to 1944 the REA borrowed from the Reconstruction Finance Corporation (RFC) at an interest rate of 3 per cent. The REA relationship with the RFC was discontinued in 1947, and loan funds were thereafter borrowed from the U.S. Treasury. By memorandum of agreement the interest rate was set at the average rate paid on all marketable securities, with a maximum of 2 per cent. The rate of interest paid by REA borrowers thus has been generally lower than rates paid by other public utility firms.

Loan funds advanced by the REA from its inception in 1935 to 1963 were about $4,800 million. Total outstanding on January 1, 1963, was $3,800 million. Losses have been negligible, and the main cost to government is money appropriated for administration, which totaled $154.8 million from 1935 to 1963, and a somewhat smaller amount to subsidize the low-interest-rate borrowing.

The effect of the REA program is far-reaching. When the program began in 1935, about 11 per cent of the farms in the United States were served with central-station electricity; by 1953 about nine out of ten farms were being so served; and by 1963 an estimated 97.6 per cent of all farms in the United States were included. About one-half of these were customers of REA borrowers. The REA policy has been to provide "area coverage," that is, to extend electrical facilities into fringe areas and to supply all customers in a given area. Consequently, a large part of the clientele served by the REA is nonfarm, and this is a major source of recent and potential growth. Other power companies have probably developed more rapidly as a result of REA competition, and rural electrification has proceeded much more rapidly than would have been the case without this government program. Additional investment as the result of power availability is probably on the order of $5,000 to $10,000 million in the farm sector and possibly as much as $3,000 million elsewhere.

Agricultural credit covers a wide variety of situations and needs. It is provided by three general types of lenders: individuals and commercial agencies, government-sponsored cooperatives, and government agencies which make direct loans. How much credit is needed or should be provided and which system is best are matters of social objectives and judgment. Certainly, however, agricultural credit will continue to play a crucial role in agricultural and economic development.

HAROLD G. HALCROW

[See also AGRICULTURE, particularly the articles on CAPITAL and DEVELOPING COUNTRIES; LAND TENURE, article on LAND REFORM.]

BIBLIOGRAPHY

BELSHAW, HORACE 1959 Agricultural Credit in Economically Underdeveloped Countries. Rome: Food and Agriculture Organization of the United Nations.
COMMISSION ON MONEY AND CREDIT 1961 Money and Credit: Their Influence on Jobs, Prices, and Growth: Report. Englewood Cliffs, N.J.: Prentice-Hall.
LAND ECONOMICS INSTITUTE, UNIVERSITY OF ILLINOIS 1960 Modern Land Policy: Papers. Urbana: Univ. of Illinois Press.
SAULNIER, RAYMOND J.; HALCROW, HAROLD G.; and JACOBY, NEIL H. 1958 Federal Lending and Loan Insurance. A Study by the National Bureau of Economic Research. Princeton Univ. Press.

CRIME

I. CAUSES OF CRIME   Donald R. Cressey
II. OFFENSE PATTERNS   Leslie T. Wilkins
III. WHITE-COLLAR CRIME   Marshall B. Clinard
IV. HOMICIDE   Marvin E. Wolfgang

I
CAUSES OF CRIME

The contemporary literature on crime causation theory is closely linked with the more general literature in anthropology, psychiatry, social psychology, and sociology. Since criminal acts and crime rates are similar to other acts and rates studied by social scientists, the alliance of criminology with more general scientific disciplines is not surprising. Although some of the scholars specializing in the study of crime and criminals (criminologists) are concerned with penal legislation, with the sociology of the criminal law, or with simple fact finding, the majority of them are directly or indirectly concerned with crime causation.

This concern has been expressed in two principal forms. First, criminologists have studied the processes by which persons become criminals and have developed theories of criminality. Second, criminologists have studied the relation of crime rates to variations in culture and social organization and have developed theories of crime. The theories of criminality are theories about social learning and personality development and thus are necessarily related to more general theories about these phenomena. Theories about the distribution of crime rates are theories about social systems and, consequently, are closely related to more general theories of social structure.

Although theories of criminality are sometimes considered psychological theories, whereas theories about crime rates are viewed as sociological, it is clear that sociologists have contributed significant theories of criminality as well as significant theories regarding the distribution of crime rates. Accordingly, there is no distinct division of labor between the sociologist–criminologist and others. The theoretical work of criminologists has developed most significantly in the last half century. Although there were some happy exceptions, little systematic theoretical research on criminality or crime was conducted until the twentieth century, and most of the books written on these subjects prior to that century were written by persons outside academic circles, such as theologians, physicians, and reformers. Most of these writers were attempting to find a panacea for criminal behavior, and they often merely selected a general "cause" of all criminality and then sought to convince their readers that elimination of that cause would eradicate crime both by reforming criminals and by preventing future criminality. There was little attempt to "make sense," by means of a theory, of the known facts about criminals or about variations in crime rates, in part because few facts were known.

Near the end of the nineteenth century, sociology was making its way into the curricula of American universities and colleges, and a survey conducted in 1901 indicated that criminology and penology were among the first courses offered under the general title "sociology" (Tolman 1902–1903). From that time to the present, the main American contributions to crime causation theory have been made by sociologists, among whom the tendency has been to develop and state theories of crime causation that are consistent with, but nevertheless separate from, more general sociological and social psychological theory. On the other hand, the tendency among psychologically trained and psychiatrically trained persons is to assume that general knowledge of clinical psychology and psychiatry is a sufficient basis for understanding criminality, with the result that few psychological theories specifically directed toward explanation of criminality have been stated.

Theoretical requirements. Ideally, a theory that explains social behavior in general, or a specific kind of social behavior like crime, should deal with both the individual conduct and the epidemiology involved (Cressey 1960). Thus, in a theory of crime causation, there should be a statement that explains the statistical distribution of criminal behavior in time and space (its epidemiology) and that can be used to derive predictive statements about unknown statistical distributions. But the same theory also should be concerned with criminality and should identify, at least by implication, the processes by which individuals come to exhibit criminality and from which can be derived predictive statements about the behavior of individuals. We shall review the principal theories that attempt, in varying degrees, to integrate explanation of the epidemiology of crime with explanation of individual criminality. This arbitrary limitation eliminates from our immediate concern the older biological theories, which held that individual criminality is inherited or caused by nonhereditary biological conditions. It also eliminates from consideration those theories of crime that are based on economic or cultural determinism and that, therefore, have only slight implications for explanation of the behavior of individual criminals.

The multiple-factor approach. Perhaps the most popular approach to integrating explanation of crime rates and explanation of individual criminality is not, in the strict sense of the term, a theory at all. William Healy's early emphasis upon multiple causation in the cases of individual delinquents (1915, pp. 33–125, 130–138), combined with the then prevalent attempts to discount biological explanations of criminality, played an important part in the development of the multiple-factor approach in criminology. A revolt against stressing one cause for all criminality led to production of extensive lists of causes of criminality, each one of which was at first said to produce a portion of all criminals (Burt [1925] 1944, p. 600). The idea that criminality is the result of multifarious influences has persisted to the present, but the specific "factors" said to be important have shifted from time to time, becoming progressively more social in nature (Jones [1956] 1962, pp. 57–74).

Since a theory of crime causation consists of a logical generalization about facts pertaining to crime and criminality, the multiple-factor approach actually is not a theory. In recent years the approach has taken on two separate aspects. Some workers who use the approach in the study of individual criminality maintain that one case of criminality results from one configuration of factors, while another case of criminality results from a different configuration of factors. This is not the same as the earlier multiple-factor notion that one kind of criminality is caused by one kind of factor and another type of criminality is caused by a different kind of factor. For example, this early approach solved the heredity versus environment controversy by maintaining that some crimes are caused by hereditary factors, some by environmental factors. The current idea is that each case of criminality results from a peculiar, if not unique, combination of factors, each with its own degree of weight. The factors may be assigned equal weight, or one factor may be classified as major while another is classified as minor. For example, one author observed that delinquency is caused by a combination of hereditary factors and environmental factors and then was able to conclude that heredity accounts for about 60 per cent of the influence and environment about 40 per cent (Hirsch 1937, pp. 55–56). Another author has commented that the logic behind this kind of conclusion "is about on a par with that which would be involved if the assumption were made that the element hydrogen is twice as important as the element oxygen in the compound water . . ." (Vold 1958, pp. 101–102). Broken home, alcoholic parents, poverty, defective intelligence, poor education, and emotional immaturity are examples of the factors contemporarily used in this kind of approach.

When the multiple-factor approach is used in the study of crime rates, the investigator merely lists conditions (factors) that are statistically associated, to a high or low degree, with crime. Generally speaking, the higher the degree of association, the more importance is ascribed to the particular condition. In this kind of study, there is little attempt to make sense of the statistical findings by showing that they are consistent or inconsistent with a theoretical scheme. Reckless has advocated the use of this method under the name "actuarial approach" (1943, p. 74).

Critique of the multiple-factor approach. In one of the best critiques of the multiple-factor approach, Albert K. Cohen (1951, pp. 5–13) identified three principal errors. First, there is confusion between explanation by means of a single theory and explanation by means of a single factor. A single theory is a logical statement showing how variations in one phenomenon (variables) are linked with variations in other phenomena. Statements of fact are made in terms of the values of variables, but such statements of fact are not theories of crime causation, whether they are concerned with the relationships between criminality or crime and the values of one variable (say, income) or with the relationship between criminality or crime and the values of a number of variables (income, age, sex, education, parental discipline). Further, the fallacy that "evil causes evil" usually characterizes the multiple-factor approach, although it is not peculiar to it. The fallacy consists in thinking that effects that are viewed as undesirable (criminality and high crime rates) must have antecedents that are undesirable (alcoholism, psychopathic personality, poverty, class discrimination). When this fallacy is present, "explanations" of criminality and crime are likely to be statements that merely attribute causal power to a list of ugly and sordid conditions that any "decent citizen" must deplore. Finally, factors are confused with causes, and each factor is assumed to contain within itself a fixed amount of crime-producing power. For example, the fact that a person has a low income is said to have some criminality-producing power; the fact that he is a young adult pushes him further in the direction of criminality; and the fact that he is a male is the last straw. Sometimes the basis for imputing causal power to a factor in an individual case is high statistical association between the factor and crime rates—if in a city the areas of poor housing are also the areas of high crime rates, a person who lives in a substandard house is considered on the road to crime. Statisticians have regularly pointed out the fallacy of such reasoning, and it is not part of the "actuarial" approach. But, equally important, sometimes the basis for imputing causal power to a factor is based only on the subjective judgment of the person doing the imputing and cannot be determined at all by others.

Psychological theories. Among psychologists such attention as has been given to the problem of epidemiology has been directed toward locating social conditions that affect the personal traits said to produce criminality. Thus, psychological interest in criminality has been logically akin to psychiatric interest in finding unusual conditions producing abnormal traits in the make-up of criminals. However, in psychology this interest has been expressed principally in attempts to measure objectively the degree to which criminals are psychologically different from noncriminals.

Intelligence testing came into vogue in the years just after World War I, and the newly devised intelligence tests were rather indiscriminately given to delinquents and criminals. One result was a widespread belief that low intelligence is an important cause of criminality. However, more recent studies indicate that criminals are not intellectually inferior to noncriminals. Nevertheless, the assump-

tions that led to the attempts to differentiate criminals from noncriminals on the basis of intelligence test scores are still maintained. They now are most evident in attempts to differentiate criminals from noncriminals on the basis of scores on tests of personality. Generally speaking, the work in this area has been fragmentary in character, in the sense that studies of criminals' scores on personality tests have been made without reference to a systematically developed theory of criminality (Schuessler & Cressey 1950).

Psychiatric theories. With the development of psychiatry in the last half century, there has been an increasing tendency to apply psychiatric and psychoanalytic techniques and theories to the problem of criminality, especially by such practitioners as prison, probation, and parole workers. William Healy's *The Individual Delinquent* (1915) stressed multifarious influences on the criminal, but it also freed psychiatric criminology from Lombrosian preconceptions and thus opened the door to theorizing about the nature of individual criminal conduct. Bernard Glueck (1918) provided another impetus to the psychiatric study of individual offenders when he published the results of a study of 608 inmates of Sing Sing Prison.

The early preoccupation of psychiatrists concerned with criminality was the assumption that criminals constitute an inferior type, characterized by mental disorders, alcoholism, neuroticism, and the like (Hakeem 1958). In more recent years, this concern with serious mental defects and disorders among criminals has continued, but there also has been a trend toward inclusion of numerous minor emotional traits within the scope of the conditions held to be significant in producing criminality. Psychiatrists are also moving away from the notion that there is an undue amount of deviation from the normal among criminals and are moving toward descriptions of processes involved in the development of criminal mentalities. Thus, criminality is viewed as an adjustment to an emotional problem, and the criminal act is therefore considered as a symbol or a symptom. Consistently, there is an increasing concern with explanation of crime rates, although attention continues to be focused on individual criminality. For example, psychiatrists are beginning to study the epidemiology of mental disorders and, as a by-product, to develop explanations for the high incidence of crime among men as compared to women, among city dwellers as compared to rural dwellers, among lower-class persons as compared to upper-class persons, and the like. One popular theory is that such variations are due to differences in child-rearing processes, but other theories are closely allied with the sociological "cultural" and "social structure" theories, which account for the distribution of various forms of deviancy.

Sociological theories. The central theme running through criminological studies conducted by sociologists and social psychologists is that crime and criminality are products of the same kinds of social conditions and processes that produce noncriminal social behavior. The sociological attempts to define and identify the processes by which persons become criminals have involved the use of such social psychological concepts as imitation, role playing, differential association, differential identification, compensation, self-conception, and frustration–aggression. The sociological attempts to link variations in the crime rates of societies, subsocieties, and groups with variations in social organization and culture have led to theoretical concern for such processes as mobility, competition, and culture conflict; political, religious, and economic ideologies; population density and composition; and the distribution of wealth, income, and employment. This kind of structural analysis and the theoretical propositions based upon the analysis declined in popularity after about 1940, principally because investigators became aware of the great hazards in making generalizations about crime rates as measured by conventional crime statistics. At present, however, sociologists are again studying the relationships between crime rates and social organization and developing theories to account for the variations observed.

Differential association. Edwin H. Sutherland hypothesized that persons acquire patterns of criminal behavior in the same way they acquire patterns of lawful behavior. It is his idea that "criminal behavior is learned in interaction with persons in a pattern of communication," and the specific direction of motives, drives, rationalizations, and attitudes—whether in the direction of anticriminality or criminality—is learned from persons who define the legal codes as rules to be observed and from persons whose attitudes are favorable to the violation of legal codes. "A person becomes delinquent because of an excess of definitions favorable to violations of law over definitions unfavorable to violations of law" (Sutherland & Cressey 1960, p. 78). Sutherland named the process of giving and receiving these definitions "differential association" because the content of what is learned in the process of association with criminal behavior patterns differs from the content of what is learned in the process of association with anticriminal behavior patterns. Differential association refers to a ratio of associations with both criminal behavior patterns and anticriminal behavior patterns. Daniel Glaser (1956) has modified this theory of criminality by placing stress on the process of receiving criminal and anticriminal behavior patterns rather than on the process of donating them, thus changing the basic concept from differential association to "differential identification."

Differential social organization. When it is applied to the variations in the crime rates of nations, cities, or groups, the theory of differential association and differential identification becomes a theory of differential social organization. A high crime rate in a city, for example, is the end product of a situation in which a relatively large number of persons have received an excess of criminal behavior patterns as compared with anticriminal behavior patterns. From this it can be reasoned, as Sutherland did, that a group with a high crime rate is organized *for* crime at the same time that it is organized *against* crime. Whether the crime rate is high or low depends upon the degree to which the organized system for presenting anticriminal behavior patterns is counteracted by the organized system for presenting criminal behavior patterns. In contemporary societies the social conditions in which the influences on a person are relatively inharmonious and inconsistent are themselves a form of social organization, and there are wide variations in the degree of conflict between criminal and anticriminal norms. Since the rates of criminality vary with the degree of normative conflict, they can be attributed to differential social organization.

Culture conflict. Like the theory of differential association and differential social organization, the culture conflict theory developed by Thorsten Sellin (1938, pp. 21–32) stresses the importance of conflicts between conduct norms. According to this theory, both criminality and noncriminality of individual persons are attributable to the kinds of conduct norms that have been experienced. But learning of divergent conduct norms presupposes the existence of a society in which the conduct norms of one group are in conflict with the conduct norms of another. Thus, a condition of culture conflict underlies a condition of high crime rates, for it is only when there is culture conflict that persons can learn conduct norms that permit the reaction to some situations to be one of criminality.

Sellin proposes that criminologists should not restrict their attention to criminality and crime but instead should study the conflicts of conduct norms that exist when divergent rules of conduct govern the specific life situations in which a person may find himself. These rules "prohibit and conversely enjoin specific types of persons, as defined by their status in (or with reference to) the normative group, from acting in a certain specified way in certain circumstances" (Sellin 1938, pp. 32–33). Conduct norms arise as a group reaction to behavior that is not in the interests of the social group and acquire validity when they are incorporated into the personalities of the group members. Hence, the differentiation of the personality structure or growth process of the violator over and against that of the conformist is closely allied with variations in the degree of culture conflict and, therefore, with variations in crime rates.

Criminogenic cultures and social structure. Where the theories of differential association and culture conflict stress the importance of transmission of criminal and delinquent behavior patterns from one person to another, a different type of sociological theory extends beyond the individual and his personal groups to the broader culture of a people. This kind of theory is directed more to the problem of explaining why one nation, group, or class has a high crime rate as compared with another nation, group, or class than to the problem of identifying the processes by which individuals become criminals.

One cultural theory, for example, links the relatively high American crime rates with conditions and processes in the American culture that are criminogenic in their influence (Taft [1942] 1956, pp. 336–349, 754–755). Among these are the culture's dynamic, complex, and materialistic qualities, the tradition of the frontier, the breakdown of primary-group relationships, and political corruption and inefficiency. Variations in crime rates among different groups, classes, and categories within nations are attributable to the differential impact of the criminogenic culture on those groups, and individual criminality and noncriminality are attributable to differential impact of these conditions on individuals (Reckless [1950] 1961, pp. 335–359). For example, the theory explains that the excess of crimes by men is due to the relative protection of women from the stresses of competitive economic life and to their different moral codes and social roles. More generally, such factors as relative economic welfare, relative isolation from competition, and families that give security and affection will isolate individuals from the criminogenic culture and will, thus, keep crime rates low in some groups.

A "social structure" theory of crime causation has been developed by Robert K. Merton (1938) as part of a more general theory of deviance. Although the theory has been modified in some respects by Merton himself ([1949] 1957, pp. 161–194), by Albert K. Cohen (1955), and by Richard A. Cloward and Lloyd E. Ohlin (1960), the basic notion is that high crime rates are a reflection of a situation in which a society places great emphasis upon the goal of individual "success" while effectively blocking, for some part of the population, the paths to achievement of that goal. In this kind of social system, the generally approved rules of the game may be known to those individuals who evade them, but the emotional supports that accompany conformity to the law are offset by the emphasis placed upon achieving success. Consequently, it may be said that the social structure frustrates some individuals but does not provide mechanisms of social and personal control (Reiss 1951) that enable them to release their frustration legitimately.

Limited theories. The theories outlined above are directed at explanation of criminality and crime in general. Such general theories are desirable because they organize, integrate, and make sense of the factual data on crime and criminals. However, it also is desirable to break crime down into homogeneous units, and develop theories to explain each unit. Crime in general consists of a great variety of criminal acts; and except for the fact that such acts are all violations of law, they may have very little in common. Consequently, a theory that attempts to explain all of them must necessarily be quite general in nature. Such general theories can be, and have been, supplemented with theories about specific units within the broad area of crime and about specific units within the legal definitions of types of crime, such as embezzlement, robbery, and murder.

General theories about criminal behavior as a whole can guide the research and theory directed at explaining particular kinds of crime and criminal behavior, and studies of particular kinds of crime and criminal behavior can lead either to strengthening or to modifying the general theories. In this sense, explanation of crime is like explanation of disease. A theory purporting to explain all disease must be quite general, but such theory is quite useful in understanding the origin and transmission of illness. Nevertheless, even general theories of disease, like the germ theory, do not apply to all diseases, and theories about specific diseases have been developed to supplement them. In criminology, important specific theories of this kind have been developed to explain embezzlement (Cressey 1953), forgery (Lemert 1953; 1958), gang delinquency (Cohen 1955), homicide (Henry

& Short 1954; Wolfgang 1958), professional theft (Conwell 1937), vandalism (Clinard & Wade 1958), and white-collar crime (Sutherland 1949).

DONALD R. CRESSEY

[*See also* CRIMINOLOGY; PENOLOGY; *and the biography of* SUTHERLAND.]

BIBLIOGRAPHY

BURT, CYRIL L. (1925) 1944 *The Young Delinquent.* 4th ed. Univ. of London Press.

CLINARD, MARSHALL B.; and WADE, ANDREW L. 1958 Toward the Delineation of Vandalism as a Sub-type in Juvenile Delinquency. *Journal of Criminal Law, Criminology, and Police Science* 48:493–499.

CLOWARD, RICHARD A.; and OHLIN, LLOYD E. 1960 *Delinquency and Opportunity: A Theory of Delinquent Gangs.* Glencoe, Ill.: Free Press.

COHEN, ALBERT K. 1951 Juvenile Delinquency and the Social Structure. Ph.D. dissertation, Harvard University.

COHEN, ALBERT K. (1955) 1963 *Delinquent Boys: The Culture of the Gang.* New York: Free Press.

CONWELL, CHIC 1937 *The Professional Thief: By a Professional Thief.* Annotated and interpreted by Edwin H. Sutherland. Univ. of Chicago Press. → A paperback edition was published in 1960.

CRESSEY, DONALD R. 1953 *Other People's Money: A Study in the Social Psychology of Embezzlement.* Glencoe, Ill.: Free Press.

CRESSEY, DONALD R. 1960 Epidemiology and Individual Conduct: A Case From Criminology. *Pacific Sociological Review* 3:47–58.

GLASER, DANIEL 1956 Criminality Theories and Behavioral Images. *American Journal of Sociology* 61: 433–444.

GLUECK, BERNARD 1918 Concerning Prisoners. *Mental Hygiene* 2:85–151.

HAKEEM, MICHAEL 1958 A Critique of the Psychiatric Approach to Crime and Correction. *Law and Contemporary Problems* 23:650–682.

HEALY, WILLIAM 1915 *The Individual Delinquent: A Text-book of Diagnosis and Prognosis for All Concerned in Understanding Offenders.* Boston: Little.

HENRY, ANDREW F.; and SHORT, JAMES F. JR. 1954 *Suicide and Homicide: Some Economic, Sociological, and Psychological Aspects of Aggression.* Glencoe, Ill.: Free Press.

HIRSCH, NATHANIEL D. M. 1937 *Dynamic Causes of Juvenile Delinquency.* Cambridge, Mass.: Sci-Art Publishers.

JONES, HOWARD (1956) 1962 *Crime and the Penal System: A Textbook of Criminology.* 2d ed. London: University Tutorial Press.

LEMERT, EDWIN M. 1953 An Isolation and Closure Theory of Naive Check Forgery. *Journal of Criminal Law, Criminology, and Police Science* 44:296–307.

LEMERT, EDWIN M. 1958 The Behavior of the Systematic Check Forger. *Social Problems* 6:141–149.

MERTON, ROBERT K. (1938) 1957 Social Structure and Anomie. Pages 131–160 in Robert K. Merton, *Social Theory and Social Structure.* Rev. & enl. ed. Glencoe, Ill.: Free Press. → First published in the *American Sociological Review.*

MERTON, ROBERT K. (1949) 1957 *Social Theory and Social Structure.* Rev. & enl. ed. Glencoe, Ill.: Free Press.

RECKLESS, WALTER C. 1943 *The Etiology of Delinquent and Criminal Behavior.* New York: Social Science Research Council.

RECKLESS, WALTER C. (1950) 1961 *The Crime Problem.* 3d ed. New York: Appleton.

REISS, ALBERT J. JR. 1951 Delinquency as the Failure of Personal and Social Controls. *American Sociological Review* 16:196–207.

SCHUESSLER, KARL F.; and CRESSEY, DONALD R. 1950 Personality Characteristics of Criminals. *American Journal of Sociology* 55:476–484.

SELLIN, THORSTEN 1938 *Culture Conflict and Crime.* New York: Social Science Research Council.

SUTHERLAND, EDWIN H. (1949) 1961 *White Collar Crime.* New York: Holt.

SUTHERLAND, EDWIN H.; and CRESSEY, DONALD R. 1960 *Principles of Criminology.* 6th ed. New York: Lippincott. → E. H. Sutherland was the sole author of the first edition, published in 1924 as a textbook under the title *Criminology.*

TAFT, DONALD R. (1942) 1956 *Criminology.* 2d ed. New York: Macmillan. → A 4th edition was published in 1964 by Macmillan.

TOLMAN, FRANK L. 1902–1903 The Study of Sociology in Institutions of Learning in the United States. *American Journal of Sociology* 7:797–838; 8:85–121, 251–272, 531–558.

VOLD, GEORGE B. 1958 *Theoretical Criminology.* New York: Oxford Univ. Press.

WOLFGANG, MARVIN E. 1958 *Patterns in Criminal Homicide.* Philadelphia: Univ. of Pennsylvania Press.

II

OFFENSE PATTERNS

The concept of crime is an unusually difficult one, since it is difficult to find any definition of crime that does not have a large element of circularity. In general, crimes are defined as events and actions that are proscribed by the criminal law of a particular country. This reduces to the definition of crime as being "what the criminal law says it is." The boundaries of a legal system are usually those of the nation-state, but the national boundaries are not exactly similar to cultural boundaries. England and Wales, for example, have a different legal system from that of Scotland. Yet it would be difficult to define the difference in culture between border towns.

Legal fictions are useful within any legal system; but since they vary across nations and cultures, they are not very satisfactory concepts in behavioral science when comparison is made across cultures or nation-states. Almost all actions of which mankind is capable have, at some time, at some place, been defined as "criminal"; and almost all acts now defined as criminal have, at some time, at some place, been socially approved by the culture of the time and hence not proscribed by the law.

Crime involves at least two essential actors, the victim and the offender. Crime may be perceived and defined differently according to the role of either of them. In the Soviet Union crime is made to mean something different from what is understood as crime in Western cultures. There are many reasons for this, not the least of which is the fact that the "victim," by reason of the social and economic system, must frequently be the state.

Most crime in most countries consists of offenses against property. It is difficult, in modern society, to imagine it otherwise, even in very different cultures. But when property is owned by the state, crime involving property involves the state as the victim, and, if the state has a philosophy regarding property, crime against property will be seen as crime against the state. If, on the other hand, wealth is privately owned, crime against such ownership is seen as an attempt to obtain the wealth of another by *illegal means.*

But the mere transfer of wealth does not constitute a crime. Fair exchange is not crime. But what is fair exchange is not determined by the same considerations as those used to determine what is crime in terms of other forms of behavior, as, for example, an assault on a person. Moreover, the type of exchange that is defined as legitimate may be determined more by the nature of a country's economy than by its moral values.

Crime is always defined in terms of the social institutions and their organization in a society. The crimes will be defined through some organized process as behavioral deviations from the values as institutionalized in the norms and rules. There could be no crime in any society where all persons behaved in the same way, no matter how they behaved.

In the Western world we are concerned in our definitions of crime mainly with what is sometimes a very fine distinction between legitimate and illegitimate means of acquisition of wealth. Thus, the ownership of private wealth is valued—the "wrong" in stealing consists only in the *means* of acquisition of wealth. When the line between legitimate and illegitimate becomes very thin, different subcultures within the same legal system may perceive the distinction differently.

To draw a sharp distinction between what is criminal and what is noncriminal does not make sense. Crime is human behavior. But not all human behavior is the same. Presumably all human actions form a frequency distribution of actions and can be placed on an imaginary continuum from the most saintly to the most sinful, or from acts incurring the greatest degree of public acclaim to those acts which attract the greatest amount of public disapprobation. There are very few extremely sinful acts committed in this world, and there are very few extremely saintly acts; most of the actions taking place throughout any culture are just "normal." The continuum of ethical content of our actions may be cut for purposes of definition at any point, thereby including or excluding a proportion of marginal acts. The cutting points, as defined, may change from time to time, depending upon changes in statutes, cultural meanings attached to their language, or customs' allowing statutes to lapse. This process of change may go unnoticed by most observers in the culture, since it is often gradual.

Crimes and criminals

It will be obvious that "crime" and "criminals" are two different concepts. Often these two are confused, particularly when reference is made to criminal statistics. It is necessary always to inquire closely into exactly what figures relating to "crime" refer to. A "crime" (illegal action) can occur without there being an identifiable criminal, and a criminal can commit a number of crimes even in the course of one actual action or event. A person removing a motor vehicle without the owner's consent may break a large number of laws in this one act, or, less frequently, there are multiple acts which are subsumed under the definition of one crime. To some extent crimes committed by persons under the legally defined age of "criminal responsibility" are crimes without defined criminals. If a crime is not detected or otherwise "cleared up," there is always a chance that it may be an outcome without a criminal.

The problem of definition of crime is closely related to the problem of measurement of crime. Can we measure crime and express it in numbers? Certainly there are plenty of numbers in the U.S. *Uniform Crime Reports,* in *Criminal Statistics,* published in England and Wales, and in similar reports published in all Western countries. But do these numbers measure what we are speaking about when we speak about "crime"?

Sutherland and Cressey ([1924] 1960) have criticized criminal statistics on the grounds that it is impossible to determine with accuracy the amount of crime in any jurisdiction at any time. But the difficulty is not a statistical difficulty; it is a difficulty relating to problems of definitions.

Figures are available for "indictable offenses known to the police" in England and Wales, and there are similar figures for other countries; figures are available for the numbers of persons proceeded against in courts; there are figures for persons found guilty, figures for persons arrested (in the

United States), and many other sets of figures. Are any of these figures measurements of "crime"? Undoubtedly not. But as numbers representing what they claim to represent, they are not *necessarily* to be impugned as the most unreliable of statistics. It is not the statistical data that claim to be what they are not; rather, it is the people who make use of these data who may be regarded as "unreliable."

There are a large number of points at which it is possible to intercept events or persons and to make counts of them. Whether these counts are correctly and efficiently made is one problem, but whether the figures represent what we are speaking about is another problem. It is necessary to keep these two problems separate.

Any one event in the continuum ranging from sinful to saintly may trigger off a series of events. Processes involving human behavior, whether defined in law as "criminal" or not, are dynamic processes. If the event is definable in law as criminal, the processes from the commission of the act, so defined, to the reception of the convicted offender in a penal institution are many and varied. Different decisions are made at different points in this process, and each decision may be considered as a "gate" which opens or closes and diverts the "offender" from one channel to another—into or out of the system. Each of these decision "gates" can provide an efficient count of the "gate passages" (Wilkins 1964). Whether a record of any or all of these decisions at any or all of these points would be a measure of what we are speaking about when we speak about "crime" is debatable.

It is obvious that counts and measurements at different points along the process continuum will give different numbers, and these different numbers will measure different things. It may be desirable to examine some of these distinctions.

Crimes known to the police. It will be clear that figures collected at some points along the continuum from the commission of the offense to the disposal of the offender by a court or by other means are likely to be more reliable than others. But perhaps the more reliable the figures can be, the less informative they may be regarded as being on other matters, such as the volume of crime. For example, it is often considered important to know about the amount of "juvenile delinquency," but it is difficult, in practice, to measure the amount of juvenile delinquency in any area or country. Clearly, the age of the offender cannot be known until a crime has been detected and an offender identified who is presumed to have committed it. Thus, to measure juvenile delinquency, some action must already have been taken by society regarding a

reported crime or behavior. Some writers have proposed methods for questioning children themselves about their acts, and such methods overcome this difficulty but raise many others of a different kind (see Sutherland & Cressey [1924] 1960; Reiss & Rhodes 1960).

In the general criminal statistics, it would appear that data relating to persons are more reliable than data relating to events. For example, the number of persons received into prison under sentence in any one year is a figure which it is possible to know exactly, as also is the population of any country's prisons on any day or an average of days. There will be problems of what is meant by "prison," and perhaps what is meant by "person" and by "under sentence," but these terms may be dealt with by means of operational definitions. Nonetheless, such numbers, even though absolutely accurate, do not necessarily relate to a question about crime, unless we are careful to speak in exactly the same terms as those used to determine the counting procedures.

It has been suggested by some authorities that the value of a crime index decreases as the distance from the crime itself in terms of procedure increases (Short & Nye 1957–1958). This means that figures which relate to "crimes known to the police" provide a better index of crime than figures relating to arrests, persons proceeded against or found guilty, or various other figures relating to the later processing of persons defined as offenders. In other words, and reminding ourselves of the distinction between crimes and criminals, it is often claimed that the most meaningful figures, from a criminological point of view, are figures relating to events (crimes) and not those relating to persons (criminals). If one is speaking about events, one should not use data relating to persons, but it is doubtful whether data relating to events can be obtained in any satisfactory way. A person is simply defined by his own physical identity. If persons pass through any decision point and that point has a counting mechanism, there can be little doubt about the number of such persons. But whenever an event is imagined independently of a specific person and a specific decision point, or a concept is discussed which has no relation to a specific activity or decision which can be observed, there is far more chance of uncertainty.

In the definition of crime we are concerned with the cutting points in a continuum, not a gate decision system. If we wish to discuss crime, it is necessary to consider the working of the system of definitions that may vary the cutting points in the continuous distribution of actions from evil to good.

It is, of course, obvious that the police do not get to know of crimes by some direct process of "knowing" or observation. Criminals usually go to great pains to make this difficult for the police. Crimes "known to the police" are usually reported to them by the public, most frequently by the victim. This means that an event must first of all be *defined by a member of the public*, with no special legal knowledge, as an event requiring that the police do something about it. That is to say, a crime is usually first defined by a *democratic* process as "something that the police ought to do something about." It may be that events defined by an ordinary citizen as a "crime worth reporting to the police" may not be a crime within the legal code of the country concerned, and, although the event is reported because it is *perceived as a crime*, the police will not record it. Although they may still take action to remedy the problem, they would not record an event as a crime simply because the reporter viewed it as such. On the other hand, there are many events known to the same citizen which he does not define as "something that the police ought to do something about" although they are in fact crimes under the law.

It would, of course, be possible to define as "crimes" all events which become known to ordinary citizens and are thought by them to be worthy of reporting to the police in the expectation of some action to remedy their complaint. Such events generally are called "complaints known to the police," but not "crimes." It might, however, be more useful operationally to define "crimes" as "complaints," since this would amount to defining crimes as events that give rise to a level of disapproval on the part of the victim or other members of the public such that they actively seek the assistance of the forces of social defense.

Criminal statistics.   At present the figures relating to "crimes known to the police" (in countries where these are available), although nearest to the event which is regarded as "criminal," provide an *amended* record of events believed by the general public to be crimes, plus some additional events where the police obtain direct evidence and where information regarding one event leads to disclosure of another. In most countries there are events which are crimes according to the law but which the average citizen does not define as anything that the police should know about. Similarly, in most countries there are events which are perceived by average citizens as crimes against their culture but which are not acknowledged in law.

In most democratic societies the law will tend to be amended to agree with public opinion, but the relationship between public opinion and legal definitions is not a one-to-one correlation. An example of public disapprobation leading to new legislation may be cited—the Offensive Weapons Act of England and Wales, which made it a crime for persons to offer certain types of knives for sale. In the other direction, attempted suicide, for a long time not a criminal offense in Scotland, has recently been removed from the criminal definition in England and Wales also.

Legal definitions of crimes, while very suitable for legal processes, are not directly translatable into sociological and psychological terms. Behavior usually regarded as "normal" includes some acts that are crimes by legal definition, while at the extreme end of a distribution are crimes that all sane persons, even offenders themselves, regard as such.

Crimes and morals.   It is often argued that the cause of an increase in crime is a decline in moral standards of the population. If this argument is not circular (crime being held to be a reflection of morals), it is possible to throw some light on the relationship between moral values and crimes. Perhaps the layman who assumes, when he hears that crime has increased, that he is in greater risk of an attack upon his person or property is nearer to equating morals with crime than the official definitions allow. Indeed, it seems possible, and even probable, that any *improvement* in moral values would show in the official records of crime as an *increase* in the number of crimes known to the police and perhaps also as an increase in the number of arrests.

Any change in the social definition of an event worth notification of the police will, even in stable conditions, influence the bias of the sample of crimes represented by the "crimes known" figures. If a society is becoming more "moral," it is possible to suggest that that society is becoming more stringent and requiring more conforming standards of behavior. If this occurs, the democratic definition of "things which the police ought to do something about" will tend to agree more closely with the legal definition of crime for the majority of events that are defined in the criminal law as crimes.

It is simpler to demonstrate the effect of change in public opinion in regard to expected levels of behavior where the criminal statistics are based on "crimes known to the police" than where data are derived from arrests. It may be supposed, however, that the police as public servants are aware of public pressure, and, of course, they are themselves members of the culture that forms the definitions to which they operate in their official capacities.

In England and Wales and some other countries,

what is a "crime" to be included in the "crimes known" figures is determined by whether the offense is "indictable." The definition of an "indictable offense" depends upon the way in which an adult person accused of the offense might be tried. Special provisions for the juvenile (persons under 17 years of age in England and Wales and certain states in the United States) are ignored for purposes of this definition. Perhaps the criterion of recording as crimes only indictable offenses was at one time related to levels of public disapprobation. Today it has no very strong association with public opinion, particularly in the distinction between offenses of larceny and vandalism. In England and Wales, larceny of any value is an indictable offense, but vandalism is a misdemeanor. For example, it would be regarded as an indictable offense for a person to open the doors of a parked car and remove a half-empty package of cigarettes from the glove pocket, but not an indictable offense to carve his name on the windshield or twist off the door handles. This illustration is not universally applicable, but in all legislations some similar event can be found.

The problem of trends and comparisons

It is generally agreed that precise cross-cultural comparisons of crime are impossible. Attempts have been made by committees of the United Nations to establish some form of comparison for the most serious offenses, like homicide and robbery, but even at this level of seriousness no strictly comparable basis can be found. In the case of murder, the social significance of weapons differs among countries, and vestigial traces of the dueling cultures of the past still remain in the legal codes of many countries. Comparisons have been attempted in terms of legal definitions, because it is believed that the legal basis for crime cannot be avoided. It might be possible to find some basis for comparisons if crimes were described in terms of exactly *what happened*, as perceived in the current cultural setting, but even this would be difficult. Add to the difficulty of cultural differences, which are current in their effects, traces of history preserved to greater or lesser degrees in the laws of different countries, and exact cross-cultural comparisons are impossible.

For legal purposes, and not without good reason, there is a tendency to try to preserve a law that has worked in the past to suffice for the newer conditions for as long as possible. The horse was a factor to be considered in relation to economic and criminal behavior in the past, but it is very doubtful whether the transition from horse to "horseless carriage" is a sufficiently direct one for the continuity of legal definition and sociological and psychological inferences based on this transition.

Perhaps the main problem in the study of trends arises from the fact that changes in the law can be made only in discrete steps, whereas the processes of technological change are continuous. Changes in perceptual processes that follow upon and are related to technological changes as well as value systems are also continuous changes. Some items in legal classifications must, no matter how much the law is changed, be out of step with social and economic conditions. The changes will be made in different countries and different states at different rates and with respect to different parts of the law. But these discrete adjustments immediately prejudice the study of trends. Trends seem to require a stable definition, but changes are essential if the law is to have any meaning in a changing society.

Clearly, the law cannot be in a process of continuous change if it is to function for the protection of society, although society, in order to preserve itself, must be continuously adjusting to change.

Changes within a culture. It may be thought that although the problem of trends and comparisons is difficult and complex when cross-cultural analysis is being attempted, something more positive may be said about trends within a culture. But even here there are serious problems.

It may seem a simple matter to adjust the figures for crime within a country or state according to changes in the population. The total amount of crime is expected to change because, if the population of a country increases and the definitions remain constant and are constantly interpreted, more persons would be expected to commit more crimes. But in some parts of the world it is not possible to estimate the population with any degree of accuracy during the years between censuses. In the United States this is particularly true for states with a rapidly growing or declining population. Even an accurate estimate of the total population may not provide sufficient information for adjustment of crime data to be meaningful. It is obvious that a better crime rate is provided if the crude number of crimes is modified by the number of persons available to commit them. The rate per 100,000 of population (the conventional rate) provides something which is obviously better than rates that make no allowance for population size. But the obviousness of the improvement may be a snare and a delusion. The majority of crimes, so far as is known from the persons identified as criminals, are committed by younger male persons. In all Western countries females commit from one-fifth to one-tenth of the amount of crime committed by males. Further, persons of either sex over thirty years of age commit (or are found guilty of) relatively few offenses.

Thus, if the age structure of a population is changing and if there are increasingly more young people in the population, then even with a constant population an increased amount of crime would be expected. The converse is also true. If a population is becoming older, the crime rate can be expected to drop, even if every person, age for age and sex for sex, remains as criminal as before. This argument assumes, of course, that crimes for which offenders are identified are similar, in respect to age and sex distribution, to crimes which are not "cleared up." (The rate of clear-up varies between types of crimes and from place to place but is seldom greater than 50 per cent for crimes where the victim does not see the offender in a face-to-face situation.)

Taking all these points and bearing in mind others which could be raised, it is regarded as unsafe to make any statements about the state of crime or crime trends over time or between different countries, states, or districts, except perhaps in the crudest possible terms.

Crime and opportunity

Adjustments for changes in population are usually regarded as obvious and sound. But there are few crimes that relate to a basis of persons. Perhaps the number of murders may be expected to change in proportion to the number of persons available to commit murders or to be the victims of murder, but if adjustments are obviously necessary for persons whose crimes affect persons, why are other adjustments not equally obvious? If, for example, there are more cars available to be stolen, why should not the number of cars stolen be expected to rise proportionally to availability? If there is more money available for legitimate transfer, why should not the number of illegitimate transfers of money be expected to rise proportionally?

Some data relating to certain indictable offenses known to the police, adjusted for population, are given in Table 1. It will be observed that the adjusted number of murders has remained reasonably constant over the years from 1946 through 1959, whereas housebreaking has shown a fall and a rise, and embezzlement an almost continuous rise. Indeed, the figures for murder do not show

Table 1 — Certain indictable offenses known to the police, adjusted for population changes, England and Wales, 1946–1959

	Murder[a]	Burglary	Embezzlement	Housebreaking
1946[b]	131	4,220	799	31,270
1947	134.5	3,872	1,052	30,285
1948	146.3	4,153	1,732	31,417
1949	118.1	3,712	1,734	26,770
1950	121.2	3,592	2,153	26,057
1951	122.4	3,711	2,333	26,164
1952	134.7	3,811	2,894	28,195
1953	129.2	3,659	2,842	26,479
1954	134.5	3,126	2,981	22,782
1955	121.5	2,862	2,833	21,435
1956	142.7	2,836	3,091	22,705
1957	144.6	3,516	2,563	27,775
1958	118.2	4,316	2,756	34,569
1959	134.6	4,387	3,533	35,874

a. Uncorrected for cases subsequently found to be manslaughter, infanticide, and so on.
b. Base year 1946 = actual figures.

Source: Adapted from Wilkins 1964, based on Criminal Statistics of England and Wales, *Annual Report.*

any variation in excess of chance, whereas other offenses show considerable and significant variation. This raises the question of whether the murder figures remain constant because the factor used to compute these adjusted figures is based on the relevant "population at risk." If equally meaningful bases could be used to construct rates for other crimes, it might even be discovered that the total amount of crime in this and other societies remains constant. However, it seems unreasonable to deny that major changes can occur in the long run; what is needed is a better understanding of both short-term fluctuations and long-term trends.

The problem of heterogeneity. It is possible to examine the problem of the heterogeneity of current definitions of crime in a number of ways. It may be postulated, for example, that if all types of crime tend to increase and decrease simultaneously over time, it does not matter which type of crime is selected as an index or whether all crimes are added together. It might seem desirable to select an offense that presents as little difficulty as possible in identification and classification. Another method is provided by an area analysis. It could be suggested that if different areas show different interrelationships between crimes, an index of crime should not mask these differences. But neither of these methods can begin with any finer breakdowns of the data than are provided by the original classifications. It is true that the law may subdivide into different crimes types of actions that may be sociologically and psychologically similar, but it may also place together into one category crimes that are dissimilar in other dimensions. Once information has been lost by coding it, it cannot be recovered without a basically new encoding system.

Despite these limitations, the writer has used both a historical analysis and an area analysis to gain information regarding ways of classifying similar crimes together and separating those which do not show similar patterns. The following classification system is proposed (Wilkins 1963a):

I. Homicide
  (a) Murder
  (b) Manslaughter
II. Serious crimes against the person (including sex offenses and violence)
III. Serious crimes against property (burglary, breaking and entry, robbery, etc.)
IV. Social disorganization (drunkenness, disorderly conduct, petty larceny, etc.)

In terms of variations over time and variations between districts, these categories tend to show different patterns and thus to suggest heterogeneity. In many jurisdictions the legal classification does not discriminate by degree of seriousness. Robbery, for example, will generally cover a bank robbery at one end of the scale and a small boy tripping another and stealing his pocket money at the other. Thus, the dividing line between serious and nonserious offenses against the person is not fixed in terms of injury to the victim or period of medical treatment occasioned. The perception of what is "serious" may well vary from time to time and from place to place according to the social attitudes of the culture in which the events occur.

Two comparisons. It would be unsatisfactory to leave the impression that all forms of research into crime which involve cross-cultural comparisons or even comparisons within one culture are invalid. It is true that it is difficult to sustain the common concept of crime and to make valid comparisons, and the legal definitions only make the problem the more difficult. Nonetheless, two examples will be given of comparisons that seem to be legitimate, and these may serve to indicate methods through which some positive contributions may be made.

Comparisons require well-defined and specific forms of behavior, and, with existing data, these are few. Larceny from motor vehicles and drug addiction are the examples used, the former for a comparison within one culture and the latter for a cross-cultural analysis.

Offenses of larceny from motor vehicles which

Table 2 — Larceny from motor vehicles, adjusted for number of vehicles, England and Wales, 1940–1961

	Registered private motor vehicles, in thousands	Larceny from motor vehicles*	Rate per 100 vehicles
1940	1,423	16,849	1.2
1941	1,503	15,672	1.0
1942	858	12,180	1.4
1943	718	11,084	1.5
1944	755	14,509	1.9
1945	1,487	26,520	1.8
1946	1,770	32,546	1.8
1947	1,943	33,984	1.7
1948	1,961	32,665	1.7
1949	2,131	30,297	1.4
1950	2,258	33,156	1.5
1951	2,380	43,127	1.8
1952	2,508	41,125	1.6
1953	2,762	39,739	1.4
1954	3,100	39,398	1.3
1955	3,526	43,304	1.2
1956	3,888	50,782	1.3
1957	4,187	54,937	1.3
1958	4,549	68,466	1.5
1959	4,966	79,899	1.6
1960	5,526	92,704	1.7
1961	5,979	112,671	1.9

* Crimes known to the police.

Source: Adapted from Criminal Statistics of England and Wales, Annual Report.

were recorded as "known to the police" in England and Wales during the period from 1938 through 1961 are shown in Table 2, together with the number of motor vehicles registered. It will be noted that when we use as a divisor the number of motor vehicles "at risk," the "crime rate" for this category of offenses shows a very different picture from that which would be obtained by dividing by the population. Were the moral values in England and Wales at a low ebb in the years 1944 to 1946, 1951, and 1961, when thefts from cars reached an index of 1.8 per cent or more? Or have moral values tended to deteriorate more or less steadily since the end of World War II? Is the base of "opportunity" a meaningful base? Could thefts from other sources be better interpreted against the changes in the gross national product or some other economic measure of affluence? In this case, the highest rate of larcenies per 100 vehicles is only 1.9 times the lowest rate, although the largest absolute number of larcenies in any year is about ten times the lowest number. Would similar results be obtained for other crimes, or do these results represent a tendency toward a constant factor in crime after adjustment of crude figures to a suitable base? Whether any of these questions are answered one way or another, it would certainly seem to be meaningful to explore *divergencies* from the "constant" rather than to examine figures unadjusted by "vehicles exposed to risk."

Can the study of crime be separated from economics and other forms of study of human behavior? Moral explanations are obviously not sufficient—unless it is seriously held that moral values have deteriorated (and improved) strictly proportional to the number of cars! Before there can be serious discussion of trends in crime, much more sophisticated models must be sought than the simple cause–effect models that have been considered so far. If "crime" concerns economic behavior, then other aspects of economic behavior must be considered in assessing its cause. If legitimate opportunities are increasing in any culture, it will usually mean that illegitimate opportunities are also increasing. If a society wishes to generate change in criminal behavior, it seems highly likely that it will have to consider changes also in economic behavior—at least insofar as the balance between legitimate and illegitimate opportunities for the exchange of wealth is concerned.

The need for more complex models seems to be illustrated by the cross-cultural comparison of drug addiction. The United States, and particularly the major cities on the east and west coasts, have a very serious problem of addiction. England has no such problem. Yet it is often claimed that the system of drug control in England is almost exactly the same as that in the United States. This point is argued, but it would appear that the difference in the addiction rates cannot be due to the small procedural differences—that is, if similar causes must have similar effects. But there are types of models, called "deviation amplifying systems," in which similar causes can have different effects (Wilkins 1964). In order to illustrate such a model, let us reverse the present example and suggest how England might find itself with a drug addiction problem. One way could be if an attempt were made to reduce the number of addicts (at present about five hundred) by more stringent control. The existing "image" of addicts as sick persons might then be changed by increased pressure from the police authorities. The difference between the image of a sick person and a sinner may be unsubstantial, but it might generate considerable differences in behavior. No one goes out of his way to become sick, but sinning has some attractions! The deviation-generating model is very often found in economic behavior: what, for example, causes prices to fall on the stock exchange—a fall in con-

fidence? Or does a fall in prices cause a drop in confidence? Clearly this is a mutual causal system where a small instability can cause a major deviation to be generated. The concepts of "image" and "confidence" are extremely similar; indeed, confidence in the market may be described as the "image" of the market.

Leslie T. Wilkins

[*See also* Government statistics; Statistics, descriptive; *and the biography of* Sutherland.]

BIBLIOGRAPHY

Criminal Statistics of England and Wales *Annual Report.* → Published since 1923.

Reiss, Albert J. Jr.; and Rhodes, A. L. 1960 The Distribution of Juvenile Delinquency in the Social Structure. *American Sociological Review* 25:720–732.

Short, James F. Jr.; and Nye, F. Ivan 1957–1958 Reported Behavior as a Criterion of Deviant Behavior. *Social Problems* 5:207–213.

Sutherland, Edwin H.; and Cressey, Donald R. (1924) 1960 *Principles of Criminology.* 6th ed. New York: Lippincott. → First published as a textbook, *Criminology,* under the sole authorship of Edwin H. Sutherland.

Wilkins, Leslie T. 1963a The Measurement of Crime. *British Journal of Criminology* 3:321–341.

Wilkins, Leslie T. 1963b What Is Crime? *New Society* 2, no. 42:15–16.

Wilkins, Leslie T. (1964) 1965 *Social Deviance: Social Policy, Action, and Research.* Englewood Cliffs, N.J.: Prentice-Hall.

III
WHITE-COLLAR CRIME

The concept of white-collar crime covers law-breaking among the middle and upper (or "white-collar") socioeconomic classes. This type of criminal behavior differs from that of the lower socioeconomic classes in several important respects; different, also, are some of the legal sanctions for the two classes of offenses. To include white-collar violations within criminology, crime must be defined in terms broad enough to cover any behavior punishable by the state, regardless of whether the penalty is criminal, civil, or administrative, and regardless of the offender's social status.

Lawbreaking can be divided into two categories: *conventional* crimes (burglary, for example, or larceny), which are usually punishable under the criminal law, and *white-collar* crimes, which are not usually punishable in this manner. An apprehended burglar or robber is punished by a jail sentence, a fine, or probation; a doctor may be punished through revocation of his license. Penalties imposed on businessmen include enjoinment by the government, the levying of civil damages, suspension of license to do business, or (as in impure food cases) the seizure and destruction of commodities. All of these sanctions imply that the behavior is socially injurious; in each case, punishment is involved and society stigmatizes the offender.

History of the concept. The concept of white-collar crime is a relatively new addition to criminological theory, although the need for such a term had been apparent to at least one of the founders of American sociology (Ross 1907) and was re-affirmed in the 1930s (see, for instance, Morris 1934). However, the term itself did not gain wide currency until 1940, when Edwin H. Sutherland published a paper entitled "White-collar Criminality." In it he developed the concept and outlined its widespread implications for criminology (Sutherland 1940). Nine years later, he published the first major study of white-collar crimes: those committed by seventy of the two hundred largest nonfinancial corporations in the United States (Sutherland 1949).

After World War II, Clinard (1946; 1952) and Hartung (1950) published studies of white-collar crime in the form of black-market violations of price and rationing laws by United States businessmen during the war. Other offenses dealt with by social scientists that have the same general kind of orientation include employers' violations of labor laws (Lane 1953), embezzlement and other violations of trust (Cressey 1953), violations of pure-food laws (Newman 1957), and illegal activities of pharmacists (Quinney 1963). Theoretical articles on white-collar crime have been written by a number of American and European criminologists. But, with a few exceptions, such as Great Britain and Germany (see Mannheim 1946; 1965; Grygier et al. 1965; *Strafrechtspflege* . . . 1961; Zirpins & Terstegen 1963; Middendorff 1959), research in this field has remained a unique contribution of American criminologists, although white-collar crime occurs in nearly all countries.

Social status of the offenders. Sutherland used the term "white-collar crime" to refer to violations of the law by persons of relatively high social and occupational status. "White-collar crimes" are those crimes committed by "respectable" persons in connection with their occupations. The concept, therefore, does not include such conventional crimes as murder or robbery, offenses that are defined in the same way regardless of the status or occupation of the persons committing them. Nor does it include legal acts that are considered "unethical"; it cannot be a white-collar crime unless it is punishable in some manner by the state.

Sutherland was not specific about which occu-

pations should be included in the concept, and as a result there has been considerable confusion. In his study of black-market violations, Clinard included all gasoline-station operators and anyone who rented property. Newman suggested that "farmers, repairmen, and others in essentially non-white-collar occupations could, through such illegalities as watering milk for public consumption, making unnecessary 'repairs' on television sets, and so forth, be classified as white-collar violators" (Newman 1958, p. 737). Others feel that white-collar crime should be restricted to those in high status positions and that those with non-high status positions in the middle class should be dealt with separately (Mannheim 1965, p. 474). Consequently, some have suggested that it would be advisable to change the emphasis of the concept from "white-collar crime" to "occupational crime" (Quinney 1964); it would not include all violations of law by white-collar persons, such as income-tax evasion and rent-control violations, unless they occurred in connection with the violator's occupational role.

White-collar criminal activities. Common forms of white-collar crime by businessmen include illegal activities of reorganization committees in receiverships and bankruptcies; restraint of trade, such as monopoly, illegal rebates, and infringement of patents, trade-marks, and copyrights; misrepresentation in advertising; unfair labor practices; financial manipulations; and wartime crimes, such as black-marketeering. In developing countries, businessmen are especially prone to violations of the income-tax laws, import and export regulations, and currency-control measures.

Embezzlement is an especially common form of white-collar crime. One classification of embezzlers identifies three types (Cressey 1953): "Independent businessmen" is the name given to violators who convert "deposits" entrusted to them for specific purposes while at the same time maintaining their regular businesses. The second group, the "long-term violators," consists of employed individuals who convert funds belonging to their employers, or to their employers' clients, by taking relatively small amounts over a long period of time. "Absconders" are persons who violate their trust by removing funds or goods entrusted to them and then severing connections with the trustor by leaving his employment or leaving the vicinity.

Politicians and government employees commit various white-collar offenses, including direct misappropriation of public funds as well as the indirect acquisition of these funds through padded payrolls, the placement of relatives on a payroll, or monetary payments from appointees. Their illegal activities are usually more subtle than this, however. Politicians and government employees make financial gains by granting favors to business firms, such as illegal commissions on public contracts, the issuance of fraudulent licenses or certificates, and tax exemptions or underestimated tax evaluations. Labor union officials engage in such criminal activities as the misappropriation or misapplication of union funds; failure to enforce laws affecting their unions; collusion with employers to the disadvantage of the union members; and the use of fraudulent means to maintain control over the union.

Doctors may illegally prescribe narcotics, perform illegal abortions, make fraudulent reports in accident cases, and split fees. Fee-splitting, wherein a doctor gives part of his fee to the doctor referring the case, is illegal in many places in the United States because of the danger that such referrals might be based on the fee rather than the practitioner's ability. Lawyers engage in such illegal activities as the misappropriation of funds in receiverships; the securance of perjured testimony from witnesses; the practice known in the United States as "ambulance chasing," that is, investigating as many accidents as possible soon after they occur in order to secure the damage-suit business of the victims; and collaboration in making fraudulent claims for damages. In these cases, an apprehended offender is more likely to be disbarred from practice than prosecuted.

Extent of white-collar crime.   Obviously, to restrict the definition of "crime" solely to conventional crimes results in an underestimation of the extent of crime and its effect on society. Studies have indicated the widespread nature of white-collar crime; however, these crimes are far more difficult to tabulate than ordinary crimes. The categories of offenses covered by the term are not as precise as in conventional crime; the criteria for determining the social class of the offender are often not clear; and the criminal law, with few exceptions, makes no distinction regarding the social class of offenders (Caldwell 1958). National crime statistics, such as the *Uniform Crime Reports* of the Federal Bureau of Investigation in the United States, tabulate only violations of criminal law and not those of administrative and civil law, and therefore include very little about white-collar crime. Some of the latter information may be obtained from reports of various other government agencies and investigations, but this requires considerable effort, and often the required information is not fully available. The financial losses to society in a single case of white-collar crime may be equal to the total amount

involved in thousands of larcenies, burglaries, and robberies. However, society does not conceive of the white-collar criminal as a true criminal; this is reflected in the fact that poor and relatively uneducated offenders are usually sentenced to prison, whereas white-collar criminals are seldom imprisoned.

Sutherland's study (1949) of 70 large nonfinancial corporations reported a total of 980 decisions rendered against them for violation of government regulations, an average of 14 per corporation. Restraint of trade, infringement of patents, and unfair labor practices were the most frequent violations. Sixty per cent of these decisions were rendered during a ten-year period (1935 through 1944) of increased government enforcement of business regulations. Although only 158 cases were dealt with by the criminal courts, crimes were actually committed in 779 of the 980 cases. Two-thirds of these corporations had been convicted in criminal court with an average of 4 convictions each; 97 per cent of the corporations were repeaters.

Violations of rationing and price-control laws by businessmen (black-marketeering) were a serious problem in many countries during World War II. Clinard (1952) found that approximately one in fifteen of the three million U.S. business concerns were punished for such violations, but only 6 per cent involved the criminal sanction. Of the 250,000 concerns selling gasoline in the United States during the war, one in sixteen was punished for rationing violations, most of which were complex, evasive, and willful. A significant case of white-collar crime involved conspiracy in price-fixing and price-rigging violations of the federal antitrust laws by many leading U.S. electrical concerns (Herling 1962). Twenty-nine companies were convicted of illegalities in sales of heavy electrical equipment to both government and private purchasers; the federal court imposed fines totaling $1,924,000. Of the 45 company executives who were convicted, 7 at the policy-making level were sentenced to 30 days in jail, and 24 others received suspended sentences. These sentences, and the severity of the fines, are fairly unusual punishments for white-collar crimes. Civil suits involving millions of dollars were brought against many of the firms to recover damages.

The case of the electrical companies does serve, however, as a reminder that white-collar crime in many areas is a well-organized affair, ranging from the comparatively simple reciprocal relationships involved in doctors' fee-splitting to the more complex illegal activities of large corporations. Most techniques of violation are, of course, selected because they involve the smallest danger of detection, but they may also recommend themselves, especially to a corporation, because the violators are confident that the case will either not be prosecuted, or not result in a conviction, or receive a minor penalty. Indeed, they may even hope to change the law itself, or at least demonstrate that it is unenforceable.

Punishment for white-collar crime. The punishments for white-collar offenses vary considerably, but almost without exception they differ from those given for ordinary offenses. One of the most significant of the many factors involved in this variation is the fact that many of these acts were not made illegal until recent years. For instance, the following practices were not made illegal in the United States until the beginning of the nineteenth century: restraint of trade, false advertising, insolvency of banks due to fraud or negligence of officials, sale of fraudulent securities, and misuse of trade-marks. Previously, the philosophy of laissez-faire (and its time-honored companion, the slogan *caveat emptor*) had completely dominated public thought and policy. Legislation directed toward controlling the more powerful economic groups was an inevitable, although somewhat tardy, outcome of industrialization, as the entrepreneur was gradually displaced by the corporation and large-scale labor unions began to appear on the economic scene. Public recognition of the socially injurious nature of white-collar crime has also developed slowly. White-collar crimes are usually both more complex and diffused over a longer period of time than ordinary crimes; and so the essential criminality of the acts tends to be obscured. Furthermore, the type of publicity given white-collar crimes, as contrasted with the more overt crimes like burglary or larceny, seldom creates much public resentment. It is therefore difficult to create and sustain the kind of public pressure needed for the enactment of stronger legislation designating this type of behavior, however antisocial, as "criminal."

Most statutes outlawing white-collar crime differ from conventional criminal laws in five ways: origin, determination of responsibility or intent, philosophy, enforcement and trial procedures, and sanctions against violators (Newman 1958, p. 738). Responsibility for enforcement is delegated primarily to specially created agencies. The administrative process of hearing cases closely approximates juvenile court procedures, and the actions taken are more often remedial in nature—injunctions, for example, rather than fines or imprison-

ment. In fact, there has been a tendency in the United States to enact rather lenient statutes and then to enforce them in similar fashion, with favoritism shown to offenders of high social status. Even when criminal sanctions are included, they have generally been used hesitatingly. Criminal action against corporations presents difficulties, for even after long litigation, often the only result is a fine that is modest by corporate standards or a sentence for an officer that is light when matched against the gravity of the offense. Some of the specific legal problems connected with white-collar crime have been discussed by Mannheim (1965, pp. 481–484).

Criticisms of the legal concept. Some law professors and sociological criminologists have criticized the expansion of the concept of crime beyond the criminal law, stressing the criminal law's more rigorous procedures, greater stability, and greater capacity to stigmatize the offender (Tappan 1947; Caldwell 1958). Such critics think that "crime" and "criminal" relate only to overt acts of ordinary convicted offenders: "there is an obvious and basic incongruity involved in the proposition that a community's leaders and more responsible elements are also its criminals" (Vold 1958, p. 253). Mannheim has pointed out that the basic issue involves the elements of conviction and stigma. He feels that the legalistic view that only punishable acts dealt with by criminal law are crimes and the view that punishable acts are always crimes are both unsatisfactory: "What is needed is an injection of sociological thinking into the whole administration of criminal justice to insure that the present incongruities between stigma and conviction will be reduced to an unavoidable minimum" (Mannheim 1965, p. 33).

It is true, of course, that the criminal law is more integrated into the mores than civil law, since the latter is more recent and derives largely from the prevailing economic system. But the boundaries have also expanded; indeed, the nature of modern criminal law has been used as evidence in favor of a concept of criminality that includes almost any behavior showing "a lack of a developed social feeling and ethical code" (Hurwitz [1947] 1952, p. 31). Such a view certainly includes white-collar crime, but it neglects the crucial factor of legality, which is an essential part of the definition (see Clinard 1952, pp. 226–262; Mannheim 1965, pp. 30–31). The concept of white-collar crime is not as tendentious and moralistic as has been claimed by some of its critics (see, for instance, Jones 1956, p. 8). It was not Sutherland who designated these types of behavior as undesirable; they had already been so designated by laws in the United States and elsewhere. We must therefore conclude that the white-collar offender is indeed a criminal; what kind of criminal remains to be seen.

Typologies of white-collar crime.   The study of white-collar crime has been handicapped by subsuming under this term a large variety of behaviors needing different causal explanations. To avoid this, it has been suggested that white-collar crimes be separated into three categories: those committed by relatively autonomous professionals, such as lawyers or doctors; those committed by employees against corporations, for example, embezzlement; and those committed in the form of policy-making decisions by officers of corporations (Bloch & Geis 1962). Whatever scheme is adopted, there seems to be a need for some classification according to the occupational status of the offender. Geis has thought that white-collar crimes should be concerned with more homogeneous occupational groups; he therefore has restricted the concept to "corporate violations" (1962).

Quinney has argued that more homogeneous occupational units would be desirable, but that they have to be delineated by the researcher, since the construction and explanation of occupational crime rates is a task that has been largely neglected by sociologists. He therefore suggests concentrating on studies both of the violation of legal norms and of deviation from *occupational* norms; both types of deviance could then be related to occupational behavior in general. Occupations change, and so do the types of crime and other deviance associated with them; thus an increase in the extent of an occupational practice hitherto considered merely deviant may evoke a law that renders it illegal. In distinguishing categories of crime based on occupation, one should consider the kind of occupation, its position in the occupational structure, the occupational role of the offender, and the nature of the institutional setting. The researcher should also acquaint himself with the effect of the law on that particular occupation and with the relevant norms and values embodied in the law (Quinney 1964).

Theories of white-collar crime.   The concept of white-collar crime, in the fifteen years since it became current, has had little effect on the theory and research of criminologists in the field of psychiatry and psychology. But a useful theory of crime should apply alike to the ordinary criminal and the white-collar criminal. Most current studies of ordinary criminals have largely disregarded this fact. On the basis of studies of offenders, chiefly of the lower socioeconomic groups, various theories have attempted erroneously to explain criminal behavior as the result of childhood emotional insecurity, unrepressed primitive desires, guilt feelings, and the like. Similarly, attempts have been made to explain crime as a result of poverty, poor housing, broken homes, and feeble-mindedness. Such writings have made almost no references to the contradictory evidence presented by white-collar offenders.

Sutherland stated that white-collar crime could be explained within the general framework of criminal behavior as a process of *differential association*, wherein the behavior is learned from those who consider it favorable, in isolation from those who do not. For example, lawbreaking may be normative in certain business concerns, and persons who are isolated from other situations may learn values, rationalizations, and techniques that will enable them both to violate the law and to feel justified in so doing. Several factors isolate businessmen from unfavorable definitions of illegal activity. The media of mass communication usually treat white-collar crime leniently as compared with their treatment of conventional crime. Furthermore, government officials often shield businessmen from severe criticism, since many of the officials either were formerly in business or may have accepted political contributions from business sources. In addition, businessmen associate chiefly with other businessmen, both at work and in their social activities, so that the implications of white-collar crime are removed from outside scrutiny (Sutherland 1949).

Clinard (1952) has pointed out that most white-collar violations appear to originate in behavior learned through association with others. But this does not explain why some persons engage in such behavior and others do not. Such an explanation would require an examination of the roles played by the individual. Also, some violations may involve the independent invention of complex techniques without learning from others.

Cressey (1953) has developed what he believes to be a universal explanation of trust violations by individuals entrusted with funds or property, although not an explanation of white-collar crime generally. He has identified three essential elements in a trust violation: a "nonshareable" financial problem, knowledge of how to violate, and rationalizations about the violations. Financial problems which are experienced as nonshareable include business reversals and important obligations involving the person's status or sense of personal responsibility. Trust violators are aware that these problems can be resolved secretly by violating their positions of trust, and they have acquired knowledge of the techniques to do so. They define the situation through rationalizations in terms that enable them to regard their criminal behavior as essentially noncriminal. For example, they explain that they were "only borrowing," that their behavior is part of the "general irresponsibility" for which they are not completely accountable, or that their behavior is due to unusual circumstances. Unfortunately, Cressey's study does not describe the characteristics of trust violators and does not specify the situations that most often result in violations. Future studies may enable us to predict more accurately which persons will be violators and what situations are most conducive to violations.

Conception of self. The white-collar criminal is set apart by his distinctive conception of himself. He generally regards himself as a "respectable citizen" rather than as a "criminal"; at most, he sees himself as a "lawbreaker." In this sense, he is similar to some offenders convicted of such crimes as statutory rape, nonsupport, and drunken driving. The white-collar criminal gains support for this image of himself from the general public, which, although it does not necessarily condone his activities, finds it hard to conceive of them as being associated with "real" criminal behavior. Moreover, the white-collar offender usually suffers little loss of status among his associates. Although some of them may frown upon his behavior, others may even admire it, especially if his transactions reveal considerable shrewdness. This last reaction may be related to a general contempt for laws affecting them as well as for government (especially government personnel) as a whole on the part of large sections of an occupational group.

Role orientations. So far, we have emphasized characteristics that the white-collar offender shares with other kinds of criminals. But there is one important aspect in which he differs from them: he may play a variety of other, noncriminal roles, and the degree to which he recognizes the existence of conflict between these roles and his criminal role may vary considerably.

The theory of differential association, especially if there has been continuous and intimate association with unethical and illegal norms and some isolation from other norms, cannot explain why many people never become white-collar criminals at all, even though they are likely to have both the means and the opportunity to do so, as well as the inducement. Nor it is enough to say that most people are "honest," but some are not. The known

variations in individual rates of deviance cannot be explained simply in terms of the differential acceptance of general social values, although this is of course an important fact. The best available empirical evidence shows that people appear to accept or reject opportunities for white-collar crime according to their orientations toward the various roles they play in society, especially their occupational role.

But most criminologists interested in white-collar crime have been concerned more with establishing its existence than with studying variations in offense rates within various occupations. Quinney, who did study such variations among retail pharmacists, found that prescription violations are related both to the structure of the occupation and to the differential orientation of retail pharmacists toward it. The retail pharmacist was found to have two divergent occupational role expectations—that of the professional and that of the businessman; the structural strain inherent in this situation is usually met by the adoption of an "occupational role organization" that, in both including and emphasizing the "professional" aspect of the occupation, tends to restrain the pharmacist from violating the prescription laws. On the other hand, pharmacists who emphasize the "businessman" aspect of the occupation tend to have the highest violation rate, whereas those who emphasize neither aspect have a rate somewhere between those of the two other groups (Quinney 1963).

White-collar crime and the social structure. White-collar crime cannot be fully understood without reference to the value conflicts presented to people in higher-status positions. These vary according to the social structure and value system of society. For instance, the values involved in the state regulation of commercial transactions in the United States may conflict with those of the American free-enterprise system. When such conflicts occur, attitudes that are involved in selective obedience to a "good" or "bad" law become the key to compliance. "The demand for law arises out of the conflicts in cultures; and because there is a conflict in cultures, the law is not effective as a deterrent upon the other groups that did not at first demand the law" (Sutherland [1929] 1956, p. 108). Further research should focus on the conditions that lead to a definition of behavior as criminal and to a definition of the way in which legal norms intersect and are integrated with the norms of other institutional structures (Jeffery 1956). Study of the values, norms, and other aspects of middle- and upper-class subcultures and occupations may help to explain white-collar crime in much the same way that knowledge of the subculture of the lower class and the culture of poverty is necessary to understand many conventional crimes.

The recent concern of sociologists with white-collar crime brings into focus a long-neglected relationship between criminal behavior, criminal law, penal sanctions, and social structure (Aubert 1952). Studies of white-collar crime in highly differentiated societies have focused on the ambivalent attitudes of average citizens toward the law, with the result that structured conflicts have been discovered between social roles and the larger social system. In this way, as Cressey (1961, p. xii) has emphasized, there is need for study of the entire society if we are to understand why white-collar crime is often not reported or studied. White-collar crime can often be viewed as violation of laws which are not part of the moral values of the groups concerned (Fuller 1942).

MARSHALL B. CLINARD

[*See also* PUNISHMENT *and the biography of* SUTHERLAND.]

BIBLIOGRAPHY

AUBERT, VILHELM 1952 White Collar Crime and Social Structure. *American Journal of Sociology* 58:263–271.

BLOCH, HERBERT A.; and GEIS, GILBERT 1962 White-collar Crime. Pages 379–404 in Herbert A. Bloch and Gilbert Geis, *Man, Crime, and Society: The Forms of Criminal Behavior.* New York: Random House.

CALDWELL, ROBERT G. 1958 A Reexamination of the Concept of White Collar Crime. *Federal Probation* 22, no. 1:30–36.

CLINARD, MARSHALL B. 1946 Criminological Theories of Violations of Wartime Regulations. *American Sociological Review* 11:258–270.

CLINARD, MARSHALL B. 1952 *The Black Market: A Study of White Collar Crime.* New York: Holt.

CLINARD, MARSHALL B. (1957) 1963 *Sociology of Deviant Behavior.* 2d ed. New York: Holt.

CRESSEY, DONALD R. 1952 Application and Verification of the Differential Association Theory. *Journal of Criminal Law, Criminology, and Police Science* 43:43–52.

CRESSEY, DONALD R. 1953 *Other People's Money: A Study in the Social Psychology of Embezzlement.* Glencoe, Ill.: Free Press.

CRESSEY, DONALD R. 1961 Foreword. In Edwin H. Sutherland, *White Collar Crime.* New York: Holt.

FULLER, RICHARD C. 1942 Morals and the Criminal Law. *Journal of Criminal Law and Criminology* 32:624–630. → Now called the *Journal of Criminal Law, Criminology, and Police Science.*

GEIS, GILBERT 1962 Toward a Delineation of White Collar Offenses. *Sociological Inquiry* 32, no. 2:160–171. → The journal of the Alpha Kappa Delta National Sociology Honor Society.

GRYGIER, TADEUSZ; JONES, HOWARD; and SPENCER, JOHN C. (editors) 1965 *Criminology in Transition: Essays in Honour of Hermann Mannheim.* London: Tavistock. → See especially "White Collar Crime," by John C. Spencer.

HARTUNG, FRANK E. 1950 White-collar Offenses in the Wholesale Meat Industry in Detroit. *American Journal of Sociology* 56:25–34.

HARTUNG, FRANK E. 1953 White Collar Crime: Its Significance for Theory and Practice. *Federal Probation* 17, no. 2:31–36.

HERLING, JOHN 1962 *The Great Price Conspiracy: The Story of the Antitrust Violations in the Electrical Industry.* Washington: Luce.

HURWITZ, STEPHAN (1947) 1952 *Criminology.* London: Allen & Unwin. → First published in Danish.

JEFFERY, CLARENCE R. 1956 The Structure of American Criminological Thinking. *Journal of Criminal Law, Criminology, and Police Science* 46:658–672.

JONES, HOWARD (1956) 1962 *Crime and the Penal System: A Textbook of Criminology.* 2d ed. London: University Tutorial Press.

LANE, ROBERT E. 1953 Why Business Men Violate the Law. *Journal of Criminal Law, Criminology, and Police Science* 44:151–165.

MANNHEIM, HERMANN 1946 *Criminal Justice and Social Reconstruction.* London: Routledge.

MANNHEIM, HERMANN 1965 *Comparative Criminology: A Text Book.* 2 vols. London: Routledge.

MERTON, ROBERT K. (1938) 1957 Social Structure and Anomie. Pages 131–160 in Robert K. Merton, *Social Theory and Social Structure.* Rev. & enl. ed. Glencoe, Ill.: Free Press. → First published in the *American Sociological Review.*

MERTON, ROBERT K. 1957 Continuities in the Theory of Social Structure and Anomie. Pages 281–386 in Robert K. Merton, *Social Theory and Social Structure.* Glencoe, Ill.: Free Press.

MIDDENDORFF, WOLF 1959 *Soziologie des Verbrechens: Erscheinungen und Wandlungen des asozialen Verhaltens.* Düsseldorf (Germany): Diederich.

MORRIS, ALBERT 1934 *Criminology.* New York: Longmans.

NEWMAN, DONALD J. 1957 Public Attitudes Toward a Form of White Collar Crime. *Social Problems* 4:228–232.

NEWMAN, DONALD J. 1958 White-collar Crime. *Law and Contemporary Problems* 23:735–753.

QUINNEY, EARL R. 1963 Occupational Structure and Criminal Behavior: Prescription Violation by Retail Pharmacists. *Social Problems* 11:179–185.

QUINNEY, EARL R. 1964 The Study of White Collar Crime: Toward a Reorientation in Theory and Research. *Journal of Criminal Law, Criminology, and Police Science* 55:208–214.

RECKLESS, WALTER C. (1950) 1961 White-collar Crime and Black-marketing. Pages 207–229 in Walter C. Reckless, *The Crime Problem.* 3d ed. New York: Appleton.

ROSS, EDWARD A. 1907 *Sin and Society.* Boston: Houghton Mifflin.

Strafrechtspflege und Strafrechtsreform. 1961 Wiesbaden (Germany): Bundeskriminalamt. → See especially pages 81–118.

SUTHERLAND, EDWIN H. (1925–1951) 1956 *The Sutherland Papers.* Edited by Albert K. Cohen et al. Indiana University Publications, Social Science Series, No. 15. Bloomington: Indiana Univ. Press.

SUTHERLAND, EDWIN H. (1929) 1956 Crime and the Conflict Process. Pages 99–111 in Edwin H. Sutherland, *The Sutherland Papers.* Edited by Albert K. Cohen et al. Bloomington: Indiana Univ. Press.

SUTHERLAND, EDWIN H. 1940 White-collar Criminality. *American Sociological Review* 5:1–12.

SUTHERLAND, EDWIN H. 1941 Crime and Business. American Academy of Political and Social Science, *Annals* 217:112–118.

SUTHERLAND, EDWIN H. 1945 Is "White Collar Crime" Crime? *American Sociological Review* 10:132–139.

SUTHERLAND, EDWIN H. (1949) 1961 *White Collar Crime.* New York: Holt.

TAPPAN, PAUL W. 1947 Who Is the Criminal? *American Sociological Review* 12:96–102.

VOLD, GEORGE B. 1958 *Theoretical Criminology.* New York: Oxford Univ. Press.

ZIRPINS, WALTER; and TERSTEGEN, OTTO 1963 *Wirtschaftskriminalität: Erscheinungen und ihre Bekämpfung.* Lübeck (Germany): Schmidt-Römhild.

IV
HOMICIDE

Homicide is the killing of one human being by another and may be criminal or noncriminal. *Noncriminal* homicide is considered to be either excusable, that is, accidental or in self-defense, or justifiable, such as when a police officer shoots a felon or an executioner carries out a penalty of death. *Criminal* homicide, on the other hand, may be murder (first-degree or second-degree) or manslaughter (voluntary or involuntary). The legal distinctions are important because the sanction imposed on the offender in each case is a function of the adjudged degree of criminal homicide.

Among the different state and federal jurisdictions in the United States, there is considerable similarity in the meaning of these degrees of homicide, partially because the Pennsylvania homicide statute of 1794 was used as a model. *First-degree* murder generally means premeditated killing, "by lying in wait" or by poison, and with malice; all the states but Alaska, Hawaii, Iowa, Maine, Michigan, Minnesota, New York, North Dakota, Rhode Island, Vermont, West Virginia, and Wisconsin retain the death penalty as the maximum sanction. In addition, by statute any death that occurs during the commission of one or more types of felonies, which vary among the states, is a first-degree murder. Although some states include all felonies under this "felony–murder rule," most restrict it to rape, arson, burglary, robbery, and kidnaping.

Second-degree murder refers to a killing without premeditation but with malice and in the heat of passion. A maximum sentence of 20 years is common. *Voluntary* (or nonnegligent) manslaughter is a killing that occurs with the presence of intent to do bodily harm; and *involuntary* (or negligent) manslaughter is unintentional killing, usually during commission of some criminal act other than a felony or through negligence during an act that is otherwise noncriminal.

Legal codes of other countries reflect different juridical situations. *Mord* and *Totschlag* have meant murder and manslaughter, respectively, in the German code. *Meurtre* in the French code is not murder but manslaughter, and premeditated homicide is assassination (*assassinat*), which is a common designation in Latin countries. The Italian penal code distinguishes between *omicidio doloso* (willful killing, which may be aggravated by premeditation or other circumstances); *omicidio preterintenzionale* (the intent is not to kill, only to do harm, but death results); and *omicidio colposo* (no intent, but death occurs by negligence or the like).

Homicide statistics

Like other crimes, criminal homicides may be reported by the police as the number of offenses known or the number of persons arrested, by the courts as the number of persons convicted, or by the prisons as the number of persons committed. Unlike most other crimes, offenses may be counted by the number of persons victimized; if two persons are killed in a single criminal event, the public authorities will generally count two criminal homicides even though there is only one offender. Moreover, because there is a death, governments at almost all levels, using the international list of causes of death, will record the act under the title of homicide in the mortality statistics.

Valid international statistical comparisons are difficult to make because of differences in the legal definition of criminal homicide and the range of variations encompassed by the term. Hence, all such references must be examined with caution and understanding of these variations. The *Demographic Yearbook* of the United Nations reports homicide data for many countries; in 1960 the rates (per 100,000 population) ranged from 34.0 for Colombia to 0.2 for Ireland (United Nations 1961). Although the United States does not have a criminal-homicide rate as high as those of Mexico, Colombia, and several other nations, the contrast with England, which is one of the leading low-rate countries, is dramatic. For example, the city of Philadelphia (population two million) has about the same number of criminal homicides each year as all of England, Scotland, and Wales combined (population 45 million). Yet the rate per unit of population for Philadelphia is about the same as that for the United States as a whole.

For the United States, one of the major sources of criminal homicide data is the *Uniform Crime Reports,* published annually by the Department of Justice. These are compilations of information submitted voluntarily by police departments throughout the country, and they provide interesting breakdowns by city size and region. The New England states consistently have the lowest rates; the southeastern states, the highest rates. In 1960 the regional rates (per 100,000 population) varied from 1.5 for New England to 9.7 for the South Atlantic states (U.S. Federal Bureau of Investigation 1960). The criminal homicide rate in the United States has been declining since 1933, when the rate was 7.1. Although there were some slight upward changes in 1945 and 1946, the rate gradually fell to 5.1 in 1960; this rate still means that as many as 9,136 persons met death as a result of murder and nonnegligent manslaughter. A breakdown by murder and manslaughter or degrees is not available on a national level. In Standard Metropolitan Statistical Areas (county or counties having at least one core city of 50,000 or more inhabitants), the rate was 4.9 in 1960. All other cities had a lower rate of 3.8, and rural areas had a higher rate of 6.4 (U.S. Federal Bureau of Investigation 1960).

Patterns in criminal homicide

Research has shown that although criminal homicide is largely an unplanned act, uniformities and patterns exist nonetheless. There is, for example, a statistically significant association between criminal homicide and the *race* and *sex* of both victim and offender. Negroes and males involved in homicide far exceed their proportions in the general population of the United States, and rates for these two groups are many times greater than the rates for whites and females. In a study of criminal homicides in Philadelphia from 1948 to 1952, the rate per 100,000 by race and sex of offenders was in the following rank order of magnitude: Negro males (41.7), Negro females (9.3), white males (3.4), and white females (0.4) (Wolfgang 1958). The association between race and homicide is statistically more significant than that between sex and homicide. Thus, the proportion (but not the rate) of female offenders is much higher in England than in the United States; it has been suggested that in those countries with high homicide rates the proportion of female offenders is low, while in countries with low homicide rates the proportion of female offenders is high (Verkko 1951, pp. 55–56). In fact, it seems likely that there is a greater constancy to female homicide.

Variations by age. Among offenders the age group 20–24 predominates, while the highest rate for victims is in the age group 25–34. Victims are generally older than their offenders; the median age of the former, in the Philadelphia study, was

35.1 years and of the latter, 31.9 years. The race differential by age is particularly striking; the lowest five-year age-specific rates for Negro males and females are similar to, or higher than, the highest five-year age-specific rates for white males and females, respectively. Although males of both races more frequently commit criminal homicide during their twenties than during any other period of life, Negro males in their early sixties kill as frequently as do white males in their early twenties. Sociocultural and psychological evidence appears to offer the best explanations for these age–race differentials.

Variations by method. Methods of inflicting death vary, but about one-third of criminal homicides in the United States are shootings, one-third are stabbings, and the remainder are mostly beatings, with a small percentage involving miscellaneous methods, such as poisoning. There appears to be some cultural preference for particular weapons: males, if Negro, usually stab and are stabbed, if white, beat and are beaten; females generally stab their victims with a butcher knife, but are themselves often beaten to death.

Temporal variations. Although homicides tend to increase during the hot summer months, there appears to be no significant association by seasons or months of the year (Brearley 1932, pp. 189–190; Wolfgang 1958, pp. 98–100). But homicide is significantly associated with days of the week and hours of the day. The weekend in general and Saturday night in particular are related to homicide, as are the hours between 8 P.M. and 2 A.M. In one study (Wolfgang 1958, pp. 106–110) it was pointed out that about two-thirds of all homicides occur during the weekend, as compared to one-third from Monday to Friday.

The social significance of the weekend period as a time of increased social intercourse between persons of similar groups is even more strikingly revealed by data on the use of alcoholic beverages by both victims and offenders. Either the victim or offender or both had been drinking immediately prior to the slaying in nearly two-thirds of the 588 cases in the Philadelphia study (Wolfgang & Strohm 1956); other studies have shown slightly different proportions. Caution must be exercised in evaluating the presence of alcohol in homicides, because drinking—particularly on Saturdays, the day of highest incidence of homicide—is an integral part of the mores of the lowest socioeconomic group, whose members are most likely to be involved in this crime. The consumption of alcohol is involved in a significantly higher proportion of weekend homicides than of homicides occurring during the remainder of the week.

Victim and offender. Criminal homicide usually results from a domestic quarrel, jealousy, argument over money, robbery, or some more vaguely defined altercation. These are the "motives" that are commonly recorded by the police and that have been mentioned with only slightly varying terms and classifications in many studies over time and space (Gillin 1946; Hentig 1948). Most victim–offender relationships may be classified as "primary-group" relations, or those that include intimate, close, frequent contacts. Close friends and relatives alone usually account for more than half of the known relationships that involve male offenders, and much more than half of those that involve female offenders. Mate slayings are common and may constitute as much as one-fifth of the cases in some areas. Wives killed by their husbands make up nearly half of all female victims, but husbands slain by their wives rarely constitute more than 10 per cent of all male victims. When a woman commits homicide she is more likely than is a man to kill her mate; and when a man is killed by a woman, he is most likely to be killed by his wife. With rare exceptions, criminal homicide is an intragroup phenomenon; where there is racial heterogeneity, as in the United States, victims and offenders are of the same race in more than 90 per cent of the cases.

Previous criminal records. Many studies report that participants in homicide do not generally have previous criminal records (Brearley 1932, pp. 85–86; Gillin 1946, p. 551). They have also proved to have good disciplinary records in prison and are among the best risks for parole. However, the definition of "previous record" is often unclear in reported studies and sometimes refers to prior police or arrest record, other times to prior conviction or prior institutional commitment. In contrast to earlier research, the Philadelphia study revealed that nearly two-thirds of the offenders and almost half of the victims had a previous arrest record, and that more male victims than female offenders had such a record. Moreover, when an offender had a previous record, it was more likely to be one of offenses against the person than against property; and when he had a record of offenses against the person, he was more likely than not to have a record of having committed a serious assaultive offense.

Rates of clearance and conviction. Among serious offenses, homicide has the highest rate of "cleared by arrest," that is, the taking into custody by the police of one or more suspects held for prosecution. In the United States, among the seven offenses used by the *Uniform Crime Reports* to construct a crime index, the over-all "clearance rate" is usually less than 30 per cent, but that for homicide is consistently about 90 per cent. The intragroup, unplanned, primary-group character of the offense partially explains this high rate. However, the rate of conviction among persons charged with homicide is relatively low, often less than 50 per cent. The seriousness of the charge, the severity of the penalty, the greater use of a jury trial, the greater strain placed on the meaning of "reasonable doubt," and the greater probability that cases of homicide will be disposed of by ways other than a conviction all contribute to a low conviction rate. Those who commit suicide (usually directly after homicide) and those who plead insanity may together constitute as much as 8 to 10 per cent of offenders known to the police. Homicide–suicide is relatively uncommon in the United States, however, for studies show that only about 2 to 4 per cent of offenders kill themselves after killing others. In England homicide–suicide has reached very high proportions: as much as half the homicide cases in 1939 and, not uncommonly, as much as one-fourth to one-third each year (Grünhut 1952). About the same proportions appear to hold for both the United States and England in regard to homicide offenders declared to be insane.

Theories about criminal homicide

There are more studies using descriptive data and case reports of homicide than there are acceptable theories. Unfortunately, there is little interdisciplinary theory or research, and most "explanations" of homicide are limited to the biological, psychological, or social aspects of the problem.

The published anthropometrical and medical studies are few and contribute little to explanation. It is generally asserted (Buss 1961) that the causative chain of aggression is traced back to stimuli that are *external* to the organism and that, although there may be individual differences in the reactivity to external stimuli evoking aggression, these inner characteristics do not by themselves explain aggressive, particularly homicidal, behavior.

Psychometric studies. With few exceptions, psychometric studies of homicide have not emerged from testable hypotheses; furthermore, they have failed to distinguish different types of homicides and have neglected the use of control groups and adequate statistical analysis. Most studies on the differential psychology of homicide have been exploratory and tentative. The intelligence of homicide offenders in different countries has generally been noted to be lower than that of property offenders (Berg & Fox 1947; Lazzari et al. 1958).

However, the differences are not very discriminative, and the intragroup differences are greater than the differences between various criminal typologies.

Personality tests have been used to some descriptive advantage, indicating, for example, that with the Thematic Apperception Test, "heroes" of an antisocial type and themes of rebellion and impulsivity occur with high frequency (Paolella 1960). In a careful study of an aggressive-content scale applied to the TAT, Stone (1956) found that the scale was able to correctly identify murder cases. Most psychometric studies have used the Rorschach test; leading traits of homicide offenders as obtained from Rorschach protocols appear to be introversion, impulsivity, and explosive emotions. In summarizing several Rorschach studies of homicide, Endara (1960) stated that one of the most important findings is the fact that those who commit homicide produce about half the number of "human-content" responses as compared to other criminals, which indicates a lack of empathy and the presence of hostility and rebelliousness against authority. However, as Buss (1961) claimed in his review of studies assessing aggression through projective techniques and questionnaires, the tests appear to measure behavioral, not latent, aggression. Moreover, as Schuessler and Cressey (1950) earlier had stated in their criticism of studies on the personality characteristics of criminals, the studies generally apply a personality test without reference to any hypothesis about the relation of personality elements and criminal behavior.

Frustration–aggression theory. The frustration–aggression theory (Dollard et al. 1939) was readily accepted by many sociologists and psychologists as a useful theoretical framework, but few psychologists today would assert that the presence of frustration inevitably leads to aggression or specifically to homicide. In a review of the literature on the social psychology of aggression (McNeil 1959) it was concluded that scientific research on this theory is difficult because of the nearly inherent problems of circular logic. However, Leonard Berkowitz (1962), using the theory, has been doing some very interesting experimental research on violence in general, and Lewis Coser (1962) in a theoretical paper demonstrated that violence can be viewed from a sociological perspective.

Henry and Short (1954) and, to a more limited extent, Palmer (1960) have used elements of the frustration thesis in specific analyses of homicide. Henry and Short assume that in American society such lower status groups as Negroes, females, and the elderly are socially deprived of upward status

mobility opportunities; hence frustration will lead them to aggression. The hypothesis, they contend, is supported by data relative to Negroes but not to all females. Suicide has higher incidence among the aged than does homicide. They further argue that the degree of internal restraints is greater for members of the upper social classes, who commit suicide more frequently than members of the lower social classes. External restraints operate more among lower social classes, for whom other-oriented aggression is legitimized and manifested frequently as homicide. There is some theoretical connection in these terms to Reckless' containment theory (1950) of criminal and noncriminal behavior. Palmer's study (1960) defines frustration in such a general way that items like epilepsy, severe measles, head trauma, are taken as "frustrating" factors, with no concern for the aggressive personality deformations that they can cause by themselves, exclusive of any "frustration" hypothesis. Moreover, Palmer's study lacks the more systematic logic and analytical consistency of the study by Henry and Short and is methodologically inadequate in many ways.

In sum, frustration, it is generally agreed, is an inevitable and necessary part of the socialization process. The frustration–aggression thesis is challenging and should not be abandoned, but its present value for research purposes in homicide studies appears to be limited (Buss 1961; McNeil 1959).

Homicide and suicide. Much the same may be said of the concept of anomie, although Bohannan (1960) has provided a taxonomy of homicide in primitive societies that follows the "anomic," "egoistic," "altruistic" classification earlier proposed for suicide by Durkheim (1897). It should be noted that theory and research on suicide and homicide often have considered these two phenomena to be related—either as complementary phenomena, as similar manifestations of the same stream of aggression, or as the antithesis of one another (Henry & Short 1954; Verkko 1951; Hentig 1948, chapter 12; Wolfgang 1959).

The subculture of violence

A sociopsychological theory of a subculture of violence has been suggested as an explanation for homicides, most of which are crimes of passion or violent slayings that are not premeditated or psychotic manifestations (Wolfgang 1958, pp. 188–189; Wolfgang & Ferracuti 1962). The empirical data have shown that homicide rather consistently occurs with highest frequency among certain social groups and that in these groups there is close contact between offender and victim. The group members' characteristics and expected responses to certain stimuli, their perceptual differences in the evaluation of the stimuli, and the limited importance they place upon human life in the scale of values appear to be conducive to the use of violence as a principal way to solve everyday problems. If there exists among these certain social class–sex–age groups a subculture of violence, it is further suggested that the greater the degree of integration of the individual into this subculture, the higher the probability that his behavior will often be violent; or, that there is a direct relationship between rates of homicide and the degree of integration into the subculture of violence to which the individual belongs.

This thesis has been used to view the high rates of homicide among nonwhites in American society. As a group nonwhites have been segregated both physically and socially and thus constitute to some extent a "subcultural" area. This subgroup is characterized by poor housing, high population density, overcrowded home conditions, and often by a system of values that condones violence and physical aggression, all the way from child-rearing processes to adult interpersonal relationships, which sometimes end in criminal slayings. To a lesser degree, whites in the lower socioeconomic class also are part of a subculture of violence and participate in criminal homicide. By the dispersal of this culturally isolated group and the integration of its members into the general community of morality and values, there may occur some reduction of the violence that results in homicide.

Finally, this theory contains working hypotheses that can be tested by psychological tools. The fact that an individual belongs to a deviant subculture, which is reflected in commitment to a set of values that is characterized by the ready use of violence, will cause him to adopt a differential perception of the environment and of its stimuli. In this subculture of violence, the continuous challenges and daily frustrations that are faced and solved by the adaptive mechanisms of the individual have a greater chance of being perceived and reacted upon as menacing, aggressive stimuli, which call for immediate defense and counteraggression. Such a hypothesis lends itself to objective study through appropriate psychological methodologies.

A review of homicide studies tends to reaffirm the contention of many criminologists that meaningful and significant contributions to an understanding of the phenomenon can occur only through parsimonious, integrated theory that generates hypotheses to be tested by the collection of data from allied disciplines.

MARVIN E. WOLFGANG

[See also AGGRESSION, *article on* PSYCHOLOGICAL ASPECTS; FEUD; SUICIDE.]

BIBLIOGRAPHY

BENSING, ROBERT C.; and SCHROEDER, OLIVER JR. 1960 *Homicide in an Urban Community.* Springfield, Ill.: Thomas.

BERG, IRWIN A.; and FOX, VERNON 1947 Factors in Homicides Committed by 200 Males. *Journal of Social Psychology* 26:109–119.

BERKOWITZ, LEONARD 1962 *Aggression: A Social Psychological Analysis.* New York: McGraw-Hill.

BOHANNAN, PAUL (editor) 1960 *African Homicide and Suicide.* Princeton Univ. Press.

BREARLEY, HARRINGTON C. 1932 *Homicide in the United States.* Chapel Hill: Univ. of North Carolina Press.

BUSS, ARNOLD H. 1961 *The Psychology of Aggression.* New York: Wiley.

COSER, LEWIS A. 1962 Violence and the Social Structure. Unpublished manuscript. → Paper presented at the meeting of the American Association for the Advancement of Science.

DOLLARD, JOHN et al. 1939 *Frustration and Aggression.* Yale University Institute of Human Relations. New Haven: Yale Univ. Press.

DURKHEIM, ÉMILE (1897) 1951 *Suicide: A Study in Sociology.* Glencoe, Ill.: Free Press. → First published in French.

ENDARA, J. 1960 Degradazioni e devitalizzazioni nei criminali, rilevabili per mezzo del test di Rorschach. *Quaderni di criminologia clinica* 1:21–36.

GILLIN, JOHN L. 1946 *The Wisconsin Prisoner: Studies in Crimogenesis.* Madison: Univ. of Wisconsin Press.

GRÜNHUT, MAX 1952 Murder and the Death Penalty in England. American Academy of Political and Social Science, *Annals* 284:158–166.

HARLAN, H. 1950 Five Hundred Homicides. *Journal of Criminal Law and Criminology* 40:736–752.

HENRY, ANDREW F.; and SHORT, JAMES F. JR. 1954 *Suicide and Homicide: Some Economic, Sociological, and Psychological Aspects of Aggression.* Glencoe, Ill.: Free Press.

HENTIG, HANS VON 1948 *The Criminal and His Victim.* New Haven: Yale Univ. Press.

LAZZARI, RENATO; FERRACUTI, F.; and RIZZO, G. B. 1958 Applicazione della scala di intelligenza Wechsler-Bellevue, Forma 1 su un gruppo di detenuti italiani. Volume 8, pages 449–456 in Convegno Internazionale di Criminologia Clinica, *Atti.* Rome: The Congress.

McNEIL, ELTON B. 1959 Psychology and Aggression. *Journal of Conflict Resolution* 3:195–293.

MORELAND, ROY 1952 *The Law of Homicide.* Indianapolis, Ind.: Bobbs-Merrill.

PALMER, STUART 1960 *A Study of Murder.* New York: Crowell.

PAOLELLA, ALFREDO 1960 Resultats au T.A.T. chez des homicides. Pages 669–670 in International Congress on Applied Psychology, Thirteenth, Rome, 1958, *Proceedings.* London: International Association of Applied Psychology.

PORTERFIELD, AUSTIN L. 1949 Indices of Suicide and Homicide by States and Cities: Some Southern–Non-Southern Contrasts With Implications for Research. *American Sociological Review* 14:481–490.

RECKLESS, WALTER C. (1950) 1961 *The Crime Problem.* 3d ed. New York: Appleton.

ROBIN, GERALD D. 1963 Justifiable Homicide by Police Officers. *Journal of Criminal Law, Criminology, and Police Science* 54:225–231.

SCHUESSLER, KARL F.; and CRESSEY, DONALD R. 1950 Personality Characteristics of Criminals. *American Journal of Sociology* 55:476–484.

SELLIN, THORSTEN 1959 *The Death Penalty: A Report for the Model Penal Code Project of the American Law Institute.* Philadelphia: American Law Institute.

STONE, HAROLD 1956 The TAT Aggressive Content Scale. *Journal of Projective Techniques* 20:445–452.

SVALASTOGA, KAARE 1956 Homicide and Social Contact in Denmark. *American Journal of Sociology* 62:37–41.

UNITED NATIONS 1961 *Demographic Yearbook.* New York: United Nations. → See especially pages 398–471, Table 17, on "Deaths and Death Rates by Cause, and Percentage Medically Certified: 1955–1960."

U.S. FEDERAL BUREAU OF INVESTIGATION 1960 *Uniform Crime Reports for the United States.* Washington: Government Printing Office. → See especially page 33, Table 1, on "Index of Crime, United States, 1960" and pages 36–37, Table 2, on "Index of Crime by Geographic Divisions and States, 1959–1960."

VERKKO, VELI K. 1951 *Homicides and Suicides in Finland and Their Dependence on National Character.* Copenhagen: Gad.

WERTHAM, FREDERIC 1949 *The Show of Violence.* Garden City, N.Y.: Doubleday.

WOLFGANG, MARVIN E. 1958 *Patterns in Criminal Homicide.* Philadelphia: Univ. of Pennsylvania Press.

WOLFGANG, MARVIN E. 1959 Suicide by Means of Victim-precipitated Homicide. *Journal of Clinical and Experimental Psychopathology and Quarterly Review of Psychiatry and Neurology* 20:335–349.

WOLFGANG, MARVIN E.; and FERRACUTI, FRANCO 1962 Subculture of Violence: An Interpretive Analysis of Homicide. *International Annals of Criminology* [1962]: 52–60.

WOLFGANG, MARVIN E.; and STROHM, ROLF B. 1956 The Relationship Between Alcohol and Criminal Homicide. *Quarterly Journal of Studies on Alcohol* 17:411–425.

WOOD, ARTHUR L. 1961 Crime and Aggression in Changing Ceylon. American Philosophical Society, *Transactions* New Series 51, part 8.

CRIMINAL LAW

Criminal law, in the substantive sense, is a body of norms, formally promulgated through specified governmental organs, contravention of which warrants the imposition of punishment through a special proceeding maintained in the name of the people or the state. Criminal procedure is formalized official activity that authenticates the fact of commission of a crime and authorizes punitive treatment of the offender. These are at best core definitions; they do not comprehend all legal systems, all stages in the development of a legal system, or all elements within a given legal system.

Substantive criminal law

Substantive criminal law embodies both specific prohibitions and the general principles within which those prohibitions are construed. From the specific prohibitions one may glean the particular problems about which the society that produced them is concerned or at least has been concerned in the past. From the penalty provisions one can ascertain whether the community believes that punishments should be meted out in exact retribution for harm done or believes that flexible periods of segregation suit its needs best. From the statement of general principles in a penal code one can learn the factors or circumstances that the lawmakers view as significant in deciding whether punishment shall be mitigated or eliminated entirely in an individual case.

Moreover, how one views the context of a penal code depends on his view of law in general. Typically, legislators and judges appear to believe that legal norms are self-executing, so that the important thing is enactment of a law on any subject about which there is current concern. To make certain that citizens listen to it, the legislature usually attaches relatively heavy penalties to its enactments. The fact of enactment is usually equated with actual control.

At the other end of the philosophical spectrum, however, stand those who maintain that legal norms, including those embodied in the criminal law, are valid only to the degree that they express the generally accepted values in the community and thus are enforceable only for whatever period of time the community's attitudes toward these values remain basically unchanged. In support of this approach, one need only cite the mass of outmoded sections or statutes that are typically part of a state's legislation. The traditionalist will insist that statutes like these are still law, while the functionalist will say that they are not law at all because they are never invoked.

Furthermore, when law is viewed as a pragmatic effort to cope with contemporary problems, the primary problem is less that of identifying what must be controlled than that of ascertaining the most effective means of achieving control over that minority in the group which does not conform through group pressures or inculcation of group standards. Therefore, according to the functional approach, controls in the nature of license revocation, administrative penalties, and, in some instances, preventive detention are usually far more efficient means of control than are criminal penalties. There is implicit, if not explicit, in this view a repudiation of the classical deterrent theory, according to which the threat of future harshness administered through legal agencies outweighs the immediate sense of pleasure or benefit that the actor contemplates as a result of his act. In short, in a society-oriented framework of criminal law, one identifies first the interest or value that the group wishes to promote, second the most efficient means of effecting promotion of the value, and last the most effective methods of either rehabilitating the offender or segregating him indefinitely from the community.

Criminal codes are generally organized according to one of two patterns. One is an alphabetical listing of offenses. This has the advantage of any good index, that is, ease of access from a known starting point; but it places definitions in strange contexts. The other, and more common, arrangement involves a division into general principles and specific problems, under the established headings "The General Part," "The Special Part," and a further categorization of specific crimes according to the type of harm sought to be prevented. Each crime, therefore, appears in an identifiable context that facilitates its application to concrete problems. Though in form the general part precedes the special part, a layman often finds it less difficult to comprehend criminal law concepts if he first considers concrete problems; for that reason we will start with the special part.

The special part. One primary aim of the special part is to protect the existence of government itself and its ordinary operations. Laws evidencing this aim include those against treason, sedition, counterfeiting, theft and intentional destruction of government property, obstruction of public officials in the exercise of their office, bribery, and official oppression or coercion. In addition, prohibitions against perjury safeguard the investigative functions of government.

A second major category of crimes includes crimes against public order, health, and morals: unlawful assembly, riot, interference with lawful group meetings, vagrancy, public intoxication, solicitation to sexual acts, prostitution, and traffic in obscene materials. Public health considerations underlie prohibitions against prostitution and traffic in narcotics and, to a degree, support regulation of traffic in alcoholic beverages and tobacco products. The latter two commodities, however, have such revenue potential that it is usually only the traffic in which the state has no financial interest that is outlawed.

A third very important grouping comprises crimes against the person, including intentional homicide or murder, manslaughter, assaults of various kinds, and rape; the last often includes intercourse obtained through fraud or misrepresentation of identity, as well as sexual activity with certain classes of women who are viewed as incapable of consent, such as mentally ill persons or girls below a certain age.

A fourth category is that of offenses against property. It includes theft or larceny, burglary or other criminal intrusion into premises, arson, malicious destruction of property, robbery, extortion, and forgery. In some of these offenses (e.g., arson, burglary, and robbery) protection of life and limb looms as large as or larger than protection of property, while in others (e.g., theft) only property interests are protected.

A fifth category of offenses against family relationships is common to all codes: bigamy and polygamy, incest, extramarital and nonmarital intercourse, homosexuality, abortion, infanticide, and child abuse and nonsupport.

A final grouping comprises crimes relating to businesses and occupations, including public health controls. There are few occupations that are not subjected to controls through criminal law penalties, at least in form.

The general part. The general part provides the framework into which the particular offense must fit. In some applications it indicates when the court is competent to act or has jurisdiction. It states whether the legislature has intended citizens or aliens to be penalized for acts done outside the geographical limits of the state in which trial is held (the forum state). It decrees when the state has lost the power to prosecute because of certain limitations: that is, because the period of prescription or the statute of limitations has run, or because a prior prosecution by the same state, or perhaps by another state, requires application of either the double-jeopardy concept (in Anglo–American law) or the principle of *non bis in idem* or that of *non bis poena in idem* (in the civil law).

Retroactive punishment prohibited. The general part, in civil-law codes at least, also requires that all crimes be stated in law before penalties may be imposed (the principle of *nullum crimen, nulla poena sine lege*). Anglo–American statutes sometimes state the same principle, but equivalent control is usually achieved indirectly through the constitutional requirement that criminal statutes not be vague and indefinite, so that a man may be apprised of the legality of projected activity before he engages in it. The common-law tradition of judge-created criminal law, however, transgresses this principle. An expansion of criminal law by judicial decision is retroactive in the case in which the decision is given. What is forbidden to the legislature is thus assumed proper for a court. Perhaps all one can say in justification of this is that the extension of doctrine is usually so gradual that there may be very little hardship in most cases and that in fact the same process occurs in civil law, in which the broad terms of a statute are often expanded by judicial interpretation. The conceptual difference, however, is still appreciable. What is common to both systems is the difficulty of developing a meaningful application and adaptation of succinct formulations of law to the amorphous context of the society within which legal rules are to be utilized.

Elements of an offense. The general part defines the structure of a crime: it requires that there be an act, including an omission or failure to act—accompanied by a certain subjective state of mind (intent, or *mens rea*)—by a person, including legal entities like corporations or associations, that causes a specified harm or injury for which penalties may be imposed through prosecution. This provides a guide to interpretation of each crime in the special part.

Intent element of crimes. The sections on intent, or *mens rea*, embody the greatest verbal differences between the Anglo–American and the Roman-derived systems of law. Both systems punish acts done purposely to inflict any injury that the penal statute is designed to prevent. The act may warrant punishment if the actor knows there is a substantial likelihood that the harm or injury delineated in the statute will be inflicted if he acts; this principle is embodied in the *dolus eventualis* concept of the civil law and the "reckless disregard of known consequences" of Anglo–American law. But the systems diverge in the matter of whether (*a*) "negligence" can be the basis for exacting criminal penalties or (*b*) "strict" or "absolute" liability can be imposed for the doing of an act, despite the actor's unawareness of its dangerousness or undesirability. Anglo–American common law has long utilized negligence as a basis of criminal liability in manslaughter and certain other offenses against the person, but it has not used it in property crimes, even serious crimes like arson. Legislatures, however, have increasingly included negligence as a basis for imposing punishment for property crimes and offenses involving government activities. Moreover, "strict liability" is a common ingredient of crimes regulating the economy. An entrepreneur, for example, may be liable to criminal penalties if the commodity that he produces does not meet statutory requirements, though he may in good faith have believed that it does. In contrast, most civil-law commentators deny that strict liability is either possible under their law or compatible with criminal-law theory, penalizing as it does ignorance and not purpose.

Is the civil-law position preferable? As a matter of abstract criminal-law theory, the careless person is certainly not as "evil" as one who either intends

harm or is willing to ignore the almost certain consequences of his activity, that is, consequences of which he is fully aware. Criminal penalties are crude instruments to promote knowledge or caution. If, however, enforcement is stressed, strict liability may be necessary in some cases. In most serious offenses, purpose may be inferred from activity. For example, if a man stabs another, he usually does so with intent to kill or severely injure. But one who sells a commodity may not know that it is adulterated or mislabeled; common experience may not equate act with intent. To require the state to prove "intent" in the first instance may not significantly impair the enforceability of the statute, because the act usually purports intent. A similar requirement, however, may render the second statute totally unenforceable. If a standard of "strict liability" is imposed, by which knowledge of impropriety is rendered superfluous, prosecutions are easy; this position assumes that most persons in fact know what they are doing, and therefore only a few "innocent" criminals are numbered among the many "guilty."

Nevertheless, to give the "innocent" an opportunity to explain, should the legislature, as an alternative, make the doing of an act "prima-facie evidence" of the required intent, and permit the defendant to persuade the tribunal that he did not in fact have the *mens rea* (guilty mind) which merits imposition of criminal penalties? Certainly many American statutes embody this compromise between the ideals of pure legal theory and the realities of law enforcement.

Furthermore, many civil-law scholars in effect evade the issue by equating "penal law" with the "penal code," thus completely ignoring a broad array of penal legislation (outside the penal code) that imposes strict liability or a separate code of "economic offenses" that parallels Anglo–American strict liability legislation. Though comparison of the two systems, civil and common-law, is rendered difficult because Anglo–American law embodies the jury system and the complicated doctrines of evidence law, including presumptions, which it has engendered, and the civil law does not, there is still a decided similarity in penal economic legislation in legal systems the world over, whatever the theoretician may say.

Legal significance of mistake. The general part also lists special states of mind that affect criminal responsibility. One is ignorance or mistake, of either fact or law. Mistake of fact, which means nonknowledge of a factor or circumstance known to others, affects the mental element of the crime, not the objective elements. If the actor's error suggests lack of purpose to inflict harm, but he is punished anyway, he is punished for his ignorance only. But this can hardly be distinguished from negligence, which embodies a failure to know what the "reasonable man" would know. Therefore, if only "reasonable" mistakes of fact are taken into account as extenuating, negligence extends to all crimes. Civil-law codes usually recognize this by saying that any "honest," that is, nonperjured, claim of mistake is to be considered in its impact on the required state of mind, unless the crime is based on negligence, in which case only a "reasonable" mistake excuses. Anglo–American law is somewhat more ambivalent: some judicial interpretations require that all mistakes be "reasonable," but others recognize "good faith" claims of mistake.

Mistake of law involves either ignorance of the existence of the statute under which the prosecution is maintained or ignorance of a collateral doctrine of law affecting, for example, property, contracts, or marriage. Few systems permit an absolute defense based on ignorance of the existence of the criminal law under which the defendant is prosecuted, but civil-law codes commonly authorize mitigation of penalty. Collateral mistake of law that negates a required specific intent warrants acquittal, if not under a general provision to that effect, then because the trier cannot find that intent to have existed as a fact.

Mental conditions negating criminality. The other most important states of mind affecting criminal responsibility are unconsciousness, insanity, and intoxication. Civil-law codes usually state only that if a person is either unconscious or irresponsible because of insanity, mental illness, mental deficiency, and the like when he commits a criminal act, he is not to be punished. Expert data are received as a matter of course, but courts do not generally explain in detail what underlies their use of code labels of unconsciousness, mental illness, or mental deficiency.

Anglo–American law, however, has had to formulate legal tests for insanity, primarily because the jury must be formally instructed as to what "insanity" is. That term, it must be noted, is a legal, not a medical, term. The prevailing test is the so-called M'Naghten Rules, under which a man is deemed insane if he does not know that he is performing an act or, assuming he has that awareness, if he does not know that the act is "wrong," which traditionally means legally rather than morally wrong. The original formulation of this test also included a third alternative—"insane delusion"—according to which a defendant is excused if the facts as he deludedly believed them to be would have

justified an acquittal; it might be called an "insane mistake of fact" test. This test lingers on in a handful of American states. Many states have added the alternative of "irresistible impulse": that is, if the defendant was uncontrollably impelled by his mental condition to do the act with which he is charged, he is to be viewed as nonaccountable.

These tests have been violently criticized by behavioral scientists as scientifically outmoded and as embodying value judgments that a psychiatrist or psychologist cannot be called upon to make in his professional capacity. It is indisputable that expert testimony is distorted, in the typical case, because of insistence that the expert testify in conclusory terms. The emphasis on "right–wrong" and "knowledge–nonknowledge" has caused medical opinion and lay opinion to be used indiscriminately, which in turn has prevented the development of a scientifically sound concept of legal insanity. Accordingly, several new tests have been formulated, though as yet they have not been widely adopted. They stress mental defect or disorder, beyond the actor's control, that causes the act on which the criminal charge is based. All demand qualified expert data and exclude lay opinion.

The value of these modern tests does not rest on the legal terms in which they are couched but on the freedom which they offer the expert to describe the defendant in scientific terms. A change in terminology is useful chiefly because it requires judges and lawyers to re-evaluate what they do. Statutory changes may, therefore, be in order in civil-law countries; however, there the problem in regard to the concept of legal insanity arises from legislative understatement rather than from outmoded overstatement, as in common-law countries.

Intoxication and criminal responsibility. Intoxication and the broader problem that it presents, namely addiction, are ambivalently dealt with in both civil-law and common-law systems. Whenever the defendant is identified only circumstantially, evidence of intoxication is always relevant to prove that he was not physically able to commit the crime with which he is charged. However, intoxication is relevant as a matter of formal law only when the defendant is admittedly the actor and the issue is that of his intent. Logically, if the defendant is unable because of intoxication or addiction to entertain the required state of mind, he ought not to be punished. His addiction as such would be more appropriately controlled through protective custodial treatment than through punishment. But most codes view intoxication and addiction as, if anything, aggravating factors; and thus they either require increased punishment for intoxicated persons or demand that the judge exclude from consideration the actual impact of intoxication on the defendant's state of mind and decide the case on the assumption that the defendant was in full control of his acts.

Defenses to criminality. The general part also takes account of external circumstances that affect criminality, including duress, consent of the victim, defense of self or others, defense or protection of property, the needs of law enforcement, and other extraordinary circumstances, such as famine or extreme peril to life, that can be avoided only by acts against the life or property of others. These concepts most commonly apply to homicide and assault, though some defenses based on necessity affect property crimes. In effect, the actor's motive for forming an otherwise prohibited intent or purpose serves to eliminate or mitigate the criminal punishment provided for the act and intent in the special part. Common-law courts recognize only certain stereotypes of necessity, like self-defense. Codes, however, may include a more general clause on necessity based on a "choice of evils," so that the harshness of the standards in the special part may be tempered in unusual cases.

Punishable attempts. Yet another function of the general part is to identify preparatory conduct which, though it does not eventuate in the ultimate harm prohibited by one or more criminal provisions, comes close enough to warrant punishment. This is called "attempt." Though efforts are made to develop legal standards to control its application, the concept of attempt is simply a device for extending the coverage of a criminal statute beyond its literal scope. It may be applied if the actor has done enough to evidence his criminal purpose, if his attitude and purpose suggest that he is likely to try again in the future with perhaps greater success, and if the harm which he sought to inflict is of appreciable gravity. The decision is basically one for the individual case. Conspiracy is also penalized as one form of preparatory activity, that of agreement to commit a crime.

Punishment of accomplices. The general part authorizes imposition of punishment on others than the actor himself, by imposing vicarious responsibility for the acts of the principal on those who have induced him to act, conspired with him in the conception of the act, or aided or encouraged him in its commission. Some codes reach backward into a criminal transaction to punish unsuccessful solicitation to commit a crime, and some reach forward in time to punish those who, as accessories after the fact, harbor or aid the criminal

actor after the specific crime has been committed. The latter, however, is a special crime of obstructing the administration of criminal justice.

Disposition of offenders. Last, the general part grades offenses according to seriousness and creates standards by which sentence is determined in the individual case. Some civil-law codes include in this portion of the general part the so-called protective or security measures, by which a defendant is channeled into special institutions for mentally ill persons, alcoholics, or youthful offenders. Recidivism may also call for special forms of incarceration as well as increased maximum and minimum terms of imprisonment.

Criminal procedure

It is difficult to equate and compare civil-law and common-law proceedings on the basis of the legal terms that each embodies. But there are certain stages and functions common to both, even though the details of procedure differ.

Investigation. The first function of criminal procedure is investigation. Civil-law codes of criminal procedure delineate fairly precisely the relative roles of police and prosecutor in investigations of crime. The primary responsibility to investigate is with the police, but the public prosecutor has power to supervise and intervene. The police have only a limited power to arrest; advance judicial authorization is required unless the offender is caught in the act or unless there are special circumstances that make it difficult or impossible to obtain judicial permission to arrest beforehand. Special statutes or regulations may permit "preventive detention," but they are usually comprehended as one aspect of administrative law.

Civil-law codes strictly limit the period for which an arrested person can be held in police custody. A judicial order of detention is required after a few hours; this order is valid for only a brief period while a formal charge is prepared. After the filing of the formal charge, a court through a more formal proceeding may authorize continued detention pending trial. Bail or some other form of provisional release may be proper after the suspect or accused has been detained on judicial authority, but this tends to be limited to the period after formal accusation and then is at the discretion of the court.

In civil-law codes judicial control extends not only to arrest and detention but also to acquisition of evidence. Police and public prosecutors have limited power to search for and seize contraband and evidentiary material, but for the most part they must seek a judicial warrant before entering buildings or seizing matter in the hands of third parties. In some systems a special investigating judge takes the initiative of ferreting out evidence, while in other systems it is incumbent on the public prosecutor or command police officers to apply for authorization to search, specifying what is sought. Acquisition of evidence includes formal questioning of witnesses, whose statements under oath are preserved for later use. In some civil-law codes the defense may also ask that evidence be preserved for its benefit, but in others the defense may only inspect whatever the state has taken the initiative in gathering.

The Anglo–American system places much greater responsibility on the police and makes relatively little use of warrants. Warrants are available for arrest, search, or seizure, but there is no duty to apply for them. Police are authorized to arrest without warrant if they "reasonably believe" that a felony has been committed by the arrestee or if any offense is committed in their presence. If a valid arrest has been made, the arrested person and his immediate surroundings may be searched and evidentiary matter seized. If an arrest is made, the police must produce the arrestee before a magistrate within a short period of time; delays for the purpose of interrogation are usually viewed as contravening this requirement. The magistrate may then commit the arrested person, pending a preliminary hearing to determine if there is some basis for the charge levied against him. In most American jurisdictions bail must be set in all but very serious cases. Anglo–American law has done very little to develop a systematic means of impounding evidentiary material under judicial supervision. The preliminary examination or grand jury proceeding may be used for this purpose by the state, but it is not often useful to the defense. Discovery, by which one or both parties are required by court order to make evidence in its hands accessible to the opponent before trial, is in a rudimentary stage but may in time serve to permit acquisition and preservation of evidence for later trial use by either the state or the defense.

Preparation of the formal charge. The second function of criminal procedure is preparation of the formal charge. Here, too, one must identify where discretion to charge lies, for not all arrested or suspected persons are brought to trial. In some systems the police have sole control, and in all systems they in fact dispose of many cases without trial or other formal proceedings. Private citizens control some prosecutions; if, for example, prompt complaint of rape must be made by the victim, or if only the offended spouse can complain

of adultery, nonaccusation by the citizen for whose benefit the criminal statute exists bars all proceedings. In most countries the public prosecutor has discretion whether to press charges, though in some instances he may have to obtain judicial concurrence. In those parts of the Anglo–American world where the grand jury survives, that body exercises substantial discretion to refuse prosecution. In some civil-law countries the police and public prosecutor are required to refer the material they have gathered, together with the draft of a pleading, to a judge or court, which then determines whether the trial shall occur. In the last-mentioned system, a person moves from "suspect" status to "accused" status to "defendant" status; where discretion is vested in police or public prosecutor, only "suspect" and "defendant" statuses are formally recognized.

If discretion is acknowledged in a legal system, controls must be placed on its exercise. Thus, though a private citizen may determine that certain cases shall not be pursued, the public prosecutor has discretion over those prosecutions which are desired by private citizens, some of which will not be carried through. A grand jury indictment can be dismissed on motion of the district attorney; on the other hand, a refusal to indict can be circumvented by presenting the same matter to another, presumably more tractable, grand jury. Sometimes a judge may order the institution of prosecution despite the prosecutor's refusal to do so, or an advisory body of citizens may be called upon to review that refusal. Whatever the primary allocation of discretion, however, at some point the judiciary has the final word.

The code of criminal procedure also specifies the contents of the pleading. Legal rules differ primarily as to how much detailed information the defendant requires to prepare an adequate defense and as to the extent to which the pleading can be amended during the proceedings. Civil-law pleadings are usually more detailed than common-law pleadings but may also be amended and changed with greater freedom; this comparison suggests a balance of function at about the same point in each system. The defendant is not usually required to submit a formal answering pleading, but this may be modified in the case of certain special defenses, such as insanity or alibi.

Trial procedure. The third major phase of criminal procedure is trial. In each system the place of trial must be fixed. Civil-law codes permit one case to be brought simultaneously in more than one court, based on place of the crime, residence of the defendant, or place of arrest; one court is then selected on the basis of convenience. Common-law crimes are to be prosecuted where they are committed; in theory this means one court only, but in practice it permits some choice of court. The civil law provides for further transfer of a case for reasons both of convenience and of bias, while the common law usually acknowledges only the latter, and then often only if the defendant asserts it. However, the differences between the systems are less in application than they are in theory. Another factor involved in properly assigning a case for trial is the gravity of the offense: the court that is selected must, of course, be authorized by law to adjudicate criminal cases of the gravity of the offense charged.

Lay participation in criminal trials. The civil law and the common law differ in outward form in the degree of lay participation in trials. In some legal systems, particularly after a revolution, all judges are laymen; at times, indeed, the community as a group both accuses and tries, as it is reputed to have done in more primitive eras. In most modern systems, however, the judiciary is a professionally trained career group, and the issue is one of whether judges are to be joined by laymen. Some countries place sole responsibility on the judge or on a multiple-judge, or collegiate, court. Others utilize lay assessors who sit with judges over a period of weeks or months while many cases are tried. At times laymen join judges to try one case only, as voting members of the tribunal.

The Anglo–American system relies on a lay jury selected by lot to hear the particular case and to make a "final" determination of guilt. The judge supervises the conduct of the trial and instructs the jury about relevant law, while the jury determines the facts and whether, under the judge's instructions, the defendant is guilty. However, the jury is not necessarily as independent as common-law tradition would have it. In minor cases there is no jury. Moreover, even if a jury sits and convicts, the trial judge may repudiate its verdict and either discharge the defendant or order retrial. Only an acquittal is final. This, however, is a safeguard to the citizen which should not be underestimated, for acquittal and the protection of the double-jeopardy concept which it produces have been very strong protections against overzealous public officials who have prosecuted minorities for their beliefs.

Procedural guarantees to the defendant. The outward trappings of the trial are also important. There has been a strong reaction in most countries against secret proceedings, so that most codes require public trial. Some civil-law statutes permit *in absentia* proceedings, though it is usually possible for the defendant to procure a rehearing that he can attend. *In absentia* proceedings are prohibited in common-law countries, except perhaps for minor traffic offenses. Moreover, the trier must be impartial. Therefore, most codes permit challenge of prejudiced judges, assessors, or jurors. It is important, at least in theory, that a defendant be represented by counsel. Certainly common-law lawyers are vocal in urging this as a primary factor in assuring fairness of trial. Whether representation by counsel is important, however, cannot be determined solely by whether a lawyer attends and participates. He may not be trained as an advocate and may view himself only as a special attaché to the court. The primary responsibility for interrogating witnesses and evaluating data may rest with the court or with the court and public prosecutor, so that defense counsel has little to do. Sometimes the controlling stage of the proceeding is at an earlier time, when evidentiary material is assembled and a decision reached whether to carry forward the prosecution. If defense counsel does not participate at this earlier stage, then his activity in the later "formal" trial has little impact on the formal adjudication of guilt by the court. The heavy reliance by the court on the data presented to it by the prosecutor at the time he institutes prosecution means that the decision to prosecute in effect guarantees a judgment of guilt. At best defense counsel may be able to call extenuating circumstances to the attention of the court. In this field, also, function and not form is important.

The two major systems differ in regard to the material received to support the final adjudication and in regard to the responsibility to marshal and present it. The common law embodies elaborate rules of evidence, by which some data can be utilized only for limited purposes and other matter cannot be used at all. The responsibility to gather and present evidence is on the person who wishes to make affirmative use of it. Evidence must be presented either through witness testimony given in open court or through documents, the authenticity and contents of which are vouched for by witnesses testifying under oath. The opponent must be given an opportunity to cross-examine the proponent's witnesses; the defendant's right of confrontation ensures that this be done by him or in his presence in the case of prosecution witnesses. The judge is a neutral arbiter, who intervenes in the questioning only to clarify the testimony.

In contrast, in civil-law systems the judge plays the predominant role in the trial; he weighs evidence solely in terms of its probative value, not its admissibility. However, whether the systems are as dissimilar in function as in form is doubtful. Strict as common-law rules of evidence may appear, most evidence can in fact be submitted either under one of the many exceptions to the rule forbidding hearsay or as "lay" opinion evidence. Though the judge may caution the jury to consider evidence for a limited purpose only, there is neither guarantee nor probability that jurors will so limit their use of it. Moreover, strict invocation of rules of evidence characterizes only the portion of the trial in which the jury participates. Strict rules of evidence do not apply to pretrial and procedural matters. No limitations apply to material bearing on sentence; the judge relies principally on hearsay documents. In the civil-law tradition, the trial aims primarily at final approval of the material gathered through earlier proceedings and at pronouncement of sentence. Thus, rules of evidence play no more useful a role in civil-law trial procedure than they do in American pretrial and postconviction proceedings; the opportunity to contest and offer counterdata is what matters most. Lay participation is also a less critical part of the system; and perhaps the distrust of the jury is less prevalent than it has been in the common-law system, so that little purpose is served by creating rules of evidence. Here, too, the differences are probably greater in form than in application.

When fact-finding ends—which in some systems, such as that of the Japanese, may be after a series of intermittent hearings—the case proceeds to judgment. In all modern systems the burden is heavily on the state to establish guilt. In the common-law tradition the jury is told that it must be persuaded of the defendant's guilt "beyond a reasonable doubt," while the classical statement in the civil law is that "all doubts are resolved in favor of the accused" (*in dubio pro reo*). Neither term is capable of precise definition, but both are similar in application, in that a man acquitted under one system would very probably have been acquitted under the other.

The form of the judgment differs in the two traditions. The common-law judgment records the bare conclusion of guilt or innocence and the sentence; no explanations of any kind are appended by either jury or judge. The civil-law judgment, in contrast, contains a fairly elaborate recital of the facts that suggest guilt, the statutory provisions that have been invoked, and the factors that have led the court to impose the particular sentence. This difference in the form of the judgment in turn indicates a functional difference. In the civil law

there is no division of the proceedings into guilt-ascertainment and sentence-assessment; both are done simultaneously and embodied in the same judicial document. In the common-law tradition the jury ascertains guilt, and the judge then assesses sentence.

Appeal. The final major phase of judicial proceedings is appeal, including extraordinary remedies after the time for ordinary appeal has elapsed. Appeals may be designed to relieve the defendant or the state from prejudicial error in earlier proceedings, to ensure procedural regularity by dictating compliance with law on the part of lower courts, or to perform a didactic function of instructing the population concerning their rights and duties under law. Anglo–American law places formal emphasis only on the first, and then solely for the defendant's benefit. Civil-law appeals permit one review for relief against hardship, but review beyond that point promotes only regularity and purity in legal processes themselves. Both systems formally disclaim any purely didactic purpose, but in practice many American and Japanese opinions are judicial essays intended for public edification.

After judicial activity is exhausted, there may still be administrative relief against court-imposed penalties, in the form of pardon, amnesty, or parole. It is usually through these devices that society adapts its simple but sweeping rules of law to the requirements of common sense and justice in the individual case, and works a meaningful integration between criminal law and other relevant areas of law.

Criminal law and welfare law

Traditional criminal law and procedure presuppose a rational actor who exercises considerable free will. The legal order encourages acceptable choices of conduct; it contemplates that the criminal will cooperate in his own rehabilitation. If, however, the actor is totally or substantially incapable of cooperation, criminal-law processes falter and must be either adjusted or replaced. Three problems—mental disorder, addiction, and immaturity—account for much of the current difficulty in administering traditional criminal-law machinery.

Criminal law and mental illness. Mental disorder manifests itself in many ways, some of which concern only a diagnostician but others of which affect the peace and order of the community. When a mentally ill person injures other people or their property, disturbs the peace, offends community sensibilities, or acts so as to imperil himself, official activity almost certainly results. That activity becomes stereotyped, and new legal doctrines develop. Most systems of law recognize voluntary hospitalization as legal; in others the family acknowledges a responsibility to control its own mentally ill members. Some mentally ill persons, however, must be coerced into hospitalization. All legal systems, therefore, recognize some form of civil commitment, either judicial or administrative, resulting in hospitalization of the afflicted person until he may safely be released.

Nevertheless, a number of mentally ill persons will have been apprehended as "criminals" before their mental abnormality is recognized. Since their acts have already been tentatively characterized as "crimes," ordinary civil commitment proceedings are considered inappropriate, and special procedures based on their mental condition are developed within criminal procedure itself. The defendant may be characterized as "incompetent to stand trial" because of his inability to comprehend the nature of the proceedings against him and to participate in his own defense, and thus he may be confined indefinitely in a mental institution for the "criminally insane" until an administrator certifies him "competent" and returns him for trial on the original charge. Or he may be denominated a "criminal sexual psychopath" or a "defective delinquent" under a special statute and confined to an institution, again usually a hospital for the "criminally insane." If he is tried, he may be found "not guilty by reason of insanity" or, in some systems, "guilty but insane," in which case, too, under a special statute he is committed to the same facility for the "criminally insane" that receives men in the preceding two categories. In yet other cases, the defendant may be found "sane" in the legal sense and sent to prison. However, from the prison he may be administratively transferred to the same institution for the "criminally insane" to which he would have gone if he had been acquitted by reason of insanity, though he remains there only for the maximum term of his sentence.

Mental abnormality ought always to be ascertained through a civil commitment proceeding, which should supplant criminal proceedings if the defendant's otherwise criminal act is symptomatic of a pattern of activity that is caused by mental illness or abnormality. If that activity endangers public safety or order, the actor should be committed to a treatment-oriented hospital or, if no treatment is possible, to some form of custodial institution. A person too disoriented to stand trial manifests a mental condition that probably accounted for his "criminal" activity. Only the accident of arrest may explain why no civil commitment proceedings have been undertaken. To permit criminal charges to sleep while the defendant is hospitalized as "incompetent to stand trial" makes a fair trial at a later time almost impossible; prosecutorial or judicial discretion is probably not a sufficient safeguard to him. Moreover, a mentally abnormal person in a prison disrupts prison administration. Much wasted activity would be avoided if final disposition were made soon after the mentally abnormal actor has been first placed under restraint.

Reform, however, is difficult. For one thing, it is less expensive to maintain a "hospital" prison than a treatment hospital. For another, lawyers, judges, and private citizens fear any system in which psychiatrists, psychologists, and social workers make the critical diagnosis; thus, instead of supporting modifications in traditional procedure or the development of new but fair procedures, they oppose change altogether. Moreover, a treatment-oriented hospital system requires open institutions and outpatient treatment. Most citizens are apprehensive enough about "lunatics" who have been civilly committed; to contemplate that "criminal" mentally ill persons may be placed in ordinary hospitals with "civil" patients and released on outpatient status is almost unbearable.

Nonetheless, the older traditions are beginning to crumble; in many jurisdictions efforts are under way to develop a single state hospital system and early, final coordination of criminal prosecutions and civil commitments. Success, however, will require major capital expenditures, for to relabel a "prison" a "hospital" makes no major difference so far as the average inmate is concerned.

Criminal law and addiction. Another dilemma for traditional law is drug or alcohol addiction. Indeed, since addiction is increasingly viewed as symptomatic of serious mental disturbance, it may be that this is ultimately a specific instance of the broader problem of mental illness. But other explanations of addiction stress socioeconomic factors, so that addiction may have to be viewed as an independent problem in itself. Criminal law, particularly in the United States, has considered narcotics addiction a result of free choice and has relied on increasingly heavy penalties to deter citizens from using narcotics, particularly from trafficking in them. The legal significance of intoxication has already been touched on. But repression achieves only the illusion of control. Narcotics users and alcoholics constitute a fairly constant percentage of the populace, whatever the legal prohibitions may be. Prohibition, however, forces the price of narcotics upward, so that the addict must commit crime to obtain money to buy narcotics through illicit channels. Therefore, the system developed in England and western Europe, by which addicts receive drugs under medical supervision, makes pragmatic sense, if only because crimes committed by addicts for gain tend to diminish under that system. If addiction is a symptom and not a separate condition, then the causes of addiction must be isolated before addiction itself can be controlled. Exclusive reliance on the criminal law not only produces hardship in particular cases, except as unfettered police and prosecutor discretion may invisibly ameliorate it, but also fosters in the community an illusion of effective control that militates against developing more efficient means of control. Here, also, there are some signs of change, but the successful integration of criminal-law processes with administrative public health and economic measures lies further in the future than integration of criminal-law and mental-health procedures.

Criminal law and immaturity. There was a time when immaturity had only limited significance in traditional criminal law: one who had not reached a certain chronological age at the time he acted was either not within the coverage of the criminal law or was presumed incapable of forming the requisite criminal intent. But the age at which full criminal responsibility was imputed was so low (usually 13 to 15 years) that many adolescents were processed through the courts and incarcerated or executed with adult criminals. The reaction to this was the creation of special juvenile courts and treatment facilities.

The new system, however, has proved at best a mixed blessing. Special detention facilities are often nothing more than juvenile prisons, in some instances with fewer educational or vocational facilities than adult prisons. In the enthusiasm for eliminating the grosser aspects of a criminal trial, important safeguards have also been discarded. Minors are often given no notice of the allegations against them, are at times not permitted to be present in court or represented by counsel, are usually not given even a summary of the data on which the court's findings are based, and are often consigned to a custodial institution for a longer period than an adult would be for the same act. In general, there is also a failure to differentiate between juvenile neglect cases, in which some informality is perhaps in order, and juvenile delinquency cases, in which specific acts form the basis for an adjudication against the minor. Even in neglect proceedings the procedural rights of the parents or custodian of the child are minimized and the child disposed of on the basis of anonymous reports or the recommendations of welfare agencies whose representatives either do not appear or are not required to substantiate their reports.

A countertrend has appeared, however; there is increasing judicial scrutiny of juvenile court proceedings. This has brought about insistence on advance notice of the allegations against the parent or juvenile, participation by attorneys in the adjudicative process, and appellate review of findings, which themselves must be specific and supported by relevant data. Nevertheless, even this measure of reform is ineffective if the community does not provide adequate treatment facilities. The past history of juvenile court practice and standards forecasts the direction that new efforts to dispose of the mentally ill and the addicted may take, as well as the resources that must be expended and the procedural standards that must be created if unfairness and hardship are to be avoided.

B. J. George, Jr.

[*See also* Crime; Law; Legal systems; Penology; Punishment.]

BIBLIOGRAPHY

In 1966 the American Law Institute in Philadelphia was known to be preparing a model penal code, publication of which was expected in 1967.

American Bar Foundation 1961 *The Mentally Disabled and the Law: The Report on the Rights of the Mentally Ill.* Edited by Frank T. Lindman and Donald M. McIntyre. Univ. of Chicago Press.

The American Series of Foreign Penal Codes. Edited by Gerhard O. W. Mueller. 1961— Hackensack, N.J.: Rothman; London: Sweet & Maxwell. → Each volume contains an introductory essay by an authority on the law of the individual country concerned.

Andenaes, Johannes (1956) 1965 *The General Part of the Criminal Law of Norway.* Hackensack, N.J.: Rothman; London: Sweet & Maxwell. → First published as *Alminnelig strafferett.*

Archbold, John F. (1853) 1962 *Criminal Pleading, Evidence and Practice.* 35th ed. London: Sweet & Maxwell.

Berman, Harold J. 1966 *Soviet Criminal Law and Procedure; the RSFSR Codes: Introduction and Analysis.* Harvard University, Russian Research Center, Study No. 50. Cambridge, Mass.: Harvard Univ. Press.

Crime and the American Penal System. 1962 American Academy of Political and Social Science, Annals 339.

Dando, Shigemitsu 1965 *Japanese Law of Criminal Procedure.* Hackensack, N.J.: Rothman.

Eldridge, William B. 1962 *Narcotics and the Law: A Critique of the American Experiment in Narcotic Drug Control.* New York: American Bar Foundation.

Feldbrugge, F. J. 1964 *Soviet Criminal Law: The General Part.* Volume 9: Law in Eastern Europe. Leiden (Netherlands): Sythoff.

Hall, Jerome (1935) 1952 *Theft, Law and Society.* 2d ed. Indianapolis, Ind.: Bobbs-Merrill.

HALL, JEROME (1947) 1960 *General Principles of Criminal Law.* 2d ed. Indianapolis, Ind.: Bobbs-Merrill.

INTERNATIONAL CONFERENCE ON CRIMINAL LAW ADMINISTRATION, CHICAGO, *1960* 1962 *Police Power and Individual Freedom: The Quest for Balance.* Chicago: Aldine.

MORELAND, ROY 1952 *The Law of Homicide.* Indianapolis, Ind.: Bobbs-Merrill.

MORELAND, ROY 1959 *Modern Criminal Procedure.* Indianapolis, Ind.: Bobbs-Merrill.

MORRIS, NORVAL; and HOWARD, COLIN 1964 *Studies in Criminal Law.* Oxford: Clarendon.

MUELLER, GERHARD O. W. (editor) 1961 *Essays in Criminal Science.* Hackensack, N.J.: Rothman; London: Sweet & Maxwell.

PERKINS, ROLLIN M. 1957 *Criminal Law.* Brooklyn, N.Y.: Foundation Press.

WILLIAMS, GLANVILLE (1953) 1961 *Criminal Law: The General Part.* 2d ed. London: Stevens.

CRIMINOLOGY

It is proper to use the term *criminology* to designate either (*a*) a body of scientific knowledge about crime, including its causes and prevention, the handling of offenders, and the pursuit of such knowledge regardless of where it stems from; or (*b*) a didactic discipline, which assembles, analyzes, and integrates the findings of criminological research in all scientific disciplines and indicates the best way in which they can be applied in practice to secure socially desirable ends.

Since Raffaele Garofalo (1885) invented the term, no agreement has been reached on the definition of criminology. Traditionally, it has concerned itself with the study of violations of the criminal law and of those who commit them, but opinions vary on the nature and scope of such study. Some hold that it should concentrate on the scientific investigation of the causes of crime and form a subclass of a more general catch-all discipline called "criminal science." Criminal science would be composed of many specialized branches of study, some concerned with etiology—criminology, further subdivided into biological, psychological, and sociological criminology—and others with police science, substantive and procedural legal problems, and penology. By contrast, there are those who would regard all these branches as parts of criminology, a view reflected in American textbooks in particular, which consequently employ the term merely as a pedagogical device. This custom is opposed by those who see in criminology an empirical and naturalistic science, but even this more restrictive view raises problems. This is because the scientific study of offenses, offenders, and the whole complex of penal and law-enforcing institutions is carried on by researchers in a variety of scientific fields, each having its own theories, hypotheses, and techniques of investigation, which are often poorly understood, misunderstood, or rejected by researchers in other fields—either in principle or because of faulty interdisciplinary communication arising from increasing specialization in research activity. One cannot, therefore, speak of a science of criminology in the narrow sense of a discipline that possesses universally accepted theoretical concepts.

The search for causes

It is in the search for an understanding of why people commit crime that most research has occurred. The history of such inquiries can be said to have begun with the nineteenth century, which witnessed the development of the psychological and social sciences. Previously, indeed going back to antiquity, the problem of criminal conduct occupied the minds of natural philosophers and protoscientists, and various theories were advanced to explain it. Observers of the social scene also speculated on the causes of criminality long before sophisticated inquirers with more adequate sources of data began their studies. Generally speaking, one might say that the search for the causes of crime has either been made by those who believe that criminal conduct can be explained chiefly by the biological or mental characteristics of offenders, or by those who believe that environmental conditions and circumstances are the chief operative factors. We shall call the former the individualists and the latter the environmentalists.

The individualists. Attempts to interpret the significance of relationships between body and mind led in ancient times to the development of *physiognomics*. This method of character diagnosis survived well into the Middle Ages, and one of its practitioners, Giambattista della Porta (1536–1615), may have been the first criminologist. He is said to have made anthropometric measurements on criminals in order to establish a typology. These medieval studies are not unlike some that appeared in the last century, and della Porta's drawings comparing human and animal faces have found counterparts in relatively recent studies by responsible scientists working with different underlying hypotheses. However, physiognomics soon fell into disrepute and remained so until Lombroso revived it in a new connection.

A different approach to the explanation of crime was that of Franz Joseph Gall (1758–1828), the greatest brain anatomist of his age, who was influenced by the faculty psychology of the time. His study of the brain and the nervous system caused him to propound a theory of the localization of brain functions, each operating through an organ in a cluster of other organs distributed over the outer layer of the brain. Criminal conduct then occurred if an overdeveloped organ of combativeness or acquisitiveness, for instance, was too stimulated. In vogue for a few decades, Gall's theory was abandoned, but it called attention to the necessity of studying the offender in order to understand his conduct. Following Gall's lead, Lauvergne (1841) studied prisoners at Toulon and described a criminal type that Lombroso later was to call a criminal by nature.

Psychiatrists were also interested in the etiology of crime. Benjamin Rush (1786), a Philadelphia physician, published an essay on the influence of physical causes on the moral faculties, in which he described persons who, although in other respects normal, became criminals because their moral faculty was impaired, a disease he called anomia. This theory, later elaborated by Philippe Pinel and Jean E. D. Esquirol, given the name "moral insanity" by James C. Prichard, and strongly defended by Prosper Despine and Henry Maudsley, took on a new lease of life in the late 1930s, when the notion of the constitutional psychopathic inferior aroused a discussion that seems likely to continue. [See PSYCHOPATHIC PERSONALITY.]

The political revolutions of the eighteenth century may have proclaimed the equality of man, but scientists of the period were fully aware of the great variations within the human species. The prevalence of physical and mental defects, ill-health, poverty, and criminality gave rise to B. A. Morel's theory of "degeneration" (1857), which held that all these phenomena were the results of a progressive pathological process in which heredity played an important role. This process led to the formation of a variety of human types, which he described in a monograph (Morel 1864) that contained many of the ideas later adopted by the Lombrosians. He also suggested the need for a science of "morbid anthropology." Dugdale's study of the Jukes (1877) shows some affinity with Morel's ideas.

In 1876 a work with the title *L'uomo deliquente* ("The Criminal Man"), by Cesare Lombroso (1835–1909), introduced a new variant among individualistic theories—the most important one, judging from its ultimate influence rather than its intrinsic value. On the basis of clinical and anatomical studies of criminals, Lombroso was convinced that the criminal was a throwback (atavism), a person who has the body and mind of our primitive ancestors, a kind of vestigial survivor from a day when mankind stood on a lower rung of the ladder of evolution, who, acting in a way natural to such a person, breaks the laws of modern society. The theory is a perfect example of the confluence of many contemporary sources of ideas. Jacob Moleschott and Friedrich K. C. L. Büchner supplied the materialistic doctrine, Charles Darwin the framework, Ernst H. Haeckel's biogenetic principle of recapitulation the mechanism that, interfered with, would account for the atavism (Mendel's discovery was still unknown), psychiatrists the concepts of moral insanity and degeneration, Paul Broca the techniques and instruments of anthropometry, the psychophysicists the methods of psychometrics, and Joseph A. de Gobineau the documentary data on the customs of primitive man.

Lombroso's theory aroused both support and opposition among researchers, not to mention the clergy or the laity represented by the legal profession. The first serious attempt to test it was done by C. B. Goring (1913), who found no support for it, and the last by E. A. Hooton, who failed to substantiate the claims he made for it. It no longer survives anywhere in its original formulation, but the orientation it represents, namely the stress on the importance of biological factors, still dominates criminological thought in Italy, the Iberian peninsula, and the Latin American countries.

A parallel avenue has been followed by the constitutionalists, seeking a correlation between somatic body types and criminality. The rediscovery of Mendel's hypothesis and the development of new psychometric devices such as intelligence tests led to numerous researches on the relationship of hereditary or psychological factors in delinquency, best demonstrated in studies of identical twins. It is within this context that we should appraise the psychoanalytic theories advanced in explanation of crime. Biological theories also fall under this head; indeed, it looks as if ancient beliefs in the role of body fluids in shaping temperaments have reappeared in a new guise in physiological studies of endocrine influences on behavior. As each new hypothesis of a biological or psychological nature has appeared, or new diagnostic devices have been found (the electroencephalograph or projective psychological tests, for instance), attempts have been made to determine their usefulness in research explaining criminal conduct.

The environmentalists. The earliest environmentalists were probably the astrologers who believed that traits ascribed to planets were mysteriously transmitted to humans, and that persons born when certain planets were in ascendancy or conjunction were doomed to crime. In later ages, such primitive conceptions were replaced by beliefs in the effect of climate on behavior (cf. Montesquieu), systematized less than a century ago by Enrico Ferri (1881a) in his discussion of telluric factors in the etiology of crime. Today, observed seasonal changes in criminality are recognized but explained in social terms. Indeed, the contributions of the environmentalists to an understanding of criminality have been predominantly sociological. Their ideas, at first based on commonplace experience and observation, have undergone many different, if not always basic, changes, because of improved sources of data, greater methodological sophistication, and the stimulus of scientific developments of the behavioral sciences in general.

It is said that Galen, noting the malpractice of Roman physicians, claimed that their conduct was made possible only by the anonymity of city life. Had they lived in small towns, where everybody would have known them, they could not have persisted in their conduct. The effect of poverty on crime was seen by Sir John Fortescue in the fifteenth century, and described by Sir Thomas More and Juan Luis Vives in the sixteenth century. The economic and social consequences of the Black Death and the endemic wars of the following three centuries created a criminal class, the existence of which was attributed to social causes. Eighteenth-century writers like Bernard Mandeville, Henry Fielding, and Patrick Colquhoun cited police corruption, the moral contagion of prisons, poor law enforcement, gambling, the saloon, illiteracy and ignorance, etc. as responsible for criminality. Both Fielding and Colquhoun gave graphic descriptions of organized crime, as did Avé-Lallemant in Germany half a century later.

It is during the last three quarters of the nineteenth century that we discern in the social sciences a development paralleling that already described in our discussion of the individualists. In 1825 France set up the first system of judicial criminal statistics. It was to be imitated by most other European countries. These annual series of data inspired the first important statistical studies by Charles J. M. Lucas (1827) on the relation of education to crime, by Adolphe Quetelet in 1831 on the relation of age to criminality, and by André M. Guerry (1833) on economic conditions, education, sex, etc. as related to crime. To facilitate the understanding of their tables, they presented maps of France showing the distribution of some of the phenomena they investigated, a technique much employed by contemporary and later authors and revived in the present century by American social ecologists.

The socioeconomic consequences of the industrial revolution were seen as criminogenic by numerous authors, especially those influenced by the economic theories of Karl Marx. Indeed, two of them, Napoleone Colajanni (1889) and Enrico Ferri (1881b), produced the first treatises on criminal sociology. Ferri's work became particularly influential. His effort to reconcile the divergent views of the social scientists and the criminal anthropologists led to a multiple-factor approach to the study of causation, which took account of anthropological, telluric, and social factors. His earliest studies (Ferri 1881a) were statistical analyses of criminality in France since 1825.

Two French sociologists were to have considerable influence on criminological thought—Gabriel Tarde (1843–1904) and Émile Durkheim (1858–1917). Both presented sociological theories of criminality worthy of comparison with the biological theories of men like Morel and Lombroso, and the dates of their formulation are evidence of the comparatively later maturation of sociological thought. Tarde (1890) held that as a special activity criminality was explained by the laws of imitation. The criminal represented a social type. Forms of crime originated in the upper classes and spread downward by imitation; thus an individual might be born vicious, but societal influences make him a criminal. Durkheim's best contribution was his theory of anomie, a condition that he held to be created by social evolution, as it transforms homogeneous societies into heterogeneous ones by the increasing division of labor, and by the rise of more and more social groups with divergent norms that may be in conflict with legal norms. Both of these authors, and especially Durkheim, have influenced the thinking of American criminologists.

Criminology in modern times

In this brief review, scores of names of scholars and scientists who have engaged in criminological research and who have assisted in enriching it have necessarily been omitted. And it will be noticed that, with one exception, Benjamin Rush, only Europeans have been mentioned. This is because in the United States, until the present century, studies of criminality or criminals only imitated work done abroad. The poverty of criminal statistics, which is still a problem, made the kind of social investigations done in Europe impossible. Psychologists and psychiatrists faced no such problem; the publication of Healy's *The Individual Delinquent* (1915) marked the beginning of a new era for their studies. Sociologists had to find different approaches. Before World War I, no leading

American sociologist, except perhaps Charles H. Cooley, Franklin H. Giddings, or E. A. Ross, showed any theoretical interest in criminology. Courses in criminology were offered in many American colleges and universities by 1905, but they were largely concerned with social reform. Only in the last forty years has a scientific orientation grown up in American sociological research on crime, as in other sociological areas of inquiry. Such research has tended to focus on the causation of crime. Psychiatric research in criminology, clinically oriented, has also increasingly come to recognize the significance of social and cultural influences on criminal conduct. [*See* CRIME, *article on* CAUSES OF CRIME.]

Whereas in the United States criminological research has been done mostly by sociologists, elsewhere clinical criminology, practiced mainly by psychiatrists, dominated research until World War II. In most countries of basically Latin culture, this is still the case. Since then, however, sociological research has been gaining in importance in many countries and has reversed the psychiatric dominance, especially in northern Europe. This process has been largely due to the phenomena of postwar criminality and delinquency and to the growing familiarity with the products of American empirical criminological research, which before World War II seemed to be almost unknown outside the United States.

Sociologists have also become interested in the study of correctional institutions seen as social systems; significant research in that connection has been conducted in the United States, England, and Norway. The effectiveness of various forms of correctional treatment is being studied in many countries. Such research may be expected to have an influence on legislation on crimes, their sanctions, and correctional administration. Attempts are also being made in some countries to develop prognostic instruments useful in spotting future delinquents among young children, in the selection of offenders for placement on probation or parole, and in the assignment of prisoners to different types of treatment programs. In this connection, the central diagnostic clinics established by many state or national correctional departments, of which California, France, and Italy offer good examples, have aided in bringing about closer cooperation among staff representatives of the various disciplines concerned with criminal conduct.

Concurrent with the growth of scientific research activity and with the proliferation, especially in the United States, of state or local programs and agencies for the prevention of crime and delin-quency and for the treatment of offenders has been the increase in the demand for criminologically trained research and treatment personnel. Pedagogical institutes of criminology, aiming to broaden the knowledge of the judiciary and of correctional administrators or candidates for such civil service offices, have existed for more than half a century at law schools in many foreign countries. Institutes combining staff research and teaching have appeared more recently. The most active are those at Cambridge, England, and Vaucresson, France. In the United States, a few universities offer programs of graduate study leading to advanced degrees related to criminology. Such courses are, with rare exceptions, designed to train teachers of criminology or correctional administrators rather than researchers; the same holds true for the offerings of the institute recently established in Japan by the United Nations.

THORSTEN SELLIN

[*Directly related are the entries* CRIME; PENOLOGY. *Other relevant material may be found in* DELINQUENCY; DRUGS, *article on* DRUG ADDICTION: SOCIAL ASPECTS; *and in the biographies of* DURKHEIM; HOOTON; LOMBROSO; MANDEVILLE; MONTESQUIEU; QUETELET; RUSH; SUTHERLAND; TARDE.]

BIBLIOGRAPHY

No adequate history of criminology exists, and the textbooks give scanty information. A broader view may be gained from Niceforo 1941; Kan 1903; Bonger 1905; Bernaldo de Quirós 1898; Antonini 1900; Montes 1911; Fink 1938; Vold 1958; Mannheim 1960. *The discussion of the scope and nature of criminology continues unabated, as witnessed by such works as* Bianchi 1956; Pelaez 1960. *Two national dictionaries of criminology are worthy of note:* Elster & Lingemann, Handwörterbuch der Kriminologie 1933–1936; *and the* Dizionario di criminologia 1943. *Good bibliographical tools are now available; especially useful are the* International Review of Criminal Policy; International Bibliography on Crime and Delinquency; Annales internationales de criminologie; Excerpta criminologica; Current Projects in the Prevention, Control and Treatment of Crime and Delinquency. *Textbooks are numerous. Among the many current American ones, all written by sociologists, the best known is* Sutherland & Cressey 1924. *Of foreign texts, among the leading titles are* Agge 1955; Greeff 1946; Hurwitz 1947; Bemmelen 1942; Pinatel 1963. *Many criminological journals are being published; among them, in the United States, are the* Journal of Criminal Law, Criminology, and Police Science; Archives of Criminal Psychodynamics; Journal of Research in Crime and Delinquency.

In England, the leading publication is the British Journal of Criminology. *In Germany, the* Archiv für Kriminologie *and the* Monatsschrift für Kriminologie und Strafrechtsreform *are both well-established journals, as are the Belgian* Revue de droit pénal et de criminologie, *the Dutch* Nederlands tijdschrift voor criminologie, *and the Swiss* Revue internationale de criminologie et de police technique. *France and Italy, both of which have long traditions of criminological research, produce, respectively, the* Revue de science criminelle et de droit pénal comparé *and the* Quaderni di criminologia clinica. *More extensive listings of journals will be found in* International Society of Criminology 1961. *The teaching of criminology in different countries, including the United States, is described in* International Society of Criminology 1957. *Also worth reading in this connection is* Radzinowicz 1961. *National societies for the study and promotion of scientific criminology exist in many countries. International exchange between criminologists has been organized since the late nineteenth century; no fewer than seven international congresses of "criminal anthropology" were held between 1885 and 1911. The International Society of Criminology, organized in 1937, has held such congresses in 1938, 1950, 1955, 1960, and 1965.*

AGGE, IVAR et al. 1955 *Kriminologi.* Stockholm: Wahlström & Widstrand.

Annales internationales de criminologie. → Published by the Société Internationale de Criminologie. From 1951 to 1961 it was called the *Bulletin* [of the International Society of Criminology].

ANTONINI, GIUSEPPE 1900 *I precursori di C. Lombroso.* Turin (Italy): Bocca.

Archiv für Kriminologie: Unter Besonder Berücksichtigung der naturwissenschaftlichen Kriminalistik. → Published since 1898.

Archives of Criminal Psychodynamics. → Published since 1955.

BEMMELEN, JACOB M. VAN (1942) 1958 *Criminologie: Leerbock der misdaadkunde.* 4th ed. Zwolle (Netherlands): Tjeenk Willink.

BERNALDO DE QUIRÓS, CONSTANCIO (1898) 1911 *Modern Theories of Criminality.* Boston: Little. → First published as *Las nuevas teorías de la criminalidad.*

BIANCHI, HERMANUS 1956 *Position and Subject-matter of Criminology: Inquiry Concerning Theoretical Criminology.* Amsterdam: North-Holland Publishing.

BONGER, WILLIAM A. (1905) 1916 *Criminality and Economic Conditions.* Boston: Little. → First published as *Criminalité et conditions économiques.*

BRANHAM, VERNON C.; and KUTASH, SAMUEL B. (editors) 1949 *Encyclopedia of Criminology.* New York: Philosophical Library.

British Journal of Criminology. → Published since 1960 by the Institute for the Study and Treatment of Delinquency. From 1950 to 1960 published as *British Journal of Delinquency.*

COLAJANNI, NAPOLEONE 1889 *La sociologia criminale.* 2 vols. Catania (Italy): Tropea.

Current Projects in the Prevention, Control and Treatment of Crime and Delinquency. → Published from 1962 to 1964 by the National Council on Crime and Delinquency. Now published by the National Clearing House for Mental Health Information, U.S. Department of Health, Education and Welfare, Public Health Service.

Dizionario di criminologia. 2 vols. Edited by E. Florian, A. Niceforo, and N. Pende. 1943 Milan (Italy): Vallardi.

DUGDALE, RICHARD L. (1877) 1910 *The Jukes: A Study in Crime, Pauperism, Disease and Heredity.* 4th ed. New York: Putnam.

ELSTER, ALEXANDER; and LINGEMANN, HEINRICH (editors) 1933–1936 *Handwörterbuch der Kriminologie und der anderen strafrechtlichen Hilfswissenschaften . . .* Berlin: de Gruyter.

Excerpta criminologica. → A journal of abstracts, published since 1961 by the Excerpta Criminologica Foundation, Amsterdam.

FERRI, ENRICO 1881a *Studi sulla criminalità in Francia dal 1826 al 1878.* Rome: Botta.

FERRI, ENRICO (1881b) 1917 *Criminal Sociology.* Boston: Little. → First published as *I nuovi orizzonti del diritto e della procedura penale.* Title later changed to *Sociologia criminale.*

FINK, ARTHUR E. 1938 *The Causes of Crime: Biological Theories in the United States, 1800–1915.* Philadelphia: Univ. of Pennsylvania Press. → A paperback edition was published in 1962 by Barnes & Noble.

GAROFALO, RAFFAELE (1885) 1914 *Criminology.* Boston: Little. → First published in Italian.

GORING, CHARLES B. 1913 *The English Convict: A Statistical Study.* London: H.M. Stationery Office.

GREEFF, ÉTIENNE DE (1946) 1947 *Introduction à la criminologie.* 2d ed. Brussels: Vandenplas.

GUERRY, ANDRÉ M. 1833 *Essai sur la statistique morale de la France.* Paris: Crochard.

HEALY, WILLIAM 1915 *The Individual Delinquent: A Text-book of Diagnosis and Prognosis for All Concerned in Understanding Offenders.* Boston: Little.

HURWITZ, STEPHAN (1947) 1952 *Criminology.* London: Allen & Unwin. → First published in Danish.

International Bibliography on Crime and Delinquency. → Published since 1963, first by the National Research and Information Center on Crime and Delinquency, National Council on Crime and Delinquency, now by the National Clearing House for Mental Health Information, U.S. Department of Health, Education and Welfare, Public Health Service.

International Review of Criminal Policy. → Published since 1952 by the United Nations, Department of Social Affairs. Contains an extensive international bibliography of criminology.

INTERNATIONAL SOCIETY OF CRIMINOLOGY 1957 *The University Teaching of Social Sciences: Criminology.* Paris: UNESCO.

INTERNATIONAL SOCIETY OF CRIMINOLOGY 1961 *Selected Documentation on Criminology.* Social Science Clearing House, Reports and Papers in the Social Sciences, No. 14. Paris: UNESCO. → A selective bibliography for each of 25 countries.

Journal of Criminal Law, Criminology, and Police Science. → Published since 1910 under various titles.

Journal of Research in Crime and Delinquency. → Published since 1964 by the National Council on Crime and Delinquency and the Center for Youth and Community Studies, Howard University.

KAN, JOSEPH VAN 1903 *Les causes économiques de la criminalité: Étude historique et critique d'étiologie criminelle.* Paris: Storck.

KINBERG, OLOF 1935 *Basic Problems of Criminology.* Copenhagen: Levin & Munksgaard. → A French revision was published in 1960 as *Les problèmes fondamentaux de la criminologie.*

LAUVERGNE, HUBERT 1841 *Les forçats considérés sous le rapport physiologique, moral et intellectuel.* Paris: Baillière.

LUCAS, CHARLES J. M. 1827 *Du système pénal et du système répressif en général, de la peine de mort en particulier.* Paris: Béchet.

MANNHEIM, HERMANN (editor) (1954–1960) 1960 *Pioneers in Criminology.* London: Stevens. → A collection of biographies that first appeared separately in the *Journal of Criminal Law, Criminology, and Police Science.*

MANNHEIM, HERMANN 1965 *Comparative Criminology: A Text Book.* 2 vols. London: Routledge.

MIDDENDORFF, WOLF 1959 *Soziologie des Verbrechens.* Düsseldorf (Germany): Diederich.

Monatsschrift für Kriminologie und Strafrechtsreform. → Published since 1904 under various titles.

MONTES, JERÓNIMO 1911 *Precursores de la ciencia penal en España: Estudios sobre el delincuente y las causas y remedios del delito.* Madrid: Suarez.

MOREL, BENEDICT A. 1857 *Traité des dégénérescences physiques, intellectuelles et morales de l'espèce humaine et des causes qui produisent ces variétés maladives.* Paris: Baillière.

MOREL, BENEDICT A. 1864 *De la formation du type dans les variétés dégénérées: Ou, nouveaux éléments d'anthropologie morbide pour faire suite à la théorie des dégénérescences dans l'espèce humaine.* Paris: Baillière.

Nederlands tijdschrift voor criminologie. → Published since 1959.

NICEFORO, ALFREDO (1941) 1949 *Criminologia.* Volume 1: Vecchie e nuove dottrine. Milan (Italy): Bocca.

PELAEZ, MICHELANGELO 1960 *Introduzione allo studio della criminologia.* Milan (Italy): Giuffré.

PINATEL, JEAN 1963 *Criminologie.* Volume 3 in Pierre Bouzat and Jean Pinatel, *Traité de droit pénal et de criminologie.* Paris: Dalloz.

Quaderni di criminologia clinica. → Published since 1959.

RADZINOWICZ, LEON (1961) 1962 *In Search of Criminology.* Cambridge, Mass.: Harvard Univ. Press.

Revue de droit pénal et de criminologie. → Published since 1907.

Revue de science criminelle et de droit pénal comparé. → Published since 1936 by the Centre Français de Droit Comparé, Université de Paris, Institut de Criminologie.

Revue internationale de criminologie et de police technique. → Published since 1947.

RUSH, BENJAMIN (1786) 1839 *Inquiry Into the Influence of Physical Causes Upon the Moral Faculty.* Philadelphia: Cist. → Speech delivered before the American Philosophical Society, February 27, 1786. First published as *An Oration . . . Containing an Enquiry Into the Influence of Physical Causes Upon the Moral Faculty.*

SELLIN, THORSTEN; and SAVITZ, LEONARD (1935) 1963 A Bibliographical Manual for the Student of Criminology. 3d ed., rev. *International Bibliography on Crime and Delinquency* 1, no. 3.

SUTHERLAND, EDWIN H.; and CRESSEY, DONALD R. (1924) 1960 *Principles of Criminology.* 6th ed. New York: Lippincott. → First published as a textbook under the title *Criminology* with E. H. Sutherland as sole author.

TARDE, GABRIEL (1890) 1912 *Penal Philosophy.* Boston: Little. → First published as *La philosophie pénale.*

TULLIO, BENIGNO DI 1945 *Trattato di antropologia criminale.* Rome: Criminalia.

VOLD, GEORGE B. 1958 *Theoretical Criminology.* New York: Oxford Univ. Press.

CRISIS

"Crisis" is a lay term in search of a scholarly meaning. Some scholars treat it synonymously with stress, panic, catastrophe, disaster, violence, or potential violence. Others, adhering to the medical connotation, regard it as a "turning point" between a fortunate and an unfortunate change in the state of an organism. In decision-making analysis, it is one kind of situation or event. The concept is used by historians, sociologists, political scientists, and psychologists.

Because of its varied meanings the term "crisis" has not been useful in building "systematic knowledge" about social phenomena. Terms that cover almost any situation are not helpful in analysis that emphasizes variables and the relations among variables. If many different kinds of situations are labeled crises, then the factor becomes a constant and cannot be related to variations in other aspects of social process.

Uses of the term are *substantive* and *procedural*. Substantive uses specify the content of a policy, problem, or situation. Procedural conceptions emphasize generic characteristics of situations, without regard to whether a particular case involves, for example, an international crisis, a political crisis, or an individual crisis.

Substantive definitions. Among substantive definitions the most elaborate is that of Kahn (1965), who enumerated 44 distinguishable steps in political–military escalation, from a minor provocation to full-scale nuclear holocaust. His conception is a helpful instrument of policy making because it suggests that military and political decision makers have available many stages through which to increase pressure on an adversary, without, however, necessarily converting a hastened escalation into full-scale nuclear war. (This presumes that both adversaries have similar perceptions of the scale.) The theoretical potential of this definition is, however, limited because it is confined to nuclear crises and, at least at present, calls for far more data than are likely to be found.

Procedural definitions. Procedural definitions identify elements that occur in any crisis. These uses have been reviewed in two papers. Wiener and Kahn (1962) enumerated 12 generic dimensions: (1) Crisis is often a turning point in an unfolding sequence of events and actions. (2) Crisis is a situation in which the requirement for action is high among participants. (3) Crisis threatens the goals and objectives of those involved. (4) Crisis is followed by an important outcome whose consequences shape the future of the participants. (5) Crisis consists of a convergence of events that results in a new set of circumstances. (6) Crisis produces uncertainties in assessing a situation and in formulating alternatives for dealing with it. (7) Crisis reduces control over events and their effects. (8) Crisis heightens urgency, which often produces stress and anxiety among participants. (9) Crisis is a circumstance in which information available to participants is unusually inadequate. (10) Crisis increases time pressures for those involved. (11) Crisis is marked by changes in the relations among participants. (12) Crisis raises tensions among participants, especially in political crises involving nations.

Miller and Iscoe (1963) reviewed traits of crises as used in psychological and sociological studies: (1) A crisis situation is acute rather than chronic, although its length is usually unspecified. (2) Crisis results in behavior that is frequently "pathological," such as inefficiency or scapegoating. (3) Crisis threatens the goals of persons involved. (4) Crisis is relative; what is a crisis for one party or participant may not be for another. (5) Crisis causes tension in the organism, including physical tension and anxiety.

Studies by Wiener and Kahn and by Miller and Iscoe identified some of the same traits of crisis. Both studies list threat to goals and pathological effects, such as frustration and anxiety. Both adhere to a bias that appears in scholarly writings on crisis, as well as in the more conventional conception of crisis taken by participants and laymen, namely, that crisis is something to be avoided.

Several political analysts have experimented with different definitions in their empirical research. Robert North and his associates (including Richard Brody, Ole Holsti, and Dina Zinnes) have engaged in extensive studies of the crisis resulting in World War I and of more recent Sino–Soviet and Soviet–American crises, including the Cuban crisis of 1962. North and his colleagues adhere to the original Greek meaning, which persists to this day in the medical conception of the term (North et al. 1963, p. 4). This definition identifies crisis as a "turning point" that distinguishes the outcome of an event favorably or unfavorably, between life or death, violence or nonviolence, and resolution or protracted conflict. The difficulty with this conception is the obverse of that with Kahn's definition. Whereas Kahn's refined 44 stages are too numerous for theory building, the conception of crisis as a turning point is too restricted. An event is either a crisis or it is not; it is either a turning point or it is not; it is either a favorable outcome or an unfavorable outcome. Such categories are too gross.

These difficulties reveal a familiar dilemma that occurs in the development of new concepts. Definitions are either extraordinarily precise and specific, and hence not widely applicable to a variety of situations, organizations, and subjects; or they are so unrestricted in meaning that, in this case, it is difficult to distinguish crisis from noncrisis.

Crisis as a decision situation. Robinson (1962) set forth a threefold conception of crisis founded on a number of case studies of political decisions. This provisional characterization of crisis as a decision situation or as an occasion for decision (Barnard 1938; Snyder et al. 1962) included: (1) identification of the origin of the event—whether external or internal for the decision makers; (2) the decision time available for response—whether short, intermediate, or long; and (3) the relative importance of the values at stake to the participants—whether high or low. The origin of the situation was selected because of apparent differences between such crises as the Korean invasion of 1950, which surprised American foreign policy makers, and the Bay of Pigs crisis of 1961, which was precipitated by the United States. It was recognized that a crisis for one party may not be a crisis for another and that the existence of crisis may depend upon whether the decision unit precipitated the crisis or was confronted by it.

Decision time was regarded as important because of apparent consequences for the content of decisions. For example, Snyder and Paige (1958) reported that the number of alternatives available to the United States in the Korean decision were few and that they were quickly reduced to one in an effort to meet the action that the situation seemed to demand. In contrast, the Marshall Plan, developed during 15 weeks in 1947 in response to rapidly deteriorating economic and political stability in western Europe, offered a longer period to search for ways to deal with the problem (Jones 1955). Different from both the Korean invasion and the Marshall Plan was the settlement of the Japanese peace treaty, which was negotiated for several years and which allowed for extensive search for alternatives and for the exploration of the acceptability of alternative treaty formulations (Cohen 1957).

Relative importance of the values at stake was selected because crisis confronts decision makers with potential consequences of profound importance. In international affairs, the stakes may be violent or nonviolent, and between violent outcomes, they may involve "conventional" warfare or varying degrees of nuclear war. In crises other than international political ones, the stakes may be economic stability or instability, or varying degrees of either; organizational survival or demise; personal well-being or illness, *inter alia*.

Working initially with this typology of crisis situations, Charles Hermann (1963) reviewed organizational studies and theorized about consequences of crisis for organizational viability and decision making. For purposes of simulating foreign policy crises through internation simulation,

Hermann (1965) categorized occasions for decisions as either anticipated or unanticipated, as involving short or long response time, and as involving low, medium, or high threat to the goals or objectives of the decision-making unit. Because of limitations in the simulation technique, he arbitrarily dichotomized anticipation and response time and trichotomized threat. Obviously, these three dimensions could be scaled in a more refined fashion, but their combination yielded 12 occasions for decision, which was expected to be a practicable number for analysis. Later, however, it was discovered that the simulation technique was not rich enough to deal with this many and that it was necessary to compromise by comparing most crisislike with least crisislike situations. [*See* SIMULATION, *article on* POLITICAL PROCESSES.]

Decision time. Consideration of this conception of crisis uncovered serious difficulties with the element response time. Robinson and Snyder (1965, pp. 440–442) emphasized the relative effect that time may have in different decisions. What is a short time for one decision may be a long time for another. The complexity of tasks confronting decision makers may require different amounts of time for identification, alternative search and selection, and, in different cases, implementation.

Decision time should not, therefore, be equated with clock time. There are two reasons for treating decision time differently. The first is that time has varying meanings and effects for different decision makers. Owing to variations in cognitive capacity or decision-making styles, some individuals need a short amount of time to work on a task for which others require a longer period. Decision makers differ in reflectiveness and decisiveness. The same decision may be taken by the reflective as by the decisive, but their personal procedures for deciding may not be the same. This problem can be overcome by relating personality variables to crisis variables and by treating the problem-solving or decision-making characteristics of individual decision makers elsewhere than in the conception of crisis.

Another difficulty with clock time, however, cannot be so arbitrarily disposed of or transferred conceptually. When calendar time is long, the decision may be so complicated that many tasks need to be performed in formulating a policy. A case that illustrates this is the set of British decisions concerning membership in the Common Market. Between 1960 and 1963, the British Foreign Office confronted a wide range of detailed tasks in an effort to negotiate entry into the European Economic Community (Young & Robinson 1962). Although the calendar for negotiation was nearly three years, it was crowded by demands and competition.

Decision time, therefore, should not be treated as an absolute. It varies with the intricacies of the decision and with the number of participants. [*See* LEADERSHIP, *article on* POLITICAL ASPECTS.]

Related terms. Stress, conflict, tension, panic, catastrophe, and disaster are terms used more frequently by social scientists than crisis (C. Hermann 1965, p. 23). Like crisis, they too have many meanings, as Horvath (1959) showed with respect to stress. The most common usage of stress is probably that formulated by Lazarus and Baker (1956): thwarting some motive state or potentially thwarting, resulting in effective arousal. "Negative affect" is a frequent consequence of stress and constitutes a collective term for anxiety, fear, frustration, hostility, and tension. The difficulties with using stress synonymously with crisis center on the one-dimensional character of stress. As a threat to goals, it is only one of the major elements of crisis, as we have formulated the term.

Similar problems arise for a term like conflict. Conflict is an incompatibility between parties with respect to a goal (Boulding 1962, p. 5; North et al. 1960, p. 356). This is the same as threat to an objective, one of the three major aspects of crisis. [*See* CONFLICT.]

Tension is another related concept. It, however, is a consequence of crisis and not a characteristic of crisis. It seems useful not to include in the conception of crisis the outcomes or effects of crisis.

Panic, catastrophe, and disaster, although subject to study in important social contexts, are less technical terms and ordinarily have not been the subject of investigation in organizational and political contexts.

Another limitation of related concepts is that, with only a few exceptions (for example, M. Hermann 1965), they have been investigated in problem-solving rather than decision-making research. Problem-solving experiments typically present subjects with situations for which alternatives are given and for which a determinate and "best" solution exists. Decision making differs from problem solving in that decisions are not confined to the selection among alternatives but rather extend to the search for alternatives and to the formulation and negotiation of alternatives. Moreover, these stages of the decision process probably consume a larger share of the time for making a decision than does selection among alternatives (Simon's article in Easton 1966).

In addition, many decisions are not subject to determinate and "best" solutions. Routine, recurring decisions may be subject to linear programming or other computational techniques that result in near-determinate solutions. The kinds of situations that crisis ordinarily connotes, however, are not. Accordingly, the relevance of problem-solving experiments to crisis decision making is limited. Dahl (1961, p. 98) and Wood (1961, p. 17) caution against applying findings from nondecision-making experiments (such as problem solving) to political arenas in which policy decisions are taken.

In addition to these limitations on stress as a synonym for crisis, others apply to panic, catastrophe, and disaster. These concepts usually have been used to study mass behavior and other responses dissimilar to decision-making processes.

The state of theory. Although no theory of crisis has been developed as yet, theorizing about this phenomenon has already begun. Charles Hermann (1963; 1965) inductively reviewed hypotheses and placed them in a chain of independent, intervening, and dependent variables. In addition, Hermann (1965) advanced *ad hoc* predictions about some of the relations among crises and other variables. In some cases, however, the *ad hoc* predictions were arbitrary, and contradictory reasons could be given for opposite predictions. However innovative this effort was for testing hypotheses, it indicates the lack of a rich deductive theory or theories involving crisis.

Not only is crisis theory barren, but theories of decision making rarely accommodate explicit reference to crisis. For example, the theory of games, which deals with decision making under varying conditions, does not treat the concept. The critical aspects of decision with which game theory deals are conflicts between parties under conditions of uncertainty. Conflict is only one dimension of crisis (threat to values). It is important to note also that uncertainty is a variable. The amount of uncertainty in situations or occasions for decision varies, and all crisis decisions involve uncertainty. Because the theory of games treats uncertainty as a parameter, not as a variable, it is difficult to draw probable hypotheses that will apply to both game theory and crisis.

Theories of psychotherapy, including those of Erikson (1959, pp. 50–100) and Dabrowski (1964), regard crisis as inevitable in the development of the identity of individuals. The relevance of this for a theory of crisis is not immediately apparent, except for its suggestion of "positive" effects of crisis in the development and evolution of personality. Likewise, in theorizing about negotiation, as in labor–management bargaining, crisis has been identified as an inevitable and positive occurrence that precedes resolution or settlement (Douglas 1962).

Most studies, however, emphasize the "negative," pathological aspects of crisis. Communication theories concerned with the processing of information, with the possibilities of overloading networks of messages, and with selective perception and distortion of content bear on crisis (Deutsch 1963; Meier 1963; Pool & Kessler 1965). With respect to one dimension of crisis, that of anticipation or unanticipation, the processing of information in an organization may determine whether warnings about impending events reach top level decision makers. The "level of crisis" is a category for analysis in the conceptual scheme of "the policy science orientation" where variations in the crisis level are associated with variations in the outcomes and effects of social processes (Lasswell & Kaplan 1950).

Crisis will become a useful concept when it plays a part in theoretical formulations. Just as a fact is regarded as without meaning apart from a theory, so a concept can hardly be productive if it does not relate to other variables in a theory.

JAMES A. ROBINSON

[*See also* CRISIS GOVERNMENT; STRESS. *Other relevant material may be found in* DECISION MAKING; DECISION THEORY.]

BIBLIOGRAPHY

BARNARD, CHESTER I. (1938) 1962 *The Functions of the Executive.* Cambridge, Mass.: Harvard Univ. Press.

BOULDING, KENNETH E. 1962 *Conflict and Defense: A General Theory.* A publication of the Center for Research in Conflict Resolution at the University of Michigan. New York: Harper.

COHEN, BERNARD C. 1957 *The Political Process and Foreign Policy: The Making of the Japanese Peace Settlement.* Princeton Univ. Press.

DABROWSKI, KAZIMIERZ 1964 *Positive Disintegration.* Boston: Little.

DAHL, ROBERT A. (1961) 1963 *Who Governs? Democracy and Power in an American City.* New Haven: Yale Univ. Press.

DEUTSCH, KARL W. 1963 *The Nerves of Government: Models of Political Communication and Control.* New York: Free Press.

DOUGLAS, ANN 1962 *Industrial Peacemaking.* New York: Columbia Univ. Press.

EASTON, DAVID 1953 *The Political System: An Inquiry Into the State of Political Science.* New York: Knopf.

EASTON, DAVID (editor) 1966 *Varieties of Political Theory.* Englewood Cliffs, N.J.: Prentice-Hall. → See the article by Herbert A. Simon.

ERIKSON, ERIK H. 1959 Identity and the Life Cycle: Selected Papers. *Psychological Issues* 1, no. 1.

FESTINGER, LEON 1964 *Conflict, Decision, and Dissonance.* Stanford Studies in Psychology, No. 3. Stanford Univ. Press.

FESTINGER, LEON; RIECKEN, H. W.; and SCHACHTER, STANLEY 1956 *When Prophecy Fails.* Minneapolis: Univ. of Minnesota Press.

HERMANN, CHARLES F. 1963 Some Consequences of Crisis Which Limit the Viability of Organizations. *Administrative Science Quarterly* 8:61–82.

HERMANN, CHARLES F. 1965 *Crises in Foreign Policy Making: A Simulation of International Politics.* Contract N123 (60530) 32779A. China Lake, Calif.: U.S. Naval Ordnance Test Station.

HERMANN, MARGARET G. 1965 Stress, Self-esteem, and Defensiveness in an Inter-nation Simulation. Ph.D. dissertation, Northwestern Univ.

HORVATH, FRED E. 1959 Psychological Stress: A Review of Definitions and Experimental Research. *General Systems: Yearbook of the Society for General Systems Research* 4:203–230.

JONES, JOSEPH M. 1955 *The Fifteen Weeks: February 21–June 5, 1947.* New York: Viking.

KAHN, HERMAN 1965 *On Escalation.* New York: Praeger.

KAPLAN, ABRAHAM 1964 *The Conduct of Inquiry: Methodology for Behavioral Science.* San Francisco: Chandler.

LASSWELL, HAROLD D.; and KAPLAN, ABRAHAM 1950 *Power and Society: A Framework for Political Inquiry.* Yale Law School Studies, Vol. 2. New Haven: Yale Univ. Press. → A paperback edition was published in 1963.

LAZARUS, RICHARD S.; and BAKER, ROBERT W. 1956 Personality and Psychological Stress: A Theoretical and Methodological Framework. *Psychological Newsletter* 8:21–32.

LINDBLOM, CHARLES E. 1965 *The Intelligence of Democracy: Decision Making Through Mutual Adjustment.* New York: Free Press.

LUCE, R. DUNCAN; and RAIFFA, HOWARD 1957 *Games and Decisions: Introduction and Critical Survey.* New York: Wiley.

MEIER, RICHARD L. 1963 Information Input Overload: Features of Growth in Communications-oriented Institutions. *Libri* 13:1–44.

MILLER, KENT; and ISCOE, IRA 1963 The Concept of Crisis: Current Status and Mental Health Implications. *Human Organization* 22:195–201.

NORTH, ROBERT C.; KOCH, HOWARD E.; and ZINNES, DINA A. 1960 The Integrative Functions of Conflict. *Journal of Conflict Resolution* 4:355–374.

NORTH, ROBERT C. et al. 1963 *Content Analysis: A Handbook With Applications for the Study of International Crisis.* Evanston, Ill.: Northwestern Univ. Press.

POOL, ITHIEL DE SOLA; and KESSLER, ALLAN 1965 The Kaiser, the Tsar, and the Computer: Information Processing in a Crisis. *American Behavioral Scientist* 8, no. 9:31–38.

ROBINSON, JAMES A. 1962 *The Concept of Crisis in Decision-making.* National Institute of Social and Behavioral Science, Symposia Studies Series, No. 11. Washington: The Institute.

ROBINSON, JAMES A.; and SNYDER, RICHARD C. 1965 Decision-making in International Politics. Pages 435–463 in Herbert C. Kelman (editor), *International Behavior: A Social-psychological Analysis.* New York: Holt.

SIMON, HERBERT A. (1947–1956) 1957 *Models of Man; Social and Rational: Mathematical Essays on Rational Human Behavior in a Social Setting.* New York: Wiley.

SNYDER, RICHARD C.; BRUCK, H. W.; and SAPIN, B. (editors) 1962 *Foreign Policy Decision Making: An Approach to the Study of International Politics.* New York: Free Press.

SNYDER, RICHARD C.; and PAIGE, GLENN D. (1958) 1961 The United States' Decision to Resist Aggression in Korea: The Application of an Analytical Scheme. Pages 193–208 in James N. Rosenau (editor), *International Politics and Foreign Policy: A Reader in Research and Theory.* New York: Free Press. → First published in Volume 3 of the *Administrative Science Quarterly.*

WIENER, A. J.; and KAHN, H. 1962 *Crisis and Arms Control.* Harmon-on-Hudson, N.Y.: Hudson Institute.

WOOD, ROBERT C. (1961) 1964 *1400 Governments: The Political Economy of the New York Metropolitan Region.* Garden City, N.Y.: Doubleday.

YOUNG, ROLAND; and ROBINSON, JAMES A. 1962 Parliamentary Decision-making in Great Britain: The Case of the Common Market. Paper delivered at the annual meeting of the American Political Science Association, Washington, D.C. Unpublished manuscript.

CRISIS GOVERNMENT

The concept of crisis government is founded on the assumption that in certain situations of political, military, or economic emergency the system of limitation and balance of power typical of a constitutional government has to give way before the enlarged power of the executive or even the military.

There exist, however, vast differences of opinion as to the theoretical foundation and the range of practical measures, as well as to their legal interpretation and political justification. Moreover, historical experience shows that the institution of crisis government can often bring about the very consequences of political and social crisis that it was designed to prevent. If employed prematurely, it may impede further attempts at solving the problems by the means of constitutional government. Provisions of crisis government may thus invite dictatorial ambitions of political parties, groups, and persons. When practiced over a longer period, those provisional emergency arrangements designed for the protection of the existing constitutional order may even become tools for pseudolegal revolution and dictatorial domination at the cost of that order.

Historical examples. For reasons of political logic and practical experience, the problem of crisis government has occupied political theory from its beginning, but in particular since the rise of the modern state. In antiquity the constitutional framework of the Roman Republic, with its emergency provision of a temporary dictator, represented the most elaborate attempt at institutionalizing crisis government, as distinct from Oriental despotism and unlimited tyranny. The concept of "constitutional dictatorship" contained, however, the ever-present danger of turning into permanent dictatorship. The Roman institution of a temporary dictator nominated for a period of six months by the acting consul—who alone had the power to proclaim or prolong the state of emergency that gave the dictator his special powers—was applied successfully during the earlier history of the republic. However, with the emergence of revolutionary generals in the civil wars of the first century B.C., it was turned into a permanent regime leading to the dictatorships of Caesar and his successors.

Modern constitutional arrangements reflect the same lack of distinction between constitutional emergency provisions and legalized dictatorial regimes. The transition from the first republic in France to the regime of Napoleon is a classical example of a pseudo-revolutionary turnover. Between the two world wars, many feeble democracies surrendered to the same tendency. The proclamation of a protectionist dictatorship to meet crisis situations determined developments in Italy (Mussolini), Poland (Pilsudski), Turkey (Kemal Atatürk), Spain (Primo de Rivera and Franco), Portugal (Salazar), Germany (Papen and Hitler), Austria (Dollfuss and Schuschnigg), and the Balkan countries; in South America, such developments belonged to everyday politics.

In Germany, Hitler's coming to power was a clear result of use and misuse of the emergency powers given to the president of the Weimar Republic. Under article 48 of the constitution he had the right to subsede normal parliamentary legislation by crisis decrees and to apply military force for the execution of such federal decrees in the states. In 1923, under a democratic president (Ebert), this power was exercised as a strictly temporary measure for the protection of the republic; after 1930, under Hindenburg, emergency government became gradually institutionalized, and parliamentary controls were paralyzed by successive dissolutions of parliament. It was at this very point that antidemocratic forces of the right succeeded in breaking up the constitutional government. The Nazi dictatorship was founded and legalized by posing as a presidential crisis government, before Hitler managed to override parliament and to suppress the non-Nazi groups, which until the last party elections (March 1933) commanded a majority of German votes.

Although these examples demonstrate the dangers contained in the institution of crisis government, many exponents of constitutional theory maintain that emergency provisions remain essential to the existence and maintenance of democratic regimes. The discussion distinguishes between emergency situations caused by exterior forces (military threat, war) and revolutionary situations conditioned by domestic developments. Since disturbances in the operation of parliamentary governments can hardly be cured by extraparliamentary provisions, it remains open to discussion whether emergency articles should be formally included in a constitution and how far they should be applied to either external or internal crises. Consequently, constitutional structure and political practice in modern democracies have attempted many varied solutions. In substance, the problem is always how far civil rights may be restricted and to what degree such increased executive power should be transferred to certain bureaucratic, political, or even military authorities.

Contemporary provisions. In such Western democracies as the United States, Great Britain, and Switzerland, the constitutions contain no explicit clauses regarding crisis government. To meet emergency situations, either parliament is expected to convey necessary powers to the government or constitutional theory agrees on implied and inherent powers for the president (as in the United States). By common understanding, however, the controls by the courts and parliamentary legislation are not to be curtailed by such concentration of power.

The constitution of the semiauthoritarian French Fifth Republic (1958), which is reminiscent of the dualistic, parliamentary–presidential structure of the Weimar Republic, contains far-reaching emergency powers conferred on the president "when the institutions of the Republic, the independence of the Nation, the integrity of its territory or the fulfillment of its international obligations are threatened with immediate and grave danger, and when the regular functioning of the constitutional governmental authorities is interrupted" (France, Constitution, 1958, art. 16).

Such sweeping stipulations, while leaving everything to the personal qualities and intentions of the president, contain all the dangers discussed above. This certainly does not present a strong case for institutionalized emergency provisions. Nevertheless, there are strong efforts in West Germany to change the constitution of 1949 and to add an "emergency constitution" that would allow for restrictions on civil rights and suspension of parliamentary legislation by government decrees, with controls remaining (as a compromise formula) in a small committee of the two houses of parliament. In the author's opinion, this contradicts the original intentions of the Bonn constitution, which was designed to avoid the mistakes of Weimar by substituting for emergency provisions strong regulations against antidemocratic activities as well as regulations supporting stable governments and working majorities in parties and parliament.

Problems of crisis government. The basic problems posed by any attempt to provide, by constitutional and institutional means, for strong crisis government may thus be summarized in five questions.

(1) *Who is to be in charge of proclaiming the state of emergency, or the need for crisis government?* A widespread view, often justified with technical reasons and arguments of greater efficiency, tends to leave it to the executive. This coincides with a general tendency toward the bureaucratic administrative state; yet it contradicts the practice of proved democracies to maintain the responsibilities of parliament. The right to declare a state of emergency should be reserved to an organ not invested with the powers derived from that state. For the same reason, this requires a qualified majority larger than the governing majority.

(2) *When does the state of crisis eventuate, and how can it be defined?* In general, the practice of confining crisis government to the case of war appears the least dangerous way. All attempts to apply it to situations of "imminent danger" (as in recent German drafts) or domestic problems (as in the Weimar Republic and Fifth French Republic) will lead into a jungle of divergent interpretations inviting misuse of power and enabling the overthrow of democratic government by one-party systems or military dictatorship, thus paving the way to authoritarian or totalitarian regimes.

(3) *What does crisis government really mean?* Here again the basic distinction would be between (*a*) a concentration of power functions, with some simplification of the governmental process in the framework of responsible government that leaves intact the competence of legislatures and courts; and (*b*) the concept of temporary dictatorship, which, suspending the democratic system and the rule of law, aims at empowering the executive to enact laws on its own authority. In the first case, the parliament may temporarily yield power to the executive by passing "enabling acts," but retains its prerogatives; in the second case, the executive

commands emergency powers to be mobilized by a proclamation of a state of emergency and effected by decrees. However, there is wide agreement that the constitution should not be changed during the period of emergency.

(4) *Which controls are to remain or should be introduced to reduce the dangers inherent in any of these solutions?* The answer again depends on the degree to which responsible government is abandoned in favor of a bureaucratic and dictatorial interregnum. If crisis government means merely a strengthening of democratic government by bipartisan politics or an all-party coalition government, no basic changes in the system of controls seem necessary. On the other hand, any serious shift in function between the legislative and executive agencies, even if only for a restricted period, requires special controls designed to meet the dangers of unrestricted government with its tendencies to perpetuate and extend the anomalous power situation.

Among the institutions granting a minimum of essential control, so that the efforts to defend democracy do not destroy the very existence of democracy are parliamentary committees and councils representing various groups, an independent position for the constitutional courts, and the widest possible freedom of the press. The question remains whether the principle of voluntary cooperation and self-restriction as practiced in countries without fixed emergency provisions (e.g., Switzerland or Britain during the war) is not more effective than the most elaborate schemes of crisis government, since these will never be able to foresee all the actual forms of emergency measures necessary in a future crisis.

(5) *How is crisis government ended?* The end of crisis government poses a final problem that all constitutions with emergency provisions have to meet with special care. Considering the crucial danger of constitutional dictatorship—its perpetuation and transformation into a new regime—the question of who, how, and when an emergency government is to be terminated and must relinquish its powers is the acid test of any institutionalized crisis government. Such a decision can certainly not be left to the executive enjoying his increased power; it appears as the particular function of the parliament. But this implies a continuity of parliamentary life during the period of suspension. In fact, unlike the Weimar constitution, that of the Fifth Republic makes the dissolution of parliament impossible during the period of emergency government. After specifically limited periods, par-

liament must always be in a position to decide on the end (or continuation) of emergency politics.

Crisis government and democracy.   Any review of the problems arising from the attempts, old and new, to design safe and effective forms of crisis government leaves doubts as to their compatibility with democratic systems. In many cases, such attempts have been favored by exponents of political theory or practice who turned out to be more interested in nondemocratic rule. One well-known example is Carl Schmitt, the German professor of public law who started by posing perfectionist demands to the democratic state, then concentrated on the "decisionist" superiority of emergency government (decision before constitution), only to become the outstanding protagonist of Hitler's totalitarian dictatorship. In other cases, as in present-day France or West Germany, the antiparty effect of a great man or the perfectionism of a bureaucracy may be the prime mover behind the schemes for institutionalizing crisis government, advocated as they may be by arguments of military threat, anticommunism, socioeconomic problems, or the failure of parliamentarism.

But historical experience as well as political reasoning favor the other side. In times of crisis, government should be founded on as broad a basis as possible, with parliament, parties, and a free press participating in, not eliminated from, the political mastering of the problems. This contradicts the widespread assumptions that democracy is feasible during "normal" times only; that the stronger a state has to be the less democratic it can be; that security can be achieved by constitutional perfection and elaborate precautionary measures; and that bureaucratic government without parliamentary interference would grant a higher degree of efficiency in handling emergency situations.

Constitutional possibilities, once established, always produce an appetite to use them. What is more, they tend to seduce the responsible authorities—parties and parliament—to escape from difficult or unpopular situations by leaving the field to emergency measures that do not have to be justified to the public. Such political and psychological consequences can hardly be avoided, unless all elements of the democratic state remain fully incorporated into the mechanism of emergency rule. Crisis government remains a task of democratic cooperation and trust in the final superiority of free societies with responsible governments, rather than a matter of reshaping constitutions and suspending basic rules of democracy. Good as the

purpose of such experiments may be, the way back to a normal situation is most difficult once the road toward dictatorial forms of government has been pointed out.

KARL DIETRICH BRACHER

[*See also* CRISIS; DELEGATION OF POWERS; DICTATORSHIP; *and the biography of* SCHMITT.]

BIBLIOGRAPHY

ALLEN, CARLETON K. (1945) 1956 *Law and Orders: An Inquiry Into the Nature and Scope of Delegated Legislation and Executive Powers in English Law.* 2d ed. London: Stevens.

ARNDT, ADOLF; and FREUND, MICHAEL 1962 *Notstandsgesetz—aber wie?* Cologne (Germany): Wissenschaft und Politik.

BALLREICH, HANS (editor) 1955 *Das Staatsnotrecht in Belgien, Frankreich, Grossbritannien, Italien, den Niederlanden, der Schweiz und den Vereinigten Staaten von Amerika.* Cologne and Berlin: Heymann.

BRACHER, KARL D. (1955) 1960 *Die Auflösung der Weimarer Republik.* 3d ed. Villingen (Germany): Ring.

BRACHER, KARL D. 1964 *Deutschland zwischen Demokratie und Diktatur.* Bern: Serz.

DULLEMEN, A. A. L. F. VAN 1945 *Staatsnoodrecht en Rechtsstaat.* Alphen aan den Rijn (Netherlands): Samson.

DULLEMEN, A. A. L. F. VAN 1947 *Staatsnoodrecht en Democratie.* Alphen aan den Rijn (Netherlands): Samson.

DUVERGER, MAURICE 1962 *Les institutions françaises.* Paris: Presses Universitaires de France.

FAURE, JOHN 1937 *Le droit de nécessité de l'état; étude du droit public fédéral: Les pouvoirs extraordinaires des autorités fédérales.* Lausanne (Switzerland): Payot.

FOLZ, HANS-ERNST 1962 *Staatsnotstand und Notstandsrecht.* Cologne and Berlin: Heymann.

FRANCE, CONSTITUTION 1958 *The French Constitution: Adopted by the Referendum of September 28, 1958 and Promulgated on October 4, 1958.* French text and English translation. New York: French Embassy, Press and Information Division.

FROMME, FRIEDRICH K. 1960 *Von der Weimarer Verfassung zum Bonner Grundgesetz: Die verfassungspolitischen Folgerungen des parlamentarischen Rates aus Weimarer Republik und nationalsozialistischer Diktatur.* Tübingen (Germany): Mohr.

GANSHOF VAN DER MEERSCH, W. J. 1953 Les états d'exception et la constitution belge. *Annales de droit et des sciences politiques* 1953:49–124.

GIACOMETTI, ZACCARIA 1945 *Das Vollmachtregime der Eidgenossenschaft.* Zurich: Polygraphischer Verlag.

GROSSHUT, F. S. 1962 *Staatsnot, Recht und Gewalt.* Nuremberg (Germany): Glock & Lutz.

HESSE, KONRAD 1955 Ausnahmezustand und Grundgesetz. *Die öffentliche Verwaltung* 8:741–746.

HESSE, KONRAD 1960 Grundfragen einer verfassungsmässigen Normierung des Ausnahmezustandes. *Juristen Zeitung* 15:105–108.

HEWITT, DESMOND J. 1953 *The Control of Delegated Legislation.* Sydney (Australia): Butterworth.

JENNINGS, WILLIAM I. (1942) 1961 *The British Constitution.* 4th ed. Cambridge Univ. Press.

LAMARQUE, JEAN 1961 La théorie de la nécessité et l'article 16 de la constitution de 1958. *Révue du droit public et de la science politique en France et à l'étranger* 77:558–628.

MORRISON, HERBERT (1954) 1959 *Government and Parliament.* 2d ed. Oxford Univ. Press.

PESTALOZZI, RICHARD 1944 *Die Notgesetzgebung.* Zurich: Fluntern.

REBER, KURT 1938 *Das Notrecht des Staates.* Zurich: Polygraphischer Verlag.

RIDDER, HELMUTH; and STEIN, EKKEHART 1963 *Der permanente Notstand.* Göttingen (Germany): Vandenhoeck & Ruprecht.

ROCHE, JOHN P. 1952 Executive Power and Domestic Emergency: The Quest for Prerogative. *Western Political Quarterly* 5:592–618.

ROSSITER, CLINTON L. 1948 *Constitutional Dictatorship: Crisis Government in the Modern Democracies.* Princeton Univ. Press. → A paperback edition was published in 1963 by Harcourt.

ROYAL INSTITUTE OF PUBLIC ADMINISTRATION 1957 *The Organization of British Central Government 1914–1956: A Survey by a Study Group.* Edited by Daniel N. Chester and F. M. G. Willson. London: Allen & Unwin.

SCHMITT, CARL (1921) 1928 *Die Diktatur von den Anfängen des modernen Souveränitätsgedankens bis zum proletarischen Klassenkampf.* 2d ed. Munich and Leipzig: Duncker.

SCHMITT, CARL 1940 *Positionen und Begriffe im Kampf mit Weimar–Genf–Versailles: 1923–1939.* Hamburg (Germany): Hanseatische Verlagsanstalt.

SIEGHART, MARGUERITE A. 1950 *Government by Decree: A Comparative Study of the History of the Ordinance in English and French Law.* London: Stevens.

SPEISER, THOMAS M. 1953 *Vom Notrecht in der Demokratie: Der neue Artikel 89 bis der schweizerischen Bundesverfassung.* Zurich: Füssli.

STURM, ALBERT L. 1949 Emergencies and the Presidency. *Journal of Politics* 11:121–144.

TÖNDURY, GIAN R. 1947 *Der Begriff des Staatsnotstands im Staatsrecht.* Zurich: Jun.

WATKINS, FREDERICK M. 1939 *The Failure of Constitutional Emergency Powers Under the German Republic.* Cambridge, Mass.: Harvard Univ. Press.

CROCE, BENEDETTO

Benedetto Croce (1866–1952) was a writer with an unusually wide-ranging mind who dominated Italian intellectual life from the eve of World War I to the middle of the twentieth century. His more than sixty volumes embrace history, literary criticism, political polemic, and formal philosophy, particularly ethics, aesthetics, and the philosophy of history. It is in this last capacity that he is of concern to social scientists. As a philosopher of history, Croce, while continuing the idealist tradition of Droysen and Dilthey, eliminated a number of the problems that perplexed his German predecessors and contemporaries: he made a radical separation between science (including social science) on the one hand—dismissing it as arbitrary and "practical" in its aim—and the realm of history and

philosophy on the other. But rather than impose philosophy on history, as Hegel had done, Croce *included* philosophy *within* history, as the methodology of history. He asserted that this philosophical type of history is supreme among intellectual disciplines and that the "truth" of history lies in the logic applied by the historian himself and in his skill in reconstituting in his own mind the thoughts and actions of past generations.

Born of Neapolitan parents, Croce chose to spend virtually his entire life in Naples. His substantial independent means freed him from the necessity of a university career, and he remained a private scholar, largely self-taught and supremely confident in his chosen role as the thinker who would "de-provincialize" Italian intellectual life and bring it into the mainstream of European thought. The most urgent task, he believed, was to combat the vulgarized positivism which pervaded Italian writing and teaching in the last quarter of the nineteenth century and to re-establish the concept of the "spirit" in human affairs. Starting his career as an antiquarian-scholar of his beloved Naples, Croce naturally encountered the writings of his fellow Neapolitan Giovanni Battista Vico, who became his most influential intellectual guide (but as the founder of history philosophically understood, rather than as a schematizer of the past—something with which Croce had little patience). After a brief encounter with Marxism at the turn of the century, and after a more sustained interest in Hegel (although he never became more than a qualified Hegelian), Croce, just before World War I, put together the four systematic volumes of his *Filosofia come scienza dello spirito* (1902–1917; "Philosophy of the Spirit"), on which his reputation primarily rests. These volumes deal respectively with aesthetics, logic, economics and ethics, and historiography.

The latter part of Croce's life brought him into closer touch with public events and partisan politics. Appointed a senator of the realm in 1910 and having served from 1920 to 1921 as minister of public instruction, Croce ranked from the mid-1920s onward as the chief intellectual opponent of Mussolini's fascist regime. Concomitantly, in his writings he began to concern himself with the question of value judgments, which he had earlier neglected, most notably in four substantial volumes of history published between 1925 and 1932 and in his last major philosophical work, *History as the Story of Liberty* (1938). In these books he argued that the *vita morale* ("ethical life") is the central thread of history and that, consequently, history, as "the story of liberty," is necessarily liberal in character. With the fall of Mussolini in 1943 Croce emerged as Italy's leading citizen. Too old, however, to give a clear direction to the course of events, he was able to participate only in the first postfascist governments, retiring from active politics shortly after the end of World War II.

Croce's influence on subsequent generations of historians and philosophers of history has been widely ramifying, although his reputation in the English-speaking world has suffered from the fact that his chief interpreter, R. G. Collingwood, pushed his teaching to extreme conclusions. Certainly Croce ranks as the single most important member of the twentieth-century idealist school. Some of the difficulties his theory presents are characteristic of most idealist argumentation—a tendency to denigrate science, both natural and social, and to give no clear account of the processes the historian follows in arriving at historical understanding. (In this connection, it is important to note that Croce was largely ignorant of the twentieth-century philosophy of science and that he paid only scant attention to the work of such leading contemporaries as Freud and Max Weber.)

Other difficulties are peculiarly Croce's. His most celebrated dictum that "every true history is contemporary history" has proved most illuminating in showing how contemporary relevance lifts historical writing above mere antiquarianism. But his approach has raised two crucial problems. First, Croce's concern with values and with what he called ethico-political history led him, in the later part of his life, to stress the abstractions of "reason" and "liberty" as against that understanding of the past in its own terms which had been central to traditional idealist historiography. Nor did Croce ever satisfactorily explain whether he considered these values absolute or relative. Second, although Croce's work was more consistently rationalistic than that of most idealists (with the significant exception of Hegel), he offered no more than a metaphorical validation (for example, a "lightning-flash" of understanding) for the truth of a given historical interpretation. The paradoxical result is that what started as a rationalist theory terminated in an "act of faith."

H. STUART HUGHES

[*For the context of Croce's work, see* HISTORY, *article on* THE PHILOSOPHY OF HISTORY; *and the biographies of* DILTHEY; HEGEL; VICO.]

WORKS BY CROCE

(1902–1917) 1954–1958   *Filosofia come scienza dello spirito.* 4 vols. Bari (Italy): Laterza. → Volume 1: *Estetica come scienza dell' espressione e linguistica generale,* (1902) 1958. Volume 2: *Logica come scienza del concetto puro,* (1905) 1958. Volume 3: *Filosofia della practica: Economica ed etica,* (1908) 1957. Volume 4: *Teoria e storia della storiografia,* (1917) 1954.

(1905) 1917   *Logic as the Science of the Pure Concept.* London: Macmillan. → A translation of Volume 2 of Croce 1902–1917.

(1917) 1960   *History: Its Theory and Practice.* New York: Russell. → A translation of Volume 4 of Croce 1902–1917.

(1938) 1962   *History as the Story of Liberty.* London: Allen & Unwin. → First published as *La storia come pensiero e come azione.*

SUPPLEMENTARY BIBLIOGRAPHY

CAPONIGRI, A. ROBERT   1955   *History and Liberty: The Historical Writings of Benedetto Croce.* London: Routledge.

CORSI, MARIO   1951   *Le origini del pensiero di Benedetto Croce.* Florence (Italy): La Nuova Italia.

FLORA, FRANCESCO (editor)   1953   *Benedetto Croce.* Milan (Italy): Malfasi.

HUGHES, H. STUART   1958   *Consciousness and Society: The Reorientation of European Social Thought, 1890–1930.* New York: Knopf.

NICOLINI, FAUSTO   1962   *Benedetto Croce.* Turin (Italy): Unione Tipografico.

CROSS PRESSURE

Cross pressure refers to that social situation in which an intrapersonal conflict arises when the motives affecting a decision are incompatible. Two broad categories of such conflicts can be distinguished—attitudinal and affiliative. Attitudinal conflict may occur when a person is faced with a choice between alternative beliefs or courses of action under conditions which bring into play attitudes motivating different and opposing choices. Affiliative conflict can result from a person's attachment to several groups which have preferences for different alternatives. These two types of conflict can be illustrated by voting behavior, the field of study to which the cross-pressure hypothesis has most frequently been applied. If a voter who generally agrees with the foreign policy of one party prefers another party's domestic policy, his voting decision will be affected by *attitudinal* cross pressure. If his personal friends belong to one party and his business associates to another, his voting choice may be subject to *affiliative* cross pressure. While the two types of cross pressure are not mutually exclusive and frequently occur together, they are based on different psychological mechanisms. In attitudinal conflict the individual is assumed to be striving for consistency between his actions and the various relevant parts of his attitude structure, whereas in affiliative conflict he is trying to adjust satisfactorily to various relevant parts of his social environment.

The concept of cross pressure is typically used to link the choice-behavior of individuals to social processes. This implies that the sources of cross pressures are part of the social world. That is, in the case of attitudinal cross pressure the conditions to which the individual responds must have objective reality. To illustrate, the specific domestic policies which motivate a person to vote for a political party must actually be the policies of that party or at least the policies which public opinion generally attributes to that party, not merely those the individual alone attributes to it. In the case of affiliative cross pressure, the attitudes which the individual imputes to his various relevant groups must actually be the attitudes which characterize them. Again, the voting preferences a person imputes to friends or business associates must be their real voting preferences. If this assumption of objective social reality were not made, there would be no reason to treat cross pressure as a special phenomenon apart from the general field of internal psychological conflict.

While the causes of attitudinal cross pressure include a large variety of social, individual, and situational factors, the etiology of all kinds of affiliative cross pressure reduces itself to what Riecken (1959, p. 178) calls "social transition." The term covers both vertical and horizontal mobility, as well as certain processes of culture change, i.e., acculturation and cultural evolution.

There are special problems of definition with respect to affiliative cross pressures. In Simmel's usage the term "social circle" (which Bendix translated as "group") referred to any kind of social aggregate, from the most intimate primary group to the community and from involuntary social groups to voluntary associations (Simmel [1908] 1955, pp. 127–130). More recent writers have sometimes broadened or restricted the meaning of the term "group." In their Erie County voting study, Lazarsfeld, Berelson, and Gaudet (1944) dealt chiefly with broad social strata such as classes, religious sects, and residents of urban or rural areas. In their more recent study in Elmira, N. Y., Berelson, Lazarsfeld, and McPhee (1954, pp. 118–127) put greater stress on the voter's personal associates (his friends, family, co-workers). They believe that these personal associations translate the more abstract group memberships into concrete personal experience and thus make them effective. The mechanism which accounts for conflict, then, is that of primary group attachment, i.e., the individual's need to maintain a sense of belonging to groups of close associates by conforming to their basic values and attitudes. Yet another version of the affiliative cross-pressure hypothesis holds reference groups accountable for the generation of conflicts. Campbell et al. (Michigan, University of . . . 1960, pp. 370–380) regard the individual as subject to cross pressure if he identifies with a social stratum to which he does not belong according to objective criteria. Other definitions of cross pressure include conflict between group norms or preferences and internalized values and between group and mass-media pressures.

Effects on individuals.   Simmel ([1908] 1955, pp. 140–143) saw cross pressures as the social mechanism which leads to the development of individuality. In a complex society, he argued, each person stands at the "intersection" of a large number of social circles. To the extent that the "interests" of these "circles" are not identical—to the extent that they are in conflict—the person has freedom of choice, and the particular set of choices he makes establishes him as an individual distinct from all others. Thus, in Simmel's view cross pressures stimulate innovation, although he acknowledged that they may also have inhibitory effects and occasionally lead to "psychotic breaks."

Some researchers dealing with acculturation processes support Simmel's views. Thus Lerner (1958, pp. 49–54) describes the "transitional"—the person exposed to both the traditional and the contemporary culture—as the chief agent of change. There are, however, other reports which point to the destructive or debilitating effects of cultural cross pressures (cf. Opler 1959).

Students of voting behavior have shown that cross pressures are associated with a reduction of partisanship and interest in both the election campaign and its outcome. Voters under such cross pressures tend to make up their minds late in the campaign; they tend to split their ticket; and more of them fail to vote than in the general population.

Effects on society.   Cross pressure is believed to reduce social tensions and political conflict, since cross-pressured individuals serve as bridges between social and political groups.

For instance, an individual who identifies with a social class different from his own tends to vote according to the norms of the chosen class rather than those of his social environment (Michigan, University of . . . 1960, pp. 369–375). This prevents the polarization of society into status groups. Similarly, cross pressures arising from multiple-group membership tend to restrain interest groups from extreme and uncompromising stands (Truman 1951, p. 158). Workers whose *locus* in society keeps them in a state of relative isolation are more strike-prone than workers subject to social cross pressures (Kerr & Siegel 1954). And since individuals under cross pressure are likely to be the members of society who are most directly involved in processes of social change, their presence in the system makes for flexibility and ability to accommodate to new conditions (Parsons 1959, p. 98).

Second, cross pressures are believed to stabilize the political system by strengthening dominant opinion. Cross-pressured voters tend to resolve their conflicts in favor of the party or policy which commands majority support or is otherwise dominant in the community (Berelson et al. 1954, p. 100). Lipset et al. (1954, pp. 1133–1134) further believe that the cross-pressure mechanism contributes to the maintenance of existing power relations, since lower-class people are subject to the pressures of both their lower-class culture and the upper-class-controlled mass media; for upper-class people, there is no such divergence between affiliative and mass-media pressures.

Critique. The main burden of the cross-pressure hypothesis is the postulated decrease in interest, partisanship, and other forms of involvement as the pressures upon the individual become more evenly balanced: the notion is that such pressures then tend to cancel each other. This physical analogy carries over into the realm of social and political relations: the lower the aggregate energy potentials carried by all its members, the less the tensions in the society.

The seeming obviousness of this physical analogy may have prevented theorists from specifying the exact conditions under which the hypothesis can be expected to hold. Clearly, it is possible to imagine cases in which a strong attachment to a congruent set of attitudes or to groups with congruent attitudes goes with low interest in both the decision process and the outcome. Thus, a person firmly attached to the moral conventions of his society or to a variety of groups committed to society's ethical code may routinely choose the conventionally correct alternative course of action without evincing any involvement in either the decision process or its outcome. Conversely, a person not so firmly attached and thus experiencing greater conflict may be more deeply involved.

Therefore, two conditions appear to be necessary for the cross-pressure hypothesis to be applicable: the outcome of the impending decision must have emotional significance; and the outcome must be delayed or uncertain. Emotional significance in social decisions is usually supplied by the presence

of social dissensus over norms or policies. Delay or uncertainty gives rise to the anxious expectations or anticipations of reward which stimulate involvement. The cross-pressure hypothesis thus applies mainly to situations of social conflict or political competition.

If so restricted, the cross-pressure hypothesis may seem a tautology: it argues that people whose attitudes or group attachments make them hesitate between two alternatives are not very partial to either of them. Certain psychological theories suggest, however, that the reaction to internal conflict can be, quite to the contrary, an exaggerated commitment to one of the alternatives. In such a case, the unpleasant consequences of internal conflict are eliminated by blocking out the other alternative—for example, by selective perception or selective exposure to the situational stimuli (Festinger 1957, pp. 123–176).

This possibility is clearly present in cases of attitudinal conflict. In a less direct way, it may apply to affiliative conflict as well. Some individuals experiencing strong internal conflict may overcome their discomfort by selective perception of their associates' attitudes or by one-sided selection of primary groups. Others, similarly conflicted, may rationalize their indecision by (rightly or wrongly) attributing divergent views to the members of their several primary groups. The existing evidence on voting behavior does not preclude such interpretations, since it relies exclusively on the reports of subjects about their associates, not upon direct testing of these associates themselves (Luce 1959, pp. 349–352). Thus, some individuals whose primary groups do in fact diverge in their attitudes may escape from the psychological pressures resulting from such affiliations by taking extremely partisan positions and falsely attributing similar positions to all of their associates.

Neither version of the cross-pressure hypothesis contains any theoretical notions, nor are there any data that might help in deciding how an individual will react to cross pressure—by an increase in, or a reduction of, one-sided commitment. Thus, it is not possible to assert unconditionally that cross pressures will always reduce social and political tensions. Three types of response to cross pressures seem possible: (1) withdrawal or alienation (as hypothesized in the voting studies); (2) overreactive affirmation of, or extreme commitment to, one of the alternatives (Festinger's hypothesis); and (3) careful weighing of all alternatives with possible innovation as a solution (Simmel's hypothesis). Which of these responses will actually occur may be a matter of the individual's ability to tolerate internal conflict. It has been suggested that such ability to tolerate "ambiguity" or "dissonance" is a part of personality structure (Frenkel-Brunswik 1949; Festinger 1957, pp. 268–270). Furthermore, threatening social situations may reduce such ability among the general population. Both the frequency of personality types with high and low conflict-tolerance and the frequency of threatening situations may have historical antecedents and thus be rooted in a given culture. If this is true, then it is not possible to predict any particular effects on the individual or society only from the knowledge of patterns of cross pressures. Rather, certain personality characteristics, the frequency of their occurrence in a given society, and their distribution over the structure of social roles must be considered contributory sources of variability.

FRANK A. PINNER

[See also COGNITIVE THEORY; ELECTIONS; POLITICAL BEHAVIOR; PUBLIC OPINION; SOCIALIZATION.]

BIBLIOGRAPHY

BERELSON, BERNARD; LAZARSFELD, PAUL F.; and McPHEE, WILLIAM N. 1954 Voting: A Study of Opinion Formation in a Presidential Campaign. Univ. of Chicago Press.

CAMPBELL, ANGUS; GURIN, GERALD; and MILLER, WARREN E. 1954 The Voter Decides. Evanston, Ill.: Row, Peterson.

FESTINGER, LEON 1957 A Theory of Cognitive Dissonance. Evanston, Ill.: Row, Peterson.

FRENKEL-BRUNSWIK, ELSE 1949 Intolerance of Ambiguity as an Emotional and Perceptual Personality Variable. Journal of Personality 18:108–143.

KERR, CLARK; and SIEGEL, ABRAHAM 1954 The Interindustry Propensity to Strike: An International Comparison. Pages 189–212 in Arthur W. Kornhauser, Robert Dubin, and Arthur M. Ross (editors), Industrial Conflict. New York: McGraw-Hill.

LANE, ROBERT E. 1959 Political Life: Why People Get Involved in Politics. Glencoe, Ill.: Free Press. → A paperback edition was published in 1965.

LAZARSFELD, PAUL F.; BERELSON, BERNARD; and GAUDET, HAZEL (1944) 1960 The People's Choice: How the Voter Makes Up His Mind in a Presidential Campaign. 2d ed. New York: Columbia Univ. Press.

LERNER, DANIEL (1958) 1964 The Passing of Traditional Society: Modernizing the Middle East. New York: Free Press.

LIPSET, SEYMOUR M. et al. (1954) 1959 The Psychology of Voting: An Analysis of Political Behavior. Volume 2, pages 1124–1175 in Gardner Lindzey (editor), Handbook of Social Psychology. Cambridge, Mass.: Addison-Wesley.

LUCE, R. DUNCAN 1959 Analyzing the Social Process Underlying Group Voting Patterns. Pages 330–352 in Eugene Burdick and Arthur J. Brodbeck (editors), American Voting Behavior. Glencoe, Ill.: Free Press.

MICHIGAN, UNIVERSITY OF, SURVEY RESEARCH CENTER 1960 The American Voter, by Angus Campbell and others. New York and London: Wiley.

OPLER, MARVIN K. (editor) 1959 Culture and Mental Health: Cross-cultural Studies. New York: Macmillan.

PARSONS, TALCOTT 1959 Voting and the Equilibrium of the American Political System. Pages 80–120 in Eugene Burdick and Arthur J. Brodbeck (editors), American Voting Behavior. Glencoe, Ill.: Free Press.

RIECKEN, HENRY W. 1959 Primary Groups and Political Party Choice. Pages 162–183 in Eugene Burdick and Arthur J. Brodbeck (editors), American Voting Behavior. Glencoe, Ill.: Free Press.

SIMMEL, GEORG (1908) 1955 Conflict and The Web of Group Affiliation. Glencoe, Ill.: Free Press. → Two essays first published as "Der Streit" and "Die Kreuzung sozialer Kreise" in Simmel's Soziologie.

TRUMAN, DAVID B. (1951) 1962 The Governmental Process: Political Interests and Public Opinion. New York: Knopf.

CROSS-SECTION ANALYSIS

Empirical analysis is concerned with the establishment of quantitative or qualitative relations between observable variables. From a temporal point of view two kinds of data are used in empirical analysis—cross-section data and time series data. Cross-section data are observations on variables at a point of time, whereas time series data are observations covering several time periods. Sometimes the two kinds of data are used together to overcome some specific difficulties.

The unit of observation in a cross section is generally, although not necessarily, elementary, such as a firm or a consumer; the unit of observation in a time series is generally an aggregate. The empirical association between the type of data and the level of aggregation contributes to differences in the results obtained with the two kinds of data.

While cross-section analysis is used in many of the social sciences, this article focuses on applications of cross-section analysis in economics. [For other applications, see SURVEY ANALYSIS.]

Some of the more important areas of economics in which cross-section data have been used are the estimation of Engel curves (Liviatan 1964; Prais & Houthakker 1955), the estimation of consumption functions (Friedman 1957), the estimation of production functions (Bronfenbrenner & Douglas 1939), and the estimation of investment functions (Kuh 1963).

Reasons for using cross-section data. There are several reasons why cross-section data are often superior to time series data for estimating economic relations.

(1) Cross-section data contain large variations

in some variables whose variations over time are only moderate and often subject to trend. For instance, there is a much larger variation in income among consumers at a particular point of time than in average per capita income over time. Likewise, there are wide variations in productive capacity and sales among firms in a cross section, but only relatively small variations in these variables in a time series.

(2) The size of a cross-section sample of data can usually be increased enough to make sampling variance relatively negligible (Kuh 1963).

(3) Multicollinearity among variables in a cross section is often less acute than among corresponding variables in a time series.

(4) The problem of interdependent disturbances, which frequently arises in the analysis of time series because of trends in time series data, usually does not arise in the analysis of cross-section data, simply because the order of the observations has no meaning.

(5) In some cases cross-section data are more reliable; and the variables that can be measured in a cross section often correspond more closely to the variables defined and studied in economic theory. For instance, cross-section data on consumer budgets furnish a precise account of consumption by commodity, and such data can be more useful than time series data for estimating demand functions. On the other hand, some variables are subject to larger errors in a cross section, although the errors are of a different nature than those encountered in a time series. For example, the discrepancy between observed income and permanent income is larger in a cross section than in an aggregate time series (Friedman 1957). This problem is discussed below.

(6) The distinction between the individual economic unit and the market, which is basic in economic analysis, leads to different classifications of variables at the microeconomic and macroeconomic levels of analysis. For instance, prices can be assumed to be given (exogenous) for a consumer, but they should be considered as dependent (endogenous) variables when markets are analyzed. Cross-section analysis usually deals with the behavior of microeconomic units; therefore it can often proceed on the basis of a simpler economic model than time series analysis of macroeconomic data.

It should be noted that cross-section analyses had been undertaken long before the statistical advantages of cross-section data were recognized; and in some cases, such as the study of Engel curves, cross-section analyses also preceded the rationale that was to be provided for them by economic theory (Staehle 1934–1935; Stigler 1954).

The scope of cross-section analysis. The explanatory variables appearing in economic relations can be divided into three groups: (1) variables that vary in a cross section and over time; (2) variables that are stable in a cross section and vary over time; (3) variables that vary in a cross section and are stable over time.

It is the existence of the first group that makes cross-section analysis valuable in economics. For instance, income is an important variable in consumption functions, and its impact on consumption can be learned from cross-section analysis. If income did not vary in a cross section, cross-section analysis of consumption functions would be impossible; if income did not vary over time, the results of cross-section analysis would be of little interest.

The existence of the second group implies that cross-section analysis by itself is not sufficient to explain the variations of many economic variables. For example, variations in consumption resulting from changes in income can be determined by cross-section analysis, since income varies in a cross section; but variations in consumption resulting from changes in prices cannot be determined by cross-section analysis, since prices generally do not vary in a cross section. Thus, to obtain complete economic relations, variables in the second group must be included in the relations, and the coefficients of these variables must be estimated by time series analysis.

The variables in the third group may be very important in explaining variations of economic variables in a cross section. For instance, age and sex and their interaction may explain more of the variations in consumption of certain commodities among individuals than does income. Yet they may be relatively unimportant variables to consider in most economic decisions or predictions, since neither the average age nor the sex composition of the population varies much over time.

The variables in the third group are largely noneconomic, that is, they are not endogenous variables in current economic theory. Among the important variables in this group are those measuring the uncertainty faced by decision-making units, particularly firms. According to the theory of the firm facing no uncertainty, the amount of a good supplied by a firm and the amounts of productive factors demanded by a firm depend on the price of the good and on the prices of the productive factors.

Given input and output prices, the firm should choose the input–output configuration that maximizes its profits. But in many empirical analyses of cross-section data, it is found that prices explain only a small proportion of variations in input demands and output supplies among firms. The unexplained variations may be attributable to differences in the degree of uncertainty among firms or to differences in the response to uncertainty among firms. Firms may be certain of the prices that will prevail when they execute their decisions, but they may be uncertain of the quantity of output that can be sold or the amounts of inputs that can be purchased at those prices.

Given uncertainty of this kind, a firm may deviate from its profit maximizing input–output configuration, so as to avoid partially the costs that would be incurred if plans cannot be realized, e.g., the costs of undesired inventory accumulations. In such cases a firm might consider all input–output configurations that yield profits greater than a preassigned fraction, say 95 per cent, of maximum profits and select one of these configurations for final execution. The range of acceptable configurations may be very large. Hence, firms may differ considerably in their decisions, the differences resulting from variations in uncertainty and in the response to uncertainty among firms.

From these considerations it is evident that economic variables may well explain only a small fraction of the variations of a dependent variable in a cross-section relation and that other variables that appear or should appear in the relation will perform the major explanatory role. Thus, there is no a priori requirement that cross-section relations produce high degrees of explanation or that, if they do, their explanatory powers result from the economic variables included (Grunfeld & Griliches 1960). Yet when all individuals are taken together, the noneconomic variables generally offset each other, and economic variables, such as prices, may turn out to be the important explanatory variables.

The problem of multiperiod relations. In general, the time horizon of economic decisions extends beyond a single period. Consequently, "true" economic relations contain variables of several periods; but in cross-section analysis one can usually observe only the current variables, and the problem of inferring a complete relation from such partial information arises. To illustrate, according to the permanent income hypothesis the consumption function is a relation between permanent consumption and permanent income. While permanent consumption may be approximately equal to observed consumption, permanent income is an average of incomes of several periods. Hence, consumption in any given year will depend, apart from errors, on a stream of income which, except for its current component, is unobserved. Similarly, in deciding whether to invest in durable assets, a firm takes into account the profits that the assets will yield not only in the year of the investment but also in future years. Thus, in order to ascertain empirically the determinants of business investment, it is necessary to take into account firms' expectations of the future, which are unobservable.

The nature of the problem can also be seen by expressing an economic relation as

$$f(\boldsymbol{x}_0, \boldsymbol{x}_1, \cdots, \boldsymbol{x}_t, \cdots) = 0,$$

where $\boldsymbol{x}_t$ is the vector of variables from period t that enter the relation. The problem discussed above exists when observations are available only for a particular $\boldsymbol{x}_t$ (as is the case in cross-section analysis) and when f is not separable with respect to that $\boldsymbol{x}_t$. In such cases the estimated cross-section relation is subject to bias resulting from the omission of the unobserved variables. This is all that can be said at this level of generality.

More specific conclusions can be arrived at when the underlying theory is more specific with respect to the economic relation to be estimated and with respect to the relationships between the observed and the unobserved variables. For instance, in the case of the permanent income hypothesis the stream of income over time in the true relation is replaced by one unobserved variable—permanent income. For purposes of estimation it is assumed that observed income measures permanent income with an unsystematic error. With specifications of the properties of the error term, the estimation problem reduces to a regression problem with errors in the variables, and the appropriate statistical methods are applied [see LINEAR HYPOTHESES, article on REGRESSION].

It should be noted that if the measurement errors are unsystematic, then aggregating the observations will reduce the measurement errors. Thus, while measurement errors are a serious problem in estimating most multiperiod relations with cross-section data, they usually do not present much of a problem in estimating such relations with aggregate time series data.

In studying multiperiod relations, considerable information can be gained by taking repeated observations on microeconomic units over time. Liviatan (1963) used such information to perform a rich variety of tests of the permanent income hypothesis.

The study of multiperiod relations is further

complicated by the existence of uncertainty in the decisions of microeconomic units. Consumers and firms do not have complete information on the future values of the variables exogenous to them. In such cases observed values of variables cannot be identified with expectations, and the utilization of repeated observations does not solve this problem. Assumptions must be made regarding the formation of expectations and regarding the behavior of individuals under uncertainty. Some of the consequences of uncertainty were noted in the preceding section.

Estimation. An initial step in estimating cross-section relations is choosing the explanatory variables to be included. Returning to the classifications noted above, variables in the second group obviously cannot be included, since they do not vary in a cross section. Variables in the first group should be included for two reasons. First, their variations in the cross section may contribute to explaining the variations in the dependent variable of the relation. Second, since they vary over time, cross-section estimates of their coefficients will be useful in making intertemporal forecasts with the estimated relation. Variables in the third group, which are specific to the cross section, may be of little interest for forecasting intertemporal changes in the dependent variables. However, if they are correlated with variables in the first group, they should also be included in the relation, to avoid bias in the estimates of the coefficients of the variables in the first group. For example, the size of the family is included as a variable in cross-section studies of Engel curves, even though it may have little to contribute in making intertemporal forecasts (Liviatan 1963; Prais & Houthakker 1955).

Sometimes the variables in the third group are not quantifiable but their attributes can be specified. They are then introduced into the analysis by grouping individuals according to the attributes and estimating separate relations for each group. For example, in studying consumption functions one of the variables in the third group might be "place of residence." Individuals in a cross-section sample might then be grouped according to geographical areas. After fitting the relation to each group, one may test the hypothesis that individuals in all groups behave in the same manner, i.e., that the same relation holds for all the groups and that the so-called group effects are insignificant. Covariance analysis provides the statistical framework for testing the equality of intercepts and the equalities of some or all of the slopes in the group relations. In such analysis, within-group variations of the variables (deviations of observations in the group from the group mean) are utilized, so at least two observations per group are required.

It may happen that the appropriate groups are identical to the units of the observations. For example, managerial ability is not quantifiable but must be allowed for in a cross-section study of production functions. However, the unit of observation may be the firm, and managerial ability probably differs for each firm. In that case, covariance analysis is impossible with just one cross section, since there is only one observation per group. If managerial ability is to be handled by the use of covariance analysis, repeated observations over time must be made on each firm. Since this calls for a combination of time series and cross-section data, some of the variables in the second group must also be included in the relation. If some of these variables are not directly quantifiable, their effects may be allowed for by introducing different intercepts and slopes for the various years in the sample (Mundlak 1963).

Analysis that is based merely on within-group variations of the variables ignores the between-group variations (deviations of the group means from the mean of all the observations), which are often much larger. The between-group variations can be utilized if the explanatory variables in the estimated relations are not correlated with the group effects. For example, if income is uncorrelated with "place of residence," then the mean consumptions of the groups can be regressed on the mean incomes of the groups. This is particularly desirable when the variables are subject to unsystematic measurement errors (as is the case when testing the permanent income hypothesis), because averaging observations for each group will eliminate most of the measurement errors. [See LINEAR HYPOTHESES, *article on* ANALYSIS OF VARIANCE.]

The problem of measurement errors is also handled in cross-section analysis by the use of instrumental variables [*see* SIMULTANEOUS EQUATION ESTIMATION]. For instance, in estimating the consumption function it is assumed that observed income measures permanent income with error. If this error is not serially correlated, the income of one year may be used as an instrumental variable for estimating the consumption function in another year. Note that this again calls for repeated observations over time on the incomes of the microeconomic units.

When variables in the relation to be estimated are jointly determined, the explanatory variables in the relation may not be independent of the disturbance term. For instance, factor inputs may not be independent of the disturbance term in a production function (Mundlak 1963; Walters 1963). In such cases estimating the relation by direct least squares will result in biased estimates of the coefficients. Various multiequation estimation procedures are available to overcome least-squares bias. However, they depend fundamentally on restrictions that may be satisfied only over time and not in a cross section. An exception is the instrumental variables method which, for example, uses lagged (or lead) factor inputs as instrumental variables in estimating a production function.

Special problems exist in estimating dynamic cross-section relations that involve adjustment processes [*see* DISTRIBUTED LAGS]. The empirical implications of many of the currently used adjustment models may be more applicable to group behavior than to individual behavior. While individuals facing uncertainty may not react instantaneously to changes in the variables on which they base their decisions, changes in their decisions may be discrete rather than continuous. It may be advantageous for them to make larger adjustments less often. However, the adjustment models employed in empirical work generally assume continuous adjustment. Since the frequency and size of adjustments may vary among individuals, continuous adjustment might be the result for the group. Here again, repeated observations over time on individuals can be utilized to surmount this difficulty.

Problems of application. The application of cross-section estimates of economic relations to intertemporal predictions of aggregates is subject to several difficulties. The cross-section estimates may depend on the values of the variables that are constant in the cross section but vary with time. Presumably this problem should be solved by a correct specification of the estimated relations, so that the variables that are stable in the cross section will not affect the estimates of the coefficients of the cross-section variables. For instance, income coefficients should be independent of prices, so that an estimated income coefficient will be applicable to periods with different prices. While such independence may nearly exist for income coefficients and prices, it may not exist in relations such as investment functions, where less regularity is the rule.

Furthermore, estimation of the coefficients of variables that are constant in a cross section but vary over time requires time series data. In estimating their coefficients by time series analysis, it is possible to use cross-section estimates of the coefficients of the variables in the first group in the time series relation. This of course can be done only if the cross-section estimates do not vary much from year to year. Income elasticities estimated from cross-section analysis are often grafted onto time series demand equations (Tobin 1950).

Finally, the transformation of estimates obtained for individuals to estimates applicable to markets is somewhat problematic. Aggregation over individuals is sensitive to the distribution of the explanatory variables among individuals and may lead to aggregate relations that differ in form from the individual relations (Houthakker 1955; Tobin 1950).

YAIR MUNDLAK

BIBLIOGRAPHY

BRONFENBRENNER, MARTIN; and DOUGLAS, P. H. 1939 Cross-section Studies in the Cobb–Douglas Function. *Journal of Political Economy* 47:761–785.

FRIEDMAN, MILTON 1957 *A Theory of the Consumption Function.* National Bureau of Economic Research, General Series, No. 63. Princeton Univ. Press.

GRUNFELD, YEHUDA; and GRILICHES, Z. 1960 Is Aggregation Necessarily Bad? *Review of Economics and Statistics* 42:1–13.

HOUTHAKKER, HENDRIK S. 1955 The Pareto Distribution and the Cobb–Douglas Production Function in Activity Analysis. *Review of Economic Studies* 23, no. 1:27–31.

KLEIN, LAWRENCE R. 1953 *Textbook of Econometrics.* Evanston, Ill.: Row, Peterson. → See especially pages 211–241.

KUH, EDWIN 1963 *Capital Stock Growth: A Micro-econometric Approach.* Contributions to Economic Analysis, 32. Amsterdam: North-Holland Publishing.

LIVIATAN, NISSAN 1963 Tests of the Permanent-income Hypothesis Based on a Reinterview Savings Survey. Pages 29–59 in *Measurement in Economics: Studies in Mathematical Economics and Econometrics in Memory of Yehuda Grunfeld.* Stanford Univ. Press. → A "Note" by Milton Friedman and a reply by Liviatan appear on pages 59–66.

LIVIATAN, NISSAN 1964 *Consumption Patterns in Israel.* Jerusalem: Falk Project for Economic Research in Israel.

MICHIGAN, UNIVERSITY OF, SURVEY RESEARCH CENTER 1954 *Contributions of Survey Methods to Economics.* Edited by Lawrence R. Klein. New York: Columbia Univ. Press.

MUNDLAK, YAIR 1963 Estimation of Production and Behavioral Functions From a Combination of Cross-section and Time-series Data. Pages 138–166 in *Measurement in Economics: Studies in Mathematical Economics and Econometrics in Memory of Yehuda Grunfeld.* Stanford Univ. Press.

PRAIS, S. J.; and HOUTHAKKER, H. S. 1955 *The Analysis of Family Budgets With an Application to Two British Surveys Conducted in 1937–1939 and Their Detailed Results.* Cambridge Univ. Press.

STAEHLE, HANS 1934–1935 Annual Survey of Statistical Information: Family Budgets. *Econometrica* 2:349–362; 3:106–118.

STIGLER, GEORGE J. 1954 The Early History of Empirical Studies of Consumer Behavior. *Journal of Political Economy* 62:95–113.

TOBIN, JAMES 1950 A Statistical Demand Function for Food in the U.S.A. *Journal of the Royal Statistical Society* Series A 113, part 2:113–141.

WALTERS, ALAN A. 1963 Production and Cost Functions: An Econometric Survey. *Econometrica* 31:1–66.

CROWDS

See COLLECTIVE BEHAVIOR; MASS PHENOMENA; QUEUES; *and the biography of* LE BON.

CULTS

See SECTS AND CULTS *and the biography of* TROELTSCH.

CULTURAL ADAPTATION

See *under* CULTURE.

CULTURAL ANTHROPOLOGY

See *under* ANTHROPOLOGY.

CULTURAL COOPERATION

See INTERNATIONAL CULTURAL COOPERATION.

CULTURAL DIFFUSION

See *under* DIFFUSION.

CULTURAL ECOLOGY

See *under* ECOLOGY.

CULTURAL EVOLUTION

See *under* EVOLUTION.

CULTURAL INTEGRATION

See *under* INTEGRATION.

CULTURAL LAG

See CULTURE, *article on* CULTURE CHANGE; SOCIAL CHANGE.

CULTURAL RELATIVISM

See *under* CULTURE.

CULTURE

The articles under this heading deal primarily with the nature and history of the concept of culture. The study of cultural and social anthropology is discussed under the heading ANTHROPOLOGY; *the development of the concept of culture and its applications are reviewed in* CULTURE AND PERSONALITY; DIFFUSION; ECOLOGY; EVOLUTION; HISTORY, *article on* CULTURE HISTORY; SOCIAL STRUCTURE. *Culture patterns and configurations are described in* INTEGRATION, *article on* CULTURAL INTEGRATION, *and in the biography of* BENEDICT. *Other utiliza-* *tions of the concept are reviewed in* POLITICAL CULTURE *and* STRATIFICATION, SOCIAL, *article on* CLASS CULTURE. *The biographies of* BOAS; KROEBER; MALINOWSKI; *and* TYLOR *should also be consulted.*

I. THE CONCEPT OF CULTURE   *Milton Singer*
II. CULTURAL RELATIVISM   *David Bidney*
III. CULTUROLOGY   *Leslie A. White*
IV. CULTURAL ADAPTATION   *Robert L. Carneiro*
V. CULTURE CHANGE   *Evon Z. Vogt*

I
THE CONCEPT OF CULTURE

In his charter definition of the anthropological concept of "culture," Tylor stated: "Culture or Civilization, taken in its wide ethnographic sense, is that complex whole which includes knowledge, belief, art, morals, law, custom, and any other capabilities and habits acquired by man as a member of society" ([1871] 1958, vol. 1, p. 1). His definition does not distinguish social organization and social institutions from a general concept of culture.

This inclusive use of the term "culture" was continued by Boas, Malinowski, and other ethnologists. In other respects the later usage differs from Tylor's in the new emphasis on the plurality of local cultures as functioning and organized wholes and in the loss of interest in the long-run evolution of discrete customs and institutions. With these many focuses, the three axioms of ninetenth-century anthropology—the psychic unity of mankind, the unity of human history, and the unity of culture— began to fade away. If such unities existed, it was thought, they would have to be laboriously pieced together from the comparative and intensive studies of many individual societies and cultures. Such universal principles could not be invoked as explanatory postulates.

This pluralistic and relativistic conception of culture, a product of the "Boas revolution" in anthropology, has characterized anthropological thought for almost fifty years, at least until the early 1950s, when a revival of interest in universalistic theories occurred. In its relativized form, anthropology did not, however, devote itself exclusively to the study of Tylorian culture. Under the leadership of Radcliffe-Brown social anthropology developed and was made the basis for a separation between social anthropology as the comparative study of "social structures" and ethnology and cultural anthropology, which study cultures comparatively or historically. This separation was probably first dramatized in a famous debate between W. H. R. Rivers, the teacher of Radcliffe-Brown, and A. L. Kroeber on the proper interpretation of L. H. Morgan's distinction between classificatory and descriptive kinship systems. Out of this debate about the nature of kinship systems grew the two major rival anthropological theories of culture—the theory of "culture patterns," best represented by Kroeber, and the theory of "social structure," best represented by Radcliffe-Brown.

This rivalry is still very much alive, although some anthropologists have tried to moderate it with peacemaking formulas and with new, integrated theories. It has mobilized the major factions in modern anthropology and sociology, so that in Great Britain, Malinowski and his followers are regarded as students of culture and of cultural anthropology, while Radcliffe-Brown and his followers are regarded as students of social structure and of social anthropology. In the United States the contrast between culture and social structure has symbolized the institutional rivalry between anthropologists and sociologists. Not until 1958 did the dean of American anthropologists, A. L. Kroeber, and the dean of American sociologists, Talcott Parsons, agree to sign a nonaggression pact in which both culture and society are recognized (Kroeber & Parsons 1958).

British social anthropologists usually set themselves off from American anthropologists who have, with few exceptions, until recently emphasized studies of culture and cultural anthropology (Murdock 1949; Firth 1951). The national labels are out of place, since the "British" Radcliffe-Brown derives from the work of Morgan and the French sociological school, while the "American" cultural anthropologists derive from Tylor and, through Boas, the German diffusionists. Bronislaw Malinowski wrote the article on culture for the *Encyclopaedia of the Social Sciences* (1931), placing emphasis on culture as a functioning, active, efficient well-organized unity, which must be analyzed into component institutions in relation to one another, in relation to the needs of the human organism, and in relation to the environment, man-made as well as natural. This concept of culture became the "common sense" of an entire American generation of anthropologists in the 1930s and 1940s. Similarly, in the 1950s and 1960s, much of British social anthropology became the common sense of a younger generation of American anthropologists.

Behind this rivalry there are, of course, intellectual issues; however, in order to separate the genuine issues from the spurious, we cannot take at face value what the members of one school say about the views of another, nor can the chapter headings in an ethnographic monograph—religion and art, family and marriage—tell us whether the material is treated in a framework of culture patterns or of social structure. The decisive criterion is the general framework of theory which is used for the interpretation and explanation of a particular set of facts. There are two frameworks to discuss, that of "culture patterns" and that of "social structure."

The pattern theory of culture

A significant text for pattern theory is the historical and critical review by A. L. Kroeber and Clyde Kluckhohn of several hundred definitions of culture and their heroic effort to arrive at a summary formulation which, they believed, would be acceptable to most social scientists:

Culture consists of patterns, explicit and implicit, of and for behavior acquired and transmitted by symbols, constituting the distinctive achievement of human groups, including their embodiments in artifacts; the essential core of culture consists of traditional (i.e., historically derived and selected) ideas and especially their attached values; culture systems may, on the one hand, be considered as products of action, on the other as conditioning elements of further action.   (1952, p. 181)

This represents a condensation of much of what American anthropologists, at least in the 1940s and 1950s, would call culture. And it is certainly a richer and more adequate formulation than the well-known formula of the 1920s and 1930s, "culture is learned behavior," which seemed so satisfying then. For as Kroeber and Kluckhohn observed, while the logical construct of culture is based on the study of behavior and behavioral products and makes behavior intelligible,

culture is not behavior nor the investigation of behavior in all its concrete completeness. Part of culture consists in norms for or standards of behavior. Still another part consists in ideologies justifying or rationalizing certain selected ways of behavior. Finally, every culture includes broad general principles of selectivity and ordering ("highest common factors") in terms of which patterns of and for and about behavior in very varied areas of culture content are reducible to parsimonious generalization.   (*ibid.*, p. 189)

A. Irving Hallowell, himself one of the first anthropologists to apply learning theory to the study of culture, has come to a somewhat similar conclusion in a recent discussion of personality, culture, and society in behavioral evolution: "Cultural adaptation cannot be equated with learned and socially transmitted behavior, although it is one of the necessary conditions underlying it. Equally important in behavioral evolution is how much is learned and what is learned, relative to the psychological capacities and total life adjustments of the animal" (1963, p. 492). But even if we accept the Kroeber and Kluckhohn definition of the culture concept, as they themselves say: "But a concept, even an important one, does not constitute a theory. . . . In anthropology at present we have plenty of definitions but too little theory" (1952, p. 181).

There are, as they also point out, adumbrations of a general theory of culture in the works of Boas (1911), Sapir (1927), Benedict (1934), Linton (1936), Bateson (1936), Kluckhohn (1941), Kroeber ([1923] 1948, chapter 8; 1952; see also "Anthropological Horizons" 1962), White (1949), Opler (1945; 1946; 1959), and others. Essentially this general theory emphasizes the study of pattern, form, structure, and organization in culture rather than discrete culture traits and culture content. While influenced by biological analogies, the pattern theory is also closely affiliated with the nineteenth-century German school of cultural history and with gestalt psychology. Culture patterning is an "emergent" of human creativity transcending the limits of biology and the natural environment.

Different spheres of social life differ in susceptibility to patterning, and culture patterns differ in degrees of consciousness and complexity as well as in kind. The simplest patterns are the explicit and more or less objective patterns of behavior expressed in customs of dress, diet, work, and salutation, and in artifacts. Then there are the more complex patterns underlying social, political, and economic organization and the systems of religion, language, law, philosophy, science, and the arts. Among these Kroeber has distinguished those "basic" or "systemic" patterns in different fields of culture which have persisted (at least in their cultural descendants) for several thousand years as coherent organizations of traits with functional value (e.g., the alphabet, plow agriculture, monotheism), and the "secondary" patterns (of formal social organization, systems of thought, etc.), which are subject to greater variety and instability. Different again from all these kinds of culture patterns are those qualities of cultural organization which come to pervade all or most spheres of some cultures and give them a distinctive individual "slant." Such are the implicit and unconscious configurations which Ruth Benedict described in her *Patterns of Culture* (1934). Kroeber saw these configurations as "patterns of patterns" in those cultures which have achieved stylistic integration. Acknowledging that they may have psychological correlates in personality traits, he preferred to analyze these total cultural patterns in cultural and historical terms.

The totality of human culture also contains an element of patterning that provides the general framework for individual cultures and represents a historical summation of those cultures which have segregated themselves out as crystallized historical configurations of culture. The "universal pattern" of human history, in either sense, is not yet known but can only be gradually discovered through comparative-historical studies of the systemic, secondary, and configurational patterns in all cultures, primitive and civilized (Kroeber & Kluckhohn 1952, p. 185; "Anthropological Horizons" 1962).

There are no absolute units or natural boundaries for cultural–historical studies. "The lines of demarcation of any cultural unit chosen for description and analysis are in large part a matter of level of abstraction and of convenience for the problem at hand. Occidental culture, Graeco–Roman culture, nineteenth-century European culture, German culture, Swabian culture, the peasant culture of the Black Forest in 1900—these are all equally legitimate abstractions if carefully defined" (Kroeber & Kluckhohn 1952, p. 185).

Culture patterns tend to persist as organized bodies of custom in spite of changes in items of culture content. Changes in individual items can be explained as selections and rejections consistent with the cultural patterns. But the patterns themselves are also subject to change. There is a cultural orthogenesis, in which "the direction of at least some culture change is more predetermined by earlier forms of the culture than caused by environmental press and individual variability" (*ibid.*, p. 189). Sapir called this "cultural drift": "Whenever the human mind has worked collectively and unconsciously, it has striven for and often attained unique form. The important point is that the evolution of form has a drift in one direction, that it seeks poise, and that it rests, relatively speaking, when it has found this poise" (quoted in *ibid.*, p. 182).

The relevance of "cultural drift" to studies of cultural continuity and change is obvious. Eggan (1963) has recently applied it to an analysis of cultural changes in the Philippines, and Redfield and the present writer have suggested ways in which the role of cities in cultural change may be interpreted as the product of "orthogenetic" and "heterogenetic" processes (see the article by Redfield & Singer in Redfield 1962; also see Singer 1959).

Another important kind of pattern change has been analyzed by Kroeber in his *Configurations of Culture Growth* (1944). In this and in later discussions Kroeber showed that the rise and the decline of civilizations can be viewed as phases in the growth and realization of stylistic configurations. The clustering of the peak periods of cultural creativity in each civilization within limited time periods suggests the importance of critical periods of "ripeness" in the process of cultural growth and innovation (Kroeber 1957; 1963).

Pattern theory assumes that culture is created by individuals and groups and interacts with them as well as with the environment. However, these interactions of biology, psychology, and geography are the given conditions and starting points for cultural growth but not its determinants. Such a theory views the process of cultural growth as a historical process, as Boas emphasized, a "growing together" of elements of culture content from different sources, which have become associated in a historical configuration. The end result of this historical process, at any given time, is an associated set of patterns, a precipitate of the history of a particular group, of its past choices, conscious and unconscious. Culture is this precipitate "present in persons, shaping their perceptions of events, other persons, and the environing situation in ways not wholly determined by biology and environmental press. Culture is an intervening variable between human 'organism' and 'environment'" (Kroeber & Kluckhohn 1952, p.186). It is "an abstract description of *trends toward* uniformity in the words, acts, and artifacts of human groups" (*ibid.*, p. 182).

Culture pattern theory has also been used in acculturation studies (Spicer 1962) and in studies which try to relate culture patterns to personality structure (reviewed in Singer 1961; and in Mead 1962) or to changes in environment and demography (Steward 1955).

Applications of pattern theory tend to avoid causal hypotheses, because culture is so intricate, multiple and cumulative that there seems no point in looking for specific external causes of specific cultural forms, either in deterministic laws or in cross-cultural statistical correlations. The primary research task of a pattern theorist is to delineate culture patterns and, beyond that, to compare and classify types of patterns as well as to distinguish the most fundamental and constant patterns from the secondary and variable ones.

Social structure as a theory of culture

The theory of social structure was first developed in an important series of papers by Radcliffe-Brown in the 1930s and 1940s and has since been considerably extended. "Social structure," is defined by Radcliffe-Brown as a network or system of social relations including persistent social groups and differentiated social classes and social roles. In Radcliffe-Brown's formulation the theory follows the organic analogy very closely; thus comparative social morphology is concerned with studying and classifying the different types of social structure and social physiology with studying how particular types of social structure function. It is assumed as a working hypothesis that each structural system is a functional unity in which all the component parts contribute in a harmonious way to its existence and continuity. To test this hypothesis all kinds of social phenomena—morals, law, etiquette, religion, government, economics, education, language—need to be studied "not in abstraction or isolation, but in their direct and indirect relations to social structure, i.e. with reference to the way in which they depend upon, or affect the social relations between persons and groups of persons" (Radcliffe-Brown 1952, p. 195).

The study of how particular types of social structure change into new structural types forms a third branch of the theory of social structure. This study requires assistance from history and archeology to trace the actual processes in the formation and transformation of particular structural types. Radcliffe-Brown suggested that the hypothesis of social evolution, which he accepted as plausible, should be defined "as the process by which wide-range systems of social structure have grown out of, or replaced, narrow range systems" (*ibid.*, p. 204).

Radcliffe-Brown's formulation of the theory of social structure is universal; it is intended to apply to societies of all kinds, at all places and times. In practice, Radcliffe-Brown and others at first restricted social anthropology to a comparative study of the social structure and social physiology of contemporary nonliterate and simple societies. Since primitive societies were assumed not to have histories or historical records, the study of structural change was also restricted to cases of contact with civilized societies. These limitations led to a definition of social anthropology as the intensive study of the structural systems of small, nonliterate communities, or "primitive isolates."

Developments in social anthropology have since relaxed these restrictions, and studies of structural change in primitive and simple societies have undertaken to combine history and archeology with structural–functional analysis (as in the work of Eggan, Evans-Pritchard, and M. G. Smith) or to restudy the same society at different periods (as in the work of Redfield, Firth, and others); the study of structural conflicts in simple societies was undertaken and the assumption of stability was dropped (Leach, Gluckman, Fallers); and studies of the social structures of peasant and modern communities and of civilizations were begun (Redfield, Warner, Geertz, Firth, Schneider, M. Freedman, E. Wolf and others).

These developments have broadened social anthropology and have brought it closer to the original universal scope of the theory of social structure. The expansion of social anthropology to include macrostructural studies of peasant societies, modern communities, and civilizations has gone more smoothly in comparative social morphology than in social physiology. The reasons for this are obvious—it is relatively easier to trace networks of social relations, social classes, and social groups in a large-scale society than it is to demonstrate how such a macrostructural system constitutes a functioning, integrated unity. To demonstrate the existence of such a functional unity requires consideration of the results of different approaches, such as economics, political science, literary studies, and art history, each of which has made some specialized aspect or subsystem of the total society its peculiar subject matter. Structural changes, on the other hand, are easier to trace at this level because of the longer time perspectives and data provided by historical and archeological studies.

The boundaries and identity of the unit of study also became more problematic when social anthropology moved beyond the primitive isolate. Radcliffe-Brown was very much aware of this difficulty: "It is rarely that we find a community that is absolutely isolated, having no outside contact. At the present moment of history, the network of social relations spreads over the whole world, without any absolute solution of continuity anywhere" (*ibid.*, p. 193).

If this is so, what then is a unit society, asks Radcliffe-Brown? "Is the British Empire a society or a collection of societies? Is a Chinese village a society, or is it merely a fragment of the Republic of China?" The answer is pragmatic: "If we take any convenient locality of a suitable size, we can study the structural system as it appears in and from that region, i.e. the network of relations connecting the inhabitants amongst themselves and with the people of other regions" (*ibid.*).

Thus, finding the suitable and convenient unit of society becomes a matter of the problem at hand and the resources one has available for dealing with it. In effect, then, there is no "natural" unit of society most suitable for structural analysis which can be defined at the beginning of fieldwork; natural units emerge in the form of structural types only as the results of intensive field studies, comparison, abstraction, classification, and generalization.

Radcliffe-Brown and other adherents of the theory of social structure tended to avoid using the term "culture" after the early 1930s. This avoidance is based on the claim that social anthropology studies social structure, not culture. This claim is misleading. In fact, the theory of social structure both explicitly and implicitly incorporates a concept of culture. Fortes, for example, writes that social structure and social organization are not just "an aspect of culture but the entire culture of a given people handled in a special frame of theory" (1953, p. 21). Fortes uses "culture" in almost precisely the same sense as Kroeber and Kluckhohn. In this frame "the facts of custom—the standardized ways of doing, knowing, thinking, and feeling—universally obligatory and valued in a given group of people at a given time" are then seen "as symbolizing or expressing social relations" (*ibid.*).

This special frame of theory is obviously Radcliffe-Brown's social physiology. Without using the word "culture" Radcliffe-Brown acknowledges the concept when he defines a social system as "the total social structure of a society together with the totality of social usages in which that structure appears and on which it depends for its continued existence" (1952, p. 181). These social usages include morals, law, etiquette, religion, government, education, and every kind of social phenomenon which is a part of "the complex mechanism by which a social structure exists and persists" (*ibid.*, p. 195). Social physiology, in other words, is a frame of theory which tries to relate all aspects of culture, in Tylor's sense, to social structure as a network of social relations.

That a concept of culture is implicit in the theory of social structure is usually overlooked because of the notion that social anthropology deals with "actually existing social relations" and not with such abstractions as culture. Radcliffe-Brown, who occasionally writes in this vein (e.g., *ibid.*, pp. 189–190), nevertheless makes it quite clear that while actually existing social relations may provide the raw data of observation, they are not the same thing as the social structure, which is derived from them by abstraction and generalization.

In the study of social structure the concrete reality with which we are concerned is the set of actually existing relations, at a given moment of time, which link together certain human beings. It is on this that we can make direct observations. But it is not this that we attempt to describe in its particularity. . . . What we need for scientific purposes is an account of the form of the structure. For example, if in an Australian tribe I observe in a number of instances the behaviour towards one another of persons who stand in the relation of mother's brother and sister's son, it is in order that I may be able to record as precisely as possible the general or normal form of this relationship, abstracted from the variations of particular instances, though taking account of these variations. (*ibid.*, p. 192)

A social structure, then, is not something directly observed but an abstraction of structural forms from the actually existing relations, which are observable. These abstracted "structural forms" or "normal forms of social relations" cannot be described or understood without reference to culture: "Social relations are only observed, and can only be described, by reference to the reciprocal behaviour of the persons related. The form of a social structure has therefore to be described by the patterns of behaviour to which individuals and groups conform in their dealings with one another" (*ibid.*, p. 198).

Such behavior patterns sound very much like Kluckhohn and Kroeber's explicit and implicit patterns: "These patterns are partially formulated in rules which, in our own society, we distinguish as rules of etiquette, of morals and of law. Rules, of course, only exist in their recognition by the members of the society; either in their verbal recognition, when they are stated as rules, or in their observance in behaviour" (*ibid.*).

At the very heart of the theory of social structure we find the concept of culture as a set of rules, implicit or explicit, of standardized modes of behavior and thought. The concept of culture is also implicit in Radcliffe-Brown's definition of "a social relation" as a mutual adjustment of interests between persons: "Whenever we say that a subject has a certain interest in an object we can state the same thing by saying that the object has a certain value for the subject. Interests and values are correlative terms, which refer to the two sides of an asymmetrical relation" (*ibid.*, p. 199).

This conception of a value as any object of any interest, derived from the American philosopher R. B. Perry, is extended by Radcliffe-Brown to a definition of "a social value" as the object of a common interest. This leads Radcliffe-Brown to the position that values—and their correlative interests —are the determinants of social relations, and hence of social structure. The foundations of the theory of social structure are thus two intangibles —social values and psychological interests.

It is now clear why the theory of social structure can dispense with the word "culture": it has incorporated the culture concept into the core of the theory, for the theory of social structure deals with social relations not simply as concrete actually existing objects of observations but as institutionalized and standardized modes of behavior and thought whose normal forms are socially recognized in the explicit or implicit rules to which the members of a given society tend to conform.

Culture patterns and social structure as parallel and as complementary

There is a striking formal parallelism between the theory of culture patterns and the theory of social structure. Both are holistic theories in the sense that they try to cover all aspects of society and culture—law, politics, economy, technology, kinship and social organization, art, literature, language, religion, philosophy, science, and so on. Fortes' formulation applies to both theories: each provides a special frame of theory to handle the entire culture of a people. Or, to put it a little differently, each theory incorporates Tylor's omnibus concept of culture in a different frame. Both theories are universalistic: they are intended to apply to all kinds of societies and cultures, and not to just one special kind. Each theory defines its basic concepts in such a way that it is possible to deal with different levels and hierarchies of pattern and structures, including the possibility of a single world-wide culture pattern and a world-wide network of social relations.

The early field studies of "primitive" and small-scale societies and cultures were in part associated with two kinds of theoretical interests: the lingering interest in the origins and evolutionary place of "contemporary primitives" and the belief that primitive societies and cultures are instances of simple, functionally integrated units. It was in the latter connection that both the theory of culture patterns and that of social structure came to be thought of as essentially theories of the primitive isolate. As both theories were extended to peasant villages and to modern urban communities, however, the primitive isolate gradually faded as a natural unit; thus liberated, both theories were applied to morphological, functional, and historical studies of both the culture patterns and the social organization of civilizations.

The parallels between the theory of culture patterns and the theory of social structure are numerous and striking. Both theories have explanatory aims, although each finds different factors to be primary.

The relation between basic and secondary patterns, on the one hand, and between the "substructure" of social relations and the "superstructure" of culture, on the other, is not necessarily causal, but it has explanatory value. This, therefore, is the parallelism between the two theories; the difference arises from the fact that the pattern theory does not specify which aspects of culture and society are most likely to form basic patterns—they may be matters of religion, technological invention, or ideas—while the structural theory assigns basic explanatory value to social relations. This difference, in relation to a particular individual society or culture, is not very great, because the structural theory considers an "explanation" achieved when it has shown how each part contributes functionally to the existence and continuity of a particular type of social structure, while the pattern theory's desideratum for "explanation" is to show how each part fits into an over-all configuration or stylistic pattern of the culture.

The difference between the two concepts is not that one is an abstraction and the other a concrete, observable unit of behavior, for both are abstractions of regularities from observations of actual behavior, whether these regularities are implicit and unconscious or explicit and verbalized. That social structure, too, is an abstraction and not a directly observable, concrete reality was first effectively argued by Bateson (1936) and subsequently reaffirmed by Fortes (1949), Firth (1951), Kroeber and Kluckhohn (1952), Nadel (1951), Eggan (1955), Redfield (1955; 1956), Lévi-Strauss (1953), Leach (1954), Schneider (1965), and others. Radcliffe-Brown himself in an earlier paper acknowledged this when he wrote:

In human society the social structure as a whole can only be *observed* in its functioning. Some of the features of social structure, such as the geographical distribution of individuals and groups can be directly observed, but most of the social relations which in their totality constitute the structure, such as relations of father and son, buyer and seller, ruler and subject, cannot be observed except in the social activities in which the relations are functioning. (1952, p. 181)

A particularly concise and lucid formulation of the issue has been made by Firth:

If . . . society is taken to be an organized set of individuals with a given way of life, culture is that way of life. If society is taken to be an aggregate of social relations, then culture is the content of those relations. Society emphasizes the human component, the aggregate of people and the relations between them. Culture emphasizes the component of accumulated resources, immaterial as well as material, which the people inherit, employ, transmute, add to, and transmit. (1951, p. 27)

Both Eggan (1955) and Redfield (1962) have systematically analyzed the differences and similarities between the complementary abstractions, culture and social structure. Eggan's summary includes the essential points: social structures are more limited in variety of forms and more predictable in terms of change than culture patterns and may vary independently; social relations are more abstract and more difficult to grasp than are cultural forms and less likely to be borrowed; social integration and cultural integration are defined by different criteria and can vary independently of one another; cultural integration is perhaps the more essential for personality integration, although the integration of the individual into groups is also important; the data and forms of culture seem to be more amenable to historical study, and social structures more amenable to classification and comparison, although the method of controlled comparison can and should be applied both to social structure and to culture patterns in a given historical framework (Eggan [1955] 1962, pp. 490–501).

Eggan explains the major differences between British social anthropology and American ethnology in terms of the emphasis given to one or the other side of this complementarity:

The British social anthropologists tend to think of themselves as sociologists concerned primarily with the social structures and institutions of primitive societies, or they utilize social structure as a frame for the organization and interpretation of cultural phenomena; most American ethnologists consider culture as the major concept and point of departure and subordinate social structure to it, if they utilize this concept at all, preferring to operate with concepts of culture pattern and cultural form. (*ibid.*, p. 490)

Yet Eggan, along with everyone else who has stressed the complementary nature of the concepts of social structure and culture, emphasizes that these

two aspects of social behavior—social structure and cultural pattern—cannot exist independently of one another in human society: society and culture are mutually dependent, and social relations are carried, or exemplified, only in cultural behavior. Social institutions partake of both aspects: they are composed of individuals organized through recurring social relationships into a social structure, with a set of attitudes, beliefs, and behavior patterns through which the structure is exemplified and the institutional ends achieved. (*ibid.*, p. 492)

If the complementarity between social structure and culture pattern is so intimate and interdependent, how is it possible to construct a global theory of either concept by itself? Eggan suggests that the actual field studies by British social anthropologists and American ethnologists show fewer differences than their theoretical formulations would lead one to expect. This is probably true, but leaves the theoretical formulations in doubt. For if social structure and culture pattern are complementary abstractions, then it follows that a theory of social structure must also make a place for the concept of culture pattern and that a theory of culture patterns must make a place for the concept of social structure. Each is a comprehensive theory which includes both concepts, but not on a basis of equality. The pattern theory subordinates social structure to culture, and the structural theory reverses the subordination. Acceptance of the complementarity of the two concepts is consistent with both theories and does not, therefore, account for the difference between the structural and pattern theories of culture.

Cultural versus structural explanations of kinship systems

The best clue to the difference between the pattern theory and the structural theory is to be found in the Rivers–Kroeber–Radcliffe-Brown debate over Morgan's distinction between "classificatory" and "descriptive" kinship systems. This debate is well known in the history of kinship studies and served to crystallize the difference between the concepts of a kinship system as a "cultural system" and as a "social system" and the difference between a pattern and a structural theory of culture. All the issues in this debate are by no means dead, so far as can be judged from the revival of Kroeber's earlier position in the recent development of "componential analysis" of kinship by Goodenough and Lounsbury and, to some extent, in Lévi-Strauss's "structuralism." We shall deal briefly with the debate here only insofar as it stimulated both Kroeber and Radcliffe-Brown to sharpen the difference between structural and cultural explanations of kinship systems, and, a fortiori, of other systems as well.

Kroeber's 1909 paper, "Classificatory Systems of Relationship," in addition to criticizing Morgan's conception of classificatory kinship systems, proposed to compare and classify all kinship terminologies in terms of a limited number of categories of relationship and the degree to which these categories are recognized and expressed in different terminological systems. Kroeber identified eight such categories: difference in generation, difference of age in generation, difference between lineal and collateral relatives, sex of relative, sex of speaker, sex of connecting relative, difference between relation by marriage and by blood, and condition of life of connecting relative. In the 1909 paper he used these categories to compare English kin terms and those of several North American Indian languages. His conclusion from this comparison was that while the English terms give expression to a smaller number of the categories, each set of terms forms a consistent and self-contained system. From the comparison he also drew a more general conclusion—that one cannot reconstruct specific social institutions and forms of marriage from specific systems of kinship terms, as was the common practice, because "terms of relationship reflect psychology not sociology," and are "determined primarily by language and can be utilized for sociological inferences only with extreme caution" (p. 84).

Under the pressure of criticism from Rivers and later from Radcliffe-Brown, both of whom defended the "sociological" theory, Kroeber clarified what he meant by "psychological" and "linguistic" determination of systems of kinship terms. He meant, he explained later, that the systems were "clean-cut made-to-order patterns of culture, speech, and conceptualization" (1952, p. 174). Certainly, kinship terminologies are part of a language, and as such they are classifications, and classifications are based on categories. The categories are conceptual categories subject to the patterning of "unconscious logic." The result is "a pattern of semantic classification for thinking and speaking of blood relationship." Some of these patterns may possess "a surprising historical tenacity," as Kroeber shows in the case of the Philippine kinship system. Such semantic patterns, or "logical schemes," may also correspond to social institutions, as in the Philippine system, but the correspondence is between the total pattern of terminology and the total pattern of institutions, and reflects the underlying logical scheme rather than any exact detailed causality between kin terms and institutions. The correspondence of the terminology with the general level of culture—language and religion, for example—may be even looser. A kinship terminology, in Kroeber's view, is primarily a semantic pattern, that is, a pattern of speech and thought, and only secondarily and in special cases is it correlated with a pattern of social institutions.

Kroeber was interested in linguistic and logical systems for their own sake and believed that culture was too intricate to be easily unraveled according to any formula of exact causal determinism. He saw kinship terminologies, like other aspects of culture, as historically developed and, to some extent, independent, stylistic patterns. Patterns of formal social structure, such as clans, moieties, totems, and unilateral groups, are also examples of such stylistic differentiation and secondary elaboration of the primary patterns of subsistence and residence. Kinship terminologies and formal social structures are kinds of culture patterns which, among primitive peoples, express the impulse toward cultural play, innovation, and unconscious experiment. The extent of their mutual correspondence is a matter of historical and functional adjustment and varies from culture to culture. "Kinship terminologies are pattern systems of semantic logic, highly variable in detail and historically derivable, but also classifiable" into "natural types" (*ibid.*, p. 172). In this respect they are analogous to linguistic families and biological types.

Radcliffe-Brown was stimulated by the Rivers–Kroeber debate to develop a concept of kinship system which differed from both of these and which became the foundation of his structural theory. Radcliffe-Brown included in his concept several of the components suggested by Kroeber; he agreed with Kroeber that the terminology of kinship is an intrinsic part of the system and an important starting point for its study. He accepted the position that kin terms designate "categories of relation," although Radcliffe-Brown did not restrict his analysis to Kroeber's underlying eight categories. For Radcliffe-Brown, however, a set of kinship terms and associated categories did not constitute a kinship system as it did for Kroeber in the form of a relatively independent semantic system. Radcliffe-Brown agreed that terms and categories do reflect the way a people generally think and feel about kinship, but he believed that social institutions also reflect such general modes of thought and should also be included in the conception of a kinship system. On this point he sided with Rivers rather than with Kroeber: social practices, including forms of marriage, are regularly connected with kinship terminologies. Radcliffe-Brown's distinctive contribution was the way in which he analyzed these connections. He did not accept Rivers' causal analysis of the connections or their use for historical reconstruction; kin terms and social institutions are, for him, related, not as cause and effect, but as component and interdependent parts of a *structural system*. Within such a system the kin terms are used to establish and recognize particular categories of relatives, and the categories fix the actual social relations between the relatives who belong to these categories. The particular behavior manifested in the social relations between relatives is defined by legally formulated rights and duties or by socially approved usages. In this functionally interdependent system, there is no line or direction of causality running either from kinship terminology to standard kinship behavior or conversely. Both terminology and behavior are reflections of the underlying structural principle or principles by which the system is organized and characterized. These principles, such as that of sibling solidarity or solidarity of the patrilineal lineage, need to be discovered by intensive study and comparison of different kinship systems. Why some societies differ in the structural principles they have selected as the basis of their kinship systems and of their respective social structures can only be answered by historical study of how the systems developed in particular environments.

The difference between Kroeber's and Radcliffe-Brown's ideas of a kinship system is an illustration and source of the difference between the pattern theory of culture and the structural theory. A kinship system for Kroeber is one of several kinds of culture pattern—as a semantic system it is governed by an inner logic, is historically derived, and has some functional significance. Its relation to social institutions and to other aspects of culture is not causal and not entirely accidental but is rather the relation of one culture pattern to other culture patterns which have become historically associated with it and which have undergone some mutual adjustments. In this paradigm, social structure is subordinated to culture only in the sense that social institutions are also subject to the patterning of the experimental play impulse of human creativity.

The Radcliffe-Brown structural paradigm, on the other hand, obviously includes culture as a component of the system. Culture is subordinated to social structure only in the sense that both kin terms and the social usages defining socially approved behavior between relatives are brought together into a single system organized by structural principles. Although history is considered essential for understanding how a system came to be organized the way it is, the morphology and functioning of the system can be understood without reference to its history. If Kroeber's pattern theory makes social institutions subject to patterning, Radcliffe-Brown's structural theory makes culture a component of a structural system, that is, subject to "structuring."

The social organization of culture

Both Kroeber and Radcliffe-Brown regarded kinship systems as natural systems. This was so for Kroeber if they could be shown to be systemic culture patterns and for Radcliffe-Brown if they could be shown to conform to a type of social structure. The natural systems, whether culture patterns or structural types, emerge in the course of field studies and comparative analysis; the boundaries of such systems are relative to the problem being studied.

Thus we may study the culture patterns or the social structures of villages, towns, cities, regions, nations, civilizations, as well as of occupations, social classes, castes, religious sects, or of any groups that may turn out to have them. The interrelation of patterns and structures in groups of different size and composition may also be traced, albeit with extensions and modifications of the methods of analysis that have been used to study the cultural patterns or social structures of relatively small, isolated, and homogeneous groups. How is this extension to be made?

In 1948 Kroeber wrote that "perhaps *how it comes to be* is really more distinctive of culture than what it is" (see [1923] 1948, p. 253). And in 1949 and 1952 Radcliffe-Brown talked of culture as "the process by which a person acquires, from contact with other persons or from such things as books or works of art, knowledge, skill, ideas, beliefs, tastes, sentiments" (1952, pp. 4–5). In a particular society one may discover processes of cultural tradition and "in complex modern societies there are a great number of separate cultural traditions. By one a person may learn to be a doctor or surgeon, by another he may learn to be an engineer or an architect" (*ibid.*, p. 5).

"Culture" is thus reintroduced by Radcliffe-Brown as the process by which, in a given social group or social class, learned ways of thinking, feeling, and acting are transmitted from person to person and from one generation to the next. He does not, however, reinstate it as an independent concept but assimilates it to the social process.

Neither Radcliffe-Brown nor Kroeber developed his respective theory further to take into account those processes of interpersonal interaction by which, in a particular society, separate cultural traditions are formed, transmitted, and modified or those processes by which communication is established among separate local cultural traditions, one with another and with wider regional and national cultural traditions. It was Robert Redfield who suggested that these problems might be fruitfully studied through a study of the institutionalized social relations involved in the transmission of cultural traditions. He formulated his suggestion in the concept of "the social organization of tradition," which he defined as "the way in which elements of action are put together in any particular case of transmission of tradition." In analogy with Firth's distinction between social organization

and social structure (1951) and Radcliffe-Brown's distinction between organization and structure (1952, p. 11), the social organization of a cultural tradition represents the expression in concrete, organized activities of "the social structure of tradition," or, in Redfield's words, "those persisting and important arrangements of roles and statuses appearing in such corporate groups as castes and sects, or in teachers, reciters, ritual leaders of one kind or another, that are concerned with the cultivation and inculcation of the great tradition" (1956, p. 101). Redfield also generalized these concepts of the social organization and structure of cultural traditions to a conception of a civilization as a structure of different levels and kinds of cultural traditions ("little" and "great") in mutual contact and communication. Civilizations have both a "societal structure" and a "cultural structure" (Redfield 1962).

These conceptions have proved very fruitful for the study of civilizations, particularly in India which, indeed, has been the major empirical source and proving ground, and they are beginning to be applied to other civilizations. They have stimulated studies of how specific networks of social relations (marriage, trade, political administration, etc.) also serve as channels of cultural transmission; of "cultural performances" as the chief vehicles for discovering and expressing a sense of "cultural identity"; of the roles of different kinds of "cultural specialists" and "cultural policy makers" in forming and changing "cultural identities"; and of continuity and change in the cultural traditions of a historic civilization, and so on (see Singer 1964a, for a review of some of these studies). One reason why this approach is fruitful is that it bypasses the older antinomies—"How can one culture pattern produce another without the intervention of specific agencies?" or "How can 'social structures' be causally correlated with 'culture patterns'?" By concentrating on the institutionalized social relations, media, and functionaries which transmit specific cultural traditions from person to person and from group to group, this approach is at once both structural and cultural.

This approach to the study of culture is sometimes criticized for being too humanistic, too subjective and evaluational in contrast to the alleged objective and value-free character of other approaches. This is an unjustified criticism. All definitions of culture have contained implicit positive evaluations of the elements of culture and have not been neutral and objective. To bring these implicit evaluations to the surface it is only necessary to conduct the experiment of turning the elements of any of the definitions into their opposites or to ask why, if culture is a neutral concept, one would not think of applying it to a group that lacked the elements of the definition—for example, language, art, knowledge, and skills. The implicit evaluation is that culture consists of positive achievements and desirable characteristics. Even in the context of evolutionary discussions, where one problem is to differentiate human culture from animal behavior, the ostensibly objective definition of culture as learned behavior in contrast to instinctive behavior has not proved very differentiating. And it will not be very useful until, as Hallowell and others have pointed out, we can specify what and how much has been learned and how the learning is transmitted and modified; in other words, until we can tell how learn*ed* is learned behavior.

George Stocking, Jr., is probably correct in linking the normative elements in Tylor's definition of culture to nineteenth-century humanistic discussions such as are to be found in Matthew Arnold's *Culture and Anarchy* (Stocking 1963). But Stocking's highly illuminating article tends to understate the differences between the Tylor conception and that of Arnold. For what was distinctive about Tylor's conception of culture was not its nonnormative character—Stocking is quite right to challenge this myth—but the *breadth* of its application. Tylor and anthropologists after him have been able to find evidences of culture among the most primitive and lowly peoples, but many humanists are not yet prepared to accept this finding. In spite of his apparently ethnocentric preference for nineteenth-century English institutions, Tylor sought "to treat mankind as homogeneous in nature, though placed in different grades of civilization," without regard to hereditary differences. From this broad perspective he could see "scarce a hand's breadth difference between an English ploughman and a negro of Central Africa."

Some humanists have come to accept the anthropologists' broad use of the term "culture." T. S. Eliot, for example, in his *Notes Towards the Definition of Culture* is very close to this anthropological usage when he writes that in his usage "it includes all the characteristic activities and interests of a people," among the British, for example, "Derby Day, Henley Regatta, Cowes, the twelfth of August, a cup final, the dog races, the pin table, the dart board, Wensleydale cheese, boiled cabbage cut into sections, beetroot in vinegar, nineteenth century Gothic churches and the music of Elgar" ([1948] 1949, p. 30).

The problem then in studies of the social organization of cultural traditions and of the relations between the "little traditions" of the uneducated and the "great traditions" of the learned, is not to avoid the normative aspects of culture, an impossible task in any case, but to develop further the methods for observing and analyzing specific cultural traditions within a framework of a general theory of culture.

I have not referred to recent studies of the social organization of cultural traditions in order to introduce still a third general theory of culture to compete with the pattern and social structure theories. On the contrary, these studies illustrate one of the ways in which these two general theories can be extended, with a little modification, to the study of culture in composite societies and in complex historic civilizations.

Current developments—the new ethnography

In the 1930s and 1940s, Radcliffe-Brown's analysis of kinship systems as social systems tended to prevail over Kroeber's analysis of them as semantic patterns, even among American anthropologists who had accepted the pattern theory of culture in preference to a structural–functional theory. This situation was later reversed by a return to Kroeber's semantic analysis of kinship systems. The revival of the semantic analysis of kinship is largely the result of new developments in linguistics and is in turn generating a new theory of culture to compete with structural–functional theory.

Componential analysis. In their papers on the componential analysis of kinship terms, both published in 1956, Goodenough and Lounsbury acknowledge Kroeber's precedent. The more immediate sources of componential analysis, however, probably come from the methods of phonemic analysis. The analysis of kinship terminologies into their necessary and sufficient conceptual components resembles Kroeber's earlier efforts to identify a minimal list of conceptual categories of relations and results in a similar conception of a kinship system as a semantic or cognitive system. Methods analogous to componential analysis have been applied to other kinds of folk terminologies—for plants, diseases, colors, directions—in order to determine the underlying semantic structures of the cognitive systems.

These extensions of componential analysis have been regarded as applications of a new method in ethnography and even as a new discipline, "ethnoscience." Underlying these extensions and the programs of the "new ethnography" is a theory of culture, most explicitly formulated by Goodenough. According to his formulation, culture "is not a material phenomenon; it does not consist of things, people, behavior, or emotions. It is rather an organization of these things. It is the forms of things that people have in mind, their models for perceiving, relating, and otherwise interpreting them" (Goodenough [1957] 1964, p. 36).

The externals and observables—what people say and do, their social arrangements and events—are "products . . . of their culture as they apply it to the task of perceiving and dealing with their circumstances" (ibid.). Culture then consists of the "concepts" and "models" which people have in their minds for organizing and interpreting their experiences. Goodenough believes that "it is obviously impossible to describe a culture properly simply by describing behavior or social, economic, and ceremonial events and arrangements as observed material phenomena. What is required is to construct a theory of the conceptual models which they represent and of which they are artifacts" (ibid.).

Since the theory is to be empirical, Goodenough proposes as tests of its validity that it predict how informants will behave in response to what goes on in the community as well as in response to the ethnographer's behavior. In operational practice, however, the concepts and models of a culture are learned "when we learn the system of meanings for which its linguistic forms stand. Much descriptive ethnography is inescapably an exercise in descriptive semantics" (ibid., p. 39). This is as true of every human being learning his own culture as it is of the ethnographer trying to learn another's culture. Accordingly, "language is not only a part of culture" but "a major instrument for learning it" (ibid.).

This approach does not exclude the nonlinguistic aspects of culture, since "nonlinguistic forms have systematic relationships to each other in paradigms and combine in accordance with principles analogous to those of linguistic morphology and syntax" (ibid.). To one who knows the culture, the nonlinguistic aspects "are also signs signifying the cultural forms or models of which they are the material representations" (ibid., p. 36).

Goodenough's semantic and conceptual theory of culture bears a resemblance to Kroeber's pattern theory. Kroeber's semantic analysis, however, was explicitly applied only to the linguistic aspects of culture, to language, and to kinship terminologies. He did not explicitly extend this kind of analysis to other kinds of culture patterning, for example, to patterns of social structure. In Goodenough's theory, and in the new ethnography, the semantic analysis is generalized to all aspects of culture. All patterns in a culture are conceptual patterns, and

if some of the conceptual patterns are not directly expressed in the vocabulary of the language, their semantic structure can nevertheless be determined by analyzing the nonlinguistic forms as "artifacts" and "signs" of the conceptual patterns. All culture thus becomes cognitive and conceptual, and since, according to Goodenough, an individual can know only the concepts in his own mind, his "private culture" is more real than any "public culture."

The new structuralism. The componential analysis of kinship terminologies treats social structure explicitly only insofar as it can be reduced to a semantic structure and only in terms of a corresponding "cognitive structure." More direct attention is given to social structure in Lévi-Strauss's structural anthropology. This theory combines features of both Kroeber and Radcliffe-Brown and adds some original elements of its own. As in the other cases, the analysis of kinship systems is paradigmatic of the general theory. Lévi-Strauss accepts Radcliffe-Brown's views that there is a relation of interdependence between kinship terminologies and kinship behavior and attitudes and that the interdependence is not one of linear causality. In agreement with Kroeber, however, he does not believe that the relations of interdependence are point-for-point correspondences. Terminologies, on the one hand, and behavior and attitude, on the other, can be analyzed as separate systems and compared with one another as well as with other kinds of systems, such as those of social organization, religion, myth, ritual, and political ideology. These comparisons can be made within a single society or culture as well as between different societies and cultures. A single culture is "a fragment of humanity which, from the point of view of the research at hand and of the scale on which the latter is carried out, presents significant discontinuities in relation to the rest of humanity" (Lévi-Strauss [1953] 1963, p. 295).

So far this sounds very much like the pattern theory—a kinship terminology is one kind of culture pattern related by varying degrees of morphological and historical relations to other kinds of culture patterns. Lévi-Strauss introduces, however, a far more abstract and mathematical notion of system and structure than either Radcliffe-Brown or Kroeber. Lévi-Strauss makes explicit the distinction in Radcliffe-Brown's analysis between networks of social relations as the raw materials of observation and social structure as an abstract model of these relations; he goes on to generalize the concept of structure to its mathematical and logical level, as the regular order of relations among elements of any kind. Distinguishing the relationship between kinship terminologies and kinship behavior is thus a problem of constructing structural models for systems of kinship terminologies and for systems of kinship behavior and then investigating whether the relations existing between the structures are homologous, contradictory, and so on. Lévi-Strauss believes that the relations between the structures of kin terms and behavior are dialectical and functional; while behavior and attitudes reflect the terminological classification somewhat, they are at the same time responsive to contradictions created by the terminological classification. Resolving these contradictions leads to terminological changes that call for new behavior patterns, and so on (*ibid.*, pp. 310–311). He has made a similar analysis of the dialectical relations between the structures of myths and the structures of rituals and believes the analysis can be extended to other kinds of structures as well.

The existence of contradictions between different structures and the resolution of these contradictions through changes in the structures is not usually conscious to the participating members of a society. The structures and their relations exist at a deep unconscious level and reflect, in their particular modalities of space and time, universal mental processes. In some societies, however, there may be "home-made" conscious models of these structures, which need to be taken into account by the social anthropologist because they may be accurate and, in any case, form an important part of the data (see, e.g., Leach 1954).

Lévi-Strauss does not believe that all aspects of a culture and society are equally structured or that every culture has a single all-embracing structure. The degree and kind of structuring is a matter for anthropological investigation. He believes the following possess well-ordered structures—language, kinship, social organization, law, religion, myth, ritual, art, etiquette, cooking, and political ideology. Other domains are either not structured or at least their structures have not yet been discovered. The structures of specific domains are not microcosms of the whole society or culture but are "partial expressions of the total society."

Although he uses a general mathematical–logical concept of structure, Lévi-Strauss has acknowledged the important influence of structural linguistics, especially as developed by Jakobson and Trubetzkoy, and game theory and cybernetics as developed by Von Neumann and Wiener. Both kinds of models are used in his structural analysis, not to establish the identity of language and culture or

the identity of communication and society, but as formal analogies only, whose methodological fruitfulness depends on the existence of structural homologies among language, culture, and society. This is the sense, I suggest, in which the exchange of messages, the exchange of goods and services, and the exchange of women all represent, as Lévi-Strauss says, different levels of the communication process and the sense in which culture itself consists of "*rules* stating how the 'games of communication' should be played both on the natural and on the cultural levels" ([1953] 1963, p. 296).

Summary and conclusion

We can now summarize the major conclusions of the analysis in a series of brief propositions:

(1) Tylor's omnibus conception of culture is still the basis of most modern anthropological theories of culture, although the conception has been refined and developed in several different directions.

(2) Two theories of culture which have dominated anthropological thinking from about 1900 to 1950 are the process-pattern theory derived from Boas and best represented by Kroeber and the structural–functional theory derived from Malinowski and Radcliffe-Brown.

(3) While the process-pattern theory takes the concept of culture pattern as basic and the structural theory takes social structure as basic, both theories cover the full range of Tylor's culture concept.

(4) Each theory is holistic and universal, each seeks to explain all aspects of culture within a single theoretical framework, and each intends to apply that framework to societies and cultures of any kind, from small primitive societies to complex civilizations.

(5) The difference between the two basic theories cannot be derived from the complementary character of the two basic concepts—culture pattern and social structure—since each theory accepts this complementarity but deals with it in a different way.

(6) The difference between the two theories is to be found in the different ways they connect culture and social structure within explanatory systems.

(7) The precise nature of these explanatory systems may be inferred from a paradigmatic model of the analysis of kinship systems. According to pattern analysis, a kinship system is a terminological system which expresses a system of classification and an underlying unconscious logic. The relation of a kinship system, so defined, to social

institutions and other aspects of culture is the relation of one kind of culture pattern to others and varies with the history and mutual association of the patterns within particular places and times.

(8) In the structural analysis, a kinship system is a social system which includes a network of social relations, as expressed in customary modes of behavior, feeling, and thought, as well as a set of terms and categories of relations classified by the terms. The interrelation within the system is one of functional interdependence among the parts. The terms express and establish specific categories of relation and the categories fix and regulate specific modes of behavior and feeling in accordance with a limited number of structural principles around which the system is organized.

(9) These different analyses of kinship systems are both examples and models for cultural and structural analysis of all kinds and, hence, for two general theories of culture.

(10) Neither theory attempts to explain the nature of cultural or structural systems in terms of linear causality. Each regards such systems as outcomes of the multiple influences of biology, psychology, and the natural environment, as well as of historical processes and of the creative human responses to these "givens."

These propositions suggest an underlying convergence of the pattern theory and the structural–functional theory of culture. Although the pattern theory has probably been influenced more by study of language, literature, and the arts and the structural–functional theory more by biological and organic analogies, the direction taken by both kinds of theory has been the same. In closing, it may be useful to characterize this trend as it represents the mainstream of culture theory since Malinowski's 1931 article and also represents many recent theoretical developments.

Most characteristic is a shift away from a theory of discrete culture traits within a framework of universal cultural history or cultural evolution to a study of the functions, patterns, and structures of cultural forms within a plurality of organized contexts. There has been a corresponding shift from an interest in artifacts and other external manifestations of material culture to an almost overriding interest in social culture and in mental culture.

The definition of culture in terms of learned behavior (or standardized behavior) seemed at first to promise a unified theory of social and mental culture. But with the failure of behavioristic learning theories to account for the differentiated processes and kinds of learning involved in the acquisi-

tion of language, kinship systems, and other aspects of culture, this promise has not been fulfilled. Anthropologists, linguists, and psychologists interested in higher mental processes have begun to look to genetics, neurophysiology, maturation theory, ethology, and ego psychology for the mechanisms that enable organisms to acquire, transmit, and modify culture (see, e.g., Hallowell 1963; Chomsky 1959).

Recent definitions and analyses of culture have grown progressively more abstract, formal, and conceptualistic. Behavior, observed social relations, and material artifacts may provide the raw data for a construct of culture but are not themselves considered the constituents of culture. Rather, the patterns, norms, rules, and standards implicit in the behavior, social relations, and artifacts are considered as the constituents of culture. They are the systems of meanings, ideologies, conventionalized understandings, and cognitive and unconscious structures, which may be recognized in a given society with varying degrees of consciousness and explicit verbal formulation but which, in any case, are to be brought to conscious awareness and precise formulation by anthropological studies (see, e.g., the work of Goodenough).

Those social anthropologists who have been influenced by the theories of Durkheim, Weber, and Parsons are producing a fruitful synthesis of the pattern and structural theories of culture (see, e.g., the work of Fallers, Geertz, and Schneider).

The new ethnography, ethnolinguistics, and ethnoscience and Lévi-Strauss's new structuralism, share this new emphasis on cultures as abstract structures. They differ only in the procedures they propose for discovering the unconscious structures —in the form of codes, models, rules of the game— which determine the underlying cognitive structures (see, e.g., Romney & D'Andrade 1964; Lévi-Strauss 1953).

Taken as a working hypothesis the cognitive conception of culture offers a promising program of research, the results of which should improve cross-cultural understanding. Taken as a definition of the nature of man or as a general theory of human culture, however, it seems just as narrow and one-sided as previous definitions and theories. That man is a rational animal was long ago enunciated by Aristotle. And it is perhaps timely that anthropology, after neglecting this aspect of man's nature for over fifty years while it explored causal and structural models of culture, should now explore a logical model. This exploration will not forget, we hope, that there is more to human rationality than how different people classify kin, colors, plants, and diseases and that there is more to human culture than knowledge and the logic of classification. Even Tylor, whose theory of culture has so often been criticized for being too intellectualistic, left room in his omnibus concept, and in his writings, not only for science and language but also for all "the arts of life," "the arts of pleasure," religion, all forms of social organization, history, and mythology, and any other capabilities and habits acquired by man as a member of society. It is going to take more than one kind of theoretical model to do justice to the variety, complexity, and richness of human culture.

MILTON SINGER

BIBLIOGRAPHY

Anthropological Horizons: Report on a Symposium Organized and Chaired by Professor A. L. Kroeber. 1962 *Current Anthropology* 3:79–97.

BATESON, GREGORY (1936) 1958 *Naven: A Survey of the Problems Suggested by a Composite Picture of the Culture of a New Guinea Tribe Drawn From Three Points of View.* 2d ed. Stanford Univ. Press.

BENEDICT, RUTH 1934 *Patterns of Culture.* Boston: Houghton Mifflin. → A paperback edition was published in 1961.

BOAS, FRANZ (1896) 1955 The Limitations of the Comparative Method of Anthropology. Pages 270–280 in Franz Boas, *Race, Language and Culture.* New York: Macmillan. → First published in Volume 4 of *Science.*

BOAS, FRANZ 1911 Introduction. Part 1, pages 1–83 in Franz Boas (editor), *Handbook of American Indian Languages.* U.S. Bureau of American Ethnology, Bulletin No. 40. Washington: Government Printing Office.

CHICAGO, UNIVERSITY OF, COMMITTEE FOR THE COMPARATIVE STUDY OF NEW NATIONS 1963 *Old Societies and New States: The Quest for Modernity in Asia and Africa.* Edited by Clifford Geertz. New York: Free Press.

CHOMSKY, NOAM 1959 [A Review of] B. F. Skinner's *Verbal Behavior. Language* 35:26–58.

COHN, BERNARD S. 1962 Political Systems in Eighteenth Century India: The Banaras Region. *Journal of the American Oriental Society* 82:312–320.

DRIVER, HAROLD E.; and MASSEY, WILLIAM C. 1957 Comparative Studies of North American Indians. American Philosophical Society, *Transactions* 47:165–456.

DURKHEIM, ÉMILE (1893) 1960 *The Division of Labor in Society.* Glencoe, Ill.: Free Press. → First published as *De la division du travail social.*

DURKHEIM, ÉMILE (1895) 1958 *The Rules of Sociological Method.* 8th ed. Edited by George E. G. Catlin. Glencoe, Ill.: Free Press. → First published as *Les règles de la méthode sociologique.*

DURKHEIM, ÉMILE (1912) 1954 *The Elementary Forms of the Religious Life.* London: Allen & Unwin; New York: Macmillan. → First published as *Les formes élémentaires de la vie religieuse, le système totémique en Australie.* A paperback edition was published in 1961 by Collier.

EGGAN, FRED (1955) 1962 Social Anthropology: Methods and Results. Pages 485–551 in *Social Anthropology of North American Tribes.* Univ. of Chicago Press.

→ This article first appeared in the 1955 enlarged edition.

EGGAN, FRED 1963 Cultural Drift and Social Change. *Current Anthropology* 4:347–355.

ELIOT, T. S. (1948) 1949 *Notes Towards the Definition of Culture.* New York: Harcourt.

EVANS-PRITCHARD, E. E. (1937) 1965 *Witchcraft, Oracles and Magic Among the Azande.* Oxford: Clarendon.

EVANS-PRITCHARD, E. E. (1951) 1956 *Social Anthropology.* London: Cohen & West; Glencoe, Ill.: Free Press.

FALLERS, LLOYD A. 1956 *Bantu Bureaucracy: A Study of Integration and Conflict in the Political Institutions of an East African People.* Cambridge: Heffer.

FALLERS, LLOYD A. (editor) 1964 *The King's Men: Leadership and Status in Buganda on the Eve of Independence.* Oxford Univ. Press.

FIRTH, RAYMOND W. 1951 *Elements of Social Organization.* London: Watts. → A paperback edition was published in 1963 by Beacon.

FIRTH, RAYMOND W. (editor) (1957) 1964 *Man and Culture: An Evaluation of the Work of Bronislaw Malinowski.* New York: Harper.

FIRTH, RAYMOND W. 1959 *Social Change in Tikopia: Re-study of a Polynesian Community After a Generation.* New York: Macmillan; London: Allen & Unwin.

FORTES, MEYER (1949) 1963 Time and Social Structure: An Ashanti Case Study. Pages 54–84 in Meyer Fortes (editor), *Social Structure: Studies Presented to A. R. Radcliffe-Brown.* New York: Russell.

FORTES, MEYER 1953 The Structure of Unilineal Descent Groups. *American Anthropologist* New Series 55:17–41.

FORTES, MEYER 1955 Radcliffe-Brown's Contributions to the Study of Social Organization. *British Journal of Sociology* 6:16–30.

FRIEDRICH, P. 1964 Semantic Structure and Social Structure. Pages 131–166 in Ward H. Goodenough (editor), *Explorations in Cultural Anthropology: Essays in Honor of George Peter Murdock.* New York: McGraw-Hill.

GEERTZ, CLIFFORD (1960) 1964 *The Religion of Java.* New York: Free Press.

GEERTZ, CLIFFORD 1966 Religion as a Cultural System. Pages 1–42 in Association of Social Anthropologists of the Commonwealth, Conference on New Approaches in Social Anthropology, 1963, Cambridge, *Anthropological Approaches to the Study of Religion.* Edited by Michael Banton. London: Tavistock; New York: Praeger.

GLUCKMAN, MAX 1963 *Order and Rebellion in Tribal Africa.* New York: Free Press.

GOODENOUGH, WARD H. 1951 *Property, Kin, and Community on Truk.* Publications in Anthropology, No. 46. New Haven: Yale Univ. Press.

GOODENOUGH, WARD H. 1956 Componential Analysis and the Study of Meaning. *Language* 32:195–216.

GOODENOUGH, WARD H. (1957) 1964 Cultural Anthropology and Linguistics. Pages 36–39 in Dell H. Hymes (editor), *Language in Culture and Society: A Reader in Linguistics and Anthropology.* New York: Harper.

HALLOWELL, A. IRVING 1963 Personality, Culture, and Society in Behavioral Evolution. Volume 6, pages 429–509 in Sigmund Koch (editor), *Psychology: A Study of a Science.* New York: McGraw-Hill.

HYMES, DELL H. (editor) 1964 *Language in Culture and Society: A Reader in Linguistics and Anthropology.* New York: Harper.

JARVIE, I. C. 1964 *The Revolution in Anthropology.* London: Routledge.

KLUCKHOHN, CLYDE (1941) 1960 Patterning as Exemplified in Navaho Culture. Pages 109–130 in *Language, Culture and Personality: Essays in Memory of Edward Sapir.* Salt Lake City: Univ. of Utah Press.

KLUCKHOHN, CLYDE 1954 Culture and Behavior. Pages 921–976 in Gardner Lindzey (editor), *Handbook of Social Psychology.* Cambridge, Mass.: Addison-Wesley.

KROEBER, ALFRED L. 1909 Classificatory Systems of Relationship. *Journal of the Royal Anthropological Institute of Great Britain and Ireland* 39:77–84.

KROEBER, ALFRED L. (1923) 1948 *Anthropology: Race, Language, Culture, Psychology, Prehistory.* New ed., rev. New York: Harcourt. → First published as *Anthropology.*

KROEBER, ALFRED L. 1944 *Configurations of Culture Growth.* Berkeley: Univ. of California Press.

KROEBER, ALFRED L. 1952 *The Nature of Culture.* Univ. of Chicago Press. → A collection of essays that were first published between 1901 and 1951.

KROEBER, ALFRED L. 1957 *Style and Civilizations.* Ithaca, N.Y.: Cornell Univ. Press.

KROEBER, ALFRED L. 1960 Statistics, Indo-European, and Taxonomy. *Language* 36:1–21.

KROEBER, ALFRED L. 1963 *An Anthropologist Looks at History.* Berkeley: Univ. of California Press.

KROEBER, ALFRED L.; and KLUCKHOHN, CLYDE 1952 *Culture: A Critical Review of Concepts and Definitions.* Harvard University Peabody Museum of American Archeology and Ethnology Papers, Vol. 47, No. 1. Cambridge, Mass.: The Museum. → A paperback edition was published in 1963 by Vintage Books.

KROEBER, ALFRED L.; and PARSONS, TALCOTT 1958 The Concepts of Culture and of Social System. *American Sociological Review* 23:582–583.

LEACH, EDMUND R. 1954 *Political Systems of Highland Burma: A Study of Kachin Social Structure.* A publication of the London School of Economics and Political Science. London School of Economics and Political Science; Cambridge, Mass.: Harvard Univ. Press.

LEACH, EDMUND R. 1961 *Rethinking Anthropology.* London School of Economics and Political Science Monographs on Social Anthropology, No. 22. London: Athlone.

LÉVI-STRAUSS, CLAUDE 1949 *Les structures élémentaires de la parenté.* Paris: Presses Universitaires de France.

LÉVI-STRAUSS, CLAUDE (1953) 1963 *Structural Anthropology.* New York: Basic Books. → First published in French.

LINTON, RALPH 1936 *The Study of Man: An Introduction.* New York: Appleton.

LOUNSBURY, FLOYD G. 1956 A Semantic Analysis of the Pawnee Kinship Usage. *Language* 32:158–194.

LOUNSBURY, FLOYD G. 1964 A Formal Account of the Crow- and Omaha-type Kinship Terminologies. Pages 351–393 in Ward H. Goodenough (editor), *Explorations in Cultural Anthropology: Essays in Honor of George Peter Murdock.* New York: McGraw-Hill.

LOWIE, ROBERT H. 1937 *The History of Ethnological Theory.* New York: Farrar & Rinehart.

MALINOWSKI, BRONISLAW (1916–1941) 1948 *Magic, Science and Religion, and Other Essays.* Glencoe, Ill.: Free Press. → A paperback edition was published in 1954 by Doubleday.

MALINOWSKI, BRONISLAW (1922) 1960 *Argonauts of the Western Pacific: An Account of Native Enterprise and Adventure in the Archipelagoes of Melanesian New Guinea.* London School of Economics and Political Science Studies, No. 65. London: Routledge; New York: Dutton. → A paperback edition was published in 1961 by Dutton.

MALINOWSKI, BRONISLAW 1931 Culture. Volume 4, pages 621–645 in *Encyclopaedia of the Social Sciences.* New York: Macmillan.

MALINOWSKI, BRONISLAW 1944 *A Scientific Theory of Culture and Other Essays.* Chapel Hill: Univ. of North Carolina Press.

MALINOWSKI, BRONISLAW (1945) 1949 *The Dynamics of Culture Change: An Inquiry Into Race Relations in Africa.* New Haven: Yale Univ. Press. → A paperback edition was published in 1961.

MARRIOTT, McKIM (editor) 1955 *Village India: Studies in the Little Community.* Univ. of Chicago Press. → Also published as Memoir No. 83 of the American Anthropological Association, which was issued as *American Anthropologist,* Volume 57, No. 3, Part 2, June 1955.

MEAD, MARGARET 1962 Retrospects and Prospects. Pages 115–149 in Anthropological Society of Washington, Washington, D.C., *Anthropology and Human Behavior.* Washington: The Society.

MURDOCK, GEORGE P. 1949 *Social Structure.* New York: Macmillan. → A paperback edition was published in 1965 by the Free Press.

NADEL, SIEGFRIED F. (1951) 1958 *The Foundations of Social Anthropology.* Glencoe, Ill.: Free Press.

NADEL, SIEGFRIED F. (1957) 1958 *The Theory of Social Structure: With a Memoir by Meyer Fortes.* Glencoe, Ill.: Free Press.

OPLER, MORRIS E. 1945 Themes as Dynamic Forces in Culture. *American Journal of Sociology* 51:198–206.

OPLER, MORRIS E. 1946 An Application of the Theory of Themes in Culture. *Journal of the Washington Academy of Sciences* 36:137–166.

OPLER, MORRIS E. 1959 Component, Assemblage, and Theme in Cultural Integration and Differentiation. *American Anthropologist* New Series 61:955–964.

PARSONS, TALCOTT 1951 *The Social System.* Glencoe, Ill.: Free Press.

PERRY, R. B. (1926) 1954 *General Theory of Value: Its Meaning and Basic Principles Construed in Terms of Interest.* Cambridge, Mass.: Harvard Univ. Press.

RADCLIFFE-BROWN, A. R. (1922) 1948 *The Andaman Islanders.* Glencoe, Ill.: Free Press.

RADCLIFFE-BROWN, A. R. (1952) 1961 *Structure and Function in Primitive Society: Essays and Addresses.* London: Cohen & West; Glencoe, Ill.: Free Press.

RADCLIFFE-BROWN, A. R. 1958 *Method in Social Anthropology: Selected Essays.* Edited by M. N. Srinivas. Univ. of Chicago Press. → Published posthumously.

REDFIELD, ROBERT 1941 *The Folk Culture of Yucatan.* Univ. of Chicago Press.

REDFIELD, ROBERT 1950 *A Village That Chose Progress: Chan Kom Revisited.* Univ. of Chicago Press. → A paperback edition was published in 1962.

REDFIELD, ROBERT 1953 *The Primitive World and Its Transformations.* Ithaca, N.Y.: Cornell Univ. Press. → A paperback edition was published in 1957.

REDFIELD, ROBERT 1955 Societies and Cultures as Natural Systems. *Journal of the Royal Anthropological Institute of Great Britain and Ireland* 85:19–32.

REDFIELD, ROBERT 1956 *Peasant Society and Culture: An Anthropological Approach to Civilization.* Univ. of Chicago Press. → A paperback edition, bound together with *The Little Community,* was published in 1961 by Cambridge Univ. Press.

REDFIELD, ROBERT 1962 *Human Nature and the Study of Society.* Univ. of Chicago Press.

RIVERS, WILLIAM H. R. 1914 *Kinship and Social Organi-*

sation. London School of Economics and Political Science Studies, No. 36. London: Constable.

ROMNEY, A. KIMBALL; and D'ANDRADE, ROY GOODWIN (editors) 1964 Transcultural Studies in Cognition. *American Anthropologist* New Series 66, no. 3.

SAHLINS, MARSHALL D.; and SERVICE, ELMAN R. (editors) 1960 *Evolution and Culture*. Ann Arbor: Univ. of Michigan Press.

SAPIR, EDWARD (1927) 1958 The Unconscious Patterning of Behavior in Society. Pages 544–559 in *Selected Writings of Edward Sapir in Language, Culture and Personality*. Edited by David G. Mandelbaum. Berkeley: Univ. of California Press.

SCHNEIDER, DAVID M. 1965 Some Muddles in the Models. Pages 25–85 in Association of Social Anthropologists of the Commonwealth, Conference on New Approaches in Social Anthropology, 1963, Cambridge, *The Relevance of Models for Social Anthropology*. Edited by Michael Banton. London: Tavistock; New York: Praeger.

SCHNEIDER, DAVID M.; and GOUGH, KATHLEEN (editors) 1961 *Matrilineal Kinship*. Berkeley: Univ. of California Press.

SINGER, MILTON (editor) 1959 *Traditional India: Structure and Change*. Philadelphia: American Folklore Society.

SINGER, MILTON 1961 A Survey of Personality and Culture Theory and Research. Pages 9–90 in Bert Kaplan (editor), *Studying Personality Cross-culturally*. Evanston, Ill.: Row, Peterson.

SINGER, MILTON 1964*a* The Social Organization of Indian Civilization. *Diogenes* 45:84–119.

SINGER, MILTON 1964*b* The Social Sciences in Non-Western Studies. American Academy of Political and Social Science, *Annals* 356:30–44.

SPICER, EDWARD H. 1962 *Cycles of Conquest*. Tucson: Univ. of Arizona Press.

SPIRO, MELFORD E. 1956 *Kibbutz: Venture in Utopia*. Cambridge, Mass.: Harvard Univ. Press.

SRINIVAS, MYSORE N. 1952 *Religion and Society Among the Coorgs of South India*. Oxford: Clarendon.

STEWARD, JULIAN H. 1955 *Theory of Culture Change: The Methodology of Multilinear Evolution*. Urbana: Univ. of Illinois Press.

STOCKING, GEORGE W. 1963 Matthew Arnold, E. B. Tylor, and the Uses of Invention. *American Anthropologist* New Series 65:783–799.

TYLOR, EDWARD B. (1871) 1958 *Primitive Culture: Researches Into the Development of Mythology, Philosophy, Religion, Art and Custom*. 2 vols. Gloucester, Mass.: Smith. → Volume 1: *Origins of Culture*. Volume 2: *Religion in Primitive Culture*.

WHITE, LESLIE A. 1949 *The Science of Culture: A Study of Man and Civilization*. New York: Farrar, Straus. → A paperback edition was published in 1958 by Grove.

WHITE, LESLIE A. 1959 *The Evolution of Culture: The Development of Civilization to the Fall of Rome*. New York: McGraw-Hill.

WOLF, ERIC R. 1964 *Anthropology*. Englewood Cliffs, N.J.: Prentice-Hall.

II
CULTURAL RELATIVISM

Cultural relativism is to be understood as (1) a method in ethnology and social anthropology; (2) a theory of cultural determinism and a philosophy of cultural reality; (3) a guide to the evaluation of value systems, especially ethics, politics, and aesthetics; and (4) an attitude toward practical problems of sociocultural reform and change.

Relativism as a method

Cultural relativism may be described as the method whereby social and cultural phenomena are perceived and described in terms of scientific detachment or, ideally, from the perspective of participants in or adherents of a given culture. Further, cultural phenomena are evaluated in terms of their significance in a given cultural and social context. The methodology of cultural relativism rests on the assumption that the ethnologist is able to transcend, or to eliminate for the moment, his own cultural conditioning and values and to assume the subjective, ethnocentric attitudes and mentality of an adherent of or a participant in the culture. This requires a measure of imagination and empathy on the part of the observer so that he can see others as they see themselves or as they wish to be seen. The anthropologist is required to report what actually happens and to attempt to interpret his data from the standpoint of his subjects. This may, and usually does, lead the observer to participate in the very institutions he is describing in order to get the "feel" and emotional concomitants of the behavior he observes. He must also collect ethnographic statements, narratives, typical utterances, and items of folklore, inasmuch as they reflect ideology. Thus, although he is objective in collecting his data and observations of cultural phenomena, the anthropologist also tries to identify with his subjects so as to perceive their mentality and their vision of society and the world about them.

The social anthropologist tries to evaluate the artifacts, socifacts, and mentifacts of a culture in relation to given institutions; he seeks to appreciate the "function" a given object or act performs in satisfying the needs of the society. When the anthropologist observes how a given artifact is used and for what purposes in a given context, he is able to provide a relative evaluation of the artifact through its function; he does not rely on the observation of the form alone. Similar detachment is required when he observes and reflects upon the long-range consequences of a ritual act. In evaluating the function of an institution from this impersonal, objective standpoint, the social anthropologist often introduces his own mental construct or hypothesis, which he tests against his observations. To the extent that social scientists tend to differ in their analyses of the function of a given institution—for example, "magic"—they introduce a new subjective and relativistic factor of their own.

All anthropologists are in agreement on the

value of the method of cultural relativism and the relative objectivity required to report and interpret data from the perspective of the adherents of the culture. There is considerable disagreement in the use of the method of impersonal, objective, functional evaluation.

Relativism as a theory and philosophy

Cultural relativism is a controversial doctrine that was quite fashionable in the second quarter of the twentieth century but that has since lost much of its support. Melville Herskovits (1948), the most articulate contemporary exponent of a philosophy of cultural relativism, found support for his approach in the Neo-Kantian historical idealism of Ernst Cassirer. According to Cassirer's "spiritual anthropology" (1944), man lives in a symbolic universe of his own creation. There is, for him, no reality other than the symbolic forms, and hence all reality is cultural or symbolic reality. The physical world is discerned through the screen of enculturation; perception of time, distance, weight, size, and other "realities" is mediated by the recognized conventions of any given group (Herskovits 1955, p. 35). All reality *as known* is cultural reality, and all human experience is culturally mediated. And if all human experience is structured by enculturation, it follows that all cultural judgments, perceptions, and evaluations are a function of, and are relative to, a given cultural system. Moral values are but one element in cultural experience, and moral relativism is only one aspect of a general theory of cultural relativism.

It should be noted, however, that the theory of cultural determinism originated with Auguste Comte and Herbert Spencer, both of whom postulated levels of natural phenomena, with social phenomena constituting the top level of phenomenal reality. In America A. L. Kroeber (1917) adopted Spencer's term "the superorganic" and applied it to culture, which he at first identified with the level of social phenomena. Culture was regarded as an entity *sui generis*, subject to its own laws of evolutionary development. As such, it was viewed as a closed system in which all cultural phenomena were to be explained only through other cultural phenomena and not by "reduction" to a lower order of reality. After 1948 Kroeber virtually abandoned his old theory of the superorganic and came to think of culture as essentially an abstraction from human behavior. Leslie A. White, however, has continued to uphold the doctrine of the cultural superorganic under the banner of "culturology."

The point to be marked here is that a theory of cultural relativism can be derived from, and is compatible with, a variety of philosophical approaches: First, as in the case of Herskovits, it may be explained by a theory of Neo-Kantian historical idealism. Cassirer's own philosophy of symbolic forms was based on the essential postulate of human freedom and creativity. Although Herskovits has utilized Cassirer's "spiritual anthropology," it is not necessary to adopt Cassirer's philosophy of cultural idealism in order to explain the facts of cultural conditioning. Second, as in the case of White, cultural relativism depends on a philosophy of historical materialism. Historical materialism is also a philosophy of cultural determinism whereby the economic core of a culture determines its ideational manifestations and values. Third, for Kroeber (as for Comte and Spencer) cultural relativism depends on a positivistic philosophy of science that postulates the autonomy of cultural phenomena. If human behavior is determined by culture, there is little scope for individual freedom and for creative innovation. All individuals participate in the culture of their society and their age; individual differences are insignificant when compared with the over-all pattern or configuration of a given culture.

Modern ethnology has made us aware of the role played by social institutions in culturally conditioning the personality and experience of the individual. As a result of cultural conditioning, there is *some degree* of cultural relativism that differentiates the participants in diverse cultures. The philosophical problem is to explain systematically how this diversity of cultural conditioning is to be understood. It is not necessary to subscribe to historic idealism, historic materialism, or evolutionary positivism in order to account for the facts of cultural relativism. All that is really necessary is to recognize that culture is one essential condition of human experience and that all experience is to *some extent* culturally mediated. It is equally important to recognize other dimensions of reality, those of nature, both human and cosmic, that provide human experience with a common frame of reference within which to test its cultural constructs. In the last analysis, *culture is not* the measure of all things, *but nature is*, and there are more things in nature than are ever grasped through our human, cultural symbols. Culture is but our human means of adjusting to nature and utilizing its powers in the service of mankind. This postulate of a *metacultural reality* renders scientific progress possible and saves us from *the culture-centric predicament* of historic idealism, historic materialism, and evolutionary positivism. Cultural relativism is a fact of human experience as conditioned by culture. However, a scientific methodology that includes the comparative study of diverse cultures enables men to transcend some ethocentric limitations and to live in a common world of reality.

Validation and evaluation of values

The principle of cultural relativism affirms that all values are a function or product of their culture and reflect the interests of their society and culture. The fundamental assumption of both sociological determinism and relativism is that society is a newly emergent self-explanatory reality through which all the values of cultural life are to be explained historically. All cultural values are thought to be functions of social organization and to vary with the modes and interests of society. The work of the sociologists Émile Durkheim and William Graham Sumner is devoted to the demonstration of this thesis.

Moral or ethical relativism is one element in a general theory of cultural relativism. It is possible, however, to maintain a theory of moral relativism without subscribing to total cultural relativism. For example, Friedrich Nietzsche in his *Genealogy of Morals* transvaluated traditional moral values by indicating how they served the respective interests of masters and slaves. Similarly, the contemporary communist ideology rests on the relativity of cultural values to the class interests of capitalists and proletarians.

Furthermore, one may adhere to a theory of moral relativism on psychological and epistemological grounds rather than on those of social and cultural relativism. For example, Edward Westermarck (1932) maintains that moral evaluations are expressions of individual emotions and have no objective basis in fact. His argument, like that of the philosopher David Hume and some modern logical positivists, rests on the assumption of the subjective origin of value judgments, which renders all value judgments relative to the emotional preferences of the individual.

Insofar as moral relativism is considered to be a function of society and culture, it may be said to rest on two distinct postulates or assumptions. First, all value judgments are culturally conditioned or determined, and this limits their validity to the social and cultural context in which they originate. Second, it is impossible to establish any universally acceptable criterion for measuring and comparing values. Hence, all value systems are to be regarded as having equal validity.

This practical assumption of the equality of disparate value systems leads to the prescription of tolerance as a prime virtue. Reverence for cultural values, rather than reverence for life, becomes the absolute virtue advocated by the cultural relativist. Intolerance is said to be a product of an ethnocentric, uncritical prejudice in favor of the absolute validity of one's own cultural values.

It should be noted, especially, that the cultural and moral relativist does not advocate moral skepticism and nihilism. Those, he would say, are philosophical diseases to which he is not subject. Morality is a cultural universal and is essential for the corporate existence of any society. The members of any given society are obligated to conform to the rules and norms of their society on the practical, utilitarian ground that without such obedience social life would be impossible. Pragmatically, the individual must conform to the rules of his society, and each society must tolerate the codes of other societies in the interest of mutual survival. Obedience and conformity are cultural imperatives once a code of behavior is accepted.

The cultural and moral relativist differentiates between moral universals and moral absolutes. Morality as a whole is a cultural universal in the sense that all cultures have some system of morality. Within all systems of morality there is a limited number of universal values, such as a standard of what constitutes a "good" man, a standard of truth, and some appreciation of beauty. However, the criteria for evaluating and delimiting the content of these values are culturally defined. The cultural relativist would argue that there are no absolute, universal norms that are valid for all cultures. The only possible exception would be the prohibition of incest.

Against this universal formalism of the moral relativist it may be argued that some of the actual values reflected in cultural systems are much the same everywhere and that differences arise over the relative importance of particular values and the extent of their application. In all cultures the perpetuation of the society takes precedence over the life of the individual, and hence no society tolerates treason, murder, rape, and incest. All societies recognize mutual rights and duties in marriage and condemn acts that threaten family solidarity. Similarly, all societies give recognition to some personal property and provide some techniques for the distribution of economic surplus to the needy. The fact of common cultural values provides a basis for mutual understanding between adherents of diverse cultures.

The point at issue is whether, following the cultural relativist, we recognize only empty, formal, universal categories of value with unlimited diversity of content or whether a comparative study of cultures reveals some common content in universal values. As Malinowski, Linton, Kluckhohn, and Redfield have advocated, there is an actual common core of cultural values in all societies, which derives from the universal functions certain acts fulfill in satisfying human needs and aspirations. There are concrete cultural, universal values because there are universal needs, biological, derived, and integrative, common to all societies. These cultural universals are not merely abstract categories but actual regulative modes of conduct and norms of conduct common to all cultures. Such transcultural values may be called absolutes as well as universals. Cultural relativists tend to stress cultural differences but neglect the uniformities and common elements based on the imperatives of a universal human nature.

The cultural relativist is very much concerned lest we commit *the fallacy of ethnocentrism*, which consists in the attitude that "one's way of life is to be preferred to all others." Hence, he prefers not to judge others at all.

Here again it is necessary to distinguish between the fact of ethnocentrism and its value. If by ethnocentrism is meant judgments based on irrational preferences incapable of rational validation, then it is a fact that some degree of ethnocentrism is to be found in all societies and cultures. Modern theories of racism and extreme nationalism are vicious forms of ethnocentrism. Uncritical preference for one's own culture and its mores and prejudice against alien cultures, the notion that one's own ethnic society has a true appreciation of spiritual values of civilization whereas other groups and states are debased by materialistic values—these are expressions of ethnocentrism. It is not, however, the mere fact of preference for one's own cultural values that constitutes ethnocentrism but, rather, the uncritical prejudice in favor of one's own culture and the distorted, biased criticism of alien cultures. The only antidote to ethnocentric prejudice is comparative knowledge of one's own and other cultures. This implies that it is possible to transcend the limits of cultural conditioning by empirical observation of cultural behavior.

The cultural relativist, like the skeptic, maintains that cultural determinism leads to ethnocentrism in value judgments but, strangely enough, need not lead to ethnocentrism in judgments of fact. The anthropologist, by profession, is not subject to ethnocentrism so long as he reports the actual facts of behavior and belief of his subjects; he becomes ethnocentric only when he indulges in value judgments and comparative evaluations of values. If it is admitted, however, that cultural relativism does not preclude objective judgments of fact with transcultural, universal validity, why should it preclude judgments of value that have similar objectivity and validity? Only the prejudice induced by a positivistic philosophy of science, which divides the world of phenomena into facts and values, prevents recognition of the factual objectivity of values.

The advocates of cultural relativism counsel us to suspend comparative judgment and to grant, in principle, the equality or equivalent value of all value systems. This assumed ability to doubt and suspend judgment presupposes, as Descartes recognized long ago, an inherent freedom of judgment that liberates the mind from its own prejudices and past cultural conditioning. Hence, the exercise of freedom of judgment and rational analysis in accord with empirical data is as much a fact of human behavior as is cultural determinism. Were it not for man's innate ability freely to evaluate and verify the truth of his ideas by subjecting them to empirical and critical tests, it would be impossible to overcome ethnocentric prejudices in any way whatsoever. Man would be the prisoner and victim of his own cultural conditioning, and a science of anthropology would, in effect, be impossible. The cultural relativist, in the interests of a science of culture, stresses cultural determinism but completely overlooks the primary, ineluctable fact that freedom of judgment and cultural creativity are absolutely essential for an understanding of the very existence of cultural phenomena.

Pragmatic attitude and cultural ideal

It is necessary to distinguish between the universal *fact* of cultural relativism and the *ideal value* of cultural relativism advocated by the liberal ethnologist. The fact of cultural relativism coexists, and is historically compatible, with the very ethnocentrism the ethnologist deplores. As a result of cultural conditioning, especially if it is of a puritanic, dogmatic nature, a people may come to regard their own values as absolute and to disparage those of other societies as inferior to theirs. In an "enlightened" society, however, people will be conscious of the facts of cultural relativism and believe that there is no criterion for making comparative value judgments. Such enlightened people will readily infer that they should treat all other cultural values as equal and equivalent to their own. Cultural relativism may thus be viewed as an ideal postulate of liberal culture which is tolerant of all other cultures. It is assumed implicitly that there is a kind of pre-established harmony of cultures that makes it possible for all to coexist in a pluralistic cultural world. It has taken the shock of World War II, with its brutalities, to awaken this romantic cultural optimism of our modern Candides to the reality of cultural crises and the actual conflict of cultures.

Thus, the *ideal* of cultural relativism is to be contrasted with the *real*, ethnocentric cultural relativism of history. As an idealist, the culturologist may ask other liberals to transcend and shed their ethnocentric prejudices, and especially their predilections for absolute values. He infers from the facts of cultural relativism the ideals of cultural reverence and tolerance. In Kantian terms, he might describe a new cultural imperative: so act as to treat all cultures as ends and never as means. We are not informed, however, how this leap from the ethnocentric real to the ideal of relative objectivity is to be made. It is equally logical, as many a philosopher has seen, to reach the conclusion of nihilism and to treat all cultural values as equally worthless.

Cultural relativism involves tolerance based on skepticism of universal, objective standards of value as well as of the idea of progress. The comparative study of cultures has made us conscious of the dangers of uncritical ethnocentrism, but it has also provided us with the materials and the incentive to transcend the limitations of both cultural relativism and ethnocentrism through the pursuit of scientific truths concerning facts and values.

DAVID BIDNEY

[*Directly related are the entries* CULTURE, *article on* CULTUROLOGY; EVOLUTION, *article on* CULTURAL EVOLUTION; OBSERVATION; VALUES, *article on* VALUE SYSTEMS.]

BIBLIOGRAPHY

BENEDICT, RUTH 1934 *Patterns of Culture.* Boston: Houghton Mifflin. → A paperback edition was published in 1961 by Houghton Mifflin.

BIDNEY, DAVID 1953a The Concept of Value in Modern Anthropology. Pages 682–699 in International Symposium on Anthropology, New York, 1952, *Anthropology Today: An Encyclopedic Inventory.* Edited by A. L. Kroeber. Univ. of Chicago Press.

BIDNEY, DAVID 1953b *Theoretical Anthropology.* New York: Columbia Univ. Press.

CASSIRER, ERNST (1944) 1956 *An Essay on Man: An Introduction to a Philosophy of Human Culture.* New Haven: Yale Univ. Press.

DURKHEIM, ÉMILE (1895) 1950 *The Rules of Sociological Method.* 8th ed. Translated by Sarah A. Solovay and John H. Mueller, and edited by George E. G.

Catlin. Glencoe, Ill.: Free Press. → First published in French.

HERSKOVITS, MELVILLE J. 1948 *Man and His Works: The Science of Cultural Anthropology.* New York: Knopf.

HERSKOVITS, MELVILLE J. 1955 *Cultural Anthropology.* New York: Knopf. → An abridged revision of *Man and His Works,* 1948.

KLUCKHOHN, CLYDE (1937–1960) 1962 *Culture and Behavior: Collected Essays.* Edited by Richard Kluckhohn. New York: Free Press.

KLUCKHOHN, CLYDE 1949 *Mirror for Man: The Relation of Anthropology to Modern Life.* New York: McGraw-Hill.

KROEBER, A. L. (1901–1951) 1952 *The Nature of Culture.* Univ. of Chicago Press.

KROEBER, A. L. (1917) 1952 The Superorganic. Pages 22–51 in A. L. Kroeber, *The Nature of Culture.* Univ. of Chicago Press. → First published in the *American Anthropologist.*

LINTON, RALPH 1952 Universal Ethical Principles: An Anthropological View. Pages 645–660 in Ruth N. Anshen (editor), *Moral Principles of Action: Man's Ethical Imperative.* New York: Harper.

LOWIE, ROBERT H. 1960 Empathy, or "Seeing From Within." Pages 145–159 in Stanley Diamond (editor), *Culture in History: Essays in Honor of Paul Radin.* New York: Columbia Univ. Press.

McEWEN, WILLIAM P. 1963 *The Problem of Social-scientific Knowledge.* Totowa, N.J.: Bedminster Press.

MALINOWSKI, BRONISLAW (1922) 1960 *Argonauts of the Western Pacific: An Account of Native Enterprise and Adventure in the Archipelagoes of Melanesian New Guinea.* London School of Economics and Political Science, Studies, No. 65. London: Routledge; New York: Dutton.

MAQUET, JACQUES J. 1964 Objectivity in Anthropology. *Current Anthropology* 5:47–55.

MEAD, MARGARET 1963 Socialization and Enculturation. *Current Anthropology* 4:184–188.

NORTHROP, FILMER S. C.; and LIVINGSTON, HELEN H. (editors) 1964 *Cross-cultural Understanding: Epistemology in Anthropology.* New York: Harper.

WESTERMARCK, EDWARD A. 1932 *Ethical Relativity.* New York: Harcourt. → A paperback edition was published in 1960 by Littlefield.

WHITE, LESLIE 1949 *The Science of Culture: A Study of Man and Civilization.* New York: Farrar, Straus. → A paperback edition was published in 1958 by Grove.

III
CULTUROLOGY

Culturology is the branch of anthropology that treats culture (institutions, technologies, ideologies) as a distinct order of phenomena, organized upon principles of its own and behaving in terms of its own laws. The culture process is regarded as self-contained and self-determined. Variations in culture are explained in cultural terms, rather than biological or psychological terms. The science of culture had, of course, to wait upon the development of a scientifically adequate concept of culture. Preliterate peoples have been aware of differences of custom, speech, and belief among themselves. But even so sophisticated a people as the Greeks of Aristotle's day had no word equivalent to our term *culture*. The term was borrowed by E. B. Tylor, the great pioneer in English anthropology, from German culture historians. Tylor defined culture as "that complex whole which includes knowledge, belief, art, morals, law, custom, and any other capabilities and habits acquired by man as a member of society" (Tylor 1871, vol. 1, p. 1). He made it clear that culture was the exclusive possession of the human species.

The symbolic process. Numerous and varied definitions of culture have been formulated since Tylor's day, but his is substantially the one that prevails today. Culture is the name of those behavioral traits that distinguish man from other species: articulate speech; institutions; codes of ethics and etiquette; ideologies; a continuous, cumulative, and progressive tool process; etc. Man is unique in that he alone possesses the ability to symbol, i.e., to bestow, freely and arbitrarily, meaning upon things and events, objects and acts. Articulate speech is the most characteristic and important form of symboling. All culture was produced and has been perpetuated by symboling in general and by articulate speech in particular.

But things and events that are dependent upon symboling (called symbolates) may be, and commonly are, considered in two different contexts. In a somatic context, their significance lies in their relationship to the human organism, and as such constitute *behavior*. In the extrasomatic context, symbolates are significant, not in terms of their relationship to the human organism that produces them, but in relationship to other symbolates. In this context they are *culture*. Thus, mother-in-law avoidance is to be regarded as *behavior* when viewed in terms of the concepts, acts, and attitudes of human organisms; it is *culture* when considered in its relationship to other customs, such as forms of marriage, place of residence of the newly married couple, roles of the sexes in subsistence, offense and defense, etc. Culture, therefore, is a class of things and events dependent upon symboling, considered in an extrasomatic context.

Prior to the emergence of culturology in the expansion of the scope of science (White 1949), naturalistic (i.e., nonmythological, nontheological) explanations of the behavior of peoples were biological, psychological, or sociological. Accordingly, peoples behaved as they did because of their physical type; or because of the way their minds worked; or as a consequence of certain processes of social interaction. In all these explanations, man, individually and collectively, was the independent vari-

able; his customs, institutions, beliefs, etc., the dependent variable. Man was the cause; culture, the result.

The culturological explanation. The culturological revolution reversed this kind of interpretation. Culturology asserts that peoples behave as they do because they have been born and reared in particular cultural traditions. The behavior of a people is determined, not by its physical type or genetic constitution, nor by its ideas and desires and hopes and fears, nor by processes of social interaction, but by external, extrasomatic cultural tradition. Peoples born into a Tibetan linguistic tradition will speak Tibetan, not English. A people practices monogamy, polygyny or polyandry, or loathes milk, avoids mothers-in-law, or uses the multiplication table, because they are obliged to react to these cultural traditions. The behavior of a people is a function of its culture.

If the behavior of a people is determined by its culture, what determines the culture? The answer is that it determines itself. Culture may be regarded as a process *sui generis*. It is a process in which culture traits interact with one another, forming new permutations, combinations and syntheses. One trait, or combination of traits, is the result of antecedent and concomitant traits and the cause of subsequent traits and trait combinations. One form of language, writing, social organization, technology, or of culture as a whole, grows out of a previous stage or emerges from an anterior condition.

Every sociocultural system is of course affected by its terrestrial and celestial environment. Climate, topography, flora, fauna, and mineral resources may or do exert influences upon cultural systems. But environments merely permit or prohibit the existence of certain elements or features of culture; they do not determine them. The influence of environmental factors finds expression only in and through cultural means; consequently, they may be dealt with culturologically. Certain elements present in the environment, such as iron or petroleum, do not enter the culture process except at certain stages of development. Finally, in dealing with cultures in general, or with culture as a whole, the factor of environment may be considered a constant and therefore disregarded in explanation of the culture process.

Although culturology treats the culture process without regard to the biological and psychological processes of human beings, the culturologist recognizes the intimate and necessary relationship between culture in general and man in general. Generically, culture is what it is because man is the kind of animal that he is. If man, the animal, were different, his culture would be different. If man did not have spectroscopic, chromatic vision, his culture would be different. If he could subsist only upon meat or cereals, his culture would be different. If he had a rutting season, or reproduced with litters rather than individuals, his culture would be different. Culture was brought into being by the human species, and it functions to serve the needs of this species. Thus, when one considers the question of the origin and functions of culture one must take biological man into consideration. But once culture has come into being, its subsequent variations—its changes, its growth, its additions and subtractions—are to be explained without reference to the animal man, either individually or collectively. We do not need to invoke man when we consider such questions as the evolution of mathematics or currency, sociocultural processes of integration and disintegration, the relationship between social systems and technological systems, the diffusion and distribution of the keystone arch, etc. To be sure, these cultural processes could not take place without people. But it is their culture, not their innate natures, that causes them to behave as they do. Man is necessary to the existence and functioning of the culture process, but he is not necessary to an explanation of its variations.

An atom cannot be understood merely by a consideration of its components; an atom is a system that must be understood in terms of itself. The properties of sugar cannot be discovered in its component atoms of carbon, hydrogen, and oxygen; the molecule functions as a molecular system. A living cell cannot be understood in terms of its component molecules; a biological organism cannot be understood in terms of its cells. Individual organisms do not reveal the properties of societies. Every kind of system exists in terms of its own structure and functions, in terms of its own principles and laws. In the human species, societies are *cultural*; i.e., sociocultural systems. Like other kinds of systems, they must be understood in their own terms.

Linguistic systems are comprehended in terms of lexicon, grammar, syntax, phonetics, and so on. Languages can, of course, have no existence without human beings. But linguistic science proceeds as if mankind did not exist. So it is with culture as a whole. The evolution of culture can be worked out as a cause-and-effect sequence of cultural events. The influence of technologies upon social systems, the interrelationships among technologies, social systems, and ideologies can be ascertained and measured without reference to the human car-

riers of these systems. Such problems as the evolution of mathematics or of tribal confederacies, processes of integration and disintegration of social systems, or the mechanisms of the regulation and control thereof can be attacked and solved without regard to human organisms as such. We could not have symphonic music, trial by jury, or the Decalogue were it not for respiration and metabolism, but a consideration of these physiological processes does not in the least help us to understand these cultural phenomena.

The phenomena of culture, like biological and physical phenomena, are to be treated scientifically from four standpoints. Our point of view may be temporal or nontemporal, generalizing or particularizing. If we combine these two dichotomies, we get a fourfold classification of scientific interpretation, or treatment of cultural or any other kind of natural phenomena, as shown in Table 1.

Table 1

	TEMPORAL	NONTEMPORAL
PARTICULARIZING	Historical	Descriptive ethnography
GENERALIZING	Evolutionist	Functional–Structural

Consideration of cultural things and events from a temporal–particularizing point of view results in culture history. The temporal–generalizing approach yields evolutionist interpretations. The nontemporal–generalizing interpretation deals with the structures and functions of sociocultural systems. And the nontemporal–particularizing treatment is descriptive ethnography. Thus, all the schools of ethnological theory are embraced by this classification of kinds of interpretation: mere ethnographic description; the historical schools of Graebner, Elliot Smith, Boas; the evolutionist schools of Tylor, Morgan et al.; the functionalist schools of Malinowski and Radcliffe-Brown, and their successors, the structuralists of modern British social anthropology. Culturology employs, therefore, these four ways of treating cultural phenomena.

The culturological point of view has encountered considerable opposition from various quarters. Many scholars have insisted that it is people, not cultures, that meet and interact. The culturologist is accused of "reifying" culture into a mystic entity that exists apart from society.

To consider culture—languages, institutions, ideologies, and technological systems—as distinct orders of phenomena, explainable in terms of themselves, is not to reify them. They are real, observable things and events in the external world, just as atoms, cells, and stars are.

The origin and development of culture traits,

such as jury trials, firearms, constitutional government, the theory of relativity, etc., cannot be accounted for psychologically; they can be explained only in terms of a developmental culture process. Again, people are necessary for the existence of cultural events, but they are not necessary to an explanation of their origins or variations.

The psychosocial explanation. Émile Durkheim contrasted psychological and culturological interpretations of human behavior and institutions. When "one sees in the organization of the family the logically necessary expression of human sentiments inherent in every mind, the true order of facts is reversed. On the contrary, it is the social organization of the relationships of kinship which has determined the respective sentiments of parents and children" (Durkheim [1893] 1960, p. 340). "Every time that a social phenomenon is directly explained by a psychological phenomenon, we may be sure that the explanation is false" (Durkheim [1895] 1958, p. 104). We may properly substitute "cultural phenomenon" for social phenomenon in the preceding quotation. Race prejudice, war, capitalism, etc. are not to be explained as "the logically necessary expression of concepts and sentiments inherent in the human mind." On the contrary, it is the structure and behavior of the extrasomatic culture process that establishes racial, marital, and capitalistic ideas and sentiments in the minds of individuals.

The sociologist tends to regard culture as the product of social interaction. One kind of social interaction produces polygyny, another kind, polyandry; one kind produces capitalism, another, communism. But if social interaction alone could produce culture, we would find it among baboons. The institutions of polygyny and polyandry cannot be explained as consequences of the interaction of individuals. But the interaction of one man (husband) and more than one woman (wives), or one woman (wife) and more than one man (husbands) can be explained as a consequence of the influence of external, extrasomatic cultural structures upon them. And these institutions must be explained—in their origins and variations—in terms of other cultural elements, such as the requirements of the sex division of labor, customs of residence, occupational hazards and death rates of the sexes, wealth and prestige, etc.

There is, and can be, no justifiable conflict between the science of psychology and the science of culturology; these sciences complement, rather than conflict with, each other. Both are essential to a complete comprehension of anything that man does as a human being. Just as the origins of institutions must be explained culturologically, the experiences that people undergo within these institutions is the concern of psychology. What are the conceptions and attitudes held by the individuals most directly involved in the mother-in-law taboo, namely, a man, his wife, and his wife's mother? Are they imbued with supernaturalism, or are they naturalistic in character? Are they attitudes of respect, fear, or contempt? What is it like to be a wife in a polygynous household? Or a husband in a polyandrous one? These are questions for the psychologist rather than the culturologist.

The anthropocentric viewpoint. The opposition to culturology arises principally from the age-old and deeply entrenched philosophy of anthropomorphism and anthropocentrism. Man has been conceived as a prime mover, as a first cause, and is often endowed with free will. This is expressed by Sapir: "It is always the individual that really thinks and acts and dreams and revolts." There have also been others who insist that culture originates in the creative acts of individuals, or that only the individual is real.

This anthropocentric conception receives support from the fact that the behavior of all nonhuman species is a function of their respective biological constitutions. The biological principle applies to ducks, sharks, sunflowers, and all other nonhuman species. But it does not apply to human beings, who live in a symbolic environment and respond to different kinds of extrasomatic traditions. The institutions of man are to be explained in terms of culture.

The anthropocentric point of view receives support also from the fact that, as a biological organism, man is a dynamic system. He reacts positively to his terrestrial habitat and to his enveloping culture. But with regard to the latter, he can respond only within the limits set by his culture. Although physically and biologically a thermodynamic system, man is, and remains, a puppet of his culture.

LESLIE A. WHITE

BIBLIOGRAPHY

The first explicit, self-conscious formulation of a scientific study of culture as a distinct order of phenomena was made by Tylor 1871. *As early as 1909, the German chemist and philosopher Wilhelm Ostwald coined the term "culturology," which he defined as the science of cultural, i.e., specifically human activities. Leslie A. White gathered many of his earlier articles and lectures in a single volume,* The Science of Culture 1949. *The essays in this collection expound the scope, principles, and objectives of culturology. They include "The Symbol: The Origin and Basis of Human Behavior," "The Expansion of the Scope of Science," "Culturological vs. Psychological Interpretations of Human Behavior," "Energy and the Evolution of Culture," and a sketch on "The Science of Culture."*

Dole, Gertrude E.; and Carneiro, Robert L. (editors) 1960   *Essays in the Science of Culture: In Honor of Leslie A. White, in Celebration of His Sixtieth Birthday and His Thirtieth Year of Teaching at the University of Michigan.* New York: Crowell.

Durkheim, Émile (1893) 1960   *The Division of Labor in Society.* Glencoe, Ill.: Free Press. → First published in French as *De la division du travail social: Étude sur l'organisation des sociétés supérieures.* The extract in the text was translated by L. A. White.

Durkheim, Émile (1895) 1958   *The Rules of Sociological Method.* 8th ed. Translated by Sarah A. Solovay and John H. Mueller and edited by George E. G. Catlin. Glencoe, Ill.: Free Press. → First published as *Les règles de la méthode sociologique.*

Kroeber, A. L. (1917) 1952   The Superorganic. Pages 22–51 in A. L. Kroeber, *The Nature of Culture.* Univ. of Chicago Press. → First published in the *American Anthropologist.*

Lowie, Robert H. 1917   *Culture and Ethnology.* New York: Boni & Liveright.

Lowie, Robert H. (1936) 1960   Cultural Anthropology: A Science. Pages 391–410 in Robert H. Lowie, *Selected Papers in Anthropology.* Berkeley: Univ. of California Press. → First published in Volume 42 of the *American Journal of Sociology.*

Murdock, George P. 1932   The Science of Culture. *American Anthropologist* New Series 34:200–215.

Ostwald, Wilhelm 1909   *Energetische Grundlagen der Kulturwissenschaft.* Philosophisch–soziologische Bücherei, Vol. 16. Leipzig: Klinkhardt.

Sapir, Edward (1910–1944) 1949   *Selected Writings in Language, Culture, and Personality.* Edited by David G. Mandelbaum. Berkeley: Univ. of California Press.

Sapir, Edward 1917   Do We Need a Superorganic? *American Anthropologist* New Series 19:441–447.

Tylor, Edward B. (1871) 1958   *Primitive Culture: Researches Into the Development of Mythology, Philosophy, Religion, Art and Custom.* 2 vols. Gloucester, Mass.: Peter Smith. → Volume 1: *Origins of Culture.* Volume 2: *Religion in Primitive Culture.*

White, Leslie A. 1949   *The Science of Culture: A Study of Man and Civilization.* New York: Farrar, Straus.

White, Leslie A. 1959a   The Concept of Culture. *American Anthropologist* New Series 61:227–251.

White, Leslie A. 1959b   *The Evolution of Culture: The Development of Civilization to the Fall of Rome.* New York: McGraw-Hill.

White, Leslie A. 1962   Symboling: A Kind of Behavior. *Journal of Psychology* 53:311–317.

White, Leslie A. 1963   The Culturological Revolution. *Colorado Quarterly* 11:367–382.

IV

CULTURAL ADAPTATION

Culture, a uniquely human attribute, is something which man interposes between himself and his environment in order to ensure his security and survival. As such, culture is adaptive.

This way of looking at culture, uncommon a few decades ago, has within recent years won increasing support among anthropologists. Leslie A. White (1949, p. 360), for example, speaks of culture as "a specific and concrete mechanism employed by a particular animal organism in adjusting to its environment," and Ralph Piddington ([1950] 1952, p. 219) holds that "culture is essentially an adaptive mechanism, making possible the satisfaction of human needs, both biological and social."

As this attitude has gained currency, cultures have ceased to be treated as unique constellations of traits, each the fortuitous product of history. A culture is now more frequently thought of as the resultant of a parallelogram of forces—forces whose identity can be ascertained and whose effects can be weighed.

Within culture as a whole, anthropologists have generally recognized the adaptive function of technology. As Robert Lowie succinctly expressed it, the purpose of an ax is to fell trees. Some anthropologists, however, have seemed unsure of the function of social organization. Lowie ([1920] 1947, p. 439) said it had "unknown ends," and A. L. Kroeber ([1923] 1948, p. 307) found many of its manifestations "strange, unpredictable, . . . [and] unreasonable." To Kroeber (1938, p. 308), "the phenomena of formal social organization . . . represent a field of experimentation or play on the part of cultures . . . ."

That social life is not something mysterious or capricious, but that like technology it is adaptive, has long been appreciated by biologists. The ecologist Angus Woodbury (1954, p. 412) recognized that social life is an adaptation for efficient use of time and space upon the earth. The existence of a social life, he thought, was forced upon members of a group by their need to cooperate in order to succeed in the struggle for existence. The zoologist William Etkin (1954, p. 134) wrote of the essential role played by social behavior in an animal's adaptation to its environment and stated that various forms of group behavior were as necessary to survival as any of an animal's physiological or structural characteristics. In their joint work, *Life: Outlines of General Biology,* J. Arthur Thomson and Patrick Geddes (1931, vol. 1, pp. 120–126) listed seven advantages of social life, and in *Natural Communities,* Lee R. Dice (1952, pp. 285, 287) enumerated nine such advantages.

Social organization, generally, is the way in which the individuals of a group within an animal species coordinate their behavior in adapting to the exigencies of life. Human social organization is simply the way in which human beings, through cultural means, do the same thing. As White has observed: "Human beings have to be related to each other in an effective manner in order to carry on the business of life successfully. Social, political, ethical, artistic, ecclesiastical, and educational systems operate to accomplish this purpose. They are means of coördinating, integrating, regulating, and directing human endeavor toward the goal of all life: a secure and agreeable existence" (1947, p. 183).

But granting that social organization is adaptive, can the same be said, for example, of rituals and ceremonies? Some anthropologists have held them to lie outside the realm of the rational and the functional, and therefore to be nonadaptive. Yet it is possible to examine rituals and ceremonies in the context of a broader theory of adaptation, and the results of such analyses have been to throw new light on them.

The celebrated potlatch of the Northwest Coast Indians provides an example of this. It has always been regarded by anthropologists not only as non-adaptive but also as ostentatiously wasteful. Suttles (1960, p. 304), however, writing of the potlatch among the Coast Salish, concludes that "the drive to attain high status is clearly not the explanation of the potlatch. Nor is the production of surplus. Nor the cooperation achieved by the potlatching community. The potlatch is a part of a larger socio-economic system that enables the whole social net-work, consisting of a number of communities, to maintain a high level of food production and to equalize its food consumption both within and among communities. The system is thus adaptive in an environment characterized by the features indicated before—spatial and temporal variation and fluctuation in the availability of resources."

Another example may be cited. After taking a second look at the practice of scapulimancy among the Montagnais–Naskapi, who used this form of divination in selecting hunting routes, O. K. Moore (1957, p. 73) suggested that "it is in essence a very crude way of randomizing human behavior under conditions where avoiding fixed patterns of activity may be an advantage." In other words, by leading them to hunt randomly over their territory, and thus preventing the overhunting of any one area, the practice of divination may well contribute to the preservation of game animals and thus ulti-mately to improved chances for the survival of the Montagnais–Naskapi themselves.

Acknowledging, then, that all aspects of culture may contribute to the ecological adjustment of a society, let us examine the process of cultural adaptation more closely. Basically, societies adapt to their environment by three means: technological, organizational, and ideational.

Technology, which may be taken to include tools, machines, utensils, and weapons, along with the techniques associated with their use, is the most directly adaptive facet of culture. Man's occupancy

of every corner of the earth could not have come about without the implements necessary to cope with the peculiar problems posed by each habitat. This is especially well illustrated by harsh environ-ments. To survive in their Arctic habitat the Es-kimo must rely on such sophisticated and specialized traits as the igloo, the kayak, the seal-oil lamp, the dog sled, the harpoon with bladder float, and snow goggles.

Other cultures in other environments furnish us with additional examples of highly specialized and effective technical adaptations. The boomerang of the Australian aborigines, the bolas of the Pata-gonian guanaco hunters, the snowshoe of the sub-Arctic, the blowgun of Malaysia and South America, pemmican among the Plains Indians, the outrigger canoe of Polynesia, the manioc squeezer of Ama-zonia, and the agricultural terraces of the Incas are only a few of the illustrations that could be cited.

In addition to implements of subsistence, tech-nology includes weapons of war. Hostile relations often prevail among neighboring societies, and mil-itary technology may at times be as important as subsistence technology.

In bronze age China, the invention and use of the *ch'i*, a combination of the halberd and the spear, is credited with helping the state of Ch'in to defeat its rivals and to unify China for the first time (Li 1957, p. 58).

Stirrups, an Asiatic invention which reached Europe in the eighth century, had a profound effect on warfare during the Middle Ages. "The use of stirrups enabled an armored horseman, carrying a lance at rest under his right arm, to brace himself in the saddle so firmly that the shock of his attack could combine the momentum of horse and rider. This feature made the mounted knight the most powerful instrument of medieval warfare, render-ing obsolete the older Roman and Germanic mili-tary tactics of fighting on foot in close order" (Homans 1962, p. 396).

The second major aspect of culture is the organ-izational. While it is logically distinguishable from the technological aspect, in actuality it is closely related to it. Indeed, White maintains that "social systems are social means of operating technological systems" (1947, pp. 182–183). It is certainly true that cooperation in human societies, especially sim-pler ones, exists principally for the purpose of pro-curing food, providing shelter, and meeting the demands of offense and defense. Accordingly, all forms of social organization involved in achieving these ends must be regarded as adaptive. Going beyond this, however, it can be argued that forms of organization developed to deal with an increased population are also adaptive, since they contribute to a society's integration and, therefore, to its survival.

Plains Indian cultures afford a striking example of how seasonal aggregations of population connected with subsistence can lead to an elaboration of social organization. During most of the year, bands of a typical Plains tribe were dispersed over a wide area, subsisting separately from other bands and acting independently of them. The band chief had little authority, and the socioceremonial life of the band was simple. For the summer buffalo hunt, however, the bands came together and assumed a form of tribal organization that was distinctly more complex. Band chiefs, previously without superiors, now formed themselves into a council from which a paramount tribal chief was selected. The tribal chief wielded considerably greater authority than he had as band chief; it was now his responsibility to coordinate and direct the activities of the tribe as a whole.

Men's associations, inactive during most of the year, re-formed when the bands came together and carried out activities that took place only when the entire tribe was assembled. One of these men's societies was designated by the tribal chief to serve as a police force charged with punishing violations of the strict rules that prevailed during the buffalo hunt, as well as with preserving order during the march and on the occasion of the sun dance.

That the emergence of these structural features was an adaptation to the problems created by a supraband aggregation is demonstrated by the fact that all the features—the council, the tribal chief, the men's societies, the police force, the sun dance organization—lapsed when the tribe broke up into its constituent units in the autumn.

The adaptiveness of a society's internal organization, tested repeatedly by the food quest, may be tried even more severely by warfare. Survival is the ultimate measure of fitness, and however well adapted a society may be in other respects, if it is unable to stand up to its enemies, it must be found wanting in its over-all adaptation. Superiority in military technology may be the decisive factor in armed conflict, but where the weapons of war are alike on both sides, success may well go to the society better organized to wage war.

Continual and successful involvement in war tends to leave its stamp on all segments of a society, sometimes to a remarkable degree. The ancient Spartans afford a classic example of this. Everything in the life of a Spartan was subordinated to his military obligations. The institutions of war were paramount, and other institutions were adjusted accordingly. Among preliterate peoples, the Zulu and Masai of Africa and the Northern Cayapó of South America provide examples of the same phenomenon.

The ideational aspect of culture also serves to adapt a society to the prevailing conditions of existence. For example, it has been noted of nomadic peoples like the Eskimo, Tehuelche, and Lengua that even when the food supply is unusually plentiful, after a band has spent more than a few days or weeks in one spot, everyone becomes restless and anxious to be on the move. Ecological necessity has developed in them a psychology of nomadism. By being mentally adapted to normal ecological conditions, the individuals in a culture are always ready, and even eager, to make what is ordinarily the most appropriate response. The matter may be put this way: a sociocultural system works best when it makes people *want* to do what they *have* to do.

A question that remains to be answered is how cultural adaptation is related to cultural evolution. The two are not synonymous: adaptation is the adjustment of a society to its external and internal conditions of existence, while evolution is change by which a society grows larger, more heterogeneous, and more coherent. While adaptive changes are usually evolutionary, they are not necessarily or always so. Adaptation may sometimes involve simplification, as when deteriorating environmental conditions force a society to split into smaller groups, move its settlements more often, and give up some of its ceremonies. Here, although the chances of survival under worsened conditions have increased, complexity has decreased, so that while the changes are adaptive, they are not evolutionary. Nevertheless, most adaptive changes undergone by a society do tend to render it more complex and better integrated—in a word, more evolved.

An evolutionary advance characteristically begins with an adaptive solution to an ecological problem and is followed by a series of readjustments whereby cultural elements successively further removed from the source of the change are affected by the change and accommodate themselves to it. Wittfogel (1957) has suggested that the need to establish or extend irrigation systems in certain heavily populated and arid parts of the world brought about basic changes in the economic and political institutions of several of the early civilizations and that these basic changes eventually ramified throughout their entire social systems.

During the course of these kinds of readjustments within a culture, new traits appear which are alternative to, and therefore competitive with, existing ones. In this competition traits are subjected to the cultural equivalent of natural selection: the better adapted traits survive and expand, and the less fit decline and disappear.

Competition, selection, and displacement among traits can readily be illustrated from contemporary American culture. We see them exemplified by the diesel engine replacing the steam locomotive and by the corporation replacing other forms of large-scale business enterprise. The operation of this process was recognized and expressed years ago by E. B. Tylor when he wrote: "the institutions which can best hold their own in the world gradually supersede the less fit ones, and . . . this incessant conflict determines the general resultant course of culture" ([1871] 1958, vol. 1, p. 62).

ROBERT L. CARNEIRO

[*Directly related are the entries* ECOLOGY; EVOLUTION, *articles on* CULTURAL EVOLUTION *and* SOCIAL EVOLUTION; TECHNOLOGY.]

BIBLIOGRAPHY

DICE, LEE R. 1952 *Natural Communities.* Ann Arbor: Univ. of Michigan Press.

ETKIN, WILLIAM 1954 Social Behavior and the Evolution of Man's Mental Faculties. *American Naturalist* 88:129–142.

HOMANS, GEORGE C. 1962 [Review of] *Medieval Technology and Social Change,* by Lynn White, Jr. *American Journal of Sociology* 68:396–397.

KROEBER, ALFRED L. (1923) 1948 *Anthropology: Race, Language, Culture, Psychology, Prehistory.* New rev. ed. New York: Harcourt. → First published as *Anthropology.*

KROEBER, ALFRED L. 1938 Basic and Secondary Patterns of Social Structure. *Journal of the Royal Anthropological Institute of Great Britain and Ireland* 68: 299–309.

LI, CHI 1957 *The Beginnings of Chinese Civilization: Three Lectures Illustrated With Finds at Anyang.* Seattle: Univ. of Washington Press.

LOWIE, ROBERT H. (1920) 1947 *Primitive Society.* New York: Liveright. → A paperback edition was published in 1961 by Harper.

LOWIE, ROBERT H. (1934) 1952 *An Introduction to Cultural Anthropology.* Rev. ed. New York: Farrar & Rinehart.

MOORE, OMAR K. 1957 Divination: A New Perspective. *American Anthropologist* New Series 59:69–74.

PIDDINGTON, RALPH (1950) 1952 *An Introduction to Social Anthropology.* 2d ed. Vol. 1. Edinburgh: Oliver & Boyd.

SUTTLES, WAYNE 1960 Affinal Ties, Subsistence, and Prestige Among the Coast Salish. *American Anthropologist* New Series 62:296–305.

THOMSON, J. ARTHUR; and GEDDES, PATRICK 1931 *Life: Outlines of General Biology.* 2 vols. London: Williams & Norgate.

TYLOR, EDWARD B. (1871) 1958 *Primitive Culture: Researches Into the Development of Mythology, Philosophy, Religion, Art and Custom.* 2 vols. Gloucester, Mass.: Smith. → Volume 1: *Origins of Culture.* Volume 2: *Religion in Primitive Culture.*

WHITE, LESLIE A. 1947 Evolutionary Stages, Progress, and the Evaluation of Cultures. *Southwestern Journal of Anthropology* 3:165–192.

WHITE, LESLIE A. 1949 Ethnological Theory. Pages 357–384 in Roy W. Sellars et al. (editors), *Philosophy for the Future: The Quest of Modern Materialism.* New York: Macmillan.

WITTFOGEL, KARL A. 1957 *Oriental Despotism: A Comparative Study of Total Power.* New Haven, Conn.: Yale Univ. Press. → A paperback edition was published in 1963.

WOODBURY, ANGUS M. 1954 *Principles of General Ecology.* New York: Blakiston.

V
CULTURE CHANGE

Culture change is the conceptual formulation that refers to the many ways in which societies change their patterns of culture: Internal factors such as new inventions may lead to an increased food supply and population growth, or external factors such as conquest by another society may bring about culture change. We know from the records of prehistory and history that the patterns of culture of every human society are constantly changing. The rate and type of change may be slow and gradual, as it was during the Paleolithic, or fast and drastic, as it has been in contemporary societies. The basic problem is a question of how and why there are shifts in rate and type of change, rather than a question of static versus changing cultures.

Our knowledge about culture change may be summarized in four basic questions: (1) What are the internal or external factors that generate shifts in rates and types of culture change? (2) What are the processes by which culture change takes place? (3) What models and methods are now available for the study of culture change? (4) How is the concept of culture change related to the closely associated phenomena of diffusion, innovation, evolution, acculturation, and nativism?

Factors influencing culture change. The data on change do not yet permit any easy generalizations concerning the relative primacy of various factors that may generate significant shifts in rates and types of culture change. Some anthropologists favor a basically Marxist, or Neo-Marxist, interpretation and give primacy in their theories to such factors as "the amount of energy harnessed per capita per year" (White 1949). Some, such as Steward (1955), place emphasis upon ecology and stress the "adaptation of a culture to its environment" as the primary factor. Other scholars emphasize the importance of "religious ideology" (Weber 1922), cultural "themes" (Opler 1945), and "cultural focus" (Herskovits 1955) or, like Geertz (1957), point to inherent incongruities and tensions in social and cultural systems that generate constant pressure for change. Still others have developed more specialized theories, such as Murdock (1949, p. 199), who concludes that "... social organization is a semi-independent system comparable in many respects to language, and similarly characterized by an internal dynamics of its own," or Hallowell (1955) and Wallace (1961), who stress the psychological aspects of culture change.

Whatever special emphasis may characterize a theory, it is useful to isolate three general factors that can influence change in a given culture:

(1) Any change in the ecological niche occupied by a society influences culture change. Such a change may occur as a result of either (a) natural environmental changes, e.g., the gradual desiccation of the great basin of Utah and Nevada following the retreat of the last glaciation; or (b) the migration of a society from one ecological niche to another, e.g., the movement of southern Athabascans from the subarctic territory of interior Canada and Alaska to the arid southwestern United States. New cultural adaptations are always required for survival in the case of such shifts in ecological niche.

(2) Any contact between two societies with different cultural patterns influences change in both societies. The diffusion, or borrowing, of cultural elements that occurs has made these exchanges important in culture change throughout history. More profound and sustained cultural contact, usually called "acculturation," generates even more significant shifts in the rates and types of change in the two cultures.

(3) Any evolutionary change occurring within a society is obviously a factor of critical importance. Following Murdock (1949, p. 184), "evolution" is used here simply to designate "processes of orderly adaptive change." For example, when a society with a food-gathering economy has domesticated its plants and animals and has thereby increased its food surplus potential, the requirements of the new food-producing technology and the ensuing population growth pose critical problems. The need for division and specialization of labor, social control, and distribution of the surplus leads to adaptive changes in the cultural patterns. Or if a society (for whatever reasons) shifts from matrilocal to patrilocal residence, then again there are adaptive changes in a whole range of cultural patterns, as Murdock (1949) has demonstrated.

Processes of culture change. The study of the processes of culture change refers to the actual social mechanisms by which the change takes place. Some scholars take the position that the basis of all culture change is located in changes in the attitudes and behavior of individual members of a society. This point of view is found in Barnett (1953), who focuses upon the individual innovator in a society and analyzes the cultural conditions that stimulate him to innovate, the incentives that motivate him, and the mental processes he experiences in innovation. In this study Barnett also treats the basic innovative processes in terms of recombinations, identifications, substitutions, etc., in mental configurations. He finds those who accept innovations are likely to be individuals who are "dissident," "disaffected," or "resentful."

Other scholars take the point of view that although individuals are the carriers of a culture, there are processes of change in social and cultural systems which have dynamic properties of their own that can be isolated and studied. Thus, we can study the mechanisms of "cultural evolution" (White 1949; Sahlins & Service 1960), the "configurations of culture growth" (Kroeber 1944) over long time spans, or the "evolution of social organization" (Murdock 1949) over at least several generations.

Systematic theories interrelating processual phenomena observed in changes in both individual behavior and social and cultural systems are currently one of the outstanding problems for future research and analysis. Firth (1951, p. 40) differentiates between "social structure," which he views as providing the principle of continuity in society, and "social organization," in which lies the principle of variation or change "... by allowing evaluation of situations and entry of individual choice." Herskovits (1955, pp. 497–514) emphasizes "individual variation," which is found even in the most isolated and primitive societies, and the importance of this variation in the mechanisms of culture change. Wallace (1961, pp. 143–152) attempts to combine individual personality and cognition with changes in cultural systems in his study of "revitalization" processes, in which he has described "... a common process structure which can be conceptualized as a pattern of temporally overlapping, but functionally distinct, stages."

Other recent contributions to the conceptual mapping of processes of culture change include Herskovits' formulation (1955, p. 492) of "reinterpretation" as the process by which old meanings are ascribed to new elements or by which new values change the cultural significance of old forms; Firth's description (1951, p. 86) of the process of "social convection," by which individuals not directly involved in a change in the first instance tend to modify their behavior to adjust to the change, and the process of "social conduction," by which an innovation brings unforeseen results that must be adapted to; and Vogt's distinction (1960, pp. 21–22) between "recurrent processes," found in micro time-scales, which characterize the daily, seasonal, annual, and generational life of a society, and "directional processes," found in macro time-scales, which involve nonrepetitive, cumulative shifts in the structures of social and cultural systems.

Models for the study of culture change

Culture change can be studied as it occurs over long time spans (e.g., the analysis of cultural evolution in human societies from the Lower Paleolithic to the twentieth century) and in the microscopic sense, as it occurs in short periods of time (e.g., the analysis of how individual American Indians altered their behavior patterns during one generation of education in Indian Service schools). The more specific methods for the study of culture change always require a comparative framework of some type. Sequences of change in individual behavior, in social structure, or in stages of cultural development are compared in order to yield systematic statements reaching beyond the concrete case.

Stable equilibrium versus constant change. From the writings of earlier social theorists such as Durkheim and Radcliffe-Brown, students of culture inherited a conceptual image of human society based upon an organismic analogy that emphasized the ways in which a custom, institution, or social activity preserved or maintained the social order. This conceptual image has led us to assume that social and cultural systems tend to maintain equilibrium unless they come into contact with some force from the outside, or develop some inner strain that disturbs the equilibrium. The problem then is to discover how the equilibrium is restored.

From the writings of other theorists, notably Max Weber (1922), students of change inherited a more dynamic image of society. The adequacy of the stable equilibrium model as a conceptual framework for the analysis of culture change has been questioned by such writers as Firth (1951), Leach (1954), Herskovits (1955), and Vogt (1960), who all maintain that the basic tendencies in social and cultural systems are toward change, rather than toward states of equilibrium. Furthermore, it can now be demonstrated from our accumulated archeological and historical data that a culture is never static, but rather that one of its most fundamental properties is change.

The problem for students of culture change has therefore become one of describing, conceptualizing, and explaining a set of ongoing processes of change that occur at varying rates, move in varying directions, and that are triggered and maintained by complex interactions of ecological, technological, social, cultural, and psychological variables.

Macroscopic models. The most inclusive models, with respect to both cultural coverage and time span, are those utilized by White (1949) and Childe (1951) for the study of cultural evolution. Both deal with trends and stages in the culture of mankind as a whole. White's most significant proposition is that technological development expressed in terms of man's control over energy underlies social changes and cultural achievements (1949, pp. 363–396). Childe is especially noted for his formulation of the important shift from food-gathering to food-producing societies in early human history. These models, dealing with what Steward (1955) has called "universal evolution," advance propositions about world culture as a whole but cannot explain particular features of particular cultures. An attempt to solve this conceptual and methodological difficulty has more recently been proposed by Sahlins and Service (1960), who differentiate between "general" and "specific" cultural evolution. They write:

General cultural evolution . . . is passage from less to greater energy transformation, lower to higher levels of integration, and less to greater all-around adaptability. Specific evolution is the phylogenetic, ramifying, historic passage of culture along its many lines, the adaptive modification of particular cultures. (p. 38)

In his model, Steward proposes a different methodological solution described as "multilinear evolution," in which "regularities in culture change" are studied by comparing sequences of change in a series of particular cultures. His classic paper (1955, pp. 178–209) utilizing this model is his comparison of the development of "irrigation civilizations" in five arid or semiarid areas of the world: Peru, Mesoamerica, Mesopotamia, Egypt, and China. Although more recent empirical evidence has not supported his generalizations concerning irrigation works as the crucial factor in all these areas, the comparative framework he proposes is a fruitful one that can be utilized on other ranges of culture change data.

Another model that involves social and cultural changes over relatively long time spans is that of Redfield, whose classic study (1941) of the shift from "folk" to "urban" society has stimulated many further studies of culture change, including the present interest in the emergence of and changes in "peasant society." Drawing upon the earlier ideas of Durkheim, Maine, Morgan, and Tönnies, Redfield designed a field study that compared four communities in Yucatan: a tribal village, a peasant village, a town, and a city. Using degree of isolation and degree of homogeneity in culture patterns as the independent variables, he shows how three types of culture change accompany lessening isolation and homogeneity: disorganization of the culture, secularization, and individualization.

Redfield's model generates a number of interesting propositions. Perhaps the major methodological difficulty in his Yucatan study was that two quite different types of phenomena were inextricably intertwined. Although his cases certainly range from "folk" to "urban" types of society, they are also cases that have involved a massive confrontation between the Mayan Indian and the Spanish cultural traditions. It is difficult to distinguish between changes that have derived from a shift in type of society from folk to urban and changes that have derived from the contact between Mayan Indians and Spaniards.

A more recent model dealing with sweeping changes in societies over long time spans is that of Rostow (1960), whose formulation of the stages of socioeconomic growth ranging from "a traditional society" to a stage of "durable consumers' goods and services" is currently influencing anthropological thought about the processes of culture change in the modern nations of the world. Other aspects of this long-range process of growth and development (at least in our own Western society) are treated in such studies as Riesman's characterization (1950) of the sequence of "tradition-directed" to "inner-directed" to "other-directed" systems.

Microscopic models.   Among the many models that are less extensive in scope, but still focused upon changing social and cultural systems, are those of Murdock (1949) and Leach (1954). Murdock (1949, pp. 201–221) is mainly concerned with changes in social organization, and he singles out the "rule of residence" as the aspect of social structure that acts as a filter, capable of responding to a variety of quite diverse external stimuli but in only a limited number of ways. He proposes that change in a social system regularly begins with a modification of the rule of residence, and other changes in kinship structure and terminology follow in predictable order. Leach, on the other hand, utilizes what might be called an "oscillation

model" in his description of Kachin society, where there is a regular oscillation between two polar types of political value systems to which the people can appeal and still be considered members of the society.

On a still more modest scale of comparative analysis, there are models for the study of changes in individual and group behavior within one culture. An example of such a model is that of Spindler and Goldschmidt (1952), who present an experimental design for the study of sociological and psychological variables in the changes that are occurring in individual and group behavior among the Menominee Indians of Wisconsin.

Finally, mention should be made of the "genetic model" proposed by Romney (1957), which provides for the analysis of culture change a comparative framework that offers the possibility of controlling geographical and historical factors to the maximum extent and of utilizing the full range of linguistic, archeological, and ethnographic data as these become available. The model, building upon earlier suggestions by Sapir (1916) and Eggan (1954), assumes that genetically related tribes, as determined by related languages, common physical type, and shared systemic patterns, form a "genetic unit" that derived from a small protogroup with a protoculture at some time in the past. The term "genetic" implies nothing beyond a concern with origins and mode of development of a unit of culture history. It is not assumed that all the people in the genetic unit necessarily descend from the ancestral group in a strict biological sense; biological mixture is expected wherever people of the genetic unit are in contact with other groups. What is required is a distinguishable physical type that converges, rather than diverges, as one goes back in time.

The model resembles that of the zoologist who views a certain species of animal as evolving and making an adaptive adjustment to a given ecological niche and then radiating from this point as the population expands into neighboring ecological niches. As the population moves into different ecological settings, further adaptive variations occur in the species. But these variations are traceable to the ancestral animal, or, in other words, back to the prototype. In applying the model to human populations, we may assume that a small protogroup succeeds in adapting itself efficiently to a certain ecological niche and in developing certain basic systemic patterns, which constitute the basic aspects of the protoculture. Once the adaptation proves to be efficient, the population expands, and the group begins to radiate from this point of dispersal. As members split off from the protocommunity, move into neighboring ecological niches, and come into contact with alien cultures, they make appropriate adaptations to these new situations and begin to differentiate—that is, there are adaptive variations from the prototype as the members of the genetic unit spread from the dispersal area. The use of this model not only makes possible the controlled comparative study of prehistoric and historic sequences of culture change in a geographically and historically meaningful unit but also sets the stage for more precise structural–functional comparisons of the various branches of the genetic unit as these continue to undergo change in the contemporary world. An example of a recent application of the model may be found in Vogt (1964).

EVON Z. VOGT

BIBLIOGRAPHY

BARNETT, HOMER G. 1953 *Innovation: The Basis of Cultural Change.* New York: McGraw-Hill.

CHILDE, V. GORDON 1951 *Social Evolution.* New York: Schumann.

EGGAN, FRED 1954 Social Anthropology and the Method of Controlled Comparison. *American Anthropologist* New Series 56:743–763.

FIRTH, RAYMOND W. 1951 *Elements of Social Organization.* London: Watts. → A paperback edition was published in 1963 by Beacon.

GEERTZ, CLIFFORD 1957 Ritual and Social Change: A Javanese Example. *American Anthropologist* New Series 59:32–54.

HALLOWELL, A. IRVING 1955 *Culture and Experience.* Philadelphia: Univ. of Pennsylvania Press.

HERSKOVITS, MELVILLE J. 1955 *Cultural Anthropology.* New York: Knopf. → An abridged revision of *Man and His Works,* 1948.

KEESING, FELIX M. 1953 *Culture Change: An Analysis and Bibliography of Anthropological Sources to 1952.* Stanford Anthropological Series, No. 1. Stanford Univ. Press.

KROEBER, ALFRED L. 1944 *Configurations of Culture Growth.* Berkeley: Univ. of California Press.

LEACH, EDMUND R. 1954 *Political Systems of Highland Burma: A Study of Kachin Social Structure.* A publication of the London School of Economics and Political Science. London School of Economics and Political Science; Cambridge, Mass.: Harvard Univ. Press.

MURDOCK, GEORGE P. 1949 *Social Structure.* New York: Macmillan. → A paperback edition was published in 1965 by the Free Press.

OPLER, MORRIS E. 1945 Themes as Dynamic Forces in Culture. *American Journal of Sociology* 51:198–206.

REDFIELD, ROBERT 1941 *The Folk Culture of Yucatan.* Univ. of Chicago Press.

RIESMAN, DAVID 1950 *The Lonely Crowd: A Study of the Changing American Character.* New Haven: Yale Univ. Press. → An abridged paperback edition was published in 1960.

ROMNEY, A. KIMBALL 1957 The Genetic Model and Uto-Aztecan Time Perspective. *Davidson Journal of Anthropology* 3, no. 2:35–41.

ROSTOW, WALT W. (1960) 1963 *The Stages of Economic Growth: A Non-Communist Manifesto.* Cambridge Univ. Press.

SAHLINS, MARSHALL D.; and SERVICE, ELMAN R. (editors) 1960 *Evolution and Culture.* Ann Arbor: Univ. of Michigan Press.

SAPIR, EDWARD (1916) 1949 Time Perspective in Aboriginal American Culture: A Study in Method. Pages 389–462 in Edward Sapir, *Selected Writings in Language, Culture and Personality.* Edited by D. Mandelbaum. Berkeley: Univ. of California Press.

SPINDLER, GEORGE; and GOLDSCHMIDT, WALTER 1952 Experimental Design in the Study of Culture Change. *Southwestern Journal of Anthropology* 8:68–83.

STEWARD, JULIAN H. 1955 *Theory of Culture Change: The Methodology of Multilinear Evolution.* Urbana: Univ. of Illinois Press.

VOGT, EVON Z. 1960 On the Concept of Structure and Process in Cultural Anthropology. *American Anthropologist* New Series 62:18–33.

VOGT, EVON Z. 1964 The Genetic Model and Maya Cultural Development. Pages 9–48 in Conference on the Cultural Development of the Maya, Burg Wartenstein, Austria, 1962, *Desarrollo cultural de los Mayas.* Edited by Evon Z. Vogt and A. Ruz Lhuillier. University City: Universidad Nacional Autónoma de México.

WALLACE, ANTHONY F. C. 1961 *Culture and Personality.* New York: Random House.

WEBER, MAX (1922) 1963 *The Sociology of Religion.* Boston: Beacon. → First published in German. A paperback edition was published in 1964.

WHITE, LESLIE 1949 *The Science of Culture: A Study of Man and Civilization.* New York: Farrar, Straus. → A paperback edition was published in 1958 by Grove.

CULTURE AND PERSONALITY

Culturally constituted social groups are as necessary for human existence as are any of man's vital organs. Nevertheless, as even cursory observation of children reveals, the acquisition of culture is often accompanied by conflict and struggle; and conformity with cultural rules and norms is frequently associated with frustration and tension. These two facets of culture—its capacity for both gratifying and frustrating human needs—constitute the basis for the two major axes of social science inquiry, stability and change; together, they constitute the generic problems of culture-and-personality research: What are the psychological conditions that promote persistence and innovation in human social and cultural systems?

Historical background

Despite the evident importance of its problems, culture-and-personality, as a formal discipline, is the youngest and smallest branch of anthropology. With some few exceptions, it hardly exists outside of the United States. Culture-and-personality, like biochemistry, falls between two academic stools, in this case anthropology on the one hand and the psychological sciences on the other. Thirty-five years ago there was no way of bridging the gap between them. Anthropology, to the extent that it was theoretically oriented, was concerned with such macroproblems as historical developments and evolutionary trends, for which the concepts of academic psychology were, or were deemed to be, irrelevant. The psychological sciences, on the other hand, were tied to the *a*historical, *a*cultural laboratory; their molecular concepts were obviously unrelated to the sociocultural concepts of anthropology. Only psychoanalytic psychology—not part of the academic establishment—seemed to see a bridge between the data obtained in the clinic and the social sciences. Earlier, Freud had made periodic forays into anthropology, but attempts to link the disciplines met with strong opposition on the part of social scientists.

The raw data of anthropological field work exposed living human beings in all their complexity, acting within a specified historical–cultural matrix. It is no accident that it was the field anthropologists, confronted with the necessity of relating traditional, descriptive cultural constructs to the ongoing social life about them, who first attempted to build this bridge in their search for the psychologically "genotypic" bases of their "phenotypic" cultural constructs. It is no accident, either, that psychoanalytic theory, however modified, was seized upon first as a possible theoretical tool. For psychoanalysis, unlike academic psychology, is concerned with molar rather than molecular psychological variables. Despite its *a*historicism, psychoanalysis anchors its patients in their own ontogenetic histories, thereby providing a link with the anthropological notion of culture as a configuration of learned customs. Hence, Edward Sapir, the generally acknowledged founder of the field, was influenced by his personal contacts with the psychiatrist H. S. Sullivan; Margaret Mead, by her contacts with E. H. Erikson; Ralph Linton and Cora DuBois, by collaboration with Abram Kardiner.

Personality studies 35 years ago were unsystematic; and cultural studies, with their heavy descriptive and empirical emphases, were self-consciously nontheoretical. Hence, a large share of culture-and-personality theory was, and continues to be, devoted to the exploration of empirical and analytic relationships. At that time, anthropologists had few techniques for the study of personality. The time-honored techniques of gross observation and informant interviews were inadequate for personality investigation. Again anthropology looked to the psychological sciences for assistance: depth interviews, Rorschach tests, doll-play, dreams, life

histories, systematic observation of family interaction, and other techniques were borrowed in whole or in part from clinical psychology and psychiatry. Where disciplinary boundaries are rigidly drawn, this influx of exotic tools—combined with the exotic concepts of psychoanalytic theory and learning theory—could hardly have been expected to attract discipline-bound researchers.

Some anthropologists avoided culture-and-personality because of the imprecise and inconclusive nature of its findings. This is not to say, as is sometimes charged, that its studies are "soft," or lacking in rigor—the best of its studies are certainly as rigorous, conceptually and methodologically, as their counterparts in other branches of social and cultural anthropology. It is, rather, that the very nature of its problems, given the research tools available, results in findings that sometimes lack the unqualified conviction characteristic of research in more structured fields.

As the field has matured, its initial period of heavy borrowing has come to an end. Methods and theories borrowed from other fields have become transformed by the new discipline for its own problems and its specific theoretical aims—and, although it continues to be catholic in its sources of stimulation, it has been developing its own. Increasingly, data cited in favor of a theory, and theories used for hypothesis derivation, originate in culture-and-personality research, rather than in the psychiatric clinic or the experimental laboratory. Moreover, as data accumulate, it is becoming increasingly possible to test hypotheses statistically by means of large-scale, cross-cultural samples. Although these studies, pioneered by Whiting and Child (1953), have been subjected to serious criticism, their findings have been sufficiently suggestive to hazard the prediction that such studies will increase both in number and in importance.

Despite its small number of practitioners, culture-and-personality has been extraordinarily diversified in its research interests. Although culture-and-personality has explored many topics that have been neglected by other anthropologists, it has also explored many of the topics that are of greatest interest to them. In both cases, psychological variables have played a prominent role in its research. The rationale for this emphasis must be sought within the explanatory framework of anthropological thought.

Explanation in anthropology

Anthropological theory has, in general, been cast in four explanatory modes—historical, structural, causal, and functional—that, when analyzed, can be reduced to the causal or the functional mode. Thus, historical explanations, to the extent that they are scientific explanations rather than uncontrolled speculations, are really causal explanations. The mere listing of a series of events that are chronologically prior to the appearance of the custom to be explained does not constitute explanation, unless it can be shown that one or more of these events was a condition—either necessary and/or sufficient—for the appearance of the custom. If this can be demonstrated, the explanation of the custom's origin is causal, the fact that it originated in the past being incidental to the theoretical aim, which is to provide an explanation for a certain type of social or cultural innovation.

Structural explanations can also be shown to be either causal or functional. Those which show the configuration (or interrelationships) in a set of customs are essentially descriptive. The data are ordered according to a coherent plan. If a theory is offered to explain the configuration (structure), then this theory is necessarily either causal or functional. Structural explanations that purport to explain a custom or set of customs in terms of some "principle" that it embodies are either verbal labels, serving to classify a set of data according to a heuristic scheme (such as the "principle" of the unity of the sibling group), or phenomenological principles of the actors (cognitive maps), in which case they are members of a cognitive subset in a set of causal variables. Similarly, explanations that stipulate either the structural requirements of a system or its structural "implications" are either causal or functional. Causal explanations are concerned with the antecedents of a system; functional explanations, with its consequences.

If anthropological explanations can be classified as either causal or functional, what role has culture-and-personality played in either or both types of explanation?

The human social order as a normative order

Social systems are characterized by a configuration of reciprocal roles that are shared by the members of a social group and are acquired from a previous generation. These roles serve to satisfy the three functional requirements of any society—adaptation, adjustment, and integration. Within zoological perspective, the unique feature of human social systems does not reside in the fact that their constituent roles are acquired through learning—for this is probably characteristic, although not to the same degree, of all mammalian social systems—but that many of the customs comprising these roles are based on rules and norms.

A custom, as this term is used by anthropologists, refers to any socially acquired behavior pattern that is widely, if not uniformly, performed by the members of a society or by one of its constituent social groups. In general, it is possible to distinguish two types of customs. First, there are those customs whose occurrence is based on prescriptive or proscriptive norms. Their performance may thus be characterized as being *isomorphic* with a norm or set of norms. These may be termed Type-1 customs. Second, there are customs whose occurrence, although not based on norms, nevertheless reflects them. If a norm, or set of norms, is proscriptive with respect to one subclass of behavior patterns but permissive with respect to all other members of the class, the latter, if they occur, reflect the norms but are not isomorphic with them. For example, marriage with any female not included in incest proscriptions reflects, but is not isomorphic with, the proscriptive norms. These customs may be termed Type-2 customs.

Although the occurrence of Type-1 customs is mandatory and the occurrence of Type-2 customs is voluntary, the performance of the latter is also normative in the sense that behavior falls within a normative, i.e., permissible, range of variability. Type-2 customs are also governed by socially shared rules that define proper performance. In the absence of such rules, behavior patterns are habits that describe individual action; they are not customs, which describe social interaction. Knowledge of habits and customs enables us to predict behavior.

The human social order as a cognitive order

Culture, as a normative system, is a functional requirement of a human social order. Because of the enormous degrees of biological plasticity and cognitive ingenuity that, together, produce the broad variability characteristic of human behavior, the absence of this normative dimension would render human social systems impossible. The range of behavior patterns potential in any individual is much broader than the limited range required for the performance of any custom or set of customs. Beyond a certain critical point, whose limits are still unknown, variability in behavior precludes the very possibility of custom. In other words, human societies have had to set limits (by means of prescriptive and proscriptive norms, and of rules) to the range of permitted variability in customary behavior. The cultural dimension of human social systems is made possible by the very capacity for symbolization. It is to human societies what limited plasticity and biological determination are to insect and mammalian societies. By selecting the optimal range required by the operation of a particular social system, from the potential range of variability characteristic of the species, it ensures an important degree of uniformity and predictability, thereby rendering social order possible. In short, the invention of culture allowed man to combine the short-run adaptive value of social order with the long-run advantage of flexibility.

A human social order, then, is a cognitive order. The set of customs that comprise the constituent roles of a human social system consist, in the first instance, of a set of norms and rules—cognitive variables—that either prescribe or regulate behavior. These norms and rules must be cognized by the members of the society if the social system is to be maintained. The acquisition of cognitions, then, as well as of complete cognitive maps, is a necessary psychological condition (cause) for the performance of single customs and for the maintenance of an entire social system. Cognitions can regulate behavior, but they are not identical with it. The conventional statement "Social behavior is learned" implies two kinds of learning, cognitive and behavioral. That is, the performance of a custom requires that the actors learn about the custom (acquisition of cognitions) and that they learn to perform what they have learned (acquisition of behavior). In general, culture-and-personality has devoted less attention to the former type of learning than to the latter. Nevertheless, the recent interest in cognition and in ethnoscience, and the development of such techniques as componential analysis, will probably redress the balance.

Since customary behavior is governed by rules, proper performance of customs requires that the actors be capable of evaluating and regulating their own behavior in terms of these rules. Evaluation, then, is yet another cognitive basis for the maintenance of social systems, although it has received little attention from culture-and-personality.

Despite their importance, cognition, learning, and evaluation do not constitute necessary and sufficient psychological prerequisites for the performance of customs. For, although anthropological informants are entitled to explain their own behavior by the ubiquitous "It is our custom," anthropologists cannot abdicate their scientific responsibility by this obviously redundant explanation. Customs cannot compel the occurrence of behavior; they can only channel behavior once it occurs. Unless the actors are more highly motivated to perform a custom than to perform competing, alternative behavior patterns that compose their behavioral repertoire, the learning of a custom, however normative, will not ensure its performance. In short, the performance of customs, like other forms of behavior, must be instigated by the intention or expectation of satisfying a need or set of needs. A great deal of culture-and-personality research has been devoted to the study of motivation and its ontogenesis in the socialization process.

In sum, cognition, learning, motivation, and evaluation—all psychological variables—constitute necessary and sufficient conditions (causes) for the proper performance of customs and, hence, for the maintenance of social systems. This analysis becomes much more complicated when it is observed that the relationship between the performance of customs and the satisfaction of needs is not always a simple one. For Type-2 customs—in which "performance" means the practice of personally preferred behavior patterns—this analysis, with proper qualifications, will serve as a simplified model. For Type-1 customs, in which "performance" means compliance with prescriptive or proscriptive norms, further elaboration is required.

The human social order as a moral order

A normative order, it has been indicated, consists of two related, but discrete, variables: norms and rules. "Norms" prescribe the occurrence of behavior; proscriptive norms prescribe avoidance behavior. "Rules" regulate or govern behavior (whether it is prescribed or permissive) once it occurs. Norms and rules ensure the uniformity, and hence the predictability, of behavior. Rules are ethically neutral; norms implicitly incorporate a set of moral values and, therefore, also function to preclude the overt expression of motives that are, or are deemed to be, socially harmful or disruptive. Norms also ensure the performance of activities that are, or are deemed to be, socially desirable, if not necessary. In terms of the moral order, deviation from norms is viewed as an offense to the social order. The limits that norms impose on behavioral variability are intended to ensure the occurrence of *culturally* normative behavior, as well as to regulate the performance of *socially* normative behavior.

Because of man's plasticity and cognitive ingenuity, what any actor *must* do, as defined by cultural norms, in order to participate in his social system is not the same as what he *can* do; thus, what he must do may conflict with what he would *like* to do. Hence, tension between personal needs and cultural norms, as well as the internal pressures to eliminate this tension, are omnipresent in any society. In general, tension is resolved in favor of the norms, resolution being mediated by anxiety. This will be moral anxiety, if the norms have been internalized (superego); or social anxiety, if punishment is known to be the consequence of deviation. Although anxiety can serve to motivate compliance with Type-2 customs, the source of deviation (the original need) is inhibited but not extinguished. For the existence of these norms implies that the motivational systems of the actors are either indifferent to, or opposed to, the prescriptive or proscriptive behavior. If the latter is the case, the frustration of the proscribed motive has important consequences for cultural stability and change.

Frustration, sociocultural persistence, change

If the expectation of gratifying drives, including anxiety, constitutes a necessary (although not a sufficient) condition for the persistence of social systems, the frustration of drives constitutes a necessary (although not a sufficient) condition for the disruption of and change in these systems. Cultural norms, which proscribe the satisfaction of certain drives, constitute one importance source of frustration. The social structure is another important source. For example, if a structural arrangement such as stratification prevents certain groups in society from satisfying culturally approved needs by denying them access to those roles whose performance can satisfy these needs, the attendant frustration may be as great as frustration induced by proscriptive norms. Both types of frustration constitute potential sources of social and cultural deviation, innovation, and change.

Paradoxically, they also constitute sources of cultural and social persistence. If motives cannot be satisfied directly, because of cultural or social impediments, need-frustration may be averted by distortions in any of the motive's four dimensions—drive, goal, act, and agent. These changes may sufficiently alter the original meaning of the motive so that, in its disguised form, the need may seek gratification in indirect, but culturally approved, ways. Frequently, the means for such distortion of motives, and consequent gratification of needs, are found in elements of the social and cultural systems. Although customs—and even roles—making up the social system are often used in this fashion, it is the cultural system that, *par excellence*, serves the function of gratifying these forbidden motives. For example, forbidden dependency or hostility motives are often disguised and, consequently, gratified in subservient or dominant political roles, respectively. Religion, art, folklore, ritual, and the like may function as culturally constituted defense mechanisms by which frustrated motives may be disguised and, hence, gratified in a culturally approved manner. This, of course, is not their only function. They have other latent, not to mention manifest, functions of a nondefensive character. When elements of the social and cultural systems serve to gratify otherwise frustrated and potentially disruptive needs, the needs, in turn, constitute powerful motivational causes for the persistence of these systems. Culture-and-personality research has only begun a systematic exploration of this important field of research.

Sometimes, however, socially and culturally induced need-frustrations are not resolved in this manner; and this frustration results in deviation, either cultural or psychological. In defending the self against internal conflict, some defense mechanisms are adopted in which the cognitive distortion of motives is of sufficient magnitude to cause behavior that, psychologically bizarre and/or socially disruptive, may be diagnosed as mental illness. In other cases, defense mechanisms may be avoided in favor of direct expression of forbidden motives, resulting in crime and delinquency. This type of deviation has received less attention from culture-and-personality research than has psychological deviation, probably because its incidence is much less frequent in the primitive societies whose study has engaged traditional anthropological attention.

Need-frustration is a necessary (but not a sufficient) condition for social and cultural change, as well as for psychological and cultural deviation. Indeed, the border line between change and deviation is often a tenuous one. If certain cultural norms or structural arrangements systematically frustrate important needs, indigenous or borrowed innovations in norms or in social structure, which might otherwise have been ignored or labeled as deviation, become the basis for sociocultural cumulation and change. In general, culture-and-personality research has paid more attention to dramatic change than it has to gradual change. (This is found, for example, in studies of nativistic and revivalistic movements.)

If motivation is a necessary stimulus to change, cognition is a necessary basis for change. Any change entails cognitive restructuring; the more dramatic the change, the greater the restructuring required. Although cognitive maps, or perceptual sets, seems to be highly resistant to change, it is frequently observed that the acceptance of innovations is impeded by cognitive blocks. If innovations are accepted, they are sufficiently assimilated to traditional cognitive orientations, often rendering dramatic changes that are more apparent than real. Culture-and-personality has devoted relatively little attention to cognitive variables in studies of sociocultural change.

Psychological variables, such as learning, cognition, perception, and motivation, are as important in causal explanations of change in sociocultural systems as they are in explanations of structural persistence.

Functionalism in culture-and-personality

Culture-and-personality theory, by the very nature of its explanatory concepts, is both causal and functional in character. If customs are performed because of the expectations of satisfying needs, at least one of their functions (manifest and/or latent) is the satisfaction of the biological and psychological requirements of the actors. However, customs are units within a sociocultural system; functionalism, as a theory that purports to explain the maintenance of social and cultural systems, is concerned with the functional requirements of social groups taken collectively. Since the functional requirements of group existence are satisfied not by the *existence* of customs but by their *performance*, and since performance is caused by the expectation of satisfying needs (personal functions), social functions are served in the process of serving personal functions. Obviously, an explanation of the latter is contingent upon an explanation of the former. Thus, when personal functional requirements are not satisfied by the performance of customs, these customs may not occur. When this happens, their functions are not served, and changes and/or disruptive influences may take place in both the social and the cultural systems.

Personality variables, although always causal, may not always be important for understanding social functions. If all of the functions of a custom are recognized (manifest functions), motivation may be taken for granted; an understanding of a custom's social functions does not entail explicit knowledge of the needs that instigate its performance. This is not true of unrecognized (latent) functions, especially of those which are served by the performance of customs whose motivation is at least partially unconscious. Since unconscious motives are frequently expressed in the performance of customs whose manifest functions are unrelated to these motives, and since the motives are disguised because of the disruptive sociocultural impact of their undisguised expression, the latent social functions served by the performance of these customs are of the utmost importance for an understanding of sociocultural persistence.

MELFORD E. SPIRO

[*Other relevant material may be found in* COGNITIVE THEORY; CULTURE; LIFE CYCLE; SOCIALIZATION; *and in the biographies of* BENEDICT *and* SAPIR.]

BIBLIOGRAPHY

BENEDICT, RUTH 1934 *Patterns of Culture.* Boston and New York: Houghton Mifflin. → A paperback edition was published in 1961.

DuBois, CORA A. (1944) 1960 *The People of Alor: A Social-psychological Study of an East Indian Island.* Cambridge, Mass.: Harvard Univ. Press.

HALLOWELL, A. IRVING 1955 *Culture and Experience.* Philadelphia: Univ. of Pennsylvania Press.

HARING, DOUGLAS (editor) (1948) 1956 *Personal Character and Cultural Milieu: A Collection of Readings.* 3d rev. ed. Syracuse Univ. Press.

HSU, FRANCIS L. K. (editor) 1961 *Psychological Anthropology: Approaches to Culture and Personality.* Homewood, Ill.: Dorsey Press.

KAPLAN, BERT (editor) 1961 *Studying Personality Cross-culturally.* Evanston, Ill.: Row, Peterson.

KARDINER, ABRAM 1939 *The Individual and His Society: The Psychodynamics of Primitive Social Organization.* New York: Columbia Univ. Press.

KLUCKHOHN, CLYDE et al. (editors) (1948) 1953 *Personality in Nature, Society, and Culture.* 2d ed., rev. & enl. New York: Knopf.

LaBARRE, WESTON 1954 *The Human Animal.* Univ. of Chicago Press.

MEAD, MARGARET 1939 *From the South Seas: Studies in Adolescence and Sex in Primitive Societies.* New York: Morrow.

OPLER, MARVIN K. (editor) 1959 *Culture and Mental Health: Cross-cultural Studies.* New York: Macmillan.

SAPIR, EDWARD (1910–1944) 1949 *Selected Writings in Language, Culture, and Personality.* Edited by David G. Mandelbaum. Berkeley: Univ. of California Press.

SIEGEL, BERNARD J. (editor) 1959–1962 *Biennial Review of Anthropology.* 2 vols. Stanford Univ. Press.

WALLACE, ANTHONY F. C. 1961 *Culture and Personality.* New York: Random House.

WHITING, JOHN W. M.; and CHILD, IRVIN L. 1953 *Child Training and Personality: A Cross-cultural Study.* New Haven: Yale Univ. Press. → A paperback edition was published in 1962 by Yale University Press.

CULTURE AREA

Culture areas are geographical territories in which characteristic culture patterns are recognizable through repeated associations of specific traits and, usually, through one or more modes of subsistence that are related to the particular environment. As one formulation within the general school of historical particularism that has developed in anthropology in the United States, the concept of culture area reflects the theoretical position that each culture, on whatever level it may be analyzed, must be examined with regard to its own history and also with regard to the general principles of independent invention, culture borrowing, and cultural integration. Although many factors at the base of any recognizable culture area are ecological in nature, the culture-area concept is one that conforms to the doctrine of limited possibilities rather than to a simple geographic determinism.

Viewed in this light and assessed according to the size and character of the geographic units and the degree of complexity of cultural similarities within, and differences beween, the units, the culture-area concept takes shape as a classificatory device of marked utility in describing the cultural regions of the world. Since "culture" and "area" are both generalized terms, their use in combination gives no real clue as to precise meaning, which must be specified. When contrasting one culture area with another, the level of abstraction must be the same.

In its original formulation the culture-area concept applied primarily to the ethnographic present and occupied an important niche in the natural-history phase of anthropology that was concerned with the orderly description of the cultures of the world. The geographic distribution of culture traits within such areas served as indirect evidence for the reconstruction of cultural histories. The formulations for each of the major continents were used for convenience in the ordering of ethnographic descriptions but were otherwise ignored or discarded as being too limited in time, too static in concept, and too generally conceived to be of much use to the developing trends of concern with interpersonal and social dynamics. The steady expansion of archeological research, which furnishes direct evidence for the construction of the historical chronicle in local terms, reduced the role of indirect evidence furnished by contemporary data in the reconstruction of culture history. Although the culture-area concept went into temporary eclipse as a tool for theoretical research, it was still retained for the arrangement of museum collections, for which it was originally devised, and for the presentation of descriptive data on the classroom level (e.g., Herskovits 1955; Keesing 1958). It should, however, be noted that efforts to sketch a culture-area map of Asia persisted into the 1950s, as a move to complete the world picture. The organization of data in culture-area terms persists in standard anthropological works of the present day (e.g., Gibbs 1965; Murdock 1959). The utility of the concept with regard to cultural dynamics and other current interests appears in Service's discussion of differences in acculturation in colonial Latin America that were conditioned by the aboriginal culture-area patterns (1955) and in such studies as those of Hallowell (1946) and Devereux (1951), which deal with personality types characteristic of specific culture areas and their survival through time and acculturation.

The culture-area concept can add insight to the processes of culture history by filling in the archeological record (see, for example, Steward 1955, chapter 11); in the mapping of culture areas or of trait or trait-complex distributions for successive periods, the same general areas or boundaries show tendencies to survive (Bennett 1948; Kroeber 1944; Smith 1952) or recur (Ehrich 1956; 1961). Culture-area mapping must initially be done with regard to single periods, but it is the repeated geographical and distributional patterns that give some intimation of physiographic and ecological influences, and the dynamic processes of cultural formation and adjustment must in each case be separately analyzed and evaluated.

Wissler is generally considered to have formulated the culture-area approach during the course of arranging the ethnological exhibits of the North American Indians for the American Museum of Natural History; his first major work on the subject appeared in 1917. Kroeber (1939, pp. 4–8), although describing Wissler's approach as of gradual, empirical, almost unconscious growth, gives him full credit for the codification and development of then current usages, the recognition of the stabilizing effects of environment on cultural patterns, and the foundation of the idea of temporal culture climax by his enunciation of spatial culture centers.

Driver (1962), however, points out that as early as 1904, Kroeber himself dealt with areal subdivisions of California, and that Wissler first mentioned the culture area in 1906. Also in 1904 Livingston Farrand suggested a seven-part classification of North American Indians, including considerations of both geography and culture, and then discussed them at some length (1904, pp. 101–194). Holmes (1903), writing on museum exhibits, mapped the North American Indians according to 19 geo–ethnic groups, which correspond well to the groupings in the later work of both Wissler and Kroeber. Furthermore, Kroeber (1939, p. 7, note 6) cites an article by O. T. Mason, published in 1896, that recognizes 18 culture areas or environments in the Western Hemisphere. Museum exhibits of ethnographic materials had been geographically organized for some years (Wallace 1887), and this approach to ethnographical data was clearly derived from zoogeography.

It is significant that the initial growth and formulation of the culture-area concept took place with regard to the North American Indians, for whom the documented ethnographic evidence was reasonably full and for whom the environmental settings were contrasting and limiting.

Methodological considerations. The initial objective of the culture-area concept as a classificatory device is the organization of the vast number of individual cultures into a coherent system of units that can be analyzed and compared. Such an ordering of data is a preliminary step in the study of cultural dynamics and culture history, and it is static only insofar as one wishes to treat its descriptive categories as ends in themselves.

Although there is a general tone or pattern to a culture area, the distributions of its elements are not necessarily uniform, and Kroeber's concept of climax (1939, pp. 4, 5, 222 ff.) refers to peaks of intensity. The boundaries between areas are not necessarily distinct, for recognizable cultures within a given area may contrast with those of neighboring ones, and if the boundaries are not sharply delineated, zones of composite culture or blended traits may make the transition from one to another a matter of gradation. Within a single area, however, as in the southwestern United States and in the Congo region of Africa, quite different ways of life may coexist as characteristic patterns.

In a hierarchical classification the criteria selected as determinants become more numerous and more detailed as the levels of categories become more specific. In this sense, Kroeber's 84 divisions in "Cultural and Natural Areas of Native North America" (1939) are a more detailed elaboration of Wissler's original major culture areas; and Murdock's article on South American culture areas (1951), using nine major types of positive information, does not merely attempt to revise Steward's formulation (1946–1959) but also actually increases the number of recognizable subareas. It seems at least in part to be a matter of categorical level that leads to divergence in the assessment of the theoretical significance of the concept. Thus, Naroll, in discussing the major culture areas of Asia, writes, in support of Wissler's theoretical interpretations, that "while the environment does not of itself either produce or determine cultural patterns, it does have a powerful influence on them; it not merely states the economic problems which people must solve, but in each ecological region it tends to standardize some particular pattern which the people have chosen as a solution" (1950, p. 186). On the other hand, Murdock, while minimizing its theoretical importance, describes it as "nearly as useful in ordering the immense range of ethnographic variation as is the Linnaean system in the ordering of biological forms" (1951, p. 415).

Operationally, it makes little difference whether one's original approach is through the somewhat intuitive recognition of similarities and differences in integrated patterns viewed as cultural wholes, whether it is based on detailed distribution studies of traits and trait complexes, or whether it stems from a delineation of geographic and ecological factors. All three procedures must be brought into play, and distributional studies, such as cross-cultural surveys and the Human Relations Area Files documentation, can serve as controls.

Kroeber's recognition of areal distinctions preceded the extensive work on trait-element distributions in California (Driver 1962). On the other hand, the Midwestern Taxonomic System of archeological classification (McKern 1939), although not originally concerned with spatial considerations, did show the areal distributions of "aspects" in a methodology that seems clearly derived from the California studies. Although distributions of specific North American Indian traits, as mapped in Driver and Massey (1957), did not result in an automatic delineation of culture-area boundaries, correlations of traits did fall consistently into areal clusters (Driver 1962, p. 23). On the other hand, Naroll (1950, p. 186) paid as much attention to ecological frontiers as to cultural. An additional factor seems to be that geographical entities such as river systems or plains areas may focus human contacts inward, resulting, on the one hand, in a form of isolating mechanism that establishes consistency in culture patterning, while at the same time tending to delimit independent trait and trait-complex diffusion (Ehrich 1956). Also to be noted are continued attempts to produce temporally flat geographic maps of culture patterns at given points in time.

Time depth. Although much of the work on culture-area analysis and delineation has been carried out with relation to the ethnographic present or to particular periods, some attempts have been made to consider the concept with relation to time depth. These efforts have two major orientations.

(1) The first of these is the persistence of the same culture patterns or configurations in given areas over long periods. One aspect of continuity analysis is implicit in Kroeber's *Configurations of Culture Growth* (1944), in which he uses configurations to apply to long-continuing traditions in the civilizations of the Old World, particularly with regard to their geographical locations. The changing interests and bursts of energy that occur at various times, he isolates as temporal climaxes within the main stream of the localized configuration.

Another aspect is the persistence of established traditions or substrata that may have conditioning effects upon the direction of acculturation. Writing on the northwest coast of North America and on Latin America, respectively, Smith (1952) and Service (1955) bring into focus the influences of traditions typical of particular areas upon the local patterns of culture change.

Into a third category of continuities falls Bennett's development of the "co-tradition" as formulated for Peru, as applied experimentally to the archeology of the southwestern United States, and as suggested for Mesoamerica (1948). The Bronze Age culture of mainland Greece, Crete, and the Cyclades would also seem to fall within the "co-tradition" pattern. The concept is one of somewhat similar and related, although recognizably distinct, cultures that persist for reasonably long periods within an area. The term "tradition" connotes persistence, and the significance is that of cultural linkage, either of enduring parallels descending from common or related origins and remaining in contact or of strong acculturation or convergence.

(2) A second orientation of the culture-area concept with regard to time bears no relation to the continuity of cultural tradition. It is becoming evident, especially in archeological contexts, that the mapping of culture areas at different periods reveals regions and boundaries that persist or reappear, even when peoples with distinctly different culture patterns overrun the territory. Sooner or later the same geographic lines tend to re-establish themselves. A striking example of this thesis is the close correspondence between the regionalization of contemporary Anglo-American civilization in the United States and the culture areas of the North American Indians. Here we have the replacement of a population by new peoples with a new technology, but the geographical and ecological factors have reasserted themselves. This would seem to indicate a form of geographic uniformitarianism that, despite cultural discontinuities, brings about the persistence or the re-emergence of areas and boundaries at various times, from the period of earliest settlement onward. Similar processes have marked the culture history of the Mediterranean and the Middle East and of Europe (Ehrich 1956; 1961).

The culture-area concept is a means of organizing a vast amount of variegated ethnographic data into comprehensible units within a classificatory system. Like all such systems, it depends upon an increasing number of criteria or determinants in the isolation of units in a descending order of magnitude. Major considerations in recognizing these areas and subareas are ecological zones, patterns of

cultural integration, and correlations of independently diffused traits. Although initial recognition may depend in part upon familiarity and intuition, distribution studies serve as effective controls. Important determining processes seem to be cultural adjustments to the environment and the inward focusing of contacts within an area, caused by regional topographic patterns which produce cultural isolates. These factors persist through time and find expression either in the continuities of cultural traditions or in the reappearance of the same areas and boundaries, even when the local culture history is discontinuous.

The concept is far from static and orders cultural information in a form that makes it useful for comparative analyses and an understanding of cultural dynamics, processes, and cultural history.

ROBERT W. EHRICH AND
GERALD M. HENDERSON

[See also AFRICAN SOCIETY; CARIBBEAN SOCIETY; ECOLOGY; ETHNOLOGY; INDIANS, NORTH AMERICAN; MIDDLE AMERICAN SOCIETY; OCEANIAN SOCIETY.]

BIBLIOGRAPHY

ARMILLAS, PEDRO 1948 A Sequence of Cultural Development in Meso-America. Pages 105–111 in Wendell C. Bennett (editor), A Reappraisal of Peruvian Archaeology. Society for American Archaeology, Memoir No. 4. Menasha, Wisc.: The Society for American Archaeology and the Institute of Andean Research. → The historical chronicle as generalized from archeological sources within the framework of a single major culture area. See also Kirchhoff 1943 and Steward 1955.

BACON, ELIZABETH 1946 A Preliminary Attempt to Determine the Culture Areas of Asia. Southwestern Journal of Anthropology 2:117–132.

BENNETT, WENDELL C. 1948 The Peruvian Co-tradition. Pages 1–7 in Wendell C. Bennett (editor), A Reappraisal of Peruvian Archaeology. Society for American Archaeology, Memoir No. 4. Menasha, Wisc.: The Society for American Archaeology and the Institute of Andean Research. → The initial statement on "co-tradition" as part of a culture-area analysis.

BENNETT, WENDELL C.; and BIRD, JUNIUS B. (1949) 1964 Andean Culture History. 2d ed. Garden City, N.Y.: Doubleday. → See especially pages 1–65. Sketches the main culture areas of South America before discussing the archeology of the Andean region.

COON, CARLETON S. (1951) 1961 Caravan: The Story of the Middle East. Rev. ed. New York: Holt. → Treats north Africa and the Middle East as a major culture area.

DEVEREUX, GEORGE 1951 Reality and Dream: Psychotherapy of a Plains Indian. New York: International Universities Press. → Personality types as characteristic of a particular culture area.

DRIVER, HAROLD E. 1961 Indians of North America. Univ. of Chicago Press. → Culture traits and subjects treated mainly in a culture-area framework. A fuller and reoriented discussion of much of the material in Driver and Massey 1957.

DRIVER, HAROLD E. 1962 *The Contribution of A. L. Kroeber to Culture Area Theory and Practice.* Indiana University Publications in Anthropology and Linguistics, No. 18. Baltimore, Md.: Waverly Press. → Good discussion and bibliography.

DRIVER, HAROLD E.; and MASSEY, WILLIAM C. 1957 Comparative Studies of North American Indians. American Philosophical Society, *Transactions* 47: 165–456. → Outlines subsistence and culture areas. Emphasizes trait distributions, which are given in a series of maps. Culture areas are adumbrated by concentrations of overlapping rather than shown by coterminous boundaries.

EHRICH, ROBERT W. 1956 Culture Area and Culture History in the Mediterranean and the Middle East. Pages 1–21 in Saul S. Weinberg (editor), *The Aegean and the Near East: Studies Presented to Hetty Goldman on the Occasion of Her Seventy-fifth Birthday.* Locust Valley, N.Y.: Augustin. → The culture area as a classificatory system; its recurrence through time, with applications to the major areas mentioned.

EHRICH, ROBERT W. 1961 On the Persistences and Recurrences of Culture Areas and Culture Boundaries During the Course of European Pre-history, Protohistory, and History. Pages 253–257 in International Congress of Prehistoric and Protohistoric Sciences, Fifth, Hamburg, 1958, *Bericht über den V. Internationalen Kongress für Vor und Fruhgeschichte, Hamburg vom 24, bis 30 August 1958.* Berlin: Mann. → A restatement of culture-area classification and recurrence and a suggested application to temperate Europe.

Europe and Its Cultures. 1963 *Anthropological Quarterly* 36, no. 3 (Special Issue). → Symposium papers by Conrad M. Arensberg, Michael M. Kenny, Donald S. Pitkin, Robert K. Burns, Jr., and Joel M. Halpern.

FARRAND, LIVINGSTON (1904) 1964 *Basis of American History: 1500–1900.* New York: Ungar. → An early discussion of North American Indian culture areas.

GIBBS, JAMES L. JR. (editor) 1965 *Peoples of Africa.* New York: Holt. → Organized in accordance with Herskovits' culture areas. See especially maps on end papers and pages viii–ix.

GOLDENWEISER, ALEXANDER A. (1937) 1942 *Anthropology: An Introduction to Primitive Culture.* New York: Appleton. → Contains a discussion of culture areas, particularly with relation to trait diffusion and local integration.

HALLOWELL, A. I. 1946 Some Psychological Characteristics of the Northeastern Indians. Pages 195–225 in Frederick Johnson (editor), *Man in Northeastern North America.* Papers of the Robert S. Peabody Foundation for Archaeology, Vol. 3. Andover, Mass.: Phillips Academy; The Foundation. → Psychological factors as distinctive of a particular culture area and as persistent through time.

HERSKOVITS, MELVILLE J. 1930 The Culture Areas of Africa. *Africa* 3:59–77.

HERSKOVITS, MELVILLE J. 1955 *Cultural Anthropology.* New York: Knopf. → An abridged revision of *Man and His Works,* 1948. See pages 396–410 for a good textbook treatment and review of culture areas.

HERSKOVITS, MELVILLE J. 1962 *The Human Factor in Changing Africa.* New York: Knopf. → See especially pages 56–112 and the map on page 57 for culture-area orientation.

HOLMES, WILLIAM H. 1903 Classification and Arrangement of the Exhibits of an Anthropological Museum. Pages 253–278 in Smithsonian Institution, *Annual Report of the Board of Regents of the Smithsonian Institution . . . for the Year Ending June 30, 1901.* Washington: Government Printing Office. → See especially pages 268–269 for a list of the geo-ethnic groups in North America and a map.

KEESING, FELIX M. 1958 *Cultural Anthropology: The Science of Custom.* New York: Holt. → See pages 107–137 for a good textbook treatment and review of culture areas.

KIRCHHOFF, PAUL (1943) 1952 Mesoamerica: Its Geographic Limits, Ethnic Composition and Cultural Characteristics. Pages 17–30 in Sol Tax (editor), *Heritage of Conquest: The Ethnology of Middle America.* Glencoe, Ill.: Free Press. → First published in *Acta americana.*

KROEBER, ALFRED L. (1939) 1963 *Cultural and Natural Areas of Native North America.* Berkeley and Los Angeles: Univ. of California Press. → First published in Volume 38 of the University of California *Publications in American Archaeology and Ethnology.* → A classic work.

KROEBER, ALFRED L. 1944 *Configurations of Culture Growth.* Berkeley and Los Angeles: Univ. of California Press.

KROEBER, ALFRED L. 1947 Culture Groupings in Asia. *Southwestern Journal of Anthropology* 3:322–330.

LINTON, RALPH 1928 Culture Areas of Madagascar. *American Anthropologist* New Series 30:363–390.

LINTON, RALPH; and WINGERT, PAUL S. 1946 *Arts of the South Seas.* New York: The Museum of Modern Art. → See especially the maps on the end papers and on pages 7–9.

McKERN, W. C. 1939 The Midwestern Taxonomic Method as an Aid to Archaeological Culture Study. *American Antiquity* 4:301–313.

MURDOCK, GEORGE P. 1951 South American Culture Areas. *Southwestern Journal of Anthropology* 7:415–436.

MURDOCK, GEORGE P. 1959 *Africa: Its Peoples and Their Culture History.* New York: McGraw-Hill. → A culture-area treatment is implied but is not specific.

NAROLL, RAOUL S. 1950 A Draft Map of the Culture Areas of Asia. *Southwestern Journal of Anthropology* 6:183–187.

PATAI, RAPHAEL 1951 Nomadism: Middle Eastern and Central Asian. *Southwestern Journal of Anthropology* 7:401–414.

PATAI, RAPHAEL 1952 The Middle East as a Culture Area. *Middle East Journal* 6:1–21.

SERVICE, ELMAN R. 1955 Indian–European Relations in Colonial Latin America. *American Anthropologist* New Series 57:411–425. → The effect of differences in cultural patterns characteristic of different culture areas upon the course of acculturation.

SMITH, MARIAN W. 1952 Culture Area and Culture Depth: With Data From the Northwest Coast. Pages 80–96 in International Congress of Americanists, 29th, New York, 1949, *Selected Papers.* Edited by Sol Tax. Volume 3: Indian Tribes of Aboriginal America. Univ. of Chicago Press. → Emphasizes historical time depth in the formation, survival, and continuity of culture areas under acculturation.

STEWARD, JULIAN H. (editor) (1946–1959) 1963 *Handbook of South American Indians.* 7 vols. U.S. Bureau of American Ethnology, Bulletin No. 143. New York: Cooper Square. → See especially Volume 1, page 12, and Volume 5, pages 669–772, for South American culture areas.

STEWARD, JULIAN H. 1955 *Theory of Culture Change: The Methodology of Multilinear Evolution*. Urbana: Univ. of Illinois Press. → Deals with regularities in cultural development within similar natural environments, thus implicitly bringing into focus cultural depth and continuities which characterize geographic regions as culture areas. An aspect of multilinear evolution. Also contrasts culture-area with culture-type studies.

TAX, SOL (editor) 1952 *Heritage of Conquest: The Ethnology of Middle America*. Glencoe, Ill.: Free Press. → Contains Kirchhoff 1943. The concept of Meso-america is basic throughout the book. See especially the map on page 304.

WALLACE, ALFRED R. (1887) 1900 American Museums. Volume 2, pages 16–58 in *Studies Scientific and Social*. London and New York: Macmillan. → First published in the *Fortnightly Review*. Indicates the organization of museum collections, e.g., the Peabody Museum of Harvard University, by geographical area prior to the formulation of the culture-area concept.

WISSLER, CLARK (1917) 1957 *The American Indian: An Introduction to the Anthropology of the New World*. 3d ed. Gloucester, Mass.: Smith. → A pioneer and classic work on the formulation and application of the culture-area concept.

CULTURE CHANGE
See under CULTURE.

CULTURE HISTORY
See under HISTORY.

CULTUROLOGY
See under CULTURE.